FAMILY VIOLENCE ACROSS THE LIFESPAN

SECOND EDITION

To the victims of family abuse and to the dedicated individuals in every walk of life who are working to end the violence

FAMILY VIOLENCE
ACROSS THE LIFESPAN
An Introduction
SECOND EDITION

WITHDRAWN

Ola Barnett
Pepperdine University
Cindy L. Miller-Perrin
Pepperdine University
Robin D. Perrin
Pepperdine University

SAGE Publications
International Educational and Professional Publisher
Thousand Oaks ▪ London ▪ New Delhi

For information:

Sage Publications, Inc.
2455 Teller Road
Thousand Oaks, California 91320
E-mail: order@sagepub.com

Sage Publications Ltd.
1 Oliver's Yard
55 City Road
London EC1Y 1SP
United Kingdom

Sage Publications India Pvt. Ltd.
B-42, Panchsheel Enclave
Post Box 4109
New Delhi 110 017 India

Printed in the United States of America

Library of Congress Cataloging-in-Publication Data

Barnett, Ola W.
Family violence across the lifespan : an introduction / by Ola W. Barnett,
Cindy L. Miller-Perrin, and Robin D. Perrin.—2nd ed.
     p. cm.
Includes bibliographical references and index.
ISBN 0-7619-2755-7 (Cloth : alk. paper)—ISBN 0-7619-2756-5 (pbk. : alk. paper)
   1. Family violence. I. Miller-Perrin, Cindy L. (Cindy Lou), 1962- II. Perrin, Robin D.
III. Title. HV6626 .B315 2005 362.82′92—dc22

                                                    2003024429

This book is printed on acid-free paper.

04   05   06   07   08   10   9   8   7   6   5   4   3   2   1

Acquisitions Editor:	Jerry Westby
Editorial Assistant:	Vonessa Vondera
Copy Editor:	Judy Selhorst
Production Editor:	Kristen Gibson
Typesetter:	C&M Digitals (P) Ltd.
Proofreader:	Elizabeth Larson
Indexer:	Teri Greenberg
Cover Designer:	Janet Foulger

BRIEF CONTENTS

Detailed Contents

PREFACE

F amily violence is not a new phenomenon—it has probably existed since the beginning of time. Only in modern times, however, have societies begun to recognize violence against family members as a social problem. In 2002, the World Health Organization recognized violence between family members and intimates as a global health problem (Krug, Dahlberg, Mercy, Zwi, & Lozano, 2002).

Many grassroots organizations as well as mental health workers, researchers, lawmakers, legal and medical professionals, criminal justice authorities, authors, and the news media have mobilized efforts to draw attention to and understand the phenomenon of family violence. Over the past three decades, the general public in the United States has become familiar with family violence through news coverage of highly publicized cases, television programs, and movies. At the same time, researchers have made great strides in recognizing the scope of family violence and the contexts in which it occurs.

We have written this textbook in an effort to continue the "discovery" of this social problem. We hope to help bring the topic of family violence into the mainstream of public knowledge. To achieve our goals, we have drawn together the research literature that describes the magnitude, consequences, and causes of family violence as well as methods for assessing this phenomenon. In this second edition of *Family Violence Across the Lifespan*, we review the substantial body of research conducted in this field since the first edition was published in 1997, broaden our scope to present more data about marginalized groups, and consider in detail the practice and policy implications of the research findings reported in the literature. We also include in this edition a new final chapter that addresses the role that individuals might play in helping to alleviate the problem of family violence. While primary authorship alternated from chapter to chapter (Ola W. Barnett, Chapters 2 and 8–12; Cindy L. Miller-Perrin, Chapters 3–7; and Robin D. Perrin, Chapters 1 and 13), the coauthors worked collaboratively, exchanging drafts and commenting on each other's work throughout the revision process.

Because of the breadth of the topic and the enormous amount of literature available, we have organized the information in this volume to present a broad overview and summary of research findings. Throughout the book, we attempt to keep our commitment to responsible scholarship by presenting information relevant to both sides of debatable issues. Along the way, we enliven our statistical accounts with graphic case histories, and we highlight a number of current controversies within boxed inserts. For readers who are interested in obtaining further details on specific topics, we include a list of resources in Appendix A, and more information is available at the link for this volume on the Sage Publications Web site (http://www.sagepub.com/book.aspx?pid = 10013; click on the "Additional Materials" button).

Throughout this volume we also feature interviews that we have conducted with nationally and internationally recognized experts. These interviews help to demonstrate the wide variety of philosophies and forms of training found among the many professionals working in the field of family violence. Our aim is to acknowledge this diversity and to point out that individuals with different backgrounds and points of view can and must work together to eradicate family violence.

We hope that we have presented the content in such a way that readers will find their own personal roles in the struggle to end family violence. We invite you, our readers, to contact us to express your impressions of the book, to send us your personal case histories, and to inform us about additional references and resources. Furthermore, we hope that the information provided here will help both victims and perpetrators of family violence to change their lives for the better. Finally, we hope that this text in some measure decreases the isolation and suffering of victims and ultimately contributes to solutions to the problem of family violence.

—Ola W. Barnett

—Cindy L. Miller-Perrin

—Robin D. Perrin

ACKNOWLEDGMENTS

We have many people to thank for their contributions to this text. First, we wish to acknowledge Jerry Westby, acquisitions editor at Sage Publications. Without his support and guidance, we could not have brought this book to the public. His expertise guided and shaped the changes we have made in this edition, enabling us to create a text that appeals to the needs of a broad group of potential readers. We also want to thank Vonessa Vondera, editorial assistant in Sage's Acquisitions Department, for her cheerful attitude as she helped us to assemble all the materials needed for production. We are indebted as well to Judy Selhorst for her careful copyediting. Another person who deserves credit is Carol V. Harnish, who read and reread chapters from a layperson's perspective and helped us to add clarity to our scientific writing style. She collected current case histories and up-to-date newspaper stories that helped to bring the topic of family violence to life. She also served as an invaluable creative consultant by advancing ideas about the selection of information to be presented in the text.

The instructor-reviewers deserve credit for their analytic reading of the first edition. Their extensive knowledge of the field and constructive comments provided us with new insights and directions. They also offered considerable feedback about the selection of information and the appropriate framework for its presentation. We gratefully acknowledge the contributions of the following individuals: Eve Buzawa, University of Massachusetts, Lowell; Barbara Carson, Minnesota State University; David Chandler, University of Hawaii, Manoa; Phil Davis, Georgia State University; Maureen Donohue-Smith, Elmira College; Jean Giles-Sims, Texas Christian University; C. Terry Hendrix, APSAC Board of Directors, Executive Committee; E. Diane Hiebert-Murphy, University of Manitoba; Catherine Lemieux, Louisiana State University; Sharon G. Portwood, University of Missouri–Kansas City; Claire M. Renzetti, Saint Joseph's University; and Arlene Weisz, Wayne State University.

We are especially indebted to the scholars who granted our requests to interview them. Their professionalism in conveying their personal and sometimes controversial viewpoints within a field where final truths have yet to emerge is commendable. Although they sometimes disagree with each other when it comes to research methodologies and interpretations of study findings, these professionals are totally united in their commitment to end family violence. They serve as models for the generation of scholars to follow.

We wish to thank the staff members at both Sage Publications and Pepperdine University who executed the many detailed tasks that accompany the publication of a book this size. We would also like to thank our many friends and colleagues who provided both intellectual and emotional support throughout the publication process. Finally, we wish to thank our families for their encouragement and support while we undertook this long project.

1

History and Definitions of Family Violence

August 19, 2003, Baltimore Sun (Maryland): Police charged a 63-year-old Baltimore woman with attempted murder after her 8-month-old great-grandson was found on the street with a comb down his throat and a shoestring wrapped around his neck (Stiehm, 2003).

August 20, 2003, Alameda Times-Star (California): Adult protective services rescued a 79-year-old woman who was found lying in her own feces and urine with a plate-sized bedsore and cigarette burns on her back. Police arrested her two unemployed sons, who had been living off her Social Security checks ("Horrific Images," 2003).

August 21, 2003, Richmond Times Dispatch (Virginia): A judge sentenced the parents of a 5-year-old to 10 years in prison for locking the boy in a dog cage to keep him from getting food from the kitchen. A former landlord reported that the refrigerator in the home was chained and that the six children who lived there often complained of being hungry ("Parents Guilty," 2003).

August 22, 2003, Newsday (New York): A jury found the father of three young boys, ages 8, 9, and 10, guilty on 31

charges of sexual abuse, ranging from possession of child pornography to first-degree attempted sodomy (Chaudhry, 2003).

August 23, 2003, Houston Chronicle (Texas): Child protective services fired a caseworker after she mishandled a child abuse report in a case that eventually resulted in the death of a 2-year-old girl. Police charged the child's father with murder (Rendon & Horswell, 2003).

August 24, 2003, San Francisco Chronicle (California): Soon after being released from prison and successfully completing an intervention class for batterers, Tari Ramirez killed his 28-year-old ex-girlfriend. Neighbors discovered the woman after her 10-year-old son ran outside screaming that his mother had been stabbed (Marech, 2003).

August 25, 2003, New York Times (New York): Reactions to death of ex-priest John Geoghan continued to make front-page headlines. The 68-year-old convicted sexual abuser was brutally murdered in his prison cell in Massachusetts. The Geoghan case opened the door to the sexual abuse crisis in the Catholic Church (Zezima, 2003).

The newspaper articles cited above represent a sample of the stories about interpersonal violence that appeared across the United States in one 7-day period, from August 19, 2003, through August 25, 2003. These seven stories illustrate the diverse forms of **family violence**. There is no reason to

believe that this particular week, selected at random, was in any way unique.

Child abuse comes in many forms: physical, sexual, and psychological. Child neglect is also considered to be a form of abuse. The story of the 8-month-old infant who was found bleeding on the sidewalk likely illustrates a case of physical abuse. The child's great-grandmother told police, however, that she drank a half-pint of whiskey and fell asleep with the baby on her lap. She claims not to know how the baby got outside (Stiehm, 2003). If her story turns out to be true, this may be a case of neglect rather than physical abuse. Neglect, which is an act of omission rather than commission, is the most common form of child abuse. The parents who locked their child in a dog cage are likely guilty of psychological abuse, although the withholding of food for an extended period of time is also an example of neglect. Child sexual abuse can include a variety of behaviors, but the father convicted of abusing his three children is guilty of the most egregious forms of sexual abuse. Police in Suffolk County called it the worst case of sexual abuse and neglect by a parent they had ever seen (Chaudhry, 2003).

The elderly woman who was rescued from her two sons was placed in a nursing home, but she died 6 months later, never having fully recovered from her abuse. Her sons spent only a short amount of time in jail and inherited their mother's home. Alameda County authorities used the publicity surrounding the case to create a campaign to educate the public about the prevalence of elder abuse, which they assert is a rapidly growing problem ("Horrific Images," 2003).

Many homicides occur within families, and the case cited above of the woman killed by her ex-boyfriend is not unusual. In fact, perhaps as many as one-half of all female homicide victims are killed by intimates or family members. This particular case attracted national attention because the woman had turned to the criminal justice system for help, and the system failed her. She had secured numerous protective orders and her former boyfriend had completed a batterer intervention program. Her murder raised questions about the ability of the system to protect women and to treat abusers (Marech, 2003).

The case of the fired child protective services (CPS) worker also raises questions about the ability of the system to protect vulnerable family members (Rendon & Horswell, 2003). The mistakes of CPS workers and the shortcomings of CPS agencies are laid bare whenever a child who is known to CPS is killed. Cases like the one described above have caused many to question our society's commitment to protect children from abuse.

Finally, we include the story about John Geoghan and the sexual abuse scandals that have rocked the Catholic Church in recent years (Zezima, 2003) with the other stories above to introduce the fact that in this volume our discussions of family violence will sometimes lead outside the family to violence within other intimate relationships.

News media accounts of family violence are not always representative of typical cases encountered by authorities. Those that receive news coverage are undoubtedly the most sensational cases. In this book, however, we focus not on the sensational but on the common and often accepted violence that occurs within families. Newspaper and other media accounts cannot provide the depth of information one needs to comprehend the complex nature of family violence. If one hopes to understand the causes and consequences of family violence in its various forms, one must examine the topic comprehensively and scientifically.

Our aim in this book is to provide readers with accurate, empirically based information on family violence. After completing the final chapter, readers should have a good understanding of many different issues associated with family violence, including definitions and estimates of the problem, the physical and psychological consequences of family violence, the various theories that have been developed to explain family violence, and policy recommendations aimed at stopping family violence. We begin this first chapter by considering two important questions: When (and how) did family violence come to be recognized as a social problem? and How is family violence defined?

VIOLENCE IN FAMILIES

It is easy to think of the family as being relatively immune from violence, a place of safe harbor, a place of sustenance and care. The idea that a parent or a spouse would intentionally and knowingly inflict injury on a loved one is counterintuitive. A parent is supposed to protect and care for a child. Spouses are supposed to love and cherish each other. We know, however, that often the family is a source of maltreatment and violence. We read about maltreatment within families in the newspapers, and we see news stories about it on television. Many of us know people who have been abused by family members or we ourselves have been abused, or we have witnessed abuse between our parents. We know family violence exists.

How common is family violence? For a variety of reasons (which we discuss in detail in Chapter 2), this is a very difficult question to answer. Measuring family violence is inherently problematic, first of all, because there is little agreement among those who gather data as to exactly what constitutes family violence. Even if there were definitional consensus, however, the fact remains that most family violence occurs behind closed doors. It is often hidden, unnoticed, or ignored. Most family violence does not come to the attention of authorities and therefore does not turn up in the official estimates computed by the FBI and the U.S. Department of Health and Human Services (U.S. DHHS). When researchers try to address the question of the frequency of family violence by using self-report surveys, such as the National Crime Victimization Survey (NCVS), the information they gather is inevitably incomplete. Adult victims may not recall childhood abuse, and, as Rennison (2001) notes, children and spouses who have been abused, especially those who are currently in abusive relationships, may "not view, may not wish to view, or may be unable to report the behavior" they have experienced as abuse (p. 6). Given these numerous problems, any statistics on family violence should be interpreted with a degree of caution. There is simply no way we can know with certainty how much family violence exists in our society.

The data that are available from a number of sources, however, can give us a sense of the scope of the problem. The U.S. Department of Health and Human Services (2002b) estimates, for example, that in 2001 approximately 1,200 children died in the United States as a result of abuse and neglect.[1] Of these children, 45% were under the age of 1 year and 85% were under the age of 6. Most of their abusers were their parents or other family members.

The data on adult homicides suggest a similar picture. According to an FBI report, of the 13,752 homicides reported in the United States in 2001, 2,387 (17%) were committed by family members, boyfriends, or girlfriends of the victims. Keep in mind, however, that the assailants remain unknown in almost half (45%) of the total homicides; thus the actual proportion of intrafamily homicides is no doubt considerably higher, likely well over 20% (U.S. Department of Justice, 2002).[2]

Women are especially vulnerable within the family. Although they represent a relatively small percentage of all homicides in any given year (about 25% annually), women make up approximately three-quarters of all victims of intimate homicide (Rennison, 2001). Nearly one-third (32%) of female homicide victims in 2001 were killed by intimates (i.e., husbands, ex-husbands, boyfriends, or ex-boyfriends). Once again, it should be noted that the actual proportion is probably considerably higher, given that so many homicides go unsolved (U.S. Department of Justice, 2002). It is not unreasonable to speculate that the proportion of female homicide victims who are killed by intimates or other family members may be as high as 50%, a figure that is consistent with historical evidence on intimate homicide (Dobash & Dobash, 1979).

According to the U.S. Department of Health and Human Services (2002b), in the year 2000 social service agencies across the United States received approximately 3 million reports of child maltreatment, a rate of 12.2 per 1,000 children. This figure includes all reports of physical and sexual abuse, neglect, and psychological maltreatment. Approximately 900,000 of these 3 million reports were **substantiated** upon investigation (i.e., child protective services determined that the alleged abuse had likely occurred). Of these substantiated cases, the most common form of abuse was neglect (62%), followed by physical abuse (19%), sexual abuse (10%), and psychological abuse (8%). The rate of abuse in 2000, of 12.2 per 1,000 children, was slightly higher than the rate in the previous year but below the all-time high of 15.3 per 1,000, which was recorded in 1993. Parents were the perpetrators of the abuse in 84% of these cases, with mothers the most likely perpetrators in physical abuse and neglect cases and fathers the most likely perpetrators in sexual abuse cases.

Keep in mind, however, that these data represent *reported* child maltreatment. How much violence and maltreatment occurs that is never reported? This is, of course, a very difficult question to answer. Findings from national surveys, for example, suggest that three-fourths of parents report using some method of physical violence during the rearing of their children. Although most of this violence consists of minor acts such as spanking, slapping, and pinching, studies suggest that nearly *half of all parents* engage in more severe violence, including hitting children with objects such as sticks or belts, slapping children's faces, hitting children with fists, kicking children, or throwing/knocking children down (Straus, Sugarman, & Giles-Sims, 1997). Findings from the National Violence Against Women Survey indicate similar rates of child abuse, with 52% of adult women and 66% of adult men in the survey sample reporting that they were assaulted as children by adult caretakers (Tjaden & Thoennes, 2000b).[3]

Data from the National Violence Against Women Survey also suggest that violence between married and dating partners, or **intimate partner violence** (IPV), is not uncommon. Using a modified version of the Conflict Tactics Scale, which measures a range of behaviors from relatively minor violence (e.g., pushes, slaps) to very serious violence (e.g., using a gun), the researchers found that 22% of women and 7% of men reported experiencing violence at some point in their lifetimes. Approximately 1% of men and women in the survey sample reported being physically assaulted by a current spouse/partner in the preceding year. The survey also found that rape within intimate relationships is not uncommon, with nearly 10% of women reporting having been raped by intimate partners at some time in their lives (Tjaden & Thoennes, 2000b).[4]

Additional data on IPV comes from the National Crime Victimization Survey, a survey conducted by the U.S. government to gather data for use in estimating the frequency and severity of criminal victimizations. According to the NCVS, women are the victims in 85% of intimate violence, and the overall rate of 6 victimizations per 1,000 women. Younger women aged 16–24 were especially vulnerable, with victimization rates at nearly 16 per 1,000 (Rennison, 2001).

According to the Centers for Disease Control and Prevention, one in four Americans is directly affected by family violence (Melton, 2002). The U.S. Department of Justice estimates that the likelihood of victimization by an acquaintance, friend, relative, or intimate is twice that of victimization by a stranger (Greenfeld et al., 1998). Levesque (2001) maintains that family violence is the most widespread form of violence in the United States and is the leading cause of injury and death among women and children. Empirical estimates like these have led some to conclude that "family violence in the US is a problem of mind-boggling, soul searching scope" (Melton, 2002, p, 576). One could reasonably make the claim that women and children are more likely to be victimized in their own homes than they are on the streets of America's most violent cities (Bachman & Saltzman, 1995; Hotaling, Straus, & Lincoln, 1990).

As social scientists and advocates, we argue that the statistics cited above offer sufficient reason to study family violence. We need to understand the scope of the problem and its causes and consequences in order to intervene and protect our most vulnerable citizens. For those who are not sufficiently motivated by these reasons, however, we offer a more practical rationale: Family victimization is a significant causal factor in a number of the personal and societal problems that affect American society, and preventing family

violence may help to alleviate some of these problems. Perhaps the most obvious example is violent criminal behavior. Although many factors contribute to violence in society, research has shown family influence to be the single greatest determinant of an individual's level of violence outside the home. Children who are abused, or who witness abuse, are far more likely to engage in violence themselves, both as children and later in their lives. In a 4-year longitudinal study of 1,000 adolescents conducted by the Office of Juvenile Justice and Delinquency Prevention (OJJDP, 1995), 38% of youths from nonviolent families reported that they had perpetrated some type of violence; in contrast, 78% of youths exposed to maltreatment, violence by parents, and a general family climate of hostility reported having perpetrated violent acts. Although care in interpreting these data is warranted, given that the relationship between childhood victimization and subsequent perpetration is far from perfect, there is every reason to suspect that childhood victimization plays a profound role in producing the next generation of violent offenders. Indeed, the adage "Violence begets violence," although no doubt overly simplistic, seems generally true. According to OJJDP administrator Shay Bilchik, the research seems clear: "If we can reduce family violence—not just abuse and neglect—we can prevent future violence by its young victims" (quoted in "Violence in Families," 1995, p. 6).

WHY ARE FAMILIES VIOLENT?

All families have tensions, and all families sometimes resolve these tensions in inappropriate ways. Even the best parents and the most loving couples sometimes lose their tempers, say intentionally hurtful things to one another, raise their voices when arguing, and even lash out at loved ones physically. Given this reality, it is fruitful to consider the many social and cultural conditions that contribute to physically violent and verbally aggressive family interactions. As we will see, in many respects, aggression is a "normal" (i.e., common and culturally approved) part of family life. Why is this so? And why are women and children so overrepresented in victimization data?

Many structural factors make families particularly prone to violence. One of these is the amount of time family members spend together, which increases the opportunity for violence. Another factor is that family interactions are often emotional, and so especially volatile. In addition, power differentials often exist among family members: Children are subordinate to parents, elderly parents may be subordinate to their adult children, and wives may be subordinate to husbands. The result is that the powerless sometimes become targets of aggression. Further complicating matters is the fact that children (and to some degree women as well) cannot fight back. Nor can they always choose with whom they will or will not interact. Whereas many interpersonal conflicts can be resolved simply through the dissolution of relationships, family relationships are protected by law and are not so easily severed. Wives can easily feel trapped by the cultural, legal, and economic constraints of marriage. Children are dependent on their parents. Even when child maltreatment comes to the attention of authorities, states are reluctant to break up families and parents are often given every opportunity to change. And finally, the privacy and autonomy traditionally granted to families in our society make violence relatively easy to hide (Brinkerhoff & Lupri, 1988).

Levesque (2001) asserts that the problem begins with an idealized notion of the family that offers families rights and protections that are sometimes undeserved. The apparent reasonableness of this notion serves to "justify what otherwise could be construed as violent, abusive, and worthy of intervention. Much violence remains hidden and justified in families viewed as precious" (p. 5). This image of the family includes several beliefs: (a) that parental rights supersede children's rights and that parents can and should have control over the development of their children; (b) that family members will act in the best interests of children and elderly parents who are not capable of caring for themselves; (c) that families rooted in traditional cultures are "strong families," even though some of their cultural customs justify family violence; and (d) that families have the right to privacy and autonomy, even though this right often results in harm to vulnerable members (this assumed right may also indirectly result in society's reluctance to provide social service assistance).

There is little doubt that family norms contribute to a certain amount of family aggression. In national surveys conducted by the National Opinion Research Center (1998), for example, 73% of Americans surveyed agreed or strongly agreed that it is "sometimes necessary to discipline a child with a good hard spanking." Although aggression between spouses is less acceptable, many survey participants agreed that sometimes aggression between husbands and wives "just happens." There is, of course, considerable debate about the appropriateness of different forms of family aggression,

and we address the various viewpoints on these issues in subsequent chapters. However, beyond opinions concerning the use of corporal punishment, or marital pushing, or siblings hitting one another, there can be little doubt that the more a society accepts aggression as "appropriate" or "inevitable," the more likely it is that serious violence (i.e., abuse) will occur. The problem is that aggression generally deemed "legitimate" in American society (e.g., a slap on the hand of a misbehaving child) and aggression deemed "illegitimate" (e.g., a fist to the face of a misbehaving child) exist on the same continuum. It stands to reason that the more society encourages and condones some forms of violence as legitimate, the more illegitimate violence will occur. Many abusive parents report, for example, that they lost their tempers while disciplining their children and did not "mean" to cause physical harm (Straus, 1994). Interestingly, many social scientists maintain that societal acceptance, encouragement, and glorification of violence *in general* also contribute to abuse in the family. Society's tolerance for aggression may have a "spillover effect," raising the likelihood of violence in the home (Tolan & Guerra, 1998).

DISCOVERING FAMILY VIOLENCE: HOW SOCIAL CONDITIONS BECOME SOCIAL PROBLEMS

Presumably, few would question our assertion that family violence is a serious social problem. Television and the print news media routinely report on disturbing stories of family violence. The academic community has included coverage of the topic in textbooks on social problems and deviant behavior, and increasingly colleges and universities are offering specific courses on family violence. In the past 20 years, several new journals related to family violence have appeared, including *Child Abuse & Neglect; Child Maltreatment; Child Welfare; Journal of Child Sexual Abuse; Journal of Elder Abuse & Neglect; Journal of Family Violence; Journal of Interpersonal Violence; Aggression and Violent Behavior; Trauma, Violence, & Abuse;* and the *Journal of Religion and Abuse.* Articles reporting on family violence research have also become increasingly common in mainstream journals in the fields of psychology, sociology, social work, law, and criminal justice. In addition, numerous social movement organizations and federal agencies are devoted to researching and preventing family violence.

Concern about family violence has also increased around the world, and several international treaties explicitly include mention of the human right to protection from violent family members. The 1989 United Nations Convention on the Rights of the Child declares that all children should be protected from "physical or mental violence, injury or abuse, neglect or negligent treatment, maltreatment or exploitation including sexual abuse, while in the care of parent(s), legal guardian(s) or any other person who has the care of the child" (quoted in Levesque, 2001, p. 7). The U.N.'s Declaration on the Elimination of Violence Against Women, adopted in 1994, condemns any "act of gender-based violence that results in, or is likely to result in, physical, sexual, or psychological harm or suffering to women, including threats of such acts, coercion or arbitrary deprivation of liberty, whether occurring in public or private life" (quoted in Levesque, 2001, p. 7). In these documents, the United Nations rejects cultural relativism, declaring that all U.N. member countries must eliminate any cultural practices or customs that contribute to the abuse of women or children.

Clearly, the problem of family violence is an increasingly universal concern, occupying a very high position on the social agendas of the United States and many other nations. It is important to recognize, however, that concern about family violence is a fairly recent phenomenon. Indeed, even a cursory look at human history reveals that family violence was a social condition long before it was recognized as a social problem. When and how did family violence come to be seen as a social problem?

According to many sociologists, social conditions become social problems through a process of **social constructionism** (Loseke, 2003; Spector & Kitsuse, 1977). From this perspective, *societal reactions* are central to the process through which a social condition is redefined as a social problem. Societal reactions can come from many sources: individual citizens, religious groups, social movement organizations, political interest groups, and the media, to name but a few. Through their reactions to particular social conditions, individuals and institutions play a crucial role in transforming public perceptions.

A social condition becomes a social problem when various interest groups actively engage in the process of raising awareness about that condition. The term *claims-making* has been applied to the activities of such groups; it refers to the "activities of individuals or groups making assertions of grievances or claims with respect to some putative condition" (Spector & Kitsuse,

1977, p. 75). Generally speaking, the process begins when the members of an interest group, or **claims-makers**, express concern about a particular condition that they see as unacceptable. Claims-makers may have vested interests in the outcomes of their protests, or they may be "moral entrepreneurs" engaged in what they see as purely moral crusades (Becker, 1963). As the cause of a particular claims-making group comes to be recognized by society more generally, the social condition comes to be defined as a social problem. Social problems, then, are essentially "discovered" through this process of societal reactions and social definition. From this perspective, social problems come and go as societal reactions to given conditions and responsive behaviors change.

The social constructionist perspective helps to explain cross-cultural variations in definitions of family violence. That is, what is condemned as abuse in one culture is not always condemned in another. For example, the Sambia of Papua New Guinea believe that the only way a boy can grow into manhood is by orally ingesting the semen of older boys and men. In other words, a boy becomes masculine, strong, and sexually attractive to women only by performing fellatio (Herdt, 1987). In the United States such behavior is nonnormative and illegal, but for the Sambia it is not. Perhaps in the future the Sambia might redefine this behavior as deviant, but for this social change to occur, claims-makers would have to challenge the cultural practice. The practice will come to be perceived as a problem only if claim-makers can succeed in redefining it as such.

The social constructionist perspective also helps to illustrate how research is used in ongoing debates about social problems such as family violence. Family violence research is one of the most contentious areas of social science, and disagreements among scholars are often intense. Is family violence increasing or decreasing? Are men as likely as women to be the victims of intimate partner violence? Should parents be allowed to hit their children? What constitutes rape? Although one might hope that research findings could settle the debates surrounding such topics, the reality is that the data that researchers collect are often interpreted differently by competing claims-makers. Those on both sides in any given debate typically arm themselves with their own sets of empirical findings, which they espouse as "the truth." From a social constructionist perspective, the nature of social problems and the "facts" about those problem are defined for the general public by the "winners" of such debates (Best, 2001).

The social constructionist perspective on social problems is important because it gives us a theoretical framework within which to understand the discovery, definition, and extent of family violence in the United States and around the world. This perspective helps us understand what is recognized as a problem and how it came to be recognized as such. It does not, however, help us to distinguish right from wrong, and it should not be mistaken for the extreme relativist perspective, which suggests that cultural norms supersede human rights. Indeed, just because a practice is culturally condoned, that does not make it right, a point the United Nations and other international claims-making organizations have increasingly emphasized (Levesque, 2001).

Discovering Child Maltreatment: The Historical Context

> This history of childhood is a nightmare from which we have only recently begun to awaken. The further back in history one goes, the lower the level of child care, and the more likely children are to be killed, abandoned, beaten, terrorized, and sexually abused. (deMause, 1974, p. 1)

Contemporary conceptions of children and childhood in the United States—that childhood is a special phase of life and that children should be loved, nurtured, and protected from the cruel world—emerged only within the past few hundred years. As Empey, Stafford, and Hay (1999) note, what we call children today were, in previous times, "regarded more as small or inadequate versions of their parents than as sacred beings in need of special protection" (pp. 6–7). One illustration of the previous indifference to children as a group of special status is found in the historical practice of infanticide, which some scholars maintain was the most frequent crime in all of Europe and remained a relatively common practice until about 1800 (Piers, 1978). Given modern-day conceptions of the importance of the mother-child bond, such widespread practice of infanticide seems unbelievable; it also reminds us that this bond is, to some degree, culturally defined.

Over the centuries, the value of children grew in developed societies, and by the 1900s in the United States, the government's interest in the welfare and control of children had resulted in child labor laws, the creation of a juvenile court system, mandatory education requirements, and child protection laws. Although these changes likely reflect an increase in the value U.S. society placed on children, they no doubt also came about because of the state's interest in protecting itself from troubled children and the troubled adults these children often become (Pfohl, 1977).

Discovering child physical abuse. In many ways, the indifference to childhood evidenced in previous centuries is not difficult to explain. The harshness of life, the high rates of disease, and the visibility of death all contributed to a general devaluation of life and of children's lives in particular. In addition, children were politically powerless, without independent status or rights; most societies thus regarded children as the property of their parents, who were allowed to treat their property as they saw fit. In some cases, parents probably viewed their children as economic liabilities—as little more than extra mouths to feed (Walker, Bonner, & Kaufman, 1988; Wolfe, 1991).

In the 17th century, Protestant reformers in the New World had mixed perceptions of children, suggesting that children were valued gifts of God but also possessed "wrong-doing hearts" and were "inclined to evil." The result was a preoccupation with both the need to nurture and protect children and the necessity to break them of their incorrigible nature (Empey et al., 1999; Rice, 1998). It was these reformers who enacted the first laws against child abuse. Massachusetts's Body of Liberties (1641), for example, prohibited parents from "any unnatural severitie" toward children (quoted in Pleck, 1987). However, because children were seen as innately inclined toward evil, the child protection laws were enforced only in those cases where the child was seen as completely blameless. The Body of Liberties, in fact, permitted the death sentence for any child over the age of 16 who had cursed or struck a parent. According to Pleck (1987), there is no evidence that a child was ever executed for such insubordination, but the fact that the law existed illustrates the Puritans' intolerance of stubbornness and disobedience in children.

Many scholars trace the actual discovery of child abuse in the United States to the "house of refuge" movement of the early 1800s. In large part a reaction to growing industrialization and urbanization, this movement was guided by the medieval principle of parens patriae—that is, the right and responsibility of the state to protect those who cannot protect themselves (Pfohl, 1977). As a result of reforms brought about by the movement, children in the early to mid-1800s who were neglected, abused, or otherwise "on the road to ruin" were housed in one of many state-supported institutions. The house of refuge movement represents the government's first attempt to intervene in neglect and abuse cases (Empey et al., 1999).

Probably the most famous early court case involving child abuse was tried in 1874. Church social worker Etta Wheeler discovered that 8-year-old Mary Ellen Wilson was being beaten and starved by her stepmother. After unsuccessfully seeking help to remedy the situation from several sources, Wheeler took the case to Henry Bergh, founder of the Society for the Prevention of Cruelty to Animals. Mary Ellen was, after all, a member of the animal kingdom. A courtroom full of concerned New Yorkers, many of them upper-class women, heard the shocking details of Mary Ellen's life. She had been beaten almost daily and had not been allowed to play with friends or to leave the house. She had an unhealed gash on the left side of her face, where her stepmother had struck her with a pair of scissors. The jury took only 20 minutes to find the stepmother guilty of assault and battery (Pleck, 1987).

The case of Mary Ellen attracted considerable attention, and the resulting public outcry eventually led to the founding of the Society for the Prevention of Cruelty to Children in 1874 (Pagelow, 1984). This organization, and the larger child-saving movement of which it was a part, advocated for dramatic changes in society's treatment of children. Increasingly, child protection advocates argued that children need to be loved and nurtured, and that they need to be protected by the state when their parents fail to do so. They argued, in effect, that parents should not have complete authority over their children (Finkelhor, 1996).

As Finkelhor (1996) notes, two social changes that took place during the 20th century directly contributed to the success of the child-saving movement. First, a large group of specialized professionals—nurses, social workers, schoolteachers and counselors, legal advocates, and family counselors—took on the task of protecting children. And second, as women gained more freedom in their personal lives and more power in the workplace, they felt more empowered to advocate for children.

Largely as a result of the claims-making of child advocacy groups, many state legislatures passed child protective statutes in the early 1900s, criminalizing parents' abusive and neglectful behavior and specifying procedures for meeting the needs of abused and neglected children (Pleck, 1987). Although there was considerable movement toward child protection during this time, sociolegal reactions to the problem of child abuse remained somewhat sporadic. For example, no laws existed to make the reporting of suspected child abuse mandatory for certain professionals, so most such abuse remained unacknowledged.

The full recognition of child abuse as a social problem in the United States was not complete until the 1960s, when Dr. C. Henry Kempe and his colleagues first described the "battered child syndrome" and suggested that physicians should report any observed cases of abuse (Kempe, Silverman, Steele, Droegemueller, & Silver, 1962). Kempe et al. defined child abuse as a clinical condition with diagnosable medical and physical symptoms resulting from deliberate physical assault. This work was important not simply because the researchers identified and defined child abuse—indeed, child abuse had been identified and defined before—but because it marked the addition of the considerable clout of the medical community to claims-making about the child abuse problem. When medical doctors combined forces with other professionals and advocacy groups already fighting for child protection, the movement rapidly gained momentum. Before the end of the 1960s, every U.S. state had created laws mandating that professionals report suspected cases of abuse, and in 1974, Congress enacted the Child Abuse Prevention and Treatment Act, which provided federal funding to help states fight child abuse.

Discovering child sexual abuse. Throughout history, and particularly in certain cultures, sexual interactions involving children have been commonplace. These interactions have often been seen as appropriate; in some cases, they have been believed to be healthy for children. In his disturbing review of the history of abuse of children, deMause (1974) notes that the children of ancient Greece, especially the boys, were often sexually exploited. Aristotle, for example, believed that masturbation of boys by adult males hastened their manhood. Greek authors made reference to "adults feeling the 'immature little tool' of boys" (p. 44). Although it is not clear how common these practices were, their matter-of-fact depiction in the literature and art of the time suggests that they were not widely condemned.

Despite dramatic changes since that time, condemnation of sexual contact between adults and children is far from universal. One extreme minority perspective is that of the North American Man/Boy Love Association (NAMBLA), an organization founded in 1978 that supports "the rights of all people to engage in consensual relations, and opposes laws which destroy loving relationships merely on the basis of the age of the participants" (NAMBLA, 2002). Robert Rhodes, a NAMBLA spokesperson, made the following comments when asked whether the organization views itself as an advocacy group for children:

> Yes. Considering the legitimacy of sexual relationships with children, there are two main theories that you can work from. One was the classical Greek theory—that is to say that the older partner in a sexual relationship served as initiator and tutor of the younger partner. You can also take a children's liberationist viewpoint—that is to say that children insofar as is possible—and it's far more possible than the current structure allows—should be given liberty to run their own lives as they choose, including the ability to determine how and with whom they should have sex. (quoted in Hechler, 1988, pp. 193–194)

These views effectively illustrate the role that claims-making groups have played in the discovery and definition of family violence. NAMBLA's perspective represents a minority view, of course—and in the United States the acts that NAMBLA promotes are criminal acts. From a historical perspective, however, the views espoused by NAMBLA are not that unusual.

Discovering child neglect and child psychological maltreatment. Child neglect has been referred to as the "most forgotten" form of maltreatment (Daro, 1988). The limited interest in neglect is surprising, given that it is far more common than physical or sexual child abuse. Psychological maltreatment is also pervasive; indeed, it is a central component in all child maltreatment. Although physical wounds may heal, psychological wounds often run deep. Why do child neglect and psychological maltreatment receive less attention than other forms of abuse? The most obvious reason is that physical and sexual abuse are far more likely to result in observable harm. Child physical abuse tends to be defined only by the physical harm the child experiences. Sometimes neglect results in signs of physical harm (e.g., malnutrition), but often the negative effects of neglect and psychological maltreatment never become fully apparent to observers outside the family.

As is true of all forms of child maltreatment, child neglect is not a new phenomenon. It was not until the 20th century, however, that neglect of children's basic needs came to be acknowledged and defined as a social problem (Wolock & Horowitz, 1984). Psychological maltreatment of children has received even less recognition. Professionals have tended to view psychological maltreatment as a side effect of other forms of abuse and neglect, rather than as a unique form of maltreatment. Only since the early 1990s have experts recognized psychological maltreatment as a discrete form of child maltreatment (see Hart & Brassard, 1993; Loring, 1994; Wiehe, 1990). Surveys suggest that Americans have come to consider psychological maltreatment a serious problem, with 75% indicating that exposure to "repeated yelling and swearing" is harmful to a child's well-being (Daro & Gelles, 1992).

Discovering Intimate Partner Violence: The Historical Context

> WOMAN'S RIGHTS CONVENTION. A Convention to discuss the social, civil, and religious condition and rights of women, will be held in the Wesleyan Chapel, at Seneca Falls, N.Y., on Wednesday and Thursday, the 19th and 20th of July, current; commencing at 10 o'clock am. ("Seneca Falls Convention," 1848)

Social conditions in the United States were not conducive to the discovery of wife abuse until the subordination of women was discovered as a result of the "woman movement" of the mid- to late 1800s. This movement, which was followed by the suffragist movement of the early 1900s and the feminist movement of the mid- to late 1900s, was an important precursor to the discovery of marital violence.

The seed for a women's rights movement was planted in 1848 in a Wesleyan Methodist church in Seneca Falls, New York. The Seneca Falls Convention was organized by Lucretia Mott, the wife of an anti-slavery reformer and Quaker preacher, and women's rights advocate Elizabeth Stanton. In the days prior to the convention, Stanton wrote the convention's "Declaration of Sentiments," a document modeled after the Declaration of Independence. The declaration begins with the following pronouncement:

> We hold these truths to be self-evident; that all men and women are created equal; that they are endowed by their Creator with certain inalienable rights; that among these are life, liberty, and the pursuit of happiness; that to secure these rights governments are instituted, deriving their just powers from the consent of the governed. (*Seneca Falls Convention*, 1848)

In surprisingly strong language, the document asserts that throughout history men have injured and controlled women in hopes of establishing "absolute tyranny" over them. It concludes: "In view of this entire disfranchisement of one-half the people of this country . . . we insist that they have immediate admission to all the rights and privileges which belong to them as citizens of the United States."

Through the early 1900s, the struggle for women's rights in the United States focused mainly on securing for women the right to vote, because it was assumed that with this right women would gain the power to challenge many injustices, including violence in the family (Ashcraft, 2000). The efforts of the suffragist movement culminated with the passage of the 19th Amendment to the U.S. Constitution in 1920. Despite its success, many have argued that the single-mindedness of the women's suffrage movement proved somewhat costly to women more generally, for once they gained the right to vote, the equality movement lost steam (Cott, 1988). During the 1960s, however, interest in women's rights was revived as a new feminist movement gained momentum. This time, the movement's major concerns included the subordination and victimization of women within the family.

Discovering battered women. Many historians have noted that early marriage laws actually gave men the legal right to hit their wives (Dobash & Dobash, 1979). English common law held that women were inferior to men, and that a married woman had no legal existence apart from her husband, who in effect owned and controlled her and was considered responsible for her actions. Because husbands were expected to control their wives, the law allowed them a great deal of latitude in using force to do so (Sigler, 1989). Early British rape laws also reflected the status of women as property, stating that when a woman was raped, restitution should be paid to her husband (or, if she was unmarried, to her father) (Sigler, 1989).

The reformers of the "woman movement" of the late 1800s fully recognized the vulnerability of women within the family. In the Declaration of Sentiments for the Seneca Falls Convention, Elizabeth Stanton argued that the rights of women should be acknowledged in all spheres of life. In doing so, she listed a number of "facts submitted to a candid world," several of which related specifically to the family:

> He has made her, if married, in the eye of the law, civilly dead. He has taken from her all right in property, even to the wages she earns.
>
> In the covenant of marriage, she is compelled to promise obedience to her husband, he becoming, to all intents and purposes, her master—the law giving him power to deprive her of her liberty and to administer chastisement.

> He has so framed the laws of divorce, as to what shall be the proper causes, and in case of separation, to whom the guardianship of the children shall be given, as to be wholly regardless of the happiness of women—the law, in all cases, going upon a false supposition of the supremacy of man, and giving all power into his hands. (*Seneca Falls Convention*, 1848)

Despite the efforts of Stanton and other influential reformers, the problem of wife abuse attracted little attention in the first half of the 20th century. As Pleck (1987) has noted, the campaign was, "compared to the child abuse movement of roughly the same time period, an abysmal failure" (p. 109).

The modern feminist movement that arose in the 1960s renewed public interest in the problem of the subordination of women, including the issue of inequality in marital relationships. However, leaders of the movement, including the National Organization for Women (NOW), founded in 1966, for the most part ignored the topic of wife abuse early on. Instead, NOW focused on passage of the Equal Rights Amendment, elimination of discrimination against women in the workplace, public funding for child care, and abortion rights. To the degree that feminists did advocate for battered women, their claims were often dismissed by a public suspicious of a movement it perceived to be radical and antifamily (Pleck, 1987).

The battered women's movement gained momentum when Chiswick Women's Aid, the first shelter for battered women to gain widespread public attention, opened in England in 1971. Chiswick's founder, Erin Pizzey, published the influential book *Scream Quietly or the Neighbours Will Hear* in 1974. The publicity that surrounded the book, and the subsequent radio and television exposure it generated, helped to spread the battered women's movement in Europe. American activists, some of whom visited Chiswick in the early 1970s, were anxious to open similar shelters in the United States. A flood of media attention in the mid-1970s further increased public awareness of the domestic violence problem (Dobash & Dobash, 1978, 1979; Pleck, 1987).

In 1976, NOW decided to make wife battering a priority issue. The organization announced the formation of a task force to examine the problem and demanded government support for research and shelter funding. As battered women moved higher up the list of feminist concerns, women's organizations more effectively exerted pressure on police and government officials to protect abused women. Advocacy organizations such as the National Coalition Against Domestic Violence, founded in 1978, effectively voiced the concerns of battered women on a national level, and this led to improvements in social services for battered wives and changes in legal statutes that were inadequate to protect women (Studer, 1984). Several organizations, including the Displaced Homemakers Network, the National Association of Women and the Law (in Canada), the National Organization for Victim Assistance, the National Clearinghouse for the Defense of Battered Women, and the National Council on Child Abuse and Family Violence, actively fought for the rights of women. These organizations did not all share a particular social and political agenda, but their combined efforts raised awareness of the significance of domestic violence against women as a social problem.

Discovering battered men? One of the most vigorous ongoing debates in the field of family violence concerns the issue of intimate partner violence by women against men: Does such violence constitute a serious social problem? The debate can in many respects be traced to survey data from the 1970s and 1980s that suggest that wives are violent toward their spouses as frequently as husbands are (Gelles & Straus, 1988; Straus, Gelles, & Steinmetz, 1980). Most of these data were collected by researchers who used the Conflict Tactics Scale (CTS), which measures the frequency of various kinds of violent interactions that might occur between couples through respondents' self-reports (see the discussion of the CTS in Chapter 2). For example, findings from the National Family Violence Resurvey indicate that 12% of the women and 11% of the men surveyed engaged in at least one act of violence in the previous year (most of these were minor acts of violence, such as pushing, slapping, or kicking). "Cultural spillover" theorists such as Gelles and Straus (1988) assert that the overall prevalence of marital violence— both men hitting women and women hitting men—is problematic because it is indicative of implicit societal acceptance of violence as a legitimate means of settling disputes.

The assertion that the data show that women are as violent as men angers many advocates for battered women who perceive the "real" marital violence problem to be wife battering. Critics charge that the CTS, especially the first version of the scale (CTS1), fails to measure the degree to which women who report committing violent acts may be acting in self-defense or out of fear of abusive husbands (Kurz, 1989). The

dialogue between the two sides in this debate has sometimes been quite heated, and, as Migliaccio (2002) notes, the findings of Straus and his colleagues have "embroiled the CTS in controversy" (p. 28). Kurz (1991), for example, charges that Straus and others have used "large amounts of federal money for research whose conclusions have vastly underestimated the harm done to women and greatly exaggerated their responsibility for that violence and ha[ve] provided a distorted picture of this problem to policy makers" (p. 158).

Straus and his colleagues (1980) have acknowledged that the problem of wife abuse is more severe than that of husband abuse, and they have stated that it would be unfortunate if the data on wife-to-husband violence "distracted us from giving first attention to wives as victims as the focus of social policy" (p. 43). Arguably, however, the data that have come from their research have fed a backlash against the battered women's movement. Armed with these data, critics of the movement have charged that women are just as abusive as men and that the battered women's movement has received an unjustified amount of attention and resources (George, 2003).

Despite the controversy, the issue of women's violence against men has for the most part been pushed into the background, and the problem of marital violence has been defined almost exclusively as the problem of woman battering. Recently, however, the issue of male victimization seems to be attracting renewed attention. Several researchers, most of whom are sensitive to the plight of battered women, have raised the question of why the hitting of husbands by wives cannot also be seen as a social problem. For example, in an examination of the case histories of 12 male victims of domestic violence, Migliaccio (2002) notes that "commonalities found in past research on wife abuse can be used in the analysis of husband abuse, regardless of the size and the strength of the individual" (p. 47). After reexamining evidence from studies using the CTS, George (2003) recently concluded that domestic violence against men is a reality, and that the academic controversy that has surrounded the issue is "unnecessary and counterproductive" (p. 23).

Although the victimization of women continues to dominate the domestic violence discussion (as is evident in the research we review in this book), competing claims-makers continue to negotiate the scope of the domestic violence problem, and perceptions of the nature of the problem may well change in the next few years. No doubt the debate will continue.

Discovering marital rape. The women's movement has been influential in the relatively recent discovery of another form of domestic violence: marital rape. Historically, rape laws have pertained only to sexual assault outside of marriage. In the 1700s, Sir Matthew Hale, a chief justice of the Court of Kings Bench in England, originated the marital exemption law, which held that by mutual matrimonial consent and contract, a wife had given her consent to sexual intercourse with her husband and could not retract it. Hasday (2000) argues that women's sexual rights were a concern of women's rights activists from the beginning of the "woman movement" in 1848. Early reformers viewed a woman's right to control her own body as key to her subordination, and, according to Hasday, they waged "a vigorous, public, and extraordinarily frank campaign against a man's right to forced sex in marriage." In addition to feminist advocacy of the late 19th century, instructional literature at the time maintained that a wife's right to say no to sex is essential to a happy marriage and urged men to acknowledge women's sexual rights. Early feminist attempts to change marital exemption laws, however, were unsuccessful, and there were no attempts made in the 19th century to charge a husband criminally for raping his wife (Hasday, 2000; Pleck, 1987).

Not until the modern feminist movement of the 1960s and 1970s did marital rape once again become a significant topic of debate. Contemporary defenders of marital exemption have challenged feminist claims-making during the past 40 years, arguing that the state has no business intervening in the private affairs of married couples. Keeping the judicial system out of the bedroom, they argue, serves the interests of both the husband and the wife by protecting the privacy of the marital union. They also assert that exemption laws facilitate reconciliation and are ultimately good for the family. As Hasday (2000) notes, they claim that once the state intervenes, "the delicate shoots of love, trust, and closeness in a marriage will be trampled in a way unlikely ever to be undone." A less common defense of marital exemption is that the husband needs to be protected from a "vindictive wife" who might be tempted to use marital rape as leverage in a divorce case.

Discovering dating violence. In 1981, Makepeace published the results of a seminal study on dating violence. The apparent similarity in the victimization of women in dating relationships and marital unions led advocates for battered women to view dating violence as just one more example of male domination of women

(Dobash & Dobash, 1979). Many family violence researchers began to see dating violence as a microcosm of the larger problem of marital violence. Advocates and researchers have been quite successful in their claims-making, and today many high school and college campuses offer programs aimed at educating students about dating violence (Levy, 1991).

Date rape has also come to be recognized as a social problem only in recent years. Historically, the common perception of rape has been that of violent sexual assault committed by a stranger. In recent years, however, advocates for women have sought to redefine rape, asserting that a woman may be at far greater risk of being assaulted by an acquaintance at a party than by a stranger who attacks her as she walks home from that party.

According to some observers, date rape was not fully discovered as a social problem until the late 1980s, when the results of a study called the *Ms.* Magazine Campus Project on Sexual Assault were published in a series of articles by University of Arizona psychologist Mary Koss (e.g., 1992b, 1993). The study, which was funded by the National Institute of Mental Health, found that 27% of the college women surveyed (a sample of 6,159 women on 32 college campuses) had been victims of rape (15%) or attempted rape (12%). Although critics questioned these findings as "advocacy statistics" (Gilbert, 1998; Roiphe, 1993), the research put date rape on the map. The findings were widely cited in the popular press, the study was the subject of a 1991 U.S. Senate hearing on sexual assault, and the estimate that one in four college women is likely to be a victim of rape or attempted rape became the mantra of rape awareness programs on college campuses around the country. Young women were warned to be careful about who they date, to stay sober, to take their own cars and go only to public places on dates, and to be assertive in informing their dates of their physical boundaries (Gilbert, 1998).

Another form of abuse that is loosely related to dating violence is stalking, which Tjaden and Thoennes (2000b) define as "visual or physical proximity; nonconsensual communication; verbal, written, or implied threats; or a combination thereof that would cause fear in a reasonable person" (p. 5). Stalking has always existed, but it was largely ignored in criminal codes until the 1990s. Largely as a result of the advocacy of women's groups, stalking has attracted considerable media and scholarly attention in recent years, and today it is a criminal offense in all 50 states (Rosenfeld, 2000).

Discovering elder abuse. Elder abuse has been one of the last forms of family violence to receive societal attention, following the discovery of child abuse in the 1960s and marital violence in the early 1970s (Wolf & Pillemer, 1989). The first research on family elder abuse did not appear in the *Social Science Index* until 1981–1982 (Baumann, 1989). It was not until 1989 that a scholarly journal dedicated solely to the topic of elder abuse, the *Journal of Elder Abuse & Neglect,* began publishing.

The earliest federal government involvement in attempts to address elder abuse in the United States came in 1962, when Congress authorized payments to states to provide protective services for "persons with physical and/or mental limitations, who are unable to manage their own affairs . . . or who are neglected or exploited" (U.S. DHHS, as quoted in Wolf, 2000, p. 6). In 1974, Congress mandated adult protective services (APS) programs for all states. Public concern about elder abuse as a pervasive social problem began to grow in 1978, when a congressional subcommittee heard testimony on "parent battering." The image of the stressed and burdened adult daughter abusing an elderly parent linked elder abuse to child abuse and resulted in considerable media attention. Following the child abuse model, claims-makers successfully advocated for laws that make the reporting of suspected elder abuse mandatory for certain professionals (Wilber & McNeilly, 2001).

International Issues in the Discovery of Family Violence

Most Americans probably did not know much about Osama bin Laden, the Taliban, or the views of radical Islamic fundamentalists prior to the terrorist attacks on New York City and Washington, D.C., on September 11, 2001. These attacks not only awakened Americans to the threat of terrorism, they served to raise awareness about another shocking reality: the oppression of women around the world. Although human rights organizations had been publicizing the atrocities of the Taliban regime for some time before September 11, 2001, only after the attacks did the mistreatment of women in Afghanistan make headlines in major U.S. newspapers and magazines.

The mistreatment of women, however, is not unique to radical Islamic fundamentalism as practiced in pre-September 11 Afghanistan. Women and girls around the world have been and continue to be victimized by a vast array of cultural practices, including genital mutilation, foot binding, dowry death, child abandonment and infanticide, selective abortion of female fetuses, sexual exploitation, forced prostitution, and violent pornography (Holloway, 1994; Levesque, 2001).

Many of these practices continue today essentially as "customary laws"—that is, customs that predate international legal reforms and are still widely observed (Levesque, 2001). Although no longer legally endorsed, these customs are deeply rooted in some cultures and continue to influence contemporary practices. In China, for example, the cultural devaluation of girls and the state's one-child policy (which penalizes urban married couples for having more than one child and rural couples for having more than three) have combined to lead to speculation that infanticide has become widespread. Demographers estimate that approximately 12% of Chinese girl infants go "missing" each year (Riley, 1996). Another example of a cultural practice that indirectly contributes to abuse is India's dowry system. Because a bride's family must make long-term payments to the groom and the groom's family, some families may view female children as an unwanted burden, which may lead to female infanticide. Wives who cannot pay dowries are often abused and sometimes killed by their husbands or their husbands' families. The dowry system also likely contributes to high rates of suicide among young brides. Another cultural practice that victimizes women is the custom of female genital mutilation, in which prepubescent girls are subjected to the removal of the clitoral prepuce and the labia minora, presumably to ensure their virginity before marriage and their fidelity after marriage (Levesque, 2001). This practice continues today in parts of Africa and the Middle East.

Levesque (2001) cites estimates made by the United Nations that between 17% and 38% of the world's women are victims of intimate violence, with rates as high as 60% in developing countries. McWhirter (1999) reports that in Chile, "private violence" probably affects 25% of wives and 60% of families, but the country's cultural history of machismo, alcohol use, and acceptance of violence in general has hindered efforts to reduce private violence. According to Levesque (2001), criminal penalties for wife abuse in Chile apply only if the abuse resulted in 14 days of hospitalization for the victim or her loss of work, so prosecutions are rare, and in Brazil, the courts routinely acquit husbands and boyfriends who have killed women suspected of infidelity. In Russia, domestic violence rates are estimated to be four to

five times the rates
Approximate
year by inti
in any We
increase sin

New and Em

Violence betw
interpartner
attract atten
ners. Resear
homo
withi
attent
Stock
be tha
leave violent r
wives can leave th
ering violent relations
homosexuals, in part because   n a.   .ated
from their families of origin   isolated. In
addition, homosexual victims of .....ate partner violence stay in violent relationships for many of the same
reasons heterosexual victims do (Merrill & Wolfe, 2000).

Cross-cultural factors. As interest in cultural diversity
within the United States has grown, researchers, social
services providers, and health and mental health practitioners have increasingly come to recognize some of
the subtleties of cultural influences that they need to
consider when responding to accusations of family
violence. For example, Latino cultures generally place
high value on the closeness of extended family, on family obligation, and on respect for older people. Latino
children are expected to be obedient to their elders and
to represent the family well. Latino parents, therefore,
tend to be relatively authoritarian and are more likely
than Anglo-American parents to punish their children
physically for public displays of disrespect or disobedience. Latino families in the United States are also more
likely than Anglo families to live in poverty and to experience the stresses associated with recent immigration—factors that are likely to contribute to violence in
the family. Thus Latino families are especially likely to
come into contact with CPS agencies. As Fontes (2002)
notes, however, the vast majority of these families are
not dysfunctional or abusive, and they do not need the
strong arm of the state. What they need are counselors
who can explain to parents the dangers of punishing
children physically, who can teach them nonviolent

.arenting skills, and who can help them to cope with
isolation and other stressors often experienced by
.c minority families. Increasing awareness of cul-
.ifferences will help social services professionals
.rstand how best to help parents and protect

the case in child rearing, norms concerning
.tal relationship vary across ethnic and racial
.nd the higher levels of stress, poverty, low
.m, and substance abuse sometimes associ-
. minority status may contribute to violence.
.ant women may be socially isolated and
.ically dependent, and thus especially vul-
.e to violence in their intimate relationships
.olette & Barnett, 2000).

DEFINING FAMILY VIOLENCE: UNDERSTANDING THE SOCIAL CONSTRUCTION OF DEVIANCE DEFINITIONS

Just as the claims-making process is an important
part of the history and discovery of family violence, it
plays an important role in how family violence is
defined as well. Indeed, as Best (1989) notes, "claims-
makers do more than simply draw attention to particular social conditions. Claims-makers *shape our
sense of just what the problem is*" (p. xix; emphasis
added). Because competing claims-makers disagree
on exactly what constitutes abuse, any given definition
is rarely accepted as objectively correct. The debates
are important, however, because the winner essentially
earns the right to define family violence.

Two examples help to illustrate this point. Many
social scientists and child advocates believe that
corporal punishment is morally wrong and harmful
to children. Some go so far as to argue that corporal
punishment should be condemned as a form of child
maltreatment (Straus, 1994). It is important to recognize that all of these claims-makers make their arguments in an attempt to influence societal definitions
of child maltreatment. At present, theirs is a minority
opinion, as evidenced by the fact that surveys have
shown that a majority of U.S. parents spank, and every
U.S. state protects the right of a parent to spank as
long as the child is not injured. But if the voices
of these claims-makers become louder and more persuasive, spanking could conceivably be criminalized
in the United States, as it is in some Scandinavian
countries (Straus, 1994).

Equally controversial is the issue of the definition of rape. Currently, the FBI defines rape as "carnal knowledge of a female forcibly and against her will" (U.S. Department of Justice, 2002). *Carnal knowledge* has typically been defined very narrowly as forced penetration of the vagina by a penis, which essentially excludes other sexual acts (oral or anal sex) from the definition of rape. In the past 20 years, feminists have convincingly argued that all forced sexual acts should be legally condemned, and most states have in recent years rewritten and expanded their legal definitions of rape. Feminists have also advocated, with some success, for a broadening of the interpretation of "against her will," arguing that where there is no female desire or explicit consent there is, by definition, male coercion. From this more inclusive perspective, a woman whose ability to consent to sexual intercourse is compromised by the influence of alcohol or drugs or through some form of coercion is a victim of rape. Competing claims-makers criticize this perspective, saying that the definition of rape loses any meaning when it is expanded so much (Gilbert, 1998). The point here, for our purposes, is that claims-making influences what society defines as deviant behavior. What constitutes rape? The answer to that question depends, at least in part, on whom you ask. Whoever wins the debate earns the right to define the behavior and estimate its prevalence.

In the following subsections, we briefly examine some of the general issues critical to the process of defining family violence. We address specific definitions in greater detail in subsequent chapters.

What Is a Family?

In general, the term *family violence* refers to violence that takes place between immediate family members: husbands hitting wives, wives hitting husbands, parents hitting children, children hitting each other. Yet consideration of the topic of family violence invariably leads to the discussion of interpersonal violence outside the bounds of the traditional family. Cultural and legal definitions of what constitutes a family are changing, and as a result it is increasingly difficult to discuss marital violence, for example, without also considering violence between unmarried intimates, such as adult cohabitors, dating partners, and same-sex intimates. Until recently, the terms *marital violence* and *domestic violence* were usually used to refer to violence between spouses and sometimes between cohabiters. Today, the term *intimate* is more commonly used to refer to anyone in a very close

personal relationship, frequently a sexual relationship. The U.S. Bureau of Justice and the Centers for Disease Control and Prevention currently use the term *intimate partner violence* to refer to violence between spouses, ex-spouses, or separated spouses; between cohabitors or ex-cohabitors; between boyfriends or ex-boyfriends and girlfriends or ex-girlfriends; and between same-sex partners or ex-partners.

Many of the forms of violence that we discuss in this volume occur outside of families as well as within them. Child sexual abuse often occurs within the family, but not always. Elders may be abused by family members, but they are also neglected by society more generally. Although our primary focus here is on the family, in the following chapters we include discussions of some abusive situations that exist outside the family unit.

What Is Violence?

Violence may be defined as "an act carried out with the intention of, or an act perceived as having the intention of, physically hurting another person" (Steinmetz, 1987, p. 729). Although this definition offers a clear and concise starting point, for our purposes it presents problems. On one hand, it is too narrow, because it fails to include some forms of maltreatment—such as psychological abuse and child neglect—discussed in this book. On the other hand, it is too broad, because some forms of physical aggression—for example, corporal punishment—are not generally considered to be family violence. There is some risk in defining family violence too broadly, because as the definition comes to encompass more and more behaviors, it may come to lose any real meaning (see Box 1.1).

To illuminate the matter further, Gelles and Straus (1979) have proposed that family violence may be conceptualized along two separate continua. One continuum, legitimate-illegitimate, represents the degree to which social norms legitimate violence. The other continuum, instrumental-expressive, represents the degree to which violence is used as a means to an end—"to induce another person to carry out or refrain from an act" (p. 557)—or as an end in itself (e.g., hitting someone out of anger). These two continua provide the basis for a four-cell taxonomy of family violence. *Legitimate-expressive violence* is cathartic for the person who uses the violence. This is reflected in the belief, however misguided, that it is sometimes better to express your anger physically than to hold it in, as long as it is expressed in culturally acceptable ways. *Legitimate-instrumental*

Box 1.1 Distinguishing Family Maltreatment From Family Violence

Despite past relative indifference to the victimization of women and children in the family, today family violence is nearly universally condemned. Most countries have enacted laws that explicitly protect women and children, and the ones that have not are under considerable international pressure to do so (Levesque, 2001). The question of how to define family violence, however, remains a matter of considerable debate. In recent years, activists have tended to advocate for "violence-free" families, and in doing so they have defined more and more behaviors as abusive. Emery and Laumann-Billings (1998) point out that these ever-broadening definitions are problematic and note that they are "troubled by the potential for overreaching in defining family violence" (p. 121). They suggest making a distinction between *family maltreatment*, defined as abuse that involves minimal physical or sexual endangerment, and *family violence*, defined as abuse that results in serious physical injury or sexual violation.

It is important to make this distinction for two reasons. First, if the trend toward broadening the definition of family violence continues, the term will essentially become meaningless. Surveys indicate, for example, that an overwhelming majority of children are pushed, grabbed, or hit by their siblings. This "sibling violence" was the focus of increasing concern during the 1990s (Finkelhor & Dziuba-Leatherman, 1994). If one chooses to define sibling aggression as family violence, Emery and Laumann-Billings (1998) argue, then almost all children are victims (and perpetrators) of abuse. After all, how many siblings *don't* push, shove, or occasionally hit one another? If sibling pushing constitutes abuse, then the meaning of *abuse* is diluted. Emery and Laumann-Billings maintain that however inappropriate sibling pushing and hitting may be, it is common behavior that probably should be clearly distinguished from more serious forms of child abuse.

The second reason it is important to make a distinction between family maltreatment and family violence is that such a distinction should help social service agencies to identify appropriate interventions. Through the 1980s and 1990s, as Americans became more aware of child abuse and definitions of child abuse broadened, reports of child abuse increased. This meant that a higher percentage of child protective services resources went to policing and investigating reports, two-thirds of which went unsubstantiated. This shift in focus came at the expense of social service agencies' historic commitment to offering support to families in need. Most parents reported for child maltreatment are not guilty of severe endangerment, and such parents are more likely to "benefit from interventions designed to support them through the challenges of parenting than from interventions that first label them as abusive" (Emery & Laumann-Billings, 1998, p. 125). A clear distinction between families with problems of maltreatment and violent families could also help CPS agencies to identify and respond to cases of severe family violence more decisively, possibly saving lives. According to some estimates, between 30% and 50% of child maltreatment fatality victims are children who were already known to CPS or law enforcement officials, a problem that is sometimes blamed on an overburdened system.

---

violence is culturally accepted, means-to-an end violence. This is the form of violence most often defended by family advocates who endorse spanking as an effective means of controlling behavior but believe that parents should administer such punishment only when they are not angry.

Illegitimate-instrumental violence is any culturally condemned form of violence that the actor claims is necessary to curb bad behavior on the part of the victim. Finally, *illegitimate-expressive violence* involves lashing out in anger; this is the most recognized and condemned kind of family violence.

A Definition of Family Violence

The above conceptualization of family violence is problematic for our purposes. For one thing, because it includes violence that is not typically condemned in American society (e.g., parents spanking children, siblings hitting one another), it is probably too broad. Although we will consider the potential consequences of culturally condoned violence in this volume, our primary interest is in violence that crosses the legitimacy line—violence that has been successfully labeled *abusive* by claims-makers.

In addition, limiting the definition of family violence to acts that result in physical harm to individuals fails to capture the full range of harmful interactions that can take place within the family. Sexual abuse, for example, may only occasionally involve physical violence but can have damaging effects that last a lifetime. Child neglect and emotional abuse are forms of maltreatment that can be even more devastating than physical violence. A woman can be psychologically tormented and controlled by a man who never touches her. Elders can be harmed through neglect rather than physical assault. Rape, both within and outside of marriage, can be void of physical violence or restraint.

In the end, then, we need a definition of family violence that is narrow enough to avoid labeling every family potentially violent and broad enough to include the concept of nonphysical violence. Roger Levesque (2001) offers just such a definition: "Family violence includes family members' acts of omission or commission resulting in physical abuse, sexual abuse, emotional abuse, neglect, or other forms of maltreatment that hamper individuals' healthy development" (p. 13). This is only a starting point, however. In the following chapters, we address in detail the definitions of specific forms of family violence. As will quickly become obvious, the ongoing debates concerning definitions and methods for assessing family violence are among the most contentious in the social sciences (see Hamberger, 1994).

Family Violence and the Law

Ultimately, societal norms concerning family violence are formalized in laws, and every U.S. state has struggled with this difficult task. Not all forms of family violence are equally difficult to define legally. In general, child sexual abuse laws focus on *perpetrator actions,* which results in far less ambiguity concerning the "legitimate-illegitimate" distinction than is the case with other forms of child maltreatment. Legal definitions of physical marital violence are also relatively unambiguous, because adult assault laws apply to married couples. Essentially, at least in the eyes of the law, there is no legitimate marital violence.

The laws concerning physical abuse, neglect, and psychological abuse, in contrast, tend to focus on *injury outcomes* and, as a result, are far less clearly defined. The "harm" caused by psychological abuse of a child or elder is rarely externally visible. As a result, the legal distinction between, for example, legitimate and illegitimate forms of verbal punishment is far from clear. "Harm" may be more easily measured in cases of neglect, but with neglect the problem becomes one of making a legal distinction between parents who have neglected their children and parents who are guilty of nothing more than being poor.

PRACTICE, POLICY, AND PREVENTION ISSUES

Because societal recognition of family violence has grown over time, it is impossible to pinpoint exactly when this issue attained the status of a social problem. One could reasonably argue that, despite growing awareness between the mid-1800s and the mid-1900s, family violence was still widely tolerated until the 1960s and 1970s, when it came to be seen as a full-fledged problem. With this recognition came the connected belief that family violence should not be tolerated. Any history of the discovery of family violence, therefore, should conclude with a discussion of the numerous policies and practices introduced in recent years to help prevent family violence.

As with the prevention of crime more generally, family violence prevention is confronted with two pervasive tensions. The first concerns the relative importance of prevention versus **intervention.** *Prevention* refers to social support and education programs designed to prevent family violence from occurring in the first place. *Intervention* refers to societal responses to family violence after it occurs; such responses include programs to identify and protect victims, criminal justice sanctions for perpetrators, and various treatment options for offenders and victims.

The second tension relates more specifically to competing perspectives on intervention. Should society focus on protecting victims and punishing offenders, or on providing treatment and services for offenders and victims? The justice and protection response is reflected in a number of policies—**mandatory reporting laws**, **mandatory arrest laws**, increased criminal sanctions, restraining orders—that have been implemented to identify abuse, protect victims, and punish perpetrators.

History helps to put the current social policy debates in context. Once family violence became fully recognized in the 1960s and 1970s, the most immediate and urgent concerns of authorities were the identification and protection of abuse victims and the punishment of offenders. Given the prior history of indifference toward family violence, this policy emphasis on protection and justice seems reasonable. However, this response has often come at the expense of a societal commitment to **primary prevention** and efforts to help abusive families. With most of the resources available to combat family violence committed to the criminal justice response, little is left for the support and services needed by vulnerable families.

Table 1.1 lists a number of family violence prevention and intervention strategies targeted toward children and adults. In the discussion that follows, we introduce these strategies briefly; we consider each in more detail in subsequent chapters.

Prevention of Family Violence

It is possible to approach the subject of family violence prevention on many different levels. One might begin with a discussion of the social problems directly or indirectly related to family violence (e.g., poverty, unemployment, inadequate housing, illegitimacy). Although these enduring and complicated problems are causally relevant, they are, for the most part, well beyond the scope of our discussion in this book. More manageable are the various prevention strategies that focus specifically on community education and social services for families.

Family support and training programs. A teenager cannot legally drive an automobile without first receiving appropriate training and passing a test to obtain a license, but the same teenager can become a parent without any interference from the state. No doubt it has to be this way, but the fact remains that many who assume the role of parent are not adequately prepared to do so. In recent years, family support and training programs have become increasingly common as part of community efforts to enhance the knowledge and competence of new parents. Although these programs

vary, many involve home visits with at-risk (i.e., poor, single, young) parents of newborns or expectant mothers. These contacts give the service providers opportunities to evaluate the home setting and to work with the parents in a safe, nonconfrontational environment. Such programs provide at-risk families with networks of support in hopes of preventing the social isolation that often contributes to abuse. The goals of such primary prevention programs typically include increasing parents' knowledge about child development, child management (including nonviolent approaches to child discipline), positive family functioning, and triggers of abuse (National Clearinghouse on Child Abuse and Neglect, 1998b). Sometimes programs also provide parents with help and advice on physical and mental health, job training, and treatment for drug and alcohol problems (Godenzi & De Puy, 2001). Evaluation research on some of these programs has been very promising, suggesting many positive outcomes (Daro & Donnelly, 2002; Guterman, 2001).

Although in-home intervention programs typically focus on child abuse prevention, it is important to note that they could potentially influence marital violence rates as well. Because child abuse and marital violence are correlated and share many risk markers, families identified as being at high risk for child abuse are also likely to be at high risk for marital violence. To the degree that programs provide families with networks of support and emphasize positive family functioning, violence-free interactions, and recognition of the triggers of violence, they might have ameliorative effects on rates of marital violence (Wolfe & Jaffe, 1999).

School-based programs. School-based programs have obvious appeal because they are an inexpensive way to reach many children, teens, and college students. The most common programs target school-age children (ages 6–12) and emphasize primary prevention and detection of sexual abuse (Reppucci, Land, & Haugaard, 1998). The overwhelming majority of school districts in the United States offer sexual abuse programs, and research suggests that these programs are successful in increasing children's knowledge and in teaching prevention skills. Schools can also be suitable places for teaching young children about marital violence and for identifying children exposed to marital violence (Wolfe & Jaffe, 1999). Whether school-based programs actually reduce the incidence of sexual abuse is a matter of some debate (Wurtele, 2002).

Many scholars see the adolescent years (13–18), when children often form their first intimate

Table 1.1   A Model for Prevention and Intervention

Age Group Targeted	Prevention (Designed to Stop Violence Before It Occurs)	Intervention (Response to Victims and Offenders)
Infants and preschoolers (ages 0–5)	*Family support and training programs:* Education and social support for at-risk families	*Family support and training programs:* Intervention services for marginally abusive families *Foster care and adoption programs:* Provide alternative homes when conditions warrant removal *Treatment programs:* Programs for victims
School age to high school (ages 6–17)	*School-based education:* Programs to educate young children about inappropriate touching; programs to educate junior high and high school students about violence-free intimate relationships	*Foster care and adoption programs:* Provide alternative homes when conditions warrant removal *Treatment programs:* Programs for victims and offenders
College age and adults (over age 17)	*College-based education:* Programs on violence-free intimate relationships and rape *Community awareness campaigns:* Campaigns to promote awareness about family violence	*Mandatory reporting policies:* Professional mandates to report child abuse, elder abuse, and, in some states, domestic violence *Mandatory arrest and no-drop policies:* Policies that essentially force police and the courts to arrest and prosecute offenders *Treatment programs:* Programs for offenders and victims

SOURCE: Adapted from Wolfe and Jaffe (1999, p. 137).

relationships, as an ideal time to teach children about the importance of violence-free intimate relationships (Godenzi & De Puy, 2001). High schools commonly offer a variety of learning opportunities—school assemblies, lectures, videos, drama groups, discussion groups—in hopes of promoting healthy relationships and reducing dating and marital violence. Evaluation research suggests that such programs result in positive changes in knowledge and attitudes, and some reduction of violence perpetration. At this point, however, the long-term benefits are unknown (Wekerle & Wolfe, 1999).

At the college level, discussions about the importance of healthy relationships can be broadened to include date rape. Date rape programs can have both primary prevention and intervention goals, including teaching definitions of date rape and providing information on its prevalence; consciousness-raising regarding the sexual rights of women, rape myths, and traditional sex roles; and assertiveness training for women (Holcomb, Savage, Seehafer, & Waalkes, 2002). Although less common, school-based programs designed to educate parents have also been presented (Hebert, Lavoie, & Parent, 2002).

Community awareness campaigns. One of the easiest and most cost-efficient family violence prevention techniques is public education through advertisements and public service announcements. Many of the social movement organizations and federal agencies devoted to the family violence problem see themselves, at least in part, as public educators. One prominent example is the Family Violence Prevention Fund, which, in collaboration with the Advertising Council, has initiated several public service campaigns. Among these is "Teach Early," a domestic violence campaign directed toward men that sends the message, "What they learn as boys, they do as men. That's why we need to teach our sons and other boys in our lives that violence against women is wrong. Now, when they need to hear it most." The campaign includes a 30-second television announcement, radio and print spots, and a toll-free information number (Family Violence and Prevention Fund, 2002). Evaluation research on education campaigns like this one have found that following the periods of the campaigns, people have more knowledge about family violence and are more willing to report family violence (Wolfe & Jaffe, 1999).

Another example comes from Canada, where the "Violence—You Can Make a Difference" campaign attempted to raise awareness about both child and adult family violence. Television and radio advertisements, along with "fact sheets" distributed nationally, provided tips on anger management, how to help abuse victims, safety plans, coping with family violence, and getting help. The campaign focused specifically on identifying early warning signs of violence, especially from the perspective of the aggressor (Godenzi & De Puy, 2001).

It is becoming increasingly common for companies to take an active interest in the family lives of their employees. Employer-based initiatives aimed at preventing family violence include conscious attempts to facilitate stress-free working environments, given the awareness that work-related stress often spills over into the family. More common, however, are workplace education and information campaigns designed to help employees who are dealing with family violence. Many of these programs focus specifically on IPV, in part because of the potential costs of reduced employee performance that result from such violence (Urban & Bennett, 1999).

Intervention Strategies

Mandatory reporting laws. Within 5 years following the publication of Kempe's influential research on the "battered child syndrome," every U.S. state had enacted laws mandating that professionals report all cases of suspected child abuse. Arguably, no other kind of legislation has been as widely and as rapidly adopted in the history of the United States (Zellman & Fair, 2002). Initially, the laws pertained primarily to medical personnel who suspect physical abuse, but since their initial passage the list of professionals required to report has grown, as has the list of abusive behaviors they must report. Today, doctors, nurses, social workers, mental health professionals, and teachers and other school staff are required to report any suspected physical, sexual, or emotional child abuse.

Mandatory reporting protections for adult victims have also become more common. Almost all states, for example, now require medical and social services professionals to report suspected cases of elder abuse (Moskowitz, 1997), and a few states mandate the reporting of suspicions of marital violence (Hyman, Schillinger, & Lo, 1995).

Mandatory reporting laws have generally been heralded as a triumph of family violence advocacy. No doubt the benefits of these laws include increased identification of abuse, which has led to improvements in protecting the powerless and holding perpetrators accountable. Increasingly, however, such laws have been the source of some controversy. Critics point to a number of unintended consequences. Some advocates for women, for example, have expressed concern that mandatory reporting laws might inhibit women from seeking care or make them vulnerable to retaliation (Hyman et al., 1995). These laws also often put people in the helping professions in a difficult position, essentially forcing them to violate the confidences of their clients. Many professionals who are required to report suspected abuse see themselves as better equipped to help needy families than the overburdened CPS and APS systems, so they choose to ignore the reporting laws (Melton, 2002; Zellman & Fair, 2002). Research evidence suggests that the more professionals know about the child protection system (i.e., the more formal training they have), the *less* likely they are to report suspected cases of child maltreatment (Melton, 2002).

Family preservation, foster care, and adoption. One of the most controversial issues within child protection circles is the question of when children should be temporarily or permanently removed from their homes. Child protective services agencies are mandated to make child protection their top priority, and no one questions this mandate. But when a child is being abused, what course of action will serve the best interests of the child? Should CPS attempt to maintain the family unit, offering support and training in hopes that abuse will not occur again in the future? Should CPS remove the child from the home and place him or her in a temporary setting with the hope of eventually returning the child to the home? Or should the state seek a more permanent solution for the child, such as adoption or placement in an orphanage?

Proponents of the family preservation model maintain that the best place to raise a child is in a nuclear family, and that children can be safely left in their homes *if* their communities offer vulnerable families the social services and training they need. These advocates point out that the foster care system is not a panacea, noting the relatively high rates of abuse in foster families (U.S. DHHS, 2000). They also praise the successes of various family preservation programs around the country, such as Homebuilder. This program, which began in Washington and has now been implemented in several states, provides vulnerable families with intensive in-home help in the areas of financial management, nonviolent discipline, anger management, and education (Melton, 2002).

The commitment to family reunification is not without its critics, of course. Several highly publicized child deaths in recent years have served as reminders of the potential dangers of reuniting children with parents who have been abusive in the past. However, not all critics of family reunification embrace foster care as an alternative to keeping children in possibly dangerous homes. Some, in fact, advocate placing children in orphanages instead (see, e.g., McKenzie, 1998).

Criminal justice issues. Despite the fact that domestic violence has long been recognized as a crime, police discretion in making arrests—combined with family privacy norms, cultural tolerance, and the reluctance of women to press charges—has meant that criminal sanctions have often been the exception rather than the rule. For example, as late as the 1980s, only about 1 in 10 police interventions in domestic violence situations resulted in arrest (Gelles & Straus, 1988). Many researchers and women's advocates saw these data as a sign of societal indifference to and continuing tolerance of the abuse of women. Citing the deterrence doctrine (see Chapter 2), they argued that a society that punishes violent family members should have less family violence. A husband who hits his wife is guilty of criminal assault, and he should be punished as a criminal. Punishing family offenders would begin, these advocates argued, with the limiting of discretion in the criminal justice system. Mandatory arrest policies soon became the most widely implemented and

highly publicized way of placing limits on justice system discretion in cases of domestic violence.

The mandatory arrest movement was given empirical legitimacy in 1984, when sociologists Lawrence Sherman and Richard Berk published their findings from the Minneapolis Domestic Violence Experiment, a pioneering study of the deterrent effects of arrest. Sherman and Berk devised a system by which suspects in domestic disturbances were randomly assigned to one of three police interventions: mediation, separation, and arrest. Subsequently collected self-report and arrest data revealed that suspects who had been arrested were less likely to reoffend than were suspects in either of the other two groups. The results of this study were widely disseminated and had a significant impact on police department policies around the country. By the late 1980s, many state and local governments were strongly encouraging or requiring their police departments to make arrests in domestic violence cases when probable cause existed (Ferraro, 1989). Although subsequent research has produced mixed results (for a review, see Garner & Maxwell, 2000), the impact of social science research on criminal justice policy is difficult to question.

Criminal justice system discretion in domestic violence cases is also limited by "no-drop" prosecution policies, which require prosecutors to move forward with criminal proceedings even if the victim has recanted or asked that the prosecution cease (for a review, see Robbins, 1999). Although some praise no-drop policies as a move forward in protecting women, others suggest that such policies disempower women by treating them as helpless victims (Epstein, 1999).

Treating offenders and victims. The deterrence doctrine assumes that people rationally weigh the costs and benefits of their actions. From this perspective, the increased legal costs that offenders incur as a result of mandatory arrest and no-drop policies should lead to lower rates of violence. Increasingly, however, the notion that perpetrators freely choose to commit violence has been challenged by researchers and mental health professionals who argue that perpetrators are psychologically disordered and need treatment for their deviance.

The interest in treatment is part of a more general trend toward *medicalization,* in which deviant behaviors that have historically been defined as "sinfulness" or "badness" requiring punishment have been redefined as "sickness" or "disease" requiring treatment (Conrad & Schneider, 1992). This trend has been the source of some controversy because, taken to its extreme, medicalization suggests that the perpetrators of violence have little or no control over their behavior. How can offenders be punished for behavior over which they have no control? Most of the people who advocate for treatment, however, do not take the illness assumptions quite this far. In fact, it is very common for advocates to argue that family violence perpetrators should be both punished and treated. The punishment communicates that violence will not be tolerated, and the treatment helps the perpetrators to recognize why they are prone to violence.

Discussion of the various methods of treating perpetrators of family violence is well beyond the scope of this chapter; suffice it to say for now that there are numerous treatment responses to violent families and individuals, and many of these treatments are the subjects of some debate. (We discuss many different treatment methods in detail in subsequent chapters.) Treatments for the perpetrators of child physical abuse, emotional abuse, and neglect most often focus on the unlearning of inappropriate parenting techniques as well as on anger control and stress management (Miller-Perrin & Perrin, 1999). In treatments for perpetrators of sexual abuse, the illness model is more uniformly endorsed, with some employing drug therapies designed to control sexual impulses (Maletzky & Field, 2003).

One continuing debate in the treatment of IPV concerns whether couples' therapy is appropriate for violent partners or whether treatment should focus on modifying the behavior of the batterer. Those who support the use of couples' therapy argue that intimate partner violence is often mutual and is often a product of a couple's interaction patterns (Margolin & Burman, 1993). Many advocates for abused women, on the other hand, maintain that U.S. society's patriarchal nature is the primary explanation for men's violence against women, and so treatment emphasizing couple interactions is misguided and potentially harmful (Trute, 1998).

Treating victims can also sometimes reduce subsequent rates of violence by empowering victims to take an active role in preventing the abuse from happening again. A battered women may learn in counseling, for example, that she is not responsible for the violence, that her children are adversely affected by the violence, and that she can and should take steps to protect herself and her children.

Shelters and hotlines. Perhaps the most visible form of intervention in domestic violence is the battered women's shelter. Since the first such shelter opened in England in the early 1970s, battered women's shelters have become commonplace. Today, most large metropolitan areas have shelters that provide numerous services, including counseling, social support groups, child care, economic support, and job training. The U.S. government took an active role in promoting the shelter movement in 1994 when it passed the first Violence Against Women Act (VAWA). The VAWA, which was reauthorized in 2000, has provided funding for shelters and established the National Domestic Violence Hotline (1-800-799-SAFE). Some observers have argued that although implementing VAWA provisions has been expensive, the law meets the needs of battered women so effectively that it may have saved U.S. taxpayers billions of dollars in medical costs and social services (Clark, Biddle, & Martin, 2002).

Coordinated community responses. Many communities have attempted to coordinate the implementation of a number of the kinds of prevention and intervention strategies listed in Table 1.1. Such a coordinated community response to child abuse prevention, for example, might include education campaigns to raise awareness, in-home visitations of at-risk and marginally abusive families, school-based education on sex abuse, and treatment programs for victims and offenders. A truly communitywide effort of this magnitude would involve doctors, nurses, social workers, police, lawyers, judges, and others in the community willing to take an active role.

The most commonly cited coordinated community response to the problem of domestic violence is the Domestic Abuse Intervention Project (DAIP), which was implemented in the 1980s in Duluth, Minnesota. The DAIP was the first community project to coordinate the responses of police, lawyers, and judges in an effort to limit justice system discretion and ensure at least a minimum legal reaction against perpetrators and the protection of victims. The "Duluth model," as the design of the DAIP has come to be known, has also been influential in the creation of community education and treatment programs for male batterers. Various aspects of this model have been adopted in communities across the United States, and the model has been the subject of much discussion and research (Shepard & Pence, 1999).

Box 1.2 Common Myths About Family Violence

Family violence is a topic that generates many opinions. These opinions, however, are not always well-informed. Without sufficient knowledge, people are likely to develop "commonsense" understandings that may not be accurate. Overly simplistic explanations for the occurrence of family violence are sometimes repeated so often that they become accepted as fact (Gelles & Cornell, 1990). In part because some myths contain elements of truth, they are often difficult to dispel. Providing accurate information regarding such myths is one important role of the social scientist.

Myth 1: Family Violence Is Uncommon

Because family violence is hidden, subjectively defined, and difficult to measure, it is impossible to estimate precisely how frequently it occurs. However, the fact that it is rarely seen and difficult to measure should not be taken to mean that it rarely occurs. In fact, if there is one point about which all family violence experts seemingly agree, it is that family violence is far more common than is generally realized (Gelles & Cornell, 1990).

Perhaps the best way to understand this point is by envisioning our fears about crime and violence. What do we fear? Whom do we fear? Parents may fear that their children will be snatched from their bedrooms or from a playground. Women may fear that strangers will jump from behind bushes and rape them at knifepoint. Since September 11, 2001, many Americans may fear that they will be victims of further terrorist attacks. People may deal with their fears in any of a number of ways, perhaps by installing home security systems, buying guns, carrying pepper spray, or even storing gas masks. Because acts of random crime do happen, we know that our fears are not completely unfounded. Yet are these the kinds of things we should fear the most?

True, there have been several widely publicized child abductions and murders in recent years. The overwhelming majority of child homicide victims, however, are not snatched from their homes. Approximately 1,200 children die annually as a result of abuse or neglect, and an estimated 50% of all homicide victims under the age of 10 are killed by family members (U.S. Department of Health and Human Services, 2002b). True, many women are raped by strangers, but rape statistics show that one can reasonably argue that a woman is far more vulnerable at a party where the alcohol is flowing than she is on any city street. And although approximately 3,000 people died on September 11, 2001, in what is one of the saddest days in American history, it is important to remember that in the same year, 2,387 people were killed by family members or by their boyfriends or girlfriends. As no doubt some of the more than 6,000 murder victims in 2001 whose assailants are unknown were also killed by family members, the annual number of homicides committed by intimates is likely over 3,000 (U.S. Department of Justice, 2002). The loss of life on September 11 was an anomaly, an aberration, but the number of intimate homicides in 2001 was normal. Every year, in fact, some 3,000 Americans are killed by family members. Again we ask, What, exactly, should we fear?

We could expand the analogy, of course, to include less severe forms of violence. In the end, the conclusion is the same: What we fear and what we *should* fear are not always the same things. Violence in the United States is, perhaps more than society cares to acknowledge, often intrafamilial. The risk of victimization and injury, at least for women and children, is likely greater at home than on the most dangerous city streets.

Myth 2: Family Violence Has Reached Epidemic Levels

Given all that Americans read and hear today about the "increasingly serious" problem of family violence in newspapers and on television news broadcasts and newsmagazines, along with the frightening statistics publicized by some organizations devoted to addressing family violence, it is tempting to assume that the prevalence of family violence has reached an all-time high and is getting worse. As observers have noted, a problem that is getting worse is more likely than less pressing issues to receive public attention, generate concern, and motivate people to action (Best, 2001).

Even a cursory look at the history summarized in this chapter, however, serves as a reminder to us that family violence is likely not a problem that is getting worse. Compared to children in the past, in fact, today's children are probably exposed to far less neglect and mistreatment. The "good old-fashioned whippings" that our grandparents may have received when they were young would probably not be considered an acceptable form of discipline by most Americans today. Given the history of power differences between "man and wife," we might similarly conclude that wives today are less likely to be victims of violence in their homes than they were in past times.

But what about more recent trends? In our idealized *Leave It to Beaver* image of the 1950s family, it is hard to imagine abuse. Somehow, in today's modern, urbanized, anonymous world, family violence seems more feasible. Or one might hypothesize that family violence seems a natural by-product of the so-called breakdown of the family. On the other hand, given that the social and legal costs of family violence have risen dramatically in recent years, perhaps it would be more reasonable to hypothesize that rates of family violence have declined.

The empirical evidence on this topic is inconclusive. It is true that the past 50 years have seen dramatic increases in the reporting of family violence, but these increases reflect changes in professional and legal responses more than anything else. Self-report survey data from the 1970s and 1980s suggest declines in the rates of family violence, leading some of the most well-known family violence advocates and researchers to conclude that the problem is actually decreasing (Gelles & Straus, 1988).

Whatever the actual pattern, there is no evidence of a contemporary family violence epidemic. It is important to note, however, that one does not have to be convinced that a problem is getting worse in order to be concerned about the problem. Individuals and organizations devoted to addressing family violence should not be threatened by the possibility that rates of family violence are declining. This is good news; it suggests that the prevention efforts of the past 50 years have been somewhat successful. Reductions in the problem need not, and should not, reduce society's resolve to eliminate the problem.

Myth 3: Risk Markers Cause Family Violence

Despite the fact that statisticians repeatedly caution us not to do so, it is tempting to equate correlation with causation. It is equally tempting to assume that a correlate of family violence, even if its causal significance is empirically and theoretically justified, is *the* cause of family violence. The presence of certain risk markers may increase the probability of family violence, but risk markers alone do not completely explain family violence.

Two examples may help to illustrate this point. First, the link between family violence and low socioeconomic status is largely unquestioned, but this empirical connection should be interpreted with a degree of caution for a couple of reasons: (a) People who are poor and lack other resources may be more likely than those who are better-off to turn to police and social service agencies, and therefore are more likely to be represented in official estimates of family violence (Hampton & Newberger, 1988); and (b) even if we acknowledge the statistical viability of social class as a risk marker, the evidence does not suggest that only poor families are violent or that poor families are always violent.

A history of family violence is also a commonly recognized correlate of family violence. Studies have consistently found that abusive adults have been exposed to significantly more childhood violence than nonabusive adults (Egeland, 1993). As with socioeconomic status, however, one must be careful not to overinterpret these data. A childhood history of abuse is neither a necessary nor a sufficient cause of adult violence. At best, the data suggest that individuals who were abused as children, or who witnessed abuse in childhood, are more likely to be abusive adults. They are not predetermined to be abusive adults. In fact, the majority of abused children do not grow up to be abusive adults (Widom, 1989b).

Myth 4: Victims "Ask For It"

Some have chosen to explain family violence by focusing on the victims. A woman is beaten because she "nags" or "drinks too much," or perhaps she comes from a "dysfunctional family" (Tilden, 1989). Or perhaps she is a "masochistic martyr" who actually enjoys being beaten (Shainess, 1979). Those who blame battered women for not "just leaving" violent men often make such criticisms. Implicit in many of these assertions are assumptions that something must be wrong with battered women, that they somehow deserve the violence directed at them, and that they should do something to alleviate the violence. This shifting of the blame from the perpetrator to the victim is inherently unfair (see Hotaling & Sugarman, 1990). No one deserves to be hit. No one "asks for it." The perpetrator, not the victim, bears responsibility for the abuse.

Myth 5: Family Violence Sometimes "Just Happens," and We Should Not Make Too Much of It

Some believe that family members can be expected to "lose control" from time to time, that parents and spouses sometimes need to "blow off steam." They may rationalize that a man who hits his wife is not really violent, he just had a bad day at work and lost his temper. Or they may rationalize that a woman is generally a good mother, but her kids were really acting up and she only hit them because she lost control temporarily. Some people believe that such actions are inevitable—even "natural"—and are hardly worthy of serious societal reaction.

The ludicrous nature of the "it just happens" justification becomes clear, however, when one recognizes that stranger violence is not so easily dismissed (Gelles & Straus, 1988). When one stranger assaults another, we do not allow the assailant to dismiss his actions as a momentary loss of control, a need to blow off steam, or a reaction to a bad day at work. Nor do we allow the assailant to blame the victim. We are appropriately intolerant of stranger violence. According to Gelles and Straus (1988), family members hit family members because "they can." That is, because society has generally accepted the "it just happens" justification, the social and legal costs attached to family violence are very low.

Myth 6: Minor Acts of Family Violence Are Always Trivial and Inconsequential

Although we should be careful not to equate minor acts of violence with severe violence (Emery & Laumann-Billings, 1998), it is not true that minor violence is always trivial and inconsequential. Parents who push, shove, and occasionally hit one another are implicitly endorsing such violence as the way to settle disagreements. The same can be said for parents who condone pushing and hitting between siblings and for parents who hit their chil-

The potential negative effects of minor violence within the family, including corporal punishment, have long been the subject of considerable debate, and we discuss this issue in more detail in subsequent chapters. We should note here, however, that social scientists are increasingly willing to condemn the use of "legitimate violence," in large part because of the belief that such violence sometimes "spills over" into other forms of violence both within and outside the family (Straus, 1994).

Myth 7: Women Who Claim Date Rape Are "Lying," "Deserve What They Got," or Were "Asking for It"

Feminists have argued, with some success, that all forced and coerced acts of sex should be legally condemned as rape. They have also encouraged us to think more broadly about the notion of "against her will" and to include in definitions of rape various nonviolent ways in which a woman might be coerced into sex. This trend has contributed to some observers' belief that women who report date rape were not "really" raped. They suggest that perhaps the woman "led him on" and was essentially asking for it. Or perhaps she feels guilty about a sexual experience she now sees as negative and alleges rape out of vindictiveness. There is, however, no evidence to indicate that changing definitions of rape have led to a wave of rape accusations. In fact, although self-report estimates of rape rates are obviously much higher with the more inclusive definitions (Koss, 1988), accusations of rape remain very *uncommon* on college campuses (Gilbert, 1998). Rape is such an underreported crime that exaggeration and false reports seem especially unlikely.

Box 1.3 Personalizing Family Violence Research

Academic discussions of social problems have a way of depersonalizing those problems. Social scientists are trained to be scientific and to approach any given topic with a degree of objectivity. As a result, as you read this book, you may find it easy to distance yourself from the words on the page, to think of the victims and perpetrators discussed as mere statistics or participants in research studies. It is important to remember, however, that behind every research finding and every generalization there are real people. In reading the following chapters, don't forget that family violence affects real victims.

The media accounts at the opening of this chapter serve as reminders of the human tragedy of family violence. Each of these stories was unique enough, or horrific enough, that it made headlines in the national press. There are, of course, thousands upon thousands of other stories that never attract media attention. Behind each of these stories there is sadness. In our own work as teachers and counselors we often encounter terrible stories personally. Consider the case of Markus, a cute and precocious 7-year-old boy who went to live with his father and stepmother in 1990 after his biological mother abandoned him. Markus's father asked that the boy be admitted to the inpatient psychiatric unit of a local hospital because he and his wife were unable to keep him from running away from their home in the middle of the night. Markus's father admitted that they had sometimes resorted to "shackling" Markus to his bed so he would not run away. His stepmother also revealed that she and her husband had never really wanted Markus to move into their home but that they had to take him because his biological mother had rejected him. Young Markus had now been rejected by his mother, father, and stepmother. Imagine being 7 years old and facing the realization that your mother and father neither love you nor want you. No wonder he wanted to run away.

We sometimes wonder what became of Markus. He came in and out of our lives, and we moved on to other matters very quickly. But for Markus it was likely not so easy to move on. He would be in his 20s now—a grown man. We can only hope and pray that he survived and made a life for himself. But even if Markus's life now includes success and happiness, we must acknowledge that the impact of his childhood experiences will be with him forever. Does one ever recover from parental rejection?

GOALS OF THIS BOOK

We have many reasons for writing this book. First, we want to summarize the available research on the topic of family violence so that our readers will gain substantive knowledge. In the process, we also want to challenge many common myths about family violence (for discussion of some of these myths, see Box 1.2). Second, we want to foster an understanding of the magnitude of the problem and the devastation it causes (see Box 1.3). Finally, we hope that our book will help to alleviate the problem of family violence by providing practical information on prevention and policy, and by motivating people to get involved. We trust that by providing numerous sources of information, we will help to give students, researchers, social workers, psychologists, policy makers, and advocates who have an interest in family violence a better foundation for their work. Just as we have felt compelled to write this book, we anticipate generating interest and concern among our readers. We hope that they find this exploration of the field of family violence to be stimulating and worthwhile.

CHAPTER SUMMARY

Our intent in this chapter, in part, is to impress on the reader the significance and prevalence of family violence in U.S. society. The United States is one of the most violent industrialized countries in the world, and a remarkably high proportion of this violence occurs within families.

It is important to understand the history of family violence as a social problem and the role of claims-making in defining social conditions as social problems. History is filled with accounts of the mistreatment of children and women. The mistreatment of children began to receive serious attention during the child-saving movement of the mid- to late 1800s, and the research community essentially ignored child abuse until the 1960s. The victimization of women was similarly ignored until the late 1800s, and the social problem of woman battering was not fully discovered until the early 1970s. Other forms of family violence—sibling violence, dating violence, marital rape, date rape, stalking, and elder abuse—came to be acknowledged as social problems in the 1980s.

The claims-making process is also important in the construction of definitions of deviance. Definitions of family violence are, to some degree, subjective and always evolving. Words such as *abuse, battering, assault, maltreatment,* and *violence* are commonly used in discussions of family violence, but there is sometimes little agreement on exactly what these words mean. Their meanings are negotiated by claims-makers, and the winners in these negotiations earn the right to define particular behaviors and estimate their prevalence. Definitions, however, are a crucial part of any research or social policy endeavor. Social scientific progress in the field of family violence depends, to some extent, on a shared understanding of what constitutes family violence.

Any history of the recognition of family violence as a social problem is incomplete without a consideration of the prevention and intervention strategies that have been introduced to address this problem. Prevention efforts are attempts to keep family violence from occurring in the first place, whereas intervention strategies are responses to family violence after it occurs. To date, U.S. social policies have tended to emphasize intervention rather than prevention, and many of the intervention strategies have focused on protecting victims and deterring perpetrators from committing further violence.

DISCUSSION QUESTIONS

1. Why do you think families are violent?
2. It is often said that women and children in the United States are in more danger at home than on the streets of the most violent cities. Is this an empirically defensible claim?
3. In the discussion above, we assert that children are more valued today than at any time in history. Is this is a defensible claim?
4. Some observers have claimed that the marriage license is a hitting license. Is this an empirically defensible claim or feminist advocacy?
5. What claims-making have you heard about family violence?
6. How is family violence defined? Who defines family violence? Why is it important to examine the influence of claims-making on definitions of social problems?
7. Should family violence be defined broadly or narrowly? What are the advantages and disadvantages of broad versus narrow definitions?
8. Why have greater societal resources been directed toward intervention in cases of family violence than toward prevention?
9. Do you have any perceptions about family violence that have been challenged by anything you have read in this opening chapter?

RECOMMENDED READING

Best, J. (2001). *Damned lies and statistics: Untangling numbers from the media, politicians, and activists.* Berkeley: University of California Press.

Daro, D., & Donnelly, A. C. (2002). Charting the waves of prevention: Two steps forward, one step back. *Child Abuse & Neglect, 26,* 731–742.

deMause, L. (Ed.). (1974). *The history of childhood.* New York: Psychotherapy Press.

Dobash, R. E., & Dobash, R. P. (1979). *Violence against wives: A case against patriarchy.* New York: Free Press.

Gelles, R. J., & Straus, M. A. (1988). *Intimate violence.* New York: Simon & Schuster.

Levesque, R. J. R. (2001). *Culture and family violence.* Washington, DC: American Psychological Association.

Loseke, D. R. (2003). *Thinking about social problems: An introduction to constructionist perspectives* (2nd ed.). New York: Aldine de Gruyter.

Melton, G. B. (2002). Chronic neglect of family violence: More than a decade of reports to guide US policy. *Child Abuse & Neglect, 26,* 569–586.

Tjaden, P. & Thoennes, N. (2000). *Full report of the prevalence, incidence, and consequences of violence against women: Findings from the National Violence Against Women Survey* (NCJ Publication No. 183781). Washington, DC: U.S. Department of Justice.

NOTES

1. These are estimates based on data from CPS agencies and coroner's offices. Some of these suspected child abuse deaths may not (or may not yet) have been the subjects of court proceedings to determine cause of death (U.S. DHHS, 2002b).

2. Of the 7,616 homicides in which the relationship between the offender and the victim was known, 2,387 (31%) were committed by a family member, boyfriend, or girlfriend (U.S. Department of Justice, 2002).

3. Assault, as measured by a modified version of the Conflict Tactics Scale (see Chapter 2), includes minor acts such as "throw something at you that could hurt," "push, grab, or shove you," and "pull your hair" as well as very serious acts such as "used a gun on you" (Tjaden & Thoennes, 2000b).

4. Rape was defined as use of force or threat of force to penetrate the victim's vagina or anus with a finger, tongue, object, or penis or to penetrate the mouth with a penis. The definition included both attempted and completed rape (Tjaden &Thoennes, 2000b, p. 4).

5. Researchers are not sure whether the dramatic increase since 1989, when 1,623 Russian women were reported killed by intimates, reflects an actual increase in homicide or a reluctance to report domestic homicides during the Soviet era.

2

Research Methodology, Assessment, and Theories

Investigating the Problem of Family Violence

Case History: Juanita's Broken Heart and Broken Body

When I was a child, my father switched my legs when I failed to clean my room right, and he belted me if I "ran my mouth." My mother said nothing about my father's "discipline."

When I was 17, I met Miguel at school. He told me I was beautiful and that he couldn't live without me. He said he loved me. He was always gentle and kind and we did everything together. He transformed my whole world.

Everything was perfect, like living in a dream. When Miguel said he wanted to marry me, I knew that I was going to have a home of my own where I would be loved and protected. It was the happiest time of my life.

When I was 18, Miguel and I got married. The week after the wedding, Miguel slapped me across the face and pushed me to the floor. I couldn't believe it. Why? Why? Why? I couldn't figure it out. What had gone wrong? I was stunned and heartbroken. I still loved him. I didn't know what to do. I decided Miguel must have been upset and that he probably wouldn't hit me again.

After we had been married about 3 months, Miguel no longer made love to me. Instead, he forced me to have sex whenever he wanted and he made me do some things I still can't talk about. He told me I was an ugly slut, the house looked like a pigpen, and the food wasn't fit for a dog to eat. He told me what to wear and where I could go. Once he socked me and blackened my eye. After that, I was afraid of him. My older brother and father guessed what was going on and threatened to beat up Miguel. I begged them not to, and they didn't. Actually, no one did anything. When I got pregnant, Miguel was really angry and he took to punching me in the stomach. He kept saying that the baby wasn't his, and if it wasn't, he was going to kill me.

Sometimes he woke me up in the middle of the night, screaming, "Who is the baby's father?" He said I wasn't fit to be a mother. He told me he hoped the baby would die, and he forbade me to see a doctor. One time he hit me so hard I began hemorrhaging. A neighbor took me to the doctor.

Miguel started going out without me and staying out all night with other women. He said I was a fat slob and he couldn't stand to be seen with me. I felt alone . . . unloved, afraid . . . very, very sad. I sometimes thought he hated me. I cried a lot, but I kept it to myself. Finally, I went to our priest and told him about Miguel. He told me to pray and try harder. It was my duty to obey my husband. So I tried harder to make Miguel happy. I kept the house clean and cooked good meals. I told him how much I loved him. Nothing changed. I did not know what to do, where to turn. One thing I did know was that going back home wouldn't help.[1]

This case history contains many elements that exemplify the issues encompassed by family violence research. How would you, as a researcher or practitioner, define and measure the types of experiences that Juanita endured? How would you assess Miguel's behavior or explain why Juanita did what Miguel told her to do or why she kept trying to make him happy? Who could Juanita have told about her predicament? What would you do if you were in Juanita's situation? What would you do if you had ever acted like Miguel?

To grasp the difficulties of conducting research in the field of family violence, you will find it helpful to keep this case history in mind. This chapter presents an overview of family violence research. It describes the various kinds of specialists working in the field, the different theories used to explain family violence, the methodologies that family violence researchers employ, and practice and policy issues associated with family violence. In doing so, the chapter delineates the extreme difficulties that family violence researchers often encounter and illuminates some of the different approaches they use in attempting to understand family violence. Researchers differ not only in their methods but in their assumptions about the causes of family violence. These differences ultimately affect their conclusions about which intervention and/or prevention strategies and policies are most effective for reducing family violence.

Studying Family Violence: A Multidisciplinary Effort

No single social institution or group has been able to come to grips with the enormity of family violence in the United States, although many have tried, including the criminal justice system, the medical and mental health communities, social welfare agencies, schools, and researchers. The diversity of approaches has resulted in a knowledge base that looks very much like a colossal jigsaw puzzle: Some parts of the picture are relatively clear, some are obscured, some do not fit together, some seem as if they will never fit together, and some are totally missing.

As interest in family violence has heightened, the field has expanded beyond its initial academic borders. Among the disciplines that are highly involved in the study of family violence are criminology, psychology, social work, sociology, and public health. Also connected to the field are such tangentially related disciplines as family studies/sciences, political science, victimology, and women's studies. In addition, professionals in the areas of law and medicine, especially nursing, pediatrics, obstetrics, and psychiatry, are actively engaged in family violence research.

Advocates for the victims of family violence have emerged as a forceful group with a specific value-centered and political agenda. Whereas academic researchers who study family violence have spent years in graduate school learning the procedures they use in their work, activists have spent years "on the firing line" trying to awaken the public, legislators, and law enforcement personnel to the plight of victims. As a group, these advocates deserve recognition and appreciation.

The interest of so many divergent groups in the same subject has posed a serious challenge to the field of family violence research in terms of accommodating opposing points of view (e.g., Jacobson, 1994b). Contentious debates have arisen between experts schooled within different academic disciplines and among researchers, clinicians, and victims' advocates. Various factions have formulated their own definitions and theoretical frameworks, applied differing research methodologies, and developed specialized interventions. The interviews with leading experts that appear throughout this book illustrate these distinctive points of view. As noted in Chapter 1, these dissonant perspectives are examples of claims-making, the process through which groups and individuals with differing views compete for society's attention.

Thoughtful diversity of opinion is one cornerstone of science, but fractious debate generated by opposing academic and political groups is detrimental. In the field of family violence, conflict has exceeded customary levels and has occasionally created an atmosphere of distrust and acrimony (see Gelles & Loseke, 1993). In an extreme instance, Dr. Murray Straus of the Family Violence Laboratory at the University of New Hampshire received a bomb threat from someone who was trying to stop a presentation of his research findings (see Straus, 1991d). Apparently, Straus's stance on gender equivalence, which flows from his research, infuriates some groups. (For a more thorough description of these problems, see Box 2.1.)

The greatest rancor among various factions in the field of family violence has erupted primarily over the issue of the causes of family violence and over the question of gender mutuality in adult intimate partner violence (IPV). Such disputes among factions intensify

Box 2.1 Conflicting Goals of Researchers and Practitioners: The Need for Collaboration

Through their training, researchers learn to value as ideal a number of procedures related to implementing the scientific method. In particular, they want to test large samples, recruit suitable comparison groups, and be able to control variables such as age, socioeconomic status, and minority status of subjects and the timing of tests. They may also have other incentives, such as winning research grants, obtaining academic promotions, or gaining status in their field. Most, if not all, family violence researchers are strongly committed to the mission of preventing or ending family violence through the application of research findings.

Practitioners who work with the victims of family violence, in contrast, are principally concerned with improving their clients' functioning, such as helping them cope with anger. Therapists want to protect their clients from undue intrusions and from emotionally upsetting experiences. Practitioners often must consider whether using valuable clinical time for research purposes is warranted. They may have reservations about collaborating with researchers if the studies proposed appear to be irrelevant to their clients' current needs. Participating in research also generates added paperwork and responsibility for clinicians.

Because of these differences in priorities, clashes sometimes arise between researchers and clinicians in agencies such as those that administer shelters or outreach programs (Levin, 1999). Researchers may unthinkingly expect clinical staff to conduct their investigations for them or to supervise students as they conduct research-related interviews. Some investigators with higher-level academic degrees may behave as though they believe they are superior to master's-degree-level clinical personnel.

In addition, the two factions may hold different opinions about various issues associated with family violence, especially about treatments. Researchers may appear insensitive to the needs of agency staff, as they frequently fail to grasp the fact that agency personnel face endless tasks and responsibilities, such as answering hotlines and supervising trainees. Agency personnel, on the other hand, may experience difficulties in attempting to fulfill a research role. They may not allow investigators to interact with research participants directly, yet neglect to administer tests on behalf of the investigators when scheduled. They may fail to keep notes on clients who do not participate or fail to keep data in a locked location. On occasion, overworked practitioners may even lose research data. Some agency personnel may go so far as to cancel a research agreement when other obligations become more compelling.

Some agency directors have become hostile to researchers in general. Such directors might require would-be investigators to supply vast quantities of written materials as part of requesting permission for research access, knowing that they intend all along to reject their requests.

In recent years, the strain between practitioners and researchers has motivated some who work in the field of family violence to promote a significant shift in conceptualization—the need to establish a collaborative culture (see Mohr, 1998). Within such an environment, investigators, practitioners, and victims' advocates can reach agreement on fundamental standards, encourage individual contributions, learn how to listen to each other, value different perspectives, develop trust in each other, and work toward equalizing power and making joint decisions (Block, Engel, Naureckas, & Riordan, 1999; Murphy & Dienemann, 1999).

when the interested parties must compete for limited resources (Dobash & Dobash, 1988; Schechter, 1988). The issue of child molestation provides an illustration: Should the tax and charitable money available to address this problem go to treatment programs for child molesters, who, without treatment, will go on to molest hundreds of children, or should it go to treatment programs for molested children whose lives have been shattered by their victimization and whose futures are in jeopardy?

Sociological Research

Sociologists were the first social scientists to grapple with the problem of family violence. Sociologists conducting research in this field often survey large numbers of people about their experiences with interpersonal violence and use the data they gather to examine the relationships between these experiences and variables such as age, gender, and socioeconomic class (e.g., Steffensmeir & Hayne, 2000). They also conduct surveys with smaller samples to study a vast array of related topics, such as gender-role conflicts among immigrants and the impact of IPV on women's employment (Browne, Salomon, & Bassuk, 1999; Min, 2001).

Social Work Research

Specialists with degrees in social work often investigate family violence using handy clinical samples. Some of the topics they have considered include the effects of poverty and welfare on rates of abuse, the effectiveness of parenting classes, and the functioning of child protective services (e.g., Barber & Delfabbro, 2000; Busch & Wolfer, 2002; Edleson, 1999). Additionally, clinical social workers are frequently on the front lines of treatment, working in agencies that serve individuals affected by interpersonal violence.

Criminological Research

Criminologists who study family violence are most often sociologists who focus on family crime. Frequently, these researchers analyze the very large banks of crime statistics gathered and published by government agencies such as the Federal Bureau of Investigation. It is important to note, however, that criminologists did not categorize violent acts between family members as crimes until the 1970s (Ohlin & Tonry, 1989). Typical kinds of criminological inquiry into family violence are investigations of the role of the police or the criminal justice system in domestic violence cases (e.g., Buzawa, Hotaling, & Klein, 1998; Finn & Stalans, 2002; Gaarder & Belknap, 2002). (For a recent analysis of topics covered in a criminology convention, see Robinson, 2002.)

Psychological and Psychiatric Research

Psychologists and psychiatrists who study family violence usually collect data from clinical samples, although some conduct large surveys. They customarily evaluate the effects of individual factors, such as psychopathology or the dynamics of interpersonal functioning, on the treatment and prevention of family violence. These specialists have also conducted research concerning such issues as the role of alcoholism in violent behavior (e.g., Feiring, Deblinger, Hoch-Espada, & Haworth, 2002; Huss & Langhinrichsen-Rohling, 2000).

Medical, Nursing, and Public Health Research

Family violence researchers based in the field of medicine often study clinical samples, and public health specialists tend to conduct epidemiological studies. As one might anticipate, the subjects of interest to these researchers include the role that health care providers can play in preventing or intervening in family violence, the nature of victims' injuries, the mental and physical effects that stem from family violence, and the training that providers of health care services receive (e.g., Isaac & Enos, 2001; McNutt, Carlson, Rose, & Robinson, 2002).

Legal Research

Because of the escalation of family violence reports in recent years, along with mounting public pressures for authorities to prevent such violence, growing numbers of legal scholars have redoubled their involvement in the field. Many such researchers have conducted reviews of both family violence laws and the academic literature, and they have worked to change laws where needed (Barata & Senn, 2003). Some legal scholars have delved into controversial issues, such as whether battered women should be charged with failure to protect their children because the children have been exposed to IPV. Some other areas of legal research have concerned the financial abuse of elders and the identification of legal steps needed to end stalking (e.g., Anand, 2001; Biernath, 2000; Trepiccione, 2001).

Expansion of Federal Government Research

Government researchers, statisticians, and epidemiologists working in the field of family violence often design surveillance systems and collect data on crimes and other violence-related incidents from very large population samples. In recent years, government agencies have increasingly funded family violence research and expanded their collaborations with other experts and agencies. (For a list of surveillance surveys from which data are available concerning violence against women, click on the "Additional Materials" button at the link for this volume on the Sage Publications Web site, http://www.sagepub.com/book.aspx?pid=10013.)

SECTION SUMMARY

Scholars and practitioners in the field of family violence come from a wide range of academic disciplines and professions. In the past decade, the U.S. government has become proactive in improving surveillance systems, and groups and institutions with disparate agendas have begun to unite behind their shared desire to find solutions to family violence.

THEORETICAL EXPLANATIONS FOR FAMILY VIOLENCE

In many respects, family violence is seemingly incomprehensible. How could a husband who supposedly loves his wife be physically violent toward her? How could a mother purposely hurt her infant? In considering family violence, it may be fruitful to look at the many social and cultural conditions that make such violence not only comprehensible but also, in some respects, a normal (or at least culturally approved) part of family life. Researchers' and practitioners' ideological convictions are pivotal because they typically dictate the selection of research designs and preferences for intervention (Hamby, 1998; Kim & Ahn, 2002). (For overviews of theories used to explain family violence, see Ellis & Walsh, 1999; O'Neill, 1998.)

Just as no single measure of family violence is a true reflection of all violence between family members, no one theory can fully explain what causes family violence. A **theory** may be defined as "an integrated set of ideas that explain a set of observations"

(O'Neill, 1998, p. 459). Without empirical support, theories are only speculations that leave scholars free to dispute their merits. So far, no one has evaluated how theories about the causes of family violence compare across the many disciplines that contribute to this field. Thus identical theories may exist in different subfields, their agreement obscured by variations in terminology. The micro and macro framework described below is useful for organizing the existing theoretical formulations for understanding family violence.

The case history at the opening of this chapter can serve as a basis for the following discussion of theories. What caused the IPV in Juanita and Miguel's relationship? Why did Miguel change after marriage and start hurting Juanita? Why did Juanita put up with the abuse?

Macrotheory: Explaining Patterns of Family Violence

The task of a macrotheory of family violence is to identify the broad cultural and structural factors that make families prone to violence. Macro-level explanations incorporate cultural factors, social-structural variables (e.g., poverty), structural characteristics of the family (e.g., family stresses), and issues of deterrence (e.g., punishment and costs of family violence).

Cultural factors. On many levels, family violence is an accepted, encouraged, and even glorified form of cultural expression in the United States (O'Neill, 1998). Social approval of **corporal punishment**, for example, is consonant with the moral obligation that parents have to use enough force to train, protect, and control their children. From this point of view, hitting children is normative (Ellison, Bartkowski, & Segal, 1996; Flynn, 1996). Striking a spouse may be viewed as less tolerable than striking a child, and presumably hitting a woman is less acceptable than hitting a man (Bookwala, Frieze, Smith, & Ryan, 1992; Felson, 2000). A sizable minority of Americans, however, still think that slapping an intimate partner is permissible under certain circumstances, such as when a partner has been unfaithful (Klein, Campbell, Soler, & Ghez, 1997; Simon et al., 2001). In one study of East Asian and Southeast Asian immigrants to the United States, approximately one-fourth to one-third of the study sample agreed that marital violence is justified under certain circumstances (e.g., nagging) (Yoshioka, DiNoia, & Ullah, 2001).

In many ways, complaints about the patriarchal nature of U.S. culture have been the foundation on which the American anti–domestic violence movement has been built. In a patriarchal culture, men hold greater power and privilege in the social hierarchy than do women. In its extreme form, patriarchy literally gives men the right to dominate and control women and children (Dobash & Dobash, 1979). In an article published in 1976, Murray Straus identified four cherished cultural standards in the United States that not only permit but encourage husband-to-wife violence: (a) the greater authority that men have, compared with women, in the culture; (b) male aggressiveness, along with the notions that aggression positively correlates to maleness and that aggression is not only an acceptable tool for a man but a way to demonstrate male identity; (c) the wife/mother role as the preferred status for women; and (d) male domination and orientation of the criminal justice system, which provides little legal relief for female victims.

There is little doubt that in many countries, men have the power to kill, imprison, punish, or enslave women and children with impunity (see Levesque, 2001). The patriarchal nature of U.S. culture is insufficient, however, to account for the IPV perpetrated by American husbands. Although many Americans hold patriarchal values, the influence of patriarchy is not all-embracing. Only 10–11% of American men can be classified as "wife beaters" (Dutton, 1994), and no more than 30% of American men ever abuse their female partners (Straus & Gelles, 1990).

Feminist theories regarding family violence typically include four principal perspectives: (a) the relationship between gender and power and its utility in accounting for IPV; (b) the historical importance of the family as a social institution; (c) the importance of understanding and validating women's experiences; and (d) the use of family violence research findings to help women (Bograd, 1988). Feminists decry the widespread use of so-called gender-neutral research methodologies that they argue contain a patriarchal bias and therefore are damaging to women (Yllö, 1993). The selection of research questions provides an illustration of this premise. If it were not for feminists, some questions would never be asked. Until Russell (1982) and Finkelhor and Yllö (1982) conducted their landmark surveys in the early 1980s, the law did not recognize marital rape, and academicians did not study it. Despite the salutary effects that feminism has had on U.S. society as a whole, and on academia in particular, the scope of feminist theory concerning family violence is confined almost entirely to male-to-female IPV. Feminist scholars have not yet offered satisfactory

accounts of other types of family violence, such as child abuse or same-sex aggression (see Ash & Cahn, 1994; Waldner-Haugrud, Gratch, & Magruder, 1997).

In a modern application of an older theory, Smith (1991) has hypothesized that male peers compose a subculture of violence by approving and supporting violence against women (but not against children). In a survey of Canadian male college students, DeKeseredy and Kelly (1993) identified two patterns of peer support that explained a small portion of the variation they found in male-to-female dating abuse: peers' patriarchal attitudes (e.g., general approval of male-to-female violence) and informational peer support (e.g., advising a male friend to maintain his authority over a romantic partner by using physical force).

Social-structural variables. Theories based in social-structural formulations link family violence to certain socially defined classifications, such as low income, minority status, and gender. Although abuse occurs at every social-structural level, a large volume of research has identified all of the aforementioned factors as correlates of IPV (Harmon, 2001; Magdol et al., 1997; Rennison & Welchans, 2000; Waters, 2000). Also, the presence of stressors such as unequal opportunity and poverty produces high levels of personal frustration, which increase the risk of aggression (e.g., Copenhaver, Lash, & Eisler, 2000; Mazerolle & Piquero, 1997; McLeod & Kessler, 1990).

Early on, scholars identified another cluster of factors woven throughout family living that make families especially prone to violence (Brinkerhoff & Lupri, 1988; Gelles & Straus, 1979). Some of these typically stress-producing elements of family life are close proximity, emotional investment, privacy issues, and power imbalances. Two obvious power imbalances in the family are the subordination of children to parents and, frequently, the subjugation of women to men. These family stressors foster conflict and aggression (see Brinkerhoff & Lupri, 1988; Lambert & Firestone, 2000). Nevertheless, social-structural explanations fall short of accounting for the fact that the vast majority of lower-class family members do not assault each other.

Deterrence theory: the low cost of family violence. From a social control standpoint, deviant behavior is common when it does not engender many social or legal costs. According to Hirschi (1969), humans are held in check by their "stakes in conformity"—that is, by their commitments to conventional goals, involvement in conventional activities, attachments to significant others, and beliefs that violence is wrong. Sherman, Smith, Schmidt, and Rogan (1992) applied a deterrence framework to interpret their distinctive finding that arrest reduced wife assault only in men who were employed (that is, men who had a stake in conformity). For revised interpretations of their findings, see Maxwell, Garner, and Fagan (2001).

Deterrence theory is the backbone of the criminal justice system. According to this theory, intensifying the legal consequences for a given **antisocial behavior** should lessen its frequency. Many logicians argue that the reason family violence is so common is that the potential costs of committing a family-violent act are almost nonexistent. Arrest and prosecution are unlikely, and incarceration or other punishments are even less probable (Healey, Smith, & O'Sullivan, 1998; National Institute of Justice & American Bar Association, 1998; Office for Victims of Crime, 1999). Contradicting deterrence theory, research evidence has shown that criminal justice interventions with batterers are not necessarily effective (e.g., Gondolf, 2000b).

Microtheory: Explaining the Behaviors of Violent Family Members

Theories that take broad cultural belief systems into account help to explain why families within certain societies are violent, but they are insufficient to explain violence on an individual level. For example, selling teenage girls into prostitution is an acceptable and widespread practice in some African countries, yet many parents do not sell their daughters. Several types of theories address individual proclivities toward aggression, including learning theories, individual (intrapersonal) differences theories, and interpersonal interaction theories.

Socialization and learning theories. A large body of research extending across academic disciplines has documented the importance of childhood socialization in the development of family-violent offenders. Abusive parents provide children with a classroom for learning specific forms of abusive behaviors, particular attitudes, and distinct cognitions that justify violence (Dunlap, Golub, Johnson, & Wesley, 2002; Ritter, Stewart, Bernet, Coe, & Brown, 2002; Widom & Maxfield, 2001). (For a discussion of socialization effects based on the findings of a **longitudinal study**, see Moffitt & Caspi, 1999.)

Over the years, researchers have expanded applications of basic learning principles to a broad repertoire of behaviors. The following paragraphs explain and provide examples of the principles of modeling (social imitation), classical conditioning (emotional learning), and operant conditioning (modification of behavior), including the overarching principles of reinforcement and punishment.

A widely accepted account of how socialization plays a role in family violence hinges on social learning principles. At the core of this theory is a process called *modeling,* in which people learn social and cognitive behaviors by simply observing and imitating others (Bandura, 1977). The popularity of social learning theory rests on two major lines of evidence. First, a wealth of laboratory experiments with humans lends strong validation to the claim that aggression can be learned through modeling (e.g., Bandura, Ross, & Ross, 1961). Second, research has shown that violence tends to be perpetuated from one generation to the next (e.g., Widom & Maxfield, 2001). Abuse during childhood is associated with later dating violence, marital violence, and the abused person's eventual abuse of his or her own children (e.g., Carr & VanDeusen, 2002; Frias-Armenta, 2002; Green, 1998; Miller & Bukva, 2001). The stability of these findings reaffirms intergenerational accounts of family violence, even though the magnitudes of the relationships are not uniformly robust (Stith et al., 2000). In a recent 20-year longitudinal, prospective study, Ehrensaft et al. (2003) uncovered very strong intergenerational effects for partner violence. The models of both victim and perpetrator behavior provide social learning opportunities. As applied specifically to family violence, the observation of violence (e.g., father hits mother for "mouthing off") and reinforcement of violence within a social context (i.e., mother "shuts up") teaches children exactly how to be abusive and how to be victims.

Although the social learning theory explanation for family violence has many proponents, some skeptics find this explanation to be overstated or too narrow, and others believe that the research thus far has had methodological shortcomings (Kaufman & Zigler, 1993; MacEwen, 1994; Newcomb & Locke, 2001). Also counting against this theory is the fact that many, if not most, individuals exposed to violent family models do not go on to emulate abusive behaviors later in life (e.g., Mihalic & Elliott, 1997).

Another type of learning, classical conditioning, concerns the emotional changes that take place in an individual as a result of experience. Fear, for example, can be classically conditioned in humans through the

An Interview with Kersti Yllö

"I feel that I have become a translator between mainstream sociologists and those concerned with feminist analysis."

Kersti Yllö, a widely recognized feminist scholar, teaches and conducts sociological research at Wheaton College in Norton, Massachusetts, just outside of Boston. She is Henrietta Jennings Professor of Sociology, an endowed chair that is awarded for outstanding teaching. She has published primarily on the topics of the status of women and wife abuse, marital rape, and feminist analysis of domestic violence. She completed her undergraduate work at Denison University, and in 1980 she earned her Ph.D. in sociology from the University of New Hampshire (UNH), where she also held a postdoctoral fellowship in the Family Violence Research Program.

Q: What sparked your interest in the area of family violence?

A: While I was an undergraduate, I took the first course ever offered in women's studies at Denison University and a family course that looked at power issues, and I began to see a connection. When I later entered graduate school in sociology at the University of New Hampshire, it was at a time when Murray Straus was just beginning his national survey work on family violence. I was given the opportunity to obtain an NIMH [National Institute of Mental Health] predoctoral grant with the stipulation that my work be connected to family violence. I found the topic of family violence to be the most compelling focus of family power issues, and I've been fascinated with the topic ever since.

Q: Looking back, what is your most influential contribution to the area of family violence?

A: One area is my work with David Finkelhor and our book *License to Rape: Sexual Abuse of Wives* [1987]. At the time we began our work, there were no published articles on marital rape, although legislatures were beginning to debate whether marital rape should be criminalized. Many people thought of marital

pairing of a signal (e.g., angry voice) with a subsequent frightening and painful event (e.g., assault). Thus theories of family violence that encompass the idea of classical conditioning can explain the intense levels of fear experienced by battered women (see O'Keefe & Treister, 1998). If a husband repeatedly comes home drunk and then threatens his wife with a beating, the wife will learn to fear her husband's drunken arrival.

A third type of learning, operant conditioning, involves the individual's understanding of the relationship between his or her actions and their consequences. Some scholars theorize that individuals learn to be violent through operant conditioning (which shapes their behavior in a step-by-step fashion). An obvious application of operant conditioning is a perpetrator's use of violence (actions) to coerce a victim's compliance (consequences). Victim compliance reinforces (rewards) the perpetrator's aggression. When abusive persons get what they want by mistreating others, they are likely to become even more violent (see Felson, 1992; Ganley, 1989). Similarly, when abusive persons are not punished for their violent behavior, they gain further opportunities to hone their aggressive skills (Patterson, 1982). (For further discussion of the applications of learning theory principles, see Chapters 10 and 11.)

Individual (intrapersonal) differences theories. In their attempts to define the etiology of family violence, some scholars have searched for answers in individual differences among offenders and sometimes among victims, including psychopathology, psychological traits, and psychobiological mechanisms. Countering these theories is research evidence showing that although many abusive individuals manifest unusual personal characteristics, most do not.

rape as a "contradiction in terms." Our in-depth interviews with women provided such a rich source of data that we ended up testifying before lawmakers in support of criminalization. Through the work of many women's advocates, marital rape has finally been criminalized in all 50 states. Unfortunately, the laws stop short of full criminalization by incorporating many restrictions, time limits, and allowing too many loopholes. The laws still do not treat marital rape like "real" rape.

Q: How do you see marital rape as intersecting with power issues?

A: I think that marital rape at its core is about the use of sexuality in a power relationship, whether it occurs in the midst of a very violent, injurious attack, whether it is a means of humiliation and degradation, or whether it is a nonviolent coercive action, the one way for the husband to win a power battle. Marital rape actually receives very little attention from researchers or anyone.

Q: What do you see as your role in the field of family violence, where you have been, and where you are going?

A: Working at University of New Hampshire and with people like Murray Straus, I became well acquainted with the mainstream approach of sociologists, and I understand their thinking. Although I disagree with some of the tenets of this school, Murray has always been supportive of work and my approach. I also disagree with those who feel that the mainstream approach has done more harm than good. I think that these kinds of criticisms by feminists and other family violence researchers have been very hurtful to the people at UNH. On the other hand, I understand the viewpoint of those involved in feminist analysis. I am very close to this group of feminist researchers. I feel that I have become a translator between these two groups—the mainstream sociologists and those concerned with feminist analysis.

Q: What is the focus of your current work?

A: My current work is focused on expanding the feminist framework, to address more adequately race, ethnicity, and global issues. I still believe that gender remains a critical concept in our understanding of violence, but our work needs to become more nuanced, incorporating the differences among women as well as our commonalities. I also think that family violence researchers need to connect to others doing related work. On the issue of marital rape, for example, I am trying to link to those addressing HIV/AIDS. Unless the issue of sexual coercion within marriage is taken seriously, our efforts to stem this epidemic will be limited. Given the legality and cultural acceptance of marital rape globally, this is an enormous but critical challenge before us.

One recurrent explanation for family violence is psychopathology (mental disorders) in perpetrators, victims, or both. These theories propose that individuals who mistreat children, dating partners, spouses, elders, or other family members are seriously disturbed. Their psychopathology may distort their view of the world or serve as a disinhibitor to prohibited behavior. Over the years, scientifically sound studies have supported the mental illness model by demonstrating higher rates of mental disorders in family violence offenders relative to subjects in comparison groups. **Narcissism**, depression, and **antisocial personality disorder** are examples of psychopathology typical of family violence offenders (e.g., see Kessler, Molnar, Feurer, & Appelbaum, 2001; Krueger, Moffitt, Caspi, Bleske, & Silva, 1998). Some of these disorders (e.g., antisocial personality disorder) are extremely difficult to treat effectively.

Other research has focused on psychological traits of persons involved in family violence that are not defined as psychopathological. Some authorities have theorized that certain personality traits typical of offenders (e.g., high hostility) contribute to their perpetration of family violence. Such characteristics help to explain (but do not justify) abusive behaviors (Barnett & Hamberger, 1992; Blanchard, 2001; Harmon, 2001). Although traits are simply constructs (labels) that do not exist in reality, they describe characteristic ways in which people behave in different situations. This formulation alleges that traits reside within the individual and are not situation specific. For example, a person who has the trait of cheerfulness would be cheerful at home, at work, and in other settings. According to this viewpoint, the quantification of traits based on questionnaire data can help practitioners to predict individuals' behavior and can also provide a clear point of therapeutic intervention.

Taking trait formulations a step further, social scientists concentrated heavily in the 1990s on devising patterns of traits, or typologies (Holtzworth-Munroe & Stuart, 1994). (For a review of typology research, see Dixon & Browne, 2003.) As one illustration, trait research has found that perpetrators of child sexual abuse tend to exhibit feelings of vulnerability, dependency, inadequacy, and loneliness and to experience cognitive distortions (e.g., Hanson, Gizzarelli, & Scott, 1994). Offenders with these traits typically satisfy their own needs by seeking out children instead of adults as sexual partners. Studies have also identified several psychological traits in assaultive partners and abusive parents that are correlated with aggression, including low self-esteem, anger, hostility, emotional dependency, and poor problem-solving skills (e.g., Sedlar & Hansen, 2001; Sidebotham, Golding, & ALSPAC Study Team, 2001).

Until the early 1990s, possible psychobiological bases for family violence escaped scrutiny for the most part (DiLalla & Gottesman, 1991). Illustrative of this approach is research showing that physical child abusers exhibit hyperresponsive physiological activity to both positive and negative child stimuli (Milner & Chilamkurti, 1991). Such unusual physiological responses might contribute to diminished tolerance for proximity to children in such individuals, which in turn elicits physical aggression. Investigators have also explored possible links between the hormone testosterone and aggression (for a meta-analysis, see Book, Starzyk, & Quinsey, 2001).

Finally, some specialists have found evidence of genetic bases for such correlates of family violence as antisocial personality disorder, aggression, and alcoholism (Lesch & Merschdorf, 2000; van den Bree, Svikis, & Pickens, 1998). Understanding how genetic determinants are related to aggression is important, because the presence of such determinants suggests that alternative interventions, such as drug treatments, may be successful in reducing family violence (Paris, 2001).

Interpersonal interaction theories. Some researchers and clinicians assume that family violence is a product of interactions between individuals in specific relationships (systems theory). Proponents of this view think that violence in a relationship is not the result of the behavior of only one person, such as the perpetrator (Giles-Sims, 1983). Rather, as Lane and Russell (1989) contend, one cannot separate victim from victimizer, dominance from submission, or aggression from passivity. In other words, certain aspects about specific relationships, in and of themselves, may instigate family violence. Feminist theoreticians deplore such explanations because they place a portion of the blame on victims, and thus fail to make perpetrators totally responsible for their violence.

A number of researchers have pinpointed marital dysfunction (dyadic/relationship stress) as a factor that promotes IPV. The supposition is that a violent partner's behavior may be a response to the other partner's conduct. Accordingly, it is the interactions of both partners that preserve the homeostatic balance (e.g., violence) of the relationship (another concept from systems theory; see Johnson & Lebow, 2000; Tyrell, 2002). Support for this premise comes from research that has shown that both partners in abusive relationships experience high rates of discord or have deficits in communication skills. The frequent replication of findings that dyadic stress and aggression are closely linked raises the age-old question of directionality: Is aggression an antecedent or a consequence of dyadic stress? (See, e.g., Babcock, Waltz, Jacobson, & Gottman, 1993; Good, Heppner, Hillenbrand-Gunn, & Wang, 1995; Marcus & Swett, 2002.)

Evidence contradicting dyadic stress (marital dysfunction) formulations demonstrates that men scoring above the median on marital satisfaction tests may still beat their wives, and some of those scoring below may not (e.g., Barnett & Hamberger, 1992; Rosenbaum & O'Leary, 1981). In other words, men who are abusive may or may not be satisfied with their marital interactions. Furthermore, longitudinal data on early marriages demonstrate that relationship discord does not inevitably precede the occurrence of aggression; sometimes, the reverse may be true (O'Leary et al., 1989).

Researchers have also applied interpersonal transaction theories to child abuse and neglect. According to such theories, the reciprocal nature of the parent-child relationship initiates and maintains abusive and neglectful patterns of behavior (Wolfe, 1987). In fact, some evidence suggests that child abuse results when the behavior problems of a parent interact with the conduct of a hard-to-manage child (e.g., U.S. Department of Health and Human Services, 1993).

Research findings in several areas allude to the occurrence of disturbed patterns of **attachment** in abusive and neglecting families (e.g., Kolko, 1992). For example, experts have consistently observed defective patterns of attachment in physically abused, neglected, and psychologically maltreated children (Kolko, 1992; for a Japanese study, see Rothbaum, Weisz, Pott, Miyake, & Morelli, 2000). (*Infant attachment* refers to the enduring emotional bond that develops between a dependent infant and his or her primary caretaker during the first year of life; see Bowlby, 1980.)

Failure to form a secure attachment early in life may carry over into adulthood, causing distress in romantic relationships (Corvo, 1992; McCarthy & Taylor, 1999). According to some theorists, an inadequately attached adult suffers anxiety and anger when faced with a partner who threatens to leave, and these intense feelings may fuel an assault against that partner (Bookwala, 2002; O'Hearn & Davis, 1997).

Again, however, a lack of clarity about the sequence of romantic attachment and anxiety makes interpretation of the research findings uncertain. A primary advantage of this theory is its ability to explain not only the co-occurrence of love and violence but variability in commitment to a relationship. It can account for a partner's "on-again, off-again" romantic behavior as well as the stress it generates (e.g., Billingham, 1987). In addition, adult persistence in an abusive relationship can be linked with emotional attachment (love and dependence) to the violent partner (Griffing et al., 2002; Henderson, Bartholomew, & Dutton, 1997). (See Table 2.1 for additional information on microtheoretical frameworks.)

Table 2.1 Additional Family Violence Microtheory Explanations

Explanation	Description
Social exchange theory	Explores interactions between victim and perpetrator from a cost-benefit point of view, assuming that humans enter and maintain relationships only when they judge that the benefits (such as love and security) outweigh the costs (such as increased workload) (Gelles, 1983). Social exchange principles may apply to several family and intimate relationships, including adult child-elder parent, parent-child, husband-wife, and boyfriend-girlfriend. When benefits outweigh costs, one member of the pair may perceive the relationship as inequitable and terminate it (see Blum, 1997; Call, Finch, Huck, & Kane, 1999; Sprecher, 2001). When termination is impossible, the aggrieved party experiences frustration and may become aggressive (frustration-aggression hypothesis; see Rodriguez & Henderson, 1995; Worden, 2002).
Symbolic interactionism	Emphasizes the symbolic communication between humans. Within the ongoing process of social interactions, the actors construct and reconstruct their own social reality, which, in turn, propels behavior. From this point of view, it is simplistic to assume that human behavior can be understood merely on the basis of objectively specifiable variables, such as the actors' background characteristics or external stimuli (see Felson & Tedeschi, 1993; Snow, 2001). Through this lens, the key to understanding family violence can be found in the meanings that family members attach to various interactions. A real-life illustration of this "meaning in the making" process is a case in which an infant-abusing mother interprets her baby's crying as repetitive complaints about the mother's ineptitude. Refusing to be labeled "bad," the mother decides to shut the baby up by hitting her (for an application, see Hill & Amuwo, 1998).
Routine activities theory	Especially useful for explaining stalking patterns (Tjaden & Thoennes, 1998b). Cohen and Felson (1979) define routine activities as "any recurrent and prevalent activities which provide for basic population and individual need (e.g., working, schooling, leisure outings, shopping" (p. 590). Schwartz and Pitts (1995) have applied parts of this theory to explain sexual assault of college women. Presumably, women's regular attendance at classes, restaurants, and other settings makes it easier for men to target them.

Multidimensional Theories

Multidimensional models endeavor to integrate several unidimensional theories. Attempts to develop such models flow logically from the failure of single-concept frameworks to account for family violence. The need for a multidimensional theory is especially salient when one is attempting to interpret the causes of family violence in other cultures or when one is striving to delineate a worldview (Perilla, Bakeman, & Norris, 1994). The complexity of family violence, however, has so far confounded social scientists who have tried to posit an inclusive model (see Shotland, 1992).

As a comprehensive illustration, suppose that a very hostile man (psychological trait) who was abused as a child (learning), who is currently unhappily married (interpersonal interaction), who has inherited a genetic predisposition for antisocial personality disorder (psychopathology), and who has just lost his job (stress) uses male privilege (patriarchy) as a justification for assaulting his wife. Clearly, no singular etiological framework fully explains his violence.

SECTION SUMMARY

Macrotheories account for family violence by explaining how broad, cultural forces allow or even promote it. Cultural acceptance ideology assumes that family violence is the product of widespread social acceptance of violence. Patriarchal formulations attribute family violence to male privilege and power in a society. Peer-group influence theories suppose that male peers support male-to-female aggression and domination. Feminist analysis focuses on gender inequality. Through this lens, men beat women because they can get away it. Social-structural explanations assert that certain conditions, such as low social class and the structure of the family, create stress and anger, which lead to aggression. Deterrence theory presumes that the criminal justice response to assaults against family members is too minimal to be effective.

Microtheories are narrower in scope than macrotheories. They explain family violence on an individual level. Socialization (learning) explanations take note of children's strong tendency to be influenced by parents, peers, the media, and other factors. Social learning theory proposes that children model specific family-violent behaviors and attitudes, conflict resolution styles, and alcohol misuse. Modeling leads to an intergenerational theory of family violence. Some theories incorporate classical and operant conditioning principles, many of which have been extrapolated to humans from the findings of laboratory studies with animals. The concept of classical conditioning explicates how individuals learn emotional reactions such as fear. Operant conditioning, which involves the use of reinforcement and punishment, is useful in accounting for victims' compliance with perpetrators' demands and entrapment.

Psychopathological explanations for family violence assume the presence of mental illness in perpetrators. Psychological traits theories attribute family violence to individual variation in personality traits such as empathy. Psychobiological theories posit that certain physiological abnormalities are at the core of family violence. Interpersonal interaction formulations, such as dyadic stress (systems) theory, hold that the actions of both perpetrator and victim interact to promote violence. Attachment theory asserts that children who have bonded insufficiently with their primary caregivers are at risk for abuse. Such early difficulties with attachment may set the stage for later anxieties about adult romantic attachments.

Given that no single-concept theory has been able to explain the complex phenomenon of family violence fully, the development of multidimensional theories should be a priority for scholars in this field.

METHODOLOGY: HOW RESEARCHERS TRY TO ANSWER QUESTIONS ABOUT FAMILY VIOLENCE

Conducting research in the field of family violence is a daunting challenge for investigators. Gathering data is especially problematic because of the delicate and private nature of the subject matter. In addition, by reporting subjects' experiences, researchers may stigmatize or shame individual research subjects, or generate fears of reprisal or even legal sanctions (Weis, 1989). Consequently, researchers must employ considerable diplomatic and social skills, in addition to academic expertise, in recruiting study participants.

The earliest investigations of family violence tended to be exceedingly weak methodologically. The first researchers in this area "swept with a wide broom," desperately searching for commonalities in hopes of gaining insight into the phenomenon. This approach led to a proliferation of essentially pilot studies that failed to produce the crucial information researchers so eagerly sought (Rosenbaum, 1988). Among the many shortcomings of the early research mentioned throughout the literature are the following: (a) the researchers' lack of understanding of ethical principles, (b) inadequate methods for obtaining data, (c) underdeveloped theory, (d) imprecise definitions and methods of measurement, (e) faulty sampling, (f) failure to use optimal comparison groups, (g) over-reliance on descriptive and cross-sectional investigations, (h) the use of univariate rather than **multivariate methods** of analysis, (i) failure to replicate studies or integrate findings, and (j) insufficient adjustments for cultural and ethnic differences. Overall, the research on family violence to date has been "extensive but not definitive" (see Gartner, 1993; Ohlin & Tonry, 1989). This section elaborates on the deficiencies of the research.

In an effort to pinpoint defects in the family violence research, two groups of investigators recently employed computer searches of the literature. In a fascinating computer review of papers on youth violence in the PsycINFO database, Acosta, Albus, Reynolds, Spriggs, and Weist (2001) uncovered two particularly bothersome trends. First, descriptive statistics do not provide information that can be generalized to other samples of research participants. Between 1980 and 1999, Acosta et al. found, approximately 63% of the research published was descriptive (not inferential) or assessment related, about 24% was treatment oriented, and 13% was concerned with prevention. Second, researchers tend to focus on some topics while neglecting others. Gordon, Holmes, and Maly (1999) searched PsycINFO for publication productivity in the areas of child abuse and intimate partner violence for the years 1990 through 1996 and found that just a few institutions were responsible for the majority of investigations. They also found an imbalance in topics: Experts studied physical child abuse less than sexual child abuse and, conversely, studied adult IPV more than adult sexual assault.

Although researchers have made methodological advances in the past 10 years, deficiencies are still the rule rather than the exception. Of great promise, however, are the growing numbers of working partnerships between researchers in the private sector and those working within federal government agencies such as the National Institutes of Health, the National Institute of Mental Health, the National Institute of Child Health

and Development, and the Centers for Disease Control and Prevention. With federal funding, these researchers have undertaken a number of large-scale, representative surveys and other highly significant studies (Felson, Messner, Hoskin, & Deane, 2002; Tjaden & Thoennes, 1998a, 2000a). Government agencies also accumulate all types of health and violence information that is often generalizable across large regions (see Box 2.2).

Sources of Data

Data on family violence come from several kinds of sources. Weis (1989) separates these into five major types: (a) *Official records* come from FBI summaries of police department reports and reports from social service agencies and reflect amounts of "officially" reported family violence; (b) *self-reports* are mail, phone, or face-to-face surveys about violence in the family conducted with members of the general public; (c) *victimization and perpetration surveys* are mail, phone, or face-to-face surveys conducted with individuals involved in family violence; (d) *informant reports* are mail, phone, or face-to-face surveys conducted with observers (e.g., parents) of violent behaviors (e.g., fights between siblings) that do not inquire directly of the individual agents involved (e.g., siblings); and (e) *direct observations* are empirical observations (e.g., measurement of physiological responses during a quarrel) made by social scientists in a laboratory. No one type of data source is inherently superior to the others; rather, each has its own strengths and weaknesses (Verhoek-Oftedahl, Pearlman, & Babcock, 2000). (For descriptions of government and large private surveys from a criminological perspective, see Buzawa & Buzawa, 2003.)

Official statistics reflect the rates of reported intimate violence—that is, cases reported to police or to other public agencies. The Federal Bureau of Investigation's *Uniform Crime Reports (UCR)* are the most commonly cited sources of official data. These reports, which are published annually, include data on all reported crimes and arrests made for those crimes across the United States. Government statisticians also track injuries recorded by hospital emergency department personnel through the National Electronic Injury Surveillance System. Another newer data collection tool is the National Incident-Based Reporting System (Centers for Disease Control and Prevention [CDC], 2000; Orchowsky & Weiss, 2000). State agencies such as those devoted to adult protective services and child protective services accumulate reports of family

Box 2.2 Issues Related to Family Violence Research

Research results rest on a number of factors that may vary widely from study to study. This extensive variability makes it difficult to interpret findings and affects their generalizability. The following questions illustrate some of the issues faced by family violence researchers:

1. Who asks the questions? (Researcher, practitioner, government interviewer, medical personnel, school personnel, police officer?)

2. What questions are asked? (Items about abuse, sexual assault, or neglect; identity of perpetrator(s); questions about frequency, duration, severity, or outcomes of abuse?)

3. What referent period of abuse is selected? (Last month, last 6 months, last 12 months, last 2 years, over a lifetime, during relationship, other time frame or historical period?)

4. How are the questions asked? (By an interviewer, over the phone or in person, by mail, on a paper questionnaire, in an online questionnaire?)

5. What is the context of the questions asked? (Length of the questionnaire and terminology, items within the context of conflict resolution, criminal acts, violence against women, sexual abuse, health problems, human rights abuses?)

6. What is the setting in which questions are asked? (Shelter, emergency room, home, classroom, university laboratory, prison or other institution, military setting? With others present or respondent alone?)

7. What is the cultural context? (Language spoken, reading ability, freedom to speak honestly, views of women and children, roles of men and women?)

8. What is the purpose for asking the questions? (For information on victims' perspectives, utility of perpetrators' arrest, prevalence and incidence rates, effects of violence on physical and mental health?)

9. When are the questions asked? (On arrival at a shelter, following an assault, several years after the incident, when the victim is pregnant, drunk, injured, or afraid?)

10. Who answers the questions? (Child, man, woman, mother, father, stepparent, brother, sister, husband, wife, cohabitor, same-sex partner, dating partner, racial or ethnic minority group member, elder, immigrant, institutionalized person, homeless person, non–English speaker, doctor, nurse, social worker, agency personnel?)

11. What relationship factors exist between abusers and victims? (Parent-child, stepparent-stepchild, acquaintances, siblings, dating partners, intimate partners—cohabiting, divorced, separated; duration and quality of relationship, degree of relationship intimacy, previous battering relationships?)

12. What historical data are gathered? (Respondent's abuse as a child, criminal victimization, exposure to interparental aggression, criminal arrest record, education, employment, welfare recipient status, children and their health status, religious preference, injuries, illnesses, other events?)

13. What types of sociodemographic data are gathered? (Age, race, socioeconomic status, education, area of residence?)

violence against vulnerable groups. (For a full list of national sources for data on family violence, click on the "Additional Materials" button at the link for this volume on the Sage Publications Web site, http://www.sagepub.com/book.aspx?pid=10013.)

It should be noted, however, that official statistics on family violence are plagued by a number of flaws. The most glaring of these is that individuals report only a small proportion of the violence that takes place within families. The violence that is reported, furthermore, tends to be the most serious, and therefore it is not representative of family violence as a whole (Chalk & King, 1998). Other problems with official data include the failure of government agencies to track criminal acts against children under the age of 12 (Finkelhor & Ormrod, 2001).

Occasionally, government agencies have categorized certain kinds of acts of family violence as other types of crimes (Steinman, 1991). Agencies collecting data have often merged specific information on the relationships between offenders and victims (e.g., boyfriend-girlfriend, spouses, ex-spouses) into two less precise offender categories: stranger and non-stranger. Gradually, however, the FBI has modified the crime classifications in the *UCR* and has improved the coverage, reliability, and detail of these reports (Jensen & Karpos, 1993).

In self-report perpetration surveys, respondents answer questions about their own violent behavior directed toward other intimates (children, spouses, partners, parents). The obvious advantage of such surveys is that they provide access to information about violence that is not reported to official agencies. They are especially useful for gathering information on subabusive behavior, such as corporal punishment or pushing between marital partners. These reports also have some inherent problems, one of which arises because of their retrospective nature—respondents may not answer questions accurately because of memory lapses. Other drawbacks include the possibility for differential interpretations of questions and motivated or unconscious response errors. That is, perpetrators might lie, underreport, or minimize the severity of their violent acts (Kessler et al., 2001; Riggs, Murphy, & O'Leary, 1989). Research has shown that a number of reporting biases can influence respondents' answers in such surveys, such as the tendency to perceive one's own violence as justified and therefore not reportable (see Kruttschnitt & Dornfeld, 1992).

Victimization (and perpetration) surveys are especially useful for gathering data about crimes such as spouse abuse and date rape, in which the victims may be reluctant to talk to police but may be willing to share information about the crimes in anonymous surveys. The most commonly cited data source of this kind in the United States is the National Crime Victimization Survey, a survey of 60,000 households conducted semiannually by the U.S. Bureau of the Census. Victimization surveys also have their drawbacks, however. Because they ask respondents about specific time periods (e.g., the previous 6 months), for example, they generally fail to tap the chronic and repetitive nature of victimization that is typical of family violence (Weis, 1989). Moreover, like respondents on self-report perpetration surveys, victimization survey respondents are likely to underreport the violence they have experienced. Even though they are promised anonymity and confidentiality, they may not tell the truth because they think what they have gone through is "a private matter," because they have already "reported it to another official," or because they fear retaliation (U.S. Bureau of Justice Statistics, 1992b). The relationship between victim and perpetrator strongly influences reporting: Victims often do not want to report violence perpetrated on them by family members (Harris, 1991; Waltermaurer, Ortega, & McNutt, 2003). In addition, research has shown that the interviewer's gender has strong effects on reporting, with women revealing sexual assault more readily to female interviewers (Sorenson, Stein, Siegel, Golding, & Burnam, 1987). (For an expanded discussion of the drawbacks of self-report surveys, see the link for this volume on the Sage Publications Web site at the URL noted above.)

The gathering of informant data requires that individuals report the use of violence they have observed by others; for example, children might report on violent acts that have taken place between their parents (e.g., Cronin, 1995; O'Brien, John, Margolin, & Erel, 1994). Although seemingly valid at first glance, informant reports may lack validity because informants (e.g., teachers) may not always know the extent of the behavior about which they are reporting (e.g., children's sexualized behaviors with peers). In fact, researchers in the area of children's exposure to parental violence more frequently ask parents to report on their children's behaviors than they ask children to provide self-report data (Peled & Davis, 1995; Wilkens, 2002). These reports may also be biased for other reasons, such as informants' defensiveness or level of psychological distress (DeVoe & Smith, 2002; Levendosky, Huth-Bocks, Semel, & Shapiro, 2002).

Direct observation of violent acts is a rarely used mode of data collection, but it may provide unusual insight into the dynamics of interpersonal violence (Weis, 1989). Direct observation also circumvents overreliance on self-reports. Urquiza and Timmer (2002) recommend that family violence researchers videotape study participants' social interactions or observe the interactions directly. As an illustration, researchers might watch couples as they quarrel in their own homes (Margolin, Burman, & John, 1989) or monitor the physiological responses of couples as they quarrel in laboratory settings (Jacobson & Gottman, 1993).

Assessment and Research Design Issues

Given the record of the 1980s and early 1990s, it is clear that progress in understanding family violence depends on improvements in the quality of research. The discussion below calls attention to the extraordinary difficulties of conducting family violence research in the field and proposes some solutions. Although researchers may well be aware of the value of including certain elements in their study designs, they typically must compromise some of their goals. Access to appropriate research subjects, for instance, may be extremely limited (Kinard, 2001). On the other hand, researchers often appear oblivious to research design defects that they could avoid with a reasonable amount of forethought.

Lack of theoretical foundation. Even though causation of family violence may be the most hotly contested issue in the field, a surprisingly large number of family violence studies lack any stated theoretical premise. By proposing a conceptual base and then testing it within a controlled study, a researcher can put forward the basic determinants of family violence. Because selection of treatment flows from etiological conceptions, debates concerning the causes of family violence spill over into quarrels about interventions.

Definitional disagreements. Without a doubt, the most problematic issue in family violence research is the lack of well-established and agreed-upon definitions. Overcoming this obstacle is challenging (see Fincham, 2000; O'Leary, Slep, & O'Leary, 2000). Definitions of abuse need to be sufficiently comprehensive to capture the experiences of victims, yet not so broad as to encompass behaviors that cannot be validly assessed (CDC, 2000). Some scholars have tailored their definitions very restrictively, and others have employed definitions that are quite broad. Family violence researchers' definitions of ancillary terms such as *child, neglect,* and *date rape* have also been vague or inconsistent. In some studies, for instance, the appellation *child* may refer to an individual under age 12, whereas in others it may include all persons up to age 18 (Goldman & Padayachi, 2000). Appel and Holden (1998) have outlined a prototypical outcome of definitional uncertainty, reporting that in 31 articles

covering the co-occurrence of physical child abuse and IPV, they found 15 different definitions of abuse.

It is essential that researchers differentiate **battering** (repetitive, severe physical and psychological abuse accompanied by fear and control) from normative abuse or common couple violence (a few slaps or shoves, not accompanied by fear or control) (Johnson, 2000; Schumacher, 2002). Family violence scholars' failure to reach accord on the meanings of such terms has significantly handicapped scientific inquiry, limited interpretations of research findings, restricted generalizations across studies, and impeded understanding of the very nature of family violence. In many circumstances, lack of standardized definitions has precluded the development of effective preventions and interventions (Portwood, 1999; Tatara & Kusmeskus, 1999).

Populations sampled. Family violence researchers have recruited widely divergent samples of people to examine, including the following: (a) individuals randomly chosen from the general population; (b) volunteers recruited from clinics or through door-to-door or telephone solicitation, or by advertisement; (c) individuals who are members of special groups, such as military recruits, college students, or postpartum mothers; and (d) people referred by agencies, such as elders. Researchers have also examined the records of hospital emergency room visits and police calls to gather sample data. Obviously, systematic differences exist between any two such sample populations, and this noncomparability hampers comparisons across studies (see Ohlin & Tonry, 1989).

The representativeness of study samples is another issue in family violence inquiries. A representative sample is one in which the sample's characteristics are proportionally similar to those of the population from which the sample was drawn. Representative samples, such as those used in the National Family Violence Surveys, the National Crime Victimization Survey, and the National Violence Against Women Survey, can be used to make inferences about entire populations. Some supposedly representative samples, however, may still exclude some kinds of people, such as those who have no telephones or who fall into circumscribed categories (e.g., gay men, non–English speakers, homeless people, and those living in institutions) (CDC, 2000). Nonresponse is also a complication, because it may raise questions about the representativeness of a sample (Koss et al., 1994).

Another type of sample, a clinical sample, can be drawn from any number of sources. In the case of family violence research, typical sources might be group homes for abused children, shelters for battered women, prisons, criminal justice records, and social service agencies. Clinical samples are small "handy" samples, but data gathered from them provide little knowledge about the broader population. Data derived from clinical samples commonly lack generalizability, even within small subgroups of the population. Findings based on data gathered from children living in battered women's shelters, for example, cannot be generalized to children living in violent homes or in foster care. Notwithstanding these serious limitations, research conducted with clinical samples provides useful information about the dynamics and causes of abuse and often generates initial impressions about prevention and treatment (see Weis, 1989).

Comparison groups. Most family violence research designs have failed to include satisfactory comparison groups of subjects. Comparison groups provide critical details about how target groups differ from or are similar to other groups. Without them, it is difficult to present a useful interpretation of research findings (see Chalk & King, 1998). When researchers have used comparison groups, moreover, they have all too frequently failed to conceptualize sufficiently the kinds of individuals appropriate for comparison. This has led to serious errors in the classification of subjects and, in turn, meaningless results (Smith, Thornton, DeVellis, Earp, & Coker, 2002). For example, as Rosenbaum (1988) has noted, in a study of maritally violent men, a suitable comparison group is not simply men who are maritally nonviolent, but rather men who are both unhappily married and maritally nonviolent. Some researchers have contrasted maritally violent men with generally violent men (Fagan, Stewart, & Hansen, 1983; Mowat-Leger, 2002).

When researchers cannot readily obtain comparison group data, they sometimes use normative data (i.e., data from published test standards). As an illustration, a researcher might initially obtain a clinical sample of foster mothers' ratings of children on the Child Behavior Checklist (CBCL), a standardized instrument designed to measure a variety of behavior problems (Achenbach & Edelbrock, 1983). The investigator might then compare the foster mothers' ratings with CBCL ratings obtained previously from a representative sample of mothers from the general population (the normative group ratings).

A disadvantage of relying on normative group scores is that the comparison does not control for any confounding variables (e.g., drug abuse) inherent in the target group. This critique can apply to comparisons between any naturally occurring groups. That is, when the researcher does not randomly assign participants to the conditions that are being compared, such as children in foster care versus children not in foster care, confounds may affect the results on dependent variables (e.g., CBCL ratings) (see Randolf & Conkle, 1993). Of course, researchers cannot randomly assign children to foster care or non–foster care conditions. Consequently, they settle for methods such as those described above, which are basically correlational in nature.

Longitudinal (outcome) studies. Experts generally advocate the use of research designs that extend over time, rather than cross-sectional designs, even though the data are still correlational (National Research Council, 1993). Without random assignment, causal inferences are difficult to make. To identify causal models, researchers may use advanced statistical procedures such as structural equation modeling.

Longitudinal investigations are expensive and difficult to conduct, in part because it can be hard to recruit sufficient numbers of research participants and attrition (or dropout) rates among participants are high. As might be expected, longitudinal studies also may have serious flaws. Typical of such shortcomings are instances in which test score variations can be attributed to children's age differences over time (e.g., Lauritsen, 1999; Yoshihama & Gillespie, 2002). (For an impressive example of a longitudinal analysis conducted by family violence researchers, see Runyan, Curtis, et al., 1998; and for a review of recruitment and retention problems in IPV research, see Dutton et al., 2003.)

Diversity awareness. Although the American Psychological Association has in recent years made cultural sensitivity a hallmark of its organizational goals, implementing these policy changes is a "work in progress" (Crawford, 2002). American family violence scholars have systematically indulged in what Hall (1997) calls "cultural malpractice." Individuals from certain communities (e.g., immigrants) have been understudied and underserved (Daniels, 2001; DeKeseredy, 2000; for a review, see Harway et al., 2002). To improve their studies of family violence, investigators must employ research designs that include minority groups. To help improve researchers' cultural sensitivity, the American Psychological

An Interview With K. Daniel O'Leary

"We may have to accept the very clear possibility that not all aggressive individuals may be amenable to treatment, and we need to have greater emphasis on helping young couples stop their physical aggression in its nascent stage."

K. Daniel O'Leary is a prolific researcher in the area of dating and marital violence. He is Distinguished Professor of Psychology at the State University of New York at Stony Brook, where he has supervised the dissertations and postdoctoral training of many clinical psychology students whose subsequent careers have been quite noteworthy. He serves on the editorial boards of the *Journal of Family Violence*, *Family Psychology*, and *Behavior Therapy*. He currently has a National Institute of Mental Health research grant (with Drs. Susan O'Leary and Amy Slep) to evaluate the extent and ways in which physical aggression toward partners and aggression toward children overlap. He is also an investigator on an NIMH grant (with Dr. Evelyn Bromet) on the prevalence of partner abuse and mental disorders in the war-ravaged Ukraine. He received his bachelor's degree in psychology at Pennsylvania State University and his Ph.D. in clinical psychology at the University of Illinois (1967).

Q: What has shaped your approach to the field?

A: Much of my early training included a mixture of cognitive and behavioral methodologies, and work with partners on marital and family issues certainly prompted me to see some aspects of partner aggression in a family context. In addition, my training as a clinical psychologist also prompted me to try to understand how individual psychopathology, like alcohol abuse and personality disorders, affects partner violence.

Q: What is your current research focus?

A: Currently, my research focus is on the etiology and treatment of physical aggression in relationships (the etiology of wife abuse). I see partner aggression as influenced by many factors, and David Riggs and I

Association (2003) has issued a set of guidelines on multicultural education, training, research, and organizational changes.

Family Violence Scales and Measurement Issues

Just as research design features are important, it is equally important that researchers address measurement issues. Incorrect or inadequate measurements lead to faulty assumptions about family violence that narrow understanding. Family violence scholars have had many disagreements about measuring family violence because optimal assessment methods remain uncertain.

Conflict Tactics Scale (CTS1). As noted in Chapter 1, the most widely used measure in family violence research is the Conflict Tactics Scale (Straus, 1979). The construction of the first version of this scale, or CTS1, represented an impressive leap forward in identification and quantification of specific violent interpersonal behaviors. Respondents to the CTS1 instrument indicate how many times in a given period (the previous year, the individual's lifetime) they used reasoning and argument, verbal and symbolic aggression, or physical aggression during interpersonal disagreements.

A slightly modified version of the scale is available for use by children and teenagers. For IPV assessment, investigators interview one or both members of a randomly selected couple. Overall, the scale has served as the basis for estimating family violence in a variety of groups, including adolescents, college students, same-sex partners, and elders. In a surprising turn of events, some researchers who have used CTS1 to examine published a background-situational model of partner aggression in 1996 that shows that background factors (e.g., violence in the family of origin and personality variables like aggression and impulsivity) operate along with more current situational variables (e.g., relationship discord, communication problems, and psychological aggression) to predict partner aggression. Variants of this model have been validated with several different samples, and we are trying to understand how some variables may play different roles in different populations.

Q: Which of the many articles that you have written in the last 10 years has attracted the most attention?

A: A longitudinal study of physical aggression in marriage in 1989 coauthored with Julian Barling, Ileana Arias, Alan Rosenbaum, Jean Malone, and Andrea Tyree. This study showed that physical aggression by men and women occurred in over one-third of young married couples. The fact that women themselves reported acts of physical aggression like pushing, slapping, and shoving at a rate equal to or greater than rates of their male partners was very surprising to some and controversial to most. Sequels to that study have basically replicated our results in community samples. These results do not imply that physical aggression is more common by women in all samples, and, in fact, in samples of battered women, one would not expect such. However, our results with high school students, college students, community couples, and marital clinic samples all show that physical aggression by women is as common as physical aggression by men (and such is the case even when you only rely on the reports of women about themselves and their partners).

Q: What are your future research goals?

A: I would like to be able to classify types of men and women who might respond to different types of treatment, and to classify those who might not respond to any psychological intervention. Aggression is a very stable phenomenon in both children and adults, in fact, as documented in a 1979 article by Daniel Olweus, almost as stable as intelligence. Thus we may have to alter our sights to reasonable treatment and change goals—accepting the very clear possibility that not all aggressive individuals may be amenable to treatment.

Q: What policy recommendation would you like to make?

A: To reduce levels of physical aggression in our society, of which partner aggression is simply one facet, we need to take broad preventive approaches. Like the approaches to alcohol and smoking, the prevention efforts have to start early. Given the intractability of the problem, prevention efforts need to be given much greater priority, as is beginning to be the case at the federal level. Psychological treatments should be evaluated for what they can and cannot do, and legal punishments should receive continuing evaluations. We also need to address gender issues in a straightforward manner with less volatility.

---

rates of IPV initially reported that women are as interpersonally violent as men (Magdol et al., 1997; O'Keefe & Treister, 1998).

The use of CTS1 has generated concerns that seem to represent a microcosm of the many problems inherent in family violence research. First and foremost, experts have argued that CTS1 misplaces violence questions within the context of family conflict. The assumption that IPV occurs *only* in the context of settling interpersonal disputes overlooks the very real occurrence of unprovoked aggression and aggression in the service of social control (Yllö, 1993). Critics have contended that, among several other limitations, CTS1 does not measure important aspects of family violence, such as the antecedents and consequences of violence (Koss et al., 1994; M. D. Schwartz, 2000).

Several empirically based inquiries have revealed that CTS1 does not measure men's IPV as adequately as it does women's (see Cascardi, Avery-Leaf, O'Leary, & Slep, 1999; Nazoo, 1995; Schafer, 1996). Findings anchored on CTS1 data have led to heated exchanges over the exclusion of contextual factors (e.g., fear) and claims of gender equivalence (Archer, 2000; DeKeseredy & Schwartz, 1998; White, Smith, Koss, & Figueredo, 2000).

Revised Conflict Tactics Scale (CTS2). With the revised version of the Conflict Tactics Scale, or CTS2, Straus and his colleagues attempted to remedy CTS1's perceived weaknesses. CTS2 assesses IPV more broadly than does CTS1. Its improvements on CTS1 include clarified wording, improved differentiation between minor and severe degrees of violence, and a simplified format. CTS2 includes five subscales: negotiation, psychological aggression, physical assault, sexual coercion, and injury. All but the negotiation subscale incorporate both minor and severe forms of violence (Straus, Hamby, Boney-McCoy, & Sugarman, 1995). To examine the psychometric properties of CTS2, scholars have used the scale with a variety of populations, including incarcerated women. Several factor-analytic inquiries have demonstrated excellent matches between empirically derived clusters of items and subscales of CTS2 (see Jones, Ji, Beck, & Beck, 2002; Lucente, Fals-Stewart, Richards, & Goscha, 2001).

In addition to any other issues raised by CTS1 and CTS2, scholars have found that the use of these scales poses research design dilemmas. Researchers, for example, have shown substantial dissimilarities in their categorization of research participants into violent and nonviolent groups based on CTS scores. Whereas some researchers may accept one use of minor violence over a lifetime as the criterion for placement in a violent group, others may not consider subjects violent unless their CTS scores indicate two or more severe acts of aggression (Schumacher, Feldbau-Kohn, Slep, & Heyman, 2001). A respondent to CTS2 is asked to rate the frequencies of his or her own behaviors or those of someone else, such as a boyfriend or girlfriend. The following statements are similar in nature to the items found in CTS2:

- You discussed the disagreement calmly.
- You refused to talk about your feelings.
- You threw a hard object at your partner.
- You punched your partner in the face.
- You threatened your partner with a weapon.
- You coerced your partner to have unwanted sex.
- You had to see a doctor because you were injured.

The items on the Parent-Child Conflict Tactics Scale, which is known as CTSPC (Straus, Hamby, Finkelhor, Moore, & Runyan, 1998), are similar to the following:

- Mother told me why some things were bad to do.
- Father spanked me with a belt or chain.
- Father threatened to burn me but didn't do it.
- Mother pushed me down the stairs.
- Father told me I was really stupid.
- Mother left me alone in the house without a babysitter.

Growing recognition of psychological abuse. In recent years, ever-expanding numbers of individuals concerned about family violence have called for additional recognition of psychological (emotional) abuse that goes beyond what the CTS scales measure (e.g., Elliston, 2001; O'Leary, 1999; Tang, 1997). These advocates argue that understanding the parameters of emotional abuse is essential because this kind of maltreatment appears to be even more damaging than physical abuse (e.g., Coker et al., 2002; Harned, 2001).

Although constructs of child and adult psychological aggression overlap, distinctions remain. Some forms of psychological abuse, such as rejection, may have comparable effects across ages and genders (e.g., shame or sadness). Other forms of abuse, such as inducing an individual to engage in antisocial behavior (e.g., bullying), may produce dissimilar outcomes across the same variables. As one might suspect, it is even more difficult for family violence researchers to reach accord about defining and measuring psychological abuse than it is for them to agree about measurements of physical abuse (Schumacher, Slep, & Heyman, 2001b). Should scholars assess the construct of emotional abuse in terms of frequency, intent, duration, perceptions of victims, or harm done to victims? Who has the authority to decide the true meaning of the construct? Will empirical research resolve the issue?

Need for multiple measurements. Because no single scale is sufficient to gauge every dimension of family violence, researchers should use multiple measures. They also should obtain both quantitative and qualitative data. Interview data, for instance, yield more comprehensive information than do data gathered through the examination of records kept by health agencies (Smith, Smith, & Earp, 1999; Verhoek-Oftedahl et al., 2000). Furthermore, questionnaires designed to measure given constructs (e.g., abuse) sometimes yield disparate results (Hamby, Poindexter, & Gray-Little, 1996). Analogously, clinicians should use multiple measures when assessing clients, especially when their findings will be used to make decisions that may alter the clients' lives (e.g., decisions concerning recommendations for placement in foster or institutional care) (Budd, Felix, Poindexter, Naik-Polan, & Sloss, 2002).

Cultural competence in assessment. For many years, family violence researchers have often excluded persons who belong to racial or ethnic minority groups from research samples. To make matters worse, when researchers have recruited minority study participants, they have usually assessed them using inappropriate questionnaires or inappropriate test administration. It is important, for example, that researchers use correct appellations for minority groups and that they test minority group members in ways that meet with these individuals' cultural mores. Of course, it is expensive and time-consuming to translate existing tests into other languages and to validate the translated versions, but this may not be the only reason researchers have tended to ignore minority populations. Rather, scholars' disinterest in minorities may actually lie at the heart of the oversight. (For a set of guidelines concerning multicultural education and other variables, see American Psychological Association, 2003.)

In recent years, government funding and other inducements have allowed social scientists to make some inroads into the evaluation of family violence among more diverse populations. Representative of these fledgling efforts are studies of American Indian families (Stubben, 2001), families in developing countries (Marenin, 1997), Blacks and Hispanics (Cunradi, Caetano, & Schafer, 2002), and Asian American immigrants (Dasgupta, 2000; Yoshihama, 2001). Clinicians also have an obligation to become culturally competent so that they can assess the needs of their clients who are members of underserved groups.

Estimating rates of family violence. Family violence is such a complex multidimensional problem that no single set of numbers or statistics can adequately capture the phenomenon (U.S. Department of Justice, 2000). Researchers, students, and members of the lay public need to recognize that statistical estimates of the prevalence and incidence of various forms of family violence are not empirical facts. Rather, they are conjectures based on quantitative data that are easily influenced by many factors, such as the nature of the sources and types of samples from which they come. Note, for example, that estimates of the proportion of U.S. families in which violent acts occur range from 20% to 55%, and estimates of severe acts of violence extend from 1% to 9% (for a minor review, see Gordon, 2000). The wide span of these appraisals is a clear indication that nobody knows exactly how much family violence takes place.

In discussing family violence, scientists typically report **prevalence** rates, **incidence** rates, or both. Family violence research, however, has been plagued by considerable confusion over the precise meanings of these terms (Brownridge & Halli, 1999). In general, *prevalence* of family violence refers to the number of people in the population of interest who are affected by the occurrence of family-violent acts. *Incidence* refers to the frequency of family-violent acts occurring within this subgroup of affected individuals.

Statistical and Evaluation Matters

In addition to the pitfalls described above, statistical analysis is another area of methodological weakness in the family violence research.

Researcher training. Some statisticians have denounced the ways social science researchers in general analyze and present their data, implying that the basic problem is inadequate training on the part of the researchers. The American Psychological Association's Task Force on Statistical Inference has asserted that scholars need to learn the importance of describing their data fully, characterizing their analyses thoroughly, scrutinizing the results of their analyses carefully for anomalies, and reporting the magnitude of relationships (cited in B. Azar, 1997). The task force also recommends that researchers employ research designs and analyses that are as simple as possible. Other observers have noted that the academic training researchers receive in conducting longitudinal studies appears to be suboptimal (Stouthamer-Loeber, van Kammen, & Loeber, 1992). Finally, some scholars have suggested that, in order to meet the needs of policy makers, researchers should translate their findings into simple terms and illustrate them with graphs. They should also offer clear policy recommendations based on their findings. Frequently, legislators lack sufficient staff to search through journals and Web sites for research applicable to their needs (Feldman, Nadash, & Gursen, 2001).

Univariate versus multivariate designs. Although simplicity in research designs is commendable, overreliance on single-variable (e.g., gender) analyses tends to fragment and narrow family violence researchers' findings in the field. Comparisons based on multiple variables (e.g., gender, age, abuse type), in contrast, can deepen researchers' understanding of the dynamics of violent families (Williams, 1992).

Assessments of **risk markers** are multivariate approaches that allow statisticians to pinpoint the degree of association between antecedent and consequent variables. Emblematic of this approach is a risk-factor study that uncovered several precursors of sexual offending, such as childhood emotional abuse and family dysfunction (Lee, Jackson, Pattison, & Ward, 2002). Another multivariate technique useful for making sense of vast quantities of data derived from individual studies is **meta-analysis,** which has been described as a set of "quantitative procedures for summarizing or integrating findings obtained from a literature review of a subject" (Vogt, 1993, p. 138). By combining findings from a large number of studies, meta-analysis brings clarity to areas where individual studies have had conflicting results. (For a meta-analysis of child sexual abuse data, see Bouvier et al., 1999.)

Case histories and qualitative studies. Case histories such as those presented throughout this book enliven researchers' dissemination of information about family violence. Qualitative studies accomplish similar goals by adding richness and meaning to quantitative data. As Vogt (1993) observes, "Qualitative components are crucial to most good quantitative research, which begins with theories, concepts, and constructs" (pp. 183–184). (For a qualitative comparison of Anglo-American and African American women's experiences in ending abuse in their relationships, see Moss, Pitula, Campbell, & Halstead, 1997; and for an extensive evaluation of research practices in family violence, see Chalk & King, 1998.)

Ethical Issues

The most central ethical requirement of any form of research with human subjects is the protection of those subjects (M. D. Schwartz, 2000). Fears regarding the possibility that human research participants may somehow be harmed as a result of their participation have so far prompted four U.S. states (California, Maryland, New York, Virginia) to create regulations governing the procedures that researchers must follow when working with human subjects (Kessler, 2002). In fact, when someone is injured while participating in a medical or psychological inquiry (e.g., receives the wrong medicine dosage, is made to feel stupid), a legal response may ensue.

Although ethical constraints are necessary, there is no denying that they hamper the progress of research (e.g., researchers cannot compel anyone to participate in their studies). In working with human subjects, family violence researchers must meet several important ethical requirements: (a) ensure the safety of research participants, investigators, and mental health workers; (b) obtain informed consent from all research subjects and make sure that those giving consent are competent to do so; (c) guarantee anonymity (where possible) and confidentiality to research participants and use methods that honor this pledge; (d) disclose research findings carefully, describing methodology, conclusions, and limitations of the work meticulously and with political sensitivity; (e) implement the legal duty to warn and protect certain groups endangered by violent subjects; and (f) display cultural competence in working with participants whose cultures are different from the researchers' own (e.g., members of ethnic minority groups, immigrants, disabled persons, or gay, lesbian, bisexual, and transgendered persons).

The number of publications devoted to the ethical issues involved in research and practice with human research participants has mushroomed over the past few years. (For a list of some of these resources, see the link for this volume on the Sage Publications Web site at the URL noted above.)

Universities have been at the forefront of the movement toward improved ethical standards in research and practice with human subjects. Indeed, psychology instructors are finding ways to incorporate the subject of research and practice ethics across the entire curriculum (e.g., Balogh, 2002; Benson, 2002; Kitchener, 2000). The American Psychological Association commissioned a task force to formulate recommendations for ethical guidelines for those who work in the field of family violence (Harway et al., 2002). Other disciplines associated with family violence research, such as criminal justice, counseling, psychiatry, education, medicine, and nursing, have also expanded the emphasis on ethics in their curricula (see Hyman, 2000; McSkimming, Sever, & King, 2000; Orb, Eisenhauer, & Wynaden, 2000).

An example of questionable ethical behavior in family violence research would be a researcher's requiring a child victim in a child sexual assault study to spend time alone in the same room with the perpetrator of the abuse. Looking back at the case history that opens this chapter, how do you think it would have worked out if a researcher had interviewed Juanita in her living room while Miguel was reading in the adjacent dining room? How would Juanita have felt if a male interviewer had asked her whether she had been raped by her husband? Would it be ethical for interviewers to quiz Juanita and Miguel's neighbors about the couple's marriage? Would it be safe for an investigator to check on Juanita's situation 36 months later?

PRACTICE, POLICY, AND PREVENTION ISSUES

Practice Issues

The literature covered in this chapter has several implications for practice. Family violence scholars could improve their contributions to the field by doing the following: (a) keeping abreast of emerging ethical and legal issues and applying them in their work, (b) improving their own cultural sensitivity, (c) finding ways to collaborate with other researchers more harmoniously, and (d) improving their awareness of their own personal preferences for interventions and the empirical foundations of those interventions.

Policy Implications

Policy makers can contribute to progress in the field of family violence by doing the following: (a) improving funding for longitudinal studies; (b) requiring ethics education in applicable graduate schools; (c) encouraging collaborative efforts among researchers, practitioners, and advocates at all levels; and (d) convening symposia to reach agreement on definitions.

CHAPTER SUMMARY

Academicians, professionals, and activists from diverse disciplines have embraced the issue of family violence and have worked diligently to deepen society's understanding of this problem. The U.S. government has become more actively involved over the past decade by funding more research, developing new surveillance systems, and convening panels of experts to confer about important issues. Regrettably, the individual nature of research conducted in separate academic fields has resulted in a disorganized representation of family violence.

Logicians have promulgated numerous theories to explain and unify disparate research findings. No one conceptual framework adequately explains family violence, but evidence has emerged that supports several theories. One practical organization classifies theories into two major groups: macrotheories and microtheories. Macrotheories concerning family violence are broad-based conceptions; they include theories based in cultural acceptance of violence, patriarchal determinants, peer influences, and

feminist analysis. Social-structural factors (e.g., poverty and family stress) and deterrence theory (the low cost of family violence) are other useful explanations.

Microtheories, in contrast, are anchored in individual behaviors. Learning explanations for family violence, the most empirically grounded of this group of theories, rest primarily on the concepts of social learning (modeling) and classical and operant conditioning. Learning principles form the basis for arguments concerning the intergenerational transmission of violence. Individual intrapersonal theories (psychopathology, psychological traits, psychobiological traits) and interpersonal interaction theories (dyadic stress, parent-child stress, and insecure attachment) complete the microtheory category. Although family violence research would benefit from the development of multidimensional theories, the complexity of the family violence problem has made such theories elusive.

Conducting research in the field of family violence is daunting in part because of the sensitivity of the topic and the need to shield at-risk target populations. Much of the research in the field has been methodologically weak, but it is now slowly improving. Many variables (e.g., sample selection, type of questionnaire employed, relationship between victim and perpetrator) influence study results. Researchers in various family violence subfields collect data from a wide variety of sources that are compatible with their expertise. Despite long-standing differences in their goals, family violence researchers and practitioners have recently begun to work more collaboratively.

An initial deficiency in family violence research has been the lack of a theoretical footing. In addition, at the core of criticisms of research across the entire field has been the lack of uniform definitions. Without such definitions, meaningful comparisons among studies are not possible. Furthermore, many studies have employed either representative samples or small clinical samples, and so their findings have proved insufficient to improve scholars' understanding of the prevalence and incidence of family violence. Other shortcomings of family violence research include the lack of appropriately conceived and assessed comparison groups in research designs, the limited number of longitudinal studies conducted, and the failure to include members of marginalized groups in study samples.

Measurement issues have become a focal point, if not a rallying cry, for various subgroups of researchers. The original Conflict Tactics Scale has been the most widely used instrument for measuring family-violent behaviors. Straus and his colleagues have revised this scale to include questions about injury outcomes and sexual assault. Both CTS1 and CTS2 assess violent behaviors through self-reports of perpetrators, victims, and informants. Despite their extensive use and excellent psychometric properties, these scales have drawn the criticism of skeptics who assert that they decontextualize family-violent behaviors and their meanings.

In recent years, family violence researchers have increasingly recognized the need to incorporate the phenomenon of emotional abuse into definitions of family violence. Both researchers and practitioners need to use multiple measures in their assessments in order to gather information on all forms of abuse. Several new and improved government surveillance systems have expanded to cover reports of violence within special populations. These large studies hold great promise for the field.

Statisticians have asserted that researcher training in statistical analysis is faulty. As true experimental studies are impermissible in family violence research, more quasi-experimental studies are needed. Currently, there is an overreliance on univariate designs when multivariate designs are needed. The use of sophisticated statistical techniques, such as risk assessment and meta-analysis, has begun to help explain disparate research findings.

The current heightened emphasis on the protection of human research subjects, although necessary, has impeded the application of rigorous research methodologies. The past few years have seen the publication of an avalanche of new or updated ethical guidelines for research with human subjects.

In the final analysis, it is important to note that despite the many methodological limitations of research on family violence, a large and growing body of research worthy of academic consideration has emerged, and scholars have established a modest core of principles that have met with general acceptance.

DISCUSSION QUESTIONS

1. In which major academic and professional fields can one find researchers and practitioners who are concerned with understanding and eliminating family violence?

2. Why do family violence researchers and practitioners sometimes have difficulty working together effectively?

3. What is the difference between macrotheories and microtheories of family violence? Select one theory in each category and evaluate it.

4. Why does the field of family violence pose extraordinary problems for the conduct of research?

5. What kinds of issues arise when researchers attempt to define and assess family violence?

6. How important is it that definitions of family violence incorporate the concept of emotional abuse?

7. Think of a population you would like to study or know more about in relation to family violence. Propose a research design that would answer your specific questions of interest about that population.

8. What ethical issues are associated with family violence research? Why are ethical guidelines for researchers necessary?

9. How can investigators study cases such as that of Juanita and Miguel (presented at the opening of this chapter)? Why did violence occur in Juanita and Miguel's relationship? What should Juanita do?

10. How might society prevent violence in intimate relationships?

RECOMMENDED READING

American Psychological Association. (2003). Guidelines on multicultural education, training, research, practice, and organizational change for psychologists. *American Psychologist, 58,* 377–402.

Barata, P., & Senn, C. Y. (2003). When two worlds collide: An examination of the assumptions of social science research and law within the domain of domestic violence. *Trauma, Violence, & Abuse, 4,* 3–21.

Centers for Disease Control and Prevention. (2000, October 27). Building data systems for monitoring and responding to violence against women. *Morbidity and Mortality Weekly Report, 49,* 1–19.

Feindler, E. L., Rathus, J. H., & Silver, L. B. (2003). *Assessment of family violence: A handbook for researchers and practitioners.* Washington, DC: American Psychological Association.

Feldman, P. H., Nadash, P., & Gursen, M. (2001). Improving communication between researchers and policy makers in long-term care: Or, researchers are from Mars; policy makers are from Venus. *Gerontologist, 41,* 312–321.

Harway, M., Geffner, R., Ivey, D., Koss, M. P., Murphy, B. C., Mio, J. S., & O'Neil, J. M. (2002). *Intimate partner abuse and relationship violence.* Washington, DC: American Psychological Association.

National Institute of Justice & American Bar Association. (1998). *Legal interventions in family violence: Research findings and policy implications* (NCJ Publication No. 171666). Washington, DC: U.S. Department of Justice.

U.S. Department of Justice. (2000). *Measuring violence against women: Recommendations from an interagency workshop* (NCJ Publication No. 184447). Washington, DC: Author.

Ward, S., & Finkelhor, D. (2000). *Program evaluation and family violence research.* Binghamton, NY: Haworth.

NOTE

1. Unless otherwise noted, all of the case histories presented in this volume come from our own personal knowledge of the cases described, which we have gathered through our experience as researchers and practitioners in the field of family violence. Also unless otherwise noted, all of the names used in these case histories are pseudonyms.

3

CHILD PHYSICAL ABUSE

Case History: Kevin Fell Off of His Razor

Kevin was placed in foster care because his community's Department of Child Protective Services determined that his family was "in conflict." The placement was made after 10-year-old Kevin was seen at the local hospital's emergency room for bruises, welts, and cuts on his back. According to his mother's report to emergency room personnel, the boy "fell off of his Razor" (scooter) while riding down a hill near the family home. Kevin was very quiet during the visit, never speaking but occasionally nodding his head in affirmation of his mother's report. The attending physician, however, believed that Kevin's injuries were unlikely to have occurred as the result of such a fall. Rather, they appeared consistent with the kinds of injuries a child might have from being slapped repeatedly or possibly whipped with a belt or other object.

Initially, Kevin's mother persisted in her story that Kevin had fallen from his Razor, but after the doctor told her that the injuries could not have resulted from such an accident, she confessed that her boyfriend of several years, Sam, had some strong opinions about how children should behave and how they should be disciplined. She reported that Sam had a "short temper" when it came to difficult behavior in children and that he sometimes "lost his cool" in disciplining Kevin. She also suggested that Kevin's behavior could often be very difficult to control. She said that Kevin had numerous problems, including difficulties in school (e.g., trouble with reading) and with peers (e.g., physically fighting with other children); she described both acting-out behaviors (e.g., setting fire to objects, torturing and killing small animals, stealing) and oppositional behaviors (e.g., skipping school, refusing to do homework, breaking curfew, being noncompliant with requests).

In interviews with a child protective services worker, Kevin revealed that he was, in fact, experiencing physical abuse inflicted by his mother's boyfriend. Kevin reluctantly acknowledged that Sam frequently disciplined him by repeatedly slapping a belt across his back. Kevin reported that on these occasions he tried hard not to cry, but that often the whippings hurt so much that he couldn't help himself. He also talked about an incident that had taken place when he was several years younger. He had been playing with some baby ducks that lived in the pond in his backyard, trying to teach the ducks to "swim underwater." When Sam saw Kevin submerging the ducklings' heads under the water, he became very angry and "taught Kevin a lesson" by holding Kevin's head underwater repeatedly. Kevin was tearful as he told this story and stated that at the time, he thought he was going to drown.

After Kevin had been in foster care for several weeks, his foster mother indicated that he was doing very well and described him as a "remarkably adaptive child." She said she found him to be a "warm, loving kid," and he had not exhibited "any behavior problems other than what you might expect from a 10-year-old boy." She reported also that Kevin "hoped to go home soon" because he "missed his mother and Sam." He believed that he was placed in foster care because he was disobedient toward his mother and her boyfriend, and because he hadn't been doing well in school.

The experiences of children such as Kevin, and their likely feelings about their abuse, are well reflected in the lyrics of the song "Hell Is for Children," as recorded by Pat Benatar in the 1980s:[1]

They cry in the dark so you can't see their tears.
They hide in the light so you can't see their fears.
Forgive and forget.
All the while, love and pain become one in [sic] the same in the eyes of a wounded child.

Because hell, hell is for children.
And you know that their little lives can become such a mess.
Hell! Hell is for children.
And you shouldn't have to pay for your love with your bones and your flesh.

It's all so confusing this brutal abusing.
They blacken your eyes and then apologize.
Be Daddy's little girl and don't tell Mommy a thing.
Be a good little boy and you'll get a new toy.
Tell Grandma you fell off the swing.

The case history presented above and these lyrics poignantly describe the world of the abused child. Until the 1960s, society was relatively unaware of the "hell" characteristic of abused children's lives. Child maltreatment was considered a mythical or rare phenomenon that occurred only in some people's imaginations or in "sick" lower-class families. As is now more widely known, however, child maltreatment is an ugly reality for millions of children. In 1990, the U.S. Advisory Board on Child Abuse and Neglect described the level of child maltreatment in the United States as a national emergency.

In this chapter, we focus on one form of child maltreatment: child physical abuse (CPA). We first examine issues related to the definition of the physical abuse of children and the use of official estimates and self-report surveys for determining the magnitude of the problem. We then shift our attention to some of the characteristics that research has found to be typical of physically abused children and the adults who abuse them. We also present evaluations of the short-term and long-term consequences associated with CPA. We conclude the chapter with a discussion of the major theories concerning the causes of CPA and recommendations for addressing the problem.

Scope of the Problem

What Is Child Physical Abuse?

One of the most significant issues in understanding the problem of CPA is that of defining the term *child physical abuse*. Consider the following situations:

- Jimmy, a 3-year-old, was playing with his puppy in his backyard when he tried to make the puppy stay near him by pulling roughly on the dog's tail. Jimmy's father saw the child vigorously pulling on the puppy's tail and yelled at him to stop. When Jimmy did not respond quickly, his father grabbed Jimmy's arm and pulled him away from the dog. The father then began pulling on Jimmy's ear, actually tearing the skin, to "teach him a lesson" about the appropriate way to treat a dog.
- Angela's baby, Maria, had colic from the day she was born. This meant that from 4:00 in the afternoon until 8:00 in the evening, every day, Maria cried inconsolably. No matter what Angela did, she could not get Maria to stop crying. One evening, after 5-month-old Maria had been crying for 3 hours straight, Angela became so frustrated that she began shaking Maria. The shaking caused Maria to cry more loudly, which in turn caused Angela to shake the infant more vigorously. Angela shook Maria until the baby lost consciousness.
- Ryan and his brother, Matthew, were playing with their Power Rangers in Ryan's bedroom when they got into a disagreement. Both boys began hitting each other and calling each other names. Their mother heard the commotion and came running into the room and separated the two boys. She then took each boy, pulled down his trousers, put him over her knee, and spanked him several times.

These vignettes portray a range of behaviors, from actions that are clearly abusive to some that may or may not be considered abusive. Acts of violence perpetrated by adults against children and adolescents range from mild slaps to extremely injurious attacks. Researchers and practitioners concerned with CPA have also discovered that violence against children sometimes takes unusual forms, as in cases of the disorder known as **Munchausen by proxy**, in which adults falsify physical and/or psychological symptoms in a child in order to meet their own psychological needs (see Box 3.1). Prior to the 1960s, however, few, if any, of the adults' actions in the above scenarios would have been labeled abusive.

Box 3.1 Munchausen by Proxy

In recent years, family violence researchers and practitioners have focused attention on the underrecognized form of child maltreatment known as *Munchausen by proxy* (MBP; also sometimes called *Munchausen syndrome by proxy*). Munchausen syndrome is a factitious disorder in which adults seek medical treatment for no apparent purpose other than to assume the role of patient. Meadow first used the term *Munchausen syndrome by proxy* in 1977 to describe a constellation of behaviors by an adult in which a child is used as the vehicle for fabricated illness. MBP includes two diagnostic components: the presence of pediatric condition falsification in the child victim and the presence of factitious disorder by proxy in the adult perpetrator (Ayoub, Alexander, et al., 2002). As Ayoub, Alexander, and colleagues (2002) explain, pediatric condition falsification is "a form of child maltreatment in which an adult falsifies physical and/or psychological signs and/or symptoms in a victim, causing the victim to be regarded as ill or impaired by others" (p. 106). The fourth edition of the *Diagnostic and Statistical Manual of Mental Disorders* defines the essential features of factitious disorder by proxy as the "deliberate production or feigning of physical or psychological signs or symptoms *in another person* who is under the individual's care," motivated by "a psychological need to assume the sick role by proxy" (American Psychiatric Association, 1994, p. 725; emphasis added).

Typically, children who are victims of MBP are "paraded before the medical profession with a fantastic range of illnesses" (D. A. Rosenberg, 1987, p. 548). Jones (1994) describes the principal routes that caregivers with MBP take to produce or feign illness in children, including the fabrication of symptoms, alteration of laboratory specimens (e.g., urine or blood), and direct production of physical symptoms or disease. For example, caregivers have been known to contaminate children's urine specimens with their own blood and claim that the children have been urinating blood (D. A. Rosenberg, 1987). One mother repeatedly administered laxatives to her child, causing severe diarrhea, blood infection, and dehydration (Peters, 1989). In another case, a mother injected feces into her child's intravenous line to produce illness in the child (D. A. Rosenberg, 1987).

Recent evidence also suggests that adults with MBP may not only actively induce illness in their children but may engage in indirect methods of falsification, such as over- or underreporting physical symptoms and/or coaching the child victims or others to misrepresent the children as ill (Ayoub, Alexander, et al., 2002; Feldman, Stout, & Inglis, 2002). In some cases, adults may fabricate or exaggerate psychological, psychiatric, or developmental symptoms in children, although the falsification of nonphysical symptoms appears to be less common (Schreier, 1997). In one recent study, Ayoub, Schreier, and Keller (2002) found that mothers with MBP falsified educational disabilities (e.g., attention-deficit/hyperactivity disorder, learning disabilities, and/or behavioral difficulties) in their children in attempts to meet their own needs to be perceived as "exceptionally interested and invested parents" or as persons who are "competent and self-sacrificing" (p. 150).

Until relatively recently, very little was known about MBP other than the anecdotal information presented in case reports. As recognition of the condition has increased, however, several studies have assessed the characteristics of adults with MBP and their child victims. The children are typically quite young, most in their preschool years, although the onset of MBP victimization frequently occurs in infancy (Feldman et al., 2002; D. A. Rosenberg, 1987). The victimizing adults are most often the mothers of their victims, and these women often have considerable experience or knowledge in health-related areas (Meadow, 1990). Evidence suggests that such individuals frequently suffer from additional disturbances, such as Munchausen syndrome, personality disorders, reported histories of abuse in childhood, drug and alcohol problems, eating disorders, and mental illness (Bools, Neale, & Meadow, 1994; Feldman et al., 2002). The majority of the conditions that MBP caregivers inflict on children involve the gastrointestinal, genitourinary, and central nervous systems (American Psychiatric Association, 1994). Exaggerated complaints of real and common illnesses have also been documented, including asthma, allergies, sinopulmonary infections (e.g., ear and sinus infections), and drug reactions/sensitivities (Feldman et al., 2002). Some have suggested that another characteristic of MBP victims is having had siblings die under unusual circumstances (e.g., multiple sibling deaths; Meadow, 1990).

An adult's production or feigning of illness in a dependent child is considered abusive, in large part, because of the serious physical consequences to the child. The procedures that MBP caregivers use to produce illness in children often cause the children physical discomfort or pain. For example, McClung, Murray, and Braden (1988) describe cases in which caregivers administered ipecac to children to produce symptoms (e.g., recurrent and chronic vomiting and diarrhea). Such behaviors on the part of caregivers sometimes results in children's deaths. One review of MBP cases found that 9% of the children in the study sample died as a result of the procedures inflicted on them by their parents (D. A. Rosenberg, 1987). In addition, children victimized by MBP are often subjected to unnecessary, painful, and potentially harmful medical procedures as physicians attempt to diagnose and treat the symptoms described by the children's caregivers (Malatack, Wiener, Gartner, Zitelli, & Brunetti, 1985; Meadow, 1977). Such children are also at risk for later psychiatric and psychological problems (Ayoub, Deutsch, & Kinscherff, 2000; McGuire & Feldman, 1989).

It is important that MBP families receive treatment, because MBP behaviors are likely to continue over time if left untreated (McGuire & Feldman, 1989). Sanders and Bursch (2002) have recently outlined several recommendations for case management and treatment of MBP families: First, treatment teams should be created that allow for open and continual communication among child protective services, foster care parents, physicians, and therapists; second, foster care placement should be seriously considered for all children, given the risk of continued abuse or death for children in such families; third, strict guidelines should be observed (e.g., parents should not be allowed to give their children candy or medicine or to discuss health-related issues with them) and regular monitoring should be incorporated into all parental visits with their children; fourth, parents should be required to engage in a medical monitoring plan to enhance the identification of any reoccurrence of MBP behaviors and to ensure that any medical treatments are properly authorized; fifth, efforts should be made to integrate the children into full-time school programs that may include individualized educational programming; and sixth, psychotherapy is indicated for the children as well as for both parents, and long-term follow-up with social services is strongly recommended.

With the "discovery" of child abuse during the 1960s (Kempe, Silverman, Steele, & Droegemueller, 1962) and the increased interest in child protection that followed in the United States, definitions of child abuse changed rapidly. For the most part, the definitions that first emerged focused on acts of violence that cause some form of observable harm. Therefore, although recognition of CPA was increasing, the definition of physical abuse was still restrictive. As Gelles and Cornell (1990)

point out, "If a father takes a gun and shoots at his child and misses, there is no physical injury. There is, of course, harm in a father's shooting and missing, but the act itself does not qualify as abuse" (p. 21).

In 1988, the National Center on Child Abuse and Neglect broadened the definition of abuse to include both a **harm standard** and an **endangerment standard** (U.S. DHHS, 1988, 1996). The harm standard recognizes children as CPA victims if they have observable injuries that last at least 48 hours. Children without observable injuries may also be recognized as abuse victims if they are deemed substantially *at risk* for injury or endangerment. Despite relatively inclusive definitions such as this one, controversy continues to exist regarding which specific behaviors should be labeled *violent* or *abusive*. As we have noted in Chapter 1, most family violence experts and researchers define *violence* as an act carried out intentionally (or nonaccidentally) to cause physical pain or injury to another person (Gelles & Cornell, 1990). *Acts* of violence, however, can range from a slap on the hand to a cigarette burn on the face to an attack so violent that the result is death. What range of behaviors should be included under the umbrella of CPA?

Physical punishment and child rearing. In Chapter 1, we made a distinction between legitimate and illegitimate violence. At one extreme of the continuum are those practices considered to be "normal" violence, including commonplace physical acts such as slapping, pushing, and spanking. Many people consider such acts to be acceptable as part of the punishment of children in the course of child rearing. Indeed, survey data suggest that most Americans do not label such behaviors as abusive and that the behaviors are quite common. In surveys of parents, for example, 75–90% have reported that they use some form of physical punishment with their children (Straus, Hamby, Finkelhor, Moore, & Runyan, 1998; Wauchope & Straus, 1990). Similar studies of young adults have shown comparable rates, with 93–95% reporting having experienced some physical punishment as children or adolescents (Bryan & Freed, 1982; Graziano & Namaste, 1990). As Graziano and Namaste (1990) state:

> Slapping, spanking, paddling, and, generally, hitting children for purposes of discipline are accepted, pervasive, adult behaviors in U.S. families. In these instances, although anger, physical attack, and pain are involved between two people of vastly different size, weight, and strength, such behavior is commonly accepted as a proper exercise of adult authority over children. (pp. 459–460)

Many who study child maltreatment find this level of acceptance of "normal" violence appalling. Perhaps the most significant critic of the cultural acceptance of corporal punishment is Murray Straus, who has attracted considerable attention in recent years for his research and views on spanking (see, Straus, 1991c,

1994). Straus argues that spanking is harmful for two reasons. First, the use of spanking legitimates violence: When authority figures spank, they are, in essence, condoning the use of violence as a way of dealing with frustration and settling disputes. Second, the implicit message of acceptance of this form of violence contributes to violence in other aspects of society. According to Straus's (1991c) "cultural spillover theory," violence "in one sphere of life tends to engender violence in other spheres" (p. 137).

The research evidence tends to support this perspective, indicating that spanking is positively correlated with other forms of family violence, including sibling abuse and spouse assault. On the basis of findings from the first National Family Violence Survey, Straus (1991c) estimated that children who had been physically punished during the previous year were three times more likely to have assaulted a sibling during that year. Spanking is also correlated with crime outside the home, including self-reported delinquency, arrest, and homicide (Straus, 1991c). Straus's most recent research focuses on the relationship between spanking and antisocial behaviors such as cheating, telling lies, and disobedience in school. His findings suggest that parents who use spanking to punish antisocial behavior are actually contributing to subsequent antisocial behavior in their children (Straus, Sugarman, & Giles-Sims, 1997). Especially problematic, according to Straus and Mouradian (1998), is impulsive corporal punishment, in which parents lash out in anger, without forethought or control. A recent meta-analysis of corporal punishment research confirms many of the conclusions that Straus and his colleagues have drawn; Gershoff (2002a) examined 88 studies and found associations between corporal punishment and several negative outcomes in childhood as well as adulthood, including deficits in moral internalization, poor mental health, and increased aggression, antisocial behavior, and abusive behavior toward others.

As many observers have noted, however, two variables can be correlated without necessarily being causally connected (e.g., Baumrind, Larzelere, & Cowan, 2002; Gershoff, 2002a; Straus, 1994). Perhaps children with problem behaviors, who tend to be spanked more than other children, also tend to go on to lives of crime in any case. It is also possible that the main reason spanking and other forms of violence are correlated is that CPA and violence are correlated. That is, because children who are physically abused are presumably likely to be spanked, spanking might appear to be a causal contributor to violence when it is

An Interview With Murray Straus

"We have to change the culture of communities before parents will feel free to bring up children without violence."

Murray Straus, one of the world's preeminent family violence researchers, can be credited with organizing the field after the initial impetus provided by medical research on child abuse. He is Professor of Sociology and Codirector of the interdisciplinary Family Research Laboratory at the University of New Hampshire. He has authored or coauthored more than 200 articles and 15 books related to the family. His latest book is the second edition of *Beating the Devil Out of Them: Corporal Punishment in American Families and Its Effects on Children* (2001). He has served as president of several professional organizations, such as the National Council on Family Relations, and has received one prestigious honor after another, including the 1992 Distinguished Contribution Award from the New Hampshire Psychological Association. He received both his B.A. in international relations and his Ph.D. in sociology (1956) from the University of Wisconsin.

Q: What sparked your interest in family violence?

A: It was the old scientific principle: If you come across something interesting, drop everything else and study it. In my case, it was the discovery in 1979 that one-quarter of my students had been hit by their parents during their senior year in high school, and another quarter had been threatened with being hit. Somehow, it clicked with me that this kind of parental violence might be one of the roots of the violence that came to national attention during the Vietnam War era, a period of riots and assassinations, and the rising murder rate.

not. Despite the potential limitations of the research, many experts are convinced by the data that spanking is harmful, and many label spanking a form of child abuse. For a majority of Americans, however, spanking remains a common practice; in the minds of the general public, it is certainly not a behavior worthy of the abuse label. Indeed, many U.S. states explicitly exclude acts of corporal punishment from their child abuse statutes (see Chapter 13 for a more detailed summary of the debate about corporal punishment).

Legal perspectives. Legal definitions of CPA are different from conceptual definitions but come with their own set of difficulties. Daro (1988) has identified several problems involved in the development and operationalization of state statutes aimed at addressing CPA, which include but are not limited to the following: how to define abuse in as objective a manner as possible, how to balance children's rights

with parental rights, and how to apply the legal system to such a complex set of human behaviors.

Unfortunately, no uniform law defines CPA for all jurisdictions within the United States. Instead, each of the 50 states, and the District of Columbia, has its own legal definition of CPA and corresponding reporting responsibilities. In general, all states acknowledge that CPA is physical injury caused by other than accidental means that results in a substantial risk of physical harm to the child. Other key features of states' definitions vary according to the specificity of the acts included as physically abusive (Myers & Peters, 1987; Stein, 1993). Most emphasize the overt consequences of abuse, such as bruises or broken bones. In addition, most states generally allow parents to use "reasonable" corporal punishment with their children (Myers, 1992). The California statute, for example, states that CPA "does not include reasonable and age appropriate spanking to the buttocks where

Q: What is your current research focus?

A: After more than 20 years of studying wife beating, I returned to just where I started in family violence 27 years ago—research on spanking and other legal forms of corporal punishment. My colleagues and I did a major revision of the Conflict Tactics Scale [CTS], and we have developed a test to measure 22 "risk factors" for family violence—the Personal and Relationships Profile. These instruments are tremendously important because they make possible studies that would otherwise not be undertaken, such as the consortium of researchers I organized in 34 countries to study violence in the dating relationships of university students.

Q: What would you like to do if you had a large grant?

A: I would do a community experiment on corporal punishment. Corporal punishment will take a long time to end if we deal only with parents. Convincing them that they are more likely to have well-behaved children if they never spank tends to get undone when the inevitable misbehaviors occur and their friends and relatives say that what that child needs is a good spanking. We have to change the culture of communities before parents will feel free to bring up children without violence.

Q: What research would you like to see others undertake?

A: I think it is important to study violence by women against their partners. Almost everyone is afraid to deal with this issue despite data showing that women strike out physically against their partners as often as do men, and they also hit first just as often as men. My concern with the issue is partly because I think the evidence is clear that when women engage in what they call "harmless" violence, it is not. True, the man is rarely harmed, but it tremendously increases the risk that the woman will be.

Q: What should be done to reduce child physical abuse?

A: A great deal of my research has been on parents spanking children who persist in a misbehavior and on women slapping a partner who persists in doing something outrageous. These are physically aggressive behaviors that our culture defines as permissible, and in some circumstances as necessary or required. Moreover, most members of our society define these behaviors as harmless. Spanking a child or slapping a male partner may not be physically harmful, but it does tremendous psychological and social harm. Among other things, these behaviors are part of the root causes of physical abuse of children and wife beating. Consequently, changing these two aspects of the culture to redefine them as immoral, outrageous, and harmful is among the many steps needed to reduce the level of violence in families and in the society generally. Neither has yet been the focus of public education efforts or legal changes in the USA, in contrast to such legislation banning spanking in Sweden. When that occurs in our country, we will have taken a major step toward prevention of all types of violence.

---

there is no evidence of serious physical injury" (cited in Myers, 1992, p. 141).

How Common Is Child Physical Abuse?

Despite problems in defining CPA, researchers have made numerous efforts to determine the scope of the problem. Within the United States, researchers generally use one of two methods of estimation: Official estimates come from government agencies, based on the numbers of cases of CPA reported to law enforcement and social service agencies; other estimates come from self-reports of victims and perpetrators as gathered by survey research.

Official estimates. The number of child abuse cases officially reported to child protective services (CPS) agencies in the United States has increased every year since the U.S. government began collecting data on child abuse. The National Incidence Study (NIS), conducted by the National Center on Child Abuse and Neglect, is designed to measure the number of cases of CPA reported to investigative agencies, schools, hospitals, and other social service agencies. The first NIS (known as NIS-1), the results of which were published in 1981, found 199,100 reported cases of CPA, for a rate of 3.1 per 1,000 children in the United States (U.S. DHHS, 1981). In 1986, NIS-2 found approximately 311,500 cases of CPA, for a rate of 4.9 per 1,000 children (Sedlak, 1990). NIS-3, published in 1996, found that the number of reported cases of CPA had nearly doubled between 1986 and 1993, with 614,000 children reported for CPA in 1993 (a rate of 9.1 per 1,000 children) (Sedlak & Broadhurst, 1996).

Other organizations have attempted to determine the scope of CPA by aggregating reports to CPS agencies across the 50 states and the District of Columbia. Since 1976, the American Association for Protecting

Children (AAPC), a division of the American Humane Association, has conducted an annual survey called the National Study of Child Neglect and Abuse Reporting. This survey of official reports of child maltreatment documented by CPS agencies has also found that between 1976 and 1987 there was a threefold increase in child maltreatment reporting overall (AAPC, 1989). In the majority of instances, CPS caseworkers classified the children's injuries as minor (e.g., minor cuts, bruises, and welts) rather than major (e.g., brain damage, bone fracture, internal injuries, poisonings, and burns and scalds; see AAPC, 1988).

According to the most recent figures available, reported by the National Child Abuse and Neglect Data System, CPS agencies across the United States received approximately 3 million reports of child maltreatment (including physical and sexual abuse, neglect, and psychological maltreatment) in 2001. Of these reports, approximately 903,000 were substantiated, which converts to a rate of 12 out of every 1,000 children (U.S. DHHS, 2003a). Approximately 168,000 (or 19%) of these cases were specific instances of CPA. Data from the same survey also indicate that in 2001, approximately 242 children died as a result of CPA only, 327 children died as a result of physical neglect only, and another 255 children died as a result of physical abuse in combination with some other type of maltreatment (U.S. DHHS, 2003a).

Self-report surveys. Surveys of individuals and families across the United States also provide researchers with data they can use to estimate rates of CPA. In one form of such self-report surveys, parents in the general population are asked to estimate and report on their own use of various kinds of physical violence with their children. The most significant survey of this type to date is the second National Family Violence Survey, which was conducted in 1985 (Gelles & Straus, 1987, 1988). In this telephone survey, which used the Conflict Tactics Scale (CTS) to measure abuse, parents reported on the conflict techniques they used with their children in the past year, selecting their responses from a scale that ranged from mild forms of violence (e.g., slapped or spanked child) to severe forms of violence (e.g., beat up child, burned or scalded child, used a knife or gun).

Some 75% of the parents in the reporting sample admitted to having used at least one violent act in rearing their children. Approximately 2% of the parents had engaged in one act of abusive violence (i.e., an act with a high probability of injuring the child) during the year prior to the survey. The most frequent type

of violence in either case was slapping or spanking the child; 39% of respondents reported slapping or spanking their children more than two times in the previous year.

The Parent-Child Conflict Tactics Scale (known as the CTSPC) was designed to improve on the limitations of the CTS for measuring violence between parents and children (Straus et al., 1998), as the original CTS was created to assess behavior between partners in adult relationships. In addition to its revised psychological aggression and physical assault scales, the CTSPC expands on the CTS by including new scales designed to measure nonviolent discipline, child neglect, and sexual abuse.

Straus and his colleagues (1998) recently administered the CTSPC to a nationally representative sample of 1,000 parents who reported on the disciplinary methods they use with their children as part of a survey sponsored by the Gallup Organization. The CTSPC distinguishes three levels of physical assault: *minor* assault (i.e., corporal punishment), *severe* assault (i.e., physical maltreatment), and *very severe* assault (i.e., severe physical maltreatment). Nearly two-thirds of the parents surveyed reported using at least one physical assault tactic during the previous year, and three-fourths reported using some method of physical assault during the rearing of their children. The CTSPC items that accounted for most of the reporting of physical assaults by parents were those considered minor assaults, such as spanking, slapping, and pinching. As Straus and his colleagues point out, however, although the majority of physical assaults were in the minor assault category and included corporal punishment tactics, *nearly half* of all the parents surveyed said that they had engaged in behaviors from the severe physical assault subscale at some point during their parenting. These behaviors included hitting the child with an object such as a stick or belt, slapping the child on the face, hitting the child with a fist, kicking the child, and throwing/knocking down the child. Each of the very severe physical assault tactics (e.g., "beating up" or burning the child or threatening the child with a knife or gun) was used by less than 1% of the sample.

In another form of self-report survey, adults in the general population are asked to report on their own childhood experiences with various forms of physical violence from adult caretakers. The most significant survey of this type to date is the National Violence Against Women Survey, which was conducted in 1995–1996 (Tjaden & Thoennes, 2000b). In this telephone survey, a random U.S. sample of 16,000 adults

(8,000 women and 8,000 men) responded to a modified version of the Conflict Tactics Scale. The respondents were asked to report on the kinds of physical assaults they had experienced as children at the hands of their adult caretakers. Nearly half reported having experienced at least one physical assault by an adult caretaker, with the acts of violence ranging from relatively minor forms of assault (e.g., being slapped or hit) to more serious forms (e.g., being threatened with a knife or gun). For both men and women, most of the assaults consisted of pushing, grabbing, shoving, slapping, hitting, or being hit with an object, although men were at greater risk than women of having experienced these forms of violence.

Is the rate of child physical abuse increasing? It is difficult to know whether the rate of CPA is currently increasing in the United States because several problems interfere with researchers' ability to estimate the frequency of CPA. Perhaps the most significant of these is the lack of definitional consensus. Because definitions of abuse change through time and across studies, estimates of the frequency of abuse also vary. Depending on how one defines an abusive act, for example, the rate of abuse could range from nearly all children (i.e., those who are spanked) to very few children (e.g., those who are threatened with a gun). The rate of abuse one finds also varies depending on one's definition of harm. Abuse estimates that include children who are at risk for harm are higher than estimates that include only those children with observable injuries. With specific regard to official estimates, there is the obvious problem that CPA is a hidden crime that often goes unreported. Another problem stems from the differing ways in which cases of abuse are counted. Some states, for instance, count individual children in estimating the amount of CPA, whereas others use the family as the unit of analysis; the latter method is likely to underestimate the frequency of abuse, because more than one child may be maltreated per family. In addition, the retrospective nature of self-report surveys— as well as the possibility that respondents may forget or fail to admit their past abusive behavior—may limit their validity.

In addition to contributing to the difficulty in determining whether CPA is increasing, the methodological problems noted above produce considerable debate among scholars (e.g., Besharov, 1990; Finkelhor, 1990). Whether one believes that CPA is increasing or not seems to depend on whether one examines official estimates or the data from self-report studies.

According to official estimates, rates of CPA have long been increasing dramatically. Between 1980 and 1993, the number of reported cases in the United States more than tripled (Sedlak & Broadhurst, 1996; U.S. DHHS, 1981, 1988). Gelles and Straus (1987) suggest that official estimates indicate that rates of CPA have increased because of increased popular media and research attention to the problem of child abuse, which has resulted in higher rates of reporting. Changes such as broadened definitions of abuse, mandatory reporting laws, 24-hour hotlines for reporting of abuse, and state and national media campaigns have all contributed to increases in reports of CPA.

Although the increase in reporting primarily reflects greater public awareness and concern, there has likely been some actual increase in CPA, particularly in recent years. The results of the most recent National Incidence Study, for example, indicate that although the number of less severe cases of child abuse remained stable between 1986 and 1993, the number of serious cases quadrupled (Sedlak & Broadhurst, 1996). These findings seem to suggest an increase in reporting due to more than enhanced awareness and concern; otherwise, increases would be evident in reporting across all levels of abuse severity.

Although official statistics show an increase in the number of reports of CPA, particularly for serious cases, in recent years, the *rate* of increase has declined (Gelles & Cornell, 1990; Wang & Daro, 1997). In addition, data from self-report studies have not shown increases in reports of parental violence directed at children. The National Violence Against Women survey, for example, found evidence that childhood physical assault by caretakers, as reported during adulthood, remained relatively unchanged over time (Tjaden & Thoennes, 2000b). In this survey, younger adults (age 25 or younger at the time of the survey) were just as likely as older adults (age 50 or older) to report having experienced physical assault by caretakers during childhood. Gelles and Straus (1987) replicated their 1975 nationwide survey 10 years later and found that the estimated rate of violence toward children actually declined from 1975 to 1985. The most substantial decline was in the use of severe and very severe violence, which was 47% lower in 1985. Severe violence, defined as "kicking, biting, punching," "hitting or trying to hit with an object," "beating, threatening with a knife or a gun," or "using a knife or a gun over the past 12 months," declined from 1975 to 1985. It is unclear, however, to what degree *reporting* rates reflect *true* rates of CPA. Presumably, many parents who are abusive would not report this fact to researchers. Because child abuse arguably came to be more strongly socially condemned between 1975 and 1985, one has to wonder whether decreasing self-report rates of child abuse might reflect increasing instances of dishonesty in reporting.

SECTION SUMMARY

Society has not always recognized physical violence directed at children as abusive, but today CPA is illegal in every U.S. state. Most state statutes and experts in the field recognize that CPA includes a range of acts carried out with the intention of harm that puts a child at considerable risk for physical injury. Disagreement continues to exist, however, regarding behaviors that do not result in any physical signs of injury (e.g., spanking) or that fall somewhere between "normal" and excessive corporal punishment. Effective legal statutes that address CPA depend on objective definitions; in addition, they balance children's rights with parental rights and include provisions for the enforcement of workable solutions for this complex human problem.

CPS agencies receive hundreds of thousands of reports of CPA each year, and the numbers of reports have increased steadily during the past two decades. Official estimates as well as data collected through self-report surveys indicate that violence toward children in the home occurs frequently. In one survey of parents, some 75% reported using at least one violent act toward their children at some point during child rearing. Current debates about whether the rate of CPA is increasing focus on the differences between official statistics, which show a yearly increase in reports of CPA, and self-report survey data, which generally show stable or declining rates of CPA.

SEARCHING FOR PATTERNS: CHARACTERISTICS OF VICTIMS AND PERPETRATORS

Are children of one gender or children with particular behavioral characteristics or from specific ethnic backgrounds more likely than others to be victims of CPA? What specific characteristics and traits have been found to be common among adults who perpetrate violent acts against children? Scholars have drawn a great deal of information on the sociodemographic characteristics of victims and perpetrators of CPA from data provided by agencies that receive official reports of abuse and by surveys conducted with representative samples of the U.S. population. Clinical as well as empirical studies have also provided information about the psychological characteristics of CPA perpetrators. Although these data are limited by the biases discussed above, they nonetheless shed some light on the most common characteristics of child victims and adult perpetrators of CPA (for a review, see Black, Heyman, & Slep, 2001a).

Demographic Characteristics of Children Who Are Physically Abused

Age. Much evidence suggests that the risk of maltreatment in childhood declines with a child's increasing age (U.S. DHHS, 1998, 2002b); this pattern appears to be true of CPA. Statistics from the AAPC (1985), for example, indicate that for all types of officially reported physical abuse, the majority of child victims fall between the ages of 0 and 5 years (51%), followed by children ages 6 to 11 (26%), and then children ages 12 to 17 (23%). Although age differences in child maltreatment have become somewhat attenuated in recent years, it appears that nearly half of all physical abuse victims are 7 years old or younger (Sedlak & Broadhurst, 1996; U.S. DHHS, 1998). Self-report surveys, on the other hand, suggest no decrease in CPA as children grow older (Straus et al., 1998; Wauchope & Straus, 1990). One explanation for this inconsistency could be that higher rates of CPA in official estimates reflect greater risk of *injury* present among young children rather than greater risk of *assault* (Wauchope & Straus, 1990). Assaults that produce injury are certainly more likely to be reported to professionals.

Young children are not the only age group at risk for abuse. Official estimates, for example, indicate that approximately 32% of all CPA reports are for adolescents between 12 and 17 years (U.S. DHHS, 1998). Until relatively recently, little attention was paid to adolescent CPA victims. Gelles and Cornell (1990) suggest that this lack of attention may have reflected societal perceptions that adolescents share some complicity when they are abused because of their size and strength, and because of their often difficult behavior. Consequently, violent acts perpetrated on teens by parents may have been viewed as legitimate attempts to maintain parental control. In addition, compared with younger children, adolescents may appear to be less physically vulnerable or in danger of bodily harm (Powers & Eckenrode, 1988).

Gender. Boys are generally at slightly greater risk for CPA than are girls, according to the results of the second National Family Violence Survey (Wolfner & Gelles, 1993), the National Violence Against Women Survey (Tjaden & Thoennes, 2000b), and official reports on 1996 data gathered by the National Child Abuse and Neglect Data System (U.S. DHHS, 1998). There is some evidence, however, that gender distributions may vary with the severity of violence and age of the victim. With regard to severity of violence, statistics from the AAPC (1988) indicate that boys and girls are equally at risk for minor acts of physical abuse, but boys are at slightly greater risk for major acts of physical abuse. Consistent with these data, findings from the NIS-3 indicate that

FROM:

cant predictor of CPA (Chaffin, Kelleher, & Hollenberg, 1996; Connelly & Straus, 1992; Ross, 1996).

Race. Studies intended to evaluate the relationship between race and CPA are fraught with methodological difficulties (Asbury, 1993), and their findings should be interpreted cautiously. According to the most recent official statistics published by the National Committee to Prevent Child Abuse, 56.1% of CPA reports in 1997 involved Caucasian children, 27.7% involved African American children, and 13.6% involved Hispanic children (Wang & Daro, 1998). Compared with 1996 census data (U.S. Bureau of the Census, 1997), these figures suggest that African Americans and Hispanics are overrepresented and Caucasians are underrepresented in CPA reports. In contrast, results from the National Incidence Studies, which are subject to fewer reporting biases, indicate an absence of race differences in rates of CPA (Sedlak & Broadhurst, 1996; U.S. DHHS, 1981, 1988). Methodological difficulties no doubt contribute to the equivocal findings in these studies.

The data on race gathered through national self-report studies of CPA are also mixed. The first National Family Violence Survey found that rates of CPA for Caucasians and African Americans were consistent with the sizes of the two groups in the U.S. population at large, but that being of Native American or Asian heritage was a risk factor (Straus, Gelles, & Steinmetz, 1980). The second National Family Violence Survey found African American families to be at greatest risk for CPA (Wolfner & Gelles, 1993).

Additional characteristics. Many researchers in the field of CPA have argued that special characteristics may put some children at increased risk for abuse and neglect. Several studies, for example, have found an association between CPA and birth complications such as low birth weight and premature birth (Brown, Cohen, Johnson, & Salzinger, 1998; Parke & Collmer, 1975). Research findings have also implicated physical, mental, and developmental disabilities as risk factors for CPA (e.g., Ammerman, Van Hasselt, Hersen, McGonigle, & Lubetsky, 1989; Sullivan & Knutson, 1998). In contrast, other research has failed to find any evidence that prematurity or disabilities are risk factors for abuse or that these factors increase a child's risk above and beyond parent characteristics (e.g., Ammerman, 1991; Benedict, White, Wulff, & Hall, 1990).

The National Center on Child Abuse and Neglect addressed the incidence of child abuse among children with disabilities (e.g., mental retardation, physical impairments such as deafness and blindness, and serious emotional disturbance) by collecting data from a nationally representative sample of 35 CPS agencies (U.S. DHHS, 1993). The results of that analysis indicated that the incidence of child maltreatment was almost twice as high (1.7 times higher) among children with disabilities as it was among children without disabilities. For children who were physically abused, the rate of disability was 2.1 times the rate for maltreated children without disabilities (versus 1.8 for sexually abused and 1.6 for neglected children). The most common disabilities noted were emotional disturbance, learning disability, physical health problems, and speech or language delay or impairment.

One difficulty in interpreting these data hinges on the specification of the sequence of these events. Were children disabled before the abuse, or did their disabilities result from abuse? CPS caseworkers reported that for 47% of the maltreated children with disabilities, the disabilities directly led to or contributed to child maltreatment; for 37% of the children, abuse presumably caused the maltreatment-related injuries (U.S. DHHS, 1993).

Demographic Characteristics of Adults Who Physically Abuse Children

Age. There is some evidence that younger parents are more likely than older parents to maltreat their children physically (Brown et al., 1998; Connelly & Straus, 1992; Straus et al., 1998). It also appears that abusive parents often begin their families when they are relatively young, with many being in their teens when their first children are born (American Humane Association, 1984; U.S. DHHS, 1981).

Gender. Authorities receive slightly more CPA reports for females than for males (55% female, 45% male; U.S. DHHS, 1998). Some have suggested that this gender disparity is present because mothers spend more time with their children than do fathers (Gelles & Cornell, 1990). The gender distribution of CPA perpetrators may depend, however, on the specific relationship between perpetrator and child. The NIS-3, for example, found that children who had been physically abused by birth parents were more likely to be abused by mothers (60%) than by fathers (48%), but the reverse was true when the perpetrators were nonbiological parents or parent substitutes (90% male and 19% female; Sedlak & Broadhurst, 1996). Self-report studies have also found that gender results vary depending on other factors. In the second National Survey on Family Violence, for example, female caretakers reported a higher rate of

minor violence compared with male caretakers, but gender differences for severe violence were nonexistent (Wolfner & Gelles, 1993). The most recent nationally representative self-report studies, however, found no significant relationship between parent gender and the likelihood of a parent's engaging in minor or severe forms of violence toward children (e.g., Chaffin et al., 1996; Straus et al., 1998).

Relationship to the abused child. Official statistics indicate that physically abused children's birth parents are the perpetrators of the abuse in the majority of reported cases (85%; U.S. DHHS, 2001). Only a small minority of child maltreatment cases involve strangers or outsiders (10%; U.S. DHHS, 1998). Official statistics are difficult to interpret, however, because many states, by definition, report only on those child abuse cases in which perpetrators are in caretaking roles.

Speculation about whether single parents and stepparents are particularly likely to abuse the children in their care has prompted several investigations. Both official report data and survey data show that single parents are overrepresented among abusers (Brown et al., 1998; Gelles, 1989; Sedlak & Broadhurst, 1996). The NIS-3 found that children living in single-parent families had a 63% greater risk of CPA than children living in two-parent families (Sedlak & Broadhurst, 1996). As Gelles (1989) points out, however, it is possible that the greater risk evident among single parents is not a function of raising children alone but rather a function of the high rates of poverty and stress in such families.

Societal stereotypes also suggest that stepparents are particularly likely to abuse their nonbiological children. The "wicked stepmother" figure common to many fairy tales is a prime example of the way some people view stepparents. Neither self-report surveys nor official estimates, however, indicate that stepparents are any more likely than biological parents to abuse children physically (Gelles & Harrop, 1989; Sedlak & Broadhurst, 1996).

Psychological, Interpersonal, and Biological Characteristics of Adults Who Physically Abuse Children

Many studies have attempted to determine whether adults who physically abuse children share any particular characteristics (for reviews, see Black et al., 2001a; Milner, 1998; Milner & Dopke, 1997). Early studies of CPA perpetrators identified several characteristics of abusive adults, such as emotional and behavioral

Table 3.1 Psychological, Interpersonal, and Biological Characteristics of Adults Who Physically Abuse Children

Characteristics	*Examples*
Emotional and behavioral difficulties	Self-expressed anger Depression Low frustration tolerance Low self-esteem Rigidity Anger control problems Deficits in empathy Anxiety Perceived life stress and personal distress Substance abuse/dependence Deficits in problem-solving skills
Family and interpersonal difficulties	Spousal disagreement, tension, abuse Parental history of abuse in childhood Deficits in positive interactions with children and other family members Verbal and physical conflict among family members Deficits in family cohesion and expressiveness Isolation from friends and the community
Parenting difficulties	Unrealistic expectations of children Disregard for children's needs/abilities Deficits in child management skills View of parenting role as stressful Negative bias/perceptions regarding children Poor problem-solving ability with regard to child rearing Intrusive/inconsistent parenting Low levels of communication, stimulation, and interaction with children High rates of verbal and physical aggression toward children
Biological factors	Reports of physical health problems and disabilities Physiological overreactivity Neuropsychological deficits (e.g., problem solving, conceptual ability)

SOURCES: A representative but not exhaustive list of sources for the information displayed in this table includes the following: Bousha and Twentyman (1984); Cantos et al. (1997); Cappell and Heiner (1990); Caselles and Milner (2000); Chan (1994); Coohey (2000); Crowe and Zeskind (1992); Dore, Doris, and Wright (1995); Kelleher et al. (1994); Lahey et al. (1984); Nayak and Milner (1998); Tuteur et al. (1995); Whipple and Webster-Stratton (1991).

difficulties, interpersonal problems, low levels of intelligence, and lack of child development knowledge (e.g., Hunter, Kilstrom, Kraybill, & Loda, 1978; Smith, Hansen, & Noble, 1974; Steele & Pollock, 1968). These studies were primarily descriptive in nature, based on the observations of clinicians. As a result, they provided little information about whether the characteristics observed were unique to physically abusive parents. Later studies were more scientifically sound,

employing comparison groups of nonabusive parents as well as standardized measurement instruments. Although these studies' use of more sophisticated methodology cannot definitively establish whether certain characteristics *cause* a parent to abuse a child physically, information about characteristics seen in abusers can be helpful for guiding treatment efforts. Table 3.1 lists the most common characteristics of adult perpetrators of CPA described by researchers.

Emotional and behavioral characteristics. Studies comparing nonabusive parents with physically abusive parents have confirmed several characteristics typical of abusive parents that were noted in earlier clinical studies, such as anger control problems, hostility, low frustration tolerance, depression, low self-esteem, substance abuse or dependence, deficits in empathy, and rigidity (e.g., Chaffin et al., 1996; Christensen et al., 1994; Kelleher, Chaffin, Hollenberg, & Fischer, 1994). Many studies have also found that physically abusive adults report more anxiety, life stress, and personal distress than do nonabusive adults (e.g., Chan, 1994; Lahey, Conger, Atkeson, & Treiber, 1984; Whipple & Webster-Stratton, 1991). Other studies have shown that physically abusive adults demonstrate deficits in problem-solving skills (Cantos, Neale, O'Leary, & Gaines, 1997). Such negative emotional and behavioral states may increase the risk of CPA by interfering with the ways these parents perceive events, by decreasing their parenting abilities, or by lowering their tolerance for specific child behaviors (Hillson & Kupier, 1994; Lahey et al., 1984; Milner, 1998).

Family and interpersonal difficulties. Physically abusive adults are more likely than nonabusive individuals to exhibit family and interpersonal difficulties such as isolation from family and friends, spousal conflict, and negative family interactions. Abusive and high-risk individuals report more verbal and physical conflict among family members, higher levels of spousal disagreement and tension, and greater deficits in family cohesion and expressiveness (e.g., Justice & Calvert, 1990; Merrill, Hervig, & Milner, 1996; Mollerstrom, Patchner, & Milner, 1992). Studies have also demonstrated a significant relationship between the occurrence of CPA and domestic violence between parents (Appel & Holden, 1998). In addition, compared with nonabusive parents, abusive parents engage in fewer positive interactions with their children, such as playing together, providing positive responses to their children, and demonstrating affection (e.g., Alessandri, 1992; Bousha & Twentyman, 1984; Lahey et al., 1984). Abusive parents also report more conflict in their families of origin (e.g., their own child abuse) than do nonabusive parents (Cappell & Heiner, 1990). Another group of studies indicates that perpetrators of CPA report more interpersonal problems outside the family—such as social isolation, limited support from friends and family members, and loneliness—than do nonperpetrators (e.g., Chan, 1994; Coohey, 2000; Kelleher et al., 1994).

Parenting difficulties. Studies comparing abusive and nonabusive parents have also evaluated other variables, such as the context of the abusive family and characteristics of parenting. Compared with nonabusive adults, abusive individuals have been found to have unrealistic expectations and negative perceptions regarding their children (Azar & Siegel, 1990; Milner & Robertson, 1990). Such parents often regard their children as bad, slow, or difficult to discipline and view their children's behavior as if it were intended to annoy them. An abusive parent may expect a child to be toilet trained at an unreasonably early age, for instance, and so interpret the child's soiling of diapers as deliberate misbehavior.

Several studies have found that abusive parents tend to view the parenting role as stressful and dissatisfying, and that such parents exhibit numerous deficits in child management skills (Mash, Johnston, & Kovitz, 1983; Trickett, Aber, Carlson, & Cicchetti, 1991; Trickett & Kuczynski, 1986). Compared with nonabusive parents, physically abusive parents interact with their children less; when they do interact with their children, they display higher rates of directive, critical, and controlling behavior and a higher frequency of verbal and physical aggression (Bousha & Twentyman, 1984; Caselles & Milner, 2000; Whipple & Webster-Stratton, 1991). Tuteur, Ewigman, Peterson, and Hosokawa (1995) observed mother-child dyads at a public health clinic, with each dyad spending 10 minutes in a private room equipped with toys, a table, and paper and crayons. The researchers asked each mother to sit at the table with her child, who was allowed to use the paper and crayons but was not permitted to play with the toys. They found that abusive mothers, compared with nonabusive mothers, used more negative and rigid control (e.g., chased child under the table) rather than positive control (e.g., comfortably directed child) and made requests of their children that were either neutral (e.g., "Keep going") or negative (e.g., "Draw a circle right now") rather than positive (e.g., "Can you please draw a circle for Mommy?").

Biological factors. Several researchers have suggested that biological factors may distinguish physically abusive parents from nonabusive parents. Some theorists, for example, have proposed that physically abusive parents possess a physiological trait that predisposes them to hyperreactive responses, or heightened physiological reactions, to stressful stimuli, such as the crying of a child (Bauer & Twentyman, 1985). Many studies have examined physiological reactivity in perpetrators of CPA, and the findings have consistently demonstrated that these individuals are hyperresponsive to child-related stimuli (e.g., Disbrow, Doerr, & Caulfield, 1977; Frodi & Lamb, 1980; Milner & Chilamkurti, 1991). Frodi and Lamb (1980), for example, measured the physical responses of physically abusive mothers and a control group of nonabusive mothers who were presented with three videotapes: one showing a crying infant, one showing a quiet but alert infant, and one showing a smiling infant. Comparisons revealed that although both the abusive and the nonabusive mothers responded to the crying infant with increased heart rate, blood pressure, and skin conductance, the abusive mothers displayed greater increases in heart rate. In addition, only the abusive mothers showed increased physiological reactivity in response to the smiling infant, suggesting that abusive parents may view their children as aversive regardless of how the children behave.

These findings have been replicated in studies comparing nonabusive but high-risk participants with low-risk participants and in studies using stressful non-child-related stimuli (e.g., Casanova, Domanic, McCanne, & Milner, 1992; Crowe & Zeskind, 1992). Although it appears that abusive parents exhibit a general physiological overreactivity, it is unclear exactly how this pattern contributes to parents' physical maltreatment of their children. It may be that heightened physiological reactivity influences the way a parent cognitively processes or perceives a child's behavior or the way a parent subsequently reacts to a child (Milner, 1993). It is also difficult to determine whether this physiological pattern is the result of a genetic trait that predisposes parents toward abusive behavior or whether the physiological pattern develops as a *result* of continuing negative parent-child interactions.

Several studies that have evaluated additional biological risk factors have demonstrated that adults who abuse children report more health problems and physical disabilities than do nonabusing adults (e.g., Conger, Burgess, & Barrett, 1979; Lahey et al., 1984). Other research has found evidence that particular neuropsychological factors are characteristic of physically abusive parents. Nayak and Milner (1998), for example, found that mothers at high risk for CPA performed worse than mothers at low risk for CPA on measures of problem-solving ability and conceptual ability as well as on measures of cognitive flexibility. Researchers need to evaluate the variables of physical health and neurological functioning further before they can determine the precise nature of the link between biological risk factors and CPA.

SECTION SUMMARY

The sociodemographic characteristics of the victims of CPA do not suggest that any particular subpopulation of children is the primary target of violence. Both girls and boys are maltreated, and victims are found in all age groups. CPA victims also come from diverse ethnic backgrounds. Although studies show that CPA is reported more often for African American and Hispanic children than for children of other ethnicities, cautious interpretation of these data is warranted. There is evidence, however, that some characteristics place certain individuals at more risk than others. Young children, for example (birth to age 7), are at particularly high risk for CPA, as are children who are economically disadvantaged. Children with special needs, such as those with physical or mental disabilities, also appear to be at higher risk for abuse than other children.

A relatively large volume of literature exists concerning the characteristics of perpetrators of CPA. Although no single profile exists, research findings indicate that several attributes may represent elevated risk for CPA. High rates of abuse are associated with individuals who begin their families at young ages. In the overwhelming majority of reported cases, perpetrators are the parents of the victims. Single parenthood is also associated with abuse. The relationship of stepparenting to abuse has been examined, but the findings are not definitive. Data regarding perpetrator gender are mixed, although it is clear that CPA is committed by both males and females. Studies aimed at determining whether particular psychological characteristics and biological factors are associated with CPA perpetrators have found that numerous factors differentiate abusive parents from nonabusive parents, including depression, anger control problems, parenting difficulties, family difficulties, and physiological overreactivity. Although research has identified many characteristics of perpetrators, it is important to note that not every individual possessing such risk factors is abusive. Additional research efforts are needed to identify potential mediating variables.

CONSEQUENCES ASSOCIATED WITH CHILD PHYSICAL ABUSE

Children who experience physical maltreatment are more likely than their nonabused counterparts to exhibit physical, behavioral, and emotional impairments (for reviews, see Azar & Wolfe, 1998; Kaplan, Pelcovitz, & Labruna, 1999; Wolfe, 1999). In some cases, the negative consequences associated with abuse continue to affect these individuals well into adulthood (for reviews, see Glod, 1993; Malinosky-Rummell & Hansen, 1993). Table 3.2 displays the most frequently reported problems associated with CPA for children as well as for adolescents and adults.

Effects Associated With the Abuse of Children

Until relatively recently, research examining the effects of CPA on children was limited to measures of physical harm. Investigators ignored the subtle, yet significant, social and psychological effects of CPA, focusing only on visible signs of trauma, such as physical injuries. More recent research indicates that CPA is also associated with detrimental effects on victims' emotional, social, and intellectual functioning. It is important to interpret the findings of this research with considerable caution, however. The issue of effects is complicated, and, as a result, the consequences of CPA are not well understood. Most of the findings we discuss in this subsection are correlational, which means that one cannot necessarily assume that CPA is the cause of the various problems observed in CPA victims. Child physical abuse often occurs in association with other problems within the family or in the environment, such as marital violence, alcohol or drug use by family members, parental depression, psychological maltreatment, and low SES. It is therefore difficult to conclude with any certainty that the psychological problems associated with CPA result solely, or even primarily, from violent interactions between parent and child. Certainly, it would not be surprising to find that an abused child who regularly witnesses violence between his or her drunken parents, who is abused by an older sibling, and who is poor is having problems in school. It would be surprising if such a child were *not* having difficulties. Determining which factors, or combination of factors, in the child's environment are responsible for those problems, however, is a difficult task.

Medical and neurobiological problems. The medical consequences of CPA are numerous and range from minor physical injuries (e.g., bruising) to serious physical disfigurements and disabilities. In extreme cases, CPA can result in death. Bruises are one of the most common types of physical injuries associated with CPA. Although nonabused children also incur bruises, physically abused children have bruises in uncommon sites (e.g., buttocks, back, abdomen, and thighs; Schmitt, 1987). CPA victims may also have other marks on their bodies as the result of being grabbed or squeezed or of being struck with belts, switches, or cords. When a child has a series of unusual injuries, this is often an indication of CPA (Myers, 1992).

One of the most dangerous types of injury seen in cases of CPA is head injury, the most common cause of death in abused children (e.g., Smith, 1994). Various actions on the part of an abuser can result in head injury, including a blow to the child's head by an object, punching the head with a fist, compressing the head between two surfaces, and throwing the child against a hard surface. Grasping the child and vigorously shaking him or her can result in a particularly dangerous type of head injury known as **shaken baby syndrome** or *shaken impact syndrome.* Shaking a child violently can cause the child's brain to move within the skull, stretching and tearing blood vessels (Bruce & Zimmerman, 1989); the end result can be severe injury, coma, or death. Commonly, parents who bring their children into emergency rooms with nonaccidental head injuries report that the children were hurt when they fell from some item of furniture (e.g., crib, couch, bed). Such parental claims are not credible, given that the research on injuries from accidental falls has shown that these events typically result in minor injuries (e.g., bruises or cuts) or no injuries at all (Lyons & Oates, 1993).

Other common physical injuries associated with CPA include chest and abdominal injuries, burns, and fractures (Myers, 1992; Schmitt, 1987). Victims may incur abdominal injuries by being struck with objects, by being grabbed tightly, or by being punched or kicked in the chest or abdomen, which can result in organ ruptures or compressions. Burns, which are often inflicted as punishment, can result from immersion in scalding water or from contact with objects such as irons, cigarettes, stove burners, and heaters. Finally, fractures of bones in various areas of the body often result from CPA. Any of a number of actions can

Table 3.2   Possible Effects Associated With Physical Child Abuse for Children, Adolescents, and Adults

Age Group	Effects	Examples
Children	Medical and neurobiological complications	Bruises; head, chest, and abdominal injuries; burns; fractures; compromised brain development; alteration of biological stress system
	Cognitive difficulties	Decreased intellectual and cognitive functioning; deficits in verbal abilities, memory, problem solving, and perceptual-motor skills; decreased reading and math skills; poor school achievement; increase in need for special education services
	Behavioral problems	Aggression; fighting; noncompliance; defiance; property offenses; arrests
	Socioemotional deficits	Delayed play skills; infant attachment problems; poor social interaction skills; peer rejection; deficits in social competence with peers; avoidance of adults; difficulty making friends; deficits in prosocial behaviors; hopelessness; depressive symptoms; suicidality; low self-esteem
	Psychiatric disorders	Major depressive disorder; oppositional defiant disorder; conduct disorder; attention-deficit/hyperactivity disorder; borderline personality disorder; posttraumatic stress disorder
Adolescents	Aggressive and antisocial behavior	Violent interpersonal behavior; delinquency; violent and criminal offenses
	Deficits in social competence	Low levels of intimacy; increased levels of conflict and negative affect in interpersonal interactions; decreased levels of social competence
	Psychiatric disorders	Major depressive disorder; disruptive behavior disorders; substance abuse
	Other	Attentional problems; deficient school performance; increased daily stress; low self-esteem; suicidal behavior; sexual risk taking
Adults	Criminal/violent behavior	Arrests for delinquency; violent and/or criminal behavior; marital violence (for adult males); received and inflicted dating violence; physical abuse of own children; prostitution
	Substance abuse	Abuse of alcohol and other substances
	Socioemotional problems	Self-destructive behavior; suicidal ideation and behavior; anxiety; hostility; dissociation; depression and mania; unusual thoughts; interpersonal difficulties; poor self-concept
	Psychiatric disorders	Antisocial and other personality disorders; disruptive behavior disorders; major depressive disorder; posttraumatic stress disorder

SOURCES: A representative but not exhaustive list of sources for information displayed in this table includes the following: Bryant and Range (1997); Chu et al. (1999); Cicchetti and Barnett (1991); Coohey and Braun (1997); de Paul and Arruabarrena (1995); Downs and Miller (1998); Eckenrode et al. (1993); Fantuzzo et al. (1998); Glod (1993); Haskett (1990); Kaplan et al. (1997); Kaufman and Cicchetti (1989); Langeland and Hartgers (1998); Lopez and Heffer (1998); Malinosky-Rummell and Hansen (1993); Pelcovitz et al. (1994); Rogosch et al. (1995); Widom (1989a); Wodarski et al. (1990).

cause fractures, including punching, kicking, twisting, shaking, and squeezing.

Researchers have reported several neurobiological consequences associated with CPA, including compromised brain development and alterations of the biological stress systems within the body. Some research suggests that abuse-related brain injury results in impaired neurological functioning; victims may exhibit deficits in language skills, memory, spatial skills, attention, sensorimotor functioning, cognitive processing, and overall intelligence (e.g., Lewis, Lovely, Yeager, & Femina, 1989; Miller, 1999). The experience of child maltreatment can also result in impaired physiological functioning, as reflected in the disruption of various chemicals in the body such as **neurotransmitters** and hormones (De Bellis, 2001; Hart, Gunnar, & Cicchetti, 1996; Miller, 1999). In one study, for example, researchers found that a sample of physically and sexually abused children exhibited greater concentrations of urinary dopamine, norepinephrine, and free cortisol than did children in a control group (De Bellis et al., 1999). They also found that a number of specific brain regions were smaller in the abused children. Changes in neurobiological systems can have negative impacts on the physical and cognitive development of maltreated children as well as on their ability to regulate both emotional and behavioral responses (De Bellis, 2001).

Cognitive problems. Studies have shown that physically abused children exhibit lower intellectual and cognitive functioning relative to comparison groups of children on general intellectual measures as well as on specific measures of verbal facility, memory, **dissociation**, verbal language, communication ability, problem-solving skills, and perceptual motor skills (e.g., Fantuzzo, 1990; Haskett, 1990; Macfie, Cicchetti, & Toth, 2001). Academic performance is another area of substantiated difficulty in physically abused children. Compared with nonabused children, victims of CPA display poor school achievement and adjustment, receive more special education services, score lower on reading and math tests, exhibit more learning disabilities, and are more likely to repeat a grade (de Paul & Arruabarrena, 1995; Eckenrode, Laird, & Doris, 1993; Salzinger, Kaplan, Pelcovitz, Samit, & Krieger, 1984). Researchers have found that many of these differences in cognitive ability remain even after they have statistically controlled for the effects of socioeconomic disadvantage (Kurtz, Gaudin, Wodarski, & Howing, 1993; Wodarski, Kurtz, Gaudin, & Howing, 1990). The

cognitive deficits that have been observed in physically abused children, however, may be the results of direct physical injury (e.g., head injury), environmental factors (e.g., low levels of stimulation and communication), or a combination of both. Additional research is needed to determine the precise nature of the relationship between CPA and the cognitive problems observed in abused children.

Behavioral problems. Physical aggression and antisocial behavior are among the most common correlates of CPA. In most studies, abused children have been found to show more aggression than nonabused children, even after the researchers have statistically controlled for the poverty, family instability, and wife battering that often accompany abuse (e.g., Fantuzzo, 1990). In other words, abuse seems to have effects on behavior independent of the potential contribution of other factors. This negative behavioral pattern has been observed across a wide variety of settings, including summer camps (Kaufman & Cicchetti, 1989) and preschool and day-care programs (Alessandri, 1991), in which researchers have used a variety of data collection procedures (e.g., Feldman et al., 1995, used adult ratings; Bousha & Twentyman, 1984, used observations). Other behavioral difficulties displayed by CPA victims include drinking and drug use, noncompliance, defiance, fighting in and outside of the home, property offenses, and arrests (e.g., Hotaling, Straus, & Lincoln, 1990).

Socioemotional difficulties. Additional problems frequently observed in physically abused children are internalizing behavioral symptoms that include social as well as emotional difficulties. Several studies have documented higher levels of internalizing symptoms among physically abused children compared with nonabused children (Fantuzzo, delGaudio, Atkins, Meyers, & Noone, 1998; Wolfe, 1999).

In terms of social difficulties, some researchers argue that victims of CPA suffer from problems related to attachment to caregivers. They suggest that the violence that occurs between parent and child in such families might disrupt the development of healthy parent-child relationships. There is growing evidence that the quality of the parent-child bond consistently reflects insecure attachments (e.g., increased avoidance of and resistance to the parent) in infants exposed to CPA (Cicchetti & Toth, 1995; Kolko, 1992). Evidence from recent research suggests that child maltreatment is also associated with a form of attachment referred to as **disorganized attachment**, or *Type D*, which is characterized as insecure as well as disorganized and disoriented (Barnett, Ganiban, & Cicchetti, 1999). For these children, the parent-child relationship presents an "irresolvable paradox" because the caregiver is at once the child's source of safety and protection and the source of danger or harm (Hesse & Main, 2000).

These early patterns of parent-child interaction may also lay the foundation for subsequent difficulties in social interactions for older children. Physically abused children exhibit poor social interactions with peers as well as adults (e.g., Fantuzzo, 1990; Salzinger, Feldman, Hammer, & Rosario, 1993). Their problems include difficulty in making friends, deficits in prosocial behavior (e.g., smiling) with peers, peer rejection, and delays in interactive play skills (e.g., Alessandri, 1991; Prino & Peyrot, 1994; Rogosch, Cicchetti, & Abre, 1995). Some research suggests that the interpersonal problems CPA victims experience may be the result of specific social-cognitive skills deficits, such as problems with perspective taking, inability to generate alternative solutions to social problems, and difficulty understanding appropriate affective responses in interpersonal situations (Haskett, 1990; Howes & Espinosa, 1985; Rogosch et al., 1995).

Studies have also demonstrated a higher incidence of emotional difficulties in physically abused children relative to comparison children. School-age CPA victims, for example, have been found to display lower levels of self-esteem (Allen & Tarnowski, 1989; Kaufman & Cicchetti, 1989). Finally, evidence suggests that physically abused children exhibit feelings of hopelessness, depressive symptoms, suicidality, and feelings of low self-worth (Allen & Tarnowski, 1989; Fantuzzo, 1990; Finzi et al., 2001).

Psychiatric disorders. The various cognitive, behavioral, and socioemotional difficulties described above may sometimes form a constellation of symptoms characteristic of specific psychiatric disorders. A number of studies have examined rates of psychiatric disorders in samples of physically abused children and have found that CPA victims are at increased risk for such problems (Famularo, Fenton, & Kinscherff, 1992; Famularo, Fenton, Kinscherff, Ayoub, & Barnum, 1994; Flisher et al., 1997). In their review, Kaplan et al. (1999) conclude that approximately 40% of CPA victims will meet criteria for major depressive disorders during their lifetimes, and at least 30% will meet criteria for **disruptive behavior disorders**, such as oppositional defiant disorder or **conduct disorder.** A history of CPA has also been associated with **attention-deficit/hyperactivity disorder** as well as borderline personality disorder (Famularo et al., 1992; Famularo, Kinscherff, & Fenton, 1991).

Other studies have documented the presence of **posttraumatic stress disorder** (PTSD) in victims of physical abuse. Famularo et al. (1994), for instance, found that 36% of CPA victims in their sample met criteria for PTSD. Other researchers have examined the presence of diagnoses of PTSD in CPA victims as compared with nonabused children and as compared with victims of other forms of child maltreatment. Dubner and Motta (1999), for example, examined rates of PTSD among three groups of children in foster care: sexually abused children, physically abused children, and nonabused children. They found that both the sexually abused children (64%) and the physically abused children (42%) were more likely than the nonabused children to receive diagnoses of PTSD.

Effects Associated With the Abuse of Adolescents

Although researchers have shown extensive interest in the consequences associated with CPA for young children, they have focused much less attention on the physical, social, and psychological effects of CPA on adolescents. It can be difficult to determine the precise effects of CPA on adolescents, because in some cases the abuse begins in adolescence, whereas in others the abuse is of longer duration, having begun in childhood. Nonetheless, some scholars have argued that the effects of CPA may be expressed somewhat differently in adolescents than they are in younger children (e.g., Williamson, Borduin, & Howe, 1991).

Findings from the few studies that have examined the consequences of physical maltreatment for adolescents suggest that deviant or problematic behavior in adolescence is often associated with childhood abuse. Adolescents who were abused when they were younger often display a number of aggressive and antisocial behaviors (Kaplan, Pelcovitz, Salzinger, Mandel, & Weiner, 1997; Pelcovitz, Kaplan, Goldenberg, & Mandel, 1994; Wolfe, Wekerle, Reitzel-Jaffe, & Lefebvre, 1998). In addition, research indicates that physically abused adolescents often exhibit violent interpersonal behavior, such as coercion and violence in dating relationships and aggression toward parents and siblings (Dodge, Bates, & Pettit, 1990; Kratcoski, 1984; Wolfe et al., 1998). Abused adolescents also have higher rates of delinquency than are found in the general population as well as in poverty samples (e.g., Alfaro,

1981; Kratcoski, 1984; Zingraff, Leiter, Myers, & Johnsen, 1993). Studies that have examined the interpersonal and social competence of physically abused adolescents have also revealed that these teens tend to have some specific deficits compared with their nonabused peers, such as lower levels of intimacy, increased levels of conflict and negative affect, and lower levels of social competence (Parker & Herrera, 1996; Pelcovitz et al., 1994). Other consequences associated with CPA for adolescents include internalizing behavior problems, suicidal behavior, attention problems, poor self-esteem, substance abuse, depressed school performance, and high levels of daily stress (e.g., Kaplan et al., 1997; Pelcovitz et al., 1994; Williamson et al., 1991; Wodarski et al., 1990).

In the past decade, several studies have examined rates of psychiatric disorders in samples of physically abused adolescents. They have found that adolescent CPA victims are at increased risk for a number of the same psychiatric disorders found in younger victims of CPA. A history of CPA has been found to be associated with depression, disruptive behavior disorders (e.g., conduct disorder, oppositional defiant disorder, attention-deficit/hyperactivity disorder), and drug abuse in adolescents (Kaplan et al., 1997; Pelcovitz et al., 1994). Although the relationship between PTSD and physical abuse in younger children has been examined frequently and is well established, few systematic studies concerning PTSD have been carried out with physically abused adolescents. One exception is the work of Pelcovitz et al. (1994), who conducted a well-controlled study of adolescent physical abuse and psychiatric diagnoses. They found that adolescents who had been physically abused did not exhibit a higher proportion of PTSD than did adolescents in a normal control group. In contrast, in a study based on a large national telephone sample, Boney-McCoy and Finkelhor (1995) found evidence of an association between parental physical violence and heightened PTSD-related symptoms (these researchers did not, however, determine formal diagnoses). Clearly, further research is necessary before scholars can draw any definitive conclusions about the relationship between PTSD and CPA in adolescents.

The correlates of adolescent CPA described thus far have been identified in studies that used cross-sectional designs; that is, the adolescents studied were assessed at one point in time. As we have noted previously, this research method is limiting because it does not enable researchers to establish cause-and-effect relationships. In such a study it is unclear, for example, whether the psychological effects observed are the result of abuse that occurred during an individual's childhood, abuse that occurred during his or her adolescence, or some other factor present in the individual's life (e.g., other life stressors). Prospective longitudinal studies that evaluate CPA victims at several points in time over long periods, however, can help to alleviate some of the limitations associated with cross-sectional designs. Ellen and Roy Herrenkohl and their colleagues have conducted several such longitudinal studies, and their findings confirm many of the results obtained in cross-sectional studies of adolescents with histories of CPA. They have found that the characteristics of adolescent CPA victims include decreased social and school competence, violent and criminal behavior, and sexual risk-taking behavior (e.g., Herrenkohl, Egolf, & Herrenkohl, 1997; Herrenkohl, Herrenkohl, Egolf, & Russo, 1998; Herrenkohl, Herrenkohl, Egolf, & Wu, 1991).

Possible Long-Term Effects

Only a few studies have empirically examined the long-term sequelae associated with CPA. There is some evidence that many of the psychological and social difficulties that emerge in childhood CPA victims are also evident in adults with histories of CPA (Malinosky-Rummell & Hansen, 1993). It is further believed that many of the social and behavioral impairments that begin in childhood and persist in adulthood as a result of CPA may contribute to the intergenerational transmission of abuse (Wolfe, 1999).

Criminal and violent behavior. One of the most frequently discussed long-term consequences of CPA is criminal behavior. Widom (1989a) compared a sample of validated cases of child abuse and neglect (identified 20 years earlier by social service agencies) to a sample of matched comparisons, evaluating juvenile court and probation department records to establish occurrences of delinquency, criminal behavior, and violent criminal behavior. Widom did not distinguish among various forms of maltreatment, but she found that the subjects in the abused-neglected group had a higher likelihood of arrests for delinquency, adult criminality, and violent criminal behavior than did those in the comparison group. In follow-up studies, Widom and her colleagues found support for these original findings as well as evidence that victims of abuse or neglect are more likely than nonvictims to have lifetime symptoms of antisocial personality disorder (Luntz & Widom, 1994; Maxfield & Widom, 1996; Widom & Kuhns, 1996). These researchers also found, however, that a majority of the individuals with histories of abuse or neglect in these studies did not exhibit offenses or symptoms, indicating that the link between abuse and antisocial behavior is far from perfect.

Other research suggests that the interpersonal relationships of adults with childhood histories of physical abuse are more likely than those of nonabused persons to be characterized by violence. Adults with histories of CPA are more likely both to receive and to inflict dating violence (Marshall & Rose, 1990; Riggs, O'Leary, & Breslin, 1990). In addition, male adults who were physically abused as children are more likely to inflict physical abuse on their marital partners (Rosenbaum & O'Leary, 1981). Researchers have also found that adults who were victims of physical abuse as children are more likely to be perpetrators of CPA as adults (Coohey & Braun, 1997; Ross, 1996; Straus, 1994). In addition, there is some evidence of a link between the degree to which college students use violent strategies toward their parents and the degree to which their parents used violence in disciplining them in earlier years (Browne & Hamilton, 1998). The proportion of adults who were abused as children who later go on to abuse others, however, is not 100%. Once again, it is important to remember that a history of childhood abuse alone is neither a necessary nor a sufficient cause of adult perpetration.

Recently, a team of researchers working in England, New Zealand, and the United States examined the potential role of genetic makeup as a contributor to aggressive, antisocial, or violent behavior in adults who were abused or maltreated as children (Caspi et al., 2002). These researchers speculate that the relationship between childhood maltreatment and violent behavior in adulthood depends on variations in a gene that helps to regulate neurotransmitters in the brain that are implicated in antisocial behavior. They assessed a group of 442 boys in New Zealand for antisocial behavior periodically between the ages of 3 and 28 years and found that maltreated children with a "protective" version of the gene were less likely to develop antisocial problems in adulthood. In contrast, 85% of maltreated children who had the less protective version of the gene later became violent criminal offenders. Although the implications of these findings for social policy could be significant, the researchers warn against the simple conclusion that genes alone determine behavior. Indeed, they note that the relationship between child maltreatment and later antisocial behavior is likely a complex interplay among a number of different genes and a variety of environmental factors.

Substance abuse. The topic of substance abuse rates in adults with histories of CPA has also attracted scientific attention. In a review of the literature linking adult substance abuse with CPA, Malinosky-Rummell and Hansen (1993) reached the following conclusions: (a) Adults who abuse substances report a higher incidence of childhood physical abuse than that found in the general population; (b) male alcoholics with histories of abuse report more problematic drinking and social and medical difficulties than do nonabused alcoholics; and (c) inpatients with histories of CPA tend to experience more alcoholism and substance abuse than do nonabused inpatients. Most of the research on substance abuse, however, has used cross-sectional methods and has focused primarily on alcohol abuse in men. In one exception, Widom, Ireland, and Glynn (1995) examined gender differences in alcohol use in a longitudinal study of adults who were abused or neglected in childhood. They found that the abused women in their sample, but not the abused men, exhibited greater alcohol use than did nonabused controls. A recent review of the literature has also confirmed the presence of alcohol problems in women with histories of CPA (Langeland & Hartgers, 1998).

Socioemotional difficulties. Little information is available on the long-term socioemotional consequences of physical maltreatment in childhood compared with other forms of abuse (e.g., sexual). Nonetheless, some recent cross-sectional research suggests a relationship between CPA and psychological adjustment in adulthood. Evidence to date indicates that adults with histories of CPA exhibit more significant emotional problems (e.g., higher incidence of self-destructive behavior, suicidal thoughts and behavior, anxiety, hostility, depression, and mania) than do nonabused adults (e.g., Bryant & Range, 1997; Downs & Miller, 1998; Levitan et al., 1998; Wind & Silvern, 1994). Reports also confirm that a history of CPA is associated with greater dissociation, poor self-concept, and negative feelings about interpersonal interactions (e.g., Chu, Frey, Ganzel, & Matthews, 1999; Downs & Miller, 1998; Lopez & Heffer, 1998).

Recent prospective longitudinal studies have confirmed some of these findings, including those that point to the presence of suicidal ideation and behavior as well as symptoms of anxiety and depression in adults with histories of CPA (Brown, Cohen, Johnson, & Smailes, 1999; Silverman, Reinherz, & Giaconia, 1996). Longitudinal studies also confirm the presence of various psychiatric diagnoses in these adults. Cohen, Brown, and Smailes (2001), for example, assessed mental disorders from early childhood to adulthood in a community sample of individuals who were later identified as having CPA histories either by official records or by self-reports. Their findings indicated that adults with official records of CPA exhibited elevated symptoms of disruptive disorders (e.g., conduct disorder, attention-deficit/hyperactivity disorder, oppositional defiant disorder), personality disorders, major depressive disorder, and substance abuse relative to the normative sample. Widom (1999) found evidence of lifetime PTSD in her sample of adults who had experienced CPA, and the relationship between CPA and PTSD symptoms persisted when she controlled for other potential confounding variables (e.g., family, individual, and lifestyle factors). Horwitz, Widom, McLaughlin, and White (2001) also evaluated the impact of childhood maltreatment on measures of mental health in a prospective sample of adults, although they did not distinguish between individuals with histories of abuse and those with histories of neglect. These researchers found that the men in their sample who were maltreated as children exhibited more **dysthymia** and antisocial personality disorder than did matched controls, whereas the women who were maltreated as children exhibited more symptoms of dysthymia, antisocial personality disorder, and alcohol problems. Once Horwitz et al. controlled for stressful life events, however, they found that childhood maltreatment had little impact on mental health outcome.

Mediators of Abuse Effects

To add to the uncertainty regarding the effects of CPA, it is also true that CPA victims do not respond to being abused in consistent or predictable ways. For some, the effects of their victimization may be pervasive and long-standing, whereas for others their abuse experiences may not be invariably negative or disruptive. For example, the severely abused children in the small sample that Elmer initially described in 1967 and reevaluated in 1992 evidenced scores within the normal range on measures of mood, self-esteem, and aggression (Martin & Elmer, 1992).

What factors might contribute to the variability researchers have found in the effects associated with

CPA? One appears to be the severity and duration of the abuse. The assumption is that the more severe and/or chronic the maltreatment, the more negative the outcomes. Although empirical data on this topic are sparse, some evidence supports this contention (e.g., Wind & Silvern, 1992). In addition, some researchers have suggested that the greater the number of subtypes of maltreatment (e.g., physical abuse, sexual abuse, neglect) to which a child is subjected, the more negative the outcomes will be for the individual in both childhood and adulthood (Kurtz, Gaudin, Howing, & Wodarski, 1993; Wind & Silvern, 1992).

Researchers have also begun to evaluate the importance of the **attributions** that children make with regard to their abuse experiences. Brown and Kolko (1999) found that specific attributions as well as general attributional style were predictive of the level of psychopathology exhibited by CPA victims, above and beyond the influence of the level of severity of the abuse experienced. Children who tended to blame themselves for the abuse, for example, exhibited greater internalizing symptoms. These findings suggest that not only are the specific characteristics of a child's abuse important potential mediators of the effects of CPA, but the child's *perceptions* of those events may also serve an important mediating role.

Other research suggests that the negative effects of abuse are greatest for children in families in which there are high levels of stress and parental psychopathology (e.g., schizophrenia) or depression (Kurtz, Gaudin, Howing, & Wodarski, 1993; Walker, Downey, & Bergman, 1989). Reports are also beginning to appear that demonstrate the influence of sociocultural and family variables (e.g., SES and the quality of the parent-child interaction) on negative outcomes (Herrenkohl, Herrenkohl, Rupert, Egolf, & Lutz, 1995). Finally, recent studies have suggested that certain factors, such as high intellectual functioning in the CPA victim (Herrenkohl et al., 1991) and the presence of a supportive parent figure (Herrenkohl et al., 1995), may have a protective influence.

SECTION SUMMARY

The problems associated with CPA include negative physical and psychological effects for child and adolescent victims as well as for adults with childhood histories of CPA. Possible negative effects for children include medical, neurobiological, cognitive, behavioral, and socioemotional problems. Although less is known about the negative consequences associated with the physical abuse of adolescents, the available research indicates that possible effects range from antisocial and violent behavior to poor self-esteem and substance abuse. Relatively recent research also suggests that both child and adolescent victims of CPA are at risk for developing a variety of psychiatric disorders, such as PTSD, major depressive disorder, and disruptive behavior disorders. Many of the same social and behavioral impairments found in child and adolescent victims are also found in adults with histories of CPA, including criminal and violent behavior, substance abuse, and socioemotional difficulties.

Not all CPA victims are affected in the same ways, however. Specific characteristics of victims' families or their abuse experiences may serve to mediate the effects of abuse. For example, victims whose families are characterized by high stress and whose abuse experiences are more severe tend to exhibit greater levels of psychological distress. On the other hand, victims with high levels of intelligence and supportive parent figures appear to be protected from many negative consequences and exhibit fewer psychological symptoms.

Explaining Child Physical Abuse

Unfortunately, with the knowledge currently available it is impossible to specify the exact circumstances that lead to CPA. There are several reasons for this difficulty. First, CPA consists of a complex set of interacting behaviors that are influenced by many different factors. Second, methodological problems have plagued the research in this area. Most studies to date have been retrospective, which means that the information provided by subjects could be biased by the subjects' perceptions or inaccurate memories. In addition, sample sizes have often been small and nonrandom, calling into question the validity and generalizability of findings. The definition of what constitutes abuse has also varied across studies, contributing to difficulties in interpreting results. In addition, little is known about cause-effect relationships because experimental study designs, which could help establish cause-effect relationships, are rarely feasible—researchers obviously cannot randomly assign some children to abusive

parents and others to nonabusive parents. Finally, it is clear that physically abusive adults and children who are abused vary widely in their psychological, social, and demographic characteristics, so it is unlikely that any one theory regarding the causes of abuse could account for all, or even most, cases of CPA.

Despite the difficulties noted above, scholars have developed several models intended to explain the causes of CPA. Since the early 1960s, views on the primary causes of child abuse have expanded to move beyond disturbed adults or children to include the more pervasive influences of parent-child relationships, the family environment, socioeconomic disadvantage, and cultural sanctioning of violence and corporal punishment. Most recently, scholars have incorporated these influences into multidimensional, interactional theories that emphasize the interplay among various individual factors. In the subsections below, we describe the major models of CPA and discuss the contemporary theories that build on these models in an attempt to explain the processes and transactions that underlie CPA.

The Individual Pathology Model

As we have noted in Chapter 1, many observers trace the discovery of child abuse to the 1962 publication of Kempe et al.'s article "The Battered Child Syndrome," in which the authors argued that adults who physically abuse children are "psychopathic" and in need of psychiatric treatment. They also suggested that CPA is a rare social problem, which facilitated the assumption that perpetrators are disturbed individuals who must be "crazy" or "sick." As CPA has come to be defined more broadly to include greater numbers of adults as perpetrators, however, it has become increasingly difficult to view "child abusers" as people who suffer from mental illnesses, personality disorders, alcohol or drug abuse, or any other individual defect. Although research has identified a subgroup of severely disturbed individuals who abuse children, only a small proportion of abusive parents (less than 10%) meet criteria for severe psychiatric disorders (Kempe & Helfer, 1972; Straus, 1980; Walker et al., 1989). As we have noted above, however, adults who physically abuse children often do exhibit specific nonpsychiatric psychological, behavioral, and biological characteristics that distinguish them from nonabusive parents, such as anger control problems, depression, parenting difficulties, physiological hyperreactivity, and substance abuse.

The Role of Child Behavior Problems

Other theorists have focused on child behavior as a contributing factor to CPA. As we have noted above, children with certain characteristics (such as physical and mental disabilities and young age) appear to be at increased risk for abuse. Researchers have also suggested that difficult behavior and specific temperaments in children may contribute to abusive incidents (e.g., Youngblade & Belsky, 1990). Some parents may lack the skills to manage children who are annoying, argumentative, defiant, or vindictive, for example, and this may lead to abusive interactions. Some recent research evidence has linked child maltreatment to these kinds of behavior patterns in children. One study found that children with oppositional defiant disorder had much higher rates of child maltreatment than did children with other psychological disorders (Ford et al., 1999). It is sometimes difficult, however, to determine whether such traits are the results or the precipitants of abuse. Mental disability in a child, for example, could have existed at birth or could have resulted from abuse (e.g., severe blows to the head).

Regardless of the cause of a child's behavior, CPA is associated with especially demanding and difficult child care. We want to emphasize, however, that the behavior of a child should never be accepted as an excuse for an adult's violent behavior. When an adult inflicts injury on a child, he or she is legally responsible for that behavior. Children cannot be held responsible for their own victimization. Legal statutes governing adult behavior, furthermore, do not grant adults the right to inflict physical injury on children who are difficult. In addition, it is important to remember that although characteristics of the child are important, they are only one factor among many that contribute to CPA. Sidebotham and Heron (2003), for example, conducted a large prospective study that examined characteristics of children that might predispose them to child maltreatment. They found that although child factors were significant, parental attitudes toward the child played a more significant role in child maltreatment.

Parent-Child Interaction

Parent-child interaction theories suggest that difficult child behaviors interact with specific parental behaviors to result in CPA (Cerezo, 1997; Crittenden, 1998). That is, it is the behavior of both parent and child, rather than the behavior of either alone, that promotes violence. Studies have repeatedly demonstrated, for instance, that punitive parenting is associated with negative child behavior and outcomes (e.g., Denham, Renwick, & Holt, 1991; Dowdney & Pickles, 1991). Likewise, deviant child behaviors have contributed to parental abuse (Biringen & Robinson, 1991; Youngblade & Belsky, 1990). Such findings raise what is known as the directionality question: Who affects whom? Clearly, parenting practices have direct effects on children. A child's behavior, however, also contributes to a parent's response to that child (Bell & Chapman, 1986).

Some experts have suggested that difficulties in parent-child relations develop during the abused child's infancy, when early attachments between parent and child are formed (Erickson & Egeland, 1996; Malinosky-Rummell & Hanson, 1993). A child may be born with a particular characteristic, such as a difficult temperament or a physical disability, that creates an excessive challenge for a parent and interferes with the development of a secure attachment between the parent and child. This vulnerability may in turn lead to further difficult child behaviors and increased challenges for the parent. Such a pattern may escalate and result in physical abuse when the challenges exceed the parent's tolerance or capability threshold. Several studies have found that, compared with nonmaltreating parents, maltreating parents more frequently have insecure attachments to their infants (e.g., Crittenden, Partridge, & Claussen, 1991; Egeland & Sroufe, 1981). In addition, findings from several studies support a theory of negative escalation in abusive parent-child dyads (for reviews, see Cerezo, 1997; Crittenden, 1998).

Social Learning Theory

Many retrospective studies have demonstrated that a significant percentage of adults who abuse children were abused themselves as children (e.g., Cappell & Heiner, 1990; Gelles, 1973; Hunter et al., 1978). In one relatively recent study, Coohey and Braun (1997) found that a history of abuse by one's own mother or father distinguished physically abusive from nonabusive mothers. These adults presumably learned, through experiences with their own parents, that violence is an acceptable method of child rearing. In addition, adults with histories of CPA missed the opportunity as children to learn appropriate and nurturing forms of adult-child interaction.

The findings from some prospective studies support the notion that parenting styles are passed from one generation to the next. Crittenden (1984) found that children as young as 2 years of age interacted with their infant siblings in ways that were similar to those exhibited by their mothers, who demonstrated a range of parenting styles that included abusive, neglecting, inept, and sensitive patterns of interaction. Others have found a relationship between the parental practices of grandparents and adults' subsequent use of harsh parenting practices (Simons, Whitbeck, Conger, & Wu, 1991).

Evidence also suggests that even children who do not experience abuse directly may learn violent interpersonal interaction styles. Through witnessing negative interactions between the significant adults in their lives, children learn maladaptive or violent methods of expressing anger, reacting to stress, and coping with conflict (Jaffe, Wolfe, & Wilson, 1990; Kalmuss, 1984; we discuss children who observe marital violence further in Chapter 6). Studies have consistently demonstrated that adults who abuse children are more likely to come from homes characterized by considerable marital discord and violence (Gelles, 1980; Hotaling & Sugarman, 1986; Kalmuss, 1984).

As we have noted in Chapter 2, however, most abused children do not become abusive adults. Kaufman and Zigler (1987) reviewed the empirical literature on this question and concluded that the rate of intergenerational transmission is approximately 30%. This means that 70% of those who were abused as children do not go on to become abusive adults. Given that not all children who experience CPA become physically abusive adults, what factors mediate these intergenerational patterns? Egeland, Jacobvitz, and Sroufe (1988) found that mothers who were physically abused but did not abuse their own children were significantly more likely than abusing mothers to have received emotional support from a nonabusive adult during childhood, to have participated in therapy during some period in their lives, and to have been involved in nonabusive, stable, emotionally supportive, and satisfying relationships with mates. Nonabusive mothers with histories of CPA are also reportedly less anxious, dependent, dissociative, immature, and depressed than abusive mothers, as well as more flexible in how they view their children (e.g., Caliso & Milner, 1994; Egeland et al., 1988; Egeland & Susman-Stillman, 1996).

Situational and Societal Conditions

During the 1970s, interest in the contexts of abusive behavior led researchers to examine social and cultural factors that might foster abuse. Sociological models of abuse focused on factors such as economic conditions, societal and cultural values, and social systems. Contemporary views of CPA consistently include discussion of these situational and societal conditions and the roles they play in CPA (e.g., Hillson & Kupier, 1994; Krug, Dahlberg, Mercy, Zwi, & Lozano, 2002; Wolfe, 1999).

Economic disadvantage. Gil (1970) was one of the first to point out that a high proportion of abused children come from poor and socially disadvantaged families. Subsequent research has supported these early findings, indicating that CPA is more common among low-income families and families supported by public assistance than among better-off families (Sedlak, 1991; U.S. DHHS, 1996). Studies have also found that blue-collar workers are more likely than white-collar workers to engage in physical punishment and abuse of children (Straus et al., 1980; Wolfner & Gelles, 1993). Children whose fathers are unemployed or work part-time are also at greater risk for abuse than children whose fathers have full-time employment (McCurdy & Daro, 1994b; Wolfner & Gelles, 1993). In addition, SES is associated with physical abuse more than it is with sexual abuse or child neglect (Gillham et al., 1998).

Social isolation. Another factor associated with CPA is social isolation, including a lack of extended family or peer support network. Research suggests that, compared with nonabusive parents, abusive parents have relatively fewer contacts with peer networks as well as with immediate family and other relatives (e.g., Coohey, 2000; Whipple & Webster-Stratton, 1991). Corse, Schmid, and Trickett (1990) evaluated social support networks, both within and outside the family, in terms of the presence of family social support, child-rearing help, and the size of any existing support networks. They found that CPA mothers reported less family social support as well as less child-rearing help from peers and professionals than non-CPA mothers, but no less child-rearing help from family members. CPA mothers also reported having smaller peer networks than did non-CPA mothers, but the groups did not differ in terms of the sizes of other social networks (e.g., nuclear family, extended family).

Using official reporting statistics, Zuravin (1989) measured social isolation in maltreating families by evaluating community variables. Results indicated a significant relationship between physically abusive families and communities with high proportions of single-family dwellings and vacant housing. According to Garbarino and Crouter (1978), single-family housing serves as a physical impediment to social networks by isolating families from one another and decreasing the number of social supports available. Other researchers have found that maltreating families engage in few social or recreational activities and do not use available community resources (e.g., Corse et al., 1990; Smith, 1975).

These findings are consistent with research and theory suggesting the importance of the role of "social capital" (i.e., the degree of solidarity and cohesion existing within a community; Runyan, Hunter, et al., 1998) in mitigating CPA. Children who live in communities with low social capital appear to be at greater risk for CPA than children who live in communities with well-developed social networks and community connections (Krug et al., 2002).

Other situational factors. Research indicates that some situational variables, particularly as they affect the levels of stress within families, are associated with CPA. In their recent review of the literature, Black et al. (2001a) found that CPA is generally associated with high numbers of stressful life events as well as stress associated with parenting. Stressful situations that appear to be risk factors for CPA include the presence in the family of a new baby, illness, death of a family member, poor housing conditions, and larger-than-average family size (e.g., Gil, 1970; Starr, 1982; Straus et al., 1980; Wolfner & Gelles, 1993). Other situational variables associated with CPA include high levels of stress in the family from work-related problems and pressures, marital discord, conflicts over a child's school performance, illness, and a crying or fussy child (Barton & Baglio, 1993; Gelles, 1973).

Cultural approval of child physical abuse. Some scholars have suggested that specific cultural factors play a role in conditions leading to CPA. The pervasiveness of violence in a society, in general, might create a context that fosters the physical abuse of children. Indeed, various forms of social violence (e.g., availability of weapons, war) occur in many parts of the world and are associated with family violence (Djeddah, Facchin, Ranzato, & Romer, 2000). The general acceptance of corporal punishment as a method of discipline is another cultural factor that is conducive to violence in general and to CPA more specifically. Because corporal punishment puts the child at risk for physical injury, it is at least indirectly connected to CPA (Gershoff, 2002a).

Unequal power differentials in the structure of a society, particularly within the family, might also contribute to CPA (Gelles & Cornell, 1990). Children are abused, in part, because they are unable to defend themselves against stronger and more powerful adults (e.g., financially, emotionally, and physically). Some evidence consistent with this idea is found in official estimates of CPA that suggest the rates of physical abuse decrease with child age—that is, as the child becomes older and stronger and more capable of self-defense (Gelles & Hargreaves, 1981).

In their edited volume on violence and health worldwide, Krug et al. (2002) list additional cultural factors that may contribute to child abuse: (a) the role of cultural values and economic forces in determining family decisions; (b) gender and income inequalities; (c) cultural norms associated with gender roles, family privacy, and parent-child relationships; (d) public policy related to children and families; (e) the role of preventive health care in the identification of child abuse and neglect; (f) the strength of the social welfare system; (g) the role of the criminal justice system in social protection; and (h) the influence of larger social conflicts and war. Most of these broad cultural and social factors have not yet been examined empirically; future research should evaluate their potential influence on the problem of child physical abuse.

Contemporary Theories of Child Physical Abuse

In the past decade, experts have formulated several theories of child physical abuse that build on the models just described and take into account the risk factors known to be associated with CPA. Most of these theories focus on the interplay among individual factors, parent-child interaction factors, family environment factors, and situational and societal factors. Table 3.3 displays the multiple risk factors implicated in the empirical literature as playing important roles in the physical abuse of children.

Contemporary theories can be divided into two categories: process theories and transactional theories. **Process theories** emphasize specific precursors that lead to abuse and, in some cases, the specific processes that serve to maintain abuse. **Transactional theories**, in contrast, emphasize the interactions among **risk factors** and **protective factors** associated with child physical abuse. Unfortunately, both kinds of theories currently have only limited empirical support. Efforts directed toward conceptualizing such theories,

Table 3.3   Risk Factors Associated With Physical Child Abuse

Risk Factors	*Examples*
Factors associated with individual pathology	
Characteristics of perpetrators	Self-expressed anger and anger control problems
	Depression
	Low frustration tolerance
	Low self-esteem
	Rigidity
	Deficits in empathy
	Substance abuse/dependence
	Physical health problems
	Physiological reactivity
Factors associated with the parent-child relationship	
Characteristics of the child	Difficult child behaviors
	Young age
	Physical and mental disabilities
Characteristics of the adult	Deficits in parenting skills
	Unrealistic expectations of children
	Viewing the parenting role as stressful
	Negative bias/perceptions regarding children
Factors associated with family environment	
Characteristics of the family	Current abusive family practices (e.g., spouse abuse)
	Intergenerational abusive family practices (e.g., child abuse)
	Marital discord
	Few positive family interactions
Factors associated with situational and societal conditions	
Situational conditions	Low socioeconomic status
	Single-parent household
	Public assistance
	Blue-collar employment
	Unemployment or part-time work
	Situational stress (e.g., large family size)
	Social isolation and lack of social capital
Societal conditions	Cultural approval of violence in society, generally
	Cultural approval of corporal punishment
	Power differentials in society and the family

SOURCES: A representative but not exhaustive list of sources for information displayed in this table includes the following: Black et al. (2001a); Bousha and Twentyman (1984); Cappell and Heiner (1990); Caselles and Milner (2000); Coohey (2000); Gelles and Cornell (1990); Krug et al. (2002); McCurdy and Daro (1994b); Tuteur et al. (1995); Whipple and Webster-Stratton (1991); Wolfner and Gelles (1993); Youngblade and Belsky (1990); Zuravin (1989).

however, are a positive first step in understanding the origins of CPA.

Process theories. One example of a process theory of CPA is the stress and coping model described by Hillson and Kupier (1994). This model suggests that physically abusive behavior by a parent toward a child results from a sequence of events that includes the parent's perceptions of stressful events as well as his or her ability to cope with stressful events. According to this model, the initial event is the parent's exposure to a specific environmental event (e.g., a child's crying). The parent then appraises the situation and interprets the event as either a stressor or a nonstressor. If the parent perceives the event as stressful (e.g., as a threat), he or she then engages in a secondary appraisal process, evaluating his or her own internal resources (e.g., specific abilities to cope with the threat). This appraisal can be influenced by a variety of factors related to the child (e.g., some form of disability, difficult child behavior), the parent (e.g., personality, parenting skills), and ecological factors (e.g., social isolation, unemployment). In the final step in the model, the parent engages in some type of coping behavior, which is typically influenced by the availability (or lack of availability) of external supports. The specific methods that parents use for coping with stressful events vary and can lead to either adaptive (e.g., appropriate caregiving behavior) or maladaptive (e.g., physically abusive, neglectful) forms of parenting.

Wolfe (1999) has also developed a process theory to explain the origins of child physical abuse. In this model, CPA results from a three-stage process in which a set of destabilizing factors leads to a negative outcome in the parent-child relationship or a set of compensatory factors leads to a positive outcome. Stage 1 is characterized by a reduction in the parent's stress tolerance and disinhibition of aggression. Destabilizing factors that might lead to a negative outcome include stressful life events and poor child-rearing preparation. Compensatory factors that might lead to a positive outcome include socioeconomic stability and social supports. Stage 2 is characterized by the parent's poor management of acute crises. Destabilizing factors during this stage include multiple sources of anger/aggression and the perception that the child's behavior is harmful or threatening. Compensatory factors during this stage include good coping resources and improved child behavior. Stage 3 in the process is characterized by chronic patterns of anger and abuse. Destabilizing factors during this stage include an escalation in problem child behavior and parental success in using strict control techniques. Compensatory factors during this stage include parent dissatisfaction with using strict control techniques and availability of community resources.

Transactional theories. Belsky's (1993) developmental-ecological model of child maltreatment is perhaps the best-known transactional theory. This model emphasizes the contribution of several independent factors.

One set of factors that contribute to CPA is made up of developmental or individual factors, such as the characteristics of a child (e.g., difficult child behaviors, a child's young age) or parent (e.g., unrealistic expectations of a child, deficient parenting skills). A second set of factors is associated with interpersonal interactions, including specific parenting practices and characteristics of the parent-child interaction. Belsky's model also considers broader contextual factors and their role in CPA, such as situational variables (e.g., low SES) and culture (e.g., societal tolerance for violence). Cicchetti and Lynch (1993) have developed a similar transactional theory that focuses on the importance of independent factors such as characteristics of the individual, the family, the community, and culture. They suggest that child maltreatment results when potentiating factors that increase the likelihood of maltreatment outweigh various compensatory factors that decrease the risk for maltreatment at each ecological level. These transactional theories are unique in that they not only describe various factors that might contribute to CPA, they emphasize the role of the interaction of these factors in the etiology of child maltreatment.

SECTION SUMMARY

Scholars' views on the primary causes of CPA vary widely, from those that focus on the psychiatric disturbance of abusers (e.g., mental illness, personality disorder, substance abuse) to those that suggest the problem is rooted in dysfunctional parent-child interactions (i.e., increased risk of abuse because of parental frustration, stress, and impatience). Evidence suggests that children learn to model violent behavior merely by witnessing negative interactions, and this perpetuates intergenerational cycles of violence. Nevertheless, issues that have been raised regarding the reliability of information about the causes of CPA (e.g., methodological problems, sample sizes, definitions of abuse, ethical issues, the use of heterogeneous groups in study samples) have affected research in the field.

A significant shift in the conceptualization of the causes of CPA occurred with the birth of sociological models that focus on the situational and social context of abuse. These models emphasize the possible contributions to CPA of the factors of socioeconomic disadvantage, social isolation, situational stressors, and cultural approval of violence. Contemporary theories of CPA include both process and transactional theories that conceptualize CPA as a complex problem resulting from multiple interacting factors from many domains, including the adult perpetrator, parent-child interactions, family environment, and situational and social conditions.

—————•◆•—————

PRACTICE, POLICY, AND PREVENTION ISSUES

It is clear from the material presented in this chapter that CPA is a serious and pervasive social problem. Proposed solutions to this problem include both intervention and prevention strategies that vary in emphasis depending on the etiological frameworks of the proponents. Those who explain CPA in individualistic terms advocate strategies that focus on the individual child or adult, whereas those who explain CPA from a process or transactional perspective propose strategies that focus on disturbed marital relationships or the parent-child interaction. Others who explain CPA in structural or ecological terms emphasize community intervention and prevention strategies aimed at the alleviation of social problems connected with CPA (e.g., poverty and social isolation).

Intervention Strategies for Child Physical Abuse

The psychopathology-based view of CPA initially led to treatment efforts directed primarily at individual parents. Such methods have been criticized for being too narrow in scope, ignoring the other serious contributors to and consequences of CPA (Graziano & Mills, 1992). Current approaches are broader and include not only adult interventions but child-focused and family interventions (Kolko, 1998, 2002; Oates & Bross, 1995; Wolfe & Wekerle, 1993). Several community interventions commonly serve as adjuncts to some of these other intervention methods. The idea behind community interventions is that it is important to address directly the multiple factors believed to contribute to CPA, such as social isolation, financial stress, and excessive child-care demands.

Treatment for physically abusive adults. Since the 1970s, interventions aimed at abusive parents have increasingly used multiple approaches, including some form of training that centers on skills in anger management, child management, or stress management (for reviews, see S. T. Azar, 1997; Schellenbach, 1998). The most frequently used behavioral approach is to train parents in the use of nonviolent child management skills (i.e., parent training). Such training involves educating parents about the effects of reinforcement and punishment on children's behavior and the importance of consistency in discipline. Parents learn how to deliver both appropriate reinforcement and appropriate punishment for child behaviors. Programs achieve these goals by providing parents with written information, supplying them with appropriate parenting models through demonstrations (on video or live), helping them to learn problem-solving approaches for increasing child compliance, and giving them opportunities to practice their new skills through role-playing (e.g., MacMillan, Olson, & Hansen, 1991).

Some programs have used cognitive-behavioral techniques to address abusive parents' cognitive distortions and the negative emotions associated with parenting. Treatment efforts that target parents' cognitive distortions attempt to help the parents change their distorted beliefs and attributions and improve their problem-solving skills (Azar & Wolfe, 1998). Parents learn anger control techniques that are intended to reduce their negative emotional responses and thoughts and enhance their coping ability (e.g., Acton & During, 1992). These programs help parents to identify events that increase negative emotions and teach them how to replace anger-producing thoughts with more appropriate ones. Anger control programs also attempt to teach parents self-control skills in an effort to reduce their impulsive expressions of anger. Programs with a stress management component typically teach parents relaxation techniques, ways to reduce psychological stress, and methods for coping with stressful interactions with their children (e.g., Egan, 1983).

Empirical studies that have evaluated the effectiveness of interventions for adults who abuse children have found that parent-focused approaches consistently demonstrate improvements in parenting skills, such as positive interactions with, and perceptions of, their children; effective control of unwanted behavior; and decreases in negative, coercive, or physically punitive management techniques (e.g., Fennell & Fishel, 1998; Graziano & Mills, 1992; Wolfe & Wekerle, 1993). These techniques are also effective in enhancing anger control, reducing stress, and increasing coping and problem-solving skills (Acton & During, 1992;

Whipple & Wilson, 1996). Parent-focused programs also exhibit some collateral effects by decreasing aggressive or negative behavior in the children of abusive parents and by increasing family members' social skills and support networks (Oates & Bross, 1995; Wolfe & Wekerle, 1993). The findings of some evaluation studies indicate that changes in parent behavior are maintained through time, although more researchers need to incorporate follow-up measures in their research designs (Schellenbach, 1998).

Treatment for physically abused children. In extreme cases, physically abused children may exhibit such severe psychological and behavioral difficulties that they require hospitalization. Most child interventions, however, involve therapeutic day treatment programs, individual therapy, group therapy, and play sessions. Therapeutic day treatment programs typically provide abused children with group activities, opportunities for peer interactions, and learning experiences to address developmental delays (Culp, Little, Letts, & Lawrence, 1991; Parish, Myers, Brandner, & Templin, 1985). Individual therapy often incorporates training in relaxation skills, problem-solving strategies, and anger management techniques, as well as efforts to improve self-esteem (Walker et al., 1989). Group therapy may include sharing experiences, anger management, and social skills training (see Swenson & Kolko, 2000). Play sessions include opportunities for informal interaction between abused children and adults and/or peers (e.g., Davis & Fantuzzo, 1989).

Unfortunately, very few studies have examined the effectiveness of treatment services directed toward victims of CPA. Those that have evaluated child-focused treatment interventions, however, indicate that these programs can be successful in decreasing aggressive and coercive behaviors in CPA victims and in improving social behavior, cognitive development, and self-esteem in these children relative to controls (Fantuzzo et al., 1996; Oates & Bross, 1995; Wolfe & Wekerle, 1993). Unfortunately, most of the studies that have been conducted to date have focused on preschool-age or young children to the exclusion of school-age and adolescent victims and have not distinguished among various forms of maltreatment. In addition, few researchers have performed extended follow-up assessments to determine whether the benefits that have been seen are maintained through time.

Family interventions. Limited information is available regarding CPA interventions that target the family,

such as marital or family therapy approaches. One exception is a study in which Brunk, Henggeler, and Whelan (1987) compared 33 maltreating families who were randomly assigned to either parent training or family therapy. The researchers found that both treatments were associated with decreases in psychological complaints, perceived stress, and overall severity of identified problems in the families. In a more recent study, Kolko (1996b) randomly assigned physically abused children and their parents to either family therapy or separate individual cognitive-behavioral treatments for the child and parent, and then compared these two groups with families who received routine community services. Both family therapy and cognitive-behavioral treatment were found to be superior to routine community services in reducing child-to-parent violence, child behavior problems, and parental distress. Family therapy was also shown to be effective in reducing levels of parental anger and physical discipline or force, although not as effectively as cognitive-behavioral treatment (Kolko, 1996a).

Intensive family preservation programs constitute another family-oriented approach that has received a great deal of attention in the literature. In such programs, professionals or community volunteers provide a variety of short-term intensive and supportive interventions during regular visits to abusive parents, either in the family's home or in another location that is familiar to the child. Advocates for family preservation have developed these programs as part of their efforts to prevent out-of-home placement of abused and neglected children. Most such programs focus on training parents in child development and parenting skills, as well as in stress reduction techniques and anger management (Wasik & Roberts, 1994). Several evaluations of intensive family preservation programs conducted in the 1990s demonstrated the success of such programs in preventing out-of-home placement of children (e.g., Bath & Haapala, 1993; Fraser, Walton, Lewis, & Pecora, 1996; Schwartz, AuClaire, & Harris, 1991). In reports on two more recent reviews, however, the authors conclude that family preservation programs are not effective either in reducing out-of-home placements or in protecting children who are at risk for abuse (Gelles, 2000; Lindsey, Martin, & Doh, 2002). Lindsey et al. (2002) assert that earlier reports of the success of family preservation programs were based on methodologically flawed studies and the exaggerated enthusiasm of program advocates. The controversy surrounding family preservation programs is far from settled, and additional research using sound methodology is needed before professionals in the field can draw any firm conclusions about the effectiveness of such programs.

Community interventions. Because research has found that many abusive parents are socially isolated, some observers advocate providing them with assistance in developing social support networks made up of personal friends as well as community contacts. The kinds of community contacts that could benefit these families vary depending on their particular needs, but they might include crisis hotlines, support groups (e.g., Parents Anonymous), and educational resources (e.g., Wolfe, Edwards, Manion, & Koverola, 1988). Programs that involve home visits offer another avenue of support to abusive parents. Through home visits, social service agency workers can provide parents with knowledge about child development and management as well as social support (see Amundson, 1989; Roberts, Wasik, Casto, & Ramey, 1991).

Abusive families often need assistance with basic necessities of living, such as food and shelter. Unfortunately, very few CPA prevention programs are designed to address such macro-level concerns (Hay & Jones, 1994). Assistance of this kind might come from service organizations such as the Salvation Army or from individual families' caseworkers. Professionals working with families at risk of abuse might also make job and educational referrals for parents, but additional support may be necessary to combat the economic difficulties faced by these families (Hay & Jones, 1994). Parents may also need help to complete government forms that will allow them to obtain food stamps, state funds for child support, and Temporary Assistance for Needy Families (which has replaced Aid to Families with Dependent Children).

Because abusive parents often find the parenting role challenging and have fewer child-care options than other parents, programs that offer child care can provide relief for overly burdened parents who need a break (Hay & Jones, 1994; Thompson, Laible, & Robbennolt, 1997). For abused children, therapeutic day-care centers provide environments similar to those found in traditional day-care programs but additionally provide services that target the developmental delays and behavioral disorders associated with child maltreatment. Some programs enroll at-risk children in preschool or Head Start, and some offer families respite care services (e.g., home aides). Research has shown that such programs are successful in enhancing abused children's functioning (Daro & McCurdy, 1994).

Multiservice interventions address the complex and interactive nature of CPA by targeting multiple systems and integrating complementary services. Most multiservice interventions have an ecological emphasis—that is, they offer diverse community services with the aim of improving the family's social environment (Corcoran, 2000). Such programs attempt to alter the social factors that increase stress and affect a family's ability to function effectively. Project 12-Ways is a noteworthy example of a multiservice intervention; it includes a variety of services for families, such as parent-child training, stress reduction, marital counseling, employment assistance, and training in money management (Lutzker, Bigelow, Doctor, Gershater, & Greene, 1998). In a recent analysis of several different family preservation programs, MacLeod and Nelson (2000) identified specific program components that appear to increase program effectiveness, including high levels of participant involvement, an emphasis on family strengths, and the inclusion of social support. Although studies of families' participation in such programs have documented improvements in some parent behaviors and lower reabuse rates among parents in comparison with controls, initial evaluations have also found that these improvements are not maintained through time (Lutzker, 1990b; Lutzker et al., 1998; Nelson, 1994).

Preventing Physical Abuse of Children

Most experts in the field of child maltreatment agree that, to be successful, strategies for preventing CPA must be aimed at all levels of society (e.g., family, community, social service institutions). Proponents have designed and implemented a wide variety of prevention approaches, but to date surprisingly little research has investigated their effectiveness. In addition, consensus is lacking regarding which specific services prevention programs should offer. This state of affairs reflects, in part, the difficulty inherent in measuring and interpreting outcomes for a problem as complex as CPA. With these caveats stated, we offer below some brief descriptions of the most common prevention efforts currently being implemented. We also review the research evidence available concerning the effectiveness of some of these efforts.

Parental competency programs. A number of programs have as their main goals the improvement of parenting practices and the provision of support for families. The many home visitation programs currently in operation attempt to achieve these goals by bringing community resources to at-risk families in their homes. It has been estimated that as many as 550,000 children are reached annually by such programs directed at pregnant women and families with young children (Gomby, Culross, & Behrman, 1999). These programs, which are rooted in attachment theory, are designed to facilitate the development of positive and secure attachments between parents and their children. They achieve this goal through parent education provided by program workers during home visits. In addition, caseworkers attempt to improve family functioning by supplying needed information, support, and access to other services. Home visitation programs have been identified as one of the most promising avenues for the prevention of child abuse and neglect (Krug et al., 2002). (We discuss these programs and research evaluating their effectiveness in greater detail in Chapter 5.)

Another common approach to improving parental competency is that of providing education and skills training through parent education programs and parent support groups. In contrast to home visitation programs, in this approach services are typically provided outside the home, through school or community organizations. Programs of this kind focus on educating parents about child development, improving parenting skills, and providing settings where parents can share their concerns and work on problem solving with one another (Carter & Harvey, 1996; Rodriguez & Cortez, 1988). Although most of these programs are intended for high-risk populations, some experts argue that all parents or prospective parents might benefit from this type of education and training (Krug et al., 2002). Evaluations of these types of programs have shown evidence of the effectiveness of this approach for improving parental psychological adjustment, increasing parenting skills, improving parents' beliefs about child development and age-appropriate interventions, reducing parent-child conflict, improving child behavior, increasing parents' use of social supports, enhancing self-efficacy, and reducing the risk of child maltreatment (e.g., Daro, 1993; Hoelting, Sandell, Letourneau, Smerlinder, & Stranik, 1996; Peterson, Tremblay, Ewigman, & Saldana, 2003).

Community awareness campaigns. Another approach to the prevention of CPA, and child maltreatment more generally, is that of educating the public about the problem of CPA through mass-media campaigns. Such campaigns employ public service announcements on radio and television; in newspapers, magazines, and brochures; and on posters and billboards. The rationale behind this approach is that increasing knowledge and awareness about the problem of CPA will result in lower levels of abuse. The reduction of CPA occurs directly, when abusive parents learn that their behavior is inappropriate and take action to change their behavior. Community awareness campaigns may also indirectly reduce rates of abuse as professionals and laypersons begin to recognize the signs and symptoms of CPA and begin reporting suspected abuse to authorities.

Some research evidence indicates that public education campaigns are effective in reducing CPA. As noted previously, between 1980 and 1993, the number of reported cases of CPA in the United States more than tripled (Sedlak & Broadhurst, 1996; U.S. DHHS, 1981, 1988). Just prior to this dramatic increase in reporting, several local and national media campaigns were implemented to increase public awareness about child maltreatment (Daro & Gelles, 1992). More compelling evidence for a link between public education and increased reporting comes from a multimedia campaign conducted in the Netherlands in 1991–1992 (Hoefnagels & Baartman, 1997; Hoefnagels & Mudde, 2000). The campaign employed a variety of media and educational efforts, including a televised documentary, televised public service announcements, a radio program, teacher training, and various printed materials (e.g., posters, newspaper articles). In an evaluation of the campaign, Hoefnagels and Baartman (1997) found that it was effective in increasing awareness of abuse, as shown by the dramatic increase in the number of calls received by a national child abuse hotline in the period after the campaign (Hoefnagels & Baartman, 1997).

CHAPTER SUMMARY

The physical abuse of children is a complex problem that is not well understood despite nearly four decades of research. The complexity of CPA is evident in attempts to define what specific circumstances constitute abuse. Although most experts agree that CPA includes a range of behaviors that cause observable harm to children, there is less agreement about the boundary between CPA and "normal" parenting practices, or behaviors that do not result in observable harm. Despite definitional ambiguities, it is clear that thousands of children are subjected to the harm associated with CPA each year.

Research examining the characteristics of physically abusive adults and physically abused children has demonstrated the heterogeneity of both victim and offender populations, which encompass both genders and all ages, races, and socioeconomic groups. A number of risk factors, however, have been consistently associated with CPA. Children who are physically abused are often quite young (i.e., 5 years old or younger), and children with special needs (e.g., those with physical or mental disabilities) also appear to be at high risk for abuse. Physically abusive adults are found disproportionately among economically disadvantaged groups, and their environments include additional stressors such as having children at a young age and single parenthood. Many adults who inflict violence on children also display other common characteristics, including depression, anger control problems, parenting difficulties, family difficulties, and physiological overreactivity.

CPA is associated with a number of negative physical and psychological effects for child and adolescent victims, as well as for adults with childhood histories of CPA. These consequences affect a variety of areas of functioning, including physical, emotional, cognitive, behavioral, and social domains. The experience of CPA, however, does not affect all victims in the same way. Specific factors can mediate the effects of CPA; for example, factors associated with increased negative impact of CPA include the severity of abuse, the duration, and the number of forms of abuse experienced.

The causes of CPA are not well understood, and scholars have proposed a number of models in their attempts to improve the state of knowledge about the violence that occurs between adults and children. Early theories focused on psychiatric disturbances in abusers, whereas more recent theories implicate dysfunctional parent-child interactions. A significant shift in the conceptualization of CPA occurred with the birth of sociological models, which emphasize the situational and social factors associated with abuse, including the roles of socioeconomic disadvantage, social isolation, situational stressors, and cultural approval of violence. The most recent conceptual models of CPA attempt to explain the phenomenon as a process involving multiple, interacting factors associated with the child, the parent, parent-child interaction, family situation, and society.

Proposed solutions to the CPA problem include both intervention and prevention efforts. Because of the complexity of CPA, any single intervention or treatment is unlikely to be successful, particularly with high-risk families. Psychological approaches for children and their families target parenting skills, anger control and stress management, social and developmental skills, and child-centered, marital, and family interactions. Some families may need additional treatment interventions that focus on psychiatric disorders, substance abuse problems, or in-home services (e.g., crisis intervention and assertiveness training). Furthermore, community interventions have expanded to address situational and social factors that might contribute to CPA, such as social isolation and economic stressors. Efforts to prevent CPA have focused primarily on parental competency programs that include home visitation, parent education, and parent support. Such programs operate on the assumption that by enhancing parental support and parents' knowledge about parenting and child development, they can improve family functioning, which will result in lower levels of physical abuse. Public education campaigns have also used the mass media effectively to increase awareness, recognition, and understanding of the CPA problem. Although evaluation studies suggest that many intervention and prevention strategies are promising, additional research is needed to enhance the current state of knowledge about solutions to the CPA problem.

DISCUSSION QUESTIONS

1. Why have researchers found defining CPA to be such a challenge? Describe the distinction between *harm* and *endangerment* standards.
2. Should corporal punishment be considered a form of child physical abuse?
3. What is the relationship between CPA and Munchausen by proxy?
4. Is the rate of CPA currently increasing in the United States?
5. Considering what is known about the general characteristics of physically abused children (e.g., age, gender, SES), how would you describe a prototypical physically abused child?
6. Considering what is known about the general characteristics of adults who physically abuse children (e.g., age, gender, psychological, interpersonal, and biological characteristics), how would you describe a prototypical adult who abuses children?
7. What physical, psychological, and socioemotional effects have been associated with CPA in the research literature? How do these effects vary across developmental periods (e.g., childhood, adolescence, adulthood)?
8. Describe the different models that scholars have developed to attempt to explain the causes of CPA. Which model or models seem most useful for explaining why CPA occurs?
9. What are the various intervention strategies currently used in the treatment of adults who physically abuse children? What intervention strategies are used to help children who have been abused? Are such interventions effective?

10. What kinds of approaches have communities and government agencies implemented in their efforts to prevent CPA?

RECOMMENDED READING

Black, D. A., Heyman, R. E., & Slep, A. M. S. (2001). Risk factors for child physical abuse. *Aggression and Violent Behavior, 6,* 121–188.

Cerezo, M. A. (1997). Abusive family interaction: A review. *Aggression and Violent Behavior, 2,* 215–240.

Gershoff, E. T. (2002). Corporal punishment by parents and associated child behaviors and experiences: A meta-analytic and theoretical review. *Psychological Bulletin, 128,* 539–579.

Krug, E. G., Dahlberg, L. L., Mercy, J. A., Zwi, A. B., & Lozano, R. (Eds.). (2002). *World report on violence and health.* Geneva: World Health Organization.

MacLeod, J., & Nelson, G. (2000). Programs for the promotion of family wellness and the prevention of child maltreatment: A meta-analytic review. *Child Abuse & Neglect, 24,* 1127–1149.

Straus, M. A., Hamby, S. L., Finkelhor, D., Moore, D. W., & Runyan, D. (1998). Identification of child maltreatment with the Parent-Child Conflict Tactics Scales: Development and psychometric data for a national sample of American parents. *Child Abuse & Neglect, 22,* 249–270.

Teicher, M. H. (2000, March). Scars that won't heal: The neurobiology of child abuse. *Scientific American,* pp. 68–75.

Trickett, P. K., & Schellenbach, C. J. (Eds.). (1998). *Violence against children in the family and the community.* Washington, DC: American Psychological Association.

Widom, C. S. (1999). Posttraumatic stress disorder in abused and neglected children grown up. *American Journal of Psychiatry, 156,* 1223–1229.

Wolfe, D. A. (1999). *Child abuse: Implications for child development and psychopathology* (2nd ed.). Thousand Oaks, CA: Sage.

NOTE

1. From "Hell Is for Children," by P. Benatar, N. Geraldo, and R. Capps, 1981. Rare Blue Music, Inc./Neil Geraldo (ASCAP), Red Admiral Music Inc./Big Tooth Music Co. (BMI), Rare Blue Music Inc./Muscletone Music (ASCAP). (1980). Used with permission.

4

CHILD SEXUAL ABUSE

Case History: Sashim's Secret

Sashim, an only child, was 6 years old when her parents divorced. Her father had been physically violent toward both Sashim and her mother, and they broke off all ties with him after the divorce. The next 3 years were difficult for Sashim because she rarely saw her mother, who had to work two jobs to make ends meet. When Sashim was 9 years old, her mother became romantically involved with Bhagwan, a 39-year-old construction foreman. Shortly after Sashim's mother met Bhagwan, he moved in with the family and took a serious interest in Sashim. He took her to movies, bought her new clothes, and listened to her when she complained about difficulties at school. He seemed to provide her with the parental attention that she had missed for so many years.

Over the course of several months, Bhagwan's behavior toward Sashim gradually changed. He became much more physical with her, putting his arm around her when they were at the movies, stroking her hair, and kissing her on the lips when he said good night. He began to go into her bedroom and the bathroom without knocking when she was changing her clothes or bathing. He also began "checking on her" in the middle of the night. During these visits, he would stroke and caress her body. In the beginning, he touched only her nonprivate areas (e.g., shoulders, arms, and legs), but after several visits, he began to touch her breasts and genitals. Eventually, he began to kiss her sexually during his touching, all the while telling her how much he loved her and enjoyed being her father. He warned her that she should not tell anyone about their time together because others would not understand their "special" relationship.

One night, Bhagwan attempted to have sexual intercourse with Sashim, and she refused. A few days later, one of Sashim's favorite teachers noticed that Sashim seemed very quiet and asked if something was bothering her. Sashim began crying and told her teacher everything that had happened. Sashim's teacher reassured her that she believed her and would help her. The teacher called child protective services and reported her conversation with Sashim. Two social workers came to Sashim's school and listened to Sashim as she told her story. Bhagwan was arrested. Sashim's mother could not believe that Bhagwan could do such things or that the things Sashim described could occur without her knowledge. She refused to believe Sashim, calling her a liar and a "home wrecker."

As a result, Sashim was placed in a foster home. Shortly thereafter, she was diagnosed with leukemia; the doctors estimated that she had only 6 months to live. Her only request was that she be able to die at "home" with her foster parents, to whom she had become quite attached. The hospital, however, was unable to grant Sashim's request without the consent of her biological mother, who still had legal custody of Sashim. Her mother refused to consent unless Sashim agreed to recant her story about Bhagwan.

As this case history demonstrates, child sexual abuse (CSA) is a multifaceted problem, extraordinarily complex in its characteristics, dynamics, causes, and consequences. This chapter examines the major issues that contribute to this complexity. We begin by addressing issues related to defining the scope of CSA, including definitions and estimates of the rates of CSA in the United States. We then focus on the typical characteristics of CSA victims and perpetrators as well as additional factors noted in the research. We also address the dynamics of CSA and the consequences of this form of maltreatment for victims. We conclude the chapter with an analysis of potential causes of CSA and responses to the problem. Although we focus our discussion on CSA within the broad context of family violence, we do not limit our attention to intrafamilial (i.e., incestuous) sexual abuse, because a substantial proportion of CSA is extrafamilial.

SCOPE OF THE PROBLEM

What Is Child Sexual Abuse?

As discussed previously, one of the greatest barriers to understanding different forms of child maltreatment is the difficulty inherent in defining particular problems. This is the case with CSA. Indeed, as Haugaard (2000) notes, "child sexual abuse has never been unequivocally defined," and this lack of consensus among professionals in the field "continues to inhibit research, treatment, and advocacy efforts" (p. 1036). To illustrate the complexities in defining CSA, consider the following scenarios:

- Jamie, a 15-year-old, frequently served as babysitter for his neighbor, 4-year-old Naomi. Each time Jamie was left alone with Naomi, he had her stroke his exposed penis while they watched her favorite video.
- Manuel and Maria frequently walked around nude at home in front of their 5-year-old son, Ernesto.
- Richard, an adult, repeatedly forced his nephew Matt to have anal intercourse with him when Matt was between the ages of 5 and 9 years. After the abuse stopped when he was 10, Matt frequently sneaked into his 6-year-old sister's room and had anal intercourse with her.
- Sally, at 16 years old, was a self-proclaimed "nymphomaniac." She had physical relationships (e.g., kissing, fondling, and sexual intercourse) with numerous boyfriends from school with whom she had physical relationships. One evening when Sally was home alone with her 45-year-old stepfather, he asked her if she would like to "mess around." Sally willingly agreed to have sexual intercourse with him.
- Dexter, a 30-year-old man, invited 7-year-old Jimmy to his house frequently for after-school snacks. After their snacks, Dexter asked Jimmy to undress and instructed him to assume various sexual poses while Dexter videotaped him. Dexter sold the videos for profit.

Which of these interactions should be described as CSA? The above vignettes illustrate two important questions concerning the definition of CSA. First, what behaviors are culturally defined as inappropriately *sexual*? Second, under what circumstances do sexual interactions become *abusive*?

Cultural context. As noted in Chapter 1, sexual interactions between children and adults have occurred throughout history. Only relatively recently, however, has CSA been recognized as a social problem. It is thus apparent that any definition of CSA is dependent on the historical period in question, the cultural context of the behavior, and the values and orientations of specific social groups (Wurtele & Miller-Perrin, 1992). To define CSA today in the United States, it is essential to know something about what types of behaviors are generally regarded as acceptable within American families. Would most people consider Manuel and Maria abusive for walking around nude in front of their 5-year-old son? What if their son were 13 years old? How much variation in nudity, touching various body parts, and kissing on the lips is socially acceptable between adults and children?

Unfortunately, few studies have focused on normal patterns of touching and physical contact in families. One exception is the research of Rosenfeld and colleagues, who examined typical family patterns of bathing and touching (Rosenfeld, Bailey, Siegel, & Bailey, 1986; Rosenfeld, Siegel, & Bailey, 1987). Survey responses of 576 parents revealed that the parents rarely bathed with their children at any age, particularly with children of the opposite sex (e.g., mothers with sons), after the children were 3 to 4 years old. Children's touching of mothers' and fathers' private areas (e.g., genitals or breasts) was relatively common among preschoolers but declined as the children became older. More recent research confirms these findings and indicates that some types of sexual behavior are common in nonabused children (e.g., children touching their own sex parts), whereas more explicit sexual behaviors (e.g., inserting objects into the anus or vagina and oral-genital contact) are extremely rare (Davies, Glaser, & Kossoff, 2000; Friedrich, Grambusch, Broughton, Kuiper, & Beilke, 1991; Sandnabba, Santtila, Wannas, & Krook, 2003). Additional research is necessary to determine the average frequency of other family behaviors, such as sleeping patterns, nudity, privacy, and other types of touching (e.g., kissing and hugging), as well as cultural differences in such behaviors.

Conceptual issues. The National Center on Child Abuse and Neglect published one of the earliest definitions of child sexual abuse in 1978:

> Contacts or interactions between a child and an adult when the child is being used for the sexual stimulation of the perpetrator or another person. Sexual abuse may also be committed by a person under the age of 18 when that person is either significantly older than the victim or when the perpetrator is in a position of power or control over another child. (p. 2)

This definition, which is consistent with most current legal and research definitions of CSA, incorporates four key components that are generally regarded as essential in defining CSA. First, definitions of CSA are typically broad enough to include extrafamilial abuse as well as intrafamilial abuse (i.e., incest). Such broad definitions have both advantages and disadvantages. As we have noted in Chapter 3 in regard to child physical abuse, broad definitions of abuse lead to the labeling of greater numbers of interactions as abusive. Haugaard (2000) asserts that one consequence of broad definitions of abuse has been increased public concern resulting from reports of high rates of abuse. In contrast, all-encompassing definitions of abuse can be practically meaningless (Emery & Laumann-Billings, 1998). In addition, such broad definitions can lead some to believe that reports of high rates of abuse are merely exaggerated claims, producing skepticism and possible dismissal of the problem rather than concern (Perrin & Miller-Perrin, 2004).

Second, definitions of CSA often include sexual experiences with children that involve both physical contact and noncontact activities. For example, CSA may include physical contact such as fondling or intercourse, as described in the vignettes above about Jamie, Matt, and Sally, but it can also include noncontact forms, as in the scenario involving Dexter and Jimmy. Controversy continues to exist, however, regarding what specific behaviors should be deemed abusive, regardless of whether those behaviors are classified as contact or noncontact experiences. Is parental nudity, a noncontact behavior, abusive? One way to distinguish between abusive and nonabusive behaviors is to evaluate the intent of the perpetrator. Many definitions of CSA, for example, include the requirement that the sexual activities are intended for the sexual stimulation of the perpetrator, thus excluding normal family and caregiving interactions (e.g., nudity, bathing, displays of affection). In practice, however, determining whether a behavioral intention is

sexual or nonsexual can be difficult. How can one determine whether a grandfather kisses his granddaughter out of innocent affection or for his sexual gratification? Furthermore, some experts argue that caregiving behaviors can go beyond normal experiences and become abusive, such as when children are repeatedly exposed to genital examinations or cleanings (Berson & Herman-Giddens, 1994).

A third important component of CSA definitions emphasizes the adult's exploitation of his or her authority and power to achieve sexual ends. Implicit in this component is the assumption that children are incapable of providing informed consent to sexual interactions with adults for two reasons: (a) Because of their developmental status, children are not capable of fully understanding what they are consenting to and what the consequences of their consent might be; and (b) children might not be in a position to decline involvement because of the adult's authority status. The vignette above about Sally and her stepfather illustrates a case of abuse because, despite Sally's sexual experience and "consent" in this situation, she is not mature enough to understand the ramifications of having sexual intercourse with her stepfather. As Haugaard and Reppucci (1988) point out, "The total legal and moral responsibility for any sexual behavior between an adult and a child is the adult's; it is the responsibility of the adult not to respond to the child" (p. 193).

The fourth and final component of CSA definitions addresses the age or maturational advantage of the perpetrator over the victim. Although many definitions limit abuse to situations involving an age discrepancy of 5 years or more between perpetrator and victim (e.g., Conte, 1993), others include children and adolescents as potential perpetrators if a situation involves the exploitation of a child by virtue of the perpetrator's size, age, sex, or status. Broader definitions of CSA include circumstances such as those described in the second scenario above between 10-year-old Matt and his 6-year-old sister. An increasing number of reports involving both adolescent offenders and children victimizing children younger than themselves are beginning to appear (e.g., Abel & Rouleau, 1990; Gomes-Schwartz, Horowitz, & Cardarelli, 1990; Saunders, Kilpatrick, Hanson, Resnick, & Walker, 1999).

Legal issues. All U.S. states have laws prohibiting the sexual abuse of children, but the specifics of criminal statutes vary from state to state (Myers, 1998). CSA laws typically identify an age of consent—that is, the age at which an individual is considered to be capable of consenting to sexual contact. In most states, the age of consent falls somewhere in the range from 14 to 18 years. Sexual contact between an adult and a minor who has not reached the age of consent is illegal. Most states, however, define incest as illegal regardless of the victim's age or consent (Berliner & Elliott, 2002).

Criminal statutes also vary in how they define sexual contact between an adult and a minor. Most define CSA in relatively broad terms. In the state of Oregon, for example, "abuse" of a child is defined by a number of inappropriate behaviors, including "sexual abuse," "rape of a child," and "sexual exploitation" (National Clearinghouse on Child Abuse and Neglect Information, n.d.). In the Oregon statute, "sexual abuse" is not further defined. In contrast, California law defines CSA very specifically: "Sexual abuse" includes both "sexual assault" and "sexual exploitation," and both of these terms are explicitly defined (National Clearinghouse on Child Abuse and Neglect Information, n.d.). In the California statute, sexual assault includes anal or vaginal penetration by the penis or another object, oral-genital and oral-anal contact, touching of the genitals or other intimate body parts whether clothed or unclothed, and genital masturbation of the perpetrator in the presence of a child.

Estimates of Child Sexual Abuse

Despite problems in defining CSA, researchers have made numerous efforts to determine the scope of the problem. In the United States, researchers generally gather data on which to base their estimates from one of two kinds of sources: official government reports and the results of self-report surveys of adults who have been asked about their experiences with sexual victimization during childhood.

Official estimates. Some official estimates of rates of CSA come from annual surveys of child protective services (CPS) agencies conducted by government and other organizations to assess the numbers of official reports of CSA in the United States. For example, in 1986, approximately 50,714 cases of CSA were reported to CPS agencies, according to the American Association for Protecting Children (1988). In 1997, this figure increased to 223,650 cases (Wang & Daro, 1998). As noted previously, official estimates—such as those published by the U.S. Department of Health and Human Services—are difficult to interpret because

most child maltreatment never comes to the attention of CPS. Victims and their families often do not report abuse, and many professionals who are mandated to report abuse often fail to do so (e.g., Kalichman, Craig, & Follingstad, 1989; Russell, 1983). Sedlak (1990) estimates that professionals under mandate to report abuse (e.g., psychologists, social workers, and physicians) fail to report approximately half of the maltreatment cases they identify.

The three National Incidence Studies (NIS-1, NIS-2, and NIS-3) have attempted to avoid some of the problems associated with underreporting of CSA by including cases of abuse encountered by community professionals as well as reports to CPS (Sedlak, 1990; Sedlak & Broadhurst, 1996; U.S. DHHS, 1981, 1988). According to the findings of NIS-1, 42,900 children under the age of 18 were sexually abused in the United States in 1980 (a rate of 0.7 per 1,000 children). NIS-2 found that 133,600 children were sexually abused in 1986 (a rate of 2.1 per 1,000 children), and NIS-3 estimated that 300,200 children were sexually abused in 1993 (a rate of 4.5 per 1,000 children).

Data from both CPS reports and the NIS indicate an increase in reporting rates for child sexual abuse during the 1980s and early 1990s. A very different picture emerges during the mid-to-late 1990s, however, as data indicate a marked *decline* in reporting rates of CSA. Substantiated cases of sexual abuse decreased by 31% from 1992 to 1998, for example (U.S. DHHS, 2001). The proportion of sexual abuse cases represented among all types of maltreatment reported has also declined. Whereas CSA cases represented 15% of reports in 1991 (National Center on Child Abuse and Neglect, 1993), the most recent data indicate that 10% of children found to be victims of child maltreatment in 2001 were sexually abused (U.S. DHHS, 2003).

Many factors contribute to fluctuating reporting rates, making the interpretation of official statistics difficult (we return to this issue later in the chapter). The particular definition of CSA employed is one such factor. In NIS-2, for example, rates were higher when teenagers, in addition to adults, were considered perpetrators of abuse (U.S. DHHS, 1988). Another factor is that official statistics also often include duplicate reports or reports made only to CPS.

Self-report surveys. Researchers use self-report victimization surveys to determine the proportions of persons in particular populations who acknowledge having experienced sexual abuse during childhood. Compared with official statistics, self-report surveys have the potential to present a clearer picture of the "true" rate of victimization. Such surveys, however, are not without their problems. First, in order to be able to generalize survey results to given populations, researchers must use random samples. Many of the studies that have been conducted have relied on clinical samples, and so the findings are not generalizable to the public at large. Second, self-report surveys about CSA likely underestimate actual rates, because some men and women who were victimized as children may not remember their experiences or may be reluctant to report them as adults (see Williams, 1994). Finally, because measurement requires definition and operationalization of the ambiguous term *sexual abuse,* estimates can vary dramatically from one study to the next. In one review of college student and community studies, for example, the prevalence rates for child sexual abuse ranged from 7% to 62% for females and from 3% to 16% for males (Wurtele & Miller-Perrin, 1992).

In a national random sample of 1,000 adults who participated in a telephone survey sponsored by the Gallup Organization, Finkelhor, Moore, Hamby, and Straus (1997) asked respondents two questions about their own childhood experiences of sexual abuse. Overall, 23% of the respondents reported having been "touched in a sexual way" or "forced to have sex" before the age of 18 by a family member or by someone outside the family. The women in this survey sample were nearly three times as likely as the men to self-report child sexual abuse. These results are similar to those found in the most representative and methodologically sound self-report surveys in the literature, which indicate that at least 20% of women and between 5% and 10% of men in North America experienced some form of sexual abuse as children (Finkelhor, 1994a).

Is child sexual abuse increasing or decreasing? Official estimates indicate that reports of CSA increased dramatically during the 1980s. Do these estimates reflect a true rise in the rate of CSA during that period? It is certainly possible that sexual abuse increased in the 1980s because of changes taking place within the family, such as increased divorce rates (leading to increased presence of stepfathers) and increased numbers of women in the workforce (leading to increased presence of babysitters). It is also possible that what actually increased was public awareness about CSA, resulting in a greater number of reports of abuse. Some observers have argued that official reports were inflated during this period by false allegations stimulated by social hysteria about CSA (Rabinowitz, 1990). The issue of whether or not children are likely to fabricate reports of CSA has generated considerable controversy among researchers and in the mass media, although the research evidence suggests that false allegations by children are rare (for more on this topic, see Box 4.1).

Box 4.1 Do Children Fabricate Reports of Child Sexual Abuse?

Each year, there are persons who go to jail and lose their life savings, their homes, their reputations, and their jobs because social workers, psychologists, prosecutors, jurors, and judges believe what young children tell them about being sexually molested. Hundreds of thousands of individuals each year are accused falsely of child abuse. (Besharov, quoted in Emans, 1988, p. 1000)

The statement that "hundreds of thousands of individuals each year are accused falsely of child abuse" is typically attributed to Douglas Besharov, the first director of the National Center on Child Abuse and Neglect and keynote speaker at the first conference held by the organization Victims of Child Abuse Laws (Hechler, 1988). Besharov (1985) has asserted that large numbers of false allegations are attributable to the massive publicity that has surrounded CSA. Has there been an epidemic of false allegations? Do parents and other individuals who interact with children need to be concerned that they may be accused of CSA?

Based on television news coverage and newspaper stories, one might be tempted to conclude that the answer to both of these questions is a resounding yes. A number of well-publicized cases have contributed to some people's perception that there is an epidemic of false allegations. Celebrities such as Woody Allen and Michael Jackson have claimed that they were falsely accused of CSA. One case that received a great deal of attention in the 1990s was that of Dale Akiki, a mentally and physically disabled child-care worker who lived in San Diego. Akiki was accused of sexually abusing, torturing, and kidnapping nine preschool-age children. The grand jury refused to indict Akiki, however, and issued a report that rebuked therapists, parents, and prosecutors involved in the case of being "overzealous" and using improper investigative procedures. The report concluded, "Lawyers should try cases, not causes" (quoted in Mydans, 1994, p. A7).

A few years earlier, one of the longest and most costly criminal trials in U.S. history, the McMartin Preschool case, similarly ended without convictions. In this Southern California case, seven child-care workers (Ray Buckey; his mother, Peggy McMartin Buckey; and five others) were accused of sexually abusing some 360 children at the McMartin Preschool over the course of several years (Victor, 1993). As in the Akiki case, the defendants were said to be "devil worshipers" and were accused of many bizarre and unspeakable acts (for further discussion of this topic, see Box 7.4 in Chapter 7). The district attorney's office, citing the "leading questions" of many of the social workers who counseled the children, eventually dropped the charges against everyone except Ray and Peggy Buckey. In January 1990, 7 years after the case began, the Buckeys were acquitted on 52 of the 65 counts against them. Later that year, the prosecution dropped the remaining charges against Ray Buckey.

Highly publicized CSA cases such as these might lead one to conclude that *most* accusations of CSA made by children are fabricated. Whether children are likely to fabricate experiences of sexual abuse, however, is a very complicated question. Available research suggests that children rarely lie about sexual abuse (Lanning, 2002). Researchers in the field of child development have examined children's general capacity to lie at various ages and have found that children under age 7 are unlikely to be successful at telling lies (Morency & Krauss, 1982).

Another relevant issue is whether children have the capacity to form and recall accurate memories of events. Some research suggests that children may not intentionally fabricate stories of CSA, but may make false reports as a result of developmental limitations or because they are led to do so by parents and professionals, such as doctors and therapists. Recent studies of memory in children indicate that it is related to both language skills and the ability to order and interpret events, skills that are not usually well developed in young children (Hewitt, 1998; Saywitz, Goodman, & Lyon, 2002). Some researchers have examined the suggestibility of children by exposing them to different kinds of events and then asking the children about those events. Most such studies have found that young children, such as preschoolers, are more suggestible than older children and adults (Ceci & Bruck, 1993). By age 10 or 11, however, children are no more suggestible than adults (Saywitz & Snyder, 1993).

It is clear that several factors can contaminate the memories of young children (Ceci & Bruck, 1998; Lyon, 1999; Saywitz et al., 2002). Loftus and Ketcham (1991), for example, describe research in which preschool and kindergarten children were shown 1-minute films and subsequently interviewed about what they saw. The children who were asked leading questions such as "Did you see a boat?" and "Didn't you see a bear?" responded affirmatively that they had seen these objects in the films. Because there was no boat or bear in the films, the researchers concluded that they were able to alter the children's responses, or possibly even "create" memories in the children, simply by asking leading questions.

It is difficult to determine, however, how well such results generalize to research related to false allegations of CSA, because the circumstances in experimental situations are different from those surrounding actual events of sexual abuse. One factor that distinguishes experimental situations from actual CSA situations is that the latter are generally *traumatic* for the child. Some researchers who study how memory works have hypothesized that stress has a debilitating effect on memory, whereas others have argued that memory is enhanced for salient or stressful events. Several studies that have examined memories for stressful events among both adults and children suggest that individuals generally retain core features of stressful events, although they may not retain some less significant details (e.g., Bidrose & Goodman, 2000; Christiansson, 1992; Goodman, Hirschman, Hepps, & Rudy, 1991). In addition, there appear to be significant differences among individuals in the ways they remember stressful events (Saywitz et al., 2002).

The most direct research evidence associated with false allegations of CSA comes from studies that have examined samples of cases reported to CPS agencies or other professionals. Most official estimates of CSA indicate that approximately 40–50% of reported cases are unsubstantiated (Wang & Daro, 1998; Wiese & Daro, 1995). Confusion continues to exist, however, regarding what constitutes an unsubstantiated case. Although some observers equate "unsubstantiated" cases with false allegations, this is misleading. A case may be labeled unsubstantiated in official records for several reasons, including a finding of insufficient evidence. That is, the cases appearing in official statistics as "unsubstantiated" theoretically include false allegations of abuse as well as reports of true cases for which authorities found insufficient evidence to charge any perpetrators.

Estimates of false allegations of abuse range from 3% to 8% of sexual abuse reports (Everson & Boat, 1989; Jones & McGraw, 1987). For example, Jones and McGraw (1987) reviewed 576 reports of alleged sexual abuse made to the Denver Department of Social Services in 1983. Of those reports, 53% were confirmed (substantiated), 17% were unsubstantiated but categorized by the reporters as representing legitimate suspicions, and 24% were categorized as having insufficient information to make a determination about the abuse. The remaining 6% of reports were categorized as false allegations. Of the false allegations, 26 were reports from adults and 8 were reports from children or adolescents (5 of these 8 reports were made by disturbed adolescents who had been sexually victimized by adults in the past). Of the false allegations made by adults, the large majority arose in the context of child custody or visitation disputes. (It should be noted, however, that other studies have shown that allegations of sexual abuse are not part of the overwhelming majority of custody disputes; Faller, 1993.) The most recent official estimates available suggest that in those states that identify malicious reports of CSA, approximately 1% of unsubstantiated reports are intentionally false (U.S. DHHS, 1998).

The results of such studies should be interpreted cautiously for several reasons. For one thing, rates of false allegations of CSA vary depending on the types of populations sampled (Everson & Boat, 1989). In addition, whether a report is considered true or false depends on the criteria used, which can vary from the consensus of clinicians to the disposition of CPS to a judge's opinion. Such judgments are fallible, so the "true" rate of false allegations could be either somewhat higher or somewhat lower than estimated. Despite these methodological limitations, across studies the rate of false allegations has been found to be consistently low, representing a minority of reports. Even the smallest percentage of false positives, however, warrants continued research focusing on the methods of validating charges of sexual abuse, such as increasing the accuracy of validation attempts, improving interview techniques, and enhancing training for evaluators. By clearly identifying false allegations of CSA, researchers and others will not only prevent the harm that is done to those falsely accused but refocus attention on identified victims of abuse.

It seems most likely that the actual occurrence of CSA is not increasing. As noted above, the reporting rates of CSA have been decreasing steadily since the early 1990s. It may be that the increased reporting in the 1980s reflected legislative changes and increases in public and professional awareness associated with CSA. The current declines may be the result of similar social forces, such as changes in public attitudes and policies (U.S. DHHS, 2001). Alternatively, declines in CSA reports could be an indication that the actual incidence of child sexual abuse is decreasing, possibly as the result of the public awareness campaigns, prevention and criminal justice efforts, and treatment interventions that have been introduced over the past two decades (Jones & Finkelhor, 2003).

Although official reporting statistics provide some information about trends over time, self-report data may provide a more accurate picture because they also indicate the sources of such trends (Jones & Finkelhor, 2003). Feldman and colleagues (1991) examined self-report estimates by comparing English-language studies from the 1970s and 1980s with those of the 1940s. When the researchers controlled for variations in methodology across studies (e.g., definitions of abuse and upper age limits used for victims), they found that prevalence figures in 1940 were not significantly different from prevalence estimates of the 1970s and 1980s (e.g., 12% versus 10% to 12%, respectively, for females younger than 14 years of age). This absence of a decline in sexual abuse might reflect the fact that the 1970 and 1980 cohorts would not have benefited from social changes occurring during the 1980s and 1990s.

In another study, Bagley (1990) surveyed younger age cohorts regarding childhood experiences of CSA and found that 18- to 19-year-olds recalled proportionately less sexual abuse than did 20- to 27-year-olds. Finkelhor and Jones (in press) also report the findings of two self-report surveys of children that are consistent with declines in reports of CSA. Both surveys were conducted during the 1990s and support the notion that in recent years there has been a significant decline in CSA.

SECTION SUMMARY

Sexual interactions between children and adults have existed throughout history, but most societies have not recognized these types of interactions as abusive until relatively recently. Although any definition of CSA is time and culture bound, current definitions focus on types of behaviors and the intent involved as well as age and/or power discrepancies between offenders and victims. Legally, it is assumed that children are incapable of providing informed consent to sexual interactions with adults. Although all states have laws prohibiting the sexual abuse of children, criminal statutes vary from state to state. CSA includes both contact and noncontact experiences, events that occur both within and outside the family, and behaviors that involve the exploitation of authority, status, and physical size to achieve the perpetrator's sexual interests.

Although the actual number of children victimized by CSA is unknown, it is apparent that sexual victimization in childhood is a common experience. Indeed, there is good reason to speculate that official and self-report data underestimate the extent of the problem. The actual rate of child sexual abuse remains elusive because of the reluctance of victims and families, as well as professionals, to report abuse. The variability of both official and self-report estimates is due to a number of factors, including the type of population sampled and the definition of abuse employed. Research during the past several years has documented significant decreases in rates of reported CSA, but it is unclear whether these changes are attributable to social factors or to an actual decrease in the incidence of abuse.

SEARCHING FOR PATTERNS: CHARACTERISTICS OF VICTIMS AND PERPETRATORS

Research evaluating the demographic characteristics associated with CSA has addressed several questions about victims and perpetrators of this form of abuse. Studies have focused on the ages and genders of the adults and children involved, on the relationships between perpetrators and victims, and on specific risk factors associated with CSA (for a review, see Black, Heyman, & Slep, 2001b).

Characteristics of Sexually Abused Children

Age. Definitions of CSA typically limit the upper age range of victims to 16 to 18 years, but children as young as 3 months have been reported as victims (Ellerstein & Canavan, 1980). Cases on the extreme ends of the age continuum are less common than cases in the middle, and most clinical studies indicate the mean age of CSA victims as 9 to 11 years (e.g., Gomes-Schwartz et al., 1990; Ruggiero, McLeer, & Dixon, 2000). Retrospective studies conducted with adults support the finding that middle childhood (approximately 7 to 12 years of age) is the most vulnerable period for CSA (Finkelhor, 1993; Finkelhor, Hotaling, Lewis, & Smith, 1990; Saunders et al., 1999). It is probable, however, that some abuse of very young children goes undetected because these children are less likely, or less able, than older children to report abuse (Hewitt, 1998), and adults responding to self-report surveys may not remember abuse that occurred early in their childhoods (Williams, 1994). Indeed, recent official reporting statistics indicate that the rates of sexual abuse show little variability across ages for children from birth to 17 years of age (U.S. DHHS, 2001).

Gender. Data from both official sources and self-report surveys indicate that the majority of CSA victims are female (Finkelhor et al., 1990; U.S. DHHS, 2001). Girls are three times more likely than boys to be sexually abused, according to NIS-3 findings (Sedlak & Broadhurst, 1996) as well as data from a nationally representative community sample (Boney-McCoy & Finkelhor, 1995). Many experts believe that, in reality, boys may be abused more often than the data indicate, because males appear to be less likely to report sexual abuse. Self-report surveys of adult males, for example, have found that male victims are less likely to disclose abuse (e.g., Finkelhor, 1981). Several societal norms may contribute to this underreporting, including (a) the expectation that boys should be dominant and self-reliant; (b) the notion that early sexual experiences are a normal part of boys' lives; (c) fears associated with homosexuality, because most boys who are abused are abused by men; and (d) pressure on males not to express helplessness or vulnerability (Nasjleti, 1980; Rew & Esparza, 1990; Romano & De Luca, 2001). Some research evidence suggests that the proportion of males being abused is higher than previously thought. Data from self-report surveys of adults, for example, indicate higher rates of CSA for males than do official reporting statistics (Larson, Terman, Gomby, Quinn, & Behrman, 1994).

Additional risk factors. In efforts to identify and describe the risk factors associated with CSA, several researchers have compared victims and nonvictims on characteristics other than age and gender. They have found that a number of family and social characteristics are associated with increased risk for CSA, such as the presence of a stepfather, living without both natural parents for extended periods, interparental violence, family isolation and residential mobility, and a parents' prior history of sexual abuse (Brown, Cohen, Johnson, & Salzinger, 1998; Finkelhor et al., 1997; McCloskey & Bailey, 2000). Other risk factors include having a mother who is employed outside the home or who is disabled or ill; living with parents whose relationship is conflicted; living with parents who have alcohol, drug abuse, or emotional problems; having few close friends; and having a poor relationship with one or both parents (e.g., Brown et al., 1998; Finkelhor, 1984; McCloskey & Bailey, 2000). There is also some evidence that children with cognitive vulnerabilities are at increased risk for CSA. The incidence of CSA among children with cognitive disabilities, for example, is 1.75 times the rate for children with no such disabilities (U.S. DHHS, 1993). Researchers have also evaluated other variables that have been suspected of being linked to CSA, such as social isolation, ethnicity, and socioeconomic status, but so far these studies have produced mixed results (e.g., Doll, Joy, & Bartholow, 1992; Finkelhor et al., 1990, 1997; Laumann, Gagnon, Michael, & Michaels, 1994; Sedlak & Broadhurst, 1996; Wyatt, 1985).

Characteristics of Individuals Who Sexually Abuse Children

Many people have the impression that CSA perpetrators are frightening strangers or "dirty old men." Research findings concerning the demographic characteristics of CSA perpetrators, however, suggest that these stereotypes are rarely accurate.

Age. Research shows that CSA offenders vary widely in age. In 1988, the American Association for Protecting Children found that the mean age of reported perpetrators was 32 years. Since that time, however, growing research evidence has suggested that juvenile perpetrators may be underestimated among reported cases and may constitute a significant segment of the CSA offender population (Barbaree, Marshall, & Hudson, 1993; Saunders et al., 1999). General population surveys, for example, have found that adolescents represent up to 40% of offenders (Saunders et al., 1999). Clinical data from victim surveys also suggest that a substantial proportion of offenders are adolescents (Gomes-Schwartz et al., 1990). Other studies of perpetrator samples suggest that most sexual offenders develop deviant sexual interests prior to age 18 (e.g., Abel & Rouleau, 1990). Furthermore, increasingly large numbers of adolescents are being referred for treatment for sexual offenses against children (Ryan & Lane, 1991). For the most part, other than age, the characteristics of juvenile CSA offenders are similar to those of adult offenders: Most are male, and they represent all ethnic, racial, and socioeconomic groups (Margolin & Craft, 1990; Ryan & Lane, 1991).

Gender. As we have noted, most CSA perpetrators (75% or more) are male (Finkelhor, 1984; Russell, 1983; U.S. DHHS, 1996, 1998). In addition, there is evidence that a significant minority of the general male population in the United States has committed a sexual offense against a child. In a nationwide random sample survey, Finkelhor and Lewis (1988) found that between 4% and 17% of the male respondents acknowledged having molested a child. Similarly, Briere and Runtz (1989) found that 21% of male undergraduate students in their study sample reported having experienced sexual attraction to children, and 7% indicated some likelihood of having sex with a child if they could avoid detection and punishment.

Female perpetration of CSA may be more common than the available data suggest. Because of culturally prescribed definitions of child sexual abuse, many Americans may fail to recognize women as potential offenders (see Box 4.2). Abuse by females may go unnoticed, for example, because inappropriate sexual contact may occur in the context of culturally approved routine child care. Even when such contact comes to light, it may simply be labeled as "inappropriate affection" (Lawson, 1993; Saradjian, 1996; Schetky & Green, 1988).

Box 4.2 The Letourneau Case: Love or Abuse?

When a 36-year-old teacher at Shoreline Elementary School confessed to having had sex with a former student in the summer of 1997, the community of Burien, Washington, was understandably shocked. The teacher was married and had four children, was well liked in the community, and was considered one of the better teachers in the school. The sexual affair had been "consensual," but the child, who had just turned 13 when the affair started, was hardly in a position to offer consent. In the state of Washington, sex with a minor aged 12 to 16 is "rape of a child," a serious felony that carries a maximum penalty of 89 months in prison (Cloud, 1998). Because both the teacher and student confessed to the affair, there was no doubt about the guilt of the teacher.

Although the sexual abuse of students by teachers is not widely studied and is certainly not the most common form of sexual abuse, it is probably more common than many people realize. In one of the few studies conducted on the topic to date, Shakeshaft and Cohan (1995) found that more than 50% of school superintendents in the state of New York indicated that they had been called on to address cases of sexual abuse between school personnel and students. In Washington State, the superintendent of public instruction receives between 75 and 100 accusations of teacher sexual misconduct annually (Montgomery, 1996). Indeed, cases such as the one in Burien, although unusual, are not unheard of. Only a year before the Burien case made headlines, junior high teacher Mark Billie was convicted of raping a 15-year-old student in the neighboring community of Kirkland (Bartley, 1998).

The Burien case, however, received far more attention than other similar cases of sexual abuse in the schools. The story was told and retold in all the nation's major newspapers and magazines and was featured on countless television newsmagazine programs. From the *Globe* to the *Washington Post,* and from *20/20* to *Dateline NBC,* this case was big news. Why the interest? The rapist was a woman.

Mary Kay Letourneau first met Jimmy when he was a student in her second-grade class at Shoreline Elementary School.[1] Jimmy was in her class again 4 years later, when he was a sixth grader. During his sixth-grade year, Jimmy and Letourneau became quite close.

When Jimmy had problems at home or at school, he could always talk with Letourneau. She was his mentor and confidant. Their relationship was so close that sometimes when Jimmy's mother had to work late, Jimmy would spend the night at Letourneau's home. During this time, Letourneau may have been in need of a confidant herself. She and her husband, Steve, had been forced to file for bankruptcy and were having marital problems. On top of that, her father was very ill (Cloud, 1998).

During the latter part of Jimmy's sixth-grade year, the relationship began to change. Jimmy began to write love letters to Letourneau and apparently asked her to have sex with him. At first she refused. Then, in the aftermath of a particularly heated fight with her husband, she had sex with Jimmy for the first time (Cloud, 1998). The relationship lasted for 8 months and was discovered only after Letourneau told her husband she was pregnant. Knowing that he was not the father, Steve Letourneau confronted Jimmy, who confessed to the affair. The police arrested Mary Letourneau in February 1997.

Letourneau pleaded guilty to second-degree child rape and was sentenced to 7½ years in prison. Judge Linda Lau, however, was reluctant to put her in prison for so long. Letourneau's defense lawyer had argued that Letourneau suffered from bipolar disorder, otherwise known as manic depression, and that she was in need of treatment rather than punishment. Letourneau had no criminal record, and she seemed unlikely to reoffend. Not even the boy's mother was pushing for prison time. Standing before Judge Lau, Letourneau begged for mercy: "I did something that I had no right to do morally or legally," she said. "It was wrong, and I am sorry. I give you my word that it will not happen again" (quoted in Fitten, 1997, p. 3). The judge ultimately showed leniency, suspending all but 6 months of the sentence. She did, however, set two conditions: Letourneau would have to undergo treatment as a sex offender, and she could have no contact with Jimmy (Santana, 1998).

Despite her statements before the judge, Letourneau apparently saw herself as more a victim than a criminal. She resented the label "child rapist" as well as having to attend counseling in a sex offender treatment program. She claimed that she had fallen in love with a 13-year-old, and he had fallen in love with her—she failed to see what was so wrong with that (Cloud, 1998). Only 4 weeks after Letourneau was released from prison after serving her 6-month sentence, police found her and Jimmy together in her car. Because this was a violation of the conditions of her release, Judge Lau immediately reimposed the 7½-year prison sentence, saying, "These violations are extraordinarily egregious and profoundly disturbing. This case is not about a flawed system. It is about an opportunity that you foolishly squandered" (quoted in Santana, 1998, p. 5). Finally, in March 1998, just when it seemed that this case could not get any more bizarre, Letourneau's attorney announced that Mary was 6 weeks pregnant (Santana, 1998).

At first glance, this may seem like a strange case to include in a chapter on child maltreatment. After all, it does not represent a typical example of child sexual abuse. It is atypical because it involves a male victim and a female perpetrator, demographic characteristics especially uncommon in reported cases of sexual abuse (U.S. DHHS, 1996). Many professionals in the field, however, argue that female perpetration of CSA is underrecognized (e.g., Saradjian, 1996).

One reason female perpetration may go unrecognized is society's reluctance to define sexual interactions between women and children as abuse. The Letourneau case provides a good illustration of the process by which societies come to define some interactions between adults and children as abusive. From the beginning, the reactions of the U.S. public as to whether the Letourneau case was *really* a case of sexual abuse were mixed. Media accounts emphasized that Jimmy pursued Letourneau, that he was especially mature, and that he knew exactly what he was doing. Likewise, some observers asserted that Letourneau was not a sex offender, but simply a vulnerable woman in a shaky marriage who happened to fall in love. Although these kinds of reactions to the case represented the views of many Americans, many child advocates were not nearly so reluctant to define Letourneau's behavior toward Jimmy as abusive. Regardless of whether she was pretty or psychologically disturbed, and regardless of whether he was precocious, they stated, this was child abuse. As one noted:

> Lots of 13-year-old kids are physically mature, very intelligent. But this business of a 35-year-old woman making a love commitment with a 13-year-old boy is hard to fathom. What 13-year-old has the capacity for that kind of love. . . . I have no sympathy for her. When we hear it here—the proclamation of love—it is a rationalization. Did she care about his welfare, about what could happen to him by becoming a father at 13? I don't see where she's acted in [the boy's] best interest. That's not love—that's a big emotional party. (Florence Wolfe, codirector of Seattle-based Northwest Treatment Associates, quoted in Fitten, 1997, pp. 2–3)

The vast majority of reported CSA perpetrators are male, and that may have contributed significantly to many people's reluctance to recognize Letourneau's actions as abuse. It is men, for example, who are supposedly physiologically programmed to seek as many partners as possible (McDermott, 1997). On the surface, it seems nearly impossible for a woman to be sexually attracted to a 13-year-old boy. This may have been the thought of the police officers who initially found the couple together in June 1996, some 8 months before Letourneau's eventual arrest. Letourneau and Jimmy were lying together, late at night, underneath a blanket in the back of Letourneau's parked van. The officers who found them there talked with Letourneau and with Jimmy's mother and became convinced that nothing had happened, as Letourneau claimed; they decided not to take any action. If the same police officers had found a 35-year-old *male* teacher lying in the back of a parked van with a 13-year-old *female* student, their reaction would likely have been different.

Note

1. Jimmy is not the boy's real name. We have elected not to reveal his identity, although the *Globe* and several other news outlets have done so.

Increasing numbers of researchers have begun to evaluate various characteristics of female perpetrators of CSA (for a review, see Grayston & De Luca, 1999). Preliminary results suggest that female offenders can be described by any of a number of typologies (see Elliott, 1993; Mitchell & Morse, 1998; Saradjian, 1996). Most female perpetrators are (a) accomplices to male perpetrators, (b) lonely and isolated single parents, (c) adolescent babysitters, or (c) adult women who develop romantic relationships with adolescent boys (Elliott, 1993; Finkelhor, Williams, & Burns, 1988; Margolin & Craft, 1990; Saradjian, 1996). There is some evidence that female offenders are more likely to be caretakers to their victims than to be strangers and that they tend to abuse younger children than do male offenders. The severity of abuse, however, does not appear to differ between male and female perpetrators (Rudin, Zalewski, & Bodmer-Turner, 1995).

Researchers who have examined possible causal factors associated with female perpetration of CSA have uncovered some common characteristics, including a troubled childhood (e.g., sexual victimization), specific personality traits (e.g., need for nurturance and control), mental illness, drug addiction, and disturbed sexual and social relationships (for a review, see Saradjian, 1996). Caution in interpreting the results of these studies is necessary, however, because most of the research has been based on case studies. Additional research using appropriate comparison groups and adequate samples is needed before firm conclusions can be drawn.

Relationship to the abused child. Perpetrators of CSA are generally divided into two categories: those who commit intrafamilial (within the family) abuse and those whose abuse is extrafamilial (outside the family). Official reporting statistics suggest that intrafamilial abuse is more common, as male parents acting alone are the perpetrators in the greatest proportion of reported sexual abuse cases (U.S. DHHS, 2001). In contrast, large-scale community surveys of women reporting childhood histories of abuse suggest that extrafamilial abuse is more common. In 1983, for example, Russell published the results of a survey conducted with a probability sample of 930 women living in the San Francisco area. She found that 11% of the sexual victimizations experienced by respondents involved fathers or stepfathers; 45% involved acquaintances, friends, or family friends; 20% involved other relatives; and 11% involved strangers.

Thus the CSA that comes to the attention of authorities and is substantiated tends to be almost completely intrafamilial, whereas that identified in the general population through self-report surveys tends to be primarily extrafamilial (Bolen, 2000). The most comprehensive and unbiased information regarding the victim-perpetrator relationship in CSA encounters comes from the first national survey of adults reporting histories of CSA (Finkelhor et al., 1990). In this study, percentages for victim-perpetrator relationships for female and male victims, respectively, were as follows: strangers, 21% and 40%; friend or acquaintance, 41% and 44%; and family member, 29% and 11%. In this sample, males were more likely to have been abused by strangers, whereas females were more likely to have been abused by family members. These data suggest that although extrafamilial CSA is more common, the perpetrator of either form of abuse is a person familiar to the child in the majority of cases.

SECTION SUMMARY

One of the most consistent findings of the research evaluating risk factors associated with CSA is that females are more likely than males to be victims of CSA, and males are more likely than females to be perpetrators. Relatively recent research suggests, however, that significant proportions of female perpetrators and male victims may go undetected by researchers, practitioners, and reporting agencies.

Research has shown that widely held stereotypes of CSA perpetrators and victims are inaccurate. For example, rather than being "dirty old men," CSA perpetrators vary in age (although research suggests that most sexual offenders develop deviant sexual interests prior to age 18). CSA perpetrators are also less likely to be strangers to their victims than is often imagined. Most develop trusting relationships with their victims, and many are acquaintances or friends of the victims, or fathers, other parental figures, or other family members. Child and family variables that may increase the risk of CSA victimization include victim's age (i.e., 7 to 12 years old), family composition (e.g., presence of a stepfather), maternal availability, and family conflict (e.g., parents with emotional or drug-related problems).

Populations of victims and offenders are heterogeneous, suggesting that sexual abuse occurs in virtually all demographic, social, and family circumstances. Furthermore, because the majority of research has focused on female victims and male perpetrators, most research findings do not pertain to male victims or female perpetrators. As a final caveat, it is important to acknowledge the difficulty in determining whether the variables found to be associated with CSA are actual risk factors for abuse, consequences of abuse, or correlates of abuse history.

DYNAMICS AND CONSEQUENCES ASSOCIATED WITH CHILD SEXUAL ABUSE

Dynamics of Child Sexual Abuse

To develop a comprehensive understanding of CSA, it is necessary to examine the characteristics of the victimization experience itself. Much of what is known about the victimization experience comes from cases reported to CPS agencies and from studies of CSA victims and perpetrators.

Types of sexual activity. Both adults and children have provided descriptions of the types of sexual behaviors they encountered in incidents of CSA. Although the range of sexual activities theoretically extends from exhibitionism to intercourse, the questions posed by researchers have influenced the variability in the types of activities actually reported. In addition, the research procedures employed (e.g., face-to-face versus anonymous interviews or surveys) and the types of samples studied (e.g., community samples of adults or children reported for abuse, clinical populations, and college students) have affected the proportions of victims reporting various types of abuse.

Russell (1983) distinguishes three types of sexual activity: *very serious* abuse (e.g., completed or attempted vaginal, oral, or anal intercourse; cunnilingus; and analingus), *serious* abuse (e.g., completed and attempted genital fondling, simulated intercourse, and digital penetration), and *least serious* abuse (e.g., completed and attempted acts of sexual touching of buttocks, thighs, legs or other body parts, clothed breasts, or genitals; and kissing). Of the 930 women in her sample, 38% reported having had childhood experiences involving one of these forms of sexual abuse. Of that 38%, 38% experienced very serious abuse, 34% experienced serious abuse, and 28% experienced less serious abuse. In another study of 156 sexually abused children, Gomes-Schwartz et al. (1990) assessed specific sexual behaviors and found that 28% experienced either vaginal or anal intercourse, 38% experienced oral-genital contact or object penetration, 23% experienced fondling or mutual stimulation, and 6% experienced some form of attempted sexual contact (i.e., the offender requesting that the child touch his genitals), touching, or voyeurism. The types of abuse reported in different studies tend to vary by the types of populations sampled. Not surprisingly, respondents in nonclinical samples have tended to experience less severe forms of abuse than those in clinical samples (e.g., Ruggiero et al., 2000; Saunders et al., 1999).

Initiation of abuse. Preliminary reports from men incarcerated for CSA or participating in treatment programs for CSA offenders have provided some information about the techniques perpetrators use to identify and recruit child victims (e.g., Budin & Johnson, 1989; Conte, Wolf, & Smith, 1989; Elliott, Browne, & Kilcoyne, 1995). Perpetrators do not molest every child to whom they have access; instead, they generally select children who are vulnerable in some way. These may include children who are passive, quiet, trusting, young, unhappy in appearance, needy, or living in a divorced home.

Once a perpetrator has identified a target child, he or she may desensitize the child to sexual activity through a "grooming" process that involves a progression from nonsexual to sexual touch in the context of a gradually developing relationship. The typical scenario begins with seemingly accidental or affectionate touches and then proceeds to sexual touches. Offenders tend to misrepresent moral standards or misuse their authority or adult sophistication to seduce children (e.g., "It's okay, you're my daughter"). In addition, perpetrators report employing a range of coercive tactics to initiate relationships with children, such as separating the children from other protective adults, conditioning the children through reward (e.g., money, toys, candy, and clothes) and punishment (e.g., threatening to hit the child or to hurt loved ones), forcing the children to observe violence against their mothers, and using physical force or threatening gestures.

To avoid overreliance on data derived solely from acknowledged perpetrators, researchers have also asked CSA victims directly about their abuse experiences. Berliner and Conte (1990), for example, interviewed child victims (10 to 18 years of age) about the processes of their own sexual victimization. The children's accounts closely resembled those provided by perpetrators. The children reported that their perpetrators initiated sexual activity by gradually shifting from normal affectionate contact or physical activities (e.g., bathing, hugging, massaging, wrestling, and tickling) to more sexual behaviors (e.g., genital touching). The children also reported that their perpetrators made statements in which they attempted to justify the sexual contact. Most commonly, the perpetrators claimed that the behavior was not really sexual, or if they acknowledged that the behavior was sexual, they asserted that it was acceptable (e.g., "I'm just going to look, I won't touch"; "I'm teaching you about sex").

Maintenance of abuse. Studies that have examined victim and perpetrator perspectives on the process of CSA also shed light on the strategies that perpetrators use to keep children engaged in sexual activities over prolonged periods. Central to a perpetrator's maintenance of sexual activities with a child is the perpetrator's ability to convince the child that the activities should be kept secret so that other adults cannot intervene to terminate the abuse. Studies of child victims as well as adults who were victimized as children indicate that the majority of victims do not disclose their abuse immediately, and a significant number do not disclose for years (Elliott & Briere, 1994; Gomes-Schwartz et al., 1990; Timnick, 1985).

Perpetrators report using a range of coercive activities to maintain abusive relationships, including bribes, threats, and physical aggression. A child may maintain silence about being abused, for example, because the offender has offered the child attention, money, or purchases of special toys in exchange for his or her silence (e.g., Elliott et al., 1995). Perpetrators also often use threats to silence their victims; they might threaten to harm or kill the child, a significant other, or a pet; to send the victim to a frightening place; or to show the child's parents pictures of the child involved in sexual acts. Finally, perpetrators often employ overt acts of aggression, such as physically overpowering the child, to reinforce secrecy (Budin & Johnson, 1989; Conte et al., 1989; Lang & Frenzel, 1988). Some research suggests that sexual offenses against children are most often nonviolent; Timnick (1985), for example, has estimated that physical violence accompanies only approximately 20% of CSA incidents. Other findings, however, suggest that offenders are more frequently aggressive and often use physical threats (Becker, 1994; Briere & Elliott, 1994; Stermac, Hall, & Henskens, 1989).

Exploitation through the Internet. Another form of sexual exploitation of children described in the research literature in recent years is sometimes referred to as "cyberexploitation" or "online crimes against children." Kreston (2002) describes the variety of ways that children who use the Internet may be at risk. First, they may be propositioned online for sexual activity. Such propositions may be explicit proposals, or perpetrators may take a more indirect approach, using an online version of the grooming process described above to establish and maintain contact with children. Some children may provide their names, addresses, and telephone numbers to individuals they correspond with online, and may even agree to meet with them. Second, children may be exposed to various forms of sexually explicit material on the Internet via links that come up when they use search engines, through their own misspelling of Web addresses, or through unsolicited e-mails and pop-up ads. Third, children may experience online harassment. This can include a variety of behaviors, such as "threatening or offensive behavior targeting the child or sharing information or pictures on-line about the targeted child" (Kreston, 2002, p. 13).

Researchers at the Crimes Against Children Research Center recently conducted the Youth Internet Safety Survey in an attempt to determine the magnitude of online exploitation of children (Finkelhor, Mitchell, & Wolak, 2000). The survey was administered to a national U.S. sample of 1,501 children and adolescents ages 10 to 17 years. The respondents were asked about their experiences online with unwanted sexual solicitation, exposure to sexual material, and harassment within the past year. Of the children in this sample, 1 in 5 reported

having experienced an unwanted sexual solicitation, 1 in 4 had experienced unwanted exposure to sexual material, and 1 in 17 had been threatened or harassed. Adolescents in the sample (ages 14 to 17) were more likely than younger children to have had these experiences online. As Finkelhor et al. (2000) point out, however, it is important that one view these findings from an appropriate perspective. Although the findings from this survey suggest that children are at risk for this form of exploitation, such victimization constitutes only a small proportion of the sexual abuse, exploitation, and other crimes to which children are vulnerable. In addition, the results of this survey suggest that most of the solicitations made online by potential CSA perpetrators fail; they do not result in offline sexual assault or illegal sexual contact. Although no successful solicitations were found in this survey, such cases have been investigated and confirmed by law enforcement agencies (Finkelhor et al., 2000).

Scholars have proposed several approaches to combating the problem of Internet exploitation of children. A first step is to educate children, parents, and professionals who work with children and families about the potential dangers the Internet poses to children and adolescents and how they can protect against this form of exploitation. Parents need to be educated, for example, about ways in which they can limit their children's Internet access (e.g., browser access controls, software filters). In addition, as Kreston (2002) recommends, families should place any computers with Internet access in family living areas rather than in private rooms, and parents should instruct their children not to enter Internet chat rooms without parental permission. The National Center for Missing and Exploited Children has implemented an education and awareness campaign about the dangers of the Internet targeted toward parents and children. The campaign, which has reached millions of children and families in homes and classrooms, emphasizes parental knowledge about computers and the Internet as well as the importance of parents' involvement in the lives of their children (Finkelhor et al., 2000).

Legislation is also needed to address the issue of online exploitation of children. Currently, several countries have laws in place that are intended to protect children from such exploitation. The United States, for example, has established an $11 million federal program that includes Internet Crimes Against Children Task Forces, which are developed to assist state and local law enforcement agencies in conducting undercover investigations, provide technical assistance and training, and develop prevention and education materials. In addition, the Child Online Privacy Protection Act was developed to protect children from explicit sexual advertising practices online and from registration of their personal information without parental consent. Additional efforts are necessary, however, to ensure that federal and state child abuse statutes, most of which were written prior to the development of the Internet, apply to illegal behaviors carried out online (Finkelhor et al., 2000).

Organized Exploitation

Of all the major forms of child maltreatment discussed in this book, child sexual abuse is the one that is most likely to occur between a child and an adult who is not a family member. Organized exploitation is one form of CSA that is typically extrafamilial, although recent reports suggest that some elements of organized exploitation may also occur within the family (Itzin, 1997). The term *organized exploitation* typically refers to the sexual maltreatment of groups of children for the sexual stimulation of one or more perpetrators, for commercial gain, or both. This form of child maltreatment includes sex rings, pornography, and prostitution, activities that are often interrelated. To date, research on the organized sexual exploitation of children is limited.

Child sex rings. In a child sex ring, a number of children are sexually abused by one or more perpetrators. Using various modes of deception, enticement, and manipulation, the perpetrators interest children in joining the group and then require that the children fulfill sexual demands in order to be accepted (Burgess, Groth, & McCausland, 1981; Lanning & Burgess, 1984). Burgess and her colleagues distinguish among three types of child sex rings: *solo rings,* which consist of single adults involved with small groups of children; *syndicated rings,* which consist of multiple adults in well-structured organizations that exist to recruit children, produce pornography, deliver direct sexual services, and establish networks of customers; and *transitional rings,* which consist of one or more adults and several children but do not include any organizational aspect, although such rings may eventually move toward organizational status (e.g., selling pornographic photographs) (see Burgess & Hartman, 1987; Burgess, Hartman, McCausland, & Powers, 1984).

One core element of sex rings is the inclusion of pornographic activities, which are sometimes used to stimulate and instruct children in these groups (e.g., Burgess et al., 1984). In addition, the sexual activities

of children in sex rings are often photographed or videotaped, and some researchers believe that a child sex ring may be the first phase in the development of an organization devoted to child prostitution and pornography (Creighton, 1993; Hunt & Baird, 1990; Wild, 1989).

Child pornography. The National Center for Missing and Exploited Children (n.d.) notes that federal law defines child pornography as "a visual depiction of any kind, including a drawing, cartoon, sculpture, or painting, photograph, film, video, or computer or computer-generated image or picture, whether made or produced by electronic, mechanical, or other means, of sexually explicit conduct" involving a minor. Until the late 1970s, there were no laws against child pornography in most U.S. states. In 1978, the U.S. Congress passed the Protection of Children Against Sexual Exploitation Act in an attempt to halt the production and dissemination of pornographic materials involving children. Soon thereafter, several other countries adopted prohibitions against child pornography as well (Doek, 1985; Tyler & Stone, 1985). In addition, the Child Sexual Abuse and Pornography Act of 1986 provides for federal prosecution of individuals engaged in child pornography, including parents who permit their children to engage in such activities (Otto & Melton, 1990). Several U.S. states have also passed legislation that requires commercial film and photo processors to inform authorities when they discover suspected child pornography during the processing of film (Wurtele & Miller-Perrin, 1992).

Determining the number of children involved in child pornography is extremely difficult, given that the production, distribution, and sale of child pornography are cloaked in secrecy. U.S. government subcommittees that have investigated the problem of child pornography, however, have determined that significant numbers of children are sexually exploited in this way, with an estimated 7% of the pornographic industry in the United States involving children in sexual activities (cited in Pierce, 1984). In recent years, some have argued that the advent of the Internet has led to significant increases in the numbers of children exploited by the child pornography industry (Virginia Department of Social Services, 2003).

Child pornography is clearly abusive in and of itself, but it may also contribute to the problem of child maltreatment by stimulating adult sexual interest in children (Rush, 1980; Russell, 1988). Results of studies that have examined the role of pornography in affecting perpetrators' likelihood of offending against children have been equivocal. Some researchers have found that CSA perpetrators use pornography more than do comparison groups, whereas others have found no relationship between CSA perpetration and pornography (Carter, Prentky, Knight, Vanderveer, & Boucher, 1987; Howe, 1995; Malamuth & Briere, 1986). There is no doubt, however, that child pornography contributes to the exploitation of children by creating a market for the victimization of children and by serving as a tool that perpetrators use to educate and stimulate victims or to blackmail victims into maintaining secrecy about abusive activities (Burgess & Hartman, 1987; Hunt & Baird, 1990; Tyler & Stone, 1985).

Little has been written about attempts to address the problem of child pornography outside the enactment of federal and state legislation that prohibits the use of minors in the production of pornographic material. Although such laws have been somewhat successful in curtailing the problem within the United States, complete elimination of the problem of child pornography will require worldwide prohibitions (Tyler & Stone, 1985; Virginia Department of Social Services, 2003). With the advent of the Internet and the widespread availability of personal computers, the problem has become increasingly complex, as access to child pornography has become a worldwide problem of considerable magnitude (Durkin & Bryant, 1995; Esposito, 1998; Hughes, 1996).

Child prostitution. Of all the various forms of organized sexual exploitation of children, child prostitution has received the most attention from researchers. The findings of surveys conducted with adult female prostitutes suggest that significant numbers of these women began to work as prostitutes when they were children. Silbert and Pines (1983) surveyed 200 San Francisco street prostitutes and found that 70% reported that they were less than 21 years of age when they began prostitution. Of these, 60% reported they were under age 16 when they started work as prostitutes. Other studies have found child prostitutes as young as 10 years of age, with a median age for entry into prostitution at age 14 (e.g., Nadon, Koverola, & Schludermann, 1998).

Characteristics of adolescent prostitutes that have been documented repeatedly in the literature include a history of childhood maltreatment (such as physical and sexual abuse and exposure to interparental violence), personal and parental alcohol or drug abuse, and poor family functioning (e.g., Bagley & Young, 1987; Earls & David, 1990; Silbert, 1982). One of the most common factors in the backgrounds of adolescent prostitutes, however, is runaway youth status,

whether because of the death of a parent, because of being kicked out of the family home, or because of alcoholism or abuse in the home (Nadon et al., 1998).

Like child sex rings, child prostitution is associated with child pornography. Silbert and Pines (1983) found that 38% of their sample of San Francisco adult prostitutes said that someone had taken sexually explicit photographs of them for commercial purposes when they were children, and 10% described being used in pornographic films when they were children. Child pornography and prostitution have also been linked in reports of international trafficking of women and children for sexual purposes. In a practice sometimes referred to as *sex tourism,* individuals purchase "vacation travel packages" that include the sexual services of women or children (Itzin, 1997; Joseph, 1995). According to Muntarbhorn, the United Nations recently concluded that child prostitution and pornography represent "a vast national and transnational problem" (cited in Itzin, 1997, p. 62).

Effects Associated With Child Sexual Abuse

Since the initial recognition of CSA as a societal problem, scholars have argued about the effects on children of adult-child sexual interactions in the context of secret relationships. Some have suggested that children who are sexually exploited by adults do not suffer harm, either while they are children or in adulthood (e.g., Yorukoglu & Kemph, 1966; Rind, Tromovitch, & Bauserman, 1998). The majority of research evidence, however, suggests that CSA victims are more likely than nonvictims to exhibit a variety of negative psychological, behavioral, and interpersonal problems (see reviews by Neumann, Houskamp, Pollock, & Briere, 1996; Paolucci, Genuis, & Violato, 2001; Trickett & Putnam, 1998; Tyler, 2002). The consequences associated with CSA can be classified as either initial effects (occurring within 2 years following the abuse) or long-term effects (consequences beyond 2 years subsequent to the abuse).

Initial effects. Investigators have identified a wide range of emotional, cognitive, physical, and behavioral effects in CSA victims within 2 years of the abuse. The specific manifestation of symptoms appears to depend on the developmental level of the victim (Hewitt, 1998; Kendall-Tackett, Williams, & Finkelhor, 1993; Wurtele & Miller-Perrin, 1992). Table 4.1 displays the most common initial effects associated with CSA for preschool, school-age, and adolescent children.

Table 4.1   Possible Initial Effects Associated With Sexual Abuse in Preschool, School-Age, and Adolescent Children

Behavioral Effects	Emotional Effects	Cognitive Effects	Physical Effects
Preschool children			
Regression/immaturity	Anxiety[a]	Learning difficulties	Bruises
Social withdrawal	Clinging		Genital bleeding
Sexualized behavior[a]	Nightmares[a]		Genital pain
Sexual preoccupation[a]	Fears		Genital itching
Precocious sexual knowledge*	Depression		Genital odors
Seductive behavior[a]	Guilt		Problems walking
Excessive masturbation[a]	Hostility/anger		Problems sitting
Sex play with others[a]	Tantrums		Sleep disturbance
Sexual language	Aggression		Eating disturbance
Genital exposure			Enuresis
Sexual victimization of others[a]			Encopresis
Family/peer conflicts			Stomachache
Difficulty separating			Headache
Hyperactivity			
School-age children			
Regression/immaturity[a]	Anxiety	Learning difficulties[a]	Stomachache
Social withdrawal	Phobias	Poor concentration	Headache
Sexualized behavior	Nightmares[a]	Poor attention	Genital pain
Sexual preoccupation	Fears[a]	Declining grades	Genital itching
Precocious sexual knowledge	Obsessions	Negative perceptions	Genital odors
Seductive behavior	Tics	Dissociation	Problems walking
Excessive masturbation	Hostility/anger		Problems sitting
Sex play with others	Aggression[a]		Sleep disturbance
Sexual language	Family/peer conflicts		Eating disturbance
Genital exposure	Depression		Enuresis
Sexual victimization of others	Guilt		Encopresis
Delinquency	Suicidality		
Stealing	Low self-esteem		
Poor peer relations			
Hyperactivity[a]			
Adolescents			
Social withdrawal[a]	Anxiety	Learning difficulties	Stomachache
Self-injurious behavior[a]	Phobias	Poor concentration	Headache
Sexualized behavior	Nightmares	Poor attention	Genital pain
Sexual preoccupation	Obsessions	Declining grades	Genital odors
Precocious sexual knowledge	Hostility/anger		Genital itching
Seductive behavior	Depression[a]		Problems walking
Promiscuity	Guilt		Problems sitting
Prostitution	Suicidality[a]		Pregnancy
Sexual language	Low self-esteem		Eating disturbance[a]
Sexual victimization of others			Sleep disturbance[a]
Delinquency[a]			Possible immune
Running away[a]			system dysfunction
Early marriage			Dysregulated cortisol
Substance abuse[a]			Increased
Truancy			catecholamine level
Dropping out of school			
Stealing			
Poor peer relations			

SOURCES: A representative but not exhaustive list of sources for the information displayed in this table includes the following: Ackerman, Newton, McPherson, Jones, and Dykman (1998); Boney-McCoy and Finkelhor (1995); De Bellis, Burke, Trickett, and Putnam (1996); De Bellis, Chrousos, et al. (1994); De Bellis, Lefter, Trickett, and Putnam (1994); Dubowitz, Black, Harrington, and Verschoore (1993); Friedrich, Grambusch, and Damon (1992); Kaufman and Widom (1999); Lanktree, Briere, and Zaidi (1991); Mennen and Meadow (1994); Mian, Marton, and LeBaron (1996); Putnam, Helmers, and Trickett (1993); Trickett, McBride-Chang, and Putnam (1994); Tyler (2002); Wells, McCann, Adams, Voris, and Ensign (1995).

a. Most common symptoms for this age group.

In a review of 45 empirical studies on initial effects of CSA, Kendall-Tackett et al. (1993) found that one of the two most common symptoms identified in sexually abused children is sexualized behavior (e.g., overt sexual acting out toward adults or other children, compulsive masturbation, excessive sexual curiosity, sexual promiscuity, and precocious sexual play and knowledge). The sexual behaviors of sexually abused children are often associated with intercourse, such as mimicking intercourse and inserting objects into the vagina or anus (Friedrich et al., 2001). Sexualized behavior is also believed to be the behavioral symptom that is most predictive of the occurrence of sexual abuse (Friedrich, 1993).

The other most frequent problems noted in sexually abused children are symptoms of posttraumatic stress disorder (PTSD). These include nightmares, fears, feelings of isolation, inability to enjoy usual activities, somatic complaints, autonomic arousal (e.g., heightened startle response), and guilt feelings. Several studies have demonstrated that sexually abused children consistently report higher levels of PTSD symptoms relative to comparison children and are more likely to receive a diagnosis of PTSD than are other maltreated children (e.g., Dubner & Motta, 1999; McLeer et al., 1998).

In addition to the myriad symptoms documented in sexual abuse victims, CSA has been associated with a wide range of psychopathology. Of the victimized children studied by Gomes-Schwartz et al. (1990), 17% of the preschool group (4 to 6 years of age), 40% of the school-age group (7 to 13 years of age), and 8% of the adolescent group (14 to 18 years of age) evidenced clinically significant pathology, indicating severe behavioral and emotional difficulties. Using a checklist of parent-reported behaviors to assess the effects of sexual abuse on 93 prepubertal children, Dubowitz, Black, Harrington, and Verschoore (1993) found that 36% had significantly elevated scores on the Internalizing Scale (e.g., depression and withdrawn behavior) and 38% had elevated scores on the Externalizing Scale (e.g., acting-out behaviors). Similar levels of dysfunction would be expected in only 10% of the general population of children.

Overall, evidence to date strongly suggests that CSA results in disturbing psychological sequelae in a significant proportion of child victims. Based on their review, Browne and Finkelhor (1986) concluded that from 20% to 40% of abused children seen by clinicians manifest pathological disturbance. Most of the types of symptoms demonstrated in victims of CSA, however,

are no different from the difficulties seen in clinical samples of children and adolescents more generally. In degree of symptomatology, sexually abused children generally exhibit significantly more psychological symptoms than nonabused children, but fewer symptoms than children in clinical samples. The only exceptions to this pattern are findings indicating that sexually abused children exhibit more sexualized behavior and PTSD symptoms than both nonabused children and children in clinical groups (Beitchman, Zucker, Hood, daCosta, & Akman, 1991; Kendall-Tackett et al., 1993).

Long-term effects. The psychological consequences of childhood sexual victimization can extend into adulthood and affect victims throughout their lives. A history of CSA has been associated with a variety of long-term symptoms, such as emotional reactions including depression and anxiety (e.g., Gold, Lucenko, Elhai, Swingle, & Sellers, 1999; Peters & Range, 1995; Weiss, Longhurst, & Mazure, 1999). According to Berliner and Elliott (2002), depression is the most common symptom reported by adults who were sexually abused as children. Additional effects include problems with interpersonal relationships (DiLillo & Long, 1999), PTSD symptoms (Saunders et al., 1999), problems with sexual adjustment (Bartoi & Kinder, 1998; Bensley, Eenwyk, & Simmons, 2000), and behavioral dysfunction (e.g., substance abuse, eating disorders, and self-mutilation; see Briere & Gil, 1998; Saunders et al., 1999; Smolak & Murnen, 2002). Several longitudinal studies have found elevated rates of various mental disorders in adults who were sexually abused as children (e.g., Cohen, Brown, & Smailes, 2001; Widom, 1999). Table 4.2 summarizes the long-term effects associated with CSA.

Explaining the Variability in Effects

The research findings discussed above suggest that no single symptom or pattern of symptoms is present in all victims of CSA. Many CSA victims exhibit no symptoms at all, at least in the short term. Based on their review of CSA effects, Kendall-Tackett et al. (1993) concluded that approximately 20% to 50% of CSA victims are asymptomatic at initial assessment, and only 10% to 25% become symptomatically worse during the 2 years following victimization. Why is it that some victims are severely affected, others are moderately affected, and still others are relatively unscathed by the experience of CSA? Furthermore, why do some victims

Table 4.2   Possible Long-Term Effects Associated With Child Sexual Abuse

Type of Effect	Specific Problem	Specific Symptoms
Emotional	Depression	Depressed affect Suicidality Low self-esteem Guilt Poor self-image Self-blame
	Anxiety	Anxiety attacks Fears Phobias Somatic symptoms Migraine Stomach problems Aches and pains Skin disorders
Interpersonal		Difficulty trusting others Poor social adjustment Social isolation Feelings of isolation, alienation, insecurity Difficulty forming/maintaining relationships Parenting difficulties Sexual revictimization Physical victimization
Posttraumatic stress disorder (PTSD) symptomatology	Reexperiencing	Intrusive thoughts Flashbacks Nightmares
	Numbing/avoidance	Dissociation Amnesia for abuse events Disengagement ("spacing out") Emotional numbing Out-of-body experiences Poor concentration
Sexual adjustment		Anorgasmia Arousal/desire dysfunction Sexual phobia/aversion Sexual anxiety Sexual guilt Promiscuity Prostitution Dissatisfaction in sexual relationships
Behavior dysfunction	Eating disorders	Bingeing Purging Overeating
	Substance abuse	Alcoholism Use of illicit drugs
	Self-mutilation	Cutting body parts Carving body areas Hitting head or body with or against objects

SOURCES: A representative but not exhaustive list of sources for the information displayed in this table includes the following: Bartoi and Kinder (1998); Bensley et al. (2000); Briere and Gil (1998); Cole, Woolger, Power, & Smith (1992); D. M. Elliott (1994); Elliott and Briere (1992); S. N. Gold et al. (1999); Neumann et al. (1996); Noll et al. (2003); Saunders et al. (1999); Springs and Friedrich (1992); Steiger and Zanko (1990); Urquiza and Goodlin-Jones (1994); Weiss et al. (1999); Widom (1995); and Zanarini, Ruser, Frankenburg, Hennen, and Gunderson, 2000.

manifest anxiety in response to their abuse and others show physical symptoms or depression?

One reason it is difficult to answer these questions is that methodological weaknesses have plagued the research in this area (see Briere, 1992). Definitions vary across studies, many studies have failed to include comparison groups, and some research has relied on interview and assessment devices that are unstandardized. The samples used in the research are also problematic. College student samples, for example, tend to be nonrepresentative of the general public in terms of intelligence, social class, and motivational aspects. Clinical samples of CSA victims are also biased because they include only CSA cases referred for treatment services, so the results may not be generalizable to all cases of CSA (e.g., such samples may not include less symptomatic children or undisclosed victims). Finally, research findings concerning psychological symptoms in adolescents or adults who were abused as children do not establish a definitive causal relationship between those symptoms and the subjects' histories of CSA. In the absence of longitudinal studies that begin before abuse occurs, it is difficult to determine whether observed characteristics result from early sexual abuse or some other variable, such as family dysfunction. Although studies conducted within the past 10 years have achieved greater empirical precision by using larger numbers of participants, multiple measures, comparison groups, and longitudinal designs (e.g., Erickson, Egeland, & Pianta, 1989; Gomes-Schwartz et al., 1990; Noll, Trickett, & Putnam, 2003), more research is needed to clarify the specific effects of CSA for given individual victims.

Researchers attempting to understand the effects associated with childhood sexual victimization have explored associations between characteristics of the sexually abusive situation or its aftermath and differential psychological effects. Are the psychological effects of CSA victimization by a father figure, for example, more severe than those seen when the abuser is an uncle? Are the effects more severe when the child's disclosure is met with disbelief? Researchers have evaluated the relationships between CSA effects and a number of factors, including the circumstances of the abuse, postabuse characteristics, and victim perceptions of the abuse. Table 4.3 lists many of the variables that have been examined and their influence on the effects of CSA.

Several aspects of CSA situations are associated with increased symptoms in both child victims and adult survivors. Perhaps the most consistent finding is that threats, force, and violence by the perpetrator are linked with increased negative outcome (Beitchman et al., 1992; Gomes-Schwartz et al., 1990; Tyler, 2002). Studies have also demonstrated that the least serious forms of sexual contact (e.g., unwanted kissing or touching of clothed body parts) are associated with less trauma than are more serious forms of genital contact (e.g., vaginal or anal intercourse; Bagley & Ramsay, 1986; Elwell & Ephross, 1987; Mennen & Meadow, 1995). Most studies indicate that when abuse is perpetrated by a father, father figure, or other individual who has an intense emotional relationship with the victim, the consequences are particularly severe (Beitchman et al., 1991, 1992; Briere & Elliott, 1994). In addition, when victims are exposed to multiple forms of child maltreatment (e.g., sexual and physical abuse), they exhibit increased symptoms (e.g., Ney, Fung, & Wickett, 1994).

Research has also found that specific postabuse events (e.g., the ways in which family members and institutions respond to disclosure) are related to the effects of CSA. It is well established that responses toward the victim by parents, other relatives, teachers, and other adults have significant effects on the trauma associated with CSA as well as victims' recovery. Studies have consistently found that negative responses tend to aggravate victims' experience of trauma (e.g., Gomes-Schwartz et al., 1990; Runyan, Hunter, & Everson, 1992). In contrast, the availability of social supports following the disclosure of abuse, such as maternal support or a supportive relationship with another adult, appears to mitigate negative effects and play a protective role (e.g., Conte & Schuerman, 1987; Gomes-Schwartz et al., 1990). Lack of social supports has also been associated with increased psychological problems in adults who experienced sexual abuse as children (Herman, 1992; Springs & Friedrich, 1992).

Additional mediators of the effects of CSA that have received considerable attention in recent years are victims' cognitive appraisals and attributional styles (e.g., Hazzard, 1993; Miller-Perrin, 1998; Williams, 1993). Williams (1993), for example, found in her sample of 531 adult victims that the victim's perception of the severity of the abuse was the major determinant of subsequent adjustment or maladjustment. Spaccarelli and Fuchs (1997) also found that victims' negative appraisals of the abuse experience were related to poorer outcomes. Greater distress has also been found in those who blamed themselves for their abuse, experienced high levels of shame, perceived themselves to be different from their peers and less believed, and viewed their abusive experiences as threatening

Table 4.3   Potential Mediators of the Effects of Child Sexual Abuse

Potential Mediators	Influence on Child Sexual Abuse Effects
Abuse characteristics	
Duration and frequency	Results are mixed for research evaluating child victims; increased duration is associated with more negative effect for adults abused as children.
Type of sexual activity	More severe forms of sexual activity (e.g., penetration) are associated with more negative effect.
Age at onset	Results are mixed.
Child-perpetrator relationship	More negative effect is associated with fathers, father figures, and intense emotional relationships.
Number of perpetrators	Results are mixed for research evaluating child victims; a greater number of perpetrators are associated with more negative effect for adults abused as children.
Victim gender	Results are mixed, with some findings showing similarities between genders and some suggesting more externalizing symptoms for males and internalizing symptoms for females.
Force or physical injury	Presence of force or physical injury is associated with greater negative effect.
Multiple forms of abuse	Different combinations of child maltreatment are associated with more negative effect.
Postabuse characteristics	
Response toward the victim	Negative reactions are associated with greater negative effect.
Court involvement	Results are mixed.
Out-of-home placement	Results are mixed.
Available social support	Increased social support is associated with less severe effect.
Perceptions of abuse	
Perceived severity	Increased perceived severity of abuse and negative appraisals of the abuse experience are associated with greater negative effect.

SOURCES: A representative but not exhaustive list of sources for the information displayed in this table includes the following: Beitchman et al. (1991, 1992); Calam, Horne, Glasgow, and Cox (1998); Conte and Schuerman (1987); Feinauer (1989); Gomes-Schwartz et al. (1990); Henry (1997); Holmes and Slap (1998); Kendall-Tackett et al. (1993); Mennen and Meadow (1995); Noll et al. (2003); Ruggiero et al. (2000); Spaccarelli & Fuchs (1997); Tremblay, Hebert, and Piche (1999); Tyler (2002); Williams (1993); and Young, Bergandi, and Titus (1994).

(e.g., Feiring, Taska, & Lewis, 1996; Mannarino & Cohen, 1996a, 1996b; Morrow, 1991). Future research should examine additional potential mediators, particularly those that might decrease the negative effects of CSA.

———◆•◆———

SECTION SUMMARY

Greater numbers of empirical studies of the dynamics of CSA victimization are beginning to appear that describe the types of sexual activities involved and how abuse is initiated and maintained, as well as various forms of organized exploitation. The sexual activities of CSA perpetrators range from exhibitionism to various forms of penetration. Perpetrators appear to target children who are vulnerable in some way and initiate abuse by desensitizing children to increasingly sexual types of contact. To initiate and maintain abuse, perpetrators may use coercive tactics such as verbal threats or overt aggression.

A relatively new area within CSA research concerns the sexual exploitation of children via the Internet. Such exploitation may include propositions for sexual activity, exposure to sexually explicit material, and sexual harassment. Although researchers have only recently begun to explore this problem, findings to date indicate that this form of victimization constitutes only a small proportion of CSA.

Organized exploitation, another form of child maltreatment, involves groups of children who are abused for the sexual stimulation of one or more perpetrators and often for commercial gain. This form of CSA includes three interrelated activities: child sex rings, pornography, and prostitution. Children who become involved in prostitution and pornography are often runaways attempting to escape dysfunctional or abusive home environments. Interventions aimed at alleviating the problem of organized exploitation have focused primarily on policy initiatives and legislation designed to protect children from these activities. Although these approaches have met with some success, more efforts are needed.

Numerous empirical studies have shown that myriad psychological consequences are associated with childhood sexual victimization. These include both short-term and long-term difficulties of an emotional, physical, cognitive, and behavioral nature. Victims exhibit a wide range of effects, with some having few problems and others experiencing significant psychopathology. This heterogeneity in the effects of CSA plus methodological weaknesses in many of the studies conducted have led researchers to equivocal findings. Nevertheless, it appears that the factors most likely to increase the trauma experienced by CSA victims include long duration of abuse, exposure to multiple forms of abuse, the presence of force and/or violence during the abuse, abuse by someone who is a father figure or otherwise emotionally close to the victim, abuse that involves invasive forms of sexual activity, and negative reactions by significant others once the abuse has been revealed. Recent research has also examined potential mediators of the effects of CSA, such as the victim's subjective perceptions of the events and the availability of social support following disclosure.

EXPLAINING CHILD SEXUAL ABUSE

The victims and perpetrators of CSA are characterized by a great deal of diversity, and the dynamics and consequences of abuse show similar variability. Such heterogeneity contributes to the difficulty in answering one of the central questions about CSA: Why do some individuals sexually abuse children? Another factor that makes it hard to answer this question is the paucity of high-quality research on the topic. Despite these limitations, scholars have developed theoretical formulations that focus on different individuals or systems involved in CSA, including the victim, the perpetrator, the abusive family, and society. Table 4.4 displays the risk factors associated with each of these systems.

Focus on the Abused Individual

Early explanations for the occurrence of CSA focused on the victim's culpability for encouraging or "allowing" the sexual abuse to occur. Researchers asserted that victims seductively encouraged perpetrators or that they enjoyed the abuse (for a discussion of these viewpoints, see Faller, 1988a). Little evidence, however, exists to support these positions. Admittedly, many CSA victims exhibit sexualized behavior, but most experts believe that such behavior is the result, rather than the cause, of the abuse. In addition, the idea that children encourage or "want" the abuse experience is contradicted by research evidence: Only a minority of victims report that their abuse had pleasurable or positive characteristics (e.g., that they felt loved during the abuse; Faller, 1988a). Whether a CSA victim can be viewed as culpable also depends on the definition of sexual abuse that is applied. As previously discussed, current perspectives on CSA preclude victim culpability because, by definition, children are viewed as developmentally incapable of consenting to take part in sexual activities with adults.

Culpability is distinct from vulnerability, however. It is possible to argue that certain attributes of children might make them special targets for molesters. Young, female children who have few close friends or who have many unmet needs appear to be particularly susceptible to the attentions of potential molesters. At particular risk are children described as passive, quiet, trusting, young, unhappy or depressed, and needy. CSA victims also often appear to have strong needs for attention, affection, and approval (Berliner & Conte, 1990; Erickson et al., 1989; Finkelhor et al., 1990).

Focus on the Offender

Some theorists implicate perpetrators in their efforts to determine the roots of CSA. The majority of research that has attempted to discern why particular individuals sexually abuse children has included only male subjects, and, as a result, the findings cannot be generalized to female perpetrators. The earliest

Table 4.4   Risk Factors Associated With Child Sexual Abuse

System Level	Risk Factor
Child	Female gender
	Prepubescent age
	Few close friends
	Passivity
	Quietness
	Trustingness
	Unhappy appearance
	Depressed affect
	Neediness
Perpetrator	Male gender
	Childhood history of sexual and physical victimization
	Antisocial disregard for concerns of others
	Poor impulse control
	Passivity
	Sensitivity about performance with women
	Deficient heterosocial skills
	Feelings of dependency, inadequacy, vulnerability, loneliness
	Sexual attraction to children
	Use of alcohol/drugs
	Use of cognitive distortions to justify behavior
	Fantasies about sexual activity with children
Family	Divorced home
	Unhappy family life
	Poor relationships of children with parents
	Parents in conflict
	Home with a stepfather or without natural father
	Mother employed outside of home
	Mother not a high school graduate
	Mother disabled or ill
	History of sexual abuse in mother
Sociocultural	Sanctioning of sexual relations between adults and children
	Neglect of children's sexual development
	Male-dominated household
	Oversexualization of normal emotional needs
	Socialization of men to be attracted to younger, smaller, more vulnerable sexual partners
	Blocking of the development of empathy in males
	Socialization of stoicism in males
	Objectification of sexual partners
	Child pornography

researchers who investigated the traits of CSA perpetrators relied on the psychiatric model, assuming that the causes of abuse stem from the individual psychopathology of male abusers. Later attempts focused additionally on deviant patterns of sexual arousal and childhood history. Contemporary theories attempt to integrate several factors that might contribute to sexual offending against children.

Offender pathology. Early theorists viewed CSA perpetrators as psychotic, brain-damaged, senile, or mentally retarded individuals who could not control their own behavior (Weinberg, 1955). Subsequent research, however, has suggested that severe psychiatric, intellectual, and neurological problems characterize only a small minority of offenders (National Center for Prosecution of Child Abuse, 1993; Williams & Finkelhor, 1990).

The perpetrators of CSA have been found to have a variety of less severe forms of psychopathology, however, including antisocial tendencies such as disregard for the interests and concerns of others and lack of empathy and impulse control (e.g., Bresee, Stearns, Bess, & Packer, 1986; Phelan, 1995; Yanagida & Ching, 1993). Such findings suggest that these offenders have a willingness to exploit others and to violate social norms (Williams & Finkelhor, 1990). Some researchers have described child molesters as passive; as having feelings of vulnerability, inadequacy, and loneliness; as displaying deficits in intimacy; as being overly sensitive about their sexual performance with women; and as exhibiting deficits in heterosocial skills (e.g., Cortoni & Marshall, 2001; Hayashino, Wurtele, & Klebe, 1995; Seidman, Marshall, Hudson, & Robertson, 1994). Perpetrators of CSA also generally demonstrate ineffective means of coping with stress (Marshall, Serran, & Cortoni, 2000). Presumably, such difficulties may lead them to avoid the demands of adult relationships by turning to children to have their social and relationship needs met.

Deviant sexual arousal. Some theorists propose that CSA perpetrators seek out sexual encounters with children primarily because they are sexually attracted to children (Abel, Becker, & Cunningham-Rathner, 1984; Marshall, Barbaree, & Butt, 1988). The origins of such deviant sexual arousal, however, are undetermined. Some researchers have suggested that biological factors may be a cause, such as abnormal levels of male hormones called androgens (Bradford, 1990). Learning theorists, on the other hand, have proposed that deviant sexual arousal develops when it is reinforced through fantasies of sexual activity with children and masturbating to those fantasies (Cortoni & Marshall, 2001; Laws & Marshall, 1990; Marshall & Eccles, 1993). Although some support exists for each of these theories, the research has yielded inconsistent results (e.g., Bradford, 1990; Hunter, Goodwin, & Becker, 1994; Langevin, Lang, & Curnoe, 1998; Salter, 1988).

Regardless of the cause of deviant sexual arousal, the procedure most often used to determine whether a CSA perpetrator has an unusual sexual arousal to children is called penile plethysmography. In this procedure, a circular gauge is placed around the base of the perpetrator's penis in the privacy of a lab or clinic. The subject then views slides or videotapes of different types of people who might be potential sexual partners (e.g., individuals the same age as the subject, people of the same sex and the opposite sex, young male chil-dren, adolescent females) or listens to audiotaped descriptions of different types of sexual encounters (e.g., consenting nonviolent sex with a same-age opposite-sex partner, nonconsenting violent sex with a male child). The gauge registers even small increases in the circumference of the penis, and the percentage of arousal is recorded by the plethysmograph.

Investigators have compared the sexual responses of child molesters, incest offenders, and nonoffending men with mixed results. Freund and his colleagues, who conducted some of the first studies, found that molesters were significantly more aroused by slides of both female and male children interacting with adults than were nonoffending males (e.g., Freund & Langevin, 1976). Subsequent studies examining sexual arousal in specific categories of perpetrators have yielded conflicting results. Quinsey, Chaplin, and Carrigan (1979) found that incestuous fathers exhibited more appropriate adult sexual arousal than did nonincestuous child molesters. In contrast, Marshall, Barbaree, and Christophe (1986) found that although incest offenders paralleled comparisons by showing low arousal to children, they showed no dramatic arousal increase to adult females. Indeed, the incest offenders in their sample exhibited less arousal to adult females than did members of the control group. The nonincestuous offenders, on the other hand, showed considerable arousal to children up to age 9, minimal arousal for 11- to 13-year-olds, and increased arousal again to adult females. Taken together, these findings suggest that some subgroups of CSA perpetrators, primarily extrafamilial child molesters, exhibit deviant sexual arousal toward children. The pattern of sexual arousal exhibited by incestuous offenders is less clear.

Because not all individuals who are sexually aroused by children act on their feelings, researchers have hypothesized that other factors, usually referred to as *disinhibitors,* must be operating. One possible disinhibitor is alcohol, which may affect perpetrators' ability to maintain self-control over their sexual impulses toward children (Finkelhor, 1984; Peugh & Belenko, 2001). Cognitive distortions may also be disinhibitors. That is, perpetrators may rationalize and defend their behavior through distorted ideas or thoughts, such as "Having sex with children is a good way to teach them about sex" or "Children need to be liberated from the sexually repressive bonds of society" (Abel et al., 1984, 1989; Segal & Stermac, 1990). Research evidence indicates the presence of cognitive distortions in CSA perpetrators (Hayashino et al., 1995; Segal & Stermac, 1990).

In evaluating research on deviant sexual arousal, it is important to view such studies within the confines of their conceptual and methodological limitations. Many studies, for example, have mixed the types of perpetrators within groups (e.g., natural fathers, step-fathers, and adoptive fathers in a single incest sample). Other limitations include the use of small and unrepresentative samples. The penile plethysmography procedure itself has also been questioned because of findings of false positives and false negatives and the ability of some molesters to inhibit sexual arousal in the lab (Conte, 1993). In examining the relationships of deviant sexual arousal, alcohol and drug use, and cognitive distortions to CSA, it is important to note that these factors may not play roles in all cases of CSA. It is also unclear to what degree such variables cause, rather than result from, the abuse.

Childhood history of sexual abuse. Many researchers have suggested that childhood sexual victimization contributes to adult perpetration. Perpetrators may have experienced abuse directly in the past themselves or they may have observed or been aware of the abuse of other family members. Overholser and Beck (1989) found that 58% of their sample of child molesters reported having been molested as children, compared with 25% of their rapist group and only 5% of matched controls. In a similar study, Glasser and colleagues (2001) found that the overall rate of past victimization among perpetrators was 35%, whereas the rate among nonperpetrators was 11%. The relationship between perpetration and a history of previous sexual victimization holds for adolescent sexual offenders as well (Becker, Kaplan, Cunningham-Rathner, & Kavoussi, 1986; Johnson, 1989; Katz, 1990). Several studies have also found frequent reports of sexual abuse against some other family member in offenders' families of origin, and others have noted a relationship between CSA perpetration and high rates of physical abuse in the backgrounds of offenders (Williams & Finkelhor, 1990).

Why would a history of victimization lead an individual to become a perpetrator of CSA? One possible explanation is that such a person abuses children in an effort to resolve, assimilate, or master the anxiety resulting from his or her own abuse (Hartman & Burgess, 1988). As we have noted above, victims of CSA often engage in inappropriate sexual behaviors with others (see Table 4.1). Another explanation is that the adult perpetrator who was abused as a child lacked a nurturing parental relationship, experienced betrayal

as a child, and suffered the subordination of his or her own needs to those of an abuser, all factors that preclude the development of empathy or sensitivity toward others (Ginsburg, Wright, Harrell, & Hill, 1989). Still others have suggested that repeatedly having one's needs subordinated and having one's body invaded or manipulated may result in feelings of powerlessness that later lead to a need to exploit others to regain personal power and control (Wurtele & Miller-Perrin, 1992). A final possibility is that, having experienced victimization, the offender has learned through modeling that children can be used for sexual gratification (Laws & Marshall, 1990; Veneziano, Veneziano, & LeGrand, 2000).

Some scholars have questioned the research on intergenerational transmission of sexual abuse on methodological grounds, pointing to overreliance on retrospective designs, self-report data, and correlational studies. The research findings to date are also difficult to interpret because of the lack of appropriate comparison groups and the possibility that perpetrators report histories of abuse to rationalize their own behaviors. It is likely that although some association exists between having been abused and becoming an abuser, most children who are sexually abused do not grow up to abuse other children, and some individuals without histories of abuse become CSA perpetrators.

Contemporary integrative theories. Until relatively recently, most models and theories attempting to explain the behavior of CSA perpetrators focused on only one possible perpetrator characteristic (e.g., psychopathology or deviant sexual arousal or a childhood history of abuse). Contemporary theories, however, attempt to explain sexually abusive behavior by focusing on the integration of multiple contributing factors. Covell and Scalora (2002), for example, have developed a model of sociocognitive deficiencies in sexual offenders that contribute to sexually assaultive behavior. According to this model, deficits in a variety of abilities—including social skills, interpersonal intimacy, and cognitive processes—may have an impact on the development and expression of appropriate empathy and lead to sexually assaultive behavior. Marshall and Marshall (2000) have proposed a comprehensive etiological model of sexual offending that incorporates multiple components, including biological, social, and attachment processes. According to their theory, the early developmental environment of a sexual offender includes several stressful events, such as poor **attachment** between parent and child, low self-esteem, limited coping abilities, low-quality relationships with others, and a history of sexual abuse. The presence of such stressors leads the child to rely on sexualized coping methods, including masturbation and sexual acts with others, as a way to avoid current stressors. Eventually, the individual is conditioned to rely on sexualized coping mechanisms and, when other factors are present (e.g., access to a victim, disinhibition owing to alcohol use), is predisposed to engage in sexually abusive behavior.

Focus on the Family

From the perspective of family dysfunction models, CSA is a symptom of a dysfunctional family system. These theories hold that the family in general, or one of its members (e.g., typically the perpetrator or a nonoffending adult), contributes to an environment that permits and possibly encourages the sexual victimization of children.

A number of family system theories focus on how a mother's behavior may contribute in some way to her child's victimization. Early theories held mothers responsible for sexual abuse of their children, blaming them for having poor marital relationships—in particular, infrequent marital sex. According to this view, infrequent marital sex increased a husband's sexual frustration and "drove" him to seek satisfaction elsewhere in the family (e.g., Justice & Justice, 1979). Other early theories viewed mothers as culpable for their children's abuse because of the mothers' failure to protect the victims from the offenders. As noted previously, maternal employment outside the home and maternal disability or illness are known risk factors for CSA. Such theories, however, have often relied on clinical impressions or retrospective data and have not been supported by research. In addition, many of the so-called contributing characteristics ascribed to mothers in these theories could be the results of living with CSA perpetrators.

Contemporary family system explanations for CSA view the mother's role in the context of contributing to a child's vulnerability, rather than of being responsible for the abuse. Research suggests that mothers of sexually abused children may actually be covictims rather than coconspirators. Mothers in incestuous families are often physically and emotionally abused by the perpetrators themselves and also frequently have childhood histories of CSA (e.g., Faller, 1989; Gomes-Schwartz et al., 1990; Strand, 2000). According to this view, mothers may contribute to their children's vulnerability by withdrawing from their children or being unavailable to them (either emotionally or physically) because the mothers lack an adequate representation of a secure mother-child relationship themselves (Friedrich, 1990). Faller (1988a, 1989) has also suggested that these women may gravitate toward men who are similar to their own abusers or who will not make sexual demands on them because the men are sexually attracted to children.

Other family systems theorists have focused on general characteristics of the family as a unit rather than on individual members. Some who take this perspective have identified significant levels of dysfunction in families of CSA victims, although the nature of the dysfunction is unclear because of conflicting research findings (Crittenden, 1996). Many researchers have found that abusive families exhibit conflicted relationships, including marital conflict in the home, poor relationships between children and parents, divorce, and spouse abuse (e.g., Boney-McCoy & Finkelhor, 1995; Lang, Flor-Henry, & Frenzel, 1990; Paveza, 1988). Others have confirmed that CSA families are frequently disorganized, lacking cohesion and involvement between members; they are also deficient in community involvement and generally more dysfunctional than non-CSA families (e.g., D. M. Elliott, 1994; Madonna, Van Scoyk, & Jones, 1991; Ray, Jackson, & Townsley, 1991). The most common difficulties in CSA families appear to be problems with communication, lack of emotional closeness, and inflexibility (Dadds, Smith, Weber, & Robinson, 1991).

Theorists have proposed several explanations for how poor family relations might be related to CSA. To reduce the tension that exists within the marital relationship, for example, a father might distance himself from his wife by turning his sexual and emotional attention toward his daughter. This distancing stabilizes the marital conflict and reduces the likelihood of a breakup. Gruber and Jones (1983) have suggested that marital conflict may play a role in extrafamilial CSA as well, in that a child living in an unstable home may seek some sense of emotional stability through relationships outside the home, such as with a potential offender. Others have theorized that families lacking in cohesion, concern between members, and organization may fail to supervise children adequately, thus exposing them to opportunities for sexual abuse. In their study of a nationally representative sample, Finkelhor et al. (1997) found that parent reports of leaving a child without adequate supervision were associated with CSA.

Focus on Society and Culture

Some researchers have examined the broad context of societal and community forces that may play roles in the etiology of CSA. Current theories target social attitudes and child pornography. Sociocultural theories remain largely speculative, awaiting confirmation through empirical investigation.

Societal attitudes. One theory views CSA as a problem stemming from the inequality between men and women that has been perpetuated throughout history by patriarchal social systems (e.g., Birns & Meyer, 1993). Rush (1980) extends the boundaries of this inequality to include children, pointing out that, traditionally, women and children have shared the same minority status and have been subject to sexual abuse by men. Some limited support for the feminist theory of CSA comes from a study conducted by Alexander and Lupfer (1987), who found that female university students with histories of incest rated their family structures as having greater power differences in male-female relationships than did female university students with histories of extrafamilial sexual abuse or no histories of abuse.

Media depictions. Other sociocultural theories implicate mass-media portrayals of sexuality and children as factors in the etiology of CSA (e.g., Wurtele & Miller-Perrin, 1992). Many depictions of sexuality in the popular media contribute to misperceptions that women and girls deserve or desire violent sexual contact (e.g., Millburn, Mathes, & Conrad, 2000). Child pornography is another type of media that may stimulate sexual interest in children. The findings of research examining the relationship between child pornography and CSA have been mixed, as noted previously, with some studies failing to support the hypothesized relationship and others indicating that child molesters do use pornography (for a review, see Murrin & Laws, 1990).

SECTION SUMMARY

Despite the work of numerous researchers, it is still unclear what causes individuals to abuse children sexually. Some theories focus on the child, in particular on characteristics that may make a child vulnerable to CSA (e.g., being passive, quiet, trusting, young, unhappy, and needy). Other theories focus on perpetrator characteristics, such as psychological dysfunction, deviant sexual arousal, and childhood history of victimization. Numerous family characteristics are also associated with CSA, including family conflict and dysfunction. Mothers in CSA families are also more likely than those in other families to have histories of CSA, and recent theories further suggest that mothers in CSA families may be victims of sexual abuse as well. Other theories propose that sociocultural forces such as social attitudes (e.g., inequality between men and women) and child pornography may contribute to CSA. Currently, no existing theory or combination of theories effectively explains CSA.

PRACTICE, POLICY, AND PREVENTION ISSUES

Throughout this chapter, we have described what is known about CSA in an attempt to explore the relevant issues thoroughly. A comprehensive understanding of any problem is a necessary first step in attempting to prevent or intervene in that problem. One of the earliest responses to the CSA problem was the establishment of programs to provide therapeutic services to victims and offenders as well as to victims' families. Several of these programs originated in the early 1970s, although they were restricted in number and focus. More recently, renewed interest in the treatment of sexual abuse victims as well as perpetrators has led to the development of treatment programs that better reflect an understanding of the complexity of the CSA problem. In addition, CSA experts have established a number of programs aimed at preventing the sexual abuse of children.

Basic Issues in Treatment Intervention

Whether treatment centers on the child victim, the adult survivor, or the perpetrator of CSA, treatment programs must take several basic issues into account. First, victims and perpetrators of CSA are diverse in their preabuse histories, the nature of their abuse experiences, and the social supports and coping resources available to them. As a result, treatment programs need to be able to tailor the services they offer to meet the particular needs of each individual client (Chaffin, 1994; Courtois & Watts, 1982). No single treatment plan will be effective for all victims, all perpetrators, or all families.

Second, therapists and others working in the field of CSA need to be aware of the issues associated with countertransference—that is, their own personal reactions toward victims, perpetrators, and victims' families. Individuals who work with a CSA perpetrator, for example, may have feelings of anger or hatred toward that individual that make it difficult for them to respond in a therapeutic manner. As Haugaard and Reppucci (1988) put it, "The image of a 5-year-old girl performing fellatio on her father in submission to his parental authority does not engender compassion" for the father (p. 191). Clinicians may also feel uncomfortable working with child victims, who sometimes behave sexually toward their therapists. In addition, studies have revealed that a significant number of

professionals who work with CSA victims have histories of CSA themselves (Feldman-Summers & Pope, 1994; Nuttall & Jackson, 1994). These experiences might affect practitioners' views of CSA and its victims, contributing to distorted perceptions of patients and also possibly to therapy-induced "memories" in patients (Beutler, Williams, & Zetzer, 1994). (For further discussion of this issue, see Box 4.3.) Therapists working with CSA families should also be aware of their own susceptibility to secondary trauma as a result of being exposed to victims and their traumatic histories (for a comprehensive discussion of secondary traumatic stress, see Chapter 7).

Box 4.3 The Repressed Memory Controversy

- **1989:** A California Court of Appeal extends the statute of limitations for CSA under the doctrine of "delayed discovery," allowing individuals who, as adults, claim histories of CSA during childhood to sue their parents. An individual bringing such a claim must be able to demonstrate that his or her memories of the abuse were repressed (by providing certification from a licensed mental health professional).

- **1990:** Holly Ramona, age 19, accuses her father, Gary Ramona, of repeatedly raping her when she was between the ages of 5 and 8. Holly's memories of the abuse surfaced while she was a college student receiving therapy for depression and bulimia. During several months of therapy, Holly experienced flashback memories of her father sexually molesting her. Just before accusing her father, Holly received the hypnotic drug sodium Amytal and recounted multiple episodes of abuse by her father. After the allegations surfaced, Gary Ramona lost his $400,000-a-year job, his daughters refused to interact with him, and his wife divorced him.

- **1991:** The False Memory Syndrome Foundation is established to provide information and support individuals who have been victimized by a "rash" of false accusations of sexual abuse (see this organization's Web site at http://fmsfonline.org). Several similar organizations are also soon established, including the British False Memory Society, FACT (Falsely Accused Carers and Teachers), Action Against False Allegations of Abuse, and VOCAL (Victims of Child Abuse Laws).

- **1994:** In Napa Valley (California) Superior Court, a jury rules that Holly Ramona's memories were "probably false" and that although her therapists did not implant the memories, they negligently reinforced them (Butler, 1994). Gary Ramona, who has sought $8 million in damages, is awarded $500,000.

- **1999:** In the first criminal trial involving charges against therapists accused of implanting false memories in a client, a mistrial is declared after 5 months of testimony when the dismissal of several jurors reduces the number of jurors to 11. The five defendants (two psychologists, two psychiatrists, and one hospital administrator) had been charged with insurance fraud and with falsely diagnosing multiple personality disorder and implanting memories of satanic ritual abuse (see Box 7.4 in Chapter 7). The judge and prosecutors in the case concluded that it would be too costly to retry the defendants, so charges are dropped (Smith, 1999).

- **2002:** Numerous cases of sexual misconduct and cover-up bring the issue of the sexual abuse of parishioners by Catholic priests to the front pages of the nation's newspapers. Although most of the cases do not involve the recovery of repressed memories, the publicity surrounding the cases once again draws attention to the repressed memory controversy. Animosities reach their peak when Paul McHugh, longtime chair of the Department of

Psychiatry at Johns Hopkins University, is appointed to a review board to monitor the Catholic Church's response to the sexual abuse scandal. Members of SNAP (Survivors Network for those Abused by Priests) are critical of the appointment because McHugh has openly supported the False Memory Syndrome Foundation and has testified for defendants in recovered memory cases. McHugh, while acknowledging that memories can be recovered, is critical of faulty psychiatric practices that have produced thousands of bogus abuse claims. Nonetheless, he stands by his record, vowing to fight child abuse "tooth and nail . . . It's possible to be on the side of the abused person and still be on the side of somebody who was falsely accused too. Not only are they compatible. They are implicit in one another" (quoted in "Religion; Psychiatrist's Appointment," 2002, p. B23).

This chronology of events illustrates some of the dilemmas associated with the repressed memory debate. Are Holly and others like her victims of CSA? Or are the accused adults the victims of false memories induced by therapists? There is little consensus regarding these questions.

In one camp are experts who believe that repressed memories are common and result from either repression of negative feelings associated with the abuse or amnesia associated with dissociative defenses (i.e., multiple personality disorder) of a traumatic event (Briere & Conte, 1993). In the other camp are critics of the concept of repressed memories, who claim that what some individuals perceive to be memories may be fantasies or illusions, the results of contextual cues or implantation by therapists or other perceived authority figures (Ganaway, 1989; Loftus, 1993). The potential consequences of the outcome of this debate are significant, because if therapists are indeed implanting false memories, then people will be falsely accused and innocent families will be ripped apart. If the critics are wrong, on the other hand, then victims of abuse will not be believed (Ost, 2003). In a world that has historically been reluctant to acknowledge many of the unthinkable acts inflicted on children, disbelieving the truth, no matter how horrendous, is unacceptable.

The disagreements between the two camps are quite heated, and sometimes personal. Historian Lloyd deMause (1994), for example, in dismissing charges that those accused of satanic ritual abuse are victims of a "witch hunt," goes so far as to say that "all members of the False Memory Syndrome Foundation are pedophiles or abusers themselves" (p. 505). Critics of the recovered memory movement, on the other hand, belittle as "feminazis" (feminists) and "the-rapists" (therapists) those who believe recovered memories are common (Ost, 2003). To be sure, the "memory wars" are far from settled.

The findings of several studies provide support for the argument that repressed memories exist. Herman and Schatzow (1987), for example, found that 64% of female incest survivor patients did not have full recall of their sexual abuse and reported some degree of amnesia. One-fourth of these women reported severe memory deficits or complete amnesia for the abuse events. Approximately 75% of the women obtained evidence to corroborate their abuse reports, such as confirmation from other family members, discovering that a sibling had also been abused, or confession by the perpetrator. Briere and Conte (1993) found a substantial rate of repressed memories (59%) in a clinical sample of sexual abuse victims. Such studies, however, are limited because of the retrospective and self-report nature of the data and because the individuals were in therapy. In an attempt to overcome these problems, Williams (1994) followed a community sample of 100 documented sexual abuse cases in which the victims were between the ages of 10 months and 12 years. When these CSA victims were questioned about their childhood histories 17 years later, 38% did not recall the previously substantiated incidents.

Critics of the concept of repressed memories, on the other hand, emphasize the limitations of such studies; specifically, they point out that participants in clinical samples are attempting to remember "a memory for forgetting a memory" (Loftus, 1993, p. 522). Some critics have suggested other potential sources for what are asserted to be repressed "nearly universal" (Bower, 1993b) and contain unvalidated claims, such as "If you are unable to remember any specific instances but still have a feeling that something abusive happened to you, it probably did" (Bass & Davis, 1988, p. 21). They assert that such statements are dangerous given the malleability of memory. Research has shown that memory is subject to distortion from stress, incentives to keep secrets, and suggestion (Loftus, 1993; Perry, 1992).

Others contend that popular writings about repressed memory encourage those who perceive themselves to be victims to undertake emotional confrontations with their alleged perpetrators (Loftus, 1993) and in general are part of a "sexual abuse industry" that exists to create victims (Travis, 1993). Since 1989, 19 U.S. states have passed legislation that allows people to sue for recovery of damages for injury suffered as a result of CSA remembered for the first time during adulthood, and an estimated 300 lawsuits involving formerly repressed memories had been filed as of September 1993 (Bower, 1993a). Some have suggested that the motivation behind these lawsuits is fame and fortune rather than justice (Davis, 1991; Lachnit, 1991).

The final argument offered by critics is that therapists may "implant" ideas that their patients then perceive to be memories, through either overt or covert suggestions. They also assert that therapists may inadvertently communicate to their clients their own beliefs that repressed memories are common, and clients might subsequently assume that they may have repressed memories of abuse (Loftus, 1993). Some have suggested that therapists may overtly implant "memories" of CSA by diagnosing abuse after too brief an evaluation, by using leading questions, or by using questionable assessment or therapeutic techniques, such as hypnosis and sodium Amytal (Butler, 1994; Loftus, 1993). Numerous laboratory studies suggest that memories can be manipulated (Loftus, 2003). For example, in one study, 50% of research subjects who were shown falsified pictures of themselves as children flying in a hot-air balloon claimed to recall some of the details of the fictitious balloon ride (Wade, Garry, Read, & Lindsay, 2002).

Unfortunately, the debate about whether some people's memories of CSA are repressed or false remains unresolved, and it is unlikely that any research will provide a clear answer in the near future. To date, there is no definitive way of knowing whether a given memory is true or false. Those on both sides of the debate agree, however, that improvement of the methods available to assess and treat victims of CSA is crucial, and that researchers must continue to seek empirical knowledge to uncover the truth about the nature of repressed memories. In his review of several books on the topic, British psychologist James Ost (2003) suggests that there is plenty of room for middle ground. He notes that scholars on both sides of the debate generally acknowledge that victims of sexual abuse usually remember the abuse, that abuse can sometimes be forgotten and then remembered, and that it is possible to construct false memories. An American Psychological Association task force (made up of both skeptics and believers) appointed to examine what is known about repressed memories reached essentially the same conclusion:

> Both ends of the continuum on people's memories of abuse are possible. . . . It is possible that under some cue conditions, early memories may be retrievable. At the other extreme, it is possible under some conditions for memories to be implanted or embedded. (DeAngelis, 1993, p. 44)

At the same time, however, there remains a tendency for the two sides to talk past one another:

> Both sides in the "memory wars" are paying lip service, at least, to the principle that *both* recovered "memories" *and* false "memories" are a reality. However, the very terminology of *false* or *recovered* "memory" is divisive, rather than inclusive, and explicitly defines two extreme positions at the opposite ends of a spectrum. Terms such as *false* memory and *recovered* memory may be a necessary evil in the courtroom but they do not promote or facilitate clear communication and understanding between researchers or clinical professionals. (Ost, 2003, p. 133)

Therapy for Child and Adult Survivors

Many different kinds of mental health professionals conduct therapy with child victims and adult survivors of CSA, including master's degree–level therapists, clinical social workers, psychologists, and psychiatrists. Treatment can take a variety of forms, such as individual counseling, family treatment, group therapy, and marital counseling, and often includes various combinations of these (e.g., individual counseling and group therapy).

Despite the diversity of treatment modalities, several goals of therapy are common to most approaches. One goal of therapy is to alleviate any significant symptoms presented by the individual child or adult (Courtois & Watts, 1982; Lipovsky & Elliott, 1993; Osmond, Durham, Leggett, & Keating, 1998; Rust & Troupe, 1991). The variability of responses to CSA dictates the therapist's need to develop a specialized treatment strategy to meet each individual's needs. A child victim who presents with self-injurious behaviors, for example, might benefit from a behavior modification program designed specifically to alleviate such behaviors. An adult who presents with a specific sexual dysfunction might respond to a modified sex therapy technique.

Other symptoms of CSA victimization are so common that therapists should expect to address them in the majority of child victims and adult survivors. For example, therapists will likely need to help victims overcome negative attributions and cognitive distortions such as guilt, shame, and stigmatization. Here, therapists often undertake some form of cognitive restructuring to help victims change their perceptions that they are "different" as well as somehow to blame for the abuse and appropriately relocate the responsibility for the abuse to the offender (Cahill, Llewelyn, & Pearson, 1991; Jehu, Klassen, & Gazan, 1986; Osmond et al., 1998). Many experts believe that group therapy is a particularly effective modality in which to counter victims' self-denigrating beliefs and to confront issues of secrecy and stigmatization because participants are able to discuss their experiences with peers who have also been abused (Berman, 1990; Cahill et al., 1991; Celano, 1990; Corder, Haizlip, & DeBoer, 1990).

Anxiety and fear are also common symptoms among CSA survivors, and one task of therapy is to give victims the opportunity to defuse these feelings by talking about their abuse experiences in the safety of a supportive therapeutic relationship (Berliner, 1991; Courtois & Watts, 1982). Adults are often able to

process their abusive experiences simply by discussing them with their therapists. With children, however, therapists may need to explore other avenues, such as reenacting the abuse through play. Therapists need to teach both adult survivors and child victims the strategies they will need for managing the fear and anxiety that may accompany the processing of the abuse, such as relaxation techniques, problem-solving skills, and how to use positive coping statements and positive imagery (Berliner, 1991; Meichenbaum, 1977).

Another goal of therapy is to teach the client to express anger in appropriate ways (Blake-White & Kline, 1985; Jones, 1986). To combat depression and low self-esteem in CSA victims, many therapists use cognitive and interpersonal exercises and role-plays to emphasize the clients' survival skills and personal strengths (e.g., Corder et al., 1990; Courtois & Watts, 1982). In addition, CSA victims may gain a sense of empowerment through sex education and training in self-protection skills that may also prevent any further victimization (Berliner, 1991; Damon, Todd, & MacFarlane, 1987).

To date, relatively little is known about the effectiveness of victim-oriented interventions for CSA because of the dearth of systematic evaluations (for reviews, see Becker et al., 1995; Price, Hilsenroth, Petretic-Jackson, & Bonge, 2001; Saywitz, Mannarino, Berliner, & Cohen, 2000). Most reports of therapy outcomes consist of descriptive data and nonstandardized approaches that show only modestly positive or nonsignificant results (Beutler et al., 1994; Kolko, 1987). Although few studies have examined treatment efficacy, the available research suggests that both individual and group treatments for child and adult victims of CSA are effective (Price et al., 2001; Saywitz et al., 2000). Some studies have found positive self-reported behavioral change, whereas others have demonstrated improvements in social, emotional, and behavioral functioning on standardized measures (e.g., Cohen & Mannarino, 1993; Friedrich, Luecke, Beilke, & Place, 1992; Roth & Newman, 1991).

One treatment approach that is receiving increasing attention is abuse-specific cognitive behavioral therapy. This form of therapy targets a variety of the symptoms associated with sexual abuse victimization, including negative attributions, cognitive distortions, fear, anxiety, and other posttraumatic stress reactions. The treatment includes a number of components: psychoeducation (e.g., providing accurate information about the problem of sexual abuse), techniques to reduce fear and anxiety, exposure therapy (e.g., including exposure to elements of the abuse experience in order to decondition negative emotional responses to memories of the abuse), and cognitive therapy techniques that target negative attributions and distorted cognitions associated with the abuse (Cohen, Berliner, & Mannarino, 2000). Researchers who have evaluated the effectiveness of abuse-specific cognitive behavioral therapy have found that this form of treatment is effective, particularly for reducing posttraumatic stress symptoms in children (American Academy of Child and Adolescent Psychiatry, 1998; Cohen et al., 2000; Saywitz et al., 2000).

Although a growing body of research suggests that treatment for sexual abuse victims can be helpful in reducing abuse-related symptoms, several questions remain unanswered. Some research indicates, for example, that not all abuse survivors benefit from, or need, treatment. In a longitudinal study, Tebbutt, Swanston, Oates, and O'Toole (1997) found that although most of the CSA-victimized children in their sample received treatment, few showed reductions in symptoms. Others have questioned whether every CSA survivor needs a full course of treatment (Saywitz et al., 2000). Researchers have also begun to evaluate variables that enhance or inhibit treatment efficacy and have found that the following factors affect treatment outcome: therapist and victim gender, victim's current social supports, victim's educational level, and victim's relationship to the perpetrator (e.g., Alexander, Neimeyer, & Follette, 1991; Fowler & Wagner, 1993; Friedrich, Luecke, et al., 1992). Additional research is needed to determine the specific conditions under which CSA survivors are likely to benefit from therapy.

Treatment Interventions for Offenders

The primary treatment goal in working with CSA offenders is to reduce the likelihood of recidivism, or repeated offenses. It is difficult to study the outcomes of offender treatment, because the measurement of recidivism is complex. It is often difficult, for example, for researchers to determine whether particular convicted offenders commit subsequent offenses unless they can monitor those offenders through indefinite long-term follow-ups. In a study that included follow-ups over 10 years, Romero and Williams (1995) found that only 27% of the offenders in their sample did not reoffend for 4 or more years after their release from prison.

Numerous methodological problems also characterize the research examining treatment outcomes with CSA offenders, including nonrandom assignment to treatment conditions, biased samples, and attrition among treatment participants (see Becker, 1994; Marshall & Pithers, 1994). Despite these difficulties, Becker (1994) asserts that advances in treatment approaches "provide definite grounds for optimism about the responsiveness of some segments of the offender population to existing treatment modalities" (p. 188). A variety of treatment approaches exist for CSA offenders, including medical approaches, traditional and family systems therapies, and cognitive-behavioral techniques (e.g., Becker, 1994; Marshall, Jones, Ward, Johnston, & Barbaree, 1991).

Medical approaches. Medical approaches for treating sexual offenders include castration (surgical removal of the testicles), brain surgery, and drug therapy (e.g., Bradford, 1990; Maletzky & Field, 2003; Marshall et al., 1991). Most medical treatments are based on the notion that some sort of biological mechanism affects the offender's sex drive and causes the abusive behavior. Early approaches focused on castration and removal of certain brain areas (e.g., hypothalamus) in attempts to control sexual behavior. Although some outcome studies show that these techniques resulted in a reduction in sex offenses, the presence of methodological problems in the evaluations, ethical concerns, and negative side effects cast doubt on the usefulness of these techniques (Maletzky & Field, 2003; Marshall et al., 1991; Rosler & Witzum, 2000).

Newer medical approaches to treating CSA perpetrators focus on the use of medications to reduce sexual drive. This type of treatment, sometimes referred to as *chemical castration,* usually involves the administration of hormonal agents that reduce sexual drive. One particular drug that has received considerable attention in Canada and Europe is cyproterone acetate, a synthetic steroid that reduces testosterone levels. Unfortunately, no well-controlled research has yet been carried out to determine the efficacy of this treatment. Because there is no clear evidence of the drug's efficacy, and because it may have long-term negative effects on liver functioning, cyproterone acetate cannot be prescribed in the United States (Maletzky & Field, 2003). Another hormonal agent employed to reduce testosterone levels is medroxyprogesterone acetate, which is generally known by its brand name, Depo-Provera. This drug is available in injectable form in a long-acting formula (i.e., the substance is slowly released into the bloodstream). Several outcome studies have evaluated the efficacy of Depo-Provera treatment for

An Interview With Lucy Berliner

"Finally, although child maltreatment is associated with other social ills, it is possible to make a difference for children and families without requiring fundamental societal change. We need to be realistic and practical as well as idealistic."

Lucy Berliner is a licensed social worker and Clinical Associate Professor at the University of Washington Graduate School of Social Work and Department of Psychiatry and Behavioral Sciences, and Director of the Harborview Center for Sexual Assault and Traumatic Stress in Seattle, Washington. She has published extensively on topics associated with child sexual abuse victimization and offending and is actively engaged in administering clinical interventions to victims of violence and trauma and their families, conducting research on various aspects of victimization of children, and promoting public policy on behalf of victims. She serves as an associate editor of two journals devoted to the topic of interpersonal violence and also serves on the boards of a number of organizations concerned with child maltreatment, such as the National Center for Missing and Exploited Children. She received her B.A. in Spanish from Earlham College in Indiana and her M.S.W. from the University of Washington.

Q: What sparked your interest in the area of child maltreatment?

A: As a graduate student intern in the early 1970s, by sheer serendipity, I ended up working graveyard shifts in the emergency department of Harborview Medical Center, Seattle's regional trauma center. I also worked days in the hospital's newly established program for sexual assault victims. The program was funded to provide crisis support to rape victims to increase the women's cooperation with the criminal justice system. These experiences provided me with up-front, personal exposure to the impact of interpersonal violence and ignited an enduring interest in developing effective clinical and social policy responses to such violence. Although children were not my initial focus, it soon became apparent that children constitute a substantial percentage of victims. I have always been concerned with child maltreatment within the larger context of interpersonal violence.

Q: What would you describe as your most influential contribution to the field of child maltreatment?

sexual offenders, and although clinical evidence suggests that it is somewhat effective in reducing sexual crimes, controlled and methodologically rigorous studies are lacking (Maletzky & Field, 2003). The authors of two reviews of the literature on treatment of sexual offenders have concluded that drug therapy with agents such as Depo-Provera may be beneficial for some offenders but should be used conservatively in conjunction with other treatments or as a temporary method until psychological treatments can begin (Maletzky & Field, 2003; Marshall et al., 1991)

Traditional and family systems approaches. Insight-oriented approaches to therapy for CSA offenders primarily involve individual counseling for offenders.

The general purpose of such therapy is to help the perpetrator to understand the role sexual abuse plays in his or her life. Studies that have evaluated the outcomes of various insight-oriented approaches to CSA offender treatment have been mixed (Prendergast, 1979; Sturgeon & Taylor, 1980), probably because of methodological differences across studies. According to one survey of sex offender treatment programs, individual counseling techniques are used in only approximately 2% of such programs (Knopp, Freeman-Longo, & Stevenson, 1992).

Other treatment programs for offenders emphasize family systems approaches. Giarretto (1982) pioneered the comprehensive Child Sexual Abuse Treatment Program, which uses a sequence of therapies for incest

A: I think my strength, and unique contribution, is my ability to integrate clinical experience, research findings, and social policy considerations to create better ways of helping child victims and their families recover from abuse experiences and obtain justice. My ideas almost always come directly from personal experiences with victims, encounters with other professionals involved within the field, or my work in the community focused on improving system responses or legislation. As a result, my ideas are grounded in real life and usually have credibility, even with those who may have a different point of view. In addition, I think I have been a good model for the importance of learning from other disciplines, seeing the other side of arguments, acknowledging when mistakes have been made, and being open to new ways of approaching issues.

Q: What should be done to help solve the problem of child maltreatment?

A: Professionals need to come up with better methods to obtain the common citizen's support for efforts to prevent and respond to child maltreatment. To make this happen, professionals need to be more effective in addressing the contrast between how the public feels about child abuse in the abstract and the personal reactions to child maltreatment when it occurs in one's own family or immediate community. One mistake professionals can make, for example, is to be righteous and assume that others are not as concerned about child maltreatment as themselves. Although legislators and citizens may not always accept or support policy recommendations, it is not necessarily because they do not care about maltreated children. Everyone realizes that abuse happens and that it is bad, yet it is clear we have not hit on the best way to get broad community support for solutions. Finding ways to "get on the same page" with regular citizens would help professionals' efforts to prevent and respond to child maltreatment.

Q: What type of policy recommendations are most needed in the field of child maltreatment?

A: I think that what is needed to solve the problem of child maltreatment are better ways of going about achieving policy goals. We are too quick to see passing a law or getting the government to give more money as the primary mechanism. More resources are definitely needed, but it is also true that we could do a better job with current funding. First, we need to use our knowledge base more responsibly. Many of the key principles for effective individual and community interventions, for example, are known and can inform the development and implementation of policies and programs in diverse individual and community settings. Second, we need to establish and embrace empirically supported interventions. We have a tendency to promote programs and interventions simply because we like them, despite a lack of empirical support for some programs. Now that we have a body of knowledge on preventing and ameliorating child maltreatment, it is reasonable for the government or other funding agencies to expect us to provide evidence of the efficacy of our programs. A useful policy recommendation, for example, would be to tie services funding to interventions that have empirical support for their effectiveness and that demonstrate improved outcomes. Finally, although child maltreatment is associated with other social ills, it is possible to make a difference for children and families without requiring fundamental societal change. We need to be realistic and practical as well as idealistic.

families, including individual counseling for the child victim, mother, and perpetrator; mother-daughter counseling; marital counseling; perpetrator-victim counseling; group counseling; and family counseling. Hewitt (1998) describes a family approach that includes a series of meetings with individual family members (e.g., nonoffending parent, the child victim, and the alleged abuser) and between family members (e.g., nonoffending parent and child victim; alleged abuser and child victim) in an effort to reunify families in which sexual abuse has occurred. Typical themes addressed in family-oriented therapies include the parents' failure to protect the victim from abuse, feelings of guilt and depression resulting from the abuse, the inappropriateness of secrecy, the victim's anger toward the parents, the perpetrator's responsibility for the abuse, appropriate forms of touch, confusion about blurred role boundaries, poor communication patterns, and the effect the abuse has had on the child (Giarretto, 1982; Hewitt, 1998; Osmond et al., 1998; Sgroi, 1982; Wolfe, Wolfe, & Best, 1988). Family therapy may also address the needs of family members indirectly affected by the abuse, such as the nonoffending parent and siblings, as well as disruptions caused by the disclosure of abuse, such as incarceration, financial hardship, and parental separation (Wolfe, Wolfe, & Best, 1988). It should be noted that whenever therapists see victims and abusers together in therapy, they must pay special attention to protecting the victims from intimidation. Although to date few studies have evaluated the outcomes of the family therapy approach to treating CSA perpetrators, and none have included long-term follow-up, the research that is available appears to demonstrate the effectiveness of the approach (Giarretto, 1982).

Cognitive-behavioral techniques. Cognitive-behavioral approaches to treatment are the most widely available and actively researched forms of therapy for CSA offenders (for a review, see Marshall et al., 1991). Behavioral interventions are primarily concerned with altering the deviant sexual arousal patterns of CSA perpetrators. Most behavioral approaches use some form of aversive therapy. For example, Abel, Becker, and Skinner (1986) report on a process called masturbatory satiation. In this technique, the perpetrator is instructed to reach orgasm through masturbation as quickly as possible using *appropriate* sexual fantasies (e.g., sexual encounters between two mutually consenting adults). Once he has ejaculated, he is told to switch his fantasies to images involving children and continue to masturbate until the total masturbation time is 1 hour. The reasoning behind this technique is that it reinforces the appropriate fantasies through the pleasurable feelings of orgasm and diminishes the offender's inappropriate fantasies by associating them with nonpleasurable masturbation that occurs after ejaculation. Cognitive therapies, in contrast, are designed to teach offenders how to recognize and change their inaccurate beliefs (e.g., that the perpetrator is simply "teaching" the victim about sex; Abel et al., 1986).

Many CSA offender treatment programs use multidimensional approaches that combine both cognitive and behavioral techniques with other components (e.g., improving social and life skills) (e.g., Marshall & Barbaree, 1988). Consistent with these multidimensional approaches, some experts have recommended that treatment of CSA offenders should focus on their nonsexual difficulties, such as antisocial behavior, in addition to their offending behavior (e.g., Chaffin, 1994; Scavo, 1989). One component of some multidimensional treatment programs that is gaining increasing support is relapse prevention. Programs that include a relapse prevention component attempt to assist perpetrators in identifying patterns in their behavior that are precursors to abuse and provide long-term, community-based supervision (Marques, Nelson, West, & Day, 1994; Miner, Marques, Day, & Nelson, 1990; Pithers & Kafka, 1990). In their review of the treatment literature, Marshall and Pithers (1994) endorse multidimensional

treatment programs, noting that "implementation of a single therapeutic intervention, even by the most highly skilled practitioners, cannot be considered sufficient treatment for most sex offenders" (p. 25).

Most experts agree that the therapeutic value of cognitive-behavioral approaches has been clearly demonstrated (Marshall et al., 1991; Marshall & Pithers, 1994). Others have argued that such a conclusion is premature given the methodological limitations of most studies (Quinsey, Harris, Rice, & Lalumiere, 1993). One criticism of outcome studies is that although some treatment approaches have been shown to alter CSA perpetrators' arousal patterns to pictures and/or stories of children, such changes do not necessarily apply to actual children. Other methodological limitations include limited follow-up information, overreliance on self-report data, and lack of appropriate comparison groups. In his review of the treatment outcome literature, Chaffin (1994) concludes:

> Despite previous skepticism regarding the efficacy of offender treatment, there are good data to support its effectiveness with the kinds of patients often seen in outpatient settings. This suggests that practitioners can justify favorable prognoses for less severe patients. The data are less optimistic regarding the outlook for severe populations. (p. 233)

Prevention of Child Sexual Abuse

Efforts aimed at eliminating child sexual abuse through prevention have focused primarily on equipping children with the skills they need to respond to, or protect themselves from, sexual abuse. Such approaches include programs that educate children about the problem of CSA as well as teach them specific methods for coping with potentially abusive situations. Some CSA prevention programs are geared toward parents, who are often in a position to empower children to protect themselves.

Education programs for children. During the 1980s, school-based empowerment programs to help children avoid and report victimization became popular across the United States. Such programs generally teach children knowledge and skills that experts believe will help them to protect themselves from a variety of dangers. Most focus on sexual abuse and emphasize two goals: *primary prevention* (keeping the abuse from occurring) and *detection* (encouraging children to report past and current abuse) (Reppucci, Land, & Haugaard, 1998). Empowerment programs have obvious appeal because they are an inexpensive way to reach many school-age children, who, for the most part, are eager to learn (Daro & McCurdy, 1994). A 1990 survey of elementary school districts found that 85% of districts offered CSA education programs, with 65% of those programs mandated by law (Breen, Daro, & Romano, as cited in Finkelhor, Asdigian, & Dziuba-Leatherman, 1995). In their National Youth Victimization Prevention Study, a telephone survey of 2,000 children and their caretakers, Finkelhor et al. (1995) found that 67% of children reported being exposed to victimization prevention programs, with 37% reporting participation within the previous year.

Evaluations of school-based victimization prevention programs suggest that, in general, exposure to such programs increases children's knowledge and protection skills. The National Youth Victimization Prevention Study, for example, found that children who were exposed to comprehensive school-based prevention programs were more knowledgeable about the dangers of sexual abuse and more effectively equipped with protection strategies than were children who had not been exposed or who were only minimally exposed (Finkelhor et al., 1995). In a recent meta-analysis, Davis and Gidycz (2000) examined 27 school-based prevention programs and found that children who participated in prevention programs scored higher on measures of prevention-related knowledge and skills than did children in comparison groups. In addition, this study's results suggest that long-term programs (e.g., four or more sessions) and programs that involved participants physically are most effective. Unfortunately, no research has demonstrated a relationship between prevention programs and a decline in actual numbers of victimizations.

CSA prevention programs are not without their critics. Reppucci et al. (1998), among other researchers, have questioned whether the "relatively exclusive focus on children as their own protectors is appropriate" (p. 332). Many children may not be developmentally ready to protect themselves, and an overreliance on these types of programs may give parents and society a false sense of security. At the same time, it seems reasonable to conclude that

> children and adolescents have a right to be enlightened about sexuality and sexual abuse and to know about their right to live free from such abuse. The more pertinent question is not *whether* to educate children about sexual abuse but rather *how* to do so in an effective, sensitive manner. (Wurtele & Miller-Perrin, 1992, p. 89)

Many experts have noted that for prevention efforts to be most effective, they should include both primary prevention goals (e.g., preventing abuse before it occurs) and secondary prevention goals (e.g., preventing abuse in high-risk groups, identifying abusive situations and intervening early so as to minimize harm, and increasing disclosures by victimized children) (Miller-Perrin & Wurtele, 1988; Wurtele & Miller-Perrin, 1992). Some researchers have speculated that school-based CSA prevention programs might lead to increased disclosure (Wurtele & Miller-Perrin, 1992), and a few studies have assessed the effects of such programs on rates of disclosure. In one study, school counselors from five of six schools received 20 confirmed reports of inappropriate touching during the 6 months following the implementation of prevention programs, compared with no reports from one control school (Kolko, Moser, & Hughes, 1989). Although these findings are promising, currently insufficient data are available to confirm the hypothesis that CSA prevention programs increase victim disclosures (Daro & McCurdy, 1994; Wurtele & Miller-Perrin, 1992). Additional research is needed.

The parental role in child empowerment. Secondary prevention efforts also include programs that attempt to target adults who can help children avoid sexually abusive experiences (Miller-Perrin & Wurtele, 1988; Wurtele & Miller-Perrin, 1992). Parents, of course, play an important role in empowering their own children to protect themselves. Because parents are the most likely offenders for most forms of child maltreatment, efforts that include parents focus primarily on sexual abuse, the form of child maltreatment most often perpetrated by individuals outside the child victims' own families.

Prevention efforts that focus on parents primarily attempt to educate them about CSA. Various prevention program formats designed for parents include audiovisual materials, books, and educational workshops (see Wurtele & Miller-Perrin, 1992). One such program, the Child Assault Prevention Project, helps parents empower their children through an educational workshop that focuses on sexual abuse in general (Porch & Petretic-Jackson, 1986). It also informs parents about specific responses their children can make to prevent abuse (e.g., saying no or screaming when confronted by a potentially abusive situation). Studies indicate that parents not only want to be involved in preventing CSA but also are effective in teaching their children about sexual abuse and appropriate protective skills (Wurtele, 1993; Wurtele, Kast, &

Melzer, 1994; Wurtele, Kvaternick, & Franklin, 1992). Parents are particularly effective if they are given specific instruction in how to talk to their children about sexual abuse (Burgess & Wurtele, 1998).

In addition, parents can play other roles in child maltreatment prevention. As Wurtele and Miller-Perrin (1992) note, for example, parents might interrupt abuse by learning to identify behaviors in children that are associated with CSA. Parents also play an important role when a child victim discloses abuse, because by responding appropriately they can reduce the child's feelings of self-blame, isolation, and anger. These prevention roles can also effectively be extended to other adults in a child's environment, such as teachers. Teachers can of course provide children with information about sexual abuse and self-protection skills, but in addition they are in a unique position, given their daily contact with children, to detect possible abuse by learning to identify behaviors indicative of abuse (Renk, Liljequist, Steinberg, Bosco, & Phares, 2002). To date, no research has evaluated the effectiveness of CSA prevention programs specifically targeting teachers. Future research should assess the effectiveness of these programs as well as programs that attempt to help other adults identify CSA and respond appropriately.

CHAPTER SUMMARY

No one knows exactly how many children experience sexual abuse each year. The difficulty in determining accurate rates of CSA stems from the problems inherent in defining and studying any complex social problem. Although no precise figures are available, it is clear that adults sexually exploit large numbers of children. Conservative estimates derived from the most methodologically sound studies suggest that in the United States 20% of women and between 5% and 10% of men have experienced some form of CSA.

Research has demonstrated the heterogeneity of CSA victim and offender populations. Victims are both male and female, range in age from infancy to 18, and come from a variety of racial and socioeconomic backgrounds. Perpetrators represent all possible demographic and psychological profiles. A number of risk factors, however, have been consistently associated with CSA. Victims often are female, have few close friends, and live in families characterized by poor family relations and the absence or unavailability of natural parents. Perpetrators of CSA are most often male,

and they are often relatives or acquaintances of their victims.

Perpetrators and victims provide consistent descriptions of the dynamics that characterize CSA situations. Perpetrators usually target children who are vulnerable or needy in some way and involve the children in a grooming process that involves a gradual progression from nonsexual to sexual touch. Perpetrators also use a variety of coercive tactics to initiate and maintain the abuse, such as threats, bribes, and physical force. New research is examining the sexual exploitation of children via the Internet, although initial findings suggest that this form of exploitation constitutes only a small proportion of CSA victimization. Organized exploitation, another form of child maltreatment, involves groups of children who are abused for the sexual stimulation of one or more perpetrators and often for commercial gain. Organized exploitation includes child sex rings, pornography, and prostitution.

The psychological sequelae for victims associated with CSA are variable and consist of short-term as well as long-term effects. Difficulties associated with CSA include a variety of symptoms that affect emotional well-being, interpersonal functioning, behavior, sexual functioning, physical health, and cognitive functioning. Variability in outcome for victims is associated with a number of factors, including the severity of the sexual behavior, the degree of physical force used by the perpetrator, the response the victim received following disclosure, and the relationship of the perpetrator to the victim.

The heterogeneity of victim and perpetrator populations has contributed to scholars' difficulty in establishing a single explanation for the occurrence of CSA. One perpetrator may abuse a certain type of child for one reason, and another may abuse a different type of child for a different reason. Etiological theories have focused on different individuals and systems involved in CSA. Some center on the role of the victim or the victim's mother, whereas the majority emphasize some form of offender dysfunction associated with personality, deviant sexual arousal, or childhood history. Some theories have also proposed that specific characteristics of the family system (e.g., parental conflict and family disorganization) might contribute to CSA. Finally, several theories have implicated sociocultural factors that might play contributory roles.

In recognition of the significance of the CSA problem, many professionals are involved in responding to the needs of victims and the treatment of perpetrators. Researchers and mental health practitioners have developed an array of treatment interventions in an effort to address the multiple causes and far-reaching consequences of CSA. Regardless of the type of approach, the therapeutic goals for child victims and adult survivors of CSA generally include addressing significant symptoms as well as common emotions associated with abuse, such as guilt, shame, anger, depression, and anxiety. Group therapy has been recommended as a beneficial intervention for victims to reduce self-denigrating beliefs, secrecy, and stigmatization. Treatment programs for offenders include a variety of approaches but most typically incorporate cognitive and behavioral components to reduce deviant sexual arousal and cognitive distortions associated with abuse. These approaches demonstrate some promise, but further studies are needed to address the limitations of extant research methodologies and potential alternative treatments (e.g., improving social and life skills) to accompany therapeutic interventions.

The prevention of child sexual abuse begins with social awareness, plus the recognition that expertise, energy, and money are needed to alleviate the conditions that produce CSA. Many experts maintain, however, that society has not yet sufficiently demonstrated a commitment to prevention. In most communities, monetary resources are tied up in responding to, rather than preventing, CSA. Increasing commitment to the prevention of CSA, however, is evidenced in the many prevention programs appearing across the United States. Several of the strategies employed in these programs seem especially promising. School-based CSA education for children is appealing because it has the potential to reach large numbers of young people. Parental competency programs target at-risk parents (poor, young, single) and at-risk children with the goal of providing training and social support before any abuse can occur. Although additional evaluations are needed, available research indicates that these programs have tremendous positive potential.

DISCUSSION QUESTIONS

1. What are the four key conceptual components of most current definitions of child sexual abuse?
2. How common is CSA? Are rates of CSA currently increasing or decreasing?
3. Do children commonly fabricate reports of CSA?
4. What is generally known about the characteristics of sexually abused children (e.g., age, gender, additional risk factors)? Using these characteristics, describe a prototypical child who has been sexually abused.
5. What is generally known about the characteristics of adults who sexually abuse children (e.g., age, gender, relationship to the victim)? Describe a prototypical perpetrator of child sexual abuse.
6. What are the dynamics of CSA? Describe the types of sexual activity that may be involved, factors associated with the initiation of abuse, and factors associated with the maintenance of abuse.
7. What are the various forms of organized sexual exploitation discussed in the research literature?
8. What are the potential initial and long-term effects associated with CSA?
9. What are the various etiological models that attempt to explain why children are sexually abused? Which model or models best explain why CSA occurs?
10. What are the common goals of therapy for child and adult survivors of CSA?
11. Which treatment interventions appear to be most promising for CSA offenders?
12. What kinds of approaches have been implemented in efforts to prevent CSA? How effective are these approaches?
13. What are the arguments made by the two sides in the repressed memory controversy?

RECOMMENDED READING

Berliner, L., & Elliott, D. M. (2002). Sexual abuse of children. In J. E. B. Myers, L. Berliner, J. Briere, C. T. Hendrix, C. Jenny, & T. A. Reid (Eds.), *The APSAC handbook on child maltreatment* (2nd ed., pp. 55–78). Thousand Oaks, CA: Sage.

Haugaard, J. J. (2000). The challenge of defining child sexual abuse. *American Psychologist, 55,* 1036–1039.

Hewitt, S. K. (1998). *Small voices: Assessing allegations of sexual abuse in preschool children.* Thousand Oaks, CA: Sage.

Maletzky, B. M., & Field, G. (2003). The biological treatment of dangerous sexual offenders: A review and preliminary report of the Oregon pilot Depo-Provera program. *Aggression and Violent Behavior, 8,* 391–412.

Price, J. L., Hilsenroth, M. J., Petretic-Jackson, P. A., & Bonge, D. (2001). A review of individual psychotherapy outcomes for adult survivors of childhood sexual abuse. *Clinical Psychology Review, 21,* 1095–1121.

Renk, K., Liljequist, L., Steinberg, A., Bosco, G., & Phares, V. (2002). Prevention of child sexual abuse: Are we doing enough? *Trauma, Violence, & Abuse, 3,* 68–84.

Saradjian, J. (1996). *Women who sexually abuse children: From research to clinical practice.* Chichester, Eng.: John Wiley.

Saunders, B. E., Kilpatrick, D. G., Hanson, R. F., Resnick, H. S., & Walker, M. E. (1999). Prevalence, case characteristics, and long-term psychological correlates of child rape among women: A national survey. *Child Maltreatment, 4,* 187–200.

Saywitz, K. J., Mannarino, A. P., Berliner, L., & Cohen, J. A. (2000). Treatment for sexually abused children and adolescents. *American Psychologist, 55,* 1040–1049.

Tyler, K. A. (2002). Social and emotional outcomes of childhood sexual abuse: A review of recent research. *Aggression and Violent Behavior, 7,* 567–589.

5

CHILD NEGLECT

Case History: Will and Mark—Where Are the Parents?

Will and Mark arrived at the psychiatric unit of the county hospital after they had been apprehended by the police the night before. Their clothes were covered with dirt, and the odor emanating from their bodies indicated that they had not bathed in quite some time. Both were thin and immediately asked the nursing staff for some food. An interview revealed that they were brothers and part of a family of seven, although many other "friends of the family" often stayed in their house. Neither of their parents worked, and Will and Mark stated that they often had the responsibility of bringing home money for their parents. Their father had taught them how to beg for money on various street corners around the city.

After the interview, the events of the previous evening were clear. Mark and Will had been out "killing time" by wandering around the neighborhood. After roaming the city for hours, they spotted a pickup truck and took it for a ride. After a short drive, they stopped at a local furniture store, broke in, and began to vandalize the merchandise, using Will's knife. A woman from the community spotted the intruders and called the police. She told the police that two young boys, probably somewhere between 7 and 9 years of age, had broken into a local business.

The events of this case history clearly reflect parenting practices that are less than ideal. Such behaviors, however, would not be characterized as physical or sexual abuse as previously defined in this volume. Rather, this vignette illustrates another form of child maltreatment: child neglect. In contrast to physical and sexual abuse, child neglect is typically viewed as an act of *omission* rather than an act of *commission*. Child neglect may sometimes be unintentional, but that does not make it any less detrimental to a child's development than intentional abuse or neglect.

Like all forms of child maltreatment, child neglect is not new. It was not until the early 20th century, however, that the neglect of children's basic needs was acknowledged or defined as a social problem in the United States (Wolock & Horowitz, 1984). In more recent times, widespread recognition of this form of child maltreatment, and subsequent empirical attention

directed toward it, has taken a backseat to concerns about physical and sexual child abuse (Berliner, 1994; Dubowitz, 1994). Historically, child neglect has been cast in the role of stepchild to the more tangible forms of child maltreatment. Indeed, scholars often refer to child neglect as the "most forgotten" form of maltreatment (e.g., Daro, 1988). Wolock and Horowitz (1984) coined the phrase "the neglect of neglect" to describe the disinterest in this topic shown by researchers and professionals as well as society in general. Dubowitz (1994) suggests several reasons for the historical inattention to child neglect among scholars and professionals in the field of family violence:

1. Some erroneously believe that neglect does not result in serious consequences.

2. Many may feel that it is inappropriate to judge parents involved in poverty-related neglect.

3. Many may be reluctant to become involved in the problem of child neglect because it seems insurmountable.

4. Some may find other forms of child maltreatment more compelling.

5. Some may be confused by the vagueness of many definitions of child neglect.

6. Some may be uncomfortable with the topic of child neglect because it provokes negative feelings.

The complex nature of child neglect has led to a serious lack of information about the characteristics, consequences, and causes of this form of child maltreatment. The relatively recent realization that child neglect is the most frequently reported form of child maltreatment (U.S. DHHS, 1996, 1998; Wang & Daro, 1998), however, has served to increase clinical and research efforts directed at the problem. In this chapter we address what is currently known about child neglect by examining issues related to defining child neglect and determining the magnitude of the problem. We then shift our attention to the characteristics researchers have found to be associated with neglectful parents and their children before focusing on an evaluation of the short-term and long-term consequences associated with child neglect. The chapter concludes with a discussion of potential intervention and prevention strategies for addressing the problem.

SCOPE OF THE PROBLEM

In response to increasing interest in the phenomenon of child neglect, scholars have focused on defining the parameters of child neglect and determining the magnitude of the problem. As is true of other forms of child maltreatment, reaching consensus regarding conceptual and operational definitions and determining the rates of the problem are two of the greatest challenges to the field.

What Is Child Neglect?

- Mark, who is 8 years old, is left to care for his 3-year-old sister, Maria, while their parents go out.
- Margaret fails to provide medication for her 10-year-old daughter, who has a seizure disorder.
- Jonathan refuses to allow his 16-year-old son into the family's home and tells him not to return.
- Tyrone and Rachel live with their three children in a home that is thick with dirt and dust, smells of

urine, and has nothing but rotting food in the refrigerator.

- Alicia leaves her 10-month-old infant unattended in a bathtub full of water.

The scenarios above portray a range of behaviors that may fall under the label of child neglect. The way that child neglect is defined is critical, because definitions influence how researchers, practitioners, and others conceptualize the problem for purposes of conducting research, reporting neglect, understanding the causes of neglect, and formulating interventions as well as prevention strategies.

Current definitions. Defining child neglect, both conceptually and operationally, is one of the greatest challenges in the field. Most experts generally agree that deficits in meeting a child's basic needs constitute child neglect. Gaudin (1993), for example, states, "Child neglect is the term used most often to encompass parents' or caretakers' failure to provide basic physical health care, supervision, nutrition, personal hygiene, emotional nurturing, education, or safe housing" (p. 67). There is less agreement, however, about various aspects of the scope and specificity of children's needs and parental behaviors.

One unresolved issue concerns how much importance a definition should place on intentionality with regard to parental failure to provide. Definitions of child neglect that emphasize parental blame, parental responsibility, or both may focus narrowly on the role of the caretaker in child neglect, limiting understanding of the problem. In the second scenario above, for example, Margaret may not provide her 10-year-old with medication for her seizure disorder because she cannot afford to pay for the medication, not because she has any intention of harming her child. If professionals designing child neglect interventions focus exclusively on the negative intent or failures of neglecting parents, they might confine their strategies to improving parental behaviors and thereby fail to address other important contributors to neglect, such as poverty.

Several researchers have called for a comprehensive definition of child neglect that incorporates a variety of factors, in addition to a parent's failure to provide, that might lead to neglect (e.g., Dubowitz, Black, Starr, & Zuravin, 1993; Helfer, 1990; Paget, Philp, & Abramczyk, 1993). Dubowitz (1999), for example, has argued for a definition of neglect that focuses on the unmet needs of the child, regardless of parental intentions. The definition of child neglect used in the second and third National Incidence Studies (Sedlak & Broadhurst, 1996 [NIS-3]; U.S. DHHS, 1988 [NIS-2]) included various forms of physical neglect, such as refusal of health care, abandonment, inadequate supervision, and inadequate nutrition, clothing, and hygiene. In addition, it distinguished between parental failure to provide when options are available and failure to provide when options are not available. The definition excluded situations in which the parents or caretakers were involved in acts of omission because of financial limitations (e.g., inability to afford health care). The penal codes of several states include definitions of child neglect that exclude neglect associated with limited financial resources. Such definitions call attention to additional social factors potentially involved in neglectful behaviors, which encourages awareness about the complexity of child neglect. Understanding the multidimensional nature of child neglect may, in turn, help scholars and practitioners to be effective in their research, prevention, and intervention efforts.

Another serious challenge to establishing consensus on a definition of child neglect is lack of agreement about exactly what constitutes a child's basic needs. Are the parents of Mark and Maria, described in the first scenario, negligent because they leave an 8-year-old boy to care for his 3-year-old sister? Obviously, the answer to that question depends on the specific circumstances. What if Mark were responsible for Maria's care for 5 minutes while she played on the floor? For 5 minutes while she played in the bathtub? For one evening between 9 p.m. and 1 a.m.? For every evening between 9 p.m. and 1 a.m.? What if Mark were responsible for Maria's care while their parents took a 2-week vacation? A given behavior can be interpreted as neglectful or not depending on several factors, including the consequences to the child, the duration and frequency of the behavior, and the cultural context in which the behavior occurs.

Severity of consequences. Many scholars have argued that the severity of the consequences of neglect is an important but overlooked variable in attempts to define child neglect (Crouch & Milner, 1993; Erickson & Egeland, 1996). The severity of neglect is typically assessed according to the magnitude of the consequences for the child or the degree of demonstrable harm (Dubowitz, Black, Starr, & Zuravin, 1993; U.S. DHHS, 1981). A case in which a child dies from bleach poisoning, for example, might be considered more severe than a case in which a child receives a minor burn

from an iron, although the same parental behavior (i.e., lack of supervision) contributed to both injuries.

One problem with including a criterion of demonstrable harm in a definition of child neglect is that some negative outcomes of neglect are difficult to measure (e.g., emotional consequences), and there may be no immediate harm from some forms of neglect. The three children of Tyrone and Rachel, described in the fourth scenario above, may suffer no demonstrable immediate harm as a result of living in unsanitary conditions for a month, but the parents' behavior could still be considered neglect. Zuravin (1988) found that only 25% of neglected children reported to a CPS agency suffered immediate physical harm. In recognition of this dilemma, the U.S. Department of Health and Human Services (1988) broadened its definition of child neglect in the NIS-2 to include a category titled *endangered.* This new category allowed for the reporting of cases in which children demonstrated no actual harm (i.e., present evidence of injury) but in which it was reasonable to suspect potential harm (i.e., future risk of injury). The laws in most U.S. states include risk of harm or endangerment in their definitions of child neglect (Myers & Peters, 1987).

As Dubowitz, Black, Starr, and Zuravin (1993) have noted, there are two difficulties in considering potential harm: how to predict the likelihood that harm will actually occur and how to determine whether that potential harm is significant. An illustration is the potential for harm present each time a person gets into a car, crosses a street, or consumes foods high in cholesterol. In each case, there is uncertainty about whether actual harm will result and whether such harm will be significant. Professionals who investigate cases of alleged child neglect face a continuum of behaviors and must use their human judgment in making determinations. Thus the definitional process attached to child neglect may be even more subjective than those associated with the other forms of child maltreatment discussed in this book. We agree with Dubowitz et al. that definitions of child neglect should take into consideration potential harm that is probable and severe in its consequences. Leaving a 10-month-old unattended in a bathtub full of water, as Alicia did in the last scenario above, for example, could potentially result in severe injury or even death.

Frequency and duration. The frequency and duration of neglecting behaviors are also important definitional considerations (Claussen & Crittenden, 1991; Dubowitz, Black, Starr, & Zuravin, 1993). A single incident of neglectful behavior or an occasional lapse in adequate care is usually considered a normal characteristic of parenting or parental error rather than an indication of serious child neglect. Few would allege child neglect if a child occasionally misses a bath or a meal. In contrast, a pattern of frequent and repeated deficits in child care (e.g., few baths and numerous missed meals) is likely to be considered neglectful (Daro, 1988; Dubowitz, Black, Starr, & Zuravin, 1993).

Some scholars have argued that the frequency and chronicity of neglecting behaviors should be evaluated in the context of the severity of the potential harm of those behaviors (Dubowitz, Black, Starr, & Zuravin, 1993; U.S. DHHS, 1988; Zuravin, 1991). Some isolated incidents or brief omissions in care can result in serious consequences. If a caretaker leaves a young child or infant alone just once near a swimming pool, for example, that child may drown. If a parent fails to buckle a young child into a car seat properly just one time, that child may die in a car accident. Some have argued that "an omission in care that harms or endangers a child constitutes neglect, whether it occurs once or a hundred times" (Dubowitz, Black, Starr, & Zuravin, 1993, p. 18). In the third scenario above, in which Jonathan throws his 16-year-old son out of the family home and tells him not to return, the behavior occurs only once, but that single behavior could prove to be quite harmful to the child.

Distinctions based on frequency and chronicity are helpful not only for defining child neglect but for improving understanding of the characteristics and causes of child neglect. Nelson, Saunders, and Landsman (1990), for example, have reported finding differences between chronically and nonchronically neglectful families. The chronically neglectful families in their study sample were characterized by multiple problems and deficits, including lack of knowledge, skills, and tangible resources. Nonchronically neglectful or "new neglect" families had experienced recent significant crises (e.g., parental divorce or illness) that appeared to overwhelm their normally sufficient coping abilities. These researchers suggest that the characteristics of nonchronically neglectful families indicate they would benefit from short-term crisis, stress management, and support group interventions, whereas chronically neglectful families need multiple treatment interventions of long duration.

Cultural issues. Societal reactions largely determine the point at which child care moves from adequate to inadequate. These reactions communicate and clarify cultural and community values. The age at which a minor is considered capable of being responsible for preparing his or her own meals, for example, differs among cultural groups and for various claims-making groups within any culture. Some groups might condemn the notion of a 12-year-old taking on this responsibility, whereas others might approve of it. Thus, ultimately, societal reactions distinguish adequate from inadequate care. The social context of a family's culture and beliefs is an important factor to consider in both defining and intervening in child neglect, because knowledge of culturally driven reasons for neglectful behavior might inform treatment and prevention approaches.

Research examining North American communities indicates that cultural views of what constitutes household cleanliness, appropriate medical and dental care, and adequate supervision vary little across sociodemographic variables. Polansky and colleagues have evaluated nonmaltreating mothers with various sociodemographic backgrounds using the Childhood Level of Living scale to assess the importance of basic standards of child care, including cognitive, emotional, and physical care. Their results have consistently indicated that there is strong agreement about the basic elements of child care, with similar standards of care found for rural, urban, working-class, and middle-class individuals (Polansky, Ammons, & Weathersby, 1983; Polansky, Chalmers, & Williams, 1987; Polansky & Williams, 1978).

In a study conducted in Israel with a group of parents from a low-income deprived neighborhood and a group of parents from a middle-income neighborhood, Shor (2000) found similar results. No group differences appeared in terms of the parents' level of acceptance for, or degree of harm associated with, the behaviors of parents in vignettes portraying lack of parental supervision. When Shor evaluated the rationales for parents' responses, however, group differences emerged. Parents from the low-income neighborhood believed that the lack of supervision was unacceptable and harmful for reasons related to the child's physical safety, whereas parents from the middle-income neighborhood believed it was unacceptable and harmful because of its effects on the child's developmental needs. Shor suggests that it might be helpful to consider the adaptive nature of parenting behaviors within their socioecological contexts.

Forms of neglect. Additional efforts to define the precise nature of child neglect have led researchers to propose numerous typologies to clarify the various situations that constitute child neglect. Most experts agree that child neglect exists in many forms, such as physical neglect, educational neglect, developmental neglect, and emotional neglect. Some experts in the field have proposed an additional category, prenatal neglect, for neglect that occurs even before a child is born (see Box 5.1).

Box 5.1 Neglecting the Unborn Child

The term *prenatal neglect* refers generally to any actions of a pregnant woman that can potentially harm her unborn child. Most conceptualizations of prenatal neglect focus on women who abuse illicit drugs and alcohol during pregnancy, exposing infants to the effects of these substances in utero. Estimates of the numbers of drug-exposed infants in the United States vary widely because none of the states requires the uniform testing of infants for drug exposure. In its annual national survey, the National Committee to Prevent Child Abuse found that in 1993, 6,922 infants were reported for drug exposure (McCurdy & Daro, 1994b). This figure increased to 7,469 in 1994 (Wiese & Daro, 1995). According to some estimates, approximately 11% of all women who have given birth in the United States used illegal drugs while pregnant (e.g., Jones, 1992).

Most of the concern about prenatal drug exposure has arisen because increasing numbers of studies have demonstrated a relationship between prenatal drug exposure and negative child developmental outcomes (see reviews by Chiriboga, 1993; Ondersma, Simpson, Brestan, & Ward, 2000). The most compelling evidence comes from studies that have examined the effects of fetal exposure to alcohol. Research has consistently demonstrated that children born of mothers who consumed large quantities of alcohol during pregnancy face definitive and irreversible effects, including growth deficiency, anomalies of brain structure and function, mental retardation, and abnormalities of the head and face (Streissguth, 1997). *Fetal alcohol syndrome* is the established term for this constellation of symptoms. More limited exposure of the infant to alcohol during pregnancy has been shown to result in subtler outcomes; these are termed fetal alcohol effects.

The findings of research examining the link between fetal harm and prenatal use of illicit drugs such as heroin, cocaine, and marijuana have been more equivocal. Much of this research has focused on the possible negative effects of cocaine on developmental outcome for exposed infants. Although cocaine's relation to short-term effects such as jitteriness and irritability in newborns appears to be well established, some controversy exists with regard to possible long-term effects of prenatal cocaine exposure (Ondersma et al., 2000). In a recent review of the potential effects of cocaine exposure, for example, Kelley (2002) notes that "research findings over time have failed to substantiate pervasive long-term adverse effects of cocaine exposure" (p. 109). In contrast, Ondersma and colleagues (2000) reviewed the available literature on illicit drugs and found that "subtle but meaningful long-term behavioral and cognitive deficits may result from prenatal drug exposure, especially in the area of attention and habituation" (p. 97).

One explanation for these equivocal findings may be the many methodological constraints on this research, which limit the establishment of definitive cause-effect relationships between prenatal drug exposure and negative developmental outcome. The quantity of cocaine that pregnant women consume, for example, may determine whether any negative effects manifest in their infants (Schuler & Nair, 1999). Maternal drug use also often occurs in association with poor maternal nutrition, so it is difficult to determine which variable is responsible for negative developmental outcomes. Results of such studies are also difficult to interpret when researchers do not consider the influence of environment on infants' development subsequent to birth. Recent research findings suggest that the postnatal environment influences the developmental outcomes of drug-exposed infants. Characteristics of a drug-exposed infant's environment that contribute to negative developmental outcomes include high levels of parental stress, continued parental substance abuse, and postnatal drug exposure (Kelley, 2002). A child may be exposed to cigarette or marijuana smoke in utero, for example, as well as in the environment after birth when the mother continues to smoke.

Despite inconsistent research findings, many observers have called for drug testing of newborns, asserting that such testing could identify infants at risk for developmental problems. Several problems are associated with infant drug screening, however. Drawbacks to both universal testing (testing of all newborn infants) and targeted testing (testing of specific groups of infants identified as high risk) include financial costs, potential avoidance of medical care by pregnant drug users, the limited ability of some tests to detect certain substances, and the potential for discriminatory screening practices (Ondersma et al., 2000). As of 1998, one national survey of public health policy directors found that 12% of U.S. states had policies of mandatory drug testing for pregnant women (Chavkin, Breitbart, Elman, & Wise, 1998).

Some observers argue that substance-abusing pregnant women should be held criminally liable for any ill effects their substance abuse causes their children. Punishment could include legal sanctions, court-ordered treatment, and removal of the infant from the home. Many states currently require medical and other professionals to report drug-exposed infants or substance-abusing pregnant women to child protective services. As of 1994, 27 states required the reporting of drug-exposed babies, an increase from 19 states in 1993 (Daro & McCurdy, 1994; Wiese & Daro, 1995). Although some states explicitly define infants born with positive drug toxicology as abused or neglected, most do not. In one national survey, 35% of state public health policy directors reported that positive neonatal drug toxicology is legally defined as child abuse or neglect in their states (Chavkin et al., 1998).

Successful criminal prosecutions of prenatal neglect (conducted under child abuse and neglect statutes) are rare (Garrity-Rokous, 1994; Sovinski, 1997). Civil proceedings resulting in removal of drug-exposed infants from their homes (rather than prison sentences for their mothers) are more likely outcomes for substance-abusing pregnant women. In many cases, courts have intervened to protect drug-exposed newborns on the basis that the circumstances of their births are probative of child neglect (Myers, 1992). Prosecutors have also sometimes used statutes other than those addressing child abuse and neglect (e.g., laws concerning involuntary manslaughter and prohibitions against delivering drugs to minors) to charge women who abuse substances during pregnancy, although they have generally been unsuccessful in obtaining criminal convictions on such charges (Garrity-Rokous, 1994; Sovinski, 1997).

One reason for the lack of uniformity in states' responses to prenatal neglect is the ongoing debate surrounding the relative significance of the rights of the unborn child versus the rights of the pregnant woman (Fleisher, 1987; Garrity-Rokous, 1994). Another source of confusion is the ambiguity of some states' statutes concerning the circumstances under which a pregnant woman can be legally sanctioned for causing possible harm to her fetus. In addition, a number of scholars have questioned the use of punitive responses toward substance-abusing pregnant women on practical, constitutional, therapeutic, and empirical grounds (e.g., Garrity-Rokous, 1994; Sovinski, 1997). Although the problem of prenatal neglect continues to be the focus of much theoretical discussion and empirical research, solutions will likely remain elusive for some time.

Despite general agreement regarding the broad categories of neglect, disagreement exists regarding the precise behaviors that should be included under each category. The strongest consensus exists for *physical neglect,* which is generally defined as failure to provide a child with basic necessities of life, such as food, clothing, and shelter. The NIS-2 and NIS-3 broadened the concept of physical neglect to include refusal to seek or delay in seeking health care, desertion or abandonment, refusing custody (e.g., throwing a child out of the house or not allowing a runaway to return home), and inadequate supervision (Sedlak & Broadhurst, 1996; U.S. DHHS, 1988). In the NIS-3, an example of physical neglect included a 2-year-old who was found naked and alone, wandering on the street late at night (Sedlak & Broadhurst, 1996). *Educational or developmental neglect* is generally defined as failure to provide a child with the experiences necessary for growth and development, such as intellectual and educational opportunities (Sedlak & Broadhurst, 1996). An example of educational neglect is a child who is chronically truant or not enrolled in school.

The category of *emotional neglect* has stimulated the greatest disagreement among scholars in terms of defining what it encompasses. Although most agree on broad conceptual parameters of emotional neglect that include failure to provide a child with emotional support, security, and encouragement, they disagree on the specific operationalization of such behaviors. Recent attempts to delineate the behaviors that constitute emotional neglect include situations that many have traditionally viewed as physical, educational, or developmental neglect. The NIS-3, for example, included in the definition of emotional neglect the delay or refusal of psychological care for a child, a behavior that others have classified as developmental neglect (e.g., Hegar & Yungman, 1989; Sedlak & Broadhurst, 1996). There is also considerable overlap between definitions of emotional neglect and psychological maltreatment. Some experts, for example, consider a parent's failure to express affection and caring for a child to be psychological maltreatment, whereas others define this behavior as emotional neglect (Hart, Brassard, & Karlson, 1996; Sedlak & Broadhurst, 1996).

Despite the disagreement and overlap in organizational frameworks, several subtypes of neglect are repeatedly reported in the literature: health care neglect, personal hygiene neglect, nutritional neglect, neglect of household safety, neglect of household sanitation, inadequate shelter, abandonment, supervisory neglect, educational neglect, emotional neglect, and fostering delinquency. Each of these is described briefly in Table 5.1.

Table 5.1   Subtypes of Child Neglect

Subtype	Description	Examples
Health care neglect	Refusal to provide, or delay in providing, physical or mental health care	Failing to obtain child's immunizations Failing to fill prescriptions for child's needed medications or to follow health care provider's instructions Failing to attend to child's dental needs Failing to obtain prescribed psychological help for child
Personal hygiene neglect	Failure to meet basic standards of personal care and cleanliness	Infrequent bathing of child Neglecting child's dental hygiene Not providing child with clothing adequate for weather conditions or of the correct size Not providing sleeping arrangements that allow child to obtain adequate sleep
Nutritional neglect	Failure to provide a sufficient and nutritionally balanced diet	Providing insufficient calories to support child's growth Providing meals for child that do not include all the basic food groups Providing child with food that is stale or spoiled

Subtype	Description	Examples
Neglect of household safety	Failure to eliminate safety hazards in and around the child's living area	Allowing structural hazards to exist in and around the home, such as broken stairs or railings, broken windows, holes in floors or ceilings Allowing fire hazards and burn threats to exist in and around the home, such as combustible materials close to heat sources, frayed wiring Leaving chemicals or drugs where they are accessible to child
Neglect of household sanitation	Failure to meet basic standards of housekeeping care and cleanliness	Allowing garbage and trash to accumulate in the home Failing to control vermin and insects Allowing surfaces in the home to become covered with dirt and filth; failing to provide clean bedding
Inadequate shelter	Failure to provide adequate physical shelter and/or a stable home	Refusing responsibilities of custody of child Not allowing runaway child to return home Failing to provide child with a stable and permanent home (i.e., homelessness) Providing child with an overcrowded home (e.g., 25 people living in a four-bedroom home) Throwing child out of the home
Abandonment	Physical desertion of the child	Placing child in a dumpster; leaving child in a park Failing to return after placing child in the care of others (e.g., babysitters, hospital personnel, relatives)
Supervisory neglect	Failure to provide a level of parental supervision necessary to avoid child injury	Leaving child in the home without adult supervision for prolonged periods Allowing child to roam the streets at night
Educational neglect	Failure to provide care and supervision necessary to promote education	Failing to enroll child of mandatory school age in school Permitting child's frequent and chronic truancy Failing to attend to child's special education needs
Emotional neglect	Failure to provide child with emotional support, security, and encouragement	Being unavailable to child emotionally Being indifferent toward or rejecting child
Fostering delinquency	Encouragement of the development of illegal behaviors in the child	Rewarding child for stealing

SOURCES: A representative but not exhaustive list of sources for the information displayed in this table includes the following: Hegar and Yungman (1989); Munkel (1994); Sedlak and Broadhurst (1996); Wolock and Horowitz (1984); Zuravin (1991).

Table 5.2   Numbers of Children Reported for Physical and Educational Neglect in the National Incidence Studies

	Physical Neglect		*Educational Neglect*	
	Number of Children	*Rate per 1,000 Childrem*	*Number of Children*	*Rate per 1,000 Children*
NIS-1	103,600	1.6	174,000	2.7
NIS-2	507,700	8.1	284,800	4.5
NIS-3	1,335,100	19.9	397,300	5.9

SOURCES: Sedlak (1990); Sedlak and Broadhurst (1996); U.S. DHHS (1981, 1988).

Estimates of Child Neglect

During the past 15 years, child neglect has emerged as the most frequently reported and substantiated form of child maltreatment (Wang & Daro, 1998). Estimates of child neglect come primarily from official reports made to professionals and CPS agencies. Recent research has also employed parent self-report techniques to determine estimates of neglecting behavior.

Official estimates. Official reporting statistics over the past several years indicate that reports of child neglect have increased steadily. In 1986, according to the American Association for Protecting Children (AAPC, 1988), child neglect cases (i.e., cases in which children experienced deprivation of necessities) accounted for approximately 55% of all child maltreatment cases reported to CPS agencies in the United States. Data from the National Child Abuse and Neglect Data System, the most recent data available, reveal that child neglect currently accounts for approximately 63% of all reported cases of child maltreatment (U.S. DHHS, 2002b).

Findings from the three National Incidence Studies indicate that the numbers of children reported for neglect have also increased in recent years, as shown in Table 5.2 (U.S. DHHS, 1996; Wang & Daro, 1998). It is not clear, however, whether these changes indicate actual increases in neglectful behavior by parents. The increase in cases reported from NIS-1 to NIS-2 reflects, for example, the broadening of the definition of child neglect in the NIS-2 to include children at risk for harm in addition to those actually harmed. Definitional variability, however, cannot account for the increases between NIS-2 and NIS-3 because the two studies used identical definitions of child neglect. Increases in the numbers of children reported for child neglect between 1986 and 1993 likely reflect increased

awareness and knowledge of child neglect on the part of community professionals, but they may also reflect a real increase in child neglect during this period (Sedlak & Broadhurst, 1996).

Self-report surveys. A study that employed a nationally representative sample of parents using the Parent-Child Conflict Tactics Scales provides self-report estimates of child neglect (Straus, Hamby, Finkelhor, Moore, & Runyan, 1998). Several questions that focused on lack of parental supervision, nutritional neglect, alcohol abuse, medical neglect, and emotional neglect defined child neglect. Of parents responding to this survey, 27% reported engaging in some form of child neglect at least once during the past year. The most common form of neglect reported was leaving a child alone even when the parent thought an adult should be present. In this sample, 11% of the parents also reported that they were unable to ensure that their children obtained the food they needed, and approximately 2% reported an inability to care for their children adequately because of problem drinking.

---•◆•---

SECTION SUMMARY

Although child neglect is not a new form of child maltreatment, traditionally it has not received as much attention, socially or empirically, as the problems of sexual and physical child abuse. Neglect may seem "less deviant" than these other forms of child maltreatment, and professionals may be reluctant to judge or blame neglectful parents (especially in cases of poverty). Difficulties in defining and identifying child neglect have also contributed to the lack of attention this problem has received.

Current research efforts concentrate on defining child neglect, both conceptually and operationally. Most experts agree that child neglect consists of failure to provide for a child's basic needs. Scholars have formulated a number of typologies of neglect in efforts to operationalize precisely what should be included among these basic needs. Current typologies include physical, educational, developmental, and emotional neglect. Researchers have also emphasized the need to incorporate several characteristics of neglect into current definitions, including severity of neglect, frequency and duration of neglecting behaviors, and community and cultural (e.g., socioeconomic) aspects of neglecting situations. Despite considerable effort, little consensus exists regarding the best way to define child neglect.

The true incidence of child neglect is unknown because of the many methodological problems inherent in attempts to study rates of child maltreatment (e.g., reporting biases, definitional variability, and failure to differentiate among subtypes of neglect). Despite these difficulties, it is clear that hundreds of thousands of children are reported for child neglect each year—so many children that child neglect is the most frequently reported form of child maltreatment, accounting for 52–55% of reported maltreatment cases.

SEARCHING FOR PATTERNS: CHARACTERISTICS OF NEGLECTED CHILDREN AND THEIR FAMILIES

What are the specific characteristics and traits of neglecting adults and their children? Agencies that receive official reports of abuse and survey data collected from representative samples of the U.S. population have provided much of the information currently available on the sociodemographic characteristics of parents and children involved in child neglect. Clinical as well as community studies have also provided information relevant to the psychosocial characteristics of neglecting parents. Much of the research that has evaluated risk factors for child neglect has been limited by methodological weaknesses. Inconsistent definitions of neglect, the retrospective nature of some data, biased sampling techniques, and overreliance on studies of mothers (rather than fathers or both parents) as perpetrators of neglect have all contributed to the difficulties in interpreting findings. Although the studies described below are limited by these biases, their findings nonetheless shed some light on the general characteristics of neglected children and their parents (for a review, see Schumacher, Slep, & Heyman, 2001a).

Characteristics of Neglected Children

Age. The mean age of neglected children in the United States is 6 years (AAPC, 1988). Several sources of estimates indicate that the risk for child neglect generally declines with age (e.g., Sedlak & Broadhurst, 1996; U.S. DHHS, 1998, 2001). Recent data from the National Center on Child Abuse and Neglect (NCCAN) indicate that 51% of reported child neglect victims are under 5 years of age and that, of those reports, 34% are for children under 1 year of age (U.S. DHHS, 1994). Serious injuries and fatalities from neglect are also more common for younger children than for older children (Wang & Daro, 1998). This general pattern, however, varies for different subtypes of neglect. Findings from the NIS-3, for example, indicated that older children were more likely than younger children to be victims of emotional neglect (Sedlak & Broadhurst, 1996).

Gender. Few differences appear between genders in rates of child neglect (U.S. DHHS, 1988, 1994, 2001). The NCCAN found, for example, that the children in 51% of reported cases were males and in 49% of cases they were females (U.S. DHHS, 1998). Research findings vary with regard to gender, however, when subtypes of neglect are examined. The NIS-3, for example, found that boys were more likely than girls to be emotionally neglected (Sedlak & Broadhurst, 1996).

Race. Studies that have attempted to determine racial differences in rates of child neglect have been fraught with methodological difficulties, and, as a result, their findings should be interpreted cautiously (Asbury, 1993). According to official reporting statistics from the AAPC (1988), 63% of child neglect reports in the United States in 1986 involved Caucasian children, 20% involved African American children, and 12% involved Hispanic children. Comparison of these data with census data indicates that the risk of neglect appears to be higher for African American and Hispanic children. Indeed, in more recent official statistics, 44% of all medical neglect reports involved African American children (U.S. DHHS, 1998). The significance of these patterns is unclear, however, because race is also associated with socioeconomic status (SES).

Characteristics of Neglecting Parents

Demographic characteristics. Data from the NIS-3 indicate that birth parents are the primary perpetrators of child neglect, accounting for 91% of reported cases (Sedlak & Broadhurst, 1996). Consistent with these findings are the most recent data gathered through the National Child Abuse and Neglect Data System, which demonstrate that parents are the perpetrators in approximately 92% of child neglect cases (U.S. DHHS, 2001).

Limited information is available with regard to age characteristics of neglecting parents. As of 1986, the mean age of parents reported for child neglect was 31 years, according to a study conducted by the AAPC (1988). Other studies have compared the ages of neglecting versus nonneglecting parents and found mixed results. For example, Zuravin (1987) found that neglecting mothers were older than nonneglecting mothers in their sample, whereas Chaffin, Kelleher, and Hollenberg (1996) found the reverse to be true. Such discrepancies may be due to variability in sampling procedures (e.g., mothers reported to CPS for neglect versus self-identified neglectful mothers) and definitions of neglect.

With regard to parent gender, the majority of research findings indicate that females are significantly more likely than males to be reported for neglect (AAPC, 1988; U.S. DHHS, 1996, 1998). The NCCAN, for example, found that females were reported as the perpetrator in 72% of cases (U.S. DHHS, 1998). In addition, the most recent reporting statistics indicate that both parents are reported for neglect in only 19% of child neglect cases (U.S. DHHS, 2001). It is not uncommon in two-parent families for only mothers, and not fathers, to be labeled as neglectful (Azar, Povilaitis, Lauretti, & Pouquette, 1998).

The higher proportion of females reported for neglect may reflect the general social attitude that mothers, rather than fathers, are responsible for meeting the needs of their children (Turney, 2000). In fact, both the mother and the father may be equally responsible for child neglect in a particular home, but the mother might be more likely to be *reported* for neglectful behaviors because of social stereotypes. Chaffin et al. (1996) examined this issue by evaluating risk factors for child neglect in a representative community sample of parents who were not reported or referred to treatment for child neglect. They identified a group of parents who did not self-report neglect of their children at initial assessment and then reassessed the parents a year later and identified a group who self-reported neglect of their children. The researchers then evaluated the social risk factors associated with the onset of self-reported neglect, including gender, and found that parent gender was not predictive of child neglect.

Psychological and behavioral characteristics. A number of researchers have examined the psychological and behavioral characteristics of neglecting parents. Most research in this area has attempted to distinguish characteristics of neglectful parents compared with physically abusive or nonmaltreating parents. The findings from the majority of these studies indicate that neglectful parents exhibit some unique psychological characteristics as well as behavioral deficits.

One consistent finding is that, compared with nonneglecting parents, neglecting parents generally interact less with their children, and when they do interact, the interactions are less positive. Neglectful parents, for example, engage in less verbal instruction and play behavior with their children, show their children less nonverbal affection, and exhibit less warmth in discussions with their children (e.g., Bousha & Twentyman, 1984; Crittenden, 1993; Polansky, Gaudin, & Kilpatrick, 1992). There is also evidence that neglecting parents are involved in more negative behaviors with their children, including issuing commands and engaging in verbal aggression (Bousha & Twentyman, 1984; Burgess & Conger, 1978).

Some researchers have suggested that neglecting parents may perceive their children and the parent-child relationship differently than do nonneglecting parents. Twentyman and Plotkin (1982), for example, found that neglectful parents' expectations of their children were less accurate than those of their nonneglectful counterparts. Several other studies, however, have failed to find differences between neglectful and nonneglectful parents on measures of parental expectations. Williamson, Borduin, and Howe (1991), for example, assessed mothers' expectations with regard to the appropriate timing of several child development milestones and found no differences between neglectful and nonneglectful mothers.

Other researchers have focused on the relationship of parental personality and psychopathology to neglectful behavior, but their findings are difficult to interpret. Some data indicate that neglecting mothers report depressive symptoms, impulsivity, low self-esteem, low empathy, and parental stress at higher levels than do nonneglecting mothers (Christensen et al., 1994; Ethier, Lacharite, & Couture, 1995; Polansky et al., 1992; Shahar, 2001). Williamson et al. (1991), however, found no differences between neglectful and nonneglectful mothers on a measure of psychiatric symptoms. Chaffin et al. (1996) evaluated specific psychiatric diagnoses, such as substance abuse, depressive disorders, and obsessive compulsive disorder, and found that neglectful parents in their sample were more likely to receive such diagnoses than were nonneglectful parents. It may be that psychiatric disorders or particular underlying personality styles (e.g., limited empathic capacity) are risk factors for neglectful parenting, rather than specific individual psychiatric symptoms or independent personality dimensions (Schumacher et al., 2001a).

Some researchers have investigated the hypothesis that neglecting parents are neglectful because they received inadequate parenting in childhood. Several studies have reported childhood histories of both neglect and abuse in adults who neglect their children (e.g., Widom, 1989b). It is difficult to determine, however, which form of maltreatment is the likely contributor to current neglecting behavior. Few studies have examined the intergenerational transmission hypothesis with groups of adult subjects who experienced child neglect only. One exception is a study in which Ethier compared the childhood histories of physically abusive mothers with those of neglectful mothers (cited in Ethier, Palacio-Quintin, & Jourdan-Ionescu, 1992). Results indicated that neglectful mothers were more likely to have been victims of neglect, both physical and emotional.

Family Structure and Functioning

Research has also shown that family size and structure are associated with neglect. Children of single parents are at greater risk for all types of neglect compared with children living with both parents (Brown, Cohen, Johnson, & Salzinger, 1998; Drake & Pandey, 1996; Sedlak & Broadhurst, 1996). In addition, at-risk percentages are considerably higher for neglected children compared with both sexually and emotionally abused children (Sedlak & Broadhurst, 1996). Child neglect is also related to the number of dependent children living in the family. In NIS-3, children in the largest families (four or more children) were two to three times more likely to be neglected (Sedlak & Broadhurst, 1996). In addition, mothers who have a greater number of children during their teen years or who are younger at the birth of their first child were at

increased risk for neglecting their children. Furthermore, teenage mothers whose first child was premature or had a low birth weight were more likely to neglect their children than were older mothers whose infants were healthier (Zuravin & DiBlasio, 1992).

Researchers have also evaluated the relationship between family functioning and child neglect. Williamson et al. (1991) compared levels of overall stress, family adaptability, and family cohesion between neglecting and nonneglecting families. The results varied depending on whether the neglected adolescents or their neglecting parents were providing family ratings. Neglected adolescents, for example, perceived their families as being less cohesive than did nonneglected adolescents. In contrast, neglectful mothers' ratings of both family adaptability and family cohesion did not differ significantly from ratings of nonneglectful mothers. When the researchers assessed levels of family and daily stress, however, they found that both neglected adolescents and their mothers were more likely to report high levels of stress than were nonneglected adolescents and their mothers.

Social and Community Factors

Socioeconomic status. Although child neglect occurs at all levels of U.S. society, studies indicate that rates of neglect are higher in families characterized by very low income, unemployment, and dependence on social assistance (Brown et al., 1998; U.S. DHHS, 1996). Indeed, SES is a stronger predictor of child neglect than of any other form of child maltreatment (Sedlak & Broadhurst, 1996). In an ecological investigation of risk factors for child neglect conducted by Drake and Pandey (1996), communities with the highest rates of poverty had 18 times as many reports of neglect incidents as did communities with the lowest rates of poverty. Income level has also been associated with severity of neglect, with higher-income families generally associated with less severe forms of neglect (see Claussen & Crittenden, 1991).

Although child neglect is consistently reported more frequently in families of low SES, it is possible that higher rates of reported neglect among the lower classes reflect, in part, a reporting bias. Poor and disadvantaged families may be more likely to come to the attention of professionals through reporting or treatment referrals. That is, child neglect may not *occur* more frequently in low-SES groups, it may simply be *reported* more often among the disadvantaged. Chaffin et al. (1996) addressed the possibility of reporting bias in their

An Interview With Patricia Crittenden

"Unfortunately because we think of children as victims, parents are consequently labeled as perpetrators. As a result, we become tempted to punish such 'perpetrators' and thus reduce our ability to help either the parents or their children."

Patricia Crittenden is a prolific scholar who has published several books and more than 80 journal articles and book chapters on issues related to child maltreatment. She has a multidisciplinary background, having earned an M.Ed. in special education and an M.A. in developmental psychology, both at the University of Virginia. She received her Ph.D. in family and developmental psychology from the University of Virginia in 1983 and held a postdoctoral fellowship at the University of New Hampshire in the Family Research Laboratory. She has been involved in a variety of professional activities, including college and graduate-level instruction, social work case management, infant intervention, parent education, psychotherapy, administration of the Miami Child Protection Team, and instruction of normal and special education high school, elementary, and preschool students. Her current work involves theory development, clinical research and case consultation, graduate and postgraduate teaching, and development of clinical assessments for disorders of attachment.

Q: What sparked your interest in the area of child maltreatment?

A: Like many turns in my career, my interest in maltreatment was unintended but fortuitous. In the 1960s, I began working with low-income, disadvantaged children. As I worked my way down in age toward a greater focus on prevention, I began to work with infants at risk for developmental delay. As it turned out, most of the referrals were of maltreated infants and their mothers. Hence I needed to learn about child abuse and neglect.

Q: What would you describe as your most influential contribution to the field of child maltreatment?

A: I wish I could say that I changed people's views of maltreating adults to a nonblaming, compassionate attitude toward these individuals who are distressed themselves and who have been victimized far longer than their children. I think the United States, however, is still predominantly concerned with who

community sample of parents who were not identified through reporting or referral. Their results suggest that reporting biases do not completely explain the relationship between SES and child neglect. Individuals who self-identified as neglectful in Chaffin et al.'s study had lower scores on an SES composite score than did parents who did not self-identify as neglectful. In addition, SES remained a significant predictor of child neglect when the researchers controlled for other social and psychiatric risk factors. The impact of SES in the analysis was relatively weak, however, suggesting that SES may play only a small role with regard to risk for child neglect when other factors are considered.

Community integration and social support. Social factors such as a family's level of community integration

and social support may also play a role in child neglect. Polansky, Ammons, and Gaudin (1985) found that, compared with a control group, neglecting mothers were less involved in informal helping networks, exhibited less participation in social activities, and described themselves as more "lonely." In addition to reporting less involvement in social networks, neglecting mothers perceived themselves as less supported in terms of receiving material aid as well as advice and guidance from others, and in terms of being included in social activities (Williamson et al., 1991). Polansky, Gaudin, Ammons, and Davis (1985) also investigated perceptions of social support for neglecting families by interviewing 152 neglecting and 154 nonneglecting families receiving Aid to Families with Dependent Children (AFDC). They compared responses of families officially did what to whom and whether it was right or wrong. So, at one level, I think I have fallen short in my intended goal of helping others to understand developmental processes in a nonjudgmental and compassionate way. Possibly, however, I have assisted others to see patterns in children's behavior that were not formerly apparent. That is, I hope I have assisted professionals in seeing the strategic and self-protective organization that underlies some disturbed behavior, as well as the pain that underlies some apparently "resilient" behavior.

Q: What should communities do to assist child victims of maltreatment?

A: I think our society has become too focused on children as "victims" of child maltreatment. Conceptualizing oneself as a victim is not good for one's mental health and does not do justice to the active coping strategies used by children who have been endangered. We need to (a) look at what mal-treated children do to cope with their situations, (b) create nonthreatening environments for maltreated children, and (c) teach maltreated children to recognize the difference between the two (thus enabling them to develop strategies for safety). Further, any real help for the great majority of maltreated children must include assistance to their parents. Unfortunately, because we think of children as victims, parents are consequently labeled as perpetrators. As a result, we become tempted to punish such "perpetrators" and thus reduce our ability to help either the parents or their children. If we eliminate the notion of victims, we can view all people as individuals having to cope with a range of dangers. This perspective would promote supporting endangered parents and children so that they might live in safer environments and learn to use strategies suitable for safety. Put another way, I think we need a strengths approach to troubled families.

Q: What should be done to diminish child maltreatment?

A: I would focus on prevention by making environments safe at the cultural/community level, by supporting couples to make family life safe, and by teaching parents and children strategies for reduc-ing danger. Although I resist single-issue approaches, the prevention of child maltreatment demands both severe reduction of firearms in homes and also wide use of birth control. The teaching of strate-gies for safe interpersonal behavior should begin in kindergarten and continue to graduation as a basic part of the curriculum on family life (in the positive sense, not as techniques for identifying, reporting, and protecting oneself from abuse). Universal screening of mother-infant dyads at 6 weeks, 15 to 18 months, and 30 months could help focus group and individual prevention efforts. In all cases, I would respect parents enough to understand their goals and to assist them to find more effec-tive means of meeting them. Concurrently, I would cease to respond punitively toward parents who harm their children and would reduce greatly the use of foster care while increasing equally the avail-ability of family-centered intervention. If forced to choose between prevention and extensive treat-ment, I would choose prevention. No other choice has the possibility of reducing the problem of child maltreatment in the future.

designated as neglecting, a comparison group of non-neglecting AFDC families, and a group of adults who were the next-door neighbors of the neglecting families. They found that neglectful mothers viewed their neighborhoods as less supportive than did both their next-door neighbors and the comparison mothers. In contrast, Chaffin and colleagues (1996) did not find differences between self-identified neglectful and nonneglectful mothers and fathers on a self-report measure of availability of confidants. The inconsistency in these findings may be due to methodological issues (e.g., assessing mothers only versus both mothers and fathers; assessing referred versus nonreferred neglect-ing adults) or to the specific type of social support investigated. The availability of assistance and advice with regard to child care may be more salient for neglecting parents than the availability of confidants (Schumacher et al., 2001a).

SECTION SUMMARY

Official estimates of child neglect, despite their limita-tions, provide most of the available information on the subject. Research has demonstrated that the majority of children reported for neglect are under the age of 5 and that risk for and severity of child neglect generally decrease with age. Studies have found no appreciable differences between genders in rates of child neglect. Furthermore, the role of racial differences is unclear because of confounding factors such as SES and methodological difficulties.

Official statistics concerning demographic, psychological, and behavioral characteristics of neglecting parents are preliminary and so should be viewed cautiously. One of the strongest predictors of child neglect is economic disadvantage, and low-income families with unemployed parents and children residing in single-female-headed households are at greatest risk. Consistent findings indicate that neglecting mothers have low levels of positive interactions with their children and high levels of emotional and psychological distress. The most consistent findings with regard to family and community factors suggest that neglecting families exhibit high levels of daily stress and family stress and low levels of community integration and social support. Future studies should attempt to replicate current findings while improving methodology and should also evaluate the characteristics of fathers in neglecting families.

CONSEQUENCES ASSOCIATED WITH CHILD NEGLECT

Although considerable research has evaluated the negative consequences associated with other forms of child maltreatment, relatively little has examined the unique effects of child neglect on children's functioning. The limited research in this area is surprising given that child neglect is the most frequently reported form of child maltreatment and can have serious consequences for children. Indeed, child neglect may be associated with more serious harm than physical or sexual abuse (e.g., Erickson & Egeland, 2002; Ney, Fung, & Wickett, 1994).

The findings of many of the studies conducted to date on the effects of child neglect are of limited usefulness because of small sample sizes, the use of unstandardized measures, definitional variability, and the lack of comparison groups. An additional problem is that the victim samples in most studies have been heterogeneous—that is, they have included victims not only of child neglect but of other forms of abuse. The overlap that exists between various forms of child maltreatment represents a general problem for this kind of research. Because many children experience more than one of the major forms of maltreatment (e.g., physical abuse and child neglect) as well as subtypes of maltreatment (e.g., physical neglect as well as emotional neglect), it is difficult to determine which

specific effects are associated with the various forms of child neglect.

Most studies that have examined the effects associated with child neglect have focused on developmental outcomes for infants, children, and adolescents (for reviews, see Crouch & Milner, 1993; Hildyard & Wolfe, 2002). Collectively, these studies have consistently uncovered several problems associated with child neglect, including social difficulties, intellectual deficits, emotional and behavioral problems, and physical consequences. Many of these problems manifest in unique form when compared with problems associated with child physical abuse (Hildyard & Wolfe, 2002). In addition, evidence is accumulating that suggests that the effects associated with child neglect may endure into adulthood. Table 5.3 provides a summary of the possible negative effects that have been found to be associated with child neglect.

Developmental Considerations

Because children are rapidly developing and changing, any examination of the effects associated with child neglect should consider the age and developmental level of the child. Some researchers have attempted to tease out the effects of development by using cross-sectional research designs to examine outcome differences among children of various ages at one point in time (e.g., evaluating academic difficulties among preschoolers, school-age children, and adolescents who have all experienced neglect). Others have examined neglected children using longitudinal study designs, following children for long periods across different stages of development. One example of a developmentally sensitive study is the Minnesota Mother-Child Project, a prospective longitudinal study that followed the development of 267 children born to first-time mothers identified as being at risk for parenting problems (Egeland, 1997). In this study, the researchers identified several child maltreatment groups as well as a comparison group of nonmaltreated children. They then defined two of the child maltreatment groups as neglected based on maternal behaviors. "Neglectful" mothers included those who were *physically neglectful* (e.g., failed to provide adequate physical care or protection for their children) as well as those who were *emotionally neglectful* (e.g., exhibited emotional detachment and unresponsiveness to their children's needs for care). The researchers assessed neglected children and a comparison group of nonmaltreated children during different developmental periods,

Table 5.3   Possible Negative Effects Associated With Child Neglect

Effects	*Examples*
Social and attachment difficulties	Disturbed parent-child attachment (e.g., anxious and disorganized) Disturbed parent-child interactions (e.g., child is passive and withdrawn; parent exhibits low sensitivity to and involvement with child) Disturbed peer interactions (e.g., deficits in prosocial behavior, social withdrawal, isolation, few reciprocal friendships)
Cognitive and academic deficits	Receptive and expressive language deficits Low academic achievement and grade repetitions Deficits in overall intelligence Low level of creativity and flexibility in problem solving Deficits in language comprehension and verbal abilities
Emotional and behavioral problems	Apathy and withdrawal Low self-esteem Ineffective coping Difficulty recognizing and discriminating emotion Negative affect (e.g., anger, frustration) Physical and verbal aggression Attention problems Conduct problems and noncompliance Personality disorder symptoms Psychiatric symptoms (e.g., anxiety and depression)
Physical consequences	Death Failure to thrive
Long-term consequences	Cognitive deficits (e.g., low IQ scores and reading ability) Illegal behavior (e.g., delinquency, prostitution, violent assault) Psychiatric disorders (e.g., dysthymia, PTSD, major depressive disorder, disruptive disorders, antisocial personality disorder) Alcohol problems

SOURCES: A representative but not exhaustive list of sources for the information displayed in this table includes the following: Bolger et al. (1998); Cohen et al. (2001); de Paul and Arruabarrena (1995); Erickson and Egeland (2002); Hildyard and Wolfe (2002); Kaufman and Widom (1999); Kendall-Tackett and Eckenrode (1996); Manly et al. (2001); Pollak et al. (2000); Widom (1999); Widom and Kuhns (1996); Williamson et al. (1991).

including infancy, preschool, elementary school, and adolescence. The results of the Minnesota Mother-Child Project and similar developmentally sensitive studies suggest that the experience of child neglect results in significant developmental problems that are cumulative across development and that the negative outcomes are similar across developmental stages (Hildyard & Wolfe, 2002).

Social and Attachment Difficulties

One of the most frequently cited problems associated with child neglect is difficulty in social adjustment.

As evidence of such difficulties, a number of studies suggest a relationship between neglect and disturbed patterns of infant-caretaker attachment. Mothers and children in the Minnesota Mother-Child Project, for example, participated in a series of situations designed to allow the researchers to assess the quality of attachment between mother and child during the first 2 years of life (Egeland & Sroufe, 1981; Egeland, Sroufe, & Erickson, 1983). Investigators observed mother-infant pairs during several interactions, including feeding and play situations, a stressful situation in which a stranger was introduced into the environment, and a problem-solving task. Results indicated that, compared with children in the control group, a significantly higher proportion of neglected children were anxiously attached (e.g., overly dependent, clingy, and prone to crying) at both 12 and 18 months, and the social difficulties these children experienced continued throughout elementary school (Erickson & Egeland, 2002). Recent evidence suggests that in addition to **anxious attachment** styles, child neglect is associated with disorganized styles of attachment (Hildyard & Wolfe, 2002). Other indications of disturbed parent-child interactions have appeared, demonstrating the deficits in communication, increased aggression, and poor involvement characteristic of the interactions between neglecting mothers and their children (Bousha & Twentyman, 1984; Christopoulos, Bonvillian, & Crittenden, 1988; Crittenden, 1992a).

Neglected children also show deficits in peer interactions and social adjustment, with many exhibiting more socially withdrawn behavior, decreased prosocial behavior, greater conflict with friends, and fewer reciprocated friendships than nonneglected children (e.g., Bolger, Patterson, Kupersmidt, 1998; Crittenden, 1992a; Prino & Peyrot, 1994). Crittenden (1992a), for example, observed children interacting with their siblings and found that neglected children tended to be more isolated than nonneglected children during periods of free play.

Cognitive and Academic Deficits

An additional area of functioning often affected by neglect in childhood is intellectual ability. Findings from a large group of studies comparing neglected infants, children, and adolescents with matched comparisons have indicated that neglect victims show deficits in language abilities, academic skills, intelligence, and problem-solving skills (e.g., Erickson & Egeland, 2002; Kendall-Tackett & Eckenrode, 1996; Wodarski, Kurtz, Gaudin, & Howing, 1990). Wodarski et al. (1990), for example, evaluated 139 school-age and adolescent physically abused, neglected, and nonmaltreated children and found that both neglected and abused children evidenced significantly poorer overall school performance and math skills than their nonmaltreated peers. The neglected children, but not the abused children, also had lower scores on measures of language and reading skills than did the nonmaltreated children. These intellectual deficits continued even after the researchers controlled for the influence of socioeconomic disadvantage. In addition, a 3-year follow-up study demonstrated that these patterns in performance were generally stable over time (Kurtz, Gaudin, Wodarski, & Howing, 1993). Based on their review of developmental outcomes associated with child neglect, Hildyard and Wolfe (2002) conclude that neglected children generally display more severe cognitive and academic deficits than do children who have been physically abused.

Emotional and Behavioral Problems

Child neglect victims frequently exhibit emotional and behavioral difficulties. Studies have demonstrated that neglectful mothers are more likely than nonmaltreating mothers to rate their children as having behavioral problems in general (Erickson & Egeland, 2002; Rohrbeck & Twentyman, 1986; Williamson et al., 1991). Researchers have also documented differences in specific behavioral and emotional problems between nonneglected and neglected adolescent, school-age, and preschool children (e.g., Johnson, Smailes, Cohen, Brown, & Bernstein, 2000; Manly, Kim, Rogosch, & Cicchetti, 2001; Shields, Ryan, & Cicchetti, 2001; Toth, Cicchetti, Macfie, Maughan, & Vanmeenen, 2000; see Table 5.3). Neglected children have also been found to have difficulty in recognizing and discriminating the emotions (e.g., happiness, sadness) of others (Pollak, Cicchetti, Hornung, & Reed, 2000). In summarizing the findings of their longitudinal research on physically and emotionally abused and neglected children, Egeland et al. (1983) say about the neglect group, "This is an unhappy group of children, presenting the least positive and the most negative affect of all groups" (p. 469).

In contrast, other researchers have failed to find differences in behavioral and emotional adjustment between neglected and nonmaltreated children(e.g., Rohrbeck & Twentyman, 1986; Wodarski et al., 1990). These conflicting findings demonstrate the difficult nature of studying the complex effects associated with child neglect. One reason for the differences in findings could be sampling variability. Studies that have not found differences in adjustment between neglected and nonmaltreated children, for example, might have used samples of less severely neglected children than did studies in which such differences were evident. Bias may be another reason for the differences in findings. Differences found between groups may be accounted for by the fact that neglected children are likely to come from low socioeconomic groups, which experience high levels of environmental stress. The behavioral differences observed could be due to SES rather than to neglect per se. Wodarski and colleagues (1990), for example, found no substantial differences between neglected and nonmaltreated children on measures of overall behavioral functioning or on measures assessing specific behaviors (e.g., self-concept, aggression, self-help skills, and delinquency) after they controlled for SES.

Physical Consequences

Child neglect also has physical consequences for victims. The most serious physical consequence, of course, is death. In 2001, an estimated 1,300 children died in the United States as a result of child abuse and neglect. Of these, approximately 36% died as the result of child neglect, the form of maltreatment most often associated with death (U.S. DHHS, 2003a). An additional physical consequence often associated with neglect is **failure to thrive** (FTT), a syndrome characterized by marked retardation or cessation of growth during the first 3 years of life (Kempe, Cutler, & Dean, 1980). Because FTT also includes nonphysical components, its designation as a consequence of physical neglect versus psychological maltreatment is controversial (for more on this, see Box 5.2).

Box 5.2 Failure to Thrive

One of the most extreme consequences of child maltreatment is a clinical disorder known as *failure to thrive*. This term was initially coined to describe infants and young children hospitalized or living in institutions in the early 1900s who exhibited marked deficits in growth as well as such abnormal behaviors as withdrawal, apathy, excessive sleep, unhappy facial expressions, and self-stimulatory behaviors, including body rocking or head banging (e.g., Bakwin, 1949; Kempe & Goldbloom, 1987). Some cases of FTT are organic in nature, resulting from kidney or heart disease, for example. More controversial are FTT cases believed to be nonorganic in nature, resulting from "psychosocial diseases" such as physical and emotional neglect.

Although most experts agree that nonorganic FTT results from psychosocial difficulties that reduce a child's caloric intake, the nature of the psychosocial difficulties has been the subject of considerable debate. Some professionals focus on the physical aspects of the syndrome, such as the lack of nutrients, and therefore view FTT as primarily a medical condition resulting from physical child neglect (e.g., adult caretakers' failure to supply a child with adequate food and nutrition). Medical professionals have operationalized the physical aspects of FTT as height and weight gain below the third to the fifth percentile on standardized growth charts of expected development (e.g., Kerr, Black, & Krishnakumar, 2000; Marino, Weinman, & Soudelier, 2001). FTT has traditionally been viewed as a physical or medical condition because the physical problems associated with the syndrome (e.g., malnutrition) often bring the child to the attention of medical professionals.

Mental health professionals, in contrast, have begun to focus on the psychological aspects of FTT, such as lack of stimulation in the child's environment and disrupted mother-child relationships. From this viewpoint, FTT is primarily a psychological condition resulting from emotional neglect. Numerous studies have demonstrated a relationship between nonorganic FTT and maternal deprivation or disturbed mother-child interactions (e.g., Ward, Lee, & Lipper, 2000). Researchers who have evaluated differences between nonorganic FTT infants and normally developing infants, for example, have found that the interactions between FTT children and their mothers are characterized by negative behavior and affect, mother's insensitivity toward the child, and discomfort between mother and child (e.g., Ayoub & Milner, 1985; Benoit, 1993; Hegar & Yungman, 1989). Drotar, Eckerle, Satola, Pallotta, and Wyatt (1990) found that mothers of nonorganic FTT infants demonstrated less adaptive social interactional behavior, less positive affect, and more arbitrary terminations of feedings than did mothers in a control group. Disturbed patterns of attachment also characterize the mother-child relationships of FTT children. Wekerle and Wolfe (1996) found that more than 90% of FTT children in their sample exhibited insecure attachments to their mothers, compared with less than 50% of non-FTT children.

Theoretical and research advances have broadened conceptual understanding of nonorganic FTT. Although most studies of FTT have focused on mothers as parents, for example, some research suggests that fathers also play a significant role. Gagan, Cupoli, and Watkins (1984) found that the family dynamics associated with nonorganic FTT are characterized by both maternal and paternal deprivation. To gain a broader understanding of FTT, researchers should focus on the role of parental deprivation as well as on deficits in the parent-child relationship.

Kempe and Goldbloom (1987) have argued that the term *nonorganic FTT* should be replaced with *malnutrition due to neglect*, as the latter term is more likely to direct professionals to "more precise descriptions of deficits in nutrition and growth, weight and height levels, and the individual developmental and behavioral characteristics of a given child" (p. 312). Many scholars have additionally argued that diverse factors interact to cause nonorganic FTT, including a number of environmental variables related to feeding and nurturance in addition to organic factors (e.g., Dubowitz & Black, 2002; Hathaway, 1989; Lachenmeyer & Davidovicz, 1987). Additional environmental variables that appear to be related to nonorganic FTT include parents' lack of education or knowledge about child rearing as well as conditions associated with poverty (Marino et al., 2001). Efforts to develop treatments for nonorganic FTT should focus not only on enhancing a child's nutritional status and improving the parent-child relationship but on additional environmental variables as well.

Long-Term Consequences

Very few studies have examined the unique effects of neglect in childhood on long-term adult functioning. Based on findings from the few studies that do exist, it is evident that many of the psychological and social difficulties that emerge in neglected children are also evident in adults with histories of childhood neglect. Much of what is known about the long-term effects associated with child neglect comes from the prospective longitudinal research of Widom and her colleagues. Recall from the discussion in Chapter 3 on the consequences of child physical abuse that these researchers compared a sample of validated cases of child abuse and neglect (identified 20 years earlier by social service agencies) with a sample of matched comparisons. Over much of the course of their study, however, the investigators did not distinguish between individuals with histories of abuse and those with histories of neglect. Their findings demonstrated a link between child maltreatment and deficits in cognitive abilities (e.g., lower intelligence test scores and reading ability), increased illegal behavior (e.g., delinquency, criminal behavior, violent criminal behavior), and increased likelihood of running away from home (Kaufman & Widom, 1999; Perez & Widom, 1994; Widom, 1989a; Widom & Kuhns, 1996).

Other studies investigating the long-term effects of child neglect have examined the relationship between maltreatment in childhood and personality and psychiatric disorders in adulthood. Widom and colleagues once again provide much of the evidence, which links child neglect with dysthymia, antisocial personality disorder, and alcohol problems in adults, although once the researchers controlled for stressful life events, they found that childhood maltreatment had little impact on mental health outcome (Horwitz, Widom, McLaughlin, & White, 2001). Widom (1999) also found evidence of lifetime PTSD in her sample of adults who had experienced child neglect specifically. Additional prospective longitudinal studies have also confirmed the presence of various psychiatric diagnoses in adults with histories of child neglect. Cohen, Brown, and Smailes (2001), for example, assessed mental disorders from early childhood to adulthood in a community sample of individuals who were later identified by official reports. Findings indicated that adults with official records of child neglect exhibited elevated symptoms of disruptive disorders and major depressive disorder relative to adults in the normative sample. The cases of child neglect in this study, however, showed some partial remission in symptoms from adolescence to adulthood.

SECTION SUMMARY

Relative to other forms of maltreatment, less research has examined the unique effects of child neglect on children's functioning, although an increasing number of methodologically sound investigations are appearing. This oversight is troubling, given the high frequency with which neglect occurs and the serious consequences associated with this form of child maltreatment. Available research to date suggests that child neglect is associated with a variety of problems, including social difficulties, cognitive and academic deficits, behavioral and emotional problems, and physical dysfunction. Studies that have evaluated child neglect victims of various ages (e.g., infants, school-age children, and adolescents) consistently demonstrate that experiences of child neglect result in significant developmental problems and negative outcomes that are similar across developmental stages. Research also indicates that the effects associated with child neglect are cumulative and extend into adulthood. Long-term effects that have been documented include cognitive deficits, illegal behaviors, and psychiatric disturbances. Future studies should continue to be sensitive to developmental issues and also attend to additional variables potentially associated with child neglect outcome, such as the victim's gender, the severity of neglect, and various subtypes of neglect.

PRACTICE, POLICY, AND PREVENTION ISSUES

Treatment of Child Neglect

Researchers and practitioners have proposed few interventions that are unique to child neglect versus other forms of abuse (for reviews, see Becker et al., 1995; Corcoran, 2000; Kolko, 1998). Indeed, many of the interventions described previously (e.g., interventions with adults to enhance parenting skills, interventions with children to reduce effects associated with maltreatment, economic assistance, and multiservice interventions) have been suggested for child neglect. In addition, much of the research directed at interventions specifically for neglected children and their families has suffered from a variety of methodological limitations, including single-subject research designs, exceedingly small sample sizes, nonstandardized assessment methods, and biased samples (Gaudin, 1993). Another limitation is that most intervention programs directed at neglect include services for parents but offer few direct services for children (Cohn & Daro, 1987; Kolko, 1998). Available interventions for neglected children focus primarily on improving their social interaction skills. There appears to be consensus among researchers and clinicians in the field that currently available interventions intended to address child neglect are ineffective, being successful with no more than 50% of neglecting families (Erickson & Egeland, 2002; Gaudin, 1993).

Despite these limitations, one approach to intervention that has shown promise with neglecting families is the parent-directed approach. Intervention programs taking this approach use behavioral techniques to teach neglecting parents specific skills. Lutzker, Lutzker, Braunling-McMorrow, and Eddleman (1987), for example, investigated the use of simple prompts to increase appropriate affective responses by mothers during interactions with their children. Mothers who received prompts to increase affective responses demonstrated more affective responses with their children than did mothers who received no prompting. Other studies have demonstrated that training can result in skills improvements in neglecting mothers, including problem-solving skills, personal hygiene skills, nutrition skills, and infant stimulation skills (e.g., Dawson, DeArmas, McGrath, & Kelly, 1986; Lutzker, Campbell, & Watson-Perczel, 1984; Lutzker, Megson, Dachman, & Webb, 1985; Sarber, Halasz, Messmer, Bickett, & Lutzker, 1983). Neglecting mothers have also learned to reduce the numbers of hazards in their homes (Barone, Greene, & Lutzker, 1986).

Another form of intervention for neglecting families that has proven effective is the promotion of social support (for a review, see DePanfilis, 1996). Given that social isolation and lack of social support have been identified as significant risk factors for child maltreatment, some programs have been designed to increase the social support available to neglecting families. Although research examining the effectiveness of such programs is limited, a variety of approaches to enhancing the social connections of neglecting families appear promising. These range from programs that teach parents how to establish and maintain their own social support systems to programs that provide social support to families individually, in the form of personal parent aides (e.g., DiLeonardi, 1993; Witt & Sheinwald, 1992). Given the limited social competency of neglectful parents, Crittenden (1996) recommends that programs use as few individuals as possible to deliver such services to a family and that they deliver the services for an extended period.

Multiservice intervention approaches are ideal for neglecting families because of the multiproblem nature of such families (Daro, 1988; Fortin & Chamberland, 1995). Multiservice interventions typically include the delivery of a broad range of services, including individual, family, and group counseling; social support services; behavioral skills training to eliminate problematic behavior; and parenting education. An example of this type of program is Project SafeCare, which provides, among other services, training in safety and accident prevention and the promotion of healthy parent-child interactions (cited in Kolko, 1998).

Evaluation studies of such programs have reported some positive results. Evaluations of a series of multiservice projects funded by the NCCAN and directed at chronically neglectful families have found that a combination of parenting groups, intensive in-home counseling, and supportive interventions (e.g., paraprofessional aides) has been effective in improving neglectful parenting practices (Landsman, Nelson, Allen, & Tyler, 1992). Other research has shown family-focused, multiservice projects to be effective interventions for neglecting families (e.g., Daro, 1988; Lutzker, 1990a; Wesch & Lutzker, 1991). Two studies suggest, however, that the outcomes of interventions for neglecting families are less positive than the outcomes of interventions aimed at abusive families or families of delinquents (Berry, 1991; Yuan & Struckman-Johnson, 1991). At present, it is unclear why these differences exist.

Prevention of Child Neglect

Emmanuelle, an 18-year-old high school senior, was desperate. The father of her child had abandoned her, she was unable to support herself and her child with her waitress job, and her family was unwilling to help. With nowhere to turn, she left her two-and-one-half-year-old child at a Brooklyn hospital with a note:

To Whom It May Concern:

I am an 18-year-old student and I also work. I can't handle the pressure. I sometimes take it out on her. I love her and would not like to hurt her. Please find her a good home where she'll get the love she desires.

The next day Emmanuelle realized she had made a mistake and called the hospital to ask for her baby back. When she arrived, she was arrested and charged with child abandonment. (Fontana & Moohnan 1994, pp. 227–228)

For Fontana and Moohnan (1994), the case of Emmanuelle illustrates the need for societal intervention in cases of child neglect rather than punishment. Emmanuelle was a young mother with no support. When her cries for help were not heard, she chose to abandon her baby at the hospital. When she realized she had made a mistake, she was arrested. Fontana and Moohnan argue that with help, Emmanuelle might have been able to care for her child, whereas prosecuting her merely put "one more young woman in jail and another child in the city's already overstretched foster care system" (p. 229). In addition, Emmanuelle's situation sent a message to other needy parents: "Don't dare come out and ask for help, because you'll be thrown into prison and your baby will be taken away! Stay in your closet and beat up your kid or get rid of her. You'll be safer that way!" (p. 229).

According to Wekerle and Wolfe (1998), in recent years there has been a shift away from sickness or evil models that emphasize legal punishments for neglecting parents and toward a contextual approach that emphasizes parental competence and relieving parental stress. This shift in perspective is evident, for example, in the passage of "safe-haven" laws in the majority of U.S. states in recent years. These laws allow biological mothers to give up their newborn infants anonymously in specific safe locations (e.g., hospitals, fire stations) with full immunity from prosecution. Since 1999, when Texas's "Baby Moses" safe-haven law was passed, more than 40 other states have passed similar legislations. Although such laws have their detractors, they do provide a solution that protects children from abandonment that could lead to death.

Research examining contextual approaches to preventing child neglect that emphasize parental competence and relieving parental stress suggest that the best way to prevent neglect is to meet the needs of at-risk families. Many neglectful parents, for example, may not know how to be good parents or may be experiencing pressures that make effective parenting difficult. They may be young and immature, have economic pressures, and be socially isolated. They or their children may have physical problems, or their children may have especially difficult temperaments. Programs that teach parents how to be effective at the parenting role should help to reduce child neglect. Such programs could have some indirect benefits as well. According to attachment theory, child maltreatment is more common when the parent-child relationship is weak and unrewarding (Wekerle & Wolfe, 1998). As noted previously in this chapter, a significant proportion of child neglect victims are insecurely attached to a parent (e.g., the mother is not a responsive, nurturant, and sensitive caregiver), and any program that enhances parenting effectiveness in general should indirectly improve attachment bonds between parents and children, leading to lower rates of neglect.

Home visitation programs. Home visitation programs aimed at preventing child neglect typically connect at-risk parents with mentors who come to their homes and provide social support, parenting suggestions, and help with life decisions (for reviews, see Daro & Donnelly, 2002; Guterman, 2001). Although the specifics of the parental education and support efforts of such programs vary, the National Clearinghouse on Child Abuse and Neglect Information (1998b, p. 4) has identified several general goals:

- Increasing parents' knowledge about general child development, child management techniques, and positive family functioning
- Improving parents' overall child-rearing skills
- Increasing parents' empathy for and awareness of others' needs
- Improving the positive self-concept and self-esteem of all family members
- Improving family and parent-child communication
- Building family support and cohesion
- Increasing parents' knowledge about the triggers of abuse
- Increasing parents' use of nonviolent approaches to child discipline

Many home visitation programs attempt to identify high-risk parents in a community (i.e., those who are young, low-income, and single) and intervene during pregnancy, before the first child is born. Such programs, especially those that incorporate early intervention, are gaining considerable support. The U.S. Advisory Board on Child Abuse and Neglect has cited home visitation of at-risk parents as the one policy the government could implement right now to reduce rates of child maltreatment (Krugman, 1995). More than half of the nation's states currently have parent support initiatives under way. Early intervention programs have received not only considerable state and federal support, but the support of several important private foundations (such as the Carnegie Corporation of New York, the Commonwealth Fund, and the Ronald McDonald House Charities) (Daro, 1998).

One such effort, the Hawaii Healthy Start Program, began in 1985. The program is part of a series of programs known as Healthy Families America (HFA), a joint effort of the National Committee to Prevent Child Abuse and the Ronald McDonald House Charities (Daro, 1998). Initially created by the Hawaii Family Stress Center in Honolulu, the Healthy Start Program has since expanded across the state and now serves 50–55% of the state's population (Daro, McCurdy, & Harding, 1998). The program offers a variety of voluntary services to high-risk parents, as identified by a list of 15 demographic and socioeconomic factors (e.g., marital status, education, family support, limited prenatal care, and history of substance abuse). Although the specifics of individual HFA programs vary, in general they begin before at-risk mothers give birth, are intensive (at least once a week), and provide social support for parents as well as instruction on parenting and child development (Daro et al., 1998; Healthy Families America, 1994). HFA has a lofty goal: "to offer all new parents nation-wide support around the time their first baby is born" (Daro, 1998, p. 6). As of fall 1998, HFA programs were operating in two-thirds of U.S. states and more than 300 communities (Daro, 1998).

In a carefully controlled evaluation of the Hawaii Healthy Start Program, Daro et al. (1998) randomly assigned families who qualified for the program into one of two groups. Those families whose children had been born on even-numbered days were offered Healthy Start services, and those with children born on odd-numbered days were not offered services. Data collected 12 months after birth indicated that when compared with controls, Healthy Start mothers were more involved with their children and sensitive to their children's needs, and the children were more responsive to their mothers. Healthy Start children were also at less risk of physical abuse. A second component of the study examined long-term effects of the program by comparing the family functioning of former Healthy Start clients with established norms. Healthy Start families had average to above-average scores on measures of parental functioning, positive parent-child interaction, and social support. In addition, Daro et al. identified several less quantifiable results, including emotional and social support from the para-professional visitor, increased access to medical and child-care services, and information about child development and parenting. Only half of the parents reported using corporal punishment, for example, and those who did so tended to use mild forms (e.g., a slap on the hand). Some parents reported that others in their households (e.g., grandparents, partners, and friends) were critical that they did not use more corporal punishment.

Another well-known home visitation program centers on pairing young single mothers with public health nurses (Olds, Henderson, Tatelbaum, & Chamberlain, 1986). This program, the Prenatal/Early Infancy Project, began in the 1970s and is highly regarded as an important success story in child maltreatment prevention (Wekerle & Wolfe, 1998). Research suggests that poor, young, single parents are less likely than more affluent, older, and married parents to have healthy children and to be capable caregivers. The Prenatal/Early Infancy Project provides prenatal and early childhood services to young mothers to help them understand child health and development and to strengthen their confidence in themselves and in their capacity for change. Specifically, the program is designed to accomplish the following goals: (a) improve the health of the infant, (b) improve parental caregiving, and (c) provide life-course development support (e.g., educational, occupational, and pregnancy planning) (Olds, 1997). In the first implementation of the project, conducted in Elmira, New York, a nurse visited each mother an average of 9 times during the pregnancy and 23 times during the first 2 years of the child's life (Olds, 1997).

Research evaluating the effectiveness of home visitation programs has shown that such programs are generally successful in meeting many of their goals. Follow-up evaluations of the Prenatal/Early Infancy Project, for example, revealed that the mothers in the study spent more quality time with their children, were less likely to abuse their children, had fewer children, waited longer to have subsequent children, spent less time on welfare, and had fewer arrests than did mothers in the control group (Emery & Laumann-Billings, 1998;

Olds et al., 1986). Studies of other home visitation programs have found similar positive outcomes, including enhanced parenting knowledge and skills, fewer injuries to children, and less use of corporal punishment among program participants than among controls (for reviews, see Daro & McCurdy, 1994; Wekerle & Wolfe, 1993).

Despite these positive outcomes, however, many in the field remain cautiously optimistic about the potential of home visitation programs for preventing child maltreatment. Daro and Donnelly (2002) recently outlined several reasons "the full promise of prevention has yet to be realized" (p. 737). One limitation associated with home visitation programs, for example, is that a significant number of families drop out of treatment before service goals are fully met. In addition, there is little evidence that changes associated with participation in such programs continues over the long term. It is also unclear whether home visitation programs fulfill their broader goal of integrating families into their communities, so they can access community resources. It is important that researchers continue to examine these issues. In addition, future research should attempt to determine the specific conditions associated with program success, such as the types of families that benefit and the specific components of intervention that are effective. Some evidence indicates, for example, that families experiencing interparental abuse in addition to child abuse and neglect may receive limited benefits from participation in home visitation programs (Eckenrode et al., 2000).

Programs for parents with high-risk children. Also relevant, but far less common than the kinds of programs described above, are programs that attempt to prevent child neglect by helping parents of high-risk children. All other things being equal, children who are demanding, aggressive, or intense, or who cry a lot, are more likely to be victims of maltreatment than are children without these characteristics (Dore & Lee, 1999; Wekerle & Wolfe, 1998). It is important to remember, however, that characteristics of the child are only one factor among many that contribute to child neglect. Sidebotham and Heron (2003), for example, examined characteristics of children from a large cohort study that might predispose them to maltreatment. They found that although child factors were significant, parental attitudes toward their children played a more significant role in child maltreatment.

As discussed in Chapter 3, the interaction of difficult child behaviors and particular parent characteristics can lead to negative parent-child interactions. Helping parents learn how they can best respond to behaviorally challenging children should help to reduce abuse and neglect. In working with a sample of Dutch parents with irritable children, van den Boom (1994, 1995) observed that the parents often approached the children during times when the children were fussy and ignored the children when the fussiness stopped. Through time, the parent-child interactions became increasingly negative. To test his observations, van den Boom randomly assigned parents of irritable children into experimental and control groups. Parents in the experimental group attended information sessions and received home visitation, the purposes of which were to promote parent-child attachment and to teach parents how to respond to their children appropriately. Evaluations after 12 months and 18 months indicated that, compared with the control group, mothers in the experimental group were more responsive and attentive, and their children were more securely attached (van den Boom, 1994, 1995; cited in Wekerle & Wolfe, 1998).

CHAPTER SUMMARY

Child neglect is one of the most elusive forms of child maltreatment and, as a result, has received less attention than other forms. The vague nature of child neglect is evident in the fact that a significant proportion of the research devoted to this topic has focused on definitional issues. At present, no single definition of child neglect is universally accepted. Although experts generally agree on conceptual definitions of child neglect (i.e., failure to provide for a child's basic needs), little consensus exists regarding operational definitions.

Given these definitional complexities, the true incidence of child neglect is largely undetermined, as are the characteristics of child neglect victims. Researchers have obtained much of their information about rates and correlates of child neglect from official reports made to CPS agencies. Although such reports are limited for several reasons (e.g., lack of definitional consensus among researchers), it is clear that hundreds of thousands of cases of child neglect are reported each year in the United States. Child neglect is the most frequently reported form of child maltreatment, accounting for 45–55% of reported maltreatment cases. The majority of child neglect victims are under age 5, and the risk for neglect appears to decline as children become older. Children whose families are

experiencing a variety of financial stressors (e.g., low income and unemployment) are at higher risk than children in financially better-off families. For this form of child maltreatment there appears to be little difference in risk between boys and girls.

Studies that have examined the negative effects associated with child neglect have so far been limited in both number and quality, making the interpretation of findings difficult. Nonetheless, this research has consistently shown a variety of problems to be associated with child neglect, including social difficulties, intellectual deficits, and emotional and behavioral problems. Although many scholars believe that the negative effects of child neglect extend into adulthood, more research is needed to establish the relationship between childhood history of neglect and adjustment problems in adulthood.

In attempting to establish the causes of child neglect, researchers have often applied many of the same theories proposed to explain the physical and sexual abuse of children (e.g., environmental factors, parent-child interaction, and intergenerational transmission). Several studies have distinguished neglectful from nonneglectful parents on various characteristics. One consistent finding in families of neglect is that parent-child interactions are disturbed and parents have increased levels of stress, with few social supports and limited integration into the community. Neglecting parents are also characterized by low educational achievement and often have become parents at a young age. Further research is needed to determine additional factors contributing to child neglect, given that not all parents with the characteristics noted neglect their children.

Few intervention and prevention strategies have been devised to address the unique aspects of child neglect, and, as a result, research evaluating the effectiveness of interventions for victims of this form of maltreatment is limited. Preliminary efforts directed at neglecting parents have been effective in increasing positive parent-child interactions, improving parents' problem-solving abilities, and enhancing parents' personal hygiene and nutrition skills. Few programs offer services directly to neglected children, but research shows that some have been successful in improving such children's social interaction and developmental skills. Multiservice approaches to intervention have demonstrated some effectiveness. There is also evidence that home visitation programs targeting high-risk parents, as well as programs targeting parents with high-risk children, are generally effective in meeting many of their goals.

DISCUSSION QUESTIONS

1. Why is child neglect often referred to as the "most forgotten" form of child maltreatment? What factors have contributed to scholars' historical lack of interest in the topic of child neglect?

2. Why has defining child neglect been such a challenge? Discuss the roles of the following factors in definitions of child neglect: severity of consequences associated with neglect, frequency and duration of neglect, and cultural issues associated with neglect.

3. What are the various forms or subtypes of child neglect described in the research literature?

4. What is prenatal neglect? Should prenatal neglect be considered a form of child neglect?

5. What are the general characteristics of neglected children and their parents (e.g., demographic characteristics, psychological and behavioral characteristics, characteristics of family structure and functioning)? Describe a prototypical family of child neglect.

6. What role do social and community factors play in the problem of child neglect?

7. What are the short- and long-term effects (e.g., cognitive, behavioral, emotional) associated with child neglect?

8. What are the potential physical effects associated with child neglect? Describe FTT and distinguish between organic and nonorganic subtypes.

9. What are some of the intervention strategies currently being used to help neglected children and their families?

10. What are the primary components of home visitation programs? How effective are such programs in preventing child neglect?

RECOMMENDED READING

Chaffin, M., Kelleher, K., & Hollenberg, J. (1996). Onset of physical abuse and neglect: Psychiatric, substance abuse, and social risk factors from prospective community data. *Child Abuse & Neglect, 20,* 191–203.

Corcoran, J. (2000). Family interventions with child physical abuse and neglect: A critical review. *Children and Youth Services Review, 22,* 563–591.

Daro, D., & Donnelly, A. C. (2002). Charting the waves of prevention: Two steps forward, one step back. *Child Abuse & Neglect, 26,* 731–742.

Dubowitz, H. (Ed.). (1999). *Neglected children: Research, practice, and policy.* Thousand Oaks, CA: Sage.

Dubowitz, H., Black, M., Starr, R., & Zuravin, S. J. (1993). A conceptual definition of child neglect. *Criminal Justice and Behavior, 20,* 8–26.

Eckenrode, J., Ganzel, B., Henderson, C. R., Smith, E., Olds, D. L., Powers, J., Coles, R., Kitzman, H., & Sidora, K. (2000). Preventing child abuse and neglect with a program of nurse home visitation: The limiting effects of domestic violence. *Journal of the American Medical Association, 284,* 1385–1391.

Erickson, M. F., & Egeland, B. (2002). Child neglect. In J. E. B. Myers, L. Berliner, J. Briere, C. T. Hendrix, C. Jenny, & T. A. Reid (Eds.), *The APSAC handbook on child maltreatment* (2nd ed., pp. 3–20). Thousand Oaks, CA: Sage.

Hildyard, K. L., & Wolfe, D. A. (2002). Child neglect: Developmental issues and outcomes. *Child Abuse & Neglect, 26,* 679–695.

Horwitz, A. V., Widom, C. S., McLaughlin, J., & White, H. R. (2001). The impact of childhood abuse and neglect on adult mental health: A prospective study. *Journal of Health and Social Behavior, 42,* 184–201.

Schumacher, J. A., Slep, A. M. S., & Heyman, R. E. (2001). Risk factors for child neglect. *Aggression and Violent Behavior, 6,* 231–254.

6

CHILD PSYCHOLOGICAL MALTREATMENT

Case History: Tough Love or Psychological Maltreatment?

By most outward appearances, the Machnicks were a typical all-American family. Grady Machnick was a sergeant with the Los Angeles County Sheriff's Department, and Deborah Machnick was an elementary school principal. They were raising three children, including a 14-year-old boy, Grady Machnick's biological son and Deborah Machnick's stepson. The Machnicks lived in a two-story home in a well-kept Southern California neighborhood. In the fall of 2001, however, Orange County prosecutors charged Grady and Deborah Machnick with child abuse. At the time the charges were filed, Grady Machnick denied any inappropriate mistreatment of his son, and Machnick's attorney stated that "any actions that were taken were appropriate to the circumstances of disciplining a teenager."

The Machnicks' case made national headlines, in part because the circumstances were so unusual. Indeed, a deputy district attorney involved with the case stated, "It's very, very bizarre. I have not seen this type of conduct in my entire career." The allegations included the following:

- *The parents required the teenage boy to spend nights outside, sleeping on a dog mat, as punishment for not completing his homework.*
- *The parents did not allow the teen to use the bathroom located in the home, instead requiring him to use a public restroom at a nearby park.*
- *The parents poured water on the teen to wake him from sleep.*
- *The parents sent the teen to school with dog feces in his backpack as punishment for not cleaning up after the family dog.*
- *The parents forced the teen to strip and be photographed naked as a form of punishment.*
- *The parents forced the teen out of the house at 3:30 a.m. when the parents needed to go out because, they said, he could not be trusted in the home alone.*
- *The parents confiscated the teen's belongings (e.g., clean clothing) and required that he "earn" the items back through good behavior.*
- *The parents withheld the teen's lunch money.*

At trial, Grady and Deborah Machnick testified that they employed the parenting practices they did because they were attempting to discipline their defiant son. The teen reportedly earned poor grades in school, refused to help with chores at home, and was often caught lying and stealing (e.g., shoplifting, taking money from his parents). Grady Machnick summed up his son's behavior by testifying that his son "reminded him of inmates." Throughout their trial, the Machnicks insisted that their efforts at discipline were designed to keep their son from continuing to engage in questionable behavior.

In December 2002, the Machnicks were acquitted on felony charges of conspiring to abuse their teenage son. The jurors agreed that the parents' discipline was inappropriate and inconsistent with their own parenting practices, but they were reluctant to condemn the Machnicks' behavior as criminal or to judge the couple based on their own value systems. Although the jurors agreed that the Machnicks' behavior did not rise to the level of a felony, they could not agree on whether to convict the Machnicks of the lesser charge of misdemeanor child abuse. One juror who voted to convict both parents stated in an interview: "Breaking someone down mentally, that's what they tried to do. There were no bruises, but the whole behavior of Grady and Deborah was to break him down mentally."

In his closing argument, one of the Machnicks' attorneys described the couple's parenting behavior as follows: "It's not a great parenting technique. If you're grading, A, B, C, D or F, maybe it's an F. But it's not a crime." At the time of this writing, a judge has ruled in favor of the Machnicks' being retried on the lesser charge of misdemeanor child abuse, but the case has not gone forward.[1]

Most individuals have witnessed or heard about interactions between parents and their children that seemed inappropriate. The child whose parents are the subjects of this case history may not be physically or sexually abused or neglected. Despite the lack of overt physical aggression, sexual behavior, or physical signs of maltreatment in this case, however, most observers would probably agree that the type of interaction between parents and child described above is inappropriate and likely harmful. Cases such as this have led researchers to address child psychological maltreatment, a form of child maltreatment that differs from the other forms discussed in this volume.

Psychological maltreatment was not recognized as a distinct form of child maltreatment until quite recently. Historically, scholars have tended to marginalize child psychological maltreatment in much the same way they have marginalized child neglect. They have viewed psychological maltreatment as a side effect of other forms of abuse and neglect, rather than as a unique form of child maltreatment. O'Hagan (1993) articulates several reasons researchers may often have overlooked child psychological maltreatment, noting that psychological maltreatment is "slow and protracted, will create no stir, pose no threat of scandal nor media scrutiny, and has little political significance for the managers of child care bureaucracies" (p. 15).

What other explanations might there be for researchers' greater focus on child physical and sexual abuse than on psychological maltreatment? The most obvious answer is that physical abuse and, to a lesser degree, sexual abuse result in immediate and observable harm. The negative consequences of psychological maltreatment are much more elusive. A single act of psychological maltreatment is unlikely to result in significant and immediate harm, but the cumulative effects of this form of abuse are insidious. Research has shown that child psychological maltreatment is associated with negative consequences for victims that are just as serious, if not more so, than those related to physical and sexual abuse (Crittenden, 1992a; Ney, Fung, & Wickett, 1994).

Several scholars have suggested that psychological maltreatment may be the most destructive and pervasive form of child abuse (Brassard, Germain, & Hart, 1987; Garbarino, Guttman, & Seely, 1986). Imagine the potential consequences to children who grow up hearing constantly that they are worthless or stupid or ugly. Consider the potential damage to a child whose parents refuse to demonstrate love through physical affection. In what has become known as the Thomas theorem, famed social psychologist W. I. Thomas once concluded that *situations defined as real are real in their consequences* (Thomas & Thomas, 1928). In other words, when children regularly hear that they are worthless, stupid, unlovable, or ugly, they come to believe these things are true. After all, as sociologists and psychologists have discovered, individuals perceive themselves as others see them. Perhaps even more tragic, children who are exposed to such maltreatment may begin to *act* as though they are worthless, stupid, unlovable, or ugly.

Child psychological maltreatment has also received less attention than other forms of abuse because of the difficulties associated with defining this form of maltreatment. Defining child physical abuse and child sexual abuse involves some ambiguities, particularly at the less extreme ends of the two continua, but understanding what constitutes psychological maltreatment poses even greater problems. Where should the line be drawn between less-than-adequate parenting, or parental error, and psychological maltreatment? Many of the specific behaviors noted in definitions of psychological maltreatment are less "deviant" than the behaviors associated with other forms of child maltreatment. Many, if not most, parents ignore, criticize, or are unsupportive of their children from time to time. As a result, it is necessary to consider under what circumstances these behaviors constitute psychological maltreatment.

Related to definitional ambiguities is the problem of overlap between psychological maltreatment and other forms of child abuse. Psychological maltreatment rarely occurs in isolation as a "pure" form of maltreatment; rather, it often coexists with other forms of child maltreatment (e.g., Ney et al., 1994; Osofsky, 2003). This is a unique characteristic of psychological maltreatment, which in the broadest sense exists as a component of all forms of maltreatment. Some scholars have suggested that every form of child abuse and neglect includes a psychological maltreatment component, because every form might be potentially damaging to a child's feelings of self-worth and self-esteem (e.g., Hart & Brassard, 1991).

Given that child psychological maltreatment is a complicated phenomenon and has only recently been recognized as a social problem, it is not surprising that little information is available about the characteristics, consequences, and causes of this form of child maltreatment. The realization that psychological maltreatment may be the most pervasive and damaging form of child maltreatment, however, has spurred research interest in the topic in recent years. In the following sections, we first address the current state of knowledge regarding child psychological maltreatment. Much of the literature to date aims at clarifying definitional issues, and our discussion reflects that emphasis. Although research evaluating this form of maltreatment is in its infancy, we also attempt to address what the research so far reveals about children who experience psychological maltreatment, the characteristics of maltreating parents, and the consequences associated with psychological maltreatment. We conclude the chapter with descriptions of various prevention and intervention strategies that scholars have proposed to address the problem.

SCOPE OF THE PROBLEM

Recent community surveys indicate that Americans in general are concerned about the psychological maltreatment of children. The National Center for Prosecution of Child Abuse, for example, conducted a nationally representative public opinion poll between 1987 and 1992 and found that approximately 75% of adults who were surveyed during this period viewed "repeated yelling and swearing" at children as harmful to the children's well-being (Daro & Gelles, 1992).

Within the past decade, scholars have also increasingly recognized psychological maltreatment as a discrete form of child maltreatment worthy of scientific study (see Binggeli, Hart, & Brassard, 2001; Hart, Brassard, Binggeli, & Davidson, 2002; Loring, 1994).

In response to these new viewpoints, researchers have focused on defining the parameters of child psychological maltreatment and determining the magnitude of the problem. As is true of other forms of child maltreatment, two of the greatest challenges researchers face are those of reaching consensus regarding conceptual and operational definitions and determining the rates of the problem.

What Is Psychological Maltreatment?

- A mother locks her 3-year-old son in a dark attic as a method of punishment.
- A father shackles his 7-year-old son to his bed at night to prevent him from getting out of bed repeatedly.
- A mother says to her daughter, "You are the stupidest, laziest kid on earth. I can't believe you're my child. They must have switched babies on me at the hospital."
- A father tells his daughter that he will kill her new puppy if she or the puppy misbehaves.
- A mother and father provide alcohol and marijuana to their 16-year-old son.
- A mother refuses to look at or touch her child.
- A father repeatedly states to one of his children, "I don't love you."

Would you characterize the behaviors depicted in all of these vignettes as "abusive"? Why or why not? The difficulty in determining what behaviors constitute psychological maltreatment may contribute to the idea that psychological maltreatment is the most ambiguous form of child abuse (Daro, 1988). It is likely that nearly all parents, at some level, psychologically mistreat their children at some time by saying or doing hurtful things they later regret. Such mistakes are a characteristic of most intimate relationships. Few assert, however, that most children are victims of psychological maltreatment. How, then, does one determine when child psychological maltreatment has occurred? Which verbal interactions are abusive, which behaviors are psychologically neglecting, and which interactions are a necessary part of parenting?

Conceptual issues. Professionals have proposed many conceptual definitions for psychological maltreatment to guide research, clinical practice, and social policy. According to one generic definition, as offered by Hart, Brassard, and Karlson (1996), psychological maltreatment is a "repeated pattern of behavior that conveys to children that they are worthless, unloved, unwanted, only of value in meeting another's needs, or seriously threatened with physical or psychological violence" (p. 73). Much disagreement exists, however, about how psychological maltreatment should be operationally defined. This inconsistency stems, in part, from the variety of purposes to which definitions of psychological maltreatment are put (e.g., to make legal decisions, to conduct interventions with victims, to determine incidence figures). As a result, there is much debate and confusion in the literature regarding what exactly constitutes child psychological maltreatment.

Some researchers offer broad definitions and argue that child psychological maltreatment is pervasive. Some have suggested that psychological maltreatment is embedded in all major forms of child abuse and neglect (Garbarino et al., 1986; S. N. Hart et al., 1996; Hart, Germain, & Brassard, 1987). Others have suggested even broader definitions that include ecological factors such as racism, sexism, and war-zone environments (Hart et al., 1987; Jones & Jones, 1987). Such broad definitions are clearly problematic: At worst, they make everyone a victim of psychological maltreatment; at best, they fail to distinguish psychological maltreatment as a unique form of child maltreatment.

One conceptual dilemma that scholars face in defining psychological maltreatment is whether to focus on child outcomes or parental behaviors. Some, for example, have defined the results of such maltreatment as "mental injury" or "impaired psychological functioning and development" (Hamarman, Pope, & Czaja, 2002; Hart et al., 2002). Although research to date has documented a variety of emotional and psychological impairments in victims of psychological maltreatment (to be reviewed later in this chapter), several problems are associated with this approach. One of these is that a definition requiring demonstration of harm precludes the possibility of preventing the harm before it occurs (Glaser, 2002). In addition, definitions that require a harm standard fail to recognize that the harm associated with psychological maltreatment may not be evident immediately; it could take months or even years to develop. Despite these limitations, many U.S. states require evidence of harm in cases of child psychological maltreatment (Glaser, 2002).

Alternatively, child psychological maltreatment can be defined as a group of specific abusive behaviors on the part of adults. The American Professional Society on the Abuse of Children supports this approach in its recently published *Guidelines for the Psychosocial Evaluation of Suspected Psychological Maltreatment in Children and Adolescents* (1995). These guidelines list six categories of parental behaviors that constitute child psychological maltreatment:

- Spurning (e.g., verbal and nonverbal hostile rejecting/degrading behaviors)
- Terrorizing (e.g., caregiver behaviors that harm or threaten harm to a child or child's loved ones or possessions)
- Exploiting/corrupting (e.g., encouraging inappropriate behaviors in a child)
- Denying emotional responsiveness (e.g., ignoring a child's needs or failing to express positive affect toward a child)
- Isolating (e.g., denying a child opportunities to interact/communicate with others)
- Mental health/medical/educational neglect (e.g., failing to provide for a child's needs in these areas)

Although a growing body of empirical research has validated the usefulness and credibility of this approach (e.g., Hart et al., 2002), some experts have criticized this conceptualization on theoretical, conceptual, and empirical grounds (e.g., Glaser, 2002; McGee & Wolfe, 1991). Glaser (2002) has recently proposed an alternative framework for conceptualizing child psychological maltreatment that does not focus exclusively on either parent behaviors or child outcomes. Rather, Glaser's approach is based on various elements that constitute a child's psychosocial being and defines psychological maltreatment as the violation or failure to respect the elements of a child's psychosocial being. Every child, for example, is a social being and needs to experience interaction and communication with other human beings in a variety of settings. Parents who fail to respect this element of a child's psychological being (e.g., by isolating the child or by denying the child emotional responsiveness) are committing psychological maltreatment. This conceptual framework emphasizes the *interaction* between parent and child.

At the core of the conceptual problems associated with defining child psychological maltreatment is a lack of clarity concerning the meaning of the term *psychological*. There has been a great deal of disagreement among scholars regarding whether this term refers to behavior on the part of perpetrators or to the consequences that result for the child victim. McGee and Wolfe (1991) have constructed a matrix to explain the

Table 6.1 Conceptual Perspectives on Psychological Maltreatment

Consequences to the Child	Parent Behaviors	
	Physical	*Nonphysical*
Physical	Physical abuse	Psychological maltreatment
	Example: Choking a child results in injury to the child's trachea.	*Example:* A parent's lack of supervision results in a child's being poisoned.
Nonphysical	Psychological maltreatment	Psychological maltreatment
	Example: Repeatedly beating a child leads to low self-esteem in the child.	*Example:* Repeatedly yelling and screaming at a child leads to low self-esteem in the child.

SOURCE: Adapted from McGee and Wolfe (1991, p. 5).

multiple conceptual perspectives from which scholars view psychological maltreatment. Table 6.1 displays a modified version of this matrix, which shows various combinations and possibilities for understanding the concept of psychological maltreatment, depending on the type of parent behavior and the consequences to the child. As this matrix shows, parent behaviors can be physical or nonphysical and can result in either physical or nonphysical (e.g., psychological or emotional) consequences to the child. Parent behaviors that are physical and result in physical consequences (e.g., touching a child with a cigarette that results in a burn) fit the commonly accepted view of child physical abuse. According to McGee and Wolfe, researchers have defined psychological maltreatment using the remaining combinations of parenting behaviors and psychological outcomes. Some would classify as psychological maltreatment a situation in which a parent engages in physical behavior (e.g., touching a child with a cigarette) that results in physical as well as nonphysical outcomes (e.g., anxiety and fear) (e.g., Garbarino et al., 1986). On the basis of this model, additional physical behaviors carried out by parents (such as sexual abuse or physical neglect) that result in negative psychological outcomes would also be considered psychological maltreatment.

In contrast, some parental behaviors can be nonphysical in nature and still result in either physical or nonphysical harm to the child. For example, insensitive parenting (e.g., not responding to a child's needs for nurturance and attention), which is often labeled as a form of neglect (and which we describe in Chapter 5), has been linked to both physical (e.g., malnutrition) and nonphysical (e.g., deficits in cognitive development) negative outcomes in children. Finally, the combination of nonphysical parental behavior (e.g.,

swearing at a child) and nonphysical outcomes (e.g., decreased self-esteem) reflects the conceptualization of psychological maltreatment as a distinct or "pure" form of child maltreatment (Garbarino et al., 1986; McGee & Wolfe, 1991).

The consensus among those who have debated the conceptual issues is that psychological maltreatment should be defined primarily on the basis of specific parental behaviors rather than on the basis of the effects those behaviors may produce (Hamarman & Bernet, 2000). Some scholars who support this approach, however, also emphasize the need to consider secondarily the effect of maltreatment (Hart & Brassard, 1991). It might be difficult to define psychological maltreatment in the absence of information on its effects on child victims, given that parental behaviors lie on a continuum. Although not all parental behaviors consisting of criticism are abusive, for example, some may be. One way to distinguish between abusive and nonabusive behaviors might be to consider particular behaviors' negative effects on child development. Effects on child functioning, however, need to be determined by research, as do additional variables, such as the specific characteristics of psychologically maltreating behaviors (e.g., frequency, intensity, and duration; Hart & Brassard, 1991; McGee & Wolfe, 1991).

Subtypes of psychological maltreatment. In an effort to define specific parental behaviors more precisely, several researchers have developed organizational frameworks that identify various subtypes of psychological maltreatment (e.g., Baily & Baily, 1986; Garbarino et al., 1986; Hart & Brassard, 1991; O'Hagan, 1995). Table 6.2 summarizes many of the subtypes of child psychological maltreatment reported in the literature.

Table 6.2   Subtypes of Child Psychological Maltreatment

Subtype	Description	Examples
Rejecting	Verbal or symbolic acts that express feelings of rejection toward the child	Singling out a specific child for criticism and/or punishment Refusing to help a child Routinely rejecting a child's ideas
Degrading (i.e., verbally abusing)	Actions that deprecate a child	Insulting a child or calling a child names Publicly humiliating a child Constantly criticizing a child Continually yelling or swearing at a child
Terrorizing	Actions or threats that cause extreme fear and/or anxiety in a child	Threatening to harm a child Threatening to harm a child's loved one Exposing a child to spouse abuse Setting unrealistic expectations for a child, with threat of loss/harm Punishing a child by playing on normal childhood fears Threatening suicide or to leave a child
Isolating	Preventing a child from engaging in normal social activities	Locking a child in a closet or room Refusing to allow a child to interact with individuals outside the family Refusing to allow a child to interact with other relatives
Missocializing (i.e., corrupting)	Modeling, permitting, or encouraging antisocial behavior in a child	Encouraging delinquent behavior in a child Encouraging alcohol or substance abuse in a child Indoctrinating a child in racist values
Exploiting	Using a child for the needs, advantages, or profits of the caretaker	Treating a child as a surrogate parent Using a child for child pornography or prostitution Using a child to live the caretaker's unfulfilled dreams
Denying emotional responsiveness (i.e., ignoring)	Acts of omission whereby the caretaker does not provide a child with necessary stimulation and responsiveness	Behaving toward a child in a detached and uninvolved manner Interacting with a child only if absolutely necessary Failing to express affection, caring, and love toward a child Refusing to look at a child or call a child by name
Close confinement	Restricting a child's movement by binding limbs	Tying a child's arms and legs together Tying a child to a chair, bed, or other object
Other	Forms of psychological maltreatment not specified under other categories	Withholding food, shelter, sleep, or other necessities from a child as a form of punishment Chronically applying developmentally inappropriate expectations to a child (sometimes referred to as *overpressuring*)

SOURCES: A representative but not exhaustive list of sources for the information displayed in this table includes the following: Baily and Baily (1986); Garbarino et al. (1986); Hart and Brassard (1991); Hart et al. (1987); U.S. DHHS (1988).

Scholars have consistently identified eight subtypes: rejecting, degrading (i.e., verbally abusing), terrorizing, isolating, missocializing (i.e., corrupting), exploiting, denying emotional responsiveness (i.e., ignoring), and close confinement.

An example of an organizational framework is the typological system provided in the third National Incidence Study (NIS-3; Sedlak & Broadhurst, 1996), which distinguished among various forms of psychological maltreatment, including psychological forms of abuse as well as neglect. *Emotional abuse* included close confinement and verbal or emotional assault as well as miscellaneous other behaviors. *Close confinement* referred to torturous restriction of movement, such as tying a child's limbs together or tying a child to a heavy object. *Verbal or emotional assault* included belittling, denigrating, threatening harm, and other forms of hostile or rejecting treatment. Other miscellaneous behaviors included extreme forms of punishment (e.g., withholding food or sleep) and economic exploitation (e.g., prostitution). *Emotional neglect* included a variety of behaviors ranging from inadequate nurturance and affection to permitted drug or alcohol abuse. *Psychological neglect* was defined as allowing a child to witness extreme or chronic domestic violence, permitting maladaptive behavior (e.g., chronic delinquency), and refusing or delaying obtainment of needed psychological treatment for a child.

The typology displayed in Table 6.2 illustrates the subjective nature of definitions of child psychological maltreatment. Definitions and typological systems represent compilations of the various behaviors and circumstances that researchers in the field have identified. As such, these conceptualizations reflect the values of those who created them, with various advocates and researchers determining the types of parent-child interactions that "should be" considered inappropriate. For example, one researcher may see "refusing to help a child" as abusive, whereas another may see such behavior on the part of a parent as important in helping a child gain independence.

McGee and Wolfe (1991) offer criticisms of several other current typologies of child psychological maltreatment. The psychological maltreatment subtypes in some typologies, they argue, fail to include all potentially psychologically abusive and neglectful behaviors. Some typologies omit inconsistent parenting practices, for example, despite the research demonstrating the detrimental effects of such inconsistency on children's development. Another problem with many classification systems is that the subtypes are not mutually exclusive: One behavior can be categorized under more than one subtype. Insulting a child by shouting, "You're nothing but a fat, lazy pig," for instance, could be considered not only an act of degrading but also an act of rejecting. McGee and Wolfe's final criticism of many existing typologies of child psychological maltreatment is that they include some subtypes that are defined by their outcomes. *Corrupting,* for example, is defined as stimulating the child to engage in destructive and antisocial behavior.

Despite the numerous difficulties in defining child psychological maltreatment, there are reasons to be hopeful that progress will continue in this area of research. For example, research has supported distinctions among several subtypes of psychological maltreatment (e.g., Crittenden, 1990; Hart & Brassard, 1991; Hart et al., 2002). Scholars have also demonstrated that both laypersons and professionals are consistently able to identify adult-child interactions that have been conceptually defined as child psychological maltreatment. Burnett (1993), for example, surveyed 452 social workers and 381 members of the general public regarding their opinions about 20 vignettes depicting possible child psychological maltreatment. Both groups generally agreed that the adults' behaviors in 18 of the 20 vignettes constituted psychological maltreatment. In another study, Schaefer (1997) asked parents and mental health professionals to rate the acceptability of 10 categories of verbal behavior of parents toward children and found 80% agreement between the groups about the definition of these categories as "never acceptable."

Children exposed to interparental violence. Research has shown that children suffer psychological maltreatment not only directly, but also indirectly, from exposure to violence between others. A growing literature focuses on children's exposure to violence between family members, primarily parents. Such exposure may take several forms: Some children, for example, may directly observe violent acts, some may overhear violent behaviors, and some may see the results of assaults (e.g., bruises). This exposure to violence is often conceptualized as a specific form of child maltreatment. Some experts classify exposure to interparental violence as psychological neglect (e.g., Sedlak & Broadhurst, 1996), whereas others consider it a form of psychological abuse (e.g., S. N. Hart et al., 1996). There is a considerable amount of debate, however, on the issue of whether such classifications are conceptually and legally sound (see Box 6.1).

An Interview With Marla R. Brassard

"I found the area of psychological maltreatment even more compelling than child sexual abuse because we have all experienced some level of psychological maltreatment in our close relationships."

Marla R. Brassard is Associate Professor of Psychology and Education at Teachers College, Columbia University, where she conducts research, teaches, and supervises students in clinical work. Her research focuses on the mental injuries and behavioral problems that result from parental psychological maltreatment and the contextual factors that moderate the effects of maltreatment, particularly the role of schools, teachers, and peer relationships. She has published two books on this topic: *Psychological Maltreatment of Children and Youth* (1987, coedited with Robert Germain and Stuart N. Hart) and *Psychological Maltreatment of Children* (2001, coauthored with Nelson J. Binggeli and Stuart N. Hart). She has also played a key role in the development of instruments for assessing psychological aggression/maltreatment, including the Psychological Maltreatment Rating Scales and the Teacher Psychological Aggression Scale. She is currently completing a longitudinal study funded by the Spencer Foundation titled "Modifiable Risk Factors for Aggression in Middle Schools." In her clinical practice she has worked in a variety settings, including a prison, preschools, public schools, and clinics with disabled, maltreated, and other troubled children and youth. She received her B.A. in psychology from Whitworth College in Spokane, Washington, and her Ph.D. in school psychology from Columbia University.

Q: What sparked your interest in the area of psychological maltreatment?

A: I had never thought much about child abuse and neglect until I was recruited to do some psychoeducational assessments for children in a respite care home program in Salt Lake City for families at risk for maltreatment. That led to coleading a children's group for the local Parents United group [an organization for families receiving court-ordered treatment for sexual abuse] and research with participating families. I found the area of maltreatment and related family dynamics interesting and emotionally compelling. Around that time, Professor Stuart Hart of Indiana University–Purdue University at Indianapolis became president-elect of the National Association of School Psychologists. He obtained funding for an International Conference on Psychological Abuse. I was one of the very few people within school psychology with experience and publications in the area of child maltreatment, and so he asked me to join him in coordinating the conference. I found the area of psychological maltreatment even more compelling than child sexual abuse because we have all experienced some level of psychological maltreatment in our close relationships. The conference was a success, and shortly thereafter we published a book of papers from the conference titled *Psychological Maltreatment of Children and Youth*.

Q: What would you describe as your most influential contribution to the field of child maltreatment?

A: I would say that our most important contribution has been in bringing psychological maltreatment the prominence and attention it has deserved. We did this by (a) holding the first conference on the topic and inviting all of the researchers and clinicians with published work in the area; (b) widely distributing the definition that emerged from the conference through other articles, book chapters, and presentations/workshops; (c) operationally defining psychological maltreatment through our research with the Psychological Maltreatment Ratings Scales; (d) writing and editing public interest pamphlets/comics for parents, teachers, and children; (e) demonstrating the devastating developmental consequences of psychological maltreatment independent of other forms of maltreatment though a critical review of the literature; and (f) developing guidelines for the forensic evaluation of cases of suspected psychological maltreatment for the American Professional Society on the Abuse of Children's *Guidelines for Psychosocial Evaluation of Suspected Psychological Maltreatment in Children and Adolescents* [1995].

Q: What has been the most rewarding experience you have had working in the field of child maltreatment?

A: It has been the close relationships I have developed with an interdisciplinary group of professionals and child maltreatment survivors working in this area. Maltreatment researchers and clinicians are an extraordinarily interesting and decent group of people. They put their concerns for children and their families above their own ego involvement in their work. They have a complex, nuanced view of human beings embedded within relationships—a view that does not diminish their moral commitment to protect and care for children. I have also benefited enormously from my involvement with families participating in our research. I have learned a lot about the human experience from our interactions.

Q: What is your current research focus?

A: One project is a continuation of my work with Stuart Hart on assessment issues in psychological maltreatment. With other colleagues and governments we are developing forensic quality measures of psychological maltreatment and the mental/emotional injuries that can result from all forms of maltreatment. We are refining observational measures of parent-child interaction for use in the home (what parents typically do) and clinic (what parents can do when on their best behavior, and how well they cope when challenged). Similarly, we are developing structured interviews of caring and maltreatment experiences for parents, older children, and other knowledgeable informants that include psychological maltreatment. We are also developing a protocol and select measures for the assessment of cognitive/emotional injury. Once parental psychological maltreatment, or any form of maltreatment, has been substantiated, an assessment for emotional/cognitive injury needs to occur. This is important because (a) many legal jurisdictions require evidence of injury in order to substantiate a case for emotional abuse and neglect, and (b) maltreated children suffer from significantly higher rates of mental health, behavioral, learning, and physical health problems. These problems can only be identified and treated if routine assessments in these areas occur.

Q: What type of policy recommendation is most needed in the field of child maltreatment?

A: I will mention one recommendation in particular, that is dear to my heart. Because I am a school psychologist, I would like to see the schools used more actively in intervening with the problem of child maltreatment. And because we have evidence that children respond to treatment, even if that treatment doesn't necessarily stop the maltreatment the child is experiencing, the school setting might be ideal as a compensatory and treatment environment for children and adolescents. Preschool and elementary school teachers could be provided with support and supervision to enhance their relationships with maltreated children, serving as secure attachment figures, role models, and supports for positive peer relationships and mastery of the curriculum. Working collaboratively, school mental health professionals in secondary schools, child protective services, and agencies that contract with them could develop and implement a variety of interventions for older children and adolescents. These interventions would not only address maltreatment-specific issues, but would also support social and academic competence and the decision-making skills that adolescents need to shape their life course. Interventions could include individual and group psychotherapy, mentoring by a favorite teacher or coach, personal skill development classes, and encouragement to participate in art, music, athletics, academics, or social groups. Schools that give maltreated and other at-risk students a sense of competence and self-worth through such activities have significantly better student outcomes than those that do not.

Box 6.1 Is Exposure to Interparental Violence a Form of Child Maltreatment?

Historically, the fields of child maltreatment and domestic violence have developed as separate entities. As Graham-Bermann (2002) notes, "Researchers in the areas of child abuse and domestic violence have occupied different spheres of inquiry, used disparate sources of data, received funding from different agencies, reported results at different conferences, and published their work in different journals" (p. 119). In recent years, however, there has been a high degree of overlap between research on child maltreatment and research on other forms of family violence. There is considerable evidence, for example, that interparental violence and child physical abuse co-occur in families at a significant rate (Appel & Holden, 1998). As a result of the recognition that child and spouse abuse are interconnected, several scholars have begun to consider what place children's exposure to interparental violence should occupy within the field of child maltreatment, from both conceptual and legal perspectives. Consider the following scenarios that depict the experiences of children who are exposed to interparental violence:

- Alice, a 4-year-old, hears shouting and arguing between her parents on a daily basis.
- On numerous occasions, 8-year-old Manuel observes his father using his fists to violently beat Manuel's mother.
- Emilio, who is 12, listens in as his mother repeatedly swears at and degrades his father.
- Late one evening, 6-year-old Elizabeth witnesses her father brutally raping her mother.

Many experts in the field of child maltreatment have suggested that children who are exposed to experiences such as these are indeed victims of child maltreatment, in part because of the emotional harm associated with exposure to such events. Indeed, a number of controlled studies have found that children exposed to marital violence experience a variety of negative psychosocial problems (see the subsection in this chapter headed "Effects Associated With Children's Exposure to Interparental Violence"). Some would argue that the harm that befalls such children is the result of an omission in care, and thus exposure to interparental violence should be classified as child neglect. Children who are exposed to interparental violence, more specifically, are seen as neglected due to parental failure to provide the children with a safe environment (Kantor & Little, 2003). Others would argue that the emotional harm that such children experience results from a parental act of commission, and thus exposure to interparental violence should be viewed as a form of psychological maltreatment. These observers assert that such exposure is a form of terrorizing, whereby parental actions or threats cause a child to experience extreme fear and anxiety (Somer & Braunstein, 1999).

The way that researchers and scholars conceptually define exposure to interparental violence is important, because definitions of such problems have significant social and legal implications. Several U.S. states, for example, have recently adopted laws that make exposing a child to interparental violence a form of criminal child abuse (Kantor & Little, 2003). One issue that is unclear about such laws, however, is who would be identified as the perpetrators of child abuse in such cases. Would the father who physically abuses his wife in the presence of their child be culpable? Would the mother be culpable? Would the mother be culpable if she chooses to reunite with her abuser or continues to reside with her abuser despite her child's having witnessed multiple abusive episodes? Should both parents be held culpable? These are difficult questions that will need careful consideration. It is particularly important that researchers examine these questions in light of the special circumstances of battered individuals and the potential obstacles associated with leaving a violent relationship (Berliner, 1998; Kantor & Little, 2003).

Another significant issue related to defining exposure to interparental violence as child abuse per se is the impact that such a definition would have on already overburdened child protective services systems (Hart et al., 2002; Kantor & Little, 2003). Currently, all U.S. states mandate that certain professionals report suspected cases of child abuse, but only a few states mandate reporting of marital violence (Hyman, Schillinger, & Lo, 1995). Defining exposure to interparental violence as criminal child abuse would result in a dramatic increase in the number of referrals to CPS, requiring millions of dollars to fund additional caseworkers to process and investigate the influx of new cases.

Defining exposure to interparental violence as child maltreatment involves complex issues that require greater knowledge than is currently available, particularly with regard to the implications associated with both conceptual and legal definitions. Important practice and policy initiatives, for example, might take on different forms depending on whether exposure to parental violence is conceptualized as an act of omission or an act of commission. When exposure to marital violence is viewed as an act of omission, responsibility for failure to protect the child from such exposure generally falls on the mother, who is frequently a victim herself. Many in American society are quick to blame a woman who knowingly allows her child to be exposed repeatedly to her partner's violence (Wilson, 1998). Others would argue, however, that society should hold the violent person accountable rather than placing the blame on victims, regardless of whether the victims are children or adults (Edleson, 1998). Conceptualizing exposure to marital violence as an act of commission shifts the focus onto the perpetrator of marital violence.

It may be best to classify exposure to interparental violence broadly, as a form of psychological maltreatment that could involve acts of omission, acts of commission, or both. In addition, legal statutes that define exposure to interparental violence as child abuse per se need further examination. Rather than defining all cases of exposure to interparental violence as child abuse, legislators and others may find it more useful to consider the specific circumstances under which exposure should be defined as criminal child abuse. Kantor and Little (2003), for example, recommend that CPS caseworkers ask themselves the following questions when attempting to determine what interventions are in the best interests of the child in such circumstances:

1. What types of injuries have both the parent victim and the child sustained?
2. How frequent and severe is the interparental violence?
3. What is the victim parent's ability to nurture the child?
4. How has the victim parent attempted to protect the child?

Recent years have seen a number of gains in terms of increasing collaboration between domestic violence and child abuse programs and between battered women advocates and CPS workers (Edleson, 1998; Findlater & Kelly, 1999). Several innovative strategies include cross-networking in which domestic violence specialists and CPS workers consult on individual cases or domestic violence programs refer battered women to appropriate family preservation services (Findlater & Kelly, 1999). Although progress in coordinating the efforts of both these fields is growing, greater collaborative efforts are needed. In addition, further research is needed to determine what conceptualization of the relationship between interparental violence and child maltreatment will best serve children exposed to such violence.

Regardless of the particular classification system used, it is clear that children exposed to interparental violence experience multiple threats. Children in these violent homes fear for themselves as well as for the parent who is the direct recipient of violence. In addition, these children are likely to experience direct forms of abuse and neglect (e.g., Appel & Holden, 1998; Holden, 2003; McCloskey, Figueredo, & Koss,

1995). Such experiences are of concern, in part, because of the potential negative effects they have on children. Consider the following excerpt from a paper written by one of our college students:

> The topic of marital violence and its effects on children who observe that violence is of exceptional interest to me. I chose this topic because I desire a better understanding of the problem, primarily because of my younger siblings who live in a home where violence, both physical and verbal, is far from uncommon. This scenario does not reflect the common situation of marital violence in which the male abuses the female; rather the abuser is my stepmother. For reasons that could constitute an entire paper on its own, my stepmother relieves her frustration through physical violence directed at my father. I can't count how many times I have seen her become angry and hit or throw things at my father. She even uses various objects to hit him.
>
> Initially, I was worried about my dad's safety, however, I realized he is a big man and would be all right. After they had my brother Jordan, now 7, however, I began to worry about what effects the abuse would have on him. I wondered if he would learn to believe this kind of behavior is acceptable. My wondering has sadly proven correct. Jordan is an aggressive boy and is often in trouble for his problem behavior.
>
> Two years after Jordan's birth, my parents had another child, Max, who is now 5. Max has watched the violence between my parents continue during his childhood. In contrast to Jordan, though, Max's interaction with family and friends portrays a picture of a little boy who is self-conscious, has low self-esteem, and lacks confidence. I love him so much and it breaks my heart to see him develop this sort of low self-image. He is a loving, generous, and sweet child and in spite of the "little brother abuse" he receives, he still looks up to his big brother, Jordan.
>
> My parents have recently had a third child, my sister, Amy. I now wonder, what will happen to my beautiful baby sister? I want to know more about the topic of children who are exposed to marital violence so that I can provide my father with empirical proof of the repercussions of such a situation. Hopefully, he will do something about the violence in his home and my little brothers and sister will benefit.

The student who wrote these words has an interest in child maltreatment because his personal experience tells him what it is like to observe interparental violence and that such experiences are potentially very harmful. Social recognition that children exposed to interparental violence are in need of services has grown in the United States because of the work of advocates, clinicians, and researchers since the late 1970s. Before that time, the public and the scientific community seemed to ignore the possibility that marital violence might have negative effects on children (Rossman, 1994). Although the problem of children's exposure to interparental violence has received increasing recognition in the intervening years, many factions within society still fail to acknowledge this form of violence as problematic for children. A 1994 report from the American Bar Association acknowledged, for example, that despite its obligation to protect children living in violent households, the law has generally failed even to recognize their exposure as a problem (Davidson, 1994). Indeed, some authors have described children in such homes as "the 'forgotten,' 'unacknowledged,' 'hidden,' 'unintended,' and 'silent' victims" of family violence (Holden, 1998, p. 1).

Legal issues. As the case history that opens this chapter illustrates, although many Americans acknowledge that the psychological maltreatment of children is potentially harmful and represents less-than-ideal parenting, many do not consider such maltreatment to be worthy of legal intervention. State reporting statutes, for example, do not always specifically cover psychological maltreatment, although most include some reference to the concept. The 1974 federal Child Abuse Prevention and Treatment Act refers to psychological maltreatment as "mental injury" and delegates the responsibility for more specific definitions to the individual states. In addition, few court decisions have addressed cases in which psychological maltreatment has occurred in the absence of any other form of child maltreatment, such as physical or sexual abuse (Hart et al., 2002).

At the root of the problem of defining psychological maltreatment from a legal perspective is the ambiguity associated with the term *mental injury.* How do state legislatures define this term? Some emphasize harm to the child rather than focusing on parental actions. Pennsylvania, for example, provides a specific and narrow definition for its category of "serious mental injury": "a psychological condition . . . which renders the child chronically sick and severely anxious, agitated, depressed, socially withdrawn, psychotic, or in fear that his/her life is threatened" (quoted in Garbarino et al., 1986). Other states require that a child's injuries be *substantial* and *observable.* The state of Oregon added a broad definition of mental injury to its child abuse reporting law in 1985. This law states that any mental injury to a child "shall include only observable and substantial impairment of the child's mental or psychological ability to function caused by cruelty to the child, with due regard to the culture of the child" (ORS 418.740). It goes on to say, "It will not suffice for a reporter to imagine a child might possibly be injured later by a particular course of parental behavior" (quoted in State of Oregon, 1991, p. 4). Legal statutes that include requirements for identifiable harm are problematic because the effects of psychological maltreatment may only rarely be identifiable, or they may be identifiable only after years of maltreatment.

Other state definitions emphasize the parental actions that lead to child injury. Minnesota's statute, for instance, includes injury that results from either overt acts of commission that are consistently and deliberately inflicted or a parent's omissions in caring for a child (Minn. Stat. Ann. 260C.007). Florida's statute provides even greater definitional specificity with regard to which parental acts of commission and omission should be regarded as psychological maltreatment. For example, it recognizes various forms of isolation as psychological maltreatment, such as the use of unreasonable restraints or subjecting the child to extended periods of isolation in order to control the child (Fl. Stat. Ann. 39.01).

The lack of clear and consistent legal definitions likely contributes to problems in identifying child psychological maltreatment, inaccuracies in reporting such maltreatment, and limitations in the ability of child protective services to intervene to protect children who are psychologically maltreated (Hamarman et al., 2002; Hart et al., 2002). In a recent study, for example, Hamarman et al. (2002) found that specific aspects of state statutes influence the identification and reporting of child psychological maltreatment. For instance, states in which the laws recognize inclusive caretaker culpability report higher rates of psychological maltreatment than do other states. Clear legal definitions and definitional consensus concerning child psychological maltreatment are needed across the United States so that lawmakers can develop appropriate statutes to identify children at risk and intervene effectively.

Estimates of Psychological Maltreatment

Given the definitional complexities described above, it is no surprise that the actual rates of child psychological maltreatment are unknown. Despite definitional problems, however, several researchers have attempted to investigate the scope of the problem.

Official estimates. National reporting statistics have consistently demonstrated that psychological maltreatment is the least common form of reported and substantiated child maltreatment. Estimates vary, however, and are influenced by definitional and methodological variability across studies. The American Association for Protecting Children (1988) found that psychological maltreatment (defined as *emotional maltreatment*) accounted for approximately 8% of all official reports of child maltreatment in the United States in 1986. Data from the National Center on Child Abuse and Neglect indicated that psychological maltreatment accounted for 6% of reported child maltreatment cases in 1996 (U.S. DHHS, 1998). The most recent statistics available indicate that in 8% of reported cases of child abuse, psychological maltreatment (as distinct from physical abuse, child neglect, and so on) is the primary form of abuse (U.S. DHHS, 2002b).

The National Incidence Studies suggest considerably higher rates (Sedlak & Broadhurst, 1996; U.S. DHHS, 1981, 1988). In NIS-2, the 391,100 reported cases of psychological maltreatment (including psychological abuse and emotional neglect) accounted for 28% of all cases of child maltreatment (Sedlak, 1990). NIS data indicate that between 1980 and 1986, the rate of psychological abuse increased by 43%, and the rate of emotional neglect more than doubled. Results of NIS-3 indicated that the rate of both psychological abuse and emotional neglect nearly tripled between 1986 and 1993 (Sedlak & Broadhurst, 1996). Rates of psychological maltreatment are obviously higher when definitions are broadened to include potential harm.

As is the case concerning other forms of child maltreatment, many professionals believe that psychological maltreatment is underreported. Many individuals in a position to report it may fail to do so because they do not define questionable parental behaviors as psychological maltreatment, or because psychological maltreatment often co-occurs with other forms of abuse (Claussen & Crittenden, 1991). That psychological maltreatment is the least reported form of child abuse may reflect nothing more than that it is usually the least visible form of abuse experienced by a particular child. Although psychological maltreatment is the least common form of child maltreatment reported to CPS agencies, it is the most commonly reported form of child maltreatment among families involved in therapeutic treatment programs for child abuse and neglect (Daro, 1988).

Self-report surveys. Daro and Gelles (1992) examined the parenting practices of a nationally representative sample of 1,250 American parents surveyed each year between 1988 and 1992. Although rates fluctuated during the 6 years of data collection, 45% of the parents in this sample reported insulting or swearing at their children in 1992.

Analysis of data from the second National Family Violence Survey provides additional information on self-report estimates of psychological maltreatment (Vissing, Straus, Gelles, & Harrop, 1991). In this survey, psychological maltreatment was defined to include both verbal (e.g., insulting or swearing) and nonverbal (e.g., sulking or refusing to talk) forms of interaction with a child. Approximately 63% of the parents surveyed reported using one of these forms of interaction with their children at least once during the preceding year. An analysis of the frequency of these types of interactions found that the average number of instances was 12.6 per year, with approximately 21% of parents reporting more than 20 instances.

Parent self-reports of psychological maltreatment were even higher in a nationally representative sample of parents using the Parent-Child Conflict Tactics Scales. Straus, Hamby, Finkelhor, Moore, and Runyan (1998) found that approximately 86% of the parents in their sample reported using some form of psychological aggression toward their children (e.g., yelling, screaming or shouting, using threats, and swearing) at least once during the preceding year. The parents who reported engaging in such behaviors did so an average of 22 times during the preceding 12 months. The most common form of psychological aggression used by parents in this study was verbal—shouting, yelling, or screaming at the child. In addition, psychological aggression was almost as common in this sample of parents as nonviolent means of discipline, such as distraction or time-outs.

Estimates of children exposed to interparental violence. Published estimates of the numbers of children in the United States exposed to interparental violence range from 3.3 million to nearly 10 million (Carlson, 1984; Straus, 1991a). The disparity in these estimates reflects the fact that they depend on researchers' methods of data collection and definitions of exposure to interparental violence.

Some researchers have used retrospective study designs, questioning adults about their childhood memories of interparental violence. On the basis of data from the 1985 National Family Violence Survey, Straus (1992) has estimated that more than 10 million American children witness physical assaults between their parents. This study measured exposure to interparental violence (using the original Conflict Tactics Scale, or CTS-1) by asking adult respondents whether they recalled one or both parents hitting the other during the respondents' teenage years. Nearly 13% recalled observing at least one incident of marital violence between their parents. In presenting these figures, Straus notes that they likely underestimate the true amount of such experiences, because most parents try to avoid physical fights when their children are present and because these figures represent only the violence that respondents observed between parents during the respondents' teenage years. Indeed, when the adults in the 1985 National Family Violence Survey were asked about interparental violence in their own relationships, 16% reported such violence within the previous year, whereas 30% reported violence with their spouses at some time during their marriages (Gelles & Straus, 1988; Straus, Gelles, & Steinmetz, 1980).

Retrospective studies of college students using the CTS-1 have yielded similar results. Gelles (1980) found that 16% of college students reported exposure to at least one incident during the past year in which one of their parents had physically abused the other. Silvern et al. (1995) also surveyed college students and found that 37% of the 550 undergraduates in their sample reported exposure to some form of interparental violence while growing up. The most common types of violence reported were one partner's throwing an object at the other, pushing, shoving, and slapping.

Other researchers have questioned parents involved in marital violence, primarily women residing in shelters, and found variable results. In a national survey of battered women, for example, Tomkins et al. (1994) found that less than 25% thought their children had *directly observed* the interparental violence within their homes. In contrast, other inquiries of battered women have indicated that two-thirds or more of children living in violent homes were exposed to the violence, either by directly observing the violence or by witnessing its aftermath (Hilton, 1992; Holden & Ritchie, 1991). Some scholars have questioned the estimates obtained from parents in violent relationships on the grounds that individuals involved in such relationships may underestimate their children's exposure, perhaps from shame or guilt, stress or trauma, or lack of awareness that their children were present (Elbow, 1982; Hilton, 1992). A recent study that examined data from multiple informants (both parents and children), for example, found that mothers' reports of children's exposure agreed with fathers' reports fairly well, but there was much less agreement between parents' and children's reports (O'Brien, John, Margolin, & Erel, 1994).

Given the problems in collecting data from parents involved in violent relationships, researchers have also directly questioned children from community samples regarding their experiences with interparental violence. O'Brien et al. (1994) interviewed 8- to 11-year-old children about whether they had witnessed physical aggression between their parents, and approximately one-fourth of the children reported witnessing both husband-to-wife aggression and wife-to-husband aggression. Using a narrower definition of violence, McCloskey et al. (1995) found that 20% of the children in their community sample had seen their fathers slap their mothers within the past year. These data are limited, however, to specific age groups of child victims as well as nonrandom samples of children (Margolin, 1998).

SECTION SUMMARY

Many scholars have described psychological maltreatment as the most difficult form of child maltreatment to define. Disagreement originates in the problem of determining how to define the term *psychological*. Some experts emphasize nonphysical behaviors toward children on the part of adults, such as failing to respond to a child's needs for nurturance and attention, terrorizing a child, or insulting or swearing at a child. Others focus on the nonphysical consequences to the child victim, including a variety of emotional and cognitive symptoms (e.g., anxiety and fear). Still others define psychological maltreatment broadly to include a combination of physical and nonphysical parental actions that result in negative psychological consequences for the child. Although researchers have described numerous subtypes of psychological maltreatment, significant variability in definitions continues to exist, with little consensus regarding the most appropriate definition. Definitional ambiguity complicates the efforts of legislators to set specific legal standards to address child psychological maltreatment. The frequency, intensity, duration, and context of psychologically maltreating behaviors need additional study.

The true rate of psychological maltreatment is difficult to determine and largely unknown. Official estimates derived from reporting agencies indicate that between 3% and 28% of reported cases of child maltreatment are for psychological maltreatment, distinguishing psychological maltreatment as the least reported form of child maltreatment. Some evidence, however, suggests that psychological maltreatment is underreported. Self-report surveys also suggest that parents frequently engage in negative behaviors consistent with psychological maltreatment. Children's exposure to interparental violence is one specific form of child psychological maltreatment that is receiving increasing attention. How such exposure should be defined constitutes another challenge for scholars and lawmakers. Although it is clear that significant numbers of children are exposed to violence between their parents, precise estimates of the incidence and prevalence of this problem are lacking. Published estimates of the numbers of children exposed to interparental violence annually in the United States currently range from approximately 3 million to 10 million.

SEARCHING FOR PATTERNS: CHARACTERISTICS OF VICTIMS AND PERPETRATORS

Characteristics of Psychologically Maltreated Children

Most of the available information about sociodemographic characteristics of psychological maltreatment victims comes from official reports made to CPS agencies and other mandated reporters of child abuse as well as community samples of parents. Due to a lack of definitional consensus across studies and the small percentage of psychological maltreatment cases reported, however, the current knowledge about sociodemographic characteristics of psychological maltreatment victims is tentative at best (for a review, see Black, Slep, & Heyman, 2001).

Age and gender. Findings from NIS-2 (Sedlak, 1997), with its broad definition of psychological maltreatment, as well as recent data from the U.S. Department of Health and Human Services (1998), indicate that reports of psychological maltreatment increase with child age. Results from the National Family Violence Survey support this finding. Vissing and colleagues (1991) found that children ages 7 to 17 were more likely to be psychologically abused (defined as having experienced verbal aggression such as being yelled at and/or insulted) than were children 6 years old or younger.

Official estimates and community surveys have reported mixed findings with regard to gender differences associated with rates of psychological maltreatment. Recent data from the National Child Abuse and Neglect Data System indicate that girls (53%) are slightly more at risk than boys (47%) for psychological maltreatment (U.S. DHHS, 1998). In a community sample of parents, however, Vissing et al. (1991) found the opposite: Boys were more likely than girls to experience psychological maltreatment. Still other researchers have failed to find any gender differences associated with psychological maltreatment (e.g., Sedlak, 1997). Such discrepancies are likely due to methodological differences between studies, such as the different populations sampled, and the different definitions of child psychological maltreatment used (Black et al., 2001).

Other risk factors. Researchers have also demonstrated a link between psychological maltreatment and other risk factors, such as the child's race or ethnicity and family income. In NIS-2, victims of psychological maltreatment were more likely to be described as "other" in terms of racial background than as White, Black or Hispanic (Sedlak, 1997). Both NIS-2 and NIS-3 also found an association between economic factors and psychological maltreatment. In both studies, lower-income families (i.e., yearly income less than $15,000) were significantly more likely than higher-income families to be characterized by psychological maltreatment (Sedlak & Broadhurst, 1996).

Characteristics of Psychologically Maltreating Parents

To date, little research has examined the characteristics of psychologically maltreating parents. Most of the available demographic information about these parents comes from studies that have evaluated official reporting statistics. Information pertaining to the psychosocial qualities of parents who maltreat their children comes from research that primarily includes samples of psychologically maltreating parents or community samples of parents.

Age and gender. The American Association for Protecting Children (1988) found that parents are the primary perpetrators of child psychological maltreatment, accounting for 90% of reported cases, and that the average age of psychologically maltreating parents was 33 years. The gender distributions of recently reported cases indicate that females (57%) are slightly more likely to be reported as perpetrators of psychological maltreatment than are males (43%; U.S. DHHS, 1998). With regard to race, the parents of psychologically maltreated children are more likely to be Caucasian than in other forms of child maltreatment (U.S. DHHS, 1998). Information to date about the demographic characteristics of psychologically maltreating parents, however, is tentative at best given the limitations of official report data.

Psychosocial qualities. A few studies have examined the psychosocial characteristics of psychologically maltreating parents. Such parents, compared with nonabusive parents, appear to exhibit more difficulties with interpersonal and social interactions, problem solving, and psychiatric adjustment. Hickox and Furnell (1989), for example, studied a group of parents legally established as emotionally abusive and found that these parents were characterized by more problem psychosocial and background factors compared with a matched comparison group of parents identified as needing assistance with child care and management. Emotionally abusive parents had more difficulty building relationships, exhibited poor coping skills, and displayed deficits in child management techniques. In addition, emotionally abusive mothers demonstrated a lack of support networks (both personal and community) as well as greater levels of perceived stress, marital discord, and alcohol and drug use. Lesnik-Oberstein, Koers, and Cohen (1995) evaluated psychologically abusive and nonabusive mothers on a variety of measures of adjustment and found that the psychologically abusive mothers exhibited a greater number of psychiatric symptoms (e.g., depression, aggression, hostility), personality disturbances (e.g., social anxiety, neuroticism, low self-esteem), and physical illnesses. In addition, relative to nonabusive mothers, psychologically abusive mothers scored lower on a measure of verbal reasoning ability and reported engaging in fewer social activities.

Researchers in the field of child development have examined the psychological characteristics of psychologically maltreating parents from a different perspective. A number of different studies, for example, have demonstrated a link between psychiatric disturbances in mothers and parent-child interactions marked by decreased emotional responsiveness and nurturance and increased verbal aggression (e.g., Field, Healy, Goldstein, & Gutherz, 1990; Hawley, Halle, Drasin, & Thomas, 1995; Radke-Yarrow & Klimes-Dougan, 2002). Such parents often suffer from major depressive disorders or substance abuse disorders that may undermine their ability to parent their children effectively.

Another line of research has evaluated the nature of early parent-child interactions in psychologically maltreating parents to examine whether such parents are abusive because they themselves received inadequate parenting during childhood. Hemenway, Solnick, and Carter (1994) randomly sampled a group of American parents and asked them how often they were yelled at as children in addition to how often they yelled at their own children. Results indicated that the parents who were yelled at frequently (e.g., daily) in childhood were more likely than other parents to yell at their own children.

SECTION SUMMARY

Researchers have relied primarily on official reporting statistics to study risk factors associated with child psychological maltreatment. Given the limitations of such data, information to date about the demographic characteristics of psychologically maltreated children and their parents is tentative at best. Research conducted to date, however, indicates that reports of psychological maltreatment increase as children become older, with those ages 7 and above being more likely than younger children to be reported for psychological maltreatment. Research findings indicate no appreciable gender differences among victims of psychological maltreatment, nor has any clear pattern of racial differences emerged, largely because of the existence of methodological difficulties. Early studies do show a link, however, between child psychological maltreatment and low income.

Evaluations of the demographic characteristics of psychologically maltreating parents based on official statistics are also preliminary and, as a result, require cautious interpretation. Female parents are identified most often as the perpetrators of psychological maltreatment. Consistent findings with regard to psychosocial variables in psychologically maltreating parents indicate that they often exhibit interpersonal and social difficulties, poor problem-solving skills, substance abuse, and psychiatric maladjustment. Data also provide preliminary support for the hypothesis of potential intergenerational transmission of psychological maltreatment. Additional research is needed to replicate current findings and expand our understanding of the risk factors associated with psychological maltreatment.

CONSEQUENCES ASSOCIATED WITH PSYCHOLOGICAL MALTREATMENT

Both researchers and clinical practitioners have speculated about the potential consequences of child psychological maltreatment, such as antisocial behaviors, depression, withdrawal, and low self-esteem (e.g., Gross & Keller, 1992). Descriptive clinical and case study research appears to confirm that victims are subject to many of these difficulties, although such research is questionable on methodological grounds. Within the past 10 years, however, a growing number of systematic, controlled research studies have examined both the short-term effects associated with psychological maltreatment observed in infants and children and the long-term effects observed in adolescents and adults (Table 6.3 lists the effects that have received the most consistent empirical support). In addition, a significant amount of research has addressed the effects associated with children's exposure to interparental violence. In this section, we review current findings on the effects associated with child psychological maltreatment and discuss the limitations associated with this research (for reviews, see Binggeli et al., 2001; Hart et al., 2002; Rossman, 2001; Wolfe, Crooks, Lee, McIntyre-Smith, & Jaffe, 2003).

Initial Effects

The short-term effects associated with child psychological maltreatment include a variety of problems and difficulties that have been observed in infants as well as children, such as interpersonal maladjustment, intellectual deficits, and affective-behavioral problems. In the interpersonal realm, researchers have documented maladjustment in psychologically maltreated infants and children in the areas of attachment, social adjustment, and peer relationships. Psychologically maltreated children, for example, are significantly more likely than their nonmaltreated peers to be insecurely attached to a parent (e.g., Crittenden & Ainsworth, 1989; Egeland, 1997). Several investigators have also found that psychologically maltreated children exhibit lower levels of social competence and adjustment (e.g.,

Table 6.3   Possible Short- and Long-Term Effects Associated With Psychological Maltreatment

Short-Term Effects Observed in Infants and Children	
Interpersonal maladjustment	Insecure attachment to caregiver Low social competence and adjustment Difficulties making and retaining friends Difficulties with peers
Intellectual deficits	Academic problems Low educational achievement Deficits in cognitive ability Deficits in problem solving and intelligence Lack of creativity
Affective-behavioral problems	Aggression, hostility, anger Disruptive classroom behavior Noncompliant behavior Lack of impulse control Self-abusive behavior Anxiety Low self-esteem Shame and guilt Conduct disorder Hyperactivity and distractibility Pessimism and negativity Dependence on adults for help, support, and nurturance

Long-Term Effects Observed in Adolescents and Adults	
Affective-behavioral problems	Juvenile delinquency Aggression Negative life views Low self-esteem Anxiety Depression Suicidal behaviors Interpersonal sensitivity Dissociation Personality disorders Sexual problems Eating disorders

SOURCES: A representative but not exhaustive list of sources for the information displayed in this table includes the following: Claussen and Crittenden (1991); Crittenden et al. (1994); Downs and Miller (1998); Egeland (1997); Johnson et al. (2001); Herrenkohl et al. (1997); Kent and Waller (1998); Mullen et al. (1996); Spillane-Grieco (2000); Rorty, Yager, and Rossotto (1994); Vissing et al. (1991).

have trouble making friends) than do their nonmaltreated counterparts (e.g., Brassard, Hart, & Hardy, 1991; Claussen & Crittenden, 1991; Vissing et al., 1991).

Intellectual deficits also distinguish psychologically maltreated children from controls (e.g., Crittenden, Claussen, & Sugarman, 1994; Erickson & Egeland, 2002). Recall the longitudinal Minnesota Mother-Child Project described in Chapter 5. Researchers in that study included two psychologically maltreating groups

of mothers: verbally abusive mothers and psychologically unavailable mothers (Erickson & Egeland, 2002). The children of verbally abusive mothers exhibited difficulty learning and solving problems as well as low levels of creativity relative to comparison children. The children of psychologically unavailable mothers appeared to show even greater deficits, including declines in intellectual ability and low educational achievement.

Psychological maltreatment is also associated with a variety of affective and behavioral problems in children. Several studies have substantiated that psychologically maltreated children exhibit significantly more general behavior problems than do nonmaltreated children (e.g., Hart & Brassard, 1989; Hickox & Furnell, 1989; Vissing et al., 1991). Psychologically maltreated children also demonstrate higher levels of such specific problems as aggression, conduct problems, attention difficulties, disruptive classroom behavior, self-abusive behavior, hostility and anger, and anxiety (e.g., Crittenden et al., 1994; Erickson & Egeland, 1987; Vissing et al., 1991).

Long-Term Effects

Although only a limited number of studies have evaluated the potential long-term effects of child psychological maltreatment in adolescent and adult samples, the available information indicates that psychological maltreatment in childhood is associated with a number of psychological difficulties in adulthood. Johnson, Cohen, and Smailes (2001), for example, examined the relationship between child psychological maltreatment (particularly in the form of parents' verbally aggressive behaviors) and personality disorders in a community-based longitudinal study of adolescents and young adults. This study found that verbally abusive behaviors inflicted by mothers were associated with greater risk for several personality disorders in adolescence and adulthood, including borderline, narcissistic, obsessive-compulsive, and paranoid personality disorders.

Researchers have also begun to evaluate the long-term impacts of psychological maltreatment relative to other forms of child maltreatment. Many of these studies confirm that negative outcomes are associated with psychological maltreatment, in addition to suggesting that, relative to other forms of child maltreatment, psychological maltreatment is the *strongest* predictor of long-term impacts on psychological functioning. Gross and Keller (1992), for example, evaluated 260 university students identified as physically abused, psychologically abused, both physically and psychologically abused, or nonabused. On standardized instruments, psychologically abused respondents had lower self-esteem scores than nonabused respondents but did not differ significantly from them on measures of depression and attributional style. Respondents who had experienced both physical and psychological abuse, however, exhibited higher levels of depression

than nonabused respondents as well as those with histories of only one type of abuse. Regression analysis also revealed that psychological abuse was a more powerful predictor of depression, low self-esteem, and external attributional style (attributing outcomes for events to external, unstable, or specific causes) than was physical abuse. Other studies have confirmed the presence of difficulties such as low self-esteem, substance abuse, anxiety, depression, suicidal behavior, dissociation, and interpersonal sensitivity in adults with histories of childhood psychological maltreatment as well as the central role of psychological maltreatment in predicting the effects of child maltreatment (e.g., Downs & Miller, 1998; Kent & Waller, 1998; Langhinrichsen-Rohling, Monson, Meyer, Caster, & Sanders, 1998; Mullen, Martin, Anderson, Romans, & Herbison, 1996).

Effects Associated With Children's Exposure to Interparental Violence

Since the late 1970s, researchers have made progress in documenting a number of problems in children exposed to interparental violence. Research findings on the effects associated with exposure to interparental violence reveal that such children are prone to suffer problems in five general areas: emotional functioning, behavior problems, social competence, cognitive ability, and physical health. Table 6.4 displays the effects most frequently associated with children's exposure to interparental violence.

Children exposed to interparental violence tend to exhibit more emotional and behavior problems than do nonexposed children, and they often display multiple problems (Gleason, 1995; Kitzmann, Gaylord, Holt, & Kenny, 2003; Wolfe, Crooks, et al., 2003). In addition, these children often exhibit problems at a level that warrants clinical intervention. Across studies, approximately 35% to 45% of children in samples from shelters for battered women and their children have received scores within the clinically significant range (see Hughes, 1992; O'Keefe, 1994; Sternberg et al., 1993).

Similar to studies of the victims of other forms of child maltreatment, however, studies of children exposed to interparental violence have revealed that a subgroup of these children appear to be well adjusted despite their violent home environments (e.g., Hughes & Luke, 1998). Why might some children be significantly affected by such experiences whereas others appear to emerge relatively unscathed? Several factors might mediate the psychological and developmental

Table 6.4   Possible Effects Associated With Children's Exposure to Interparental Violence

Areas Affected	Examples
Emotional functioning	Anxiety/difficult temperament Low self-esteem Depression and suicide Trauma/stress reactions Negative emotions (e.g., feelings of loss, anger, sadness, self-blame)
Behavior problems	Aggression Delinquency Alcohol/drug use High levels of physical activity
Social competence	Shyness/withdrawal Social incompetence Low empathy Aggression, wariness, and hostility in interpersonal relationships
Cognitive ability	Academic and achievement problems Poor problem-solving and conflict resolution skills Cognitive deficits Negative perceptions Deficits in adaptive behavior Altered information-processing ability Increased vigilance for threat situations
Physical health	Physical symptoms/ailments Somatic complaints

SOURCES: A representative but not exhaustive list of sources for the information displayed in this table includes the following: Boney-McCoy and Finkelhor (1995); Copping (1996); Coyne, Barrett, and Duffy (2000); Ericksen and Henderson (1992); Gleason (1995); Graham-Bermann and Levendosky (1998); Hughes and Luke (1998); Jaffe, Hastings, and Reitzel (1992); Johnson et al. (2002); Kolbo, Blakely, and Engleman (1996); McKay (1994); Mertin (1992); O'Keefe (1994); Rossman (2001); Sternberg, Lamb, Greenbaum, Dawud, and Cortes (1994); Wolfe, Wekerle, Reitzel-Jaffe, and Lefebvre (1998); Wolfe, Crooks, et al. (2003).

outcomes for children exposed to interparental violence, such as the nature of the violence (e.g., severity and duration), age, gender, ethnicity, the level of stress experienced by the mother, the quality of mothering, availability of social support, the child's exposure to other forms of violence (e.g., verbal or physical abuse), and child characteristics such as temperament and self-esteem (e.g., Jouriles & Norwood, 1995; O'Keefe, 1994; Spaccarelli, Sandler, & Roosa, 1994). To date, however, research findings in this area are inconsistent; additional studies are needed to clarify what factors might increase or decrease children's likelihood of suffering particular effects as a result of being exposed to interparental violence.

Children exposed to interparental violence also continue to demonstrate psychological difficulties later in life. Several studies have examined problems in adolescents, college students, and national samples of adults that are correlated with childhood exposure to interparental violence. The long-term effects observed include depression, trauma-related symptoms (e.g., anxiety and sleep disturbance), low self-esteem, alcohol and drug use, poor social adjustment, general psychological distress, and ineffective conflict resolution skills (Choice, Lamke, & Pittman, 1995; Henning, Leitenberg, Coffey, Turner, & Bennett, 1996; Silvern et al., 1995). Other possible long-term effects include verbal and physical violence against one's own spouse, dating partner, or peers; verbal and physical abuse of one's own children; and participation in violence outside the family (e.g., arrests for criminal assault) (Cantrell, MacIntyre, Sharkey, & Thompson, 1995; Maker, Kemmelmeier, & Peterson, 1998; McCloskey & Lichter, 2003; Straus, 1992). There is also some evidence that outcomes for young adults who were exposed to interparental violence in childhood depend on whether the violence was initiated by their mothers or fathers, with father-initiated violence associated with greater risk for psychological problems (Fergusson & Horwood, 1998).

Methodological Issues
Pertaining to Effects Research

The results of studies that have examined the negative effects associated with child psychological maltreatment should be interpreted cautiously. As we have noted in previous chapters, the issue of effects is complicated, and, as a result, the consequences of child maltreatment are not completely understood. Many of the same methodological problems that have arisen in the research on other forms of child maltreatment also plague studies investigating the negative effects associated with psychological maltreatment. These methodological problems include a lack of standard definitions, the use of biased samples, and the use of limited research designs.

The lack of a standard definition of the term *psychological maltreatment* across studies is associated with a number of problems. Some researchers have used the term to refer to a broad collection of behaviors, including a number of different forms of psychological maltreatment (e.g., verbal rejection/degradation, terrorizing, denying emotional responsiveness). Others have used the term to refer to a more circumscribed set of behaviors (e.g., verbal abuse). An additional definitional problem is that some researchers have not considered the parameters of maltreatment, such as its frequency, severity, and duration, all of which might potentially influence a child's functional outcome. Future studies should employ carefully constructed operational definitions of psychological maltreatment that consider such parameters and should examine the short- and long-term effects associated with different forms of child psychological maltreatment.

Another methodological problem is that most studies to date have used small, nonrepresentative samples. The majority of studies that have examined the effects associated with exposure to interparental violence, for example, have included mothers and children temporarily residing in battered women's shelters. Such samples vary greatly from general population samples in many ways. Many researchers have also failed to control for the fact that child and adult samples often include individuals who have experienced multiple forms of abuse. Studies have often included samples of children who have observed interparental violence *in addition* to experiencing direct physical or sexual abuse (Appel & Holden, 1998;

McCloskey et al., 1995; Peled & Davis, 1995). It is therefore difficult to ascertain precisely which factors contribute to the difficulties these children experience. Such research designs preclude the possibility, for example, of separating the effects of *observing* interparental violence from the effects of *experiencing other forms* of maltreatment. When researchers have controlled for the presence of multiple forms of abuse, the findings have suggested that particular forms of child maltreatment are associated with specific problems and that specific forms of abuse have differential power to predict certain types of functioning (see Chapter 7 for a discussion of research examining multiple forms of maltreatment).

Another potential methodological problem relates to the sources of reports of children's psychological and behavioral functioning (e.g., mothers versus fathers, teachers versus parents). In one study that examined the effects associated with exposure to parental violence, for example, Sternberg et al. (1993) found that mothers' reports of the degree of their children's behavioral difficulties varied depending on whether or not the mothers were victims of spouse abuse. In this study, mothers whose children were exposed to interparental violence alone or in addition to being physically abused demonstrated significantly more behavior problems than did children in a nonabused control group. A group of physically abused children who had not been exposed to interparental violence, however, did not differ from the control group, which may suggest that mothers report higher levels of problem behavior in their children when they themselves are victims. Additional research indicates that maternal accounts of their children's difficulties are often inconsistent with fathers' descriptions as well as those of professionals (Christensen, Margolin, & Sullaway, 1992; Sternberg et al., 1993). Mothers in shelters are likely to be in a crisis situation brought on by factors such as injuries, insufficient funds, departure from their homes, depression, and posttraumatic stress disorder, and this may impair their objectivity (see Saunders, 1994; Walker, 1977). One solution to this problem would be for researchers to obtain information about children's functioning from multiple sources, including both parents and self-report measures from the children themselves.

Research on the effects associated with child psychological maltreatment has also been weakened by its correlational nature; that is, one cannot necessarily assume that psychological maltreatment is the cause of the various problems observed in children and adults reporting histories of such experiences. Children living in homes characterized by psychological maltreatment often experience additional risk factors, such as marital conflict, parental alcoholism, low income, stress, and maternal impairment (Hughes, Parkinson, & Vargo, 1989; Rossman, 2001). Without appropriate statistical controls or comparison groups (e.g., comparison groups of children who have been exposed to parental alcoholism, low income, and stress, for example, but have *not* been exposed to psychological maltreatment), it is impossible to determine which of these many factors, in addition to psychological maltreatment, contribute to the negative outcomes observed in children. Reports of several studies have recently appeared in which the researchers have either controlled for some of these confounding variables or employed a prospective longitudinal design that provides information about causality and temporal sequence (e.g., Herrenkohl, Egolf, & Herrenkohl, 1997; Maker et al., 1998; McCloskey & Lichter, 2003). Maker et al. (1998), for example, assessed psychological functioning and experiences of interparental violence along with several other risk factors (including sexual abuse, physical abuse, and parental substance abuse) among community college women. Results indicated that several psychosocial problems (e.g., depression, PTSD symptoms, antisocial behaviors, violence in dating relationships) were associated with interparental violence. In addition, when the researchers controlled for all of the other risk factors, exposure to interparental violence remained predictive of violence in the women's dating relationships.

Two final criticisms concerning much of the research to date on the effects of child psychological maltreatment are that it has rarely been driven by theory and that researchers have paid little attention to the processes that lead to behavioral problems in children and adults with histories of this form of abuse. A new wave of research, however, is addressing both theoretical and conceptual issues within the field and attempting to link findings with implications for intervention and social policy (e.g., Holden, Geffner, & Jouriles, 1998; Kent & Waller, 2000).

SECTION SUMMARY

The results of studies that have evaluated the short- and long-term effects of child psychological maltreatment

are tentative at best. This is an emerging research area, and many of the same methodological problems already discussed in the context of other forms of child maltreatment apply here also. To date, studies have indicated that child psychological maltreatment may result in a variety of problems for victims that may extend into adulthood.

Negative effects associated with psychological maltreatment in children include difficulties in interpersonal, intellectual, and affective and behavioral realms of functioning. For example, these children demonstrate more problems than comparison children in such areas as aggression, delinquency, self-abuse, anxiety, hostility, and anger. Researchers have found similar problems in adults with childhood histories of psychological maltreatment. Future research should attempt to examine the effects of development on the consequences of psychological maltreatment, the effects of psychological maltreatment alone or in combination with other forms of maltreatment, and the distinctive effects associated with various subtypes of psychological maltreatment.

A considerable body of knowledge has accumulated concerning one specific form of child psychological maltreatment: exposure to interparental violence. Studies demonstrate that such exposure is related to negative psychological difficulties that affect children's emotional, behavioral, social, cognitive, and physical functioning. It is difficult to interpret the findings of studies that have evaluated the negative effects associated with exposure to interparental violence, however, because of the large number of variables that may simultaneously influence children's behavior (e.g., parental alcoholism, low income, and maternal impairment) and the methodological problems inherent in the studies conducted to date.

PRACTICE, POLICY, AND PREVENTION ISSUES

Although researchers and practitioners have proposed a number of intervention and prevention strategies that are unique to child sexual abuse and child physical abuse, few unique research efforts have been directed toward possible solutions and interventions particularly for the problem of psychological maltreatment. Some scholars have even questioned whether adding specific interventions for psychological maltreatment is feasible given the limited success of already overwhelmed CPS systems in meeting the needs of other maltreated groups (Claussen & Crittenden, 1991). As a result, studies concerned with intervention and prevention approaches unique to psychological maltreatment have been nearly nonexistent. Exceptions to this rule have been studies conducted to evaluate programs focused specifically on children exposed to interparental violence. In the following subsections, we review these programs and the few programs that have been suggested more generally for victims of child psychological maltreatment, including treatment interventions for children and parents as well as prevention strategies.

Interventions for Psychologically Maltreated Children

Given the many forms that child psychological maltreatment can take, it is likely that no single treatment intervention will be effective for all victims of this type of maltreatment. Although currently no empirically supported treatment approaches focus on psychological maltreatment specifically, some experts in the field have recommended various targets for treatment as well as specific treatment approaches. Binggeli and colleagues (2001), for example, have recommended treatment interventions that include three domains related to the negative effects associated with psychological maltreatment: The first domain concerns intrapersonal issues, including identity, self-esteem, and dysfunctional attributions of self; the second domain focuses on social and interpersonal issues, including relationship problems and deficits in attachments to significant others; and the third domain consists of behavior and emotional problems, such as depression, anxiety, aggression, and poor impulse control.

Wolfe (1991) has proposed specific intervention strategies for child victims of both physical and emotional abuse that address several of the domains noted above. To address interpersonal issues, particularly the disruption in the relationship between parent and child, one treatment goal is to enhance the parent-child relationship. In particular, treatment strategies focus on enhancing parental sensitivity and enjoyment of the child through child observation, child-centered activities, and play and stimulation techniques. Other intervention strategies focus on the behavioral and emotional difficulties of the child as well as parental responses to the child. These strategies include

enhancing the developmental and adaptive abilities of the child, enhancing appropriate expectations for child compliance, increasing effective parenting skills, and promoting anger management techniques.

Although there is no intervention outcome literature on these treatment strategies that are designed specifically for psychological maltreatment, studies have documented the effectiveness of various treatment strategies with other child maltreatment groups (see Chapters 3, 4, and 5 for discussions of treatment outcome research for other forms of child maltreatment). These strategies, however, may not prove effective in addressing the problems associated with psychological maltreatment. In a 1987 review of various intervention projects targeting the general problems associated with child maltreatment, Cohn and Daro (1987) concluded that psychological maltreatment was the most treatment-resistant form of abuse. As Binggeli et al. (2001) point out, however, this conclusion may have been premature, because none of the programs that Cohn and Daro evaluated specifically addressed the problem of *psychological* maltreatment. Additional research is needed that focuses on intervention strategies specific to psychological maltreatment. The findings of studies in related areas of research provide some reason for optimism that strategies specific to psychological maltreatment hold promise. Studies of interventions that have included mothers with affective disorders (who often engage in inappropriate parent-child emotional interactions), for example, have demonstrated effectiveness in enhancing both positive parent-child emotional interactions and secure mother-child attachment (Beardslee et al., 1997; Lyons-Ruth, Connell, Grunebaum, & Botein, 1990).

Interventions for Children Exposed to Interparental Violence

Although children who have been exposed to interparental violence would likely benefit from involvement with various child welfare and mental health professionals, many such professionals have been slow to respond. The difficulties of these children are often overlooked because the children are often not themselves direct victims of physical or sexual abuse. Children who experience various forms of abuse directly are much more likely to come to the attention of CPS and other professionals (Elbow, 1982). A variety of new services for the children of battered women are increasingly becoming available, however, including

An Interview With David Wolfe

"While we need to maintain family privacy, we also need to get out the message about the prevalence of abuse in particular neighborhoods and to offer support to parents."

David Wolfe, one of North America's foremost researchers on child maltreatment, is the RBC Investments Chair in Developmental Psychopathology and Children's Mental Health and Professor of Psychiatry at the Centre for Addiction and Mental Health at the University of Toronto. He is a diplomate in clinical psychology certified by the American Board of Professional Psychology. He is the author of the significant book *Child Abuse: Implications for Child Development and Psychopathology* (2nd edition, 1999). Along with Peter G. Jaffe and Susan K. Wilson, he is coauthor of the best-selling family violence book *Children of Battered Women* (1990), and with Christine Wekerle and Katreena Scott, he is coauthor of *Alternatives to Violence: Empowering Youth to Develop Healthy Relationships* (1997). He is a member of the editorial boards of several journals, including *Child Abuse & Neglect, Journal of Family Violence, Journal of Consulting and Clinical Psychology,* and *Journal of Interpersonal Violence.* He is also past-president of the Division of Child, Youth, and Family of the American Psychological Association. He received his B.A. in psychology from the University of Rochester and his Ph.D. in clinical psychology from the University of South Florida.

Q: What shaped your approach to the field of child maltreatment?

A: In 1980, I met Peter Jaffe and became active in prevention of child abuse. With grant money, we designed group education and abuse prevention programs for children of battered women. We were interested in the similarities between children who witness violence and those who are abused themselves.

individual treatment, group therapy, and home visitation (see Graham-Bermann, 2002; Graham-Bermann & Hughes, 2003; Groves, 2002; Peled & Davis, 1995).

One of the most common treatments for children exposed to interparental violence is group counseling (Jaffe, Wolfe, & Wilson, 1990; Peled, Jaffe, & Edleson, 1994; Sudermann & Jaffe, 1997). The goals of such treatment for the child typically include the following: (a) labeling feelings, (b) dealing with anger, (c) developing safety skills, (d) obtaining social support, (e) developing social competence and a good self-concept, (f) recognizing one's lack of responsibility for a parent or for the violence, (g) understanding family violence, and (h) specifying personal wishes about family relationships (Hughes, 1992; Jaffe et al., 1990). Data about the effectiveness of group counseling for such children are limited, but the technique appears promising. Several studies have demonstrated positive treatment effects of group counseling, including improved social skills, increased self-esteem, and decreased problematic behaviors and symptoms (e.g., Cassady, Allen, Lyon, & McGeehan, 1987; Peled & Edleson, 1992; Wagar & Rodway, 1995).

Other interventions take the form of multiservice programs. Jouriles and colleagues (1998), for example, developed a program for mothers and their children seeking refuge at a battered women's shelter that includes weekly in-home intervention sessions over an 8-month period. The program focuses on providing mothers with social support, parent training (including child management and nurturing skills), and training in problem-solving and decision-making skills. The home-based sessions also include social support for the children: A child mentor is assigned to each mother-child dyad to serve as a "big brother" or "big sister" to the child, engaging him or her in interesting activities

Q: What are your future personal goals?

A: I would like to expand the implementation and evaluation of our "Fourth R" program, which was developed to prevent teen dating violence and related risk behaviors. This program involves a schoolwide approach to educating young adolescents (in grade 9) about healthy, nonviolent relationships. The program involves a classroom curriculum as well as teacher training and schoolwide activities. I think that child abuse, woman abuse, and other forms of interpersonal violence are "public health" concerns that require widespread prevention efforts. Another interest I have is in prenatal education. The roots of child abuse and neglect are often visible before couples have children. We need to use prenatal screening as a method for identifying parents at high risk for child abuse. We then need to apply a public health model by adopting a referral system to help these at-risk parents obtain medical services and abuse prevention education. Screening could be the first step in starting the referral service.

Q: How can society diminish family violence?

A: One area we need to focus on more is cultural values. Family privacy is such a strongly held value that society fails to intervene sufficiently. Abuse is hidden behind closed doors. While we need to maintain family privacy, we also need to get out the message about the prevalence of abuse in particular neighborhoods and to offer support to parents. Similarly, educational approaches to the abuse of women and children will help to breach the poor understanding that exists throughout North America regarding these issues.

Q: Why can't we as a society seem to eliminate child abuse?

A: It would take a change in priorities, since much of our money is tied up in responding to casualties. We spend millions of dollars on the crises caused by abuse—on crime and health costs. It would take a concerted effort to reach and educate those who will repeat the cycle across generations. As a society, we need to begin the prevention process by educating children and adolescents about healthy relationships. A proactive approach to abuse prevention would be costly initially but very cost-effective in the long run.

Q: How have governmental policies failed to prevent abuse?

A: The outdated approaches too often supported by politicians and community leaders are one of the biggest stumbling blocks to action. The existing political paradigm is one of reaction, not prevention or assistance. Politicians react to crises and may lack the necessary information and expertise it takes to draft an effective, long-range plan of reducing the incidence of abuse. We need to adopt a public health strategy to these wide-reaching phenomena, much as we do for diseases and other threats to public safety. Child and woman abuse are as much a function of our dated policies of family support and cultural respect as they are a function of an individual's behavior.

and providing positive attention and affection. Jouriles et al. conducted a preliminary outcome evaluation of the program using a randomized control group design and found that participating families demonstrated significant benefits, including reduction in child antisocial behavior, enhanced child management and nurturance skills, and decreased parental psychological distress.

Preventing Psychological Maltreatment

To our knowledge, no prevention programs have yet been established with the explicit purpose of preventing child psychological maltreatment, broadly defined. This is a curious state of affairs, particularly given the evidence that psychological maltreatment is the most pervasive form of child maltreatment. In addition, research findings consistent with the notion that psychological maltreatment is the core component

of the negative outcomes associated with all forms of child maltreatment suggest the need for prevention efforts specifically targeting this form of abuse.

There are several likely reasons for the relative lack of attention paid thus far to the development and implementation of efforts to prevent child psychological maltreatment. First, psychological maltreatment has only recently been recognized as a distinct form of child maltreatment. Indeed, many experts in the field argue that awareness of the problem continues to be limited among some professional groups (Hart et al., 2002; Kantor & Little, 2003). In addition, state and federal funding has not been available to support intervention and prevention research or program implementation (Binggeli et al., 2001; Thompson & Wilcox, 1995).

Despite the current lack of prevention programs designed to target psychological maltreatment, a number of experts in the field recommend the future development of such programs. Binggeli and colleagues (2001) argue, for example, that "efforts to prevent psychological maltreatment should be embedded in comprehensive programs designed to prevent a variety of problems" (p. 72). These researchers suggest a two-tier approach to helping families in which the first tier would focus on education and support strategies. Education and support for families could be delivered, for example, through parent education classes that focus on topics such as effective parenting skills, knowledge of child development, stress management techniques, and conflict resolution. Binggeli et al. also suggest the strategy of education through sensitization campaigns. Media campaigns such as "Words Can Hurt" could serve to educate the general public regarding the harmful nature of parent-child verbal aggression. The second tier in Binggeli et al.'s approach would consist of prevention efforts more typical of those already used by many CPS agencies, such as home visitation programs.

Some researchers have suggested the important role that schools and educators can play in overcoming the negative social environments of some children in general, and psychological maltreatment in particular (Binggeli et al., 2001; Garbarino, 1995; Pittman, Wolfe, & Wekerle, 1998). Because children spend so much of their time in school, the school setting provides a natural environment for promoting healthy interpersonal interactions. Preschool and elementary school teachers, for example, can help both children and parents by developing secure attachments with the children they encounter and by serving as models of appropriate adult-child interaction for parents (Hart et al., 2002). Schools are also ideal environments for developing and nurturing specific social and academic skills. As Hart and colleagues (2002) note, "Schools that give at-risk students a sense of competence through successful experience in academics, art, music, athletics, or social interaction and that teach them to plan and make conscious choices about important events in their lives have significantly better student outcomes" (p. 97).

Thus a first step in preventing child psychological maltreatment should be to educate the public and various professionals about the problem. Legal professionals, medical and mental health practitioners, legislators, educators, and government officials need to become aware of the existence of psychological maltreatment as an independent form of child maltreatment that is associated with detrimental child outcomes. Indeed, enhancing awareness and understanding of the problem of child maltreatment among both professionals and the lay public is a primary goal of many professional organizations (see Box 6.2). Currently, many professionals in the field of child maltreatment are working diligently to increase awareness about this social problem. Recently, for example, the American Psychological Association's Section on Child Maltreatment sponsored a congressional briefing to increase awareness about the need for prevention programs and research (Dittman, 2002). Once society at large and influential professionals become convinced of the importance of the problem, greater support for prevention efforts should emerge.

Box 6.2 The American Psychological Association's Section on Child Maltreatment

The American Psychological Association (APA) is the largest scientific and professional organization of psychologists in the world, with more than 150,000 members and 55 divisions representing the many diverse areas within the field of psychology. Each APA division contains various sections made up of members who are interested in special topics within psychology. APA's Division 37 (Child, Youth, and Family Services) is the home of members of the Section on Child Maltreatment.

The Section on Child Maltreatment is the only permanent organization within the APA specifically created to address issues related to child physical abuse, child psychological maltreatment, and child neglect. The section was established in 1994 to support and promote scientific inquiry, training, professional practice, and advocacy in the area of child maltreatment. In the few short years of its existence, the section has accomplished a great deal. A team of section members, for example, has developed curriculum guidelines to improve education and training in the area of child maltreatment at the undergraduate,

graduate, and postgraduate levels. Another team has developed a lesson plan on child maltreatment for use with high school students. Members of the section have also organized a congressional briefing on Capitol Hill in an effort to increase federal funding for child abuse prevention activities. Most recently, a section team helped to develop an amicus brief for the U.S. Supreme Court on the long-term effects of child sexual abuse.

The Section on Child Maltreatment welcomes new members who are interested in furthering research, practice, and policy issues related to the area of child maltreatment. Section members receive the section newsletter, which contains updates on section activities and section-sponsored presentations at the APA's annual conference as well as columns on best practices and case notes and other information on research and policy. Members also receive information on funding for research and treatment innovations and are eligible to receive section awards for outstanding early contributions to research and practice, outstanding dissertation proposals, and outstanding undergraduate research on child maltreatment. Interested readers can get more information on joining the Section on Child Maltreatment by contacting the APA's Division Services Office at (202) 336-6013 or by visiting the section's Web site at http://www.apa.org/divisions/div37/child_maltreatment/child.html.

CHAPTER SUMMARY

Psychological maltreatment is arguably the most elusive form of maltreatment and, as a result, has received the least amount of attention. The vague nature of this form of maltreatment is evident in the fact that a significant proportion of the research directed toward psychological maltreatment focuses on definitional issues. At present, no single definition of psychological maltreatment is universally accepted. Establishing the parameters of psychological maltreatment has proved quite difficult and confusing. Researchers disagree about whether definitions should be broad or narrow and about the relative importance of parental behaviors versus child outcomes.

Given these definitional complexities, the true incidence of psychological maltreatment is largely undetermined, as are victim characteristics associated with this form of child maltreatment. Researchers have obtained much of their information about rates and correlates of psychological maltreatment from official reports made to CPS agencies. Although the quality of information available on this problem is limited, it is clear that many children are reported as victims of psychological maltreatment each year in the United States. Psychological maltreatment, however, is the least commonly reported form of child maltreatment, accounting for only 3% to 28% of reported cases.

Research conducted to date indicates that reports of psychological maltreatment increase as children become older, beginning at age 7. The research has shown no appreciable gender differences among victims, nor is there a clear pattern of racial differences. Early studies have shown a link, however, between child psychological maltreatment and low income. Most reported cases indicate that female parents are identified most often as the perpetrators of psychological maltreatment. Consistent findings have also been observed with regard to psychosocial variables in psychologically maltreating parents, who are characterized as exhibiting interpersonal and social difficulties, poor problem-solving skills, substance abuse, and psychiatric maladjustment. Additional research is needed, however, to replicate current findings and expand understanding of risk factors associated with psychological maltreatment.

Studies of the negative effects associated with psychological maltreatment are limited in both number and quality, making interpretations of findings difficult. Research has, however, consistently uncovered a variety of associated problems in victims, including social, emotional, and behavioral difficulties and intellectual deficits. Many scholars believe that the negative effects of child psychological maltreatment extend into adulthood, but more research is necessary to establish the relationship between childhood histories of psychological maltreatment and adjustment problems in adulthood.

Few intervention and prevention approaches have been developed to address the unique aspects of child psychological maltreatment, and research evaluating the effectiveness of such approaches is limited. An exception is research concerning the intervention programs that have been developed for one specific form of child psychological maltreatment: exposure to interparental violence. Such interventions typically include group therapies for children, and some programs use a multiservice approach. Preliminary outcome evaluations suggest that such programs demonstrate significant benefits, including reductions in problem behaviors and symptoms for children and increased skills for parents (e.g., child management and nurturance skills, improved social skills). Professionals in the field of child maltreatment should focus their future efforts on increasing public awareness and understanding of child psychological maltreatment in order to garner support and resources for research efforts aimed at reducing the incidence and harmful effects associated with this form of child abuse.

DISCUSSION QUESTIONS

1. Why have researchers and practitioners frequently overlooked child psychological maltreatment?
2. Why has defining child psychological maltreatment been such a challenge? Discuss the debate about whether definitions should focus primarily on parental behaviors or on child outcomes.
3. What are the various forms or subtypes of psychological maltreatment described in the research literature?
4. Should exposure to interparental violence be considered a form of child maltreatment?
5. What are some of the legal issues relevant to the definition of child psychological maltreatment?
6. How common is child psychological maltreatment?
7. What is generally known about the characteristics of psychologically maltreated children and their parents (e.g., demographic characteristics, psychosocial qualities of the parents)? Describe a prototypical psychologically maltreating parent and a psychologically maltreated child.
8. What are the various initial and long-term effects (e.g., cognitive, behavioral, emotional) associated with child psychological maltreatment? What effects are associated specifically with exposure to interparental violence?
9. What kinds of intervention strategies are used to help psychologically maltreated children and their families?
10. What kinds of approaches have been implemented in efforts to prevent the psychological maltreatment of children?

RECOMMENDED READING

Binggeli, N. J., Hart, S. N., & Brassard, M. R. (2001). *Psychological maltreatment of children.* Thousand Oaks, CA: Sage.

Glaser, D. (2002). Emotional abuse and neglect (psychological maltreatment): A conceptual framework. *Child Abuse & Neglect, 26,* 697–714.

Graham-Bermann, S.A. (2002). Child abuse in the context of domestic violence. In J. E. B. Myers, L. Berliner, J. Briere, C. T. Hendrix, C. Jenny, & T. A. Reid (Eds.), *The APSAC handbook on child maltreatment* (2nd ed., pp. 119–129). Thousand Oaks, CA: Sage.

Groves, B. M. (2002). *Children who see too much.* Boston: Beacon.

Hamarman, S., Pope, K. H., & Czaja, S. J. (2002). Emotional abuse in children: Variations in legal definitions and rates across the United States. *Child Maltreatment, 7,* 303–311.

Hart, S. N., Brassard, M. R., Binggeli, N. J., & Davidson, H. A. (2002). Psychological maltreatment. In J. E. B. Myers, L. Berliner, J. Briere, C. T. Hendrix, C. Jenny, & T. A. Reid (Eds.), *The APSAC handbook on child maltreatment* (2nd ed., pp. 79–103). Thousand Oaks, CA: Sage.

Holden, G. W., Geffner, R. A., & Jouriles, E. N. (Eds.). (1998). *Children exposed to marital violence: Theory, research, and applied issues.* Washington, DC: American Psychological Association.

Johnson, R. M., Kotch, J. B., Catellier, D. J., Winsor, J. R., Dufort, V., Hunter, W., & Amaya-Jackson, L. (2002). Adverse behavioral and emotional outcomes from child abuse and witnessed violence. *Child Maltreatment, 7,* 179–186.

Kantor, G. K., & Little, L. (2003). Defining the boundaries of child neglect: When does domestic violence equate with parental failure to protect? *Journal of Interpersonal Violence, 18,* 338–355.

Rossman, B. B. R. (2001). Longer term effects of children's exposure to domestic violence. In S. A. Graham-Bermann & J. L. Edleson (Eds.), *Domestic violence in the lives of children* (pp. 35–65). Washington, DC: American Psychological Association.

Note

1. Sources for the details and quotes in this case history are as follows: "Judge OKs Retrial" (2003), Leonard (2001), Pfeifer (2002), and Pfeifer and Anton (2002). Grady and Deborah Machnick are the subjects' real names.

7

KEY ISSUES IN THE FIELD OF CHILD MALTREATMENT

Since Kempe's initial "discovery" in 1962 that some parents physically abuse their children, awareness of the extent and nature of child maltreatment has increased significantly. It seems that the more we learn about child maltreatment, the more we realize how complex the issues are and how little we truly understand about this social problem. Up to this point, we have focused our discussion on the major forms of child maltreatment recognized by most professionals and the general public. The increased awareness in society about child physical and sexual abuse, child neglect, and child psychological maltreatment has been accompanied by increased concern for children and their well-being more generally. Specific issues in the field cut across the boundaries of individual forms of child maltreatment, such as the criminal justice system's response to the problem of child maltreatment in the United States and cross-cultural issues. In the past 40 years, research has also confirmed that more children are maltreated than many might have expected and that this maltreatment takes on a variety of forms. The concepts of child maltreatment and exploitation have been extended to include a number of circumstances that are considered unhealthy or less than optimal for children's development. In addition, as we have noted throughout the preceding chapters, each of the various forms of child maltreatment rarely occurs in isolation. Children who are victims of maltreatment are often victimized in multiple ways. In this chapter, we address the issues noted above in addition to several issues faced by professionals who work in the field of child maltreatment.

THE CRIMINAL JUSTICE SYSTEM RESPONSE TO CHILD MALTREATMENT

In the United States, after a child has been identified as a victim of some form of maltreatment, the criminal justice system requires a number of different responses. Federal, state, and local governments all play roles in establishing policy and practice in response to child maltreatment (for a review, see Myers, 2002). Some of the criminal justice system responses to child maltreatment serve a protective function—for example, the roles of child protective services, out-of-home care, and interventions to minimize for victims the potentially traumatic effects associated with being subjected to investigative interviewing and making court appearances. Criminal justice system responses to child maltreatment also include the enactment and enforcement of laws requiring professionals in certain fields to report suspected cases of child maltreatment and the prosecution of individuals who abuse children. Below, we briefly describe these various responses of the criminal justice system, note the potential problems associated with each, and make some suggestions for improvements.

The Role of Child Protective Services

Federal and state laws provide for the protection of children who are at risk for child abuse or neglect. In most states, responsibility for child protection falls on the state department of social services. This department might be called the department of public welfare, the department of human resources, the department of human services, or something else. Regardless of the label, in most states the department of social services includes a division responsible for the protection of children, often referred to as *child protective services,* or CPS. When a child is identified as in need of protection by CPS, that protection may be implemented on either a voluntary or involuntary basis and may result in a child's remaining at home or being placed in some type of out-of-home care.

CPS agencies carry out their responsibility of protecting children in four ways: by investigating reports of maltreatment, by providing treatment services, by coordinating the services offered by other agencies in the community to child victims and their families, and by implementing preventive services (Carroll & Haase, 1987; Wells, 1994). Ideally, the goal of CPS in all cases is to prevent child abuse and neglect in children's own homes through the provision of various services. The U.S. Department of Health and Human Services (2003a) distinguishes two roles for CPS: provision of *preventive services,* which are designed to increase parental competence in child rearing and understanding of child development; and provision of *postinvestigation services,* which are designed to address child safety through assessment of families' strengths, weaknesses, and needs. Preventive services generally include day care or respite care, counseling for children and parents, parenting education, home visitor services, homemaker help, transportation, and self-help or volunteer programs such as Big Brothers/Big Sisters, Parents Anonymous, and Parents United (Daro, 1988; U.S. DHHS, 2003a; Wells, 1994). Postinvestigative services include individual and family counseling and in-home services in addition to foster care and court services (U.S. DHHS, 2003a).

In recent years, CPS agencies across the United States have come under fire because of public perceptions that they are unable to provide adequate protection and services for children who have been reported victims of maltreatment (see Box 7.1). According to the authors of one review of services for child maltreatment victims, "Services to maltreated children and their families are increasingly nonexistent, inaccessible, or inappropriate" (Faver, Crawford, & Combs-Orme, 1999, p. 89).

There is considerable evidence to suggest that at-risk children and families are not receiving the investigative or supportive services necessary to ensure the safety of these children and the integrity of their families. One study found that approximately one-third of state CPS administrators contacted by the Child Welfare League of America (1986) did not routinely investigate reports within the 24 to 48 hours mandated by child welfare legislation. The average response time from report to investigation reported in the most recent data from the National Child Abuse and Neglect Data System was 50 hours (U.S. DHHS, 2003a). In addition, the findings of the third National Incidence Study indicated that CPS investigated only approximately one-fourth of children reported under the most stringent definitions of maltreatment (Sedlak & Broadhurst, 1996).

Supportive services for children and families have also been criticized as often inappropriate or lacking altogether. The most recent data from NCANDS indicate that approximately 28 children per 1,000 received preventive services in 2001 (U.S. DHHS, 2003a). When the NCANDS data were examined in terms of the sources of funding for specific services, only approximately one-forth of children were found to be receiving preventive services from each of the individual federal funding sources. Glisson (1996) found even lower percentages in an examination of the characteristics of children in state custody. In this study, 52% of children in custody were identified as having psychosocial problems within the clinical range, suggesting significant need for services. The child welfare records of these children, however, documented mental health services for only 14%.

There is also some evidence that the services provided to children and parents are often inappropriate to their particular needs. Crittenden (1992b) found, for example, that the types of services offered to families in Florida were inconsistent with the breadth of services needed. Other researchers have noted inconsistencies between what families perceive they need in the way of services and the services deemed necessary for them by CPS workers. Pelton (1982) found that agencies tended to offer services designed to change clients, whereas the clients wanted concrete advice, material assistance, and help with interpersonal problems. As Faver et al. (1999) note, regardless of whether the perceptions of clients or agency personnel are more accurate, "if clients' stated needs are not met and the services recommended are perceived as inappropriate, clients are less likely to accept and benefit from the recommended services" (p. 95).

What factors might contribute to the difficulties the child welfare system faces in providing protection and services to victims of child maltreatment? According to

Faver et al. (1999), many of the system's problems can be attributed to the ways in which child welfare policy, funding, and resource allocation have evolved over the years. Mandatory reporting laws and public education about child maltreatment have led to consistent increases in child abuse reports and resulting increases in CPS workloads, funding shortages, and high turnover rates among well-trained social workers, many of whom are leaving the field (Hewitt, 1998; McCurdy & Daro, 1994a; Thomas, 1998). Although the recommended maximum caseload that will allow for acceptable treatment services is 17 families per caseworker (Smolowe, 1995), reports of actual caseloads are often between 30 and 50 families per caseworker (Gelles & Cornell, 1990). In addition, funding guidelines often place restrictions on service delivery. Federal funding guidelines, for instance, often influence service implementation because states receive matching dollars for some expenditures regardless of the amount spent (e.g., foster care) whereas funds for other services (e.g., treatment and prevention) are restricted to certain amounts (Faver et al., 1999).

Box 7.1 When a Child Dies, Has CPS Failed?

On October 25, 1994, Susan Smith loaded her two small boys into the backseat of her Mazda. As she drove along county roads in South Carolina, Michael (age 3 years) and his brother, Alexander (age 14 months), fell asleep. Smith pulled the car up to a boat ramp by a lake and got out; she then watched as the car rolled into the lake, floated for a few minutes, and sank beneath the surface with the boys still strapped into their car seats (Adler, Carroll, Smith, & Rogers, 1994). Susan Smith murdered her two children and shocked the nation, confirming once again that parents are indeed capable of killing their own children.

Children's deaths at the hands of their parents or other caregivers seem to represent the ultimate failure of child protective services. Although no CPS agency had previously identified Susan Smith as a parent who might harm her children, in many cases of fatal child maltreatment the families have had prior or current contact with such agencies. Some evidence suggests that between 30% and 50% of children killed by parents or caretakers are killed after they have been identified by child welfare agencies, involved in interventions, and then either left in their homes or returned home after short-term removal (Besharov, 1991; Wang & Daro, 1996, 1998).

Not every child death in a community is evidence of a faulty CPS system, however. As Carroll and Haase (1987) note, "Even in the best of social service departments and with the best of services, children, most tragically, will die. In this field of protective services, human judgments are being made; and being human, mistakes are inevitable" (p. 138). The most recent statistics available suggest that in 2001, less than 10% of child fatalities received family preservation services in the 5 years prior to the occurrence of death, and in only approximately 1% of these cases were children returned to the care of the persons who were eventually responsible for their deaths (U.S. DHHS, 2003a). Carroll and Haase assert that the important determination in such cases is whether the child's death or injury resulted from a lack of response by CPS or from incorrect human judgment.

Characteristics of child maltreatment deaths have been evaluated, and some consistencies have emerged. According to data derived from reporting agencies in 2001, approximately one-fourth of child fatalities in the United States resulted from physical abuse (U.S. DHHS, 2003a). These deaths might have been caused by cumulative beatings or single violent episodes. Another 36% of child victims died as a result of neglect (i.e., caretakers failed to provide for the children's basic needs, such as medical care or adequate supervision) and approximately 31% died as a result of multiple forms of maltreatment (U.S. DHHS, 2003a). The leading cause of death among physically abused children is death associated with some type of injury to the head (Smith, 1994). The large majority (85%) of these

#1

children are under the age of 6 years, with 44% under the age of 1 year at the time of their deaths (U.S. DHHS, 2002b).

What can be done to help prevent child maltreatment fatalities? One response to this problem that is receiving increasing support is the establishment of child death review teams. Such teams are typically composed of community professionals representing multiple agencies. Currently, child death review teams are forming across the United States, Canada, and other countries (Durfee, Durfee, & West, 2002). Although the functions of these teams vary, most review child death cases to do the following: identify the prevalence of deaths from abuse and neglect, improve the policies and procedures of CPS to prevent future child deaths and serious injuries, protect siblings of children whose causes of death are unexplained, and increase professional and public awareness of child death due to maltreatment (Block, 2002; Durfee et al., 2002; Thigpen & Bonner, 1994). The American Academy of Pediatrics (1999) recently published a policy statement outlining the following recommendations for the investigation and review of unexpected deaths:

- Pediatricians should advocate for proper investigation and death certification.
- Autopsies should be required in all questionable deaths of children younger than 18 years.
- State laws should be created to establish child death review and investigation.
- Pediatricians should be involved with child death review teams.
- The child death review process should involve multiple groups and agencies.
- Death scene investigators should have special training in child abuse, child development, and sudden infant death syndrome.
- Data from child death review teams should be used to develop initiatives to prevent child death.

Other prevention efforts have focused on the investigation of risk factors associated with child maltreatment fatalities. One study compared maltreatment fatality cases with nonfatal maltreatment cases and found several factors to be associated with fatality, such as paternal drug use, absence of a maternal grandmother in the home, ethnicity, young age of the child, presence in the home of a father or father substitute, presence of a sibling with medical problems, and prior removal of the child from the home (Fontana & Alfaro, 1987). Hegar, Zuravin, and Orme (1994) have found a child's young age to be the best predictor of severe and fatal physical abuse.

Daro and Alexander (1994) have called for a broad public health approach to preventing childhood maltreatment deaths. They recommend efforts directed at federal, state, and local levels, such as expanding available funding for programs and research, reforming judicial and child welfare policy, increasing professional and community education, and providing community-based support for at-risk families. Many experts believe that a comprehensive approach is necessary for the realization of an actual reduction in child maltreatment fatalities. As U.S. Attorney General Janet Reno noted in 1994, "The problem of child maltreatment-related deaths is not a simple one, and the solutions require the coordinated efforts of many agencies and professionals as well as the commitment of the entire community" (p. 1).

Melton and Barry (1994) have argued that the ultimate reason the child welfare system fails is that it responds to allegations, not needs. CPS often operates under the assumptions of competing goals: to protect children *and* reunify families. One goal calls for investigative services; the other calls for preventive services.

Historically, CPS agencies have narrowly focused on reporting and investigation to the exclusion of prevention and treatment efforts. At present, approximately 30% to 40% of U.S. families in which maltreatment has been substantiated do not receive any "service" other than investigation (McCurdy & Daro, 1994a; Wang &

Daro, 1998). In 1993, in reaction to the problems with the system's response to abused and neglected children, the U.S. Advisory Board on Child Abuse and Neglect formulated a new national strategy for the protection of children. Melton and Barry summarize this strategy, which includes the following elements:

1. Strengthening neighborhoods as environments for children and families

2. Refocusing the delivery of human services so that efforts are focused on services to prevent child maltreatment rather than almost exclusively on services provided after abuse has occurred

3. Reorienting the role of government in child protection so that incentives are offered for prevention and treatment rather than investigation

4. Targeting societal values that may contribute to child maltreatment, such as cultural acceptance of violence and exploitation of children

5. Increasing the knowledge base about child maltreatment through federal research programs

Clearly, the child protective system in the United States is plagued by numerous problems. Some of these problems may be inevitable, given the challenge that CPS agencies face in attempting to meet multiple goals: investigating reports of child maltreatment, providing needed services to victims, protecting children, and providing support for families. In addition, CPS workers attempt to do all these things in an environment that is very stressful. Indeed, many of the decisions that child welfare workers must make on a daily basis can have significant consequences for children and their families (Norman, 2000). Despite the difficulties with the system outlined above, however, there is reason for some optimism. In addition to the literature critiquing the system, for example, a growing body of literature is being produced by researchers who are attempting to understand the complexities of child protection and service delivery (e.g., Jonson-Reid, 2003; Maluccio, 2002; Staudt & Drake, 2002a). In addition, a number of scholars have begun to delineate the principles of good child welfare practice (e.g., Dubowitz & DePanfilis, 2000; Ferguson, 2001). Ferguson (2001) echoes this optimism and expounds the need to "move the literature of child care beyond what I call the deficit perspective, where the focus is on what does *not* get done, to one which sets out best practice as a model for developing systems and practice competencies" (p. 1).

Out-of-Home Care

Out-of-home care is one example of the kinds of postinvestigative services provided by CPS agencies. Out-of-home care for child maltreatment victims includes foster care placement, court placements with relatives (e.g., kinship care), and placement in residential treatment centers and institutions. In 1985, an estimated 276,000 American children were living in out-of-home care settings, primarily as a result of child abuse, physical neglect, parental incompetence, or abandonment (Sudia, 1986). By the early 1990s, the number had escalated to more than 400,000, with approximately 75% of these children placed in foster care (George, Wulczyn, & Fanshel, 1994; Morganthau et al., 1994). The Adoption and Foster Care Analysis and Reporting System estimated that as of June 2001, more than 500,000 children were living in foster care in the United States (U.S. DHHS, 2003b). The rise in the number of children receiving out-of-home placements has led to considerable debate in recent years about placement decisions (see Box 7.2).

Foster care is one of the child placement options most frequently employed by child protective services (Trupin, Tarico, Low, Jemelka, & McClellan, 1993). In 2001, approximately one-fifth of child maltreatment victims in the United States were placed in foster care following CPS investigation (U.S. DHHS, 2003a). Several factors likely influence whether a child victim is placed in foster care, such as the child's age, the type of abuse experienced, and whether the child has been a victim of maltreatment in the past. The NCANDS examined the factors associated with child maltreatment victims' placement in foster care and found that children who were prior victims of maltreatment were twice as likely as first-time victims to be placed in foster care. In addition, children younger than 4 years of age were likely to be placed in foster care, and child victims of sexual abuse were less likely than victims of other forms of child abuse to be placed in foster care (U.S. DHHS, 2003a).

Although state laws permit CPS to place children in out-of-home care to protect them, all states have programs to prevent the dissolution of the family when that is desirable and possible (Stein, 1993). The federal Adoption and Safe Families Act of 1997 reaffirms the principle of family reunification but also holds paramount the concern for children's safety. This act, which President Clinton signed into law on November 19, 1997, is one of the strongest statements regarding child protection ever produced in this country. It establishes

Box 7.2 Out-of-Home Placement Dilemmas

In a 1993 report, the U.S. Advisory Board on Child Abuse and Neglect concluded that "the system the nation has devised to respond to child abuse and neglect is *failing*" (p. 2). One component of that system has been receiving increasing criticism in recent years: out-of-home placement. One problem is that the number of people willing to be foster parents is decreasing, and this limits the number of placements available for children (Ladner, 2000). Other concerns are the potentially negative psychological effects on children of being displaced from their family homes, such as emotional and behavioral problems. Critics also argue that the system is harmful for children because placement in out-of-home settings puts them at increased risk for abuse.

One obvious alternative to out-of-home placement for children who have been identified as abused and neglected is to have them remain in their own homes. Proponents of family preservation believe that such children should remain in their homes while their families receive intensive services aimed at keeping the children safe. There is considerable debate in the research literature, however, regarding the value of family preservation and the effectiveness of family preservation services (e.g., Altstein & McRoy, 2000; Lindsey, Martin, & Doh, 2002). Some experts argue that the doctrine of family preservation and reunification should be abandoned and replaced by programs that focus on child protection and intervention aimed at children's needs (Gelles, 2000). Others contend that such a conclusion is premature and that additional well-designed research is needed to determine the effectiveness of family preservation programs (Staudt & Drake, 2002b).

Current concerns about the problems of out-of-home placement create a dilemma about what to do with children without homes—those who are abused, neglected, or unwanted. Reform of the child welfare system has been the topic of debate in Washington. In 1994, just before he became Speaker of the U.S. House of Representatives, Newt Gingrich recommended bringing back orphanages as one solution (Ladner, 2000). Most Americans' perceptions of orphanages are generally negative, conjuring up images of lonely and emotionally starved children. Orphanages have been likened to prisons, useful for warehousing large numbers of children who are unable, for whatever reason, to live at home (Blankenhorn, 1994). In addition to distasteful images, the notion of resurrecting the orphanage has raised concerns about the resulting effects on the physical, social, and emotional well-being of children living in such arrangements. Gates (1994), for example, presents a review of the history of the orphanage, describing the overcrowded conditions, poor nutrition, and unreasonable labor demands placed on children that were characteristic of orphanages of the 1800s. The orphanages of today, however, are group homes or residential treatment centers that feature relatively small living quarters and high staff-child ratios.

What, then, is the best alternative for maltreated children? To answer this question, society must weigh the costs and benefits of leaving abused and neglected children in their homes versus placing them in foster care versus placing them in residential living settings. An analysis of the financial costs of these three options indicates that the least expensive alternative is to keep children in their homes, followed by placing them in foster care. The maximum monthly federal program payments to parents in family preservation programs range from $253 in Alaska to $192 in Vermont (Green, as cited in Morganthau et al., 1994). These figures translate into approximately $6 to $8 a day per child. The monetary costs of foster care placement range from $12 to $16 a day per child (Spencer & Knudsen, 1992). The most expensive alternative is institutional care. For example, Boys Town, a residential group home, spends approximately $111 to $133 per day per child (Morganthau et al., 1994).

Financial expenses are not the only consideration. What about the other costs associated with these alternatives, such as the potential for negative socioemotional consequences for children and the risk for further maltreatment? The research evidence concerning these issues, unfortunately, is inconclusive. With regard to the potential psychological damage resulting from out-of-home placement, some studies have found better outcomes for children in foster care (Hensey, Williams, & Rosenbloom, 1983) whereas others have found better outcomes for children who remain at home (Lynch & Roberts, 1982). In one study, Kurtz, Gaudin, Howing, and Wodarski (1993) found no effect on child outcome for length of time spent in foster care, but they did find that greater numbers of foster care placements were associated with more negative child outcomes.

Research that has evaluated the risk for further maltreatment associated with in-home and out-of-home placement has also produced inconclusive results. Cohn and Daro (1987) found that 30% to 47% of parents continued to abuse their children while receiving treatment services. Although abuse also occurs in out-of-home placements (Poertner, Bussey, & Fluke, 1999; Rosenthal, Motz, Edmonson, & Groze, 1991; Spencer & Knudsen, 1992), research suggests that this is relatively uncommon, constituting less than 1% of confirmed abuse cases (McCurdy & Daro, 1994b). Spencer and Knudsen (1992) compared relative risk for maltreatment among a variety of out-of-home facilities and found that children in day-care centers and school facilities were less likely to be maltreated than those in foster homes, residential homes, and state institutions and hospitals.

The best placement alternative for any given child likely depends on his or her particular circumstances. Placement decisions must involve a flexible and comprehensive approach that respects the potential contributions of many types of interventions. In some instances, keeping the child in the home while the family receives intensive intervention has proven cost-effective (Daro, 1988; Walton, Fraser, Lewis, & Pecora, 1993). On the other hand, there is no question that out-of-home care is necessary for some children. Ultimately, the solution to the placement dilemma involves many challenges:

> Increased risk to children and families occurs when either protection or preservation is emphasized to the exclusion of the other. If prevention of placement or reunification is framed as the primary "success," we introduce an incentive that may endanger children. Conversely, an emphasis on protection, without providing parents in-home services at the level they need, may harm children. (Lloyd & Sallee, 1994, p. 3)

child protection as a national goal and specifies procedures for ensuring that protection. In reviewing the act, and in considering the monumental task of implementing its provisions, the National Clearinghouse on Child Abuse and Neglect Information (1998a) has highlighted a number of the act's key principles. These important insights are reproduced here in Table 7.1.

The Adoption and Safe Families Act unequivocally establishes the goal of ensuring the safety of the child in all decisions about child removal and family reunification. In doing so, the law clarifies the states' responsibility to the child, explicitly noting that children should never be left in or returned to dangerous living situations. The law also provides incentives for adoption and other permanency options (Children's Defense Fund, 1997; National Clearinghouse on Child

Abuse and Neglect Information, 1998a). According to the act, a child may be placed in out-of-home care when danger to the child is imminent or when prevention attempts are unlikely to be effective. In addition, the law defines specific situations in which states are *not* required to make "reasonable efforts" to return children to their families (e.g., when the parent has committed murder, manslaughter, or felony assault of the child or another child of the parent). Furthermore, the law affirms that children should not grow up in temporary living situations by establishing requirements for early permanency planning (e.g., timely adoption and a time frame for initiating termination of parental rights). When the state terminates parental rights, for example, the law encourages the consideration of early adoption as an alternative to foster care (Emery & Laumann-Billings, 1998).

Table 7.1   The Adoption and Safe Families Act of 1997

The safety of children is the paramount concern that must guide all child welfare services. The new law requires that child safety be the paramount concern when making service provision, placement, and permanency planning decisions. The law reaffirms the importance of making reasonable efforts to preserve and reunify families, but also it now exemplifies when states are not required to make efforts to keep children with their parents, when doing so places a child's safety in jeopardy.

Foster care is a temporary setting and not a place for children to grow up. To ensure that the system respects a child's developmental needs and sense of time, the law includes provisions that shorten the time frame for making permanency planning decisions and that establish a time frame for initiating proceedings to terminate parental rights. The law also strongly promotes the timely adoption of children who cannot return safely to their own homes.

Permanency planning efforts for children should begin as soon as a child enters foster care and should be expedited by the provision of services to families. The enactment of a legal framework requiring permanency decisions to be made more promptly heightens the importance of providing quality services as quickly as possible to enable families in crisis to address problems. Only when timely and intensive services are provided to families can agencies and courts make informed decisions about parents' ability to protect and care for their children.

The child welfare system must focus on results and accountability. The law makes it clear that it is no longer enough to ensure that procedural safeguards are met. It is critical that child welfare services lead to positive results. The law requires numerous tools for focusing attention on results, including an annual report on state performance, the creation of an adoption incentive payment for states designed to support the president's goal of doubling the annual number of children who are adopted or permanently placed by the year 2002, and a requirement for the department [U.S. DHHS] to study and make recommendations regarding additional performance-based financial initiatives in child welfare.

Innovative approaches are needed to achieve the goals of safety, permanency, and well-being. The law recognizes that we do not yet have all of the solutions to achieve our goals. By expanding the authority for child welfare demonstration waivers, the law provides a mechanism to allow states greater flexibility to develop innovative strategies to achieve positive results for children and families.

SOURCE: Reprinted from National Clearinghouse on Child Abuse and Neglect Information (1998a).

Mandatory Reporting

As we have noted previously, during the child abuse prevention movement of the 1960s, all U.S. states adopted mandatory reporting laws. These laws require certain professionals to report suspected cases of child maltreatment. Professionals who are mandated to report typically include medical personnel (e.g., physicians, dentists, nurses), educators (e.g., teachers, principals), mental health professionals (e.g., psychologists, counselors), public agency employees (e.g., law enforcement officers, probation officers), and day-care personnel. Most states require mandated reporters to contact appropriate agencies "immediately" upon suspicion of abuse, and many states also require a written report to follow within a specific time period (e.g., within 24 to 48 hours).

These laws have come under increasing criticism in recent years. The problem begins with the well-documented observation that professionals fail to report approximately 50% of the suspected cases of child maltreatment they encounter (Sedlak, 1990).

Mandated professionals might fail to report for a number of reasons, including a lack of understanding about the reporting laws, concern for the parents, hesitancy to break the client-therapist confidentiality code, and a general reluctance to get involved (Renninger, Veach, & Bagdade, 2002; Wurtele & Miller-Perrin, 1992).

An additional difficulty with mandatory reporting laws is that CPS, which is charged with the task of coordinating social services for needy families, has become overwhelmed by the responsibility to investigate abuse allegations and to coordinate placement of those children who need to be removed from their homes (Emery & Laumann-Billings, 1998; Schene, 1996). Mandated professionals are well aware of this reality, and it puts them in a difficult position when they encounter cases of suspected child maltreatment. Imagine, for example, the nature of the relationship that could develop between a clinical social worker and a troubled mother. After working together for several months, the mother, who has come to trust the social worker, confesses that she sometimes engages in behavior that the social worker would define as abusive. By law, the social worker is required to report the case to CPS. Experience tells her, however, that given the ambiguity of abuse definitions and the limited physical evidence in this particular case, it is unlikely that the abuse allegation would be substantiated. Even if it were substantiated, this is not, in the opinion of the social worker, an especially severe case of abuse that suggests removal of the children. The family needs help and wants help, and the social worker knows that she is in the best position to provide that help. If the social worker reports the case, she violates the trust she has painstakingly built. In addition, the most likely outcome would be "no provision of services, no legal action, and eventually, encouraging the family to seek treatment—exactly where they began the long, expensive, and intrusive process" (Emery & Laumann-Billings, 1998, p. 130).

In general, the consensus among legal scholars and others involved in child protection has been that mandatory reporting laws are essential to child protection (Wurtele & Miller-Perrin, 1992). Given the concerns about CPS and many professionals' corresponding reluctance to report cases, however, more and more experts are calling for modifications in mandatory reporting laws. One possible solution would be to rewrite these laws so that professionals are required to report only severe cases of child maltreatment. This would remove the reporting obligation from mental health professionals who encounter minor cases of abuse and might put them in a better position to help needy parents (Emery & Laumann-Billings, 1998).

Children and the Legal System

Another concern associated with the criminal justice system has centered on how to protect child victims from the stresses associated with involvement in the legal system, including case investigation and court proceedings. Several experts have suggested that much of the stress that child victims experience results from activities that they must endure when they come to the attention of the system, such as multiple interviews, courtroom appearances, and face-to-face confrontations with their abusers (Goodman et al., 1992; Montoya, 1993; Saywitz, Goodman, & Lyon, 2002). Imagine the fear of a 4-year-old, for example, who must sit on the witness stand in a strange courtroom in front of strangers and describe events as potentially upsetting as sexual abuse. Or imagine the 7-year-old

who is expected to testify against his abuser, who is his father. In addition, child witnesses must often endure cross-examination that is usually directed at destroying their credibility. Most adults might find such an experience distressing.

In addition to increasing child victims' discomfort, the stress associated with involvement in the criminal justice system is also believed to increase their distractibility, reduce their motivation, and possibly interfere with memory recall (Saywitz & Snyder, 1993). In a study of child witnesses in cases of child sexual abuse, for example, Saywitz and Nathanson (1993) found that the courtroom environment impaired the children's memory performance and was also associated with increased child reports of stress.

Legal professionals and mental health experts have suggested a number of approaches to minimize the stress and discomfort experienced by CSA victims. One development has been the practice of minimizing both the number of interviews and the number of interviewers that a child experiences through the use of videotaped investigative interviews with children (see Montoya, 1993). This practice is effective because the numerous professionals involved in a case of child maltreatment can view the tape rather than put the child victim through multiple interviews. The use of multidisciplinary teams may also be helpful in reducing the number of interviews to which child victims must be subjected (Pence & Wilson, 1994). These multidisciplinary teams consist of various professionals involved in the investigation and adjudication of child maltreatment cases, including law enforcement officials, health professionals, and CPS workers, who work together to pool and coordinate resources. When this approach is used, only one highly trained professional typically interviews the child while other members of the team observe from behind a one-way mirror. Most states have laws authorizing or mandating the use of such teams in cases of child maltreatment.

Special courtroom accommodations for child witnesses are another way in which some jurisdictions are attempting to reduce the stress of criminal justice system involvement for child victims. Some courts, for example, have allowed child victims to testify outside the direct presence of their abusers by permitting the submission of videotaped testimony (Montoya, 1993; Perry & McAuliff, 1993). The Sixth Amendment to the U.S. Constitution, however, protects a defendant's right to confront his or her accuser, so most states do not categorically allow child witnesses to testify in this way (Pence & Wilson, 1994). As an alternative, some courts in North America and other parts of the world have allowed children to testify via closed-circuit television from judges' chambers (Bottoms & Goodman, 1996; Myers, 1992).

Another approach to reducing stress for victims of child maltreatment as they experience criminal justice proceedings is to provide them with special preparation and support. Many practices, for example, can be implemented to help make the courtroom a less frightening place for a child witness, such as familiarizing the child with the surroundings ahead of time (e.g., through a tour of the courthouse and courtroom), closing the court proceedings to the public and press, and allowing a trusted adult to remain in the courtroom while the child testifies (Myers, 1994; Regehr, 1990; Saywitz & Snyder, 1993). Other suggestions for improving the child's experience with the legal system include giving the child specific instructions before he or she is interviewed and using innovative questioning formats (e.g., the cognitive interview, narrative elaboration) (Saywitz et al., 2002). Accumulating evidence suggests that such approaches are helpful in improving child victims' ability to answer questions, the completeness of their reports, and the consistency of their responses (Goodman et al., 1992; Saywitz & Snyder, 1993).

Prosecuting Individuals Who Abuse Children

As we have noted in previous chapters, there have been few legal and social costs to child maltreatment throughout history. For much of human history, adults have physically and sexually abused children with state endorsement. Even today, many researchers and advocates argue that the social and legal costs of such violence are too low, and that parents sometimes abuse their children "because they can" (Gelles & Straus, 1988).

According to the deterrence perspective, the way to reduce the crime of child maltreatment is to punish the criminal. A father who beats his son, for example, is guilty of assault, and he should be treated as other assault offenders are treated. If the assault is serious, the father should go to jail, the child should be removed from the home, or both. As society increasingly condemns violence in the family and increasingly censures violent family offenders, the cumulative effect should be a lower level of family violence in general (Williams, 1992).

The criminal justice response toward persons accused or convicted of child maltreatment can take many forms, including prison sentences, plea bargaining, diversion programs, and probation. Although no national statistics are available on the number of child maltreatment prosecutions in the United States annually or the number of perpetrators who are court ordered into diversion programs or who receive probation, research on selected jurisdictions provides some information about criminal justice system responses to child maltreatment.

Child maltreatment offenders are not always prosecuted for their crimes. In a report published in 1987, Chapman and Smith noted that only approximately 42% of sexual abuse allegations substantiated by CPS or reported to the police were forwarded for prosecution (cited in Finkelhor, 1994a). Many factors influence whether prosecution is initiated in an individual case (e.g., Tjaden & Thoennes, 1992). Cases involving victims younger than age 7 are less likely to be prosecuted than are those involving older children, for example, and cases in which the abuse is severe, involves force, and the perpetrators have prior criminal records are more likely to be prosecuted (e.g., Myers, 1994; Tjaden & Thoennes, 1992).

As is true of other crimes, plea bargaining is common in cases of child maltreatment. Approximately two-thirds of cases nationwide result in the perpetrator pleading guilty in exchange for reduced charges (e.g., Tjaden & Thoennes, 1992). Many jurisdictions use diversion or probation programs in cases of child maltreatment. These involve agreements between prosecutors and defendants whereby the defendants participate in some form of counseling or treatment with the understanding that charges will be dismissed if they comply (Myers, 1993). Smith, Hillenbrand, and Goretsky (1990) found that 80% of convicted child molesters in their study sample were sentenced to probation, which usually included court-mandated treatment as a condition.

Some scholars have suggested that a failure to prosecute and jail child maltreatment offenders reflects a lack of social recognition of the problem and commitment to address it (Wurtele & Miller-Perrin, 1992). Child maltreatment cases are not prosecuted for many reasons, however. As the U.S. Supreme Court stated in 1987, "Child abuse is one of the most difficult crimes to detect and prosecute because there often are no witnesses except the victim" (quoted in Myers, 1993, p. 573). In addition, physical evidence of child maltreatment is rarely available (Bays & Chadwick, 1993). The child victim's testimony is often the only evidence in a case, and the public, prosecutors, and judges are often concerned about the credibility of child witnesses (Finkelhor, 1994a; Myers, 1993, 1994).

Despite the difficulty in prosecuting cases of child maltreatment, there is some evidence that child abuse is treated much like other crimes within the American criminal justice system. The proportion of child maltreatment cases that proceed to trial, for example, is approximately 10%, which is similar to the proportion for criminal cases in general (Goodman et al., 1992; Tjaden & Thoennes, 1992). A strong criminal justice system response is also evidenced by the fact that the majority of child sexual abuse cases that go to trial result in convictions (Gray, 1993). Research has also demonstrated that the percentage of child maltreatment cases for which criminal prosecutions are initiated is higher for CSA cases than for other types of maltreatment (e.g., Tjaden & Thoennes, 1992).

The criminal justice system has also responded to CSA offenders in other ways. In 1993, President Bill Clinton signed the National Child Protection Act, which requires states to report information on child abuse arrests and convictions to the national criminal history record system of the Federal Bureau of Investigation. Three years later, President Clinton signed a federal version of "Megan's Law," which requires states to maintain systems for community notification regarding the whereabouts of known sex offenders (see Box 7.3). In addition, some states require that registered sex offenders submit specimens of body fluids for possible genetic comparison with specimens taken from victims (Myers, 1994).

Box 7.3 Megan's Law #5

Richard and Maureen Kanka will remember July 29, 1994, forever. That is the day their 7-year-old daughter, Megan, was found raped and murdered in a grassy field close to their home. The murder suspect, Jesse Timmendequas, was a twice-convicted sex offender who was living across the street from the Kankas. In May 1997, Timmendequas was convicted of first-degree murder and later sentenced to death. During the trial, detectives testified that Timmendequas had confessed to touching the young girl, strangling her with a belt, tying a plastic bag over her head, and carrying her body out of his house in a toy chest and dumping it in a nearby park ("Man Found Guilty," 1997).

The Kanka family was understandably shocked and angered by Megan's murder. Why hadn't they been informed that a child molester was living across the street? Unknown to the Kanka family at the time, Timmendequas had actually been sharing the home with two other convicted sex offenders. Didn't the Kankas and others living in the community have a right to know? Maureen Kanka was determined that Megan's death would lead to something positive, and she began to speak out publicly about the need to notify communities of the whereabouts of residents with criminal records of sex crimes. Her campaign was successful, and many states implemented community notification policies. Then, on May 17, 1996, less than 2 years after Megan's death, President Clinton signed a federal version of "Megan's Law." This law requires all states to track the whereabouts of sex offenders and to make the information available to the general public.

Because the individual states have been left to decide for themselves how they will carry out the mandates of Megan's Law, specific policies vary. In New Jersey, where Megan Kanka was killed, the law calls for mandatory notification of schools, day-care centers, and youth organizations when moderate-risk sex offenders are released from incarceration. When a high-risk offender is released into a community, police are *required* to go door-to-door and inform residents that a sex offender is living in their community (New Jersey State Attorney General's Office, 2000). In California, Megan's Law *permits* police to publicize the whereabouts of convicted sex offenders but does not *require* them to do so (Vellinga, 1997). Californians who want to know if there is a sex felon living nearby can either call a 900 telephone number (and pay $10 for up to two names) or consult the Megan's Law CD-ROM, which is available for public viewing at police stations and provides the names, aliases, photographs, physical descriptions, and residential ZIP codes of convicted sex offenders who have been released from state custody (State of California, Department of Justice, 2003). Several states have made their sex offender registries available on the Internet (Bunn, 1998).

From a social constructionist standpoint, the rapid legislative response triggered by two highly publicized and horrifying murders of children by convicted child molesters (Polly Klaas in California and Megan Kanka in New Jersey) has been fascinating to observe. The crimes greatly increased public fears concerning children's vulnerability to sexual predators. Advocates concerned about child protection, including relatives of the slain children, took their concerns to the public and to politicians. As is often the case in claims-making, the rhetoric of risk became an important tool. Advocates talked of the high recidivism rates among sex offenders,[1] the high risk to unsuspecting children,[2] and the potential benefits of registry and notification systems. With public concerns heightened, lawmakers had every reason to move quickly.

Despite overwhelming public and political support, however, Megan's Law also has many critics. Much of their disapproval centers on constitutional issues. They maintain that the law violates the ex post facto clause of the U.S. Constitution, which states that the sanctions contained in a new law cannot be imposed retroactively on someone who was convicted before the new law was enacted. Some also question whether Megan's Law violates the double jeopardy clause of the Fifth Amendment, which makes it illegal to impose a second punishment on an individual for a single offense. Supporters of Megan's Law have won most of the legal battles to date, however, arguing that the publication of information on sex offenders does not infringe on the offenders' constitutional rights because the notification itself is not punishment and does not itself restrict the offenders' freedom. A community may ostracize a released offender, but that is not due to any action by the government (Fein, 1995). The most recent legal development concerning this issue took place in March 2003, when the U.S. Supreme Court ruled that states can require sex offenders to register and can publish information (including addresses) about sex offenders on the Internet.

From a social scientific point of view, Megan's Law raises an entirely different set of questions. Discrimination, ostracism, and scorn are harsh punishments, even if they are not imposed directly by the state. Released offenders may also be the victims of harassment and vigilantism. Police departments are well aware of the potential for violence against released offenders and often remind the public that harassment is illegal and probably counterproductive.[3] Despite such warnings, however, there have been isolated cases of vigilantism around the country.[4] Given that a certain amount of ostracism, harassment, and violence toward offenders is inevitable, it is important to consider what the potential consequences of this response might be. We know that the best way to reduce criminal recidivism is to reintegrate released offenders into society. When a former prisoner finds a job, makes friends, reestablishes relationships with family, and becomes an accepted part of the community, he or she has an increased stake in conformity and a reduced probability of reoffending. When individuals must live as though they have the words Sex Offender stamped across their foreheads, such reintegration seems unlikely. Is it possible that by ostracizing released sex offenders, society may eventually lead them to repeat the very behavior that Megan's Law is intended to prevent?

Perhaps the most scathing critiques of Megan's Law come from those who see it as a "haphazard," "reactionary," "knee-jerk" overreaction that serves political interests far more than it does child protection interests. For example, Semel (1997) states:

The key to what is wrong with Megan's Law is found in its very title. We ought to be suspicious whenever politicians make haste to pass a crime bill in the name of a particular crime victim or in the wake of a personal tragedy, ostensibly to ensure that it will not occur again. . . . It seems that whenever a criminal case makes national news, it becomes instant political capital for elected officials. (p. 21)

Although this criticism may or may not be fair, it is questionable whether sex offender registries really offer children much protection. Most have been shown to be prone to errors (such as old addresses) and omissions. The majority of people included in existing registries have been convicted of molesting their own children and are relatively unlikely to reoffend, especially against individuals outside their own families. Critics maintain that publicizing offenders' names may hurt offenders' own children more than anyone else (Vellinga, 1997). Some registries also include offenders who were convicted of sex crimes as many as 40 years ago, gay men convicted of sodomy, and underage youth convicted of engaging in sex that was consensual but illegal because of their age (Bunn, 1998; Semel, 1997). Perhaps most problematic, critics charge, is that Megan's Law creates the mistaken illusion that the "real problem" in cases of child sexual abuse is "the guy down the street," when research suggests that the majority of sex offenses against children are committed by their parents or parent substitutes (U.S. DHHS, 1996). Likewise, children are much more likely to be killed by acquaintances or members of their families than by strangers. In 1994, only 15% of child homicide victims in the United States were killed by strangers, compared with 30% killed by family members and 20% by acquaintances (the offenders were unknown in the remaining cases). For children under the age of 10, the percentage of family and acquaintance homicide is even higher (Greenfeld, 1996).

The debate surrounding community notification and sex offender registries is far from over and represents a controversy with no easy answers. Personally, although as social scientists we find the arguments surrounding constitutionality, fairness, and political motivation compelling, as parents we have a strong desire to protect our children. Any parent would certainly like to know if a convicted child molester is living across the street. Laws and policies that contribute only to the *appearance* of protection, however, may do more harm than good.

Notes

1. Discussions of Megan's Law typically presuppose high recidivism rates among sex offenders, with advocate estimates ranging from 50% to 90%. Recidivism rates are difficult to calculate, however, and any simplistic statement concerning "the" recidivism rate is inevitably flawed. Recidivism estimates vary dramatically, for example, depending on whether the offenders victimized family members (lower rates) or persons outside their families (higher rates). Some studies have examined recidivism after 2 years (lower rates) and some after 25 years (higher rates). As a result of these methodological complications, actual recidivism studies suggest rates varying from 8% to 50% (see Bunn, 1998; Sheppard, 1997)—significantly lower than those often claimed by sex offender registry advocates.

2. Stranger abductions and murders, although especially tragic and horrifying, are extremely rare forms of child victimization. For advocacy groups, politicians, and the news media to suggest otherwise is somewhat misleading. As journalism professor Steven Gorelick, who specializes in the study of media coverage of crime and violence, has noted: "I'm mostly concerned about the illusion of safety that is created by public crackdowns on these kinds of crimes. It's so easy. They're horrific, and they represent a quintessential kind of evil. But the press presents this information absent of the context of how infrequently these things occur. An educated person would conclude, if he's an avid newspaper reader or television watcher, that these kinds of infrequent crimes are the things to be concerned about" (quoted in Sheppard, 1997, p. 40).

3. In California, for example, authorities try to prevent the harassment of released offenders by requiring individuals who want to view the Megan's Law CD-ROM to read the following notice: "The release of this information to the public is a means of assuring public protection and not to punish the offender. The information may not be

used to harass the offender or commit any crime against the offender. Public safety is best served when offenders are not concealing their location to avoid harassment" (quoted in Sacramento Police Department, n.d.).

4. Although most evidence suggests that vigilantism and harassment are somewhat unusual, several stories about problems encountered by released sex offenders have appeared in newspapers across the country in the past few years. In New York, a man fired five bullets into the home of a convicted rapist who had been publicly identified by police (Hanley, 1998). In New Jersey, two people broke into the house of a released sex offender and beat up a man lying on the living room couch, only to discover later that the man was not the sex offender (Sheppard, 1997). In Washington State, an offender's house was burned after his name was publicized (Sheppard, 1997). In Placentia, California, after police distributed fliers identifying a "serious sex offender" and child molester, neighbors picketed the man's house, harassed him with loud horns, and called 911 every time he left his house. When the *Los Angeles Times* ran a story about the harassment and published a picture of the man, he lost his job. "I did a wrong thing, and I paid for it," he later told a reporter. "Now I am trying to start over and I can't. Some people want me to put a gun to my head" (quoted in Sheppard, 1997, p. 38).

The punitive role of the criminal justice system in responding to child maltreatment is a subject of considerable debate. The call for increasing the costs of offending seemingly contradicts the call for a societal commitment to support and services for at-risk families. Should violent parents be helped, or should they be punished? Some observers argue that prevention and therapy, rather than litigation and sentencing, are ultimately important in responding to the problem (U.S. Advisory Board on Child Abuse and Neglect, 1993). Many advocates maintain that both are achievable goals. The key, they argue, is to work harder to distinguish different levels of abuse. Emery and Laumann-Billings (1998) argue that definitional differences between less serious and more serious forms of abuse should be clearly articulated in the law, although they acknowledge the difficulty of this task. They recommend that in less serious cases of abuse, where the parents are poor, young, stressed, and needy, family reunification should be the goal, and supportive intervention should be the means to achieving that goal. The goal of reunification can be accomplished, however, only if intervention programs are in place to help these needy families and to monitor the progress of reunified families. One such program is the Children's Safety Centers Network in St. Paul, Minnesota, which pairs families with volunteers and professionals who observe and monitor the progress of family interactions and provide suggestions for improving family relationships (Hewitt, 1998).

Most experts agree that in more serious cases, the goal of family reunification should be questioned. Indeed, advocating prosecution of offenders is not necessarily inconsistent with prevention and treatment efforts and has the added value of validating victims' innocence and society's view that child maltreatment is unacceptable (Myers, 1994; Peters, Dinsmore, & Toth, 1989; Wurtele & Miller-Perrin, 1992). Unfortunately, few systematic research studies have examined the effects of various criminal justice system responses to child maltreatment (e.g., incarceration versus plea bargain versus mandated treatment) on rates of recidivism.

Ultimately, distinguishing different levels, kinds, and causes of abuse should help settle controversies between supportive versus coercive intervention and between family reunification and termination of parental rights. As Emery and Laumann-Billings (1998) note, the idea of termination of parental rights or jail time for the offender is "far more threatening when our definitions of abuse include relatively minor acts, as they currently do" (p. 131). They suggest that distinguishing different levels of abuse would "be a first step toward the broader goal of refocusing the child protection system on supporting rather than policing families under stress, while simultaneously pursuing more vigorous, coercive interventions with cases of serious child maltreatment" (p. 131).

CULTURAL AND INTERNATIONAL ISSUES IN CHILD MALTREATMENT

Although much of the research discussed in this chapter and in the preceding chapters on child maltreatment was conducted in the United States or Canada, the view that child maltreatment is a social problem of significant magnitude is not merely a North American phenomenon. Indeed, in a comprehensive summary on the problem of violence and health, the World Health Organization has declared that "there is clear evidence that child abuse is a global problem" (Krug, Dahlberg, Mercy, Zwi, & Lozano, 2002, p. 59). Some researchers are currently increasing their efforts to examine the problem of child maltreatment from an international perspective (Levesque, 2001). Such a broad, global approach implicitly requires an understanding of the relationship between cultural factors and child maltreatment. The way that a given culture or society defines child maltreatment, for example, depends on culturally accepted principles and practices of child rearing. Below, we present estimates of child maltreatment in non–North American societies and discuss cultural variability in definitions of child maltreatment. We also address the importance of cultural sensitivity in addressing the problem of child maltreatment.

Estimates of Child Maltreatment Outside North America

Estimating the degree of child maltreatment worldwide is a difficult task. One problem is that many countries have no mandatory reporting statutes or social systems in place to keep official records of reports of child maltreatment (Krug et al., 2002). Many researchers in the past have speculated that the lack of documentation of child maltreatment in some non–North American cultures is evidence of its nonexistence (see Kashani & Allan, 1998). A more probable explanation, however, is that child maltreatment has not yet been "discovered" as a problem in those cultures.

The results of several population-based studies conducted in countries outside of North America challenge the idea that child maltreatment is confined to Western societies. These findings suggest that the rates of child maltreatment in other parts of the world are similar to, or higher than, rates in the United States (e.g., Hahm & Guterman, 2001; Ketsela & Kedebe, 1997; Tang, 1998). A recent study in the Republic of Korea, for example, found that two-thirds of parents reported whipping their children and 45% admitted to hitting, kicking, or beating their children (Hahm & Guterman, 2001). Finkelhor (1994b) examined international rates of child sexual abuse in a review of 21 nonclinical population studies, primarily from English-speaking and Northern European countries but also including studies from Costa Rica, the Dominican Republic, Spain, and Greece. He found international rates of CSA comparable with those reported in North American studies. Relatively few international studies have examined child neglect and

child psychological maltreatment, although researchers have investigated these forms of child maltreatment in England and South Africa (Brooker, Cawson, Kelly, & Wattam, 2001; Madu, 2001). It is difficult to compare estimates from these studies with estimates from other countries, however, due to the varying definitions of child neglect and psychological maltreatment employed.

Cultural Differences and Child Maltreatment

As we have noted previously, the point at which the treatment of children moves from acceptable to unacceptable is largely determined by cultural and community values. The age at which a minor is considered old enough to be left at home alone, for example, might be different for various cultural groups and for various claims-making groups within any culture. Some groups might condemn the notion of a 9-year-old staying home alone, whereas others might approve of it. Ultimately, societal reactions distinguish acceptable treatment of a child from unacceptable treatment.

Most of the research to date on culture and child maltreatment has focused on cultural differences in definitions of child abuse and neglect among North Americans. Researchers have typically asked study participants who vary on cultural or socioeconomic dimensions to read and respond to hypothetical vignettes depicting various incidents of child physical or sexual abuse or child neglect. The researchers then compare the responses of the members of different cultural or socioeconomic groups. Ahn (1994), for example, sampled 364 mothers of various ethnic backgrounds, including African Americans, Cambodians, Caucasians, Hispanics, Koreans, and Vietnamese. In response to a vignette about a 9-year-old with bruises resulting from physical discipline, a majority of Caucasians and Hispanics rated the incident as abusive, whereas 90% of Vietnamese mothers did not perceive it as abusive. Additional studies have also found cultural differences in responses to parent-child bathing practices, sleeping arrangements, and neglectful behaviors (Ahn & Gilbert, 1992; Giovannoni & Becerra, 1979; Rose & Meezan, 1995).

Other research, in contrast, has shown that cultural views concerning what constitutes household cleanliness, appropriate medical and dental care for children, and adequate child supervision vary little across sociodemographic variables. One group of researchers, for example, assessed nonmaltreating U.S. mothers with various sociodemographic backgrounds on the

An Interview With David Finkelhor

"I'd like to see a bit of redress in the balance between the interest in children as perpetrators of crime and children as victims of crime."

David Finkelhor is a renowned family violence researcher with wide-ranging interests. He is currently Professor of Sociology, Director of the Crimes Against Children Research Center, and Codirector of the Family Research Laboratory at the University of New Hampshire. He recently served as cochair of the 8th International Family Violence Research Conference. He has written extensively on topics such as sexual abuse of children and marital rape. Of the 11 books he has edited or written, the latest are *Nursery Crimes: Sexual Abuse in Daycare* (1988), coauthored with Linda Williams and Nanci Burns; and *Missing, Abducted, Runaway, and Thrownaway Children in America* (1990), coauthored with Gerald T. Hotaling and Andrea J. Sedlak. He has received grants from the U.S. Department of Justice, the National Institute of Mental Health, the Office of Child Abuse and Neglect, and other sources. Dr. Finkelhor received his B.A. in social relations and his Ed.M. in sociology from Harvard and his Ph.D. in sociology from the University of New Hampshire.

Q: How did you become interested in family violence?

importance of basic standards of child care, including cognitive, emotional, and physical care. Their results consistently indicated that there is strong agreement across backgrounds about the basic elements of child care, with rural, urban, working-class, and middle-class individuals having similar standards of care (Polansky, Ammons, & Weathersby, 1983; Polansky, Chalmers, & Williams, 1987; Polansky & Williams, 1978). A study conducted in Israel with a group of parents from a low-income deprived neighborhood and a group of parents from a middle-income neighborhood found similar results: No group differences were reported in terms of the parents' level of acceptance for, or degree of harm associated with, vignettes portraying lack of parental supervision (Shor, 2000).

Although many of the findings noted above seem to contradict each other, with some studies suggesting cultural differences in definitions of child maltreatment whereas others do not, it would appear that there is a growing definitional consensus among ethnic, socioeconomic, lay, and professional groups in terms of general definitions of child maltreatment (Dubowitz, Klockner, Starr, & Black, 1998; Portwood, 1999). When cultural differences are observed, such differences tend to reflect variability between groups in terms of what elements of inappropriate parent behavior are emphasized rather than substantive disagreements (Krug et al., 2002). Additional research is necessary to enhance scholars' understanding of the complex relationship between culture and views of child maltreatment. Additional efforts should also focus on the specific reasons for cultural differences in views of child maltreatment, however subtle these differences may be. Research should also examine other child maltreatment issues that might vary between cultural groups, such as risk factors and perceived causes of child maltreatment (see Korbin,

A: There were two factors involved. First, I was influenced by some people doing work in this area who impressed me with the kinds of research questions they were asking. Second, I felt I could combine my scientific orientation with an opportunity to solve a pressing social problem. What has kept me involved is the continuing need for valid scientific information.

Q: What has shaped your approach to the field?

A: Practitioners have been very important for me in specifying issues that needed attention. Some heated public controversies have also been influential in making me think that someone ought to be looking at these ideas more objectively. Also, my disciplinary training as a sociologist has affected my work. I've been very impressed with the ability of contemporary survey research to talk to people candidly about sensitive subjects. There have been a number of recent breakthroughs in methodology, and I feel that these methods can be applied in the area of family violence.

Q: What is your current research focus?

A: My current research interest is in child victimization, in general, and all the different kinds of ways that children get victimized inside and outside the family.

Q: What types of research or advocacy should be emphasized in the field of family violence?

A: I'd like to see a bit of redress in the balance between the interest in children as perpetrators of crime and the interest in children as victims of crime. We spend far more time discussing juvenile delinquency than we spend on discussing juvenile victimization, despite the fact that children appear before the justice system more often in the role of victim than in the role of offender.

Q: What can society do to diminish family violence?

A: I would recommend programs that support parents, including comprehensive prenatal education, home visitation, and respite care. One avenue of approach is to offer these programs within a comprehensive health care system.

Q: What is the biggest problem in trying to eliminate family violence?

A: The greatest problem is at the sociological level. The American public is not able to "swear off" violence. We tolerate violence. We believe that it is an effective method for solving problems. Violence is a part of male identity. We tend to romanticize violence. We need to discourage the use of corporal punishment, eliminate exposure to violence in the media, and help teenagers learn nonviolent problem-resolution skills.

Coulton, Lindstrom-Ufuti, & Spilsbury, 2000; Krug et al., 2002). Differences in cultures and beliefs among social groups are important factors for researchers to consider, because knowledge about such differences might inform treatment and prevention approaches in the field of child maltreatment.

Cultural Sensitivity in Addressing the Problem of Child Maltreatment

Given the cultural diversity of many U.S. communities, professionals who work with child maltreatment families may find that their own cultural values are not consistent with those of some of the families they serve. Because culture and community values are powerful influences, however, the child welfare codes in most states specifically require child welfare agencies to consider the cultural practices of parents in determining the presence of child maltreatment and in establishing interventions. In Colorado, for example, CPS workers are required to consider cultural factors both when investigating reports of child maltreatment and when assessing family needs (Colorado Revised Statutes, 1997, sec. 19-1-103[b]; cited in Levesque, 2000). Attention to cultural factors is important because, as noted above, they can influence definitions of child maltreatment. Different cultural perspectives may view a particular parenting behavior as abnormal (even deviant) or as normal and acceptable (even expected).

There is some evidence that the services provided by many states' child welfare systems are not generally culturally responsive to the needs of the families they serve. Some evidence suggests, for example, that families of color receive "differential treatment with regard to what services are provided, both in terms of quantity and quality" (Harris, 1990, p. 6). Stehno (1982) found that, compared with White children, Black children were more likely to be placed in out-of-home care, more likely to be subject to restrictive patterns of referral and diagnosis, and less likely to receive desirable out-of-home placements.

In response to the cultural insensitivity present in the child welfare system today, many scholars recommend that individuals who work within the system take steps to become "culturally competent." *Cultural competence* has been defined as "the ability to understand, to the best of one's ability, the worldview of our culturally different clients (or peers) and adapt our practice accordingly" (Abney, 2002, p. 479). Harris (1990, p. 7) offers several guidelines for individuals and agencies seeking to become culturally competent:

- Value diversity and uniqueness in differing cultures.
- Develop the capacity for cultural self-assessment.
- Understand the dynamics of difference (i.e., what happens when individuals of different cultures interact).
- Put formal processes in place for obtaining and updating cultural knowledge.
- Develop service adaptations to meet the needs of culturally diverse children and families.

Abney (2002) emphasizes the need for professionals to develop culturally sensitive treatment and service methods, such as assessment techniques that are appropriate for properly diagnosing people of color and interventions that are adapted to suit various cultures. Some observers have also argued that research in the field of child maltreatment needs to reflect cultural competence (Abney, 2002; Korbin, 2002). Although cultural diversity presents many challenges for professionals who work in the field of child maltreatment, professionals who become culturally sensitive and competent should be able to meet these challenges.

ADDITIONAL FORMS OF CHILD MALTREATMENT

Claims-makers are continually renegotiating the specific boundaries of child maltreatment. Some professionals in the field have argued that conceptualizations of child maltreatment should be broadened to include many negative circumstances that are detrimental to children's development. Some have argued, for example, that heavy exposure to televised violence should be considered a form of child maltreatment (Eron & Huesmann, 1987). Others have suggested that ecological factors such as racism, sexism, and living in war zone environments should be considered child abuse (Hart, Germain, & Brassard, 1987; Jones & Jones, 1987). These claims-makers are not, of course, in agreement on the issue of just which circumstances constitute abuse and deserve the label *child maltreatment.*

In the following subsections we discuss some of the forms of child maltreatment that have appeared in the literature in addition to the major forms already addressed. As we have noted in the preceding chapters, the overwhelming majority of child abuse is *intrafamilial* and involves physical aggression, neglect, sexual abuse, and psychological maltreatment perpetrated primarily by parents or other caretakers responsible for the welfare of children. An additional form of child maltreatment that is receiving empirical attention by researchers in the field, however, is sibling abuse—that is, negative interactions between siblings that include physical aggression, sexual behavior, and verbal aggression.

The concept of child maltreatment has also been extended to include conditions and circumstances occurring outside the family. We also focus below on some forms of child maltreatment that are primarily *extrafamilial,* such as exposure to community violence, abuse in institutions and day-care settings, and ritualistic abuse. Despite limited scientific knowledge about these forms of exploitation, their sensationalistic nature has made them popular subjects of the news and entertainment media. Media attention to alleged abuse in day-care settings and ritualistic abuse has often contributed to misperceptions among the general public about the extent of such child maltreatment. These types of child exploitation occur less commonly than those discussed in previous chapters, but frequency of occurrence alone should not determine social concern about a problem. The negative impacts that such experiences can have on children's lives can be just as significant as the impacts of other forms of child maltreatment.

Sibling Abuse

During the early 1980s, discussion of a "new" form of child maltreatment emerged: sibling abuse. Consider the following:

> I can't remember a time when my brother didn't taunt me, usually trying to get me to respond so he would be justified in hitting me. Usually he would be saying I

was a crybaby or a sissy or stupid or ugly and that no one would like me, want to be around me, or whatever. Sometimes he would accuse me of doing something, and if I denied it, he would call me a liar. I usually felt overwhelmingly helpless because nothing I said or did would stop him. If no one else was around, he would start beating on me, after which he would stop and go away. (quoted in Wiehe, 1997, p. 34)

Most individuals who have brothers or sisters can undoubtedly remember a time when they engaged in some altercation with their siblings: pulling hair, name-calling, pinching, pushing, and so on. Because such behaviors are very common, they are rarely defined as family violence (Gelles & Cornell, 1990; Wiehe, 1990). Should such interactions be labeled *abusive* and recognized as an additional form of child maltreatment? The answer to this question is a matter of some debate. Emery and Laumann-Billings (1998) have argued that although such behaviors may be inappropriate, they should not be considered a form of family violence because they are very common and largely involve relatively minor physical acts that result in little or no measurable harm. Others argue that negative interactions between siblings should be recognized as one of the most serious forms of family violence *because* they are so common (Finkelhor & Dziuba-Leatherman, 1994; Wiehe, 1997). These commentators argue that such interactions between siblings, which are often rationalized as sibling rivalry and considered a normal part of development, are deserving of more research attention. In the following paragraphs, we first attempt to distinguish between normative sibling interactions and sibling abuse and then discuss the research available on this topic. Some studies have investigated the various types and frequency of negative encounters that occur between siblings, and others have attempted to determine whether such interactions are harmful.

What is sibling abuse? Most, if not all, siblings at some time hit, slap, and/or punch each other. Siblings often call each other names. Rivalry, jealousy, and anger commonly exist between siblings as they compete for the attention of their parents. Many of the behaviors that siblings exhibit toward each other are described as the products of "normal" sibling rivalry. Siblings also sometimes engage in mutual sexual behaviors, many of which experts consider to be a normal part of exploratory play. Where should society draw the line between normal sibling aggression and exploratory sex play and those behaviors that are damaging and abusive?

As we have noted in previous chapters, child maltreatment is difficult to define. One starting point in defining sibling abuse is to define what should be considered *normal* sibling interaction. Normal behavior of any kind is often defined by a statistical standard that relies on a bell curve; in such a definition, approximately 66% of individual behavior falls within the "normal" range, within one standard deviation of the mean. In this case, abusive behavior could be defined as those behaviors falling at the outer extreme of such a distribution—that is, behaviors that are exceedingly severe or occur excessively frequently. Abusive sibling interaction defined in this way stands in stark contrast to definitional conceptualizations of sibling abuse that are so inclusive that 80% of the U.S. child population could be considered victims.

Many claims-makers prefer to define sibling abuse broadly, arguing that the time has come to redefine what society views as normal sibling behavior. From this perspective, even such common behaviors as siblings hitting or pushing one another might be considered wrong and, as a result, recognized as problematic. It is true that, in times past, many behaviors now generally considered to be wrong, such as adult-child sexual relations, were not disapproved by society (as noted in Chapter 1). Adult-child sexual interactions came to be labeled as *abusive* only in relatively recent times. Similarly, much of what we label *child physical abuse* today was viewed as merely stern discipline or punishment 25 years ago. How many of the interactions between siblings that we are aware of today does society rationalize as legitimate simply because they occur frequently?

Other scholars have argued that overly inclusive definitions of sibling abuse may make it difficult for professionals to discern appropriate interventions and, ultimately, understand this form of child maltreatment (Emery & Laumann-Billings, 1998). Consider, for example, an 8-year-old boy who frequently pushes his 4-year-old sister. His behavior is inappropriate and should be addressed, but it may not be helpful to label it *abusive,* as that may diminish the significance of the term. In response to these concerns, one approach is to delineate specific criteria against which professionals can judge sibling interactions to determine whether they rise to the level of maltreatment or abuse. Several scholars have proposed specific factors that might distinguish between sibling abuse and normal sibling rivalry and sex play (e.g., De Jong, 1989; Wiehe, 1997).

Table 7.2   Criteria That Distinguish Sibling Abuse From Nonabusive Sibling Interactions

Criterion	Description
Power disparity between siblings	Negative sibling interactions that involve significant differences in the distribution of power in age, physical size or strength, or social status
Frequency and duration of the interactions	Negative sibling interactions that occur over many months or years and that include multiple incidents
Element of pressure or secrecy	Negative sibling interactions that involve coercive pressure for involvement or that are carried out in a secretive way
Outcomes of the interactions	Negative sibling interactions that result in some type of harm to the child who is the recipient of the behavior; includes physical and psychological injury
Developmental appropriateness	Negative sibling interactions that fall outside the realm of typical sibling rivalry or normal sex play exploration
Lack of appropriate parental intervention	Negative sibling interactions that occur without appropriate intervention from parents or guardians; inappropriate parental reactions/interventions that include no response, indifference to the victim's suffering, and blame directed at the victim

Table 7.2 lists some criteria that professionals might find helpful in identifying sibling abuse. In some cases, it may be necessary for sibling interactions to meet only one of these criteria to be established as abusive. Sexual intercourse between siblings, for example, is never considered developmentally appropriate. In other cases, professionals will need to evaluate whether sibling interactions meet a number of these criteria.

The first criterion of interest is *power disparity* between the siblings. That is, is one sibling older or physically more powerful than the other, or both? In one family we know, for example, the 4-year-old sister actually displays more violent behavior (e.g., kicking and hitting) than the 8-year-old brother. Because she is both younger and physically weaker than her brother, however, by definition her violent behaviors directed toward her brother would not be considered abusive. Her behavior is inappropriate, and her parents try to respond to her aggression, but it should not be labeled as abuse. Studies that have examined sexual interactions between siblings have consistently shown significant age differences between the siblings (e.g., Adler & Schutz, 1995). Some scholars have argued that the power differential criterion should additionally include power differences based on societal stereotypes involving gender, whereby males dominate females regardless of age differences (Laviola, 1992).

The second criterion to consider is the *frequency and duration of the interaction.* Most cases of severely negative sibling interactions involve multiple incidents occurring over several months or years (Adler & Schutz, 1995; Wiehe, 1997).

The third criterion that can distinguish sibling abuse from other types of sibling interactions is the presence of an *element of pressure or secrecy.* Adults who report having experienced significantly negative sibling interactions in childhood often describe themselves as nonconsenting and unwilling participants who were pressured into the interaction (Adler & Schutz, 1995; Canavan, Meyer, & Higgs, 1992). Abusive sibling behavior also often has an element of misrepresentation or trickery (De Jong, 1989; Wiehe, 1997).

The *outcome of the interaction* is another factor that professionals should consider. In most abusive sibling interactions, there is an aspect of victimization whereby the recipient of the behavior is "hurt or injured by the action or actions of another" (Wiehe, 1997, p. 167). Hurt or injury might take a physical form, such as bruises or cuts, or it might be more psychological in nature, including feelings of anger, fear, or sadness (De Jong, 1989).

One of the most significant criteria to consider is the *developmental appropriateness of the behavior* occurring between siblings. Research on child development provides a great deal of information about appropriate sexual interactions between siblings as well as typical forms of sibling rivalry (e.g., McHale & Pawletko, 1992; Quittner & Opipari, 1994; Rosenfeld,

Bailey, Siegel, & Bailey, 1986). Kolodny, for example, found that parents of children ages 6 to 7 years reported that 83% of their sons and 76% of their daughters had participated in sex play with siblings or friends of the same sex (as cited in Rice, 1998). Exploratory behavior typically involves mutual genital display, touch, and fondling. Intercourse or attempted penetration, however, is not typical of sexual exploratory behavior in childhood (Anderson, 1979; Rosenfeld et al., 1986).

A final key criterion that distinguishes sibling abuse from nonabusive sibling interactions appears to be *lack of appropriate parental intervention*. Adler and Schutz (1995) examined sibling incest cases and found that 58% of siblings exposed to abuse experienced continued abuse because of ineffective parental intervention. Other researchers have found that parents who discover inappropriate interactions between siblings often fail to protect the victims, deny any suffering on the part of the victims, or respond negatively toward the victims with blame or disbelief (Laviola, 1992; Wiehe, 1997).

Forms of negative sibling interaction. Although the majority of research on negative sibling interactions has investigated physical violence between siblings, such interactions can also include inappropriate sexual behavior and verbal aggression. The range of forms of physical violence, inappropriate sexual behavior, and verbal aggression that can occur between siblings is similar to the range of behaviors discussed previously in this book in regard to the forms of child maltreatment perpetrated by adults. *Physical violence* between siblings, for example, occurs in a variety of forms. Consider the following:

> I was 3 or 4 years old. My family went camping often. We were out at a little lake. I was walking with my two brothers . . . my brother pushed me into the water. I couldn't swim! They just stood on the dock and laughed at me. I was gasping for air. . . . Then the next thing I remember is someone pulling me out. It was a farmer driving by on his tractor. . . . He took us all back to camp. . . . I told my parents that my brothers had "pushed" me and they said I "fell" in. (quoted in Wiehe, 1997, p. 24)

This case example focuses on a relatively severe form of physical violence. Other forms of physical violence between siblings include serious acts such as smothering, choking, beating, and stabbing with an object and less serious forms such as hitting, biting, slapping, shoving, and punching (Wiehe, 1997).

Inappropriate sexual behaviors between siblings range from fondling and genital touching to oral contact to penetration (Canavan et al., 1992; Wiehe, 1997). The most common sexual behavior between siblings appears to be genital fondling (Finkelhor, 1980; Wiehe, 1997). *Negative verbal exchanges* between siblings that may be considered abusive take the form of verbally aggressive behavior such as name-calling and verbal threats or comments intended to ridicule or degrade.

Additional behaviors defined as child psychological maltreatment in Chapter 6, such as terrorizing acts, have also been documented in sibling relationships. Wiehe (1997), for example, describes a case in which a boy's brother stabbed the boy's pet frog to death in front of him. The long-lasting impact of such an act is reflected by the fact that the victim was 37 years old when he related this incident to a researcher.

Estimates of the problem. Most researchers who have attempted to evaluate the extent of sibling abuse have focused on physical violence between siblings. On the basis of data from the first National Family Violence Survey, Straus, Gelles, and Steinmetz (1980) found that 82% of American children with siblings between the ages of 3 and 17 engaged in at least one violent act toward a sibling during the 1-year period preceding the survey. Straus et al. measured violence using the Conflict Tactics Scale and included minor acts as well as severe forms of violence. In addition, Steinmetz (1982) found that between 63% and 68% of adolescent siblings in the families she studied used physical violence to resolve conflicts with brothers or sisters. Roscoe, Goodwin, and Kennedy (1987) studied 244 junior high school students who completed an anonymous questionnaire examining negative verbal and physical interactions and conflict resolution strategies between siblings. Results indicated that 88% of males and 94% of females in the sample had been victims of sibling violence at some time in the preceding year. Likewise, 85% of males and 96% of females admitted they were the perpetrators of sibling violence.

Critics have often argued the obvious: that children are immature and impulsive, and most, if not all, siblings engage in aggressive interactions. All of the research cited above, for example, suggests that the majority of violence between siblings is minor and does not meet the criteria for abuse outlined previously. Considerable numbers of studies, however, suggest that more severe violence between siblings is not uncommon. Straus et al. (1980) found that 42% of parents reported kicking, biting, and punching between siblings; 40% reported siblings hitting or attempting to hit one another with objects; and 16% reported siblings "beating up" one another. Roscoe et al. (1987) found similar results in their sample of junior high students: 46% reported that a sibling had kicked them, 38% reported that a sibling had hit them with an object, and 37% reported that a sibling had hit them with a fist.

Other researchers have attempted to evaluate the extent to which siblings engage in sexual behavior with one another. Finkelhor (1980) surveyed 796 undergraduates at six New England colleges and found that 15% of the females and 10% of the males reported some type of sexual experience involving a sibling. Bevc and Silverman (1993) also surveyed a college student sample but included only individuals who had been raised with opposite-sex siblings. Of the 367 students surveyed, 29% reported engaging in some type of sexual activity with a sibling. Males and females were nearly equally likely to report having had such experiences. In a community sample of 930 women residing in San Francisco, Russell (1983) found that 2.5% reported experiencing some type of "exploitive sexual contact" with a sibling (5 or more years older) before their 18th birthday. The variability in these researchers' findings is no doubt due to differences in the samples studied and in the definitions of sexual activity employed.

Studies examining sexual interactions between siblings have uncovered a range of behaviors that vary in their severity. Bevc and Silverman (1993) divide sexual activities or incestuous behaviors between opposite-sex siblings into two categories: consummatory and nonconsummatory. *Consummatory acts* include some form of penetration or attempted penetration and usually culminate in ejaculation (e.g., attempted or completed genital intercourse and oral or anal intercourse). *Nonconsummatory acts* are less intrusive forms of sexual contact, such as sexual kissing or hugging, exhibiting or fondling of sex organs or private body areas, and simulated intercourse. In these researchers' sample of college students, among those who reported a history of sexual activity with a sibling, the majority (76%) reported engaging in less severe forms of nonconsummatory sexual activity. Genital penetration, considered one of the most severe forms of sexual abuse, was reported by only 2% of the students with histories of sibling sexual activity.

Not surprisingly, individuals in clinical populations are more likely to report having experienced severe forms of sibling sexual abuse. Adler and Schutz (1995) found that although fondling was the most common type of sexual behavior between siblings in their clinical sample, up to 42% experienced some form of penetration, either vaginal or anal. In two other clinical samples, O'Brien (1991) found that 46% of sibling abuse victims had experienced abuse that included penile penetration, and De Jong (1989) found that 89% had experienced attempted and/or actual vaginal penetration.

Consequences associated with negative sibling interaction. A commonly held view is that violence and sexual activity between siblings is generally benign and within the context of normal play or exploration. Some scholars maintain that even sexual interactions between siblings, particularly when the children are close in age, may be relatively innocuous (Finkelhor, 1980; Pittman, 1987; Steele & Alexander, 1981). Others contend that such interactions between siblings are always harmful (Brickman, 1984; Canavan et al., 1992). Unfortunately, little sound research has been conducted to address this question. In our review of the literature on sibling abuse, for example, we found virtually no controlled studies. Most of the research to date has relied on a small number of clinical case studies of women seeking therapy, and most studies have failed to include control groups or to use standardized assessment instruments. As a result, the research evaluating the effects of violence and sexual activity between siblings has produced inconclusive findings.

Although lacking in methodological rigor, the studies conducted so far have demonstrated some consistency in the types of difficulties that sibling abuse victims experience. Table 7.3 displays the problems most frequently reported by adults with childhood histories of negative sibling interactions. These problems are similar to those reported by victims of other forms of child maltreatment: low self-esteem, negative emotions, interpersonal problems, revictimization, and PTSD symptoms. In general, these problems have been noted in sibling abuse victims regardless of the type of abuse experienced (i.e., whether it took the form of violence, sexual behavior, or verbal aggression). One exception is sexual dysfunction, which is associated primarily with sexual interactions between siblings.

Characteristics of siblings who inflict harm. Research has found that males and females engage in violent or sexual behavior directed at siblings to a nearly equal degree (Roscoe et al., 1987; Straus et al., 1980; Worling, 1995). With regard to age, differences have been noted; research suggests that as children grow older, violence toward siblings becomes less common (Steinmetz,

Table 7.3   Problems Associated With Negative Sibling Interactions

Problem	Examples
Difficulty with relationships	Mistrust
	Suspiciousness
	Fearfulness
	Hateful feelings
	Problems relating
	Inability to form intimate relationships
	Troubled parent-child relationships
	Poor peer relationships
	Aversion to nonsexual physical contact
	Revictimization in subsequent relationships
Negative emotions	Self-blame
	Depression
	Anxiety
	Anger
	Low self-esteem
Sexual dysfunction	Avoidance of sexual contact
	Sexual compulsiveness
	Promiscuity
	Sexual response difficulties
Posttraumatic stress symptoms	Intrusive thoughts
	Flashbacks

SOURCES: Canavan et al. (1992); Daie, Witzum, and Eleff (1989); Laviola (1992); Wiehe (1997).

1982; Straus et al., 1980). Sexual interactions between siblings also occur at younger ages than do other types of sexual offenses perpetrated against children (Worling, 1995).

Researchers have also evaluated other possible characteristics of individuals who perpetrate sibling abuse. Most have relied on a small number of clinical cases in which both children and adolescents have engaged in physical violence or sexual behavior with their siblings. This research indicates that perpetrators of sibling violence share several characteristic experiences, including a history of physical child abuse and neglect, a chaotic family environment, excessive responsibility for the care of siblings, and parental absence or deprivation (Green, 1984; Rosenthal & Doherty, 1984).

The results of clinical studies of sibling sexual offenders are similar and suggest that these families are characterized by many forms of family dysfunction, such as parental absence or rejection (Becker, Kaplan, Cunningham-Rathner, & Kavoussi, 1986; De Jong, 1989; Smith & Israel, 1987), childhood physical and sexual abuse (Adler & Schutz, 1995; Becker et al., 1986; O'Brien, 1991; Smith, 1988; Smith & Israel, 1987), poor parental sexual boundaries (Canavan et al., 1992; Smith

& Israel, 1987), family secrets (Canavan et al., 1992; Smith & Israel, 1987), lack of parental supervision (Smith & Israel, 1987), family stress and dysfunction (Adler & Schutz, 1995; Canavan et al., 1992), and history of maternal sexual or physical victimization (Adler & Schutz, 1995; Kaplan, Becker, & Martinez, 1990). More methodologically sound studies that have used comparison groups and well-established reliable and valid questionnaires have confirmed these findings. Worling (1995), for example, compared 32 male sex offenders who assaulted younger siblings with 28 males who offended against nonsibling children and found that, compared with nonsibling offenders, the sibling-incest offenders reported significantly more marital discord among parents, feelings of parental rejection, histories of childhood sexual victimization, parental physical discipline, negative and argumentative family atmosphere, and general dissatisfaction with family relationships.

The families of siblings who engage in violent or sexually inappropriate behaviors appear to have several features in common. One possible explanation linking these characteristics with a pattern of abuse is that children who live with abusive and rejecting parents may turn to each other for comfort, nurturance, and support through sexual interactions (Dunn & McGuire, 1992) or may pursue some form of retribution within their families for the abuse and rejection they have suffered (Schetky & Green, 1988). Social learning theory might also apply, in that the heightened degree of marital discord, childhood sexual abuse, physical discipline, and negative communication patterns in such families may serve as a source of modeling and facilitate the attitude that family members are appropriate recipients of violence (Davis & Leitenberg, 1987; Worling, 1995).

Exposure to Community Violence

Some children experience violence not only within their own homes but also within their communities. Anyone who has watched the news on television or read a newspaper has glimpsed the violence occurring regularly within communities worldwide. Rates of violence are high in the United States, for example, with the homicide rate exceeding by several times the rate in any other Western industrialized country (Maguire & Pastore, 1994; Siegel, 1995). In addition, children around the world are exposed to violent acts of terrorism as well as traumatic war-related events (Laor, Wolmer, & Cohen, 2001; Pine & Cohen, 2002; Smith, Perrin, Yule, & Rabe-Hesketh, 2001).

Many experts have expressed concern regarding the effects on children of the significant amounts of violence within many communities (Horn & Trickett, 1998; Osofsky, 1997, 1998; Wallen & Rubin, 1997). Given the knowledge that a child's exposure to violence within the family (e.g., spouse abuse) is associated with several negative developmental outcomes, it stands to reason that exposure to violence within the community might also be detrimental to children's development. Discussion of children's exposure to community violence is relevant to the topic of family violence because family and community violence are interrelated. In one of the few studies that has directly examined the relationship between community violence and domestic violence, Osofsky, Wewers, Hann, and Fick (1993) interviewed 53 African American mothers of children ages 9 to 12 living in a low-income neighborhood. They found that levels of violence within the home, as measured by the Conflict Tactics Scale, were significantly related to children's reported exposure to community violence.

It is clear that many children are exposed to violence not only within their families but also within the larger communities in which their families reside. How often are children exposed to violence in their neighborhoods—to shootings, stabbings, and other violent acts? Are there negative effects associated with such exposure, and, if so, what can be done to protect children from those effects?

Estimates of the problem. Although no official estimates of exposure to community violence exist, recent survey data indicate that American children are exposed to violence at high rates, particularly in many inner-city neighborhoods. In a survey of sixth, eighth, and tenth graders in Connecticut in 1992, 40% reported witnessing at least one violent crime in the preceding year (Marans & Cohen, 1993). Richters and Martinez (1993b) found that 72% of fifth and sixth graders and 61% of first and second graders in an elementary school in southeast Washington, D.C., reported having witnessed at least one act of community violence.

The types of violence to which children are exposed in their communities range from relatively minor acts, such as purse snatching, to severe violence, including murder. Shakoor and Chalmers (1991) found that in their sample of 1,000 African American elementary and high school students, nearly three-fourths reported witnessing at least one robbery, stabbing, shooting, or murder. One study of African American children living in a Chicago neighborhood (second, fourth, sixth, and eighth graders) found that one in four had witnessed a stabbing, and close to one-third reported that they had seen a shooting. In an older group of 10- to 19-year-olds, 35% had witnessed a stabbing and 39% had witnessed a shooting. Nearly one-fourth of the group of older children reported witnessing a killing (Bell & Jenkins, 1991, 1993).

Although some children may witness such extreme violence on only one occasion, there is some evidence that the nature of violence exposure in many communities is chronic and repeated. Studies have found, for example, that nearly three-fourths of youth who had witnessed a shooting had witnessed not just one but multiple shootings (Jenkins & Bell, 1994; Richters & Martinez, 1993a). In addition, in neighborhoods where violence occurs, the percentage of children who report witnessing violence increases as the average age of the children increases, suggesting that the longer children reside in such neighborhoods, the more likely it is they will be repeatedly exposed to violence (Horn & Trickett, 1998).

Effects associated with exposure to community violence. It is difficult to isolate the effects of exposure to community violence because children who live in violent communities are also likely to be poor, to have a single parent, and to experience violence within the home. Several recent studies, however, have examined some of the correlates of exposure to community violence (for reviews, see Horn & Trickett, 1998; Osofsky, 1999; Wallen & Rubin, 1997). Although relatively few studies have evaluated the effects of community violence exposure on children, the results that are available suggest that such exposure is associated with a variety of psychological symptoms, including PTSD symptoms (e.g., difficulty sleeping, repetitive dreams, and pessimism about the future), depression, aggression, and low self-esteem (e.g., Attar, Guerra, & Tolan, 1994; Fitzpatrick, 1993; Freeman, Mokros, & Poznanski, 1993; Martinez & Richters, 1993; Pynoos, Frederick, Nader, & Arroyo, 1987).

Research has also determined that the greater a child's exposure to violence (e.g., nearness to the event or frequency of exposure to different types of violence), the greater the degree of difficulties he or she is likely to experience (Martinez & Richters, 1993; Pynoos et al., 1987). Martinez and Richters (1993) studied 165 African American children ages 6 to 10 years attending first, second, fifth, and sixth grades at a school located in southeast Washington, D.C. The researchers assessed exposure to community violence using the Survey of Children's Exposure to Community Violence, an interview that evaluates the frequency of a child's exposure to 20 types of violence, including shootings, muggings, and stabbings (Richters & Saltzman, 1990). Both the fifth- and sixth-grade children provided estimates of their degree of exposure to community violence by responding to the survey, and mothers of all children in the sample provided estimates of their children's exposure as well. The first- and second-grade children provided estimates of their exposure to violence by completing a similar but more developmentally appropriate interview called Things I Have Seen and Heard (Richters & Martinez, 1990). Martinez and Richter assessed psychological difficulties among the children in their sample by using parent-report measures of stress and behavior problems as well as child-report measures of distress. The results of this research indicated significant correlations between child-report measures of distress and exposure to community violence. Parents' estimates of their children's distress and exposure to violence, however, were not related to children's estimates of their own distress. These seemingly contradictory findings suggest that parents may tend to underestimate the extent to which their children are exposed to violence as well as the extent to which their children display symptoms of distress.

Related research has examined the effects on children of living through the experience of war. In their review of studies on this topic, Garmezy and Rutter (1985) found that children exposed to war-related violence might develop serious difficulties, including anxiety and fear, depression, psychosomatic complaints, and PTSD symptoms such as difficulty concentrating and sleep disturbances. The degree of psychological disturbance, however, appears to vary from child to child. Recent research suggests that both the level of exposure to dangerous events and the level of disruption of children's social support networks can influence the level of difficulties children experience (Laor et al., 2001; Smith et al., 2001). Laor et al. (2001), for example, found consistently higher levels of psychiatric symptoms in children whose families were displaced following exposure to SCUD missile attacks in Israel than among children whose families were not displaced.

Research into the effects associated with children's exposure to community violence is just beginning, and the findings that have accumulated thus far should be interpreted cautiously. The most significant problem with the research to date is that all of the studies have been correlational in nature. In addition, most have failed to distinguish between effects caused by exposure to community violence and those caused by other potentially significant factors, such as poverty, neglect, and violence within the home. As a result, the specific adverse effects of exposure to community violence are unclear. Some researchers have focused on how the effects on children of exposure to community violence may differ from those related to exposure to domestic violence (Bell & Jenkins, 1993; Garbarino, 1992; Osofsky, 1995). Initial findings suggest that, of the two, exposure to domestic violence may be more traumatic for children because of its chronic, frequent, and personal nature (Groves & Zuckerman, 1997; Horn & Trickett, 1998). Evidence from several studies suggests that violence committed in the home or by someone known to the child is more likely to evoke stress symptoms than violence occurring outside the home or committed by a stranger (Martinez & Richters, 1993; Osofsky et al., 1993; Richters & Martinez, 1993a).

Interventions. Given the negative effects associated with children's exposure to community violence, interventions of some kind are warranted for children who have witnessed extreme violence. Understandably, law enforcement and other professionals often focus on dealing with the perpetrators and addressing the needs of the direct victims of community violence, unfortunately neglecting the needs of child witnesses, who are indirect victims. Children who are exposed to community violence, for example, often encounter both delays in receiving treatment referrals and few preventive intervention programs within their communities (Osofsky, 1998).

In response to these problems, several communities have developed intervention programs aimed directly at police responses to children exposed to community violence (see Groves & Zuckerman, 1997; Marans & Cohen, 1993; Osofsky, 1997). One such program is the Violence Intervention Project, which was initiated in New Orleans in 1993. This project includes an educational program that provides police trainees and officers with information on the effects of violence on children and a 24-hour hotline that police and families can call with their concerns about children exposed to community violence (Osofsky, 1998).

Another program is the Child Witness to Violence Project, founded in 1992 at Boston City Hospital (Groves & Zuckerman, 1997). This program provides therapeutic interventions for children who witness violence in their communities by offering therapeutic and support services that focus on the child, his or her family, and additional community professionals involved with the family (e.g., schoolteachers). This program represents a multiservice intervention approach that focuses not only on providing therapeutic intervention for individual children but also on mobilizing the support that parents and other community caregivers can provide for these children.

Some observers have recommended specific public policy initiatives directed at alleviating the difficulties faced by children and families who live in violent communities (American Psychological Association, 1993; Hawkins, 1995; Osofsky, 1995, 1997). Osofsky (1997) makes the following public policy recommendations, which she believes are necessary to focus attention on youth exposed to community violence and to guide program development to solve this problem:

1. Development of a national campaign to change the social image of violence from acceptable to unacceptable

2. Education for parents, educators, criminal justice professionals, law enforcement officials, and medical and mental health professionals about the effects of violence on children and methods for protecting children from such violence

3. Development of community prevention and intervention programs to prevent violence and to address the negative consequences of violence

4. Development and enforcement of gun laws that limit children's and adolescents' access to guns

5. Provision of resources to enable the development of child and family intervention programs

Institutional Abuse

Institutional abuse of children can occur in various settings, including, but not limited to, foster homes, group homes, residential treatment centers, and licensed child-care facilities. In 1984, the issue of child abuse perpetrated by institutional personnel was dramatically brought into public view by the McMartin Preschool case in Manhattan Beach, California (see Box 4.1 in Chapter 4). Although the case resulted in no convictions, the publicity surrounding it brought institutional abuse into public focus and left many Americans with the impression that children are at increased risk of abuse in child-care settings.

Research findings concerning the extent of abuse and neglect in institutional settings suggest that child maltreatment is less common in such settings than in private homes. In their evaluation of data from the Annual Fifty State Survey, Wang and Daro (1998) found that only 3% of confirmed abuse cases in 1997 occurred in day-care centers, foster care homes, or other institutional settings (see Box 7.2), and that this pattern had remained consistent for 11 years. Finkelhor, Williams, and Burns (1988) conducted a national survey of day-care sexual abuse cases and estimated that the rate of sexual abuse in child-care centers was 5.5 per 10,000 children, compared with 8.9 per 10,000 children in private households. These researchers concluded that children are at greater risk of being sexually abused at home than in child-care centers and that child-care centers are not particularly high-risk child maltreatment situations for children.

Although institutional abuse is less common than other forms of child maltreatment, many children do suffer abuse, both sexual and physical, at the hands of individuals licensed to provide quality care for children. The majority of published research addressing child abuse and neglect in institutional settings has focused on physical and sexual abuse in child-care centers. The characteristics of child maltreatment occurring in child-care facilities differ in significant ways from those of abuse perpetrated in other circumstances (Faller, 1988b; Finkelhor et al., 1988; Kelley, Brant, & Waterman, 1993; Waterman, Kelly, Oliveri, & McCord, 1993). The proportion of women involved as perpetrators in child-care centers, for example, is higher than in other cases of child maltreatment (Faller, 1988b; Kelley et al., 1993). Findings on child-care abuse also suggest that children abused in child care are more likely than other maltreated children to be abused by multiple perpetrators (Faller, 1988b; Finkelhor et al., 1988).

The types of child sexual abuse that occur in day-care settings are similar to those perpetrated in other settings (e.g., activities ranging from fondling to sexual intercourse), but fondling appears to be the most commonly reported form of abuse in day-care settings (e.g., Bybee & Mowbray, 1993a; Finkelhor et al., 1988). Other forms of sexual abuse described in day-care settings include group sex situations (in which three or more people are involved) and pornography (e.g., taking pictures of children or children and adults engaged in various sexual activities), and more controversial claims include bestiality and ritualistic abuse (Bybee & Mowbray, 1993a; Faller, 1988b; Finkelhor et al., 1988; Kelley et al., 1993). Aspects of child physical abuse have also been described in day-care settings, including hitting, physical restraint, and food deprivation (Kelley et al., 1993).

Researchers who have examined the psychological impacts of abuse in child-care centers have found that children abused in such settings exhibit symptoms similar to children who have been abused within their own homes. In their comprehensive study of sexual abuse in preschool settings, for example, Waterman et al. (1993) found that children who reported experiencing sexual abuse in preschools exhibited more social incompetence, cognitive problems, emotional difficulties, sexualized behaviors, and total behavior problems than did children in a control group. There is also evidence that abuse involving multiple perpetrators, multiple victims, pornography, and ritualistic elements is associated with more psychological difficulties for victims (Finkelhor et al., 1988; Kelley, 1989; Waterman et al., 1993).

In response to public concerns about the problem of institutional child abuse, most U.S. states have initiated a number of policy and legislative changes. Policy makers have recommended reforms in the ways institutional care services are provided, and states have established requirements for independent investigations into any charges of institutional child maltreatment. In addition, states have revised their child abuse and neglect laws to include abuse and neglect by persons providing out-of-home care to children (Rindfleisch & Nunno, 1992). In 1984, the U.S. Congress enacted a law that required states to institute employment history, background, and criminal checks on all new out-of-home child-care employees.

Additional responses to institutional abuse have focused on improving community detection and prevention of such abuse as well as providing treatment for victimized children and their families. One obvious first step toward preventing and detecting abuse in day-care centers is to increase supervision and monitoring at day-care facilities (American Humane Association, 1993; Bybee & Mowbray, 1993b). Bybee and Mowbray (1993b) also recommend the establishment of prevention education programs for children, parents, and day-care workers. Finally, treatment should be available to all child victims of institutional abuse as well as to their families, who are also often affected by the abuse (Finkelhor et al., 1988; Kiser, Pugh, McColgan, Pruitt, & Edwards, 1991; Waterman et al., 1993).

Ritualistic Abuse

Through the late 1980s and early 1990s, many social scientists became interested in a form of child abuse that was reportedly quite insidious and shockingly common: ritualistic abuse. Finkelhor et al. (1988) have defined ritualistic abuse as "abuse that occurs in a context linked to some symbols or group activities that have a religious, magical, or supernatural connotation, and where the invocation of these symbols or activities [is] repeated over time, and used to frighten and intimidate the children" (p. 59).

The topic of ritualistic abuse has produced some of the most heated exchanges seen within the field of child maltreatment. These debates have centered on the question of whether or not this form of abuse actually exists (Jones, 1991; Putnam, 1991). Some of the most controversial claims of ritualistic abuse involve cases of sexual abuse associated with forced drug use, cannibalism, impregnation, witnessing and receiving physical abuse or torture (e.g., biting, burning, whipping, and animal mutilation), being buried alive, death threats, witnessing or being forced to participate in infant "sacrifice" and adult murder, "marriage" to Satan, and various acts involving feces, urine, and blood. Many issues remain unresolved. Several experts have questioned the foundation on which the research into ritualistic abuse is based, namely, the claims of self-reported victims (see Box 7.4).

Box 7.4 Satanic Ritualistic Abuse

Patti was 32 and her sister, Bonnie, was 45 when they began seeing Huntington Beach therapist Timothy Maas in 1988. Soon after their treatment began, both reached the conclusion that they suffered from multiple personality disorder, an unusual and controversial form of mental disorder. Their multiple personalities, they concluded, allowed them to repress three decades of abuse by their mother, 78-year-old Ellen Roe. As Patti and Bonnie's therapy progressed, they uncovered increasingly bizarre memories—black-robed satanists performing bloody rituals, animal mutilations, satanic orgies, and infant sacrifices (Weber, 1991). Eventually, the two sisters brought a civil suit against their mother. In a 10-to-2 compromise vote, the jury ruled that although the women may well have been abused by someone, at worst Ellen Roe was guilty of negligence. The sisters were awarded no money (Lachnit, 1991).

As discussed in Chapter 1, from a social constructionist perspective, a social problem is anything that has been successfully labeled as such by interest groups. A social condition becomes a social problem only after claims-makers successfully raise awareness about that condition. Because claims-making about a condition, rather than the condition itself, is the central component in the definitional process, it is possible, in principle at least, that a condition that does not actually exist could be seen as a social problem. These issues have contributed to the controversy surrounding the subject of satanic ritual abuse.

Beginning in the 1980s, many adults began reporting recovered satanic memories of devil worship, human and animal sacrifices, and sexual torment (see Box 4.3 in Chapter 4). Children also reported abuse that included ritualistic elements. The term *satanic ritual abuse* (SRA) was introduced to describe this "new" form of child abuse. (Although the term *ritualistic abuse* appeared later, it is a broader term that includes SRA as one of several forms of abuse and de-emphasizes the satanic aspects emphasized in early definitions.) During the 1980s and early 1990s, people who believed in the reality of SRA argued that thousands of children were being victimized each year in satanic rituals involving cannibalism, sexual torture, incest, and murder. Critics, however, expressed skepticism and wondered whether the so-called satanism scare was merely the result of rumor and mass hysteria.

Many observers trace widespread public interest in SRA in the United States to the book *Michelle Remembers* (1980), by psychiatrist Lawrence Pazder and his patient (and later, wife) Michelle Smith. Pazder was treating Smith when she began to remember being victimized by a satanic cult during the 1950s. Among the many claims Smith made was that she witnessed numerous ritualistic murders by the satanists. Smith also claimed that she was force-fed the ashes of a cremated victim. On another occasion, she reported that a fetus was butchered in front of her and that the bloody remains were smeared across her body (Victor, 1993).

Michelle Smith's story attracted considerable attention. Pazder and Smith were featured in *People* and the *National Enquirer*. They made numerous television and radio appearances and became nationally known as "experts" on SRA (Victor, 1993). It was Pazder who coined the term *satanic ritual abuse* in a presentation to the American Psychiatric Association in 1980. Despite the considerable attention the case received, no evidence was ever uncovered that corroborated Smith's stories. Her family, including two sisters who are not mentioned in the book, asserted that none of the SRA occurred (Victor, 1993).

Another survivor story that attracted national attention was *Satan's Underground,* by Lauren Stratford (1988). Like Michelle Smith, Stratford appeared on many television shows and used notoriety from her book to launch a career as a therapist for SRA survivors. When three writers for the evangelical magazine *Cornerstone* investigated her story, however, they concluded that it was a "gruesome fantasy" (Passantino, Passantino, & Trott, 1990). Perhaps the most outrageous claim that Stratford made was that she was impregnated by satanists on three separate occasions and that each of the children was taken from her and killed. Because Stratford had led a fairly normal public life, the *Cornerstone* writers found her claims easy to investigate. They located several people who had known Stratford in high school and college (the period during which she claims to have had the children), and all of them stated that they believed she was never pregnant. Stratford herself could produce no witness to any of her claimed pregnancies. According to the *Cornerstone* authors, no one at Harvest House, the publisher of Stratford's book, had ever bothered to check her story.

Those charged with investigating the threat that SRA might pose to children have also expressed skepticism. FBI agent Kenneth Lanning (1991), a well-respected authority on child abuse, has offered the following conclusions about SRA:

> In 1983 when I first began to hear victims' stories of bizarre cults and human sacrifice, I tended to believe them. I had been dealing with bizarre, deviant behavior for many years and had long since realized that almost anything is possible. The idea that there are a few cunning, secretive individuals in positions of power somewhere in this country regularly killing a few people as part of some ritual or ceremony and getting away with it is certainly within the realm of possibility. But the number of alleged cases began to grow and grow. We now have hundreds of victims alleging that thousands of offenders are murdering tens of thousands of people, and there is little or no corroborative evidence.

> Until hard evidence is obtained and corroborated, the public should not be frightened into believing that babies are being bred and eaten, that 50,000 missing children are being murdered in human sacrifices, or that Satanists are taking over America's day care centers. (pp. 172–173)

By the mid-1990s, skepticism about SRA had extended to the social scientific community. Most academics seemed to concur with Susan Kelley (1996), who reached the following conclusion after reviewing the literature: "The existence of a large scale network of satanic cults whose primary interest is the sexual abuse of children is clearly *not* supported by empirical findings or law enforcement findings" (p. 97).

Given the scarcity of evidence, why did so many perceive the SRA threat as real? One reason is that many of the major daytime television talk shows (e.g., *The Oprah Winfrey Show, Geraldo,* and *Donahue*) and some prime-time newsmagazine shows (e.g., *20/20*) aired programs on satanism and SRA. The 1988 special "Exposing Satan's Underground," hosted by Geraldo Rivera, which featured Lauren Stratford and her story, attracted one of the largest audiences for an NBC documentary in history. Unfortunately, it is hard to imagine that many of the 19.8 million people who saw Stratford on *Geraldo* in 1988 were aware of the *Cornerstone* investigation or would later know that Harvest House pulled her book from stores in 1990 (Richardson, Best, & Bromley, 1991; Victor, 1993).

Another reason for misperceptions of the SRA threat is that many therapists, police officers, and child protection authorities, who are often required to attend seminars on current developments in their field, were exposed to SRA "experts" in seminars around the country in the late 1980s and early 1990s. Although advertised as training workshops, these seminars tended to employ proselytizing techniques characteristic of organizations seeking recruits (Mulhern, 1991). Many well-meaning helping professionals, no doubt motivated by the desire to help abused clients, became convinced of the existence of SRA through these seminars. They brought stories of what the satanists were up to back to their communities, and the phenomenon spread. Those who believed in the existence of SRA cited the similarity of the stories told in different parts of the country as evidence. After all, they reasoned, how could so many different people be offering similar stories independently? Given that clients (through the popular media) and professionals (through training seminars) were exposed to the same theories of SRA, this thinking represents, as Frank W. Putnam (1991) of the National Institute of Mental Health notes, a "naïve and simplistic model of contagion." "The child abuse community," Putnam continues, "is particularly susceptible to such a rumor process as there are multiple, interconnected communication/educational networks shared by therapists and patients alike" (p. 177).

At the peak of the satanism scare, professionals in the field of child abuse influenced state and county governments to respond to the perceived SRA problem. In Los Angeles County, for example, the Ritual Abuse Task Force was formed in 1988 to deal with the perceived SRA threat. This task force, which was controversial from the start, received front-page attention in the *Los Angeles Times* in 1992 when many of its members claimed that satanists were attempting to silence them by pumping the pesticide Diazinon into the air-conditioning vents of their offices, homes, and cars. Although Diazinon poisoning is easy to detect, according to the epidemiologist assigned to the case, none of the 43 alleged victims of the poisoning could provide any evidence (Curtis, 1992).

One question remains unanswered: How could so many people come to believe they were personally exposed to satanic abuse? Imagine an individual who turns to a therapist to help alleviate personal struggles. Therapists have been trained to suspect a childhood history of abuse as a possible explanation for personal problems. They are also trained to listen to, and support, victim accounts of abuse. Perhaps this individual's therapist has attended a seminar on SRA and has come to believe that the threat of such abuse is real, and that many people are victims of SRA. Add to this situation the fact that memories, especially childhood memories, are extremely malleable (Loftus, 2003), and distortions are possible, maybe even likely.

It is understandable that therapists do not see the corroboration of client accounts of abuse as part of their clinical responsibilities. The therapist's role is to help the client heal and to provide a supportive environment. Raising skeptical questions could well be counterproductive to the therapist's role. Nevertheless, Bottoms, Shaver, and Goodman (1996) found in a survey of therapists that many did openly question some of their clients' SRA stories. These therapists were quick to point out, however, that they were careful not to assume the detective role and that the "facts" of these cases were essentially irrelevant. Bottoms et al. acknowledge the merit of this approach but raise questions about the consequences:

> When thousands of ritual abuse reports ignite widespread public and professional fears about a national or international satanic cult conspiracy, resulting in specific accusations of sexual abuse against preschool operators, teachers, parents, and other family members, as well as changes in state laws, it definitely *does* matter whether the cults actually exist. (p. 32)

Indeed, it is important to recognize that unfounded claims of SRA probably hinder professionals from achieving the goal of child protection. There can be little question that fabricated SRA stories have provided ammunition to skeptics who want to claim that children are rarely abused at all. Although many recovered memories may be real, for example, fabricated SRA memories feed the fires stoked by those skeptics who question the validity of *all* repressed memories. Arguably, attention to SRA during the 1980s and 1990s created additional problems for professionals dealing with child maltreatment rather than providing much-needed solutions.

Perhaps the best evidence that the satanism scare was little more than a socially constructed threat is that by the mid-1990s the social hysteria that had characterized the topic had subsided (Mulhern, 1994). Given the scarcity of evidence that any threat existed in the first place, it is difficult to explain this decline as anything more than a change in societal reaction. Today, there seem to be very few true believers in SRA. In a May 2003 review of the first 20 hits turned up by an Internet search engine for the phrase "satanic ritual abuse seminars," we found many discussions of how SRA seminars fueled the satanism scare, but no announcements of upcoming SRA seminars. Likewise, in a search of the PsycINFO database we found mostly SRA skeptics in the academic world. Psychologists Margaret Thaler Singer and Abraham Nievod (2003), for example, discuss SRA therapy in a chapter on "fad" or "new age" therapies that they claim have harmed patients. In his book *Pseudoscience and the Paranormal*, Terence Hines (2003), a neuroscientist, examines the question of why people continue to believe in phenomena for which there is no evidence, such as UFOs and astrology. He includes SRA among the phenomena for which no evidence seems to exist.

Most of the information available about ritualistic abuse comes from reports of children attending day-care centers and from the memories of adults who report histories of childhood abuse. Studies investigating the parameters of ritualistic abuse have focused on the prevalence of reported cases, the impacts of this form of abuse on victims, and the characteristics of victims and perpetrators (for a review, see Kelley, 1996). Estimates of ritualistic abuse are difficult to determine not only because of disagreement about definitional issues but also because child protection and law enforcement agencies do not uniformly recognize ritualistic abuse as a specific and separate form of child maltreatment. Most researchers who have attempted to estimate the prevalence of ritualistic abuse have examined samples of children in day-care centers, collected clinical samples, or surveyed mental health professionals about the numbers of cases they have encountered (e.g., Bottoms, Shaver, & Goodman, 1996; Goodman, Bottoms, & Shaver, 1994; Kelley, 1989; Snow & Sorenson, 1990). Although some of this research indicates that as much as 13% of all child sexual abuse cases include ritualistic elements, most studies show ritualistic abuse to be relatively infrequent (e.g., Bottoms et al., 1996; Finkelhor et al., 1988; Goodman et al., 1994). When Bottoms et al. (1996) surveyed 2,722 clinical members of the American Psychological Association about their experiences with ritualistic abuse, for example, 803 respondents indicated that they had encountered one or more cases of ritualistic or religion-related abuse.

Reports of ritualistic abuse indicate that these cases tend to involve male and female victims to an equal degree (Snow & Sorenson, 1990; Waterman et al., 1993). With regard to perpetrator characteristics, however, gender discrepancies have been observed. Compared with nonritualistic abuse cases, ritualistic abuse is more likely to involve female perpetrators, multiple perpetrators, and multiple victims (Finkelhor et al., 1988; Jonker & Jonker-Bakker, 1991; Kelley, 1989; Snow & Sorenson, 1990; Waterman et al., 1993). Initial research on the psychological impacts of ritualistic abuse on victims has found symptoms similar to those observed in sexually abused children, although the findings of several studies suggest that ritualistic abuse victims exhibit a greater degree of symptomatology than do sexually abused children (Kelley, 1989; Waterman et al., 1993).

COLLATERAL EFFECTS OF CHILD MALTREATMENT

In the preceding chapters, we have discussed the myriad negative consequences associated with being a victim of child physical and sexual abuse, neglect, and psychological maltreatment. The negative outcomes associated with child maltreatment affect not only the children who experience abuse, however, but also those who live and/or work with these children. How does the experience of child maltreatment affect the victimized child's family members, including nonoffending parents and siblings, and others who live and interact closely with the child? What are the effects on therapists and other professionals of working with child victims of maltreatment who have undergone horrific experiences and been severely traumatized as a result? What are the effects of working with the adults who have perpetrated these horrific experiences? Clearly, interacting with child victims and with adults involved in child maltreatment is potentially difficult, and many family members of maltreatment victims as well as professionals working with victims and perpetrators experience negative reactions as a result. In the following subsections we review the research findings with regard to negative collateral effects among professionals who work in the field of child maltreatment and among victims' family members. We also discuss some approaches to treating and preventing such effects.

Impacts of Child Maltreatment on Parents of Victims

Most researchers who have studied the effects of child maltreatment have focused on child victims or on adults who were abused sometime during childhood. Relatively few studies have examined the effects on nonoffending family members of victims, such as nonoffending parents and siblings. Family members of abuse victims are often referred to as "secondary victims" because they can experience a number of psychological difficulties associated with the abuse (McCourt, Peel, & O'Carroll, 1998; Strand, 2000).

Most studies in this area have been concerned with the characteristics of nonoffending mothers of children who have been sexually abused. As noted in Chapter 4, the first researchers who examined this topic tended to view mothers of sexual abuse victims as coconspirators in their children's abuse. Early researchers hypothesized that dysfunction in such mothers was a cause of the sexual abuse or problems in their children. Mothers of sexual abuse victims were viewed as "unprotective," "collusive," "inadequate," or "conspiratorial" due to their own psychopathology (Strand, 2000). Within the past 15 years, however, a greater understanding of the problem of sexual abuse has led researchers to view nonoffending mothers as covictims, rather than coconspirators, in their children's sexual abuse.

Several research findings published in the mid-1980s and early 1990s contributed to this new perspective. One line of research, including studies using a variety of samples, demonstrated that most mothers of child victims support and believe their children (De Jong, 1988; Sirles & Franke, 1989; Pierce & Peirce, 1985). Another line of research evaluated various factors that might potentially affect a mother's willingness and ability to support and believe her child. Findings from these studies indicated that nonoffending mothers were more supportive when they were no longer living with or married to the perpetrators and less supportive if they were abusing substances or had little social support following their children's disclosures of abuse (Faller, 1988a; Leifer, Shapiro, & Kassem, 1993). In addition, empirical studies that assessed mothers' pathology during this time, in contrast to earlier anecdotal studies, demonstrated mixed results with regard to maternal functioning. In one review of several empirical studies conducted between 1980 and 1995, for example, Tamraz (1996) found that the results of studies evaluating maternal psychological dysfunction were inconclusive.

Several researchers have focused on the mothers of child sexual abuse victims as secondary victims who have their own traumatic reactions to their children's disclosures of abuse. Newberger, Gremy, Waternaux, and Newberger (1993), for example, studied maternal caregivers of sexually abused children by conducting interviews with mothers soon after their families visited the emergency department at a children's hospital and then at both 6 and 12 months following the initial interviews. They found that the mothers in this sample scored significantly higher on a measure of global symptomatology than the mean for the measure's standardization sample. In addition, the researchers observed a significant decline in symptoms at the 12-month assessment, suggesting that the mothers' symptoms were reactions to the disclosure of their children's abuse rather than evidence of preexisting disorders. Timmons-Mitchell, Chandler-Holtz, and

Semple (1996) examined PTSD symptoms in mothers whose children had recently disclosed sexual abuse and found that these women displayed significantly higher levels of PTSD symptoms compared with women in a standardization sample for the measure that assessed PTSD symptoms.

Researchers have also examined factors that might play roles in predicting why some mothers react more severely than others to the knowledge that their children have experienced abuse. Mothers who have themselves been victims of child sexual abuse display more PTSD symptoms in reaction to their own children's abuse than do mothers who report no personal histories of abuse (Timmons-Mitchell et al., 1996). There is also some evidence that mothers of sexually abused children display more trauma symptoms when their husbands are the perpetrators of the abuse (Carter, 1993).

One problem with the research in this area is that studies to date have not included appropriate comparison groups. Future studies should examine whether mothers of sexual abuse victims show higher scores on symptom measures than do mothers whose children have not been sexually abused. In addition, the research conducted thus far has focused exclusively on the secondary effects on mothers of their children's sexual abuse. Additional research is needed that examines the secondary effects on nonoffending parents of other forms of child maltreatment, such as physical abuse. Researchers also need to investigate the secondary effects of child maltreatment on the siblings of victims.

Impacts of Child Maltreatment on Professionals Who Work With Victims

Child maltreatment affects not only child victims and their parents, but also the professionals who work with these children and families. Working with children who have experienced significant trauma and suffering is not an easy task, and professionals who do this kind of work are subject to a variety of negative impacts. Although researchers have been investigating this topic only for the past 10 years, the findings to date strongly suggest that many professionals who work in the area of child maltreatment experience negative emotions and reactions (Cheung & Boutte-Queen, 2000; Figley, 1995; Follette, Polusny, & Milbeck, 1994). Consider the following description by a clinical psychologist who works with child victims of abuse and neglect:

I once worked with a little girl; I'll call her Molly. She was 8 years old and was admitted to the inpatient unit of a hospital where I worked at the time. Her history showed that her biological mother abused drugs and alcohol and would leave Molly and her 2-year-old brother alone for days in their apartment. Molly's mother had a boyfriend who sexually abused Molly when he was stoned or drunk. Obviously, this was a horrible situation, and eventually Molly's biological father was given custody of Molly and her brother. Molly's father was remarried and living with his new wife and first child from that second marriage. Shortly after Molly arrived in their home, her father brought her to the inpatient unit of the hospital where I was working. The father was at his wit's end because he could not control Molly. Most recently she had tried to stab her 5-year-old stepsister while the sister was taking a bath. When Molly was admitted to the hospital she showed symptoms of anxiety, depression, enuresis, encopresis, and self-mutilation. Molly's symptoms remitted within the first 10 days of her hospital stay. She was a quiet, sweet, cooperative child who was very pleasant and easy to manage during her stay. It became clear during her hospital stay, however, that Molly's stepmother hated Molly. Molly's biological father seemed unaware of any problems between Molly and her stepmother. The stepmother, however, showed open hostility toward Molly during family sessions, continually belittling, degrading, and blaming Molly for all of the family's problems. This pattern of interaction was reported to CPS, but a formal investigation never occurred. Because the case was not investigated and all of Molly's symptoms remitted, she returned to live with her biological father and stepmother. In sending Molly back to the very same situation that was causing her so much distress, I felt as if I had failed her. I still think about this little girl and feel sad, even though it's been 12 years since I was her therapist. (from the second author's notes)

This therapist's story illustrates the high costs often paid by professionals who attempt to work with and help victims of child maltreatment. Such costs are incurred not only by those who work with the victims of child maltreatment but also by those who work with the adults responsible for child maltreatment. Balakrishna (1998) has coined the phrase "ripple effects" to describe some of the difficulties that therapists encounter in working with child sexual abuse perpetrators. Professionals who work with sexual abuse perpetrators—including therapists who provide them with treatment and legal professionals who defend them in court—may feel isolated and alienated because their clients are often ostracized from society. These professionals may face questions from friends and colleagues about their motivations in working

with such clients (Balakrishna, 1998). Professionals in many groups may be affected, such as law enforcement officials, social workers, health care providers, and teachers. The negative ripple effects of child maltreatment might even extend beyond those who provide services and protection to those who conduct research with child victims and adults who abuse children (e.g., Kinard, 1996).

Most of the research on the collateral effects of trauma has been conducted with therapists who work with children and adults who have experienced particular kinds of traumatic events, such as war or rape (Pearlman & MacIan, 1995). Among the terms that scholars have used to describe the effects on those who work with victims of trauma are *vicarious traumatization, compassion fatigue,* and *secondary traumatic stress* (Figley, 1995, 2002; Pearlman & MacIan, 1995). Pearlman and MacIan (1995) describe this type of secondary reaction as empathizing and identifying with a traumatized person or child to the point that there are "changes in the self that parallel those experienced by trauma survivors themselves."

Professionals' reactions to working with traumatized clients are referred to as *secondary* because they are not direct responses to traumatic events, but rather indirect responses due to contact with victims. As we have noted in previous chapters, many victims of child maltreatment experience symptoms of posttraumatic stress disorder, a diagnosis in the *Diagnostic and Statistical Manual of Mental Disorders* that specifies psychiatric criteria associated with experiencing traumatic events. The PTSD diagnosis in early versions of the *DSM* focused only on individuals who experienced trauma directly, but in the fourth edition of the *DSM* the symptom criteria were modified to include not only the "direct observation" of an event but also "knowledge of, or witnessing another's trauma" (American Psychiatric Association, 1994). Professionals who work in the field of child maltreatment certainly are witness to, or have knowledge of, the trauma experienced by a great number of individuals.

In recent years, a growing body of research has examined secondary traumatic stress in professionals who work specifically with victims of child maltreatment. Urquiza, Wyatt, and Goodlin-Jones (1997), for example, found evidence of trauma-related symptoms in adults who interviewed adult victims of child sexual abuse. The interviewers reported symptoms such as crying, feelings of horror, sleeplessness, and nightmares following their interview sessions. Lyon (1993) also found evidence of trauma symptoms in a sample

Table 7.4   Characteristics of Secondary Traumatic Stress in Professionals

1. The professional cannot stop thinking about abused children (e.g., intrusive thoughts and distressing images continually come to mind).

2. The professional experiences recurrent dreams and/or nightmares about general abuse themes or about specific children or families with whom he or she is working.

3. The professional experiences flashbacks or dissociation associated with personal trauma that has occurred in the professional's own life.

4. The professional experiences negative health outcomes (e.g., sleep problems, depression, psychosomatic illnesses, eating disorders, drug use).

5. The professional no longer feels safety or certainty about people and the world.

6. The professional's personal relationships are negatively affected (e.g. distrust of others, difficulty with intimacy).

7. The professional's clinical judgment becomes negatively affected (e.g., seeing potential child abuse in every child).

8. The professional's work performance is negatively affected (e.g., overinvolvement or underinvolvement in work, doubts about competency).

9. The professional becomes isolated and withdrawn from family, friends, and coworkers.

10. The professional experiences emotional exhaustion (i.e., burnout).

SOURCE: Horton and Cruise (2001).

of hospital staff who worked with adult survivors of childhood abuse. Symptoms included nightmares, intrusive and repetitive images, and somatic symptoms (e.g., headaches, nausea, and sleeplessness). In contrast, Follette, Polusny, and Milbeck (1994) assessed secondary traumatization in mental health and law enforcement professionals who provided services to sexually abused clients and found that mental health practitioners reported low levels of trauma symptomatology but moderate levels of personal stress. In summarizing the research literature on secondary traumatic stress, Horton and Cruise (2001) note several reactions commonly observed in professionals who work with trauma victims. These reactions are listed in Table 7.4.

Although many individuals who work with trauma victims in general, and with child maltreatment victims in particular, experience some symptoms of secondary traumatic stress, such professionals seem to be functioning well overall, with only mild to moderate levels of disturbance (Brady, Guy, Poelstra, & Brokaw, 1999; Pearlman & MacIan, 1995). It is apparent, however, that individual professionals' reactions to working with trauma victims vary. Several factors contribute to a given professional's responses. One factor that appears to be associated with secondary traumatic stress is whether the professional has personally experienced some type trauma. Among the mental health and law enforcement personnel in Follette et al.'s

(1994) study sample, for example, those with personal histories of abuse had higher levels of trauma symptoms than did those without histories of abuse. Other researchers have found intensified professional reactions among trauma therapists and hospital staff members with personal histories of victimization (Lyon, 1993; Pearlman & MacIan, 1995). Exposure to the trauma of others may trigger negative feelings and memories in individuals with personal histories of trauma, resulting in secondary traumatic stress.

Another factor that has been found to contribute to secondary traumatic stress in professionals is the degree of exposure to others' trauma, which may vary widely. Some therapists, for example, may come into contact with many child maltreatment victims, whereas others may have contact with only a few. In addition, some professionals may learn very few details of abusive incidents, whereas others are exposed to specific, graphic, and disturbing details. One survey of female psychotherapists, for example, found that those who had more sexual abuse clients in their caseloads, had greater exposure to graphic details of the abuse, or saw a high number of survivors over the course of their careers were more likely than other therapists to exhibit trauma symptoms themselves (Brady et al., 1999).

Professionals' degree of training and experience as well as the level of support they receive are other factors that influence the likelihood of the development of secondary traumatic stress. Pearlman and MacIan (1995) studied reactions in self-identified trauma therapists and found that the therapists with the least amount of professional experience exhibited the greatest difficulties. The use of social support as a way of coping with difficulties associated with work in the area of child maltreatment has also been linked with fewer trauma symptoms (Schauben & Frazier, 1995).

Treatment and Prevention of Collateral Effects of Child Maltreatment

There is some controversy with regard to whether all victims of secondary trauma need formal interventions to aid in their recovery (McCourt et al., 1998). Obviously, whether formal therapeutic intervention is necessary depends on a variety of factors. For professionals who work in the field of child maltreatment, these factors may include the interaction between the professionals' personal characteristics (e.g., whether they have personal histories of trauma, their level of training and experience) and the nature of their work (e.g., degree of exposure to child maltreatment cases). Many scholars recommend that therapists who work with child abuse victims seek psychological help if they find they are experiencing significant symptoms or if they themselves have unresolved histories of child maltreatment (Dutton & Rubinstein, 1995; Pearce & Pezzot-Pearce, 1997).

Short of therapeutic intervention, a number of strategies may help professionals to counteract or prevent the negative effects associated with work in the field of child maltreatment (see Figley, 1995; Horton & Cruise, 2001; Pearce & Pezzot-Pearce, 1997). Recommendations concerning many of these strategies stem from the research described above on possible factors that contribute to secondary traumatic stress. Because the degree to which professionals are exposed to trauma victims is related to secondary traumatic stress, for example, professionals would be wise to limit the number of child maltreatment cases in their caseloads (e.g., Pearce & Pearce-Pezzot, 1997). The presence of social support is associated with lower levels of secondary traumatic stress, so many experts suggest that child maltreatment professionals should receive consultation and supervision from other experienced professionals, establish supportive relationships with coworkers, and develop a variety of both professional and nonprofessional relationships (Figley, 2002; Pearce & Pearce-Pezzot, 1997; Pearlman & MacIan, 1995). These and other coping strategies are listed in Table 7.5.

Table 7.5 Prevention and Reduction of Secondary Traumatic Stress: Recommendations for the Professional

Obtain appropriate and continuing education, training, and experience about child maltreatment and the potential negative reactions that professionals who work in the field sometimes experience.

Be aware of personal issues that might contribute to negative biases, attributions, or attitudes toward child maltreatment victims.

Limit the number of child maltreatment cases and maintain a balanced caseload that includes a diversity of cases.

Understand that victims may need multiple intervention experiences before change occurs and that progress may be slow (e.g., one professional may not be able to "fix" all of a victim's problems).

Maintain ongoing supervision and consultation with other experienced professionals.

Develop relationships with coworkers that provide support and opportunities for consultation.

Maintain appropriate boundaries between personal and professional lives (e.g., pursue nonprofessional interests and relationships).

Pursue activities that promote physical and spiritual well-being (e.g., exercise, healthy eating, prayer and meditation).

Use thought-stopping techniques when overwhelmed with thoughts or feelings about a case (e.g., make a conscious effort to "turn off" unwanted thoughts or replace unwanted thoughts with positive statements such as "I have done all that I can, I'm not going to think about it tonight") (Horton & Cruise, 2001, p. 176).

Maintain a sense of humor, an attitude of hope, and a healthy perspective about work in the area of child maltreatment.

SOURCES: Brady et al. (1999); Figley (1995, 2002); Horton and Cruise (2001); Pearce and Pezzot-Pearce (1997); Pearlman and MacIan (1995).

An Interview With Linda Damon

"It is frustrating when we know that the children who cannot receive services will be at greater risk of entering the juvenile and criminal justice systems, taking an even greater toll on society than if moneys were made available to prevent the cycle of delinquency, substance abuse, and depression that can evolve in this population."

Linda Damon has been affiliated with the Child and Family Guidance Center in Southern California since 1977. She is Director of Child Abuse Prevention, Early Intervention and Trauma Services at the center, where she is in charge of more than a hundred staff members, students, and volunteers. The center provides services to children from birth to 18 years and their family members in cases of sexual or physical abuse, neglect, or exposure to domestic violence or trauma. In addition to providing clinical services, she administers, supervises, and directs training and research for students in undergraduate, graduate, and postgraduate programs. She has also coauthored more than 25 articles, chapters, videos, and books addressing the problem of child sexual and physical abuse. In addition, she was a founding member and served on the boards of directors of both the state and Los Angeles chapters of the California Professional Society on the Abuse of Children. She has served as a guest lecturer at the Universities of London and Tel Aviv and has also taught psychology courses at the University of California, Los Angeles. She received her B.A. in psychology from Connecticut College and her Ph.D. in clinical psychology from the University of California, Los Angeles.

Q: What experiences led you to become a therapist?

A: While I was an undergraduate, I completed a summer internship as a recreational therapist at a home for wards of the state, where I was first exposed to children who had been neglected and abused. My interest in child abuse intensified while I was working at a child guidance clinic early in my career with a girl who eventually shot and killed her mother. In spite of what I believed to be a strong clinical relationship, the girl had not been able tell me that her mother had been sexually molesting and abusing her for many years prior to the shooting. This tragic incident brought home to me the secrecy and shame that occurs

Family members of child maltreatment victims may or may not need professional intervention, depending in large part on the quality of their existing social supports. Individuals with supportive family, friends, and community networks and resources may not require professional help (McCourt et al., 1998). Others without such support, however, might benefit from some type of formal intervention. Most of the interventions that have been developed for family members of child maltreatment victims focus on the nonoffending parents in cases of sexual abuse. Treatment formats primarily include individual therapy as well as group therapy.

Regardless of the format, common themes that are frequently addressed in such treatment include feelings of guilt, anger, fear, confusion, betrayal, grief and loss, powerlessness, and isolation (e.g., McCourt et al., 1998; Strand, 2000; Winton, 1990). Other frequent goals of such therapy are to reframe the ambivalence that nonoffending mothers often feel (e.g., conflicted allegiance toward their partner and child) and to increase their coping skills (Strand, 2000). In situations that include reunification of the family, treatment should also focus on the nonoffending parent's responsibilities once the offender returns to live with the family. Such when there is familial abuse and spurred me on to learn more about the dynamics of child abuse. When I began to work at the Child and Family Guidance Center with a preschool population of children and their parents, I became aware of the high incidence of abuse that existed in this at-risk population. The surprisingly high incidence of sexual abuse that I observed caused me to pilot and publish a curriculum for treating young victims and their nonoffending caregivers.

Q: What has been the most difficult or challenging experience you have had working in this setting?

A: The most challenging aspect of my work over the years has been to work successfully and in concert with the judicial, law enforcement, and children's protective social services systems. When there is open communication and a willingness to listen to the input of our agency regarding the latest research on memory and suggestibility as well as our clinical impressions and observations of a case, then the goals of child protection and/or family reunification may be successfully obtained. Some of the greatest frustrations for my staff and me, however, occur when representatives of the above disciplines have preconceived notions that limit their willingness to consider our input. Frequently, they lack the time to hear and integrate our input due to their unrealistically high caseloads. The system problems in Los Angeles are compounded due to the very large size of our county, which makes it difficult to establish professional relationships with the different disciplines of professionals involved in any one case. I would like to see social policy changes that mandate and promote the mutual education of, and collaboration between, different disciplines in the child abuse field. Collaboration and interdisciplinary communication and training are critical to promote better coordination and understanding among those professionals working on behalf of maltreated children, allowing the system to operate more efficiently and kindly toward children and their family members.

It is also frustrating that we must deny help to so many families because there just isn't enough money to pay for services to help them. This is particularly discouraging when we know that the children who cannot receive services will be at greater risk of entering the juvenile and criminal justice systems, taking an even greater toll on society than if moneys were made available to prevent the cycle of delinquency, substance abuse, and depression that can evolve in this population. Resources targeted for earlier intervention would save a great deal of money and unnecessary suffering further down the road.

Q: What aspect of your work do you find most rewarding?

A: The rewards of work in this area have fortunately far outweighed the frustrations for me. The slow and steady progress that I see in the family members as they begin to trust us is very gratifying. Watching mothers learn to empathize with their children, to discipline them nonviolently and effectively, and to begin to ask their children about their opinions—this indicates that they are progressing, especially when screaming, yelling, and threatening were previously the norm. Seeing the children gradually muster the courage to tell their parents how they feel and learn to ask for a hug and tenderness in appropriate ways reassures me that we are doing something important. When teachers and child-care workers begin to tell us about children's accomplishments instead of their problems, we know we are helping. And when children and their family members can begin to identify and even brag about their strengths—that is really an accomplishment that makes this work so worthwhile.

---

responsibilities include supporting the offender's relapse prevention plan, understanding the risk factors and indicators associated with relapse, and contributing to a plan that promotes child safety (Levenson & Morin, 2001).

Unfortunately, few empirical studies have addressed the effectiveness of treatment with nonoffending parents of children who have been abused. One exception is Winton's (1990) evaluation of a support group for parents who had sexually abused children. In this study, the parents completed pre- and posttest assessments of the effectiveness of a group treatment approach that included parent education and training as well as a therapeutic component focused on disclosing, understanding, and dealing with negative feelings (e.g., guilt, anger). Some support for the effectiveness of the approach was demonstrated by a reduction of behavior problems in the group members' children and parents' positive ratings of the group and its effectiveness. Additional studies are needed to examine the effectiveness of group therapy as well as the effectiveness of individual therapy approaches.

Unifying the Field
of Child Maltreatment

Since Kempe's original "discovery" of child physical abuse more than 40 years ago, the field of child maltreatment has grown considerably. During the past few decades our understanding of this significant social problem has improved considerably as well, as Behl, Conyngham, and May's (2003) recent review of trends in the child maltreatment literature illustrates. These researchers reviewed the content of articles published in six specialty journals in the area of child maltreatment over the period extending from 1977 to 1998 and found that the annual percentage of quantitative articles increased while the annual percentage of theoretical articles decreased. Prior to the 1980s, the reverse was true—theoretical articles dominated the literature. Behl et al. assert that the pattern they found is an indication of progress, because areas of scientific investigation evolve when theories generate quantitative, empirical research.

A review of the child maltreatment literature also reveals, however, that many areas are in need of improvement and advancement. The literature suggests that the field is characterized by considerable fragmentation; some scholars have described it as lacking integration across its various subfields (e.g., Saunders, 2003; Slep & Heyman, 2001). There are several realities that might explain this state of affairs. First, the problem of child maltreatment is tremendously diverse in nature, as it encompasses a multitude of negative interactions that occur between family members. The term *child maltreatment* may be applied to a broad spectrum of behaviors, extending from physical aggression to sexual assault to various forms of psychological maltreatment. Perhaps in response to such diversity, most individuals who work in the field have tended to confine themselves to specific aspects of the problem (e.g., child sexual abuse or child neglect). Although such specialization might be beneficial for theory development and the creation of treatment protocols (Daro, 1988), it also serves to compartmentalize the field. As M. S. Rosenberg (1987) has noted, in the research literature there has been "a shifting emphasis from one type of maltreatment to another with little energy directed toward integrating findings across maltreatment areas" (p. 166).

The fragmentation that characterizes the field also undoubtedly stems from the fact that so many different kinds of professionals are engaged in family vioence research, intervention, and policy (Gelles & Loseke, 1993), including social workers, academics (in such wide-ranging disciplines as biology, psychology, sociology, criminal justice, and women's studies), criminal justice personnel, physicians, clinical and counseling psychologists, and teachers. The interests, perspectives, and goals of these various professionals often vary dramatically. The factionalism within the field has obscured the relationships among various forms of child maltreatment and contributed to the lack of a unified approach to addressing the problem. Although there may be no "cure" for this fragmentation, several approaches to studying the problem of child maltreatment might lessen its effects and promote greater unity and integration among disciplines, among professionals, and across subfields. Such approaches call for a comprehensive and integrated analysis of the field that acknowledges the effectiveness of examining the relationships between various subfields of child maltreatment and also recognizes the value of integrating research and professional interests.

The Multiple Victimization of Children

One of the unfortunate correlates of fragmentation within the field is the artificial compartmentalization of various forms of child maltreatment into separate and disparate areas of study. As a result, professionals rarely approach the issue of child maltreatment from either a comparative or an integrative perspective. In comparison to the vast amount of literature that has accumulated within each of the subfields of child maltreatment, relatively little has been written about the interrelationships among various forms of family violence in general and child maltreatment in particular (for exceptions, see Finkelhor, 1983; McKay, 1994; Williams, 2003). This is true despite the fact that some scholars have been advocating this approach for the past 20 years. In a book chapter written in 1983, for example, David Finkelhor stated, "It may be important, both for the benefit of research and theory, and also to counteract some of the divisive tendencies, for researchers on the disparate forms of family violence to see what they can find in the way of commonalities" (p. 17).

Indeed, given the considerable overlap among various forms of family violence, it is somewhat artificial and unnatural to continue to treat individual forms as separate problems. Some researchers have examined the co-occurrence of different forms of family violence within individual families, and some links (such as that between spouse abuse and child abuse) are well established (Appel & Holden, 1998; McKay, 1994). Parents who are physically violent toward each other are also likely to be physically and sexually abusive toward their children, as well as neglectful (e.g., Hartley, 2002; Osofsky, 2003). Research on domestic violence suggests that in 45% to 70% of cases of wife battering, children in the home are also abused (McKay, 1994). Other examples of different forms of abuse occurring simultaneously within one family have been documented, although less evidence is available. In families where physical abuse is occurring, for example, there is also likely to be violence among siblings (Gelles & Straus, 1988).

The co-occurrence of abuse has also been demonstrated by research findings indicating that individual child victims are likely to experience multiple forms of maltreatment. Both maltreated children and adults who report histories of child maltreatment, for example, are likely to suffer from multiple forms of abuse, including various combinations of physical, sexual, and emotional abuse as well as neglect (Claussen & Crittenden, 1991; Ney, Fung, & Wickett, 1994). Determining precisely how often children experience multiple abuse, however, is a difficult task. Most official reporting statistics are not presented in a manner conducive to evaluating multiple abuse.

A few researchers have attempted to examine the prevalence of multiple victimization by surveying college and community samples. Schaaf and McCanne (1998), for example, assessed 475 female college students for childhood histories of both sexual and physical abuse (prior to age 15). Results of this study indicated that approximately 7% of participants had experienced both physical and sexual abuse prior to age 15. Varia, Abidin, and Dass (1996) found that 11% of their community sample reported having experienced combinations of sexual, physical, and verbal abuse. Other researchers have investigated the presence of multiple forms of child maltreatment by examining correlations between maltreatment types; they have generally found a high degree of overlap between physical abuse and psychological maltreatment as well as between physical abuse and sexual abuse (Higgins & McCabe, 2001).

Higher rates of multiple abuse have been found in clinical and medical samples. Moeller, Bachmann, and Moeller (1993), for example, solicited information about sexual, physical, and emotional abuse experiences during childhood from 668 women at a gynecology clinic. Approximately 30% of the women reported one form of abuse, 19% reported two forms of abuse, and 5% reported experiencing all three forms of abuse. Brown and Anderson (1991) found that 3% of 947 adult psychiatric inpatients reported a combination of physical and sexual abuse. Ney and colleagues (1994) conducted one of the few studies to examine multiple abuse in a child sample. Children in the study self-reported physical abuse, physical neglect, verbal abuse, emotional neglect, and sexual abuse, and the results indicated that less than 5% of victimizations occurred as isolated forms of abuse.

Differences in estimates of multiple abuse are likely due to a number of factors. Studies vary in terms of the populations sampled (e.g., children versus adults, clinical versus nonclinical participants), sources of reports (e.g., self-report versus parent report), definitions of child maltreatment, and the numbers of types of child maltreatment investigated (Goodman, Bottoms, Redlich, Shaver, & Diviak, 1998). In general, studies that include broad definitions of child maltreatment and psychological forms of abuse (e.g., verbal and/or emotional) obtain higher estimates. This finding is consistent with the argument that all forms of child maltreatment involve an element of psychological abuse (e.g., Claussen & Crittenden, 1991). Another general conclusion from the research on multiple victimization is that higher rates are obtained in clinical studies. Clinical studies are limited, however, because their results are not necessarily generalizable to the entire population of children who are maltreated. Although research to date suggests that children who are victims of one form of child maltreatment are often victims of other forms as well, additional research is needed to increase knowledge about the prevalence of multiple victimization.

Comparative Effects of Various Forms of Child Maltreatment

Another area of study that represents an integrative approach to the field is the investigation of the comparative effects of various forms and combinations of child maltreatment. Researchers have examined not only comparative effects in individuals experiencing multiple forms of maltreatment but differences in outcomes among various child maltreatment victim groups.

Researchers have evaluated the detrimental effects associated with multiple forms of maltreatment by examining how various combinations of maltreatment types affect the functioning of child victims. Some studies have found that specific disorders or symptoms are associated with specific forms of abuse. In one of the first studies of this type, Egeland and Sroufe (1981) found that children who had experienced both neglect and physical abuse were more likely to display frustration than were physical abuse–only children or neglect-only children, whereas neglect-only children were more likely to display anger. Swett, Surrey, and Cohen (1990) found that sexually abused children demonstrated a higher rate of inappropriate sexual behavior than did physically abused children. In a study of adolescent victims of maltreatment, Williamson, Borduin, and Howe (1991) found that adolescent physical abuse was linked to **externalizing behaviors**, whereas adolescent sexual abuse was linked to **internalizing behaviors.**

Other researchers who have examined the effects of experiencing single forms of child maltreatment, compared with multiple forms, have found that the greater the number of childhood abuses reported, the more severe the problems. Vissing, Straus, Gelles, and Harrop (1991) evaluated children who experienced verbal aggression, severe physical violence, or a combination of both and found that the children who experienced multiple forms of maltreatment exhibited the highest rates of aggression, delinquency, and interpersonal problems. Likewise, Ney and colleagues (1994) investigated the combined effects of physical and verbal abuse, in addition to physical neglect. Results indicated that the combination of all three forms of maltreatment had the most negative impacts on children's socioemotional functioning. The co-occurrence of child abuse and exposure to interparental violence is also associated with increased levels of emotional and behavioral problems, beyond levels associated with exposure alone (Wolfe, Crooks, Lee, McIntyre-Smith, & Jaffe, 2003).

Some researchers have examined the effects of combinations of forms of child maltreatment in adults with histories of childhood abuse. Similar to research with child victims, studies exploring the long-term consequences to women who experienced multiple victimization in childhood have found specific psychosocial problems associated with specific forms of abuse. Briere and Runtz (1990), for example, examined psychological outcomes associated with psychological, physical, and sexual abuse in female college students and found unique associations between physical abuse and aggression, sexual abuse and maladaptive sexual behavior, and psychological abuse and low self-esteem, suggesting abuse-specific symptomatology. More severe problems have also been found in adults who experienced multiple childhood abuses (e.g., Gross & Keller, 1992; Higgins & McCabe, 2000).

Comparative research has examined the relationship between PTSD and various forms of child maltreatment. Dubner and Motta (1999), for example, studied three groups of children and found that 64% of the sexually abused group met diagnostic criteria for PTSD, compared with 42% of the physically abused group and 18% of the nonabused comparison group. Widom (1999) conducted a prospective study on the long-term effects associated with various forms of child maltreatment and found that, of the young adults with histories of child maltreatment in her sample, approximately 38% of the sexual abuse victims met criteria for PTSD, compared with 33% of physical abuse victims and 31% of victims of childhood neglect.

Recently, studies have begun to appear in which researchers use sophisticated statistical methods to control for one or more forms of child maltreatment while isolating another form. Johnson, Smailes, Cohen, Brown, and Bernstein (2000), for example, found that childhood emotional, physical, and supervision neglect were each associated with increased risk of personality disorders and with elevated symptoms of anxiety and depression, even after the influence of childhood physical or sexual abuse was controlled for statistically. Additional studies such as this are necessary because of the high probability that any one individual may experience multiple forms of child maltreatment and because outcomes vary depending on the form(s) of maltreatment experienced. For these reasons, contamination of samples is a reality that researchers in the field must address. Some scholars have recommended that abuse co-occurrence should be included in future research as a necessity (Miller-Perrin & Perrin, 1997; Slep & Heyman, 2001). Professionals working in the field must also be cognizant of the overlap among various forms of abuse when attempting to address the needs of victims and their families. Knowledge about the co-occurrence of abuse forms is important for both the identification and the treatment of victims.

Additional Areas of Integrative Research

In addition to studying the co-occurrence and comparative effects of various forms of child maltreatment, researchers need to address additional potential areas of integration. Although there are few examples of integrative approaches in the literature outside of those mentioned above, notable exceptions are beginning to appear. Slep and Heyman (2001), for example, discuss the patterns of risk factors across the various forms of child maltreatment based on a series of reviews that appeared in the journal of *Aggression and Violent Behavior*. These authors generally conclude that although several risk factors overlap among the various forms of child maltreatment, some risk factors are unique to specific forms of child maltreatment. Miller-Perrin and Perrin (1997) provide specific examples of overlapping risk factors associated with various forms of child maltreatment. For most forms of child maltreatment, for example, there are consistent findings of gender disparity with regard to perpetrators and victims. In the case of child sexual abuse, perpetrators are disproportionately male. Gender disparities are also found for child neglect, with females more likely to be identified as neglectful parents. Economic hardship and low socioeconomic status are also risk factors associated with most types of child maltreatment. Miller-Perrin and Perrin go beyond a discussion of common risk factors and describe other areas of commonality among the various forms of child maltreatment. They also highlight the similarities among various forms of child maltreatment in terms of etiological theories and discuss the methodological challenges of conducting research in the field.

In order to advance the field of child maltreatment, scholars need to increase their efforts to integrate research findings across subfields. Research paradigms that compare and integrate different subfields of child maltreatment are beneficial because of their emphasis on the interactive nature of the problem. Because the various forms of maltreatment are interconnected, examinations of these interrelationships should enhance understanding of this very complex problem. In addition, this type of research paradigm has an interdisciplinary focus that might offset some of the factionalism within the field by reducing competition among professionals in specialized fields. Finally, many of the commonalities observed between various forms of child maltreatment can be used as risk markers to assist in the identification of victims and to guide the development of intervention strategies. Ultimately, integrative research involving the different forms of child maltreatment should help create a better understanding of the dynamics of child maltreatment, and this understanding should lead to better approaches to intervention and prevention.

CHAPTER SUMMARY

The criminal justice system responds in several ways when a child is identified as a victim of child maltreatment. These responses include the attention of child protective services. CPS agencies, under the administration of federal, state, and local systems, aim to protect children by investigating reports of maltreatment, providing treatment services, coordinating services with other community agencies, and implementing preventive services. The CPS system has been criticized in recent years for its seeming inability to provide adequate protection and services to children. Some believe that the difficulties faced by CPS are due to problems with child welfare policy, funding, and resource allocation. Others contend that the ultimate failure of the system may be due to its primary focus on investigation rather than service provision. Mandatory reporting laws have also been criticized. Professionals required by law to report suspected cases of child abuse often fail to do so because they lack confidence in CPS's ability to respond appropriately and they question whether reporting some cases of child maltreatment will ultimately be in the best interests of the child and family. Some observers have suggested that mandatory reporting laws should be rewritten so that professionals are mandated to report only severe cases of child maltreatment.

Criminal justice system responses directed at the problem of child maltreatment sometimes include interventions designed to alleviate the stress associated with victim involvement in the investigative process and court proceedings as well as punitive responses for the perpetrators of child maltreatment. Among the practices suggested to minimize the potentially traumatic effects on victims of investigative interviewing and court appearances is to limit the number of interviews and interviewers a child encounters by videotaping interviews and using multidisciplinary teams. Several courtroom accommodations for child victims have also been recommended, including allowing them to testify via videotape or closed-circuit television. With regard to punitive responses toward perpetrators, many argue that prevention and therapy, rather than litigation and sentencing, are of ultimate importance in responding to the problem of child maltreatment. Others believe that the social and legal costs to child maltreatment offenders are too low. Although not all cases of child maltreatment result in prosecutions, many perpetrators are either prosecuted or sentenced under plea bargains. Indeed, there is some evidence that child abuse is treated much as other crimes are treated within the criminal justice system.

The problem of child maltreatment is not merely a North American phenomenon; rather, it affects children in all parts of the world. A global approach to child maltreatment implicitly requires an understanding of the relationship between cultural factors and child maltreatment. The way that members of a given society define child maltreatment, for example, depends on their culturally accepted principles and practices of child rearing. Professionals working in the field of child maltreatment must be aware of cultural differences and must provide culturally sensitive interventions when addressing the problem of child maltreatment.

The past several years have seen a conceptual broadening in American society of the circumstances that might be worthy of the label *child maltreatment*. Some of these circumstances, such as exposure to community violence, are common and have been increasingly recognized as threats to children's well-being. Estimates of the numbers of children who experience child maltreatment indirectly, through exposure to violence within their communities, are staggering. Although no official estimates are available, survey data suggest that 40% or more of inner-city youth in the United States are exposed to some type of violence within their communities. Such violence ranges from relatively minor acts such as purse snatching to severe forms of violence such as shootings, and the violence in many communities is often chronic and repeated. Exposure to community violence is an adverse situation that is frequently associated with negative emotional outcomes, including posttraumatic stress symptoms, depression, aggression, and low self-esteem. The findings of research concerning the effects associated with exposure to community violence should be interpreted cautiously, however, because of the difficulty in ferreting out the specific effects of such exposure from other potentially significant factors (e.g., poverty, neglect, and violence within the home). In reality, little is known with certainty about the effects on children of exposure to community violence. Although interventions for children and families residing in violent communities are limited, efforts designed to address the issue are appearing, including programs to enhance police responses to children exposed to violence, multiservice approaches, and public policy initiatives.

Some debate surrounds the issue of whether sibling abuse should be considered a form of child maltreatment. On the one hand, some children experience severe physical violence and inappropriate sexual behaviors at the hands of siblings. On the other hand, such abuse may not be as pervasive as some accounts suggest. As is true with all forms of child maltreatment, the extent of the problem depends on the definitions used by researchers, clinicians, and other professionals. Overly inclusive definitions of sibling abuse, for example, result in estimates that more than 80% of children are victims of sibling abuse. A number of factors have been suggested as indicative of the abusiveness of sibling interactions: the frequency and duration of negative behaviors, the degree of resulting harm, the power disparity between the siblings, elements of pressure and secrecy, the developmental appropriateness of the behavior, and the type of parental intervention initiated. Research examining the psychological sequelae associated with negative sibling interactions is limited, but findings to date indicate that the problems reported by siblings are similar to those reported by victims of other forms of child maltreatment. Additional research should focus on the parameters of sibling abuse, including incidence and prevalence rates, associated psychological symptoms, and victim and perpetrator characteristics.

Forms of child maltreatment that occur outside the family include institutional abuse and ritualistic abuse. Sensationalistic media accounts of cases involving some of these forms of child maltreatment have contributed to public misperceptions about such abuse. Institutional abuse (abuse in out-of-home settings such as foster care, residential treatment centers, and licensed child-care facilities), for example, is much less common than abuse occurring within children's own homes. Official estimates suggest that only 3% of confirmed child maltreatment cases involve institutional abuse. Most research on institutional abuse, which has focused on abuse occurring in child-care facilities, suggests that this form of abuse is more likely than other forms to involve multiple perpetrators who are female. Although some researchers have attempted to describe the parameters of ritualistic abuse (prevalence rates, associated psychological symptoms, and victim and perpetrator characteristics), this form of abuse represents one of the most controversial topics within the field of child maltreatment.

The negative outcomes associated with child maltreatment affect not only the children who experience abuse but also others who live and/or work with these children. Professional and personal interactions with children and adults who are involved in child maltreatment are potentially difficult. As a result, many family members of maltreatment victims as well as professionals working within the field of child maltreatment experience negative reactions themselves. Several studies have focused on the mothers of child sexual abuse victims as secondary victims who have their own traumatic reactions to their children's disclosures of abuse. "Ripple effects" for professionals include trauma-related symptoms as well as personal stress. Many factors are predictive of who among professionals will experience secondary trauma, such as personal history of abuse, the degree of exposure to others' trauma, amount of training and experience, and availability of social supports. Professionals can engage in a number of strategies to counteract or prevent the negative effects associated with work in the field of child maltreatment.

The field of child maltreatment has been characterized as lacking integration across its various subfields. Divisions within the field have obscured the relationships among various forms of child maltreatment and contributed to the lack of a unified approach to addressing the problem. Although there is no "cure" for the fragmentation within the field, several approaches to studying the problem of child maltreatment might lessen the factionalism. For example, researchers might investigate the multiple victimization of children as well as the comparative effects of various forms of child maltreatment. Such an approach calls for a comprehensive and integrated analysis of the field that acknowledges the effectiveness of examining the relationships among various subfields of child maltreatment and also recognizes the value of integrating research and professional interests. The adoption of a unified approach should promote more unity and integration among disciplines, among professionals, and across subfields and ultimately contribute to alleviating the problem of child maltreatment.

DISCUSSION QUESTIONS

1. What is the role of child protective services in responding to child maltreatment? How effective is the CPS system in the United States?

2. What is out-of-home care? What are the dilemmas associated with out-of-home care?

3. What are mandatory reporting laws?

4. How are child maltreatment victims affected by their involvement with the criminal justice system?

5. What is Megan's Law?

6. What are some of the cultural differences that might influence people's views concerning child maltreatment? Why do professionals who work with child maltreatment victims and their families need to be culturally sensitive?

7. What is sibling abuse? What are some of the characteristics of siblings who inflict harm? Is it legitimate to classify sibling abuse as a form of child maltreatment?

8. How are children affected by being exposed to violence within their communities?

9. What does research show about the forms of child maltreatment known as institutional abuse and ritualistic abuse?

10. What are the potential collateral effects of child maltreatment? What can be done to treat and prevent such effects?

11. What does the research literature indicate about the multiple victimization of children?

12. What are the comparative effects of the various forms of child maltreatment?

RECOMMENDED READING

Dubowitz, H., & DePanfilis, D. (Eds.). (2000). *Handbook for child protection practice*. Thousand Oaks, CA: Sage.

Emery, R. E., & Laumann-Billings, L. (1998). An overview of the nature, causes, and consequences of abusive family relationships: Toward differentiating maltreatment and violence. *American Psychologist 53*, 121–135.

Levesque, R. J. R. (2000). Cultural evidence, child maltreatment, and the law. *Child Maltreatment, 5*, 146–160.

Melton, G. B., & Barry, F. D. (1994). Neighbors helping neighbors: The vision of the U.S. Advisory Board on Child Abuse and Neglect. In G. B. Melton & F. D. Barry (Eds.), *Protecting children from abuse and neglect* (pp. 1–13). New York: Guilford.

Myers, J. E. B. (1998). *Legal issues in child abuse and neglect practice* (2nd ed.). Thousand Oaks, CA: Sage.

Osofsky, J. D. (1999). The impact of violence on children. *Future of Children, 9*(3), 33–49.

Slep, A. M. S., & Heyman, R. E. (2001). Where do we go from here? Moving toward an integrated approach to family violence. *Aggression and Violent Behavior, 6*, 353–356.

Strand, V. C. (2000). *Treating secondary victims: Intervention with the nonoffending mother in the incest family*. Thousand Oaks, CA: Sage.

Waterman, J., Kelly, R. J., Oliveri, M. K., & McCord, J. (1993). *Behind the playground walls: Sexual abuse in preschools*. New York: Guilford.

Wiehe, V. R. (1997). *Sibling abuse: Hidden physical, emotional, and sexual trauma* (2nd ed.). Thousand Oaks, CA: Sage.

8

DATING VIOLENCE, STALKING, AND SEXUAL ASSAULT

Case History: Ivana and Bruce—Teaching Her a Lesson

Ivana and Bruce met during their senior year in high school. After a few dates they fell madly in love, and by the end of high school they began talking about marriage. Most of the time, Ivana felt very proud and lucky to have "landed" Bruce. Occasionally, however, Bruce was unexpectedly moody and jealous. He voiced numerous suspicions about whether Ivana was lying to him. Eventually, he secretly began to follow Ivana. He liked to follow her unobtrusively in his car as she walked to her house after school, and later he would ask her detailed questions about her trip home. In time, Ivana noticed Bruce's car parked here and there on the route to her house. Although Bruce's angry outbursts were unpleasant, Ivana felt that his possessiveness was a sign of true love. His constant watchfulness actually made her feel secure.

On one occasion, Bruce accused Ivana of being insensitive to his feelings. After thinking it over, Ivana decided that Bruce was probably right, and she resolved to be very careful about how she treated him. This didn't seem to help Bruce feel more relaxed, however. He began complaining about Ivana's many friends, who "took up all her time." Ivana felt somewhat confused, so she discussed the situation with her best friend, who urged her to work it out with Bruce if she really loved him. Ivana decided to try even harder to please Bruce, because they had been dating for nearly a year and a half and she believed that Bruce really loved her.

Next, Bruce started to call Ivana several times a day, "just to check in." Although Ivana felt pressured by these calls, she thought that Bruce was just insecure and that he surely would finally come to believe that she loved him and no one else. She still had a lot of hope that Bruce would change.

One evening when Bruce came to pick Ivana up for a date, he became angry because she was wearing a tight sweater. He wanted to know why she was "trying to turn on other guys"; wasn't he enough for her? Ivana was shocked, but she assured Bruce that she loved only him and she would be glad to change her clothes. After all, changing into a loose blouse wasn't too much to ask, she thought. Bruce appreciated her effort and was very attentive and loving during the date, but for the first time, Ivana felt vaguely disturbed by Bruce's behavior. She also felt disappointed that he couldn't seem to trust her.

When it came time for Ivana to go on vacation with her family to Tahiti, Bruce forbade her to go. Ivana still planned to go, but she stopped talking to Bruce about the trip. One day, however, Bruce came over while Ivana was packing for the vacation. When he saw what she was doing, he searched her suitcases and removed all her bathing suits. Ivana still loved him, but she felt burdened, restricted, and uneasy. Bruce seemed to be watching her every move. She hoped that the trip to Tahiti, and the break from school and from Bruce it provided, might help her to relax and clear her mind. It didn't.

When Ivana returned home with her family, she put together an album of snapshots from the trip. Bruce visited soon after, and he decided to look through the album. When he saw snapshots of Ivana in a bikini, he "went ballistic," screaming, shaking Ivana, and finally tearing out sections of the album. Ivana broke off her relationship with Bruce with a heavy heart. She felt she had failed somehow to convince him that she really loved him.

After a few weeks, Ivana decided to accept a date with Bruce and to try again to work out their relationship. After all, he had apologized and promised never to become violent again. The date went fine until the end of the evening, when they drove out to the beach; although Bruce had seemed nonchalant up to that point, his mood suddenly turned ugly. He began to yell at Ivana, saying that she had never loved him. He called her a "no-good, f___g bitch." Although Ivana was upset and furious, she did everything she could think of to calm Bruce down. She told him that she loved him, but that simply seemed to enrage him further. Suddenly, Bruce grabbed Ivana by the throat and began to slap her and choke her. She tried to fight back by scratching him and pulling his hair, but she was no match for him. She could hardly believe what was happening. Bruce ripped off her clothes and raped her, all the time cursing at her and screaming, "I'll teach you to fool around behind my back." Finally he pushed Ivana out of the car and left her sobbing on the beach.

Ivana did not call the police or tell anyone what had happened to her that night for more than 2 years. Although Bruce eventually apologized to her for his behavior, Ivana refused to see him ever again.

The case history above contains a number of elements typical of dating violence in college-age couples. Note how Ivana wanted to please Bruce and how he felt he needed to control her. Also noteworthy is that the abuse eventually led to a sexual assault. Individuals involved in dating violence (DV), a category of violence that is often understood to include stalking (ST) and sexual assault (SA), are typically adolescents in middle school or high school (12–19 years old) or unmarried college students (18–26 years old). Research concerning DV, ST, and SA among individuals younger than 12 and among young adults who are not students is rare. Although cohabitors constitute a group of unmarried intimates, their similarities to married couples place them out of the realm of typical dating couples.

The inclusion in this volume of violence between unmarried, dating adolescents under the umbrella of family violence raises some important issues. Because interest in DV originally grew out of research on marital violence, a number of similarities are apparent in these two areas of research, in the topics covered, research methods used, explanations offered, and constructs applied. Also deserving of consideration is the fact that DV has been associated with serious physical and mental health problems and may be a bridge to future abusive relationships (Davidson, 1995; Morton & Browne, 1998; Simons, Wu, Johnson, & Conger, 1995). One major difference between DV and marital violence is the greater focus on sexual assault factors in DV. A second dissimilarity exists in the amounts and kinds of information available. Compared with marital violence, less is known about DV, ST, and SA (including date rape) and their injurious outcomes. Only recently have government agencies begun to classify intimate violence by boyfriends and girlfriends as a separate category of crime. A third difference between DV and marital violence lies in society's attitudes toward violence between adolescents compared with that between adults.

The formal beginning of research on DV appears to be Kanin's (1957) landmark study of male aggression toward female dates. It soon became clear that being young and in love does not protect adolescents and young adults from DV, ST, and SA. A sampling of the DV research reveals an emphasis on proviolence attitudes, especially in terms of sex-role attitudes, male peer-group support, the relationship between alcohol consumption and DV, and gender dissimilarities in acceptance of rape myths. Academicians have also made some headway in understanding the configurations of individual psychological and dyadic factors that promote aggression. Experts do not agree on what causes DV, although many offer a social learning explanation. Finally, advocates working in the field of DV have actively pursued programs of education and prevention.

SCOPE OF THE PROBLEM

Difficulties in research methodology have hampered scholars' attempts to understand the scope of the problem of DV. The summary of methodological defects in family violence research presented in Chapter 2 serves as a preamble to the maze of difficult-to-interpret DV, ST, and SA findings (Ferguson, 1998; Jackson, 1998). To

#2

name just a few of these obstacles: The topic is very private and personal, it is difficult to obtain permission to administer tests to adolescents, the available questionnaires are inadequate, and samples may be small and nonrepresentative. Also of concern is the limited generalizability of findings based on college samples. College students constitute a select group of highly intelligent young people whose socioeconomic status (SES) and other attributes are not representative of young people in general.

The inconsistencies in the results found in the literature on dating violence are extreme. As Lewis and Fremouw (2001) note: "The challenging aspect of identifying high-risk individuals is the extremely equivocal nature of the empirical findings. For every piece of data that supports a contention, there is evidence that contradicts the finding" (p. 123). Problems of how to interpret correlational data are also apparent in this subarea of family violence, as they are in other subareas. On a more promising note, research on DV, ST, and SA has improved each year with the inauguration of more longitudinal studies and somewhat decreased reliance on self-report measures.

Defining Forms of Interpersonal Violence in Dating Populations

In part, inconsistencies in results across studies spring from differences in definitions, which continue to evolve with scientific advances. Although consensus among scholars concerning the precise meaning of the term *dating violence* would greatly enhance research efforts, no such definition has emerged.

Defining dating violence. Researchers often assume that the term *dating violence* is so easily understood that they have no need to define it. In the same vein, they rarely bother to define the meaning of the word *dating.* Dating may be defined as involving couple interaction with emotional commitment, with or without sexual intimacy. Although, as noted above, DV is sometimes understood broadly to encompass ST and SA, scholars commonly address these behaviors separately. The definition of DV used in this text is a modified and updated version of Sugarman and Hotaling's (1989) definition: "DV involves the perpetration of physical, emotional, or threat abuse by at least one member of an unmarried dating couple" (p. 5). Dating couples may or may not be sexually intimate and may or may not be heterosexual. Defining DV broadly adds stalking and sexual assault to the other abuses.

A term related to DV is *intimate partner violence* (IPV). IPV is a relatively inclusive term that refers to violence between sexually intimate persons of almost any age, education level, marital status, living arrangement, or sexual orientation. IPV is most often understood to apply to adults. DV and IPV are not totally differentiated because they overlap along three dimensions. First, college-age young people qualify as adults, suggesting that *IPV* is the more suitable term for violence between intimates in this group. Second, college-age students are not usually married or cohabiting, suggesting that *DV* is the more appropriate term. Third, dating college students may not be sexually intimate, again implying that *DV* is the better term. Experts have not yet reached consensus on this point, but this text places interpersonally violent college-age couples within the DV category.

Some scholars conceptualize DV as a mirror of IPV and warn that making artificial distinctions between the two might result in a minimization of the seriousness of DV (e.g., Hamberger & Arnold, 1989). Others perceive some similarities between DV and IPV but assert that important elements separate the two concepts. First and foremost of these is that the many developmental changes occurring during adolescence make responding to DV especially confusing for teens (for a review, see Sousa, 1999). Levy (1991) proposes that for teenage girls, certain aspects of adolescence, such as inexperience, romanticism, and the pressure to have a boyfriend, separate DV from IPV.

Operational definitions of DV are quite similar to those developed for IPV (see Chapter 9 for more details). That is, researchers define DV in terms of the frequency and severity of interpersonally violent behaviors. The items that investigators use to assess DV are most commonly anchored in the Conflict Tactics Scale (CTS1; Straus, 1979) and the Revised Conflict Tactics Scale (CTS2; Straus, Hamby, Boney-McCoy, & Sugarman, 1995) and vary along the same dimensions. An illustration of the kind of operational definition of DV that a researcher might construct is as follows: DV occurs when at least one member of a couple perpetrates a physical assault causing injury to his or her partner two or more times within a given 12-month period. The greater the precision of the operational definitions used, the greater the replicability of the research.

Few legal definitions of DV exist, although social scientists have promulgated definitions (for a review, see Ferguson, 1998). The legal status of victims (and perpetrators) is especially relevant in regard to responses of the criminal justice system (CJS). By and large, the CJS is adult centered and fails to acknowledge the DV concerns of adolescents (for a review, see Levesque, 1997). In many jurisdictions teenagers must depend on their parents to obtain legal protections for them. Usually, statutes covering violent behaviors of teenagers do not address DV directly. Instead, they classify certain interpersonally violent acts as illegal without regard to the victim-offender relationship. Where laws governing DV exist at all, they are most often subsumed under adult IPV laws. In fact, the Violence Against Women Act of 2000 for the first time extended many provisions protecting adult women to teenage women. **Stalking** was not a crime in the United States prior to 1990, and it still is not illegal under military law (Eldridge, 2000). By 2000, however, all 50 states had antistalking laws (Rosenfeld, 2000). Stalking, like assault, is a "stand-alone" offense; it does not usually fall under the umbrella of IPV. To press charges of stalking, teenagers may need their parents to file complaints with the police.

Defining stalking. Despite the relatively recent recognition of stalking as a form of interpersonal violence, scholars have not hesitated to classify it as a form of DV or IPV when the victim-offender relationship is or was intimate. The Office for Victims of Crime (2002b) defines stalking as "the willful or intentional commission of a series of acts that would cause a reasonable person to fear death or serious bodily injury and that, in fact, does place the victim in fear of death or serious bodily injury" (p. 1). Although this represents a starting point, the conceptualization of ST is still evolving. Prohibited ST behaviors ordinarily include harassing, making nonconsensual contact, and communicating with the victim (for a longer list of prohibited behaviors, see Office for Victims of Crime, 2002b). Among the most widely agreed-upon elements of stalking are its repetitiveness, long duration (averaging 2 years) (Spitzberg, 2002), and tendency to escalate over time (Emerson, Ferris, & Gardner, 1998). Despite differences in the definitions espoused by myriad observers, ST appears "to be consistent over countries and samples" (Sheridan, Blaauw, & Davies, 2003, p. 148).

Defining sexual assault. Sexual assault or date rape within the confines of dating violence is the perpetration of sexual aggression against an (unmarried) date or acquaintance (for a comprehensive definition, see Centers for Disease Control and Prevention, 2002). SA and sexual coercion are highly charged topics that

polarize opinions, commonly along gender lines (Lonsway & Fitzgerald, 1994). These disputes and other factors have made the definition and assessment of SA especially problematic.

At the root of this dissension is the question of consent (see Margolin, Moran, & Miller, 1989). The use of powerful illegal drugs such as gamma hydroxybutyrate (GHB) and Rohypnol ("roofies")—so-called date-rape drugs—is related to this issue. By administering such drugs to stupefy potential rape victims, perpetrators seek to bypass women's ability to consent to sex. For rapists, these drugs are advantageous because they render victims unable to resist and cause memory loss (Schwartz, Milteer, & LeBeau, 2000).

There are also many less dramatic and more common examples of questions about consent. Does the way a woman dresses on a date, such as her lack of underwear, convey that she is willing to have sexual intercourse? If she has consented to sex with a particular person in the past, does she give up the right to decline on subsequent occasions? Are there circumstances, such as a woman's having had too much alcohol, that excuse SA? How would you describe Ivana and Bruce's last sexual encounter in the case history that opens this chapter?

One aspect of debate is whether it is best to define SA narrowly or broadly. For purposes of data gathering, the FBI until recently defined rape narrowly, as "sexual intercourse or attempted sexual intercourse with a female against her will by force or threat of force" (Flanagan & Maguire, 1991, p. 779). Some have asserted that this narrow definition of rape, promulgated in 1929, totally overlooks and trivializes same-sex male rape (see Stop Prisoner Rape, 2002). It also ignores an entire spectrum of forced sexual behaviors (e.g., oral sex) that the laws of most U.S. states categorize as forms of rape. The methods the U.S. Bureau of Justice Statistics used to determine SA prevalence rates for the National Crime Victimization Survey (NCVS) presumed that respondents knew when sexual encounters in which they had been involved qualified as crimes (for the NCVS questions, see Bachman & Saltzman, 1995).

Social scientists, by comparison, generally prefer to use broader assessments when determining the prevalence of SA. In the case of NCVS questions, Koss (1989) speculated that survey respondents did not implicitly know the legal definition of rape as a crime. They may have been unsure, for example, whether coerced anal intercourse qualifies as "rape." Hence many scholars recommend that surveys about rape use questions that are not phrased in legal language, but instead incorporate clear descriptions of particular SA actions. With this approach, analysts have found that rape is not a single clear-cut behavior, but rather a continuum of unwanted actions. (For a contrasting conceptualization of SA, see Testa & Dermen, 1999.)

The importance of subjective definitions of SA must be acknowledged. The point at which any individual involved in a sexual encounter will label unwanted sexual behavior as SA is strongly influenced by determinants such as age, sex, race, SES, and the person's relationship with the offender (Koss, 1985). Victims who are romantically involved with their assailants, for instance, are much less likely to characterize sexual coercion as rape (Bondurant, 2001).

To obtain a fuller understanding of subjective definitions of rape, Emmers-Sommer and Allen (1999) conducted a meta-analysis. They found that designation of a sexual encounter as rape is a function of an individual's personal attitudes and his or her perception of the situation. In a study designed to illuminate the subjectivity of definitions of rape, Hannon, Hall, Nash, Formanti, and Hopson (2000) examined disapproval of an aggressor's sexual behavior along a continuum. In this inquiry, each subject in a sample of 694 college students evaluated one of four SA vignettes from his or her own viewpoint and from both the aggressor's and the victim's viewpoints. The vignettes involved male-to-female, male-to-male, female-to-female, and female-to-male SA. From 46.6% to 55.5% of the students rated the aggressor's behavior as rape in the vignettes depicting male-to-female, male-to-male, and female-to-female SA. Only 18.7% judged the aggressor's actions as rape in the vignette describing a female-to-male assault.

Case History: Mary and Her Date at a Fraternity Bash

Mary, a freshman at Florida State University, had been drinking tequila before attending a fraternity party as the date of 23-year-old Daniel Oltarsh, a junior and member of Pi Kappa Alpha.[1] When she arrived at the fraternity house, already intoxicated, Oltarsh gave her wine and left her alone in his room. Police lab tests later placed Mary's blood-alcohol level at over .349%, a level that under some circumstances is enough to cause death.

Later, Oltarsh returned and forced Mary to have sex with him. He then took her to the fraternity house's shower room, where at least two other fraternity brothers raped her in a group and further used a toothpaste pump as a means of penetration. Afterward, they dumped her in the hallway of a second fraternity house, where members of yet a third fraternity wrote their house's initials on Mary's thigh with a ballpoint pen.

As news of these assaults got out and gossip pervaded the campus, Mary started to believe she might have been to blame for her own rape, perhaps an accessory of some sort. She tried to take measures to avoid being recognized, such as changing her hair color, but that did not lessen her notoriety. Eventually, Mary was unable to cope with her life any longer and checked into a psychiatric hospital for treatment of alcoholism, bulimia, and depression. Oltarsh was arrested and pleaded no contest to forcible rape. He received a prison sentence of one year, a stiff sentence by most standards. His fraternity brothers were allowed to plea-bargain to lesser charges.

Mary now works as a bookkeeper. In a magazine interview conducted more than a year after the rapes, she said that it had been therapeutic for her to see her assailants convicted: "These men robbed me of any pride or hope or self-esteem that I had and replaced it with anger and self-hate and fear. To see their lives affected is some vindication" (quoted in Bane et al., 1990, p. 100).

The preceding case history underscores the seriousness of SA and illustrates the widespread nature and acceptance of this type of male-to-female violence in some cultural settings. At least three men in one fraternity participated in raping Mary, men from another fraternity partook in initialing her thigh, and men from a third fraternity seemed willing to play host to still other assaults on this woman. This kind of behavior should clearly sound a cultural alarm in America.

The legal definitions used in statutes covering SA across the United States have evolved over time. In the past, for sexual acts to be considered rape, victims had to prove that they had physically resisted. Judges were prone to ruling that women had not resisted even if they required stitches as a result of being assaulted.

Further, before the 1980s, many Americans believed that once a male was fully aroused, he was not capable of stopping short of sexual intercourse (Miller & Marshall, 1987). In some states, extreme laws required any woman who claimed rape to undergo a psychiatric evaluation.

Over the past two decades, both the sensibilities of the American public and laws concerning sexual assault have shifted. By 1984, all 50 states had revised their legal definitions of rape (Largen, 1987), and the process is ongoing (Kennan, 1998). As a case in point, the California Supreme Court recently handed down a decision that further refines the definition of rape in that state. In response to a claim by a teenage girl who initially consented to sex, commenced intercourse, and then said, "Stop," the court, in a unanimous opinion, interpreted the statute defining rape "as continued penetration by a man after a consenting woman demands that intercourse stop" (quoted in Kravets, 2003, p. 4).

Estimating Prevalence and Incidence of Dating Violence and Stalking

As is true of other forms of intimate violence, when DV occurs, it usually takes place in private, so it is difficult to detect. The problems in interpersonal violence research in general that are summarized in Chapter 2 are all too obvious in estimates of DV, ST, and SA. Lack of theoretical anchors, ambiguous definitions, inadequate questions, inappropriate questionnaire contexts, and suboptimal data collection methods have impeded disclosure of DV, ST, and SA and account for the wide variability in estimates. Problems with sample selection and data analysis techniques have further obscured interpretations of findings (Hilton, Harris, & Rice, 1998). Finally, the extreme variability of estimates of DV, ST, and SA probably indicates that **moderator variables** have substantial impacts.

Box 8.1 Researching Dating Violence

Scholars need to accomplish a number of goals to improve the quality of research designs for the study of dating violence, including those listed below. Practitioners and criminal justice experts need detailed information about all these topics as well.

- Researchers need to move away from self-report surveys and avoid measurements scales that conceptualize IPV as the outcome of conflict (Koss et al., 1994).
- Researchers could enhance the usefulness of their study findings by devising new scales grounded in focus group work with young people and by conducting some qualitative studies (Jackson, 1998).
- Researchers need to use questionnaires that include measures of fear, control, and psychological abuse in assessing dating violence (see Jacobson, 1994a; Tolman, 1989).
- Researchers need to present clear sociostructural information (e.g., race, SES) about their sample populations in their publications.
- Researchers should address gender differences, separate findings by gender, study couples, and more fully tie their research results to theoretical stances (Jackson, 1998; Lewis & Fremouw, 2001).
- Researchers need to conduct more studies examining self-defensive violence (Lewis & Fremouw, 2001).
- Researchers should develop typologies of DV and SA offenders (and possibly victims) (Jackson, 1998) and search for protective factors (O'Keefe, 1998).
- In addition to conducting more evaluations of the effectiveness of medical responses to DV and SA, researchers need to examine the effects of medical personnel's responses to DV and SA victims (Thurston, Cory, & Scott, 1998).
- Researchers need to devote more resources to the examination of the problem of gang rape, which to date has received little attention (Ferguson, 1998).
- Legal researchers need to focus on the effects of revictimization and statutory definitions of stalking, as the victim's level of fear may be relevant (Jordan, Logan, Walker, & Nigoff, 2003).
- Legal experts in the U.S. armed forces need to develop antistalking legislation (Eldridge, 2000).

Sources of estimates. One obstacle to deciphering prevalence rates for DV, ST, and SA is the lack of specificity inherent in the statistical summaries published by government agencies in the past. Until relatively recently, statisticians who analyzed FBI reports put interpersonal violence data into one of two categories: "known offender" or "unknown offender (stranger)." The known offender category contained data about perpetrators who were known to the victims: spouses, ex-spouses, cohabitors/ex-cohabitors, boyfriends/girlfriends, ex-boyfriends/ex-girlfriends, and other relatives. Consequently, further designation of the relationships of couples involved in DV was not available. Data from the 1992–1993 NCVS, based on self-reports, were the first assault data available that were **disaggregated** by relationship status. Researchers were finally able to report information about dating partners (current and former combined) as a category separate from other intimate couples (Bachman & Saltzman, 1995).

In addition to the NCVS, several other government-sponsored surveys include data on adolescent DV, ST, and SA. Although some of these surveys monitor large nationally representative samples, they do not incorporate multiple questions about DV. They most commonly track occurrences such as physical aggression, sexual assault, health outcomes, and injuries. One such canvass is the National Longitudinal Study of Adolescent Health, which uses five CTS1-Form R questions to assess DV: three concerning psychological abuse of partner (name-calling, swearing, and threatening behaviors) and two concerning physical abuse of partner (throwing potentially harmful objects and pushing or shoving). Another is the Youth Risk Behavior Surveillance System, which includes two DV questions, one for victimization and the other for perpetration ("Physical Violence," 1996). Both are modified CTS1 items that inquire about hitting, kicking, and throwing someone down. (For a list of surveys that are appropriate for use across cultures, see O'Donnell, Smith, & Madison, 2002.)

In addition to government surveys, independent researchers have conducted numerous smaller studies of DV and ST. They have slowly expanded their ambit to include ethnic minorities, immigrants, and other seldom-evaluated groups in their study sample. Experts in countries other than the United States have also begun to assess DV and ST.

Psychological and physical dating violence. In a recent literature review, Lewis and Fremouw (2001) found a range of DV estimates extending from 9% to 65%, revealing again the extreme inconsistency of the findings to date. Authorities are often shocked when the results of surveys about DV among adolescents come to light. High levels of psychological and physical abuse are characteristic of teenage and college student couples. Worried experts have labeled these high estimates "alarming," "deplorable," and "unconscionable." (See Table 1 in Appendix B of this volume for a summary of estimates of rates of psychological abuse, stalking, physical abuse, injuries, and homicides.)

Stalking. For the most part, researchers have presented data on stalking that are disaggregated by gender, age, and the nature of the perpetrator's acquaintanceship with the victim. One analysis of 103 studies of stalking found that most victims are women (75%), but about a fourth are men. Perpetration rates are almost the mirror image: 79% of perpetrators are male, and 20% are female (Spitzberg, 2002). A further analysis of 32 surveys revealed that 49% of ST cases originated from relationships that had previously been romantic (Spitzberg, 2002). Another recent review of representative samples resulted in the estimate that 12% to 16% of women have been ST victims, in contrast to 4% to 7% of men (Sheridan, Blaauw, & Davies, 2003). In Tjaden and Thoennes's (1998b) survey of 16,000 individuals 18 years of age and over, 74% of ST victims fell between the ages of 18 and 39. These initial findings point to the pressing need for additional ST research. (For ST estimates by boyfriends/ex-boyfriends among female college students, see the citation of Fisher, Cullen, & Turner, 2000, in Table 1 of Appendix B.)

Homicides among teenage girls. Homicide is the ultimate price society pays for failing to prevent interpersonal violence. An examination of 90 femicide victims ages 11–18 years revealed that 19% had been raped and 4% were pregnant. An intimate partner or acquaintance of the victim was the perpetrator in 78% of these homicides. Male perpetrators were 8 years older than their victims, on average, and 59% had criminal records (Coyne-Beasley, Moracco, & Casteel, 2003). Homicide figures from the FBI's *Supplementary Homicide Reports* (*SHR*) disaggregated by relationship are incomplete because they do not include former boyfriends and girlfriends. Paulozzi, Saltzman, Thompson, and Holmgreen (2001) note that they suspect *SHR* data fail to identify approximately 10% of intimate partner homicides. Table 1 in Appendix B presents a variety of estimates along several dimensions of DV and ST for large samples of adolescents, college students, and young adults.

Estimating rates of dating violence, stalking, and sexual assault among members of ethnic/racial minority groups. Although advances are being made in the assessment of rates of DV, ST, and SA in the United States, investigators have almost completely ignored the possibility that rates may differ among various racial and ethnic minority groups. Social scientists studying DV, ST, and SA have often failed to obtain samples of young people from racial and ethnic minority groups, or they have failed to index specific information about victim and offender race/ethnicity (Lauritsen & White, 2001; Rennison & Welchans, 2000). Foshee, Linder, MacDougall, and Bangdiwala (2001) may have conducted the only reliable study of DV to date that has included race as a variable. They surveyed 1,186 American teens and found that for females (but not for males) minority status was positively related to DV perpetration.

Estimating rates of dating violence, stalking, and sexual assault across cultures. Researchers have undertaken only a few DV and SA investigations outside the United States, and even fewer on ST. Because many other cultures are primarily patriarchal, data on DV and SA emanating from abroad provide an excellent opportunity to test feminist analysis. Although the data on DV and SA collected in other countries may seem comparable with data collected in the United States, some dissimilarities do exist. For estimates of DV and SA in cultures other than the United States, see Table 2 in Appendix B.

Estimating rates of dating violence, stalking, and sexual assault among gay, lesbian, bisexual, and transgendered teenagers. Despite the potential usefulness of data on interpersonal violence among gay, lesbian, bisexual, and transgendered (GLBT) young people, data on members of this population are usually meshed with data about adult IPV. Although little information is available about GLBT youths, studies suggest that DV, ST, and SA occur

---

Box 8.2 Violence Against Women Across Cultures

Over the past few years, many Americans have become aware of atrocities committed against women in Afghanistan at the hands of the Taliban. During the time of the Taliban's rule, women could not work outside their homes or attend school. When they went outside their homes, they had to wear clothing that guaranteed they would not expose any of their skin to the eyes of others. Religious police roaming the cities did not hesitate to beat women they deemed to be insufficiently covered (Norman & Finan, 2001). Americans are less aware of the unspeakable acts of violence perpetrated against women in other parts of the world, however. This violence takes many forms and often revolves around women's and young girls' sexual behavior or men's jealousy (Fields-Meyer & Benet, 1998; Levesque, 2001).

In some Middle Eastern and African countries, female genital mutilation (i.e., clitoridectomy or sewing the vaginal opening closed) is a common practice aimed at restraining "rampant" female sexuality. In most cases, female genital mutilation is performed without anesthesia by nonmedical practitioners working in unsanitary conditions. This practice endangers the health of perhaps as many as 126 million women worldwide. Only recently have some governments begun to prohibit it (Ortiz, 1998).

In Pakistan and India, an all-too-common occurrence is the disfigurement of women's faces by men who throw acid at them. Although many of the victims of these assaults are the wives of the perpetrators, some are girlfriends who have rejected the perpetrators as marriage partners. Women assaulted in this way suffer intense physical pain at the time of the attack. Some are blinded as a result, and many are badly mutilated. Those who survive experience a lifetime of physical disability, and those who do not often face an agonizing death, lying in a barren hospital ward without medication for even the most intense pain. The offenders are seldom arrested, much less prosecuted and convicted (Abdi, 2000).

more frequently among them than among non-GLBT youths. For example, a survey of high school students in Massachusetts revealed that those who reported same-sex sexual activities were twice as likely as those reporting only heterosexual contacts to be threatened or injured (Faulkner & Cranston, 1998). In an investigation of DV conducted with 521 youths, ages 13–22, who attended a rally for gays, lesbians, and bisexuals, Freedner, Freed, Yang, and Austin (2002) asked respondents about their sexual orientations along with other questions. Data yielded the following DV victimization rates for the 171 male participants: gays, 44.6%; bisexuals, 57.1%; heterosexuals, 28.6% Comparable rates for the 350 female participants were as follows: lesbians, 43.4%; bisexuals, 38.3%; heterosexuals, 32.4%. Relative to gay and lesbian respondents, bisexuals experienced the highest level of "outing" threats (i.e., threats to expose their nonheterosexual orientation). Collectively, these findings demonstrate that bisexual males are at greater risk of DV victimization than either gay males or lesbians.

Estimates of Sexual Assault

The methodological problems involved in estimating SA exceed those outlined above for DV or ST (Johnson & Sigler, 2000). Although estimates vary with methodology, it is clear that females are more often SA victims than are males (e.g., Schubot, 2001). One U.S. government study found that 54% of identified raped women in the period examined were under 18 years old (Rennison & Welchans, 2000). Unfortunately, the researchers do not provide any information on the relationships between the victims and their rapists.

Koss's self-report survey of college students. In 1989, Mary Koss published the results of her landmark study of 3,187 female and 2,972 male college students. To appraise the incidence of rape, Koss had each student respond to a graduated series of sexual aggression items on a carefully worded questionnaire that avoided legal terminology. The items covered such topics as sexual contact by misuse of authority, intercourse under influence of alcohol/drugs, and oral/anal penetration by threat of force.

Koss's data yielded a rate of 38 rapes per 1,000 women ages 18 to 24. In stark contrast, the 1984 NCVS data derived from legal definitions of rape within a crime context indicated an annual victimization rate of 3.9 per 1,000 for women ages 16 to 19 and 2.5 per 1,000 for women ages 20 to 24 (cited in Koss, 1989).

Furthermore, men's admission of rape was two to three times higher in Koss's survey than in the NCVS. Lending credence to Koss's findings are similar rates found in a 1995 National College Health Risk Survey (Brener, McMahon, Warren, & Douglas, 1999).

The vast disparity between the NCVS data and Koss's results appears to be the outcome of important wording differences in survey items. Koss's questionnaire did not require respondents to label or legally define their experiences as criminal acts of rape. In contrast, as Koss (1989) observes, the very brief NCVS items, which were worded in legal language and often presented by male interviewers, undermined full disclosure. Koss's findings reflect the significant difference that examining a problem from a feminist perspective can make.

The revised National Crime Victimization Survey. In response to criticisms, the U.S. Bureau of Justice Statistics undertook a 10-year project to redesign the NCVS questionnaire and survey procedures. The resulting changes, which included cuing respondents about potential victimization experiences, new behavior-specific (rather than legal) wording, and use of a computer-assisted telephone interview system, increased reports of personal crimes by 44% and reports of rape by 157% (Kindermann, Lynch, & Cantor, 1997). Continuing the trend in question improvement, Fisher et al. (2000) revised the National College Women's Sexual Victimization survey to include detailed behavior-specific questions. It subsequently detected a rate of 27.7 rapes per 1,000 female college students (for the old and new screener questions used in this survey, click on the "Additional Materials" button at the link for this volume on the Sage Publications Web site, http://www.sagepub.com/book.aspx?pid=10013). For estimates of sexual assaults based on the results of large surveys, see Table 3 in Appendix B.

Decontextualized violence. The most decisive element in the disparities evident in survey findings, as discussed in Chapter 2, is that CTS1 measures the types and frequencies of violent interactions, but not their antecedents or consequences. CTS2 includes additional measures of sexual assault and injury outcomes. The divergence of results noted above provides an excellent example of the power of question terminology and context to influence respondents' answers, and thus to affect rape prevalence estimates. The following case history exemplifies the relevance of contextual elements.

Box 8.3 Debating the Scope of Sexual Assault

In a book chapter published in 1993, Neil Gilbert, a professor of social welfare at the University of California, Berkeley, critiqued the so-called advocacy statistics published by Mary Koss, professor of family and community medicine, psychiatry, and psychology at the University of Arizona. Gilbert began by pointing out the huge gap between NCVS data and Koss's research findings. He criticized Koss's inclusion in her rape estimates of the 73% of rape "victims" in her sample who did not label what had happened to them as rape as well as her inclusion of "verbal coercion" as a form of threat or force.

Koss and Cook (1993) rebutted Gilbert's criticisms by saying that the experiences of the women in Koss's sample met the legal definition of rape, even if they failed to label the assaults accurately or did not report them to authorities. Koss and Cook asserted that the women may have miscategorized their experiences as some form of serious sexual abuse. Relying on data from 4,446 randomly selected college students, Fisher, Daigle, Cullen, and Turner (2003) authenticated Koss's 1985 findings.

Gilbert also observed that 40% of the rape victims in Koss, Gidycz, and Wisniewski's (1987) survey had subsequent sexual encounters with the men who supposedly raped them. Gilbert essentially argued that if the women had "really" been raped, they would not have remained sexually involved with the perpetrators. Koss (1992a), however, has offered several explanations for these interactions, one of which is that many of the women were romantically involved with their rapists and had subsequent nonforced sexual encounters. Of the victims in Koss's study who were raped by men with whom they were romantically involved, however, 87% eventually terminated those relationships.

Case History: Tiffany—A Violent Date?

Tiffany was a beautiful 22-year-old manicurist working in Beverly Hills, where she hoped to launch a modeling career. She started dating Ralph, a 35-year-old fashion photographer. After two casual luncheon dates and an evening movie date, Ralph offered to shoot a photo layout of Tiffany as a gift for her birthday.

During the shoot, Ralph frequently approached Tiffany to tilt her chin, adjust her hair, and reposition her pose. At one point, without warning, Ralph tugged on Tiffany's blouse and asked her to remove it. She jokingly replied, "Oh, you haven't got enough money to pay me for that." After trying for a while to convince Tiffany that he really wanted to photograph her topless, Ralph became menacing. Tiffany decided to leave, but Ralph blocked the exit. She became frightened and suddenly hit him as hard as she could before running out onto the street.

If a researcher were to question Tiffany and Ralph about who inflicted DV in this instance and who was the victim, both might say that Tiffany was the perpetrator of DV. She struck Ralph first and he did not strike back, so he was the victim and she was the aggressor. The case would then become one more statistic suggesting that females behave more aggressively than do males. Without information about rationales such as self-defense, or about which CTS items do not supply, it is difficult to place gender variations within a meaningful context (see Foshee, 1996; Harned, 2001; Mouradian, 2001).

Male victims of sexual assault. In a rare survey of 173 college men, Russell and Oswald (2002) found that 36.4% self-reported using sexual coercion against their female partners, and 45% claimed their female partners sexually coerced them. In this context, the term *sexual coercion* indicates force or intimidation. Of SA perpetrators, 5 said they had used threats of physical violence, and 13 had actually used physical violence. Of SA victims, 10 said they had experienced completed or attempted intercourse as a consequence of the physical force used by their female partners. These findings are unique; they require replication before scholars can accept them.

An Interview With Mary P. Koss

The rape perpetrator is not the proverbial stranger jumping out of bushes; rather, he is a date, acquaintance, marital partner, or family member.

Mary P. Koss is Professor of Public Health in the Mel and Enid Zuckerman Arizona College of Public Health, as well as Professor of Psychology, Psychiatry, and Family and Community Medicine in the College of Social and Behavioral Sciences, College of Medicine, University of Arizona. She is a licensed clinical psychologist and an extraordinary researcher whose innovative approaches have changed the world community's understanding of and response to rape. No single academic or clinical professional has done more to bring the hidden crime of date rape into the glare of public scrutiny. Her development of the Sexual Experiences Survey put a new face on the rape perpetrator. He is not the proverbial stranger jumping out of the bushes; rather, he is a date, acquaintance, marital partner, or family member. Dr. Koss's work takes her into the halls of Congress, into the offices of government agencies such as the U.S. Department of Health and Human Services, into the boardrooms of organizations such as the National Resource Center on Domestic Violence, and into courtrooms, as well as to international conferences. In addition to her teaching, clinical work, and consulting, she is an associate journal editor, sits on the editorial boards of 19 journals, and reviews for various publications. Grants that she has won competitively fund her ongoing research projects. Her scholarly publications are numerous, and she has won many awards for them as well as for her other achievements. She earned her doctorate in clinical psychology in 1972 from the University of Minnesota at Minneapolis.

Q: How did you become interested in conducting research on sexual assault?

A: I became interested through serendipity. A senior professor at my first job said I should put my name on his grant proposal because I was a woman and therefore likely to get the grant. The review committee, he

Outcomes of Dating Violence, Stalking, and Sexual Assault

As Koss (1990) notes: "Experiencing violence transforms people into victims and changes their lives forever. Once victimized, one can never again feel quite as invulnerable" (p. 374). There are many costs related to victimization by DV, ST, and SA, and women, more than men, bear the brunt (e.g., Cupach & Spitzberg, 2000). For some victims, the worst outcome is injury or negative health consequences, for others it is long-lasting psychological damage, and for still others it is the necessity of "turning one's life upside down" by quitting school, moving, or leaving a job (e.g., Coffey, Leitenberg, Henning, Bennett, & Jankowski, 1996; Spitzberg, 2002).

Injuries and negative health outcomes. Both men and women sustain injuries as a result of DV, ST, or SA, but without exception surveys show that women receive more injuries from male intimates than the reverse (e.g., Harris & Valentiner, 2002; Molidor & Tolman, 1998). Victims also develop a host of adverse health outcomes, such as sexually transmitted diseases (STDs) or chronic headaches (Ackard & Neumark-Sztainer, 2002; Straight, Harper, & Arias, 2003). They may blame themselves for DV, ST, or SA (Mahlstedt & Keeny, 1993) or feel depressed, even suicidal (e.g., Harris & Valentiner, 2002; Spitzberg, 2002). (See Table 1 in Appendix B for injury estimates.)

Reactions of victims to dating violence, stalking, and sexual assault. It is important to understand victims' responses to being abused, stalked, or sexually assaulted. Should a victim turn to the police, seek counseling, drop out of school, or take other actions? Reactions to SA have received a lot of professional said, was discriminating against him as a male. Since he proposed to have female confederates of the experimenter pose in different sizes of padded bras and be rated for rapability by male students, I obviously thought the grant had other problems. However, I was intrigued with a small idea buried in the proposal, to survey college students about their experiences with unwanted sex. This is where I got the idea to begin my work in date and acquaintance rape.

Q: What has been the strongest influence on your career?

A: What really influenced the direction of my career was my relationship with my feminist colleagues in the Society for Feminist Psychology. This group has published special issues of the *Psychology of Women Quarterly* on methodology that articulate what the feminist approach should be.

Q: What are your present research or advocacy interests?

A: One focus of my research is the RESTORE Program. In listening to what rape victims want in terms of postassault services, I have developed a model that involves sexual assault services, university researchers, and the criminal justice system working together in a single, nonadversarial process to adjudicate these crimes, restore the victim, and rehabilitate and supervise the offender. RESTORE is a victim-driven program that voices to the perpetrator the impact of the victimization and determines what must be done to repair the damage. Another ongoing research project is a study of violence against women in preconflict, conflict, and postconflict settings in Kosovo, East Timor, and Rwanda. I also am analyzing alcohol and violence prevalence data for seven American Indian tribes. Last, the Stepping Stone project is a behavioral AIDS/HIV prevention program in 70 townships surrounding Umtata in South Africa.

Q: What has been your major contribution to the field of violence against women?

A: I think my contributions fall into four major categories: (a) improved measurement of violence against women through critical analysis of federal statistics and development of empirical methods to combat underdetection; (b) identification of the previously unrecognized phenomenon of date rape, including prevalence, causes, and risk factors; (c) reconceptualization of male violence against women as a medically relevant issue because of its many negative health effects; and (d) development of new justice responses to violence against women through implementation and evaluation of the RESTORE—Justice that Heals Program.

Q: What are a couple of applications of your research?

A: One is the use of my work in fostering the development of intervention and prevention initiatives on college campuses and working for laws that mandate public reporting of crime on campus. Another is the increasing involvement of the medical care system in responding to violence against women, including adoption of policy statements, practice guidelines, and screening tools.

Q: What do you do in your "spare" time?

A: I am Chair of the Bravo Society, Arizona Opera, and a member of the board of trustees. I also take voice lessons, and my husband and I take ballroom dancing and Argentine tango lessons.

---

scrutiny over the years, but information about reactions to DV and ST are only recently coming to light.

In the aftermath of DV, victims take a number of actions. One postassault survey of 183 high school students discovered the following reactions to DV: (a) informal help seeking, 43%; (b) breakup or threat of breakup, 37%; (c) fought back, 35%; (d) took no action, 32%; and (e) formal help seeking, 8% (Watson, Cascardi, Avery-Leaf, & O'Leary, 2001). For ST victims, the level of trauma symptoms is comparable to that reported by victims of other traumas. A summary of 19 studies revealed seven clusters of adverse symptoms: (a) general disturbance; (b) emotional reaction, such as terror; (c) cognitive changes, such as feeling confused; (d) physical health, such as alcohol consumption; (e) social health, such as avoiding certain locations; (f) resource health, such as

school disruption; and (g) resilience (Spitzberg, 2002). For a report on one very well-executed study, see Westrup, Fremouw, Thompson, and Lewis (1999).

Sexually assaulted college women suffer from a variety of postassault fears, such as sexual aversion and feelings of paranoia (e.g., "It is safer to trust no one") (Harris & Valentiner, 2002). As explained in Chapter 2, victims can become conditioned so that stimuli (e.g., the smell of the aftershave lotion worn by a rapist) evoke strong fear reactions years later. SA victimization is also related to substance abuse, unhealthy weight control, sexual risk behavior, pregnancy, and suicide (Silverman, Raj, Mucci, & Hathaway, 2001). A standard outcome of SA is the development of posttraumatic stress disorder (PTSD), a tormenting disorder typified by flashbacks, sleeplessness, and other symptoms.

Valentiner, Foa, Riggs, and Gershuny (1996), for instance, found that of 103 rape victims seeking help in an emergency room, 74% experienced PTSD. (For a surprising review of the literature showing postassault "growth," see Frazier, Conlon, & Glaser, 2001.)

SECTION SUMMARY

Social scientists have defined three basic forms of interpersonal violence occurring among adolescents, college students, and other young people: dating violence, stalking, and sexual assault. Although researchers have offered operational definitions for these forms of interpersonal violence, they do not always agree among themselves about their usefulness. Legal definitions are in some ways more important than researchers' definitions, because they influence how society officially treats victims and perpetrators.

Dating violence is violence between unmarried individuals (who may or may not be sexually intimate). DV includes physical and psychological abuse as well as murder. Stalking is a series of actions, such as harassing, following, or communicating in particular ways, that cause the victim fear for his or her bodily safety. Sexual assault takes many forms, including sexual coercion, unwanted sexual behaviors, and outright rape. Legal definitions of SA abound; most focus on the issue of consent.

In estimating the prevalence of DV, ST, and SA, scholars rely primarily on four sources of data: FBI reports, NCVS, additional government surveillance systems, and university studies. Partially because research methodologies vary, data sets about these crimes yield extremely divergent estimates, especially of SA. FBI statisticians do not routinely separate data by relationship status finely enough to allow the specification of estimates for boyfriends/girlfriends. DV, ST, and SA data for ethnic groups and gay, lesbian, bisexual, and transgendered youths are almost nonexistent. Cross-cultural estimates are slowly emerging.

Some research has indicated that DV is gender equivalent. Assessments of injury data and police arrests imply that men commit a disproportionately higher number of assaults. Although men appear to commit more murders of female DV partners than the reverse, the data are unclear because the relationship between perpetrator and victim is frequently unknown. (See the estimates in Tables 1–3 in Appendix B.)

The overwhelming number of investigations have determined that DV, ST, and SA have many negative consequences, including injuries ranging from bruises and scratches to concussions and death. Victims incur a large number of negative health outcomes, such as chronic headaches, pain, nausea, HIV, STDs, and permanent disabilities. Victims of ST may feel forced to change their entire lives by dropping out of school, moving to other locations, and quitting jobs. SA appears to cause the most severe and long-lasting reactions. Nearly all victims experience extreme fear and anxiety, and a large proportion develop PTSD. A number of victims also develop substance abuse problems or eating disorders.

SEARCHING FOR PATTERNS: CHARACTERISTICS OF PERPETRATORS AND VICTIMS OF DATING VIOLENCE, STALKING, AND SEXUAL ASSAULT

At this time, no empirically based, definitive trait profiles exist for either perpetrators or victims of DV and SA. Basing her suppositions on practitioners' observations, for instance, Ferguson (1998) lists a number of credible characteristics of DV perpetrators and victims, such as victims' claim that they are "afraid to disagree with" the offenders and offenders' behavior (e.g., "he/she is extremely jealous and possessive"; pp. 103–104). There are some indications of patterns or classifications for ST offenders.

Reciprocal/Mutual Dating Violence, Stalking, and Sexual Assault

Do men and women exhibit different patterns of interpersonal violence? Both male and female high school and college students participate in DV, ST, and SA. Whether gender discrepancies appear varies according to the type of data gathered. Self-report surveys, primarily derived from CTS scores, reveal that DV is largely reciprocal or gender neutral (Gray & Foshee, 1997; Hines & Saudino, 2003; O'Keefe & Treister, 1998). Some analysts have found even greater DV perpetration by women than by men (see Bennett & Fineran, 1998; Majdan, 1998; Moffitt, 1997). In contrast, studies based on other data sources give the impression that young men use far more DV than do young women.

Scholars concerned with accounting for CTS-based DV gender equivalence have searched for explanations beyond those generally plaguing self-report data. Following are two examples of research findings that shed doubt on the validity of men's reports: (a) Men may judge themselves as less culpable for relationship violence than women (LeJeune & Follette, 1994), or (b) men may lie, minimize the severity of violence, or underreport (Armstrong et al., 2001; Felson, Messner, Hoskin, & Deane, 2002). Results derived from other measurements, such as the revised NCVS self-reports, the FBI's accumulation of police reports, and the National Violence Against Women Survey (Tjaden & Thoennes, 1998b) substantiate large gender disparities in DV, ST, and SA. Disproportionately, boyfriends/ ex-boyfriends assault girlfriends/ex-girlfriends (Bachman & Saltzman, 1995). Typical of other findings are the results of Adams, Isaac, Cochran, and Brown's (1996) analysis of restraining orders against 757 teen batterers in Massachusetts: Of these cases, 80.8% were against boys.

Many authorities believe that among high school girls, violence tends to be self-defensive, whereas among high school boys it is not. One comparison revealed that girls' violence was self-defensive 37% of the time, and boys' was self-defensive 6% of the time (Molidor & Tolman, 1998). Others have found that girls' violence is not entirely attributable to self-defense (Moffitt, Caspi, Rutter, & Silva, 2001). In other accounts, rates of being assaulted for making sexual advances were 17.1% for boys and 3% for girls (Molidor & Tolman, 1998).

Whether or not acts of DV, ST, and SA perpetrated by women are usually acts of self-defense, the use of self-defense against a rapist appears to achieve its goal (Fisher et al., 2000). In addition to physical resistance, women take other actions to ward off rape, including telling the person to stop, pleading with the rapist, and screaming or yelling. (For discussion of other resistance techniques and rough evaluations of their effectiveness, see Fisher et al., 2000.)

Evaluating who starts an episode of DV may be an important variable in understanding DV. The majority of studies have found girls more likely to start DV than boys, but the evidence is mixed (e.g., Lewis & Fremouw, 2001). Once again, the reports question the veracity of male respondents. Molidor and Tolman (1998) found that girls claimed boys initiated abuse 70% of the time, whereas boys said girls initiated abuse 27% of the time. In contrast, Foshee (1996) found a 27% initiation rate by girls and a 15% initiation rate

by boys. The question of abuse initiation merges into the question of the degree to which DV may be self-defensive. Results are inconsistent; more research is needed.

Common Criminals Versus Intimate-Only Violent Men

Based on their interactions with the criminal justice system, there is reason to believe male stalkers are "common criminals" or "generally" violent men. One review of 346 male stalkers (both intimate and nonintimate) revealed that 27.4% had been convicted of a property crime in the same year as the ST conviction. These men had criminal records of drug arrests, resisting arrest, and other crimes suggestive of antisocial personality disorder (Jordan, Logan, Walker, & Nigoff, 2003). Such criminal patterns of behaviors, as well as criminal patterns of ST, may lay the groundwork for an ST profile (e.g., Rosenfeld, 2000).

Fraternity Men and Athletes

Off-the-field violence is seemingly a daily occurrence among some American athletes. Also making the news are reports of drunken brawls and even deaths at fraternity houses. Impressions of this sort have led to empirical examinations of SA perpetrated by fraternity brothers and members of athletic organizations. These investigations have regularly demonstrated linkages between fraternity membership and SA (Brown, Sumner, & Nocera, 2002; Humphrey & Kahn, 2000; Koss & Gaines, 1993). One explanation is that fraternity norms and practices encompass viewing sexual coercion of female acquaintances (a felony) as a sport, a contest, or a game (Martin & Hummer, 1995). Researchers have found significant correlations of an increased likelihood of SA to a number of dimensions typical of fraternities: (a) promotion of toughness, dominance, and aggressiveness (Boeringer, 1999); (b) endorsement of traditional, conservative, sex-role attitudes (Lackie & de Man, 1997); and (c) engagement in heavy alcohol consumption (Cashin, Presley, & Meilman, 1996).

Social-Structural Variables

There is some evidence that persons involved in DV, ST, and SA exhibit distinct patterns of sociostructural variables, but research findings are inconsistent (O'Keefe, 1998). One survey in Australia uncovered chronic unemployment and low educational levels as characteristics of abusive male daters (Magdol et al., 1997). (See the previous discussions on possible race and ethnicity correlates of DV, ST, and SA.)

---•·•·•·---

SECTION SUMMARY

More than other areas of family violence, with the exception of sibling abuse, DV appears more gender reciprocal. Findings about self-defensive DV and the initiation of DV are limited and equivocal. SA and ST are comparatively more likely to be male-to-female behaviors, but survey results are not definitive. The index used to assess these behaviors greatly affects the level of reported mutuality. CTS1 provides more gender equivalence than NCVS and FBI reports.

According to mounting evidence, men involved in DV, ST, and SA have characteristics similar to those of common criminals. Many perpetrators have convictions for drug arrests and other crimes. Furthermore, data from studies of fraternity men and men in athletic groups provide congruent results. DV tends to be higher and SA occurs more frequently among members of these organizations. Finally, few structural variables distinguish perpetrators of DV, ST, and SA from nonperpetrators.

---•·•·•·---

EXPLAINING DATING VIOLENCE, SEXUAL ASSAULT, AND STALKING

Case History: Claudia and Roberto's Last Dance at the High School Prom

Claudia met Roberto when she was a junior in high school. It was love at first sight. All Claudia ever wanted was a boyfriend who loved her and made her feel special. One problem Claudia and Roberto had was that they fought like cats and dogs. It didn't matter what the situation was—what movie to see, where to get a hamburger, or whether to go out on Friday or Saturday.

As the couple sat in Roberto's car one night, Claudia accused Roberto of flirting with an old girlfriend. The argument got heated, and Roberto leaned over and slapped Claudia across the face. She slapped him back. They always fought like this, just like a couple of kids, the way they thought "most" couples do. After all, don't all couples who love each other fight and hit each other?

Over the next 10 months, Claudia and Roberto continued fighting, and Claudia occasionally had bruises. One time she got a black eye. The next morning, she told her parents that the bruises on her face came from a minor car accident. She wore a long-sleeved turtleneck shirt to hide her other bruises. A month later, she was badly bruised again. In fact, Roberto bit her arm several times and pulled her hair. She tried to bite him back.

Claudia loved Roberto, and she knew he loved her. In fact, she believed that he would not hit her if he didn't love her. One thing she did to please him was give up her participation on the debate team, because Roberto hated it when she stayed after school once a week for practice. In fact, she stopped seeing nearly all of her old friends. Roberto told her that it was her "nagging" that set him off, and he had to get her to stop. She tried harder and harder to please him and thought that their quarrels would cease, especially if she stopped provoking him.

Claudia's greatest fear was not that she would get seriously injured, but that Roberto would never call her again. He was her whole world. She worried that if her parents found out about Roberto's violence, they would forbid her to see him again, and that her two brothers might decide to beat him up. Every time she got hurt, Claudia renewed her efforts to hide her injuries.

On the night of their senior prom, Claudia was ecstatic. High school was almost over. She thought that she and Roberto would get married and she would finally have everything she always wanted, but it didn't work out that way. At the prom, Claudia and Roberto got into a quarrel as usual, but this time Roberto's buddies overheard the argument and he felt humiliated because he "couldn't keep Claudia in line." Roberto decided that they should leave the prom. On the way to the car, however, Roberto got out of control. He punched and kicked Claudia over and over again, letting out all of his rage about everything in his whole life. He was so infuriated that he left Claudia in the parking lot, bleeding and unconscious.

Another couple found Claudia and called the paramedics, who took her to the hospital. When Claudia regained consciousness the next morning, her parents were in a state of shock. They could not believe that

Roberto had ever hit her. Her brothers vowed to beat him up, and the police were out looking to arrest him. Claudia was worried when the doctors told her she might lose the vision in one of her eyes. She was even more worried that she would never see Roberto again, that he would never call her again, and that he might stop loving her. Without Roberto, she thought, her life would be over.

A number of factors influenced the teens in the case history above to interact with each other as they did. Many of these variables seem related to beliefs pervading American culture. Some ethnic, racial, and cultural variables as well as socialization practices and individual psychological traits seem to promote DV, ST, and SA. Certain parameters, such as gender of the perpetrator and circumstances of the dating experience, influence people's opinions about the causes of these behaviors. Investigations of determinants of DV, ST, and SA have made notable advances in methodology.

American Cultural Variables

As is common in other subareas of family violence research, experts have hypothesized that patriarchal beliefs and attitudes encourage DV, ST, and SA. Within the dating literature, associations between cultural variables and DV and SA have been positive but weak. Plainly, American mores have not led to wholesale acceptance of DV. Most young people disavow DV in general, but find it acceptable under some circumstances (Feiring, Deblinger, Hoch-Espada, & Haworth, 2002). The same is true of SA (Hannon et al., 2000). Although the findings are certainly not definitive, endorsement of some attitudes may increase the probability that DV will occur. One such belief (among males) is that DV is acceptable (Foshee et al., 2001); another is that DV is justifiable (O'Keefe, 1997; Schwartz, O'Leary, & Kendziora, 1997). A new approach involves a seldom-studied variable, communal orientation, the belief that partners should be mutually responsive to each other's needs. In one study, college students who scored high on this scale had lower DV rates than low-scoring students (Williamson & Silverman, 2001).

A slow but steady stream of research has demonstrated that adolescent peer-group support for aggressive behavior encourages DV. Following DeKeseredy and Kelly's (1993) initial survey, newer research has continued to substantiate this premise (Williamson & Silverman, 2001).

Early on, researchers began to focus on the possibility that male-to-female violence occurs in part because of male misperceptions. Male dates often think women are more willing to have sex than they really are, and that rape is more justifiable than women think it is (e.g., Muehlenhard, 1989). Such results dovetail with common perceptions of men's sexual inclinations. Nonetheless, it still seems ominous that in a study of college men's aggression, Malamuth (1989) found that 35% reported "some likelihood" of committing rape if they were certain they could get away with it. These results complement those of a laboratory study of men's sexual arousal in response to audiotaped rape scenarios (Lohr, Adams, & Davis, 1997).

In one of the most telling accounts, Van Wie and Gross (2001) explored men's ability to discriminate female partners' entreaties to stop ongoing sexual activities. As the independent variable, 185 males listened to one of six audiotaped vignettes of an after-date scenario. The vignettes varied in intimacy levels (kissing or breast contact) and in the female's explanation for asking the man to stop his sexual advances (waiting for marriage, too soon in the relationship, fear of pregnancy). As the dependent variable, researchers measured how long it took (latency) for a participant to press a switch when he thought the woman first refused to continue. The researchers found a significant interaction effect between the woman's explanation given in the vignette, "too early in the relationship," and intimacy level described, "breast contact." Latencies were substantially longer for this vignette than for others. Van Wie and Gross interpreted these latencies as indicating that men felt the woman's resistance was not entirely sincere, or that she was indecisive and wanted to be convinced. A strength of this study was its use of objective measures generated by laboratory equipment, instead of self-reports.

A related investigation examined the role of alcohol consumption and alcohol expectancies on male perceptions of female sexual arousal. A sample of 160 male undergraduates reacted to an audiotaped rape scenario after imbibing alcohol or a placebo under varying conditions of alcohol expectancy. The four condition groups (40 men in each) were as follows: Those in Group 1 received and expected alcohol, those in Group 2 expected alcohol but got tonic water, those in Group 3 did not expect alcohol but got alcohol, and those in Group 4 did not expect alcohol and got tonic water. Relative to Groups 3 and 4, men in Groups 1 and 2 were significantly slower in recognizing women's audiotaped refusals to continue with sexual activities. Also, men in Groups 1 and 2 initially rated the woman's sexual arousal level significantly higher than did men in Groups 3 and 4 (Gross, Bennett, Marx, Sloan, & Juergens, 2001). Thus it appears that alcohol consumption or alcohol expectancy can increase male misperception of cues.

Finally, Lloyd (1991) has proposed that two major facets of the culture increase the likelihood of DV and SA: gender-related themes (i.e., male control and female dependency) and romanticism (the idea that "love conquers all"). First, young women who believe in the male control/female dependency model become more vulnerable to abuse. Second, romanticism may encourage dating partners to believe that their relationship problems are mainly situational (e.g., just an angry outburst) and will dissolve upon marriage. The case history of Claudia and Roberto represents a situation in which a young girl wants a romantic relationship no matter what the cost.

Routine Activities Theory

Routine activities theory is especially useful for explaining stalker victimization. Victims' habitual activities (their routines), such as going to classes or working at regular hours, make it relatively easy for stalkers to track them (Fisher, Cullen, & Turner, 2002). (For more information on this theory, see Table 2.1 in Chapter 2.)

Historical and Learning Factors

As delineated in Chapter 2, there is every reason to expect that abusive childhood socialization experiences are associated with later involvement in DV and SA. It is also probable that the gender of a socializing parent (or imitated parent) influences the strength of socialization effects (e.g., Avakame, 1998; Jankowski, Leitenberg, Henning, & Coffey, 1999). Dye and Davis (2003) found significant associations among harsh parental discipline, anxious attachment, and stalking. Another recent study determined that one of the strongest childhood factors associated with DV is witnessing interparental violence (Chapple, 2003). Although progression from childhood abuse to adult violence is not inevitable, it is common (Smith &

Williams, 1992; Widom & Maxfield, 2001). Illustrative of the inconsistency of research findings are the results of a 12-study meta-analysis showing that violence in an individual's childhood home is weakly linked ($r = .176$) to subsequent DV (Trebino, 1997).

Research convergent with learning principles continues to emerge, for example, in violent men's belief that aggression will be positively reinforced (i.e., rewarded) (Riggs & Caulfield, 1997). Postulating effects of negative reinforcement (e.g., removal of distress), some investigators have examined the relationship between alcohol consumption and SA. Logicians are beginning to speculate that alcohol consumption may not serve only as a precursor to SA. Some victims consume alcohol after they are assaulted, apparently as self-medication to relieve stress and pain (negative reinforcement) (see Miranda, Meyerson, Marx, & Simpson, 2002). Results of one study projected a circular pattern of behavior: SA, stress, alcohol misuse, more SA, and so forth. Although learning theory is a traditional explanation for DV and SA, evidence is not definitive (e.g., Aberle & Littlefield, 2001).

Contemporary research has repeatedly shown that family-of-origin violence is significantly related to SA for both males and females. Formation of negative opinions about women and development of male adolescent sexual promiscuity leading to SA, for example, seem spawned in violent families (see Forbes & Adams-Curtis, 2001; Reitzel-Jaffe & Wolfe, 2001; Senn, Desmarais, Verberg, & Wood, 2000). In fact, some analyses have uncovered specific associations between types of childhood abuse and involvement in DV (Sappington, Pharr, Tunstall, & Rickert, 1997).

In furtherance of the intergenerational transfer of violence theory, academicians have more recently explored specific mechanisms of transfer (Simons, Lin, & Gordon, 1998). In a longitudinal inquiry, Capaldi and Clark (1998) tested male children in grade 4 and at ages 17 to 20 and obtained data from the children's parents at specified intervals. Their results displayed the transfer effect: Boys' development of antisocial behavior was prerequisite to DV, and unskilled parenting was the major precursor to boys' antisocial behavior. In a recent review article, Serbin and Karp (2003) underscore the need for researchers to examine multiple variables, such as genetic contributions, inadequate parenting, and risk and protective factors.

The most illuminating information to date originates from a longitudinal study of youths and their mothers recruited from community samples. Data from this study specify the following predictors of perpetrating IPV: (a) development of a conduct disorder in childhood, (b) exposure to interparental violence, and (c) power-assertive punishment. Exposure to interparental violence was the most robust predictor of IPV victimization in this study sample. Receipt of child physical abuse and conduct disorder in adolescence were both powerful risks for perpetration of partner injury. Substance abuse disorder mediated the effects of adolescent conduct disorder on risks of injury perpetration. In addition, as the researchers point out, many of their findings were gender neutral (Ehrensaft et al., 2003).

Other scholars have evaluated the negative impacts of family dysfunctions, such as divorce, alcoholism, mental illness, inadequate parental monitoring of teens, and possible genetic contributions (see Chapple, 2003; Kellogg, Burge, & Taylor, 2000; Langhinrichsen-Rohling & Dostal, 1996; Lesch & Merschdorf, 2000). Another approach has been to look for mediating variables. Murphy and Blumenthal (2000) ascertained that living in a violent childhood home led to development of interpersonal problems for females in their study sample. These problems (dominance, intrusiveness, vindictiveness) served as mediating influences, eventually expressed in DV involvement. Herrenkohl, Huang, Tajima, and Whitney (2003) have developed a notable model of adolescent violence that incorporates several significantly related **mediator variables**, including childhood abuse. In brief, these researchers assert that childhood abuse "influences what children believe about violence, which, in turn, affects their involvement with antisocial peers" (p. 1203). Along with inadequate parental attachment and association with antisocial peers, gender and age have direct links with youth violence.

Gender socialization. Gender socialization represents another type of learning. Gender is an important organizing variable in explaining DV, ST, and SA, as indicated by one contemporary survey of 904 sexually active women ages 14 to 26. Of these women, 20% believed that they "never" had the right to decline sexual intercourse or to demand pregnancy protection. Women from racial/ethnic minority groups felt even less entitled than nonminority women to make such demands (Rickert, Sanghvi, & Wiemann, 2002).

As has been evident over the years, men's traditional sex-role beliefs are an element in their sexually aggressive behavior (Lackie & de Man, 1997; Lavoie, Vezina, Piche, & Boivin, 1995). One of the most informative

studies to date examined associations between several rough classifications of men's beliefs/attitudes and their behavior. These classifications were as follows: (a) masculine gender role, (b) general and sexual entitlement attitudes, and (c) rape-related attitudes and behaviors. Using a sample of 114 college men, Hill and Fischer (2001) identified these linkages by making nine assessments in a path analysis. Aspects of masculine gender role predicted general entitlement attitudes, which in turn predicted sexual entitlement attitudes, which finally predicted rape-related attitudes and behaviors. In fact, both entitlement attitudes were mediators (transmitter variables) between masculine gender role and rape-related variables.

Research has revealed that individuals use gender of the perpetrator as a guide to expected outcomes of interpersonal violence. College students, for example, almost uniformly consider male-to-female violence a far more serious threat than female-to-male violence (Bethke & De Joy, 1993; Riggs, O'Leary, & Breslin, 1990). Additionally, students tend to trivialize the severity of female-to-male violence (see Miller & Simpson, 1991; Molidor & Tolman, 1998). Both genders view self-defensive DV as justifiable, but women more so than men (Foo & Margolin, 1995).

As troubling as some of men's sex-role attitudes are, women's sex-role attitudes are equally problematic. Girls' beliefs in the importance of developing and retaining close heterosexual relationships have detrimental consequences. Such beliefs force a girl to abandon some of her selfhood, to stifle her own ambitions and personality for the sake of having a boyfriend (Woods, 1999). The socialization process used to accomplish this goal has been called the "silencing of the self" (Pipher, 1994). In concordance with these views, a recent survey found that whereas only 38% of boys thought it was important to be dating, 54% of girls thought it was important (Empower Program, 2002). One inquiry revealed that the more contemporary a college woman's attitudes are, the lower her tolerance of DV (Bookwala, Frieze, Smith, & Ryan, 1992). In general, becoming less dependent on romantic relationships is beneficial for women.

Attachment issues. Attachment to a caretaker represents another type of learning, in this case early in life. Logicians have revived childhood attachment theory (Bowlby, 1980) to accommodate adult romantic attachment in DV (Mayseless, 1991). Presumably, the quality of childhood attachment (e.g., secure, avoidant, fearful, preoccupied) extends into adulthood and profoundly affects the nature of an individual's later intimate relationships (see Feeney & Noller, 1996; Morton & Browne, 1998). Painful reactions learned in childhood, such as fear of abandonment, surface in dating relationships and may precipitate DV against a partner who threatens to leave (O'Hearn & Davis, 1997).

Attachment research has proliferated in the past decade, with most results confirming the usefulness of the attachment framework in accounting for DV, ST, and SA (e.g., Bookwala, 2002; Chapple, 2003). Evidence indicates that attachment styles vary among dating pairs (Frazier, Byer, Fischer, Wright, & DeBord, 1996), with securely attached couples reporting higher levels of relationship satisfaction than insecurely attached couples (see Bartholomew, 1997; Simpson, Rholes, & Phillips, 1996). In an Australian comparison, insecure parent-child attachment was significantly correlated with college men's antisocial dispositions, aggression, and SA (Smallbone & Dadds, 2001). Lending credence to these results, Tucker and Anders (1999) established that anxiously attached males were inept at perceiving their female partners' feelings. To explain the role of dysfunctional attachment in DV, Follingstad, Bradley, Helff, and Laughlin (2002) have proposed a model that includes a four-step sequence of events. In this model, anxious attachment to a romantic partner evokes an angry temperament, which in turn leads to efforts to control one's partner, which then leads to DV.

Revictimization. An unfortunate type of learning is evident when a response to an initial victimization is predictive of a second victimization (Fisher et al., 2000). Compared with nonvictims, crime victims endure repeated victimizations (see Banyard, Arnold, & Smith, 2000; Kingma, 1999; Sanders & Moore, 1999). Documentation of this phenomenon has spurred further investigations. One prospective study of revictimization was unable to correlate directly previous SA and a new SA within an intervening year. Instead, the findings implicated other correlates. Greater alcohol consumption and expectation of engaging in risky behavior at a first assessment (Time 1) was significantly linked with new SA a year later (Time 2). In addition, expected involvement in risky behavior at Time 1 was associated with actual participation in risky behavior at Time 2 (Combs-Lane & Smith, 2002). Miranda et al.'s (2002) study may help explain these results. Greater alcohol use at Time 1 may be a stress effect generated by previous SA.

Individual Traits and Interpersonal Interaction Factors

In addition to sociocultural variables, certain kinds of personality characteristics, such as hostility, seem to precipitate abusive behavior. Whether dating aggression stems primarily from the presence of a violent person (personality trait) or more from a violent relationship (situation) remains unresolved (see Marcus & Swett, 2002). Abbey, McAuslan, Zawacki, Clinton, and Buck (2001) recently conducted the most robust examination to date of trait-situation parameters. Their analysis of responses of 343 college men yielded a very large number of both personality traits (9 of 10 measured) and situational components (5 of 5) that discriminated between SA men and non-SA men. It further produced distinctions between types of SA (forced, coercive, attempted/completed rape), tactics of perpetrators, attributions for assault, and outcomes. Hence both traits and situations played roles in men's sexually assaultive behaviors.

Sexually aggressive men. Another comparison of 191 college men found differences between those who perpetrated severe SA and those who perpetrated less severe SA (Hersch & Gray-Little, 1998). Severely aggressive SA men, as measured by the Sexual Behavior Questionnaire (SBQ; Rapaport & Burkhart, 1984), responded differently than did less severely aggressive SA men on an assessment of psychopathology, the Schedule for Nonadaptive and Adaptive Personality (SNAP; Clark, 1993). Although they did not register scores in the diagnosable range, severely sexually assaultive men scored significantly higher on the three clinical scales of the SNAP: those designed to measure aggressiveness, manipulativeness, and impulsivity. Extreme aggressors also scored significantly higher than other men on a measure of "rape myth acceptance" (Burt, 1980).

Interpersonal control. A different line of research indicates that desire for interpersonal control of one's partner lies at the heart of DV (Davis, Ace, & Anda, 2000) and ST (Tjaden & Thoennes, 1998b). Interpersonal control can take many forms, such as "threatening to leave" in order to get one's way about living situations or sexual activities. Both patriarchy and learning theory provide compelling theoretical foundations for this view. Although males, relative to females, may use more control tactics against dating partners, women also try to control their partners (for a review, see Jackson, 1998).

Some analysts believe that perpetrators of DV, ST, and SA have high needs for control and that this need can be conceptualized as a personality trait. One thread of evidence comes from Dye and Davis's (2003) research, which found a strong association between harsh parental discipline and the need to control a dating partner through ST. Other scholars have suggested that controlling behaviors may be characteristic of both partners in dating relationships. Theoretically, a dating partner might use a dominating conflict resolution style, psychological aggression, or violence to equalize what he or she perceives to be an unbalanced relationship (see Kasian & Painter, 1992; Mayseless, 1991). To help resolve this issue, Hamby (1996) constructed an interpersonal control scale containing dimensions of authority, disparagement, and restrictiveness (similar to dominance/isolation). She found that, of the three dimensions, restrictiveness is most closely linked with DV.

Results from at least one inquiry are congruent with Hamby's dominance (restrictiveness) findings. A survey of 223 undergraduates revealed that their perceptions of partners' withdrawal and controlling behavior were significantly associated with participants' SA in both genders. Men's perceptions of dating partners' demands and psychological abuse, however, were significantly correlated with their own DV, ST, and SA. The same did not hold true for women (Katz, Carine, & Hilton, 2002). Such intriguing results call for replication.

Looking at interpersonal control through a different lens suggests that two other attitudes may be pertinent. First, feeling powerless in a relationship may instigate violence (e.g., Dutton, 1994). Along these lines, Rondfeldt, Kimmerling, and Arias (1998) discovered a link between DV and low levels of satisfaction with the level of relationship power, rather than amount of perceived power. Psychological reactance (i.e., a feeling of threat to one's personal sense of freedom; Hong & Page, 1989), may also be a component of DV. Typical items for measuring psychological reactance include "I resist attempts of others to influence me." In a sample of college students, Hockenberry and Billingham (1993) found evidence compatible with reactance theory. Students involved in DV had higher psychological reactance scores than did non-DV students.

Hypermasculinity is a recently developed trait construct that may play a role in men's anger, sexual coercion, aggression, and lack of empathy toward women (Vass & Gold, 1995). Mosher and Sirkin (1984) operationally defined hypermasculinity as a personality trait that predisposes men to engage in behaviors that assert physical power and dominance in interactions. Using a deception paradigm, Parrott and Zeichner (2003) compared college men's delivery of (presumed) "painful shocks" to fictitious female opponents. Men high in hypermasculinity (HH) were significantly more apt to administer shocks than were men low in hypermasculinity (LH). Most convincing, HH men were more likely than LH men to have abused a female during the past year. In addition, HH men's shock delivery scores correlated significantly with other trait measures: (a) adversarial sexual beliefs, (b) acceptance of interpersonal violence, and (c) hostility toward women.

In an examination of 33 college men, Eckhardt, Jamison, and Watts (2000) uncovered substantial distinctions between DV and non-DV college men on responses to the State-Trait Anger Expression Inventory (Spielberger, 1988). DV males had significantly higher scores on four subscales: State Anger (intense anger at time of test), Trait Anger (ongoing, recurrent angry feelings), Anger In (withholding of angry expression), and Anger Out (expression of anger). DV men's scores were significantly lower than non-DV men's on Anger Control (reduction of angry feelings). Replication of this study with a larger sample is warranted. In another analysis, Dye and Davis (2003) found that the level of anger-jealousy over a romantic relationship breakup was a predictor of ST behaviors.

Relationship issues. It seems intuitive that relationship factors influence DV, ST, and SA, and a few investigations have substantiated this assumption. In two comparisons, low levels of relationship satisfaction were correlated with DV (Follette & Alexander, 1992). Using **factor analysis**, Riggs (1993) identified seven underlying relationship problems. Of these, aggressive individuals reported four aspects of relationships more often than did nonaggressive individuals: jealousy, fighting, breakdown of the relationship, and interference of friends.

High stress levels typify violent couples (e.g., Good, Heppner, Hillenbrand-Gunn, & Wang, 1995). Whether violent interactions are antecedents or consequences of dyadic (i.e., couple) stress, however, is uncertain. Also, recent research indicates that communication skills are highly related to DV. Marcus and Swett (2002) found that speaking in a positive affective tone, listening, and understanding served as protective elements against DV.

Blaming one's partner for DV is another relationship dynamic in need of more research. Moore, Eisler, and Franchina (2000) examined causal attributions in a college sample of DV and non-DV men using audiotaped vignettes that varied the provocativeness of women's dating behavior. As women's provocative behavior increased, both groups of men blamed them more. DV men reported significantly higher degrees of unpleasant reactions (e.g., jealousy, rejection) to the women's behavior. In addition, moderately provocative female behavior, rather than highly provocative behavior, evoked the greatest differences between groups.

One of the most disheartening findings in the literature is that interpartner aggression occurs more frequently in relationships typified by high commitment levels. Indeed, research has shown that both length of relationship and commitment level are positively correlated with DV and SA (Caulfield, Riggs, & Street, 1999). The link between commitment and DV is surprising given that it seems logical for unmarried persons simply to break off their relationship (Carlson, 1996). After all, dating couples rarely share income or children. One explanation is that commitment in an abusive relationship may represent strong emotional feelings that can be linked with attachment and dependency needs (Griffing et al., 2002; Henderson, Bartholomew, & Dutton, 1997). Feelings about an abusive partner, especially ambivalence, seem to be a crucial element in leave/stay decisions. Such relationships acquire an "on-again, off-again" quality (intermittent reinforcement) that keeps members of the couple entrapped.

Perhaps the most intriguing finding in this area is that leaving a violent partner is not linked with a high frequency of partner negative behaviors, but with the absence of partner positive behaviors (Kasian & Painter, 1992). Truman-Schram, Cann, Calhoun, and Vanwallendael (2000) corroborated and extended these findings in a controlled comparison of women either involved or not involved in DV. Involved women who stayed had significantly elevated scores in three test areas: (a) a global measure of satisfaction, (b) Liking Scale, and (c) consensus subscales of the Revised Dyadic Adjustment Scale (Busby, Christensen, Crane, & Larson, 1995). Some dating women who stay with abusive partners find their relationships more satisfying than do women who leave.

Typologies of interpersonally violent teenagers and young people. The only typology introduced in DV articles to date is Stith, Jester, and Bird's (1992)

four-cluster model. Utilizing data on relationship functions, negotiation styles, and coping styles, these investigators identified four subtypes of DV. (For a list of traits typical of SA perpetrators, see National Center for Injury Prevention and Control, 2000.)

A relatively large volume of literature has addressed both attributes of the crime of ST and attributes of stalkers. In the 1998 British Crime Survey, Budd and Mattinson (as cited in Dennison & Thomson, 2002) found that men were offenders in 81% of reported incidents and that perpetrators were former intimates of their victims in 29% of the cases. (See Table 2 in Appendix B for U.S. estimates of ST.) Stalkers often exhibit patterns of behavior, which may be classified as follows: (a) domestic or nondomestic, (b) level of aggression, (c) delusional or nondelusional, (d) motivation for ST, and (e) victim outcome (Jordan, Quinn, Jordan, & Daileader, 2000). Another arrangement encompasses such categories as paraphilic stalkers, love obsessionals, cyberstalkers, erotomanics, and antisocial stalkers (see Radosevich, 2000; Sheridan, Blaauw, & Davies, 2003). According to Sheridan, Gillett, Blaauw, Davies, and Patel (2003), the largest subcategory of stalkers is made up of the former partners of the victims.

Alcohol Consumption and Interpersonal Violence

Use of alcohol, drugs, or both appears to be one of the most common risk factors for DV, SA, and ST (Marcus & Swett, 2003). Although research has uniformly found associations between substance abuse and interpersonal violence, one cannot assume an inevitable causal link (e.g., Combs-Lane & Smith, 2002). Two variables that may obscure the relationship between alcohol use and DV, ST, and SA are the reasons for drinking (e.g., abuse-engendered stress) and the timing of alcohol consumption (e.g., before or after abuse).

SECTION SUMMARY

Although patriarchal cultural beliefs drive DV, ST, and SA in many societies, evidence of their influence in the United States suggests a lesser impact. Young people do not endorse interpersonal violence, and they view male-to-female violence as far more detrimental than female-to-male violence. Some males find interpersonal violence more acceptable and justifiable in some circumstances than do others. Although available evidence is inconclusive, endorsement of traditional male gender attitudes may propel some men toward DV, ST, and SA. Similarly, accepting more modern sex-role attitudes may encourage women not to tolerate DV. A communal orientation, the standard that couples should be responsive to each other's needs, has some footing in U.S. culture.

Peer support of male-to-female violence, beliefs of one's friends, and male misperceptions of female behavior are associated with DV and SA. Males are generally more likely than females to perceive a dating partner's behavior both as giving consent and as sexual. Romanticism, the belief that "love conquers all," may prompt some individuals to accept DV on the grounds that their dating partners may change. Routine activities theory explains ST from the perspective that a person's habitual comings and goings make him or her vulnerable.

Historical variables such as direct or indirect exposure to family violence show some relationship to DV and SA. Principles of reinforcement, social learning theory, and the concept of intergenerational abuse help explain DV and SA, but alone may not be determinative. Peer influences are especially strong. Researchers more frequently search for the mechanisms of transmission. A developing application of attachment theory to dating aggression ties feelings of anger and insecurity learned in childhood with later fears of abandonment that subsequently elicit male-to-female DV, ST, and SA. An especially widespread and disturbing finding is that any victimization in childhood, adolescence, or young adulthood increases the likelihood of continued victimization in subsequent years.

Although trait research has only just begun, several studies have shown that certain interpersonal traits are related to DV, ST, and SA. Furthermore, certain situations are associated with these forms of interpersonal violence. Men who perpetrate severe SA show more signs of psychopathology than do perpetrators of less severe SA. What meager information is available implies that individuals with high needs to control others, with feelings of powerlessness, and with needs to protect their own personal freedom are more likely to be involved in DV and SA than others. The same is true of men high in hypermasculinity and male anger.

Relationship variables also influence DV levels. Dyadic stress levels and communication skills both play roles in DV and SA. It is also true that members of couples tend to blame their partners (and sometimes themselves) for DV or SA. Both level of commitment and level of satisfaction are related to DV and SA and to stay/leave decisions. The greater the commitment level and the higher the level of satisfaction, the longer the women remain. Clusters of traits describing "types" of abusers have emerged for stalkers, but not as clearly for DV and SA perpetrators or victims.

Last, alcohol use is related strongly to SA and moderately to DV, although it is a mistake to assume that this link is causal. Given that no theory thus far presented has proved entirely adequate to explain DV, ST, and SA, a multidimensional model is needed.

PRACTICE, POLICY, AND PREVENTION ISSUES

In the United States, several societal institutions and agencies have obligations to respond to DV, ST, and SA. Lack of empirical evidence about how best to intervene creates uncertainty among those attempting to ameliorate the problems, however. Counselors in schools, community agencies, and private practice play the largest role in treatment. Schools, medical facilities, law enforcement agencies, advocates, and community organizations are on the front lines in terms of prevention. Legal scholars and legislators have obligations to devise and pass legislation aimed at protecting victims and rehabilitating offenders.

Disclosure Problems

Case History: Dominique's Blind Date and Campus Regulations

Dominique decided to go out on a double date with a guy who was a buddy of her girlfriend, Carol. Later, the two couples went to Dominique's dorm room to cap off their fun evening at a rock concert. After Carol and her boyfriend left, Dominique and her date, Greg, started kissing and petting. When Dominique eventually tried to stop Greg's advances, he wouldn't stop, and he forced Dominique to have sex.

Because Dominique felt guilty and ashamed, she did not report the incident to campus authorities. Indeed, she initially tried to keep it a secret. She was afraid authorities would discover that she had broken school rules by allowing her date into the dorm after 11:00 p.m. She did tell a counselor, however, and with the counselor's support, she finally reported the rape to both the local police department and the campus police.

After reflecting on this case, campus authorities decided to change the school's rules. Although they maintained the dorm curfew, they announced that they would no longer pursue sanctions against women caught in situations like Dominique's. Instead, they encouraged women who had been raped in a similar manner to come forward so that the police could apprehend the rapists. They even went so far as to install alarms throughout the university's buildings and grounds so that women in danger would have better opportunities to call for help. In addition, the university's Inter-Greek Council inaugurated an SA awareness program on campus, even though the student who raped Dominique came from another campus and was not in a fraternity.

Dominique's story reflects some of the difficulties in revealing DV, ST, and SA. A complicating aspect of addressing DV, ST, and SA is lack of disclosure and help-seeking actions on the part of victims. One outcome of nondisclosure is that community professionals, police, parents, and teachers have little opportunity to respond. In a survey of 1,262 high school students, 32% of women and 23.5% of men said they had been victims of some form of abuse. Of these, only 22% said that they had told someone about the event (all told a friend). In addition, they disclosed abuse to the following people: (a) to both parents, 4.4%; (b) to a counselor, 1.4%; (c) to a teacher, 0.5%; and (d) to a clergyman, 0.3% (Bergman, 1992). An analysis of somewhat older individuals, 130 female victims 18–31 years of age, yielded a different pattern of disclosure. These women often made multiple disclosures: (a) to friends, 80%; (b) to their sisters, 47%; (c) to their mothers, 43%; and (d) to criminal justice authorities, 9% (Mahlstedt & Keeny, 1993). Failure to disclose interpersonal violence to anyone other than untrained peers leaves those peers as first responders.

In regard to ST, two American studies have found similar rates of reporting to police: (a) 42% of stalked college students (Westrup et al., 1999) and (b) 54.6% of a representative sample of 16,000 people 18 years of age and older (Tjaden & Thoennes, 1998b). A British crime survey determined that more women (8–16%) than men (2–7%) report ST to authorities (cited in Dennison & Thomson, 2002).

Finally, SA is one of the most underreported crimes by any standard. One estimate is that only 12% of rape victims report the crime (Foubert & McEwen, 1998). Whether individuals involved in a sexual encounter even define the event as SA is the first step toward disclosure. In a controlled comparison of raped college women, Bondurant (2001) found that 64% did not acknowledge the rape, much less report it. Women who are most likely to acknowledge rape may differ from those who do not. According to Bondurant's data, declarers endured higher levels of rape violence. They also recognized the contrast between acquaintance rape and a so-called blitz rape scenario (a violent attack by a stranger), and they tended to blame their own behavior for the rape.

Many reasons affect women's decisions not to inform others about their SA victimization. These include privacy concerns, embarrassment, lack of understanding, and feelings of self-blame and failure. Typically, a victim does not want her family to know, or she fears that others will blame her partner, pressure her to end the relationship, take over for her, or blame her (Fisher et al., 2000; Mahlstedt & Keeny, 1993). Fears of stigmatization, inability to offer proof of abuse, or being treated with hostility are issues for victims who contemplate reporting to officials (Bachman & Saltzman, 1995; Fisher et al., 2000; Koss & Cook, 1993). For some groups, such as GLBT youths, disclosure may be especially unlikely (Sousa, 1999).

In an exploratory study of help-seeking behaviors among 165 African American middle schoolers, Black and Weisz (2003) arrived at disparate results. Study participants of both genders asserted that they were willing to seek help for possible DV victimization or perpetration from the following people: (a) mother or father, (b) other family members, (c) school counselor, (d) friend or teacher, or (e) police officer. Responses to disclosure vary. Mahlstedt and Keeny (1993) found that the most common responses from victims' social networks to DV disclosures were understanding, advice giving, listening, and stopping victim self-blame. Ullman's (1999) survey of responses revealed that peers commonly offered the most supportive responses. Some other groups, however, not only failed to offer support but also engaged in harmful responses (e.g., blaming victim). Formal responders, such as police officers and physicians, were least helpful.

Treatment and Policy Issues
Concerning Teenage Interpersonal Violence

Many practitioners emphasize the necessity of treatment for DV, SA, and ST victims because of the long-lasting adverse effects of such victimization (see Burgess, 1995; Henning, Leitenberg, Coffey, Turner, & Bennett, 1996). Others believe that intervention in violent premarital relationships is crucial in order to prevent patterns of conflict and violence from carrying over into marriage (e.g., Carr & VanDeusen, 2002; Frias-Armenta, 2002; Miller & Bukva, 2001). Professionals can and should intervene in DV because of the possibility of child endangerment (Sleutel, 1998). Schools should offer services to victims (Advisory Council on Violence Against Women, 1996), and treatment strategies should take note of gender differences (Foshee et al., 2001).

Dating violence. Once victims are in treatment, their therapists need to help them with "safety planning." The next therapeutic task might be to help victims label their own or their partners' behavior as a form of violence, because these young people are unlikely to be aware of their belief systems (Sousa, 1999; Truman-Schram et al., 2000). Service providers themselves may need to adjust their attitudes toward DV victims (Foshee & Linder, 1997).

Other important treatment topics are the need to avoid control by others and the need to modify victims' beliefs about the legitimacy of physical aggression. Based on one analysis, an important therapeutic intervention appears to be helping victimized women adopt appropriate coping methods (Coffey et al., 1996). Another target area should be an exploration of the victim's satisfaction with his or her investment in the relationship (Truman-Schram et al., 2000). Herrenkohl et al. (2003) recommend that prevention programs address issues related to the developmental trauma caused by abuse.

It also appears to be worthwhile for treatment to focus on romantic attachment styles. The finding that individuals who feel secure in their adult romantic relationships are less likely to be involved in dating violence suggests that treatment (and prevention) might focus on helping insecure daters to feel more secure (McCarthy & Taylor, 1999). Sometimes it is appropriate for a therapist to encourage and empower a victim (or even a perpetrator) to leave a violent relationship (see Rosen & Stith, 1995). Outcome studies of treatment effectiveness are extremely rare (Foshee et al., 2000; Krajewski, 1996).

Sexual assault. SA treatment has attracted extensive research attention. Whereas some of the counseling techniques mentioned above might be suitable for SA victims, others may not. Counseling for SA occurs most commonly at rape crisis centers, but crisis intervention is far from sufficient (Campbell, Wasco, Ahrens, Sefl, & Barnes, 2001). Medical responses to SA victims, especially in emergency rooms, are in need of improvement. An illustration of current efforts at such improvement are sexual assault nurse examiner (SANE) programs, which employ highly trained nurses who gather evidence and attend to victims' other medical, emotional, and legal problems. As promising as these programs seem to be, they remain unevaluated (Ahrens et al., 2000).

An especially irritating lapse in CJS practices is the mishandling of crime evidence in rape cases. It was a big step forward for women when emergency rooms began routinely using rape kits to collect DNA evidence. When this practice became widespread, members of the public, victims' advocates, and SA victims all assumed that crime labs would analyze the samples gathered and try to identify perpetrators. Not so. As of 2002, across the United States 180,000 rape kits were in storage awaiting analysis, presumably because of cost constraints (the processing of each kit costs approximately $40) (Hewitt, Podesta, & Longley, 2002).

Stalking victims and offenders. Because ST victimization takes many forms and symptoms vary, therapists can best serve ST victims by helping them to enhance their general coping skills and finding ways to help them decrease their vulnerability (Blaauw, Winkel, Arensman, Sheridan, & Freeve, 2002). Currently, no specific psychological treatments exist for the perpetrators of ST (Rosenfeld, 2000). For the subgroup of stalkers who have diagnosable mental disorders, psychotropic medicine may be beneficial (Sheridan, Blaauw, & Davies, 2003). It is probable, however, that laws protecting the mentally ill would shield ST perpetrators from forced medication (Rosenfeld, 2000). Given these obstacles, criminal and civil options may be the only choices available. Restraining orders, however, are quite ineffective in stopping ST (e.g., Hall, 1998). Spitzberg (2002) examined 32 studies and found that stalkers violated restraining orders 40% of the time.

The current state of affairs dictates the need for antistalking legislation. The most obvious improvement would be the modification of current laws to enable victims to obtain lifetime protection orders. A second would be the modification of bail rules to keep stalkers off the streets, and a third would be the passage of legislation to stop cyberstalking (Merschman, 2001). The phenomenon of cyberstalking also raises the need for improvements in law enforcement training, as most police officers are inexperienced in investigating this type of crime ("Police Agencies," 2001; "Successes Seen," 2003).

Improving the criminal justice response. One policy recommendation is to help the CJS adequately protect victims of DV, ST, and SA. As Jordan et al. (2000) point out, "Both culturally and statutorily, victims of crimes which have historically been perpetrated against women, such as rape, domestic violence and stalking, have received a focus in a way no burglary, robbery or other crime has" (p. 513). To reiterate, the CJS has tended to overlook crimes against women and to treat them very differently than other crimes. There are several causes for this state of affairs. First, there is the historical lack of attention paid to violence between intimates. Second, there is the failure of adults to recognize the seriousness of teenage violence. Third, antivictim, antiwoman biases exist throughout the CJS (e.g., Sousa, 1999; Spohn & Holleran, 2001).

The principal stumbling block in providing legal protections to teens has been the adult-centered nature of the CJS. Suarez (1994) argues that "at a minimum, legal protections now available to adult victims should be made available to teenagers" (p. 423). In a giant step forward, when Congress reauthorized the Violence Against Women Act in fall 2000, the legislation extended the act's protections to teenage victims of DV ("Congress Votes," 2000). Typical of progressive laws and programs is California's Safe at Home program, a coordinated system that works to protect the addresses of all victims of IPV and ST (see California Secretary of State, 1998).

Prosecutorial discretion in cases involving interpersonally violent crimes has received mixed reviews. As is true for other crimes, police and prosecutors use discretion in their decisions to make arrests and to prosecute offenders in cases of DV, ST, and SA. Although discretion may be necessary, its use in DV, ST, and SA cases often comes across as bias. In one analysis, Spohn and Holleran (2001) found that prosecution was less likely in assault cases if the victim was acquainted with the accused than if the perpetrator was a stranger. Prosecutors also used "extralegal" information (e.g., victim's "character") to guide their

decision making. Further research indicates that victim characteristics (e.g., drunk when police arrived) may overshadow the strength of the evidence as to whether a crime is classified as a simple or aggravated assault (Spears & Spohn, 1997).

Prevention

As Lewis and Fremouw (2001) note, the "ultimate purpose of the empirical study of dating violence is prevention" (p. 123). Society should more carefully evaluate the degree to which legal intervention, school prevention programs, and other supports are made available to young couples and single women (e.g., DeKeseredy & Hinch, 1991; Jaffe, Sudermann, Reitzel, & Killip, 1992). DeKeseredy (1996) has assembled two lists of actions that individuals can take to turn an unsafe campus learning environment into a safe place. One is made up of suggestions for personal actions (e.g., "Put a 'Stop Woman Abuse' bumper sticker on your car"), and the other suggests collective strategies (e.g., "Insist that woman abuse prevention courses be required for all males"). School education and prevention programs are proliferating, but treatment and intervention programs are scattered. (For a comprehensive source of information on prevention, see Centers for Disease Control and Prevention, 2001.)

Goals of prevention programs. Prevention programs have myriad goals, many of which reflect beliefs about causation. Some proposals are as follows: (a) Offer clinics for victims of childhood abuse(s) and at-risk daters; (b) alert college women to the dangers of interpersonal control; (c) provide guidance about avoiding date-rape drugs; (d) address sexist attitudes and problems of peer-group support for aggression; (e) teach anger management, conflict resolution skills, and stress-reduction skills; (f) present antidrug messages and alcohol misuse awareness programs (Eckhardt et al., 2002; Krajewski, 1996; Lewis & Fremouw, 2001; Rickert et al., 2002; Schwartz et al., 2000; Smith & Welchans, 2000; Weisz & Black, 2001).

School/university prevention programs. Schools and universities have the responsibility to make their campuses safe for women by evaluating and modifying their services as needed (Advisory Council on Violence Against Women, 1996). Federal legislation supporting these goals includes the 1992 Campus Sexual Assault Victim's Bill of Rights and the Student Right-to-Know and Campus Security Act of 1990, which requires schools to give students access to campus crime reports (see Ferguson, 1998). These laws may encourage reporting of violence, and thus facilitate efforts to help victims and to make perpetrators accountable (Advisory Council on Violence Against Women, 1996). Some universities now routinely present violence prevention programs to incoming students, partly to avoid liability (Marcus & Swett, 2003; Senn et al., 2000). Another strategy that would be helpful on college campuses is to discourage alcohol misuse (Wechsler, Lee, Kuo, & Lee, 2000).

Colleges could offer more courses in family violence and interpersonal relationships. One focus of attention should be college women's unrealistic fears. One survey of 564 college women revealed "perceptions of fear that were incongruent with associated actual risk of victimization" (Hughes, Marshall, & Sherrill, 2003, p. 43). These college women were unaware, for example, that being drunk around little-known acquaintances is far more dangerous than encountering an angry driver. Finally, some experts believe that schools should consider preparing teens to be peer counselors for abused friends (Creighton & Kivel, 1993), because teens are most likely to disclose abuse to their peers.

One progressive and successful DV prevention program is Safe Dates, which combines ongoing school (e.g., theater production) and community activities (e.g., support groups). In order to evaluate this program, researchers gave a control group community activities only. A 1-year follow-up assessment revealed a 25% reduction in emotional abuse and a 60% reduction in SA among Safe Dates participants (Foshee et al., 1998, 2000). A Canadian study covering a 2-year period examined a DV prevention program that included education about both healthy and abusive relationships, help with conflict resolution and communication skills, and participation in social action activities. The program did not produce significant changes in the development of healthy relationships, but it did reduce physical and emotional abuse incidents (Wolfe, Wekerle, et al., 2003).

In their infancy, the vast majority of college rape prevention programs addressed women's responsibilities to take precautionary measures (Parrott, as cited in O'Donohue, Yeater, & Fanetti, 2003). Program designers rarely conducted evaluations of program outcomes. Given that it is basically male behaviors that necessitate change if rape is to be prevented, focusing on women's conduct seems ill conceived in retrospect. In the past two decades, rape prevention programs aimed at male college students have mushroomed. As Berkowitz (2000) points out, "All institutions of higher education have the responsibility to devote significant resources to programs that engage men in the task of preventing sexual assault" (p. 67).

Cumulatively, outcome data indicate that prevention efforts aimed at all-male groups are more successful in changing attitudes than are those aimed at mixed-gender groups (e.g., Foubert & Marriott, 1997). An all-male peer education program named How Men Can Help a Sexual Assault Survivor: What Men Can Do significantly reduced behavioral intent to rape and acceptance of rape myths. Encouraging as these results are, they are certainly not definitive. As Foubert and McEwen (1998) point out, methodological problems undermine the validity and limit the generalizability of the findings. Some programs fail to have any impact on students' attitudes at all (Gidycz et al., 2001).

An evaluation of one rape prevention program showed that it had improved participants' knowledge about sexual coercion and had favorable impacts on some behavioral indices (e.g., willingness to recommend the program) (Heppner, Humphrey, DeBord, & Hillenbrand-Gunn, 1995). No research has demonstrated that prevention programs reduce the actual incidence of rape (Brecklin & Forde, 2001; Breitenbecher, 2000). Last but not least, university education and prevention programs must refrain from excluding male victims of same-sex rape (Scarce, 1997). (For an outline of elements of sound SA prevention programs, see Berkowitz, 2000. The American College of Obstetricians and Gynecologists offers prevention materials on its Web site at http://www. acog.org, and for a summary of recommendations for addressing teen DV, see Sousa, 1999.)

One policy recommendation centers on the preferential treatment often given to athletes accused of DV, ST, and SA. Advocates call for stricter rules regulating the athletic eligibility of students. Universities tend to ignore crimes against women in their quest to maintain strong athletic teams that draw important revenue. As Reed (1999) notes, violence against women is "serious misconduct," at least as serious as drug use or gambling. Why not deny eligibility to athletes who assault women?

Community collaborations. In some cases, prevention should be collaborative. In the case of ST, for example, the focus should be on victims, perpetrators, and CJS responses combined (Sheridan, Blaauw, & Davies, 2003). One innovative idea is for community agencies to partner with schools in order to offer stand-alone after-school programs that empower youths to end DV. Agencies that might participate include child protective services, youth support services, and organizations that specialize in shelters for victims of battering and batterer treatment (Grasley, Wolfe, & Wekerle, 1999). One noteworthy prevention program is the Massachusetts Teen Dating Violence Intervention and Prevention Program, which funds the implementation of DV programs in public schools (Massachusetts Department of Education, 2001). At the foundation of this mandate is the formation of community collaborative boards, which are similar to task forces. The predominant goal of these boards is to promote safe, positive, and abuse-free school environments through recommendations and written policies. Funding must include training of certain individuals, such as school administrators, staff, and students, about DV and early warning signs of DV.

Violence screening by physical and mental health providers. Clinical screening for DV, ST, and SA can identify teens involved in violence so that professionals can find ways to assist them. In such medical and psychological screening, professionals ask teens questions about the violence in their lives and then respond appropriately. Family violence experts provide physicians and counselors with a research-tested screening instrument accompanied by a list of appropriate behavioral responses. A professional asks the teenage client a series of questions from the screening test and follows up by selecting actions from the response list. One question might be "Has anyone hurt you?" or "Are you afraid of any of your acquaintances?" An appropriate response by the professional to an affirmative answer to such a question might be "No one deserves to be hit" (Hamberger & Ambuel, 1998).

In one survey, teenagers strongly endorsed medical screening, even if they did not feel like disclosing abuse at the time. A configuration of factors influence DV disclosure among teens: personal factors (e.g., fear of retaliation), patient-provider factors (e.g., trusting relationship), and provider factors (e.g., explaining screening procedures) (Freed, Gupta, Hynes, & Miller, 2003). Professionals also need to reach out to GLBT youths. Medical providers seldom query teenage patients about same-sex violence, nor do youths usually disclose their sexual orientations to their providers. Future research should investigate how professionals can best communicate with GLBT teens (Hoffman, Swann, & Freeman, 2003).

It is essential that teenagers have mental health care available to them. Variables such as race and lack of insurance coverage prevent many teens with psychological problems from obtaining help. Obviously, one policy recommendation would be to modify policies so that teens have access to mental health professionals (Kodjo, Auinger, & Ryan, 2002).

Public awareness. Education of the public about the realities of rape is essential if victims are ever to receive justice. A substantial problem in obtaining SA convictions is jurors' misperceptions of rape. Despite judges' instructions and other courtroom procedures, jurors' subjective impressions of rape are incredibly different from legalistic definitions, and these impressions affect jurors' decisions (Churchill, 1993). Illustrative of this problem is that jurors may fail to define nonconsensual intercourse as rape if the victim had consented to sex with the rapist on a previous occasion. Just like police and prosecutors, jurors take extralegal information into account when making their judgments. That is, a jury might find a rape defendant not guilty because the victim wore a miniskirt to court or because the victim was acquainted with the rapist (Candell, Frazier, Arikan, & Tofteland, 1993; Goldberg-Ambrose, 1992).

CHAPTER SUMMARY

This chapter has described dating violence, stalking, and sexual assault and presented information about the prevalence of these crimes. Definitional ambiguity and methodological variations across studies have led to a lack of consensus about interpersonal violence among teenagers and college students. For the most part, police departments have little accurate information about the prevalence of DV, ST, and SA, partially because of victim nondisclosure, and partially because records do not adequately categorize offender-victim relationships. In addition, some self-report surveys have only recently employed questionnaires sensitive enough to capture the desired data. Very few researchers have conducted studies of DV, ST, or SA with samples including members of ethnic/racial minority groups or GLBT youths. In addition, few have conducted studies outside of the United States.

Through surveys using self-report questionnaires, researchers have ascertained that DV is very common. Whereas NCVS data estimate male serious assault rates at 16% and female assault rates at 2%, other studies based on CTS data with high school samples provide estimates of roughly 12–40% for couples over their dating lifetimes. Injury data from the U.S. Bureau of Justice Statistics show that adolescent women going to an emergency room suffer almost 21% of injuries caused by current/ex-dates compared with men, who suffer 2.75%. ST by an intimate victimizes 4.8% of young women 18–29 years and 0.6% of men. SA occurs less frequently, but according to research findings it ranges for female victims from 1.8% of college women (within a 7-month period) to 20.4% lifetime prevalence rates. DV and SA are common in other countries other than the United States as well. (For more detailed estimates, see Tables 1–3 in Appendix B.)

DV, ST, and SA cause many injuries, negative health outcomes, and psychological sequelae, such as PTSD. Victims take various actions, including breaking up with abusive partners and dropping out of school. Certain patterns of abuse seem to be typical of particular groups. Some data suggest that male perpetrators of DV, ST, and SA are akin to ordinary street criminals. Other data indicate that some forms of these crimes are gender reciprocal. Fraternity men and members of all-male athletic organizations are more likely than other men to abuse women. Because much of the information is available only in the form of **aggregate data**, it is difficult to obtain estimates of the rates of these crimes among particular racial/ethnic or SES groups.

Some cultural variables, such as differential weighting of male-to-female violence, may work to decrease male-initiated violence. Other variables, such as patriarchal attitudes and peer support for violence against women, may be related to an increase in DV and SA. Although findings should be accepted tentatively, certain attitudinal dimensions, such as male sex-role traditionality, may also fuel dating abuses. Dimensions such as romanticism, gender differences about issues of consent, and attributions about responsibility for DV and SA influence the occurrence of these forms of interpersonal violence.

DV, ST, and SA are associated with experiences of direct childhood abuse or exposure to violence, but the associations are not uniformly substantial. Closely related is the question of whether DV is either a stepping-stone to or a training ground for marital violence. Gender-role socialization and insecure attachment may trigger DV, ST, and SA. On the whole, evidence shows several links between these variables, but these findings do not allow assumptions of causality.

Individual personality traits such as need for control, reactance, feelings of powerlessness, hypermasculinity, and anger seem related to DV, ST, and SA, but more research is needed to establish such generalizations. The relationship variables of dyadic stress, communication skills, attributions of blame, and level of commitment appear related to DV, ST, and SA as well as to whether a couple stays together or breaks up.

By and large, dating partners who are involved in DV, ST, or SA do not inform either helping professionals or CJS agencies about their encounters. Victims most frequently confide in peers. Consequently, formal sources of community support have little opportunity to offer assistance. Victims perceive these resources as partially helpful and partially hurtful. Improved training for professionals may be needed to ensure that victims find their interactions with helping agencies more satisfactory.

Treatment programs are scarce, but prevention programs are expanding. Schools are becoming more involved in prevention and intervention. Medical and counseling professionals need to screen teenagers for problems with DV, ST, and SA in order to intervene and prevent violence. These professionals, among others, need to include members of marginalized groups, such as racial/ethnic minorities and GLBT teens, under their umbrella of concern. Bringing DV, ST, and SA into the open may be a first step in coping with these forms of violence.

DISCUSSION QUESTIONS

1. What crucial elements should be included in definitions of dating violence, stalking, and sexual assault?
2. How do the measurement instruments used affect research results?
3. What cultural variables best explain DV, ST, and SA?
4. What should peers do to help couples like Claudia and Roberto (see the case history "Claudia and Roberto's Last Dance at the High School Prom")?
5. Can a man be raped by a lone woman? Can males be sexually coerced?
6. What should society do to prevent DV, ST, and SA?
7. If you were planning to conduct research, which of the topics covered in this chapter would you like to pursue? *Military*
8. How would you assist a friend who informed you she had been raped?
9. What advice would you give your son or daughter about alcohol use and fraternity membership?
10. Should society hold a man responsible for date rape if the woman asserts she did not consent but she was dressed in a provocative way?

RECOMMENDED READING

Abbey, A., McAuslan, P., Zawacki, T., Clinton, A. M., & Buck, P. O. (2001). Attitudinal, experiential, and situational predictors of sexual assault perceptions. *Journal of Interpersonal Violence, 16,* 784–807.

Brewster, M. P. (2003). *Stalking: Psychology, risk factors, interventions, and law.* Kingston, NJ: Civic Research Institute.

Feeney, J. A., & Noller, P. (1996). *Adult attachment.* Thousand Oaks, CA: Sage.

Ferguson, C. U. (1998). Dating violence as a social phenomenon. In N. A. Jackson & G. C. Oates (Eds.), *Violence in intimate relationships: Examining sociological and psychological issues* (pp. 83–118). Woburn, MA: Butterworth-Heinemann.

Lloyd, S. A., & Emery, B. C. (2000). *The dark side of courtship: Physical and sexual aggression.* Thousand Oaks, CA: Sage.

Patterson, G., Reid, J., & Dishion, T. (1992). *Antisocial boys.* Eugene, OR: Castalia.

Reddington, F. P., & Kreisel, B. W. (2003). *Sexual assault: The victims, the perpetrators and the criminal justice system.* Durham, NC: Carolina Academic Press.

Soitzberg, B. H. (2002). The tactical topography of stalking victimization. *Trauma, Violence, & Abuse, 3,* 261–288.

Spence-Diehl, E. (1999). *Stalking: A handbook for victims.* Holmes Beach, FL: Learning Publications.

Stenack, R. (2001). *Stop controlling me: What to do when someone you love has too much power over you.* Oakland, CA: Harbinger.

NOTE

1. In this case history, the name Mary is a pseudonym, but the name of Mary's attacker, Daniel Oltarsh, is real.

9

INTIMATE PARTNER VIOLENCE IN ADULT RELATIONSHIPS

Case History: Kree Kirkman—Getting Even With the Woman You No Longer Love

Upon learning that his wife had begun divorce proceedings, Kree Kirkman of Enumclaw, Washington, got a demolition permit and bulldozed his wife's home into shambles. The city's police dispatcher reported getting calls from men across the nation offering to set up a defense fund for Kirkman. "He's got a real cheering section out there," the dispatcher noted (quoted in Brower & Sackett, 1985, p. 108). An informal tally of opinions offered by men frequenting a bar in a nearby working-class neighborhood showed that the men thought it was "just wonderful; he really got even with her!" They seemed to ignore information that Kirkman had told his wife that he no longer loved her and that the couple had agreed jointly to a separation. The predominant feeling seemed to be that this type of violence is not only permissible, but also "macho" and praiseworthy.[1]

The above case history exemplifies several topics related to intimate partner violence (IPV). Kirkman's angry and vengeful behavior was extreme. What is more, society appears to approve of such violence. *Intimate partner violence and abuse* are the terms used for violence and abuse that occur between adult partners who are at least 18 years old, sexually intimate, married or unmarried, and currently or formerly living together. These groupings include spouses and cohabitors, whether together, separated, or divorced. In contrast, the term *dating violence* usually refers to interpartner violence among adolescents or unmarried college students. These partners may or may not be sexually intimate and may or may not be living together.

This chapter presents information on how social scientists, government agencies, and legislators conceptualize and define IPV. It also presents brief definitions of IPV suitable for special populations, such as various ethnic groups. In addition, the chapter discusses the frequency of various forms of IPV according to data derived from different sources that allow comparisons. Also included is some information about the many negative repercussions of IPV for involved individuals and for society as a whole. IPV costs U.S. society millions of dollars annually in terms of welfare, medical expenses, and criminal justice system (CJS) processing. Attempts to explain the causes of IPV cover some of the well-worn theories, such as patriarchy and learning theory. The chapter also details the responses of societal agencies expected to cope with the IPV problem, such as the religious organizations, mental and physical health agencies, and the CJS. The chapter ends with practice, policy, and prevention recommendations stemming from the review of facts presented throughout the chapter.

SCOPE OF THE PROBLEM

IPV ranges from acts of mild verbal abuse to severe physical violence and even death. This section presents definitions and estimates of frequencies of IPV within subcategories: emotional (psychological) abuse, stalking, physical assaults, sexual assaults (e.g., marital rape), injuries, and homicides. These accounts encompass facts about both heterosexual and homosexual IPV, as well as data about different ethnic/racial groups, cross-cultural groups, and a few special segments of the U.S. population.

Conceptions of Violence

One confusing aspect of discussing IPV is the terminology. There is no consensus about the precise meaning of terms such as *violence, abuse, assault, rape, sexual assault,* and *sexual coercion.* Some authors use some of these terms interchangeably, but others may not. It is possible to place all acts of IPV on a continuum ranging from mild to severe. The Conflict Tactics Scale(CTS1; Straus, 1979) and the Revised Conflict Tactics Scale (CTS2; Straus, Hamby, Boney-McCoy, & Sugarman, 1995) take this approach. They place verbal abuse first, as a mild type of IPV, and beating up, choking, and weapon use last, as severe IPV. Other scholars argue that IPV acts at different levels of severity are qualitatively different; they do not lie on a continuum. Some have conjectured that using levels of intentionality as a method for categorizing IPV would add useful information (see Marshall, 1994; Straus, 1991b; for contrasting information, see Follingstad & DeHart, 2000).

Battering: A distinct kind of intimate partner violence. Before the currently preferred term *intimate partner violence,* or *IPV,* came into common use, Adams (1986) referred to spouse abuse as *battering.* According to Adams, the battering of women is not just perpetration of a list of physically abusive behaviors. Instead, true battering includes the instillment of fear, oppression and control of the victim, and assault. This definition was helpful because it began the move toward differentiating levels of abuse. It incorporated some compelling forms of emotional and psychological factors. Following this line of reasoning, Smith, Edwards, and DeVellis (1998) define battering as "a process whereby one member of an intimate relationship experiences vulnerability, loss of power and control, and entrapment as a consequence of the other member's exercise of power through the patterned use of physical, sexual, psychological, and/or moral force" (as quoted in Smith, Thornton, DeVellis, Earp, & Coker, 2002, p. 1210).

Statistically derived categories of abuse. One way of determining categorical distinctions between different types of IPV is through statistical methods, such as factor analysis. One such analysis of data from responses to an experimenter-developed set of 54 questions yielded three abuse variables: psychological/verbal abuse, control abuse, and physical/sexual abuse (Pitzner & Drummond, 1997). In a 1992 factor analysis of CTS1 scores, Pan, Neidig, and O'Leary (1994) isolated three correlated but separate types of IPV: verbal aggression, mild physical aggression, and severe physical aggression.

Most recently, Borjesson, Aarons, and Dunn (2003) used both exploratory and confirmatory factor analyses to search for dimensions of IPV. In the first phase of their study, they asked 121 college students to list unpleasant interpersonal behaviors occurring both within and outside of intimate relationships. Along with items drawn from a literature review, the researchers identified 137 potentially abusive behaviors. In the second phase, they obtained ratings of the abusive behaviors from 1,022 other college students. A final factor analysis of these data yielded five subcategories of IPV: (a) deceptive behaviors, (b) restricting acts, (c) verbal abuse, (d) emotional abuse, and (e) overt violence.

Common couple violence versus intimate terrorism. One increasingly popular conception of IPV distinguishes minor *common couple violence* (CCV) from severe battering, or *intimate terrorism* (IT) (Johnson, 2000). (Johnson, 1995, formerly labeled IT as *patriarchal terrorism,* or *PT.*) CCV and IT serve as anchors at opposite ends of the IPV continuum. Presumably, types of assaultive acts (e.g., physical, sexual) interact with varying psychological states (apprehension, oppression, and control) to designate different points on this continuum.

At the low end of the continuum, CCV may include relatively infrequent, noninjurious fighting. CCV is the yelling or mild shoving associated with the inevitable conflicts that arise in intimate relationships. It may be mutual, and it is not especially gendered. It does not tend to victimize the partners and does not create fear. Occasionally, scholars have referred to this low-level type of abuse as *normative,* but some experts in the field find this terminology troubling. They object to the term because they are concerned that less knowledgeable individuals will assume couple violence is normal, and hence acceptable (e.g., Hamby,

Poindexter, & Gray-Little, 1996). At the high end of the continuum, IT may cluster around a pattern of assaultive, fear-producing, controlling behaviors, both criminal (e.g., physical assaults, stalking) and non-criminal (e.g., jealous monitoring of the partner's friends and activities, public humiliation of the partner). IT presumably occurs within a patriarchal framework rooted in historical and cultural conceptions of male ownership and domination of female partners.

Some logicians applaud the recognition that not every minor act of violence, such as pushing, fits into the concept of full-blown IPV. The use of CCV terminology helps integrate diverse research findings, as well as contrasting theoretical formulations and interventions (Johnson, 1995; Johnson & Ferraro, 2000). So far, few investigators have used IT as an explanatory framework. Some of Johnson's (2000) further refinements, such as violent resistance (VR) (self-defense) and mutual violent control (MVC), may enter the mainstream of family violence literature as progress continues. A 2003 study used responses from students, sheltered women, and prisoners to investigate Johnson's (1995) proposed patterns of responses. A **discriminant functions analysis** substantiated the basic dichotomy by identifying two significant functions (CCV, IT) and by classifying 75% of the cases correctly (Graham-Kevan & Archer, 2003b).

Definitions of Intimate Partner Violence and Abuse

Definitions of IPV are evolving as the science of family violence advances. In the past, scholars used the term *marital abuse* or *spouse abuse* in reference to verbal abuse, threats, and physical assaults ranging from minor to severe, including weapon use. *Sexual assault* (e.g., marital rape) constituted a separate dimension of abuse. Beginning in about 1988, the concept of psychological abuse expanded to encompass behaviors, such as damaging property, evoking fear, exploiting finances, and controlling behaviors. In the 1990s, experts began classifying stalking of intimates as abuse.

Instead of referring to interpersonal violence among adults as *domestic violence, marital violence,* or *spouse abuse,* the preferred term today is *intimate partner violence,* or *IPV.* There are many advantages to using this term. It can refer to current and former marital partners, separated marital partners, current and former cohabitors, or current and former same-sex partners, and it is gender neutral. Currently, there is some imprecision in the terminology used to refer to

violent college-age partners. Although most family violence experts categorize unmarried college students within the dating violence category, others classify them within the adult IPV group. In either case, some authors allude to any type of violence between intimates as IPV, whatever the age of the persons involved.

Comprehensive government-developed definitions. To assess interpersonal violence, the National Crime Victimization Survey (NCVS) has relied on a series of questions covering various forms of criminal acts, such as attacks, threats of violence, robberies, and rapes. In the NCVS, government specialists tabulate the following for each respondent: race, sex, age, ethnicity, education, income, marital status, location, and offender-victim relationship. As described in Chapter 2, the NCVS has not only changed some questions in recent years, but has also increased its victim-offender relationship categories to classify intimates more precisely (see Bachman & Saltzman, 1995). (For the old and new NCVS screener questions, click on the "Additional Materials" button at the link for this volume on the Sage Publications Web site, http://www.sagepub.com/book.aspx?pid=10013.)

Within the framework of violence against women, one government-convened panel of experts has suggested defining violence against intimate partners as consisting of three kinds of behaviors: (a) physical violence, (b) sexual violence, and (c) threats of physical and/or sexual violence. The panel concluded that *abuse* should be defined broadly to include the above three types of violent behaviors and two more forms: (d) stalking and (e) psychological/emotional abuse (Saltzman, Fanslow, McMahon, & Shelley, 1999). Consequently, there could be five IPV subscales.

Conflict Tactics Scales (self-reports). The CTS1 (Straus, 1979) and CTS2 (Straus et al., 1995) present questions within an interpersonal conflict context as opposed to a crime context. As explained in Chapter 2, both Conflict Tactics Scales ask respondents how they settle conflicts with others when they do not agree. CTS1 allows researchers to count frequencies of behaviors within categories of verbal abuse, minor physical abuse, and severe physical abuse. CTS2 adds sexual assault and injury outcomes. Straus and Gelles (1986) conducted two nationally representative studies of family violence in 1975 and again in 1985 using CTS1. (See the subsection below headed "Gender Perspectives on Intimate Partner Violence" for a more thorough discussion of gender issues.)

Frequency and outcome parameters. Various groups and individuals, such as health organizations, schools, and independent researchers, may devise other conceptions of IPV and use different assessment inventories. Tackling the issue from a different angle, O'Leary (1999) has proposed the following definition of IPV: "the presence of at least two acts of physical aggression within a year (or one severe act) and/or physical aggression that leads the partner to be fearful of the other or that results in injury requiring medical attention" (p. 19). This definition is consistent with the results of a factor analysis of CTS1 scores conducted previously by O'Leary and his colleagues (Pan et al., 1994). This study isolated three correlated but separate types of IPV: verbal aggression, mild physical aggression, and severe physical aggression. A major benefit of O'Leary's definition is that it excludes low-level, mild physical aggression (CCV) that should not be considered equivalent to serious assault.

Sexual assault of intimate partners. An article prepared by the Centers for Disease Control and Prevention (CDC, 2002) presents this broad definition of **sexual violence**:

> A sex act completed against a victim's will or when a victim is unable to consent due to age, illness, disability, or the influence of alcohol or other drugs. It may involve actual or threatened physical force, use of guns or other weapons, coercion, intimidation or pressure. Sexual violence also includes intentional touching of the genitals, anus, groin, or breasts against a victim's will or when a victim is unable to consent, as well as voyeurism, exposure to exhibitionism, or undesired exposure to pornography. The perpetrator of sexual violence may be a stranger, friend, family member, or intimate partner. (p. 3)

Diane Russell (1982) can be credited with drawing attention to rape among intimate partners. Her research and writing have helped dispel some of the most common myths surrounding marital rape. One such myth is that intimate partner sexual assault is rare; actually, it is the most prevalent kind of rape. A second myth is that marital rape is relatively harmless compared with stranger rape; in reality, it has serious consequences. Russell illustrates the problem of uninformed legislators and others in the 1990 revised edition of her book *Rape in Marriage*, in which she quotes a telltale statement made by California State Senator Bob Wilson: "But if you can't rape your wife, who can

you rape?" (p. 18). (For a legal review of marital rape, see Hasday, 2000.)

Psychological/emotional abuse. Some of the earliest operational definitions of emotional abuse appeared in the work of Richard Tolman (1989). Tolman developed the Psychological Maltreatment of Women Inventory (PMWI), which assesses two dimensions: dominance-isolation and emotional-verbal. Molidor (1995) has identified seven major types of psychological abuse based on the PMWI: (a) isolation, (b) monopolization (making the abuser the center of the woman's life), (c) economic abuse, (d) degradation, (e) rigid sex-role expectations, (f) psychological destabilization (making the woman feel crazy), and (g) withholding emotional responsivity.

Emotional abuse is very common and extremely damaging to victims. A number of IPV survivors have asserted that emotional abuse is worse than physical abuse and has long-lasting effects (see Currie, 1998; Lynch & Graham-Bermann, 2000). Emotional abuse is a significant predictor of posttraumatic stress disorder (PTSD), and, combined with interpersonal control, is a significant predictor of negative mood and psychosomatic complaints (see Arias & Pape, 1999; Pitzner & Drummond, 1997; Street, 1998; Tang, 1997). Psychological abuse, even without taking physical abuse into account, is related to victims' perceptions of threat and their plans to leave the relationship (Henning & Klesges, 2003).

Stalking. Stalking of celebrities has brought media attention to the behaviors typical of stalkers. When the victim-offender relationship is or was intimate, stalking is a form of IPV (see Nicole, 1997; Pearson, Thoennes, & Griswold, 1999; Tjaden & Thoennes, 1998a). Research shows that stalking is a significant predictor of femicide (McFarlane, Campbell, & Watson, 2002). (See the glossary and Chapter 8 for definitions.)

Economic exploitation. Harway et al. (2002) define economic abuse as abuse that "involves restricting access to resources, such as bank accounts, spending money, funds for household expenses, telephone communication, transportation, or medical care" (p. 10). Without funds, battered victims and their children usually cannot leave their abusers. Within the area of elder abuse, financial exploitation is all too often a type of abuse executed by family members, fraudulent businessmen, and health care workers (Nerenberg, 2000).

Definitions across cultures. For the most part, American academicians have failed to blend into their definitions of IPV nuanced interpretations of violence between intimates derived from other cultures. As one illustration, battered Japanese women emphasize unprotected sex as a particularly onerous type of IPV (Yoshihama, 2002). Unprotected sex may, of course, lead to AIDS and death. In a study of Chinese people living in Hong Kong, Tang, Cheung, Chen, and Sun (2002) ascertained that the selection of terms, such as *violence* versus *abuse*, greatly affected individuals' conceptions of whether certain actions constituted IPV.

Definitions of violence between same-sex partners. One definition of **gay intimate partner violence** is as follows: "a means to control others through power, including physical and psychological threats (verbal and nonverbal) or injury (to the victim or others), isolation, economic deprivation, heterosexist control [threats to reveal homosexuality], sexual assaults, vandalism (destruction of property), or any combination of methods" (Burke, 1998, p. 164; National Coalition of Anti-Violence Programs, 2001). Based on anecdotal evidence, some specialists have theorized the existence of a group of IPV tactics unique to same-sex partners. Lesbians and gays, for example, may use heterosexist control or convince abuse victims that they are guilty of "mutual battering" when actually they are using self-defense. Some gays also may threaten to infect their partners with HIV (see Giorgio, 2002; Hart, 1996; Letellier, 1996).

Legal definitions. Legal definitions of IPV are crucial because they are the ones most likely to have an impact on victims' lives. Victims of IPV cannot obtain orders of protection, for example, unless their experiences fall under the aegis of IPV laws. An intimate partner who is raped may not be able to seek legal redress unless her partner used physical force. Threats to lock a partner in a closet and threats to notify immigration authorities of a partner's illegal immigration status, for instance, do not count as crimes. Overall, legal definitions of IPV are so narrow that they do not capture the reality of IPV victims' lives (DeKeseredy, 2000).

Estimates of Intimate Partner Violence

Over the years, family violence researchers have attempted to estimate the prevalence and incidence of IPV. Some information is derived from crime reports made to police, whereas other information comes from self-report data. Both police reports and self-reports underestimate the amount and seriousness of IPV because of underreporting biases (see Armstrong et al., 2001; Kruttschnitt & Dornfeld, 1992; Sugarman & Hotaling, 1997).

The true amount of IPV is unknown. Scholars from various disciplines, holding dissimilar ideologies and using different research methods, have produced a multiplicity of IPV estimates. Knowledge of how the sources of information vary is useful for anyone attempting to make sense of the many disparate estimates. Generally, there are two broadly defined IPV contextual categories: a crime context and a conflict context.

Statisticians for the U.S. Bureau of Justice (U.S. BJS) and the CDC draw data from several sources set within a crime context: (a) government reports of assaults from the FBI's *Uniform Crime Reports* (*UCR*), anchored on police reports; (b) government reports of intentional injuries from the National Electronic Injury Surveillance System (NEISS), based on hospital records; (c) government reports of homicide from the FBI's *Supplementary Homicide Reports* (*SHR*), founded on police reports; and (d) government self-report surveys of crime victimization (e.g., NCVS).

Academic research projects have culled data from nationally representative self-report surveys of IPV, often set within a conflict or abuse context: (a) National Family Violence Surveys (NFVS; Straus & Gelles, 1986; Straus, Gelles, & Steinmetz, 1980), (b) National Violence Against Women Survey (NVAWS; Tjaden & Thoennes, 1998a, 2000), and (c) National Survey of Families and Households (NSFH; Zlotnick, Kohn, Peterson, & Pearlstein, 1998). Other researchers have depended on self-report data from clinical or community groups, such as women residing in shelters or visiting a doctor's office, and from the military (Cronin, 1995). Another related survey is the National Comorbidity Survey of mental health and other conditions (Kessler, Molnar, Feurer, & Appelbaum, 2001).

Prevalence and incidence data concerning nonlethal IPV arising from police reports sent to the FBI (*UCR*) are not as comprehensive as the data available on lethal assaults (*SHR*). Currently, the NCVS offers the most extensive data on IPV. Of all crimes (e.g., assaults, rapes, robberies) committed against intimates in 1998, females experienced five times as many incidents of nonfatal violence as did males (Rennison & Welchans, 2000). Of approximately 1 million violent crimes committed by current or former intimates reported in the 1996 NCVS, women were the victims in about

85% of the cases (Greenfeld et al., 1998). The rate of victimization for separated women tends to be 3 times higher than the rate for divorced women and 25 times higher than the rate for married women (Bachman & Saltzman, 1995). (For a discussion of the NCVS, see Chapter 2. For estimates of these assaults, see Table 4 in Appendix B.)

Data from the first NFVS clearly showed that IPV is extremely common (Straus et al., 1980). These compilations provided evidence supporting the impression that women commit as much IPV as men. For the faction of skeptics who have doubted gender symmetry, a more recent survey provided results that were strikingly dissimilar from those of the two National Family Violence Surveys. Tjaden and Thoennes's (1998a, 1998b, 2000) survey of 8,000 men and 8,000 women, using a modified version of CTS1, revealed that men perpetrated far more IPV than did women. Findings on stalking behavior also mirrored gender disparities; that is, there were more frequent male-to-female unwanted behaviors than female-to-male actions (Tjaden & Thoennes, 1998b). (For a summary of national violence survey data, see Table 4 in Appendix B.)

Figures from the sources noted above allow a comparison of data from official crime and injury surveys with self-report data from several non-government-sponsored conflict surveys. According to many surveys using CTS1, physical acts of IPV are most often in the "less severe" range (Aldarondo, 1996; Holtzworth-Munroe & Stuart, 1994; Straus, 1993). These episodes include hitting, throwing things, slapping, and pushing, and the resultant cuts and bruises rarely require hospitalization. Findings about IPV support Johnson's (1995) conception of common couple violence. (For a synopsis of findings, see Table 4 in Appendix B.)

Sexual assault. The preponderance of sexual assault crimes are perpetrated by men against women (Bachman & Saltzman, 1995; Rennison, 2001). Survey data from community or clinical samples of women suggest that sexual assault and rape occur rather frequently in violent marital relationships. Very few noteworthy studies have furnished estimates of marital rape. Russell (1990) determined that in a randomly selected representative community sample of 930 women, 14% of "ever-married" women had been sexually assaulted by their husbands. In another comparison of 115 battered women, 87.4% reported that their husbands thought it was their right to have sex with

their wives even against the women's will. These women suffered from various forms of extreme, sexually related degradation, such as having objects inserted (28.6%) and being sexually abused in front of their children (17.8%); 46% had been coerced into having sex immediately after being discharged from a hospital (usually after giving birth). Forced anal intercourse (52.8%) actually occurred more frequently than vaginal rape (Campbell, 1989b; Campbell & Alford, 1989; Schollenberger et al., 2003).

Bachman and Saltzman (1995) have provided the most useful estimates of intimate sexual assault because of their use of NCVS data and their ability to classify victims according to intimacy status (e.g., married). (These estimates appear in Table 4, Appendix B.) Marital rape occurs in countries other than the United States as well. Of a group of Japanese battered women, for example, 81% reported being forced to have unwanted sex, and 25% reported high levels of forced, violent sex (Yoshihama & Sorenson, 1994).

Some male-to-female partner violence occurs during pregnancy, and the literature on this crime is rather extensive. A number of medical and public health epidemiologists have surveyed patients and concluded that violence during pregnancy may be a more common problem than other conditions for which doctors routinely screen (i.e., initially check) pregnant women, such as high blood pressure. (For estimates of IPV against pregnant women by their partners, see Table 4 in Appendix B.)

Intimate partner violence among cohabitors. Research about cohabitors, as a group separate from college students or married couples, is meager. Most early studies of violence between intimates merged data from cohabitors with data from married individuals into a single category. The rationale was that cohabitors were almost indistinguishable from marrieds. This assumption now seems to have been ill founded. Based on a literature search of publications in Canada and the United States, Brownridge and Halli (2000) noted that the prevalence of IPV among cohabitors is consistently higher than that among spouses. Stets and Straus (1989) determined that the rate of severe violence in their sample, as defined by CTS1, was higher among cohabitors (22%) than among either dating partners (10.6%) or married couples (10.5%) (see also Magdol, Moffitt, Caspi, & Silva, 1998). (For a synopsis of violence estimates among cohabitors for 1990 and later, see Table 4 in Appendix B.)

Estimates of Intimate Partner Violence in Special Populations

Racism, xenophobia, classism, language barriers, cultural beliefs, and other factors have combined to render IPV invisible in certain segments of the American population. To obtain survey data on minority groups, the U.S. Congress has had to address and readdress minority issues legislatively, through the Violence Against Women Act (VAWA) of 1994 and reauthorization of that act in 2000 (see Raj & Silverman, 2002; Violence Against Women Office, 2000). These laws have included requirements to assess the levels of IPV in marginalized groups, such as Native Americans and immigrants, and to improve coverage of African Americans and Hispanics.

Same-sex pairs. In addition to heterosexual comparisons of IPV, researchers have increasingly broadened the scope and number of their investigations to include gay and lesbians populations (see Lockhart, White, Causby, & Isaac, 1994). Official reports of same-sex IPV, however, are generally lacking because police and the FBI do not have any categories suitable for classifying same-sex IPV. Instead, they place these offenders and victims into categories such as "friend" or "acquaintance." Laws against IPV in some states do not even apply to gays and lesbians because gays and lesbians cannot be legally classified as intimate partners. In one of the most distinctive surveys of gay, lesbian, bisexual, and transgendered individuals, Turell (2000) found the following lifetime percentages of physical victimization for 499 respondents: (a) physical violence, 32%; (b) forced sex, 9%; and (c) emotional abuse, 83%. Turell used a collection of 47 items from shelter-developed behavioral checklists to gauge IPV.

These outcomes suggest that the rate of violence within gay and lesbian relationships is about the same as that for heterosexual couples. Some research, however, presents a picture of same-sex victimization that is substantially higher (Bernhard, 2000; Greenwood et al., 2002). Tjaden and Thoennes (2000) found comparable results with one exception: Lesbians experienced significantly more physical violence from their female partners than heterosexual women did from their male partners. Lesbians who had at some point been in heterosexual relationships sustained even more IPV from male partners than from female partners. (For a tabular account of same-sex victimization rates, see Waldner-Haugrud, 1999.) (For additional estimates of same-sex IPV, see Table 4, Appendix B.)

Partners within ethnic/racial minority groups. Studies exploring the relationship between race and IPV have often yielded IPV prevalence rates that are higher in minority communities than in nonminority communities. NCVS data have indicated significantly higher IPV rates for Blacks in the United States relative to Whites and members of other racial groups. According to these data, Black females are victims of IPV at a rate 35% higher than that for White females and 2.5 times higher than that for other races (Rennison & Welchans, 2000). Schollenberger et al. (2003) used a modified version of the Abuse Assessment Screen (Soeken, McFarlane, Parker, & Lominack, 1998) to examine differences between two groups of Black women who received medical care at one health maintenance organization. The IPV victims ($n = 97$), compared with the nonvictims ($n = 109$), had not only significantly more health problems, but also more health problems per medical visit and more emergency room visits.

Surprisingly, Tjaden and Thoennes's (1998a) findings from their national survey of 16,000 men and women did not concur with those of the studies just described. That is, Tjaden and Thoennes did not find large differences between Blacks and Whites. They did, however, find that American Indian/Alaska Natives reported the most IPV and that Asian/Pacific Islanders reported the least. Some racial distinctions appear only when investigators aggregate data into a single category of "minorities." Otherwise, racial subgroups are likely to show significant variations among themselves and with the majority group.

Surveys generally do not uncover major differences in IPV among various ethnic groups. NCVS data have shown that non-Hispanic respondents disclose less, but not significantly less, IPV than Hispanic respondents. In a study of Caucasian women, Mexican American women born in Mexico, and Hispanic women born in the United States, Sorenson and Telles (1991) failed to find any ethnic distinctions.

A review of racial variations in rates of intimate partner homicide (IPH) shows that more minority intimates kill their partners than do nonminority intimates, but research has not routinely taken other variables, such as socioeconomic status (SES), into account. Some nonracial differences that affect IPH rates are as follows: (a) marital status, (b) current coresidency or separation, (c) large male-to-female age discrepancy between partners (Regoeczi, 2001), and (d) reporting biases (Weis, 2001). The most definitive evidence concerning disparities in IPV among different racial groups stems from NCVS data. These data reveal no significant racial differences when SES and gender of the victim are partialed out statistically (Rennison & Planty, 2003). (For estimates of IPV among different racial and ethnic groups, see Table 4, Appendix B.)

Rural populations. An analysis of calls to the National Domestic Violence Hotline (NDVH; at 1-800-799-SAFE) highlights the existence of several understudied populations, including women in rural areas (Danis, Lewis, Trapp, Reid, & Fisher, 1998). The type of IPV characteristic of some rural communities could be designated intimate terrorism. In a descriptive study of 87 rural women visiting an emergency room, Krishnan, Hilbert, and Pase (2001) determined that 41% had ever (lifetime) suffered IPV, and 29% had experienced IPV in their current intimate relationships. Of this group, 18% suffered ongoing abuse from a divorced, separated, or unmarried intimate partner. IPV screening (asking the women questions about possible IPV) by medical personnel was virtually absent in this community, as were any affirmative actions to assist these victims.

Disabled individuals. Disabled victims of IPV must overcome almost insurmountable odds to escape abusive situations. The prevalence of IPV in various disabled populations is unknown, but specialists theorize that disabled women may be 10 times more likely than nondisabled women to be abused (Sobsey, 1994; see also Sundram, 2000). One national survey of physically disabled women found no significant differences between able and disabled groups in terms of reported IPV (Nosek, Howland, & Young, 1997). It is essential to keep in mind, however, that many cognitively disabled people have limited conceptual powers and stunted vocabularies. Studies of IPV in women with severe psychiatric disorders (e.g., schizophrenia) have documented rates varying from 21% to 75% (Briere, Woo, McRae, Foltz, & Sitzman, 1997; Lipschitz et al., 1996). Handicapped women are also at risk for sexual coercion (Weinhardt, 1999).

Immigrants and cross-cultural groups. Anita Raj interviewed 167 educated South Asian women between the ages of 18 and 61 living in the Boston area about IPV. Her results indicated that approximately 35% of the women had sustained physical abuse and 19% had experienced marital sexual assault (cited in Dasgupta, 2000). A study of immigrant farmworkers (primarily Latinas) recently found that 19% had been abused or

sexually assaulted by intimate partners, companions, or family members during the preceding year. The number of assaults ranged from 0 to 70 per woman, with an average of 13.5 (Van Hightower, Gorton, & DeMoss, 2000).

Brownridge and Halli (2002) divided a representative sample of 7,115 Canadian women into three groups: (a) Canadian-born women (5,737), (b) immigrant women from developed countries (844), and (c) immigrant women from developing countries (534). Of these women, the immigrants from developing countries had experienced the highest levels of abuse. Brownridge and Halli suggest that high levels of sexual jealousy in male partners, coupled with educational achievement disparities, serve as a catalyst for IPV among immigrants from developing countries. (For estimates of IPV in these special populations, see Table 4, Appendix B.)

IPV is an immense problem all over the world. As Murphy (2003) notes, "Being born female is dangerous for your health" (p. 205). Poor reproductive and mental health consequences are obvious manifestations of gender inequity across the globe. In a 1983 report, Broude and Greene documented wife beating in 57 of 71 societies, revealing how common and unexceptional this form of violence is throughout the world.

Cultural acceptance of IPV, however, is not uniform in countries other than the United States. Singaporeans, for example, support police intervention in cases of wife assault and expect judges to treat such cases as seriously as, or more seriously than, they would treat similar crimes (Choi & Edleson, 1995). Investigations of IPV in other countries have strongly contributed to the conceptualization of family violence as an outgrowth of patriarchy. Wife assault is more likely to be permitted in societies where men control family economic resources, where conflicts are solved by means of physical force, and where women do not have an equal opportunity to divorce (Brown, 1992). The reverse is true in societies where women are equal to men under the law (Levinson, 1988). In recent years, the devaluation of women and the rampant violence perpetrated against them have become international human rights issues (Levesque, 2001).

Canadian and Australian studies have tended to replicate the findings of U.S. national family violence surveys, or sometimes have indicated even higher levels of IPV (Brinkerhoff & Lupri, 1988; Knight & Hatty, 1992). A Korean account of IPV assessed by CTS1 revealed exceptionally high victimization rates: 37.5% for wives in the year prior to the survey and

23.2% for husbands (Kim & Cho, 1992). Nonetheless, gender differences in injury-causing assaults show a consistent pattern of male-to-female partner violence, whether in Austria (Bernard & Schlaffer, 1992), Nigeria (Kalu, 1993), or Japan (Yoshihama & Sorenson, 1994).

An investigation of spousal homicides in Fiji over an 11-year period revealed that husbands were six times more likely than wives to kill a spouse (Adinkrah, 1999). (For a selection of IPV rates among various ethnic and immigrant groups, see Table 4, Appendix B.)

Gender Perspectives on Intimate Partner Violence

Case History: Mark and Cher—Running for Our Lives

Mark suddenly jumped on me from behind, knocking me to the living room floor. He started choking me and calling me a bitch. Then he forced sex on me right in front of our 12-year-old son, Danny. Danny grabbed the poker near the fireplace and hit his dad on the head, stunning him. I got up and hit Mark on the head as hard as I could with a dining room chair. Then I began to kick him as hard as I could anywhere that I could. I knew he would come after me again when he came to, so I grabbed Danny with one hand and my purse with the other and we ran for our lives.

The preceding case history exemplifies a type of self-defensive female violence. It makes vivid the significance of contextual factors associated with some battered women's violence and the confluence of their emotions: terror, intimidation, desperation, and anger. It also highlights the problems of determining the extent to which Cher's violent actions can be classified as self-defensive. The idea that men and women are equally violent has fueled a continuing debate involving mainstream sociologists (Straus, 1993), feminists (Kurz, 1993), and others. Critics suggest that CTS-defined IPV fails to incorporate the real experiences of IPV from the perspective of victims (Smith, Smith, & Earp, 1999). The phrases "the myth of sexual symmetry in IPV" and "the battered data syndrome" capture the fervor and antagonism of feminists toward claims of gender equivalence (see Dobash, Dobash, Wilson, & Daly, 1992). CTS1 data from community-based (non-clinical) surveys, nonetheless, strongly suggest that IPV is mutual—that is, women commit as much IPV as men (Archer, 2000).

As attention finally turned to issues of defining and measuring interpartner violence, skeptics of the mutual violence theory increasingly indicted CTS1 for its perceived limitations. First, CTS1 fails to account for some important gender dissimilarities, such as strength, injury differentials, and levels of fear (for a review, see White, Smith, Koss, & Figueredo, 2000). Second, some experts contend that a simple counting of violent acts between couples on CTS1 places too much emphasis on frequency and not enough on context—that is, motivations (e.g., self-defense) and outcomes (e.g., interpersonal control) (Browne, 1990). Third, Fantuzzo and Lindquist (1989) assert that the

CTS restricts acts of violence to those that occur in a conflict context; it does not count those that might be unprovoked (for a rebuttal, see Straus, 1999).

Finally, official crime surveys such as the NCVS and reports such as *UCR* and *SHR* all present markedly different findings than those based on CTS1. The latest analysis regarding the debate indicates that IPV is not monolithic. The prevalence rates of CCV or IT depend on the sample sources. Shelter, police, and hospital sources reveal much more IT than community samples (Graham-Kevan & Archer, 2003a). Women are more frequently physically and sexually assaulted, more frequently injured, more frequently stalked, and more frequently murdered by intimates (e.g., Rand, 1997; Rennison & Welchans, 2000). Relative to men, women also suffer more severe consequences from IPV, such as homelessness. Hence questions asked within a crime context do not appear to show gender parity. In response, a number of researchers either modified CTS1 or developed alternative scales (e.g., Kropp & Hart, 2000; Shepard & Campbell, 1992; Tolman, 1989), and Straus and his colleagues (1995) revised CTS1, including injury outcomes and sexual assaults in CTS2.

Many would argue that assumptions of gender equivalence in IPV have had a negative impact on battered women. Criminal justice system personnel, for example, may view women who try to defend themselves physically as being mutual combatants. Police may not identify the primary aggressor when making arrests (Avakame & Fyfe, 2001; Hofford & Harrell, 1993). There also is danger that gender symmetry conceptions may become transposed into societal perceptions that IPV is gender equivalent. Such an assumption draws attention away from the most serious IPV problem, assaults by men against women (Saunders, 2002).

Self-defensive violence. It is difficult to interpret the data gathered to assess self-defensive aggression. Interpretation hinges on the specification of the sequence of the violent events or on the measurement of other background factors (e.g., Barnett, Lee, & Thelen, 1997; Browne, Salomon, & Bassuk, 1999; Hamberger & Arnold, 1991). Clinical studies typically reveal that when assaulted female partners are violent, they are often reacting to what is being done to them, rather than initiating confrontations (Cascardi, Langhinrichsen-Rohling, & Vivian, 1992; Melton & Belknap, 2003). Women may not even use self-defensive violence frequently. An analysis of 9,919 crisis calls to a battered woman's shelter indicated that only 5% of the women had used any self-defensive counterattacks during their most recent battering. All of these self-defensive attempts were unsuccessful and resulted in even more physical injury to the women (Murty & Roebuck, 1992).

In addition to the issue of self-defensive violence, some observers have raised questions about whether women initiate abuse or take other actions. An examination of NCVS data revealed three categories of responses: (a) 43% of female IPV victims used non-confrontational methods (that is, tried to escape or called the police); (b) 34% confronted their partners (self-defense) by struggling and shouting, and 4% of this group defied their partners with weapons; and (c) 23% took no steps to protect themselves (Greenfeld et al., 1998).

A recent account of IPV among men ($n = 119$) and women ($n = 24$) in court-ordered treatment for IPV and another group of women in shelter treatment revealed significant differences. Women in both groups reported that their male partners were significantly more likely to be the first to use violence and to initiate abuse generally. This study did not find, however, that women were always the primary victims of IPV (Hamberger & Guse, 2002). In the final analysis, it may be best not to view IPV victimization as an "either/or" situation, but as a problem of "divergent proportions." Both genders can be violent, but women appear to be victimized more frequently than men.

Lack of couple concordance. It is worth noting that when couples complete surveys or interviews, their reports of IPV do not customarily agree. This lack of concordance undermines the accuracy of IPV reports.

Also, when some researchers report high levels of correspondence, it may be because couples usually do agree on the nonoccurrence of abuse. In one analysis, Caetano, Schafer, Field, and Nelson (2002) drew on 11 modified CTS items in NFVS-1995. They used an **oversampling** of Black and Hispanic couples to achieve a base of 1,635 couples. Within this population, more than half of the events would not have been classified as IPV if couple agreement had been required. The lack of couple agreement adds to the problems of estimating the prevalence and incidence of IPV (Armstrong, Wernke, Medina, & Schafer, 2002).

Fear, power, and control differentials. Fear is a strong motivator of behavior, and the level of fear generated by IPV differs dramatically by gender. Female victims report being very afraid of their violent male partners (Apsler, Cummins, & Carl, 2002; Mirrlees-Black, 1999; Smith et al., 2002), but violent male perpetrators report little fear of female IPV and almost no fear of adverse consequences from the criminal justice system (Carmody & Williams, 1987; see also Barnett et al., 1997).

Many experts have placed IPV within a context of power and control. As Worchester (2002) notes, "Violence by men and women takes place within a social, historical, and economic context in which men's and women's roles, opportunities, and social power differ" (p. 1390). Certainly, cross-cultural evidence indicates that the lower the status of women, the greater their abuse (Levesque, 2001). One review based on economic data demonstrated that women with higher educational attainments, who can equalize their occupational prestige relative to their male partners, experience fewer types of abuse than do their less educated counterparts (Lambert & Firestone, 2000).

SECTION SUMMARY

Taking into account the evolving conceptions of spouse abuse, experts have been working to develop uniform definitions. Consensus is beginning to form about the meaning of words like *violence, assault, battering,* and *abuse,* coupled with concepts such as intention, consequence, and degree of repetition. Authorities are also trying to expand or refine theories in order to capture opinions about abuse in special populations, such as diverse cultures and same-sex pairs. Researchers are beginning to adopt similar constructs encompassing various subcategories of abuse: psychological, economic, stalking, physical, and sexual.

Estimates of the frequency and severity of IPV vary according to the definitions used, the samples investigated, and the types of data collected. Estimates arise from data gathered by the FBI, the NCVS, and several other national surveys. (See Table 4 in Appendix B for summaries of estimates of IPV rates among a number of subpopulations.) Research indicates that survey data from special subpopulations and among cross-cultural groups tend to parallel those obtained from other populations. FBI crime statistics on IPV are incomplete because reporting from police departments is voluntary. Data derived from self-reports, of course, are fraught with problems, such as under-reporting and even intentional falsification. Newer surveys (e.g., NEISS) are assessing injury data.

The estimates of IPV rates from these various sources are not concordant. Surveys set within a crime context (e.g., FBI, NCVS) indicate that IPV is gendered, with males committing a disproportionate amount. National surveys incorporating a conflict context (e.g., NFVS) usually show gender equivalence. Different methods of measuring IPV and findings premised on these assessments have generated considerable debate in the field. In sum, the precise prevalence and incidence of intimate partner abuses and assaults remains unknown.

---·•◦•·---

OUTCOMES OF INTIMATE PARTNER VIOLENCE

Negative outcomes of IPV range from psychological effects (e.g., fear, low self-esteem) to monetary losses and from injuries to disability and even death. The personal and social costs of IPV in the United States are estimated to be in the billions of dollars annually. This section describes some of the injury and homicide outcomes stemming from IPV. Included is a brief reference to the psychological impact of IPV. Social and financial costs of IPV are high and encompass utilization of social service agencies, welfare and homeless agencies, medical services, and treatment programs. This section also provides an overview of criminal justice interventions. Other repercussions of IPV include the escalation of marital dissatisfaction, possibly leading to separation, divorce,

and other family disruptions. As discussed previously, children pay a heavy toll when exposed to IPV.

Injuries

Using the new version of the CTS2, Cantos, Neidig, and O'Leary (1994) demonstrated that topographically similar behaviors (e.g., slapping by a woman or slapping by a man) cause far more injuries, and more severe injuries, to women than to men. A highly gendered pattern occurs in medical injury records, with women sustaining significantly more injuries than men ("Physical Violence," 1996; Rand, 1997; Straus, 1993). The NCVS found that about 50% of female victims of partner aggression report some sort of injury, and about 20% seek medical assistance (Greenfeld et al., 1998).

In a survey of 547 rape victims, 97 of whom were raped by their husbands, 76.7% said they had been physically injured (Stermac, Del Bove, & Addison, 2001). For marital rape victims surveyed in another investigation, the most common injury-related outcome was pain (72%). Some other injuries included anal or vaginal stretching (36.1%), bladder infections (50.9%), vaginal bleeding (29.6%), leakage of urine (32.4%), missed menstrual periods (25%), miscarriages and stillbirths (20.4%), unwanted pregnancies (17.5%), infertility (7.4%), and sexually transmitted diseases (6.5%) (Campbell & Soeken, 1999; Russell, 1990).

Homicides

The relationship between the perpetrator and victim is known in only about 60–70% of homicides in the United States. As one illustration of the complications caused by unknown offender-victim relationships, the Florida Department of Law Enforcement officially recorded only 230 IPHs in 1994, compared with 281 (51 more) counted by a special mortality project that reviewed the same data (Johnson, Li, & Websdale, 1998).

Homicide is the least likely outcome of a domestic assault, but it is the most feared and is a primary basis for formulating criminal justice policy. Male intimates, rather than strangers, commit the majority of known female homicides (Bachman & Saltzman, 1995; Rennison & Welchans, 2000). When women kill, they most often kill male intimates (Greenfeld et al., 1998). Rates of IPH are higher for cohabitors (Riedel & Best,

1998), for couples in which the women are at least 10 years younger than their intimate partners (Wilson & Daly, 1992), and among minority groups (Riedel & Best, 1998; Wilson & Daly, 1992). (For the IPH estimates compiled by Greenfeld et al., 1998, see Table 4, Appendix B.)

A subcategory of lethal assault is the combined homicide-suicide. An analysis of homicide-suicide deaths in Galveston County, Texas, established that of 20 such events, 17 were consortial—that is, the victims were intimate partners of the perpetrators (wives/girlfriends). All but one of the perpetrators was male (Felthous et al., 2001). Experts in the state of Washington claim that homicide rates ought to include the collateral deaths of family and friends of IPV victims (Washington State Coalition Against Domestic Violence, 2000). (For a review of Canadian intimate partner homicides, see Regoeczi, 2001. For the most current estimates of IPH, see Table 4, Appendix B.)

Psychological Effects

Research reveals that psychological abuse is the most common form of IPV, and many experts assert that such abuse is extremely debilitating. It plays a pivotal role in diminishing victims' ability to leave abusive relationships (Follingstad & DeHart, 2000; Glaser, 2002; Mazzeo & Espelage, 2002). (For a comprehensive discussion of the devastating effects of psychological abuse, such as PTSD and revictimization, see Chapter 10.)

Monetary Costs #4

In many respects, the costs of IPV are immeasurable. One approach researchers have used to gauge costs is to estimate the financial burden of treating injuries and providing mental health care for victims. Another tactic has been to investigate the costs of IPV-related homelessness and welfare. Finally, agencies within the U.S. criminal justice system have begun to scrutinize the costs of processing battery cases. One estimate of the annual cost of IPV for American society is $5.8 billion (National Center for Injury Prevention and Control [NCIPC], 2003). (For a review of IPV costs, see Hartmann, Laurence, Spalter-Roth, & Zuckerman, 1997.)

Health care. Women victimized by IPV seek health care more frequently than do nonvictimized women (Ulrich et al., 2003). The most comprehensive estimates of the medical costs of IPV are derived from the NVAWS. This survey found that of 1,451 women who suffered physical assaults, 41.5% were injured. Of these, 28.5% received medical care as follows: (a) hospital care, 78.6%; (b) physician's care, 51.8%; (c) ambulance/paramedic care, 14.9%; (d) dental care, 9.5%; and (e) physical therapy, 8.9%. When comparable information about rapes and stalking is included, the NCIPC (2003) estimates costs at $4.1 billion annually for medical and mental health care (see also Wisner, Gilmer, & Saltzman, 1999). Total paid days lost to women for rape, physical assault, and stalking is $7,964,248 annually in the United States (NCIPC, 2003).

Homelessness. Battering also increases homelessness and welfare costs. Although unemployment and lack of education are the primary causes of homelessness in general, family violence and other forms of victimization appear to be the major causes of female homelessness (e.g., Virginia Coalition for the Homeless, 1995; Waxman & Trupin, 1997). Various researchers have estimated that IPV affects 21% to 64% of homeless shelter clients (e.g., Bassuk et al., 1996; National Low-Income Housing Commission, 1998).

It costs social agencies roughly $68 per person per day to provide housing and services for shelter clients (Raphael & Tolman, 1997). Interestingly, one contextual analysis of police responses to calls for service ascertained that "women's odds of reporting homelessness were reduced 30% if police officers responded positively" (Baker, Cook, & Norris, 2003, p. 754). Currie (1998) reports that in New Hampshire, government officials diverted some resources for battered women's shelters to a men's shelter.

Criminal justice system processing. The police, court, probation, and prison costs associated with battering are also difficult to estimate. New York City tallied 12,724 IPV arrests in 1 year at an average cost of $3,241 per arrest. Including these police costs and those for the court and detention, the city paid at least $41 million (see Zorza, 1994). A federal survey of correctional facilities established that 20,170 male prisoners were incarcerated in 1991 for harming intimate partners, at an annual average cost of $15,513 per inmate (U.S. BJS, 1992a).

Court-mandated counseling for batterers cost from $22 to $32 per session across four sites in 1995–1996. In this case, batterers bore close to 50% of the costs for these programs. Foundations and other charitable agencies funded much of the remainder. A preliminary analysis of court costs yielded an estimate of $158 per batterer plus $86 for any incremental reviews. Probation cost about $130 per year per batterer (an expense borne by taxpayers). A conviction accompanied by a sentence of 30 days in jail cost roughly $2,000 per batterer. A fine and fee for court costs to be paid by the IPV perpetrator came to $172 per batterer (Jones, 2000).

SECTION SUMMARY

The outcomes of IPV range from increased stress to negative psychological effects, as well as from injuries to death. Some problems continue over victims' lifetimes. In addition to the physical and psychological costs of IPV, the financial costs to society are very high. Victims use more medical services, and many become homeless and need shelter. Criminal justice processing of IPV offenders creates additional individual and societal expenses. In sum, not only do victims and their offspring pay a terrible price for IPV, but society also pays.

EXPLAINING INTIMATE PARTNER VIOLENCE

Examinations of possible causes of IPV often center on social-structural dimensions, such as age and gender, cultural factors, and socialization. This section addresses some of the more traditional explanations: structural characteristics (e.g., age, gender, race, SES), cultural factors (e.g., social acceptance of violence, patriarchy), socialization, and interpersonal interaction patterns (marital conflict). A discussion of these causes and two well-known correlates of IPV, alcohol use and relationship dissatisfaction, help explain how IPV occurs within a larger social context that serves to promote or inhibit its occurrence. Johnson and Ferraro (2000) argue that the ability to make distinctions is central to understanding IPV, noting that it is important to differentiate among "types of violence, motives of perpetrators, the social locations of both partners, and the cultural contexts in which violence occurs" (p. 948).

Social-Structural Variables

Researchers use structural factors such as age, gender, SES, and race/ethnicity to explain and predict family violence. It is important to remember, however, that while these factors explain patterns and variation in rates of IPV, they cannot predict precisely which individuals will or will not become perpetrators or victims.

Age and gender. The majority of studies show that youthful partners (age 16 to 24) are the most violent (Greenfeld et al., 1998). As noted previously, government estimates (*UCR, SHR,* NCVS) suggest that males, relative to females, commit a significantly greater proportion of nonlethal and lethal assault (Bachman & Saltzman, 1995; Greenfeld et al., 1998). Large representative samples using other self-report data indicate that women are as frequently violent as men and as likely as men to initiate violence toward intimates (Schafer, Caetano, & Clark, 1998; Straus & Gelles, 1986). (For estimates of assaults by gender, see Table 4, Appendix B.)

Racial/ethnic diversity. As discussed previously, when data are aggregated, rates of IPV are significantly higher among members of minority groups than among nonminorities. Otherwise, findings about racial differences are mixed. In a correlational comparison based on 60 respondents, for example, Smith and Chiricos (2003) found that the racial/ethnic makeup of Florida counties was the strongest predictor of male-to-female partner violence. Being maritally separated was the second-strongest predictor. Other investigators have questioned the relationship between IPV and race, arguing that when analyses control for demographic and socioeconomic factors, minorities are no more likely than nonminorities to be violent (Hutchison, Hirschel, & Pesackis, 1994; Lauritsen & White, 2001). One study that examined IPV frequency by African American and European American men in the military, for example, failed to find significant differences between these groups (Cronin, 1995). A different military comparison, however, indicated that Blacks used significantly higher levels of IPV than did Whites (Rosen, Parmley, Knudson, & Fancher, 2002).

Socioeconomic diversity. Although IPV occurs in every socioeconomic group, the NFVS provides self-report evidence that it is more prevalent in blue-collar and lower-class families than in others (Hutchison et al., 1994; O'Donnell, Smith, & Madison, 2002). NCVS victimization data for 1993 to 1998 also demonstrated significantly higher IPV rates for women, but not men, with annual incomes less than $7,500. These rates were seven times higher than those for women with the highest incomes, $75,000 or more (Rennison & Welchans, 2000).

Religious diversity. Very little research on IPV has included religion among the characteristics examined. Some current religious groups rob women of equality with men, going so far as to incorporate male dominance into their by-laws (Niebuhr, 1998). Furthermore, most denominations do not approve of homosexuality, thus complicating help seeking for same-sex IPV victims (Lacayo, Barovick, Cloud, & Duffy, 1998). On a more positive note, in two evaluations, female IPV victims judged spiritual beliefs to be beneficial and important (Farrell, 1996; Humphreys, Lee, Neylan, & Marmar, 1999b).

Cultural Variables in the United States

Case History: Ben and Lori—Making Up Is Not Hard to Do

At an after-theater party that Ben and Lori attended on their vacation, Ben struck up a conversation with Vanessa, a 20-year-old ingenue from the Dominican Republic. When Lori took note of Ben's "interest" in Vanessa, she began flirting with one of the theater company's young male dancers, Danny. Lori made a show of "kicking back" with Danny, requesting slow music, rubbing up against him while they danced, and asking him to bring her several glasses of wine. The next thing she knew, Ben was out of sight and so was Vanessa. Lori stormed out of the party with Danny in hot pursuit.

As Lori walked down Broadway at midnight, Ben came out of nowhere and pleaded with her to come back to the party. Lori slapped his face, screamed that he was a "cheat," and marched on toward their hotel. Ben tried to stop her by pinning her to a wall. He accused her of being "turned on" by Danny, so Lori taunted Ben, saying things like "Young guys in tight pants look good to me!" When Ben couldn't shut Lori up, he slapped her once and twisted her arm behind her back. When he let go, Lori ran crying to their hotel.

Inside their room, Lori slammed things around and insisted that Ben no longer loved her. She threw Ben's jacket to the floor and stomped all over it. Ben said that Lori ought to know that he loved her. Didn't she know that he thought she was the "sexiest woman at the party, so blond, so cool, so beautiful"? Lori burst into tears and told Ben that she wanted only him. He grabbed her and began kissing her passionately.

The "real" party lasted until 3:00 a.m. Lori and Ben had learned long ago that a few slaps "here and there" were just part of their relationship. After all, they weren't really violent, Lori said, because they loved each other and no one ever got hurt.

This case history provides an example of how many couples view a certain amount of aggression as acceptable in their relationships. Cultural factors can also be useful in explaining IPV. Some cultures accept violence; others condemn it. In some cultures, such as Brazil, a husband's violence against an unfaithful wife practically restores the husband's honor (Vandello & Cohen, 2003). Many authorities place partial blame for the widespread acceptance of violence in U.S. culture on the content of television programming as well as movies, sports, toys, and video games (Bushman & Anderson, 2001). Others cite approval of violence within the home as a contributing factor. For some, the most crucial element is cultural recognition of male dominance.

Acceptance of violence. At the same time the social problem of IPV is provoking more and more public outrage among Americans, on a more personal level its acceptance remains at surprisingly high levels. One inquiry contrasted the beliefs of 293 abused women in a given community with those of women in two comparison groups, 431 women who had an abused friend and 472 other women. In terms of the causes of IPV, the abused women clearly indicted social tolerance of IPV and men's desire to control women (Nabi & Horner, 2001). Sadly, it took the murder of Ronald Goldman and Nicole Simpson in June 1994 and the ensuing televised trial of O.J. Simpson to bring domestic abuse to the forefront of the nation's attention (Klein, Campbell, Soler, & Ghez, 1997).

In 1992 and 1995, researchers conducted two different types of public opinion polls that included questions about attitudes toward domestic violence (Klein et al., 1997). The 1992 poll found that Americans ranked domestic violence as fifth on a list of public concerns, with only 34% of the total respondents agreeing that it is an extremely important topic. By 1995, domestic violence ranked first among social concerns, with 83% of respondents evaluating it as an extremely important social issue. At that time, the respondents also thought that public intervention was necessary (82%), especially if an injury occurred (96%). The principal reason they cited for the necessity of public intervention, however, was to protect children, not women.

Cross-cultural accounts of IPV have disclosed differences in beliefs from culture to culture. In one survey of Arab Palestinian husbands, 41% agreed that "it would do some wives good to be beaten by their husbands." Another study showed that even a substantial percentage of Palestinian women (66%) still considered wife beating justified under certain circumstances, such as when a wife is sexually unfaithful or when she challenges her husband's manhood (see Haj-Yahia, 1998a, 1998b). In contrast, Canadian men show strong support for programs aimed at ending men's violence against women. In one study of Canadian men, 66% of respondents said they believed that men were not doing enough to stop violence against women, and 58% thought the Canadian government was not doing enough (White Ribbon Campaign, n.d.).

Research has indicated that men and women generally hold different attitudes and beliefs about male-perpetrated IPV. As one illustration, West and Wandrei (2002) found in a sample of college students that men were significantly more likely than women to hold attitudes condoning IPV, and that women were significantly more likely than men to condemn IPV. The men in this sample also judged female IPV victims as more provocative and more to blame for IPV than did the women.

Patriarchy. The attitude that IPV is acceptable may have its roots in patriarchy (Tiff, 1993). Male IPV perpetrators, for example, might think that they have the right to control and punish their female partners (Gamache, 1991; Sleutel, 1998). The degree to which patriarchy can be used to explain IPV, however, is questionable. Variability in attributing IPV to patriarchy originates both from the type of information utilized and the aspect of patriarchy examined (male dominance, status, privilege or power, and female dependence).

Some observers insist that patriarchal theories are inadequate to account for IPV. Dutton (1994), for example, contends that if patriarchy were the predominant cause of wife beating, nearly all men socialized in male dominance would be wife beaters. Using CTS1 data, however, Straus et al. (1980) showed that less than 30% of men in the United States had ever physically abused their female partners even once over the lifetime of their marriages. On the other hand, accounts based on female dependence seem to support patriarchal explanations of wife abuse. Rates of violence are higher among couples in which the women have little work experience, few financial resources, and few alternatives to marriage (Kalmuss & Straus, 1990).

Socialization

Socialization plays a pivotal role in transgenerational explanations for IPV. Research has frequently shown that men exposed to parental violence and men who have been abused themselves are substantially more likely to be violent toward their spouses than are men who have not been exposed to violence (e.g., Margolin, John, & Foo, 1998; Moffitt & Caspi, 1999). Although inconclusive, some evidence suggests that females exposed to interparental aggression are somewhat more likely to become victims of IPV (Doumas, Margolin, & John, 1994; Foo & Margolin, 1995). On the other hand, socialization cannot account for the number of people who perpetrate IPV but did not come from abusive homes or for the large number of people from abusive households who do not engage in IPV (Bennett, Tolman, Rogalski, & Srinivasaraghavan, 1994).

Studies are beginning to evaluate the role of socialization as it applies to the learning of cognitive or attitudinal variables that allow or encourage IPV (e.g., Barnett, Fagan, & Booker, 1991). One team of investigators, for example, has proposed that ineffective problem-solving strategies learned in childhood carry over into adult relationships and precipitate IPV (Choice, Lamke, & Pittman, 1995). Another research team found evidence linking proneness to shame learned in childhood with adult marital male-to-female violence (Dutton, Van Ginkel, & Starzomski, 1995). Fear of abandonment and emotional dependency stemming from childhood experiences may also mediate IPV (i.e., serve as an intervening variable) (Murphy, Meyer, & O'Leary, 1994).

Correlates of Intimate Partner Violence

In addition to cultural acceptance of IPV and exposure to parental violence during childhood, alcohol abuse and marital dissatisfaction are often associated with IPV. Throughout history, many individuals have blamed IPV on alcohol abuse. Also, one of the most common erroneous assumptions people make is that a happily married man would never hit his wife.

An Interview With
Claire Renzetti

"I am gravely concerned that the progress activists have made in addressing violence against women will begin—indeed, already has begun—to erode."

Claire Renzetti is Professor of Sociology at St. Joseph's University in Philadelphia. She received her doctorate in sociology at the University of Delaware. She has been the recipient of many awards, grants, and fellowships from her own university, the American Society of Criminology, the American Sociological Association, and the National Science Foundation. She was a Fulbright Senior Scholar at the Centre for Socio-Legal Studies at La Trobe University, Bundoora, Victoria, Australia, in 1993. She has written or coauthored a large number of scientific papers on a variety of topics: lesbian battering, violence against women, public housing, rape, and understanding diversity. She was the spark that ignited the interest of professionals in same-sex battering. She is active in professional organizations such as the American Society of Criminology and has served as chairperson and held other elected offices in these groups. What is most striking about Dr. Renzetti is her prolific editorial work. She has been on the editorial boards of several professional journals and is currently on the boards of *Critical Criminology, Criminal Justice: The International Journal of Policy and Practice,* and *Sociological Perspectives.* She is the founding editor of *Violence Against Women: An International and Interdisciplinary Journal.* She is coeditor of the Sage Violence Against Women book series and editor of the

Alcohol and drug abuse. Male IPV perpetrators in one survey reported using drugs and alcohol as follows: (a) 19% consumed only alcohol, (b) 18% used only illicit drugs, and (c) 30% both drank and used drugs. (Willson et al., 2000). There is little doubt that drinking can facilitate aggressive behavior (e.g., Bushman & Cooper, 1990), and Flanzer (1993) states flatly that "alcoholism causes family violence" (p. 171). Coker, Smith, McKeown, and Melissa (2000) found that drug or alcohol abuse was a significant correlate of physical, sexual, and/or emotional abuse.

Men with alcohol problems tend to perpetrate IPV more frequently and seriously than do men free of alcohol problems (Brecklin, 2002; O'Farrell, Fals-Stewart, Murphy, & Murphy, 2003). Female IPV victims living with heavy drinkers have reported that threats and assaults are strongly related to drunkenness, not just drinking (Hutchison, 1999a). In a longitudinal study, Fals-Stewart (2003) had men in treatment for IPV and IPV perpetrators entering an alcohol treatment program keep daily diaries of their IPV and alcohol consumption. These data indicated that the odds of IPV perpetration were 8 to 11 times higher on days when the men drank relative to days when they did not consume alcohol.

It appears, however, that alcohol use is not uniformly causally related to IPV (Zubretsky & Digirolamo,

Northeastern University Press book series Gender, Law and Crime. She is a frequent panelist and a popular keynote speaker at professional meetings and an avid contributor to her community.

Q: What attracted you to the field of family violence?

A: I became interested in violence against women, especially poor and marginalized women, because of my lifelong concern about inequality and social justice. In fact, this is what motivated me to conduct research on and write a book about battering in the lesbian community.

Q: What shaped your approach to the field?

A: The feminist movement of the 1970s had the greatest influence on my approach to the problem of violence against women. It raised my awareness of the many myths that hampered our understanding of the problem of violence against women and that resulted in unjust treatment of victims.

Q: What professional interests are you pursuing at this time?

A: Currently, my major research focus is on violence against women who live in public housing developments. The topics I investigate are how poverty and the life problems associated with poverty increase the risk of violent victimization among women, and how factors such as collective efficacy might lower this risk.

Q: Given your many activities, what do you think is your major contribution to the field of family violence?

A: My major contribution to the field of family violence has been to found the journal *Violence Against Women* in 1995. The journal was originally published quarterly, but went to monthly publication in 1999. The journal provides a forum for researchers, clinicians, and practitioners in various fields as well as activists and advocates to share their work with one another. A major goal of the journal is to develop dialogue across disciplines and occupations, so that people in different areas are not only aware of one another's work, but can benefit from it. It is extremely exciting and gratifying for me to facilitate this process.

Q: What concerns do you have about government policies?

A: I am gravely concerned that the progress activists have made in addressing violence against women will begin—indeed, already has begun—to erode. Politicians currently in power are not especially concerned about problems of women. Advocates, researchers, clinicians, and practitioners need to set aside their differences and disagreements and work together to preserve important legislation and programs that protect women and children from intimate violence. This includes not only the Violence Against Women Act and funding for shelters, hotlines, and other services, but also legislation such as Title IX and Title VII and court decisions such as *Roe v. Wade*—legislation and programs that empower women and girls and give them equitable access to opportunities previously afforded only to men. Efforts must also be directed toward getting women greater social assistance—for food, housing, and medical care—which will be difficult at best in an era of significantly reduced social spending and tax cuts as well as an economic downturn. Education, money, jobs, good and responsive health care—all help keep women and their children safe and reduce their risk of violent victimization and revictimization.

1994). Men who batter when they are drinking may also batter when they are sober, and the vast majority of men who consume even large quantities of alcohol never batter female partners at all (Barnett & Fagan, 1993; Fals-Stewart, 2003). Relatedly, among 180 women in one study sample, 30% experienced IPV perpetrated by male partners who had no histories of drug or alcohol use (Willson et al., 2000). In a careful critique, O'Farrell et al. (2003) enumerate several alternative explanations for their findings. They suggest that a third variable, such as antisocial personality traits, might account for the relationship between IPV and alcohol consumption. Further, stress and other factors may be antecedents to both drinking and spouse abuse (see Barnett & Fagan, 1993; Copenhaver, Lash, & Eisler, 2000).

Marital dissatisfaction. Marital dissatisfaction may play an important role in IPV. Kropp, Hart, Webster, and Eaves (1995) assert that continuing marital dissatisfaction may predict IPV recidivism. Several researchers have reported significant correlations between marital dissatisfaction and IPV (Byrne & Arias, 1997; Leonard & Senchak, 1993). Nonetheless, studies of marital satisfaction show that many partner-violent men score above the mean on marital satisfaction tests (Locke & Wallace, 1959; Spanier, 1976), and many nonpartner-violent men score below the mean (e.g., Lawrence & Bradbury, 2001; Pan et al., 1994; Sagrestano, Heavey, & Christensen, 1999). Rogge and Bradbury (1999) traced marital dissatisfaction and relationship dissolution over a 4-year period, starting with newlyweds. They demonstrated that CTS1 aggression scores discriminated between separated/divorced couples and those who were still married. Communication patterns predicted couples' scores on a measure of marital satisfaction (Locke & Wallace, 1959).

SECTION SUMMARY

Available information shows that younger people are more frequent perpetrators of IPV than older people. The extent of gender differences found in surveys depends heavily on the measurement scales employed. Whether women and men perpetrate IPV equally remains unresolved in the minds of some experts. Studies concerning rates of IPV among various racial/ethnic groups in the United States have yielded mixed results. Aggregated data clearly show substantially more IPV among minorities, but scrutiny of separate groups reveals varying levels of IPV, with Asian Americans exhibiting the lowest amount. Least certain is whether IPV occurs more frequently or with greater severity within any particular ethnic minority group.

IPV probably does occur more frequently among members of the lower socioeconomic classes. Most evidence indicates that poorer individuals suffer from more IPV than do wealthier people. Nonetheless, IPV occurs at every income level and social status. The greater documented preponderance of cases in low-SES groups and among some minority groups may partially stem from other variables, such as stress or illness. Religious beliefs of some faith communities emphasize male dominance, beliefs that may be detrimental to women. A number of concerned individuals are urging change among clergy.

Criminologists, sociologists, and anthropologists have uncovered a number of cultural factors conducive to IPV. First, American culture accepts a certain amount of relationship violence as normative, and standards are not changing rapidly. Second, patriarchal attitudes have made it possible for men to control women's lives, especially in other countries. Although patriarchy

contributes to IPV, it is not the sole cause. Research on same-sex pairs and the finding that 70% of American men probably never assault their female partners implies that patriarchy cannot totally account for IPV.

Certain socialization practices are significantly related to IPV, but social learning theory appears inadequate as a complete explanation. New approaches suggest that behaviors learned in childhood, such as inadequate problem-solving skills, function as cognitive mediators of aggression and may therefore lend support to social learning theory models.

Alcohol abuse and relationship dissatisfaction may characterize one or both members of maritally violent couples. Although marital dissatisfaction occurs frequently in male IPV perpetrators, it may not be causally related to IPV.

PRACTICE, POLICY, AND PREVENTION ISSUES

Community officials and social agencies have a responsibility to respond to IPV. This section summarizes the kinds of responses needed from groups such as the clergy, medical professionals, and agencies providing shelter services. The section also provides a brief overview of the practices and policies of the criminal justice system across the United States, both in historical perspective and in the present.

Community Responses to Intimate Partner Violence

Most professionals and the community agencies described below are "first responders" who have an obligation to determine whether violence has occurred and what services are needed (Glowa, Frasier, & Newton, 2002; Harway et al., 2002; Marshall, Benton, & Brazier, 2000). Some are more effective than others in addressing IPV.

The clergy. In a 1986 journal article, Bowker and Maurer reported that after the first battering incident, wives are more likely to contact the clergy than any other helping group except the police. The findings of two surveys, however, suggest that members of the clergy have little enthusiasm for training geared toward improving their assistance to IPV victims (Johnson & Bondurant, 1992; Reyes, 1999). Fortunately, a number of concerned individuals within faith communities are advocating that members of the clergy change their responses to IPV. Miles (2002), for instance, asserts that clergy should hold Christian men accountable for their IPV and stop blaming the victims. Neuger (2002) points out that clergy must include the topic of IPV during premarital counseling.

Health care providers and insurance companies. Health care providers, like other segments of U.S. society, have tended to view IPV as a private matter. As Barbara Seaman of the National Council on Women's Health has noted, however, the health care system should ideally be the first entry point for societal intervention in this problem (see "Focus," 1994). If medical personnel respond appropriately, by helping victims identify the problem as IPV, they may help victims begin the long road to recovery. For some assaulted IPV victims, hospital emergency room staff may be the first contacts they have regarding the abuse. Medical personnel need ongoing training to help them learn how best to screen patients for IPV and how to intervene in IPV cases (Alpert & Cohen, 1997).

In one study with 41 battered women, researchers found that medical screening for IPV had both positive and negative effects for the women. Positive effects for the victims included their recognition that the violence was a problem, decreased isolation, and feeling that the medical provider cared. Negative outcomes included the victims' feeling judged by the provider, increased anxiety about the unknown, finding the screening process cumbersome and intrusive, and disappointment in the provider's reactions to disclosure (Chang et al., 2003).

A little more than a decade ago, the Joint Commission for the Accreditation of Health Care Organizations established a policy that hospital emergency room personnel "had to identify" battered women ("Focus," 1994). In response to such policy changes, the American Medical Association now makes a booklet available for doctors' use in addressing family violence (Children's Safety Network, 1992). The literature on medical screening for IPV has also mushroomed over the past decade. (For a list of educational resources covering screening issues, click on the "Additional Materials" button at the link for this volume on the Sage Publications Web site at the URL noted above.)

Medical professionals need more training if they are to be effective in screening and referring IPV victims. Davis, Parks, Kaups, Bennink, and Bilello (2003) surveyed 1,550 emergency room patients along with their medical records and projected that 217 (14%) cases resulted from IPV. Further investigation confirmed that 27 (12.4%) of these 217 cases were IPV related. Medical personnel, however, asked only 12 patients screening questions, and only 7 received appropriate referrals. Medical professionals also require training in how to document incidents of domestic violence (Isaac & Enos, 2001). Medical schools need to expand their curricula to incorporate training about IPV and the doctor's role in helping to prevent it (Alpert & Cohen, 1997; Alpert, Tonkin, Seeherman, & Holtz, 1998; Schornstein, 1997).

Counseling responses. Psychologists and psychiatrists, as a group, have frequently failed to recognize the existence of IPV in the clients they treat. Hansen, Harway, and Cervantes (1991) used two hypothetical cases to study family therapists' ability to recognize IPV and recommend appropriate protection strategies. In one of two "test" stories, Carol told her therapist privately that she had sought an order of protection against her partner, James, because he "grabbed her and threw her on the floor in a violent manner and then struck her" (p. 235). In the other vignette, Beth claimed that Tony "punched her in the back and stomach and caused her to miscarry" (p. 235). Tony asserted that Beth tried to hit him and punched herself in the back. Of the 362 therapists in the study sample, 22% identified the problem as violence and 17% as an abusive relationship. Others classified the problem as conflict (8%), anger (5%), a power struggle (4%), lack of control (1%), or other type of conflict (4%). The remaining 39% selected nonconflict options, such as lack of communication, trust, or secrecy. Only 45% of the therapists advised crisis intervention; 48% called for further assessment, 60% suggested work on a nonviolent marital problem, and 28% recommended couples' counseling. Only 10% addressed the need for protection.

It is imperative that counselors screen clients for interpersonal violence (Heyman, Feldbau-Kohn, Ehrensaft, Langhinrichsen-Rohling, & O'Leary, 2001; Young, Barker-Collo, & Harrison, 2002). The major rationale for screening couples seeking marital therapy is that they rarely report physical violence spontaneously. In fact, in one study of 136 couples (272 spouses), less than 6% of the spouses reported IPV as a presenting problem. This was true although measurements indicated that approximately 57% were abusive in some manner (Ehrensaft & Vivian,

An Interview With
Jacquelyn Campbell

"It is crucial for the federal government to fund large research grants, such as one to investigate the interface of HIV and IPV. It is also crucial for the federal government to support more research training for doctoral students and more persons of diverse fields."

Jacquelyn Campbell is a world-recognized researcher and academician who obtained her doctorate in nursing at the University of Rochester. Currently, she is an endowed professor at Johns Hopkins University School of Nursing, where she teaches, supervises doctoral students, and conducts her own research. The breadth, quality, and creativity of her research is truly amazing. She is a pacesetter in the field of family violence, as reflected in her dedicated and effective efforts to emphasize the role of health professionals in the battle against intimate partner violence. She is a woman of many firsts: She is one of the first academicians to investigate female homicide and one of the first researchers to specify the negative health outcomes suffered by female IPV victims. She is also one of the first to include minority group women

1996). (For a list of suitable screening instruments assembled by an American Psychological Association task force on IPV [Harway et al., 2002], click on the "Additional Materials" button at the link for this volume on the Sage Publications Web site at the URL noted above.)

A number of professionals have called attention to the need for therapists to develop cultural competence in treating minority group clients (Bell & Mattis, 2000; Bonder, Martin, & Miracle, 2001; Purewal & Ganesh, 2000). If nothing else, therapists need to be sensitive to cultural differences that may contribute to IPV perpetration and victimization. Others have pointed out the need for new guidelines on multicultural education research, practice, and organizational change (American Psychological Association, 2003). It is also true that clinical experts called to testify in court concerning issues connected to family violence, such as custody cases, need to be aware of cultural differences (Jaffe & Geffner, 1998).

Shelters and safe homes. Because battered women and their children are often destitute and homeless, victims' advocates have worked to develop emergency shelters and safe homes. Many battered women are unaware of these resources, and those who know about them frequently encounter difficulty finding space available (Frisch & MacKenzie, 1991; Irvine, 1990). In an analysis of calls to the National Domestic Violence Hotline, for example, Danis et al. (1998) discovered that the greatest gap in services for IPV victims was inadequate shelter capacity. These shortages were much more prevalent in certain areas, such as rural communities, than in others.

as research participants and research colleagues. Finally, she is one of the first to collaborate with other specialists in the field and to propose methods for improved cooperation.

Q: How did you become interested in the field of family violence?

A: I became interested in domestic violence because of my master's thesis on homicide of women (1980). I found that intimate male partners killed the majority of murdered women and that intimate male partners had abused most of these women before they killed them.

Q: What shaped your interest in the field of family violence?

A: My realization that nursing could assess and intervene with battered women and thereby help prevent homicide of women and improve women's health shaped my approach to the field.

Q: What are your research and advocacy interests at this time?

A: Currently, my major research focus is the prevention of and health care interventions for intimate partner violence (including forced sex) and risk assessment for intimate partner homicide. The topics I investigate are abuse during pregnancy, intimate partner forced sex, mental health responses to IPV, other health effects of IPV, and risk of femicide.

Q: What has been your major contribution to the field of family violence?

A: My major contribution to the field has been to examine the health effects of IPV, including forced sex, identify the role of nursing in the prevention of and intervention for IPV, development of the Danger Assessment instrument, and insistence on attention to cultural influences in the field of IPV.

Q: What would you do if you had a large research grant?

A: I would like to study the interface of HIV and IPV, especially forced sex and effective interventions in health care systems in the U.S. and internationally.

Q: In your opinion, what should policy makers do? Do you have any policy recommendations?

A: It is crucial for the federal government to fund large research grants, such as one to investigate the interface of HIV and IPV. It is also crucial for the federal government to support more research training for doctoral students and more persons of diverse fields.

Shelters for battered women turn away approximately 32% of applicants because of lack of resources (U.S. Conference of Mayors, 1998). In Los Angeles County, as of 1994 there were 411 beds and cribs in 18 shelters to serve 3.5 million women over the age of 14. The shelters had to turn down requests from 8,840 families (Burke, 1995). Older women, lesbians, immigrants, and disabled women may find it nearly impossible to obtain refuge because many shelters cannot offer them suitable services (e.g., bilingual staff). In their analysis of calls to the NDVH, Danis et al. (1998) found that the third-largest gap in society's response to IPV victims is permanent, affordable housing.

Welfare services. A recent longitudinal account of 278 women leaving shelters for IPV victims established that 83% were receiving public assistance (Evans, Wells, & Chan, 2000). Nevertheless, the inadequacy of the welfare services available to many IPV victims has stunned some observers. One philosophically minded academician has suggested that it is time for the states to charter welfare departments in order to make them more accountable to clients (Stoesz, 2002).

SECTION SUMMARY

Among the professionals to whom IPV victims most often turn for help are members of the clergy, doctors, and counselors. The responses of all these community agents generally reflect insufficient knowledge and a concomitant need for training.

Because IPV victims need a large number of community services, it is important that professionals be capable of assessing the quantity and quality of services available. Clergy, medical doctors, and mental health professionals have been slow to recognize the plight of victims and to obtain the requisite knowledge about how to help. Some IPV victims find their religious beliefs helpful, but others are disappointed in the low level of help clergy offer. The role of male dominance espoused by some religions and religious leaders is worrisome to some family violence professionals, who fear that such views will be used to justify male-to-female IPV.

Health care providers need a better understanding of IPV and their potential role for intervening. One possible point of intervention occurs when IPV victims interact with hospital emergency room personnel. In 1992, the American Medical Association began distributing a booklet to help doctors recognize and handle domestic violence cases appropriately. It is imperative that doctors and other medical personnel screen patients for IPV. It would be highly beneficial if personnel could expand screening to other areas as well, such as pediatrics.

Mental health practitioners need to expand their knowledge of IPV and diminish any biases they might have toward the individuals involved. It is urgent that they use appropriate tools to screen clients for IPV. In addition, practitioners need to enhance their understanding of special populations and consider developing expertise with certain groups, such as Native Americans, people living in rural areas, immigrants, and the disabled. Mental health counselors need to make a concerted effort to become knowledgeable about IPV, to screen clients for IPV, and to become conversant with suitable treatments.

Much assistance for battered women has accrued from the efforts of advocates who have spearheaded efforts to establish shelters and safe homes. Shelter space, however, is so woefully inadequate that large numbers of families fleeing domestic assault cannot find refuge. Society needs to provide more emergency housing for victims and continue efforts to help victims survive emotionally and financially.

Criminal Justice System Responses to Intimate Partner Violence

Case History: Karen and Richard Graves

Over a year's time, 2 different police departments responded to 22 calls from Karen and Richard Graves' residence. None of the police officers involved was aware of any of the previous calls. Although Richard seriously injured Karen by hitting her with the baby's car seat, stomping on her ear, and assaulting her, several different judges set aside 6 different warrants for Richard's arrest. Karen and Richard appeared before 10 different judges (none of whom had any notification of previous cases and rulings) at 16 hearings in the local family and criminal courts.

Three different judicial officers at 8 separate hearings heard Karen's petitions for divorce, custody, and child support. Richard participated in 3 separate court-ordered counseling programs for alcohol and drug abuse and anger management. Advocates from 4 different agencies (e.g., child protective services) addressed various problems the couple had, but none of the agencies communicated with any of the others.

When Karen started seeing a new boyfriend, Richard fired a gun near Karen and made repeated death threats that Karen reported. Eventually, Karen wrote a letter to the court begging the court to read the entire file of her case, to force Richard to follow the court's directives, and to protect her and her children. Six months later, Richard killed Karen with a shotgun and then killed himself.[2]

The preceding case history is a vivid exemplar of the barriers that battered women face in seeking services from the CJS. Danis et al.'s (1998) analysis of calls to the NDVH revealed that the second most pressing problem facing IPV victims is the combination of a large gap in legal resources and inadequate response on the part of the criminal justice system. U.S. Department of Justice studies indicate that IPV victims experience significant difficulties in obtaining needed services at every level of the CJS (Hofford & Harrell, 1993). Both Feder (1998) and Parker (1997) assert that today's CJS fails to serve and protect battered women because its operation reflects historical precedents and patriarchal beliefs. Some legal scholars maintain that the CJS is too antiquated, biased, unsupportive, and underfunded to provide the services that

IPV victims need (e.g., Epstein, 1999; Goodman, Bennett, & Dutton, 1999).

Legislative reforms. Legislation should compel changes in the CJS that would ensure fair treatment of women and children and provide for their safety. Legislatures should mandate training for everyone in the system, so that they can learn to be responsive to victims and sensitive to cultural issues. State legislatures pass laws, but they often give no guidance to local officials about how to execute the directives or provide the funding they need to do so. Legislatures also may draft ambiguous statutes that force judges to "fill in the gaps" (Booth, 1999). Finally, research has shown that the more distant new legislation is from existing police or prosecutor practices, the more resistant police and prosecutors are to complying with the legislation (Ford, 1999). (For an overview of extant legal patriarchy, see "Symposium," 1997.)

Koss (2000) recommends a different type of justice response to IPV. Rather than incarcerating a batterer, a better approach may be to involve the perpetrator, victim, and community in strategies that attempt "perpetrator rehabilitation, victim restoration, and social reintegration of both victim and perpetrator" (p. 1332).

Weapons possession by batterers is a serious problem, one that the CJS needs to take very seriously. In 1997, the U.S. Congress modified the Gun Control Act of 1968 through an amendment known as the Lautenberg Amendment (after its author, Senator Frank Lautenberg). The Lautenberg Amendment bans individuals who have been convicted of domestic assault from carrying weapons, and it does not exempt law enforcement officers ("Domestic Violence Conviction," 1997). This amendment sparked investigations of IPV among law enforcement officers across the nation. One overlooked problem is that police departments need to follow the 1994 VAWA by implementing policies on officer-involved IPV. IPV by police officers is a serious problem for victims, and perpetrators are supposed to suffer severe job consequences, such as losing their licenses to carry firearms (Lonsway & Conis, 2003).

The U.S. General Accounting Office (U.S. GAO, 2002a) recently reported on continuing problems in enforcing the weapons ban for IPV offenders. The FBI has determined that between 1998 and September 2001, individuals who were not supposed to be able to purchase guns under the Brady Bill were still able to make 10,945 gun purchases. Of these, about 26% were IPV violators. The GAO report cites the 3-day limit on background checks provided in the law as the predominant stumbling block in completing background checks effectively.

Passage of the Violence Against Women Acts of 1994 and 2000 provided more help for battered women than ever before. Nonetheless, the CJS has not been able to protect women adequately from continued assault and injury (Klein, 1995; Zorza, 1995). (For descriptions of VAWA 1994 and 2000, see the link for this volume on the Sage Publications Web site at the URL noted above.)

 # 10

Confidentiality and legal service needs. Victims trying to escape their abusers by relocating have high safety needs that entail keeping their whereabouts confidential. Some observers have argued that through 1994 the CJS overlooked the privacy needs of female IPV victims. Unfortunately, courts have allowed IPV perpetrators to have access to victims' new locations through access to the women's children's schools and medical records. Two other needs are victim-counselor confidentiality and security at the courthouse (Zorza, 1995).

Under the leadership of former U.S. Vice President Al Gore, the Social Security Administration changed its policies regarding the issuance of new Social Security numbers in the fall of 1998. With adequate evidence of abuse harassment, the Social Security Administration now issues new Social Security numbers to IPV victims who need them. Along with other changes, this allows women fleeing from IPV to open new bank accounts and obtain new driver's licenses. These modifications have substantially improved victims' abilities to start new lives safely (see "Getting New," 1999).

Battered women have few affordable legal services available to them. Poor women often have to wait 2 years to obtain legal services to assist with divorce or custody issues. In cases of IPV, this means that they remain connected to their abusers in the interim. It is reassuring to note that VAWA 2000 includes provisions that should help IPV victims to get legal assistance. For example, a victim no longer has to pay a fee to obtain an order of protection ("Congress Votes," 2000).

Immigrants and the criminal justice system. As the Violence Against Women Acts and other laws against family violence have proliferated, they have increasingly included immigrants. Consequently, the courts are increasingly having to address crimes committed by immigrants whose homeland customs differ from those of the United States. Some commentators have expressed concern about cultural insensitivity toward immigrant groups and the unfairness of penalties for behaviors that are outlawed in the United States but legal in the immigrants' home countries (Murray, 1999). Defense attorneys for foreign-born people sometimes attempt to use cultural defenses (Torry, 2000), but such defenses are not uniformly acceptable. As one illustration, an immigrant father might try to force a daughter as young as 12 to marry a much older man. In the United States, the groom could be prosecuted for child sexual assault. (For a review of laws concerning special subgroups and how courts are coping, see Levesque, 2001.)

Criminal justice system reforms. Mills (1999) and other feminist legal scholars view reform of the CJS as a critical last step in ending male-to-female IPV. Several scholars assert that the principal problem in reducing IPV is not the need for new laws but the failure of the CJS to implement the laws that already exist (Feder, 1997, 1998; Lemon, 2002). Stopping IPV requires vigorous affirmative effort from everyone in the CJS: police, prosecutors, judges, defense attorneys, jurors, and court advocates. Claiming that one "cog in the wheel" (e.g., the police or the courts) is responsible for victims' plight fails to recognize the effects of other powerful agents in the system.

As a society, the United States needs to provide adequate funding for the criminal justice system to allow it to address IPV adequately. One relatively recent finding, for instance, is that although 50% of clients served through federal crime compensation programs are IPV victims, these clients received only 13% of compensation awards (Danis, 2003). A study of prosecutorial outcomes highlights the role of funding in successful prosecution of IPV cases. Differential funding of prosecutors' offices in Los Angeles County, for instance, produced broad contrasts. Prosecutors' offices with sufficient funds were able to assign specialized prosecutors to IPV cases, and those without could not. Over a 6-month period, specialized prosecutors working on 196 cases dismissed only 12.7% and successfully prosecuted 87.2%. Nonspecialized prosecutors handling 189 IPV cases dismissed 35% and successfully prosecuted 64.5%. The researchers attributed the disparate outcomes to dissimilar prosecutorial styles precipitated by funding decisions (as cited in McGreevy, 1998). (For a description of another novel program, see Davis, Smith, & Nickles, 1998.)

In summarizing the research, Davis (1998) asserts that the United States has remained incapable of devising a coherent criminal justice procedure to address IPV. In addition, several authorities have decried the CJS's missed opportunities to promote emotional benefits for individuals involved in IPV through more suitable policies (**therapeutic jurisprudence**) (Simon, 1995; Wexler & Bruce, 1996). Identification of obstacles in the CJS for IPV victims and improvement of the CJS response to IPV in general have become especially active areas of research (for an overview, see National Institute of Justice & American Bar Association, 1998).

One group of IPV experts has devised an integrated approach to batterer interventions and criminal justice strategies. This group recommends that law enforcement officers comply with four major guidelines: (a) identify the primary aggressor, (b) execute a proarrest or mandatory arrest policy, (c) gather evidence at the scene for use in prosecutions, and (d) arrange for a temporary restraining or no-contact order (Healey, Smith, & O'Sullivan, 1998).

Police services. The practices of police around the world can play a pivotal role in helping IPV victims escape by informing them of available community services. On the other hand, the police can choose to put up serious barriers that make it much harder or even dangerous for victims to leave (Grigsby & Hartman, 1997). In the United States, the literature on police responses to calls for IPV-related services reveal notable inconsistencies. Interpretations of research findings about police reactions need to include consideration of the following variables: (a) arrest policy (e.g., proarrest) in the jurisdiction studied, (b) degree of cooperation with research requests, (c) degree of implementation of new policies, and (d) whether data are derived from responses to vignettes (e.g., written hypothetical cases of IPV) or from observation of actual police behavior.

Historically, laws regarding the handling of IPV have mirrored American society's "hands-off" approach. Until the late 1970s, police in all 50 states could arrest an IPV perpetrator only if they had reason to suspect he had committed a felony or if he actually committed a misdemeanor in the presence of an officer. Police responded to IPV according to policies that protected the privacy rights of families. Police departments traditionally trivialized family violence as noncriminal, noninjurious, inconsequential, and primarily verbal "spats" (Berk, Fenstermaker, & Newton, 1988). Despite this stance, most police officers also held the erroneous and contradictory opinion that intervention in domestic violence is one of the most dangerous actions a police officer must undertake (Garner & Clemmer, 1986). Currently, some critics of the police response to IPV cases complain that officers make blaming or humiliating comments to IPV victims, such as "It's your own fault. You shouldn't have married him." Some police also may intimidate IPV victims by threatening future arrest or by having the victims' children put in foster care (Coulter, Kuehnle, Byers, & Alfonso, 1999).

The British criminal justice system has taken three paths in dealing with the problem of IPV: (a) victim choice, (b) proarrest policy, and (c) victim empowerment. The victim choice position assumes that the victim has sufficient information (options) to make a reasoned choice about whether arrest of her abuser will improve the situation. The proarrest policy implies that subsequent prosecution will be undertaken in such a way as to prevent retaliation against the victim by the perpetrator. The victim empowerment view attempts to understand the individual victim, to educate her about available services, and to find out what might work best for her, including no arrest (Hoyle & Sanders, 2000)

⚡ A popular topic among researchers who examine the CJS response to IPV has been the determination of police rationales for involvement or lack of involvement in addressing IPV. Research findings suggest that some of the following attitudes influence police decision making: (a) IPV may be the victim's fault, or "justified" (Ford, 1999); (b) if he beats her and she stays, there is no real victim (see Waaland & Keeley, 1985); (c) battered women are manipulative or unbelievable (Rigakos, 1995); (d) police involvement is not the best way to stop IPV (Feder, 1998); and (e) responding to IPV calls is not "real" police work, which is catching "real" criminals (see Mastrofski, Parks, Reiss, & Worden, 1998). Illustrative of negative police attitudes is the statement of one police officer who said during a training session that he found arresting batterers hard to accept because a perpetrator might have married a "Nazi Bitch from Hell, like I did" (quoted in Ford, 1999, p. 14).

A particularly troublesome complaint about police responses to IPV centers on a perceived double standard in determining probable cause for making an arrest: one for IPV and the other for stranger assaults. Police may fail to arrest some of the most violent IPV perpetrators, including those who have used guns, knives, or clubs, or who have thrown female partners down flights of stairs (Buzawa & Buzawa, 2003; Fyfe, Klinger, & Flavin, 1997). For whatever reasons, police

have often treated IPV perpetrators differently than they have treated other assaultive men (see Avakame & Fyfe, 2001; Bourg & Stock, 1994).

In a review of 25 studies, Erez and Belknap (1998) substantiated the hypothesis that police show leniency to IPV perpetrators—that is, police typically avoid arresting batterers compared with other violent perpetrators. According to one account, however, both police and courts appear to be more lenient with female IPV perpetrators than with their male counterparts. Police in one study were significantly more likely to issue citations to female perpetrators than to arrest them, and judges were apt to give shorter jail times to women than to men (Tollefson, 2002).

Opinions also clash over police sensitivity to female victims during on-scene handling of IPV calls. One survey ascertained that IPV victims were significantly more dissatisfied with police responses than were victims of other crimes (Byrne, Kilpatrick, Howley, & Beatty, 1999). Two more recent studies have indicated that battered women's perceptions of police responses may be improving. One study of 95 female IPV victims indicated that 75% endorsed the highest rating possible for police intervention, and only 9% endorsed the lowest rating (Apsler, Cummins, & Carl, 2003). Another qualitative investigation of 25 female IPV victims revealed that about 70% described police behavior in positive terms. The other 30% were very critical of officers' behaviors and attitudes, claiming that officers threatened them with a dual arrest or made jokes about the violence (Stephens & Sinden, 2000). An encouraging finding among immigrant victims was that 84% to 94% "felt police were responsive to their concerns" (e.g., Davis & Erez, 1998, p. 5). Similarly, some studies, but not all, have found that police treat IPV cases involving members of minority groups about the same as cases involving nonminorities (e.g., Hutchison et al., 1994)

Several studies have indicated that victims do not uniformly seek help from police. A few reporting rates follow: (a) police estimates, 50% (Greenfeld et al., 1998); (b) NCVS estimates, 54% (Rennison & Welchans, 2000); (c) 498 sheltered women, 58% (Coulter et al., 1999); (d) 329 pregnant Hispanic women, 23% (Wiist & McFarlane, 1998). Given that not all victims call the police in response to IPV, it is unwise to attribute victims' behaviors wholly to police policies (Kaukinen, 2002). To begin with, a small proportion of victims (7% of women and 15% of men) do not perceive IPV assaults as crimes, or they think of the assaults as very minor or as personal matters.

Many women do not report because of fear of reprisal (Rennison & Welchans, 2000).

In an analysis of more than 9,000 domestic violence cases, Felson, Messner, Hoskin, and Deane (2002) found that the contextual elements that make it less likely that victims will call police include privacy concerns, fear of economic or physical reprisal, threats by perpetrator to report a partner for child abuse, and victim desire to protect the offender (Wolf, Ly, Hobart, & Kernic, 2003). Circumstances that make it more likely victims will call police are self-protection needs (current and future), perception of IPV assaults as serious, victim injury, perpetrator history of abuse (see Bent-Goodley, 2001; Felson et al., 2002), and offender intoxication (Hutchison, 1999b).

Race also may be a factor in frequency of calls for police service. Most of the available data indicate that African American women are more likely than Anglo women to seek help from police and from shelters in cases of IPV (see Goodman et al., 1999; Hutchison & Hirschel, 1998; Tjaden & Thoennes, 1998a). NCVS data show that 67% of Black women, compared with 50% of White women, made reports to police (Rennison & Welchans, 2000).

Data are emerging, however, that IPV victims who call the police do not have uniform needs or expectations about police services. Not all IPV victims want their abusers arrested. Hoyle and Sanders (2000) note that victims' intentions in asking for police services may vary markedly from society's goals or, more specifically, from those of the CJS. They found that IPV victims who called police but were not seeking arrest of the perpetrators wanted the police to "tell him off" or "warn him," or they "wanted to get even." Other reasons for calling were "to shock him into straightening up," "to get advice," "to get help for the abuser (e.g., drug treatment)," and to ask police to "take the women and her children to a safe place."

Given the social climate of the 1980s and 1990s and the legacy of police inaction regarding IPV, victims' advocates became more progressive in documenting police behaviors and in trying to shape the policies of police departments. Concomitantly, the "decision to arrest" became the dependent variable researchers believed would most likely reveal police attitudes and policies (see Robinson & Chandek, 2000). Attempts to disentangle police attitudes from arrest decisions, however, produced ambiguous results. A plurality of inquiries conducted through the mid-1990s concluded that extralegal factors (e.g., victim intoxication) influenced arrest decisions (e.g., Felson et al., 2002; Finn &

Stalans, 1997; Fyfe et al., 1997; Stewart & Maddren, 1997). Another investigation, however, found that "perpetrator present (on scene)" emerged as the strongest predictor of arrest (see Robinson & Chandek, 2000).

In the mid-1990s, growing dissatisfaction with police inconsistency and leniency in handling IPV cases led to heightened preferences for arrests and eventually to demands for mandatory arrest policies. Under such policies, the police do not have the option of exercising discretion; instead, they are required to arrest any assaultive partner for probable cause. Advocates initially believed that mandatory arrest policies would guarantee aggressive police intervention on behalf of battered women. The equivocal nature of the effects of these policies, however, spawned additional inquiry. Studies uncovered continuing police resistance, if not a "backlash" effect, presumably tied to the removal of police discretion.

A few studies, such as the Spouse Assault Replication Program, detected a decrease in assaults following the introduction of mandatory arrest policies. Victim interview data from this research revealed that aggression occurred 30% less often following arrest, and police reports showed a 60% drop in reoffending during the follow-up period. However, mandatory arrest policies may not consistently exert a deterrent effect on IPV or even serve the best interests of victims. Other variables, such as drug use at the time of arrest, were related to rearrest (e.g., "Impact of Arrest," 1999).

Whatever the case may be, some social scientists believe that mandatory arrest allows judges to exert some control over perpetrators. Judges may, for example, compel offenders to seek treatment, place them under probation, or take other actions (Stark, 1993). Whether a mandatory arrest system actually serves the best interests of battered women, however, is debatable. Currently, there is insufficient research on the consequences of mandatory arrest policies to support any policy recommendations in this area. (For a comprehensive discussion of mandatory arrest outcomes, see Buzawa & Buzawa, 2003, chap. 8.)

Increasing arrest rates of women in IPV cases appear to have followed implementation of mandatory arrest policies. Some jurisdictions have implemented dual-arrest policies; that is, police must arrest both partners in response to a domestic disturbance call. Following the adoption of mandatory arrest policies, police in one state actually arrested a greater proportion of women for assault than men (34% and 23%, respectively) (Martin, 1997). In other areas, police officers are far less likely to arrest a woman for IPV, even when a man is the obvious victim (Buzawa & Hotaling, 2000). An examination of 2,670 court cases in a large midwestern jurisdiction revealed that 86.1% of IPV defendants were males, 13.9% were females, and 1.3% were same-sex couples. According to a preliminary analysis of the court transcripts in these cases, many of the women arrested and charged as IPV perpetrators were actually IPV victims (Belknap et al., 1999).

One plan for revamping police responses is to hold police accountable through performance-based systems containing identifiable criteria that measure police activities through audits (Johnson, 2003). A different approach to reducing IPV is to treat it as a unique problem requiring special police training and sensitivity. The San Diego Police Department has developed a "revolutionary" checklist for police to complete on-scene at an IPV call. The checklist, which is designed to ensure that officers collect all necessary evidence, includes places for the following information: (a) victim-perpetrator relationship (e.g., spouse, cohabitant, dating partner), (b) length of relationship, (b) medical treatment received (e.g., where, who), (c) photographs of injuries and verbal description, (d) diagram of human form for victim to mark location of injuries, (e) property damaged, (f) victim's emotional state, (g) drugs/alcohol at the scene, and (h) whether an arrest was made. Officers ask the victim to sign the sheet once it is filled out, and that signature also serves to give police permission to view the victim's medical records and records of previous IPV incidents. Armed with such complete evidence, prosecutors were able to raise IPV conviction rates 90%, and intimate partner homicide declined by 62% (see McCormick, 1999). (For a "wish list" of changes in police response to IPV, see Wolf et al., 2003.)

Prosecution of IPV perpetrators. The actions that prosecutors take can impede or enhance a battered victim's chances of escaping or even surviving. As Mimi Rose, chief assistant district attorney for the Family Violence and Sexual Assault Unit in Philadelphia, reminded an audience of court professionals, "Always remember; it's our case, but it's her life" (quoted in Ford, 1999, p. 18). Researchers who have tracked IPV cases from arrest to conviction have pinpointed a severe lack of prosecutorial follow-through (Zorza & Woods, 1994). In one inquiry, a particularly disturbing trend emerged: District attorneys prosecuted proportionately more arrested women (11%) than arrested men (6%) (Martin, 1997).

One contentious issue among prosecutors is the perception that IPV victims waste their time by seeking help and then refusing to testify (e.g., Belknap, 2000; Ford & Regoli, 1992). In some jurisdictions, IPV is a "crime against the state," so prosecutors execute their duties whether or not the victims are willing to testify. In other jurisdictions, whether to prosecute IPV perpetrators is left to the discretion of their victims. More than half the IPV victims in one survey failed to cooperate with criminal prosecution (Rebovich, 1996). Notwithstanding these findings, one in-depth analysis of 2,670 court cases ascertained that prosecutors generally view women victims as cooperative (Belknap et al., 1999). Research has uncovered several reasons battered women may not cooperate: (a) fear of retaliation by the abuser; (b) lack of tangible victim support, such as transportation and babysitting; (c) worry that the prosecutor would not prepare them adequately for testifying; (d) fear the abuser would not be found guilty; and, surprisingly, (e) prosecutor's failure to inform victims of their court dates (see Belknap et al., 1999; Goodman et al., 1999; Tomz & McGillis, 1997). IPV victims' tendency to decide not to testify against their abusers has led to the establishment in many locations of mandatory (no-drop) prosecution policies. (For a brief overview of varying opinions on no-drop policies, see Box 9.1.)

Judges' behavior and decision making. The behavior and decision making of judges play a crucial role in society's response to IPV (Carter, Heisler, & Lemon, 1991). Some judges harm female IPV victims by demeaning them. Deborah Epstein (1999) presents several accounts of shocking judicial conduct. One judge, for example, presided over a case in which testimony described the behavior of a man who doused his wife with lighter fluid and set her on fire. The judge broke into song in open court, singing, "You light up my wife," to the tune of "You Light Up My Life." Another judge expressed resentment about having to deal with a husband who pleaded guilty to killing his wife after finding her in bed with another man. The judge complained that his job was very difficult when he was "called upon to sentence noncriminals as criminals" (p. 25).

All empirical studies and criminal justice experts' analyses cite judges' lack of training in IPV as a serious problem (Burt, Newmark, Olson, Aron, & Harrell, 1997; Epstein, 1999; Family Violence Project, 1995; Zorza, 1998). Research routinely indicates, for example, that courts rarely sanction even the most

Box 9.1 Mandatory Prosecution (No-Drop) Policies

Mandatory prosecution policies (or no-drop policies) require prosecutors to process cases of intimate partner violence regardless of the victims' wishes, recantations, or objections. Conceptions about the wisdom of mandatory prosecution have ricocheted from one extreme to the other. On the one hand, some authorities argue that such aggressive policies serve IPV victims best because they help the whole CJS response to IPV run more smoothly. Police may be more willing to arrest in cases of IPV if prosecution is certain to follow. First, no-drop polices assure that IPV victims receive "equal protection under the law," thus providing a remedy to victims that prosecutors previously ignored. Second, because of extreme emotional duress evoked by battering, victims may not be sufficiently clearheaded to make appropriate decisions regarding prosecution. Therefore, the state should prosecute with or without the victim's active cooperation (for a review, see Robbins, 1999). Third, no-drop policies place less responsibility on victims for managing their own cases, and batterers might not blame victims for continuing cases. If nothing else, no-drop policies reflect society's concern about IPV and address batterers' violence (see Buzawa, Austin, & Buzawa, 1995; Hanna, 1996). Perhaps reining in a batterer is empowering to victims in and of itself. Finally, an assault against a partner is not just an isolated act of violence affecting only the victim but an affront to social standards. Violence in the home has a way of migrating out into other arenas, such as the school, workplace, and community (Robbins, 1999). Other experts contend that no-drop policies endanger or disempower battered victims. They assert that instead the best course of action is to empower battered women through consultation to make their own decisions about testifying (e.g., Dutton-Douglas & Dionne, 1991). Furthermore, some battered victims have misgivings that override prosecutorial considerations, including religious beliefs about leaving their marriages or loss of spousal economic support (for a review, see Epstein, 1999). To date, research has failed to validate the claim that no-drop policies constitute an effective strategy for reducing recidivism (Davis, Smith, & Nickles, 1998). (For information about variations in mandatory prosecution laws, see Ford & Regoli, 1992; Roth, 1998; Wan, 2000. For a review, see Mills, 1999.)

assaultive men in IPV cases. A synthesis of investigations revealed that police arrest about one-fourth of batterers, prosecutors decide to prosecute about a third of those arrested, and about 1% of those prosecuted receive jail time beyond the time served at arrest (often just a few hours) (see Coulter et al., 1999; Davis, 1998; Holmes, 1993).

An analysis of 2,670 IPV court cases revealed that 44% resulted in a guilty verdict, 5% resulted in a not guilty verdict, and the court dismissed 51% (Belknap et al., 1999). Erez and Tontodonato (1990) established that IPV perpetrators received significantly shorter sentences than did perpetrators of other crimes. A comparison of two groups of men in one community, acquaintances of an IPV victim (295) and nonacquaintances (331), uncovered significant differences in beliefs. The men with IPV victim acquaintances thought the court was less likely to treat IPV victims

fairly than did the men with no victim acquaintances (Nabi & Horner, 2001).

Judges' nonenforcement of sanctions against IPV perpetrators also extends to noncompliance with restraining orders (see Davis, 1998). A 1994 *Boston Globe* report described a database search of judicial actions in response to violations of POs (cited in Buzawa & Buzawa, 2003). Variations in judicial responses were extreme. In one Massachusetts county, judges dismissed more than 60% of cases, whereas in another county the dismissal rate was 18% ("Records Show," 1994). Furthermore, various groups have reported finding considerable antivictim and antiwoman biases in judicial rulings (Epstein, 1999; Stone & Fialk, 1999). Hemmens, Strom, and Schlegel (1998) describe a number of troublesome situations that imply bias. In their study, more than 75% of attorneys responding to a questionnaire said that judges allowed inappropriate questioning of IPV victims. Further, IPV perpetrators' defense attorneys could ask questions such as "What did you do to provoke your husband's assault?"

In addition to receiving training, judges need to assume a community leadership role to reduce IPV (Fenton, 1999). They should carefully control men with prior convictions, because research shows that such men are especially dangerous. They should adopt protocols for granting and enforcing POs in order to avoid bias in their use of discretion. As leaders in the judicial process, they should evaluate the background educations of involved court personnel (e.g., advocates, counselors, lawyers) and demand that those individuals seek appropriate training when necessary. Finally, they should set guidelines for appropriate judicial behavior and establish a judicial body (perhaps a special unit of the bar) to discipline judges whose behavior in IPV cases is outrageous.

Protection orders. A common approach to enhancing IPV victims' safety has been the recommendation that victims procure both criminal and civil orders of protection, or restraining orders, to keep their abusers away from them. There is little disagreement among social scientists and other IPV specialists that battered women acutely need access to POs (Carlson, Harris, & Holden, 1999). Indeed, one specialist suggests mandatory restraining orders following an arrest for probable cause as a technique for strengthening victims' rights (Adler, 1999). By 1994, all 50 states had legally recognized IPV victims' need for POs (Keilitz, 1994) and the full faith and credit provision of the Violence Against Women Act of 1994 required states to recognize and honor POs issued in other states.

Although POs have several functions, such as forcing an assaultive partner to vacate the family residence, their primary function is to protect victims from physical abuse, harassment, and threats. Judges can order IPV perpetrators to stay away from complaining victims, their children, and other relatives. Unfortunately, as is the case throughout the CJS, judges' decision making about POs is problematic. Many victims may simply not be able to obtain POs or keep them in effect, and obtaining a PO does not guarantee a victim's safety (Keilitz, 1994). Considering these stumbling blocks and others, some advocates have begun to urge the adoption of "permanent" POs (National Center for Victims of Crime, 2002).

There is no definitive evidence that the issuance of POs uniformly reduces IPV. In an analysis of 663 PO cases in the Quincy, Massachusetts, District Court, Carlson et al. (1999) found that almost half reported reabuse within 2 years. In another inquiry, however, these researchers found that the probability of reabuse declined significantly following issuance of POs. A 2003 investigation of 448 female IPV victims in Seattle, Washington, who obtained POs provides evidence of improved safety along several dimensions, such as fewer injuries and fewer threats (Holt, Kernic, Wolf, & Rivara, 2003). Finally, the National Center for State Courts found that 72% of 285 battered women with POs experienced no continuing problems one month after receiving the POs, but the proportion of those with no problems dropped to 65% at a later follow-up (Keilitz, Davis, & Eikeman, 1998).

Even after a victim finally gets a PO, she still may not be safe. Kane (1999), for example, found that despite Massachusetts law requiring arrest for infraction of a PO, judges did not routinely issue arrest warrants for violators. Enforcement has been so lax in many jurisdictions that women have been forced to sue police departments to make them liable for nonenforcement ("Municipal Liability," 1998). Davis (1998) concludes that if judges are not going to punish perpetrators who violate their POs, it might be best to warn women not to count on POs.

Although POs are not entirely effective in preventing reabuse, a number of women have reported feeling empowered by the process of obtaining POs (Fischer & Rose, 1995; Ptacek, 1999). Interview data from 355 women who filed petitions for POs revealed that they felt POs were worthwhile because they documented the abuse, sent a message that abuse was wrong, and punished the abuser (Stewart, 2000). In addition to crisis intervention, support groups, and children's treatment groups, some shelters for IPV victims provide services such as photographic documentation of injuries and help with obtaining POs from the courts (Gibson & Gutierrez, 1991). Shelter staff can now use Internet-based programs that aid advocates in preparing court papers properly (Zorza & Klemperer, 1999).

Community collaborations. To improve the efficiency of their responses to IPV, some jurisdictions have adopted a community collaboration approach that combines police action with social services. In this model, social service agency staff members educate themselves about the resources available to IPV victims, the functions of various agencies, and their own agencies' role in preventing IPV. They may craft an information packet to give to IPV victims that includes details about where they can go for specific services. One group of researchers evaluated the effects of responding to IPV with a multidisciplinary community response team. The program was able to provide safe housing, counseling, and explanations of CJS services and had a favorable impact on police practices. Anecdotal information indicated that the incorporation of CPS into the response team was especially beneficial. Best of all, women enrolled in the program suffered less violence (Uchida, Putnam, Mastrofski, Solomon, & Dawson, 2001).

Specialized IPV courts. Local jurisdictions would be wise to establish specialized police units or courts to address IPV cases, or to combine civil and criminal functions into a special court. When CJS personnel (police, prosecutors, judiciary, advocates, court staff) act in a coordinated fashion, arrest rates for IPV may be as high as 75% and successful prosecution as high as 70% (Buzawa, Hotaling, & Klein, 1998). In addition, IPV victims' satisfaction with the CJS appears to increase (Henning & Klesges, 1999).

Prevention

American society needs to change the lingering patriarchal practices that undermine female IPV victims' opportunities to lead violence-free lives. Society needs to transform basic conceptions of masculinity through changes in the ways in which men and boys are socialized. Men need to become women's partners rather than perpetrators of IPV. The socialization of women and girls should stress the role of education, which allows them to be self-sufficient. Women need to be less subordinate to men in general and less emotionally and economically dependent on male partners.

Americans need to become more aware of IPV in order to prevent it. Women should learn about IPV so that they can avoid relationships with violent men. Educational campaigns designed to affect beliefs about IPV in schools, clinics, the media, and courtrooms (e.g., speakers, posters, classes, and films) should continue their efforts to diminish acceptance of IPV (Chalk & King, 1998; O'Neal & Dorn, 1998; Romano & Hage, 2000; Schewe, 2002). To protect gay, lesbian, bisexual, and transgendered (GLBT) persons, the National Coalition of Anti-Violence Programs (2001) offers four recommendations: (a) Enact legally inclusive definitions of family, (b) enact GLBT-inclusive antidiscrimination legislation, (c) increase access to public and private funding for GLBT domestic violence services and research, and (d) adopt GLBT-inclusive standards of service and use training resources offered by GLBT organizations.

CHAPTER SUMMARY

This chapter has examined how conceptions and definitions of domestic violence have changed over the past decade. The most useful term for this violence is *intimate partner violence,* or *IPV,* because it is inclusive and gender neutral. IPV includes battering, or assaults accompanied by fear-producing and controlling behavior. Many experts conceive IPV as a continuum, with common couple violence on one end and intimate terrorism on the other.

Alternative ways of defining IPV have emanated from government panels and surveys, the original and revised versions of the Conflict Tactics Scale, and individuals. Common forms of IPV include physical abuse, sexual abuse, psychological/emotional abuse, stalking, and economic exploitation. Variations in meanings of IPV across cultures, for same-sex partners, and in legal determinations add nuanced understanding of IPV.

Information about the frequency, severity, and duration of IPV as well as the individuals involved originate from several sources: FBI crime data, the National Crime Victimization Survey and other national surveys (e.g., NFVS, NVAWS), and clinical or medical studies. Because definitions of IPV vary, as do sources of information about this problem, estimates of IPV often differ markedly from one another. Additional differences stem from sampling variations. Some of the subpopulations examined include same-sex pairs, ethnic/racial minority group members, people living in rural areas, disabled intimate partners, immigrants, and cross-cultural groups. This chapter has revealed the widespread nature of interpartner aggression. (Estimates of rates of abuse appear in Table 4, Appendix B.)

A strong debate continues between mainstream sociologists who advance a "gender-mutual" view of IPV and feminist researchers who promote a "gendered" view. Although many experts have argued that men commit far more IPV than women, others suggest that IPV is roughly equivalent for both genders. Feminists and experts who approach the study of IPV from the context of crime are likely to believe that women's IPV is often self-defensive. Confounding this issue are dissonant data from couples participating in IPV research.

Two related issues are that IPV frightens women more than it does men and that control of one's partner may be the central motivation for IPV.

Outcomes of IPV range from upset and humiliation for victims to severe physical and sexual assaults with consequent injuries, sometimes including death. In addition to these extremely negative personal repercussions, social consequences accrue as well. Statisticians have estimated that in the United States the monetary costs to society annually are in the billions of dollars. These funds go to offset medical expenses, to pay for shelter and welfare benefits for victims, and to process of IPV cases through the criminal justice system. Everybody loses.

Many researchers, practitioners, and laypersons have sought explanations for IPV. An examination of social-structural variables reveals that younger males are the most frequent perpetrators. Most studies, but not all, show that in the United States, IPV occurs more often among racial/ethnic minority groups and immigrant populations than among the White majority. Some variables, such as poverty, appear to be associated with these higher rates. Although IPV occurs in every socioeconomic group, most surveys indicate that it is more common in lower-SES groups. Little is known about any possible association between religion and IPV perpetration.

Certain cultural factors, such as a society's acceptance of interpersonal violence, may be catalysts for some IPV. Cultural forces that endow men with power over women promote IPV, but they are not its sole cause. Traditional sex-role socialization of both men and women are like twin pillars supporting IPV. Alcohol consumption and marital dissatisfaction are often correlated with IPV perpetration, but neither seems to be a root cause.

Members of the clergy, health care providers, counseling professionals, shelter personnel, welfare workers, and law enforcement personnel are on the front lines in dealing with the aftermath of IPV. Victims' satisfaction with the services offered by these "first responders" varies.

The criminal justice system is the major social institution involved in combating IPV. Relatively recent legislation has begun to remedy some shortcomings of the CJS response, such as the crucial need to safeguard victims' confidentiality. It is still true, however, that the CJS response to IPV has been slow to improve.

No IPV victim can feel safe if her batterer has vowed to hurt her.

The first line of defense against IPV is police intervention, but historically the police have been unwilling to intervene in IPV cases. This failure to respond to calls for protection has led to strong political action in recent years. Advocates have successfully lobbied for mandatory arrest policies in many jurisdictions, and some authorities believe that mandatory prosecution of IPV cases is helpful. Evidence remains inconclusive about the effectiveness of such policies, however.

Once IPV perpetrators are arrested, the CJS still fails to hold them accountable. Prosecution and conviction rates are very low for IPV cases. Judges need to improve their knowledge of IPV, and court support services need fine-tuning to be more supportive of battered women. Police officers also need better training to equip them to handle IPV cases. The distress that IPV victims feel as a result of their encounters with the CJS center most heavily on some police practices and especially on judicial conduct.

Although remarkable headway has been made in improving society's response to IPV over the past decade, much remains to be done. Research on IPV has extended into many areas, including medicine, counseling, education, and the legal system. Special training regarding IPV has become more and more common for professionals in this area. Taken together, these activities have begun to encourage the massive social changes needed to end IPV.

DISCUSSION QUESTIONS

1. Why is defining IPV problematic? (a) How do CTS1 and CTS2 define family violence? (b) How do crime questionnaires generally differ from conflict questionnaires? (c) How would you define IPV if you were conducting research?
2. Why are many cases of IPV never reported?
3. Why is it difficult to obtain assault data from some members of special populations?
4. What are some of the monetary costs of IPV? Who pays the costs? Who should pay them?
5. Do Americans approve or disapprove of male-to-female violence? What about female-to-male violence?
6. What role does alcohol consumption play in IPV?
7. What does screening for IPV entail? Who should screen individuals for IPV?
8. How would you describe current police and/or prosecutors' policies in responding to IPV?
9. How do clinicians appear to be falling short in regard to working with IPV victims?
10. Why is it difficult for so many women to escape IPV?

RECOMMENDED READING

Buzawa, E. S., & Buzawa, C. G. (2003). *Domestic violence: The criminal justice response* (3rd ed.). Thousand Oaks, CA: Sage.

Fals-Stewart, W. (2003). The occurrence of partner physical aggression on days of alcohol consumption: A longitudinal diary study. *Journal of Consulting and Clinical Psychology, 71,* 41–52.

Farr, K. A. (2002). Battered women who were "being killed and survived it": Straight talk from survivors. *Violence and Victims, 17,* 267–281.

Jackson, N. A., & Oates, G. C. (Eds.). (1998). *Violence in intimate relationships: Examining sociological and psychological issues.* Boston: Butterworth-Heinemann.

Jasinski, J. L., & William, L. M. (Eds.). (1998). *Partner violence: A comprehensive review of 20 years of research.* Thousand Oaks, CA: Sage.

Leventhal, B., & Lundy, S. E. (Eds.). (1999). *Same-sex domestic violence: Strategies for change.* Thousand Oaks, CA: Sage.

Ovenauf, M. (1999). The isolation abyss: A case against mandatory prosecution. *UCLA Women's Law Journal, 9,* 263–300.

Russell, D. E. H. (1990). *Rape in marriage* (Rev. ed.). Bloomington: Indiana University Press.

Sharp, P. (1996). *Crows over a wheatfield.* New York: Washington Square.

Shepard, M. F., & Pence, E. L. (Eds.). (1999). *Coordinating community responses to domestic violence: Lessons from Duluth and beyond.* Thousand Oaks, CA: Sage.

Zorza, J. (Ed.). (2003). *Violence against women.* Kingston, NJ: Civic Research Institute.

NOTES

1. The source for this case history is Brower and Sackett (1985). Kree Kirkman is the subject's real name.

2. The source for this case history is Epstein (1999). Karen and Richard Graves are the subjects' real names.

10

INTIMATE PARTNER VIOLENCE

Abused Partners

Case History: Lisa—For Better or for Worse

I believe that you stay with your partner for better or for worse. I didn't know what "worse" was when I made that promise, but I promised. I believe my husband loves me, and I'm starting to believe he could kill me. I'm not sure how long I should stay and how "bad" is "too bad." I know I don't believe I should be hit. But I do believe if my relationship is a mess, I should stay to help make it better.[1]

C hapter 9 presented discussion of many patterns of marital violence—the slaps and physical assaults, threats, and even sexual assaults that sometimes occur between married couples—as well as some explanations for this violence. It should be clear from that discussion that although both males and females are sometimes violent, women are more likely than men to be victims of injurious abuse. The focus of this chapter is the impact of marital violence (physical, sexual, verbal, and psychological) as experienced by women. The chapter begins by addressing some of the myths about battered women that have contributed to the general propensity of the public to blame battered women for being victimized. The chapter continues with descriptions of the consequences of intimate partner violence (IPV). Next, there is a consideration of the reasons women stay in abusive relationships and how they manage to survive. Finally, the discussion turns to the topic of various treatment modalities aimed at helping battered women to escape or at least reduce the violence in their relationships. Part of this discussion includes recommendations for counselors and suggestions for policy makers.

BLAMING VICTIMS OF INTIMATE PARTNER VIOLENCE

Blaming by Society

Case History: Hedda Nussbaum—When the Protector Needs Protection

One of the most notorious cases of IPV on record is that of Hedda Nussbaum and Joel Steinberg. In 1987, police arrived at the couple's apartment to find their 6-year-old adopted daughter, Lisa, beaten to death. Although left alone with the beaten and dying child for several hours, Hedda failed to take any action, such as calling 911, to save Lisa's life for fear of angering Joel. She spent much of the time free-basing cocaine, at Joel's direction.

At first, the New York district attorney booked Hedda for second-degree murder of Lisa. As the case unfolded, however, evidence of Hedda's horrifying life with Joel came to light. After the couple had been together for 2 years, Joel began to beat Hedda periodically, and the beatings continued over the ensuing 10 years. He choked her, burned her with a propane torch, beat her with a metal exercise bar, broke her knee and ribs, forced her to sleep handcuffed to a chinning bar, pulled her hair out, and urinated on her. Sometimes, he alternated his abuse with affectionate behavior. Hedda occasionally went to a hospital for medical treatment, but eventually lied about the source of her injuries for fear of the consequences at home if she told the truth. Her appearance gradually changed from that of a normal, attractive woman to one resembling a boxer, with a swollen disfigured face, and she lost her job because she was so often absent from work.

Psychiatrists explained Hedda's behavior in various ways. One said, "It's like what happens to someone in a concentration camp. They are reduced, by virtue of physical torture, to a mere existence level. They shut off normal human emotions" (quoted in Hackett, McKillop, & Wang, 1988, p. 61). Another said that Hedda "was a slave, totally submissive to this man, with no ability or will to save her own daughter" (p. 57). Others noted the gradual buildup of the abuse and the episodic nature of the abuse and affection she received from Joel.

The district attorney eventually dropped all charges against her, because he thought "she was physically and emotionally incapable either of harming Lisa or coming to her aid" (quoted in Hackett et al., 1988, p. 57). Given her state of mind, prosecutors wondered if Hedda would be able to testify against Joel, but she did manage to do so. Hedda's former acquaintances gasped and even cried at her appearance. Joel was convicted of first-degree manslaughter and sent to prison, and Hedda received inpatient psychiatric services for more than a year.[2]

Hedda Nussbaum's experience illustrates an extreme case of both child abuse and female partner abuse in which the adult female victim was unable to save herself or her child. Many nonexperts wonder why Hedda could not just take Lisa and run away. This chapter will provide information on the victimization processes that appear to be at the root of tragedies such as this.

Because women are "consenting adults," responsible for their own behavior, some commentators afford them little empathy as victims of IPV. In general, members of the lay public are unaware of the attempts battered women make to escape and how difficult escaping is. In comparison with abused children and elders, adult women victims of IPV tend to receive more blame for their own victimization. Research indicates that one reason for this is that people are often unwilling to place blame for violent behavior solely on perpetrators. Ewing and Aubrey (1987), for example, surveyed a random sample of 216 adult community members regarding their attitudes toward and attributions of responsibility to the partners in violent relationships. Each participant completed a questionnaire after reading a scenario about a violent couple. More than 40% reported that the woman in the scenario must have been at least partly to blame for her husband's assaults, even though the story provided no rationale for such a belief. More than 60% of respondents agreed that if a battered woman were really afraid, she would simply leave. There was also some tendency for respondents to believe that the woman must have been emotionally disturbed or that if she would enter counseling, she could prevent the beatings.

A survey of college students revealed varying levels of sympathy for IPV victims who remain in abusive relationships, as well as differing opinions on the justifiability of the violence and victims' locus of control. The respondents felt sympathy for the victim under a limited number of conditions. Both sympathy and justifiability ratings were higher if the victim stayed for externally imposed reasons (e.g., being threatened with death by partner if she left). Ratings were lower if the victim remained for reasons such as loneliness or because of feeling helpless to change her situation. Gender differences in victim blaming also emerged in this analysis (Follingstad, Runge, Ace, Buzan, & Helff, 2001).

Most lay observers have an even more difficult time perceiving lesbian IPV victims as "worthy" victims. There appears to be a strong reluctance within the lesbian community to acknowledge interpartner aggression. Some of the problem stems from a strong belief that intimate partners in lesbian relationships should be equal. In addition, from a feminist viewpoint, interpartner violence arises from patriarchal practices (Renzetti, 1992), and lesbian relationships should be free of patriarchal attitudes. A related problem is connected to the greater willingness of many critics to attach the label of "mutual combat" to lesbian abuse compared with heterosexual violence (Hart, 1986).

Blaming by Professionals

When negative events occur, a frequent human reaction is to search out the party or parties at fault. The extent to which people blame battered women for their own victimization has a profound effect on the treatment they receive in a number of settings, including clinics and courtrooms. Some mental health professionals, medical personnel, and police seem ready to assume that IPV victims are accomplices or at least indirectly responsible for the abuse they suffer (Whatley & Riggio, 1991).

In a survey of 121 workers at a battered women's shelter, for example, McKell and Sporakowski (1993) found that 8.4% held husband and wife equally responsible for physical violence, and 53.8% held the husband primarily responsible. Only 37.8% held the husband completely responsible. In a 1991 Kentucky survey of service providers (mental health, social services, corrections, shelters, law enforcement courts, prosecutors, and coroners), not every respondent was willing to blame perpetrators. A minority of 13.9% agreed or strongly agreed with the statement, "Victims 'ask' for it" (Wilson & Wilson, 1991).

Another group of professionals who frequently blame battered women are child protective services (CPS) workers. The primary directive of CPS is to safeguard children, to act in the best interest of the child (Edleson, 1998). In homes where fathers are abusing children, CPS expects mothers to protect their children, if necessary, by taking them and leaving the abusers. If a mother does not do so, CPS may threaten to remove the children or actually remove them (Berliner, 1998). CPS and the legal system may also classify these nonoffending mothers as "sexual abuse offenders" (Bolen, 2003). These policies do not protect children, and they do not acknowledge the plight of many mothers who are being abused by the same men who are abusing their children. Empirical evidence routinely shows that in households where children are abused, mothers are often being abused as well. (See Chapter 7 for estimates of the co-occurrence of child abuse and male-to-female interparental violence.) The assumption that women can protect their children or can do so simply by leaving their abusers, however, is not borne out by facts. Women who try to leave abusive partners may place their own lives and those of their children at risk (Morton, Runyan, Moracco, & Butts, 1998), and no government agency can guarantee their safety (e.g., Epstein, 1999; Goodman, Bennett, & Dutton, 1999). Society imposes on mothers the immense task of protecting children even when they lack sufficient means to do so, a condition that Rich (1976) calls "powerless responsibility." The effect of current legal practices is to hold battered women criminally responsible (i.e., as perpetrators) for their male partners' child abuse while simultaneously classifying these women as assault victims (see Davidson, 1995; Sierra, 1997). Conversely, society rarely, if ever, holds fathers who fail to protect their children responsible (National Council of Juvenile and Family Court Judges, 1994). Romito and Saurel-Cubizolles (2001) urge society to classify fathers who abandon children and provide no child support as guilty of "neglect," a form of child abuse. (For additional ideas on this topic, see Fleck-Henderson, 2000; Mills & Yoshihama, 2002; Pulido & Gupta, 2002; Stark, 2002; Zorza, 2003.)

The court case *In re Lonell J.*, decided in May 1998, set the standard for child welfare cases when IPV is present. The New York appellate court held that because the nonabusing mother of a minor child did not leave an abusive relationship, she was guilty of neglect, failure to exercise a minimum degree of care that resulted in physical, mental, or emotional impairment or imminent danger of impairment to the child. The decision appeared to make the mother liable for the perpetrator's abuse. In this case, the mother had called police, obtained an order of protection against the abuser, and fled to her mother's house at least once. In another New York case, *In re Glen G.*, a court found a nonabusing mother guilty of neglect for failing to protect her children from their father's sexual abuse ("Failure to Protect" Working Group, 2000). (For a more in-depth discussion of this issue, see Chapter 7.)

SECTION SUMMARY

Research indicates that many people are still willing to blame female IPV victims for their own victimization rather than hold abusers accountable. Lesbian IPV victims elicit very little sympathy from the public. Even individuals "trained" to help others in critical situations, such as mental health professionals, seem inclined to hold victims responsible. Currently, there are conflicts between CPS personnel and battered women's advocates concerning the attribution of blame for abuse of children in households where both mothers and children are being abused. CPS workers, in their zeal to protect children, may blame battered mothers for fathers' abuse of children.

CONSEQUENCES OF VICTIMIZATION

IPV is a type of violence that causes serious and long-lasting physical and psychological effects. Violence affects people and changes them forever. The most immediate feeling that most crime victims experience following an assault is helplessness. Anger, anxiety, depression, fear, posttraumatic stress disorder (PTSD), and many other negative reactions may co-occur later (see Brewin, Andrews, & Rose, 2000; Feeny, Zoellner, & Foa, 2000). The time-frame of the abuse, such as last 6 months or last year, and the victim's history of abuse with prior partners greatly influence the effects of IPV on victims (Bogat, Levendosky, Theran, von Eye, & Davidson, 2003).

Violence and Fear

Both men and women express feeling fearful of a partner's violence (e.g., Barnett, Lee, & Thelen, 1997). Generally, women express more fear of crime than men do, and their fear includes fear of victimization of their children and significant others (see Felson, Messner, Hoskin, & Deane, 2002; Mesch, 2000). It is not surprising that many battered women report high levels of fear and that women find IPV frightening although men seldom do (Gore-Felton, Gill, Koopman, & Spiegel, 1999; Healey, 1995; Short et al., 2000). Even nonphysical forms of abuse can create extraordinary levels of foreboding in victims (Jacobson, Gottman, Gortner, Berns, & Shortt, 1996). In an Israeli population survey of nearly 300 women, 10% reported that they feared violence by their male partners (Mesch, 2000). The major reason IPV generates so much fear is that the possibility of another assault is always present (e.g., Langford, 1996; Van Hightower, Gorton, & DeMoss, 2000).

In a longitudinal narrative (i.e., historical story) analysis of 10 sheltered women, Hyden (1999) differentiated several successive stages of fear: (a) extreme undifferentiated fear (general fearfulness with no target), (b) specific fear of the male partner, and (c) lesser, chronic background fear (an ambiance of fear). Hyden quotes one woman who had left her abuser and was residing in a shelter:

> If I start out with when I first came here, what I was mostly thinking about, and the worst of it was that I was so frightened. It didn't matter how many locked

doors there were, I couldn't even feel protected here, so I was really afraid. . . . It's like I just sat on a chair, and I remember I was thinking "somebody's got to come and help me now," because here I am completely paralyzed . . . completely unable to change my life . . . alone. (p. 456)

Even if a battered woman leaves her abusive partner, the necessity of having to continue to interact with him makes her apprehensive (Shalansky, Ericksen, & Henderson, 1999; Zorza, 1998). Because of conditioning (i.e., emotional learning), cues such as yelling, drinking heavily, and particular facial expressions become aversive (for a review, see Davey, 1992). These cues generalize from past assaults that were preceded by these cues to current situations, keeping IPV victims in a chronic state of fear (e.g., Nurius, Furrey, & Berliner, 1992; Pontius, 2002). One empirically sound explanation for such persisting fear responses is fear conditioning, learning that is now known to cause neurological alterations in the brain ("Emotional Judgments," 1999; Pontius, 2002; Rogan, 1997; for a discussion of fear conditioning, see Chapter 2.) Because of all these factors, family violence scholars have increasingly suggested that victim fear distinguishes IPV from lesser forms of intimate abuse and should be integrated into the definition of IPV (e.g., O'Leary, 1999).

Violence, the Hostage Syndrome, Traumatic Bonding, and Attachment

Three related theories describe how violence affects the behaviors of some victims in close relationships: the hostage syndrome (also known as Stockholm syndrome), traumatic bonding, and attachment. These theories account for the intriguing finding that love and violence may coexist (Borochowitz & Eisikovits, 2002; Kesner, Julian, & McKenry, 1997).

Hostage syndrome. One possible consequence of IPV is the development of symptoms characteristic of the hostage syndrome. The following case history describes a woman kept as a prisoner.

Case History: Sophia and Boris—Lockdown

Boris seemed to get angrier every day. He was convinced that Sophia was having an affair, even though she was 8 months pregnant. He brought some lumber home from work one day and began boarding up all the windows in the house. He also removed the telephone. When he left for work in the mornings, he locked the front door from the outside with a new lock he had installed. One day, he just never came back.

Boris went to work every day and stayed with a girlfriend at night. Actually, Boris felt sad a lot of the time, so he went out to bars after work. Although he drove by his house every night, he never checked on Sophia's situation because "she deserved what she got"; she never cared how he felt about anything. Probably the baby wasn't his, he thought, because she was a "such a whore."

Apparently, Sophia could not get out of the house, even though she screamed and tried to break through a window. There was almost no food in the house and no medicines. Sixty days later, Sophia was finally rescued; she had lost 20 pounds. A man from the Gas Company making a meter repair had heard her and called police and paramedics.

In the hospital, Sophia lay in a state of emotional and medical shock. Boris was her first visitor. He brought her flowers and apologized. When he tried to "make love" to Sophia in the hospital, a nurse caught him and called police. Boris was arrested. Although the judge did not sentence Boris to any jail time because he "was working," he did order Boris to attend a 10-week counseling program for batterers. One reason Boris agreed to counseling was that he wanted Sophia to come back.

In some circumstances of extreme threat and isolation, imprisoned men and women may exhibit strange behaviors resembling those of hostages. These behaviors, together called the *Stockholm syndrome* or *hostage syndrome,* encompass praising the abusers, denying that abuse has taken place, and blaming themselves. Such behaviors may in actuality represent a struggle for survival ("Abusive Relationships," 1991). Captor-controlled conditions of alternating threats and kindness, along with power differentials between captor and captive, appear to make hostages emotionally dependent on those who have subjugated them. Captives come to believe that the way to survive is to avoid angering their captors. Captives may even profess to love their captors (Kuleshnyk, 1984; Lang, 1974). For example, Hedda Nussbaum (see the case history on p. 283) said that she loved Joel Steinberg.

Some abusive individuals create prisonlike settings for their partners. It is not uncommon for perpetrators to confine their partners by locking them in or out of particular rooms, or in or out of their homes (Barnett et al., 1997; Sleutel, 1998). Avni (1991) describes an Israeli case in which an abuser locked his wife in their apartment and plastered the door shut whenever he went to work. Many women living in India feel they have lived in a state of prolonged captivity their entire lives, because they have no options for personal decision making (Purewal & Ganesh, 2000). Terror dictates victims' responses to all events in their lives. One victim, for instance, felt terrorized by her abuser even after she had killed him. The researchers who examined this case proposed hostage theory as a likely explanation for her strange reactions (Loring, Smith, & Bolden, 1997).

An application of the hostage syndrome to IPV victims suggests that they may adopt such survival behaviors as praising their abusers, denying their abusiveness, becoming bonded to their abusers, and blaming themselves for the violence their abusers perpetrate (Rawlings, Allen, Graham, & Peters, 1994). Threats to survival and isolation are the most powerful antecedents for predicting development of the Stockholm syndrome (Nielsen, Endo, & Ellington, 1992).

Traumatic bonding. Another possible consequence of victimization is that the victim becomes traumatically bonded to the abuser. Dutton and Painter's (1981) analysis of traumatic bonding in IPV rests on the well-established fact that intermittently rewarded behavior is extremely persistent (i.e., resistant to extinction). A cyclical pattern of loving behaviors (rewards) coupled with sporadic violence (assaults) may actually increase the abused partner's dependence on the abuser. Traumatic bonding is a negative outcome because it may play a role in a battered woman's persistence in the relationship and diminish her resolve to leave (Dutton & Painter, 1993b; Towns & Adams, 2000). (For further explanation of traumatic bonding, see LaViolette & Barnett, 2000, app. 2.)

Attachment. One factor that plays a key role in IPV leave/stay decisions is the victim's romantic attachment to the abusing partner (Griffing et al., 2002; Henderson, Bartholomew, & Dutton, 1997). Adult attachment to a romantic partner builds on childhood attachment patterns and influences the quality of adult intimate relationships (e.g., Dutton & Haring, 1999; Feeney & Noller, 1996). Concerning adult attachment, Mayseless (1991) has speculated that certain types of attachment (i.e., anxious) create fear of abandonment, which in turn leads to assaults against a partner threatening to leave. Periodic abuse, as in traumatic bonding, strengthens the romantic attachment bond and makes it more difficult for an IPV victim to leave her abusive partner permanently (Dutton & Painter, 1993b).

Violence and Learned Helplessness

Case History: She Was Her Husband's Pet

On Saturday, April 5, 2003, police arrested Jerry Thomason for aggravated assault and unlawful restraint. A witness at the school where Thomason and his wife, Patricia, dropped off their children had noticed a chain around Patricia's neck. When asked about the 25-foot chain, Jerry jerked it and told the witness that he used it so his wife could not run off.

After the witness called the police, Officer Kenny Hagen arrived at the Thomason house, where he found Patricia with the chain wrapped around her neck twice and padlocked in place. Officer Hagen said that it was difficult for Patricia to talk because she was distraught and "kinda beat down," as if she had accepted the chain as her lot in life. Police did not know how long Patricia had had the chain around her neck or if Jerry ever attached the other end to something stationary to tie her down.

Firefighters used bolt cutters to remove the chain, and doctors checked Patricia at the local hospital. When asked, Jerry said he "loved his wife," and that he had been making an effort to take care of her. Currently, he is in jail, awaiting trial; his bail is set at $53,000. The Thomason children are living with their maternal grandmother.[3]

Officer Hagan's comment in this case history that Patricia Thomason looked "kinda beat down" signifies the types of consequences that IPV victims suffer. It is possible that victims of repeated assaults become helpless, eventually developing a pattern of behavior called **learned helplessness** (LH). Gerow (1989) defines learned helplessness as "a condition in which a subject does not attempt to escape from a painful or noxious situation after learning in a previous, similar situation that escape is not possible" (p. 193). During the 1970s, Lenore Walker (1977) popularized learned helplessness theory as an explanation of battered women's failure to emancipate themselves from their abusers. According to this viewpoint, IPV victims come to believe that they cannot take actions necessary to escape, so they resign themselves to the inevitability of abuse. One recent study lends weight to LH theory by showing that 70 female IPV victims made attributions of helplessness. Victims ascribed abuse to external control factors (abuser or situation) over which they had no control (Clements & Sawhney, 2000).

Other authorities have strongly objected to the characterization of female IPV victims as helpless, because the concept seems to pathologize victims and overlook the volition they do have in the situation. Constituents of this camp further believe that the LH formulation fails to credit the numerous help-seeking activities that victims undertake to end the abuse (e.g., Campbell, Rose, Kulb, & Daphne, 1998). There is overwhelming evidence that victims systematically seek assistance, at least from friends (Goodman et al., 1999; Hutchison & Hirschel, 1998). Gondolf (1988a) found that IPV victims averaged six help-seeking behaviors (e.g., calling police or contacting a clergyman) before they entered a shelter. In a later study, Gondolf (1998c) found that partners of court-ordered batterers most frequently sought help through courts. One comparison disclosed that female IPV victims (*n* = 293) had taken significantly more helpful actions (e.g., contacted an IPV organization for advice) than had women (*n* = 431) who had friends who had been victimized (Nabi & Horner, 2001).

Contrasting findings come from a 1996 national random telephone survey of 6,766 women that identified 2,811 female survivors of partner violence, 226 of whom had been assaulted within the preceding 5 years. Women in this sample sought help from police (38%), sought restraining orders (32%), and sought medical care (31%), but many (41%) failed to access any services. Personal factors associated with failure to seek help were as follows: (a) higher income; (b) no children in the house; (c) employment, homemaker, or school activities; (d) higher educational attainment; (e) nonminority racial status; and (f) youthfulness (Hathaway et al., 1998). Coker, Derrick, Lumpkin, Aldrich, and Oldendick (2000) found that in a population-based survey of 556 South Carolinians, 57.5% of the 78 female IPV victims did not seek any professional help. Finally, some analysts have suggested that feeling helpless may be an accurate reflection of reality for IPV victims rather than a learned response (Ferraro, 2003; Webersinn, Hollinger, & DeLamtre, 1991). (For a review of the literature on LH among battered women, see Rhodes & McKenzie, 1998.)

Violence and Stress

IPV, like other forms of violence, produces stress. A task force sponsored by the American Psychological Association identified physical and sexual assault as an underdiagnosed precursor to many women's mental health problems (Russo, 1985). Stress causes temporary or even permanent changes in the brain and is manifested in a vast array of physical and emotional symptoms. Psychological reactions to stress include cognitive impairment (e.g., confusion and poor test performance), emotional responses (e.g., anxiety, anger, aggression, and depression), and physical illness (e.g., headaches and gastrointestinal problems) (Pianta & Egeland, 1994).

Rollstin and Kern (1998) ascertained that female IPV victims' stress levels are associated with the severity of their psychological and physical abuse as assessed by the Minnesota Multiphasic Personality Inventory-2 (MMPI-2). Researchers have documented the physiological toll of chronic apprehension (Weaver & Clum, 1995). Campbell and Soeken (1999) conducted a longitudinal study that revealed variations in mental health and physical health coinciding with abuse levels. One study of Nicaraguan battered women showed a clear relationship between abuse of either the wife or her child and the wife's level of emotional distress (Ellsberg, Caldera, Herrera, Winkvist, & Kullgren, 1999).

Neurological changes. Several independent studies have begun to present a picture of changes in the brain associated with fear conditioning and PTSD (Banks, 2001; Rausch, van der Kolk, Fisler, & Alpert, 1996). The same is true of changes caused by maltreatment in childhood (Teicher, 2002). Theoretically, a dual-memory representation model may provide an efficient explanation of what neurological changes occur as a result of trauma and fear. According to this model, one memory system underlies vivid or traumatic experiences and another supports ordinary (autobiographical) memory (Brewin, 2001). A large number of studies have implicated certain formations in the brain (e.g., amygdala) as structures highly involved in responding to stress reactions.

One recent analysis of brain damage among 19 female IPV victims and 9 comparison women revealed appalling results (Deering, Templer, Keller, & Canfield, 2001). Victims suffered an average of 2.8 concussions, 219.7 head blows, and 725.4 body blows during the average 5.9 years of their relationships. Furthermore,

researchers found a 35% prevalence rate of head injury occurring during IPV (Monahan & O'Leary, 1999). Valera and Berenbaum (2003) tested 57 sheltered and community female IPV victims for brain injury. Of these women, almost 74% sustained one partner-related brain injury, and 50% suffered multiple partner-related brain injuries. The researchers also found significant correlation between abuse severity and victims' psychopathology ratings.

In the Deering et al. (2002) study mentioned above, several brain-function tests revealed neurological damage in IPV victims. In contrast with nonvictims, victims exhibited significantly lower scores on the Halstead-Reitan Neurological Battery and the Wechsler Memory Scale-Revised. On the Halstead-Reitan Impairment Index, 58% of victims scored as impaired, and 53% met the impairment criterion on the Quick Neurological Screening Test. None of the comparison women evidenced impairment.

A single IPV case of considerable interest is that of a 34-year-old woman who was medically diagnosed with "shaken adult (not baby) syndrome." The woman suffered from blood clots and swelling of the brain, hemorrhaging, bleeding in one eye, vision impairment, arm bruises, apparent cigarette burns on her arms, vomiting, chest pain, and a concussion (Carrigan, Walker, & Barnes, 2000).

Physical illness. Physical illnesses are frequently associated with stress. Evidence indicating that female IPV victims suffer from IPV-related physical and mental illnesses has proliferated (Smith, Thornton, DeVellis, Earp, & Coker, 2002). In a random sample of 387 Swedish women, for example, the **odds ratio** of having a high level of common physical ailments (e.g., heartburn, headaches, back pain) was double that of nonvictimized women in the 15.6% of women in the sample who had been victimized by IPV (Krantz & Ostergren, 2000).

According to several independent analyses, IPV is significantly associated with a host of gynecological and reproductive health problems. Relative to nonvictims, IPV victims suffer from more cervical cancer, sexually transmitted diseases, unwanted pregnancies, and pelvic pain; they also have higher rates of HIV infection and greater fear about negotiating condom use with their partners (e.g., Campbell, 2002; Coker, Sanderson, Fadden, & Pirisi, 2000; Wingood, DiClemente, & Raj, 2000). Female IPV victims also report significantly more disabilities than do nonvictims (Hathaway et al., 2000). A Swedish survey found that victims took significantly longer sick leaves than did nonvictims (Hensing & Alexanderson, 2000).

IPV-related problem-solving and coping deficits. Several researchers have observed that female IPV victims are less effective problem solvers than nonvictims in some experimental settings (e.g., with everyday problems) (Launius & Jensen, 1987). In other situations (e.g., involving relationship problems), IPV victims have outperformed nonvictims (Campbell, 1989a). Problem-solving deficits in IPV victims seem to be situation specific, and some may stem from other sources. Some IPV victims may be poor problem solvers as the result of head injuries (Coffey-Guenther, 1998), for example, or because of cognitive distortions associated with PTSD. Research indicates a vast array of problems in cognitive processing, trauma memory, and appraisals in IPV victims (Halligan, Michael, Clark, & Ehlers, 2003).

Some researchers hold that IPV diminishes victims' ability to cope effectively (see Anson & Sagy, 1995; Kemp, Green, Hovanitz, & Rawlings, 1995). The findings of a recent comparison of 406 female IPV victims support this credible argument. The investigators found that the strategies these women used most often and early in their relationships to avoid violence, placating and resisting, were the least effective (Goodman, Dutton, Weinfurt, & Cook, 2003). In general, compared with nonvictims, IPV victims seem less apt to use active coping strategies (e.g., reframing stressful events, seeking spiritual support) but significantly more prone to use passive strategies (e.g., avoidance, fantasizing) (Bernhard, 2000; Valentiner, Foa, Riggs, & Gershuny, 1996). Avoidance coping is particularly common (see Kemp et al., 1995; Nurius et al., 1992; Sutliff, 1995).

A meta-analytic review of coping styles found that problem-focused styles were positively correlated with overall health (Penley, Tomaka, & Wiebe, 2002), whereas another inquiry found a relationship between problem-focused coping and decreased hopelessness (Clements & Sawhney, 2000). Coping styles such as distancing and escape-avoidance seem to be negatively associated with health outcomes (Penley et al., 2002) and positively associated with **dysphoria** (i.e., feeling unhappy/unwell) (Clements & Sawhney, 2000). One encouraging research finding is that emotionally focused coping appears to decrease over time in IPV victims after they leave their abusers, and problem-focused coping appears to increase (Lerner & Kennedy, 2000). (For an instrument designed to assess coping strategies, see Goodman et al., 2003.)

Violence, Trauma, and Posttraumatic Stress Disorder

According to the fourth edition of the American Psychiatric Association's (1994) *Diagnostic and Statistical Manual of Mental Disorders* (*DSM-IV*), a **traumatic event** is one in which the individual experiences, witnesses, or is confronted with an event or events that involve actual or threatened death or serious injury, or a threat to the physical integrity of the individual or others. The responses that such an event entails include intense fear, helplessness, and horror.

The symptoms of trauma include the following: depression, aggression, substance abuse, physical illness, lowered self-esteem, difficulties in interpersonal relationships, identity problems, and guilt and shame (Carlson & Dalenberg, 2000). Specific trauma symptoms in IPV victims are related to the level of their victimization experiences, and effects are cumulative (Follette, Polusny, Bechtle, & Naugle, 1996; Krantz & Ostergren, 2000; Kury & Ferdinand, 1997). Because the effects of trauma are cumulative, individuals' pre-trauma experiences play a significant role in the severity and duration of the symptoms experienced (Brewin, Andrews, & Valentine, 2000). Often, female IPV victims' traumatic symptoms decrease after they have been away from their abusers for 6 months to 3 years. The temptation victims often have to return to their abusers diminishes over this same period (Lerner & Kennedy, 2000).

When a traumatic event causes an acute, prolonged emotional reaction, psychiatrists designate the reaction posttraumatic stress disorder, or PTSD. PTSD is a common response to trauma and terror. Some symptoms of PTSD are reexperiencing the trauma in painful recollections, numbing of responses, an exaggerated startle response, disturbed sleep, difficulty in concentrating or remembering, anger, and avoidance of activities that rekindle memories of the traumatic event (Goldenson, 1984; Gore-Felton et al., 1999).

Many acts of IPV constitute traumatic experiences, and repeated acts of IPV increase trauma symptoms. Also, some IPV victims may have suffered from exposure to other traumatic events, such as witnessing a murder (Humphreys, Lee, Neylan, & Marmar, 1999a; Vogel & Marshall, 2001). Studies suggest that between 40% and 60% of female IPV victims suffer from PTSD (Mertin & Mohr, 2001; Saunders, 1994). A comparison of Israeli battered and nonbattered women showed that 51.6% of the battered group had "full PTSD" (Sharhabani-Arzy, Amir, Kotler, & Liran, 2003). Even psychological abuse or mild IPV can trigger PTSD. Two studies have shown that extent and severity of exposure to IPV are significantly correlated with severity of PTSD symptomatology (Houskamp & Foy, 1991; Woods & Isenberg, 2001). In a controlled comparison, Laffaye, Kennedy, and Stein (2003) found that PTSD severity was a significant predictor of future mental health. In this analysis, IPV victims with PTSD ($n = 18$) suffered significantly more impairments on quality-of-life measures (e.g., physical health, social functioning) than did IPV victims without PTSD ($n = 22$) and nonabused women in a comparison group ($n = 30$).

Battered Women Who Kill

In some cases, IPV victims become so overwhelmed by fear, feelings of helplessness, and stress symptoms that they may resort to killing their abusers, seeing this as their only means of escape. Peterson (1999) has proposed an application of Black's (1993) self-help theory as an explanation for women's intimate partner homicide. According to this thesis, women kill their intimate partners when they perceive that it is the only way they can get relief from the abuse. That is, IPV victims kill because the criminal justice system and other societal agencies fail to offer them sufficient protection.

In situations where battered women have killed their abusers to "stop the violence," their own use of violence has necessarily become the paramount issue. One fundamental reason for use of severe violence by many battered women is self-defense (e.g., Barnett et al., 1997; Mouradian, 2001). (For a discussion of the mental state of battered women who kill, see Box 10.1.)

Box 10.1 Defending Battered Women Who Kill

On March 9, 1977, Francine Hughes poured gasoline over her sleeping husband and dropped a match. She then drove herself and her children to the Sheriff's Office in Danville, Michigan, and turned herself in. As the facts in the case unfolded, it became apparent that this was not a simple case of first-degree murder. As the prosecution would later argue, Francine "premeditated" the murder; she had killed her husband while he slept. When he wasn't sleeping, however, Mickey Hughes was a violent man. For many years he had beaten and tormented his wife. Francine had children, but few job skills and few options. Over the years, Mickey's pleas for forgiveness, alternating with threats to harm her, neutralized her efforts to leave (Gelles & Straus, 1988).

Francine's defense attorney, Aryon Greydanus, did not believe that Francine was guilty of murder. Because she was not in immediate danger, however, a plea of self-defense seemed inapplicable. Instead, he entered a plea of "innocent by reason of temporary insanity." In the end, after a trial that included hours of evidence about her brutal existence, Francine was acquitted (Gelles & Straus, 1988).

The plight of Francine Hughes attracted considerable attention. She appeared on the *Donahue* show twice, and a television movie based on her life, *The Burning Bed*, drew a large viewing audience. Despite increasing awareness about the predicament of battered women during the 1980s, however, it was still difficult to win an acquittal on an insanity plea. Many battered women who killed their abusers were convicted (see Ewing, 1990). In addition, feminist legal scholars expressed concern that the insanity defense was inappropriate for battered women. Claims of insanity placed battered women in an untenable position and further contributed to general discrimination against women in society and in the courtroom (see Schneider, 1986). Why should women be put in a position of pleading insanity, advocates argued, when they had little choice but to kill?

The battered woman syndrome (BWS) defense holds that a battered woman is virtually held hostage in a violent household by a man who isolates and terrorizes her, convincing her that if she leaves, he will track her down and kill her. DePaul (1992) describes the syndrome as "the situation of a long-time victim of physical, sexual, and psychological abuse who loses self-confidence, feels trapped, and eventually strikes back, assaulting or killing the abuser" (p. 5). The BWS conception, which initially evoked widespread disagreement between professionals, is now losing favor, because the construct suffers from major flaws (e.g., Ferraro, 2003; Rix, 2001). A U.S. Department of Justice (1996) study found that even the name *battered woman syndrome* does not satisfactorily reflect the scientific knowledge accumulated and carries the implication of a malady or a single pattern of responses to battering.

Some sociologists view the concept of BWS as an example of the medicalization of deviant behavior (Conrad & Schneider, 1992). The medical model assumes that certain behaviors are symptomatic of an underlying disease process, just as certain red spots on the skin indicate the underlying disease of chicken pox. By analogy, the BWS defense suggests that the wife could not leave her husband so she had no other choice but to kill him. Members of the general public are prone to believe that female IPV victims freely choose not to leave (Feather, 1996). As with many other mental conditions, it is impossible to prove empirically that the nonobservable BWS state of mind exists. Whereas proponents of BWS argue that abuse causes battered women to believe that escape is impossible, opponents point out that such a belief is not empirically observable. It is undeniable that many battered women do get away from their abusers (e.g., Gondolf, 1988a). Presumably, the women who leave do not have BWS, and the women who do not leave have BWS—a circular argument. Obviously, these problems make BWS a controversial legal defense. Where the prosecution sees the evidence of abuse as motivation for revenge (why didn't she just leave?), the defense sees it as evidence for BWS (she was psychologically trapped and could not leave).

Feminist legal scholars also assert that the common understanding of self-defense, as requiring the immediacy of danger for justification, is gender biased. As originally written into law, the concept of self-defense seems to have applied to assault between two strangers of approximately equal fighting ability (see Schneider, 1986, 2000). The law required that the user of deadly force had to have acted to avert what "reasonably" appeared to be "imminent danger" of serious bodily harm brought about by an action of the victim. Would it have been more "reasonable," for example, for the user of deadly force to "retreat" and thus avoid a killing altogether? In consideration of BWS, the Florida Supreme Court recently removed the absolute duty of an individual to retreat (Orr, 2000).

The experiences of a battered woman, however, are very unlike those of two men fighting in a bar. She may have few options for escape (e.g., no money, no car). She may fear for her life and realize that she cannot hope to win a physical "fight" against her stronger male partner (Avni, 1991). If she tries to leave, she may place herself at greater risk for being hunted down, assaulted, or even killed by her abuser (Bachman & Saltzman, 1995; Hardesty, 2002).

A battered woman may perceive homicide as her only option for escape. "Morally and legally," argues defense attorney Leslie Abramson, "she should not be expected to wait until his hands are around her neck" (quoted in Gibbs, 1993, p. 43). Abramson (1994) has noted that she finds it disturbing that historically no one decried the "heat of passion" defense that men used when they killed their wives and their wives' lovers on finding them in flagrante delicto (in the very act of sexual intercourse). She believes that whereas men may kill out of wounded pride, women most often kill out of fear. The "reasonable man" standard needs revision to incorporate a "reasonable woman" standard (Schneider, 2000). Murdoch (2000) argues that "imminence of danger" may not always be required as part of the self-defense justification. Instead, a "necessity" rule might be a better alternative. Such a rule would be appropriate when society has failed to ensure IPV victims' safety. The idea of allowing IPV victims to make a preemptive strike bothers some legal scholars, however, because it opens the door to a defense that individuals who kill without any justification may attempt to use (e.g., Veinsreideris, 2000).

For some, the controversy surrounding BWS is part of a larger debate over the degree to which mitigating circumstances such as poverty, marital abuse, child abuse, or the influence of drugs and alcohol should be relevant in a court of law. Many observers believe that such "abuse excuses" are getting out of hand. Lorena Bobbitt was acquitted after she cut off her sleeping husband's penis. A jury could not agree on the guilt of Lyle and Eric Menendez, who, as commentator Rush Limbaugh (1994) put it, had "no choice but to gun down their wealthy parents, fake a burglary and go on a spending spree with their victims' money" (p. 56). Someone shoots a ghetto youth because of "urban survival syndrome." One teenager kills another for her coat because of "cultural psychosis." "Black rage" presumably explains Colin Ferguson's mass murder of White passengers on a New York subway (Bonfante, Cole, Gwynne, & Kamlani, 1994).

Feminist legal scholars and battered women's advocates, however, argue that the experiences of battered women are unique and that this should be explained to juries (Ferraro, 2003). Increasingly, this viewpoint is being heard in the United States, and the result is a national movement toward clemency for women who have been convicted of killing abusive husbands. Many states have reexamined cases in which abused women were convicted of homicide, and several governors have commuted the sentences of some of these women, in part because the courts involved did not allow testimony on BWS at their trials (Gibbs, 1993). In the final analysis, American society continues the struggle to find a balance between expressing compassion for victims of abuse and refusing to condone their violent responses.

The battered woman syndrome. During the 1980s, feminist clinicians began to claim that battered women often suffer from a trauma-induced condition they labeled **battered woman syndrome** (BWS; Walker, 1983). Walker (1991) conceptualizes BWS as a subcategory of PTSD. The noncontingent, cyclical nature of the perpetrator's violence creates a condition of learned helplessness in the IPV victim. The victim develops a cluster of cognitions, feelings, and behaviors that lead her to believe she cannot escape (Gleason, 1993; Walker, 1993). BWS offers an explanation for why battered women kill their abusers. BWS essentially expands the concept of legal self-defense to take into account the specific "state of mind" of a battered woman who kills.

While scholars have begun to marshal rationales for abandoning BWS, legal professionals have found more and more reasons to use the construct. On the one hand, a court's acceptance of BWS allows the defense attorney to negotiate a plea of diminished culpability for the defendant's murder of her partner (Sparr, 1996). Counterbalancing this advantage, another attorney may employ the construct to damage the defendant by proving she did not suffer from BWS,

therefore BWS could not be used to explain or mitigate her behavior. A woman who is able to hold down a high-paying job, for instance, does not fit one of the stereotypes of having BWS: being helpless. Ferraro (2003) asserts that "the persistence of the battered woman syndrome is not only a result of misrepresentations by scholars, activists, and expert witnesses, but also of the ease with which a pathological view of battered victims coexists with dominant views of crime and family relationships" (p. 126).

Is there a battered woman's defense? Despite acceptance of BWS in many quarters, there is no "battered woman's defense" per se, only expert testimony about BWS. The U.S. Department of Justice (1996) cites an extensive body of literature about the dynamics of battering and stress reactions to battering. Furthermore, expert testimony tends to increase jury members' knowledge about domestic violence and improves their ability to reach decisions. The solution is to individualize the defense under the umbrella of the "effects of battering" (Ferraro, 2003). Letendre (2000) proposes that a helpful change would be for courts to admit prior acts of domestic violence into evidence.

Other Psychological Consequences of Violence

In addition to adverse physical and stress-related effects, other negative mental effects can also co-occur with IPV (e.g., Purewal & Ganesh, 2000). Depression and low self-esteem appear to be linked to IPV variables, such as severity of abuse or specific type of abuse. A population-based study of 2,043 women ages 18 to 59 who responded to the 1998 Behavioral Risk Factor Surveillance System identified health status differences between IPV victims and nonvictims. Abused women reported significantly more depression, anxiety, sleep problems, and suicidal ideation than did nonvictims (Hathaway et al., 2000).

Depression, low self-esteem, and self-blame. A recent synthesis of studies has shown that IPV victimization is a risk factor for mental disorders, especially depression and PTSD (Golding, 1999). Physical IPV is positively related to levels of depression in both male and female victims (Zlotnick, Kohn, Peterson, & Pearlstein, 1998) and in both lesbian and heterosexual victims (Tuel & Russell, 1998). Almost without exception, researchers have documented clinical depression in battered women (e.g., Arboleda-Florez & Wade, 2001; Dienemann, Boyle, Resnick, Wiederhorn, & Campbell, 2000; Vivian & Malone, 1997). Using data from the 1985 National Family Violence Resurvey, Straus and Smith (1990) found that depression and suicide attempts were four times more likely in female victims of severe IPV than among their nonvictimized counterparts. (For a study of African American women, see Kaslow et al., 1998; for an account of Indian women, see Purewal & Ganesh, 2000.)

In a study of 1,334 Palestinian women, 54% had suffered physical abuse in the year before the survey (Haj-Yahia, 2000). Physical, psychological, sexual, and economic abuse were all significantly related to low-self esteem, as assessed by the Index of Self-Esteem (Hudson, 1982). The higher the level of abuse in each category, the lower the level of self-esteem. Level of IPV and patterns of abuse accounted for 39.3% of the **variance** in self-esteem scores, whereas sociodemographic variables (woman's education, lack of gainful employment, and years of marriage) accounted for 4.3% of the variance. Overall, researchers have not successfully explained the variance in self-esteem scores between battered women and women in comparison groups (see Haj-Yahia, 2000; Wesley, Allison, & Schneider, 2000).

A common attribution battered women make about themselves is that they somehow provoked the violence or that they should have been able to prevent it by changing their own behavior (Hyden, 1999; Towns & Adams, 2000). In one appraisal of 286 victims (of IPV, dating violence, rape, sexual assault, and physical assault), victims reported that they regretted both some of their actions (e.g., isolating themselves from sources of support) and their inactions (e.g., insufficient self-care, failure to seek knowledge) (Fry & Barker, 2001). An inquiry with a sample of Indian women revealed that a lifetime of being blamed by parents, husbands, and in-laws contributed to IPV victims' beliefs that they were ultimately responsible for managing their home lives and that they should be able to "adjust" to IPV (Purewal & Ganesh, 2000). Male IPV perpetrators contribute to women's self-blame by holding them responsible for relationship abuse (Bennett, Tolman, Rogalski, & Srinivasaraghavan, 1994).

In a British study of 286 victims of violence, Andrews and Brewin (1990) found that 53% of assaulted women still involved with the perpetrators experienced self-blame for causing the violence, compared with 35% of those who were no longer in abusive relationships. Relying on a 61-item test and two comparison groups of nonbattered women, Barnett, Martinez, and Keyson (1996) found significantly higher levels of self-blame in battered women. An example of a questionnaire item was, "I was to blame because I did not listen to him." The self-blame reported by the battered women in this study even encompassed contradictory sorts of actions, exemplifying a kind of "damned if you do, damned if you don't" mentality. As a group, for example, they blamed themselves both for "tolerating abuse" and for being "too afraid to leave" (see also Nichols & Feltey, 2003).

Other researchers have reported that IPV victims do not blame themselves for the violence in their relationships, but their studies have included only one or two self-blame items (e.g., Campbell, 1990; Langhinrichsen-Rohling, Neidig, & Thorn, 1995). An obvious cause for the lack of consensus on this issue is the inadequacy of blame conceptualizations and assessment tools (Besharat, Eisler, & Dare, 2001). (For clarification of self-blame and its relationship to anger, see Neumann, 2000; Quigley & Tedeschi, 1996.)

Repeat victimization. Vulnerability to repeat victimization appears to be another long-term consequence of abuse. One outcome of a traumatic experience is that the victim is more likely to suffer additional traumatic experiences (Sanders & Moore, 1999). Kingma (1999) was one of the first to document this phenomenon in a 25-year retrospective investigation of 9,301 male and female victims of violence who visited hospital emergency rooms. In this sample, 11.3% were repeat victims. The same pattern appeared in an Australian longitudinal study (Moffitt & Caspi, 1999). Congruent with this thesis, evidence suggests that childhood sexual abuse (CSA) places adult women at greater risk for a variety of revictimization experiences by partners and other males (Messman-Moore & Long, 2000; Noll, Horowitz, Bonnano, Trickett, & Putnam, 2003).

One study of 557 women who were screened for IPV in a medical setting reported that adult women who had been physically or sexually abused in childhood were at increased risk for adult abuse and mental health problems (e.g., depression, anxiety) (Carlson, McNutt, & Choi, 2003; Carlson, McNutt, Choi, & Rose, 2002). In a community sample of 1,490 women, 25% of CSA victims reported having suffered adult rape by an intimate, a stranger, or both (Purillo, Freeman, & Young, 2003). One comparison of 1,887 female U.S. Navy recruits revealed that rape was 4.8% more likely to occur in women with histories of CSA than in nonvictims (Merrill et al., 1999). Notwithstanding these outcomes, an Australian study of 1,168 abuse victims ascertained that a history of abuse accounted for only 25% of the variance in revictimization. Thus other factors affecting revictimization are at work (Parker & Lee, 2002). (For a review of the literature on CSA and revictimization, see Hanson-Breitenbecher, 2001.)

Psychopathology. Some research has demonstrated psychopathology in IPV survivors: elevated levels of psychosexual dysfunction, major depression, PTSD, generalized anxiety disorder, and obsessive-compulsive disorder (Gleason, 1993). A thorough comparison based on data from a nationally representative sample in the National Comorbidity Survey found that premarital mental disorders of men, but not women, predicted subsequent IPV (Kessler et al., 1994). Nonetheless, some surveys have uncovered a wide spectrum of personality disorders in female victims. In one study, more than half the female IPV victims had elevated rates of mood and eating disorders as assessed by the standards of the third revised edition of the *Diagnostic and Statistical Manual of Mental Disorders* (*DSM-III-R;* American Psychiatric Association, 1987). Two-thirds suffered from some type of diagnosable disorder in mood, eating, substance use, antisocial personality, and symptoms of schizophrenia. Further,

while these women were clearly victimized by IPV, they also were likely to be perpetrators of IPV (Danielson, Moffitt, Caspi, & Silva, 1998).

Another appraisal of 110 female IPV survivors and 50 nonabused comparison women detected significantly different scores on 4 of 9 subscales of the Structured Clinical Interview for *DSM-III-R* (Spitzer, Williams, Gibbon, & First, 1990) and the Abusive Behavior Inventory (ABI; Shepard & Campbell, 1992). Significant differences emerged on the following subscales: PTSD, major depression, alcohol abuse/dependence, and avoidant personality (Watson et al., 1997). Using MMPI-2 data from 31 sheltered women, Khan, Welch, and Zillmer (1993) identified elevations on four subscales: anxiety, alcoholism, maladjustment, and PTSD. Conversely, the women had low scores on ego strength and dominance. Length and severity of psychological abuse, as measured by the ABI, were also positively and significantly correlated with psychological distress (F scale).

SECTION SUMMARY

Violence has many consequences, one of which is chronic and long-lasting fear in victims and often in observers (e.g., children). Because of past violence, IPV victims realize that further assaults might happen at any time. Certain types of abuse, such as near-imprisonment of a victim, create odd symptoms similar to those seen in hostages (the Stockholm syndrome). Similarly, victims may form very close bonds with their abusers as a result of patterns of sporadic violence followed by periods of loving behavior. Couples involved in violent relationships often form close romantic attachments that make it difficult for abused partners to leave.

Repeated violence when no escape is possible may lead to learned helplessness, in which the victim does not try to avoid assaults. The controversy surrounding the concept of LH is difficult to resolve empirically. The most reasonable conclusion seems to be that some women respond to violence with LH, but others respond with help-seeking efforts. A victim's level of passivity or tolerance of violence probably depends on factors specific to her own situation, such as the number of escape options available.

Violence can result in many severe physical and mental conditions. Sadly, studies show that many IPV victims suffer from neurological damage as a result of the physical violence they have experienced. Stress is a very potent aspect of victimization. It can cause chronic symptoms of physical illness, and it appears to impair problem-solving difficulties. Highly stressed IPV victims often fail to find any effective methods for coping with their violent partners. Violence is traumatic and induces trauma symptoms. For many IPV victims, the trauma becomes severe enough to be labeled posttraumatic stress disorder. PTSD is a common repercussion of sexual assault and may last a very long time.

When IPV victims kill their violent partners, fear, stress, and trauma usually play important roles. A subcategorization of these symptoms, along with LH, forms a separate classification of symptoms called *battered woman syndrome.* Currently, courts in the United States almost always allow experts to inform juries about BWS when defendants in spousal homicide cases make legal claims of self-defense. Despite the legal standing of BWS and LH, however, legal scholars and others often do not accept these concepts as providing accurate or appropriate descriptions of battered women who kill. Experts on at least one government panel have suggested that a superior approach to helping an IPV victim develop a plea of self-defense is to describe the "effects of battering" rather than relying on BWS.

One of the most common correlates of IPV is depression. Another is low self-esteem. Research on these two variables is difficult to interpret, because studies cannot determine whether the traits precipitated or followed the violence. Anger is another common characteristic of victims (and perpetrators) of IPV. Victims may blame themselves for the violence they experience, but research in this area has produced inconsistent findings.

REMAINING WITH AN ABUSIVE PARTNER

"Why does she stay?" is often the first question people ask about battered women. The problem with this question is that it implicitly emphasizes the actions of the victimized woman rather than those of her abusive partner. Some commentators have suggested that instead the first questions should be "Why does he do it?" and "How can society stop him?" Or perhaps people should ask, "How did she survive the violence?"

A number of authorities prefer the term *survivors* to *victims* for women who escape IPV situations. Simply assuming that victims can leave if they "really want to" ignores a number of critical constraints these women often face.

Do Battered Victims Stay?

Several investigators have attempted to answer the question "Do battered women stay?" by examining the frequency with which abused women return to their abusers. Researchers have obtained the following return rates: (a) 33% returned after receiving treatment at a shelter (Johnson, Crowley, & Sigler, 1992), (b) 24% to 33% returned after receiving treatment at a shelter (Gondolf, 1988b), and (c) 33% of community IPV victims returned (Herbert, Silver, & Ellard, 1991). Tracking return rates over 2 years, Okun (1986) found that 30% of a sample of 187 sheltered women did leave their abusers upon exiting a shelter, and 43% left within 2 years. On average, women left and returned to their abusers five times before they left for good. Dutton-Douglas and Dionne (1991) point out that the most relevant measure is not whether a woman stays, but whether she continues to be assaulted.

Deciding to leave. Just as reasons for IPV are multidimensional, so are decisions for leaving or staying with an abuser. In reality, most female IPV victims do not want to leave; what they want is for the battering to stop (Landenburger, 1998). Some victims may perceive their relationships with their abusers not as either ongoing or over but as a continuum of involvement (Campbell et al., 1998). Deciding to leave is usually a painstakingly slow process.

In order to leave, victims must traverse several changes in beliefs: (a) acknowledging that the relationship is unhealthy, (b) realizing that the relationship will not get better, (c) experiencing some catalyst event (e.g., abuse of an infant), (d) giving up the dream of an idealized committed relationship, and (e) accepting that, to some extent, the relationship will never be over (e.g., because of the constraints imposed by shared child custody) (Moss, Pitula, Campbell, & Halstead, 1997). Other investigators have pointed out additional requirements. Female IPV victims need to gain a sense of self and hope for a nonabusive future, need to find safe places they can go to when they leave, and need to know about what community agencies are available to support their transition (Werner-Wilson, Zimmerman, & Whalen, 2000).

Recognizing the deleterious effects that being exposed to IPV can have on their children may serve as an impetus to leave for some battered women. Concern for their children is often the ultimate reason victims give for leaving their abusive partners (Hilton, 1992). In defense of their children, some battered women find the courage to mobilize their resources and change their own lives (Levendosky, Lynch, & Graham-Bermann, 2000; Pearson, Thoennes, & Griswold, 1999).

Surviving abuse-relationship satisfaction. Research has provided some ideas about the configuration of factors that make it possible for IPV victims to stay with their abusers. In a national sample of 185 survivors who had endured abuse for an average of 10 years, Horton and Johnson (1993) found only 27 who were able to retain their relationships with the men who abused them. Of these, only 16 rated themselves as feeling "satisfied" or "very satisfied" with the relationships. Compared with dissatisfied survivors in this sample, satisfied survivors tended to be younger, had been more severely abused, pursued more methods for ending the abuse, had abusive partners who became involved in the change process, sought drug and alcohol treatment more readily, were more committed to their partners, and felt more hopeful about their relationships. By comparison, dissatisfied survivors had fewer job opportunities, had a strong fear of failure, had more children, and had male partners who were more likely to sexually abuse them and physically abuse their children. In fact, dissatisfied survivors were more than three times as likely as satisfied survivors to have been forced to have sex.

Increased Physical and Sexual Assaults and Homicides

A battered woman's "just leaving" her abuser does not guarantee that she will be physically safe, or that she will experience improved emotional health (Horton & Johnson, 1993; Hyden, 1999). A popular, but erroneous, assumption is that IPV victims increase their safety by leaving assaultive partners. Unfortunately, research shows that when women try to leave, laws fail to protect them (e.g., Klein, 1995; Zorza, 1995). In 1992, the IPV victimization rate of women who were separated from their husbands was about 3 times higher than that of divorced women and about 25 times higher than that of married women (Bachman & Saltzman, 1995). For some victims the decision is not whether to leave, but whether to live (Hyden, 1999).

Heightened Fear and Postseparation Stress

Female IPV victims may not leave their partners because the abuse they have experienced has generated extremely high levels of fear (Gore-Felton et al., 1999; Healey, 1995; Short et al., 2000), and leaving a perpetrator may not put an end to fear-provoking events. Fear changes over time, and for some women contemplating leaving, actual terror comes to dominate their lives. Male partners threaten to retaliate, stalk, assault, take the children, and engage in numerous other frightening activities to force female partners to stay (Fleury, Sullivan, & Bybee, 2000). One of the most common reasons women do not leave is their sense of foreboding over the possibility of losing their children. An analysis of telephone calls to the National Domestic Violence Hotline revealed that more than half of the callers cited apprehension about revenge as their principal reason for staying with an abusive partner (Danis, Lewis, Trapp, Reid, & Fisher, 1998).

Because of increased fear and stress, leaving an abusive relationship requires courage, persistence, and support. A longitudinal study of 278 women leaving a shelter for IPV victims established that the women experienced varying amounts of stress stemming from assaults by male ex-partners, reduced income, attachment loss, and increased family responsibilities. Over the 2-year period of the study, women with the highest levels of stress became more depressed relative to less stressed women. Fortunately, social support may help offset stress and depression. The researchers found that lower levels of stress and depression were significantly associated with social support in the form of practical assistance, advice/information, emotional support, and companionship (Anderson, Saunders, Yoshihama, Bybee, & Sullivan, 2003).

Economic Dependence, Welfare, and Harassment at Work

Many researchers have called attention to the connection between economic dependence and failure to leave. Some impoverished female IPV victims may not leave their abusers because basic survival is such a struggle (Cucio, 1997). Low-income and newly divorced women are at increased risk for victimization (Byrne, Resnick, Kilpatrick, Best, & Saunders, 1999; Toews, McHenry, & Catless, 2003). Two early studies demonstrated that women either do not leave or return to abusive partners for economic reasons. In one, 58% of the study sample of abused women did not leave because of economic needs (Hofeller, 1982), and in the other, 30% stayed for that reason (Stacey & Shupe, 1983). At the macro level, large-scale government (e.g., Greenfeld et al., 1998) and nongovernment (e.g., Straus & Gelles, 1990) surveys have consistently shown an inverse relationship between rates of victimization and lifetime income. In reviewing this topic, Anderson and Saunders (2003) determined that having sufficient funds was the strongest predictor of leaving.

Of course, low employment levels among battered women factor into their economic plight. A prospective study of 2,863 female IPV victims found that unemployment and assault produced a cyclical pattern. Victimization increases women's risk for unemployment, reduced income, and divorce. Women who experienced new assaults were more than twice as likely as other women to be unemployed at the end of a 3-year test period (Byrne et al., 1999). Lack of financial resources forces many battered women to become recipients of Aid to Families with Dependent Children or other welfare programs (Honeycutt, Marshall, & Weston, 2001; Raphael & Tolman, 1997; Rodriguez, Lasch, Chandra, & Lee, 2001).

Recent investigations have shown that IPV causes victims serious problems in finding employment and holding down jobs (Meisel, Changler, & Rienzi, 2003; Romero, Chavkin, Wise, & Smith, 2003). One partial explanation for low employment of battered women is that IPV perpetrators often use physical force, threats, or other control tactics to prevent their victims from participating in the workplace. In one analysis, IPV resulted in absenteeism from work in 55% of battered women, lateness or leaving early in 62%, job loss in 24%, and batterer harassments at work in 56%. Additionally, female IPV victims in this sample reported that their abusive male partners made the following demands about work: (a) 33% prohibited their female partners from working, (b) 21% prevented them from finding work, (c) 59% discouraged them from working, (d) 24% did not allow them to attend school, and (e) 50% discouraged them from attending school. Ending the abuse, however, enabled 48% of these women to change their employment or school status (Shepard & Pence, 1988; see also Moe & Bell, 2004).

Relationship Issues

In many cultures, women accept societal expectations that they should marry, take responsibility for the quality of their marital relationships, take care of their homes and their children, and remain with their husbands no matter what happens. An IPV victim may remain with her abuser in part because she has adopted socially approved attitudes of love, hope, and commitment to the relationship (Goldner, Penn, Sheinberg, & Walker, 1990; Short et al., 2000). She loves her partner and she hopes the violence will end (see Jackels, 1997; Moss et al., 1997). Although she is aware of the discrepancy between her actual marital relationship and her ideal relationship (Shir, 1999), she has come to believe it is her duty to stay (Short et al., 2000; Towns & Adams, 2000).

Relationship commitment, hope, and loneliness. Commitment to a relationship is usually seen as a positive attribute. In recent years, numerous well-known women have demonstrated respect for their marital commitment in spite of very painful and humiliating revelations of their partners' infidelity (e.g., Hillary Clinton, Kathie Lee Gifford, and Mary Alice Cisneros). So strong is public sentiment about the virtue of marital sacrifice and fidelity that Hillary Clinton's approval ratings skyrocketed when she remained with Bill after his sexual improprieties became known (Rogers, Krammer, Podesta, & Sellinger, 1998; Schindehette, 1998). Believing that they should stay with their partners "no matter what" is significantly related to IPV victims' decisions to stay (Roloff, Soule, & Carey, 2001).

In one study, Bauserman and Arias (1992) showed that female IPV victims' commitment to their relationships was related to their level of failed investment. That is, the victims may have stayed and worked harder to make their relationships work in order to justify the time and effort they had already expended. When a relationship is not going well, frustration may motivate the victim to try even harder to work things out (see LaViolette & Barnett, 2000).

Relationship hope is an especially powerful influence on female IPV victims. Both men and women generally want their marriages to succeed. Procci (1990) has noted that the failure of a marriage to meet one's expectations causes bitter disappointment. Female IPV victims often stay in their marriages because they hope and need to believe that their abusers will stop the violence, a need that Muldary (1983) has termed "learned hopefulness." Women in Muldary's study of shelter residents listed several reasons for staying in or returning to a battering relationship. They "wanted to save the relationship" or "thought we could solve our problems." Despite the abuse, many claimed that they "loved their partners."

Pagelow (1981) found that 73% of the IPV victims in one shelter sample returned to their homes because the batterers repented and the women believed the men would change. Both Okun (1986) and Thompson (1989) discovered that the hopes of battered women were rekindled by their male partners' attendance at even one counseling session, even before the men had made any real changes in their behavior. Similarly, 95% of IPV victims whose husbands were in court-ordered counseling believed their husbands would complete the program, although only half typically do (Gondolf, 1998c). Hope also springs from the fact that an abusive male's behavior is intermittently rewarding rather than continuously abusive. IPV perpetrators can be kind, romantic, and intimate as well as intimidating and assaultive (Hastings & Hamberger, 1988). Periods of kindness interspersed with violence not only create hope but also allow the victim to deny the side of the abuser that terrifies her (Graham, Rawlings, & Rimini, 1988).

Like widows, battered women mourn the loss of their relationships. Of the female IPV victims in Turner and Shapiro's (1986) study sample, 70% said that they returned to their perpetrators because of feelings of loneliness and loss generated by the separation. Varvaro (1991) has identified 12 losses that exacerbate a battered woman's feelings of loneliness: safety, everyday routine, living in a home, personal possessions, self-esteem, a father figure for the children, love and caring from a spouse, success in marriage, hopes and dreams, trust in a mate, view of the world as a safe place, and status and support systems. Some IPV victims do not want to confront their perpetrators for fear of losing them (Roloff et al., 2001).

Interpersonal control. An individual's sense of interpersonal control is the degree to which the individual believes he or she can impose control over the environment through his or her own actions and intentions (Turner & Noh, 1983). Interpersonal control can take many forms; for example, an abusive partner might threaten to leave in order to get his way about the couple's living situation or sexual activities. One line of research indicates that desire for interpersonal control over an intimate partner plays a role in partner abuse (Davis, Ace, & Anda, 2000).

One investigation utilized data from a subsample of couples involved in IPV ($n = 401$) from the National Survey of Families and Households ($N = 5,939$) to assess control. Results demonstrated that for females (but not for males), being victimized by IPV had significant adverse effects on victims' feelings of interpersonal control (Umberson, Anderson, Glick, & Shapiro, 1998). Walker (1984) conjectures that a female IPV victim may misinterpret her focus on her batterer's happiness and her own use of coping strategies as actually having control over the IPV in her relationship. One study of abusive couples' arguments, however, showed that none of a wife's behaviors successfully suppressed a husband's violence once it began (Jacobson et al., 1994).

Social support. Unlike widows, battered women rarely have sufficient social support available to them, and this impedes their attempts to leave abusive relationships. Friends, family members, and professionals may encourage a woman to stay and tolerate the abuse, or may suggest that all she has to do is pack up and leave (Attala, Weaver, Duckett, & Draper, 2000; Rose, Campbell, & Kub, 2000; Short et al., 2000). Furthermore, social support may occur unevenly within different areas of a person's life (Davis & Morris, 1998). One recent study detected gender differences in terms of social support given to 157 crime victims (including IPV victims). Women received significantly more negative responses from family and friends than did men. These kinds of responses may place women at greater risk for negative outcomes, such as PTSD (Andrews, Brewin, & Rose, 2003).

A new study of social support among 137 sheltered women revealed that 91% disclosed their IPV victimization to family or friends. The women's questionnaire data yielded information about how family members and friends responded to their disclosures. Among the helpful responses they made were the following: (a) offered a place to stay, (b) urged victims to call police or a lawyer, and (c) urged them to seek counseling. Although positive responses were far more common than negative ones, friends and family members also occasionally did hurtful things, such as changing the subject and spending less time with the victim. Positive social support had a direct positive effect on victims' quality of life, whereas negative responses were significantly correlated with victims' depression (Goodkind, Gillum, Bybee, & Sullivan, 2003).

On the other hand, victims of family crimes may not be very open to formal support when it is offered. Gondolf (1998b) found that very few battered women involved in court cases were willing to accept support services from a shelter outreach program. Of the 1,012 reached by phone from a group of 1,895, 644 refused all services for themselves (e.g., 12-session support group, individual counseling, weekly phone counseling). None of the women in this group had ever been in touch with a shelter before. Almost half of those who refused help did so because they "did not need it." Some of the women were already in counseling, some had scheduling problems, some had left their abusers, and a few had no transportation. Some expressed worry about triggering a CPS referral if they accepted help.

The associations between a number of social support variables and their effectiveness in reducing stress and influencing coping styles are complex (see Carlson et al., 2002; Smith et al., 2002; Thompson et al., 2000). One large national survey of both men and women disclosed that victims of partner abuse received as much actual social support as nonvictimized individuals (Zlotnick et al., 1998). In a comparison of the perceptions of female IPV victims' and those of women in two nonvictim groups, victims reported receiving less social support than did the other women (Barnett et al., 1996). Apparently, judgments about receiving social support rely somewhat on subjective perceptions rather than on objective reality.

Attempts to Stop the Violence

Walker (1985) cites one myth about IPV: It is impossible to love someone who hits you. Physical aggression does not herald the demise of a marriage (Lloyd, 1988). The commonly heard claim "If he ever lays a hand on me, I'll leave" does not mirror reality. Female IPV victims reason that if they can stop the IPV, they might be able to maintain their relationships. The most common method of stopping domestic violence, however, is the physical and legal termination of the relationship (Bowker, 1983; NiCarthy, 1987).

Bowker (1993) found that women employ a variety of strategies in their attempts to end IPV. A majority of the 1,000 women in Bowker's sample used at least one of seven strategies to end IPV: (a) 868 avoided the men physically or avoided certain topics of conversation, (b) 855 covered their faces and vital organs with their hands or used other passive defenses when assaulted, (c) 758 threatened to call police or file for divorce, (d) 752 attempted to extract promises that the men would never batter them again, (e) 716 attempted to talk the men out of battering them, (f) 665 fought back physically, and (g) 651 hid or ran away when attacked.

Adaptation to violence. Another explanation for battered women's perseverance in their relationships

with their abusers is that they have learned to make numerous accommodations to the violence. A prerequisite of learning how to live with an abusive person is finding a way to make his (or her) violence acceptable. Basic psychological defense mechanisms of rationalization and denial achieve this goal. By denying that their mates harm them or even intend to, female IPV victims can negate the danger they confront (Dutton-Douglas & Dionne, 1991). These processes are not difficult to understand when one considers that in American culture many people believe that in families, a certain amount of physical force is not necessarily a repudiation of love, but can be tangible proof of it. Women in relationships come to believe, "If he didn't love me so much, he wouldn't be so jealous."

Approach-avoidance behavior and entrapment theories. Battered women are often overwhelmed by ambivalent feelings, as described by approach-avoidance behavior (for a review, see LaViolette & Barnett, 2000). One well-established conflict described by learning theorists is termed *double approach-avoidance conflict.* This type of conflict involves making a decision about an object (or person) that contains both desirable and undesirable features (the house you want to buy is affordable, but it is 70 miles from your job). People caught in this kind of conflict vacillate, first going toward one goal and then retreating, next going toward the other goal and then retreating, and so forth. On the one hand, a battered woman's relationship meets many of her emotional and economic needs, but on the other hand, it is degrading and dangerous. She wants to approach her partner's love for her, which is hopeful, and run from his IPV, which is frightening (Hyden, 1999). Should she stay or should she leave?

Some authorities refer to psychological changes brought about by various conflicts (e.g., fear and hope) as entrapment (Landenburger, 1998; Walker, 1979). Studies also find that even when such major obstacles as poverty are not present, women may still judge themselves unable to leave (e.g., Purewal & Ganesh, 2000). Although increasingly used, the word *entrapment* is bothersome to some observers because they see it as implying that battered women are unable to exercise choice. Some see the fact that many women do leave violent relationships as "proof" that battered women are not really trapped. It may be better to conceptualize the problem in terms of factors that sometimes make it extremely difficult for women to leave.

Most battered women do not stay in relationships with their abusers. Only about a third of women who leave shelters for IPV victims return to their abusive partners. Deciding to leave is a weighty proposition. Female IPV victims usually do not wish to leave; rather, they want the violence to stop. To be able to leave, they have to change their beliefs. For instance, they have to realize their abusers are not going to change. Of those who return to their abusers, some are much more satisfied with their relationships than others, depending on a number of variables, including sexual assault.

When IPV victims attempt to leave, abusers often increase their physical and sexual assaults, and abusers who are left may begin stalking their victims. Thus leaving or attempting to leave may heighten victims' levels of fear and stress, rendering them unable to take further action. Many IPV perpetrators threaten their victims with death or inform the victims that they will take the children, hurt the children, or both. Based on perpetrators' past behavior, victims have every reason to believe they will carry out their threats.

Research pinpoints economic necessity as a strong reason, if not the primary reason, many victims remain with their abusers. Most IPV victims are not employed and have no independent source of income. Many IPV perpetrators attempt to prevent their partners from working outside the home through intimidation. Victims who do manage to go to work or to school must cope with special obstacles, such as harassment on the job.

Relationship issues provide extremely compelling reasons for victims to remain with their abusive partners. Most battered women, like other women, feel committed to their relationships and want to maintain their homes. A battered woman usually loves her partner, and she keeps hoping he will "change back" to the man she married. Male IPV perpetrators are likely to exert various types of control over their victims, making them feel powerless. Victims also fear they will be lonely if their relationships end. Last, the social support that victims receive from family and friends is not sufficient to enable many victims to leave.

Another reason female victims stay with their abusers is that they gradually adjust to the battering. Approach-avoidance learning offers a different explanation for IPV victims' ambivalence. They feel attracted to their partners' loving behavior and fearful of their assaultive behavior. Victims become entrapped in abusive relationships because so many factors pressure them to stay. Violence alternated with loving behavior may prompt victims to form "traumatic bonds" with their abusers and thus become emotionally trapped in their relationships. Although psychological entrapment theories "explain" the puzzling fact that some IPV victims do not leave their abusers, acceptance of such theories is not uniform.

PRACTICE, POLICY, AND PREVENTION ISSUES

In addition to the policy considerations described previously, there are several ways to think about reducing, eliminating, and preventing IPV. Many experts, of course, focus on stopping male violence through treatment and criminal sanctions (for discussion of this approach, see Chapter 11). Others focus on helping IPV victims break free from perpetrators and begin new lives. Still others recognize that some victims very much want to save their relationships while managing to eliminate IPV. Without appropriate intervention, battered women may remain mired in abusive relationships for a considerable length of time.

This section encompasses several topics. First, it presents a small amount of information on abused male partners. Second, it addresses shelter treatments, counseling, and alcohol and drug treatment for abused female partners. Another subsection focuses on practice issues, such as screening clients, improving practitioners' cultural competence, collaboration among community agencies, and dealing with secondary trauma. The discussion then turns to recommendations for policy changes: changing gender socialization, letting battered women help guide policy, improving community services, and improving the skills of service providers. The section concludes with suggestions for prevention strategies, such as enabling women to become economically independent, improving health care services, resolving issues among various agencies and groups, and improving protection for battered women.

Male Victims of Intimate Partner Violence: How Much of a Problem?

Researchers are slowly beginning to investigate the parameters of male IPV victimization. As noted previously, Conflict Tactics Scale prevalence and incidence data derived from a broad spectrum of community-based (nonclinical) comparisons indicate that women and men commit physical and psychological IPV with almost equal frequency (Archer, 2000). Analysis of the 1985 National Family Violence Survey revealed that at least 25% of wives were the only member of a couple to have used violence during the previous year (Brush, 1990). In contrast, data collected within a crime context (National Crime Victimization Survey, *Uniform Crime Reports, Supplementary Homicide Reports*) or in clinical settings present markedly different findings. The frequencies of injury rates, emergency room visits, and calls to police, shelters, and the National Domestic Violence Hotline all suggest that women are more victimized than men (see Bachman & Saltzman, 1995; Felson et al., 2002).

Nevertheless, in 1977 Suzanne Steinmetz argued that some men suffer from a "battered husband syndrome" comparable to the battered woman syndrome, and this concept has recently received renewed endorsement (e.g., George, 2003). In a review of IPV studies, however, Saunders (2002) did not find a consensus that female-to-male partner violence is even a major social problem, let alone a behavioral equivalent to male-to-female violence. For his part, Straus (1993) has reaffirmed his position that assaults by women (e.g., "slaps") are a serious social problem, just as "slapping" a coworker would be a problem. Nonetheless, he concedes that women are more victimized than men.

All questions asked about male-to-female partner violence apply to female-to-male partner violence. Dalsbeimer (1998) convincingly speaks to some of resemblances between female-to-male partner violence and male-to-female partner violence. Some victimized men may feel or believe the following: (a) It is too embarrassing to report IPV victimization; (b) they might lose their children in a custody battle; (c) they can protect their children if they remain; (d) if they leave, they will be less financially solvent because of the costs of child support and maintaining two residences; (e) the violence is too minor to break up their families; (f) they love their wives; and (g) stress or alcohol is the real culprit. One gender disparity between victims may be a man's fear that fighting back might lead to his killing the woman.

Female-to-male partner violence may operate through the same processes as male-to-female partner violence. Female IPV perpetrators may have psychiatric conditions, such as antisocial personality disorder or mood disorders (Sommer, Barnes, & Murray, 1992). They may think violence enlivens their relationships, or they may believe it is socially acceptable for women to slap men. Dalsbeimer (1998) concludes that social agents, such as emergency room staff and mental health workers, ignore male IPV victims and fail to offer them assistance. Professional first responders, such as medical and law enforcement personnel, should find ways to help male victims through listening to their stories and referring them to helping agencies. If nothing else, Frieze (2003) asserts, researchers need to pay more attention to female-to-male partner violence. (For further descriptions of abused men, see Cook, 1997.)

Treatments for Female IPV Victims

Controversies over treatment modalities for victims of IPV cast a long shadow over the selection of treatments (see Box 10.2 for a discussion). The types of treatment offered have even become a legal issue. (See Chapter 11 for a discussion of treatments and the law.)

Box 10.2 Controversies Concerning Treatment Modalities

Debates abound over the appropriateness and effectiveness of various counseling treatments. Lundy and Grossman (2001) present a clear and comprehensive review of interventions categorized along three disciplinary lines: psychological, sociological, and feminist. They also describe integrated models. Outcome studies have not yet clarified differences in treatment effects sufficiently to allow researchers to reach firm conclusions (Chalk & King, 1998).

The most passionate debate centers on whether couples' therapy is appropriate for partners involved in a violent relationship. Therapists who recommend couples' therapy believe that when couples wish to stay together despite the violence, it may be best to treat them together, especially if the violence is not severe (Lane & Russell, 1989). Other couples' therapists contend that IPV is a product of the interactions of the partners in a specific relationship, rather than the individual behavior of one partner (Giles-Sims, 1983). Hence the presence of both partners in therapy expedites the goal of ending the violence (see Margolin & Burman, 1993). So far, studies examining the effectiveness of couples' counseling have produced inconclusive findings (Chalk & King, 1998).

Some experts voice concerns that traditional couples' and family therapists appear insensitive to the impact of gender on family relationships. They assert that some counselors may inadvertently impose a patriarchal view of the family as the standard of normal family functioning (Trute, 1998). Other counselors believe that couples' counseling places battered women in danger (Davis, 1984; Dutton-Douglas & Dionne, 1991; Hansen, Harway, & Cervantes, 1991) just at a time when the clinicians' first duty is to ensure the women's safety (Hamberger & Barnett, 1995). A woman's complaints about her male partner during a counseling session, for example, may lead to a beating later. Many think it is critical to recognize that a battering problem belongs to the person who batters (Gondolf, 1998a; Hansen et al., 1991). Consequently, couples' therapy runs the risk of changing an "individual" issue (e.g., violence) into a "family" issue (e.g., poor communication).

Shelter Treatment

The temporary separation from their abusers that shelters offer can assist female IPV victims by helping them feel safe and by providing them with people who will listen to their concerns. First and foremost, shelter programs emphasize safety planning for IPV victims planning to leave their abusers: finding a safe place to go, having money hidden in a separate account, getting a second set of keys for the car, and packing a bag with important documents in it. In one survey of female IPV victims, participants rated safety measures, such as hiding important papers, as the most helpful tactic they used to cope with IPV (Goodman et al., 2003).

Helping victims obtain temporary welfare benefits and helping them prepare for employment (e.g., referral to training programs) are usually top priorities for shelter programs and coordinated community programs (Brown, Reedy, Fountain, Johnson, & Dichiser, 2000; Dutton-Douglas & Dionne, 1991). Shelter staff often help victims complete the legal forms needed to get restraining orders, teach them (nonviolent) parenting skills, and help them enroll in substance abuse programs. Shelters are often successful in helping battered women change by helping them understand the terrible damage that exposure to interparental violence is doing to their children (e.g., McCloskey, Figueredo, & Koss, 1995; Rossman & Ho, 2000).

Helping victims achieve economic independence. Victims are more likely to escape IPV if they can get jobs or go back to school (Anderson & Saunders, 2003; for a review, see Paquet, Damant, Beaudoin, & Proulx, 1998). Shelter workers usually try to find ways to help IPV victims begin the journey toward economic independence. Female IPV victims often have few financial resources and little social support to help them surmount the host of institutional and social obstacles that impede their progress toward self-sufficiency (see Browne & Bassuk, 1997; Clarke, Pendry, & Kim, 1997).

In areas of income, employment, and child support, the American political and legal systems allow practices that undermine women's attempts to become economically independent. For example, a woman earns approximately 77 cents for every dollar a man earns, and in some occupations a man with only a high school diploma may earn more than a woman with a college degree (U.S. Bureau of Labor Statistics, 1999). Gender discrimination continues despite research showing that women are as productive on the job as men and are as committed to their jobs as men. Furthermore, women do not quit their jobs any more frequently than men do. (For a review of some factors related to gender discrimination, see Ostroff & Atwater, 2003.) Making matters worse are discriminatory practices in the court system. Ford, Rompf, Faragher, and Weisenfluh (1995) examined judges' rulings involving 174 IPV victims, for example, and found that judges ordered child support in only 13.2% of the cases. Without doubt, legislatures need to address such policies and make necessary changes. Poverty may affect men's ability to pay child support. Brown (2002) points

An Interview With Maria Michaels

"Things are going in the right direction, but there is still tolerance for family violence. We need education toward zero tolerance. There is too much pain and suffering and death and destruction. We need to keep working harder than ever to STOP THE VIOLENCE."

Maria Michaels has served as Clinical Director of Haven Hills, a shelter for battered women, and at Haven Hills II, a transitional living center located at a secondary site. She holds a bachelor's degree in psychology and a master's degree in educational psychology, and she is a licensed marriage and family therapist in California.

Q: What attracted you to the field of family violence?

A: Experiences—I remember as a child feeling a lack of power, of not being listened to or heard. Observing children as I grew and realizing the abuse and violence that too often was a secret part of their lives drew me to working with children. As the secrets of abuse of children and women began to be exposed I wanted to be part of working toward a nonviolent way of life.

Q: Why did you decide to work in a shelter?

A: When I first walked into the crisis shelter I knew this was where I wanted to be. The strength of the women and children there was remarkable. My past experiences and concerns about children and how they carry the pain of childhood abuse throughout their lives all came together.

Q: What type of work do you do at the shelter?

out that low-income men need programs that offer support, incentives, and positive affirmation, so they can better support their children.

Discrimination against women in housing complicates IPV victims' efforts to secure economic stability. Some government-subsidized housing projects have established rules that allow the eviction of tenants involved in violence, even if the tenants are the victims. In one setting, a housing authority was ordered to stop evicting female IPV victims (reported in "Federal Sex Discrimination Lawsuit," 2001).

At a practical level, shelter workers sometimes help IPV victims improve their skills by role-playing job interviewing techniques, assertion skills, and parenting skills. Shelter workers may also help victims to improve their basic apartment- or house-hunting proficiency (Holiman & Schilit, 1991). Cummings (1990) suggests that, along with other types of competency training, shelters should offer IPV victims self-defense training.

Wilson, Baglioni, and Downing (1989) have concluded that working away from home appears to be a crucial survival strategy for female IPV victims, probably because it lessens their economic, social, and emotional dependence on their abusers. An account of 162 welfare recipients disclosed that only 25% of those who were IPV victims asserted that working actually decreased their level of victimization (Brush, 2003). Further, welfare programs may reduce the level of IPV suffered by victims living in urban settings but not that

A: I supervise the staff and interns as well as counseling women.

Q: What areas of your work do you find difficult?

A: It is difficult for me and the staff to hear stories of violence, often cruel and humiliating stories that amount to torture. We hear these stories day after day, week after week, and year after year. The challenge is to remain hopeful. The threat of violence is ever present. We keep the shelter's location confidential, and we must always be vigilant.

Q: What are some of the rewarding experiences connected with your work?

A: Observing the resiliency of human beings is amazing! Seeing how women and children blossom in an environment of freedom and respect and empowerment is awesome. The struggle and pain in living through these abuses takes so much courage and energy. I often wonder if all that energy was available for other pursuits how society might benefit.

Q: What impact has your work had on you?

A: It's humbling to work with people who have experienced such horrors. As a staff we work hard to support each other. We use humor and trade ideas about managing stress. We try to "leave the work at the office." We try to pass the responsibility to the staff on duty and not take it home. When someone asks me where I work, in a social situation, I have an opportunity to educate about domestic violence, and at times this is stressful.

Q: What are your practice and policy concerns?

A: I'm part of the administration team that, with the board, sets our goals and policy. We are facing a crisis in funding at a time when we have expanded services in underserved populations and preventive services for teens. The economy—lack of affordable housing and adequate child care—make the transition to a violence-free life extremely difficult for our clients. Women are often forced to choose between poverty and abuse.

Q: What changes have you seen over the years?

A: I've worked nearly 20 years at this agency and I've seen many positive changes as a result of hard work by people in the field: clinicians, researchers, legislators, battered women, advocates, friends, concerned citizens. There have been many changes in legislation, changes in media coverage, changes in how we work with the police and courts and schools and agencies. When I first came here, the clergy often advised women to stay—"stick it out." Now they more often support a nonviolent environment and give the crisis line number to women seeking help. Things are going in the right direction, but there is still tolerance for family violence. We need education toward zero tolerance. There is too much pain and suffering and death and destruction. We need to keep working harder than ever to STOP THE VIOLENCE.

---

of victims living in rural settings (Gennetian, 2003). It is important that welfare agencies screen applicants for the occurrence of IPV and its impact in their lives in order to make case-by-case decisions about whether it is wise to encourage victims to work (Brush, 2003). Currently, only a few corporations in the United States make any effort to support employees who are IPV victims (Isaac, 1998). Although the laws are changing slowly, most states do not routinely protect women from losing their jobs because of IPV-related absenteeism (e.g., absences because of court appearances or medical treatments) (Runge & Hearn, 2000). One Swiss researcher, however, cautions social service workers not to assume that economic independence alone will protect victims from further abuse. Rather,

the criminal justice system must play a major role in protecting women (Seith, 2001).

Generally, legislators need to increase their efforts to protect IPV victims and their children so that victims can work (e.g., Brush, 2000). It is imperative that state and local governments design policies aimed at bolstering IPV victims' income and providing them with job support (Anderson & Saunders, 2003). Legislation should strengthen existing laws intended to protect women against sex- or victimization-related types of discrimination, and society should demand the enforcement of those laws. Employers may ignore signs that employees are victims of abuse, and even if they are aware of a problem, they may fail to offer supportive services.

Because of these practices, legislators need to enact laws requiring employers to assist employees who are being threatened, stalked, or harassed at work by taking preventive safety measures. Affordable permanent housing is an especially pressing need among IPV victims who have left their abusers. Government and criminal justice agencies should strengthen their efforts to make all noncustodial parents meet their child support obligations. Legislatures should also mandate the evaluation of welfare programs and job training programs for IPV victims, to be sure that these efforts succeed in helping victims learn how to earn a living.

Most corporations in the United States have not addressed the effects of IPV on employees (Isaac, 1998). Increasingly, however, states are passing employment regulations to benefit IPV victims. The Washington State Department of Economic Security, for example, has expanded IPV victims' right to leave their jobs (which may be necessary to escape their abusers) and still be eligible for unemployment insurance (Shuman-Austin, 2000). In addition, women who are seriously injured as a result of IPV may be eligible to take time off from work under the federal Family and Medical Leave Act (Runge & Hearn, 2000).

Society's agents should downplay gender differences. Gender-role socialization works against women's economic and emotional independence at the same time it advances ideas of masculinity that harm men emotionally and contribute to their violence. Every woman needs to obtain an education that will allow her to be self-sufficient. Women in general should learn to be less subordinate and less emotionally and economically dependent on men (see Nutt, 1999).

Improving shelter services. Shelters should expand their outreach to meet the needs of various groups of women: minorities, immigrants, lesbians, disabled, and older women. For example, shelters might purchase and make available to clients special telecommunication devices for the hearing impaired. (For a description of a unique shelter program in Texas, see Cameron & Abramson, 2002; for information on services for people with disabilities who have been victimized, see Office for Victims of Crime, 2002a.) Government funding policies need to incorporate funding for transitional, low-cost housing for women who do not want to return to their abusers. Such housing will allow them the time to receive more counseling, find employment, and obtain health care.

Counseling

Case History: Wendy Calls a Hotline

The third time the police arrested Wendy's husband for beating her, they handed Wendy a card with the name and phone number of a battered woman's hotline. The next day, while her cut lip was still hurting and she felt afraid and alone, she called the hotline and spoke with Judy. Judy provided Wendy with a lot of information and told her about the battered woman's outreach group she could attend on Wednesday mornings at 11:00. Although Wendy did not see how sitting around talking and listening to other battered women could possibly help her personally, she attended her first group meeting the following Wednesday. She was amazed to hear about the experiences of other women, how some were trying to get jobs, others were making plans to move in together to share expenses, and still others were seeking civil damages against their abusers in court. For the first time in 10 years, Wendy felt that maybe she really could do something to stop her husband's assaults, and she began to think more carefully about her safety needs.

As this case history illustrates, reaching out for help and interacting with other victims can be a vital link to a violence-free life for an IPV victim. Counseling is a crucial element in helping IPV victims make decisions about how to avoid further violence. Victims may be aware of their need for counseling support but may not know whom to call or what sort of assistance they might receive. Exacerbating these problems is that some counseling techniques intended to help IPV victims have, in reality, been detrimental to them

(Dutton-Douglas & Dionne, 1991; Hansen et al., 1991). A Canadian study, for example, revealed that almost 20% of IPV victims who had sought help thought that the service personnel with whom they came in contact had denied or minimized their IPV experiences (Harris et al., 2001).

Basic counseling goals. Counseling for IPV victims should include helping them to define the meaning of IPV, to understand what causes it, and to be aware of the role it plays in their lives. Therapists should help victims deal with the psychological effects of victimization, such as fear, stress, PTSD, avoidance, frustration, diminished problem-solving ability, and inept coping strategies (Kubany, Hill, & Owens, 2003). To be effective, counselors need to be experienced in recognizing victims' intense fear and its immobilizing effects (Hyden, 1999). IPV victims may exhibit strange symptoms, such as those often seen in hostages or in cases of traumatic bonding, or they may be entrapped by attachment needs (Henderson et al., 1997; Vazquez, 1996).

Because female IPV victims tend to abuse alcohol and drugs (e.g., Gleason, 1993; Wall, 1993) and because drug and alcohol use exposes victims to risk for continued IPV, sobriety treatment is urgent (El-Bassel, Gilbert, Schilling, & Wada, 2000; Salomon, Bassuk, & Huntington, 2002). Experts working jointly in the fields of substance abuse and family violence have called attention to the dangers of attempting to substitute Alcoholics Anonymous or Al-Anon for shelter programs. The "sobriety first" model applied to chemically dependent women is almost certainly doomed to failure for IPV victims. It disregards both the requisite "safety first" approach and the recognition of alcohol use as a method for coping with unremitting danger, fear, and pain (Zubretsky & Digirolamo, 1994).

Most counselors probably need more education about intimate partner rape, the effects of which are extremely damaging and long-lasting (Culbertson & Dehle, 2001; Riggs, Kilpatrick, & Resnick, 1992). As one researcher noted in testimony before the New Hampshire State Legislature, "When you are raped by a stranger you have to live with a frightening memory. When you are raped by your husband, you have to live with your rapist." Stermac, Del Bove, and Addison (2001) recently documented two important findings about intimate partner sexual assault in a community-based sample: First, husbands and boyfriends were significantly more physically violent during sexual assaults against their partners than were other males in assaults against acquaintances. Second, wives and girlfriends sustained significantly more severe injuries during sexual assaults than did women who were assaulted by friends or acquaintances. IPV victims may also need help in dealing with the effects of prior victimizations (e.g., childhood sexual abuse).

Personal empowerment strategies. The authors of many recent articles on treatment of IPV victims advise some form of personal empowerment strategy as essential to recovery (e.g., Busch & Valentine, 2000; Lempert, 1996; Peled, Eisikovits, Enosh, & Winstok, 2000). Empowerment involves two major elements: gaining power and taking action. Individual empowerment, in contrast to community empowerment, incorporates the notion of intrapsychic change. Victims often pass through several different stages before they are able to change their feelings and cognitions about IPV. They may begin with feelings of anger and powerlessness, next become aware of the danger they face, and ultimately become more assertive and self-determined.

Wetzel and Ross (1983) contend that some of the most important therapeutic work with female IPV victims is the remaking of their belief systems. Victims may erroneously believe that IPV is normative rather than abusive. They need counseling to help them stop believing that they cause or can stop the abuse. Douglas (1987) alleges that therapy can help victims accept personal responsibility for their safety while rejecting personal responsibility for the violence.

Victims might need help in evaluating whether their partners' abuse offsets their positive qualities. Marshall, Weston, and Honeycutt (2000) studied 729 female IPV victims and found compelling evidence that IPV perpetrators' positivity (e.g., affection) mediates the effects of IPV on victims. To help a victim overcome an imbalance of judgment, a therapist can first focus on the perpetrator's good qualities before discussing his violence. This technique might help the victim recognize her tendency to minimize the harm done to her.

Nabi and Horner's (2001) appraisal of female IPV victims' opinions led them to propose that policy makers should treat victims as experts in guiding policy. In a recent dissertation, West (2002) highlights the problems inherent in trying to plan a program for IPV victims without taking victims' opinions into account. A sample consisting of 4-6 victims in each of 10 focus groups evaluated a public awareness campaign about IPV. The female victims believed the information offered in the campaign was not totally accurate and suggested that the messages should have focused on enhancing early identification, empowerment, and help seeking. A different group of victims who regretted their inactions and lack of knowledge about IPV believed that public awareness campaigns emphasizing human rights would have helped them recognize IPV and take action sooner (Fry & Barker, 2001).

Training in problem-solving skills and in making self-directed decisions (see Bowen, 1982; D'Zurilla, 1986) is pivotal for helping battered women mobilize their coping capacity. An initial step may be anxiety reduction to enhance concentration (Trimpey, 1989). Similarly, therapists need to be alert to the strong probability that IPV victims suffer from PTSD, with its attendant anxiety-related symptoms. Inclusion of a support group in an overall treatment plan enhances coping capacity in battered women (Rubin, 1991; Tan, Basta, Sullivan, & Davidson, 1995). Listening to other IPV victims in a group setting describe their trauma-related symptoms and how these symptoms interfere with functioning validates a victim's experiences and tends to reassure her that she is not "crazy" (Saunders, 1994).

Social supports should help embolden a battered woman to redefine marriage as a relationship in which violence is not allowed (Bagarozzi & Giddings, 1983). Chang (1989) has theorized that supportive involvement with others is critical in the transformation of a battered woman into a self-saver rather than a wife who concentrates on either saving the relationship or helping her abuser change. For African American victims, groups should include a focus on racial stereotypes of Black women as a means of reducing isolation and providing social support (Brice-Baker, 1994). Further, social support acts as a mediator in reducing revictimization for African American women (Bender, Cook, & Kaslow, 2003). Improving victims' social support networks is crucial. Indeed, Johnson (1988) found that 63% of battered women who had little or no support returned to their abusers, whereas only 19% of those who had strong support systems returned.

Counselors need to recognize the IPV victim's grief over the loss of her abusive partner and the loss of her dreams and hopes. Most battered women feel great deprivation and loss when their relationships end (Walker, 1984). Varvaro (1991) found that assessing their losses and dealing with them in a support group enabled battered women to avoid the immobilizing effects of grief and to develop a new sense of self-determination.

Community Services and Collaborations

As Jaffe, Wolfe, and Wilson (1990) have noted, ensuring a battered woman's safety is "ultimately a community responsibility and a role of the police officers and courts" (p. 88). Victims often cannot change their lives without the support of their communities. Some victims, however, do not seek assistance. Goodman et al.'s (2003) study revealed that external sources of assistance were much more helpful than private attempts to stop the violence. At a 30-month follow-up, Gondolf (2002) questioned 278 women whose husbands were attending court-ordered treatment for batterers. A plurality (59%) said they did not seek any services because they did not need them. Along the same lines, Keilitz, Davis, and Eikeman (1998) found that almost half of the battered women in their survey turned to neighbors and friends rather than to shelters.

Victims who do seek services all too often encounter obstacles. Harris et al. (2001) list the following problems related by the women in their study: (a) cannot find service needed or service does not exist in victim's community; (b) do not know which agency to contact; (c) have difficulty contacting agencies because of language difference, literacy problem, or disabilities; (d) cannot access agency because of exigencies, such as long waiting lists or service fees; and (e) cannot receive help because agency lacks funding. In another appraisal, IPV victims reported additional problems in finding help within the community: (a) lack of services dealing with multiple barriers, (b) uneducated service providers, and (c) perpetrators' ability to use victims' barriers to further their own goals (Zweig, Schlichter, & Burt, 2002). Despite such obstacles, Whalen (1996) suggests that counselors urge IPV victims to make use of many social, psychological, legal, and political resources early in the recovery process. Victims need empowerment in terms of accessing community aid (Paquet et al., 1998).

On a more personal note, Gondolf (2002) found that 41% of 278 women who were partners of men in treatment said they did not seek help from battered women's shelters because they had negative views of shelters. Of these women, 56% developed negative views from actual experiences, and 44% relied on their perceptions only. The women held similar opinions about other community social services. From these studies and others, it is clear that the actions of certain community service providers influence women's actions and their ability to stay away from their abusers (Wuest & Merritt-Gray, 1999).

Female IPV victims themselves have formulated opinions about their needs. In terms of community service providers, battered women have reported that they need more compassion and more individualized attention (Nichols & Feltey, 2003). Battered women in one inquiry enumerated the following factors that would facilitate their leaving their abusers (Short et al., 2000): (a) laws that impose sanctions on batterers; (b) resources that allow independence, such as housing and money; (c) education about abuse; (d) more shelters; and (e) provision of interim help during the woman's decision-making phase (see also Lombardi, 1998).

Bybee and Sullivan (2002) conducted a systematically controlled longitudinal study of 267 previously sheltered female IPV victims. Their purpose was to evaluate a program aimed at helping victims access community services. Paraprofessional advocates provided a 10-week postshelter intervention to a treatment group of women. Advocates visited about twice a week to help the women obtain resources: education, legal services, health care, housing, child care, employment, services for children, financial assistance, transportation, and social support. The researchers entered "quality-of-life [QOL] data" and "reabuse reports" taken at 12 and 24 months postshelter treatment into **structural equation models**. Results indicated that women in the intervention group obtained desired community resources and increased their social support. In turn, these resources enhanced their QOL scores. Finally, enhanced QOL completely mediated a reduction in reabuse relative to nontreated comparisons at the 24-month follow-up.

A number of experts have suggested that those interested in helping battered women should focus their efforts on a holistic community response, a networking of all systems that affect families. To accomplish this goal, communities must improve the education of service providers regarding IPV, because this education can be an effective tool to begin collaborative efforts (Lia-Hoagberg, Kragthorpe, Schaffer, & Hill, 2001). Interagency collaborations are not easy to establish and maintain. Agencies attempting to work together often have different goals. In the case of IPV intervention, for instance, some agencies are concerned with batterer sanctions, some with victim advocacy, and some with family reunification. One tool that communities might use to assess the level of interagency collaboration on the problem of IPV is a community checklist of important steps to take in ending IPV (see Advisory Council on Violence Against Women, 1996).

One dilemma in interagency collaborations is that of the differing standards of ethics prescribed by various professional organizations. Typical of this quandary are the differences between social workers' duties and attorneys' duties when assisting battered women. Although both social workers and attorneys must ensure client confidentiality, social workers are mandated to report child abuse, whereas attorneys are

not. When working with battered women, attorneys need to build a confidentiality wall to protect information damaging to their clients (St. Joan, 2001).

Two groups of agency personnel that especially need to interface are shelter advocates and child protective services workers, because their differing service orientations tend to cause them to clash (see Chapter 7's focus on children). CPS workers need to assess mothers for IPV victimization as well as children for abuse. Intervening effectively on behalf of both battered mothers and children has recently emerged as a new approach to reducing family violence (Mills & Yoshihama, 2002; see also Pulido & Gupta, 2002). Chiu (2001) proposes a novel way to reduce tensions between personnel from various agencies involved in IPV intervention. She suggests that agency workers attempt to reconcile battered women's victimization effects with their ability to make decisions and carry them out. Victims may need some of the following services: counseling, shelter, protection, financial assistance, job training, relocation assistance, and legal information (see also Edleson & Beeman, 2000).

The health care community especially needs to become involved in the treatment and prevention of IPV. Victims suffer numerous physical and mental health problems that interfere with their ability to move forward in life (Attala et al., 2000; Campbell & Soeken, 1999; Ellsberg et al., 1999; Humphreys et al., 1999a). Some injuries are very debilitating and permanent. Barbara Seaman of the National Council on Women's Health has asserted that the health care system should be the first entry point for societal intervention in IPV ("Focus," 1994). The medical community can play a pivotal role by assessing, intervening, and appropriately referring battered women (Naumann, Langford, Torres, Campbell, & Glass, 1999; Schornstein, 1997; Thurston, Cory, & Scott, 1998). Without this support from health practitioners, battered women may not be able to leave their abusers.

When patients present with problems closely linked to IPV, such as PTSD and depression, doctors should screen for IPV. It would be wise for medical practitioners to expand screening for family violence beyond emergency rooms, to schools and pediatricians' offices (Sleutel, 1998). Once an IPV victim discloses her abuse, medical staff should find the time to hear her story and refer her to appropriate agencies. They should tell her that abuse is illegal, give her information about abuse, and arrange for follow-up with supportive services (Frasier, Slatt, Kowlowitz, & Glowa, 2001). Doctors can play a pivotal role in providing evidence needed by the criminal justice system to prosecute abusers. Specifically, doctors should learn how to document IPV (Isaac & Enos, 2001). Just as medical settings provide group counseling for individuals suffering from various mental health problems, they also should offer groups for IPV victims (Dienemann et al., 2000). They especially should develop and evaluate culturally sensitive programs and become culturally competent themselves (Bonder, Martin, & Miracle, 2001; Marciak, Guzman, Santiago, Villalobos, & Israel, 1999).

Practice Issues

Practitioners can change their clinical methods in several ways to improve the services they offer to IPV victims. In addition, continuing education is a must for people in the helping professions. All such professionals need to know what types of treatments are most effective.

Screening clients. Mental health practitioners working in clinics or in private practice should screen clients for IPV. As discussed previously, victims may not recognize they are being abused or may be too afraid or ashamed to tell their counselors about the violence. Laffaye et al. (2003), for example, found that identification of IPV can help to forestall development of PTSD and QOL problems. (For a list of appropriate screening instruments for IPV compiled by an American Psychological Association task force [Harway et al., 2002], click on the "Additional Materials" button at the link for this volume on the Sage Publications Web site, http://www.sagepub.com/book.aspx?pid=10013.)

Working with diverse populations. Therapists need to develop special expertise in order to offer services to individuals who are members of some particular subpopulations. Lesbians constitute one special-needs group of IPV victims. When women seek help for IPV through lesbian groups, they concurrently expose their sexual orientation, thus risking isolation and rejection (Levy, 1997). Consequently, lesbians often do not have access to two of the most common sources of help and support: family and peers (see Boxer, Cook, & Herdt, 1991; D'Augelli, 1992; Rotheram-Bokes, Rosario, & Koopman, 1991). They often find that other resources, such as access to experienced therapists, are sparse as well (Leeder, 1988; Los Angeles Department of Probation, 1998). As research on the characteristics of lesbian batterers has emerged, therapists should note the similarity of their traits to those of male heterosexual batterers. Lesbian IPV perpetrators, relative to nonperpetrators, report higher levels of childhood abuse and higher levels of alcohol problems. Their responses on the Millon Clinical Multiaxial Inventory–III indicate psychopathology: antisocial, borderline, paranoid traits, and delusional clinical symptoms (Fortunata & Kohn, 2003).

Another subpopulation in need of help is that of women living in rural communities. According to a 1998 study, the close-knit family, kinship, and friendship networks typical of rural communities greatly diminish rural IPV victims' ability and willingness to seek help (Anahita, as cited in Rural Women's Work Group, 2000). Key determinants of rural women's inability to seek help for IPV include the following aspects of rural life (in comparison with nonrural settings): more patriarchal social order, greater gun use, inadequate or no criminal justice response to incidents of IPV, and lack of confidentiality, phones, shelters, transportation, social support, and legal representation (Thompson, 1995; Websdale, 1995).

Disabled abused women (and men) constitute a group of victims who must overcome extraordinary odds to leave abusive partners (Carlson, 1997; Sundram, 2000). For conditions to improve for members of this population, universities need to include disability education in social science graduate schools (Hayward, 2002). Physical handicaps such as deafness, unclear articulation, lack of transportation, and lack of access to court buildings contribute to the particularly inadequate nature of the criminal justice response to disabled IPV victims (Reyna, 1999). Mentally ill individuals also are at risk for IPV and sexual coercion (Briere, Woo, McRae, Foltz, & Sitzman, 1997; Lipschitz et al., 1996; Weinhardt, 1999). Finally, abuse of immigrant women is exacerbated by immigration laws that make a female spouse's immigration status dependent on her marital status. Therapists must become well versed in these laws in order to help immigrant IPV victims.

Prevention Strategies

Given the serious consequences of IPV for victims, their children, and society at large, it is essential that government and nongovernment organizations take steps to prevent IPV (Osofsky, 1999). One approach would be for universities to offer more personal relationship classes within marriage and family curricula. Research has shown that even a 20-minute oral presentation to university students about domestic violence can produce some favorable changes in attitudes (O'Neal & Dorn, 1998). Public awareness programs may enable some potential victims to avoid IPV. Although several treatment modalities are available to prevent revictimization, evaluation research has yet to identify the most effective techniques. Investigators should give such research high priority (D. P. Mears, 2003).

CHAPTER SUMMARY

Society's tendency to blame victims is reflected in the general acceptance of false stereotypes about female IPV victims—that they provoke their abusers, drink too much, or are to blame in other ways. Unfortunately, professionals in several fields also attribute blame to victims instead of perpetrators, partially because of differences in these professionals' service constituencies. Currently, laws intended to protect children have the effect of criminalizing battered mothers. Instead of holding abusive fathers accountable for their abuse, agency personnel hold nonabusive mothers accountable for neglect because they did not leave.

The violence that IPV victims endure has profound effects on them. Fear becomes the dominant theme in their lives. Leaving their abusers, however, may be very difficult, because abusers tend not to accept their victims' decisions to leave. Abusers often threaten, stalk, and generally harass women who try to leave them.

Some violent relationships involve extreme perpetrator control that appears to induce strange behaviors similar to those exhibited by hostages. In other situations, intermittent loving behaviors along with intermittent assaults seem to create traumatic bonding. In violent relationships, victims sometimes become so attached to their abusers that leaving them is extremely painful emotionally. These processes tend to trap victims, making it difficult for them to leave.

IPV may evoke feelings of weakness and incapacity in victims. It is possible that some IPV victims suffer from learned helplessness. Although acceptance of the concept of learned helplessness is not uniform, some scholars assert that it makes victims passive; they become poor problem solvers and are unmotivated to change their lives. One flaw in this theory is that many IPV victims are active help seekers and do not appear helpless.

Some IPV victims suffer neurological damage as a result of assaults. Most victims suffer myriad physical ailments and have IPV-related difficulties in the areas of problem solving and coping.

Unending and unpredictable assaults also bring about trauma symptoms, such as anxiety and aggression. Such extreme stress produces PTSD in a substantial number of battered women. The symptoms of PTSD are serious and long-lasting, and they require treatment. Some experts think that extreme levels of fear, trauma, and stress create a special category of symptoms known as the battered woman syndrome, or BWS. Courts often accept expert testimony about BWS as a mitigating factor in intimate partner homicide. Most mental health specialists, however, now believe the syndrome concept is outmoded. Some suggest that a better legal approach is simply to explain the effects of battering on victims.

Research uniformly reveals that battered women are depressed, and some evidence suggests they suffer from low self-esteem, self-blame, and some forms of psychopathology. Evidence suggests that the effects of trauma are cumulative, and any victimization experience contributes to increased future vulnerability or revictimization.

Most IPV victims eventually leave their abusers, despite the difficulties they must overcome to do so. Postseparation, many victims experience heightened levels of fear. They worry that their abusers will harm them out of revenge or that the abusers will abscond with their children. Victims who remain with violent partners are at ever-increasing risk for physical and sexual assault. Economic dependence on their abusers forces many IPV victims who leave to seek public assistance for themselves and their children until they can stabilize their lives. Victims who leave their abusers are frequently unemployed, in part because their abusers may have made it difficult for them to go to work or to school.

IPV victims are committed to their relationships and seem to experience high levels of hope that their partners will change. They can easily envision the losses they will undergo without a husband/father in the home. They must deal with high levels of male-to-female interpersonal control, and they receive insufficient levels of social support to help them make the decision to leave.

To retain their intimate relationships, victims typically try a number of nonviolent strategies to end the violence. In time, some victims seem to find ways to tolerate the violence—by accepting it as normal, denying that it is a serious problem, or accepting blame themselves. Nonetheless, victims develop ambiguous feelings about their abusers—appreciating their loving qualities while rejecting their abusive behaviors—and these reactions further entrap them.

The entire topic of male IPV victims seems to evoke disbelief and derision from most members of the public. Academicians debate the prevalence of female-to-male partner violence and base their opinions on different types of data. Recently, researchers have found that a very small minority of men appear to be authentic IPV victims. These men get entrapped and stay with violent women for the same reasons women stay with violent men—commitment to marriage, fear of losing children, economic downsizing, and so forth.

Research has yet to identify the best type of treatment for female IPV victims. There is a continuing debate about the advisability of relying on couples' therapy. Many experienced shelter workers believe that working with couples is far too dangerous for victims. Other professionals believe couples' therapy is best in cases where the couple wants to stay together and the abuse is mild. Counseling can help victims learn about abuse and the extremely negative effects that exposure to IPV has on children.

Shelters effectively offer battered women safe places where they can begin to make decisions about how to change their situation. Shelter treatment initially focuses on safety needs and then expands to help victims achieve economic stability, deal with loss, and adopt different beliefs about responsibility for the violence. Shelters can also be effective in getting victims into drug and alcohol treatment programs.

Shelter staff can help victims recognize the extreme damage that living in a violent household does to children, a technique that prompts many women to leave their abusers. Shelters today are becoming increasingly aware of the need to improve their services through outreach to marginalized groups, such as lesbians, rural women, minorities, immigrants, and disabled women. Finally, shelter workers provide victims with social support and teach them practical problem-solving skills so they can begin the process of undoing the overwhelming problems engendered by IPV.

Counseling helps IPV victims learn how to make changes in their lives. Such therapy is often geared toward empowering victims. Some of the hardest work therapists must do with battered women is to help them change their belief systems. Victims need to stop accepting blame for the IPV, understand the violence in their relationships, and start believing that they can change their lives. Counselors should let victims mourn the loss of their relationships and acknowledge the positive aspects of the abusers. On a practical level, counselors usually provide victims with information about help seeking—that is, where to go in the community for various kinds of help, how to find transportation, and how to obtain housing.

In terms of practice, counselors should routinely screen clients for a number of conditions, such as depression, substance abuse, PTSD, and psychopathology. Therapists may need to seek additional education about IPV, especially in terms of working with diverse populations. There is a widespread need for staff in various community service agencies to join forces. Collaboration should lead to a more comprehensive and effective response to victims' needs. Some community service providers may be insensitive to the plight of battered women and thus may convey negative attitudes toward IPV victims. Battered women's advocates and others who are knowledgeable about IPV need to educate such providers.

Policy recommendations concerning the prevention of IPV and help for victims include the following: (a) changing gender socialization for both sexes, (b) empowering victims by letting them help fashion programs, (c) devising public outreach messages to help prevent IPV from occurring in the first place, (d) helping victims become financially independent through improvements in workplace policies, (e) improving the responses of health care professionals to IPV, and (f) working to resolve conflicts between CPS's agenda and victims' abilities to escape IPV.

DISCUSSION QUESTIONS

1. Who blames IPV victims for their victimization, and on what grounds? What is your opinion about who is to blame in cases of IPV?

2. Should battered mothers be held legally responsible for protecting their children from abusers in their households? Why or why not?

3. What forms does the fear caused by IPV take? Is such fear realistic?

4. What are the symptoms of trauma? What is PTSD? What causes it? How easily does it dissipate over time?

5. Describe the following three theories: traumatic bonding, Stockholm syndrome, and attachment. How do these theories explain an IPV victim's entrapment in the relationship?

6. What are some of the major reasons female IPV victims do not leave their abusers? How do you think you would behave if your partner became violent toward you?

7. In the context of IPV victimization, what is help seeking? Who seeks help for IPV?

8. Do community agencies and services meet most IPV victims' needs?

9. Are men abused by violent partners? What differences are there between IPV-victimized women and IPV-victimized men?

10. If an IPV victim moves away from her abuser, to another city, and gets a job and a restraining order, is she likely to be safe? Why or why not?

RECOMMENDED READING

Cook, P. W. (1997). *Abused men: The hidden side of domestic violence.* Westport, CT: Praeger.

DeKeseredy, W. S., & MacLeod, L. (1997). *Woman abuse: A sociological story.* Toronto: Harcourt-Brace Canada.

Jenkins, P. A., & Davidson, B. P. (2001). *Stopping domestic violence: How a community can prevent spousal abuse.* New York: Kluwer/Academic.

LaViolette, A. D., & Barnett, O. W. (2000). *It could happen to anyone: Why battered women stay* (2nd ed.). Thousand Oaks, CA: Sage.

Purewal, J., & Ganesh, I. (2000). Gender violence, trauma, and its impact on women's mental health. *Journal of Indian Social Work, 61,* 542–557.

Reyes, C., Rudman, W. J., & Hewitt, C. R. (Eds.). (2002). *Domestic violence and health care: Policies and prevention.* Binghamton, NY: Haworth.

Roberts, A. R. (Ed.). (2002). *Handbook of domestic violence intervention strategies: Policies, programs, and legal remedies.* New York: Oxford University Press.

Schewe, P. A. (Ed.). (2002). *Preventing violence in relationships.* Washington, DC: American Psychological Association.

Schornstein, S. L. (1997). *Domestic violence and health care: What every health professional needs to know.* Thousand Oaks, CA: Sage.

Websdale, N. (1998). *Rural woman battering and the justice system.* Thousand Oaks, CA: Sage.

NOTES

1. This case history, which was prepared by Alyce LaViolette, is quoted directly from LaViolette and Barnett (2000, p. 15).

2. The main source for the details in this case history is Hackett et al. (1988). The names used are the subjects' real names.

3. The source for this case history is "Man Held" (2003). The names used are the subjects' real names.

11

INTIMATE PARTNER VIOLENCE

Abusive Partners

Case History: Ari and Bernadette—When a Little Slap Is a Knockout Punch

Ari came into group counseling like many other men arrested and ordered into counseling. He seemed calm and collected, dressed nicely from his day's work as a department store manager. He protested his arrest, claiming that it was "all a mistake." All he did was give Bernadette a little push in the car because she wouldn't "shut up."

Ari's story was that he came home exhausted from a long day at work only to find Bernadette all dressed up and saying that she "had to get out of the house; she wanted to go out to dinner." Ari said he was too tired, but Bernadette got angry and started screaming that he only "thought of himself." Ari gave in.

It was already 8:30 by the time they pulled into the restaurant parking lot. The restaurant was crowded and noisy, and Ari was angry and sullen as they waited for their dinner. He and Bernadette each had several drinks, but Ari could not calm down. "No one ever cares about my feelings," he thought. When they returned to the car after dinner, Bernadette launched into a diatribe about Ari's "failure" to accept her 6-year-old son by a previous marriage. She kept "mouthing off as usual," and Ari's driving became erratic. As they arrived home, Ari reached across the front seat of the car and slapped her because he "had to do something to get her attention." When he went around to open the passenger-side door for Bernadette, she "fell out and hit her head on the pavement."

The neighbors called paramedics and the police, and Ari was arrested. Bernadette's medical report said that she had been "knocked out"; she did not "fall and hit her head." It took more than 10 weeks of group counseling before Ari would admit that his little slap was really a knockout punch.

Ari's behaviors in the above case history are typical spouse-abusive behaviors and illustrative of specific problems of batterers described in this chapter. To Ari, Bernadette did not seem understanding or accommodating. Note, for example, that Ari dismissed the incident as a mistake. Ari's anger and stress contributed to his assault on his wife, which he minimized. Indeed, according to Ari, Bernadette provoked his physical attack.

This chapter examines the behaviors of batterers, men who abuse and control their female partners through threats and physical, psychological, verbal, and sexual aggression. This chapter focuses on men.

Some women are violent toward their partners, and society should not overlook their violence. Men are the primary injury-producing perpetrators of intimate partner violence (IPV), however, and women are the more routinely victimized partners.

A common thread runs through the first set of topics in this chapter. Included are self-descriptions of batterers and characterizations by their partners. The next theme entails similarities between partner-only violent men and men who are violent both within and outside the family. These accounts lead to a discussion of highly scientific attempts to construct typologies of different types of violent men. The chapter then addresses etiological theories, including socialization, biological traits, relationship factors, and individual differences in personality disorders/psychopathology. The chapter concludes with a synopsis of counseling approaches used in batterer treatment, outcomes of treatment, and policy and prevention issues.

DESCRIPTIONS OF BATTERERS

One subject that has prompted experts to develop diverse solutions is how best to investigate perpetrators of IPV. The first question concerns the sources of information about IPV perpetrators. Should information be derived from victims, perpetrators, or other informants? Is it better for social scientists to make use of clinical descriptions, criminal history data, observational research, pen-and-pencil tests, or other assessments? Are IPV perpetrators a homogeneous or heterogeneous group of individuals, or is it even possible to classify perpetrators into subcategories? Allied with these questions is the issue of whether perpetrators should be characterized as a unique group of men whose violence targets family members only or whether they are simply run-of-the-mill violent criminals.

Battered Women's Descriptions of Batterers

Psychologists' earliest attempts to examine male IPV perpetrators generally consisted of descriptions provided by female IPV victims in counseling (Elbow, 1977). It is interesting to note that a 2003 study indicated that battered women's perceptions of their male partners' behaviors were excellent predictors of reassault (Gondolf & Heckert, 2003). Not long after Elbow's (1977) research, Lenore Walker's (1979) pioneering work with female victims enabled her to delineate a sequence in male spouses' battering that she termed the "cycle of violence." According to this model, IPV intensifies in degree and frequency over time and holds the people involved in an established pattern of behavior. The cycle of violence consists of three phases:

1. *Tension building:* In this phase, minor incidents of violence may occur along with a buildup of anger. This phase may include verbal put-downs, jealousy, threats, and breaking things, and can eventually escalate to the second phase.

2. *Acute or battering:* In this phase, the major violent outburst occurs. Following this phase, the couple often enters Phase 3.

3. *Honeymoon or loving respite:* In this phase, the perpetrator is remorseful and afraid of losing his partner. He may promise her anything, beg forgiveness, buy gifts, and basically seem to be "the man she fell in love with."

Battering Men's Descriptions of Themselves

When asked about their violence, men accused of IPV usually offer self-serving replies. First, they tend to blame others, especially their female partners, for their assaults. Second, they downplay the significance and seriousness of their violence, claiming they did not really hurt their female partners.

Attributions for the violence. The role of blame in a battering relationship is a critical issue. One salient factor is that men who blame their female partners are likely to be even more violent than those who do not (Byrne & Arias, 1997). Probably the most common explanation that male perpetrators give for their violence is something like this: "I told her not to do it (e.g., stay late after work). She knew what would happen if she did, but she did it anyway. She got what she asked for" (see Barrera, Palmer, Brown, & Kalaher, 1994). This scenario illustrates IPV perpetrators' propensity to formulate household rules that their female partners must obey as well as perpetrators' habits of externalizing blame and justifying their violence (e.g., Cantos, Neidig, & O'Leary, 1994).

As research advanced, several investigators began using standardized tests to examine perpetrators' attributions (i.e., explanations) for their IPV. Holtzworth-Munroe and Hutchinson (1993), for example, conducted a three-way comparison of men classified by marital violence using the Conflict Tactics Scale (CTS1; Straus, 1979) and by marital satisfaction level using the Short Marital Adjustment Test (SMAT; Locke & Wallace, 1959): (a) male-to-female partner violent, discordant in terms of marital satisfaction; (b) not-male-to-female partner violent, discordant; and (c) not-male-to-female partner violent, satisfied. Note that the latter two nonviolent groups are comparison groups. Male research participants judged women's behavior in vignettes depicting problematic marital conditions. Maritally violent, discordant men attributed more responsibility for negative behaviors to wives in the vignettes than did nonmaritally violent, satisfactorily married men. Maritally violent, discordant men also attributed more negative intentions, selfish motivation, and blame for behaviors to wives than did nonmaritally violent, satisfactorily married men. Vignettes depicting jealousy and wife's rejection elicited particularly negative attributions by the two unhappily married groups of men (see also Tonizzo, Howells, Day, Reidpath, & Froyland, 2000).

Denial and minimization. Maritally violent men tend to deny and minimize their assaultive and abusive actions, as in the case history above. Eisikovits and Enosh (1997) quote a male IPV perpetrator's explanation of his violent behavior: "You won't believe it, I could move the wall when I am in a rage. The hands get going by themselves. You can't control it. And she does this childish stuff. . . . So she deserves it. I know that legally it is forbidden, but I also know that she deserves worse" (p. 317). According to research, one reason partner-violent men behave as they do is that they may be unaware of their true intentions (Barnett, Lee, & Thelen, 1997; Yelsma, 1996). These findings suggest the usefulness of insight therapies to help perpetrators understand their behavior.

Female-to-Male Intimate Violence

Case History: Zaida and Kumar—"I Just Bopped Him One"

Zaida was one of three women arrested in one jurisdiction over a year's period for female-to-male partner violence and diverted into a counseling program. All other members of the group were men. Zaida was 57 years old and had been married for 35 years. She worked in a factory and admitted having a problem with alcohol. She looked haggard and perhaps unwell.

The evening that she completed her 26 sessions in the program, she finally opened up about her reasons for hitting Kumar. He seldom talked to her, she complained, and she was "damned mad about it." When she came home from work and saw Kumar drinking a beer in front of the TV, she often greeted him with a question, such as "What's for supper?" If she didn't like his answer, she just "bopped him one on the head." If she got "really pissed off," she grabbed his beer and threw it on the floor. Kumar never defended himself even once, but if she socked him, he would not speak to her the rest of the evening.

The therapist tactfully pointed out that he "thought he saw a connection" between Zaida's assaults and Kumar's refusal to speak to her. Zaida was stunned into silence, but she listened attentively as men in the group commented. The men told her that Kumar probably would talk to her if he didn't have to worry about getting socked. Zaida was thoughtful but said nothing more until the final good-byes. As she proudly marched off, she told the group members that they would never see her again, and they didn't.

Although male-to-female intimate partner violence (MFIPV) is by far the more serious problem, society should not overlook female-to-male intimate partner violence (FMIPV). It may be best to view IPV victimization as a problem of disparate proportions. The latest research has made it clear that although women are the primary victims of IPV, men are sometimes victims as well (Hamberger & Guse, 2002). At first, researchers emphasized the self-defensive nature of FMIPV (Cascardi, Langhinrichsen-Rohling, & Vivian, 1992; Hamberger & Potente, 1994; Saunders, 1995). Social scientists also examined motivations for abuse (e.g., Barnett et al., 1997; Browne, Salomon, & Bassuk, 1999).

Similarities and Differences Between Partner-Violent-Only Men and Other Violent Men

Advances in knowledge highlight the shortsightedness of conceptualizing abusers as a homogeneous group. For example, it has become clear that not every wife assaulter grew up in a violent home. Consequently, another approach researchers have taken in their attempts to understand wife assault has been to look for subgroups of violent men. In particular, questions have arisen about how partner-violent-only men compare with generally violent men. Generally violent men are violent toward many people: female partners, family members, acquaintances, and strangers. The question of most interest is whether these subgroups of violent men are separate or exhibit true continuities.

Differences in targets (victims). Several early investigations determined that maritally violent men were actually generally violent. In an evaluation based on interviews with 270 domestic violence victims, Fagan, Stewart, and Hansen (1983) disclosed that almost half of all spouse abusers had been arrested previously for other violence. Another survey corroborated these results by showing that male partners of women living in shelters tended to have criminal records (Dunford,

Huizinga, & Elliott, 1990). Similarly, 65% of men who had orders of protection issued against them had arrest records and appeared to be career criminals (Keilitz, Davis, & Eikeman, 1998).

In contradistinction, the 1985 National Family Violence Survey (NFVS-2; Straus & Gelles, 1990) of 6,002 households did not fully substantiate conclusions from preceding studies. Using data from 2,291 males included in the NFVS-2, Kandel-Englander (1992) identified 311 men (15%) who had been violent during the previous 12-month period. From the violent group, 208 (67%) had been violent only toward their wives, 71 (23%) had been violent only toward persons outside their families, and 32 (10%) had been violent toward both wives and nonfamily individuals. Thus the selection of the target (assaulted person) clearly differentiated these groups.

Moffitt, Krueger, Caspi, and Fagan (2000) authenticated group differences in a comparison of violent and nonviolent young adults in an Australian birth cohort consisting of more than 840 men and women. The researchers administered the Multidimensional Personality Questionnaire (MPQ; Tellegen & Waller, 2000) at age 18 and checked for IPV and criminal behavior at age 21. Tests included an experimenter-developed index of psychological and physical IPV (see Moffitt et al., 1997) and the Self-Report Delinquency Interview (SRDI; Elliott & Huizinga, 1989). The MPQ includes three dimensions: (a) Positive Emotionality (low threshold for contentment and happiness, values being close to others, feels confident), (b) Negative Emotionality (low threshold for anxiety, anger, stress, and readiness to see threat), and (c) Constraint (self-control). Approximately 53% of the study sample reported no IPV or crime. Results for violent subgroups demonstrated some distinctiveness. Responses on Negative Emotionality were correlated with violence for both partner abuse and generally violent men's crime scores. Constraint scores were associated only with crime scores for the generally violent group. That is, low self-control typified only the generally violent group. Responses on the Positive Emotionality dimension did not correlate with either group's scores. An especially interesting aspect of this study is that assessments revealed no significant sex differences. Dobash and Dobash (1992) suggest that their findings lend some support to feminist theorizing that maritally violent men are methodical batterers, selecting their targets—that is, they do not assault because of impulsive rage.

Social and behavioral differences. Other research sought to unravel social/behavioral dissimilarities between subsamples of violent men. One study found that men charged with domestic homicide experienced more behavioral problems in childhood (e.g., truancy) than did men charged with nondomestic homicide. Nonetheless, both groups were more likely than nonviolent men to have disturbed childhoods, such as a missing parent (Anasseril & Holcomb, 1985). Finally, men who are severely violent differed from less violent men on some dimensions, such as drug usage, unemployment, range of deviant acts, and psychopathology (D. S. Elliott, 1994; Huss & Langhinrichsen-Rohling, 2000; Loeber & Farrington, 1997). Buzawa and Buzawa (2003) argue that the most dangerous wife assaulters are very likely to be generally violent men who have prior arrest records. Personal characteristics of these offenders, such as pernicious drug use and impulsive rages, render them practically unfazed by arrest.

In a review of the psychopathology, antisocial personality disorder (APD), and **borderline disorder** (BD) literature, Huss and Langhinrichsen-Rohling (2000) drew parallels between maritally violent men and criminal offenders. These authors concur that psychopathy and APD are related but separate. They also advise that the Psychopathy Checklist (Hare, 1980), revised and modified as a clinical screening instrument (Hart, Hare, & Forth, 1993), should be clinicians' first choice among tests for detecting psychopathy. Huss and Langhinrichsen-Rohling note that if there is a physiological basis for psychopathy, conclusive evidence is still lacking. They assert, however, that evidence supports the existence of cognitive deficits, such as difficulty in handling delayed reward and problems in processing contextual information.

Typologies of male IPV perpetrators. Identifying commonalities among abusers provided an initial basis for intervention, but it concomitantly postponed recognition of their heterogeneity. Maritally violent men differed along several dimensions: (a) scope of their targets of violence, (b) etiology of their violence, (c) childhood experiences, (d) severity and chronicity of their violence, (e) use of drugs and alcohol, and (f) biological differences. Recognition of these dissimilarities sparked interest in typology research. Clinicians anticipated that a typology would assist them in treating IPV perpetrators more effectively.

Holtzworth-Munroe and her colleagues undertook an industrious series of research projects to search for subtypes of violent and nonviolent men (e.g.,

Holtzworth-Munroe & Stuart, 1994). They first constructed a theoretical prototype of violent men using both rational/**deductive** and empirical/**inductive** concepts culled from the literature. This work yielded three major descriptive dimensions: severity of violence, generality of violence, and psychopathology. The researchers subsequently used multiple measures to classify MFIPV perpetrators into three hypothetical subgroups: family only, dysphoric/borderline (unwell, unhappy/normality mixed with abnormality), and generally violent/antisocial (violent/little sense of responsibility, morality, concern for others). Next, they speculated how important variables, such as attachment and skill deficits, might be associated with the three purported groups.

Later, Holtzworth-Munroe, Meehan, Stuart, Herron, and Rehman (2000) confirmed their trimodal typology but also identified a fourth subtype, low-level antisocial. After this work, Marshall and Holtzworth-Munroe (2002) investigated whether any men in their samples could be classed as sexually violent only. In this comparison, they used two inventories: (a) sexual aggression questions on the Revised Conflict Tactics Scale (CTS2) and (b) items from the Sexual Experiences Survey (Koss & Gidycz, 1985; Koss & Oros, 1982). Next, they mapped these data across three husband types proposed by Monson and Langhinrichsen-Rohling (1998): (a) physically violent only, (b) sexually violent only, and (c) both physically and sexually violent. Although Marshall and Holtzworth-Munroe uncovered a sexually violent only group, it was extremely small— 3 of 105 men from the "nonviolent" comparison sample. Applying the data to Holtzworth-Munroe, Meehan, et al.'s (2000) four-group model, Marshall and Holtzworth-Munroe found that more severely partner-violent men engaged primarily in sexual coercion, whereas the generally violent/antisocial group engaged more frequently in threatened/forced sex. In their latest research, Holtzworth-Munroe, Meehan, Stuart, Herron, and Rehman (2003) determined that at follow-ups 18 months and 3 years later, a number of the assessed traits, but not all, were still present.

Other social scientists developed their own typologies, often by employing alternative statistical methods (e.g., Langhinrichsen-Rohling, Huss, & Ramsey, 2000; Tweed & Dutton, 1998; White & Gondolf, 2000). Hamberger, Lohr, Bonge, and Tolin (1996), for instance, used a **cluster analysis** of Millon Clinical Multiaxial Inventory (MCMI; Millon, 1983) data from 833 IPV perpetrators to separate violent men into three groups: (a) nonpathological, (b) antisocial, and

(c) passive-aggressive-dependent. They judged their findings to be consistent with those of Holtzworth-Munroe and Stuart (1994). In a more publicized but often criticized endeavor, Gottman et al. (1995) relied on heart rate activity to identify two types of partner-violent men. Type I men exhibited characteristics typical of criminals who commit the severest violence. Heart rate activity among these men actually lowered during exposure to a videotaped marital conflict situation. Type II men fit descriptions similar to those attributed to psychopaths. Their heart rates either increased or remained the same during observation of the videotape. While examining all typology research to date in a review of nine studies, Dixon and Browne (2003) found evidence converging with Holtzworth-Munroe and Stuart's (1994) three-dimensional model of IPV perpetrators.

SECTION SUMMARY

Battered women provided clinicians with some of the first anecdotal reports of batterers' behaviors. Investigators such as Lenore Walker continued this work by developing some provisional information about batterers' tendencies to blame others and to minimize the seriousness of their assaults. This early work set the stage for the proliferation of empirical studies that followed.

When batterers explain their own behavior, they offer accounts consistent with those that Walker outlined. They most often blame their female partners, and they further deny their violence and/or tend to minimize it.

The problem of abusive women is gaining more attention, but little information about this subgroup of abusers is available. In fact, women's violence toward male intimates has not yet reached the level of a social problem. Two reasons are that much of women's IPV is characterized as self-defensive, and men are far less injured than women. Furthermore, for various social reasons, men are much less likely to complain about being victimized by their female partners. A third explanation is that women and their children are more economically dependent on men than the reverse.

Although incomplete, available information has shown that subsamples of violent men (violent toward family only, toward nonfamily only, or toward both family and nonfamily) vary in important ways but also share some important attributes (e.g., disturbed childhoods). Data from samples of wife assaulters indicate frequent arrests for nonfamily-violent crime. New typology research has identified several subgroups of violent men that can be categorized by their assault targets: partner only, stranger only, both partner and stranger. Other characteristics, such as being diagnosed with APD, are useful in further specifying group membership. Refinement of typologies continues as researchers hope to match treatments to groups for greater therapeutic effectiveness.

BECOMING AND REMAINING A BATTERER

As Lawson et al. (2001) note, despite concerted efforts in all fields, "thorough knowledge and understanding of battering continues to elude both scholars and practitioners" (p. 86). Why MFIPV occurs is not totally clear. This section summarizes some socialization practices in the United States that appear to contribute to battering. Socialization forces are paramount in any discussion of MFIPV, because violence may be a learned behavior. Biological factors that support male aggression need further elucidation, because they too play a role in MFIPV. Research on dyadic or interpersonal relationship variables has generated a relatively large amount of data on such topics as marital dissatisfaction, verbal skills and communication styles, problem solving, stress, power and control issues, and jealousy. Finally, numerous studies have shown that MFIPV perpetrators and nonperpetrators respond differently on tests of individual differences (i.e., perpetrators show evidence of personality disorders and psychopathology). (For a list of risk factors and possible causes of MFIPV, see O'Neil & Harway, 1999.)

Socialization

A number of researchers have carefully examined socialization variables that might promote MFIPV. Generalized modeling may convey approval of violence, and specific modeling may teach that certain behaviors are acceptable and certain people are the proper targets of violence (e.g., Kalmuss, 1984). As a general rule, certain kinds of childhood abuse and trauma are capable of triggering a wide variety of problematic and long-lasting behaviors.

Childhood socialization. A relatively large volume of literature indicates that exposure to interparental violence or direct physical or sexual abuse during childhood is associated with later aggression (e.g., Trull, 2001; Widom & Maxfield, 2001). A meta-analysis of intergenerational transmission of IPV found a moderate correlation ($r = .35$) for males exposed to parental violence (Stith et al., 2000). Observing abuse, according to Hotaling and Sugarman (1986), may be a more powerful predictor of future IPV than experiencing abuse directly, and paternal violence may be a better predictor than maternal violence (see also Blumenthal, Neeman, & Murphy, 1998).

Harsh treatment in childhood may lead to development of an antisocial orientation that in turn is associated with chronic MFIPV (Simons, Wu, Johnson, & Conger, 1995). In a 20-year longitudinal study of 543 children, Ehrensaft et al. (2003) identified several risk factors for adult perpetration of MFIPV: conduct disorder, exposure to interparental violence, and power-assertive punishments. Risk for adult victimization by IPV included exposure to interparental violence.

Another longitudinal study produced compatible results. Farrington (2000) assessed 411 English males starting at 8 years of age. He used psychosocial risk factors apparent at these young ages to predict antisocial personality disorders (conduct disorders and behaviors specified in the third revised edition of the *Diagnostic and Statistical Manual of Mental Disorders* [*DSM-III-R*]; American Psychiatric Association, 1987) at ages 18 to 32 and criminal convictions between ages 21 and 40. He obtained assessments from parents, teachers, peers, criminal records, and self-reports. High-risk predictors at ages 8–10 for APD were the following: (a) convicted parent, (b) large family, (c) low intelligence or attainment, (d) young mother, and (e) disrupted family. Tests detected APD by age 32 in more than 52% of boys with a convicted parent and in 60% of high-risk boys. High-risk variables also predicted criminal convictions by age 40 in 40% of boys. APD or borderline personality organization may be the key characteristic that is transmitted across generations and, in turn, results in the well-established link between childhood abuse and adult male battering (Dutton, van Ginkel, & Starzomski, 1995; Simons et al., 1995).

Some violent men are not aware of the reasons for their behaviors (e.g., Barnett et al., 1997; Yelsma, 1996). They may have repressed many painful childhood memories that become apparent in the form of dissociative coping styles (Stosny, 1995). Braun (1988) defines *dissociation* as an extreme experience falling at the high end of a continuum of nonawareness. This

An Interview With Amy Holtzworth-Munroe

"Society needs to promote the doctrine that violence is absolutely not acceptable. I would like to see violence prevention efforts begin with young people, as we try to fashion a violence-free society."

Amy Holtzworth-Munroe is the world's most preeminent researcher on batterer typologies. She received her doctorate in clinical psychology from the University of Washington. Currently, she is a Professor of Psychology at Indiana University. Before embarking on investigations of batterer typologies, she conducted research in several areas: violent and nonviolent husbands' social information-processing skills, their marital interaction behaviors, and other correlates of male IPV, such as jealousy and attachment. She is a researcher's researcher. Her research not only follows up on her own previous work, but also advances it by creatively and comprehensively addressing additional questions. She is currently involved in a quest to identify and describe subgroups of violent men. She expects her work to lead to the development of treatments that are more effective, because they can be tailored to match problematic characteristics of subtypes of batterers. As a practitioner, Dr. Holtzworth-Munroe has been involved in establishing batterer treatment programs and in delivering services. She is a past Associate Editor of *Journal of Consulting and Clinical Psychology* and *Cognitive Therapy and Research*. She has also served as a member of grant review panels for the National Institutes of Health.

Q: How did you become interested in male-to-female intimate partner violence?

A: As a graduate student at the University of Washington, I was studying marital distress and marital therapy with my adviser, Neil Jacobson, when we read the book *Behind Closed Doors*, by Straus, Gelles, and Steinmetz [1980]. Suddenly, we thought, "I wonder if violence is a problem for any of the couples we are treating here in our marital therapy clinic?" We began administering the Conflict Tactics Scales to couples seeking therapy, and we were shocked to find out that over half the couples had experienced husband-to-wife violence. We had not even considered physical aggression in our case conceptualizations! I began

continuum runs from suppressed awareness to denial, to repression, and finally to dissociation. Numbing and detachment may generate development of a dissociative coping style that in turn allows perpetrators to carry out extremely violent MFIPV assaults (Stosny, 1995).

Working within this framework, Simoneti, Scott, and Murphy (2000) connected childhood trauma (physical abuse, sexual abuse, and witnessed abuse) with adult dissociative experiences among 47 partner-violent males. This investigation measured general dissociative experiences with the Dissociative Experiences Scale (DES; Bernstein & Putnam, 1986). An experimenter-designed scale, the Dissociative Violence Interview (DVI), assessed violence-specific dissociation. DES scores were associated with DVI scores, and both were correlated with the occurrence of MFIPV, including its frequency and severity (see also Cuartas, 2001).

reading about marital violence and sought out relevant clinical training with batterers (thanks to Peter Fehrenbach) and with battered women's support groups (thanks to Ginny NiCarthy). As I realized I needed to forge my own independent research program, I also realized how much I wanted to help women, as a budding feminist. Conducting research on violent male partners in a scientific and rigorous manner "fit the bill."

Q: What shaped your approach to the field of family violence?

A: At the time I entered the field of family violence, research on IPV was meager, and what was available often suffered from methodological flaws. What was needed was more methodologically sound research that could be published in high-quality journals. The rigorous research training I received at the University of Washington and the ongoing theoretical and research training I received as a new faculty member at Indiana University from individuals such as Dick McFall steered me along several paths. I undertook studies in social skills deficits (e.g., anger management) using strict standards of research methodology. Another strong and helpful influence on my career was the respect and support I received from more senior researchers in the field, such as Murray Straus, Kevin Hamberger, and Dan Saunders. Their inclusion of me as a bona fide batterer researcher made me feel like at long last I was "playing with the big boys." Other interactions with battered women's advocates improved my understanding of the grassroots efforts made to help battered women over the years.

Q: What do you think was your most influential article?

A: Looking back, I think my most influential article was a theoretical paper on subtypes of maritally violent men coauthored with Gregory Stuart in 1994. The article attempted to integrate findings in the field while shedding more light on the recognition that male IPV perpetrators were not a homogenous group of men.

Q: What do you think might have been your major contribution to the study of violent husbands?

A: It seems pretty clear that professionals in the field have most valued my work on typologies of male IPV perpetrators.

Q: Would you tell me a little about your advocacy efforts?

A: I have wanted to help provide a higher profile for the topic of IPV. To improve public awareness, I have given public addresses to organizations with various agendas and talked with newspaper reporters about IPV. I also have presented workshops for clinicians and other groups of professionals who wanted to know more about male IPV perpetrators.

Q: Have you given much thought to policy recommendations?

A: One thought I have is that the criminal justice system needs to accept the tentative nature of some research findings about batterers and be willing to "go back to the drawing board" when outcome studies or new research suggests further innovations. Another feeling I have is shared by all family violence researchers: Society needs to promote the doctrine that violence is absolutely not acceptable. I would like to see violence prevention efforts begin with young people, as we try to fashion a violence-free society.

Another investigation examined how parental psychopathology might be transmitted to children. In a 2001 longitudinal controlled comparison, Trull (2001) used structural equation modeling to estimate possible multiple causes of borderline personality disorder (BPD). Trull screened 5,000 18-year-old men applying for college admission for BPD features (not BPD diagnosis). He selected a sample of 421 males, half of whom met criteria for BPD features and half of whom did not. From the sample of 421 men, he randomly selected half of the BPD and half of the non-BPD men to complete several tests and interviews. Trull gathered information about parents that indicated borderline disorders, personality abnormalities, psychopathology, and other forms of mental disorders. To inquire about physical and sexual abuse during childhood, he used the Familial Experiences Interview (Orgata, 1988). From these inventory scores, he identified a number of significant precursors to BPD traits: parental psychopathology, child abuse, and two personality factors, Disinhibition and Negative Affectivity (Costa & McCrae, 1992).

Trull (2001) conducted further analyses and discovered that disinhibition and negative affectivity mediated (i.e., transmitted) the effects of parental psychopathology (e.g., BPD features). Childhood abuse measures were linked with the two personality traits and directly to BPD features among the 18-year-olds. Trull concluded that childhood trauma constitutes one etiological correlate of BPD and that personality traits of disinhibition and negative affectivity appear to be core personality traits underpinning BPD. Although replication studies are needed, such findings provide an important account of the relationship between variability in childhood experiences of abuse and adult individual differences in battering (Dutton et al., 1995).

Another set of childhood feelings that may play a role in IPV is shame or humiliation. In one study, level of IPV was strongly associated with two childhood factors expected to interfere with attachment: (a) number of separation and loss events experienced and (b) presence of paternal substance abuse (i.e., possible erratic caregiving) (Corvo, 1992). Furthermore, another appraisal correlated parent-to-child shaming and guilt inducement with chronic adult anger, trauma symptoms, IPV, and borderline personality organization (BPO) (Dutton et al., 1995). Systematic studies also linked parental rejection (as assessed using the Egna Minnen Betraffande Uppfostran [EMBU] test; Perris, Jacobsson, Lindstrom, von Knorring, & Perris, 1980) to MFIPV levels (Dutton et al., 1995; Holtzworth-Munroe, Meehan, et al., 2000).

Attachment and emotional dependency. The quality of an individual's childhood attachment to a caretaker (e.g., secure, avoidant, fearful, preoccupied) presumably affects the nature of that person's later intimate relationships. When the construct of attachment is applied to adults, it refers to an affectional bond with a romantic partner. This bond is a relatively long-lasting tie typified by wanting to be close to the partner. It also incorporates seeing the partner as unique, as an individual who is not exchangeable with any other. Being close to the partner results in feelings of comfort and security (Feeney & Noller, 1996).

Authorities have suggested that shame in adult batterers is linked with anxious attachment during childhood (Wallace & Nosko, 1993). Painful reactions learned in childhood, such as fear of abandonment,

may rise again to fuel an assault against a partner who threatens to leave. Findings indicate that MFIPV perpetrators may be justified in fearing abandonment. A male-female comparison of IPV perpetrators revealed that female partners were significantly more desirous of ending their relationships than were their male partners (Henning, Jones, & Holdford, 2003).

Evidence of the importance of adult attachment as a factor in MFIPV is mounting (e.g., Babcock, Jacobson, Gottman, & Yerington, 2000; Julian & McHenry, 1993; Kesner & McKenry, 1998). Dutton, Saunders, Starzomski, and Batholomew (1994) found that partner-violent men had significantly higher levels of two insecure types of attachment: preoccupied and fearful attachment. Nonpartner-violent men tended to report secure attachment patterns. Holtzworth-Munroe, Stuart, and Hutchinson (1997) analyzed responses of three groups of men on the Adult Attachment Interview (George, Kaplan, & Main, 1984) and the Adult Attachment Scale (Collins & Read, 1990). Researchers screened men for MFIPV and marital satisfaction level. The 58 men in the partner-violent group were significantly more insecure, preoccupied, and disorganized in their attachment patterns than the 32 nonpartner-violent, unhappily married men and the 29 nonpartner-violent, satisfactorily married men. Dutton and Starzomski (1993) have shown that certain types of attachment patterns typical of MFIPV perpetrators are linked to aggression against their female partners.

Attachment findings are congruent with research showing that partner-violent men are more emotionally dependent than other men. Murphy, Meyer, and O'Leary (1994) used two indexes to assess possible dependency needs in three groups of men: (a) male-to-female partner-violent men, (b) nonpartner-violent unhappily married men, and (c) nonpartner-violent satisfactorily married men. Scores on both the Interpersonal Dependency Inventory (IDI; Hirschfeld, Klerman, Chodoff, Korchin, & Barrett, 1976) and the Spouse-Specific Dependency Scale (Rathus & O'Leary, 1997) revealed significant differences among the groups. Holtzworth-Munroe, Stuart, and Hutchinson (1997) found similar results using the Spouse-Specific Dependency Scale. Kane, Staiger, and Ricciardelli (2000) also demonstrated higher dependency needs among 23 partner-violent males contrasted with 30 football players and 30 community service volunteers on the first scale of the IDI. Across these studies, findings revealed that MFIPV perpetrators have profound dependency needs (Dutton & Painter, 1993a) and are very sensitive to themes of abandonment (Holtzworth-Munroe & Hutchinson, 1993).

Male socialization: beliefs and attitudes. Men can be socialized to expect their wives to treat them with deference. Men's feelings of entitlement to power and their use of dominance in marital conflicts to control female partners hinge on sex-role socialization (Birns, Cascardi, & Meyer, 1994). In some ways, American society teaches men to confuse violence with sexuality and to tune out their feelings (except anger) (Harway & O'Neil, 1999; Levant, 1994, 1995). Cultural antecedents are not the sole explanation for wife abuse, however. Indeed, male-to-female violence is not universal in American society; rather, only some men use it in some relationships (Dutton, 1994). From an entirely different perspective, interesting results are emerging from analyses of twins' responses on personality dimensions. Olson, Vernon, Jang, and Harris (2001) demonstrated that 26 of 30 attitude items yielded significant genetic effects. As examples, attitudes toward "abortion on demand" revealed a strong genetic contribution, whereas "attitudes toward separate roles for men and women" demonstrated no genetic effects.

To understand the role of attitudes in MFIPV, social scientists have used several types of attitude and belief scales. A number of these indexes, however, seem unable to detect noticeable differences between male IPV perpetrators and other males. Kane et al. (2000), for example, found that male batterers, football players, and community service volunteers all judged violence against women as primarily unjustified on the Inventory of Beliefs About Wife Beating. The scale uncovered no differences (Saunders, Lynch, Grayson, & Linz, 1987). Another investigation assessed 149 college and military men on several inventories and found that only scores on the Adversarial Sexual Beliefs (ASB) scale (Burt, 1980) were significantly correlated with CTS1 scores (Hastings, 2000). High scores on the ASB scale indicate assumptions that sexual relationships will be exploitative and manipulative. Results showed that of four inventories, only scores on the ASB scale discriminated violent and nonviolent groups. Another cluster of studies has examined sexist attitudes, but found few, if any, significant differences in attitudes toward women between batterers and non-batterers (e.g., Neff, Holamon, & Schluter, 1995; Neidig, Friedman, & Collins, 1986; Stith et al., 2000).

One index of sex-role adherence measures the degree to which individuals endorse self-descriptions of masculine, feminine, undifferentiated (neither male nor female), and androgynous (both male and female) traits on the Bem Sex-Role Inventory (e.g., Bem, 1979). An early assessment on the Bem scale found that MFIPV perpetrators scored in the undifferentiated quadrant compared with normative data. Undifferentiated men lack both positive masculine skills (e.g., leadership) and positive feminine skills (nurturance) (LaViolette, Barnett, & Miller, 1984). A later meta-analysis found that batterers score significantly lower on both masculinity and femininity (Sugarman & Frankel, 1993); thus they lack important traits of both sexes.

Some surveys have found other significant differences between groups (Crossman, Stith, & Bender, 1990; Stith & Farley, 1993). Kantor, Jasinski, and Aldarondo (1994) established that approval of aggression increases the odds ratio of IPV by 2.7 times. Examination of proabuse attitudes also yielded positive results: Men who held proviolence attitudes showed more IPV than those who did not. In a meta-analysis of seven studies, Hanson and Wallace-Capretta (1998) discovered that proabuse attitudes are significantly associated with abusive behavior ($r = .25$).

A factor analysis of scores on the Abusive Behavior Inventory (ABI; Shepard & Campbell, 1992) for 123 MFIPV perpetrators yielded three subgroups: (a) Dominate and Degrade, (b) Attack and Damage, and (c) Intimidate and Punish. Using these groupings, investigators searched for correlates among results from seven inventories, including the Bias in Attitudes Survey (Jean & Reynolds, 1980). Both sex-role bias responses and childhood punishment levels (measured by an experimenter-designed scale) significantly predicted ABI scores for men placed in the Attack and Damage subgroup (Brown, James, & Seddon, 2002). A meta-analysis of results from seven studies found that assessments of sexist attitudes are significantly associated with MFIPV ($r = .20$) (Hanson & Wallace-Capretta, 1998).

Public attitudes toward batterers and arrest. Sometimes it is surprising how individuals respond to men's violence toward women. For one illustration, see Box 11.1. This discussion of the treatment of MFIPV offenders working in the Los Angeles Police Department gives some indication of that organizational culture's attitudes toward battering. On the surface, it appears that the police in Los Angeles have "circled the wagons" to protect their own. This type of behavior has appeared in other male groups as well, such as athletic teams and fraternity members. (See Chapter 8 for a discussion of this problem.)

Box 11.1 Batterers in the Los Angeles Police Department

Some police are batterers themselves, so it is interesting to see how their supervisors and coworkers react to them. Various inquiries have suggested that in the Los Angeles Police Department (LAPD), the handling of officers convicted of domestic violence is biased (Braidbill, 1997; McGreevy, 1997). In the 9,300-member LAPD, approximately 150 officers may have arrest records ("Three Deputies," 1997). A review of 84 Internal Affairs Department (IAD) incident reports disclosed that the LAPD did not make a single arrest of an officer for IPV between 1991 and 1993, even though 48 IPV victims of LAPD officers had multiple, visible injuries (Braidbill, 1997).

Under public pressure to comply with the law, the Los Angeles City Council hired additional investigators to check conviction records of all LAPD personnel. Investigator General Katherine Mader reached several conclusions (as noted in Braidbill, 1997):

1. The LAPD made arrests in only 6% of cases within its jurisdiction involving LAPD officers, whereas outside agencies made arrests in 16% of incidents in other jurisdictions.

2. Almost 90% of allegations were against male employees.

3. The IAD, charged with evaluating these accusations, judged only 38% of male employees guilty but 58% of female employees guilty.

4. Reports turned in to IAD were often flawed by inappropriate language describing and blaming victims. As an illustration, reports often described female victims as suffering from fatal attraction, whereas they described accused male officers as productive and hardworking. One report concluded that "there is no fury like a woman scorned."

5. The IAD often took almost a year to investigate domestic violence charges.

In the final analysis, investigators identified 7 convicted domestic violence abusers from the list of 150 officers, relieved them of their weapons, and assigned them to other duties (Orlov, 1997). Police union officers point out that some convictions were more than 10 years old and no longer relevant. A loophole in the law has allowed some police officers convicted of IPV to expunge their records. More than 150 officers in the LAPD have now done so ("Three Deputies," 1997). These reports lend credence to the claims of women's advocates that male privilege in some settings is still a powerful force exerting control over women's lives.

Scientific polls have gauged the attitudes of larger segments of the U.S. population toward IPV and IPV victims and perpetrators. In a 1992 poll, the general public failed to endorse arrest as the proper response to spouse abuse. At a minimum, many respondents said, a man would have to hit a woman hard (53%) to deserve arrest, but if he punched her, 94% agreed that arrest was appropriate. One disturbing and persistent belief among 38% of respondents was that "some women provoked men into abusing them" (Klein, Campbell, Soler, & Ghez, 1997). Research indicates that gender differences exist in attitudes toward IPV. In one survey, college men were significantly more likely than

college women to hold attitudes condoning partner violence, and the women in the sample were significantly more likely than the men to condemn it. The men in this study, relative to the women, also judged female IPV victims as more provocative and more to blame for IPV (West & Wandrei, 2002).

Grasmick, Blackwell, Bursik, and Mitchell (1993) ascertained minimal changes in attitudes toward IPV between 1982 and 1992 in a random community sample of 350 people. Whereas significant changes were evident over this period in attitudes toward drunk driving and littering, changes concerning IPV were more limited. Research participants responded to questions about their reactions to hurting another person. Younger males, but not older males or any-age females, said they would be worried about legal repercussions if they hurt someone else. Men also said they would be embarrassed if their friends and acquaintances found out. There were no substantial increases in feeling guilt or shame if others found out.

Violence, Biology, and Genetics

One question that has attracted increasing research scrutiny in the past decade is whether male violence might have a biological basis, rather than being simply a consequence of socialization or cultural forces. Could it be that the intergenerational transfer of abuse springs from genetic transmission (Hines & Saudino, 2002)? Newer discoveries about relationships between biology and aggression raise the age-old "nature/ nurture" controversy (now perceived as a complex dichotomy; Gottesman, 2001). Evidence suggests that biological determinants, such as hormones and neurotransmitters (brain chemicals), may drive male violence. Furthermore, criminal behavior and psychopathology may have their roots in genetic differences. One complication in unraveling genetic determinants of behavior is that psychopathic conditions are arbitrary and overlapping in the *DSM* series (Jang, Vernon, & Livesley, 2001). What is needed is for definitions of these conditions to have "genetically crisp categories" (Faraone, Tsuang, & Tsuang, 1999, p. 114). Furthermore, methodological inconsistencies, such as the time of day at which researchers gather hormone samples and how they gather those samples, undermine confidence in the findings. The subsections below provide a brief overview of biological research pertinent to IPV perpetration.

Biological hormone studies. According to Alan Mazur, the major male hormone testosterone (TST) has earned a bad reputation (cited in Bower, 2003). In a review of TST studies, for example, Harris (1999) found greater aggression in males relative to females and also found that aggression is dimorphic; that is, aggression takes different forms in men and women. One group of researchers conducted a meta-analysis of 45 independent studies covering 9,760 research participants and found that TST-aggression correlations ranged from 0.28 to 0.71. The weighted correlation was $r = 0.14$, a significant but weak correlation (Book, Starzyk, & Quinsey, 2001). Other scientists contend that TST forms part of a configuration of components contributing to a general latent predisposition toward aggression but that social factors moderate its influence (Royce & Coccaro, 2001; Soler, Vinayak, & Quadagno, 2000; Virkkunen et al., 1994). A number of social scientists believe that evolutionary biology has fashioned men to be aggressive (Daly & Wilson, 1998).

Soler et al. (2000) discovered that TST was significantly associated with verbal and physical levels of violence as measured by CTS1. Because demographic variables (e.g., age) and alcohol consumption also helped explain the variance in aggressive responses, these researchers concluded that a biosocial model best fit the data. Royce and Coccaro (2001) focused on the neurotransmitter **serotonin** in one study. Serotonin helps regulate appropriate mood states, and serotonin dysfunction or hypofunction (i.e., underproduction) is significantly correlated with impulsive aggression and suicide.

In a theoretical paper, Bernhardt (1997) credits TST with dominance-seeking behavior rather than aggression. According to Bernhardt, high TST levels heighten dominance seeking, which in turn diminishes frustration tolerance. Simultaneously, low serotonin increases responsivity to negative stimuli, thus potentiating aversive effects triggered by frustrating events. Hence the confluence of low serotonin and high TST may lead to aggressive behavior. In one meta-analysis, significantly lower serotonin levels occurred in several groups of violent antisocial men (Raine, 1993).

Brain dysfunctions. Another biological postulation is that MFIPV perpetrators may suffer from various brain disorders. A number of brain regions are involved in controlling aggression: prefrontal cortex, limbic system, septum, hippocampus, caudate nucleus, thalamus, and amygdala (Raine, 1993). A few analyses have identified the effects of damage to these regions. Volavka (1995), for instance, discovered frontal lobe dysfunction in some criminal and violent individuals. Bernstein, Newman, Wallace, and Luh (2000) have shown that psychopaths have interpersonal/affective deficits that may be related to an information-processing deficit in hemispheric arousal. In addition, a recent meta-analysis revealed that, of 39 studies encompassing 4,589 research participants, antisocial groups performed .62 standard deviations worse on executive functioning tests (frontal lobe reactions) (Morgan & Lilienfeld, 2000).

Research has also produced evidence that birth complications and head injuries contribute to crime

("Biology and Family," 1996). In a Danish investigation, Kandel and Mednick (1991) examined longitudinal data from a birth cohort. Adult data included records of both violent and property crimes. Background information included such factors as mental health classification of parents (e.g., character disorder) and pregnancy and birth complications of participants. The three comparison groups consisted of 15 violent criminals, 24 property criminals, and 177 nonoffenders. Birth complications did predict adult violent offending, but not property crimes. In an analysis of trauma effects in adult males, Rosenbaum and Hoge (1989) uncovered histories of head injury in 61% of MFIPV perpetrators in their sample (see also Warnken, Rosenbaum, Fletcher, Hoge, & Adelman, 1994).

Genetic studies. One way to evaluate biological contrasts is with genetic studies. Genetic comparisons have shown, for example, that TST level is highly heritable (Harris, Vernon, & Boomsma, 1998). One of the most accurate ways to isolate genetic from environmental contributions to criminality is with adoption studies (Walters, 1992). Children share 50% of their genetic inheritance with each biological parent and none with genetically unrelated persons, such as adoptive parents. Comparing children's behavior with both their biological fathers and their adoptive fathers constitutes an excellent test of the gene-crime relationship.

In a meta-analysis, Walters (1992) documented a low to moderate but significant association between heredity variables and indices of crime, despite methodological problems with many of the studies. Based on an analysis of 13 adoption studies, Walters suggests that the individual genetic inheritance of criminal behavior is 11% to 17%. Although these studies demonstrate a gene-crime relationship, they have not yet identified a gene-violence relationship. Two other twin studies found significant heritability for APD symptoms (Coccaro, Bergeman, Kavoussi, & Seroczynski, 1997). The overlap between MFIPV and general violence may have additional implications. The results of genetic studies of APD may, by logical extension, apply to maritally assaultive men (Dunford et al., 1990).

Relationship Factors and Problems in Living

Case History: Kevin and Kim—"She Didn't Clean the Lint Trap"

Kevin was a handsome, 32-year-old video cameraman for a local TV station. He frequently was called out of town to cover stories and even went overseas on work assignments occasionally. His beautiful wife, Kim, who earned money modeling, went with him if she wasn't working. They had no children.

On the job, Kevin felt fearful from time to time when he had to shoot at a location in a ghetto neighborhood. He was afraid that local hoods would try to beat him up, and he thought he wouldn't be able to defend himself because he was too small. He was anxious about Kim's behavior as well. Other guys were always flirting with her, and she saw nothing wrong with "just being friends" with them. Kevin saw a lot wrong with it, and he warned her to watch her step. In Kevin's mind, Kim was very sloppy around the house. No matter what he said, she was always forgetting to empty the lint trap in the clothes dryer. It was clear to him that Kim didn't care how he felt, and he was desperate to do something to make her "treat him better."

The night Kevin got arrested for beating Kim up (for the first time, according to Kevin), he had come home around 6:30 in the evening after several weeks in Australia. He had caught an early flight back to surprise Kim with an expensive pearl ring and some champagne that he bought on the way home from the airport. He really loved her, and he was looking forward to a romantic reunion.

The first thing that went wrong was that Kim was not home. Kevin was both disappointed and suspicious. Perhaps she wasn't at work, but was out having a drink with some guy who picked her up at a bar. He had never actually caught her doing this, but he thought she probably did it a lot when he was out of town. The second thing that happened was that there were some dirty dishes on the sink counter, and when he decided to do his laundry, he discovered Kim had failed to empty the lint trap again!

At 7:30, Kevin looked out a window and saw Kim coming out of the neighbor's house. He grabbed a shotgun and ran up and down the side yard, shooting into the air over the neighbor's house. He then took a sharp tool out of the garage and sliced his neighbor's tires. By the time the police arrived, Kim was on the living room floor with a broken nose and two broken ribs. Her 6-foot, 4-inch batterer was sitting on the couch sobbing. Kim was threatening to leave him. He hadn't meant to hurt her, but what other options did he have?

This case history reflects the high level of stress found in many batterers. Kevin is stressed about his wife's fidelity, her housekeeping, his job, and other factors. He cannot relax. He is miserable but does not know how to handle his feelings. He probably blames Kim for any relationship problems. As much as he loves her and needs her, he cannot get what he wants from her. His reaction is to lash out impulsively and violently and then to regret his actions. His irrational, violent behavior is probably driving her away.

For an MFIPV perpetrator, it can be a daunting challenge to form a close relationship with an intimate partner that is based on mutuality (Barnett & Hamberger, 1992). Some of the most striking problems batterers exhibit are those occurring in their personal relationships: marital dissatisfaction, poor communication, poor problem solving, power and control issues, and jealousy and lack of trust. These kinds of problems are so intolerable that they precipitate the dissolution of the marriage, the very relationship the man is striving to keep.

Investigations of marital interactions pose a number of uncertainties. If intimate partners begin yelling at and insulting each other, what might have been the proximal (i.e., most immediate) cause? Did some distal (i.e., earlier) event trigger the quarrel? Could one or both partners be responding in terms of painful childhood experiences? Do the partners have sufficient skills to resolve the issues brought up in the conflict? Are they one of the rare couples who might be able to eliminate IPV, or will they divorce (see Anderson & Schlossberg, 1999)?

Verbal skills/communication. Within the domain of couple interactions, several inept communication patterns related to IPV have come to light (Gondolf, Heckert, & Kimmel, 2002; Yegidis, 1992). Berns, Jacobson, and Gottman (1999), for example, found that IPV-involved couples show less positive communication and more negative communication than do nonviolent spouses. Relatedly, another study indicates that, compared with violent couples, when members of nonviolent couples make angry comments, their partners are much less likely to reciprocate with angry/contemptuous remarks. Instead, nonviolent partners might respond with nonhostile negative, neutral, or even positive comments. In fact, they frequently find ways to exit arguments altogether (Burman, Margolin, & John, 1993).

Feldman and Ridley (2000) studied 251 male volunteers associated with either a court-ordered domestic violence monitoring program or a public health clinic. They administered the ABI (Shepard & Campbell, 1992), the Communication Patterns Questionnaire (Christensen, 1988), and the Marital Opinion Questionnaire (Huston & Vangelisti, 1991). Relative to nonpartner-violent relationships, variables that characterized partner-violent relationships were as follows: (a) more male and female unilateral verbal aggression, (b) more male demand/partner withdraw, (c) less constructive communication, (d) less mutual problem solving, (e) poorer resolution of problems, and (f) more emotional distance after problem arguments. Taken together, the findings indicated that conflict-based communication plays a salient role in IPV (see also Sagrestano, Heavey, & Christensen, 1999).

In some cases, batterers seem unable to make their needs known verbally, and they may resort to violence as a means of control. Many partner-violent men suffer from assertion deficits (i.e., inadequacy in stating one's views forcefully or in making requests appropriately; see, e.g., Dutton & Strachan, 1987), and these deficits are associated with greater verbal hostility (Maiuro, Cahn, & Vitaliano, 1988). Across studies, research conducted during the 1980s indicated that lack of assertiveness may be a risk marker for wife assault (e.g., Hotaling & Sugarman, 1986), but findings vary depending on whether measures assess general assertiveness or spouse-specific assertiveness. MFIPV perpetrators tend to show the largest deficits in spouse-specific assertiveness. Assertion deficits, however, may be more representative of marital dissatisfaction levels than of marital assault levels (O'Leary & Curley, 1986).

Misperception of communication is yet another difficulty that violent men experience (Margolin, John, & Gleberman, 1988). In one study, partner-violent men underestimated the quality and number of caring gestures received from their wives. They saw themselves as "doing more and getting less" in their relationships (Langhinrichsen-Rohling, Smutzler, & Vivian, 1994).

Poor problem solving. Several studies have shown that, compared with nonpartner-violent men, partner-violent men are poor problem solvers (e.g., Anglin & Holtzworth-Munroe, 1997; Barnett & Hamberger, 1992; Hastings & Hamberger, 1988). Indeed, ineffective conflict resolution strategies and high marital distress may serve as mediating factors between childhood exposure to interparental violence and wife battering (Choice, Lamke, & Pittman, 1995). In particular, partner-violent men exhibit the most difficulty generating adequate responses to situations involving rejection by their wives, challenges from their wives, and jealousy.

Stress. Some batterers experience excessive levels of stress as a result of events or their own perceptions (e.g., Kevin's reaction to Kim's "poor" housekeeping in the case history above). Using the Life Experiences Survey (Sarason, Johnson, & Siegel, 1978), McHenry, Julian, and Gavazzi (1995) found that negative life events are significantly associated with MFIPV. Others have suggested that the stress of the relationship itself might trigger some degree of spousal abuse. Pan, Neidig, and O'Leary (1994) examined different types of stress in a large sample of military men ($N = 11,870$). They found that neither home stress nor occupational stress was related to aggression, but that distress about one's partner was significantly related to partner violence. Consistent with this supposition, another group of researchers demonstrated that 11 of 14 stress items (e.g., "job trouble," "small income") significantly differentiated violent from nonviolent groups (Barnett, Fagan, & Booker, 1991). The primary stressor reported by partner-violent men was the female "partner." A review of studies on the relationship between stress and IPV shows that there are multiple pathways, both direct and indirect. (For a review of the relationship between stress and IPV, see Cano & Vivian, 2001.)

Another line of inquiry concerns a unique type of stress labeled MGRS, or masculine gender-role stress. Male gender-role perceptions encompass socially mandated expectations and rules prescribing appropriate and inappropriate male behaviors. MGRS also refers to the name of a test for this type of stress (Eisler & Skidmore, 1987). Factor analysis of the MGRS test has identified types of stress-eliciting situations that comprise five dimensions: (a) Physical Inadequacy, (b) Emotional Expressiveness (c) Subordination to Women, (d) Intellectual Inferiority, and (e) Performance Failure. Researchers have found that high levels of MGRS are associated with problematic behaviors, such as physical health problems (including heart disease), psychological problems, and problems in interpersonal relationships (e.g., Copenhaver & Eisler, 1996; Lash, Copenhaver, & Eisler, 1998; Lash, Eisler, & Schulman, 1990).

Copenhaver, Lash, and Eisler (2000) evaluated 163 veterans in treatment for substance abuse on the MGRS, the CTS1, and the Trait Anger Scale (TAS; Spielberger, 1991). Correlational analyses indicated a significant correlation between MGRS and CTS1 scores ($r = .22$,

$p < .01$) and the MGRS and TAS scales ($r = .44$, $p < .001$). Regression analyses showed that TAS scores accounted for significantly more variance in CTS1 scores than did MGRS scores. An **analysis of variance** (ANOVA) revealed that high-MGRS men, relative to low-MGRS men, evidenced significantly more anger on the TAS. Other ANOVAs showed significant differences on the Verbal Abuse and Minor Physical Abuse subscales of CTS1. Simply put, MGRS may be a factor in anger evocation and MFIPV. Jakupcak (2003) included an assessment of MGRS and fear of emotions as predictors of MFIPV in an evaluation of 155 male college students. He found that fear of emotions predicted MFIPV over and above MRGS scores. Fear of emotions also mediated the link between MRGS and MFIPV.

Power and control. Issues of partner control seem to characterize most battering relationships (Tinsley, Critelli, & Ee, 1992). According to Frieze and Browne (1989), MFIPV is more common in families where husbands hold most of the power and make most of the decisions. Explanations for the relationship between power and control issues and battering depend in part on one's theoretical perspective. Feminists contend that all MFIPV is about power and control, as male-female relationships are embedded within a patriarchal society (Dobash, Dobash, Wilson, & Daly, 1992). Learning theorists point out that when aggression is instrumental in obtaining one's goal, it is reinforcing and therefore likely to increase (Felson, 1992). The results of one analysis, however, indicate that MFIPV perpetrators do not experience greater feelings of being in control than do nonperpetrators and that using IPV does not enhance their sense of control (Umberson, Anderson, Glick, & Shapiro, 1998).

Feeling controlled in marriage occurs more frequently in unhappy marriages than in happy marriages. One gender comparison revealed that women are more likely than men to believe that the motivation for IPV is control (Ehrensaft, Langhinrichsen-Rohling, Heyman, O'Leary, & Lawrence, 1999). Others conjecture that feeling powerless in the relationship may serve as a precursor to violence for some men, or that some people have a greater need for power than others. Several studies using different indexes and somewhat different samples of research participants have found that partner-violent men generate higher need-for-power themes than do nonpartner-violent men (Babcock, Waltz, Jacobson, & Gottman, 1993; Dutton & Strachan, 1987; Sagrestano et al., 1999).

Jealousy and trust. Clinicians, researchers, and shelter workers have all observed that MFIPV perpetrators suffer from inordinate jealousy. Some women have reported such extreme levels of jealousy that their violent partners did not allow them to leave their homes (e.g., Avni, 1991). Several studies have found that scores on at least one jealousy scale (Mathes & Severa, 1981) were significantly higher for partner-violent men than for nonpartner-violent men (Dutton, van Ginkel, & Landolt, 1996; Holtzworth-Munroe, Meehan, et al., 1000; Holtzworth-Munroe, Stuart, & Hutchinson, 1997). In an inquiry concerning lesbian battering, Renzetti (1992) also identified a significant relationship between level of jealousy and degree of psychological abuse of a partner.

In one investigation, jealousy correlated highly with marital dissatisfaction (Barnett, Martinez, & Bleustein, 1995), and in others it correlated with disordered attachment (see Dutton et al., 1996; Holtzworth-Munroe, Stuart, & Hutchinson, 1997). An examination of a related concept, trust (using a scale developed by Rempel, Holmes, & Zanna, 1985), produced significant results. The 58 partner-violent men in the study were significantly less trusting of their wives than were men in two nonpartner-violent groups, 32 unhappily married and 29 satisfactorily married men. Jealousy and lack of interpersonal trust appear to have some bearing on attachment disorders and dependency needs in partner-violent men. (For a review of risk factors for MFIPV, see Schumacher, Feldbau-Kohn, Slep, & Heyman, 2001.)

Individual Differences in Personality Traits and Disorders

Given that cultural explanations for IPV are incomplete, it is essential that investigators look for individual differences in personality disorders or other variables (O'Leary, 1993). In recent years, researchers have used more general personality inventories to assess a broader range of both normal and abnormal traits. Some traits that seem related to IPV levels include the following: (a) **anger** and **hostility**, (b) lack of empathy, (c) shame and guilt, (d) low self-esteem, (e), depression, and (f) trauma and posttraumatic stress disorder (PTSD). Some forms of psychopathology, such as APD and BPD, are related to MFIPV.

Anger and hostility. Specialists in wide-ranging disciplines have implicated anger as a precursor to violence. Anger may be viewed as a *trait* (i.e., a relatively stable

characteristic of some people), a *state* (i.e., temporary feelings elicited by a specific situation), or both. That is, there are individual differences in how angry people feel on an ongoing basis, and certain situations elicit more anger than others (Barbour, Eckhardt, Davison, & Kassinove, 1998). Trait anger is the disposition to regard numerous situations as unfair or threatening (Deffenbacher, 1992). Several researchers have reported significant gender differences in expression of anger.

Investigations of anger in partner-violent men have produced fairly consistent results (Eckhardt, Barbour, & Stuart, 1997). Barbour et al. (1998) found several significant differences between 31 partner-violent men and men in two nonpartner-violent groups (23 unhappily married men and 34 happily married men) as assessed by a modified version of CTS1 and the SMAT. In this comparison, partner-violent men scored significantly higher than nonpartner-violent men on two subscales of the State-Trait Anger Expression Inventory (Spielberger, 1988), the Trait Anger and Anger Out (behavioral expressions) subscales, and significantly lower on the Anger Control subscale. Partner-violent men also uttered a significantly higher number of insulting, demeaning, and belligerent aggressive verbalizations during the laboratory anger-induction test, the Articulated Thoughts in Simulated Situations (Davison & Johnson, 1983). Other investigators using other inventories have obtained higher anger scores for partner-violent men compared with nonpartner-violent men (e.g., Dutton, 1995b; Leonard & Senchak, 1993; Maiuro et al., 1988). One investigation that employed the Novaco Anger Scale (Novaco, 1975), however, did not find significantly higher scores for batterers relative to nonbatterers (Hastings & Hamberger, 1988).

Barnett et al. (1991) investigated differences on the Buss-Durkee Hostility Inventory (BDHI; Buss & Durkee, 1957) among 227 men divided into five groups: (a) partner-violent men in counseling; (b) partner-violent men not in counseling; (c) nonpartner-violent, maritally distressed men; (d) nonpartner-violent satisfactorily married men; and (e) generally violent men. Partner-violent men differed from men in either one or both of the nonpartner-violent groups on five of eight BDHI dimensions: Assault, Indirect Hostility, Irritability, Resentment, and Verbal Hostility. Partner-violent men were more hostile overall than men in any of the other groups, and nonpartner-violent men had lower mean scores on every subscale.

In a complex multimethod, dual-reporter comparison of five groups of men screened for MFIPV and marital satisfaction level, Holtzworth-Munroe, Rehman, and Herron (2000) administered anger and hostility questionnaires. They also obtained observational measures of couple discussions and coded responses to hypothetical marital and nonmarital conflict situations. Their results yielded several intriguing dissimilarities. First, measures of anger and hostility tended to correspond. Second, anger and hostility were related to level of MFIPV across groups. Third, men reported more general anger (not toward wife) than spouse-specific anger (anger toward wife) except on an inventory of trait anger. Fourth, the angriest, most hostile men were those in two groups: the borderline/dysphoric group and the generally violent group. These two groups were not significantly different from each other on every measure. (For reviews of anger and hostility studies with partner-violent men, see Eckhardt et al., 1997; Holtzworth-Munroe, Bates, Smutzler, & Sandin, 1997.)

Empathic reactions. Another line of research has explored the possibility that empathy might inhibit aggression. Given that partner-violent men are aggressive, perhaps they lack empathy. Researchers have made headway in discriminating both cognitive and affective elements of empathy (e.g., Zillmann, 1990). The cognitive component consists of the ability to take the other person's perspective, to see the situation from the other's viewpoint. Another aspect of the cognitive component is the recognition that negative consequences will occur from aggressive actions. It is possible for individuals to suffer from cognitive deficits that reduce their ability to empathize. The affective component centers on feelings of sympathy or concern for another. Zillmann (1990) has developed a model of empathy that assumes individuals can utilize perspective taking (cognitive component) if their arousal/excitation level (wanting to retaliate aggressively) is low to moderate.

According to Cox, Holzwarth, Cantrell, and Hamilton (2001), researchers have neglected to investigate variables contributing to the affective component of empathy. In the appraisal these researchers conducted, 300 undergraduates watched five videotaped vignettes of cartoon characters in emotional distress or emotional elation and rated their reactions via the Profile of Mood States (McNair, Lorr, & Droppelman, 1971). Participants responded significantly above baseline on empathic awareness in the affective domain for videos depicting emotional distress. Significant gender differences emerged: Males expressed significantly more anger in response to emotional distress than did females, and females expressed more sadness than did males. Cox et al. suggest that empathy may not develop only during a particular stage of life, but may mature over the lifetime. Although the students in this study felt empathy, their actual responses to distress were inadequate. It is possible that socialization of males strips away appropriate responses at an early age.

Over a series of three studies, Richardson, Hammock, Smith, Gardner, and Signo (1994) used a varying number of indexes and threat manipulations and reached several conclusions. First, perspective taking is able to inhibit aggression if provocation to aggress is moderate. Second, in some circumstances, empathic concern is associated with making more constructive and fewer destructive responses. In sum, these researchers assert that "any factor that enhances cognitive processing might decrease aggression" (p. 287). Even counting to 10 might be somewhat helpful in reducing aggressive responses.

Shame and guilt. Dutton et al. (1995) screened men for physical and psychological abuse using the Psychological Maltreatment of Women Inventory (PMWI; Tolman, 1989) and identified 140 abusers. The researchers then administered several inventories containing large numbers of self-report questions to these men and their female partners. The PMWI assesses psychological abuse (emotional abuse and dominance/isolation). Research participants also completed the BPO scale; the Multidimensional Anger Inventory (Siegel, 1986); EMBU scales of shame, guilt, and unlovable; and trauma items from the Trauma Symptom Checklist (TSC-33; Briere & Runtz, 1989). An extremely large number of significant relationships between scales emerged. In particular, men's recollections of being shamed by parents were linked with adult anger, abusiveness, trauma symptoms, and BPO. On the basis of additional analyses, Dutton and his colleagues determined that shame developed though parental punishments and that abuse was the central precursor to men's adult abusiveness.

In a theoretical paper about the shame-violence connection, Jennings and Murphy (2000) have formulated an explanation (not an excuse) for MFIPV in terms of humiliation, a social form of shame. These authors assert that partner violence is a result of "the disappointments of traditional male socialization and gender role training. Thus, the core pathology of male-female battering involves fundamental disruptions in male-male relations as well as male-female ones" (p. 21). That is, partner-violent men are behaving from a shame-based, esteem-deficient position. Simply put, a boy who grows up in a home characterized by public shaming, with no loving father or mentor, becomes in adulthood the sex-stereotypic "independent," "silent" male who is alienated from other males. In reality, such a man feels weak, helpless, and inadequate, conditions he must not reveal to other men for fear of humiliation. Women become his only safe outlet for need satisfaction. In need of ego building and nurturance, he must turn to his female partner, who then has the responsibility for satisfying all his security needs. She has to be his lover, mother, father, buddy, confidant, and social club. When she fails to meet all these needs, he blames her. His biggest fear is that she will leave him—he has no one else. Consequently, he must threaten her, control her, monitor her whereabouts, keep other males away, and/or assault her to make her stay. (For examples and suggestions regarding treatments for such men, see Osherson & Krugman, 1990.)

Low self-esteem. Some scholars have suggested that male IPV perpetrators engage in IPV because they suffer from low self-esteem. Indeed, two early comparisons and a more recent study found significantly lower self-esteem in partner-violent men compared with nonpartner-violent men (Goldstein & Rosenbaum, 1985; Neidig et al., 1986). More recently, a meta-analysis established a link between low self-esteem and MFIPV (Boney-McCoy & Sugarman, 1999). Murphy, Stosny, and Morrel (in press) evaluated treatments for two samples of partner-violent men that included program elements designed to raise self-esteem, as assessed by the Rosenberg Self-Esteem Scale (Rosenberg, 1979). Based on participants' self-reports, self-esteem increased while partner violence decreased over the 12- to 16-week treatment periods. Victims' reports of posttreatment MFIPV were not correlated with men's pretreatment, posttreatment, or enhancement of self-esteem during counseling. (For studies about self-esteem in relationships, see Murray, Bellavia, Rose, & Griffin, 2003; Murray, Rose, Bellavia, Holmes, & Kusche, 2002.)

Issues regarding an assumed relationship between violence and self-esteem, however, remain unresolved. One perplexing aspect of the data is that people with high self-esteem may be either aggressive or non-aggressive (e.g., Baumeister, Dale, & Sommer, 1996). Baumeister, Campbell, Krueger, and Vohs (2003) amassed evidence from their own and others' work that prompted them to call for a broad shift in thinking about an assumed link between aggression and low self-esteem. Baumeister et al. (1996) propose that "threatened egotism," rather than low self-esteem, determines aggression. In other words, a man who holds a positive view of himself may lash out at others who question or attack his self-view (see also Kirkpatrick, Waugh, Valencia, & Webster, 2002).

Depression. Most of the research conducted to date on the relationship between depression and IPV has relied on the Beck Depression Inventory (Beck, 1978). Several investigations that used comparison groups to assess moods have demonstrated that MFIPV perpetrators are substantially more depressed than non-perpetrators (Hamberger & Hastings, 1991; Julian & McHenry, 1993; Murphy, Meyer, & O'Leary, 1993). Using the *DSM-III-R* with a probability subsample of 1,738 men and 1,799 women, Kessler, Molnar, Feurer, and Appelbaum (2001) showed that partner-violent men perpetrating minor violence registered significantly higher levels of major depression than did their female counterparts. Research also indicates that depression is correlated with Modified Conflict Tactics Scale (MCTS) items of partner-violent men (e.g., Pan et al., 1994). Taken as a whole, findings suggest that partner-assaultive men who commit moderate to severe violence are significantly more depressed than nonpartner-assaultive men. Men who commit minor abuse may not be more depressed than partner-violent men (e.g., Hastings & Hamberger, 1994; Murphy et al., 1993).

Trauma and posttraumatic stress disorder. PTSD is an anxiety disorder produced by trauma, including assault and military combat. Afflicted persons have flashbacks, trouble concentrating, extreme startle reactions, and numbing of emotions (Goldenson, 1984). Some victims have symptoms for many years. Research in child abuse and wife abuse has documented high levels of PTSD in a significant number of survivors.

Using the MCMI-II, Dutton (1995b) detected a PTSD-like profile among a group of 132 partner-violent men. Unlike profiles of PTSD men, however, profiles of partner-violent men included higher scores for antisocial personality. Partner-violent males' trauma symptoms were significantly related to retrospective reports of parental treatment, especially rejection and physical abuse. More recently, Dutton (1999) has formulated a theory of intimate rage founded on a triad of traumatic childhood events. These include observation of father-to-mother violence, experiencing violence directed at the self, shaming, and insecure attachment. Presumably, taking trauma into account serves to broaden social learning theory in explaining IPV.

With increased emphasis on behavioral problems in combat veterans, however, academicians have begun to examine PTSD's relationship to aggression. One analysis of 118 Vietnam combat veterans showed that veterans with PTSD were significantly more violent than veterans without PTSD. Severity of PTSD in this group was significantly correlated with interpersonal violence (Beckham, Feldman, Kirby, Hertzberg, & Moore, 1997).

Personality traits and disorders. Some investigators have looked for individual differences (personality traits) between partner-violent and nonpartner-violent men on multidimensional personality tests. Several researchers have developed trait inventories to assess more comprehensively a number of personality dimensions. Barnett and Hamberger (1992) analyzed responses of 87 partner-violent men, 42 nonpartner-violent, maritally distressed men, and 48 nonpartner-violent, happily married men on the California Psychological Inventory (Gough, 1975). In this survey, partner-violent men clearly displayed different personality traits than nonviolent men in three general areas: intimacy, impulsivity, and problem-solving skills. Implications of this study were that batterers are less well-adjusted than nonviolent men. Partner-violent men seem to be rigid, stereotypically "masculine," and unresourceful in problem-solving techniques, and they exhibit difficulty in developing close, intimate relationships anchored on mutuality. They are also likely to be moody, impulsive, self-centered, demanding, and aloof.

Different researchers have conceptualized borderline personality disorders differently, using various tests (such as the Minnesota Multiphasic Personality Inventory, the MCMI, and the BPO scale) to assess these pathologies. From the very first, inventories of psychopathology showed that a subsample of MFIPV perpetrators are diagnosable with some form of psychological disorder (e.g., Faulk, 1974). Using the MCMI, Hamberger and Hastings (1986) contrasted 43 nonviolent community volunteers with 78 alcoholic batterers and 47 nonalcoholic batterers. They were able to classify 88% of their batterer populations as suffering from some level of psychopathology, and they identified several types of personality disorders: passive

dependent/compulsive, narcissistic/antisocial, and schizoidal/borderline.

Findings of psychopathology among IPV perpetrators continued unabated through the 1990s (Dutton & Starzomski, 1993; Flournoy & Wilson, 1991; Saunders, 1992; Vaselle-Augenstein & Ehrlich, 1992). A thorough comparison based on data from a nationally representative sample in the National Comorbidity Survey found that premarital mental disorders of men, but not women, predicted subsequent IPV (Kessler et al., 1994). Over the years, Dutton (1998) and his associates have presented data showing a correlation between BPO and partner violence in men. One of the most convincing controlled comparisons comes from an Australian cohort study of 1,037 individuals who were 21 years old when reassessed (Danielson, Moffitt, Caspi, & Silva, 1998). CTS1 scores covering the previous year and responses on *DSM-III-R*–specified behaviors uncovered a number of significant differences between partner-violent and nonpartner-violent men. More than half of partner-violent men met criteria for a mental disorder: anxiety disorder, substance abuse, or APD. (For a discussion of the causes of men's violence against women, see Harway & O'Neil, 1999.)

Partner-violent women. Henning et al. (2003) compared 2,254 male and 281 female IPV perpetrators taken from a primarily African American sample. The women in this study were more likely than the men to have previously attempted suicide, to have personality dysfunction and mood disorders, and to have taken psychotropic medications prior to arrest. More women also reported observing severe interparental violence and having received corporal punishment during childhood. The men in the sample, on the other hand, were more likely than the women to have had prior conduct disorders and substance abuse problems, and were at higher risk for substance dependence. Men, relative to women, also were significantly more likely to wish to continue their relationships with their victims. Regardless of the dissimilarities noted, the male and female perpetrators in this study obtained scores on the measures used that were more alike than different.

SECTION SUMMARY

Studies concerning the traits related to partner abuse are mostly correlational in nature and thus unable to demonstrate causality. In terms of socialization, it is clear that there are strong links between childhood exposure to violence in the home and later partner violence. Abusive men (and possibly women) are apt to come from dysfunctional homes typified by parental abuse, alcoholism, and psychopathology. Newer research has been successful in illuminating how other childhood experiences, such as being anxiously attached and emotionally dependent, are associated with MFIPV. MFIPV perpetrators' fears of abandonment are excessive. These early learning experiences probably help mold personality characteristics typical of men who batter.

Society expects men to be aggressive, and some men seem to learn that women are opportune targets for their violence. Abusive men are likely to be "undifferentiated" (have neither masculine nor feminine traits) in their sex roles. They are more prone than other men to hold sexist attitudes and to approve of aggression. The public, while becoming somewhat more intolerant of MFIPV, still favors a rather lenient approach toward partner-abusive men. Leniency is especially evident in some occupations.

Several biological elements of maleness and individual defects may exacerbate partner violence. The major male hormone, testosterone, is significantly but weakly correlated with aggression. Social factors moderate TST effects. Serotonin, a neural transmitter with calming effects, appears to be at lower levels in partner-abusive men as well, possibly leading to lower ability to tolerate frustration. Head trauma and various brain dysfunctions, observed more frequently in abusive men than in nonabusive men in some samples, also seem to influence aggression. Genetic studies demonstrate that criminal behavior and APD have genetic components. As mentioned in previous chapters and here, men with high levels of psychosocial risk at ages 8 to 10 are statistically more likely than their lower-risk counterparts to demonstrate criminal and antisocial behavior in adulthood.

Research on relationship factors has frequently shown that lack of verbal skills, stress, interpersonal control issues, jealousy, and lack of trust are related to partner violence. MFIPV perpetrators appear to be insufficiently assertive in communications and display considerable negative affect during discussions of conflictual conversations. They have inadequate problem-solving skills and consequently may become embroiled in considerable relational conflict. They frequently express feelings of "getting a raw deal," and often misperceive their partners' intentions.

Much research indicates that batterers experience high levels of stress, particularly in terms of their reactions to their female partners. Some argue that batterers are more vulnerable to stress because of childhood abuse (as noted in previous chapters). Partner-violent males also have relatively high levels of PTSD. An additional and newer conception of stress is termed *masculine gender-role stress,* or *MGRS.* High levels of MGRS are related to a number of problematic behaviors, including partner violence.

Research findings suggest that batterers use violence to control women and to get their own way. Some evidence attests to a need-for-power trait and to feelings of powerlessness among batterers. Studies using specific tests of jealousy indicate that partner-abusive men suffer from high levels of jealousy. Other types of tests reveal their inability to trust their female partners.

Correlational data from an array of single and broad-based inventories show a number of individual differences between partner-violent and nonpartner-violent men. Personality tests of anger and hostility using a variety of scales have fairly consistently demonstrated anger and extreme hostility among partner-abusive men. Investigators pursuing a different line of research have found that partner-violent men lack empathy. Consequently, they may not experience their female partners' pain to any great extent. Evidence is amassing that many partner-violent men have experienced unbearable levels of shame during childhood. Feelings of shame play a large role in these men's dependency needs. Although controversy exists about the relationship between esteem and IPV, most family violence researchers typify perpetrators as having low self-esteem. Some academicians believe that *narcissism* is a better descriptor of partner-violent males than *low self-esteem.*

In contrast, research support for depression as a batterer trait is strong. Some perpetrators are highly suicidal. Partner-abusive men score significantly higher than nonabusive men on trauma measures and suffer from significantly more PTSD. These symptoms probably relate to parental abuse experienced during childhood. Finally, IPV-perpetrating men consistently score higher than nonperpetrators on measures of personality disorders. It is clear that a significant proportion of perpetrators can be classified as suffering from some form of borderline disorder. Various sources of information, family of origin violence, assessment of biological traits, personality tests, and inventories of psychopathology all implicate APD,

BPO, and borderline disorders as the constellation of traits most typical of IPV perpetrators.

Practice, Policy, and Prevention Issues

For an abuser to make any real changes in his behavior, he must receive appropriate counseling (Dutton, 1986). Men who batter often find it difficult to acknowledge verbal and psychological abuse as abuse, and they find it difficult to change these kinds of behaviors. Much of the work that must be done in effective batterers' treatment programs revolves around recognizing these forms of intimidation and halting nonphysical as well as physical abuse.

In the late 1970s and early 1980s, batterer intervention programs (BIPs) were developing so rapidly around the world that by the mid-1980s there were more than 200 such programs in the United States alone (Stordeur & Stille, 1989). Out of this fragmented beginning grew the need for program evaluations, and from these assessments some rudimentary principles of treatment began to emerge.

Approaches to Counseling

For change to happen, basic ideological transformations must occur. In the case of MFIPV, as Adams and McCormick (1982) note, "men have a particular role to play in educating other men about the nature of abuse and how men can change" (p. 171). Glen Good (1998), president of the Society for the Psychological Study of Men and Masculinity, a division of the American Psychological Association, has brought attention to problems of masculine socialization. According to Good, "Problems like violence, substance abuse, relationship issues, parenting problems, and poor health habits need attention. We also need to develop intervention for more recently identified masculinity-related problems, such as lack of emotional competence, defensive self-sufficiency, poor sexual integrity, and uninvolved fathers" (p. 3).

Short-term group treatment is by far the most common type of treatment for IPV perpetrators (Carden, 1994). According to Jennings and Murphy (2000), group settings are preferable because they help partner-violent men work on male-male relationships. Such relationships are vital to men who experienced poor father-son relationships in childhood. Male-male relationships

are important because they spill over into male-female relationships and may contribute to IPV. In an account of standards for batterer treatment, 86% of BIP administrators stated a preference for group programs (Austin & Dankwort, 1999).

Healey, Smith, and O'Sullivan (1998) have estimated that approximately 80% of clients in BIPs attend the programs because they have been ordered to by the courts. Child abuse agency personnel and probation officers are representative of other referral sources. Some evidence suggests that batterers who are court ordered into treatment differ significantly from men who seek treatment voluntarily. In one survey, for example, men in BIPs who had no court involvement had higher levels of education, employment, and income than did court-mandated attendees, as well as higher levels of outside social support (e.g., more friends) (Barrera et al., 1994). Dutton and Starzomski (1994) found an opposite trend among a group of 38 court-referred and 40 self-referred IPV perpetrators in treatment. On the MCMI-II, the TSC-33, and other inventories, both groups exhibited problems. Self-referred men had higher scores on BPO (Oldham et al., 1985), marital conflict, anger, depression, and total trauma symptoms relative to court-referred men.

Selection of treatment type and choice of program content for MFIPV perpetrators are possibly the most contentious issues in the field. Compounding the problem is that treatments evidence minimal success (Rosenfeld, 1992). Given the variability of outcomes across studies, Hilton (1994), among others, believes that arrest and treatment decisions should match assaulter type. Of course, this idea has been the springboard for IPV perpetrator typology research. Men in a subset of psychopathic perpetrators within the generally violent group, for example, are most likely to be the most difficult to treat (Holtzworth-Munroe, Meehan, et al., 2000).

Two factions of agency personnel have undertaken the task of reducing MFIPV through treatment (usually subsequent to arrest). One group consists of trained, licensed mental health workers. The other group includes some members of these same professional organizations, as well as trained feminist advocates, or group facilitators. Disparate conclusions about the etiology of male-to-female violence (i.e., sociopolitical, interpersonal, intrapersonal, or biological) dominate the two factions' modes of facilitating change. These disagreements have polarized the field (Mankowski, Haaken, & Silvergleid, 2002). Classification of BIPs depends to a large extent on the viewpoints adopted by these various factions: feminist, cognitive-behavioral, couples, attachment, psychodynamic, and integrated (see Scott & Wolfe, 2000).

An obligation of BIPs must be consideration of battered women's safety (Hamberger & Barnett, 1995). Practitioners have the ethical and legal "duty to warn" potential victims (*Tarasoff v. Regents of the University of California,* 1976) while maintaining their primary obligation to protect clients' privacy (Chaimowitz, Glancy, & Blackburn, 2000). In an effort to ensure victims' safety, some BIPs have initiated sessions in which they provide victims with safety planning information (Hamberger & Hastings, 1990). In these sessions, experts help victims to think through various actions that will facilitate their escape from their abusers, if necessary, such as having money hidden somewhere, having a bag packed, and locating a safe home where they and their children may reside temporarily (see Dutton-Douglas & Dionne, 1991).

The Duluth model: psychoeducational approaches. Feminist theory views IPV as an extreme action falling on a continuum of behaviors through which men control and oppress women. Adherents of this perspective want to resocialize men to abandon power and control tactics as well as sexist attitudes toward women. As an illustration, a man who beats his wife because dinner is late must first learn that he has no right to order his wife to make dinner or to make it on time (Pence & Paymar, 1993). This approach also capitalizes on criminal justice sanctions as an integral part of a successful program. Such agendas do not focus on treating men's psychiatric or medical problems. Feminists believe the central point is the damage men do to women, the pain men cause women (Mankowski et al., 2002). More BIPs across the United States adhere to the Duluth model than any other (Jackson, 2003). It is important for social forces to work on changing male socialization. Men need to learn that women do not have to be subordinate to men. There is work to do on transforming basic conceptions of masculinity so that males are less violent, less controlling, more loving, more emotionally expressive, more nurturant, and more appreciative of women.

Critics question the scientific foundation of the Duluth model and consider it more of a political statement than a psychological treatment. They believe that the assumption that all men's MFIPV is motivated by issues of power and control is overbroad. In addition, scientific evidence that the Duluth model is effective is sparse (Dutton, 1994). Much to the chagrin of professionals searching for empirically based treatments, however, many U.S. states have established guidelines prescribing the feminist approach. Some professionals believe that such guidelines are ill-advised because they tend to limit program modes and research questions. In particular, many experts think that batterer treatment program staff should be licensed clinical professionals and that science, not advocacy, should guide treatment decision making (Austin & Dankwort, 1999). Of the states that have standards concerning these programs, 22% require and 46% recommend that facilitators have professional degrees. Specialized training in domestic violence is also a requirement in 95% of guidelines.

In parallel fashion, feminist scholars have criticized psychological explanations and treatments on grounds that they serve as excuses for battering (e.g., the "abuse excuse"). Batterers do not need counseling, these scholars argue; they need reeducation. Advocates of this viewpoint are outspoken in their belief that battering should be viewed not only as an individual problem, but also as a social and political problem. Male batterers are bad, not mad (Burns, 1992). When asked about causes of MFIPV, 70% of individuals adhering to the Duluth model cited patriarchy (Austin & Dankwort, 1999). Further, they label some psychological treatments, such as training to overcome "skill deficits," as misguided because, in reality, MFIPV stems from patriarchy, not miscommunication (e.g., Adams, 1988; Goldner, Penn, Sheinberg, & Walker, 1990).

Cognitive-behavioral therapy. Therapists using cognitive-behavioral therapy (CBT) apply learning principles to help clients modify behavior identified as problematic by scientific trait assessments. Simply put, a therapist might help a client restructure his thinking. The following three-stage example illustrates how a typical batterer might think before therapy: (a) Initially, he encounters external stimuli such as a wife's failure to have dinner ready on time. (b) He then internally mediates (interprets) the event (e.g., in terms of past learning, current stress, or drunkenness) as her "not caring about how he feels" and decides that he must "force her to treat him better." (c) In the final stage, he exhibits an external response, such as throwing the food in her face. CBT would focus on teaching this IPV perpetrator to reinterpret the situation so that he will perceive his wife's lateness in preparing dinner differently (e.g., she was ill) and discover other behavioral options (e.g., take the family out to a fast-food restaurant).

Other therapeutic techniques involve helping perpetrators accomplish goals such as managing adverse arousal and learning appropriate assertion and problem-solving skills (see Faulkner, Stoltenberg, Cogen, Nolder, & Shooter, 1992). Given MFIPV perpetrators' levels of stress, practitioners should teach perpetrators how to handle stress, perhaps through relaxation training (Cano & Vivian, 2001). Certain subgroups of perpetrators, such as those scoring high on antisocial measures, may do better with some variant of CBT than with other treatments (Saunders, 1996).

Therapy aimed at anger management often uses cognitive-behavioral approaches as well as anger reduction techniques (e.g., relaxation training, time-out). Anger management is an important therapeutic focus because research shows higher levels of anger among MFIPV perpetrators (e.g., Copenhaver et al., 2000; Gregory & Erez, 2002; Whatule, 2000). One anger abatement technique advocates a four-step process: preparing for change, changing, accepting and adjusting, and maintaining change (Kassinove & Tafrate, 2002). One ill-advised method of dealing with anger is "letting off steam," as catharsis may actually increase anger (Bushman, Baumeister, & Stack, 1999). Because anger can sometimes be constructive rather than destructive, it seems necessary to determine a point at which anger becomes dysfunctional (Davidson, MacGregor, Stuhr, Dixon, & MacLean, 2000; Tiedens, 2001). Therapists might also be wise to help IPV perpetrators understand gender differences in anger expression. CBT also sometimes focuses on verbal and communication skills. O'Farrell, Murphy, Neavins, and Van Hutton (2000) found that behavioral marital therapy successfully reduced verbal aggression in a sample of male alcoholics and their wives.

Suicide prevention. Depression in a partner-violent man may escalate into suicidal feelings, especially if the female partner threatens to leave. Because MFIPV perpetrators appear to be in crisis when their partners threaten to leave, counselors should inaugurate suicide prevention programs in batterer groups. Partner-violent men evidence significantly elevated rates of suicidal behavior compared with community epidemiological survey norms (Kessler, Borges, & Walters, 1999).

Conner, Cerulli, and Caine (2002) recently examined suicidal behaviors among partner-violent men whose partners were seeking orders of protection. In their sample of 101 female IPV victims, 45% reported the following suicidal behaviors among male partners:

(a) 45.5% had histories of threatened suicide, (b) 12.9% had actually attempted suicide, and (c) most recent threats clustered within the 6-month period preceding the protection order. Furthermore, partner-violent men are likely to commit especially severe IPV, as indexed by a modified version of Campbell's (1995) dangerousness scale. Despite these valid concerns about men's risk for suicide, Henning et al. (2003) point out that some evidence suggests that female IPV perpetrators are at greater risk for suicide than are male perpetrators.

Couples/family/systems therapy. The least accepted approach to batterer treatment is based in systems theory. This approach expands treatment to include marital dynamics and the whole family system as a context for marital violence. In fact, 73% of U.S. states reporting standards for IPV perpetrator treatment label couples' counseling as inappropriate (Austin & Dankwort, 1999). Underlying this approach is the value placed on preserving the family. From this stance, a batterer's violence is not isolated and ascribed to him alone, but is somehow attributable to the "relationship" (e.g., Goodyear-Smith & Laidlaw, 1999). Two assets of couples' therapy are that it improves communication and allows male and female therapists to model nonviolent behavior (Geffner & Rosenbaum, 1990). Some scholars believe such treatment is suitable under prescribed circumstances, such as when the violence is at a low level, the victim is not fearful, and the couple wants to stay together (O'Leary, 1996).

Babcock and La Taillade (2000) point out that couples' therapy inappropriately assigns a portion of blame for MFIPV to victims. Adams (1988) denigrates this approach because viewing abuse as an interactional problem of the couple runs the risk of reinforcing a batterer's belief that violence is not really his problem alone. Critics further call attention to the dearth of scientific studies documenting effectiveness of couples' therapy and voice concern that violence and safety issues may lose priority (e.g., Edleson & Tolman, 1992). Others suggest that the process can be highly dangerous if it compels battered women to continue interaction with abusive, controlling, and dangerous partners (Dutton-Douglas & Dionne, 1991; Hansen, Harway, & Cervantes, 1991). (For a brief discussion of current views of couples' therapy, see Box 10.2 in Chapter 10.)

Substance abuse treatment. Drug abuse and problems with alcohol are very prevalent in batterers.

Furthermore, evidence from several lines of research shows that certain partner-violent men commit much more severe and frequent violence when intoxicated (Fals-Stewart, 2003; O'Farrell, Fals-Stewart, Murphy, & Murphy, 2003). Men in treatment for MFIPV usually need to be in addiction treatment as well (Jackson, 2003). In fact, the probability of a dual diagnosis is high in IPV perpetrator groups. PTSD, alcoholism, and APD may be present in IPV perpetrators, thus indicating the need for thorough screening at intake. Health personnel should screen men for violence as well as for more ordinary problems, such as depression and substance abuse (Riggs, Caulfield, & Street, 2000).

Research consistently shows that spouse abusers have a number of alcohol-related problems. Both genetic components (Bower, 1994) and learning components play roles in alcohol misuse (Vaillant & Milofsky, 1982). Alcoholism and drug addiction further handicap men who need to hold down jobs. Some researcher-clinicians have speculated that unemployment fosters a sense of powerlessness that may add to men's attempts to control female partners (Tollefson, 2002). Because drunkenness can precipitate battering and may be used as an excuse, practitioners must address alcohol treatment. One myth that Zubretsky and Digirolamo (1994) have tried to debunk, however, is that treatment of alcohol or substance abuse problems alone will concomitantly eliminate problems with domestic violence. A batterer trying to stop drinking, in fact, may be more abusive because of the new, added stress of attempting sobriety. On the other hand, a treatment consisting of both behavioral marital therapy and treatment for alcoholism for alcoholic husbands and their wives has shown some promise in decreasing violence in men, especially in those who stopped drinking (O'Farrell & Murphy, 1995). Another recent treatment for alcoholism and marital violence featured a short partial hospitalization program for the men and their partners. This program attenuated alcohol use and IPV, and these improvements were apparent at follow-ups 6 and 12 months later (Stuart et al., 2003).

Psychiatric-psychotropic medication treatments. A sizable minority of IPV perpetrators suffer from psychopathology. Psychiatric or psychotropic medication treatments are indicated for this subgroup of batterers with major depressions, APD, and other psychopathologies. Psychotropic medications such as antianxiety, antidepression, antiaggression, and antipsychotic drugs should reduce associated behavioral correlates of

these conditions (see Paschall & Fishbein, 2002; Royce & Coccaro, 2001). Need for such medications also came to light in an analysis of women arrested for FMIPV (Henning et al., 2003). Psychopathic partner-violent men are poor candidates for treatment in the community, and it may be safer to treat them while they are incarcerated. Other complications might arise with community treatment. Clinicians, for instance, have a legal duty to warn intimate partners of impending danger from psychopathic male partners. Appropriate drugs to assist in alcohol cessation should be made available also.

Alternative approaches. Whether they specifically articulate the fact or not, many BIPs take an eclectic approach that includes anger management and consciousness-raising about sexist attitudes. One team of researchers developed an integrated feminist/cognitive-behavioral and psychodynamic group treatment for partner-violent men (Lawson et al., 2001). An ongoing challenge is how best to provide treatment for members of minority groups. Standards in 59% of U.S. states prescribe separate treatment for female heterosexual IPV perpetrators, and standards in 38% of states advise that lesbians and gays should receive treatment in separate groups. Although standards in 57% of states call for culturally sensitive interventions, no guidelines specify what these techniques are (Austin & Dankwort, 1999).

Counseling Outcomes

It is a truism that partner-violent men are especially difficult to treat. Looking at an entire group of batterers may mask strong resistance to change emanating from a sizable subgroup of antisocial, borderline, or psychopathic men who are not receiving adequate treatment. A number of MFIPV experts are skeptical about the quality and permanence of behavioral changes made by abusers as a consequence of counseling (e.g., Feder & Dugan, 2003; Healey et al., 1998; Tolman & Bennett, 1990). In the discussion of batterer treatment outcomes, the old catch-22 question "Are you still beating your wife?" takes on new meaning.

Research methodology issues. Many methodological and research design implementation problems occur in batterer outcome studies. The following are just a few of these complications: unreliable research measures, high dropout rates, inadequate adjustments for cultural and ethnic differences, short follow-up periods, and inconsistent program content (e.g., Gondolf, 2001; Taylor, Davis, & Maxwell, 2001). Effects of external variables represent another type of experimental confounding. Courts may override random assignment during a research project, and they usually fail to take action against treatment dropouts (see Dutton, 1998; Gondolf, 1997). In fact, Babcock and Steiner (1999) found that the courts did not punish the 63% of men in their sample who failed to attend court-ordered treatment.

Aware of these shortcomings, researchers have strenuously attempted to improve research designs, and scientific outcome studies have progressed over the past two decades (e.g., Taylor et al., 2001). At first, researchers had little opportunity to select study participants or to use comparison groups. Consequently, they based their appraisals on available variables. As an example, see Palmer, Brown, and Barrera's (1992) use of completers versus noncompleters. The second phase of the research included evaluations of perpetrators in counseling judged against perpetrators given alternative interventions, such as probation or fines (e.g., Chen, Bersani, Myers, & Denton, 1989). Most recently, researchers have relied on random assignment of perpetrators to treatment conditions, such as counseling versus community service (e.g., Taylor et al., 2001). In this area of research, using a methodologically sound research design is imperative in order to rule out effects of arrest and other powerful factors that may supplement behavioral change (Maxwell, Garner, & Fagan, 2001). (For insightful reviews of outcome studies, see Gondolf, 2001; Jackson, 2003.)

Program attrition: the dropout problem. Program attrition is an especially serious complication for BIPs. As might be expected, recidivism is higher for dropouts than for completers (e.g., Pelligrini, 2000). Completers also diverge from noncompleters in other ways. One investigation found that dropouts, relative to completers, were younger, had lower employment levels, and had higher pretreatment levels of police interaction for nonviolent offenses (Hamberger & Hastings, 1989).

The typically high rate of dropout in batterer programs undermines the generalizability of the results of program evaluations. Illustrative of this problem are Gondolf and Foster's (1991) findings in a study in which they tracked records of 200 inquiries into batterer programs (i.e., men calling about treatment). From inquiry to first intake session, the attrition rate was 73%. From inquiry to counseling attendance, attrition was 86%, and from inquiry to completion of 12 sessions, 93%. Altogether, only 1% of the original group completed the contracted 8-month treatment program. Unfortunately, the courts did not routinely intervene to prevent dropout.

One investigation following a 16-week MFIPV abatement program compared violence-free completers with violence-repeating completers (Hamberger & Hastings, 1990). Violence-free completers had fewer alcohol abuse/substance abuse problems both pre- and posttreatment, and following treatment they had lower scores for narcissism (self-centered and demanding). In contrast, variation in outcomes generated by referral (self or mandated) and record of criminal activity failed to discriminate between the two groups.

In another examination of 197 batterers (165 males and 32 females) in a state-sponsored IPV program, the attrition rate was 40%. Tollefson (2002) was able to predict dropout/completion outcomes from among 10 factors. Through **logistic regression**, he identified the 3 factors most predictive of dropout: (a) unemployment, (b) presence of an Axis II psychiatric disorder (e.g., antisocial or narcissistic personality), and (c) the individual's being under supervised probation (lower socioeconomic status, antisocial, criminal records). Although outcome studies have not all assessed the same variables, there has been a large amount of overlap. As a whole, analyses have found that variables most likely related to program attrition include low level of education, unemployment, not being ordered into treatment by the courts, and alcohol/drug problems (see Daly, Power, & Gondolf, 2001; Tollefson, 2002).

Recidivism studies. One of the first quasi-experimental studies to tackle the recidivism (i.e., reassault) problem originated in Canada. Dutton (1986) compared postconviction rates of 50 men who completed a 16-week court-mandated treatment program to those of men in a comparable group who did not receive treatment over a 3-year period. Treated men had a recidivism rate of 4% (according to police reports) or 16% (according to victim reports); nontreated assaulters had a 40% rate. Generalizability of these findings was limited by the study's nonrandom selection of participants, by customary problems inherent in self-report data, and by uncontrollable variation in police decisions to rearrest. Overall, however, Dutton's work represents a striking improvement over anecdotal reports.

In a recent controlled comparison, Taylor et al. (2001) employed randomized selection to examine outcomes for 376 male IPV perpetrators drawn from a population of 11,000 defendants. A treatment group received a 40-hour Duluth-type program, Alternatives to Violence (ATV), while a comparison group received a 40-hour community service intervention. The researchers obtained several recidivism measures at 6 and 12 months: (a) arrest reports, (b) crime complaints, and (c) 48% to 51% victims' reports (modified CTS1 index). Although of no statistical significance, problems occurred when judges overrode the researchers' random selection by assigning 14% of maritally violent men to ATV when the researchers would have assigned them to community service. Categories of outcome measures included prevalence, rate of frequency, severity, and time to first failure. Results disclosed that men in treatment had significantly less recidivism based on two sources of official data (the Criminal Justice Agency and the New York City Police Department). These analyses arrived at an estimate of a 44% reduction in recidivism attributable to treatment. Analyses of victims' reports (no new victims available) disclosed that all four measures revealed less recidivism, but no single comparison reached statistical significance. While the findings supported the value of ATV treatment, the total sample size was too small for the results to be generalizable even to the jurisdiction from which the sample was drawn.

In the study described above, Tollefson (2002) also explored factors related to recidivism. Of the sample of 167 men and women (30 others were incarcerated), 21% reoffended in the 31-month (approximate) follow-up period. Regression analysis identified the three most predictive factors: (a) substance abuse, (b) Axis II (antisocial or narcissistic) disorder, and (c) child abuse in the family of origin. The model predicted 84% of all outcomes. Replication of these findings with suitable comparison groups should be the next step (see also Murphy, Morrel, Elliott, & Neavins, 2003). As a whole, however, it is clear that MFIPV treatment programs do not uniformly produce reductions in MFIPV. Scott and Wolfe (2003) propose that determining batterers' readiness to change might lead to better treatment matching. These investigators used a stages of change model (precontemplation, contemplation, action, maintenance) to assess batterer outcomes. As predicted, men in the precontemplation stage showed minimal change over a 10-week period in an analysis that included several dimensions.

Other posttreatment changes. Batterers may not only decrease their violence posttreatment, but also make other favorable changes. In a 1-year follow-up study, Hamberger and Hastings (1989) reported a dramatic reduction in depressive symptoms for batterers following 12 CBT sessions. The inclusion of a no-treatment comparison group in this study, had one been available, would have clarified the findings further. The batterers in the sample, however, did not uniformly abandon psychologically abusive behaviors, nor did their scores on tests of pathology change.

Gondolf (2000a) explored the methods that 443 partner-violent men in four treatment programs of varied duration (3 months to 9 months) used to avoid reassault. At a 15-month follow-up, 52% of the men reported that they employed some type of interruption technique, such as leaving the room or the house. The second most frequent action, taken by 25% of the men, was some type of discussion or problem solving. From among "other" category techniques, 15% stopped drinking, went to church, and so forth. Last, 3% relied on newfound respect and empathy to refrain from assault. Most of the men in this sample used only one strategy, but 21% chose more than one, and 25% did nothing on some occasions.

A qualitative study of nine English male batterers who had completed approximately 35 intervention sessions yielded promising results. Scott and Wolfe (2000) analyzed interview data along 28 a priori–specified codes derived from theoretically grounded variables related to behavioral change. They uncovered four dimensions of change reported by more than 75% of the men interviewed: (a) increased accountability for their IPV, (b) development of empathy for their partners' suffering, (c) decreased dependence on their female partners, and (d) improved communication skills.

Batterers in the military. Heyman and Neidig (1999) examined a sample of 33,762 men and women in the military and discovered that, in comparison with 3,044 nonmilitary men and women, the military personnel had significantly higher rates of severe IPV on CTS1 measures. The number of accounts of IPV among military men and women has increased over the past few years. One analysis of 26,835 individuals (95.1% men and 4.9% women) inquired about differences in CTS1 scores of military personnel who had been deployed and those who had not. Over the 1-year period, results demonstrated a small significant difference: Compared with nondeployed individuals, those who had been deployed were more severely violent (McCarroll, Ursano, et al., 2000).

A comparison of more than 34,000 military offenders and 13,000 civilian offenders revealed significantly lower recidivism rates for the military offenders (McCarroll, Thayer, et al., 2000). Dunford (2000) compared the effectiveness of four types of 12-month treatments offered to 861 married U.S. Navy male personnel with substantiated MFIPV. Treatments were as follows: (a) a men's group, (b) a conjoint group, (c) a rigorously monitored group, and (d) a control group (no treatment). Outcome measures consisted of the MCTS, male self-reports, victims' reports (e.g., felt endangered), official police and court records, and date of first recurrence. No significant differences between groups appeared. Of the men in treatment, 83% did not reinjure their wives. The injury rate, however, was not significantly different from that for men assigned to the control group.

Rosen, Kaminski, Parmley, Knudson, and Fancher (2003) conducted one of the most interesting and complete studies of MFIPV among 713 military men. The purpose of the evaluation was to compare the combined impact of individual-level and group-level variables on MFIPV. Individual predictors of MFIPV included race, depression, poor marital adjustment, alcohol problems, and childhood abuse. Group-level predictors included lower levels of bonding between soldiers and their leaders, a culture of hypermasculinity, and lower levels of support for female spouses. The findings were congruent with previous research on increased aggression among fraternity men (Schwartz & Nogrady, 1996) and distinctions between minor and severe MFIPV (Johnson, 1995).

Conclusions about the effectiveness of counseling programs. The effectiveness of abuser counseling with or without mandatory arrest remains questionable. In a meta-analytic review of 22 carefully selected studies, Babcock, Green, and Robie (2004) found positive but very small improvement. Effect sizes indicated a 5% reduction in recidivism. Such a reduction implies that 42,000 women per year would no longer be assaulted, but these academicians also found null results in terms of effects related to treatment type, such as psychoeducational versus CBT. The most definitive effects appeared in a study of military batterers. Dunford's (2000) comparison of interventions, described above, found no positive treatment effects when measured against a control group.

Another perspective on program evaluation is consumer satisfaction. Gondolf and White (2000) asked 594 (of 840) men in treatment and 616 female partners a number of open-ended questions about their satisfaction/dissatisfaction with the male partners' programs. Approximately half of this sample made no recommendations for change. Of the 14% of men suggesting change, their wish was to have more supportive counseling. Of the 13% of women advising change, the most common requests were for greater safety and for information about the program. Men frequently wanted their partners to join them because, they asserted, the women should share the blame. (For a brief discussion of the need for agencies involved with IPV perpetrators to work together, see Box 11.2.)

Box 11.2 Community Intervention Projects: "It Takes a Village"

The critical situation that many community agencies encounter in responding to wife assault has spawned a different type of organization, the community intervention project (CIP; see Edleson & Tolman, 1992). Owing to their mutual interests, victims' rights advocates and women's groups have converged in CIPs to pressure police and to lobby legislatures to do a better job of protecting battered women. A central tenet of CIPs is that society's response to domestic violence must change (see Francis, 1993).

Historically, U.S. society has condoned, ignored, and concealed the behavior of batterers (Roy, 1982). Indeed, not everyone believes that family violence is a crime or that police should take action (see Choi & Edleson, 1995; Klein, Campbell, Soler, & Ghez, 1997). Specific situational factors, such as severity and repetitiveness of assaults, underlie public opinion about whether police should respond and in what way (Choi & Edleson, 1995). Attitudes have been changing slowly, however, and Americans are increasingly recognizing that wife assault is a criminal offense (Barrera, Palmer, Brown, & Kalaher, 1994).

CIP staff and volunteers work with abusers, victims, police, prosecutors, probation officers, and social service agencies at every level to ameliorate domestic violence (Edleson, 1991). Personnel from various agencies hold joint discussions, so that members of one group (e.g., shelter advocates) can explain to another group (e.g., CPS workers) why particular policies may be troublesome. Improved policies flow from such interactions.

A 5-year follow-up study of men participating in a CIP used the criteria of reconviction, being a subject of a restraining order, and having been a police suspect in a domestic assault case to evaluate the effectiveness of the program. The results indicated that perpetrator characteristics, rather than length or type of treatment, was the best predictor of recidivism: "Men who had been abusive for a shorter period prior to the program, court ordered for chemical evaluation, in treatment for chemical dependency, abused as children, and previously convicted for nonassault crimes were more likely to be recidivists" (Shepard, 1992, p. 167).

Policy Issues

Among other changes, researchers and practitioners should develop more individualized treatment packages for batterers (e.g., Holtzworth-Munroe, Stuart, & Hutchinson, 1997; Huss & Langhinrichsen-Rohling, 2000).

Development of new treatments. Few treatment formats employed to date have included psychodynamic (insight) therapy. Saunders (1996) found that male IPV perpetrators who had high scores on dependency improved more in a new process-psychodynamic group. It is possible that this therapy would be helpful to borderline men (as in Holtzworth-Munroe, Meehan, et al., 2000). Insight therapy is indicated for men who do not know why they batter and do not recall their painful childhoods.

Many male IPV perpetrators have attachment problems and unacknowledged emotional dependency, most likely stemming from childhood. Unfortunately, these problems seem to manifest themselves in the following attitude: "I need her so much that I can't let her leave. If I threaten and beat her she will be forced to stay." Obviously, such attitudes and behaviors are more likely to drive a female partner away. As a result of such intense feelings, partner-violent men need help with trust and relationships skills.

Batterer empowerment strategies. Batterer empowerment treatment strategies may be effective, especially with low-income batterers (Tollefson, 2002). Such approaches, however, may concern battered women's advocates who want the focus kept on victims' problems. One form of empowerment is to help batterers develop better problem-solving and employment skills (see Huss & Langhinrichsen-Rohling, 2000). Unemployment is a major problem for a sizable number of IPV perpetrators, and it is linked with treatment dropout. Education and income are also highly related to unemployment. Payment of fees for counseling may be overly challenging for some low-income offenders (Tollefson, 2002). One antidote for economic problems is to help men become more employable through job training, job-searching skills, and the like. Such efforts would probably lower treatment program attrition as well (Dalton, 2001; Tollefson, 2002). Another possible method for helping MFIPV perpetrators is through closer attention to problems of vulnerability and pain (Stoneberg, 2002).

Pirog-Good and Stets (1986) found that procedures such as allowing program clients not to pay for counseling and making use of criminal justice referrals led to higher retention levels than alternative methods. One recent study ascertained that techniques designed to improve program retention dramatically reduced attrition and subsequent recidivism. In the program evaluated, clients received reminder phone calls and handwritten notes after intake and missed sessions (Taft, Murphy, Elliott, & Morrel, 2001).

Prevention Policies

The prevention of battering has received very little attention. Public awareness campaigns concerning IPV nearly always focus on the victims, rarely providing information about what perpetrators can do to stop their violence.

Clinical and medical screening. As noted in the above discussion of counseling approaches, therapeutic models frequently employ group processes. Research has established that MFIPV perpetrators suffer from wide-ranging difficulties and are not a homogeneous group. Findings of psychopathology and neurobiological impediments in these men imply that psychiatric examinations should be added to routine screening procedures. Because neurobiological evaluations of MFIPV perpetrators may show numerous possible anomalies, such as low levels of serotonin, clinicians might need to make referrals to psychiatrists (e.g., Figueroa & Silk, 1997).

Practitioners should test IPV perpetrators thoroughly, both psychologically and forensically, and may need to refer them for medical assessment (Adams, 1996; Epperly & Moore, 2000; McCray & King, 2003). Despite the probability that partner-violent men suffer from elevated rates of PTSD, researchers have not routinely assessed men in BIPs for the disorder (see Riggs, Dowdall, & Kuhn, 1999). According to some analyses, however, it is unclear whether assessing partner-violent men as psychopaths will improve overall treatment outcomes and the situations of victims (Huss & Langhinrichsen-Rohling, 2000).

Increased court involvement. The courts must remain involved whenever they mandate counseling for IPV perpetrators. Criminal justice experts advise that a batterer should not be diverted into a counseling program and out of the justice system before a plea is entered. As long as the abuser is under the control of the court, the court can sentence him without having to reset a trial. According to a 1990 report from the Family Violence Project, without this leverage, a recalcitrant participant may be able to leave treatment with no criminal record at all (cited in Pagelow, 1992).

Almost without exception, men ordered into treatment by the courts are more likely than others to complete the necessary number of therapeutic sessions. On the other hand, counselors have noted the criminal justice system's lack of follow-through once an IPV perpetrator has been mandated to treatment. Courts do not apply any sanctions to men who fail to attend as directed. Only specialized domestic violence courts appear to monitor batterers' compliance with court orders.

Nonetheless, court-mandated treatment of MFIPV is essential to the criminal justice system's objective of reducing recidivism (Dutton, 1988). If nothing else, arrest challenges a batterer's belief that his use of violence was justified (Ganley, 1981). It also places the responsibility for change on the batterer, a stance that is compatible with deterrence themes in the criminal justice system (Fagan, 1988). Court-ordered treatment is congruent with social control models. Judges' inclusion of orders to attend counseling in their sanctions of IPV perpetrators affects the cessation of the perpetrators' assaultive behaviors. Some commentators are recommending longer jail time for batterers, given that treatment is not uniformly effective (Shepard, 1992).

Profeminist men's contributions. In some countries, men are beginning to call for greater male participation in ending MFIPV. One organization with this aim in the United States is the National Organization for Men Against Sexism (NOMAS). This group has created an umbrella Internet site, Ending Men's Violence Network (EMV.net), to provide resources, training, and support to local organizations that are combating MFIPV (see the NOMAS Web site at http://www.nomas.org). There is a substantial need for researchers to examine methods for educating men about MFIPV. In India, legislation passed in 2002 that still champions patriarchal practices, including MFIPV, has galvanized the women's movement to reject the law outright. Ahmed-Ghosh (2004) lists several policies that might prevent MFIPV in India: (a) changing the content of school textbooks; (b) organizing consciousness-raising groups for men; (c) sensitizing police, courts, and doctors to the breadth of the problem; (d) encouraging the media to produce gender-sensitive films; and (e) providing counseling for partner-abusive men.

CHAPTER SUMMARY

Research has confirmed some of the early anecdotal impressions that partner-abusive men tend to blame others for their behavior and minimize their own violence. Male IPV perpetrators attribute negative intentions to their female partners. There is growing recognition that partner-violent men are not a homogeneous group. Rather, it is becoming possible to categorize violent men into subgroups that have distinctive qualities (i.e., typologies). These men may range on a continuum extending from partner-only violent men, who select only their female partners as targets, to men who are assaultive toward a broad range of people.

There are also some data about partner-abusing women as one subtype of batterer. More research is needed on abusive women.

Childhood socialization experiences of partner-violent men contrast with those of nonpartner-violent men. Research has documented inordinately high levels of violence (e.g., harsh discipline and parental dysfunction) in the childhood homes of many violent men. It seems reasonable to assume that these early learning experiences contribute substantially to the genesis of antisocial behavior in batterers. Recent comparisons have revealed attachment difficulties and dependency needs in partner-abusive men. Presumably, the socialization of men in general requires them to display aggression. These forces add to other learning experiences that mold boys into batterers. Partner-violent men hold more sexist attitudes and approve of violence more than do nonpartner-violent men.

It is conceivable that male hormones make a nuanced contribution to aggression and that serotonin deficits further reduce batterers' abilities to avoid frustration-induced MFIPV. In addition to the possible birth complications and head injuries found disproportionately in partner-violent men, these men may also have inherited unfavorable genetic predispositions, such as antisocial personality disorder.

Batterers and nonbatterers show many dissimilarities in personalities and in interpersonal interaction styles. Batterers have high levels of marital dissatisfaction, inadequate verbal skills, unassertive communication styles, faulty problem-solving skills, high vulnerability to stress and experienced stress, and problems with power and control issues, as well as difficulties with jealousy and lack of trust. Unidimensional personality tests have linked battering to anger, hostility, lack of empathy, high levels of shame, low self-esteem, and significant depression. Trauma during childhood may still be evident in adult IPV perpetrators, and PTSD diagnoses are more common among these men than among nonperpetrators. On tests assessing dimensions of psychopathology, a majority of partner-violent men who score in the abnormal range are most likely to receive diagnoses of APD or borderline disorders.

Practitioners acrimoniously debate the causes of IPV and therefore do not agree on the most suitable type of treatment. Concerns for victims' safety, however, have garnered near-universal acceptance as the first priority for treatment programs. Feminists indict the sociopolitical system and emphasize antisexist education coupled with criminal justice sanctions under the Duluth model, a psychoeducational approach to treatment. Practitioners who advocate cognitive-behavioral therapy assume that individual variability as assessed by tests in personality and psychopathology can accurately pinpoint problem areas. They employ procedures premised on these findings to modify batterers' behavior. As a result, they focus on anger management; assertion, communication, and relaxation skills; and reframing negative attributions. CBT approaches need to include suicide prevention.

The use of couples' therapy to treat batterers presupposes that IPV is a reflection of faulty interactions between the partners that allow violence to take place. Advocates of this approach concentrate on techniques geared toward improving communication and relationship satisfaction. Some state-funded programs will not support the use of couples' therapy for IPV because advocates have been effective in influencing legislators. Dual diagnoses lead to supplementary treatments for substance abuse and other problems. More attention to screening for BPD and APD as well as medical consultation is warranted. A number of group treatment programs are eclectic, incorporating therapeutic approaches from several sources. Occasionally, they use psychodynamic approaches to help clients recognize their hidden feelings.

Treatment outcome studies are often disappointing to everyone in the field of family violence. Methodological problems beset evaluation attempts. Violence abatement programs are not uniformly successful. The ongoing problem of counseling dropouts hampers the success of treatment strategies. Some variables affecting dropout rates are batterers' unemployment, low income, and lack of supervision by the criminal justice system. Court-mandated counseling is a frequently selected judicial option, but IPV perpetrators should remain under court jurisdiction for the entire term of their treatment. New studies on IPV in the military have been equivocal. Qualitative studies might improve understanding.

Posttreatment relapse into violence remains high among batterers. Some experts believe that a subgroup of extremely violent men suffering from APD, BPD, and other pathologies may be almost untreatable with current knowledge. Typologies of batterers offer some hope that matching treatment to batterer type will be effective. Although in recidivism outcome studies batterer treatment programs have shown very little effectiveness in reducing violence, they have shown some promise in ameliorating symptoms such as depression. Substance abuse programs have also been helpful for some types of alcoholics who also perpetrate MFIPV. Some practitioners believe that treatment of MFIPV is so complex that it requires a collaborative approach. Community agencies must shoulder the responsibility for ending marital violence by working as a team. More model programs and evaluations are needed in order to stop IPV. Certainly battering will continue as long as society delegates the responsibility for finding a solution to the victim.

DISCUSSION QUESTIONS

1. Are batterers ordinary criminals or men who get into marital conflicts, lose their tempers, and strike out?
2. How would you describe the childhood of a "typical" batterer?
3. What are the major categories that experts use to explain battering?
4. What are three theories concerning the possible "causes" of battering? Explain the differences between these theories.
5. How big a problem is female-to-male battering?
6. Is there any evidence supporting the notion that batterers have biological problems that differentiate them from nonbatterers?
7. What is the evidence for assuming male batterers have personality disorders? If they do, what sort of treatment is indicated?
8. Why should medical and clinical personnel screen male patients for IPV?
9. What approach to counseling batterers do you believe is most satisfactory? Why? Which approach do you find least acceptable? Why?
10. Should poverty-stricken batterers have to pay for treatment?
11. What is the role of the criminal justice system in eliminating battering?
12. What is the biggest problem in treating batterers? What can be done about it?

RECOMMENDED READING

Aldarondo, E., & Mederos, F. (2002). *Programs for men who batter: Intervention and prevention strategies in a diverse society.* Kingston, NJ: Civic Research Institute.

Dutton, D. G. (1998). *The abusive personality: Violence and control in intimate relationships.* New York: Guilford.

Geffner, R. A., & Rosenbaum, A. (Eds.). (2001). *Domestic violence offenders: Current interventions, research, and implications for policies and standards.* Binghamton, NY: Haworth.

Harway, M., & O'Neil, J. M. (Eds.). (1999). *What causes men's violence against women?* Thousand Oaks, CA: Sage.

Holtzworth-Munroe, A., Meehan, J. C., Stuart, G. L., Herron, K., & Rehman, U. (2000). Testing the Holtzworth-Munroe and Stuart (1994) batterer typology. *Journal of Consulting and Clinical Psychology, 68,* 1000–1019.

Jackson, S., Feder, L., Forde, D. R., Davis, R. C., Maxwell, C. D., & Taylor, B. G. (2003). *Batterer intervention programs: Where do we go from here?* (NCJ Publication No. 195079). Washington, DC: National Institute of Justice.

Langhinrichsen-Rohling, J., Huss, M. T., & Ramsay, S. (2000). The clinical utility of batterer typologies. *Journal of Family Violence, 15,* 37–53.

Lindsey, M., McBride, R., & Platt, C. (1993). *AMEND: Philosophy and curriculum for treating batterers and AMEND workbook for ending violent behavior.* Littleton, CO: Gylantic.

Pence, E., & Paymar, M. (1993). *Education groups for men who batter: The Duluth model.* New York: Springer.

Schumacher, J. A., Feldbau-Kohn, S., Slep, A. M. S., & Heyman, R. E. (2001). Risk factors for male-to-female partner physical abuse. *Aggression and Violent Behavior, 6,* 281–352.

12

ABUSE OF ELDERS AND THE DISABLED

Case History: Jenny and Jeff Jr.—Dwindling Assets, Dwindling Devotion

Several years after my husband's death, my mother-in-law, Jenny, who was 91, became unable to care for herself. She went to live with my brother-in-law, Jeff Jr., and his wife, Marianne. Although my own aging mother was dying, I took time to visit Jenny, who had always been a loving mother-in-law.

Over the next year, Jeff Jr. became Jenny's guardian, and she made out a new will giving one-third of her estate to each of us—myself, Jeff Jr., and Marianne. I didn't understand this sudden change from the previous division of half for each son, but I said nothing; after all, I was a widowed daughter-in-law. As Jenny continued to deteriorate, I asked Jeff Jr. if he was planning to put Jenny in a retirement home where she would receive around-the-clock care. He said he couldn't afford to place her in a home and that he and Marianne would care for her at home. I was amazed. Jeff Jr. had sold Jenny's home for a probable yield of $150,000 in cash. Jeff Jr. and Marianne owned a mini-estate as well as stocks and bonds; they were probably worth $2 million.

I was puzzled by what was going on with Jenny and Jeff Jr., but then I became seriously concerned when I heard a number of rumors from Jenny's other relatives and friends. They said that Jeff Jr. and Marianne had offered financial advice to several aging relatives. Each had changed his or her will to name Jeff Jr. and Marianne the beneficiaries, and each had died shortly thereafter of neglect and malnutrition.

Over the next few months, I became alarmed when Jenny "refused to come to the phone" to speak to me. Marianne told me that "Jenny couldn't walk far enough to get to the phone." After 2 weeks, I drove several hours to visit her. I was appalled when I arrived. There was Jenny, sitting alone in a hot room that smelled like urine. She would not speak to me. She was in the maid's quarters, with no television and no phone. She was dirty and unkempt. There were no diapers in the room, the small refrigerator held only a piece of moldy bologna, and Jenny had not taken her medications. Later, when I expressed my concern to Jeff Jr., he said that he was going to hire a couple to come in and take care of her. I left feeling some sense of relief that Jenny's ordeal would soon be over.

A week later, I received a call from the caretaker couple. Frightened by Jenny's condition when they arrived to care for her, they had called the paramedics, who took Jenny to the hospital, and then they called me. Doctors diagnosed Jenny's condition as malnutrition, dehydration, and "neglect." The caretakers said that Jeff Jr. and Marianne had gone on a vacation, leaving no money for food or diapers, no instructions, no telephone numbers or itinerary—not even any information about when they would return. Finally, I felt compelled to call the county adult protective services (APS) agency. Someone there promised to visit the premises and soon did so. I also called some other relatives, who started making unscheduled visits to see Jenny.

Jeff Jr. and Marianne continue to take unexpected vacations to visit other aging relatives who may "need financial management services in the near future." I fear that Jeff Jr. and Marianne hope to come home someday to find that Jenny has simply "passed away in her sleep." I am constantly uneasy about Jenny's situation. I frequently call APS to see if they can do something more, and I keep "popping in" to check up on Jenny when Jeff Jr. and Marianne are away from home.

Jenny, by all accounts, is doing better now. She is clean and has food in the refrigerator. The caretakers drop in every day briefly and bring in food and diapers on their own. Jenny is still alone most of the time, and she seems too frightened to say much. As Jenny's life is slowly ending, I feel that my life is "on hold." I wish I knew for sure that everything that can be done to protect Jenny is being done. It's in God's hands now.

Violence against elders has been a perpetual feature of American social history. As with other forms of family violence, however, there has been an ebb and flow in the visibility and invisibility of elder abuse. During the 1980s, violence against elders received heightened consideration, especially violence perpetrated by informal caretakers, such as relatives (Social Services Inspectorate, 1992). The year 2002 brought international attention to elder abuse through the work of the World Health Organization (cited in Cook-Daniels, 2003b; Nelson, 2002). Only recently, however, has elder abuse attracted scholarly examination at all consonant with other subfields of family violence. As a result, there is a surprising dearth of methodologically sound research on violence against elders.

Any type of problem afflicting the elderly, of course, is likely to multiply with the rapid increase of elderly in the population. According to the U.S. Bureau of the Census (2000), in 2000 there were almost 35 million elderly (65+ years of age) in the United States, 12.4% of the total population. This figure is apt to rise through at least the first few decades of the 21st century, as the post-World War II baby boom generation ages.

Changes in economic conditions, families and family mobility, women's roles, and traditional methods of elder care appear to have contributed to increasing rates of elder abuse (see Kosberg & Garcia, 1995b; Kwan, 1995). One dilemma is that in American society there are no clear norms or moral rules about who is responsible for elder care (Phillipson, 1993). Adult children are not legally required to help elderly parents in need. Moreover, many elders are childless, homosexual elders in particular (Cahill & Smith, 2002). Because of this lack of moral and legal standards concerning responsibility for the elderly, it is difficult to know who society should hold accountable for their care or neglect. This ambiguity places the elderly in an especially vulnerable position.

Further complicating matters is the fact that even in cases of interpersonal violence involving elderly persons, it is often not clear who is the victim and who is the perpetrator. Indeed, some violence in which elders are involved can be categorized as mutual violence (e.g., Phillipson, 1992). Elders may strike out at their caregivers, for instance, in reaction to the loss of personal freedom they feel when the caregivers find it necessary to curtail the elders' behavior (e.g., when the caregiver will not let the elder leave the house alone) (Meddaugh, 1990). Taken together, these problems have generated a literature on elder abuse that lacks coherence and precision. In sum, the nascency of research on elder abuse leaves numerous gaps in current knowledge, thus creating a large number of uncertainties.

This chapter begins with perhaps the greatest uncertainty of all, namely, the lack of a clear definition of elder abuse and resulting difficulties in assessing forms and frequencies of such abuse. Other important issues include the prevalence and basic causes of elder abuse, identification of abused elders and elder abusers, strategies for treatment and prevention of elder abuse, and policy recommendations. Because many elders are disabled, this chapter also forms a nexus with information about abuse of disabled persons.

SCOPE OF THE PROBLEM

If an elderly father wishes to wear a food-stained jacket, are his offspring-caregivers supposed to enforce some sort of cleanliness standard to avoid being neglectful? What can a caregiver do if an elder decides to drink too much alcohol or otherwise act foolishly? What if an adult son decides to let his increasingly dependent father fend for himself? Is the son an abuser?

What Is Elder Abuse?

Arguably, the debate about what constitutes family violence is more pronounced in the area of elder abuse than in other subfields. State legislatures and various professional groups (e.g., in the fields of medicine and social work) all define elder abuse dissimilarly. In addition to definitional questions, additional challenges have arisen. To define elder abuse, one must, for example, specify the meanings of *elder* (i.e., age requirements), *dependency,* and *self-neglect.* The Joint Commission on Accreditation of Healthcare

Organizations (JCAHO, 2002) suggests defining an elder as someone 60 years of age or older. Congress also favors age 60 (Stiegel, 2003). (For definitions that may become standardized across the field, see JCAHO, 2002; for a glossary of terms used in the field of elder public health, see Ebrahim, 2001.)

Box 12.1 Is Self-Neglect a Form of Elder Abuse?

Johnson (1986) defines elder mistreatment as "self- or other-inflicted suffering unnecessary to the maintenance of the quality of life of the older person" (p. 180). Reports of self-neglect, as defined variously among the U.S. states, are the most frequent type of elder problem reported to APS. Based on responses from 44 states, the 2000 survey of APS agencies summarized types and proportions of alleged mistreatment as follows: (a) 39% self-neglect, (b) 19% caregiver neglect or abandonment, (c) 13% financial abuse/exploitation, (d) 11% physical abuse, (e) 10% other, (f) 7% emotional/verbal abuse, and (g) 1% sexual abuse (Teaster, 2003).

Manifestations of self-neglect may include an unsatisfactory living environment (e.g., lack of cleanliness), failure to seek or follow medical advice (e.g., rejecting necessary medications), failure to obtain psychological counseling, abuse of alcohol and other drugs, and allowing financial exploitation of oneself (Sellers, Folts, & Logan, 1992).

Should a full definition of elder/adult abuse encompass the construct of self-neglect? Inclusion of self-neglect as a form of maltreatment raises several significant issues. First, tension exists between recognition of self-neglect and recognition of an elder's right to self-determination. Who is to say that certain behaviors, which may seem foolish to some people, are forms of self-neglect? Should behaviors such as taking one bath every 11 days, eating chocolate bars for breakfast, or wearing mismatched socks be classified as self-neglect, a form of mental illness, or just a personal choice?

Second, the concept of self-neglect does not fit a definition of abuse within an interactional framework based on a victim-offender relationship (Hudson, 1994). Although self-neglect is a frequent problem for elders, it occurs without a perpetrator. It often occurs in situations where the elder is legally competent, even though mentally or physically impaired (e.g., Tatara, 1993). The question of whether self-neglect is truly elder abuse becomes more complicated when it occurs in "plain view" of an elder's family members or others. Occasionally family caretakers actually aid and abet an elder's self-neglecting conduct (e.g., by buying liquor for an alcoholic elder). More commonly, however, self-neglect results from impairment and isolation, with no one to blame for the "maltreatment" except society.

Sexual abuse. Direct forms of sexual abuse of elders encompass intercourse, molestation, sexualized kissing, oral/genital contact, and digital penetration. Indirect forms of sexual abuse include unwanted sexual discussions, exhibitionism, forced viewing of pornography, and exposed masturbation (see Ramsey-Klawsnik, 1991). A surprising newer type of sex abuse has come to light in the form of pornographic Web sites that display older victims who were too mentally incapacitated to give consent. These sites offer still photographs of elderly women posed in every conceivable sexual activity. Viewers can also play short video clips of elderly women engaged in sexual activities. These media materials are classified as pornography, but laws regarding the use of older women hinge on the adults' ability to consent. Police officers who are specially trained in child and elder sexual abuse investigate these cases (Calkins, 2003).

Financial abuse. Financial abuse of elders consists of a number of behaviors: (a) misusing a durable power of attorney, bank account, or guardianship; (b) failing to compensate transfers of real estate; (c) charging excessive amounts for goods and services delivered to an elder; (d) using undue influence to gain control of an elder's money or property; and (e) predatory lending, Internet, telemarketing, or other frauds (Sweeney, 2003).

Taxonomies of elder abuse. Boudreau (1993) distinguishes five broad categories of abuse most frequently cited in the literature: physical, psychological, financial/material, unsatisfactory living arrangement (e.g., unclean home), and violation of individual or constitutional rights. Although experts concur that physical violence constitutes abuse, they disagree over whether some behaviors, such as "violation of constitutional rights," are abuse. At what point, for example, do a caregiver's actions become a violation of an elder's constitutional rights? Does a daughter who makes her elderly mother wear a bib at dinner violate the mother's constitutional rights?

In creating a more widely acknowledged classification system, Hudson (1991) solicited opinions from 63 professionals in diverse specialties such as law, medicine, psychology, public health, and social work. Over three successive rounds of decision making, these experts attempted to reach consensus about the appropriateness of certain theoretical definitions of elder abuse. Representative of one series of judgments, participants categorized mistreatment into two major classes (elder abuse and elder neglect) with two modes of intent (unintentional and intentional). Each round resulted in greater and greater specificity with more and more subdefinitions. The final taxonomy consists of four forms of elder abuse: physical, social, psychological, and financial. With one exception, senior adults in a follow-up study agreed with the experts' definitions. Leaders in the field believe that some forms of abuse (e.g., yelling) must occur several times to reach the level of abuse, whereas the interviewed elders believed even one such occurrence is abusive (Hudson et al., 2000). It is important to acknowledge that elders find disrespect a very painful type of abuse, although it is not included in these taxonomies (Cook-Daniels, 2003b). Note that the taxonomy excludes self-neglect and does not list sexual abuse separately. Insertion of sexual abuse into the physical abuse category may be unfortunate, because sexual abuse represents a distinctive form of elder abuse. Table 12.1 presents the taxonomy of elder abuse developed by Hudson et al. (2000).

Gay, lesbian, bisexual, and transgendered elders. Although dating violence and intimate partner violence (IPV) among younger gay, lesbian, bisexual, and transgendered (GLBT) persons have gained some recognition, older GLBT individuals often go unidentified and unassisted by medical and mental health personnel. Both **heterosexism** (denigration of non-heterosexual behavior) and **homophobia** (fear or hatred of homosexual orientation) plague GLBT elders. An abusive caregiver, as one example, can threaten to "out" a gay elder if the gay elder will not comply with the caregiver's demands (see Cahill & Smith, 2002).

Elder abuse among minorities. Some racial/ethnic groups have distinctive views about elder abuse (Hudson et al., 2000). Korean Americans, for example, traditionally participate in a type of co-ownership of elder parents' financial assets, an arrangement that many African Americans and Whites consider a form of financial exploitation. Another cultural difference is that Korean Americans judge it inappropriate to tell outsiders "family business"; thus they do not report elder abuse at a rate comparable to either African Americans or Whites (Moon & Benton, 2000). Korean Americans are also especially likely to blame elder victims for their own abuse (Moon & Benton, 2000). Interestingly, as Asian immigrants' children become Americanized, they are beginning to change the habit of keeping aging parents at home and are putting them in assisted living centers (Kershaw, 2003). A survey of 2,702 White, African American, and Hispanic female victims in Illinois found some differences among types of abuse experienced. In particular, about four times as many Hispanic women and three times as many White women reported sexual abuse as did African American women (Grossman & Lundy, 2003).

Cross-Cultural Conceptions of Elder Abuse

Conceptions about elder abuse around the world are similar in some ways to those in the United States, but they also reveal some distinctions. Recognition of elder abuse worldwide has rested primarily on its "discovery" in the United States and Britain (see Kosberg & Garcia, 1995a). At first, experts in other countries tended to deny the existence of this form of abuse in their own countries (Dunn, 1995). In Ireland, for instance, the minister of health reportedly said that "no cases of abuse of the elderly were formally reported to me in 1989 or 1990" (quoted in Horkan, 1995, pp. 131–132). By the mid-1980s, however, a few reports from other countries began to trickle in (Kivela, 1995).

Table 12.1   Theoretical Definitions of Elder Mistreatment and Abuse by Delphi Panel of Elder Mistreatment Experts

Level I

Elder mistreatment	Destructive behavior that is directed toward an older adult; occurs within the context of a relationship connoting trust; and is of sufficient intensity and/or frequency to produce harmful physical, psychological, social, and/or financial effects of unnecessary suffering, injury, pain, loss, and/or violation of human rights and poorer quality of life for the older adult
Personal/social relationship	Persons in close personal relationships with an older adult connoting trust and some socially established behavioral norms, for example, relatives by blood or marriage, friends, neighbors, any "significant other"
Professional/business relationship	Persons in a formal relationship with an older adult that denotes trust and expected services, for example, physicians, nurses, social workers, nursing aides, bankers, lawyers, nursing home staff, home health personnel, and landlords

Level II

Elder abuse	Aggressive or invasive behavior/action(s), or threats of same, inflicted on an older adult and resulting in harmful effects for the older adult
Elder neglect	The failure of a responsible party(ies) to act so as to provide, or to provide what is prudently deemed adequate and reasonable assistance that is available and warranted to ensure that the older adult's basic physical, psychological, social, and financial needs are met, resulting in harmful effects for the older adult

Level III

Intentional	Abusive or neglectful behavior or acts that are carried out for the purpose of harming, deceiving, coercing, or controlling the older adult so as to produce gain for the perpetrator (often labeled *active* abuse/neglect in the literature)
Unintentional	Abusive or neglectful behavior or acts that are carried out, but *not* for the purpose of harming, deceiving, coercing, or controlling the older adult, so as to produce gain for the perpetrator (often labeled *passive* abuse/neglect in the literature)

Level IV

Physical	Behavior(s)/actions in which physical force(s) is used to inflict the abuse; or available and warranted physical assistance is not provided, resulting in neglect
Psychological	Behavior(s)/action(s) in which verbal force is used to inflict the abuse; or available and warranted psychological/emotional assistance/support is not provided, resulting in neglect
Social	Behavior(s)/action(s) that prevents the basic social needs of an older adult from being met; or failure to provide available and warranted means by which an older adult's basic social needs can be met
Financial	Theft or misuse of an older adult's funds or property; or failure to provide available and warranted means by which an older adult's basic material needs can be met

SOURCE: "Elder Mistreatment: A Taxonomy With Definitions by Delphi," by M. F. Hudson, 1991, *Journal of Elder Abuse and Neglect, 3*(2), p. 14. Copyright 1991 by Margaret F. Hudson. Reprinted with permission.

Conceptions of elder abuse vary across the globe. Some countries, for example, distinguish elder abuse from elder mistreatment, or they include a category specified as "the absence of quality care." Some authorities suggest that fear of abuse and abandonment should be included as a type of abuse (Kosberg & Garcia, 1995a). In many countries (e.g., Hong Kong, India) abandonment and neglect of elders are more significant problems than physical abuse (e.g., Kwan, 1995; Pitsiou-Darrough & Spinellis, 1995; Shah, Veedon, & Vasi, 1995). Americans also have some misconceptions about the treatment of elders in other countries. For example, whereas many Americans assume that Chinese elders hold a place of honor in their households, family members may, in reality, neglect elders, pushing them into dark corners or even cupboards (Blythe, 1969).

Conditions within a country greatly affect the rates of elder abuse found there. In South Africa, the general level of societal violence is so high that violence against elders is something of a "blip on a radar screen" (Eckely & Vilakazi, 1995). In Hong Kong, strong emigration patterns have left an ever-growing number of older people alone, with no family members to offer care (Kwan, 1995). Immigration in Israel has created a population of elderly who are predominantly foreign-born (Lowenstein, 1995). In Australia, members of the Aboriginal population have a significantly lower life expectancy than other Australians, thus elder abuse rates in this population are relatively low. In India, poverty, illiteracy, and female dependency play strong roles in elder abuse (Shah et al., 1995). The multigenerational shared housing situation in Poland seems to encourage elder neglect and psychological abuse (Halicka, 1995).

Aggression against elders exists in developing countries in ways unheard of in developed countries. According to a 2001 report published by the World Health Organization, younger adults accuse elders of witchcraft or of causing too much rain and then banish them to isolated locations. Younger adults also stigmatize elders who care for family members who are ill with HIV/AIDS (cited in Cook-Daniels, 2003b; Nelson, 2002).

Financial independence of elders tends to play a compelling role in their treatment. Income is an especially critical element when there are no government assistance programs for the elderly. Reviews in other countries show that low socioeconomic status (SES) is a strong risk factor for elder abuse (Eckely & Vilakazi, 1995). In Argentina and Bolivia, however, society considers it abusive when government pensions to elders are inadequate. Customs in some countries, such as giving away one's property as preparation for entering the next world, as the last stage of life, make financial exploitation of the elderly much easier (Shah et al., 1995). In Greece, there are no laws protecting elders with diminished capacity from financial exploitation (Pitsiou-Darrough & Spinellis, 1995).

Prevalence of Abuse

The rates of elder abuse in Australia, Canada, Great Britain, and Norway appear to be roughly similar to estimated rates in the United States (Kurrle & Sadler, 1993; Ogg & Bennett, 1992; Podnieks, 1992). The estimated proportion of Finnish elders seeking shelter from abuse is 3% to 6% (cited in Kivela, 1995). In Greece, the estimate for physical abuse is quite high, 15% (Pitsiou-Darrough & Spinellis, 1995). A recent survey of 355 elderly Chinese in Hong Kong revealed a 2% rate for physical abuse and a 20.8% rate for verbal abuse (Yan & Tang, 2001). In another study, 18% of 4,000 elderly Japanese reported knowing of an elder victim (Tsukada, Saito, & Tatara, 2001). A survey of older women ($M = 75$ years) in Ireland, Italy, and the United Kingdom suggested the elder abuse rate was approximately 20% (Ockleford et al., 2003).

In most foreign countries, elders receive support and care through informal care systems (i.e., family) rather than through formal institutions (e.g., nursing homes). In Finland, there are no government programs of any sort for elder care (cited in Kivela, 1995), and in Australia there are no adult protective services (Dunn, 1995). In Israel, only 15% of dependent elderly receive help from public authorities; the rest rely on informal sources (Lowenstein, 1995). In Greece, elder abuse is "just one more problem," and victims must wait their turn for help from social agencies (Johns & Hydle, 1995). European support services are only marginally involved in assisting elder abuse victims. Less than a third of victims report receiving any assistance, and agencies fail to collect data on elder victims who seek assistance (Ockleford et al., 2003).

Laws regarding elder abuse vary throughout the world. In contrast to the United States, many countries assign responsibility for elder care to adult children. In India, all financially able children are legally responsible for parental care (Shah et al., 1995). In Finland, however, as many as 20% of elders have no children or family of any sort to offer support (or abuse) (cited in Kivela, 1995). In Ireland, refusing to provide necessities of life to any child or any aged or sick person is a misdemeanor (Horkan, 1995). Israel has no special legal provisions for elders, but they are protected under a general Protection of Helpless Persons law (Lowenstein, 1995). As of 1994, South Africa had no laws dealing with elder abuse (Eckely & Vilakazi, 1995).

What Is Abuse of the Disabled?

APS agencies generally have responsibilities not only to protect **vulnerable adults** but also to oversee the care of many disabled individuals. Undoubtedly, a number of people under the aegis of APS are both elderly and disabled. Table 12.2 provides more

Table 12.2   Ages of Populations Served in United States Under Elder/Adult Protective Statutes

Populations Served	Number of States	% of States
Adults 60+	19	35.2
Adults 65+	11	20.4
Vulnerable/impaired adults 60+	8	14.8
Vulnerable/impaired adults 65+	8	14.8
Vulnerable/disabled adults 18–65	21	38.9
Vulnerable/disabled, all ages	33	61.1
Other	4	7.4

SOURCE: Teaster (2003).

NOTE: All states responded, and a number provided multiple responses.

detailed information on the types of populations served by APS agencies in the United States.

Over the past decade, leaders in the field have recast initial conceptions of **disability** away from the medical model of pathology, loss, and deficit. The new social paradigm maintains that "disability is a product of the intersection of individual characteristics (e.g., conditions or impairments, functional status, or personal and socioeconomic qualities) and characteristics of the natural, built, cultural, and social environments" (National Institute on Disability and Rehabilitation Research, 2003, p. 2). (For discussion of the terminology used in relation to disability, see Pledger, 2003.)

Nosek and Howland (1998) have sharpened the meaning of abuse against disabled persons by including types of abuse that are seldom used against the nondisabled. Interwoven among very common forms of mistreatment are terrorizing behaviors, severe rejection, isolation, ignoring behaviors, use of physical restraints, and deprivation of food and water. In cases of sexual abuse of the disabled, abusers frequently use deception to gain sexual access. (For descriptions of abuses against disabled victims, see Erwin, 2000.)

Estimates of Elder/Adult Abuse

Definitional disparity, along with other methodological factors, has impeded research progress to such

an extent that the scope of elder abuse is virtually unknown. Although the pace of research has improved over the past decade, very few studies have included more than 1,000 randomly sampled elders. One exception is Lachs, Williams, O'Brien, Hurst, and Horwitz's (1997) study of Boston elders. Almost no studies have included comparison groups (see Brandl & Cook-Daniels, 2002).

To date, nearly all samples in this area of research have been derived from the files of nursing homes, APS agencies, adult day health care centers, emergency rooms, and domestic violence programs. In addition to sample variations, there are verification differences (e.g., police or agency verified versus self-report) among studies and divergences in the types of data gathered (e.g., agency records, interviews, physical examinations). Although slowly improving, researchers often do not clearly state the racial/ethnic composition of their research samples and usually fail to take cultural differences into account (Moon & Benton, 2000). All of these variations contribute to divergent numerical accounts and make survey data noncomparable. As in other subfields of family violence, such diverse definitions of abuse retard scientific progress (Rosenblatt, 1996). Milberger et al. (2003) have sharpened definitions of disability by calling attention to possible distinctions between developmental and physical disability.

Because elder abuse is particularly underrecognized and underreported, prevalence estimates are complicated. Unlike children, who usually go out of the house at least to attend school, elders who live alone and seldom leave their homes are practically invisible. Although similar to other intimate violence victims in not reporting all of their mistreatment, elders are more likely than younger victims to report crimes (Klaus, 2000). The National Elder Abuse Incidence Study (NEAIS), based on APS data, showed that reports of elder abuse rose significantly over the period from 1986 to 1996. Apparently, elder abuse is not as hidden as it once was (National Center on Elder Abuse [NCEA], 1998).

Nonetheless, the NEAIS found more than five times as many unreported cases as reported cases. Some elements of reluctance to report are mental incapability, nonrecognition of abuse, fear of others' disbelief, stigma, and fear of loss of independence (Stiegel, 2001). By contrast, increased reporting rates are associated with lower SES of elders, more community training of area professionals, and higher agency service rating scores (Wolf & Donglin, 1999).

Research on abused disabled persons is acutely deficient. The few existing studies, with one exception, acquired data from convenience samples, used no comparison groups, probed few variables, and failed to include any sophisticated statistical analyses. Consequently, there are "enormous gaps" in the literature regarding abuse of disabled persons (Nosek & Howland, 1998).

Official estimates. The U.S. Bureau of Justice Statistics recently disseminated analyses of criminal victimization of persons age 65 and older averaged over the years 1992–1997. Although the research was somewhat limited by government-specified samples and methodology, statistician Patsy A. Klaus (2000) provided a large number of core findings about elder abuse. She established that, compared with younger persons, elders suffer a much smaller proportion of violent crimes, including murders—about one-tenth as many as younger people.

Klaus used the FBI's *Supplementary Homicide Reports* (*SHR*) to estimate murder rates. One unexpected factor related to eldercide is that a number of "gray murders," unrecognized murders of elderly people, have occurred. An obstacle in grappling with this issue is the low autopsy rate for elder deaths, less than 1% in recent years. Attending physicians, not pathologists, determine cause of death for most seniors, and

research has found a discordance rate of 44% between physicians' and pathologists' determinations of cause of death (Burton, as cited in Soos, 2000).

Annual homicide rates averaged over the years 1992–1997 from *SHR* analyses revealed gender and racial differences. Elder males were perpetrators of homicide at a rate twice as great as females. Blacks were overrepresented as murder victims and perpetrators. Males also committed the majority of homicide-suicides occurring at age 55+ years (Cohen, Llorente, & Eisendorfer, 1998). Dawson and Langan (1994) found in a study for the U.S. Bureau of Justice Statistics that sons and daughters commit only 11% of all homicides of victims age 60+ years. Of these patricides and matricides, sons kill fathers (53%) about as often as they kill mothers (47%), but daughters kill fathers (81%) much more often than they kill mothers (19%).

APS agencies furnish other official estimates of elder abuse. Many facets of APS practices, however, foster nonuniformity of statistical information about elder abuse: (a) definitions (age, adult, dependent), (b) investigative authority (e.g., domestic setting, institutions), (c) mandated reporters and failures to report, and (d) funding and administration. Not only do these aspects create variability in statistical compilations, but they also foster inconsistent data management. Illustrative of these impediments are missing data about age and gender in some reports.

In a survey conducted in 2000 under the auspices of the National Association of Adult Protective Services Administrators, Teaster (2003) amassed reports on elder/adult abuse from state APS agencies. The number of elder/adult abuse reports received by APS associations reached 472,813. In states that responded, APS investigated 396,398 reports, and APS workers confirmed 166,019 cases. Data from 40 states indicated that 41.9% of the unsubstantiated reports were for self-neglect, 20.1% were for physical abuse, and 13.2% were for caregiver neglect/abandonment. The amount of financial abuse of the elderly is unknown, but may affect 10.5% to 49.3% of abused elders (NCEA, 1998; Teaster, 2003).

Self-report estimates. Recognizing the need for more generalizable and inclusive data, Pillemer and Finkelhor (1988) conducted telephone interviews with 2,020 Boston area residents age 65 and older. They estimated prevalence rates of three different kinds of elder abuse: physical, psychological, and neglect. They did not, however, assess financial abuse. Using a modified version of the Conflict Tactics Scale (CTS1; Straus, 1979), they defined physical abuse as any violent act (e.g., pushed, grabbed, shoved, beat up) committed by a caregiver (spouse, child, or other coresident) since the respondent had turned 65. They defined neglect as withholding assistance with daily living (e.g., meal preparation, housework) 10 or more times in the preceding year. Finally, they designated psychological abuse as "chronic verbal aggression" (e.g., insulted, swore at, threatened) occurring more than 10 times a year.

Of 2,020 elders interviewed, 63 (3.2%) reported being abused. Specifically, 2% reported being physically abused, 1.1% reported being psychologically abused, and 0.4% reported being neglected (in the past year) (Pillemer & Finkelhor, 1988). From these figures, the researchers estimated that 701,000–1,093,560 elders were abuse victims each year in the United States. Findings of the NEAIS indicated that the number of older people abused annually was much smaller, 450,000 (NCEA, 1998). The sampling procedure for the NEAIS, however, garnered extensive criticism (e.g., Cook-Daniels, 1999; Otto & Quinn, 1999). A group of studies pinpointed the level of any elder abuse as falling between 19.1% and 59.4% (cited in Brandl & Cook-Daniels, 2002).

In addition to analyzing the *SHR* for eldercide rates, Klaus (2000) used National Crime Victimization Survey (NCVS) self-report data. She reported that from 1992 through 1997, the average annual number of nonlethal, violent crimes perpetrated against elders (65 + years) was 165,000. This figure represents a rate of 5.27/1,000. Compared with other age cohorts (27.3/1,000), elders (2.6/1,000) were victims of assault much less frequently. In regard to nonlethal victimization, males, minorities, and divorced or separated elders endured significantly more criminal violence than their counterparts. Of nonlethal perpetrators, males committed more victimization than did females, and a disproportionately larger group of Blacks perpetrated more abuse than Whites. The NCVS does not interview individuals living in institutions, such as nursing homes, and does not include financial exploitation or fraud in its list of criminal victimizations. (For details of the findings from Klaus's study, see Table 5 in Appendix B of this volume.)

As expected, nearly all elderly sexual assault victims are women and nearly all perpetrators are men. In a small study, Mouton, Rovi, Furniss, and Lasser (1999) found that husbands were guilty of forcing sex among 7% of older women. These older women had been battered throughout their lifetimes. A large percentage (80%) of sexual assault victims in a nursing home study were impaired. These women were in wheelchairs, were bedridden, or had dementia. (For more details on sexual assault of elderly victims from Klaus's [2000] analysis of NCVS data, see Table 5 in Appendix B.)

Injury estimates. Injury estimates arise from both official and self-report data. The latest official numerical summary from the National Electronic Injury Surveillance System–All Injury Program provides the most comprehensive and reliable data concerning injuries of elders seeking treatment at hospital emergency departments ("Public Health," 2003). This program furnishes national, annualized, weighted estimates of nonfatal, nonsexual, physical assaults categorized by intent. During 2001, roughly 33,026 elders received treatment in emergency departments (rate = 72/100,000). The majority of elders treated were men (55.4%). Primary injuries were as follows: (a) contusion/abrasion, 31.9%; (b) laceration, 21.1%; and (c) fracture, 12.7%. The primary sources of injury were assaults as follows: (a) by body part, 20.3%; (b) blunt object, 17.1%; (c) push, 14.4%; and (d) undetermined (31.8%). Perpetrators were most likely to be family members or acquaintances.

The 1992–1997 NCVS analysis of self-report data revealed that elders sustained 36,290 injuries annually. Relatives/intimates injured 41%, and others known to the victims caused 59% of injuries (Klaus, 2000). A different account indicates that genital injuries are exceptionally common among older sexual assault victims (age 55 +) relative to younger assault victims (ages 18–54). Of the 53 women making up the older group in this study sample, 27 sustained genital injuries compared with 7 injuries among the 53 women in the younger group (Muram, Miller, & Cutler, 1992). Another outcome for abused elders is a greater likelihood of death compared with nonabused elders, even though cause of death may not be directly traceable to injuries or ill health (Lachs, Williams, O'Brien, Pillemer, & Charlson, 1998).

Estimates of Abuse of Disabled Persons

Violence perpetrated against disabled family members is an understudied topic (e.g., Ridington, 1989). The handful of extant small studies undoubtedly suffers from underreporting. Consequently, there are no definitive prevalence estimates of individuals who are both disabled and abused. Further, investigators rarely assume that disabled women have intimate partners, so IPV often goes undetected. No one gathers adequate information about abusive family members or caretakers (see Erwin, 2000).

In the mid-1990s, the Center for Research on Women with Disabilities (CROWD) in the United States conducted the only national survey of disabled abused women to date. This study represents the most extensive scrutiny of abuse of disabled persons ever undertaken. The researchers obtained questionnaire data from 504 disabled women and 402 nondisabled women, as well as qualitative interview data from 31 women. Surprisingly, analyses failed to detect significant differences between the abused and nonabused groups. Combining all forms of abuse, including emotional, 62% of each group experienced abuse. A major group disparity, however, resided in the duration of abuse: Disabled women suffered an average of 3.9 years of physical and sexual abuse compared with 2.5 years for nondisabled women (Young, Nosek, Howland, Chanpong, & Rintala, 1997). A sample of 177 women recruited through a number of sources, such as agencies, newsletters, and contacts with rehabilitation therapists, revealed that 100 of the disabled women (56%) were abused. Thus the researchers had access to a comparison group of disabled women who had not experienced abuse. The most significant variations between groups were that the abused women, relative to the nonabused women, suffered greater proportions of hearing impairments (27% and 4%, respectively) and multiple forms of disability (40% and 26%) (Milberger et al., 2003).

SECTION SUMMARY

The term *elder abuse* covers a wide variety of commissions and omissions of various behaviors: physical abuse, psychological abuse, material (financial) abuse, and neglect. Most experts include sexual abuse either as an aspect of physical abuse or as a separate category. Financial abuse occurs frequently among vulnerable elders. Incorporating self-neglect into the meaning of elder abuse poses problems. An elder who chooses to live alone, who refuses to bathe or take life-saving medication, is a victim of neglect. but who is the perpetrator? Without norms and laws governing who should care for the elderly, society must presumably shoulder the blame. Definitions of elder abuse that include notions such as "violations of individual constitutional rights" are especially subjective and difficult to operationalize.

Very little is known about interpersonal violence against GLBT elders. Social abuse, such as obstacles to obtaining health care and laws prohibiting certain types of financial sharing among partners, exists universally. Knowledge is slowly emerging about differences in conceptions of elder abuse among American minorities and across the world. Perspectives on the proper treatment of elders in countries outside the United States influence beliefs about who is responsible for elders' care, what constitutes abuse, and how serious a social problem it is. Legal definitions of elder abuse and legal assignment of responsibility for elder care vary around the world.

Depending on how individual researchers choose to define and assess elder abuse, rates of abuse may be high or low. Data from APS agencies, NCVS, and *SHR* indicate that abuse and even murder of elders by family members are real problems. Data from these three sources are noncomparable, however, and the exact rates of these behaviors have eluded detection. Rates of physical assaults against elders are much lower than rates of assaults against individuals in younger age cohorts, and eldercide is quite rare.

SEARCHING FOR PATTERNS: WHO IS ABUSED AND WHO ARE THE ABUSERS?

Elder abuse researchers have tried to classify types of elders who may be especially vulnerable to abuse and types of individuals who are most apt to abuse elders. They have examined issues of family relationship, gender, age, and race, as well as mental health and alcohol abuse. Kosberg and Nahmiash (1996) have developed a conceptual framework for categorizing characteristics of victims and abusers that includes the following factors: living arrangements, gender, SES, health, age, psychological factors, problem behaviors, dependence, isolation, financial problems, family violence, and lack of social support. Given definitional, sampling, and methodological limitations of available research, social scientists accept identified patterns as preliminary in nature.

Characteristics of Abused Elders

Research on elder abuse has revealed few consistent differences, if any, between victims and nonvictims. In their review of the literature, Brandl and Cook-Daniels (2002) were unable to uncover any standard victim profile. Compared with members of all other age and ethnic groups, an elderly White female is the least likely person to sustain a violent victimization (Klaus, 2000). Chu's (2001) analysis of elder homicides revealed that risk factors for victimization are gender (male) and race (African American).

The American Bar Association's Commission on Legal Problems of the Elderly has outlined some risk factors, screening techniques, and remedies relevant to financial abuse of elders. Risk factors appear to be abuser dependency on elder or elder dependency on abuser, elder's physical frailty or impairment, social isolation, and substance abuse or psychiatric conditions of either abuser or elder victim (Stiegel, 2001).

Age. Because not all researchers and organizations define the status of elder in the same way, the victim characteristic of age is difficult to pin down. Some state APS agencies typically serve all adults, without regard to age, whereas others serve only elders, defined as persons 60 or 65 years of age. The fastest-growing group of elders in the United States today is made up of individuals 80 years old and older, and these elders are targets of abuse and neglect significantly more often than others (NCEA, 1998). (For a summary of age groups as reported to APS for the 2000 survey, see Table 12.2.)

Gender. The data available concerning gender are somewhat contradictory. APS reports for the 2000 survey revealed that, of substantiated cases, more than half of elder abuse victims (56.0%) were female (Teaster, 2003). In contrast, data from an older Boston self-report community survey indicated that more than half of the victims in that sample were male (52%). Even more important, the Boston study suggests that the victimization rate for men (5.1%) is double that for women (2.5%). One explanation for this finding is that 65% of the respondents were women. Equivalent numbers of male and female victims suggest that risk of victimization is greater for men (Pillemer & Finkelhor, 1988). Chu's (2001) analysis of *SHR* data points to more intimate partner homicide victimization of males than of females. Of course, a large number of offender-victim relationships of murder victims are unknown. (For a brief summary of victim-offender relationships among homicide victims, see Table 6 in Appendix B.)

Socioeconomic status and race. Some studies have found no racial disparities in rates of elder abuse (e.g., Pillemer & Finkelhor, 1988), whereas others have (e.g., Klaus, 2000). One investigation of the relationship between SES and elder abuse revealed that poor elders in the United States are no more likely to be abused than middle-class elders (Boudreau, 1993). Another appraisal found that retired elders are at no greater risk than those still working (Bachman & Pillemer, 1991). One team of researchers has suggested that members of various racial/ethnic groups may differ more in the behaviors they view as abusive than in actual frequency of abusive behaviors experienced (Moon & Williams, 1993).

Hudson and Carlson (1999) found the following abuse rates among 924 North Carolinians age 40+ years: African Americans, 9.2%; Whites, 7.7%; and Native Americans, 4.3%. One appraisal of 597 agency cases revealed that European Americans (Whites) were more likely to suffer from self-neglect, African Americans from neglect by others, and both races equally from physical or financial abuse (Longres, 1992). (For a summary of data on the race/ethnicity of victims from the APS study, see Table 7 in Appendix B.)

Other factors. Studies suggest that there may be some relationship between living arrangements and elder abuse. Several researchers have found that significant numbers of abused elders live in the same homes as their abusers (e.g., Lachs et al., 1997; Vladescu, Eveleigh, Ploeg, & Patterson, 1999). In a study of three model projects, staff rated "changes in living arrangements" as the most effective intervention strategy and "changes in the circumstances of the perpetrator" as the least effective. Of 266 cases for which data on resolutions were available, more than one-third judged the problem as "completely" resolved and another third believed that "some progress" in resolution had been made. Victim receptivity to intervention was a key variable in successful resolution, and perpetrator lack of receptivity was pivotal in unresolved cases (Wolf & Pillemer, 1989).

If elders become more isolated, however, they may become easier prey to other kinds of abuses, such as financial exploitation. Living arrangements possibly affect the likelihood of victimization in regard to gender. If elderly men are more likely to be living with someone, their rate of abuse may increase while women's decreases (see Paveza et al., 1992; Pillemer & Finkelhor, 1988). An apparent ecological risk factor for elder abuse is the rate of reported child abuse in a community. Presumably, factors that affect child abuse rates, such as community resources and differing characteristics of caseworkers, may account for this correlation (Jogerst, Dawson, Hartz, Ely, & Schweitzer, 2000).

Older IPV victims often do not leave their abusers. A recent study identified three major reasons why abused elder women stay with their abusers: (a) pragmatic concerns, such as economic insufficiency; (b) belief systems common to their generation and inadequate societal assistance; and (c) aging and health issues (Zink, Regan, Jacobson, & Pabst, 2003). Because their plight is seldom recognized by professionals, they receive little assistance toward leaving. In addition, few shelter programs nationwide are prepared to meet the needs of older battered women (see American Association of Retired Persons, 1994; Boudreau, 1993; McFall, 2000; Vinton, 1998; Vinton, Altholz, & Lobell, 1997). Shelter eligibility requirements may restrict entry to IPV victims, so that elders victimized by adult children and grandchildren are not admitted. (For a review of programs available to older abuse victims, see Brandl, Hebert, Rozwadowski, & Spangler, 2003.)

Obviously, disabled abuse victims must overcome extraordinary odds to leave abusive partners (Carlson, 1997; Sundram, 2000). Disabled women responding to interview questions related reasons that exceeded those listed above. They were unable to leave for physical reasons. Some could not leave because of architectural barriers, and others because they had no adaptive equipment, such as power wheelchairs. Further, women who had lifelong disabilities had learned to be compliant and nonassertive, so they were inclined to accept the abuse they received (Milberger et al., 2003).

Characteristics of Elder Abusers

There are so many noncontinuities among research results that a high degree of uncertainty exists about the typical characteristics of elder/adult abusers. Customary risk factors for elder homicide perpetrators are gender (male) and race (African American) (Chu, 2001). One might think, however, that women would be the most likely abusers because they provide most informal family caregiving for elders (Arber & Ginn, 1999). Several variables may be descriptive of a subset of elder abusers: (a) cognitive impairments or mental illnesses (Collins & O'Connor, 2000); (b) financial dependency on the abused elder (e.g., Bendik, 1992); (c) substance abuse problems, arrest records, and poor employment records (see Greenberg, McKibben, & Raymond, 1990); and (d) social isolation (Bendik, 1992).

Age. With only 10 states reporting on this topic, the 2000 APS survey mentioned above determined ages of elder abuse perpetrators as follows: (a) under 18 years, 5.9%; (b) 18 to 35, 18.4%; (c) 36 to 50, 24.8%; (d) 51 to 65, 10.4%; (d) 65+, 8.9%; and (e) not reported, 31.6% (Teaster, 2003). Many abusive caretakers in Pillemer and Finkelhor's (1988) community survey were over age 50 (75%), and some were over 70 (20%). Abusers who are elders themselves may suffer from dementia or other problems that render them less able to care for dependent elders and more likely to abuse those elders. Although some neglect by such elders may be conscious and premeditated, some may result from ignorance or incompetence. Accounting for intentionality of abuse in such cases is another important issue (Glendenning, 1993).

Gender. Even though women usually shoulder the major burden of elder care (Deitch, 1993), they seem not to be the primary elder abusers. With only 17 states responding, the 2000 APS survey ascertained that with the exception of neglect, most abusers were male (52%) and a third (33%) were females, with the gender of the remainder (15%) unknown (Teaster, 2003). A number of studies have found sons to be more abusive than daughters toward elderly parents (e.g., Crichton, Bond, Harvey, & Ristok, 1998; Wolf & Pillemer, 1997). One study, however, found opposite results when neglect was included as a category of abuse (Anetzberger, 1998; Dunlop, Rothman, Condon, Hebert, & Martinez, 2000).

Relationship to victim. There has been considerable discussion about which group of family members or others is most likely to abuse elders/adults. Family members consist of spouses, parents, children, grandchildren, siblings, and other relatives. Many empirical data show that adult children are the primary offenders (e.g., Brownell, Berman, & Salamone, 1999; Otiniano, Herrera, & Teasdale, 1998; Vladescu et al., 1999). The NEAIS-2000 survey of APS agencies, for instance, indicated that adult children are the largest category of abusers, 39% to 80% (NCEA, 1998).

In contrast, several other comparisons have indicated that elder abuse is primarily "spouse abuse grown old," an extension of IPV into old age (Harris, 1996). Several international evaluations have also found data congruent with the spouse abuse thesis (e.g., Halicka, 1995; Johns & Hydle, 1995; Ockleford et al., 2003). Grossman and Lundy (2003), for example, found notable discrepancies in accounts of victim-offender relationships arising from different service agencies. Although agencies serving domestic violence victims reported that husbands or ex-husbands perpetrated the largest proportion of abuse, APS organizations reported that adult children committed most of the abuse. In reality, available data cannot settle this debate with certitude. With so much ambiguity about definitions and types of reporters, not to mention underreporting biases and large gaps in data caused by nonresponding organizations, there is much room for error.

Data from the APS 2000 survey, with 25 states reporting, indicated that the majority of confirmed elder/adult abusers (61.7%) were family members (Teaster, 2003). Of family perpetrators, 30.2% were spouses or intimate partners, and 17.6% were adult children. Institutional staff committed 4.4% of abuses. A Canadian investigation of 128 elders 60+ years for whom services had been requested uncovered the following rates for abusers: spouse, 48%; adult child, 30%; and acquaintance, 22% (Lithwick, Beaulieu, Gravel, & Straka, 1999). Although most of the abuse (87%) was psychological, spouses did perpetrate most physical abuse (31%).

In an examination of 1,855 substantiated elder abuse and neglect cases from January 1993 through June 1993, the Los Angeles County Department of Community and Senior Citizen Services (1994) determined that 66% of the suspected abusers were family members (35% offspring, 18% other relationships, and 14% spouses). Other suspects were care custodians (12%), no relationship (14%), unknown (4%), and health practitioners (3%).

Lithwick et al. (1999) ascertained that adult children carried out substantially more financial abuse (59%) and neglect (49%) than did spouses (financial abuse, 13%; neglect, 23%). Acquaintances, however, perpetrated the highest amount of financial abuse (75%), but less neglect (30%) and physical abuse (7%). In a small study of 28 cases of elder sexual assault, incestuous assaults were most frequent. These included 11 adult sons, 1 grandson, and 2 brothers. Spouses were perpetrators in 7 cases. The remainder were 1 boyfriend, 2 boarders, 1 friend, 1 distant relative, and 2 unrelated caretakers (Ramsey-Klawsnik, 1991).

Little is known about abusers of the disabled. As Chenoweth (1997) has pointed out, violence against disabled women is neither "voiced nor heard." Therefore, it is even more difficult to specify the characteristics of abusers of the disabled than it is to describe elder abusers. As a case in point, Welbourne, Lipschitz, Selvin, and Green (1983, as cited in Nosek & Howland, 1998) found that various individuals had sexually assaulted

50% of women who had been blind from birth. Abusers of the disabled undoubtedly count on the fact that victims cannot identify them. Although this book has ordinarily restricted its coverage of abusers to family member, it seems necessary to widen the category of abusers of the disabled to include caregivers. The services that caregivers provide are very personal (e.g., bathing), and caregivers have access to victims over long periods of time (see Young et al., 1997).

Characteristics of Disabled Victims and Their Abusers

The most common physical and emotional abusers of disabled women may be their husbands. In one study, 26% of disabled women reported that their husbands were emotional abusers, and 18% reported that their husbands were physical abusers. This study showed that strangers were most apt to commit sexual abuse (12%) (Young et al., 1997). In a Canadian study that covered a very wide age range (18–57), 82% of cases handled at a university sexual abuse and disability project involved female victims. In 96% of cases, the victims knew the perpetrators, and in 44% of cases, the perpetrators were service providers (Sobsey & Doe, 1991). Adult disabled women may also be in need of treatment for childhood sex abuse (Monahan & Lurie, 2003).

SECTION SUMMARY

The frailty and impairments that accompany advancing age leave elders vulnerable to victimization. Data from APS agencies suggest that victims of elder abuse are predominantly females and that abusers are primarily males. A Boston community study found that males were proportionately more victimized than females. Some *SHR* data indicate that males, relative to females, are more frequent victims of intimate partner homicides. Salient sample variations, disparities in conceptualizations of abuse, survival imbalances, and other factors signify that any summarizing statements about patterns of elder abuse are still preliminary. Including financial exploitation, neglect, and self-neglect as abuse categories alters research results.

Across studies, data show no consistent significant differences in SES between abused and nonabused elders. Current studies do reveal racial disparities, however. African Americans appear to be victimized more than other groups, and they also seem to perpetrate a disproportionate amount of elder abuse. Elders living with relatives may suffer more abuse than elders living alone.

As nonrepresentative as findings based on APS data are, aggregation of data across reporting states suggests that spouses (30.2%) perpetrate more elder abuse than do adult children (17.6%). Continuities appear in *SHR* data indicating that intimate partners commit most homicides against elders. NCVS results show that intimates—including partners, family members, and relatives—commit 9.1% of assaults and rapes. Nonintimates known to victims commit an even larger proportion (27.4%) of elder abuse. Abuse of disabled victims is so hidden and research on this topic is so limited that summarizing statements based on empirical research are not available.

————— ·•·•• —————

EXPLAINING ABUSE OF
ELDERS AND DISABLED PERSONS

It is not known with any certainty why relatives abuse elders. Looking at abuse worldwide, Kosberg and Garcia (1995a) found several correlates of elder abuse: low SES, married status, substance abuse, personal problems of caretakers, isolation, female gender of victims, cultural heterogeneity, lack of housing, and societal acceptance of violence. The causal significance of these factors, however, remains unclear.

As in other subareas of family violence, there is no unicausal theory. In a review of elder abuse explanatory frameworks, Ansello (1996) featured a number of current theories: transgenerational, social exchange/ symbolic interactionism, vulnerability, excessive situational demands, and environmental press. The three theories most widely advanced in the United States to explain elder abuse are social learning theory, social exchange theory (encompassing situational stress and dependency), and psychopathology of the abuser (see Fulmer, 1991; Tomita, 1990).

Learning Theory

Because learning theory has received wide acceptance as one explanation for child abuse and spouse abuse, it seems reasonable to suggest that it may offer

a viable account of elder abuse by adult offspring. This view holds that children exposed to violence are likely to grow up to adopt proabuse norms that eventually contribute to their abusing their own parents or grandparents (Fulmer & O'Malley, 1987). Others see the learning connection more as a retaliatory response for past abuse—You hurt me then; now I'll hurt you (Phillips, 1996).

What scant research has been conducted, however, has not strongly supported a learning connection (e.g., Korbin, Anetzberger, & Austin, 1995). In one study, Wolf and Pillemer (1989) examined retrospective accounts of parent-to-child punishments. They found no significant differences between abused elders and a comparison group of nonabused elders. A study that specifically tested the theory by comparing the childhoods of adult children who abuse their elder parents with those of parents who abuse their children found no overall differences using CTS1. On severe violence items, however, child abusers relative to parent abusers had significantly higher scores of being abused as children. A contradictory finding has arisen in an attitudinal survey of Chinese elders living in Hong Kong. In this study, childhood abuse (retaliatory thesis) emerged as the strongest predictor for attitudinal acceptance of elder abuse (Yan & Tang, 2003).

Social Exchange Theory and Symbolic Interactionism

Social exchange theory assumes that "social interactions involve exchange of rewards and punishments between people, and that people seek to maximize rewards and minimize punishments in these exchanges" (Ansello, 1996, p. 17). Proponents of this theory in regard to elder abuse postulate that elders have little to offer in the way of rewards, so interacting with them is costly and rarely "pays off." From this perspective, social exchange theory rests on the well-worn learning principles of reward and punishment. Taking care of elders can be very time-consuming and unpleasant while offering few benefits to caregivers. In one survey, 150 caregivers identified several types of "costs" resulting from elders' impairment. Exemplars of these difficulties were elders' refusals of help and elders' complaints. Some "benefits" were the caretakers' improved relationships with elders and caretakers' discovery of new personal strengths (Hinrichsen, Hernandez, & Pollack, 1992). Presumably, the high costs of assuming responsibility for elder care, in combination with the few tangible rewards, can result in abuse.

Symbolic interactionism is similar to social exchange theory but focuses more centrally on the meanings of interactions. It may not be the objective difficulty of caring for an elder that causes problems, for example, but the perception that the interaction is imbalanced. Imagine the frustration of a wife who spends several hours cooking a birthday meal for her elderly, memory-impaired husband, only to have him refuse to eat the meal, insisting that it is not his birthday. Some caregivers in such a situation might surmise that the impaired elder no longer loves them, whereas others might see this turn of events as an opportunity to eat a meal in "peace and quiet."

Stress and Dependency Theories

At the foundation of the stress model of elder abuse is the belief that the elders most likely to be abused are those who create inordinate levels of stress for family caregivers. Particular impairments, such as being incontinent, being in a wheelchair, or being chronically ill, may make elders overly dependent on others. When such disabilities necessitate reliance on family members for physical, financial, or emotional support, these caregivers can experience an intolerable burden of stress. The situational stress model contends that impairment-generated stress produces abusive behavior (e.g., Harris, 1996). In fact, some experts believe that caregiver stress may be the major source of elder abuse (Steinmetz, 1993).

As an illustration of the extreme stress some elder caregivers experience, Mace (1981) coined the term "36-hour day." Others invented phrases such as the "sandwich generation" to convey the burden of middle-aged adults who must care for their own children while simultaneously caring for aging parents (Preston, 1984; Steinmetz, 1993). The expression "granny dumping" originated in England when some overburdened families simply left sick and aging elders in hospital emergency rooms (see U.S. House of Representatives, 1990). A related strain occurs when adult siblings in a given family designate a specific sibling who lives near the aging parents as "the" caretaker. Instead of elder caregiving being a "family" matter, it becomes the "individual" responsibility of one child (Janosick & Green, 1992).

The opposing viewpoint is that caregiver stress does not induce abusive behavior. According to some scholars, abusive behavior emanates from caretakers, not elder victims, but may be an interactional process (Phillips, Torres de Ardon, & Briones, 2000). The theory that caregiver stress causes elder abuse raises two questions: (a) Are abused elders significantly more dependent or impaired than nonabused elders? (b) Are caregivers of impaired elders more stressed than caregivers of nonimpaired elders?

Several comparisons of abused and nonabused elders have revealed that abused elders are not significantly more impaired or dependent than nonabused elders (e.g., Wolf & Pillemer, 1989). Lachs et al. (1997), for instance, found that impairments such as depression, incontinence, and chronic disease were not associated with abuse. In fact, dependent elders may not even depend on their abusers for assistance but ask others for help. Victims in one study were distinctly less likely to rely on their abusers (26%) for assistance than on someone else (63%) (Pillemer, 1986). Using six measures (e.g., financial, housing), Wolf and Pillemer (1989) determined that elder abuse victims were significantly less dependent on abusers than were elder nonvictims in the areas assessed.

On the other hand, several investigations have indicated that elder dependency is a strong predisposing factor for abuse (Biegel, Sales, & Schulz, 1991; Coyne, Reichman, & Berbig, 1993). Paveza et al. (1992) found that Alzheimer's-impaired elders were at greater risk for abuse than elders without the disease. It should also be pointed out that elders who are physically violent with their caregivers, presumably because of their impairments, are very likely to receive retaliatory violence (Coyne et al., 1993).

Correlational analyses have revealed a link between some burdensome caregiver tasks and measures of caregiver stress (Hinrichsen et al., 1992). One unusual measure of senior caregivers' own health (reactions to influenza vaccination) revealed differences in laboratory reports between caregiver groups. Elders caring for spouses with Alzheimer's disease were significantly less likely (37%) than those not comparably burdened (50%) to mount an effective immunological response against influenza (cited in "Stress Undercuts," 1996). Similarly, a comparison of caregivers of spouses with dementia, relative to spouses with cancer, registered significantly more stress (Clipp & George, 1993).

Arguably, it is caregiving abusers who are dependent. In one comparison, abusers were significantly more dependent on their elder victims than vice versa. In fact, two-thirds of abusers relied on their victims for help with housing, household repair, financial assistance, or transportation (Wolf & Pillemer, 1989).

Further, an evaluation of families of abused and nonabused elders indicated that stress arose from caregivers' behavior (e.g., getting arrested) rather than from strain engendered by caring for elders (Wolf & Pillemer, 1989). In reality, the victim's dependency may simply be a catalyst for abuse in a caretaker who cannot cope effectively (e.g., Movsas & Movsas, 1990; Pillemer, 1986). In other words, abusive behavior may stem from a "problem" caregiver rather than from an elder with "problems." Further, the argument that abuse stems from victim impairment and dependency may be yet one more disguised attempt to blame victims for the abusive behavior of others (Pillemer, 1993).

The use of vastly different samples and other methodological differences has most likely produced some of the divergence in findings on this issue and thus fueled the debate (Fulmer, 1990). Professional report data culled from agency samples support a caregiver-stress model (e.g., Paveza et al., 1992), whereas interview data generated from population surveys do not (Pillemer, 1986). As a final word, Brandl and Cook-Daniels (2002) state that the majority of published studies do not support the caregiver-stress model.

Individual Differences in Personality Traits and Disorders

Case History: Melvin and Charlie—The Voices Told Him to Do It

Melvin is a 79-year-old retired carpenter who currently lives with his son, Charlie. Charlie, a 53-year-old food server in a high school cafeteria, has worked for the school district for 20 years. When Charlie was 38 years old, doctors diagnosed him as having paranoid schizophrenia. At 40, Charlie went broke, spending most of his money on home security devices and car alarms that he "needed" for self-protection. Eventually, Charlie's financial problems forced him to move back in with his father.

Melvin's approach to Charlie's problems was to "set Charlie straight" whenever he told unbelievable stories about his coworkers or neighbors. Melvin accused Charlie of "talking hogwash" and of "needing medicine because he was crazy." Charlie's response was to argue with Melvin to try to convince him that his stories about other people were true. The battle between the two loomed larger and larger until Charlie's problems became the focal point of Melvin's life.

To save himself the aggravation of dealing with Charlie, Melvin began staying in his own room as much as possible. Charlie reacted by standing in front of Melvin's bedroom door, yelling and screaming at him to come out. One time, Charlie got so mad that he ripped out the telephone so neighbors could not tell Melvin lies about him. Another time, he barricaded Melvin into his room for a day, and Melvin had to break a window to escape. Melvin sank into a deep depression. He loved Charlie, but he felt humiliated, blamed, afraid, and all alone.

The next year, Melvin slipped on some ice and broke his leg. At first Charlie was the dutiful son who brought Melvin his meals, drove him to the doctor, and cleaned the apartment. Eventually, however, Charlie heard voices telling him that Melvin was plotting to have him locked up in a mental institution. One day, Charlie beat Melvin and pushed him out of his bed. Melvin lay on the floor for a day until a neighbor heard him groaning and called police.

The police kept Charlie in custody for a 3-day psychiatric evaluation and called social services. APS had Melvin admitted to a nursing home temporarily. In the psychiatric hospital, doctors started Charlie on strong antipsychotic drugs. Now, Charlie is loving, kind, and "normal," as long as he takes his medicines. At the moment, things are better for both Melvin and Charlie, but no one knows for how long.

Many researchers have concluded that it is the characteristics of the caregivers, not those of the victims, that differentiate elderly victims from nonvictims. The case history of Melvin and Charlie illustrates how the emotional and behavioral problems of adult offspring can lead to elder abuse. This perspective holds that elder abusers tend to suffer from a variety of pathologies and mood disturbances (Bendik, 1992; Movsas & Movsas, 1990). Prototypical of this problem are results generated by one study that indicated approximately 38% of abusers in three geographically different samples had histories of psychiatric illness and about 39% had alcohol problems (Wolf & Pillemer, 1988).

An impressive amount of research has linked mental health risk factors and social characteristics to abusive caretakers: clinical depression (Paveza et al. 1992), excessive dependency (Pillemer, 1993), anger and hostility (Coyne et al., 1993; Garcia & Kosberg

1992), psychiatric disorder (e.g., Collins & O'Connor, 2000), mood disturbance (Bendik, 1992), low self-esteem (Godkin, Wolf, & Pillemer, 1989), poor physical health (Bendik, 1992), inadequate communication skills (Greenberg et al., 1990), and inadequate coping skills (Godkin et al., 1989).

Public Attitudes Toward Abuse of Elders and the Disabled

Some members of society may have attitudes condoning violence against elders (Yan & Tang, 2003). Emblematic of this problem is the concept of postmaturity, the idea that elders are living too long. Some believe that older people have had their "day in the sun" and now should just "fade away" (Ansello, 1996). Kosberg and Garcia (1995b) have formulated a list of six viewpoints that promote elder abuse: ageism, sexism, proviolence attitudes, reactions to abuse, negative attitudes toward people with disabilities, and family caregiving imperatives. When caregivers hold such attitudes, they are likely to miss signs of elder abuse (Fulmer et al., 1999).

Attitudes held by some members of the current elder cohort also have the effect of hiding abuse. Several anecdotal or qualitative reports have indicated that older women may feel humiliated to admit being abused by a family member. In fact, most abused elder women and disabled women do not seek help from anyone (Brandl et al., 2003; J. Mears, 2003; Milberger et al., 2003). The elderly women served by agencies tend to believe such mottos as, "What goes on at home stays at home." They also have a strong ethic about "not being a burden" on their children. Such attitudes pose a challenge to agency personnel who wish to reach out to and help abused elders. In listening to older women's opinions, personnel at Project REACH in Maine learned to avoid using stigmatizing terms such as *domestic violence* and *battered woman* when placing advertisements about support groups. Using a trial-and-error procedure, they fashioned ads that used terminology suitable for attracting needy and isolated older women. They found that ads referring to the "concerns of older women," for example, were more palatable to their target audience than ads that mentioned the "abuse of older women" (see Brandl et al., 2003; London, 2003; J. Mears, 2003).

Various popular media tend to perpetuate stereotypes of older people, depicting them as primarily supportive of children and grandchildren or as cranky and laughable. The entertainment media include relatively few depictions of elders who lead rewarding lives (see London, 2003). Although there is no adequate research on the topic, it probably is true that most Americans find it inappropriate for elders to be sexually active. Some nursing homes make it possible for elder residents to have privacy for sexual activities by providing door locks and keys, but others make such activities impossible by allowing residents no privacy.

SECTION SUMMARY

Experts have advanced several theories to explain elder abuse. Learning theory accentuates the notion of the acquisition of abusive behaviors during childhood and their manifestation in adulthood, with the elder parent as victim. So little research has been conducted, however, that it is too early to evaluate this explanation.

Social exchange theory, as applied to elder abuse, posits that just as aging parents (or spouses) need more and more care, they are less and less able to offer rewards or benefits to those who care for them. This imbalance implies that caring for an elder "doesn't pay," so a caretaker might just as well neglect the elder. Social interactionism is related to social exchange theory but depends on elder abuse perpetrators' perceptions of an imbalance in the exchange.

A common theme in explanations of elder abuse is the situational stress of the caregiver. This model assumes that the dependency of an elder, brought about by impairments, raises the "costs" of elder care but not the benefits to the caregiver. Presumably, dependent elders' needs create such powerful feelings of stress in their caregivers that the caregivers may lose control and abuse the elders. For many middle-aged adult children caring for aging parents, the stress generated by this responsibility potentiates the stress from caring for their own children. Although most studies indicate little relationship between physical health indicators and abuse, a few have found that an elder's physical dependency clearly plays a role in vulnerability to abuse. Certainly, one might surmise that impairments of disabled persons make them vulnerable to abuse.

The individual differences (psychopathology of the abuser) theory presumes that elder abuse most likely results from the deviance and dependency of abusers. A large body of evidence demonstrates that perpetrators do tend to have far-ranging problems, such as alcohol abuse and emotional difficulties. The psychological status of abusers, in fact, may be a better predictor of elder abuse than characteristics of victims.

Given that all of these theories have limitations, it may be necessary to identify a configuration of related factors or to integrate theories. Situational stress, for example, in combination with particular personality types, might set the stage for elder mistreatment. Public attitudes toward elders, GLBT persons, and the disabled contribute to their abuse by intimates, acquaintances, and the entire health care system.

Practice, Policy, and Prevention Issues

Increasingly, government agencies and community professional groups have identified elder abuse as a social problem. The U.S. Department of Social and Rehabilitation Services began funding APS programs in the late 1960s (Quinn, 1985). In 1978, the Subcommittee on Human Services of the House Select Committee held the first congressional investigation on elder abuse (see Olinger, 1991). Following the hearings, Congress in 1981 recommended the establishment of the National Center on Adult Abuse (Filinson, 1989). By 1985, every state had some form of APS program (Quinn, 1985), and by 1989, 42 states had enacted some form of mandatory elder abuse reporting law (U.S. General Accounting Office, 1991). To read an interview with Lisa Nerenberg, a consultant in elder abuse prevention, please link to this volume on Sage's Web Site (http://www.sagepub.com/book.aspx?pid10013; click on the "Additional Materials" button).

Responses to Elder Abuse

Just as definitional ambiguity has hindered research, it has also hampered efforts to respond to elder abuse. If practitioners had a greater understanding of the precursors of elder IPV—for instance, whether it stems from desire for power and control or caregiver stress—they would probably be able to protect potential victims more readily (see Stiegel, Heisler, Brandl, & Judy, 2000).

Many of the cases that APS agencies investigate are similar to the case of Jenny and Jeff Jr., described at the beginning of this chapter. Uncertainties abound: Would a judge find Jeff Jr. and Marianne guilty of neglect? Is Jenny's situation serious enough to warrant her removal from their house? Would Jenny be happier and safer living elsewhere? What is the former daughter-in-law's appropriate role in helping Jenny? Who

should inherit the remainder of Jenny's estate when she dies? In the real world, there are no good answers, only more difficult questions.

Responses to Abuse of Disabled Persons

Services for disabled abused persons extend from nonexistent to inadequate. Pamela S. Cohen (2001), a legal expert, has advocated on behalf of disabled elderly for the right to community-based care. She is concerned with the breadth of interpretations of laws and the lack of uniformity in how the legal system implements the laws. She notes that adequate implementation of laws is contingent on "changes in the clinical, economic, political, and social spheres" (p. 234).

Available services. In a Canadian study, 15% of disabled abused women reported that no services were available or that they could not access any, whereas 10% had been able to use shelters. The majority of the women in this study (55%) had not even tried to get help (Ridington, 1989). Most shelters established for domestic violence victims are architecturally inaccessible to women with physical disabilities. Another type of inaccessibility exists for deaf clients when no sign-language interpreters are available. Unfortunately, shelter staff usually cannot offer disabled victims needed assistance with daily self-care or medications (Nosek, Howland, & Young, 1997). Among a group of 40 social service agencies, Hammond found in 1999 that very few were attuned to the problems of disabled battering victims (cited in Erwin, 2000). Of 16 agencies that responded to a set of three scenarios, 80% did not diagnose the problem correctly (see also Monahan & Lurie, 2003).

Assistive devices. If dependency or vulnerability of elders and disabled persons fosters their abuse, then the provision of needed assistive devices (such as wheelchairs, canes, and hearing aids) might reduce or eradicate abuse. Mobility training could eliminate dependency for some elders (Ansello, 1996). As Cohen and Van Nostrand (1995) observe, as the U.S. population ages, more and more elders will need help managing the activities of daily living. The proportion of elderly Americans with disabilities is likely to rise to 9.4% by 2020.

Professional Practitioners

Responding to elder mistreatment is a complex and confusing area of social work practice (Braun, Lenze

Shumacher-Mukai, & Snyder, 1993). One aspect of the problem is the continuing ambiguity concerning who is responsible for dependent elders and what kind of care (or lack of care) constitutes mistreatment. APS agencies are most commonly assigned the responsibility of implementing legal policies concerning elders. When a suspected case of elder abuse is reported, APS has several duties: (a) to determine whether the information available is sufficient to warrant an investigation, (b) to substantiate whether abuse/neglect actually occurred, (c) to assess the elder's decision-making capacity about his or her care, and (d) to evaluate what services are needed to sustain the elder (Rosenblatt, 1996). Some newly devised protocols are useful for detecting elder abuse and neglect within or outside of nursing homes (East Bay Consortium for Elder Abuse, 2001). Although APS agencies are state controlled, the federal government could provide leadership and support for the whole system (Wolf & Pillemer, 2000).

The 2000 national survey of APS organizations cited previously indicated that all U.S. states have accorded APS statutory power to investigate reported abuse in domestic settings. APS investigates abuse claims in institutional settings in 37 states, in mental health/mental retardation settings in 35 states, and in "other" settings in 37 states (Teaster, 2003). In many circumstances, the needs of elder abuse victims exceed APS agencies' functions, and other community agents, such as health care providers or law enforcement, have the responsibility to provide assistance.

In many states, APS is a subcomponent of a larger human welfare organization. One examination of APS responses offered to 204 abused elders by the Department of Aging in Illinois provides a typical picture of APS services: case management (97.5%); homemaker assistance (34.8%); legal services (24.5%); medical care or therapy (16.2%); institutional placement (14.7%); supervision and reassurance (14.2%); counseling (13.2%); home health assistance (12.3%); meals and income assistance (16.7%); housing and relocation assistance (6.4%), police, court work, and protection orders (6.9%); guardianship (3.4%); and other (6.4%) (Sengstock, Hwalek, & Petrone, 1989).

In may be a mistake for professionals charged with making decisions about placement of elders to assume automatically that family members are fit caretakers. Conducting a preplacement screening to identify high-risk elders and high-risk caretakers may prevent abuse (Kosberg, 1988). Finally, professionals would be wise to assist families with the burdens of elder care (e.g., procurement of additional home services) even if they judge their family settings to be suitable. One qualitative study investigated the effectiveness of a victim-assistance/perpetrator stress-reduction treatment. Victims did well with nursing, medical care, and home-making assistance. For abusers, individual counseling to reduce anxiety, stress, and depression was most effective in reducing abuse (Nahmiash & Reis, 2000).

In some instances, elders refuse the services offered by APS workers, and this may discourage practitioners who are trying to help. It is interesting to note that information from 40 states has recently shown that only 11% of elders contacted by APS refused services (Teaster, 2003). A small Canadian study found refusal rates among abused elders that were considerably higher and that differed by type of perpetrator and type of maltreatment (Lithwick et al., 1999). In one survey, 81% of elders who rejected intervention were women with no disabling characteristics whose sons were the caretakers/perpetrators. In Vinton's (1991) study, elders who refused care often did so because the services offered (respite care and homemaker services) did not meet their needs. What these women needed were emergency shelters and restraining orders.

Practitioner training. The three most important group targets of elder abuse education are professionals, community leaders, and the elderly themselves. University courses on family violence have often failed to include the topic of elder abuse (Otto, 2000), and service providers have rarely received any special training. In 2002, an American Psychological Association committee on aging addressed the U.S. Congress about the need for more geropsychologists (Levitt, 2002). To overcome knowledge gaps, states should require licensed professionals to take continuing education courses in health care, gerontology, elder abuse, and abuse of the disabled (Otto, 2000). Networking approaches that integrate the efforts of various community groups are a key component in successful educational programs (Weiner, 1991).

Screening elderly clients for abuse is a basic responsibility of several subgroups of professionals and others who work with the elderly. Attorneys could help safeguard dependent elders, for example, by screening their elderly clients for financial exploitation (Stiegel, 2001). Staff in adult day-care centers are also in an excellent position to screen clients for abuse. Such centers should maintain medical staff to conduct physical exams of seniors (Fulmer et al., 1999).

Cultural competence. Across the board, elderly members of marginalized groups fare worse than mainstream elders. Immigrants, for instance, are far more likely than nonimmigrants to work in hazardous jobs, and thus in old age they are more likely to be chronically ill or disabled. Language barriers and financially limited medical treatment decrease minority abused elders' chances of seeking protection from abuse. Further, immigrants may have few statutory rights and may not be eligible for services. In sum, they have little opportunity to access services in many countries, including the United States (see Biggs, Phillipson, & Kingston, 1995; Jervis, Jackson, & Manson, 2002; McFall, 2000).

Some observers claim that most professionals who work with elder abuse victims in the United States lack the competencies needed to work with members of marginalized groups. They may also need to offer outreach programs for minorities, homosexuals, and immigrants. Tomita (2000) advises practitioners to look for subtle signs of abuse, use terminology that is familiar and acceptable to victims, educate families about problem solving, and try to restore relationships that maximize the elder's potential power. Torres-Gil (as cited in Kauffman, 2002) has criticized the "one-size-fits-all" approach to recognizing diversity. Rather than aggregating data from minorities, it is more effective to study minorities in terms of characteristics such as SES, vulnerability, and adherence to cultural norms.

Needs of homosexual elders. Many policies tangential to elder abuse affect GLBT elders. Cahill and Smith (2002) found "legal" discrimination against GLBT elders in the following areas: (a) denial of senior center services; (b) noneligibility of longtime same-sex partners for spousal Social Security benefits, despite their having made payments into the system; (c) noneligibility of same-sex partners for pensions automatically set aside for spouses; (d) restriction of access to federally subsidized senior housing; and (e) barriers to receiving health care and long-term health care.

Legal Issues

Federal and state governments, and many county and city governments, have attempted to deter elder abuse through legislation. Regrettably, in addition to variations in legal definitions of elder abuse from state to state, the operating standards employed by APS agencies vary from agency to agency. Confusion about legal definitions of abuse thwarts detection of certain types of abuse (e.g., psychological abuse) and hampers intervention strategies.

In California, Section 15610 of the Welfare and Institutions Code delineates the illegal acts that constitute elder abuse as physical abuse, neglect, abandonment, fiduciary abuse, isolation, and mental suffering (see Los Angeles County Medical Association, 1992). California's statutes also encompass issues of intentionality, recklessness, and attempts to cause bodily injury (see Erwin, 2000). Further, California has enacted a law that allows for civil remedies when elder abuse occurs.

Although the federal government has not established directives about delivery of APS services, it has heightened the focus on elder abuse legislation (Stiegel, 2003). Currently pending in the Finance Committee of the Senate is the Elder Justice Act, which will change the age of an elder to 60 years, down from 65, and enact or strengthen laws protecting elders. (For a review of the bill, see the THOMAS Web site at http://rs9/loc.gov/home/thomas.html.) In addition, the Senate Judiciary Committee is fashioning the Senior Safety Act, which includes an across-the-board increase in criminal sentences related to victims' ages ("Congress Considers," 2003).

Current laws have totally failed to curb rampant Medicare and Medicaid fraud by health care workers, companies, and nursing homes (Sundram, 2003). Possibly as much as 7–10% ($100 billion) of annual U.S. health care expenditures are fraudulent. The siphoning off of these funds is an indirect form of elder abuse, because it reduces the amount of funding available for other needed elder services. Because legislatures have fallen short in their duty to enact precise laws to quell these practices, some prosecutors have relied on a very old law, the federal False Claims Act. This law allows various entities (e.g., families of abuse victims) to sue defendants (e.g., nursing homes) who obtain federal funds fraudulently. Whistle-blowers have recovered more than $800 million by invoking this fraud law successfully (Dayton, 2002).

An especially urgent legal concern is the failure of some professionals to comply with elder abuse mandatory reporting laws. Those most frequently required to report abuse under various state laws are health care professionals, such as physicians and nurses. Other frequently mandated reporters are law enforcement personnel, mental health professionals, dentists, and social workers. State social service departments are most frequently assigned the task of receiving reports of elder abuse (Wolf & Pillemer, 1989). Research indicates that some mandated reporters are failing to fulfill their obligations. The five groups most likely to report elder abuse, in descending order of report frequency, are as follows: family members, health care professionals, social service agency staff, law enforcement officers, and victims themselves (Teaster, 2003).

The lack of interagency understanding about the roles of various community agencies is at the core of many failures to report. Collaborative efforts between agencies often improve reporting. Programs built on interagency cross-training have the potential to overcome mistrust and establish successful policy guidelines. Law enforcement personnel, for example, might help social service personnel define "serious" abuse and explain various possible police reactions to reports. In return, the police may learn that they can rely on social service personnel to serve as intermediaries when elders will not cooperate with them. In one jurisdiction, such interagency cooperation led to a 300% increase in reports of elder abuse (Reulbach & Tewksbury, 1994).

Elders' access to legal services is another vital issue. Generally speaking, attorneys can provide abuse victims with services not available from other professionals. For example, attorneys can execute court and noncourt actions as well as nonlegal actions that have the potential to threaten court action. By and large, abused elders most frequently need one of four types of legal interventions: (a) an order of protection to remove the abuser from the residence; (b) guardianship of the elder and/or his or her estate; (c) a representative payeeship to safeguard certain types of the elder's income, such as social security; and (d) protection against involuntary commitment to a mental health care facility (Segal & Iris, 1989).

Although abused elders may have many unmet legal needs, they tend to make sparse use of legal resources (see Hightower, Heckert, & Schmidt, 1990; Korbin, Anetzberger, Thomasson, & Austin, 1991). They may be reluctant to instigate and become involved in the legal process, especially if the case involves family members (Pollack, 1995). Fortunately, a few alternative services are now offered to meet the legal needs of vulnerable elders. A noteworthy volunteer project sponsored by the Los Angeles County Bar Association helped approximately 1,125 elder clients obtain restraining orders in 1993 (Beitiks, 1994). Elders can help prevent their own abuse by completing a number of documents (e.g., durable powers of attorney) and keeping them updated (Overman, 1992). A Web site that originates in Ventura, California, provides a compendium of laws protecting the elderly (see M. Schwartz, 2000).

Role of Medical Personnel

Doctors, nurses, and other medical personnel can play a vital role in assisting elder abuse victims. As in other areas of family violence, medical screening of possible elder abuse victims is critical (Swagerty, Takahashi, & Evans, 1999). Most hospital and medical center emergency departments have screening protocols for identifying and reporting elder abuse, but, as Rosenblatt (1996) notes, these protocols lack uniformity. Most states have resource hotlines that doctors (or elders) can call for assistance in matters of abuse (Lachs & Pillemer, 1995). In recent years, the American Medical Association has recognized the problem and has increased its efforts to include family violence education in medical school training. Over the years, it has become clear that doctors need a forensic education (Otto, 2000). The JCAHO (2002) has produced a set of guidelines for health care settings to help professionals recognize abuse and neglect in patients of all ages.

Representative of efforts to improve medical professionals' response to the problem of elder abuse is a booklet for doctors created by the Los Angeles County Medical Association (1992) in association with several other agencies (e.g., Los Angeles City Department of Aging). The booklet covers a number of issues regarding elder abuse, such as diagnosis and clinical findings, case management, intervention, and risk management. It also presents a series of nine questions that doctors should ask elderly patients (see Table 12.3 for an excerpt from a booklet that includes such questions).

Research has suggested that medical personnel are often reluctant to report suspected cases of elder abuse (Blakely & Dolon, 1991). In one study, a significant number of interviewed doctors (36%) and nurses (60%) cited their fear of becoming involved in lengthy court appearances as a major reason for their failure to comply with mandated reporting laws. Some were simply unaware of reporting laws (O'Malley, Segel, & Perez, 1979). Other frequent reasons included beliefs that the problem is not serious enough, the evidence is insufficient, services are inadequate, and the report would disrupt family relationships (Clark-Daniels, Daniels, & Baumhover, 1989). Kosberg and Nahmiash (1996) believe that medical personnel's improved understanding of the dynamics of elder abuse would enhance their ability to detect it and presumably to report it.

Table 12.3   Assessment Interview (with patient and family member[s])

When asking the patient more direct questions pertaining to mistreatment, first explain that such questions are routine because many families experience this problem but don't know where to turn for help. The following are examples of more direct questions which may be asked of patients, depending on the individual case.

- Has anyone at home ever hurt you?
- Has anyone every touched you when you didn't want to be touched?
- Has anyone ever forced you to do something against your will?
- Has anyone taken anything that was youvu really didn't want to? Why?
- Does anyone ever talk or yell at you in a way that makes you feel lousy or bad about yourself?
- Are you afraid of anyone?
- Has anyone ever threatened you?
- Has anyone ever failed to help you take care of yourself when you needed help?

Explore each of the above affirmative responses further: How did (does) mistreatment occur? How often? Has mistreatment increased or changed over time? Explain. What precipitates mistreatment? Why does the patient think mistreatment occurs? Is patient in danger as a result of the mistreatment? How serious is the danger? How serious are the consequences of mistreatment? Can the patient protect him/herself? Does patient want to prevent mistreatment? How? If not, why? Have there been previous efforts to prevent mistreatment? If so, who helped? What happened? What would be different this time? What does the patient want to happen now?

SOURCE: Mount Sinai/Victim Services Agency, Elder Abuse Project (1988), *Elder Mistreatment Guidelines for Health Care Professionals: Detection, Assessment, and Intervention*, p. 14. Copyright by Mt. Sinai/Victim Services Agency, Elder Abuse Project. Reprinted with permission of Victim Services, New York and Mt. Sinai.

Physical and occupational therapists could play a role in the detection of elder abuse because their observation of elders with symptoms of abuse puts them in a good position to facilitate remedial and preventive services (Holland, Kasraian, & Leonardelli, 1987). Community health nurses, who go directly into homes, are another group of community service providers who, by virtue of their function and responsibilities, could become critical participants in the identification, prevention, and treatment of elder abuse (VanderMeer, 1992).

One national issue is the lack of adequate care that elders receive in America's nursing homes and the abuse that takes place in such facilities. (For a discussion of some of these shortcomings, see Box 12.2.)

Box 12.2 Abuse in Nursing Homes

No reliable estimates of the prevalence of nursing home abuse and neglect currently exist, but experts believe such abuse is extensive and vastly underreported. In some circumstances, the entire organization of nursing home practices and rules becomes a form of institutionalized abuse (Decalmer, 1993). Like a prison, a nursing home might require residents to arise at 5:00 a.m. Once awake, a resident in such a home might be placed in a wheelchair and rolled out into a corridor to wait an hour or more for breakfast.

The abuse of elders by caretakers appears to be a worldwide phenomenon. Surveys in England, Sweden, Israel, and South Africa have all found high rates of nursing home abuse (e.g., Saveman, Astrom, Bucht, & Norberg, 1999). A survey of 80 nursing home caretakers in Germany revealed very high rates of abuse occurring over the preceding 2 months: 79% of staff admitted to abusing or neglecting a resident, and 59% reported being physically or verbally abused by residents (Goergen, 2001). In addition to more commonly known types of abuse, researchers have recently uncovered the occurrence of sexual abuse of nursing home residents (Burgess, Prentky, & Dowdell, 2000).

According to a report from the Administration on Aging (1999), the top 10 complaints of nursing home residents in 1996 were as follows: (a) failure to give assistance when requested, (b) accidents and improper handling, (c) inadequate care plans, (d) staff's disrespectful attitudes, (e) inadequate personal hygiene, (f) discharge and eviction policies, (g) shortage of staff, (h) menu quality, (i) physical abuse, and (j) lost or stolen property. As Peduzzi, Watzlaf, Rohrer, and Rubinstein (1997) note, "The absence of uniform legal codes, definitions, reporting requirements, and methods of record keeping" impedes the procurement of national elder abuse rates (p. 69). In the United States, some state and federal laws are even inimical to the gathering of data on elder abuse. If a nursing home accumulates data on abuse against residents, for example, does it have to disclose the evidence to a government inspection team (Sundram, 2003)? Some laws say yes; others say no.

An adverse interweaving of private and government health care, labor, and welfare policies factor into nursing home abuse and neglect (Dawson & Surpin, 2001). As an example, the low payments that Medicare provides for acute elder care motivate hospitals to release patients "quicker and sicker." As a result, nursing homes must provide unforeseen, costly secondary care (Menio & Keller, 2000). In 1997, Medicare and Medicaid expenses for nursing home care totaled roughly $28 billion (Quin, 1999; U.S. General Accounting Office [U.S. GAO], 2002b).

Because taxpayers foot the bill for more than half of nursing home care costs, government officials are constantly searching for an improvement/cost trade-off. The resulting patchwork of funding policies and monetary constraints affects several government functions. To avoid increased costs, state officials may report that nursing homes are in compliance with government regulations when they have actually failed to meet even minimum standards of care. A section of the Medicare Web site devoted to the evaluation of nursing home quality (at http://www.medicare.gov/NHCompare/home.asp), for instance, erroneously rated 471 (of 2,549) homes as substantially in compliance with federal standards. The evaluators failed to include the 25,000 health violations documented in these homes. Federal evaluators often overlook even nursing home deaths resulting from neglect, medication errors, or asphyxia (see U.S. GAO, March 4, 2002b). According to one U.S. GAO report, the federal government "is incapable of adequately and effectively surveying, inspecting, and enforcing standards of care against long-term care facilities" (as cited in Dreher, 2002, p. 119).

Relevant to cost considerations is the selection of personnel hired to care for elders. Nursing homes limit the number of nursing aides hired, and those employed are untrained, low-wage workers. A study conducted by the U.S. Department of Health and Human Services (2002) found that more than half of nursing homes do not have enough nursing personnel to protect residents from harm, and less than 10% have enough personnel to provide good care. Estimates of additional costs to the Medicare/Medicaid budget for 2001 to improve the staff/resident ratio reached $7.6 billion (U.S. GAO, 2002b).

Certified nursing aides (CNAs), who provide approximately 90% of patient care, are the employees most likely to abuse patients. They also are the employees most likely to be abused by nursing home residents. One investigation found that two situational factors were strongly related to CNAs' propensity to abuse: staff burnout and level of staff-patient conflict (Pillemer & Bachman, 1991; Singer, 2002).

Unbelievably, states do not routinely require nursing homes to use a number of hiring safeguards that experts have recommended, such as (a) checking prospective employees for criminal backgrounds, (b) screening unlicensed employees, (c) reporting candidates with questionable abuse backgrounds to appropriate nurses' registries, and (d) reporting suspected abuse to local law enforcement agencies (see U.S. GAO, 2002b). Michigan law now requires that administrators of nursing homes with 50 or more beds meet a minimum educational standard, and that they be licensed and periodically relicensed (reported by Dayton, 2002). A national survey about abusive nursing home workers found that only 21 of 49 states reporting maintained central registries/databases of abusers (Teaster, 2003). Responses indicated multiple problems with registries, such as liability problems, cost, and undetermined effectiveness (Duke, 1999).

The most obvious solution to the problem of nursing home abuse lies in the augmentation of government subsidies for CNA salaries. Another pivotal step is better training for CNAs. Effective training consists primarily of stress and anger management, conflict resolution skills, and abuse reporting information (Menio & Keller, 2000; Pillemer & Hudson, 1993). Nursing home administrators must screen employees more thoroughly and report all abusive staff to local law enforcement and abuse registries. Last, class action lawsuits on behalf of patients may be the best approach when regulatory protection in nursing homes has failed (Golden, Roos, Silverman, & Beber, 2000; Intagliata, 2002).

Experts have also advanced several other proposals for eliminating nursing home abuse. Two studies have demonstrated methods for improving quality of care: (a) using gerontological clinical nurse specialists to support improvement (Popejoy et al., 2000) and (b) adopting national standards against which compliance could be judged empirically (Huber, Borders, Badrak, Netting, & Nelson, 2001). An untested and debatable approach is the use of electronic surveillance ("nanny cams") in patients' rooms (Galloro, 2001). Further, Nelson (2000) has theorized that rebalancing the power dynamics in nursing homes so that patients have more authority should improve care.

Without doubt, treatment of ill, frail, and demented elders in nursing homes is a critical medical and social problem. No one is held accountable for the deplorable conditions in many nursing homes. Although congressional committees decry nursing home abuse and neglect, their remedies are inadequate, frequently consisting of little more than calls for additional studies (Singer, 2002; U.S. DHHS, 2002). Advocates, researchers, practitioners, APS workers, educators, media executives, and the American public should pressure legislators to make a tectonic shift in nursing home care policies.

Shelters

Several authorities have advocated the establishment of emergency shelters for battered elderly women (e.g., Boudreau, 1993). A 1992 Florida survey of 6,026 women who were sheltered during the previous year revealed how few women over 60 ($n = 132$) gained access. Of these 132 women, 95% suffered IPV. Special programming for older women existed in only 2 of 25 shelters (Vinton, 1998). As discussed in a previous chapter, there is a need for domestic violence programs and APS agencies to collaborate (e.g., Dunlop et al., 2000; Harris, 1996). Access to battered women's shelters, however, may not be as helpful to elderly women as better access to elder care facilities. Along the same lines, Zink et al. (2003) suggest that assisted living facilities might provide emergency shelters for older women or that home health agencies might assume some of the burden of care.

There are several approaches that could make shelters more user-friendly to elders. As a case in point, local school of architecture designed special furniture for a cottage housing abused elders. Representative of the architects' volunteer efforts were beds designed with bookshelf headboards containing lights (McFall, 2000). Shelters should expand their outreach to meet the needs of marginalized groups: minorities, immigrants, lesbians, disabled persons, and older women. A model shelter might include special large-print books or telecommunication devices for the hearing impaired. (For a description of a unique shelter program in Texas, see Cameron & Abramson, 2002; for information on services for people with disabilities who have been victimized, see Office for Victims of Crime, 2002a.)

Community Involvement, Education, and Training

Communities need to make a large number of changes in practices and policies to protect vulnerable elders. One modification communities can make is to reduce the fragmentation of service delivery. Usually there is no single community agency in charge of assisting abused elders. Some agencies provide certain services, such as "Meals on Wheels," that are not available for use by other agencies, such as law enforcement. Professionals and service providers with expertise in divergent disciplines, such as APS, criminal justice, domestic violence and sexual assault, physical and mental health, religion, law, banking, and alcohol abuse, need to join forces to provide a coordinated response to elder abuse. Emergency health care teams can assist when APS workers or police discover a situation demanding immediate intervention (Watkins, 2003).

Multidisciplinary teams. Agency teamwork is the most viable form of response to the multifaceted problem of elder abuse (Nerenberg, 1996; Sanderson, 2000; Vinton, 1998). In other words, "it takes a village" to protect the vulnerable elderly. Such approaches improve victim identification as well as the quality of decision making concerning the most effective methods of intervening and which agencies are best suited to the task (Matlaw & Spence, 1994; Vinton, 2003). Experts in European countries are also calling for agency collaboration (Ockleford et al., 2003).

Discipline cross-training is the backbone of such collaborative efforts (Calkins, 2003). In Texas, for example, APS training occurs under the umbrella of the Protective Services Training Institute in conjunction with four graduate schools of social work (Urwin & McCrory, 2000). Teams have frequently formed to combat specific kinds of elder mistreatment. As one example, a few communities have formed elderly death review teams to detect "gray murders" that may go undetected (Dayton, 2002).

Teams devoted to bank fraud and the financial exploitation of the elderly are becoming more widespread. As one illustration, Wachovia, a private banking chain in Pennsylvania and the eastern seaboard, joined forces with APS to develop an antifraud unit. In time, the bank trained personnel to recognize "red flags" indicating financial exploitation of elders. Bank personnel turned over suspected cases to a loss management specialist within the bank who investigated and made referrals as needed. The bank also crafted consumer brochures to warn elders about financial fraud. This collaboration had immediate benefits, preventing actual losses of more than $200,000 and protecting assets of almost $1,500,000. The National Association of Adult Protective Services Administrators plans to promote this program nationally (Snyder, 2003).

Working with abused disabled persons. Universities must take the lead by including disability education in social science graduate schools (Hayward, 2002). The Americans with Disabilities Act of 1992 has had an impact by dictating that certain programs, such as domestic violence programs, modify shelter accessibility. From a practice perspective, Andrews and Veronen (1993) describe effective victim services for abused disabled persons in the context of four requirements: (a) adequate assessment of survivors, including disability issues; (b) recognition and appropriate response to disability needs and trauma; (c) provision of accessible or barrier-free information and facilities that are available 24 hours a day, 7 days a week; and (d) legal assistance to ensure protection from abusers.

If nothing else, it may be possible to develop some form of modified safety plans, an especially imposing challenge for disabled women (Nosek & Howland, 1998). California's Crimes Against Victims With Disabilities Initiative has developed a guide to resources that victims can use in safety planning (available on the Internet at http://www.dmh.cahwnet.gov/CVDI/docs/safety_plan_guide.pdf).

Innovative programs. In one of the few empirical studies conducted to date, Reay and Browne (2002) treated 9 individuals who had physically abused and 10 who had neglected their elderly relatives. The treatment included both an educational component and an anger management program. Using pre- and posttests, the researchers assessed the abusers via the CTS1 (Straus, 1979), Machin's Strain Scale (caregiver stress) (SS; Machin, 1984), the Beck Depression Inventory (BDI;

Beck & Steer, 1993), the Beck Anxiety Inventory (BAI; Beck & Steer, 1990), and the Cost of Care Index (problems caring for elders) (CCI; Kosberg & Cairl, 1986). Results showed that both types of abusers experienced reductions in SS, BDI, and BAI scores after each program component. Further, after anger management training, CTS1 and CCI measures also fell. These significant improvements were still evident at the 6-month follow-up.

Reports on most innovative programs aimed at reducing or preventing elder abuse have presented anecdotal accounts. Nerenberg (2003) tackled financial abuse by developing a daily money management program for elders. Weitzman and Weitzman (2003) designed a program to improve elders' communication skills, one element of which was the constructive handling of conflictual interactions.

Police and Legal System Responses

Anecdotal evidence suggests that police officers are ill trained for dealing with both older IPV victims and their abusers. Having no protocols or other guidance about dealing with frail elders, police often resort to sending alleged abusers around the block to "cool off" or advising them to stop their abuse. This approach can be dangerous for victims, who may be at risk for serious physical or sexual violence (Stiegel et al., 2000). In recent years, an enlightened group of police officers, prosecutors, sheriffs' deputies, firefighters, religious leaders, volunteers, and others developed the TRIAD program to reduce elder abuse. In addition to giving talks on elder abuse at senior centers, police in the program may "drop by" the houses of elders to chat. If an elder divulges any abuse, law enforcement personnel can initiate an investigation without the elder's having to swear out a complaint ("Congress Considers," 2003).

Physical handicaps, such as deafness, unclear articulation, lack of transportation, and nonaccess to court buildings, may contribute to particularly inadequate criminal justice responses to abuse of the disabled (Reyna, 1999). Mentally ill individuals also are at risk for abuse. When police respond to a domestic call and the victim is speech impaired, for example, they might turn to the perpetrator or to a child in the household to determine what has happened. Police also tend to dismiss cases of abuse of the disabled because they often believe disabled people are not credible witnesses (Chenoweth, 1997).

Police departments need funding to develop on-scene protocols for cases of possible elder abuse and abuse of the disabled, to purchase special transportation vehicles (e.g., for transport of wheelchair-bound victims), and to hire specialists (e.g., sign-language interpreters). At least many police departments are already providing officers with some training in recognizing mentally-ill perpetrators and where to take them (Briere, Woo, McRae, Foltz, & Sitzman, 1997; Lipschitz et al., 1996; Weinhardt, 1999). To assist police, the California State Legislature has passed directives requiring various agencies to establish medical forensic forms for use with abused elders (Dayton, 2002). Also available are several videotapes for police training (Law Enforcement Research Center, 1996).

Some observers believe that the courts lack sufficient powers to help abused elders. The slow pace of legal proceedings, coupled with elder victims' waning capacities, hinders prosecution of elder abuse. Changes in court procedures, such as allowing elders to submit testimony via videotape, would resolve situations in which elders die or lose the capacity to testify before a trial starts. Judges need to perfect monitoring practices that include the following: (a) informing guardians of their responsibilities, (b) requiring guardians to submit informative reports, (c) checking reports, and (d) holding or having the option to hold a hearing on reports (Zimny & Diamond, 1993). Without specialized training, judges may not protect elders effectively (Otto, 2000).

Collaboration between APS and law enforcement is a growing trend (Reulbach & Tewksbury, 1994). The Los Angeles Police Department has formalized the unique Elder Persons' Estate Unit within the Fiduciary Abuse Specialist Team (FAST) to curb financial exploitation of seniors. FAST includes a district attorney, a stockbroker, a bank trust officer, a retired probate judge, and public guardian staff. Some of the team's duties include training APS representatives, public guardians, and ombudsmen in how to detect financial abuse of elders. Acting as a fiduciary SWAT team, FAST sweeps into banks and other areas to safeguard seniors by suggesting that administrators put a hold on the seniors' assets. This team has recovered $31 million in homes, vehicles, and life savings since it began informally in 1987 (Nerenberg, 1995). (For an extensive list of indicators of the financial exploitation of elders, see Stiegel, 2001.)

A Research Agenda

The most essential research requirement for the field of elder/disabled adult abuse is to procure better prevalence and incidence data across states (see Dunlop et al., 2000; Ockleford et al., 2003). Although more numerical data have become available in the past 5 years, knowledge in this area is still meager and incomplete. A data collection system that compels state agencies to provide information about the ages and genders of individuals involved in elder abuse is also fundamental to improving knowledge. A comprehensive program for gathering data would not only furnish information about abused elders, but could also amass data about abused disabled adults.

Researchers cannot obtain better data without first establishing greater concordance in several areas. First, work must continue on determining the sensitivity and specificity of alternative definitions of elder/disabled adult abuse. Second, all states should provide data to government researchers using uniform definitions of *elder, adult, vulnerable,* and *disabled,* as well as uniform understandings of various types of mistreatment. Agencies should keep track of self-neglect as a dimension of elder problems even if it is not defined as abuse, because their overriding concern should be to protect elders from harm (see Mixson, 1991). Including self-neglect can be a sensitive issue, because it leaves open the possibility that APS personnel or others will encroach on elders' rights to make autonomous decisions about how to spend their remaining days.

Researchers need to answer many other questions about elder abuse as well. In 1991, an interdisciplinary group of researchers formulated a national agenda of research priorities on the subject of elder abuse. This group pinpointed the need to make the following determinations: (a) nature and extent of the problem, (b) etiology (i.e., origin, or root causes), (c) societal costs and consequences, (d) identification of abused elders, (e) prevention and treatment, and (f) legal concerns (Carp, 1999; Stein, 1991). Wolf and Pillemer (2000) assert that researchers could improve outcome measures by using risk assessment rather than simple information about case resolution (e.g., perpetrator moved) or case closure. As in other subareas of family violence, elder abuse researchers need to intensify their efforts to reach members of marginalized groups, such as homosexuals, immigrants, and those living in rural areas.

Prevention

The National Center for Injury Prevention and Control (2002) has published recommendations for preventing elder abuse that focus primarily on improving evaluations of the following: (a) efficacy of interventions, (b) strategies for changing identified cultural norms supportive of abuse, (c) training programs for elder abuse and health professionals, (d) health consequences of abuse, (e) surveillance methods used for abuse, and (f) models for integrated community services. The center also notes that it is important to examine how individuals come to be at risk for both perpetration and victimization.

One team of criminologists tested the prevention effects of a public awareness campaign, home visits, or both in a public housing project. The goal was to prevent revictimization of elders. This systematic controlled study of 403 abused elders and comparisons ascertained that interventions had no impact on victims' knowledge about elder abuse or social services and did not improve elders' psychological well-being. When victims received both treatments, however, they were more likely to call police and report abuse incidents to researchers (Davis, Medina, & Avitabile, 2001). The California State Legislature has devised a public awareness campaign to prevent elder abuse. One product to arise from the campaign is a booklet titled "A Citizen's Guide to Preventing and Reporting Elder Abuse" (cited in Cook-Daniels, 2003a). No outcome data about the effectiveness of the program are available.

CHAPTER SUMMARY

This chapter has summarized current knowledge about elder abuse and briefly described abuse of the disabled. Although investigators have made progress over the past decade, research conducted to date has been insufficient to determine the scope of elder abuse. Almost nothing is known about abuse of the disabled. Experts in the field have failed to reach consensus about the definition of elder abuse. Conceptions of what constitutes elder abuse among minority and immigrant populations vary from those of individuals in the majority. Cross-cultural studies show both similarities and differences between other countries and the United States in elder abuse. Some ecological conditions, such as poverty, increase elder abuse.

Definitional ambiguities and methodological limitations have constrained researchers' attempts to estimate the prevalence and incidence of elder abuse. Neglect—both self-neglect and neglect by others—is the most typical form of abuse, and financial exploitation of the elderly is common. Inclusion of self-neglect as an abuse category, however, remains a confound in some surveys. Rarely are the results of elder abuse lethal. Scales and interview methods for assessing abuse are varied and often inadequate, and findings across such divergent assessments are noncomparable.

The most frequent abusers of elders are family members. Relatively recent evidence suggests that intimate partners may perpetrate most abuse, although adult offspring may be almost as abusive, and in some cases more so. APS data indicate that women are the most frequent victims of elder abuse, but other types of data reveal a greater frequency of male victimization. None of the databases currently available provides sufficiently detailed information about victims and perpetrators of abuse of elders and the disabled.

Experts do not agree on the causes of elder abuse, and no single theory has proved satisfactory. Social learning may be one explanatory factor, but corroborating evidence is almost nonexistent. Social exchange theory and social interactionism propose that abusers may feel that taking care of elders is not worth the effort. Dependency and impairment of elder victims and the situational stress their care creates may provoke caregivers to abuse them. Evidence challenges this assumption, however. Research suggests instead that elder abusers have psychological and social stressors of their own (e.g., mental illness, alcoholism) that render them dependent, stressed, and unable to cope with caring for elders. Attitudes toward the elderly and disabled tend to discourage victims from reporting abuse, thus keeping the problem hidden. Many elders themselves hold counterproductive attitudes, such as "What goes on at home stays at home."

Community professionals have responded to elder abuse in a variety of ways. Social workers and law enforcement personnel are the primary guardians of the aged. In most communities, APS agencies are responsible for protecting vulnerable elders. Some APS agencies also provide oversight of disabled persons. They receive reports of abuse, investigate the charges, and determine how to intervene, if at all. APS agencies nationwide need to standardize definitions of abuse and collect and report data to national research groups.

Professionals who come into contact with elders should conduct screenings to identify cases of abuse. Social workers need to continue their training, especially in the area of working with marginalized persons, such as immigrants, GLBT elders, and the

disabled. Experts highly recommend that individuals charged with elder care and supervision receive cross-training. Universities need to offer more training in gerontology and more courses in the social sciences that include information about elder abuse.

During the past decade, elder abuse has gained increasing recognition as a legal and social problem. Legislators are beginning to strengthen laws against elder abuse and to demand greater compliance with regulations intended to protect elders in nursing homes. Ending Medicare and Medicaid fraud should be a national priority. In 42 of the 50 states, laws require certain professionals to report elder abuse either to police or to social service agencies, but not all mandated reporters comply. Attorneys have been comparatively active in providing services to elders (e.g., guardianship matters), but more advocacy seems necessary. Attorneys should routinely screen their elder clients for financial abuse and attempt to set up legal documents that protect them from exploitation.

In the past, medical personnel have been insufficiently active in identifying and referring abused elders for treatment, but today they are currently expanding efforts to comply with mandatory screening and reporting laws. Medical schools desperately need to revamp their curricula to incorporate all areas of family violence, including elder abuse.

Access to shelters is very limited and inadequate for older and disabled abuse victims. Establishment of special shelters with appropriate services for abused and disabled elders should be a high priority. Such shelters need to be user-friendly in all ways, including physical accessibility. Enhanced funding is necessary for shelters to meet these goals.

Probably the most innovative approach to intervening in elder abuse is the organization of community teams composed of professionals from multiple disciplines. Such multidisciplinary teams charged with addressing elder abuse often include social workers, law enforcement personnel, attorneys, banking personnel, health care workers, domestic violence program staff, and others who might fruitfully share experiences and work toward protecting elders. After identifying elders at risk, these teams try to furnish various types of interventions, such as homemaker services, counseling, and victim relocation.

Professionals need much more training to be able to assist abused elders and disabled adults. Elder specialists are spearheading new programs to help meet the needs of this population. Working with elder caregivers to educate them and give them support may be an effective way to reduce elder abuse. Legislators, law enforcement personnel, advocates, nursing home operators, and society as a whole must do much more to protect elders cared for in nursing homes. The current state of nursing home care in the United States is a national disgrace.

Increasingly, police departments have developed expertise in recognizing and pursuing abusers of elderly and disabled persons, and in collaborating with social workers to intervene in such cases. Police agencies cannot meet the needs of disabled abused adults without additional funding, however. They need more training and equipment to execute their societal role.

Finally, family violence researchers must broaden their scope to include scrutiny of elder abuse problems. Adopting uniform definitions is only the beginning. Improving data collection in order to standardize surveys is crucial. Just as interdisciplinary teams of practitioners are imperative, so are interdisciplinary teams of researchers. Researchers need to identify risk and protective factors for elder abuse. As in other subareas of family violence, authorities need to focus more attention on the prevention of elder abuse. Those involved in protecting elders need to follow the recent recommendations of the National Center for Injury Prevention and Control.

DISCUSSION QUESTIONS

1. What is elder self-neglect? What constitutes financial exploitation of elders? Who is responsible for elders who neglect themselves?

2. What are some of the forms of abuse that appear to be unique to disabled persons?

3. Which individuals are most likely to abuse or murder elders?

4. How is caregiver stress related to elder abuse?

5. Should society accept sexuality among elderly and disabled persons?

6. How do different societies around the world view elder abuse?

7. What factors impede effective criminal justice responses (police, prosecutors, judiciary) to elder abuse and abuse of disabled persons?

8. What elder abuse problems and responses occur in nursing homes in the United States?

9. Why do you think various agencies, professional groups, and private organizations concerned with elder abuse are collaborating more frequently today than they have in the past?

10. What innovative ideas do you have about special programs that might diminish elder abuse?

RECOMMENDED READING

Brandl, B., & Cook-Daniels, L. (2002). *Domestic abuse in later life.* Washington, DC: National Resource Center on Domestic Violence. Available from http://www.vaw.umn.edu/documents/vawnet/arlaterlife/arlaterlife.pdf

Baumhover, L. A., & Beall, S. C. (1996). *Abuse, neglect, and exploitation of older persons.* Baltimore: Health Professions Press.

Cahill, S., & Smith, K. (2002). Policy issues affecting lesbian, gay, bisexual, and transgender people in retirement. *Generations, 26*(2), 49–54.

Erwin, P. E. (2000). *Intimate and caregiver violence against women with disabilities.* Minneapolis: Battered Women's Justice Project.

Jackson, V. R. (1996). *The abusive elder: Service considerations.* Binghamton, NY: Haworth.

Klaus, P. A. (2000). *Crimes against persons age 65 or older, 1992-97* (NCJ Publication No. 176352). Washington, DC: U.S. Bureau of Justice Statistics.

National Council on Aging. (n.d.). *Healthy aging: A good investment—Exemplary programs for senior centers and other facilities.* Available from http://www.ncoa.org/attachments/healthy_living.pdf

Tobin, S. S. (2000). *Preservation of the self in the oldest years: With implications for practitioners.* New York: Springer.

Victimization of the Elderly and Disabled (newsletter; J. B. M. Otto, Ed.). Civic Research Institute, Kingston, NJ.

Wolf, R. S., & Pillemer, K. A. (1989). *Helping elderly victims: The reality of elder abuse.* New York: Columbia University Press.

13

WHAT CAN I DO TO HELP?

As we discussed in this volume's opening chapter, societal reactions play a significant role in determining which social conditions come to be seen as social problems. If interest groups and claims-makers are successful in making their case that a particular condition is unacceptable, society more generally comes to recognize that condition as a problem.

For the most part in this book we have tried to approach our subject matter as objective and empirical social scientists, and we have avoided openly engaging in claims-making. Although we have not always succeeded, with our summaries reflecting our biases from time to time, our intent has been to remain objective in our interpretation of the social *science* relating to family violence.

The tone of this final chapter, however, is somewhat different. We believe it is fitting to conclude this book with some of our *opinions* about what you, the reader, can do to help prevent family violence. Indeed, in this chapter we intend to engage in a little claims-making ourselves. Although we maintain that the suggestions we offer in this chapter are empirically grounded, we also want to acknowledge that they are influenced by our opinions. We are convinced of the soundness of our recommendations, but we retain the humility to recognize that we may not know the most effective methods for ending family violence.

CONDEMNING CULTURAL ACCEPTANCE OF VIOLENCE

One does not have to observe many American movies, cartoons, sporting events, music videos, or video games

to see that physical violence is acceptable, and that violence sells. It seems that people in this culture are, to some degree at least, entertained by violence. Equally clear is that most Americans believe a certain amount of violence in real life is inevitable and necessary. This is especially true in the family, where pushing and hitting are tolerated, and in some cases encouraged.

For social scientists, several interesting empirical questions evolve out of these observations. What are the effects of the cultural love affair with "make-believe" violence? Do violent TV programs, movies, song lyrics, and video games have any effects on rates of family violence? Likewise, does acceptance of any level of violence within the family have any effects on more serious family violence and societal violence? Many observers argue that "normative" violence has a *spillover effect,* in that it contributes to criminal violence rates in society at large and in families (Tolan & Guerra, 1998). Indeed, there is considerable agreement, at least on a theoretical level, that "violence begets violence." That is, societal acceptance and glorification of violence—everything from violent video games to corporal punishment—might potentially serve to increase the level of violence in society. At the very least, one could reasonably argue that aggression and violence in the home mirror society's tolerance for violence.

The Media and Violence

The hypothesis that media violence has detrimental effects is hotly debated and widely discussed. A thorough review of the research literature on this topic is well beyond the scope of this book, but it seems reasonable to consider briefly here the possible implications of media violence for the family. On the one hand, explanations of family violence that reduce the source of the problem to the presence of violence in the media clearly oversimplify a complex issue. However, as research evidence grows concerning the negative effects of violence in the media, the possible causal significance becomes more difficult to ignore (Comstock & Strasburger, 1990; Huesmann, Moise-Titus, & Podolski, 2003).

Perhaps the best way to illustrate the potential negative effects of violent media content is to consider two contemporary examples, both of which have received considerable attention from both the popular press and scholars. In the video game Grand Theft Auto: Vice City, players get points for having sex with a prostitute and additional points for beating her to death. The National Institute on Media and the Family, a watchdog organization, has criticized the game, as has Senator Joseph Lieberman. Lieberman and other critics of the video game industry have noted that it is especially alarming that women are increasingly becoming the targets of choice in violent games (Frommer, 2002).

The lyrics of popular rap artist Eminem provide a second illustration. Eminem has been widely criticized for the antihomosexual and antiwoman themes of some of his songs, and he has become one of the most controversial figures in the already controversial rap music world. Some of his lyrics are, in our opinion, truly shocking. For example, in the song "Kim," which appears on *The Marshall Mathers LP*, Eminem expresses his anger about his wife's infidelity by detailing his plans to beat her and kill her.

He talks about beating the s_ _ _ out of her and how she needs to shut the f_ _ _ up and get the punishment she deserves. In perhaps the most disturbing line in the song he tells of his plans to take her for a car ride. His prediction that they will be back soon but that she will be in the trunk seems to refer to his intention to kill her. The song concludes with the words "Now bleed, bitch bleed," repeated numerous times.

Both of the above examples of violence in popular media move beyond the mere glorification of violence. They are offensive and, we strongly believe, simply wrong. Clearly, however, the culture as a whole has chosen *not* to condemn Grand Theft Auto, Eminem, or any of a number of other songs, games, and movies that many might deem unacceptable. *The Marshall Mathers LP* sold 1.76 million copies in its first week of release, a clear indication that this culture does not condemn its content.

What does playing Grand Theft Auto or listening to Eminem *do* to people? The long-term effects, of course, are extremely difficult to determine empirically. Many Americans believe that Eminem has important insights to share, but what lessons do they learn from songs like "Kim"? To be sure, there is every theoretical reason to believe that content such as that described above affects individuals' attitudes and behaviors, and a growing body of empirical literature indicates that it likely does (Huesmann et al., 2003). When Comstock and Strasburger (1990) reviewed the literature on the effects of television violence in 1990, for example, they found more than 1,000 articles linking TV violence to subsequent aggressive or antisocial behavior. More recent research shows similar connections. In a recently concluded longitudinal study, Huesmann et al. (2003) found that viewing TV violence between the ages of 6 and 10 increased the probability of aggression 15 years later in their sample subjects. Wingood and her colleagues (2003) found that teenage girls who watched many hours of rap music videos were more likely to have multiple sex partners, to take drugs, to be arrested, and to hit a teacher. Some experimental research has even linked media violence to attitudes toward domestic violence. Mullin and Linz (1995) found that research subjects exposed to sexually violent films expressed less sympathy for domestic violence victims than did experimental controls.

It is important to note that most of the research on the connection between exposure to violent media and violent behavior or attitudes toward violence is correlational rather than experimental, and that most statistical correlations are minimal at best. Although experimental research on this topic is not common, most experimental studies have tended to focus on short-term attitudinal changes. The long-term behavioral effects of any single song or video game are likely negligible. Indeed, it is likely that listening to Eminem or playing Grand Theft Auto will not, by itself, substantially affect an individual's behavior. Regardless of the possible effects, however, it seems reasonable to wonder aloud whether we—as advocates of violence-free families—should support artists or games or movies that condone what we oppose. Consequently, an initial step in eliminating family violence might be to choose not to buy, play, or watch materials that condone violence, and to speak out against these materials.

A number of advocacy options are available for people interested in reducing media violence. For example, an Oregon 13-year-old's petition to get rid of violent video games in places where kids hang out (e.g., movie theaters, skating rinks) recently became part of the American Medical Association's campaign to reduce media violence (see American Medical Association, 2003). Another example is Just Think, an organization that involves teens in its campaign to encourage alternatives to violence and other mature content in media. Just Think's mission is to challenge the youth of today to think critically about the messages they are receiving from the mass media (see the Just Think Web site at http://www.justthink.org).

Questioning Culturally Accepted Family Violence

Another example of the cultural acceptance of violence in the United States is the use of corporal punishment (CP) within the family, a practice so common it goes largely unnoticed as a form of violence. In a survey of 679 college students, Graziano and Namaste (1990) found that the overwhelming majority of the respondents had been spanked in childhood (93%), believed spanking works (69%), believed parents should have the right to spank (85%), and planned to spank their own children (83%). Currently, more than 90% of American parents use CP on toddlers (Straus, 2000). Despite this overwhelming societal acceptance, social scientists and antiviolence advocates are increasingly willing to condemn the use of CP (see Finkelhor & Dziuba-Leatherman, 1994; Gershoff, 2002a; Graziano, 1994; Straus, 1994, 2000).

Experts point to several specific problems with spanking (see Box 13.1). Some note that there is an inherent contradiction between the ideal of the loving parent and the purposeful violence of CP (Graziano, 1994; Straus, 1994). In addition, CP can and often does become abuse when parents are especially angry or stressed. The distinction between a spanking and a beating is far from clear, and this definitional vagueness provides parents considerable latitude that some maintain contributes to abuse (Graziano, 1994). Perhaps most significant of all, CP is correlated with a variety of behavioral problems in children, including aggression, delinquency, low self-esteem, depression, and emotional and behavioral difficulties (Gershoff, 2002a; Straus, 1994).

Box 13.1 Ten Myths That Perpetuate Corporal Punishment

In his book *Beating the Devil Out of Them: Corporal Punishment in American Families*, Murray Straus (1994) offers the most comprehensive statement to date on the problems of spanking as a discipline technique. Straus's arguments in one of the chapters in his book, "Ten Myths That Perpetuate Corporal Punishment," are summarized below:

- *Myth 1: Spanking works better.* According to Straus, there is no evidence that spanking works better than other forms of discipline. What little evidence has been collected suggests that spanking may be less effective than nonviolent forms of discipline (e.g., timeouts or lost privileges).

- *Myth 2: Spanking is needed as a last resort.* If one accepts the argument that spanking is no better than other forms of discipline, then it stands to reason that there are no situations in which spanking is necessary. Straus argues that much of the time when parents resort to hitting, they are doing so out of their own frustration. Essentially, the parent who hits is sending a message to the child that if one is angry, hitting is justified.

- *Myth 3: Spanking is harmless.* According to Straus, hitting is so firmly entrenched in American culture that it is difficult for us to admit that it is wrong. To do so would be to admit that our parents were wrong or we have been wrong. The evidence suggests, however, that on average, spanking does more harm than good. Certainly, most people who were spanked "turn out fine," but this does not disprove the general pattern. That most smokers do not die of lung cancer does not disprove the evidence on the harmful effects of smoking.

- *Myth 4: Spanking one or two times won't cause any damage.* It is true that the evidence suggests that spanking is most harmful when it is frequent and severe. If spanking is harmful in large quantities, however, how can it be good in small quantities?

- *Myth 5: Parents can't stop spanking without training.* Eliminating spanking would be easy, Straus maintains, if society would embrace the belief that a child should never be hit. Parent educators and social scientists are reluctant to take this stand, however, because of the belief that parents cannot be expected to stop spanking unless they are presented with alternative parenting techniques. Straus maintains, however, that parents do not need training in alternative parenting techniques—they simply need to embrace the belief that spanking is wrong. Everyone agrees, for example, that directing demeaning and insulting language toward children (i.e., psychological abuse) is wrong, and no one argues that parents cannot be expected to avoid this behavior without training. "Rather than arguing that parents need to learn certain skills before they can stop using corporal punishment," Straus argues, "I believe that parents are more likely to use and cultivate those skills if they decide or are required to stop spanking" (p. 156).

- *Myth 6: If you don't spank, your children will be spoiled or will run wild.* It is true that some children who are not spanked run wild, but it is equally true that some children who are spanked run wild. The key to having well-behaved children is being a consistent disciplinarian, not being a physical disciplinarian.

- *Myth 7: Parents spank rarely or only for serious problems.* It is true that many parents perceive that they reserve spanking for serious problems, but Straus maintains that parents simply do not realize how often they hit their children. This is especially true for parents who use spanking as their primary discipline technique.

- *Myth 8: By the time a child is a teenager, parents have stopped spanking.* The national child maltreatment surveys indicate that more than half of parents of 13- and 14-year-olds had hit their children in the preceding 12 months. With teenagers, corporal punishment is more likely to be a slap to the face than a slap to the bottom.

- *Myth 9: If parents don't spank, they will verbally abuse their children.* Parents who spank frequently are actually more likely than nonspanking parents to be verbally abusive.

- *Myth 10: It is unrealistic to expect parents to never spank.* Straus is clearly frustrated by the level of acceptance of corporal punishment in the United States. He asks, Is it unrealistic to expect husbands not to hit their wives? Why is violence unacceptable between strangers but acceptable between a parent and child? Straus concedes that it is probably not feasible to criminalize spanking in this culture, but he asserts that scholars who oppose spanking can make some progress "by showing parents that spanking is dangerous, that their children will be easier to bring up if they do not spank, and by clearly saying that a child should never, under any circumstances, be spanked" (p. 162).

Straus, Sugarman, and Giles-Sims (1997) provide a good example of how researchers go about investigating the issue of corporal punishment. They interviewed more than 800 mothers of 6- to 9-year-old children and found that the greater the use of CP, the higher the level of antisocial behavior in the children 2 years later (e.g., "cheats or tells lies," "is cruel or mean to others," "is disobedient at school"). The relationships persisted even when appropriate statistical controls were added to the analysis, including the child's tendency toward antisocial behavior, the family's socioeconomic status, and emotional warmth and cognitive stimulation provided by the parents.

It is important to note that the research on the detrimental effects of spanking is far from clear, however. Critics are correct in arguing that almost all of the research to date has been correlational and that, even with statistical controls, causal inferences should be made cautiously. Also problematic is the fact that many studies have failed to distinguish appropriate CP from inappropriate CP and abuse. These critics, most notably Baumrind (1996; Baumrind, Larzelere, & Cowan, 2002) and Larzelere (1996, 2000), maintain that appropriate CP, defined as an occasional open-handed spanking of a 2- to 6-year-old, is more likely to produce positive outcomes than it is to produce negative ones.

The debate over spanking has produced interesting interactions between researchers who share the goal of promoting the well-being of children. For example, the publication of Gershoff's (2002a) widely cited report on an antispanking study in the journal *Psychological Bulletin* generated three critiques—from Baumrind et al. (2002), Holden (2002), and Parke (2002)—and a response to those critiques by Gershoff (2002b).

What, then, are we to conclude about CP? We acknowledge that the data do not support a "blanket injunction against spanking" (Baumrind et al., 2002, p. 581), and we therefore stop short of suggesting that here. At the same time, however, the correlations between CP and a variety of behavioral and psychological problems are difficult to explain away, as are the correlations between CP and abuse. CP is, arguably, inconsistent with the goal of a violence-free society. It stands to reason that a society that hits less, abuses less. In the absence of compelling evidence that CP is especially helpful, therefore, should society not err on the side of caution and discourage parents from hitting their children?

The same concerns lead us to argue against the acceptance of physical aggression in other family interactions, such as those between siblings. Parents often seem to accept a certain level of violence between siblings as something that "just happens" and that they cannot do much about. Perhaps minor and infrequent hitting between siblings produces no measurable harmful effects, but surely such violence produces nothing positive either. Research findings support the conclusion that hitting within the family, whether it be between siblings, between spouses, or between parent and child, is likely to result in more harm than good. Given this conclusion, physical aggression seems like a consistent and reasonable place to draw a line: *In this relationship, in this family, we do not hit.*

There are signs that increasing numbers of Americans are listening to criticisms of CP, because the trend is for fewer and fewer parents to spank their children (Daro, 1999). Most states have banned CP in the public schools, and the American Academy of Pediatrics has taken a stand against CP. Although in North America we are nowhere near to criminalizing spanking, as some Scandinavian countries have done (Straus, 2000), the logic of using CP is increasingly being questioned. The chances are good that your grandparents were spanked more than your parents were, and that your parents were spanked more than you were. What about your children? Perhaps they will not be spanked at all.

ADVOCATING FOR A PUBLIC POLICY COMMITMENT TO THE PREVENTION OF FAMILY VIOLENCE

It is commonly argued that the powerlessness of children contributes to violence against them, because children lack the "resources to inflict costs on their attackers" (Gelles, 1983, p. 159). To some degree, the same argument holds for vulnerable teens and adults as well. Powerlessness equals vulnerability. Ultimately, society has a responsibility to protect adults and children from family violence, both by intervening in cases of abuse and by preventing such violence in the first place. The more a society values families, the less it will tolerate victimization within the family and the more actively it will seek to protect vulnerable family members.

Given that the policy commitments discussed in this section are macro in scope, it may be difficult to see exactly how they fit into this chapter's stated aim of suggesting how you can help to alleviate the problem of family violence. We believe that concerned citizens can help to turn the policy goals outlined below into reality in any number of ways. You can educate colleagues, friends, family members, political representatives, and members of your community about the need for policy commitments to family protection by writing letters to your local, state, and federal representatives, or by visiting their offices; by writing opinion pieces for your local newspapers; by calling in to radio talk shows; and by joining organizations committed to family protection. Think about the role you can play in family protection as you read the following.

Increasing Offender Costs

Although the costs to offenders have risen dramatically in recent years, many argue that family violence remains one of the least costly crimes in the United States. Research suggests that less than 10% of all domestic assaults, for example, are reported to police. This pattern holds even for cases involving serious injury. All too often, police officers approach a domestic violence call with the intent of "handling the situation" rather than enforcing the law and protecting victims (see Buzawa & Buzawa, 2003).

The social costs to the perpetrators of family violence are sometimes quite low as well. Although there is considerable social stigma attached to designations such as *child molester, child abuser,* and *wife beater,* many family abusers somehow manage to avoid these stigmatizing labels (see Greenfeld, 1996). One interesting example of the limited social costs incurred by some abusers is the case of O.J. Simpson. In 1995, former football star O.J. Simpson was acquitted of the murder of his ex-wife, Nicole, and her friend Ron Goldman, in what was probably the most widely publicized trial in the history of the American justice system. One interesting aspect of the case is that prior to Simpson's trial, few had heard about the history of violence between Nicole and O.J. There was no public outcry or societal condemnation when Simpson pleaded no contest to spousal assault in 1989. He was not viewed, at least by most Americans, as a "wife beater." NBC, the television network that hired Simpson as a football analyst in July 1989, apparently did not worry that the abuse conviction tarnished Simpson's image. Rental car company Hertz, for which Simpson had been a spokesman for many years, was also unperturbed; a spokesperson dismissed the assault as a private issue between the couple. Reporters for *Sports Illustrated* later quoted a former employee at NBC Sports as saying, "People at NBC Sports used to always remark about the beating, shaking their heads and saying, 'Here's a man who used to beat his wife and none of America cares or remembers'" (in Lieber & Steptoe, 1994, p. 20).

Would society's reaction toward O.J. Simpson have been different had he been accused of possessing marijuana, of using racial slurs, or of assaulting another man's wife? Is Americans' tolerance of Simpson's violence indicative of societal tolerance toward domestic violence more generally? From a deterrence perspective, of course, it is clear that a society that refuses to tolerate a behavior is likely to produce fewer people who engage in the behavior. Therefore, as American society increasingly condemns violence in the family and imposes sanctions on violent family offenders, the cumulative effect should be less violence in the family.

Financially Committing to Family Protection

Discussions of a public policy commitment to the prevention of family violence often turn to the invariably controversial question of funding. Some observers believe that the federal role in child protection should be expanded, others feel the individual states should assume primary responsibility, and still others feel the problem would best be addressed by the private sector. Wherever responsibility ultimately lies, one could reasonably argue that the United States has not fully committed financially to family protection. Public awareness of family violence and the passage of mandatory reporting laws have led to increases in reporting of all forms of family violence at a time when funding for many programs has been reduced. In California, for example, resources for adult protective services declined by 35% during the 1990s. Across the country, only 20% of counties in 1998 indicated that they were able to respond to all reports made to APS agencies (Hirsch, Stratton, & Loewy, 1999).

The problem is most evident in child protective services, where system lapses that result in tragedy often receive national press attention. In 2002, Florida CPS officials struggled to explain why they ignored calls from concerned neighbors who reported that 2-year-old Alfredo Montez was a victim of abuse. When Alfredo turned up dead, beaten by his babysitter for soiling his pants, the caseworker who had been assigned to the case falsified the records to indicate that she had recently visited the child and that he seemed happy (Padgett, 2002). In another recent case, 7-year-old Faheem Williams died of starvation after being locked in a basement with his two brothers (who were themselves near death when they were rescued). When this story appeared in the news, a shocked country wondered how New Jersey's Department of Youth and Family Services could ignore repeated reports that the children were being abused. In the aftermath of this particular tragedy, the New Jersey department confessed to having lost track of more than 100 abused children as well as failing to investigate 300 reports. Michigan's CPS agency has admitted losing track of more than 300 abused and neglected children, and Florida's has acknowledged that over a 5-year period, 37 children known to CPS authorities died from child abuse–related causes (Smalley & Braiker, 2003).

Officials are likely too quick to blame lack of money and high caseloads when the child protection system fails. Tight budgets are a convenient scapegoat, but lack of funds is not the only reason child victims sometimes fall through the cracks. In the most tragic and most highly publicized cases, in fact, caseworker error is usually the most immediate reason for the system's failure (Jones & Kaufman, 2003). At the same time, however, the states' financial neglect of their CPS systems is difficult to ignore. The caseworker in the Florida case of Alfredo Montez, for example, had a caseload of 50 children and made an annual salary of only $28,000. In New Jersey, union records for the caseworker assigned to Faheem Williams indicated that during some periods she had as many as 100 cases. Current and former caseworkers in the New Jersey office where she worked complained that they were under tremendous pressure to close investigations and reduce caseloads (Kaufman & Kocieniewski, 2003). Nationally, CPS worker caseload averages are closer to 20 families and 25–30 children, but even caseloads of this size can sometimes be difficult to manage (Cyphers, 2001).

The flaws in our child protective system suggest that we Americans do not value family protection as we should. A brief examination of the dependency court (or family court) system will help to illustrate this point. Dependency courts are charged with deciding the fates of victims of child abuse and neglect—a very important task indeed. Yet, within the larger legal system, people who work in dependency courts are treated with general a lack of respect. The salaries are low and the work is difficult—sometimes overwhelming. No doubt many who pursue careers in the dependency courts do so out of concern for children, but sometimes these courts are viewed as a dumping ground for professionals who have few other options.

The problem, of course, is that there are not enough big hearts to go around, and even those with big hearts who set out to help alleviate the problem of family violence can grow disillusioned with the social service and legal systems, overwhelmed by the human tragedy they see, and burned out. We see it in our students all the time. Their hearts tell them that they want to make a difference in the world, but given the reality of workload, stress, and dealing with tragedy, combined with low salaries and low prestige, it is difficult for them to commit to working in social services. Who can blame them? After all, they have student loans to repay, families to raise, homes to purchase.

Ultimately, it is a question of what society chooses to value. When it comes to protecting families, as attorney Aron Laub (1996) argues, "you get what you pay for" (see Box 13.2). An informal browse through the Internet social service job placement site socialservice.com suggests that the salaries for entry-level positions requiring bachelor's and master's degrees in family violence–related areas rarely exceed $30,000. The American Public Human Services Association recently conducted a national survey of the child welfare workforce and found that the average salary for a CPS worker is only $33,000, with an average minimum of $27,000 and average maximum of $45,000 (Cyphers, 2001). Given that CPS workers are highly

---

Box 13.2 You Get What You Pay For

Perspective on Child Protection; Punishment by Public Penury

Aron Laub

You get what you pay for. This maxim of the marketplace is as true for government services as it is for the purchase of private-sector housing, transportation, clothing and food.

Contrary to what is currently passing for wisdom, the federal mandate for family reunification is not the cause of failures in child protection services. The true problem, the overwhelming problem, is the refusal on the part of the public to pay for the services it wants in proportion to the gargantuan size of the needs being served.

I speak from experience with just one element of the child protection system: juvenile dependency court. In California, this branch of the Superior Court oversees the provision of government services to families in which there has been child abuse. The goal in dependency court is to determine if an allegation of abuse is true, and, where it is true, to protect the child by forcing the parents to become involved in psychological counseling, parenting education classes or drug and alcohol rehabilitation programs. Often the child is separated from the parents until they have shown through their actions that the child will not be at risk if returned. If this can be shown, then the "reunification" of the family is mandated by law.

It is routine for an attorney who has worked in dependency court for a couple of years to have 300 cases. If you start with 52 weeks and subtract two weeks for sick leave, three weeks for vacation and 10 days for holidays, then multiply the remainder by 40 hours, you get 1,800 work hours per year. This allows an attorney who wastes not one minute of each eight-hour day to give six hours of effort to each case per year. If the attorney doubles his efforts and works 80 hours a week, then his cases will get 12 hours of service a year.

In that 12 hours of service, the attorney must meet with his child client, make court appearances, make and receive phone calls, write and read letters, read reports, do legal research, draft motions and petitions, interview witnesses and visit the child's home in order to view the family setting. So even doubling the workweek, giving 300 clients the service they want and deserve is humanly impossible. Each child becomes a file in a pile.

Everyone working in the dependency system is drowning. I have represented children, parents and foster parents. Few have ever received the service and respect they needed and deserved from social workers. When I first started doing this work, I wondered if the hostility that social workers so often show toward the families they are supposed to serve was an expression of some perverse personality trait common to those who choose the profession. It's not, of course. Well-intentioned, underpaid people who want to help others and who are forced to confront crisis after crisis without ever having the time needed to effectively perform their helping function eventually resent those whose demanding needs can never be met.

Do we really want to help these abused children? Government-supported child care, jobs and education for low income parents would be the most effective way to decrease the number of child abuse cases. But the public does not appear to want to make that kind of investment.

If we will not pay for prevention and must limit our spending to "protecting" children who have already been abused, then our dependency court system needs enough social workers and lawyers to do the job. This, too, will cost a lot more money than we are currently spending. Tax money. Our money. We will get only what we pay for.

SOURCE: Laub, A. (1996, February 1). Perspective on child protection; Punishment by public penury; Overwhelming and worsening caseloads in dependency court ensure that victims of abuse won't get adequate help. *Los Angeles Times*, p. 9. Reprinted with permission.

NOTE: Aron Laub is currently a criminal defense attorney in Los Angeles. Citing burnout, Mr. Laub left the dependency court shortly after this editorial was published in the *Los Angeles Times*. He remains familiar with the child protection system and believes that everything he wrote in 1996 is still true today.

educated and perform extremely stressful and important work, they are unquestionably underpaid.

Addressing Social Problems That Contribute to Family Violence

Primary prevention of family violence probably begins with an emphasis on the various social ills directly or indirectly associated with such violence. Poverty, unemployment, inadequate housing, births out of wedlock, and single-parent households are all statistically correlated with family violence, and a societal commitment to eliminating these problems would be, at least indirectly, a commitment to eliminating family violence (Willis & Silovsky, 1998). This connection, however, is lost on many. As Melton (2002) observes, although poverty and neighborhood disintegration are the two most powerful predictors of family violence, "authorities have seemed intent on maintaining ignorance of this phenomenon" (p. 577).

According to Daro and Donnelly (2002), the recognition that individual, family, and social environments are interconnected represents a "new frontier" in family violence prevention. This new frontier may begin with the neighborhood. Families that are socially connected and live in supportive communities are less likely to be abusive. A strongly integrated community is more likely to notice family violence, has the potential to influence attitudes toward family violence, and is capable of helping vulnerable families. From this perspective, anything that contributes to connectedness between the community and the family is potentially beneficial. When parks, schools, and churches are strong and poverty and unemployment rates are low, family violence rates should be low.

Committing to Primary Prevention

The most serious shortcoming of the American system of intervention on behalf of children is that it depends on a process of reporting and response that has punitive connotations and requires the dedication of massive resources to the investigation of allegations. State and county child welfare programs are not designed to get immediate help to families based on the families' voluntary requests for assistance. As a result, it is far easier for someone to get action from the system by reporting a neighbor for child abuse than by requesting help to prevent abuse in his or her own home. If the nation ultimately is to reduce the costs, in dollars and personnel, of investigating reports of family violence, more resources must be allocated to the establishment of a system that offers voluntary, nonpunitive access to help (U.S. Advisory Board on Child Abuse and Neglect, as cited in Melton, 2002, p. 571).

As Melton and Barry (1994) point out, "The system responds to allegations, not to needs" (p. 5). The police, child protective services, adult protective services, the dependency court system, and other social service agencies assigned the task of protecting families currently "investigate," "substantiate," "collect evidence," prosecute suspected offenders, and remove children from abusive homes, but they are typically not in the position to *help*. CPS agencies, for example, are supposed to protect children *and* provide services for families. Indeed, whenever possible, they are supposed to provide sufficient support and services to preserve family units. Yet increasing demands for services, insufficient staff, and excessive caseloads have transformed CPS agencies from social service providers to investigative agencies that respond primarily to cases of "imminent danger" (Hewitt, 1998; Thomas, 1998). The primary "service" that CPS workers provide is that of foster care placement for children who need to be removed from their homes temporarily. APS agencies are also understaffed and poorly funded, and so are often in no position to provide the support that many victims and vulnerable families in need. Patricia Schene (1996), who served as director of the Children's

Division of the American Humane Association for 17 years, sums up the problem this way:

> There are relatively few resources available for improving family functioning, treating the multiple service needs of abused and neglected children, and providing concrete assistance with housing, medical care, food, and other necessities, and there is almost no way for public social services to provide preventative or early intervention services to strengthen families before abuse or neglect takes hold. (p. 395)

Given the history of indifference to family violence, the societal focus on recognition and intervention is understandable. However, according to Gary Melton (2002), who served for 20 years on the board of the now defunct U.S. Advisory Board on Child Abuse and Neglect, because of the success of the mandatory reporting movement, "case finding is no longer the central problem" (p. 572). Melton maintains that the time has come for a new focus on primary prevention: "Fundamentally, a system that seldom results in delivery of services other than investigation—if indeed that can be described as a service—cannot be expected to improve victims' well-being" (p. 578).

The transformation of the system might begin with the recognition that family maltreatment is different from family violence (see Box 1.1 in Chapter 1). Many families guilty of maltreatment, defined as minimal physical, psychological, or sexual endangerment, may need support and training rather than punishment. Family violence, on the other hand, may require protection of victims and punishment of perpetrators (Emery & Laumann-Billings, 1998). Some U.S. states, conscious of these distinctions, have moved to dual-track systems that maintain mandatory reporting requirements but provide assessment and support responses rather than investigative responses for non-criminal cases (Melton, 2002).

From 1994 to 1997, Harvard University annually convened a group of child welfare professionals to consider models for redesigning the child protection system in the United States. These experts concluded that CPS cannot by itself be expected to protect children *and* provide services for families. These dual goals can be accomplished only through alliances of a variety of community partners, which must assume an active role in implementing programs to strengthen families and prevent child abuse (Thomas, 1998).

There is reason to be optimistic that a commitment to social services could prove fruitful in alleviating the problem of family violence. The success of home visitation programs such as the Prenatal/Early Infancy Project (e.g., Olds, 1997) and Hawaii's Healthy Start Program (Daro, McCurdy, & Harding, 1998) makes it clear that social service programs can work. In 1991, the U.S. Advisory Board on Child Abuse and Neglect acknowledged the potential of home visitation programs when it recommended universal home visitation services to vulnerable families. This recommendation resulted in the Healthy Families America initiative, which now serves families in more than 400 communities nationwide (Melton, 2002). Bringing such programs to every at-risk family in the country, however, is a huge task and will require a commitment to family protection that is unprecedented.

It is important to note that, although many proposed social service programs focus specifically on child maltreatment, a societal commitment to such programs would likely affect the rates of family violence of all kinds. As we have emphasized throughout this book, the same risk factors that predict child maltreatment often predict other forms of family violence as well, thus reduction in one form of family violence would likely mean a reduction in other forms. Programs that teach parents the skills they need to parent nonviolently would also encourage them to be nonviolent toward one another and toward their aging parents. Such programs would also likely lower parents' tolerance for violence in their children. Children raised in supportive and nonviolent environments would be less likely to be violent with siblings, in dating relationships, and with their own children when they become parents.

JOINING, GIVING, AND VOLUNTEERING

Surveys suggest that approximately one-half of all Americans engage in some type of volunteer work (Eckstein, 2001). Although this rate is high, at least in comparison with the rates in many other countries, volunteerism (measured in terms of both time and money) has declined significantly in the United States since 1960. Putnam (2000) suggests that the decline can be attributed to the fact that Americans have become less invested and involved in group associations. As group membership rates have declined, volunteerism has become more individualized and, ultimately, more sporadic. According to Eckstein (2001), "Giving, volunteering and joining are mutually reinforcing" (p. 830). Giving of our money and our

time often begins when we join an organization. Our voluntary associations provide us with networks of like-minded peers who encourage our giving, present us with opportunities to serve others, and provide us with the training we need to serve others. One of the ways we can serve families in need, therefore, is by becoming involved in organizations that are committed to serving families in need. Numerous national, state, and local organizations, including many faith communities, are committed to alleviating the problem of family violence.

Investing in the Life of a Child

One of the ways an individual can become personally involved in child protection is by becoming a volunteer advocate for children in family court. Such specialists—known variously as court-appointed special advocates (CASA volunteers), guardians ad litem, and child advocates—are appointed by the courts to represent children in child abuse and neglect cases. The sole purpose of a CASA volunteer is to represent the interests of the child to the court and to stand by the child until he or she is placed in a safe and nurturing home. Typically, a CASA volunteer researches a case by reviewing documents and interviewing the child, parents, teachers, and anyone else who might have information on the child. The volunteer then presents the court with a written report that outlines the actions that he or she feels will be in the best interests of the child. After the court has made a decision in the case, the CASA volunteer continues to monitor the progress of the child, making sure that the child receives the services mandated by the court. Court procedures can be very intimidating for a child, and often the CASA volunteer is the only constant in the child's life as he or she moves through the court system. (For more information, see the National CASA Association Web site at http://www.nationalcasa.org.)

Another way to become involved in helping children in need is by providing foster care. Each state has its own rules for foster parents, but typically foster parents must be at least 21 years old, must clear a variety of background checks, and must show that they can provide a stable home setting for the children in their care. The need for foster parents varies dramatically across regions because foster care systems are organized locally. Some counties have sufficient foster parents to meet their needs, but the majority struggle to find and retain competent foster parents, for several reasons. First, foster parenting can be difficult and emotionally draining work (see Box 13.3). Becoming a foster parent means being willing to offer your home and heart to a child who will be with you only temporarily. A foster parent might be asked to invest in the process of reunifying families, perhaps even working with needy parents. The monthly stipends that foster parents receive per child range from $400 to $600—not much financial incentive to take on such difficult work. A final factor in current foster parent shortages is that women, who make up the majority of foster parents, are entering the workforce in increasing numbers (Saillant & Dirmann, 2002).

More than 550,000 children are in foster care at any given time in the United States. In 2000, the mean age of foster children was 10, and the case goal in 43% of cases was reunification with parent(s) or principal caretaker(s). Of the children who left foster care in 2000, 57% were returned to parent(s) or primary caretaker(s) and 17% were adopted (other outcomes included living with another relative, emancipation, and guardianship). The mean number of months in care was 23, and the median was 12. One-half were in foster care for less than a year, and 19% for less than a month; 10% were in foster care for 5 years or more (U.S. Department of Health and Human Services, 2002a).

Box 13.3 Advice From a Foster Parent

So You Want to Be a Foster Parent?

Greg Olson

Becoming a foster parent will change your life-style. Maybe not at first, but as months and years pass you will be affected. Foster care will affect you and your family in many areas (extended family, community involvement, your personal activities, and those of your children). The changes, like life around us, range from very good to very negative.

You will find that your relatives fit into two categories when you inform them that you are going to take in a foster child. Either they proclaim you the saints of the family or just plain nuts. Whichever side of the discussion they voice their opinion on, your choice to take in foster children puts them in various dilemmas. Grandparents suffer through a multitude of questions. Besides the normal dilemma of whether to include the foster child on their Christmas list, I had a grandparent question whether they should be included in their will. If you only take one or two foster children into your home in your lifetime those questions may need an honest answer, but after ten or more foster children the questions become moot.

Foster parents are trained to respect the privacy of the foster child and their families. Relatives don't always understand why you can't tell them about their new niece or nephew. Their bewilderment only gets worse when the child acts out in an inappropriate manner and you can't justify the behavior because the past history falls into the data privacy area. For some families this leads to selective invitations, where only certain individuals, or only adults, are invited over. What do you do in those special circumstances? Cousins will get married, families will want a family portrait, what is the best way to handle special circumstances? No matter how many or what types of children you care for, the one thing that relatives will come to realize is that you are a very busy person. As the years pass, and you have to react to foster care emergency after emergency, you may find that the visits and the invitations become few and far between.

The community, your neighbors, are not much different. There may be a few who would like to blame you for every wrong that happens in the neighborhood because you brought those kids into your home. Most, though, think it's wonderful that you can do what you do, just keep them in your yard.

Our police officers know us by name and most of the teachers at the school refer to us as "that house." The ones we work with on a regular basis are supportive and complimentary, the rest just raise their eyebrows when we pass them on the street. Church members work hard to include the children in activities, but never invite the whole family over for dinner (if someone did once, it never happened twice). Foster families tend to be larger than the norm, and size alone can cause discomfort, without adding the abnormal behavior factor. Foster families are very visible to the community and can add additional pressures, whether real or imaginary. As the adult of the foster family, you will constantly find yourself surrounded by people, and yet feel very much alone.

Being a foster parent will develop your skills as an independent social director, therapist, and taxi service, to mention just a few. Activities that you took for granted as a member of the adult world will be infringed upon by the children you invited into your home. If you are physically active and participating in athletic pursuits, your activities may change when the teenager you accept into your home is too paranoid to ride a bike, skate, or go in a boat. The activities of the whole family will be tailored to fit the least adaptable member. Need for attention or preconceived fears will stimulate pseudo injuries or refusals to participate. Your social outings will be disrupted by unruly children or true emergencies (you will have more than you could imagine). The foster children you choose to bring into your home will have all the normal problems, but accelerated to an abnormal pace.

You will be on call 24 hours a day, seven days a week. The safety and welfare of the foster children will be a constant priority. Your birth children will grow up with "the street in their home." They will, at a young age, be aware of the cruelties that the children of this world face. They will endure pressures at home where they were intending to find refuge. Your choice to take in foster children will either send them on the streets in rebellion or give them skills to become outstanding young adults. It is not uncommon to find your birth children very active outside the home. They will participate in the community, not only because they choose to, but because it is a release from the constant pressure foster care places on them. Your choice to accept a foster child into your home will change your birth child for life. When you are old, no one will remember what you did. Except for:

- A child, now an adult, who has a life with a little more purpose and a lot more love.
- A child who would never have experienced an alternate "safe family" except that you chose to be a foster parent.
- A child who has a job and pays the bills because you taught them how to work.
- A child who completed school because you ensured that the homework was done.
- A child who treats their family with respect because you modeled dignity.

Thank you, from all of them!

Greg Olson, Minnesota Foster Parent

SOURCE: Reprinted with the permission of Greg Olson and the National Foster Parent Association.

During the mid-1990s, President Clinton and members of Congress became concerned about reports that children were being left in foster care for years or were being returned to unsafe family situations. The legislative result of their concerns, the Adoption and Safe Families Act (ASFA) of 1997, represents a bipartisan attempt to promote the goal of settling abused and neglected children in permanent homes. Among other things, the ASFA reaffirmed the federal government's role in protecting children, placing limits on efforts to reunite families and mandating that permanency decisions be made within 12 months. The act provides tax incentives to adoptive parents and financial incentives to states to move children who have been in long-term foster care into permanent homes.

Largely as a result of ASFA initiatives and goals, each year more and more children are adopted. Even so, many foster children who cannot return to their families are currently awaiting permanent placement. According to the North American Council on Adoptable Children (n.d.), 134,000 of the more than 550,000 children in foster care will likely never be returned to their homes. Most of these children are not infants, and many have physical and developmental problems or are emotionally scarred from abuse or neglect. It takes a unique person to adopt a child victim of abuse or neglect, and many of us would not be up to the task. Perhaps you are. Is there a special needs child in your future?

Helping Adult Victims of Family Violence

A relatively easy way to help adult victims of family violence is by joining an advocacy organization. In California, for example, the Statewide California Coalition for Battered Women coordinates prevention and intervention services for victims of intimate violence throughout the state. For a nominal fee ($10 for students, $35 for nonstudents), individuals can become members and join in the advocacy effort.

Those who desire a more hands-on opportunity to be involved might want to work for shelters in their local areas. In addition to providing food and housing, some shelters for battered women provide 24-hour hotlines to handle crisis situations, support groups for victims, legal assistance (e.g., in filing protection orders), community advocacy and education, child care, parenting classes, and exchange centers (safe locations where parents can meet to deliver and pick up children in shared custody or have supervised visits with their children).

Individuals interested in helping abused adults also have court advocacy options similar to those available in work with abused children. For example, in King County, Washington, volunteers walk victims of IPV through the legal system, help victims prepare files for their cases, and attend legal hearings (see the job description of a volunteer felony domestic violence advocate provided on the county's Web site at http:// www.metrokc.gov/proatty/Volnteer/Feladv.htm). Similar kinds of programs exist for victims of sexual assault. The Sexual Assault and Domestic Violence Center in Woodland, California, for instance, offers volunteers the opportunity to support victims of sexual assault by accompanying them through law enforcement interviews and court proceedings (information is available on the Davis [California] Community Network Web site, at http://www.dcn.davis.ca.us/YoloLINK/programs/pSexualAssaulDomest-4562.html).

Those who want to help the elderly have numerous volunteer opportunities available to them. For example, the Texas Department on Aging sponsors volunteers who visit and observe the operations of care facilities for the elderly. These volunteers also provide residents and their families with information on their rights and on the procedures they should follow to ensure their rights are respected (for a job description of an advocate for the elderly, see the University of Texas at Austin's Volunteer Information Center Web site at http://www.volunteersolutions.org/ut/volunteer/opp/one_162962.html). Other programs recruit volunteers to aid elderly patients who have been abused or are in situations that might expose them to abuse (for an example of such a program, see the Web site of the Kingston and Frontenac [California] Elder Abuse Task Force at http://www.seniorabusekingston.ca).

CHAPTER SUMMARY

In this final chapter we engage in a bit of claims-making. What can be done to reduce family violence? What can we do to help? Perhaps the best place to start is by taking a stand against mass-media content that glorifies violence. Concerned citizens can choose not to support or condone violence despite the wider culture's apparent acceptance of violent materials. We can choose not to watch or to buy, and we can encourage others to do likewise. We can also choose not to condone violence in our own families. Spouses and siblings can choose not hit one another, and parents can choose not hit their children. Admittedly, the research on the effects of culturally acceptable violence, including media violence and corporal punishment, has produced findings that are far from clear. However, in debating statistics, we may miss the point. Clearly, American culture accepts the belief that spanking is necessary, to some degree, if parents want to raise their children to be disciplined and productive. We, however, question the empirical support of this assumption. Clearly, the culture also believes that violence in the media is entertaining and harmless. We question this belief.

Although it is true that the social and legal costs to perpetrators of family violence have risen significantly in recent years, it is also true that family violence often goes unnoticed and unpunished. Indeed, it is important to recognize that most of the forms of family violence discussed in this book are against the law. Many violent family offenders are criminals, and they should be treated as criminals.

It is, however, far too simple to suggest that the problem would be solved if American society only committed to criminal sanctions for perpetrators of family violence. Some families, and some violent family members, may need help more than they need punishment. Yet the social service system often seems unprepared to provide that help. The functions of the child protection system, for example, are mostly investigative and punitive. However, as numerous experts point out, finding cases of family violence is no longer the primary problem. Are we as a society willing to commit to family protection? Even a cursory look at social worker salaries and caseloads suggests that we are not.

Individuals can support the cause of family protection and help to prevent family violence in many ways. We can give of our time and money, and the opportunities for involvement are limitless. We only need to keep our eyes open, look for opportunities to advocate for families, and look for opportunities to serve.

APPENDIX A

Resources for Individuals and Organizations Addressing Family Violence

This appendix provides names and descriptions of resources for anyone concerned with issues associated with various forms of family violence. These resources provide information, services, or both for victims of family violence, perpetrators of family violence, professionals working in the field, and other individuals interested in the topic of family violence. Please note that although the street addresses, telephone numbers, and Web addresses listed for each organization were current at the time of publication, such information is subject to change. For additional information and resources related to family violence, visit the National Criminal Justice Reference Service Web site at http://www.ncjrs.org/family_violence/additional.html.

CHILD ABUSE ORGANIZATIONS

American Humane Association, American Association for Protecting Children (AAPC)
63 Inverness Dr.
East Englewood, CO 80112-5117
800-227-4645
Fax: 303-792-5333
http://www.americanhumane.org

The AAPC promotes child protection services through training, education, and consultation. It provides national statistics on child abuse issues and publishes books, working papers, fact sheets, and a quarterly magazine. It also operates the National Resource Center on Child Abuse and Neglect (a federal agency).

American Professional Society on the Abuse of Children (APSAC)
332 S. Michigan Ave., Ste. 1600
Chicago, IL 60604
312-554-0166
Fax: 312-554-0919
http://www.apsac.org

APSAC is an organization for professionals who work within the field of child maltreatment. It is committed to improving the coordination of services in the areas of prevention, treatment, and research. APSAC sponsors professional conferences and publishes a newsletter and a journal.

Child Advocacy Resources, Life's Great
22565 Broadway PMB, No. 137
1-888-88-GREAT
Fax: 1-888-89-GREAT
E-mail: orders@lifesgreat.org

This organization provides child advocacy resources and products for professionals on community outreach and awareness, parenting programs, intervention counseling, staff training, and program marketing.

Child Welfare League of America (CWLA)
440 First St. NW, Ste. 310
Washington, DC 20001-2085
202-638-2952
http://www.cwla.org

CWLA publishes a variety of books, pamphlets, videos, and bibliographies for professionals, parents, and others concerned with the welfare of children. The organization also publishes a magazine (*Children's Voice*) as well as the journal *Child Welfare.*

Crimes Against Children Research Center
126 Horton Social Science Center
University of New Hampshire
Durham, NH 03824
603-862-1888
Fax: 603-862-1122
http://www.unh.edu/ccrc

The Crimes Against Children Research Center provides research and statistics for policy makers, law enforcement personnel, child welfare practitioners, and the public about the nature of crimes against children—including abduction, homicide, rape, assault, physical violence, and sexual abuse—and the impact of such crimes.

International Society for Prevention of Child Abuse and Neglect (ISPCAN)
401 N. Michigan Ave., Ste. 2200
Chicago, IL 60611
312-644-6610, ext. 3273 and ext. 4713
Fax: 312-321-6869
http://www.ispcan.org

ISPCAN is a membership organization that provides a forum for the exchange of information on child abuse and neglect globally. Benefits include the monthly publication *Child Abuse & Neglect: The International Journal,* a newsletter, and invitation to the biennial international congress on child abuse and neglect.

Kempe National Center for the Prevention and Treatment of Child Abuse and Neglect
1205 Oneida St.
Denver, CO 80220
303-321-3963
http://www.kempecenter.org

The Kempe Center provides clinical treatment, training, research, education, and program development to prevent and treat child abuse and neglect.

National Association of Counsel for Children (NACC)
1205 Oneida St.
Denver, CO 80220
303-322-2260
http://naccchildlaw.org

NACC is an organization for lawyers and other professionals who represent children.

National Center for Missing and Exploited Children (NCMEC)
2101 Wilson Blvd., Ste. 550
Arlington, VA 22201
703-235-3900
800-843-5678
http://ojjdp.ncjrs.org/pubs/fedresources/org.html

The NCMEC, a U.S. government agency, is a clearinghouse and resource center funded by the Office of Juvenile Justice and Delinquency Prevention. It provides a number of useful publications.

National Clearinghouse on Child Abuse and Neglect (NCCAN)
U.S. Department of Health and Human Services
P.O. Box 1182
Washington, DC 20013
703-385-7565
800-394-3366

NCCAN publishes manuals for professionals involved in the child protection system to enhance community collaboration and the quality of services provided to children and families. NCCAN conducts research, collects information, and provides assistance to states and communities on child abuse issues.

National Committee to Prevent Child Abuse (NCPCA)
332 S. Michigan Ave., Ste. 1600
Chicago, IL 60604
312-663-3520
http://www.childabuse.org

The NCPCA provides many resources (e.g., educational pamphlets) including statistical survey information across the 50 states and publishes a variety of materials on child abuse, child abuse prevention, and parenting. The NCPCA also publishes *Current Trends in Child Abuse Reporting and Fatalities: An Annual Fifty State Survey.* For a free catalog describing publications, contact NCPCA, Publications Dept., P.O. Box 2866, Chicago, IL 60690, or call 800-55-NCPCA.

WOMAN ABUSE ORGANIZATIONS

Center for the Prevention of Sexual and Domestic Violence
936 N. 34th St., Ste. 200
Seattle, WA 98193
206-634-1903
http://www.cpsdv.org/Cpsdv/contact-us.htm

This group provides rape prevention education through speakers, publications, and consultation. It provides information about marital and date rape.

Center for Women's Policy Studies
1211 Connecticut Ave. NW, Ste. 312
Washington, DC 20036
202-872-1770
Fax: 202-296-8962
http://www.centerwomenpolicy.org

This center is a feminist policy research organization that promotes equality and justice for women through research, policy analysis, and advocacy in order to bring women's voices to important political debates.

Crisis Prevention Institute, Inc.
3315-k N. 124th St.
Brookfield, WI 53005
262-783-5787
Fax: 262-783-5906
http://www.crisisprevention.com

This organization offers resources on the prevention of domestic violence. It specializes in the management of disruptive and assaultive behavior.

Minnesota Coalition for Battered Women
450 N. Syndicate, Ste. 122
Saint Paul, MN 55104
612-646-6177
Fax: 612-646-1527

This organization works to improve the availability of legal services to battered women.

Statewide California Coalition for Battered Women
6308 Woodman Ave., Ste. 117
Van Nuys, CA 91401
818-787-0072
Fax: 818-787-0073
E-mail: sccbw1@aol.com

SCCBW is a coalition of advocates and agencies throughout California dedicated to stopping domestic violence. The organization acts as a clearinghouse for information and also conducts special training.

Young Women's Christian Association (YWCA)
1015 18th St. NW, Ste. 1100
Washington, DC 20036
202-467-0801
800-YWCAUS1
Fax: 202-467-0802
http://www.ywca.org

Local branches of the YWCA offer a variety of services, such as fitness programs, infant care, children's programs, food banks, and abuse counseling. Telephone the local YWCA in your area only.

MEN'S ORGANIZATIONS

Abusive Men Exploring New Directions (AMEND)
2727 Bryant St., Ste. 350
Denver, CO 80211
303-832-6363
Fax: 303-480-9661
http://amendinc.org/index.htm

AMEND provides counseling to men who have been abusive, advocates for and supports their partners and children, and provides education to the community.

EMERGE: A Men's Counseling Service on Domestic Violence
2380 Massachusetts Ave., No. 101
Cambridge, MA 02140
617-547-9879

EMERGE provides technical assistance and training to men involved in domestic violence. It also distributes related publications.

Men Overcoming Violence (MOVE)
54 Mint St., Ste. 300
San Francisco, CA 94103
415-777-4496

MOVE provides counseling for men who have been involved in domestic violence primarily as batterers. This organization serves both gay and straight males and has a sliding scale payment plan.

National Organization for Changing Men (RAVEN)
7314 Manchester, 2nd floor
St. Louis, MO 63143
314-645-2075
http://members.tripod.com/~raventeaches

RAVEN provides educational programs that help men become nonviolent, assume personal responsibility, and behave respectfully. The organization's classes and groups explore masculinity and gender, violence and abuse, nonviolence planning, emotions and anger, relationships, and parenting.

Elder Abuse Organizations

National Academy of Elder Law Attorneys (NAELA)
1604 N. Country Club Rd.
Tucson, AZ 85716
602-881-4005
Fax: 602-325-7925

This is a professional organization for attorneys concerned with improving the availability of legal services to older persons. NAELA is striving to define the area of practice, establish practice standards, and create an information network among elder law attorneys. It distributes some publications.

National Center on Elder Abuse
810 First St. NE, Ste. 500
Washington, DC 20002-4267
202-682-2470

This organization provides training and technical assistance to adult protective service and aging agencies, publishes a quarterly newsletter, and operates the Clearinghouse on Abuse and Neglect of the Elderly (CANE). It also provides an automated information search and retrieval system and conducts national research studies.

National Committee for the Prevention of Elder Abuse (NCPEA)
UCSF/Mt. Zion Center on Aging
3330 Geary Blvd., 3rd floor
San Francisco, CA 94118
202-682-4140
Fax: 415-750-4136
http://www.preventelderabuse.org

NCPEA is an association of researchers, practitioners, and educators who conduct research and educate communities and professionals to prevent abuse, neglect, and exploitation of older persons and adults with disabilities.

Domestic Violence Organizations

Center for the Prevention of Sexual and Domestic Violence
936 N. 34th St., Ste. 200
Seattle, WA 98013
206-634-1903
Fax: 206-634-0115

This educational resource center addresses issues of sexual abuse and domestic violence. The center offers workshops concerning clergy misconduct, spouse abuse, child sexual abuse, rape, and pornography. It also distributes various materials associated with sexual and domestic violence.

Domestic Abuse Intervention Project (DAIP)
206 W. Fourth St., Rm. 201
Duluth, MN 55806
218-722-2781
218-722-4134
Fax: 218-722-1545

The DAIP is an educational resource center that provides a number of programs aimed at the problem of domestic violence. One program focuses on the provision of nonviolence classes for court-ordered individuals arrested for domestic assault. A second program offers a visitation center that is used for parents' safe exchange of children in shared custody and/or supervised visits with noncustodial parents. The center also provides training and technical assistance to domestic violence programs around the world.

Family Resource Coalition (FRC)
200 S. Michigan Ave., 16th floor
Chicago, IL 60604
312-341-0900
Fax: 312-341-9361

This organization tries to strengthen family services through prevention. FRC is also a clearinghouse and provides technical assistance.

Family Violence and Sexual Assault Institute
6160 Cornerstone Ct. E.
San Diego, CA 92121
858-623-2777, ext. 416
Fax: 858-646-0761
http://www.fvsai.org

This nonprofit organization is dedicated to promoting violence-free living by disseminating information, improving professional networking, and providing technical assistance through journals, conferences, and training.

Family Violence Prevention Fund
383 Rhode Island St., Ste. 304
San Francisco, CA 94103-5133
415-252-8900
800-313-1310
Publication orders: 415-252-8089
Fax: 415-252-8991
http://endabuse.org

This nonprofit organization is concerned with domestic violence education, prevention, advocacy, and public policy reform. Its Health Resource Center on Domestic Violence publishes public health education materials and produces training and education materials.

*National Clearinghouse on Families
and Youth (NCFY)*
P.O. Box 13505
Silver Spring, MD 20911-3505
301-608-8098

The NCFY individualizes research, provides networking, and provides updates on youth initiatives.

*National Coalition Against Domestic Violence
(NCADV)*
Membership information:
P.O. Box 34103
Washington, DC 20043-4103
202-638-6388
http://www.webmerchants.com/ncadv/default.htm
To order publications:
P.O. Box 18749
Denver, CO 80218-0749
303-839-1852

This coalition works to end domestic violence against children and women. It provides technical assistance, newsletters, and publications.

*National Council to Prevent Child Abuse and Family
Violence*
1155 Connecticut Ave. NW, Ste. 400
Washington, DC 20036
202-429-6695
800-222-2000
http://www.nccafv.org

This organization is committed to assisting victims of child abuse, spouse/partner abuse, and elder abuse and to preventing family violence through public awareness, education, and program development.

National Domestic Violence Hotline
800-799-7233

This telephone number responds in all 50 states to emergency crisis calls from battered individuals and others involved in family violence (translators are available). It also provides referrals to local batterer programs.

National Resource Center on Domestic Violence (NRC)
6400 Flank Dr., Ste. 1300
Harrisburg, PA 17112
800-537-2238
Fax: 717-545-9456
http://www.pcadv.org

The NRC is a valuable source of information, training, and technical assistance regarding domestic violence issues. It is also a clearinghouse for domestic violence resources and statistics that may be used to enhance policies and publications.

Rape, Abuse, and Incest National Network
635-B Pennsylvania Ave. SE
Washington, DC 20003
202-544-3059
800-656-HOPE
Fax: 202-544-3556
http://www.rainn.org

This network operates a toll-free hotline and offers confidential counseling along with 24-hour support for victims of rape, incest and abuse.

OTHER ORGANIZATIONS

Girls and Boys Town
14100 Crawford St.
Boys Town, NE 68010
402-498-1300
Hotline: 800-448-3000
http://www.girlsandboystown.org/aboutus/contactus/index.asp

This organization operates a variety of services for children and families, including a residential treatment center, residential services, emergency shelter, family preservation, treatment foster care, and parenting classes. The Boys Town National Training Center offers training to child-care professionals, school districts, mental health facilities, and other organizations.

Illusion Theater
528 Hennepin Ave., Ste. 704
Minneapolis, MN 55403
612-339-4944
Fax: 612-337-8042
http://www.illusiontheater.org/contact

This organization attempts to prevent child sexual abuse through the distribution of theatrical productions addressing sexual abuse, interpersonal violence, and AIDS. It also publishes sexual abuse prevention materials, a newsletter, and a video program.

National Center for Victims of Crime
2000 M St. NW, Ste. 480
Washington, DC 20036
202-467-8700
Fax: 202-467-8701
http://www.ncvc.org/index.html

This organization's main focus is to provide crime victims and witnesses with direct assistance.

PACER Center
4826 Chicago Ave. South
Minneapolis, MN 55417
612-827-2966
http://www.ed.gov/Family/ParentCtrs/pacer.html

This center offers the Let's Prevent Abuse project, which features three puppet shows for children (grades K–4) on abuse and training for professionals who work with children (birth–12) with and without disabilities. The project also offers workshops and written materials to groups and parents' organizations about child maltreatment and the increased vulnerability of children with disabilities.

Sage Publications, Inc.
2455 Teller Rd.
Thousand Oaks, CA 91320-2218
805-499-0721
Fax: 805-499-0871
http://www.sagepub.com

This publishing company provides a catalog with key resources (e.g., textbooks and workbooks) for professionals on the subject of interpersonal violence.

VOICES in Action, Inc. (Victims of Incest Can Emerge Survivors)
P.O. Box 148309
Chicago, IL 60614
773-327-1500
Fax: 773-327-4590

VOICES in Action is an international nonprofit organization working to support and empower victims of childhood sexual abuse and to educate the public about the prevalence of incest. VOICES holds annual conferences, publishes a bimonthly newsletter, and provides referrals to self-help and therapy resources.

Young Women's Christian Association (YWCA)
624 9th St. NW
Washington, DC 20001
202-626-0700
Fax: 202-347-7381
http://www.ywcanca.org

Local branches of this organization offer a variety of services such as fitness programs, infant care, children's programs, food banks, and abuse counseling. Telephone the local YWCA in your area only.

LEGAL SERVICES

American Bar Association Center on Children and the Law
740 15th St. NW
Washington, DC 20005
202-662-1720
Fax: 202-662-1755
http://www.abanet.org/child/home.html

This group provides training and technical assistance to prosecutors handling child abuse cases. State statutes, case law, and other resources are available. Advances in law and public policy to improve the circumstances of children are a goal of this group. Publications are available.

American Bar Association IOLTA Clearinghouse
541 N. Fairbanks Ct.
Chicago, IL 60611-3314
312-988-5748

This group collects funds and distributes them for programs and for support of legal personnel in special projects.

Battered Women's Justice Project
2104 Fourth Ave. South, Ste. B
Minneapolis, MN 55404
800-903-0111, criminal justice issues,
ext. 1; civil justice issues, ext. 2; defense
issues, ext. 3.
http://www.bwjp.org

This organization studies abused women in the criminal justice system, provides information to attorneys, and advocates for battered women or others working with them.

Children's Rights, Inc.
404 Park Ave. South, 11th floor
New York, NY 10016
Fax: 212-683-4015
http://www.childrensrights.org

This national program of litigation, advocacy, and education works to ensure that when government child welfare systems must intervene in the lives of troubled families and children, they do so according to constitutional and statutory standards of fairness and due process and in accordance with reasonable professional standards.

Legal Council for the Elderly (LCE)
P.O. Box 96474
Washington, DC 20090
202-434-2152
Legal hotline: 800-424-3410

This organization is a unit of the AARP that provides technical assistance, publications, training (e.g., guardianship), and referrals (some pro bono). The hotline connects callers with an attorney who will try to resolve the issues or advise the caller where to obtain help.

National Academy of Elder Law Attorneys (NAELA)
1604 North Country Club Rd.
Tucson, AZ 85716
602-881-4005

This professional organization of attorneys is concerned with improving the availability of legal services to older persons. It is striving to define the area of practice, establish practice standards, and create an information network among elder law attorneys. It distributes some publications.

National Association of Counsel for Children (NACC)
1205 Oneida St.
Denver, CO 80220
303-322-2260

The NACC is a professional organization for lawyers and other practitioners who represent children in court. It publishes a variety of materials relating to children's legal rights and sponsors child abuse training.

National Battered Women's Law Project
275 7th Ave., Ste. 1206
New York, NY 10001
212-741-9480

This organization publishes a newsletter and serves as a clearinghouse on legal issues related to family violence.

National Battered Women's Law Project at the National Center on Women and Family Law
799 Broadway, Ste. 402
New York, NY 10003
212-741-9480
http://naccchildlaw.org

This project serves as a clearinghouse for information for legal professionals and advocates. It addresses a number of specific issues, such as child custody, and provides information about case law, model briefs, and statistics.

National Center for Prosecution of Child Abuse, American Prosecutors Research Institute
99 Canal Center Plaza, Ste. 510
Alexandria, VA 22314
703-739-0321

This institute has on-staff attorneys who offer technical assistance to attorneys and other professionals working in the field of child abuse. They also provide training and publications.

National Clearinghouse for the Defense of Battered Women
125 S. 9th St., Ste. 302
Philadelphia, PA 19107
215-351-0010
Fax: 231-351-0779

This organization provides information and resources to legal personnel and assists battered women charged with crimes. It is especially concerned with women who kill in self-defense. It publishes a newsletter and networks.

National Council of Juvenile and Family Court Judges
P.O. Box 8970
Reno, NV 89507
702-784-6012
Fax: 702-784-6628

This council represents the 9,000-plus judges in the United States who exercise jurisdiction over delinquency, abuse and neglect, divorce, custody, support, domestic violence, and similar cases. It conducts or assists in conducting training programs at its headquarters training facility, the National College of Juvenile and Family Law.

NOW Legal Defense and Educational Fund
395 Hudson St.
New York, NY 10014
212-925-6635
http://www.nowldef.org

This sister organization to the National Organization for Women focuses on litigation and education in areas of gender discrimination and related issues. It sponsors women's legal rights, among other legal issues.

Project Assist, Legal Aid of Western Missouri
1125 Grand Ave., Ste. 1900
Kansas City, MO 64106
816-474-6750

Project Assist provides legal assistance to victims of family violence. This project represents a collaboration of nonprofit organizations and government agencies, including the police department, the prosecutor's office, the court, local shelters, and community agencies that treat batterers.

Quincy District Court Domestic Violence Prevention Program
Quincy Division District Court Department
10 Granite St.
Quincy, MA 02169
617-471-1650

This program is a model of an integrated police, prosecution, and court response to family violence. A key strategy is to empower victims of domestic violence and provide them with maximum protection.

Resource Center on Domestic Violence: Child Protection and Custody, National Council of Juvenile and Family Court Judges
Family Violence Project
P.O. Box 8970
Reno, NV 89507
800-527-3223
Fax: 702-784-6160

This organization provides information and technical assistance on topics such as child abuse and neglect, the foster care system, and child custody disputes. It distributes a number of publications (e.g., model codes and court programs) to assist judges and others on family violence.

MEDICAL RESOURCES

American Academy of Pediatrics, Department C
P.O. Box 927, SW
Elk Grove Village, IL 60009-2188
708-228-5005
http://www.aap.org/default.htm

This academy publishes information on issues such as child sexual abuse, identification, and effects on victims.

American College of Obstetricians and Gynecologists
409 12th St.
Washington, DC 20024
202-638-5577
http://www.acog.com

This group provides a pamphlet about abused women patients.

American Medical Association, Department of Mental Health
515 N. State St.
Chicago, IL 60610
312-464-5066
http://www.ama-assn.org

This association of doctors provides referrals and brochures containing help for doctors treating family violence victims.

Domestic Violence Project of the American Academy of Facial Plastic and Reconstructive Surgery
1110 Vermont Ave. NW, Ste. 220
Washington, DC 20005
800-842-4546
http://www.facial-plastic-surgery.org

This group, along with the National Coalition Against Domestic Violence (202-638-6388), provides some free facial reconstructive and plastic surgery for victims of family violence.

Family Violence Prevention Fund, Health Resource Center on Domestic Violence
383 Rhode Island St., Ste. 304
San Francisco, CA 94103-5133
415-252-8900
800-595-4889
Fax: 415-252-8991
http://endabuse.org

This organization attempts to strengthen the health care response to domestic violence. It provides publications and technical assistance.

SUBSTANCE ABUSE AND SELF-HELP GROUPS

Children of Alcoholics Foundation
164 W. 74th St.
New York, NY 10023
212-595-5810, ext. 7760
http://www.coaf.org

The foundation promotes public and professional awareness of children of alcoholics' problems and develops programs and materials to break the cycle of family alcoholism.

National Clearinghouse for Alcohol and Drug Information (NCADI)
11426 Rockville Pike, Ste. 200
Rockville, MD 20852
301-468-2600
800-729-6686

NCADI is part of the Center for Substance Abuse Prevention. It provides information on research, publications, and prevention.

MISCELLANEOUS RESOURCES

National Coalition for Low-Income Housing
1012 14th St. NW, Ste. 1200
Washington, DC 20005
202-662-1530

This coalition of shelters provides temporary housing to appropriate clients when vacancies are available and also provides some help with extended housing.

RESOURCE CENTERS AND CLEARINGHOUSES (PUBLICATIONS)

American Humane Association, American Association for Protecting Children (AAPC)
63 Inverness Dr. East
Englewood, CO 80112-5117
800-227-4645
Fax: 303-792-5333
http://www.americanhumane.com

The AAPC promotes child protection services through training, education, and consultation. It provides national statistics on child abuse issues. It also operates the National Resource Center on Child Abuse and Neglect (a federal agency).

Boulder County Safehouse
835 North St.
Boulder, CO 80304
303-449-8623
http://www.bouldercountysafehouse.com

This group publishes books in English and Spanish on children and family violence. These books are especially useful to parents, teachers, and health care workers.

Clearinghouse on Child Abuse and Neglect Information
P.O. Box 1182
Washington, DC 20012
703-385-7565
800-394-3366

This clearinghouse offers annotated bibliographies and can provide statistics.

Family Resource Coalition
200 S. Michigan Ave., 16th floor
Chicago, IL 60604
312-341-0900
Fax: 312-341-9361

This group attempts to strengthen families through prevention. The coalition is also a clearinghouse and provides technical assistance.

Family Violence and Sexual Assault Institute
1310 Clinic Dr.
Tyler, TX 75701
903-595-6799
Fax: 903-595-6799

This nonprofit organization is committed to education, networking, and the dissemination of information to reduce and prevent domestic violence and sexual assault. It makes available a large number of unpublished articles (e.g., convention papers) and references to published articles. The organization prepares special bibliographies and treatment manuals and publishes a quarterly newsletter that reviews books and media and announces conferences.

Higher Education Center Against Violence and Abuse
386 McNeal Hall
1985 Buford Ave.
St. Paul, MN 55108-6142
612-624-0721
800-646-2282 (within Minnesota)
Fax: 612-625-4288
http://www.mincava.umn.edu
E-mail: mincava@umn.edu

This Minnesota-based organization provides training for professionals in higher education. It provides technical assistance, plans conferences, and helps fund pilot projects. It also provides an electronic clearinghouse for colleges, universities, and career schools.

National Battered Women's Law Project at the National Center on Women and Family Law
799 Broadway, Ste. 402
New York, NY 10003
212-741-9480

This project serves as a clearinghouse for information for legal professionals and advocates. It addresses a number of specific issues, such as child custody, and provides information about case law, model briefs, and statistics.

National Center for Missing and Exploited Children (NCMEC)
2101 Wilson Blvd., Ste. 550
Arlington, VA 22201
703-235-3900
800-843-5678

The NCMEC, a government agency, is a clearinghouse and resource center funded by the Office of Juvenile Justice and Delinquency Prevention. It provides a number of useful publications.

National Clearinghouse on Child Abuse and Neglect information (NCCAN)
U.S. Department of Health and Human Services
330 C Street SW
Washington, DC 20447
703-385-7565
800-394-3366

NCCAN publishes manuals for professionals involved in the child protection system and to enhance community collaboration and the quality of services provided to children and families. NCCAN conducts research, collects information, and provides assistance to states and communities on child abuse issues.

National Clearinghouse for the Defense of Battered Women
125 S. 9th St., Ste. 302
Philadelphia, PA 19107
215-351-0010

This clearinghouse is a communications service of the Center for Substance Abuse Prevention. It provides information on research, publications, prevention and education resources, and prevention programs. A catalog is available on request.

National Clearinghouse on Families and Youth
P.O. Box 13505
Silver Spring, MD 20911-3505
301-608-8098
Fax: 301-608-8721
http://www.ncfy.com

This clearinghouse individualizes research, provides networking, and provides updates on youth initiatives.

National Clearinghouse on Marital and Date Rape
2325 Oak St.
Berkeley, CA 94708-1697
510-524-1582

This clearinghouse offers fee-based phone consultations ($15 individuals, $30 organizations, $7.50/minute).

National Coalition Against Domestic Violence (NCADV)
To order publications:
P.O. Box 18749
Denver, CO 80218-0749
303-839-1852
Fax: 303-831-9251
http://www.ncadv.org

This coalition works to end domestic violence against children and women. It provides technical assistance, newsletters, and publications.

National Committee to Prevent Child Abuse (NCPCA)
332 S. Michigan Ave., Ste. 1600
Chicago, IL 60604
312-663-3520

The NCPCA provides many resources (e.g., educational pamphlets), including statistical survey information across the 50 states.

National Institute of Justice
U.S. Department of Justice
National Criminal Justice Reference Service
P.O. Box 6000
Rockville, MD 20849-6000
301-251-5500
800-851-3420
E-mail: askncjrs@ncjrs.aspensys.com

The National Institute of Justice develops research and collects information about crime. Part of the U.S. Department of Justice, it provides the largest clearinghouse of criminal justice information in the world and many related services. The National Criminal Justice

Reference Service provides electronic versions of many documents.

National Resource Center on Domestic Violence
6400 Flank Dr., Ste. 1300
Harrisburg, PA 17112-2778
800-537-2238
Fax: 717-545-9456
http://www.nrcdv.org

This center furnishes information and resources to advocates and policy makers.

National Self-Help Clearinghouse
Graduate School of City University of New York
365 5th Ave., Ste. 3300
New York, NY 10016
212-354-8525
212-642-2944
http://www.selfhelpweb.org

This organization lists self-help groups and makes referrals to national self-help groups for those needing assistance.

CULTURE-SPECIFIC RESOURCES

United States

American Indian Institute (AII)
College of Continuing Education and Public Service
University of Oklahoma
555 Constitution St., Ste. 237
Norman, OK 73072-7820
405-325-4127
Fax: 405-325-7757
http://tel.occe.ou.edu/aii/index.htm
E-mail: aii@cce.occe.ou.edu

This institute serves North American Indian tribes and bands through workshops, seminars, and consultation and technical assistance on state, regional, national, and international levels. The AII also cosponsors the annual National American Indian Conference on Child Abuse and Neglect.

COSSMHO
1501 16th St. NW
Washington, DC 20036
202-387-5000
Fax: 202-797-4353
http://www.buscapique.com/latinusa/buscafile/wash/cossmho.htm

COSSMHO is a national nonprofit coalition of Hispanic organizations serving the Mexican American, Puerto Rican, Cuban, and other Latino communities in health and human services, substance abuse prevention, and family strengthening. Coalition affiliates include 220 local agencies in 32 states, the District of Columbia, and Puerto Rico.

Domestic Abuse Intervention Project (DAIP)
206 W. Fourth St., Rm. 201
Duluth, MN 55806
218-722-2781
Fax: 218-722-1545

This organization distributes training materials and conducts training seminars. It provides specialized training materials for those working with Native American families.

Mending the Sacred Hoop (MSH)
STOP Violence Against Indian Women Technical Assistance Project
202 E. Superior St.
Duluth, MN 55802
218-722-2781
Fax: 218-722-5775
http://www.msh-ta.org

MSH is a Native American women's organization that helps tribal governments and agencies improve their response to Native American victims of violence against women by crafting strategies at local levels that reflect available resources and cultural perspectives.

National Black Child Development Institute, Inc.
1001 15th St. NW, Ste. 900
Washington, DC 20005
202-387-1281
Fax: 202-234-1738
http://www.nbcdi.org/start.asp

This institute, together with its 42 affiliates composed of volunteers, works to improve the quality of life for African American children and youth through public education and services in child care, education, child welfare, and health. It also makes available publications on issues in the above areas.

National Latino Alliance for the Elimination of Domestic Violence
1730 N. Lynn St., Ste. 502
Arlington, VA 22209
800-342-9908
Fax: 800-600-8931
http://www.dvalianza.com

This organization includes Latino advocates, community activists, practitioners, researchers, and survivors of domestic violence working together to eliminate domestic violence in Latino communities. It serves as a national forum for ongoing dialogue, education, and advocacy.

People of Color Leadership Institute (POCLI), Center for Child Protection and Family Support
714 G St. SE
Washington, DC 20003
202-544-3144
Fax: 202-547-3601
http://www.centerchildprotection.org

POCLI has developed an agency self-assessment tool that allows agencies to assess their level of cultural competence, as well as a staff training curriculum guide. Both are available at cost. POCLI staff also provide training in the fields of child abuse and neglect, attitude competence, domestic violence, substance abuse, and family support preservation.

Turning Point for Families, Inc. (TPFFI), Alternatives to Violence: East Hawaii
P.O. Box 10448
Hilo, HI 96721-7798
808-969-7798

This nonprofit organization provides domestic violence intervention, support services, and education to battered victims, children, and adults and youth perpetrators on the Big Island. It has been serving the County of Hawaii for more than 24 years.

Women of Nations
P.O. Box 4637
St. Paul, MN 55104
612-222-5830

This organization provides information on American Indian women involved in domestic violence.

Canada

London Family Court Clinic
254 Pall Mall St., Ste. 200
London, ON N6A 5P6
Canada
519-679-7250
http://www.lfcc.on.ca/index.htm

This clinic provides educational pamphlets on violence prevention for schoolchildren and teenagers.

Metro Action Committee on Public Violence Against Women and Children (METRAC)
158 Spadina Rd.
Toronto, ON M5R 2T8
Canada
416-392-3135
Fax: 416-392-3136
http://www.metrac.org

METRAC attempts to prevent violence against women and children by promoting research on violence, services for survivors, and legal system reform. The organization publishes informational packets as well as books.

National Clearinghouse on Family Violence (NCFV)
Family Violence Prevention Division, Social Services Programs, Health Canada
Finance Bldg., 1st floor
Tunney's Pasture
Ottawa, ON K1A 1B5
Canada
800-267-1291
http://www.hc-sc.gc.ca/hppb/familyviolence

The NCFV is a national resource center providing information about violence within the family. It supplies Canadians with research findings and information on all aspects of prevention, protection, and treatment concerning family violence.

Hotlines

Girls and Boys Town National Hotline
800-448-3000

Girls and Boys Town provides many services for children, families, and professionals, including the operation of a national toll-free hotline providing 24-hour response for crisis, resource, and referral.

Legal Council for the Elderly (LCE)
800-424-3410

This hotline connects callers with attorneys who will try to resolve issues or advise callers about where they can obtain help.

National Battered Woman's Hotline
c/o Texas Council on Family Violence
8701 North MoPac Expressway, Ste. 450
Austin, TX 78759
512-794-1133
800-525-1978

This organization, along with many state coalitions and local shelters, has a hotline for calls about domestic violence. Some hotline counselors are fluent in a second language (e.g., Spanish).

National Child Abuse Hotline
800-422-4453, or 800-4-A-CHILD

This hotline provides crisis counseling, child abuse reporting information, and information and referrals for every county in the United States and the District of Columbia. The hotline is staffed 24 hours a day, 7 days a week, by mental health professionals.

National Directory of Hotlines and Crisis Intervention Centers
800-999-9999
800-999-9915

The directory is a 24-hour nationwide hotline for runaways and troubled youth and their families. The hotline offers referrals to services in a caller's local area.

National Domestic Violence Hotline
800-799-7233

This number responds to emergency crisis calls from battered individuals, women, and others involved in family violence. It also provides referrals to local batterer programs.

Note: To locate additional hotlines, look in the nonbusiness section of a telephone directory under "Social Service Agencies," "Shelters," and "Women's Organizations."

GENERAL CRIME VICTIM ORGANIZATIONS

National Organizations for Victim Assistance
2000 M St. NW, Ste. 280
Washington, DC 20036
202-232-6682
http://www.ncvc.org/index.html

This group runs public education programs, provides direct services to victims, and develops public policy and training programs for policy makers and health care providers.

National Victim Center
555 Madison Ave., Ste. 2001
New York, NY 10022
800-FYI-CALL

This organization provides research, education, training, advocacy, and resources for those working with crime victims. It also offers some publications (e.g., on stalking).

National Victims Resource Center
P.O. Box 6000
Rockville, MD 20850
800-627-6872

This center is the primary source of information on U.S. crime victims. The organization is responsible for distributing all publications of U.S. Department of Justice programs on victim-related issues, including domestic violence victims.

RELIGIOUS INFORMATION

California Professional Society on the Abuse of Children (CAPSAC)
2449 Beacon St.
Orange, CA
619-773-1649
http://www.apsac.org

Phone to obtain CAPSAC's *Anthology of Sermons* (1996).

Center for the Prevention of Sexual and Domestic Violence
2400 N. 34th St., Ste. 10
Seattle, WA 98103
206-634-1903
http://www.cpsdv.org

This center provides educational materials for religious organizations preparing sermons for clergy and lessons for Sunday school classes. It educates clergy about child abuse and inappropriate behaviors of clergy.

Promise Keepers
10200 W. 44th Ave.
Wheatridge, CO 80033
303-964-7600
800-501-0211
http://www.promisekeepers.org

This interfaith Christian group for men only has a number of local organizations that hold conventions. The purpose of the organization is to encourage male bonding and to provide sermons about the commitment men need to make to their families.

RELEVANT DIRECTORIES

*National Directory of Children, Youth and Families
Services*
To order:
National Directory of Children, Youth and Families
Services
14 Inverness Dr. East, Ste. D-144
Englewood, CO 90112
800-343-6681
http://www.childrenyouthfamilydir.com

This directory, which is produced annually, lists
more than 30,000 agencies, including human/social
services, health, mental health/substance abuse, and
juvenile justice agencies, as well as treatment centers
and specialized hospitals.

National Directory of Domestic Violence Programs
To order:
National Coalition Against Domestic Violence
P.O. Box 18749
Denver, CO 80218
303-831-9251

This directory is a guide to community shelter, safe
home, and service programs concerned with domestic
violence. It also contains a list of national information
and resource centers as well as military programs.

*The 1994 North American Directory of Programs for
Runaways, Homeless Youth and Missing Children*
To order:
American Youth Work Center
1200 17th St. NW, 4th floor
Washington, DC 20036
202-785-0764

This directory lists 500 programs designed to
protect street children from potentially abusive and
exploitative situations.

TREATMENT RESOURCES

Adults Molested As Children United (AMACU)
P.O. Box 952
San Jose, CA 95108
408-453-7616

AMACU is a self-help program for adults who were
sexually abused as children. The program, developed
by Parents United, attempts to help resolve the problems experienced by the victims of child sexual abuse.

To find a local AMACU group, or for referrals to local
sexual abuse treatment specialists, contact the office
listed above.

Children of Alcoholics Foundation
164 W. 74th St.
New York, NY 10023
212-754-0656
800-359-2623
http://www.coaf.org

This foundation seeks to promote public and
professional awareness of the problems of children of
alcoholics and disseminates new research findings
to break the vicious cycle of family alcoholism. The
foundation operates a help line that provides referrals
to national and local self-help and counseling groups
and treatment agencies.

Incest Survivors Anonymous (ISA)
P.O. Box 17245
Long Beach, CA 90807-7245
310-428-5599

ISA provides information on self-help meetings
that are Twelve-Step and Twelve-Tradition or spiritu-
ally oriented for survivors of incest. Check local listings
or check local social service agencies for information
about meetings in your area.

National Adolescent Perpetrator Network
1205 Oneida St.
Denver, CO 80220
303-321-3963

This network of people involved in identification,
intervention, and treatment of sexually abusive youth
facilitates communication, referrals, training, and
research. The network is a program of the C. Henry
Kempe National Center for the Treatment and
Prevention of Child Abuse and Neglect.

Parents Anonymous
National Parents Anonymous
675 W. Foothill Blvd., Ste. 220
Claremont, CA 91711
909-621-6184
http://www.parentsanonymous.org

Parents Anonymous has 2,100 local groups across
the United States, and many of these have groups for
adult survivors of child abuse. To locate a group in
your area, look in the white pages of your telephone
directory under "Parents Anonymous" or contact the
national office listed above.

Shield Abuse & Trauma Project
39-09 214th Pl.
Bayside, NY 11361
718-229-5757, ext. 216
Fax: 718-225-3159
http://www.shield.org

The Shield Abuse & Trauma Project provides a unique program of services to individuals with developmental disabilities who have experienced abuse or other traumatic experiences resulting in emotional, behavioral, or interpersonal difficulties. The project provides individual and group treatment services in addition to organizational training and consulting services. Organizational training and consulting are geared to help agencies understand the impact of abuse and/or trauma on these individuals and to assist in creating more effective intervention in all settings.

WEB SITES

American Bar Association on Domestic Violence
http://abanet.org/domviol/home.html

This Web site provides information on domestic violence-related conferences and meetings, national domestic violence resource center information, and materials related to culturally diverse and immigrant domestic violence groups.

American Psychological Association, Children, Youth, and Families Office
http://www.apa.org/pi/cyf

This Web site offers links to free publications, online documents, government agencies, and news concerning the welfare of children and families.

Domestic Violence Project
http://www.growing.com/nonviolent

This Web site offers a variety of resources, including materials directed at victims (e.g., information about keeping safe, domestic violence hotlines, support) as well as professionals (e.g., information on books journals, and conferences).

Law Enforcement Resource Center
http://www.lerc.com

This Web site provides materials on domestic violence for law enforcement departments within the United States, including police training videos, CD-ROMs, DVDs, and written materials.

National Electronic Network on Violence Against Women
http://www.VAWnet.org

The purpose of this Web site is to disseminate information on domestic violence and sexual assault and related issues. The site includes publications, help and safety information, and other resources.

Michael Schwartz' Compendium of Elder Abuse Law
http://www.elderabuselaw.com

This Web site provides legal information in the area of elder abuse.

Resource Center on Domestic Violence: Child Protection and Custody
http://www.nationalcouncilfvd.org

This Web site provides information, materials, consultation, and technical assistance related to child protection and custody within the context of domestic violence.

Violence Against Women Online Resources
http://www.vaw.umn.edu

This Web site provides law, criminal justice, advocacy, and social service professionals with up-to-date information on interventions to stop violence against women. The site includes a documentation library containing the latest research in the field, promising practice approaches, and information on child custody and child protection issues.

Appendix B

Interpersonal Violence Incidence Estimates

Table 1 Estimates of Dating Violence, Stalking, and Homicide for Large Samples of Adolescents, College Students, and Young Adults, 1990 and Later

Researchers	Sponsoring Organization	Reported by	Sample Type	Sample Size	Assessment Instrument	Outcome (Rate)
Psychological abuse						
White & Koss (1991)		University	College men and women	4,707	CTS1, 5 items, verbal/symbolic	From age 14 Males Females Victimization 81.9% 86.8% Perpetration 80.8% 87.7%
Foshee (1996)	CDC	University	Adolescents (grades 8 and 9)	1,965	4 items, specific behaviors Threats Monitor Insults Manipulate Threats Monitor Insults Manipulate	Lifetime Cronbach's alpha Males Females Victimization .74 .82 .72 .85 .70 .72 .77 .84 Perpetration .79 .73 .76 .66 .72 .58 .77 .74
Halpern et al. (2001)	NICHD	National Longitudinal Study of Adolescent Health	Adolescents (ages 12–21)	7,500	CTS1, 3 items	18 months Males Females Victimization 28.0% 29.0%

Researchers	Sponsoring Organization	Reported by	Sample Type	Sample Size	Assessment Instrument	Outcome (Rate)
Harned (2001)	Office of Women's Programs	University	College students	1,139 (874 daters)	Abusive Behavior Inventory	1 year Males Females Victimization 87% 82% Perpetration 84% 85%
Stalking						
Tjaden & Thoennes (1998b)	NIJ and CDC National Center for Injury Prevention and Control	Center for Policy Research	Men and women (18–29) Years	8,000 men, 8,000 women	8 screen items, stalking	Lifetime Males Females Victimization by intimate 0.6% 4.8%
Fisher et al. (2000)	NIJ U.S. BJS	NIJ	College women (ages 17–22)	4,432 women	1 item	Last 7 months Victimization Females: 13.1% By boyfriend or ex-boyfriend: 42.5% (of 13.1%)
Physical abuse						
White & Koss (1991)	University	University	College men and women	4,707	CTS1, 5 items, physical	From age 14 Males Females Victimization 38.7% 32.4% Perpetration 36.7% 35.1%

(Continued)

Table 1 (Continued)

Researchers	Sponsoring Organization	Reported by	Sample Type	Sample Size	Assessment Instrument	Outcome (Rate)
Bourg & Stock (1994)		University		1,870	Police reports	1 year only Boyfriend or girlfriend Charged: 51.5% Arrested: 39.0%
Bachman & Saltzman (1995)	U.S. Bureau of the Census and U.S. BJS	U.S. BJS	Current/ ex-daters	Not given	NCVS	1-year average Males Females Victimization 2.0%s 16.0%
Foshee (1996)	CDC	University	Adolescents (grades 8 and 9)	1,965	Violent behaviors and sexual assault	Lifetime Males Females Victimization 39.4% 36.5% Perpetration 15.0% 15.9%
Craven (1997)	U.S. Bureau of the Census and U.S. BJS	U.S. BJS	Boy-/girlfriends	593,000 crimes	NCVS, robbery and physical assaults	1 year, 1994 Victimization Males: 109,100 Females: 483,900
Halpern et al. (2001)	NICHD	National Longitudinal Study of Adolescent Health	Adolescents (ages 12–21)	7,500	CTS1, 2 items, minor physical	18 months Males Females Victimization 12% 12%
Harned (2001)	Office of Women's Programs	University	College students	1,139 (874 daters)	CTS2	1 year Males Females Victimization 21% 22%

Researchers	Sponsoring Organization	Reported by	Sample Type	Sample Size	Assessment Instrument	Outcome (Rate)
Ackard & Neumark-Sztainer (2002)	Minnesota Department of Children, Families, and Learning	University	Adolescents (grades 9 and 12)	81,247	1 item, violence by datee	Lifetime Males Females Victimization Grade 9 6.1% 6.7% Grade 12 5.7% 11.5%
Grunbaum et al. (2002)	CDC	Division of Adolescent and School Health	Adolescents (grades 9–12)	13,601 nationally representative	Youth Risk Behavior Surveillance 1	1 year only Males Females Victimization Physically hurt by date: 9.5%
Injuries						
Foshee (1996)	CDC	University	Adolescents (grades 8 and 9)	1,965	Self-reports	Lifetime percentage Males Females Victimization 51.6% 69.9% Perpetration 15.0% 15.9%
Rand (1997)	Consumer Product Safety Commission	U.S. BJS	Emergency room patients	862,000 males, 554,700 females	National Electronic Injury Surveillance System	1 year Victimization Current/ex-date Males Females 2.75% 20.90%

(Continued)

Table 1 (Continued)

Researchers	Sponsoring Organization	Reported by	Sample Type	Sample Size	Assessment Instrument	Outcome (Rate)
Homicide						
Bachman & Saltzman (1995)	FBI	U.S. BJS	Men and women, relationship known	10,351 men 3,454 women	Uniform Crime Reports	1 year Murder victims Current/ex-date Males Females 1.4% 10.3%
Greenfeld et al. (1998)	FBI	Police departments	Murdered men and women, ages 12 and over	446,370	SHR, 1976–1996	Murder victims Relationship known to police Males Females 65.5% 72.5% Percentage nonmarital partners Males Females 2.0% 9.4%
Paulozzi et al. (2001)	FBI	Police departments	Murdered men and women, ages 10 and over	35,601 intimate partner homicides 45,513 weighted cases with all data	SHR, 1981–1998	Intimate partner homicide victims Males Females 36.3% 63.7% % murdered by girlfriend/ boyfriend 32.5% 34.7%

NOTE: CTS1 = Conflict Tactics Scale; CTS2 = Revised Conflict Tactics Scale; CDC = Centers for Disease Control and Prevention; NICHD = National Institute of Child Health and Human Development; NIJ = National Institute of Justice; U.S. BJS = U.S. Bureau of Justice Statistics; NCVS = National Crime Victimization Survey; SHR = Supplementary Homicide Reports.

Table 2 Estimates of Dating Violence and Sexual Assault for Cross-Cultural Samples

Researchers	Sponsoring Organization	Reported by	Sample Type	Sample Size	Assessment Instrument	Outcome (Rate)
Jaffee et al. (1992), Canada			High school students	1,547		Lifetime victimization Physical 9.2% Sexual 9.0%
DeKeseredy & Kelly (1993), Canada	Health & Welfare Canada's Family Violence	University	College students	Males, 1,307; females, 1,835	CTS1, SES	1 year Victim-females Violence Sex 35% 45% Offender-males 17% 19.5%
Poitras & Lavoie (1995), Canada (Quebec)		University	Adolescents (15–19 years)	643	SES	Lifetime Males Females Victimization Sexual coercion 13.1% 54.1%
Magdol et al. (1997), New Zealand	NIJ, others	University	21-year-old birth cohort	941 (861 daters)	CTS1	1 year Males Females Victimization 34.1% 27.1% Perpetration 21.8% 37.2%
Lottes & Weinberg (1997), United States, Sweden	Foundation for Scientific Study of Sexuality	University	College students	Males: U.S. 129, Sweden 211 Females: U.S. 278, Sweden 359	CTS1, 3 items physical violence; 7 items physical sexual coercion	Lifetime Males Females Victimization Physical U.S. 22% 31% Physical Sweden 8% 19% U.S. Sweden

(Continued)

411

Table 2 (Continued)

Researchers	Sponsoring Organization	Reported by	Sample Type	Sample Size	Assessment Instrument	Outcome (Rate)
						Sex victim female 45% 23% Sex offender males 16% 4%
Newton-Taylor et al. (1998), Canada		University	College women	3,642	Pushed or assaulted and sexual assault and coercion	1 year only Females only Victimization Physical: 24.0% Sexual: 15.0%
Jackson et al. (2000), New Zealand		University	Adolescents (16–20 years)	304	26 items: 14 emotional 5 sex, 7 physical	Lifetime Males Females Victimization Emotional abuse 76.3% 81.5% Physical abuse 13.3% 17.5% Sexual coercion 67.4% 76.9%
Yick & Agbayani-Siewert (2000), Chinese Americans		University	College students	289 Chinese Americans and 138 White Americans	CTS1	Lifetime Males Females Victimization Chinese 25.2% 18.6% White 36.6% 289.9% Perpetration Chinese 17.0% 27.6% White 13.2% 18.8%

Researchers	Sponsoring Organization	Reported by	Sample Type	Sample Size	Assessment Instrument	Outcome (Rate)		
Hird (2000), England		University	Adolescents (13–19 years)	487	CTS1 (statistically modified)	1 year only		
						Males	Females	
						Psychological Victimization		
						49%	54%	
						Physical		
						15%	14%	
						Sexual		
						na	17.9%	
Swart et al. (2002), South Africa		University	High school (9th–12th grades)	928 males and females	CTS2, adapted 20 items	1 year only		
						Males	Females	
						Physical abuse Victimization		
						37.8%	41.7%	
						Perpetration		
						35.3%	43.5%	

NOTE: CTS1 = Conflict Tactics Scale; CTS2 = Revised Conflict Tactics Scale; NIJ = National Institute of Justice; SES = Sexual Experiences Survey.

Table 3 Estimates of Sexual Assaults for Large Samples of Adolescents, College Students, and Young Adults, 1990 and Later

Researchers	Sponsoring Organization	Reported by	Sample Type	Sample Size	Assessment Instrument	Outcome (Rate)
Bachman & Saltzman (1995)	U.S. Bureau of the Census	U.S. Bureau of Justice Statistics	Females over age 12	500,000, nationally representative	National Crime Victimization Survey	1 year average Female only rape Victimization Current/ex-date 16%
Douglas et al. (1997)	Centers for Disease Control	National Center for Chronic Disease Prevention & Health Promotion	Male and female college students (7,442 eligible)	4,838 data sets	Youth Risk Behavior Surveillance System questions	1 year Victimization Forced sex-rape Males 3.9% Females 20.4%
Abbey et al. (1998)	National Institute of Alcohol Abuse and Alcoholism	University	College men (18–59 years)	798	SES, 8 items	Lifetime Males only Perpetration 16%
Fisher et al. (2000)	NIJ	NIJ	College women	4,432, nationally representative	10 screen items + 12-item incident report	7 months only Female rape Victimization Total 2.8% By current/ ex-dates 28.7%
Harned (2001)	Office of Women's Programs	University	College students	1,130 (874 daters)	SES	1 year Victimization Males 30% Females 39%
Ackard & Neumark-Sztainer (2002)	Minnesota Department of Children, Families, and Learning	University	Adolescents (9th and 12th grade)	81,247	1 item, rape by date	Lifetime Males Females Victimization 9th grade 1.3% 1.2% 12th grade

Table 4   Statistics on Abuse of Intimates

A1. Physical Assaults

Researchers	Straus & Gelles (1986)		
Organization	Family Violence Laboratory		
Reported by	University		
Sample type	Married/divorced males/females		
Sample size	3,500		
Assessment	CTS1		
Period of time	Lifetime		
Outcome (rate)	*Percentage of perpetrators of abuse*		
		Males	*Females*
	Nonsevere abuse	11.3%	12.1%
	Severe abuse	3.0%	4.4%

A2. Physical Assaults

Researchers	Tjaden & Thoennes (1998a)		
Organization	Center for Policy Research		
Reported by	NIJ and CDC		
Sample type	Married/divorced/cohabiting/dating males/females		
Sample size	16,000 (8,000 males; 8,000 females)		
Assessment	Modified CTS1		
Period of time	Lifetime		
Outcome (rate)	*Percentage of IPV victims*		
	Males		*Females*
	7.4%		22.1%

(Continued)

Table 4 (Continued)

A3. Physical Assaults

Researchers	Bachman & Saltzman (1995)
Organization	U.S. Bureau of the Census
Reported by	U.S. BJS
Sample type	Current/former spouse and current/former boyfriend/girlfriend
Number Assaults	960,000
Assessment	NCVS questionnaire
Period of time	1 year (1992–1993)
Outcome (rate)	*Percentage of intimate victims*

Males	*Females*
15%	85%

A4. Physical Assaults

Researchers	Craven (1997)
Organization	U.S. Bureau of the Census
Reported by	U.S. BJS
Sample type	Male/female assault victims over 12
Sample size	11,068,600
Assessment	NCVS questionnaire
Period of time	1 year
Outcome (rate)	*Number victimized by gender*

	Males	*Females*
Total incidents	6,228,500	4,840,100

Percentage victimized by relationship

	Males	*Females*
Stranger	63.4%	38.4%
Known to victim	36.6%	61.6%
Current or ex-spouse or boyfriend girlfriend	2.8%	20.7%
Other relative	3.6%	6.6%
Friend/acquaintance	30.2%	34.3%

A5. Physical Assaults

Researchers	Rennison (2003)
Organization	U.S. Bureau of the Census
Reported by	U.S. BJS
Sample type	Current/former spouse and current/former boyfriend/girlfriend
Sample size	631,080 (not including robbery)
Assessment	NCVS questionnaire
Period of time	1999
Outcome (rate)	*Percentage of intimate victims*
	Males *Females*
	15% 85%

A6. Physical Assaults of Pregnant Women

Researchers	Gazmararian et al. (1996)
Organization	Prudential Center for Health Care Research
Reported by	School of Medicine
Sample type	Mothers of newborns
Sample size	12,612 from sample of 14,013
Assessment	One item: "Physically Hurt by Partner"
Period of time	12 months prior to delivery
Outcome (rate)	*Percentage pregnant women assaulted*
	3.8%–6.9%

A7. Physical or Sexual Assaults of Pregnant Women

Researchers	Amaro, Fried, Cabral, & Zuckerman (1990)
Organization	National Institute of Drug Abuse
Reported by	School of Medicine

(Continued)

Table 4 (Continued)

Sample type	Pregnant women in prenatal clinic
Sample size	1,662 from sample of 1,932
Assessment	One item: "Threatened or Physically Abused or in Any Fights or Beatings"
Period of time	When interviewed during pregnancy in clinic
Outcome (rate)	*Percentage women physically or sexually abused*
	7%

B1. Estimates of Physical Assaults Among Racial/Ethnic Minorities and Immigrants

Researchers	Greenfeld et al. (1998)	
Organization	U.S. Bureau of the Census	
Reported by	U.S. BJS	
Sample type	Females	
Sample size	Not provided	
Assessment	NCVS questionnaire	
Period of time	1 year	
Outcome (rate)	*Percentage of female victims (per 1,000)*	
	Whites	0.8%
	Hispanics	0.9%
	Blacks	1.2%
	Others (e.g., Hawaiians, Asians)	0.6%

B2. Intimate Partner Violence Among U.S. Military Men

Researchers	Rosen et al. (2002)
Organization	U.S. military
Reported by	U.S. BJS
Sample type	1,411 soldiers stationed in Alaska
Sample size	488 married soldiers

Assessment	Modified Conflict Tactics Scale (Pan et al., 1994)
Period of time	Not provided
Outcome (rate)	*Prevalence of violence against women victims*

White (n = 358)

Perpetrated

Minor aggression	22.4
Severe aggression	5.8

Received

Minor aggression	22.7
Severe aggression	12.6

Black (n = 130)

Perpetrated

Minor aggression	31.2
Severe aggression	14.4

Received

Minor aggression	25.0
Severe aggression	25.0

B3. Intimate Partner Violence Among Canadian-Born and Canadian Immigrants

Researchers	Brownridge & Halli (2002)
Organization	Statistics Canada–General Social Survey
Reported by	U.S. BJS
Sample type	25,876 men and women
Sample size	7,115 coresident heterosexual women
Assessment	9 items physical assault; 1 item threat; 1 item sexual coercion/assault
Period of time	Last 5 years (1999)

(Continued)

Table 4 (Continued)

Outcome (rate)	*Prevalence of violence against women victims*	
	Canadian-born (*n* = 5,737)	3.7%
	Immigrants–developed countries (*n* = 844)	2.4%
	Immigrants–developing countries (*n* = 534)	5.5%

B4. Intimate Partner Violence Among California Migrant Workers

Researchers	Van Hightower et al. (2000)	
Organization	U.S. Migrant Health Program	
Reported by	University	
Sample type	Adult female farmworkers (70%) and other low-income female workers seeking medical care at a migrant health center	
Sample size	1,001 adult females: 83% Latina; 4% Anglo; 1% African American; 3% Haitian; 1 Native American; 9% no data	
Assessment	Domestic Violence Assessment Form, 4 items: (a) male partner's alcohol/drug use; (b) physical abuse (hit, kicked, punched); (c) forced sex; (d) fear of abuser and identity of abuser	
Period of time	Last year	
Outcome (rate)	*Prevalence of violence against women victims*	
	Physically or sexually assaulted	19%
	Husband (only abuser)	32%
	Ex-husbands	5%
	Boyfriends	20%
	Both husbands and boyfriends	16%
	[Timing of marriage not given]	
	Companions	10%
	Family members	18%

C1. Injuries Caused by Intimate Partners

Researchers	Rand (1997)
Organization	Consumer Product Safety Commission

Reported by	U.S. BJS		
Sample type	Hospital emergency room patients		
Sample size	1,417,600		
Assessment	National Electronic Injury Surveillance System		
Period of time	1 year		
Outcome (rate)	Number of persons injured		
		Males	*Females*
		862,000	554,700
	Number and percentage injuries perpetrated by relationship		
		Males	*Females*
	Current/ex-spouse	15,400	88,400
		(1.8%)	(15.9%)
	Current/ex-boy/girlfriend	23,600	116,000
		(2.75%)	(20.9%)

C2. Injuries Caused by Intimate Partners

Researchers	Zlotnick et al. (1998)		
Organization	Center for Population Research of the National Institute of Child Health and Human Development Demography and Ecology		
Reported by	University		
Sample type	Male/female coresidents		
Sample size	7,506		
Assessment	Injury questions by telephone survey		
Period of time	1 year		
Outcome (rate)	*Percentage of sample (826) injured*		
		Males	*Females*
		27%	73%

(Continued)

Table 4 (Continued)

C3. Injuries Caused by Intimate Partners

Researchers	Tjaden & Thoennes (1998a)
Organization	Center for Policy Research
Reported by	NIJ and CDC
Sample type	Married/divorced/cohabiting/dating males/females
Sample size	16,000 (8,000 males; 8,000 females)
Assessment	Modified CTS
Period of time	Lifetime
Outcome (rate)	*Percentage of sample injured*

Males	*Females*
19.9%	41.5%

D1. Sexual Assaults of Intimates

Researchers	Bachman & Saltzman (1995)
Organization	U.S. Bureau of the Census
Reported by	U.S. BJS
Sample type	Wives and girlfriends
Sample size	500,000
Assessment	NCVS questionnaire
Period of time	1 year (1992–1993)
Outcome (rate)	*Percentage of sexual assaults*

Stranger	3%
Acquaintance/friend	40%
Total intimates	29%
Husband	9%
Ex-husband	4%
Boyfriend/ex-boyfriend	16%
Other relative	9%

D2. Sexual Assaults of Intimates

Researchers	Tjaden & Thoennes (1998a)		
Organization	Center for Policy Research		
Reported by	NIJ and CDC		
Sample type	Married/divorced/cohabiting/dating males/females		
Sample size	16,000 (8,000 males; 8,000 females)		
Assessment	Modified CTS		
Period of time	Lifetime		
Outcome (rate)	*Percentage sexually assaulted by intimate*		
		Males	*Females*
		0.2%	7.7%

E1. Homicides of Intimate Partners

Researchers	Greenfeld et al. (1998)		
Organization	FBI		
Reports by	Police departments		
Sample type	Murdered males/females over 12 years		
Sample size	2,500 (annual average)		
Assessment	Written reports		
Period of time	1976–1996		
Outcome (rate)	*Average percentage murdered by relationship to victim*		
		Males	*Females*
	Total undetermined	34.4%	27.8%
	Total known to police	65.6%	72.2%
	Spouse	3.7%	18.9%
	Ex-spouse	0.2%	1.4%
	Nonmarital partner	2.0%	9.4%
	Others (relative, acquaintance, friend, stranger)	59.6%	42.5%

(Continued)

Table 4 (Continued)

E2. Homicides of Intimate Partners

Researchers	Rennison (2001, 2003)
Organization	U.S. Bureau of the Census
Reported by	U.S. BJS
Sample type	Current/former spouse (married "group") and current/former boyfriend/girlfriend
Sample size	1,647 murders by intimates (2000) (represents 11% of all homicides; victim-offender relationship unknown in 34% of all homicides for the year)
Assessment	*Supplementary Homicide Reports*
Period of time	1993–2001
Outcome (rate)	*Murdered by intimate*

Males	*Females*
4%	33%

F1. Stalking of Intimate Partners

Researchers	Tjaden & Thoennes (1998b)
Organization	Center for Policy Research
Reported by	NIJ and CDC
Sample type	Married/divorced/cohabiting/dating males/females
Sample size	16,000 (8,000 males; 8,000 females)
Assessment	Modified CTS
Period of time	Lifetime
Outcome (rate)	*Percentage stalked (victims)*

Males	*Females*
2%	8%

G1. Violence Against Same-Sex Intimates

Researchers	Tjaden and Thoennes (2000)
Organization	Center for Policy Research
Reported by	Center for Policy Research

Sample size	79 same-sex female cohabitants from sample of 8,000; 65 same-sex male cohabitants from sample of 8,000
Assessment	Modified CTS
Period of time	Lifetime
Outcome (rate)	*Percentage victimized by rape, IPV, or stalking*

	Males (n = 65)	Females (n = 79)
Rape	—	11.4%
Physical assault	21.5%	35.4%
Stalking	—	—
Total	23.1%	39.2%

G2. Violence Against Same-Sex Intimates

Researchers	Greenwood et al. (2002)
Organization	Center for Policy Research
Reported by	Center for Policy Research
Sample type	Same-sex cohabiting males
Sample size	2,881 male cohabitants from probability-based sample of 3,700 males
Assessment	Modified CTS
Period of time	Last 5 years
Outcome (rate)	*Percentage of same-sex male victims*
Psychological/symbolic	34%
Physical	22%
Sexual	5.1%
Any type	39.2%

H1. Estimates of IPV Among Cohabitors in New Zealand

Researchers	Magdol et al. (1997)
Organization	NIJ
Reported by	University

(Continued)

Table 4 (Continued)

Sample type	941, 21-year-old birth cohort
Sample size	777 cohabiting or dating
Assessment	CTS1, 9 items + 4 items
Period of time	1 year
Outcome (rate)	*Perpetration*
	Cohabitors	52%
	Daters	27%

H2. Estimates of IPV Among Cohabitors in New Zealand

Researchers	DeMaris (2001)	
Organization	National Survey of Families and Households	
Reported by	University	
Sample type	Male and female cohabitors	
Sample size	411 cohabiting couples	
Assessment	4 violence items; verbal conflict items	
Period of time	1 year	
Outcome (rate)	*Perpetration*	
	Males	*Females*
	Violence	
	18%	20%
	Males and females combined	
	Verbal conflict	12.022%

NOTE: CTS1 = Conflict Tactics Scale; U.S. BJS = U.S. Bureau of Justice Statistics; NCVS = National Crime Victimization Survey; NIJ = National Institute of Justice; CDC = Centers for Disease Control and Prevention.

Table 3   Nonlethal and Lethal Assaults Against Elders

Researchers	Klaus (2000)
Organization	U.S. Bureau of the Census
Reported by	U.S. Bureau of Justice Statistics
Sample type	Men and women, age 65+ years
Sample size	85,000, every 6 months
Assessment	NCVS, nonlethal violence; *UCR-SHR*, murder
Period of time	5 years (1992–1997) annual average
Outcome	*Nonlethal violence against persons 65+ years*

Total number nonlethal violent crimes

	165,330
Assaults	121,100
Rapes	3,280

Victim-offender relationship (NCVS) (victims)

	Gender of victims	
	Male	Female
Assaults and rapes	7.1%	4.0%

Relative, intimate	Known by victim	Stranger	Unknown
9.1%	27.4%	56.2%	7.4%

Race/ethnicity of victims per 1,000 persons

White	Black	Other
4.8	9.8	7.1

Marital status of victims per 1,000 persons

Married	Widowed	Separated/divorced	Nevermarried	Unknown
4.4	4.4	14.4	7.5	6.3

Gender of perpetrators

Male	Female	Both
76.3	13.2	4.2

Total number nonlethal crimes

	165,330 (5.27 per 1,000)
Assaults	121,100
Rapes	3,280

(Continued)

Table 5 (Continued)

Lethal violence against persons 65+ years

1,000
0.4% all ages

Total number murders FBI (UCR-SHR) by percentages, not rate

Relative, intimate	*Known by victim*	*Stranger*	*Unknown*
26.4%	23.7%	14.6%	35.3%

Homicide perpetrators by gender

Male	*Female*	*Unknown*
59.9%	43.9%	30.7%

Homicide perpetrators by race

White	*Black*	*Other*	*Unknown*
40.2	27.2%	1.1%	31.5%

NOTE: NCVS = National Crime Victimization Survey; UCR = Uniform Crime Reports; SHR = Supplementary Homicide Reports. See Klaus (2000) for a complete summary of SHR and NCVS data analyzed for this study.

SHR homicide Data (1980–1998) for Elders 65+ Years by Relationship

Researchers	Chu (2001)
Organization	University of California, Los Angeles
Sample type	FBI (*SHR*)
Period of time	*SHR* (1980–1998)
Sample size	21,319 elder homicide victims, 1980–1998
Assessment	*SHR* (written police reports sent to FBI)
Outcome	*Male offender–female victim homicides* (SHR *data*) %

Relationship	Same age	Different age	Total
Intimate partner	94.5	19.5	28.6
Parent victim	0.0	11.7	10.3
Offspring victim	0.0	0.2	0.2
Sibling/other family victim	1.5	10.6	9.5
Friend/neighbor/acquaintance	2.5	26.4	23.5
Employee/employer	0.0	0.5	0.4
Other known victim	1.4	3.8	3.5
Stranger	0.1	27.4	24.0

Female offender–male victim homicides (SHR *data*)%

Relationship	Same age	Different age	Total
Intimate partner	95.1	36.1	39.8
Parent victim	0.0	7.8	7.3
Offspring victim	0.0	0.2	0.2
Sibling/other family victim	1.4	3.6	3.5
Friend/neighbor/acquaintance	2.8	37.1	34.9
Employee/employer	0.0	0.7	0.7
Other known victim	0.7	3.3	3.1
Stranger	0.0	11.3	10.5

SOURCE: Chu (2001, pp. 96–97).

NOTE: *SHR* = *Supplementary Homicide Reports.*

Table 7 Assaults Reported to Adult Protective Services

Researcher	Teaster (2003)		
Organization	National Association of Adult Protective Service Administrators		
Sample type	Males/females: 60+ or 65+ years only, 8 states; adults only, 8 states; younger & older, 37 states (some states include disabled adults of all ages)		
Sample size	472,813 reported cases; investigated, 396,398; substantiated, 166,019		
Assessment	Written records of state agencies, variable number states reporting on variable dimensions: adult protective services, APS, health care providers, law enforcement, family, etc.		
Period of time	Year 2000		
Outcome (rate)	*Percentage victimized by gender (elders + disabled)*		

Males	*Females*	*Unspecified*
39.0	56.0	5.0

Race/ethnicity of victims (elders + disabled)

Race/ethnicity	No. states	No. reports	% reports
Caucasian	24	56,603	65.8
African American	19	14,947	17.4
Hispanic	14	9,057	10.5
Native American	14	772	0.9
Asian/Pacific Islander	16	351	0.4
Other	9	350	0.5
Not reported	9	3,865	4.5
Total		86,045	100.0

Perpetrators by gender (substantiated) 17 state responses; 24,455 cases

Males	*Females*	*Unspecified*
52.0%	48.9%	15%

(Continued)

Table 7 (Continued)

Perpetrator relationship to victim (substantiated)

Relationship	Number of states	Number of perpetrators	% perpetrators
Spouse or partner	21	19,449	30.2
Adult child	21	11,313	17.6
Unknown	19	7,280	11.3
Other	16	6,764	10.5
Service provider	19	5,283	8.2
Other family	21	4,735	7.4
Institution staff	15	2,861	4.4
Friend/neighbor	18	1,904	3.0
Grandchild	13	1,578	2.5
Parent	16	1,389	2.2
Sibling	18	1,177	1.8
Tenants	7	104	0.2
Stranger	10	511	0.8
Total		64,348	100.1

SOURCE: Teaster (2003).

Abbreviations

AAPC   American Association for Protecting Children

ABI   Abusive Behavior Inventory

AFDC   Aid to Families with Dependent Children

APA   American Psychological Association

APD   antisocial personality disorder

APS   adult protective services

APSAC   American Professional Society on the Abuse of Children

ASFA   Adoption and Safe Families Act

BIP   batterer intervention program

BPD   borderline personality disorder

BPO   borderline personality organization

CBT   cognitive-behavioral treatment

CCV   common couple violence

CDC   Centers for Disease Control and Prevention

CJS   criminal justice system

CP   corporal punishment

CPA   child physical abuse

CPS   child protective services

CROWD   Center for Research on Women with Disabilities

CSA   child sexual abuse

CTS1, CTS2   Conflict Tactics Scales

CTSPC   Parent-Child Conflict Tactics Scale

DSM   *Diagnostic and Statistical Manual of Mental Disorders*

DV   dating violence

FBI   Federal Bureau of Investigation

FMIPV   female-to-male intimate partner violence

FTT   failure to thrive

GLBT   gay, lesbian, bisexual, and transgendered

HFA   Healthy Families America

HIV   human immunodeficiency virus

IPH   intimate partner homicide

IPV   intimate partner violence

IT   intimate terrorism

JCAHO   Joint Commission on Accreditation of Healthcare Organizations

MBP   Munchausen by proxy

MCMI   Millon Clinical Multiaxial Inventory

MCTS   Modified Conflict Tactics Scale

MFIPV   male-to-female intimate partner violence

MGRS   masculine gender-role stress

MMPI   Minnesota Multiphasic Personality Inventory

MVC   mutual violent control

NAMBLA   North American Man/Boy Love Association

NCANDS   National Child Abuse and Neglect Data System

NCCAN   National Center for Child Abuse and Neglect

NCEA   National Center on Elder Abuse

NCIPC National Center for Injury Prevention and Control

NCJRS National Criminal Justice Reference Service

NCMEC National Center for Missing and Exploited Children

NCVS National Crime Victimization Survey

NDVH National Domestic Violence Hotline

NEAIS National Elder Abuse Incidence Study

NEISS National Electronic Injury Surveillance System

NEISS-AIP National Electronic Injury Surveillance System-All Injury Program

NFVS-1, NFVS-2 National Family Violence Surveys

NIJ National Institute of Justice

NIS National Incidence Study

NOW National Organization for Women

NSFH National Survey of Families and Households

NVAWS National Violence Against Women Survey

PMWI Psychological Maltreatment of Women Inventory

PO protection order

PRWORA Personal Responsibility and Work Opportunity Reconciliation Act

PTSD posttraumatic stress disorder

QOL quality of life

SA sexual assault

SES socioeconomic status

SHR Supplementary Homicide Reports

SRA satanic ritual abuse

SSA Social Security Administration

ST stalking

STD sexually transmitted disease

SV sexually violent-only

TSC-33 Trauma Symptom Checklist

UCR Uniform Crime Reports

U.S. BJS U.S. Bureau of Justice Statistics

U.S. DHHS U.S. Department of Health and Human Services

U.S. GAO U.S. General Accounting Office

VAWA Violence Against Women Act

VR violent resistance

GLOSSARY

Aggregate data "Information about aggregates or groups such as race, social classes, or nation" (Vogt, 1993, p. 4).

Analysis of variance (ANOVA) "A test of statistical significance of the differences among the mean scores of two or more groups on one or more variables or factors" (Vogt, 1993, p. 7).

Anger (trait) A relatively stable (not temporary) tendency to perceive situations as frustrating, unfair, or threatening.

Antisocial behaviors Behaviors that suggest a disregard for the rights and feelings of others and include violating societal norms (e.g., aggression, unlawful behavior).

Antisocial personality disorder "A type of personality disorder marked by impulsivity, inability to abide by the customs and laws of society, and lack of anxiety or guilt regarding behavior [synonyms: sociopathic personality, psychopathic personality]" (Atkinson, Atkinson, Smith, & Bem, 1990, p. A-2).

Anxious attachment A form of insecure attachment between a child and a caregiver associated with insufficient attachment. Anxiously attached children are overly dependent on caregivers (e.g., clingy, fussy).

Attachment (adult) An affectionate bond with a romantic partner that is a relatively long-lasting tie typified by wanting to be close to the partner, resulting in feelings of comfort and security; also incorporates seeing the partner as unique as an individual who is not exchangeable with any other (Feeney & Noller, 1996).

Attachment (childhood) "The tendency of the young organism to seek closeness to particular individuals and to feel more secure in their presence" (Atkinson et al., 1990, p. A-2).

Attention-deficit/hyperactivity disorder A psychological disorder characterized by a consistent pattern of age-inappropriate behaviors, including inattention, impulsivity, and hyperactivity.

Attribution "The process by which we attempt to explain the behavior of other people" (Atkinson et al., 1990, p. A-2).

Battered woman syndrome (BWS) A subcategory of posttraumatic stress disorder consisting of a cluster of cognitions, feelings, and behaviors brought about by the effects of trauma, learned helplessness, and the cycle of violence that culminates in the victim's belief that she cannot escape her abuser (Walker, 1991, 1993).

Battering "A process whereby one member of an intimate relationship experiences vulnerability, loss of power and control, and entrapment as a consequence of the other member's exercise of power through the patterned use of physical, sexual, psychological, and/or moral force" (Smith, Thornton, DeVellis, Earp, & Coker, 2002, p. 1210).

Borderline disorders "A group of psychological disturbances which exhibit various combinations of normality, neurosis, functional psychosis, and psychopathy" (Goldenson, 1970, p. 172). The term *borderline* implies that there is no dominant pattern of deviance, but there are problems with impulsivity, instability of moods, and so forth. Antisocial disorder is characterized by long-standing problems, such as a disregard for the rights of others, irresponsibility, and resisting authority.

Claims-makers Interest groups and individuals actively engaged in the process of raising awareness about a particular social condition.

Cluster analysis "Any of several procedures in multivariate analysis designed to determine whether individuals (or other units of analysis) are similar enough to fall into groups or clusters" (Vogt, 1993, p. 36).

Conduct disorder One type of disruptive behavior disorder in which a child exhibits a consistent pattern of behavior characterized by antisocial behaviors, including aggression toward people or property, stealing, lying, truancy, and running away.

Corporal punishment Minor, "legitimate" violence accepted and sometimes encouraged in society because of its presumed positive effects on the behavior of children.

Deductive methods Research methods in which "conclusions [are] derived by reasoning rather than by data gathering" (Vogt, 1993, p. 64).

Disability "A product of the intersection of individual characteristics (e.g., conditions or impairments, functional status, or personal and socioeconomic qualities) and characteristics of the natural, built, cultural, and social environments" (National Institute on Disability and Rehabilitation Research, 2003, p. 2).

Disaggregate "To separate out for purposes of analysis the parts of an aggregate statistic" (Vogt, 1993, p. 70). An example would be sorting out a subgroup, such as college students, in an aggregate sample of young adults.

Discriminant functions analysis "A form of regression analysis designed for classification. It allows two or more continuous independent or predictor variables to be used to place individuals or cases into the categories of a categorical dependent variable" (Vogt, 1993, p. 71). Correlational analyses are designed to separate individuals into distinct categories based on their scores on various dependent variables. The analyses provide information on how to distinguish groups.

Disorganized attachment A form of attachment between a child and a caregiver that is characterized by insecurity and disorganization. Also referred to as *Type D attachment.*

Disruptive behavior disorders A category in the *Diagnostic Manual and Statistical Manual of Mental Disorders* (American Psychiatric Association, 1994) that includes oppositional defiant disorder, conduct disorder, and attention-deficit/hyperactivity disorder.

Dissociation "The process whereby some ideas, feelings, or activities lose relationship to other aspects of consciousness and personality and operate automatically or independently" (Atkinson et al., 1990, p. A-8; see also Braun, 1988).

Dysphoria "Generalized feeling of anxiety, restlessness accompanied by depression" (Wolman, 1973, p. 109).

Dysthymia A form of depression characterized by a chronic, rather than acute, pattern of symptoms.

Endangerment standard A standard used in defining child abuse and neglect that includes situations in which children are not yet harmed by maltreatment but have experienced maltreatment that puts them in danger of being harmed.

Externalizing behaviors A dimension of childhood behaviors typically viewed as "acting-out" behaviors, including aggressive, delinquent, and impulsive behaviors.

Factor analysis "Any of several methods of analysis that enable researchers to reduce a large number of variables to a smaller number of variables, or 'factors,' or latent variables. Factor analysis is done by finding patterns among the variations in the values of several variables; a cluster of highly intercorrelated variables is a factor" (Vogt, 1993, p. 89).

Failure to thrive A disorder in infants characterized by failure to maintain age-appropriate weight.

Family violence "Includes family members' acts of omission or commission resulting in physical abuse, sexual abuse, emotional abuse, neglect, or other forms of maltreatment that hamper individuals' healthy development" (Levesque, 2001, p. 13).

Gay intimate partner violence "A means to control others through power, including physical and psychological threats (verbal and nonverbal) or injury (to the victim or others), isolation, economic deprivation, heterosexist control, sexual assaults, vandalism (destruction of property), or any combination of methods" (Burke, 1998, p. 164).

Harm standard A standard used in defining child abuse and neglect that requires demonstrable harm to children as a result of maltreatment.

Heterosexism "An ideological system that denies, denigrates, and stigmatizes any nonheterosexual form of behavior, identity, relationship, or community" (Herek, 1990, p. 316).

Homophobia Heterosexuals' dread or fear of being in close quarters with homosexuals or aversion to non-heterosexuals or their lifestyles.

Hostility "An attitudinal disposition toward negative evaluation" (Eckhardt, Barbour, & Stuart, 1997, p. 335).

Incidence (of violence) The frequency of violent acts occurring within a subgroup of affected individuals.

Inductive methods "Research procedures and methods of reasoning that begin with (or put emphasis on) observation and then move from observation of particulars to the development of general hypotheses" (Vogt, 1993, p. 111).

Internalizing behaviors A dimension of childhood behaviors typically viewed as "inhibited" behaviors, including depression, anxiety, and low self-esteem.

Intervention (in family violence) Societal responses to family violence after it occurs, including counseling, arrest, and medical attention.

Intimate partner violence (IPV) Violence between sexually intimate couples of almost any age, education level, marital status, living arrangement, or sexual orientation.

Learned helplessness "A condition in which a subject does not attempt to escape from a painful or noxious situation after learning in a previous, similar situation that escape is not possible" (Gerow, 1989, p. 193).

Logistic regression analysis "A kind of regression analysis used when the dependent variable is dichotomous and scored 0,1. It is usually used for predicting whether something will happen or not, such as graduation, business failure, heart disease—anything that can be expressed as Event/Nonevent" (Vogt, 1993, p. 131).

Longitudinal study "A study over time of a variable or a group of subjects" (Vogt, 1993, p. 131).

Mandatory arrest laws Laws that require police to arrest violent intimates when probable cause exists; such laws currently exist in many U.S. states and local jurisdictions.

Mandatory reporting laws Laws that require certain classes of professionals to report cases of suspected child or adult abuse; such laws currently exist in all U.S. states.

Mediator (variable) "Another term for intervening variable, that is, a variable that 'transmits' the effects of another. Example: Parents' Status—Child's Education—Child's Status. Education is the mediating variable" (Vogt, 1993, p. 138).

Meta-analysis "Quantitative procedure for summarizing or integrating the findings obtained from a literature review of a subject. Meta-analysis is, strictly speaking, more a kind of synthesis than analysis. The meta-analyst uses the results of individual research projects on the same topic (perhaps studies testing the same hypothesis) as data points for a statistical study of the topic" (Vogt, 1993, p. 138).

Moderator (variable) "A variable that influences ('moderates') the relation between two other variables and thus produces an interaction effect" (Vogt, 1993, p. 142).

Multivariate methods "Any of several methods for examining multiple variables at the same time. . . . Examples include path analysis, factor analysis, multiple regression analysis, MANOVA, LISREL, canonical correlations, and discriminant analysis" (Vogt, 1993, p. 147).

Munchausen by proxy A constellation of behaviors whereby an adult uses a child as the vehicle for fabricated illness.

Narcissism "Inflated, grandiose, or unjustified favorable self-views" (Bushman & Baumeister, 1998, p. 220).

Neurotransmitter "A chemical involved in the transmission of nerve impulses across the synapse from one neuron to another" (Atkinson et al., 1990, p. A-16).

Odds ratio "A ratio of one odds to another. The odds ratio is a measure of association, but, unlike other measures of association, '1.0' means that there is no relationship between the variables. The size of any relationship is measured by the difference (in either direction) from 1.00. An odds ratio less than 1.00 indicates an inverse or negative relation; an odds ratio greater than 1.0 indicates a direct or positive relation. Also called 'cross-product ratio'" (Vogt, 1993, p. 158).

Oversampling "A procedure of stratified sampling in which the researcher selects a disproportionately large number of subjects from a particular group (stratum)" (Vogt, 1993, p. 162).

Posttraumatic stress disorder (PTSD) An anxiety disorder produced by an extremely stressful event(s) (e.g., assault, rape, military combat, death camp) and characterized by a number of adverse reactions: (a) reexperiencing the trauma in painful recollections or recurrent dreams; (b) diminished responsiveness (numbing), with disinterest in significant activities and with feelings of detachment and estrangement from others; and (c) symptoms such as exaggerated startle response, disturbed sleep, difficulty in concentrating or remembering, guilt about surviving when others did not, and avoidance of activities that call the traumatic event to mind (Goldenson, 1984).

Prevalence (of violence)   The number of people in the population of interest who are affected by the occurrence of violent acts.

Primary prevention (of family violence)   Efforts to prevent family violence from occurring in the first place. Some experts use the term *prevention* (as opposed to *primary prevention*) when referring to efforts to prevent recurrences of violence.

Process theories (of child abuse)   Theories that emphasize specific precursors that lead to child abuse and neglect and/or processes that maintain the child abuse and neglect.

Protective factor   A variable that precedes a negative outcome and decreases the chances that the outcome will occur.

Risk factor   A variable that precedes a negative outcome and increases the chances that the outcome will occur.

Risk marker   An antecedent variable that is significantly correlated with a consequent variable. The antecedent variable predicts the consequent variable. Example: Female poverty is a risk factor for female IPV victimization.

Serotonin   "A neurotransmitter in both the peripheral and central nervous systems. It is an inhibitory transmitter whose actions have been implicated in various processes including sleep, the perception of pain, and mood disorders (depression and manic-depression)" (Atkinson et al., 1990, p. A-23).

Sexual violence   "A sex act completed against a victim's will or when a victim is unable to consent due to age, illness, disability, or the influence of alcohol or other drugs. It may involve actual or threatened physical force, use of guns or other weapons, coercion, intimidation or pressure. Sexual violence also includes intentional touching of the genitals, anus, groin, or breast against victim's will or when a victim is unable to consent, as well as voyeurism, exposure to exhibitionism, or undesired exposure to pornography. The perpetrator of sexual violence may be a stranger, friend, family member, or intimate partner" (Centers for Disease Control and Prevention, 2002, p. 3).

Shaken baby syndrome   A type of brain injury in a child that results from the child's being vigorously shaken.

Social constructionism   A perspective that holds that societal reactions to a social condition are central to the process of that condition's redefinition as a social problem.

Stalking   "A course of conduct directed at a specific person involving repeated visual or physical proximity; nonconsensual communication; verbal, written, or implied threats; of a combination thereof that would cause fear in a reasonable person, with 'repeated' meaning on two or more occasions" (Tjaden & Thoennes, 2000a, p. 5).

Structural equation   "An equation representing the strength and nature of the hypothesized relations among (the 'structure' of) sets of variables in a theory" (Vogt, 1993, p. 224).

Structural equation models   "Models made up of more than one structural equation; thus models that describe causal relations among latent variable and include coefficients for endogenous variables" (Vogt, 1993, p. 224).

Substantiated (allegation of maltreatment)   "A type of investigation disposition that concludes that the allegation of maltreatment or risk of maltreatment was supported or founded by State law or State policy. This is the highest level of finding by a State Agency" (U.S. Department of Health and Human Services, 2003a, p. 92).

Theory   "An integrated set of ideas that explain a set of observations" (O'Neill, 1998, p. 459).

Therapeutic jurisprudence   A justice approach that frames an offense to include the perpetrator, the victim, and the community. Family, peers, and advocates design an individualized perpetrator rehabilitation, victim restoration, and community social reintegration of all parties involved (Koss, 2000). Also known as *restorative jurisprudence* and *communitarian jurisprudence*.

Transactional theories (of child abuse)   Theories that emphasize the interactions among risk and protective factors associated with child abuse and neglect.

Traumatic event   "A circumstance in which an individual experiences, witnesses, or is confronted with an event or events that involve actual or threatened death or serious injury, or a threat to the physical integrity of the individual or others. Responses to traumatic events entail intense fear, helplessness, and horror" (American Psychiatric Association, 1994).

Type D attachment   *See* Disorganized attachment.

Variance (explained)   The proportion of differences on one variable that is accounted for by differences in scores on another variable(s).

Violence   "An act carried out with the intention of, or an act perceived as having the intention of, physically hurting another person" (Steinmetz, 1987, p. 729).

Vulnerable adult   "A person who is either being mistreated or in danger of mistreatment and who, due to age and/or disability, is unable to protect him/herself" (Teaster, 2003, p. viii).

References

Abbey, A., McAuslan, P., & Ross, L. T. (1998). Sexual assault perpetration by college men: The role of alcohol, misperception of sexual intent, and sexual beliefs and experiences. *Journal of Social and Clinical Psychology, 17,* 167–195.

Abbey, A., McAuslan, P., Zawacki, T., Clinton, A. M., & Buck, P. O. (2001). Attitudinal, experiential, and situational predictors of sexual assault perpetration. *Journal of Interpersonal Violence, 16,* 784–807.

Abdi, S. N. M. (2000, November 27). Women's worsening plight greeted with indifference. *South China Morning Post,* pp. 14–15.

Abel, G. G., Becker, J. V., & Cunningham-Rathner, J. (1984). Complications, consent, and cognitions in sex between children and adults. *International Journal of Law and Psychiatry, 7,* 89–103.

Abel, G. G., Becker, J. V., & Skinner, L. J. (1986). Behavioral approaches to treatment of the violent sex offender. In L. H. Roth (Ed.), *Clinical treatment of the violent person* (pp. 100–123). New York: Guilford.

Abel, G. G., Gore, D. K., Holland, C. L., Camp, N., Becker, J. V., & Rathner, J. (1989). The measurement of the cognitive distortions of child molesters. *Annals of Sex Research, 2,* 135–153.

Abel, G. G., & Rouleau, J. L. (1990). The nature and extent of sexual assault. In W. L. Marshall, D. R. Laws, & H. E. Barbaree (Eds.), *Handbook of sexual assault: Issues, theories, and treatment of the offender* (pp. 9–21). New York: Plenum.

Aberle, C., & Littlefield, R. P. (2001). Family functioning and sexual aggression in a sample of college men. *Journal of Interpersonal Violence, 16,* 565–579.

Abney, V. D. (2002). Cultural competency in the field of child maltreatment. In J. E. B. Myers, L. Berliner, J. Briere, C. T. Hendrix, C. Jenny, & T. A. Reid (Eds.), *The APSAC handbook on child maltreatment* (2nd ed., pp. 477–486). Thousand Oaks, CA: Sage.

Abramson, L. (1994, July 25). Unequal justice. *Newsweek, 124,* 25.

Abusive relationships and Stockholm syndrome. (1991, September 23). *Behavior Today, 22*(39), 6–7.

Achenbach, T. M. (1997). *Child Behavior Checklist (CBCL).* Burlington: University of Vermont. (Original work published 1986)

Achenbach, T. M., & Edelbrock, C. S. (1983). *Manual for the Child Behavior Checklist and Revised Child Behavior Profile.* Burlington: University of Vermont Press.

Ackard, D. M., & Neumark-Sztainer, D. (2002). Date violence and date rape among adolescents: Association with disordered eating behaviors and psychological health. *Child Abuse & Neglect, 26,* 455–473.

Ackerman, P. T., Newton, J. E. O., McPherson, W. B., Jones, J. G., & Dykman, R. A. (1998). Prevalence of post-traumatic stress disorder and other psychiatric diagnoses in three groups of abused children (sexual, physical, and both). *Child Abuse & Neglect, 22,* 750–774.

Acosta, O. M., Albus, K. E., Reynolds, M. W., Spriggs, D., & Weist, M. D. (2001). Assessing the status of research on violence-related problems among youth. *Journal of Clinical Child Psychology, 30,* 152–160.

Acton, R. G., & During, S. M. (1992). Preliminary results of aggression management training for aggressive parents. *Journal of Interpersonal Violence, 7,* 410–417.

Adams, D. C. (1986, August). *Counseling men who batter: A profeminist analysis of five treatment models.* Paper presented at the annual meeting of the American Psychological Association, Washington, DC.

Adams, D. C. (1988). Treatment models of men who batter: A profeminist analysis. In K. A. Yllö & M. Bograd (Eds.), *Feminist perspectives on wife abuse* (pp. 176–199). Newbury Park, CA: Sage.

Adams, D. C. (1996). Guidelines for doctors on identifying and helping their patients who batter. *Journal of the American Medical Women's Association, 51,* 123–126.

Adams, D. C., & McCormick, A. J. (1982). Men unlearning violence: A group approach based on the collective model. In M. Roy (Ed.), *The abusive partner: An analysis of domestic battering* (pp. 170–197). New York: Van Nostrand Reinhold.

Adams, S. L., Isaac, N. E., Cochran, D., & Brown, M. E. (1996, December/January). Dating violence among adolescent batterers: A profile of restraining order defendants in Massachusetts. *Domestic Violence Report, 1,* 1–2, 7, 12–13.

Adinkrah, M. (1999). Spousal homicide in Fiji. *Homicide Studies, 3,* 215–240.

Adler, J., Carroll, G., Smith, V., & Rogers, P. (1994, November 14). Innocents lost. *Newsweek, 124,* 26–30.

Adler, J. R. (1999). Strengthening victims' rights in domestic violence cases: An argument for 30-day mandatory restraining orders in Massachusetts. *Boston Public Interest Law Journal, 8,* 303–332.

Adler, N., & Schutz, J. (1995). Sibling incest offenders. *Child Abuse & Neglect, 19,* 811–819.

Administration on Aging. (1999). *Long Term Care Ombudsman annual report fiscal year 1996.* Washington, DC: U.S. Department of Health and Human Services.

Advisory Council on Violence Against Women. (1996). *A community checklist: Important steps to end violence against women.* Retrieved from http://www.usdoj.gov/vawa/cheklist.htm

Ahmed-Ghosh, H. (2004). Chattels of society: Domestic violence in India. *Violence Against Women, 10,* 94–118.

Ahn, H. N. (1994). Cultural diversity and definition of child abuse. In R. Barth, J. D. Berrick, & M. Gilbert (Eds.), *Child welfare research review* (Vol. 1, pp. 28–55). New York: Columbia University Press.

Ahn, H. N., & Gilbert, N. (1992). Cultural diversity and sexual abuse prevention. *Social Service Review, 66,* 410–427.

Ahrens, C. E., Campbell, R., Wasco, S. M., Aponte, G., Grubstein, L., & Davidson, W. S., II. (2000). Sexual assault nurse examiner (SANE) programs. *Journal of Interpersonal Violence, 15,* 921–943.

Aldarondo, E. (1996). Cessation and persistence of wife assault: A longitudinal analysis. *American Journal of Orthopsychiatry, 66,* 141–151.

Alessandri, S. M. (1991). Play and social behavior in maltreated pre-schoolers. *Development and Psychopathology, 3,* 191–205.

Alessandri, S. M. (1992). Mother-child interactional correlates of maltreated and nonmaltreated children's play behavior. *Development and Psychopathology, 4,* 257–270.

Alexander, P. C., & Lupfer, S. L. (1987). Family characteristics and long-term consequences associated with sexual abuse. *Archives of Sexual Behavior, 16,* 235–245.

Alexander, P. C., Neimeyer, R. A., & Follette, V. M. (1991). Group therapy for women sexually abused as children: A controlled study and investigation of individual differences. *Journal of Interpersonal Violence, 6,* 218–231.

Alfaro, J. D. (1981). Report on the relationship between child abuse and neglect and later socially deviant behavior. In R. J. Hunter & Y. E. Walker (Eds.), *Exploring the relationship between child abuse and delinquency* (pp. 175–219). Montclair, NJ: Allanheld, Osmun.

Allen, D. M., & Tarnowski, K. J. (1989). Depressive characteristics of physically abused children. *Journal of Abnormal Child Psychology, 17,* 1–11.

Alpert, E. J., & Cohen, S. (1997). Educating the nation's physicians about family violence and abuse. *Academic Medicine, 71*(Suppl. 1), S3–S110.

Alpert, E. J., Tonkin, A. E., Seeherman, A. M., & Holtz, H. A. (1998). Family violence curricula in U.S. medical schools. *American Journal of Preventive Medicine, 14,* 273–282.

Altstein, H., & McRoy, R. (2000). *Does family preservation serve a child's best interests?* Washington, DC: Georgetown University Press.

Amaro, H., Fried, L. E., Cabral, H., & Zuckerman, B. (1990). Violence during pregnancy and substance abuse. *American Journal of Public Health, 80,* 575–579.

American Academy of Child and Adolescent Psychiatry. (1998). Practice parameters for the assessment and treatment of children and adolescents with posttraumatic stress disorder. *Journal of the American Academy of Child and Adolescent Psychiatry, 37*(10, Suppl.), 4S–26S.

American Academy of Pediatrics, Committees on Child Abuse and Neglect and Community Health Services. (1999). Investigation and review of unexpected infant and child deaths. *Pediatrics, 104,* 1158–1159.

American Association for Protecting Children. (1985). *Highlights of official child neglect and abuse reporting, 1983.* Denver, CO: American Humane Association.

American Association for Protecting Children. (1988). *Highlights of official child neglect and abuse reporting, 1986.* Denver, CO: American Humane Association.

American Association for Protecting Children. (1989). *Highlights of official child neglect and abuse reporting, 1987.* Denver, CO: American Humane Association.

American Association of Retired Persons. (1994). *Survey of services for older battered women.* Unpublished manuscript, Washington, DC.

American Humane Association. (1984). *Highlights of official child abuse and neglect reporting: 1982.* Denver, CO: Author.

American Humane Association. (1993). *Child abuse and day care* (Fact Sheet No. 11). (Available from the American Humane Association, 63 Inverness Drive East, Englewood, CO 80112-5117)

American Medical Association. (2003). Campaign to reduce media violence. Retrieved December 5, 2003, from http://www.ama-assn.org/ama/pub/category/2714.html

American Professional Society on the Abuse of Children. (1995). *Guidelines for the psychosocial evaluation of suspected psychological maltreatment in children and adolescents.* Chicago: Author.

American Psychiatric Association. (1987). *Diagnostic and statistical manual of mental disorders* (3rd ed., rev.). Washington, DC: Author.

American Psychiatric Association. (1994). *Diagnostic and statistical manual of mental disorders* (4th ed.). Washington, DC: Author.

American Psychological Association. (1993). *Violence and youth: Psychology's response* (Vol. 1). Washington, DC: Author.

American Psychological Association. (2003). Guidelines on multicultural education, training, research, practice, and organizational change for psychologists. *American Psychologist, 58,* 377–402.

Ammerman, R. T. (1991). The role of the child in physical abuse: A reappraisal. *Violence and Victims, 6,* 87–101.

Ammerman, R. T., Van Hasselt, V. B., Hersen, M., McGonigle, J. J., & Lubetsky, M. J. (1989). Abuse and neglect in psychiatrically hospitalized multihandicapped children. *Child Abuse & Neglect, 13,* 335–343.

Amundson, M. J. (1989). Family crisis care: A home-based intervention program for child abuse. *Issues in Mental Health Nursing, 10,* 285–296.

Anand, S. (2001). Stopping stalking: A search for solutions, a blueprint for effective change. *Saskatchewan Law Review, 64,* 397–428.

Anasseril, D., & Holcomb, W. (1985). A comparison between men charged with domestic and nondomestic homicide. *Bulletin of the American Academy of Psychiatry and Law, 13,* 233–241.

Anderson, D. (1979). Touching: When is it caring and nurturing or when is it exploitative and damaging? *Child Abuse & Neglect, 3,* 793–794.

Anderson, D. K., & Saunders, D. G. (2003). Leaving an abusive partner: An empirical review of predictors, the process of leaving, and psychological well-being. *Trauma, Violence, & Abuse, 4,* 163–191.

Anderson, D. K., Saunders, D. G., Yoshihama, M., Bybee, D. I., & Sullivan, C. M. (2003). Long-term trends in depression among women separated from abusive partners. *Violence Against Women, 9,* 807–838.

Anderson, S. A., & Schlossberg, M. C. (1999). Systems perspectives on battering: The importance of context and patterns. In

M. Harway & J. M. O'Neil (Eds.), *What causes men's violence against women?* (pp. 137–152). Thousand Oaks, CA: Sage.

Andrews, A. B., & Veronen, L. J. (1993). Sexual assault and people with disabilities. *Journal of Social Work and Human Sexuality, 8,* 137–159.

Andrews, B., & Brewin, C. R. (1990). Attributions of blame for marital violence: A study of antecedents and consequences. *Journal of Marriage and the Family, 52,* 757–767.

Andrews, B., Brewin, C. R., & Rose, S. (2003). Gender, social support, and PTSD in victims of violent crime. *Journal of Traumatic Stress, 16,* 421–427.

Anetzberger, G. J. (1998). Psychological abuse and neglect: A cross-cultural concern to older Americans. In Archstone Foundation (Ed.), *Understanding and combating elder abuse in minority communities* (pp. 141–151). Long Beach, CA: Archstone Foundation.

Anglin, K., & Holtzworth-Munroe, A. (1997). Comparing the responses of violent and nonviolent couples to problematic marital and nonmarital situations: Are the skills deficits of violent couples global? *Journal of Family Psychology, 11,* 301–313.

Ansello, E. F. (1996). Understanding the problem. In L. A. Baumhover & S. C. Beall (Eds.), *Abuse, neglect, and exploitation of older persons: Strategies for assessment and intervention* (pp. 9–29). Baltimore: Health Professions Press.

Anson, O., & Sagy, S. (1995). Marital violence: Comparing women in violent and nonviolent unions. *Human Relations, 48,* 285–305.

Appel, A. E., & Holden, G. W. (1998). The co-occurrence of spouse and physical child abuse: A review and appraisal. *Journal of Family Psychology, 12,* 578–599.

Apsler, R., Cummins, M. R., & Carl, S. (2002). Fear and expectations: Differences among female victims of domestic violence who come to the attention of the police. *Violence and Victims, 17,* 445–453.

Apsler, R., Cummins, M. R., & Carl, S. (2003). Perceptions of the police by female victims of domestic partner violence. *Violence Against Women, 9,* 1318–1335.

Arber, S., & Ginn, J. (1999). Gender differences in informal caring. In G. Allan (Ed.), *The sociology of the family: A reader* (pp. 321–339). Oxford: Blackwell.

Arboleda-Florez, J., & Wade, T. J. (2001). Childhood and adult victimization as risk factors for major depression. *International Journal of Law and Psychiatry, 24,* 357–370.

Archer, J. (2000). Sex differences in aggression between heterosexual partners: A meta-analytic review. *Psychological Bulletin, 126,* 651–680.

Arias, I., & Pape, K. T. (1999). Psychological abuse: Implications for adjustment and commitment to leave violent partners. *Violence and Victims, 14,* 55–67.

Armstrong, T. G., Heideman, G., Corcoran, K. J., Fisher, B., Medina, K. L., & Schafer, J. (2001). Disagreement about the occurrence of male-to-female intimate partner violence: A qualitative study. *Family and Community Health, 24*(1), 55–75.

Armstrong, T. G., Wernke, J. Y., Medina, K. L., & Schafer, J. (2002). Do partners agree about the occurrence of intimate partner violence? *Trauma, Violence, & Abuse, 3,* 181–193.

Asbury, J. (1993). Violence in families of color in the United States. In R. L. Hampton, T. P. Gullotta, G. R. Adams, E. H. Potter III, & R. P. Weissberg (Eds.), *Family violence: Prevention and treatment* (pp. 159–178). Newbury Park, CA: Sage.

Ash, M., & Cahn, N. R. (1994). Child abuse: A problem for feminist theory. In M. A. Fineman & R. Mykitiuk (Eds.), *The public nature of private violence: The discovery of domestic abuse* (pp. 166–194). London: Routledge.

Ashcraft, C. (2000). Naming knowledge: A language for reconstructing domestic violence and gender inequity. *Women and Language, 23,* 3–10.

Atkinson, R. L., Atkinson, R. C., Smith, E. E., & Bem, D. J. (1990). *Introduction to psychology* (10th ed.). New York: Harcourt Brace Jovanovich.

Attala, J. M., Weaver, T. L., Duckett, D., & Draper, V. (2000). The implications of domestic violence for home care providers. *International Journal of Trauma Nursing, 6*(2), 48–53.

Attar, B. K., Guerra, N. G., & Tolan, P. H. (1994). Neighborhood disadvantage, stressful life events, and adjustment in urban elementary-school children. *Journal of Clinical Psychology, 23,* 391–400.

Austin, J. B., & Dankwort, J. (1999). Standards for batterer programs: A review and analysis. *Journal of Interpersonal Violence, 14,* 152–168.

Avakame, E. F. (1998). Intergeneration transmission of violence, self-control, and conjugal violence: A comparative analysis of physical violence and psychological aggression. *Violence and Victims, 13,* 301–316.

Avakame, E. F., & Fyfe, J. J. (2001). Differential police treatment of male-on-female spousal violence. *Violence Against Women, 7,* 22–45.

Avni, N. (1991). Battered wives: The home as a total institution. *Violence and Victims, 6,* 137–149.

Ayoub, C. C., Alexander, R., Beck, D., Bursch, B., Feldman, K. W., Libow, J., et al. (2002). Position paper: Definitional issues in Munchausen by proxy. *Child Maltreatment, 7,* 105–111.

Ayoub, C. C., Deutsch, R. M., & Kinscherff, R. T. (2000). Munchausen by proxy: Definition, identification, and evaluation. In R. M. Reece (Ed.), *Treatment of child abuse: Common ground for mental health, medical, and legal practitioners* (pp. 213–225). Baltimore: Johns Hopkins University Press.

Ayoub, C. C., & Milner, J. S. (1985). Failure to thrive: Parental indicators, types, and outcomes. *Child Abuse & Neglect, 9,* 491–499.

Ayoub, C. C., Schreier, H. A., & Keller, C. (2002). Munchausen by proxy: Presentations in special education. *Child Maltreatment, 7,* 149–159.

Azar, B. (1997, March). APA task force urges a harder look at data. *APA Monitor on Psychology, 28,* 26.

Azar, S. T. (1997). A cognitive behavioral approach to understanding and treating parents who physically abuse their children. In D. A. Wolfe, R. J. McMahon, & R. D. Peters (Eds.), *Child abuse: New directions in prevention and treatment across the lifespan* (pp. 79–101). Thousand Oaks, CA: Sage.

Azar, S. T., Povilaitis, T. Y., Lauretti, A. F., & Pouquette, C. L. (1998). The current status of etiological theories in intrafamilial child maltreatment. In J. R. Lutzker (Ed.), *Handbook of child abuse research and treatment* (pp. 3–30). New York: Plenum.

Azar, S. T., & Siegel, B. R. (1990). Behavioral treatment of child abuse: A developmental perspective. *Behavior Modification, 14,* 279–300.

Azar, S. T., & Wolfe, D. A. (1998). Child physical abuse and neglect. In E. J. Mash & R. A. Barkley (Eds.), *Treatment of childhood disorders* (pp. 501–544). New York: Guilford.

Babcock, J. C., Green, C. E., & Robie, C. (2004). Does batterers' treatment work? A meta-analytic review of domestic violence treatment. *Clinical Psychology Review, 23,* 1023–1053.

Babcock, J. C., Jacobson, N. S., Gottman, J. M., & Yerington, T. P. (2000). Attachment, emotional regulation, and the function of marital violence: Differences between secure, preoccupied, and dismissing violent and nonviolent husbands. *Journal of Family Violence, 15,* 391–409.

Babcock, J. C., & La Taillade, J. J. (2000). Evaluating interventions for men who batter. In J. P. Vincent & E. N. Jouriles (Eds.), *Domestic violence: Guidelines for research-informed practice* (pp. 33–77). Philadelphia: Jessica Kingsley.

Babcock, J. C., & Steiner, R. (1999). The relationship between treatment, incarceration, and recidivism of battering: A program evaluation of Seattle's coordinated community response to domestic violence. *Journal of Family Psychology, 13,* 46–59.

Babcock, J. C., Waltz, J., Jacobson, N. S., & Gottman, J. M. (1993). Power and violence: The relation between communication patterns, power discrepancies, and domestic violence. *Journal of Consulting and Clinical Psychology, 61,* 40–50.

Bachman, R., & Pillemer, K. A. (1991). Retirement: Does it affect marital conflict and violence? *Journal of Elder Abuse & Neglect, 3*(2), 75–88.

Bachman, R., & Saltzman, L. E. (1995). *Violence against women: Estimates from the redesigned survey* (NCJ Publication No. 154348). Rockville, MD: U.S. Department of Justice.

Bagarozzi, D., & Giddings, C. (1983). Conjugal violence: A critical review of current research and clinical practices. *American Journal of Family Therapy, 11,* 3–15.

Bagley, C. (1990). Is the prevalence of child sexual abuse decreasing? Evidence from a random sample of 750 young adult women. *Psychological Reports, 66,* 1037–1038.

Bagley, C., & Ramsay, R. (1986). Sexual abuse in childhood: Psychological outcomes and implications for social work practice. *Journal of Social Work and Human Sexuality, 4,* 33–47.

Bagley, C., & Young, L. (1987). Juvenile prostitution and child sexual abuse: A controlled study. *Journal of Community Mental Health, 6,* 5–26.

Baily, T. F., & Baily, W. H. (1986). *Operational definitions of child emotional maltreatment: Final report* (DHHS Publication No. 90–CA-0956). Washington, DC: Government Printing Office.

Baker, C. K., Cook, S. L., & Norris, F. H. (2003). Domestic violence and housing problems: A contextual analysis of women's help-seeking, received informal support, and formal system response. *Violence Against Women, 9,* 754–783.

Baker, M. T., Miller, E. R., Johnston, F. E., Van Hasselt, V. B., & Bourke, M. L. (1998, July). *Strategies for the training of police (STOP) in domestic violence.* Paper presented at Program Evaluation and Family Violence Research: An International Conference, Durham, NH.

Bakwin, H. (1949). Emotional deprivation in infants. *Journal of Pediatrics, 35,* 512–521.

Balakrishna, J. (1998). Sexual abuse: How far do the ripples go? *Sexual and Marital Therapy, 13,* 83–89.

Balogh, D. W. (2002). Teaching ethics across the psychology curriculum. *APS Observer, 15*(7), 29, 31, 36–37.

Bandura, A. (1977). *Social learning theory.* Morristown, NJ: General Learning.

Bandura, A., Ross, D., & Ross, S. A. (1961). Transmission of aggression through imitation of aggressive models. *Journal of Abnormal and Social Psychology, 67,* 575–582.

Bane, V., Grant, M., Alexander, B., Kelly, K., Brown, S. A., Wegher, B., & Feldon-Mitchell, L. (1990, December 17). Silent no more. *People,* pp. 94–97, 99–100, 102, 104.

Banks, A. (2001). *PTSD: Relationships and brain chemistry* (Project Report No 8). Wellesley, MA: Wellesley Centers for Women.

Banyard, V. L., Arnold, S., & Smith, J. (2000). Childhood sexual abuse and dating experiences of undergraduate women. *Child Maltreatment, 5,* 39–48.

Barata, P., & Senn, C. Y. (2003). When two worlds collide: An examination of the assumptions of social science research and law within the domain of domestic violence. *Trauma, Violence & Abuse, 4,* 3–21.

Barbaree, H. E., Marshall, W. L., & Hudson, S. (Eds.). (1993). *The juvenile sex offender.* New York: Guilford.

Barber, J. G., & Delfabbro, P. (2000). The assessment of parenting in child protection cases. *Research on Social Work Practice, 10,* 243–256.

Barbour, K. A., Eckhardt, C. I., Davison, G. C., & Kassinove, H. (1998). The experience and expression of anger in maritally violent and maritally discordant-nonviolent men. *Behavior Therapy, 29,* 173–191.

Barnett, D., Ganiban, J., & Cicchetti, D. (1999). Maltreatment, negative expressivity, and the development of Type D attachments from 12 to 24 months of age. *Monographs of the Society for Research in Child Development, 64*(3), 97–118.

Barnett, O. W., & Fagan, R. W. (1993). Alcohol use in male spouse abusers and their female partners. *Journal of Family Violence, 8,* 1–25.

Barnett, O. W., Fagan, R. W., & Booker, J. M. (1991). Hostility and stress as mediators of aggression in violent men. *Journal of Family Violence, 6,* 219–241.

Barnett, O. W., & Hamberger, L. K. (1992). The assessment of maritally violent men on the California Psychological Inventory. *Violence and Victims, 7,* 15–28.

Barnett, O. W., Lee, C. Y., & Thelen, R. E. (1997). Differences in forms, outcomes, and attributions of self-defense and control in interpartner aggression. *Violence Against Women, 3,* 462–481.

Barnett, O. W., Martinez, T. E., & Bleustein, B. W. (1995). Jealousy and anxious romantic attachment in maritally violent and nonviolent males. *Journal of Interpersonal Violence, 10,* 473–486.

Barnett, O. W., Martinez, T. E., & Keyson, M. (1996). The relationship between violence, social support, and self-blame in battered women. *Journal of Interpersonal Violence, 11,* 221–233.

Barone, V. J., Greene, B. F., & Lutzker, J. R. (1986). Home safety with families being treated for child abuse and neglect. *Behavior Modification, 14,* 230–254.

Barrera, M., Palmer, S., Brown, R., & Kalaher, S. (1994). Characteristics of court-involved men and non-court-involved men who abuse their wives. *Journal of Family Violence, 9,* 333–345.

Bartholomew, K. (1997). Adult attachment processes: Individual and couple perspectives. *British Journal of Medical Psychology, 70,* 249–263.

Bartley, N. (1998, April 10). Ex-teacher pleads guilty to child rape. *Seattle Times.* Retrieved from http://www.seattletimes.com

Bartoi, M. G., & Kinder, B. N. (1998). Effects of child and adult sexual abuse on adult sexuality. *Journal of Sex and Marital Therapy, 24,* 75–90.

Barton, K., & Baglio, C. (1993). The nature of stress in child-abusing families: A factor analytic study. *Psychological Reports, 73,* 1047–1055.

Bass, E., & Davis, L. (1988). *The courage to heal.* New York: Harper & Row.

Bassuk, E. L., Weinreb, L. F., Buckner, J. C., Browne, A., Salomon, A., & Bassuk, S. S. (1996). The characteristics and needs of sheltered homeless and low-income housed mothers. *Journal of the American Medical Association, 276,* 640–646.

Bath, H. I., & Haapala, D. A. (1993). Intensive family preservation services with abused and neglected children: An examination of group differences. *Child Abuse & Neglect, 17,* 213–225.

Bauer, W. D., & Twentyman, C. T. (1985). Abusing, neglectful, and comparison mothers' responses to child-related and non-child-related stressors. *Journal of Consulting and Clinical Psychology, 53,* 335–343.

Baumann, E. A. (1989). Research rhetoric and the social construction of elder abuse. In J. Best (Ed.), *Images of issues: Typifying contemporary social problems* (pp. 55–74). New York: Aldine de Gruyter.

Baumeister, R. F., Campbell, J. D., Krueger, J. I., & Vohs, K. D. (2003). Does high self-esteem cause better performance, interpersonal success, happiness, or healthier lifestyles? *Psychological Science in the Public Interest, 4*(Suppl. 1), 1–44.

Baumeister, R. F., Dale, K., & Sommer, K. L. (1996). Relation of threatened egotism to violence and aggression: The dark side of high self-esteem. *Psychological Review, 103,* 5–33.

Baumrind, D. (1996). A blanket injunction against disciplinary use of spanking is not warranted by the data. *Pediatrics, 98,* 828–831.

Baumrind, D., Larzelere, R. E., & Cowan, P. A. (2002). Ordinary physical punishment: Is it harmful? Comment on Gershoff (2002). *Psychological Bulletin, 128,* 580–589.

Bauserman, S. A. K., & Arias, I. (1992). Relationships among marital investment, marital satisfaction, and marital commitment in domestically victimized and nonvictimized wives. *Violence and Victims, 7,* 287–296.

Bays, J., & Chadwick, D. (1993). Medical diagnosis of the sexually abused child. *Child Abuse & Neglect, 17,* 91–110.

Beardslee, W. R., Salt, P., Versage, E. M., Gladstone, T. R. G., Wright, E. M., Rothberg, P. C. (1997). Sustained change in parents receiving preventive interventions for families with depression. *American Journal of Psychiatry, 154,* 510–515.

Beck, A. T. (1978). *BDI (Beck Depression Inventory).* San Antonio, TX: Psychological Corporation.

Beck, A. T., & Steer, R. A. (1990). *Beck Anxiety Inventory.* San Antonio, TX: Psychological Corporation.

Beck, A. T., & Steer, R. A. (1993). *Beck Depression Inventory.* San Antonio, TX: Psychological Corporation.

Becker, H. W. (1963). *Outsiders.* New York: Free Press.

Becker, J. V. (1994). Offenders: Characteristics and treatment. *Future of Children, 4*(2), 176–197.

Becker, J. V., Alpert, J. L., BigFoot, D. S., Bonner, B. L., Geddie, L. F., Henggeler, S. W., et al. (1995). Empirical research on child abuse treatment: Report by the Child Abuse and Neglect Treatment Working Group, American Psychological Association. *Journal of Clinical Child Psychology, 24,* 23–46.

Becker, J. V., Kaplan, M. S., Cunningham-Rathner, J., & Kavoussi, R. J. (1986). Characteristics of adolescent sexual perpetrators: Preliminary findings. *Journal of Family Violence, 1,* 85–87.

Beckham, J. C., Feldman, M. E., Kirby, A. C., Hertzberg, M. A., & Moore, S. D. (1997). Interpersonal violence and it correlates in Vietnam veterans with chronic posttraumatic stress disorder. *Journal of Clinical Psychology, 53,* 859–869.

Beere, C. A., King, D. W., Beere, D. B., & King, L. A. (1984). The Sex-Role Egalitarianism Scale: A measure of attitudes toward equality between the sexes. *Sex Roles, 10,* 563–576.

Behl, L. E., Conyngham, H. A., & May, P. F. (2003). Trends in child maltreatment literature. *Child Abuse & Neglect, 27,* 215–229.

Beitchman, J. H., Zucker, K. J., Hood, J. E., daCosta, G. A., & Akman, D. (1991). A review of the short-term effects of child sexual abuse. *Child Abuse & Neglect, 15,* 537–556.

Beitchman, J. H., Zucker, K. J., Hood, J. E., daCosta, G. A., Akman, D., & Cassavia, E. (1992). A review of the long-term effects of child sexual abuse. *Child Abuse & Neglect, 16,* 101–118.

Beitiks, K. O. (1994, August). Violence on the homefront: A tiny step to alleviate dangers. *California Bar Journal,* pp. 1, 6.

Belknap, J. (2000). *Factors related to domestic violence court dispositions in a large urban area: The role of victim/witness reluctance and other variables* (NCJ Publication No. 184232). Washington, DC: National Institute of Justice.

Belknap, J., Graham, D. L. R., Allen, P. G., Hartman, J., Lippen, V., & Sutherland, J. (1999, October/November). Predicting court outcomes in intimate partner violence cases: Preliminary findings. *Domestic Violence Report, 5,* 1–2, 9–10.

Bell, C., & Jenkins, E. J. (1991). Traumatic stress and children. *Journal of Health Care for the Poor and Underserved, 2,* 175–185.

Bell, C., & Jenkins, E. J. (1993). Community violence and children on Chicago's South-Side. *Psychiatry, 56,* 46–54.

Bell, C. C., & Mattis, J. (2000). The importance of cultural competence in ministering to African American victims of domestic violence. *Violence Against Women, 6,* 515–532.

Bell, R. Q., & Chapman, M. (1986). Child effects in studies using experimental or brief longitudinal approaches to socialization. *Developmental Psychology, 22,* 595–603.

Belsky, J. (1993). Etiology of child maltreatment: A developmental-ecological analysis. *Psychological Bulletin, 114,* 413–434.

Bem, S. L. (1979). *Bem Sex-Role Inventory: Professional manual.* Palo Alto, CA: Consulting Psychologists Press.

Bender, M., Cook, S., & Kaslow, N. (2003). Social support as a mediator of revictimization of low-income African American women. *Violence and Victims, 18,* 419–431.

Bendik, M. F. (1992). Reaching the breaking point: Dangers of mistreatment in elder caregiving situations. *Journal of Elder Abuse & Neglect, 4*(3), 39–59.

Benedict, M., White, R., Wulff, L., & Hall, B. (1990). Reported maltreatment in children with multiple disabilities. *Child Abuse & Neglect, 14,* 207–217.

Bennett, L. W., & Fineran, S. (1998). Sexual and severe physical violence among high school students: Power beliefs, gender, and relationship. *American Journal of Orthopsychiatry, 68,* 645–652.

Bennett, L. W., Tolman, R. M., Rogalski, C. J., & Srinivasaraghavan, J. (1994). Domestic abuse by male alcohol and drug addicts. *Violence and Victims, 9,* 359–368.

Benoit, D. (1993). Failure to thrive and feeding disorders. In C. H. Zeanah, Jr. (Ed.), *Handbook of infant mental health* (pp. 317–331). New York: Guilford.

Bensley, L. S., Eenwyk, J. V., & Simmons, K. W. (2000). Self-reported childhood sexual and physical abuse and adult HIV-risk behaviors and heavy drinking. *American Journal of Preventive Medicine, 18,* 151–158.

Benson, E. (2002, March). Learning by doing: Four keys to fostering undergraduate research in your laboratory. *APA Monitor on Psychology, 33,* 42–44.

Bent-Goodley, T. (2001). Eradicating domestic violence in the African-American community: A literature review and action agenda. *Trauma, Violence, & Abuse, 2,* 316–330.

Bergman, L. (1992). Dating violence among high school students. *Social Work, 37,* 21–27.

Berk, R. A., Fenstermaker, S., & Newton, P. J. (1988). An empirical analysis of police responses to incidents of wife battery. In G. T. Hotaling, D. Finkelhor, J. T. Kirkpatrick, & M. A. Straus (Eds.), *Coping with family violence* (pp. 158–168). Newbury Park, CA: Sage.

Berkowitz, A. D. (2000, May/June). Critical elements of campus sexual assault prevention and risk reduction programs. *Sexual Assault Report, 3,* 67–68, 80.

Berliner, L. (1991). Clinical work with sexually abused children. In C. R. Hollin & K. Howells (Eds.), *Clinical approaches to sex offenders and their victims* (pp. 209–228). New York: John Wiley.

Berliner, L. (1994). The problem with neglect. *Journal of Interpersonal Violence, 9,* 556–560.

Berliner, L. (1998). Battered women and abused children: The question of responsibility. *Journal of Interpersonal Violence, 13,* 287–288.

Berliner, L., & Conte, J. R. (1990). The process of victimization: The victim's perspective. *Child Abuse & Neglect, 14,* 29–40.

Berliner, L., & Elliott, D. M. (2002). Sexual abuse of children. In J. E. B. Myers, L. Berliner, J. Briere, C. T. Hendrix, C. Jenny, & T. A. Reid (Eds.), *The APSAC handbook on child maltreatment* (2nd ed., pp. 55–78). Thousand Oaks, CA: Sage.

Berman, P. (1990). Group therapy techniques for sexually abused preteen girls. *Child Welfare, 69,* 239–252.

Bernard, C., & Schlaffer, E. (1992). Domestic violence in Austria: The institutional response. In E. C. Viano (Ed.), *Intimate violence: Interdisciplinary perspectives* (pp. 243–254). Bristol, PA: Taylor & Francis.

Bernhard, L. A. (2000). Physical and sexual violence experienced by lesbian and heterosexual women. *Violence Against Women, 6,* 68–79.

Bernhardt, P. C. (1997). Influences of serotonin and testosterone in aggression and dominance: Convergence with social psychology. *Current Directions in Psychological Science, 6,* 44–48.

Berns, S. B., Jacobson, N. S., & Gottman, J. M. (1999). Demand-withdraw interaction in couples with a violent husband. *Journal of Consulting and Clinical Psychology, 67,* 666–674.

Bernstein, A., Newman, J. P., Wallace, J. F., & Luh, K. E. (2000). Left-hemisphere activation and deficient response modulation in psychopaths. *Psychological Science, 11,* 414–418.

Bernstein, E., & Putnam, F. W. (1986). Development, reliability, and validity of a dissociation scale. *Journal of Nervous and Mental Disease, 174,* 727–735.

Berry, M. (1991). The assessment of imminence of risk of placement: Lessons from a family preservation program. *Children and Youth Services Review, 13,* 239–256.

Berson, N., & Herman-Giddens, M. (1994). Recognizing invasive genital care practices: A form of child sexual abuse. *APSAC Advisor, 7*(1), 13–14.

Besharat, M. A., Eisler, I., & Dare, C. (2001). The Self- and Other-Blame Scale (SOBS): The background and presentation of a new instrument for measuring blame in families. *Journal of Family Therapy, 23,* 208–223.

Besharov, D. (1985). "Doing something" about child abuse: The need to narrow the grounds for state intervention. *Harvard Journal of Law and Public Policy, 3,* 539–589.

Besharov, D. (1990). *Recognizing child abuse.* New York: Free Press.

Besharov, D. (1991). Reducing unfounded reports. *Journal of Interpersonal Violence, 6,* 112–115.

Best, J. (1989). Introduction: Typification and social problems construction. In J. Best (Ed.), *Images of issues: Typifying contemporary social problems* (pp. xv–xxii). New York: Aldine de Gruyter.

Best, J. (2001). *Damned lies and statistics: Untangling numbers from the media, politicians, and activists.* Berkeley: University of California Press.

Bethke, T., & De Joy, D. (1993). An experimental study of factors influencing the acceptability of dating violence. *Journal of Interpersonal Violence, 8,* 36–51.

Beutler, L. E., Williams, R. E., & Zetzer, H. A. (1994). Efficacy of treatment for victims of child sexual abuse. *Future of Children, 4*(2), 156–175.

Bevc, I., & Silverman, I. (1993). Early proximity and intimacy between siblings and incestuous behavior: A test of the Westermarck theory. *Ethology and Sociobiology, 14,* 171–181.

Bidrose, S., & Goodman, G. S. (2000). Testimony and evidence: A scientific case study of memory for child sexual abuse. *Applied Cognitive Psychology, 14,* 197–214.

Biegel, D. E., Sales, E., & Schulz, R. (1991). *Family caregiving in chronic illness: Alzheimer's disease, cancer, heart disease, mental illness, and stroke.* Newbury Park, CA: Sage.

Biernath, M. (2000). Crimes against the person: Provide protection for elderly persons and disabled adults. *Georgia State University Law Review, 17,* 93–96.

Biggs, S., Phillipson, C., & Kingston, P. (1995). *Elder abuse in perspective.* Buckingham, Eng.: Open University Press.

Billingham, R. E. (1987). Courtship violence: The patterns of conflict resolution strategies across seven levels of emotional commitment. *Family Relations, 36,* 283–289.

Binggeli, N. J., Hart, S. N., & Brassard, M. R. (2001). *Psychological maltreatment of children.* Thousand Oaks, CA: Sage.

Biology and family, partners in crime. (1996, July 6). *Science News, 150,* 11.

Biringen, Z., & Robinson, J. (1991). Emotional availability in mother-child interactions: A reconceptualization for research. *American Journal of Orthopsychiatry, 61,* 258–271.

Birns, B., Cascardi, M., & Meyer, S. L. (1994). Sex-role socialization: Developmental influences on wife abuse. *American Journal of Orthopsychiatry, 64,* 50–59.

Birns, B., & Meyer, S. L. (1993). Mothers' role in incest: Dysfunctional women or dysfunctional theories? *Journal of Child Sexual Abuse, 2*(3), 127–135.

Blaauw, E., Winkel, F. W., Arensman, E., Sheridan, L. P., & Freeve, A. (2002). The toll of stalking: The relationship between features of stalking and psychopathology of victims. *Journal of Interpersonal Violence, 17,* 50–63.

Black, B. M., & Weisz, A. N. (2003). Dating violence: Help-seeking behaviors of African American middle schoolers. *Violence Against Women, 9,* 187–206.

Black, D. (1993). *The social structure of right and wrong.* San Diego, CA: Academic Press.

Black, D. A., Heyman, R. E., & Slep, A. M. S. (2001a). Risk factors for child physical abuse. *Aggression and Violent Behavior, 6,* 121–188.

Black, D. A., Heyman, R. E., & Slep, A. M. S. (2001b). Risk factors for child sexual abuse. *Aggression and Violent Behavior, 6,* 203–229.

Black, D. A., Slep, A. M. S., & Heyman, R. E. (2001). Risk factors for child psychological abuse. *Aggression and Violent Behavior, 6,* 189–201.

Black, M., Schuler, M., & Nair, P. (1993). Prenatal drug exposure: Neurodevelopmental outcome and parenting environment. *Journal of Pediatric Psychology, 18,* 605–620.

Blake-White, J., & Kline, C. M. (1985). Treating the dissociative process in adult victims of childhood incest. *Social Casework, 66,* 394–402.

Blakely, B. E., & Dolon, R. (1991). Area agencies on aging and the prevention of elder abuse: The results of a national study. *Journal of Elder Abuse & Neglect, 3*(2), 21–40.

Blanchard, B. D. (2001). Extremes of narcissism and self-esteem and the differential experience and expression of anger and use of conflict tactics in male batterers. *Dissertation Abstracts International, 62*(05), 2476B. (UMI No. 301619)

Blankenhorn, D. (1994, December 19). Not orphanages or prisons, but responsible fathers. *Los Angeles Times,* p. B7.

Block, C. R., Engel, B., Naureckas, S. M., & Riordan, K. A. (1999). The Chicago Women's Health Risk Study: Lessons in collaboration. *Violence Against Women, 5,* 1158–1177.

Block, J. H. (1965). *Child-rearing practice report.* Princeton, NJ: Educational Testing Service.

Block, R.W. (2002). Child fatalities. In J. E. B. Myers, L. Berliner, J. Briere, C. T. Hendrix, C. Jenny, & T. A. Reid (Eds.), *The APSAC handbook on child maltreatment* (2nd ed., pp. 293–301). Thousand Oaks, CA: Sage.

Blum, L. C. (1997). The impact of the rewards and costs of family functioning on the decisions made by battered women. *Dissertation Abstracts International, 57*(11), 4928A. (UMI No. 9711021)

Blumenthal, D. R., Neeman, J., & Murphy, C. M. (1998). Lifetime exposure to interparental physical and verbal aggression and symptom expression in college students. *Violence and Victims, 13,* 175–196.

Blythe, R. (1969). *Akenfield: Portrait of an English village.* London: Allen Lane.

Bodin, A. M. (1996). Relationship conflict—verbal and physical: Conceptualizing an inventory for assessing process and content. In F. W. Kaslow (Ed.), *Handbook of relational diagnosis and dysfunctional family patterns* (pp. 371–393). New York: John Wiley.

Boeringer, S. B. (1999). Associations of rape-supportive attitudes with fraternal and athletic participation. *Violence Against Women, 5,* 81–90.

Bogat, G. A., Levendosky, A. A., Theran, S., von Eye, A., & Davidson, W. S. (2003). Predicting the psychosocial effects of intimate partner violence (IPV): How much does a woman's history matter? *Journal of Interpersonal Violence, 18,* 1271–1291.

Bograd, M. (1988). Feminist perspectives on wife abuse: An introduction. In K. A. Yllö & M. Bograd (Eds.), *Feminist perspectives on wife abuse* (pp. 11–26). Newbury Park, CA: Sage.

Bolen, R. M. (2000). Extrafamilial child sexual abuse: A study of perpetrator characteristics and implications for prevention. *Violence Against Women, 6,* 1137–1169.

Bolen, R. M. (2003). Nonoffending mothers of sexually abused children. *Violence Against Women, 9,* 1336–1366.

Bolger, K. E., Patterson, C. J., & Kupersmidt, J. B. (1998). Peer relationships and self-esteem among children who have been maltreated. *Child Development, 69,* 1171–1197.

Bonder, B., Martin, L., & Miracle, A. (2001). Achieving cultural competence: The challenge for clients and healthcare workers in a multicultural society. *Generations, 24*(1), 35–42.

Bondurant, B. (2001). University women's acknowledgment of rape. *Violence Against Women, 7,* 294–314.

Boney-McCoy, S., & Finkelhor, D. (1995). The psychosocial sequelae of violent victimization in a national youth sample. *Journal of Consulting and Clinical Psychology, 63,* 726–736.

Boney-McCoy, S., & Sugarman, D. E. (1999, July). *Self-esteem and partner violence: A meta-analytic review.* Paper presented at the Sixth International Family Violence Research Conference, Durham, NH.

Bonfante, J., Cole, W., Gwynne, S. C., & Kamlani, R. (1994, June 6). Oprah! Oprah in the court. *Time, 143,* 30–31.

Book, A. S., Starzyk, K. B., & Quinsey, V. L. (2001). The relationship between testosterone and aggression: A meta-analysis. *Aggression and Violent Behavior, 6,* 579–599.

Bookwala, J. (2002). The role of own and perceived partner attachment in relationship aggression. *Journal of Interpersonal Violence, 17,* 84–100.

Bookwala, J., Frieze, I. H., Smith, C., & Ryan, K. (1992). Predictors of dating violence: A multivariate analysis. *Violence and Victims, 7,* 297–311.

Bools, C., Neale, B., & Meadow, R. (1994). Munchausen syndrome by proxy: A study of psychopathology. *Child Abuse & Neglect, 18,* 773–788.

Booth, C. A. (1999). No-drop policies: Effective legislation or protectionist attitudes? *University of Toledo Law Review, 30,* 621–645.

Borjesson, W. I., Aarons, G. A., & Dunn, M. E. (2003). Development and confirmatory factor analysis of the abuse within intimate relationships scale. *Journal of Interpersonal Violence, 18,* 295–309.

Borochowitz, D. Y., & Eisikovits, Z. (2002). To love violently: Strategies for reconciling love and violence. *Violence Against Women, 8,* 476–494.

Bottoms, B. L., & Goodman, G. S. (Eds.). (1996). *International perspectives on child abuse and children's testimony: Psychological research and law.* Thousand Oaks, CA: Sage.

Bottoms, B. L., Shaver, P. R., & Goodman, G. S. (1996). An analysis of ritualistic and religion-related child abuse allegations. *Law and Human Behavior, 20,* 1–34.

Boudreau, F. A. (1993). Elder abuse. In R. L. Hampton, T. P. Gullotta, G. R. Adams, E. H. Potter III, & R. P. Weissberg (Eds.), *Family violence: Prevention and treatment* (pp. 142-158). Newbury Park, CA: Sage.

Bourg, S., & Stock, H. V. (1994). A review of domestic violence arrest statistics in a police department using a pro-arrest police: Are pro-arrest policies enough? *Journal of Family Violence, 9,* 177–192.

Bousha, D. M., & Twentyman, C. T. (1984). Mother-child interactional style in abuse, neglect, and control groups: Naturalistic observations in the home. *Journal of Abnormal Psychology, 93,* 106–114.

Bouvier, P., Halperin, D., Rey, H., Jaffe, P. D., Laederach, J., Mounoud, R. L., et al. (1999). Typology and correlates of sexual abuse in children and youth: Multivariate analyses in a prevalence study in Geneva. *Child Abuse & Neglect, 23,* 779–790.

Bowen, N. H. (1982). Guidelines for career counseling with abused women. *Vocational Guidance Quarterly, 31,* 123–127.

Bower, B. (1993a, September 18). Sudden recall: Adult memories of child abuse spark heated debate. *Science News, 144,* 177–192.

Bower, B. (1993b, September 25). The survivor syndrome. *Science News, 144,* 202–204.

Bower, B. (1994). Alcoholism exposes its "insensitive" side. *Science News, 145,* 118.

Bower, B. (2003, January 18). Testosterone's family ties: Hormone-linked problems reflect parent-child bond. *Science News, 163,* 36.

Bowker, L. H. (1983). *Beating wife beating.* Lexington, MA: Lexington.

Bowker, L. H. (1993). A battered woman's problems are social, not psychological. In R. J. Gelles & D. R. Loseke (Eds.), *Current controversies on family violence* (pp. 154–165). Newbury Park, CA: Sage.

Bowker, L. H., & Maurer, L. (1986). The effectiveness of counseling services utilized by battered women. *Women & Therapy, 5*(4), 65–82.

Bowlby, J. (1980). *Attachment and loss: Vol. 3. Loss.* London: Hogarth.

Boxer, A. M., Cook, J. A., & Herdt, G. (1991). Double jeopardy: Identity transitions and parent-child relations among gay and lesbian youth. In K. A. Pillemer & K. McCartney (Eds.), *Parent-child relations throughout life* (pp. 59–92). Hillsdale, NJ: Lawrence Erlbaum.

Bradford, J. (1990). The antiandrogen and hormonal treatment of sex offenders. In W. L. Marshall, D. R. Laws, & H. E. Barbaree (Eds.), *Handbook of sexual assault: Issues, theories, and treatment of the offender* (pp. 297–327). New York: Plenum.

Brady, J. L., Guy, J. D., Poelstra, P. L., & Brokaw, B. F. (1999). Vicarious traumatization, spirituality, and the treatment of sexual abuse survivors: A national survey of women psychotherapists. *Professional Psychology: Research and Practice, 30,* 386–393.

Braidbill, K. (1997, October). A deadly force. *Los Angeles Magazine,* pp. 68–69, 71, 130–132.

Brandl, B., & Cook-Daniels, L. (2002). *Domestic abuse in later life.* Washington, DC: National Resource Center on Domestic Violence.

Brandl, B., Hebert, M., Rozwadowski, J., & Spangler, D. (2003). Feeling safe, feeling strong: Support groups for older abused women. *Violence Against Women, 9,* 1490–1503.

Brassard, M. R., Germain, R., & Hart, S. N. (Eds.). (1987). *Psychological maltreatment of children and youth.* New York: Pergamon.

Brassard, M. R., Hart, S. N., & Hardy, D. (1991). Psychological and emotional abuse of children. In R. T. Ammerman & M. Hersen (Eds.), *Case studies in family violence* (pp. 255–270). New York: Plenum.

Braun, B. G. (1988). The BASK model of dissociation. *Dissociation, 1,* 45–50.

Braun, B., Lenzer, A., Shumacher-Mukai, C., & Snyder, P. (1993). A decision tree for managing elder abuse and neglect. *Journal of Elder Abuse & Neglect, 5*(3), 89–103.

Brecklin, L. R. (2002). The role of perpetrator alcohol use in the injury outcomes of intimate assaults. *Journal of Family Violence, 17,* 185–197.

Brecklin, L. R., & Forde, D. R. (2001). A meta-analysis of rape education programs. *Violence and Victims, 16,* 303–321.

Breitenbecher, K. H. (2000). Sexual assault on college campuses: Is an ounce of prevention enough? *Applied & Preventive Psychology, 9,* 23–52.

Brener, N. D., McMahon, P. M., Warren, C. W., & Douglas, K. A. (1999). Forced sexual intercourse and associated health-risk behaviors among female college students in the United States. *Journal of Consulting and Clinical Psychology, 67,* 252–259.

Bresee, P., Stearns, G. B., Bess, B. H., & Packer, L. S. (1986). Allegations of child sexual abuse in child custody disputes: A therapeutic assessment model. *American Journal of Orthopsychiatry, 56,* 560–569.

Brewin, C. R. (2001). A cognitive neuroscience account of posttraumatic stress disorder. *Behavior Research and Therapy, 39,* 373–393.

Brewin, C. R., Andrews, B., & Rose, S. (2000). Fear, helplessness, and horror in posttraumatic stress disorder: Investigating *DSM-IV* criterion A2 in victims of violent crime. *Journal of Traumatic Stress, 13,* 499–509.

Brewin, C. R., Andrews, B., & Valentine, J. D. (2000). Meta-analysis of risk factors for posttraumatic stress disorder in trauma-exposed adults. *Journal of Consulting and Clinical Psychology, 68,* 748–766.

Brice-Baker, J. R. (1994). Domestic violence in African-American and African-Caribbean families. *Journal of Social Distress and the Homeless, 3,* 23–38.

Brickman, J. (1984). Feminist, nonsexist, and traditional models of therapy: Implications for working with incest. *Women & Therapy, 3,* 49–67.

Briere, J. (1992). Methodological issues in the study of sexual abuse effects. *Journal of Consulting and Clinical Psychology, 60,* 196–203.

Briere, J. (1996). *Trauma Symptom Checklist for Children (TSCC).* Odessa, FL: Psychological Assessment Resources.

Briere, J., & Conte, J. R. (1993). Self-reported amnesia for abuse in adults molested as children. *Journal of Traumatic Stress, 6,* 21–31.

Briere, J., & Elliott, D. M. (1994). Immediate and long-term impacts of child sexual abuse. *Future of Children, 4*(2), 54–69.

Briere, J., & Gil, E. (1998). Self-mutilation in clinical and general population samples: Prevalence, correlates, and functions. *American Journal of Orthopsychiatry, 68,* 609–620.

Briere, J., & Runtz, M. (1989). The Trauma Symptoms Checklist (TSC-33): Early data on a new scale. *Journal of Interpersonal Violence, 4,* 151–163.

Briere, J., & Runtz, M. (1990). Differential adult symptomatology associated with three types of child abuse histories. *Child Abuse & Neglect, 14,* 357–364.

Briere, J., Woo, R., McRae, B., Foltz, J., & Sitzman, R. (1997). Lifetime victimization history, demographics, and clinical status in female psychiatric emergency room patients. *Journal of Nervous and Mental Disease, 185,* 95–101.

Brinkerhoff, M. B., & Lupri, E. (1988). Interpersonal violence. *Canadian Journal of Sociology, 13,* 407–434.

Brooker, S., Cawson, P., Kelly, G., & Wattam, C. (2001). The prevalence of child abuse and neglect: A survey of young people. *International Journal of Market Research, 43,* 249–289.

Broude, G. J., & Greene, S. J. (1983). Cross-cultural codes on husband-wife relationship. *Ethnology, 22,* 263–280.

Brower, M., & Sackett, R. (1985, November 4). Split. *People,* pp. 108, 111.

Brown, C., Reedy, D., Fountain, J., Johnson, A., & Dichiser, T. (2000). Battered women's career decision-making self-efficacy: Further insights and contributing factors. *Journal of Career Assessment, 8,* 251–265.

Brown, E. J., & Kolko, D. J. (1999). Child victims' attributions about being physically abused: An examination of factors associated with symptom severity. *Journal of Abnormal Child Psychology, 27,* 311–322.

Brown, G. R., & Anderson, B. (1991). Psychiatric morbidity in adult inpatients with childhood histories of sexual and physical abuse. *American Journal of Psychiatry, 148,* 55–61.

Brown, J., Cohen, P., Johnson, J. G., & Salzinger, S. (1998). A longitudinal analysis of risk factors for child maltreatment: Findings of a 17-year prospective study of officially recorded and self-reported child abuse and neglect. *Child Abuse & Neglect, 22,* 1065–1078.

Brown, J., Cohen, P., Johnson, J. G., & Smailes, E. M. (1999). Childhood abuse and neglect: Specificity of effects on adolescent and young adult depression and suicidality. *Journal of the American Academy of Child and Adolescent Psychiatry, 38,* 1490–1505.

Brown, J., James, K., & Seddon, E. (2002). The complexity of male violence: Some psychological factors and their treatment implications. *Family Violence & Sexual Abuse Bulletin, 18*(4), 7–18.

Brown, J. K. (1992). Introduction: Definitions, assumptions, themes, and issues. In D. A. Counts, J. K. Brown, & J. C. Campbell (Eds.), *Sanctions and sanctuary: Cultural perspectives on the beating of wives* (pp. 1–18). Boulder, CO: Westview.

Brown, R. M., III. (2002). The development of family violence as a field of study and contributors to family and community violence among low-income fathers. *Aggression and Violent Behavior, 7,* 499–511.

Brown, T. J., Sumner, K. E., & Nocera, R. (2002). Understanding sexual aggression against women: An examination of the role of men's athletic participation and related variables. *Journal of Interpersonal Violence, 17,* 937–952.

Browne, A. (1990, December 11). *Assaults between intimate partners in the United States: Incidence, prevalence, and proportional, risk for women and men.* Testimony presented before the U.S. Senate, Committee on the Judiciary, Washington, DC.

Browne, A., & Bassuk, S. S. (1997). Intimate violence in the lives of homeless and poor housed women: Prevalence and patterns in an ethnically diverse sample. *American Journal of Orthopsychiatry, 67,* 261–278.

Browne, A., & Finkelhor, D. (1986). Impact of child sexual abuse: A review of the research. *Psychological Bulletin, 99,* 66–77.

Browne, A., Salomon, A., & Bassuk, S. S. (1999). The impact of recent partner violence on poor women's capacity to maintain work. *Violence Against Women, 5,* 393–426.

Browne, K. D., & Hamilton, C. E. (1998). Physical violence between young adults and their parents: Associations with a history of child maltreatment. *Journal of Family Violence, 13,* 59–79.

Brownell, P., Berman, J., & Salamone, A. (1999). Mental health and criminal justice issues among perpetrators of elder abuse. *Journal of Elder Abuse & Neglect, 11*(4), 81–94.

Brownridge, D. A., & Halli, S. S. (1999). Measuring family violence: The conceptualization and utilization of prevalence and incidence rates. *Journal of Family Violence, 14,* 333–350.

Brownridge, D. A., & Halli, S. S. (2000). "Living in sin" and sinful living: Toward filling a gap in the explanation of violence against women. *Aggression and Violent Behavior, 5,* 565–583.

Brownridge, D. A., & Halli, S. S. (2002). Double jeopardy? Violence against women in Canada. *Violence and Victims, 17,* 455–471.

Bruce, D. A., & Zimmerman, R. A. (1989). Shaken impact syndrome. *Pediatric Annals, 18,* 482–494.

Brunk, M., Henggeler, S. W., & Whelan, J. P. (1987). Comparison of multi-systemic therapy and parent training in the brief treatment of child abuse and neglect. *Journal of Consulting and Clinical Psychology, 55,* 171–178.

Brush, L. D. (1990). Violent acts and injurious outcomes in married couples: Methodological issues in the National Survey of Families and Households. *Gender & Society, 4,* 56–67.

Brush, L. D. (2000). Battering, traumatic stress, and welfare-to-work transition. *Violence Against Women, 6,* 1039–1065.

Brush, L. D. (2003). Effects of work on hitting and hurting. *Violence Against Women, 9,* 1213–1230.

Bryan, J. W., & Freed, F. W. (1982). Corporal punishment: Normative data and sociological and psychological correlates in a community population. *Journal of Youth and Adolescence, 11,* 77–87.

Bryant, S. L., & Range, L. M. (1997). Type and severity of child abuse and college students' lifetime suicidality. *Child Abuse & Neglect, 21,* 1169–1176.

Budd, K. S., Felix, E. D., Poindexter, L. M., Naik-Polan, A. T., & Sloss, C. F. (2002). Clinical assessment of children in child protection cases: An empirical analysis. *Professional Psychology: Research and Practice, 33,* 3–12.

Budin, L. E., & Johnson, C. F. (1989). Sex abuse prevention programs: Offenders' attitudes about their efficacy. *Child Abuse & Neglect, 13,* 77–87.

Bunn, A. (1998, April 21). Digitizing Megan's law [Electronic version]. *Village Voice, 43,* 31.

Burgess, A. W. (1995). Rape trauma syndrome. In P. Searles & R. J. Berger (Eds.), *Rape and society: Readings on the problem of sexual assault* (pp. 239–245). Boulder, CO: Westview.

Burgess, A. W., Groth, A. N., & McCausland, M. P. (1981). Child sex initiation rings. *American Journal of Orthopsychiatry, 51,* 110–119.

Burgess, A. W., & Hartman, C. R. (1987). Child abuse aspects of child pornography. *Psychiatric Annals, 17,* 248–253.

Burgess, A. W., Hartman, C. R., McCausland, M. P., & Powers, P. (1984). Response patterns in children and adolescents exploited through sex rings and pornography. *American Journal of Psychiatry, 141,* 656–662.

Burgess, A. W., Prentky, R. A., & Dowdell, E. B. (2000). Sexual predators in nursing homes. *Journal of Psychosocial Nursing, 38*(8), 26–34.

Burgess, E. S., & Wurtele, S. K. (1998). Enhancing parent-child communication about sexual abuse: A pilot study. *Child Abuse & Neglect, 22,* 1167–1175.

Burgess, R., & Conger, R. D. (1978). Family interaction in abusive, neglectful, and normal families. *Child Development, 49,* 1163–1173.

Burke, A. (1995, July 31). Valley needs more shelter beds. *Los Angeles Daily News,* p. 6.

Burke, T. W. (1998). Male-to-male gay domestic violence: The dark closet. In N. A. Jackson & G. C. Oates (Eds.), *Violence in intimate relationships: Examining sociological and psychological issues* (pp. 161–179). Woburn, MA: Butterworth-Heinemann.

Burman, B., Margolin, G., & John, R. S. (1993). America's angriest home videos: Behavioral contingencies observed in home reenactment of marital conflict. *Journal of Consulting and Clinical Psychology, 61,* 28–39.

Burnett, B. (1993). The psychological abuse of latency age children: A survey. *Child Abuse & Neglect, 17,* 441–454.

Burns, J. (1992). Mad or just plain bad? Gender and the work of forensic clinical psychologists. In J. M. Ussher & P. Nicolson (Eds.), *Gender issues in clinical psychology* (pp. 106–128). London: Routledge.

Burt, M. R. (1980). Cultural myths and support for rape. *Journal of Personality and Social Psychology, 38,* 217–230.

Burt, M. R., Newmark, L. C., Olson, K. K., Aron, L. Y., & Harrell, A. V. (1997). *1997 report: Evaluation of the STOP formula grants under the Violence Against Women Act of 1994.* Washington, DC: Urban Institute.

Busby, D. M., Christensen, C., Crane, D. R., & Larson, J. H. (1995). A revision of the Dyadic Adjustment Scale for use with distressed and nondistressed couples: Construct hierarchy and multidimensional scales. *Journal of Marital and Family Therapy, 21,* 289–308.

Busch, N. B., & Valentine, D. (2000). Empowerment practice: A focus on battered women. *Affilia, 15*(1), 82–95.

Busch, N. B., & Wolfer, T. A. (2002). Battered women speak out: Welfare reform and their decision to disclose. *Violence Against Women, 8,* 566–584.

Bushman, B. J., & Anderson, C. A. (2001). Media violence and the American public: Scientific facts versus media misinformation. *American Psychologist, 56,* 477–489.

Bushman, B. J., & Baumeister, R. F. (1998). Threatened egotism, narcissism, self-esteem, and direct and displaced aggression: Does self-love or self-hate lead to violence? *Journal of Personality and Social Psychology, 75,* 219–229.

Bushman, B. J., Baumeister, R. F., & Stack, A. D. (1999). Catharsis, aggression, and persuasive influence: Self-fulfilling or self-defeating prophecies? *Journal of Personality and Social Psychology, 76,* 367–376.

Bushman, B. J., & Cooper, H. M. (1990). Effects of alcohol on human aggression: An integrative research review. *Psychological Bulletin, 107,* 341–354.

Buss, A. H., & Durkee, A. (1957). An inventory for assessing different kinds of hostility. *Journal of Consulting Psychology, 2,* 343–349.

Buss, A. H., & Perry, M. (1992). The Aggression Questionnaire. *Journal of Personality, 63,* 452–459.

Butler, K. (1994, June 26). Clashing memories, mixed messages. *Los Angeles Times Magazine,* p. 12.

Buzawa, E. S., Austin, T. L., & Buzawa, C. G. (1995). Responding to crimes of violence against women: Gender differences versus organizational imperatives. *Crime & Delinquency, 41,* 443–466.

Buzawa, E. S., & Buzawa, C. G. (2003). *Domestic violence: The criminal justice response* (3rd ed.). Thousand Oaks, CA: Sage.

Buzawa, E. S., & Hotaling, G. T. (2000). *The police response to domestic violence calls for assistance in three Massachusetts towns: Final report.* Washington, DC: National Institute of Justice.

Buzawa, E. S., Hotaling, G. T., & Klein, A. (1998). The response to domestic violence in a model court: Some initial findings and implications. *Behavioral Sciences and the Law, 16,* 185–206.

Bybee, D. I., & Mowbray, C. T. (1993a). An analysis of allegations of sexual abuse in a multi-victim day-care center case. *Child Abuse & Neglect, 17,* 767–783.

Bybee, D. I., & Mowbray, C. T. (1993b). Community response to child sexual abuse in day-care settings. *Families in Society, 74,* 268–281.

Bybee, D. I., & Sullivan, C. M. (2002). The process through which an advocacy intervention resulted in positive change for battered women over time. *American Journal of Community Psychology, 30,* 103–132.

Byrne, C. A., & Arias, I. (1997). Marital satisfaction and marital violence: Moderating effects of attributional processes. *Journal of Family Psychology, 11,* 188–195.

Byrne, C. A., Kilpatrick, D. G., Howley, S. S., & Beatty, D. (1999). *Female victims of partner versus nonpartner violence: Experiences with the criminal justice system* (NCJ Publication No. 178788). Washington, DC: U.S. Department of Justice.

Byrne, C. A., Resnick, H. S., Kilpatrick, D. G., Best, C. L., & Saunders, B. E. (1999). The socioeconomic impact of interpersonal violence on women. *Journal of Consulting and Clinical Psychology, 67,* 362–366.

Cabrera, Y. (1998, July 11). Refunds ordered in hospital epidural probe. *Los Angeles Daily News,* p. 4.

Caetano, R., Schafer, J., Field, C., & Nelson, S. M. (2002). Agreement on reports of intimate partner violence among White, Black, and Hispanic couples in the United States. *Journal of Interpersonal Violence, 17,* 1308–1322.

Cahill, C., Llewelyn, S. P., & Pearson, C. (1991). Treatment of sexual abuse which occurred in childhood: A review. *British Journal of Clinical Psychology, 30,* 1–12.

Cahill, S., & Smith, K. (2002). Policy issues affecting lesbian, gay, bisexual, and transgender people in retirement. *Generations, 26*(2), 49–54.

Calam, R., Horne, L., Glasgow, D., & Cox, A. (1998). Psychological disturbance and child sexual abuse: A follow-up study. *Child Abuse & Neglect, 22,* 901–913.

California Secretary of State. (1998). *How does Safe at Home work?* Retrieved November 26, 2003, from http://www.ss.ca.gov/safeathome/Safe_at_Home_how.htm

Caliso, J. A., & Milner, J. S. (1994). Childhood physical abuse, childhood social support, and adult child abuse potential. *Journal of Interpersonal Violence, 9,* 27–44.

Calkins, P. (2003, July/August). Cross-discipline gains in Indiana. *Victimization of the Elderly and Disabled, 6,* 17–18, 30.

Call, K. T., Finch, M. A., Huck, S. M., & Kane, R. A. (1999). Caregiver burden from a social exchange perspective: Caring for older people after hospital discharge. *Journal of Marriage and the Family, 61,* 688–699.

Cameron, L. A., & Abramson, W. H. (2002, July/August). Unique shelter program works to reduce violence against and exploitation of people with disabilities. *Victimization of the Elderly and Disabled, 5,* 17–18, 31–32.

Campbell, J. C. (1989a). A test of two explanatory models of women's responses to battering. *Nursing Research, 38*(1), 18–24.

Campbell, J. C. (1989b). Women's responses to sexual abuse in intimate relationships. *Health Care for Women International, 8,* 335–347.

Campbell, J. C. (1990). Battered woman syndrome: A critical review. *Violence Update, 1*(4), 1, 4, 10–11.

Campbell, J. C. (Ed.). (1995). *Assessing dangerousness: Violence by sexual offenders, batterers, and child abusers.* Thousand Oaks, CA: Sage.

Campbell, J. C. (2002). Health consequences of intimate partner violence. *Lancet, 359,* 1331–1336.

Campbell, J. C., & Alford, P. (1989). The dark consequences of marital rape. *American Journal of Nursing, 87,* 946–949.

Campbell, J. C., Rose, L., Kulb, J., & Daphne, N. (1998). Voices of strength and resistance: A contextual and longitudinal analysis of women's responses to battering. *Journal of Interpersonal Violence, 14,* 21–40.

Campbell, J. C., & Soeken, K. L. (1999). Women's responses to battering over time. *Journal of Interpersonal Violence, 14,* 21–40.

Campbell, R., Wasco, S. M., Ahrens, C. E., Sefl, T., & Barnes, H. E. (2001). Preventing the "second rape": Rape survivors' experiences with community service providers. *Journal of Interpersonal Violence, 16,* 1239–1259.

Canavan, M. M., Meyer, W. J., & Higgs, D. C. (1992). The female experience of sibling incest. *Journal of Marital and Family Therapy, 18,* 129–142.

Candell, S., Frazier, P., Arikan, N., & Tofteland, A. (1993, August). *Legal outcomes in rape cases: Case attrition and postrape recovery.* Paper presented at the annual meeting of the American Psychological Association, Toronto.

Cano, A., & Vivian, D. (2001). Life stressors and husband-to-wife violence. *Aggression and Violent Behavior, 6,* 459–480.

Cantos, A. L., Neale, J. M., O'Leary, K. D., & Gaines, R. W. (1997). Assessment of coping strategies of child abusing mothers. *Child Abuse & Neglect, 21,* 631–636.

Cantos, A. L., Neidig, P. H., & O'Leary, K. D. (1994). Injuries of women and men in a treatment program for domestic violence. *Journal of Family Violence, 9,* 113–124.

Cantrell, P. J., MacIntyre, D. I., Sharkey, K. J., & Thompson, V. (1995). Violence in the marital dyad as a predictor of violence in peer relationships of older adolescents/young adults. *Violence and Victims, 10,* 35–41.

Capaldi, D. M., & Clark, S. (1998). Prospective family predictors of aggression toward female partners for at-risk young men. *Developmental Psychology, 34,* 1175–1188.

Cappell, C., & Heiner, R. B. (1990). The intergenerational transmission of family aggression. *Journal of Family Violence, 5,* 135–152.

Carden, A. D. (1994). Wife abuse and the wife abuser: Review and recommendations. *Counseling Psychologist, 22,* 539–582.

Carlson, B. E. (1984). Children's observations of interparental violence. In A. R. Roberts (Ed.), *Battered women and their families* (pp. 147–167). New York: Springer.

Carlson, B. E. (1996). Dating violence: Student beliefs about the consequences. *Journal of Interpersonal Violence, 11,* 3–18.

Carlson, B. E. (1997). Mental retardation and domestic violence: An ecological approach to intervention. *Social Work, 42,* 79–89.

Carlson, B. E., McNutt, L. A., & Choi, D. Y. (2003). Childhood and adult abuse among women in primary health care: Effects on mental health. *Journal of Interpersonal Violence, 18,* 924–941.

Carlson, B. E., McNutt, L. A., Choi, D. Y., & Rose, I. M. (2002). Intimate partner abuse and mental health: The role of social support and other protective factors. *Violence Against Women, 8,* 720–745.

Carlson, E. B., & Dalenberg, C. J. (2000). A conceptual framework for the impact of traumatic experiences. *Trauma, Violence, & Abuse, 1,* 4–28.

Carlson, M. J., Harris, S. D., & Holden, G. W. (1999). Protective orders and domestic violence: Risk factors for re-abuse. *Journal of Family Violence, 14,* 205–226.

Carmody, D. C., & Williams, K. R. (1987). Wife assault and perceptions of sanctions. *Violence and Victims, 2,* 25–38.

Carp, F. M. (1999). *Elder abuse in the family: An interdisciplinary model for research.* New York: Springer.

Carr, J. L., & VanDeusen, K. M. (2002). The relationship between family of origin violence and dating violence in college men. *Journal of Interpersonal Violence, 17,* 630–646.

Carrigan, T. D., Walker, E., & Barnes, S. (2000). Domestic violence: The shaken adult syndrome. *Journal of Accident and Emergency Medicine, 17,* 138–139.

Carroll, C. A., & Haase, C. C. (1987). The function of protective services in child abuse and neglect. In R. E. Helfer & R. S. Kempe (Eds.), *The battered child* (4th ed., pp. 137–151). Chicago: University of Chicago Press.

Carter, B. (1993). Child sexual abuse: Impact on mothers. *Affilia, 8*(1), 72–90.

Carter, D. L., Prentky, R. A., Knight, R. A., Vanderveer, P. L., & Boucher, R. J. (1987). Use of pornography in the criminal and developmental histories of sexual offenders. *Journal of Interpersonal Violence, 2,* 196–211.

Carter, J., Heisler, C., & Lemon, K. D. (1991). *Domestic violence: The crucial role of the judge in criminal court cases.* San Francisco: Family Violence Prevention Fund.

Carter, N., & Harvey, C. (1996). Gaining perspective on parenting groups. *Zero to Three, 16*(6), 1, 3–8.

Casanova, G. M., Domanic, J., McCanne, T. R., & Milner, J. S. (1992). Physiological responses to non-child-related stressors in mothers at risk for child abuse. *Child Abuse & Neglect, 16,* 31–44.

Cascardi, M., Avery-Leaf, S., O'Leary, K. D., & Slep, A. M. S. (1999). Factor structure and convergent validity of the Conflict Tactics Scale in high school students. *Psychological Assessment, 11,* 546–555.

Cascardi, M., Langhinrichsen-Rohling, J., & Vivian, D. (1992). Marital aggression: Impact, injury, and health correlates for husbands and wives. *Archives of Internal Medicine, 152,* 1178–1184.

Caselles, C. E., & Milner, J. S. (2000). Evaluation of child transgressions, disciplinary choices, and expected child compliance in a no-cry and a crying infant condition in physically abusive and comparison mothers. *Child Abuse & Neglect, 24,* 477–491.

Cashin, J. R., Presley, C. A., & Meilman, P. W. (1996). Alcohol use in the Greek system: Follow the leader? *Journal of Studies of Alcohol, 57,* 63–70.

Caspi, A., McClay, J., Moffitt, T. E., Mill, J., Martin, J., Craig, I. W., et al. (2002). Role of genotype in the cycle of violence in maltreated children. *Science, 297,* 851–854.

Cassady, L., Allen, B., Lyon, E., & McGeehan, D. (1987, July). *The Child-Focused Intervention Program: Treatment and program evaluation for children in a battered women's shelter.* Paper presented at the Third National Family Violence Research Conference, Durham, NH.

Caulfield, M. B., Riggs, D. S., & Street, A. (1999, July). *The role of commitment in the perpetration of dating violence.* Paper presented at the Sixth International Family Violence Research Conference, Durham, NH.

Ceci, S. J., & Bruck, M. (1993). Suggestibility of the child witness: A historical review and synthesis. *Psychological Bulletin, 113,* 403–439.

Ceci, S. J., & Bruck, M. (1998). Children's testimony: Applied and basic issues. In D. Kuhn & R. S. Siegler (Eds.), *Handbook of child psychology: Vol. 2. Cognition, perception, and language* (5th ed., pp. 713–774). New York: John Wiley.

Celano, M. P. (1990). Activities and games for group psychotherapy with sexually abused children. *International Journal of Group Psychotherapy, 40,* 419–429.

Centers for Disease Control and Prevention. (2000, October 27). Building data systems for monitoring and responding to violence against women: Recommendations from a workshop. *Morbidity and Mortality Weekly Report, 49,* 1–19.

Centers for Disease Control and Prevention. (2001, December 7). School health guidelines to prevent unintentional injuries and violence. *Morbidity and Mortality Weekly Report, 50,* 1–46.

Centers for Disease Control and Prevention. (2002). *Injury fact book: 2001–2002.* Atlanta, GA: Author.

Cerezo, M. A. (1997). Abusive family interaction: A review. *Aggression and Violent Behavior, 2,* 215–240.

Chaffin, M. (1994). Research in action: Assessment and treatment of child sexual abusers. *Journal of Interpersonal Violence, 9,* 224–237.

Chaffin, M., Kelleher, K., & Hollenberg, J. (1996). Onset of physical abuse and neglect: Psychiatric, substance abuse, and social risk factors from prospective community data. *Child Abuse & Neglect, 20,* 191–203.

Chaimowitz, G. A., Glancy, G. D., & Blackburn, J. (2000). The duty to warn and protect: Impact on practice. *Canadian Journal of Psychiatry, 45,* 899–904.

Chalk, R., & King, P. A. (Eds.). (1998). *Violence in families: Assessing prevention and treatment programs.* Washington, DC: National Academy Press.

Chan, Y. C. (1994). Parenting stress and social support of mothers who physically abuse their children in Hong Kong. *Child Abuse & Neglect, 18,* 261–269.

Chang, D. B. K. (1989). An abused spouse's self-saving process: A theory of identity transformation. *Sociological Perspectives, 32,* 535–550.

Chang, J. C., Decker, M., Moracco, K. E., Martin, S. L., Petersen, R., & Frasier, P. Y. (2003). What happens when health care providers ask about intimate partner violence? A description of consequences from the perspective of female survivors. *Journal of the American Women's Medical Association, 58,* 76–81.

Chapman, J., & Smith, B. (1987). *Child sexual abuse: An analysis of case processing.* Washington, DC: American Bar Association.

Chapple, C. L. (2003). Examining intergenerational violence: Violent role modeling or weak parental controls? *Violence and Victims, 18,* 142–162.

Chaudhry, A. (2003, August 22). Dad guilty in sex abuse of sons. *Newsday* (Nassau and Suffolk ed.), p. A44.

Chavkin, W., Breitbart, V., Elman, D., & Wise, P.H. (1998). National survey of the states: Policies and practices regarding drug-using pregnant women. *American Journal of Public Health, 88,* 117–119.

Chen, H., Bersani, C., Myers, S. C., & Denton, R. (1989). Evaluating the effectiveness of a court sponsored abuser treatment program. *Journal of Family Violence, 4,* 309–322.

Chenoweth, L. (1997). Violence and women with disabilities: Silence and paradox. In S. Cook & J. Bessant (Eds.), *Women's encounters with violence: Australian experiences* (pp. 21–39). Thousand Oaks, CA: Sage.

Cheung, M., & Boutte-Queen, N. M. (2000). Emotional responses to child sexual abuse: A comparison between police and social workers in Hong Kong. *Child Abuse & Neglect, 24,* 1613–1621.

Child Welfare League of America. (1986). *Too young to run: The status of child abuse in America.* New York: Author.

Children's Defense Fund. (1997, November 20). *New law furthers safety and permanence for children.* Retrieved from http://www.childrensdefense.org/safestart_pass1.html

Children's Safety Network. (1992). *Domestic violence: A directory of protocols for health care providers.* Newton, MA: Education Development Center.

Chiriboga, C. A. (1993). Fetal effects. *Neurologic Clinics, 3,* 707–728.

Chiu, E. (2001). Confronting the agency in battered women. *Southern California Law Review, 74,* 1223–1273.

Choi, A., & Edleson, J. L. (1995). Advocating legal intervention in wife assaults: Results from a national survey of Singapore. *Journal of Interpersonal Violence, 10,* 243–258.

Choice, P., Lamke, L. K., & Pittman, J. F. (1995). Conflict resolution strategies and marital distress as mediating factors in the link between witnessing interparental violence and wife battering. *Violence and Victims, 10,* 107–119.

Christensen, A. (1988). Dysfunctional interaction patterns in couples. In P. Noller & M. A. Fitzpatrick (Eds.), *Perspectives on marital interaction* (pp. 31–52). Philadelphia: Multilingual Matters.

Christensen, A., Margolin, G., & Sullaway, M. (1992). Interparental agreement on child behavior problems. *Psychological Assessment, 4,* 419–425.

Christensen, M. J., Brayden, R. M., Dietrich, M. S., McLaughlin, F. J., Sherrod, K. B., & Altemeier, W. A. (1994). The prospective assessment of self-concept in neglectful and physically abusive low-income mothers. *Child Abuse & Neglect, 18,* 225–232.

Christiansson, S. A. (1992). Emotional stress and eyewitness memory: A critical review. *Psychological Bulletin, 12,* 284–309.

Christopoulos, C., Bonvillian, J. D., & Crittenden, P. M. (1988). Maternal language input and child maltreatment. *Infant Mental Health Journal, 9,* 272–286.

Chu, J. A., Frey, L. M., Ganzel, B. L., & Matthews, J. A. (1999). Memories of childhood abuse: Dissociation, amnesia and corroboration. *American Journal of Psychiatry, 156,* 749–755.

Chu, L. D. (2001). Homicide and factors that determine fatality from assault in the elderly population. *Dissertation Abstracts International, 62*(11), 5063B. (UMI No. 3032861)

Churchill, S. D. (1993). The lived meanings of date rape: Seeing through the eyes of the victim. *Family Violence and Sexual Assault Bulletin, 9*(1), 20–23.

Cicchetti, D., & Barnett, D. (1991). Toward the development of a scientific nosology of child maltreatment. In D. Cicchetti & W. Grove (Eds.), *Thinking clearly about psychology: Essays in honor of Paul E. Meehl* (pp. 346–377). Minneapolis: University of Minnesota Press.

Cicchetti, D., & Lynch, M. (1993). Toward an ecological/transactional model of community violence and child maltreatment: Consequences for child development. *Psychiatry: Interpersonal & Biological Processes, 56,* 96–119.

Cicchetti, D., & Toth, S. L. (1995). A developmental psychopathology perspective on child abuse and neglect. *Journal of the American Academy of Child and Adolescent Psychiatry, 34,* 541–565.

Clark, K. A., Biddle, A. K., & Martin, S. L. (2002). A cost-benefit analysis of the Violence Against Women Act of 1994. *Violence Against Women, 8,* 417–428.

Clark, L. A. (1993). *The Schedule for Nonadaptive and Adaptive Personality.* Minneapolis: University of Minnesota Press.

Clark-Daniels, C. L., Daniels, R. S., & Baumhover, L. A. (1989). Physicians' and nurses' responses to abuse of the elderly: A comparative study of two surveys in Alabama. *Journal of Elder Abuse & Neglect, 1*(4), 57–72.

Clarke, P. N., Pendry, N. C., & Kim, Y. S. (1997). Patterns of violence in homeless women. *Western Journal of Nursing Research, 19,* 490–500.

Claussen, A. H., & Crittenden, P. M. (1991). Physical and psychological maltreatment: Relations among types of maltreatment. *Child Abuse & Neglect, 15,* 5–18.

Clements, C. M., & Sawhney, D. K. (2000). Coping with domestic violence: Control attributions, dysphoria, and hopelessness. *Journal of Traumatic Stress, 13,* 221–240.

Clipp, E. C., & George, L. K. (1993). Dementia and cancer: A comparison of spouse caregivers. *Gerontologist, 33,* 534–541.

Cloud, J. (1998, May 4). A matter of hearts. *Seattle Times,* pp. 60–64.

Coccaro, E. F., Bergeman, C. S., Kavoussi, R. J., & Seroczynski, A. D. (1997). Heritability of aggression and irritability: A twin study of the Buss-Durkee Aggression Scales in adult male subjects. *Biological Psychiatry, 41,* 273–284.

Coffey, P., Leitenberg, H., Henning, K. R., Bennett, R. T., & Jankowski, M. K. (1996). Dating violence: The association between methods of coping and women's psychological adjustment. *Violence and Victims, 11,* 227–238.

Coffey-Guenther, K. M. (1998). *Assessing battered women for the presence of mild brain injuries* [CD-ROM]. Abstract obtained from ProQuest File: Dissertation Abstracts Item 9901722

Cohen, D., Llorente, M., & Eisendorfer, C. (1998). Homicide/suicide in older persons. *American Journal of Psychiatry, 155,* 390–396.

Cohen, J. A., Berliner, L., & Mannarino, A. P. (2000). Treating traumatized children: A research review and synthesis. *Trauma, Violence, & Abuse, 1,* 29–46.

Cohen, J. A., & Mannarino, A. P. (1993). A treatment model for sexually abused preschoolers. *Journal of Interpersonal Violence, 8,* 115–131.

Cohen, P., Brown, J., & Smailes, E. M. (2001). Child abuse and neglect and the development of mental disorders in the general population. *Development and Psychopathology, 13,* 981–999.

Cohen, P. S. (2001). Being "reasonable": Defining and implementing a right to community-based care for older adults with mental disabilities under the Americans with Disabilities Act. *International Journal of Law and Psychiatry, 24,* 233–252.

Cohen, R. A., & Van Nostrand, J. F. (1995). *Trends in the health of older Americans: United States, 1994.* Hyattsville, MD: National Center for Health Statistics.

Cohen, S., & Felson, M. (1979). Social change and crime rate trends: A routine activities approach. *American Sociological Review, 44,* 588–608.

Cohn, A. H., & Daro, D. (1987). Is treatment too late? What ten years of evaluation research tell us. *Child Abuse & Neglect, 11,* 433–442.

Coker, A. L., Davis, K. E., Arias, I., Desai, S., Sanderson, M., Brandt, H. M., & Smith, P. H. (2002). Physical and mental health effects of intimate partner violence for men and women. *American Journal of Preventive Medicine, 23,* 260–268.

Coker, A. L., Derrick, C., Lumpkin, J. L., Aldrich, T. E., & Oldendick, R. (2000). Help-seeking for intimate partner violence and forced sex in South Carolina. *American Journal of Preventive Medicine, 19,* 316–320.

Coker, A. L., Sanderson, M., Fadden, M. K., & Pirisi, L. (2000). Intimate partner violence and cervical neoplasia. *Journal of Women's Health and Gender-Based Medicine, 9,* 1015–1023.

Coker, A. L., Smith, P. H., McKeown, R. E., & Melissa, K. J. (2000). Frequency and correlates of intimate partner violence by type: Physical, sexual, and psychological battering. *American Journal of Public Health, 90,* 553–559.

Cole, P. M., Woolger, C., Power, T. G., & Smith, K. D. (1992). Parenting difficulties among adult survivors of father-daughter incest. *Child Abuse & Neglect, 16,* 239–249.

Collins, N. L., & Read, S. J. (1990). Adult attachment, working models, and relationship quality in dating couples. *Journal of Personality and Social Psychology, 58,* 644–663.

Collins, P. G., & O'Connor, A. (2000). Rape and sexual assault of the elderly: An exploratory study of 10 cases referred to the Irish Forensic Psychiatry Service. *Irish Journal of Psychological Medicine, 17,* 128–131.

Combs-Lane, A. M., & Smith, D. W. (2002). Risk of sexual victimization in college women: The role of behavioral intentions and risk-taking behavior. *Journal of Interpersonal Violence, 17,* 165–183.

Comstock, G., & Strasburger, V. C. (1990). Deceptive appearances: Television violence and aggressive behavior. *Journal of Adolescent Health Care, 11,* 31–44.

Conger, R. D., Burgess, R., & Barrett, C. (1979). Child abuse related to life change and perceptions of illness: Some preliminary findings. *Family Coordinator, 28,* 73–78.

Congress considers ways to stop crimes against the elderly. (2003, October 1). *Criminal Justice Newsletter,* pp. 4–5.

Congress votes to reauthorize Violence Against Women Act. (2000). *Criminal Justice Newsletter, 31*(2), 1–2.

Connelly, C. D., & Straus, M. A. (1992). Mother's age and risk for physical abuse. *Child Abuse & Neglect, 16,* 709–718.

Conner, K. R., Cerulli, C., & Caine, E. D. (2002). Threatened and attempted suicide by partner-violent male respondents petitioned to family violence court. *Violence and Victims, 17,* 115–125.

Conrad, P., & Schneider, J. W. (1992). *Deviance and medicalization: From badness to sickness.* Philadelphia: Temple University Press.

Conrad, S. D., & Morrow, R. S. (2000). Borderline personality organization, dissociation, and willingness to use force in intimate relationships. *Psychology of Men & Masculinity, 1*(1), 37–48.

Conte, J. R. (1993). Sexual abuse of children. In R. L. Hampton, T. P. Gullotta, G. R. Adams, E. H. Potter III, & R. P. Weissberg (Eds.), *Family violence: Prevention and treatment* (pp. 56–85). Newbury Park, CA: Sage.

Conte, J. R., & Schuerman, J. R. (1987). Factors associated with an increased impact of child sexual abuse. *Child Abuse & Neglect, 11,* 201–211.

Conte, J. R., Wolf, S., & Smith, T. (1989). What sexual offenders tell us about prevention strategies. *Child Abuse & Neglect, 13,* 293–301.

Coohey, C. (2000). The role of friends, in-laws, and other kin in father-perpetrated child physical abuse. *Child Welfare, 79,* 373–402.

Coohey, C., & Braun, N. (1997). Toward an integrated framework for understanding child physical abuse. *Child Abuse & Neglect, 21,* 1081–1094.

Cook, P. W. (1997). *Abused men: The hidden side of domestic violence.* Westport, CT: Praeger.

Cook-Daniels, L. (1999, May/June). Interpreting the National Elder Abuse Incidence Study. *Victimization of the Elderly and Disabled, 2,* 1–2.

Cook-Daniels, L. (2003a, July/August). Public information material. *Victimization of the Elderly and Disabled, 6,* 27–28, 32.

Cook-Daniels, L. (2003b, January/February). 2003 is the year elder abuse hits the international stage. *Victimization of the Elderly and Disabled, 5,* 65–66, 76.

Coolidge, F. L., & Merwin, M. M. (1992). Reliability and validity of the Coolidge Axis II Inventory: A new inventory for the assessment of personality disorders. *Journal of Personality Assessment, 59,* 223–238.

Copenhaver, M. M., & Eisler, R. M. (1996). Masculine gender role stress: A perspective on men's health. In P. M. Kato (Ed.), *Health psychology of special populations: Issues in age, gender, and ethnicity.* New York: Plenum.

Copenhaver, M. M., Lash, S. J., & Eisler, R. M. (2000). Masculine gender-role stress, anger, and male intimate abusiveness: Implications for men's relationships. *Sex Roles, 42,* 405–414.

Copping, V. E. (1996). Beyond over- and under-control: Behavioral observations of shelter children. *Journal of Family Violence, 11,* 41–57.

Corcoran, J. (2000). Family interventions with child physical abuse and neglect: A critical review. *Children and Youth Services Review, 22,* 563–591.

Corder, B. F., Haizlip, T., & DeBoer, P. A. (1990). A pilot study for a structured, time-limited therapy group for sexually abused pre-adolescent children. *Child Abuse & Neglect, 14,* 243–251.

Corse, S., Schmid, K., & Trickett, P. K. (1990). Social network characteristics of mothers in abusing and nonabusing families and their relationships to parenting beliefs. *Journal of Community Psychology, 18,* 44–59.

Cortoni, F., & Marshall, W. L. (2001). Sex as a coping strategy and its relationship to juvenile sexual history and intimacy in sexual offenders. *Sexual Abuse, 13*(1), 27–43.

Corvo, K. N. (1992). Attachment and violence in the families-of-origin of domestically violent men. *Dissertation Abstracts International, 54,* 1950A. (UMI No. 9322595)

Costa, P. T., Jr., & McCrae, R. R. (1992). *Revised NEO Personality Inventory (NEO-PI-R) and NEO Five-Factor Inventory (NEO-FFI) professional manual.* Odessa, FL: Psychological Assessment Resources.

Cott, N. (1988). *The grounding of modern feminism.* New Haven, CT: Yale University Press.

Coulter, M. L., Kuehnle, K., Byers, R., & Alfonso, M. (1999). Police-reporting behavior and victim-police interactions as described by women in a domestic violence shelter. *Journal of Interpersonal Violence, 14,* 1290–1298.

Courtois, C., & Watts, C. (1982). Counseling adult women who experienced incest in childhood or adolescence. *Personnel and Guidance Journal, 60,* 275–279.

Covell, C. N., & Scalora, M. J. (2002). Empathic deficits in sexual offenders: An integration of affective, social, and cognitive constructs. *Aggression and Violent Behavior, 7,* 251–270.

Cox, D. E., Holzworth, V., Cantrell, P. J., & Hamilton, J. (2001). *Tracking the cognitive, affective and behavioral elements of empathy across the age continuum.* Paper presented at the Eighth International Family Violence Research Conference, San Diego, CA.

Coyne, A. C., Reichman, W. E., & Berbig, L. J. (1993). The relationship between dementia and elder abuse. *American Journal of Psychiatry, 150,* 643–663.

Coyne, J. J., Barrett, P. M., & Duffy, A. L. (2000). Threat vigilance in child witnesses of domestic violence: A pilot study utilizing the ambiguous situations paradigm. *Journal of Child and Family Studies, 9,* 377–388.

Coyne-Beasley, T., Moracco, K. E., & Casteel, M. J. (2003). Adolescent female homicide. *Journal of Adolescent Health, 32,* 120–121.

Craven, D. (1997). *Sex differences in violent victimization, 1994* (NCJ Publication No. 164508). Washington, DC: U.S. Department of Justice.

Crawford, N. (2002, November). Upcoming diversity conference is new and improved. *APA Monitor on Psychology, 33,* 19.

Creighton, A., & Kivel, P. (1993). *Helping teens stop violence: A practical guide to counselors.* Alameda, CA: Hunter House.

Creighton, S. J. (1993, December). Organized abuse: NSPCC experience. *Child Abuse Review, 2,* 232–243.

Crichton, S. J., Bond, J. B., Jr., Harvey, C. D. H., & Ristok, J. (1998). Elder abuse: Feminist and ageist perspectives. *Journal of Elder Abuse & Neglect, 10*(3/4), 115–130.

Crittenden, P. M. (1984). Sibling interaction: Evidence of a generational effect in maltreating infants. *Child Abuse & Neglect, 8,* 433–438.

Crittenden, P. M. (1990). Internal representational models of attachment relationships. *Infant Mental Health Journal, 11,* 259–277.

Crittenden, P. M. (1992a). Children's strategies for coping with adverse home environments: An interpretation using attachment theory. *Child Abuse & Neglect, 16,* 329–343.

Crittenden, P. M. (1992b). The social ecology of treatment: Case study of a service system for maltreated children. *American Journal of Orthopsychiatry, 62,* 22–34.

Crittenden, P. M. (1993). Characteristics of neglectful parents: An information processing approach. *Criminal Justice and Behavior, 20,* 27–48.

Crittenden, P. M. (1996). Research on maltreating families: Implications for intervention. In J. Briere, L. Berliner, J. A. Bulkley, C. Jenny, & T. A. Reid (Eds.), *The APSAC handbook on child maltreatment* (pp. 158–174). Thousand Oaks, CA: Sage.

Crittenden, P. M. (1998). Dangerous behavior and dangerous contexts: A 35-year perspective on research on the developmental effects of child physical abuse. In P. K. Trickett & C. J. Schellenbach (Eds.), *Violence against children in the family and the community* (pp. 11–38). Washington, DC: American Psychological Association.

Crittenden, P. M., & Ainsworth, M. D. S. (1989). Child maltreatment and attachment theory. In D. Cicchetti & V. Carlson (Eds.), *Child maltreatment: Theory and research on the causes and consequences of child abuse and neglect* (pp. 432–463). New York: Cambridge University Press.

Crittenden, P. M., Claussen, A. H., & Sugarman, D. B. (1994). Physical and psychological maltreatment in middle childhood and adolescence. *Development and Psychopathology, 6,* 145–164.

Crittenden, P. M., Partridge, M. F., & Claussen, A. H. (1991). Family patterns of relationships in normative and dysfunctional families. *Development and Psychopathology, 3,* 491–512.

Cronin, C. (1995). Adolescent reports of parental spousal violence in military and civilian families. *Journal of Interpersonal Violence, 10,* 117–122.

Crossman, R. K., Stith, S. M., & Bender, M. M. (1990). Sex role egalitarianism and marital violence. *Sex Roles, 22,* 293–304.

Crouch, J. L., & Milner, J. S. (1993). Effects of child neglect on children. *Criminal Justice and Behavior, 20,* 49–65.

Crowe, H. P., & Zeskind, P. S. (1992). Psychophysiological and perceptual responses to infant cries varying in pitch: Comparison of adults with low and high scores on the Child Abuse Potential Inventory. *Child Abuse & Neglect, 16,* 19–29.

Cuartas, A. S. (2001). Dissociation in male batterers. *Dissertation Abstracts International, 62,* 3698A. (UMI No. 3033918)

Cucio, W. (1997). *The Passaic County study of AFDC recipients in a welfare-to-work program: A preliminary analysis.* Patterson, NJ: Passaic County Board of Social Services.

Culbertson, K. A., & Dehle, C. (2001). Impact of sexual assault as a function of perpetrator type. *Journal of Interpersonal Violence, 16,* 992–1007.

Culp, R. E., Little, V., Letts, D., & Lawrence, H. (1991). Maltreated children's self-concept: Effects of a comprehensive treatment program. *American Journal of Orthopsychiatry, 61*(1), 114–121.

Cummings, N. (1990). Issues of the 1990s. *Response, 13*(1), 4.

Cunradi, C. B., Caetano, R., & Schafer, J. (2002). Socioeconomic predictors of intimate partner violence among White, Black, and Hispanic couples in the United States. *Journal of Family Violence, 17,* 377–389.

Cupach, W. R., & Spitzberg, B. H. (2000). Obsessive relational intrusion: Incidence, perceived severity, and coping. *Violence and Victims, 15,* 357–372.

Currie, D. H. (1998). Violent men or violent women? Whose definition counts? In R. K. Bergen (Ed.), *Issues in intimate violence* (pp. 97–111). Thousand Oaks, CA: Sage.

Curtis, A. (1992, December 1). Some on ritual abuse task force say satanists are poisoning them. *Los Angeles Times,* pp. B1, B4.

Cyphers, G. (2001). *Report from the Child Welfare Workforce Survey: State and county data and findings.* Retrieved from American Public Human Services Association Web site: http://www.aphsa.org/cwwsurvey.pdf

Dadds, M., Smith, M., Weber, Y., & Robinson, A. (1991). An exploration of family and individual profiles following father-daughter incest. *Child Abuse & Neglect, 15,* 575–586.

Daie, N., Witzum, E., & Eleff, M. (1989). Long-term effects of sibling incest. *Journal of Clinical Psychiatry, 50,* 428–431.

Dalsbeimer, J. (1998). Battered men: A silent epidemic. *Topics in Emergency Medicine, 20*(4), 52–59.

Dalton, B. (2001). Batter characteristics and treatment completion. *Journal of Interpersonal Violence, 16,* 1223–1238.

Daly, J. E., Power, T. G., & Gondolf, E. W. (2001). Predictors of batterer program attendance. *Journal of Interpersonal Violence, 16,* 971–991.

Daly, M., & Wilson, M. (1998). The evolutionary social psychology of family violence. In C. Crawford & D. L. Krebs (Eds.), *Handbook of evolutionary psychology: Ideas, issues, and applications* (pp. 431–455). Mahwah, NJ: Lawrence Erlbaum.

Damon, L., Todd, J., & MacFarlane, K. (1987). Treatment issues with sexually abused young children. *Child Welfare, 116,* 125–137.

Daniels, V. (2001). Navajo male batterers' and battered Navajo females' therapeutic preferences. *Dissertation Abstracts International, 62*(03), 1570B. (UMI No. 3007081)

Danielson, K. K., Moffitt, T. E., Caspi, A., & Silva, P. A. (1998). Comorbidity between abuse of an adult and *DSM-III-R* mental disorders: Evidence from an epidemiological study. *American Journal of Psychiatry, 155,* 131–133.

Danis, F. S. (2003). Domestic violence and crime victim compensation. *Violence Against Women, 9,* 374–390.

Danis, F. S., Lewis, C. M., Trapp, J., Reid, K., & Fisher, E. R. (1998, July). *Lessons from the first year: An evaluation of the National Domestic Violence Hotline.* Paper presented at Program Evaluation and Family Violence Research: An International Conference, Durham, NH.

Daro, D. (1988). *Confronting child abuse: Research for effective program design.* New York: Free Press.

Daro, D. (1993). Child maltreatment research: Implications for program design. In D. Cicchetti & S. L. Toth (Eds.), *Child abuse, child development, and social policy* (pp. 331–367). Norwood, NJ: Ablex.

Daro, D. (1998). What is happening in the U.S. *The Link* (Newsletter of the International Society for Prevention of Child Abuse and Neglect), *7,* 6–7.

Daro, D. (1999). *Public opinion and behaviors regarding child abuse prevention: 1999 survey* (Working paper no. 840). Chicago: National Center on Child Abuse Prevention Research. Retrieved from http://www.preventchildabuse.org/learn_more/research_docs/1999_survey.pdf

Daro, D., & Alexander, R. (1994). Preventing child abuse fatalities: Moving forward. *APSAC Advisor, 7*(4), 49–50.

Daro, D., & Donnelly, A. C. (2002). Charting the waves of prevention: Two steps forward, one step back. *Child Abuse & Neglect, 26,* 731–742.

Daro, D., & Gelles, R. J. (1992). Public attitudes and behaviors with respect to child abuse prevention. *Journal of Interpersonal Violence, 7,* 517–531.

Daro, D., & McCurdy, K. (1994). Preventing child abuse and neglect: Programmatic interventions. *Child Welfare, 73,* 405–430.

Daro, D., McCurdy, K., & Harding, K. (1998). *The role of home visiting in preventing child abuse: An evaluation of the Hawaii Healthy Start Program.* Chicago: National Center on Child Abuse Prevention Research.

Dasgupta, S. D. (2000). Charting the course: An overview of domestic violence in the South Asian community in the United States. *Journal of Social Distress and the Homeless, 9,* 173–185.

D'Augelli, A. R. (1992). Lesbian and gay male undergraduates' experiences of harassment and fear on campus. *Journal of Interpersonal Violence, 7,* 383–395.

Davey, G. C. L. (1992). Classical conditioning and the acquisition of human fears and phobias: A review and synthesis of the literature. *Advances in Behaviour Research and Therapy, 14,* 29–66.

Davidson, H. A. (1994). *The impact of domestic violence on children: A report to the president of the American Bar Association* (2nd rev. ed., Report No. 549–0248). Chicago: American Bar Association.

Davidson, H. A. (1995). Child abuse and domestic violence: Legal connections and controversies. *Family Law Quarterly, 29,* 357–373.

Davidson, K., MacGregor, M. W., Stuhr, J., Dixon, K., & MacLean, D. (2000). Constructive anger verbal behavior predicts blood pressure in a population-based sample. *Health Psychology, 19,* 55–64.

Davies, S. L., Glaser, D., & Kossoff, R. (2000). Children's sexual play and behavior in pre-school settings: Staff's perceptions, reports, and responses. *Child Abuse & Neglect, 24,* 1329–1343.

Davis, G. E., & Leitenberg, H. (1987). Adolescent sex offenders. *Psychological Bulletin, 101,* 417–427.

Davis, J. W., Parks, S. N., Kaups, K. L., Bennink, L. D., & Bilello, J. F. (2003). Victims of domestic violence on the trauma service: Unrecognized and underreported. *Journal of Trauma, 54,* 352–355.

Davis, K. E., Ace, A., & Anda, M. (2000). Stalking perpetrators and psychological maltreatment of partners: Anger-jealousy, attachment insecurity, and break-up context. *Violence and Victims, 15,* 407–425.

Davis, L. (1991). Murdered memory. *Health, 5,* 79–84.

Davis, L. V. (1984). Beliefs of service providers about abused women and abusing men. *Social Work, 29,* 243–250.

Davis, M. H., & Morris, M. M. (1998). Relationship-specific and global perceptions of social support: Associations with well-being and attachment. *Journal of Personality and Social Psychology, 74,* 468–481.

Davis, M. K., & Gidycz, C. A. (2000). Child sexual abuse prevention programs: A meta-analysis. *Journal of Clinical Child Psychology, 29,* 257–265.

Davis, R. C., & Erez, E. (1998, May). *Immigrant populations as victims: Toward a multicultural criminal justice system* (NCJ Publication No. 167571). Washington, DC: U.S. Department of Justice.

Davis, R. C., Medina, J., & Avitabile, N. (2001). *Reducing repeat incidents of elder abuse: Results of a randomized experiment, final report* (NCJRS Publication No. 189086). Washington, DC: U.S. Department of Justice.

Davis, R. C., Smith, B. E., & Nickles, L. (1997). Prosecuting domestic violence cases with reluctant victims: Assessing two novel approaches in Milwaukee. In National Institute of Justice & American Bar Association, *Legal interventions in family violence: Research findings and policy implications* (NCJ Publication No. 171666, pp. 71–72). Washington, DC: U.S. Department of Justice.

Davis, R. L. (1998). *Domestic violence: Facts and fallacies.* Westport, CT: Praeger.

Davis, S. P., & Fantuzzo, J. W. (1989). The effects of adult and peer social initiations on the social behavior of withdrawn and aggressive maltreated preschool children. *Journal of Family Violence, 4,* 227–248.

Davison, G. C., & Johnson, M. K. (1983). Articulated thoughts during simulated situations: A paradigm for studying cognition in emotion and behavior. *Cognitive Therapy and Research, 7,* 7–14.

Dawson, B., DeArmas, A., McGrath, M. L., & Kelly, J. A. (1986). Cognitive problem-solving training to improve the child-care judgment of child neglectful parents. *Journal of Family Violence, 1,* 209–221.

Dawson, J. M., & Langan, P. A. (1994). *Murder in families* (NCJ Publication No. 143498). Annapolis Junction, MD: U.S. Bureau of Justice Statistics.

Dawson, S. L., & Surpin, R. (2001). Direct-care healthcare workers: You get what you pay for. *Generations, 25*(1), 23–28.

Dayton, K. (2002, November/December). Legislative roundup: New state laws protecting vulnerable adults. *Victimization of the Elderly and Disabled, 5,* 53–54, 61.

DeAngelis, T. (1993, November). APA panel is examining memories of child abuse. *APA Monitor on Psychology, 24,* 44.

De Bellis, M. D. (2001). Developmental traumatology: The psychobiological development of maltreated children and its implications for research, treatment, and policy. *Development and Psychopathology, 13,* 539–564.

De Bellis, M. D., Baum, A., Birmaher, B., Keshavan, M., Eccard, C. H., Boring, A. M., et al. (1999). Developmental traumatology part I: Biological stress systems. *Biological Psychiatry, 45,* 1259–1270.

De Bellis, M. D., Burke, L., Trickett, P. K., & Putnam, F. W. (1996). Antinuclear antibodies and thyroid function in sexually abused girls. *Journal of Traumatic Stress, 9,* 369–378.

De Bellis, M. D., Chrousos, G. P., Dorn, L. D., Burke, L., Helmers, K., Kling, M. A., et al. (1994). Hypothalamic-pituitary-adrenal axis dysregulation in sexually abused girls. *Journal of Clinical Endocrinology and Metabolism, 78,* 249–255.

De Bellis, M. D., Lefter, L., Trickett, P. K., & Putnam, F. W. (1994). Urinary catecholamine excretion in sexually abused girls. *Journal of the American Academy of Child and Adolescent Psychiatry, 33,* 320–327.

Decalmer, P. (1993). Clinical presentation. In P. Decalmer & F. Glendenning (Eds.), *The mistreatment of elderly people* (pp. 35–61). London: Sage.

Deering, C., Templer, D. I., Keller, J., & Canfield, M. (2001). Neuropsychological assessment of battered women: A pilot study. *Perceptual and Motor Skills, 92,* 682–686.

Deffenbacher, J. L. (1992). Trait anger: Theory, findings and implications. In C. D. Spielberger & J. N. Butcher (Eds.), *Advances in personality assessment* (Vol. 9, pp. 177–201). Hillsdale, NJ: Lawrence Erlbaum.

Deitch, I. (1993, August). *Alone, abandoned, assaulted: Prevention and intervention of elder abuse.* Paper presented at the annual meeting of the American Psychological Association, Toronto.

De Jong, A. R. (1988). Maternal responses to the sexual abuse of their children. *Pediatrics, 81,* 14–21.

De Jong, A. R. (1989). Sexual interactions among siblings and cousins: Experimentation or exploitation? *Child Abuse & Neglect, 13,* 271–279.

DeKeseredy, W. S. (1996). Making an unsafe learning environment safer: Some progressive policy proposals to curb woman abuse in university/college dating relationships. In C. Stark-Adamec (Ed.), *Violence: A collective responsibility* (pp. 71–94). Ottawa: Social Sciences Federation.

DeKeseredy, W. S. (2000). Current controversies on defining nonlethal violence against women in intimate heterosexual relationships. *Violence Against Women, 6,* 728–746.

DeKeseredy, W. S., & Hinch, R. (1991). *Woman abuse: Sociological perspectives.* Toronto: Thompson Educational.

DeKeseredy, W. S., & Kelly, K. D. (1993). The incidence and prevalence of woman abuse in Canadian university and college dating relationships. *Canadian Journal of Sociology, 18,* 137–159.

DeKeseredy, W. S., & Schwartz, M. D. (1998). *Measuring the extent of woman abuse in intimate heterosexual relationships: A critique of the Conflict Tactics Scales.* Retrieved December 10, 2003, from http://www.vaw.umn.edu/documents/vawnet/ctscritique/ctscritique.pdf

DeMaris, A. (2001). The influence of intimate violence on transition out of cohabitation. *Journal of Marriage and Family, 63,* 235–246.

deMause, L. (1974). The evolution of childhood. In L. deMause (Ed.), *The history of childhood* (pp. 1–74). New York: Psychotherapy Press.

deMause, L. (1994). Cult abuse of children: Witch hunt or reality. *Journal of Psychohistory, 21,* 505–518.

Denham, S. A., Renwick, S. M., & Holt, R. W. (1991). Working and playing together: Prediction of preschool social-emotional competence from mother-child interaction. *Child Development, 62,* 242–249.

Dennison, S. M., & Thomson, D. M. (2002). Identifying stalking: The relevance of intent in commonsense reasoning. *Law and Human Behavior, 26,* 543–561.

DePanfilis, D. (1996). Social isolation of neglectful families: A review of social support assessment and intervention models. *Child Maltreatment, 1,* 37–52.

DePaul, A. (1992). New laws in California aid women victimized by violence. *Criminal Justice Newsletter, 23*(2), 5–6.

de Paul, J., & Arruabarrena, M. I. (1995). Behavior problems in school-aged physically abused and neglected children in Spain. *Child Abuse & Neglect, 19,* 409–418.

DeVoe, E. R., & Smith, E. L. (2002). The impact of domestic violence on urban preschool children: Battered mothers' perspectives. *Journal of Interpersonal Violence, 17,* 1075–1101.

Dienemann, J., Boyle, E., Resnick, W., Wiederhorn, N., & Campbell, J. C. (2000). Intimate partner abuse among women diagnosed with depression. *Issues in Mental Health Nursing, 21,* 499–513.

DiLalla, L. F., & Gottesman, I. (1991). Biological and genetic contributors to violence: Widom's untold tale. *Psychological Bulletin, 109,* 125–129.

DiLeonardi, J. W. (1993). Families in poverty and chronic neglect of children. *Families in Society, 74,* 557–562.

DiLillo, D., & Long, P. J. (1999). Perceptions of couple functioning among female survivors of child sexual abuse. *Journal of Child Sexual Abuse, 7*(4), 59–76.

Disbrow, M. A., Doerr, H., & Caulfield, C. (1977). Measuring the components of parents' potential for child abuse and neglect. *Child Abuse & Neglect, 1,* 279–296.

Dittman, M. (2002). Psychologists urge Congress to support programs and research to thwart child maltreatment. *APA Monitor on Psychology, 33,* 12.

Dixon, L., & Browne, K. (2003). The heterogeneity of spouse abuse: A review. *Aggression and Violent Behavior, 8,* 107–130.

Djeddah, C., Facchin, P., Ranzato, C., & Romer, C. (2000). Child abuse: Current problems and key public health challenges. *Social Science & Medicine, 51,* 905–915.

Dobash, R. E., & Dobash, R. P. (1978). Wives: The "appropriate" victims of marital violence. *Victimology, 2,* 426–442.

Dobash, R. E., & Dobash, R. P. (1979). *Violence against wives: A case against patriarchy.* New York: Free Press.

Dobash, R. E., & Dobash, R. P. (1988). Research as social action: The struggle for battered women. In K. A. Yllö & M. Bograd (Eds.), *Feminist perspectives on wife abuse* (pp. 51–74). Newbury Park, CA: Sage.

Dobash, R. P., & Dobash, R. E. (1992). *Women, violence, and social change.* New York: Routledge.

Dobash, R. P., Dobash, R. E., Wilson, M., & Daly, M. (1992). The myth of sexual symmetry in marital violence. *Social Problems, 39,* 71–91.

Dodge, K. A., Bates, J. E., & Pettit, G. S. (1990). Mechanisms in the cycle of violence. *Science, 250,* 1678–1682.

Doek, J. E. (1985). Child pornography and legislation in the Netherlands. *Child Abuse & Neglect, 9,* 411–412.

Doll, L., Joy, D., & Bartholow, B. (1992). Self-reported childhood and adolescent sexual abuse among homosexual and bisexual men. *Child Abuse & Neglect, 16,* 855–864.

Domestic violence conviction bars gun possession by officers. (1997, January 2). *Criminal Justice Newsletter,* pp. 2–3.

Dore, M. M., Doris, J., & Wright, P. (1995). Identifying substance abuse in maltreating families: A child welfare challenge. *Child Abuse & Neglect, 19,* 531–543.

Dore, M. M., & Lee, J. M. (1999). The role of parent training with abusive and neglectful parents. *Family Relations, 48,* 313–325.

Douglas, K. A., Collins, J. L., Warren, C., Kann, L., Gold, R., Clayton, S., et al. (1997). Results from the 1995 National College Risk Behavior Survey. *Journal of American College Health, 46,* 55–66.

Douglas, M. A. (1987). The battered woman syndrome. In D. J. Sonkin (Ed.), *Domestic violence on trial: Psychological and legal dimensions of family violence* (pp. 39–54). New York: Springer.

Doumas, D., Margolin, G., & John, R. S. (1994). The intergenerational transmission of aggression across three generations. *Journal of Family Violence, 9,* 157–175.

Dowdney, L., & Pickles, A. R. (1991). Expression of negative affect within disciplinary encounters: Is there dyadic reciprocity? *Developmental Psychology, 27,* 606–617.

Downs, W. R., & Miller, B. A. (1998). Relationships between experiences of parental violence during childhood and women's psychiatric symptomatology. *Journal of Interpersonal Violence, 13,* 438–455.

Drake, B., & Pandey, S. (1996). Understanding the relationship between neighborhood poverty and specific types of child maltreatment. *Child Abuse & Neglect, 20,* 1003–1018.

Drake, B., & Zuravin, S. (1998). Bias in child maltreatment reporting: Revisiting the myth of classlessness. *American Journal of Orthopsychiatry, 68,* 295–304.

Dreher, K. B. (2002). Enforcement of standards of care in the long-term care industry: How far have we come and where to we go from here? *Elder Law Journal, 10,* 119–151.

Drotar, D., Eckerle, D., Satola, J., Pallotta, J., & Wyatt, B. (1990). Maternal interactional behavior with nonorganic failure-to-thrive infants: A case comparison study. *Child Abuse & Neglect, 14,* 41–51.

Dubner, A. E., & Motta, R. W. (1999). Sexually and physically abused foster care children and posttraumatic stress disorder. *Journal of Consulting and Clinical Psychology, 67,* 367–373.

Dubowitz, H. (1994). Neglecting the neglect of neglect. *Journal of Interpersonal Violence, 9,* 556–560.

Dubowitz, H. (Ed.). (1999). *Neglected children: Research, practice, and policy.* Thousand Oaks, CA: Sage.

Dubowitz, H., & Black, M. (2002). Neglect of children's health. In J. E. B. Myers, L. Berliner, J. Briere, C. T. Hendrix, C. Jenny, & T. A. Reid (Eds.), *The APSAC handbook on child maltreatment* (2nd ed., pp. 269–292). Thousand Oaks, CA: Sage.

Dubowitz, H., Black, M., Harrington, D., & Verschoore, A. (1993). A follow-up study of behavior problems associated with child sexual abuse. *Child Abuse & Neglect, 17,* 743–754.

Dubowitz, H., Black, M., Starr, R., & Zuravin, S. J. (1993). A conceptual definition of child neglect. *Criminal Justice and Behavior, 20,* 8–26.

Dubowitz, H., & DePanfilis, D. (Eds.). (2000). *Handbook for child protection practice.* Thousand Oaks, CA: Sage.

Dubowitz, H., Klockner, A., Starr, R., & Black, M. (1998). Community and professional definitions of child neglect. *Child Maltreatment, 3,* 235–243.

Duke, J. (1999, January/February). Summary of findings of a national survey of adult abuse central registries. *Victimization of the Elderly and Disabled, 1,* 73–74, 77.

Dunford, F. W. (2000). The San Diego Navy Experiment: An assessment of interventions for men who assault their wives. *Journal of Consulting and Clinical Psychology, 68,* 468–476.

Dunford, F. W., Huizinga, D., & Elliott, D. S. (1990). The role of arrest in domestic assault: The Omaha police experiment. *Criminology, 28,* 183–206.

Dunlap, E., Golub, A., Johnson, B. D., & Wesley, D. (2002). Intergenerational transmission of conduct norms for drugs, sexual exploitation and violence: A case study. *British Journal of Criminology, 41,* 1–20.

Dunlop, B. D., Rothman, M. B., Condon, K. M., Hebert, K. S., & Martinez, I. L. (2000). Elder abuse: Risk factors and use of case data to improve policy and practice. *Journal of Elder Abuse & Neglect, 12*(3/4), 95–122.

Dunn, J., & McGuire, S. (1992). Sibling and peer relationships in childhood. *Journal of Child Psychology and Psychiatry, 33,* 67–105.

Dunn, P. F. (1995). "Elder abuse" as an innovation to Australia: A critical overview. In J. I. Kosberg & J. L. Garcia (Eds.), *Elder abuse: International and cross-cultural perspectives* (pp. 13–30). Binghamton, NY: Haworth.

Durfee, M., Durfee, D. T., & West, M. P. (2002). Child fatality review: An international movement. *Child Abuse & Neglect, 26,* 619–636.

Durkin, K. F., & Bryant, C. D. (1995). "Log on to sex": Some notes on the carnal computer and erotic cyberspace as an emerging research frontier. *Deviant Behavior, 16,* 179–200.

Dutton, A. M., & Rubinstein, F. L. (1995). Working with people with PTSD: Research implications. In C. R. Figley (Ed.), *Compassion fatigue: Coping with secondary traumatic stress disorder in those who treat the traumatized* (pp. 82–100). New York: Brunner/Mazel.

Dutton, D. G. (1986). The outcome of court-mandated treatment for wife assault: A quasi-experimental evaluation. *Violence and Victims, 1,* 163–175.

Dutton, D. G. (1988). *The domestic assault of women.* Boston: Allyn & Bacon.

Dutton, D. G. (1994). Patriarchy and wife assault: An ecological fallacy. *Violence and Victims, 9,* 167–182.

Dutton, D. G. (1995a). A scale for measuring propensity for abusiveness. *Journal of Family Violence, 10,* 203–221.

Dutton, D. G. (1995b). Trauma symptoms and PTSD-like profiles in perpetrators of intimate abuse. *Journal of Traumatic Stress, 8,* 299–316.

Dutton, D. G. (1998). *The abusive personality: Violence and control in intimate relationships.* New York: Guilford.

Dutton, D. G. (1999). Traumatic origins of intimate rage. *Aggression and Violent Behavior, 4,* 431–447.

Dutton, D. G., & Haring, M. (1999). Perpetrator personality effects on post-separation victim reactions in abusive relationships. *Journal of Family Violence, 14,* 193–204.

Dutton, D. G., & Painter, S. L. (1981). Traumatic bonding: The development of emotional attachments in battered women and other relationships of intermittent abuse. *Victimology, 6*(1–4), 139–155.

Dutton, D. G., & Painter, S. L. (1993a). The battered woman syndrome: Effects of severity and intermittency of abuse. *American Journal of Orthopsychiatry, 63,* 614–622.

Dutton, D. G., & Painter, S. L. (1993b). Emotional attachments in abusive relationships: A test of traumatic bonding theory. *Violence and Victims, 8,* 105–120.

Dutton, D. G., Saunders, K., Starzomski, A. J., & Bartholomew, K. (1994). Intimacy-anger and insecure attachment as precursors of abuse in intimate relationships. *Journal of Applied Social Psychology, 24,* 1367–1386.

Dutton, D. G., & Starzomski, A. J. (1993). Borderline personality in perpetrators of psychological and physical abuse. *Violence and Victims, 8,* 327–337.

Dutton, D. G., & Starzomski, A. J. (1994). Psychological differences between court-referred and self-referred wife assaulters. *Criminal Justice and Behavior, 21,* 203–222.

Dutton, D. G., & Strachan, C. E. (1987). Motivational needs for power and spouse-specific assertiveness in assaultive and nonassaultive men. *Violence and Victims, 2,* 145–156.

Dutton, D. G., van Ginkel, C., & Landolt, M. A. (1996). Jealousy, intimate abusiveness, and intrusiveness. *Journal of Family Violence, 11,* 411–423.

Dutton, D. G., van Ginkel, C., & Starzomski, A. J. (1995). The role of shame and guilt in the intergenerational transmission of abusiveness. *Violence and Victims, 10,* 121–131.

Dutton, M. A., Holtzworth-Munroe, A., Jouriles, E. N., McDonald, R., Krishnan, S. P., McFarlane, J., et al. (2003). *Recruitment and retention in intimate partner violence research* (NCJ Publication No. 201943). Washington, DC: U.S. Department of Justice.

Dutton-Douglas, M. A., & Dionne, D. (1991). Counseling and shelter services for battered women. In M. Steinman (Ed.), *Woman battering: Policy responses* (pp. 113–130). Cincinnati, OH: Anderson.

Dye, M. L., & Davis, K. E. (2003). Stalking and psychological abuse: Common factors and relationship-specific characteristics. *Violence and Victims, 18,* 163–180.

D'Zurilla, T. J. (1986). *Problem-solving therapy: A social competence approach to clinical intervention.* New York: Springer.

Earls, C. M., & David, H. (1990, December). Early family and sexual experiences of male and female prostitutes. *Canada's Mental Health,* pp. 7–11.

East Bay Consortium for Elder Abuse. (2001). *Elder abuse prevention.* Alameda, CA: Author.

Ebrahim, A. B. (2001). Glossaries in public health: Older people. *Journal of Epidemiological Community Health, 55,* 223–226.

Eckely, S. C. A., & Vilakazi, P. A. C. (1995). Elder abuse in South Africa. In J. I. Kosberg & J. L. Garcia (Eds.), *Elder abuse: International and cross-cultural perspectives* (pp. 171–182). Binghamton, NY: Haworth.

Eckenrode, J., Ganzel, B., Henderson, C. R., Smith, E., Olds, D. L., Powers, J., et al. (2000). Preventing child abuse and neglect with a program of nurse home visitation: The limiting effect of domestic violence. *Journal of the American Medical Association, 284,* 1385–1391.

Eckenrode, J., Laird, M., & Doris, J. (1993). School performance and disciplinary problems among abused and neglected children. *Developmental Psychology, 29,* 53–63.

Eckhardt, C. I., Barbour, K. A., & Stuart, G. L. (1997). Anger and hostility in maritally violent men: Conceptual distinctions, measurement issues and literature review. *Clinical Psychology Review, 17,* 333–358.

Eckhardt, C. I., Jamison, T. R., & Watts, K. (2002). Anger experience and expression among male dating violence perpetrators during anger arousal. *Journal of Interpersonal Violence, 17,* 1102–1114.

Eckstein, S. (2001). Community as gift-giving: Collective roots of volunteerism. *American Sociological Review, 66,* 829–851.

Edleson, J. L. (1991). Coordinated community responses. In M. Steinman (Ed.), *Woman battering: Policy responses* (pp. 203–220). Cincinnati, OH: Anderson.

Edleson, J. L. (1998). Responsible mothers and invisible men: Child protection in the case of adult domestic violence. *Journal of Interpersonal Violence, 13,* 294–298.

Edleson, J. L. (1999). The overlap between child maltreatment and woman battering. *Violence Against Women, 5,* 134–154.

Edleson, J. L., & Beeman, S. K. (2000). *Responding to the co-occurrence of child maltreatment and adult domestic violence in Hennepin County.* Retrieved from http://www.mincava.umn.edu/link/finrport.asp

Edleson, J. L., & Tolman, R. M. (1992). *Intervention for men who batter.* Newbury Park, CA: Sage.

Egan, K. (1983). Stress management with abusive parents. *Journal of Clinical Child Psychology, 12,* 292–299.

Egeland, B. (1993). A history of abuse is a major risk factor for abusing the next generation. In R. J. Gelles & D. R. Loseke (Eds.), *Current controversies on family violence* (pp. 197–208). Newbury Park, CA: Sage.

Egeland, B. (1997). Mediators of the effects of child maltreatment on developmental adaptation in adolescence. In D. Cicchetti & S. L. Toth (Eds.), *Rochester Symposium on Developmental Psychopathology: Vol. 8. The effects of trauma on the developmental process* (pp. 403–434). Rochester, NY: University of Rochester Press.

Egeland, B., Jacobvitz, D., & Sroufe, L. A. (1988). Breaking the cycle of child abuse. *Child Development, 59,* 1080–1088.

Egeland, B., & Sroufe, L. A. (1981). Developmental sequelae of maltreatment in infancy. *New Directions for Child Development, 11,* 77–92.

Egeland, B., Sroufe, L. A., & Erickson, M. F. (1983). The developmental consequences of different patterns of maltreatment. *Child Abuse & Neglect, 7,* 459–469.

Egeland, B., & Susman-Stillman, A. (1996). Dissociation as a mediator of child abuse across generations. *Child Abuse & Neglect, 11,* 1123–1132.

Ehrensaft, M. K., Cohen, P., Brown, J., Smailes, E. M., Chen, H., & Johnson, J. G. (2003). Intergenerational transmission of partner violence: A 20-year prospective study. *Journal of Consulting and Clinical Psychology, 71,* 741–753.

Ehrensaft, M. K., Langhinrichsen-Rohling, J., Heyman, R. E., O'Leary, K. D., & Lawrence, E. (1999). Feeling controlled in marriage: A phenomenon specific to physically aggressive couples. *Journal of Family Psychology, 13,* 20–32.

Ehrensaft, M. K., & Vivian, D. (1996). Spouses' reasons for not reporting existing physical aggression as a marital problem. *Journal of Family Psychology, 10,* 443–453.

Eisikovits, Z., & Enosh, G. (1997). Awareness of guilt and shame in intimate violence. *Violence and Victims, 12,* 307–322.

Eisler, R. M., & Skidmore, J. R. (1987). Masculine gender-role stress: Scale development and component factors in the appraisal of stressful situations. *Behavior Modification, 11,* 123–136.

El-Bassel, N., Gilbert, L., Schilling, R., & Wada, T. (2000). Drug abuse and partner violence among women in methadone treatment. *Journal of Family Violence, 15,* 209–228.

Elbow, M. (1977). Theoretical considerations of violent marriages. *Social Casework, 58,* 515–526.

Elbow, M. (1982). Children of violent marriages: The forgotten victims. *Social Casework, 63,* 465–471.

Eldridge, J. P. T. (2000). Stalking and the military: A proposal to add an anti-stalking provision to Article 134, Uniform Code of Military Justice. *Military Law Review, 165,* 116–158.

Ellerstein, N. S., & Canavan, W. (1980). Sexual abuse of boys. *American Journal of Diseases of Children, 134,* 255–257.

Elliott, D. M. (1994). Impaired object relations in professional women molested as children. *Psychotherapy, 31,* 79–86.

Elliott, D. M., & Briere, J. (1992). Sexual abuse trauma among professional women: Validating the Trauma Symptom Checklist-40 (TSC-40). *Child Abuse & Neglect, 16,* 391–398.

Elliott, D. M., & Briere, J. (1994). Forensic sexual abuse evaluations: Disclosures and symptomatology. *Behavioral Sciences and the Law, 12,* 261–277.

Elliott, D. S. (1994). Serious violent offenders: Onset, developmental course, and termination. *Criminology, 32,* 1–21.

Elliott, D. S., & Huizinga, D. (1989). Improving self-reported measures of delinquency. In M. W. Klein (Ed.), *Cross-national research in self-reported crime and delinquency* (pp. 155–186). Dordrecht: Kluwer Academic.

Elliott, M. (Ed.). (1993). *Female sexual abuse of children.* New York: Guilford.

Elliott, M., Browne, K., & Kilcoyne, J. (1995). Child sexual abuse prevention: What offenders tell us. *Child Abuse & Neglect, 19,* 579–594.

Ellis, L., & Walsh, A. (1999). Criminologists' opinions about causes and theories of crime and delinquency. *Criminologist, 24*(4), 1, 4–6.

Ellison, C. G., Bartkowski, J. P., & Segal, M. L. (1996). Do conservative Protestant parents spank more often? Further evidence from the national survey of families and households. *Social Science Quarterly, 77,* 663–673.

Elliston, E. J. W. (2001). Why don't they just leave? The effects of psychological abuse on sheltered women. *Dissertation Abstracts International, 62*(07), 2570A. (UMI No. 3019516)

Ellsberg, M., Caldera, T., Herrera, A., Winkvist, A., & Kullgren, G. (1999). Domestic violence and emotional distress among Nicaraguan women. *American Psychologist, 54,* 30–36.

Elwell, M. E., & Ephross, P. H. (1987). Initial reactions of sexually abused children. *Social Casework, 68,* 109–116.

Emans, R. L. (1988). Psychology's responsibility in false accusations of child abuse. *Journal of Clinical Psychology, 44,* 1000–1004.

Emerson, R. M., Ferris, K. O., & Gardner, C. B. (1998). On being stalked. *Social Problems, 45,* 289–314.

Emery, R. E., & Laumann-Billings, L. (1998). An overview of the nature, causes, and consequences of abusive family relationships: Toward differentiating maltreatment and violence. *American Psychologist, 53,* 121–135.

Emmers-Sommer, T. M., & Allen, M. (1999). Variables related to sexual coercion: A path model. *Journal of Social and Personal Relationships, 16,* 659–678.

Emotional judgments seek respect. (1999, July 24). *Science News, 156,* 59.

Empey, L. T., Stafford, M. C., & Hay, H. H. (1999). *American delinquency: Its meaning and construction.* Belmont, CA: Wadsworth.

Empower Program. (2002, October 23). *Teen Dating Violence and Social Environment Survey: Teen opinion.* Retrieved from http://empowered.org/Press/Releases/Topline<uscore>Results.htm

Epperly, T. D., & Moore, K. E. (2000). Health issues in men: Part II. Common psychosocial disorders. *American Family Physician, 62,* 117–124.

Epstein, D. (1999). In search of effective intervention in domestic violence cases: Rethinking the roles of prosecutors, judges, and the court system. *Yale Journal of Law & Feminism, 11,* 3–50.

Erez, E., & Belknap, J. (1998). In their own words: Battered women's assessment of the criminal processing system's response. *Violence and Victims, 13,* 251–268.

Erez, E., & Tontodonato, P. (1990). The effect of victim participation in sentencing outcomes. *Criminology, 28,* 451–474.

Ericksen, J. R., & Henderson, A. D. (1992). Witnessing family violence: The children's experience. *Journal of Advanced Nursing, 17,* 1200–1209.

Erickson, M. F., & Egeland, B. (1987). A developmental view of the psychological consequences of maltreatment. *School Psychology Review, 16,* 156–168.

Erickson, M. F., & Egeland, B. (1996). Child neglect. In J. Briere, L. Berliner, J. A. Bulkley, C. Jenny, & T. A. Reid (Eds.), *The APSAC handbook on child maltreatment* (pp. 4–20). Thousand Oaks, CA: Sage.

Erickson, M. F., & Egeland, B. (2002). Child neglect. In J. E. B. Myers, L. Berliner, J. Briere, C. T. Hendrix, C. Jenny, & T. A. Reid (Eds.), *The APSAC handbook on child maltreatment* (2nd ed., pp. 3–20). Thousand Oaks, CA: Sage.

Erickson, M. F., Egeland, B., & Pianta, R. (1989). The effects of maltreatment on the development of young children. In D. Cicchetti & V. Carlson (Eds.), *Child maltreatment: Theory and research on the causes and consequences of child abuse and neglect* (pp. 647–684). New York: Cambridge University Press.

Eron, L. D., & Huesmann, L. R. (1987). Television as a source of maltreatment of children. *School Psychology Review, 16,* 195–202.

Erwin, P. E. (2000). *Intimate and caregiver violence against women with disabilities.* Minneapolis: Battered Women's Justice Project.

Esposito, L. C. (1998). Regulating the Internet: The new battle against child pornography. *Case Western Reserve Journal of International Law, 30,* 541–565.

Ethier, L. S., Lacharite, C., & Couture, G. (1995). Childhood adversity, parental stress and depression of negligent mothers. *Child Abuse & Neglect, 19,* 619–632.

Ethier, L. S., Palacio-Quintin, E., & Jourdan-Ionescu, C. (1992, June). Abuse and neglect: Two distinct forms of maltreatment. *Canada's Mental Health,* pp. 13–19.

Evans, G. W., Wells, N. M., & Chan, H. Y. E. (2000). Housing quality and mental health. *Journal of Consulting and Clinical Psychology, 68,* 526–530.

Everson, M. D., & Boat, B. W. (1989). False allegations of sexual abuse by children and adolescents. *American Academy of Child and Adolescent Psychiatry, 28,* 230–235.

Ewing, C. P. (1990). Psychological self-defense. *Law and Human Behavior, 14,* 579–594.

Ewing, C. P., & Aubrey, M. (1987). Battered women and public opinion: Some realities about myths. *Journal of Family Violence, 2,* 257–264.

Fagan, J. A. (1988). Contributions of family violence research to criminal justice policy on wife assault: Paradigms of science and social control. *Violence and Victims, 3,* 159–186.

Fagan, J. A., Stewart, D., & Hansen, K. (1983). Violent men or violent husbands? Background factors and situational correlates. In D. Finkelhor, R. J. Gelles, G. T. Hotaling, & M. A. Straus (Eds.), *The dark side of families: Current family violence research* (pp. 49–67). Beverly Hills, CA: Sage.

"Failure to Protect" Working Group of the Child Welfare Committee of New York City Inter-agency Task Force Against Domestic Violence. (2000). Charging battered mothers with "failure to protect": Still blaming the victim. *Fordham Urban Law Journal, 27,* 849–873.

Faller, K. C. (1988a). *Child sexual abuse: An interdisciplinary manual for diagnosis, case management, and treatment.* New York: Columbia University Press.

Faller, K. C. (1988b). The spectrum of sexual abuse in daycare: An exploratory study. *Journal of Family Violence, 3,* 283–298.

Faller, K. C. (1989). Why sexual abuse? An exploration of the intergenerational hypothesis. *Child Abuse & Neglect, 13,* 543–548.

Faller, K. C. (1993). Research on false allegations of sexual abuse in divorce. *APSAC Advisor, 6*(1), 7–10.

Fals-Stewart, W. (2003). The occurrence of partner physical aggression on days of alcohol consumption: A longitudinal diary study. *Journal of Consulting and Clinical Psychology, 71,* 41–52.

Family Violence and Prevention Fund. (2002, March 28). *New campaign invites men to talk to boys about domestic violence.* Retrieved from http://endabuse.org/newsflash/index.php3? Search=Article&NewsFlashID=316

Family Violence Project of the National Council of Juvenile and Family Court Judges. (1995). Family violence in child custody statutes: An analysis of state codes and legal practice. *Family Law Quarterly, 29,* 197–227.

Famularo, R., Fenton, T., & Kinscherff, R. T. (1992). Medical and developmental histories of maltreated children. *Clinical Pediatrics, 31,* 536–541.

Famularo, R., Fenton, T., Kinscherff, R. T., Ayoub, C. C., & Barnum, R. (1994). Maternal and child posttraumatic stress disorder in cases of child maltreatment. *Child Abuse & Neglect, 18,* 27–36.

Famularo, R., Kinscherff, R. T., & Fenton, T. (1991). Posttraumatic stress disorder among children clinically diagnosed as borderline personality disorder. *Journal of Nervous and Mental Disease, 179,* 428–431.

Fantuzzo, J. W. (1990). Behavioral treatment of the victims of child abuse and neglect. *Behavior Modification, 14,* 316–339.

Fantuzzo, J. W., delGaudio, W. A., Atkins, M., Meyers, R., & Noone, M. (1998). A contextually relevant assessment of the impact of child maltreatment on the social competencies of low-income urban children. *Journal of the American Academy of Child and Adolescent Psychiatry, 37,* 1201–1208.

Fantuzzo, J. W., & Lindquist, C. U. (1989). The effects of observing conjugal violence on children: A review and analysis of research methodology. *Journal of Family Violence, 4,* 77–94.

Fantuzzo, J. W., Sutton-Smith, B., Atkins, M., Meyers, R., Stevenson, H., Coolahan, K., et al. (1996). Community-based resilient peer treatment of withdrawn maltreated preschool children. *Journal of Consulting and Clinical Psychology, 64,* 1377–1386.

Faraone, S. V., Tsuang, M. T., & Tsuang, D. W. (1999). *Genetics of mental disorders.* New York: Guilford.

Farrell, M. L. (1996). Healing: A qualitative study of women recovering from abusive relationships with men. *Perspectives in Psychiatric Care, 32,* 23–32.

Farrington, D. P. (2000). Psychosocial predictors of adult antisocial personality and adult convictions. *Behavioral Sciences and the Law, 18,* 605–622.

Faulk, M. (1974). Men who assault their wives. *Medicine, Science, and the Law, 14,* 180–183.

Faulkner, A. H., & Cranston, K. (1998). Correlates of same-sex sexual behavior in a random sample of Massachusetts high school students. *American Journal of Public Health, 88,* 262–266.

Faulkner, K., Stoltenberg, C. D., Cogen, R., Nolder, M., & Shooter, E. (1992). Cognitive-behavioral group treatment for male spouse abusers. *Journal of Family Violence, 7,* 37–55.

Faver, C. A., Crawford, S. L., & Combs-Orme, T. (1999). Services for child maltreatment: Challenges for research and practice. *Children and Youth Services Review, 21,* 89–109.

Feather, N. T. (1996). Domestic violence, gender, and perceptions of justice. *Sex Roles, 35,* 115–123.

Feder, L. (1997). Domestic violence and police response in a pro-arrest jurisdiction. *Women & Criminal Justice, 8*(4), 79–97.

Feder, L. (1998). Police handling of domestic and nondomestic assault calls: Is there a case for discrimination? *Crime & Delinquency, 44,* 335–349.

Feder, L., & Dugan, L. (2003). A test of the efficacy of court-mandated counseling for domestic violence offenders: The Broward Experiment. *Justice Quarterly, 19,* 343–375.

Federal sex discrimination lawsuit settled, company agrees to end housing discrimination against battered women. (2001). *Family Violence and Sexual Assault Bulletin, 17*(7), 42.

Feeney, J. A., & Noller, P. (1996). *Adult attachment.* Thousand Oaks, CA: Sage.

Feeny, N. C., Zoellner, L. A., & Foa, E. B. (2000). Anger, dissociation, and posttraumatic stress disorder among female assault victims. *Journal of Traumatic Stress, 13,* 89–100.

Fein, B. (1995). Megan's law. *ABA Journal, 81,* 38–42.

Feinauer, L. L. (1989). Comparison of long-term effects of child abuse by type of abuse and by relationship of the offender to the victim. *American Journal of Family Therapy, 17,* 48–56.

Feiring, C., Deblinger, E., Hoch-Espada, A., & Haworth, T. (2002) Romantic relationship aggression and attitudes in high school students: The role of gender, grade, and attachment and emotional styles. *Journal of Youth and Adolescence, 31,* 173–385.

Feiring, C., Taska, L. S., & Lewis, M. (1996). Family self-concept: Idea on its meaning. In B. Bracken (Eds.), *Handbook of self-concept Developmental, social, and clinical considerations* (pp. 317–373). New York: John Wiley.

Feldman, C. M., & Ridley, C. A. (2000). The role of conflict-base communication responses and outcomes in male domesti violence toward female partners. *Journal of Social and Personal Relationships, 17,* 552–573.

Feldman, K. W., Stout, J. W., & Inglis, A. F. (2002). Asthma, allergy, and sinopulmonary disease in pediatric condition falsification. *Child Maltreatment, 7,* 125–131.

Feldman, P. H., Nadash, P., & Gursen, M. (2001). Improving communication between researchers and policy makers in long-term care: Or, researchers are from Mars; policy makers are from Venus. *Gerontologist, 41,* 312–321.

Feldman, R. S., Salzinger, S., Rosario, M., Alvarado, L., Caraballo, L., & Hammer, M. (1995). Parent, teacher, and peer ratings of physically abused and nonmaltreated children's behavior. *Journal of Abnormal Child Psychology, 23,* 317–334.

Feldman, W., Feldman, E., Goodman, J. T., McGrath, P. J., Pless, R. P., Corsini, L., et al. (1991). Is childhood sexual abuse really increasing in prevalence? An analysis of the evidence. *Pediatrics, 88,* 29–33.

Feldman-Summers, S., & Pope, K. S. (1994). The experience of forgetting childhood abuse: A national survey of psychologists. *Journal of Consulting and Clinical Psychology, 62,* 636–639.

Felson, R. B. (1992). "Kick 'em when they're down": Explanation of the relationship between stress and interpersonal aggression and violence. *Sociological Quarterly, 33,* 1–16.

Felson, R. B. (2000). The normative protection of women from violence. *Sociological Forum, 15,* 91–116.

Felson, R. B., Messner, S. F., Hoskin, A. W., & Deane, G. (2002). Reasons for reporting and not reporting domestic violence to the police. *Criminology, 40,* 617–647.

Felson, R. B., & Tedeschi, J. T. (Eds.). (1993). *Aggression and violence: Social interactionist perspectives.* Washington, DC: American Psychological Association.

Felthous, A. R., Hempel, A. G., Heredia, A., Freeman, E., Goodness, K., Holzer, C., et al. (2001). Combined homicide-suicide in Galveston County. *Journal of Forensic Sciences, 46,* 586–592.

Fennell, D. C., & Fishel, A. H. (1998). Parent education: An evaluation of STEP on abusive parents' perceptions and abuse potential. *Journal of Child and Adolescent Psychiatric Nursing, 11*(3), 107–120.

Fenton, A. E. (1999). Mirrored silence: Reflections on judicial complicity in private violence. *Oregon Law Review, 78,* 995–1060.

Ferguson, C. U. (1998). Dating violence as a social phenomenon. In N. A. Jackson & G. C. Oates (Eds.), *Violence in intimate relationships: Examining sociological and psychological issues* (pp. 83–118). Woburn, MA: Butterworth-Heinemann.

Ferguson, H. (2001). Promoting child protection, welfare and healing: The case for developing best practice. *Child and Family Social Work, 6,* 1–12.

Fergusson, D. M., & Horwood, L. J. (1998). Exposure to interparental violence in childhood and psychosocial adjustment in young adulthood. *Child Abuse & Neglect, 22,* 339–357.

Ferraro, K. J. (1989). Policing woman battering. *Social Problems, 36,* 61–74.

Ferraro, K. J. (2003). The words change, but the melody lingers. *Violence Against Women, 9,* 110–129.

Field, T., Healy, B., Goldstein, S., & Gutherz, M. (1990). Behavior-state matching and synchrony in mother-infant interactions of nondepressed versus depressed dyads. *Developmental Psychology, 26,* 7–14.

Fields-Meyer, T., & Benet, L. (1998, November 16). Speaking out. *People,* pp. 232, 234.

Figley, C. R. (Ed.). (1995). *Compassion fatigue: Coping with secondary traumatic stress disorder in those who treat the traumatized.* New York: Brunner/Mazel.

Figley, C. R. (2002). Compassion fatigue: Psychotherapists' chronic lack of self care. *Journal of Clinical Psychology, 58,* 1433–1441.

Figueroa, E., & Silk, K. R. (1997). Biological implications of childhood sexual abuse in borderline personality disorder. *Journal of Personality Disorders, 11,* 71–92.

Filinson, R. (1989). Introduction. In R. Filinson & S. R. Ingman (Eds.), *Elder abuse: Practice and policy* (pp. 17–34). New York: Human Sciences Press.

Fincham, F. D. (2000). Family violence: A challenge for behavior therapists. *Behavior Therapy, 31,* 685–693.

Findlater, J. E., & Kelly, S. (1999). Child protective services and domestic violence. *Future of Children, 9*(3), 84–96.

Finkelhor, D. (1980). Sex among siblings: A survey of prevalence, variety, and effects. *Archives of Sexual Behavior, 9,* 171–193.

Finkelhor, D. (1981). The sexual abuse of boys. *Victimology, 6,* 76–84.

Finkelhor, D. (1983). Common features of family abuse. In D. Finkelhor, R. J. Gelles, G. T. Hotaling, & M. A. Straus (Eds.), *The dark side of families: Current family violence research* (pp. 17–28). Beverly Hills, CA: Sage.

Finkelhor, D. (1984). *Child sexual abuse: New theory and research.* New York: Free Press.

Finkelhor, D. (1990). Is child abuse overreported? The data rebut arguments for less intervention. *Public Welfare, 48,* 23–29.

Finkelhor, D. (1993). Epidemiological factors in the clinical identification of child sexual abuse. *Child Abuse & Neglect, 17,* 67–70.

Finkelhor, D. (1994a). Current information on the scope and nature of child sexual abuse. *Future of Children, 4*(2), 31–53.

Finkelhor, D. (1994b). The international epidemiology of child sexual abuse. *Child Abuse & Neglect, 18,* 409–417.

Finkelhor, D. (1996). Introduction. In J. Briere, L. Berliner, J. A. Bulkley, C. Jenny, & T. A. Reid (Eds.), *The APSAC handbook on child maltreatment* (pp. ix–xiii). Thousand Oaks, CA: Sage.

Finkelhor, D., Asdigian, N., & Dziuba-Leatherman, J. (1995). The effectiveness of victimization prevention instruction: An evaluation of children's responses to actual threats and assaults. *Child Abuse & Neglect, 19,* 141–153.

Finkelhor, D., & Dziuba-Leatherman, J. (1994). Victimization of children. *American Psychologist, 49,* 173–183.

Finkelhor, D., Hotaling, G. T., Lewis, I. A., & Smith, C. (1990). Sexual abuse in a national survey of adult men and women: Prevalence, characteristics, and risk factors. *Child Abuse & Neglect, 14,* 19–28.

Finkelhor, D., & Jones, L. M. (in press). *Sexual abuse decline in the 1990s: Evidence for possible causes.* Washington, DC: U.S. Department of Justice.

Finkelhor, D., & Lewis, I. A. (1988). An epidemiologic approach to the study of child molestation. *Annals of the New York Academy of Sciences, 528,* 64–78.

Finkelhor, D., Mitchell, K., Wolak, J. (2000). *Online victimization: A report on the nation's youth.* Retrieved from the Crimes against Children Research Center Web site: http://www.unh.edu/ccrc/Youth_Internet_info_page.html

Finkelhor, D., Moore, D., Hamby, S. L., & Straus, M. A. (1997). Sexually abused children in a national survey of parents: Methodological issues. *Child Abuse & Neglect, 21,* 1–9.

Finkelhor, D., & Ormrod, R. (2001). *Child abuse reported to the police* (NCJ Publication No. 187238). Washington, DC: U.S. Bureau of Justice Statistics.

Finkelhor, D., Williams, L., & Burns, N. (1988). *Nursery crimes: Sexual abuse in daycare.* London: Sage.

Finkelhor, D., & Yllö, K. A. (1982). Forced sex in marriage: A preliminary research report. *Crime & Delinquency, 82,* 459–478.

Finkelhor, D., & Yllö, K. A. (1987). *License to rape: Sexual abuse of wives.* New York: Free Press.

Finn, M. A., & Stalans, L. J. (1997). The influence of gender and mental state on police decisions in domestic assault cases. *Criminal Justice and Behavior, 24,* 157–176.

Finn, M. A., & Stalans, L. J. (2002). Police handling of the mentally ill in domestic violence situations. *Criminal Justice and Behavior, 29,* 278–307.

Finzi, R., Ram, A., Shnit, D., Har-Even, D., Tyano, S., & Weizman, A. (2001). Depressive symptoms and suicidality in physically abused children. *American Journal of Orthopsychiatry, 71,* 98–107.

Fischer, K., & Rose, M. (1995). When "enough is enough": Battered women's decision making around court orders of protection. *Crime & Delinquency, 4,* 414–429.

Fisher, B. S., Cullen, F. T., & Turner, M. G. (2000). *The sexual victimization of college women* (NCJ Publication No. 182369). Washington, DC: U.S. Department of Justice.

Fisher, B. S., Cullen, F. T., & Turner, M. G. (2002). Being pursued: Stalking victimization in a national study of college women. *Criminology & Public Policy, 1,* 257–308.

Fisher, B. S., Daigle, L. E., Cullen, F. T., & Turner, M. G. (2003). Acknowledging sexual victimization as rape: Results from a national-level study. *Justice Quarterly, 20,* 535–574.

Fitten, R. K. (1997, July 25). Burien teacher's sex with a young student shatters the boy's family, and hers. *Seattle Times.* Retrieved from http://www.seattletimes.com

Fitts, W. H., & Roid, G. H. (1991). *Tennessee Self-Concept Scale.* Los Angeles: Western Psychological Services. (Original work published 1964)

Fitzpatrick, K. M. (1993). Exposure to violence and presence of depression among low-income, African American youth. *Journal of Consulting and Clinical Psychology, 61,* 528–531.

Flanagan, T. J., & Maguire, K. (Eds.). (1991). *Bureau of Justice sourcebook of criminal justice statistics—1991* (BJS Publication No. NCJ-137369). Washington, DC: U.S. Department of Justice.

Flanzer, J. P. (1993). Alcohol and other drugs are key causal agents of violence. In R. J. Gelles & D. R. Loseke (Eds.), *Current controversies on family violence* (pp. 171–181). Newbury Park, CA: Sage.

Fleck-Henderson, A. (2000). Domestic violence in the child protection system: Seeing double. *Children and Youth Services, 22,* 333–354.

Fleisher, L. D. (1987). Wrongful birth: When is there liability for prenatal injury? *American Journal of Diseases in Children, 141,* 1260.

Fleury, R. E., Sullivan, C. M., & Bybee, D. I. (2000). When ending the relationship does not end the violence: Women's experiences of violence by former partners. *Violence Against Women, 6,* 1363–1383.

Flisher, A. J., Kramer, R. A., Hoven, C. W., Greenwald, S., Bird, H. R., Canino, G., et al. (1997). Psychosocial characteristics of physically abused children and adolescents. *Journal of the American Academy of Child and Adolescent Psychiatry, 36,* 123–131.

Flournoy, P. S., & Wilson, G. L. (1991). Assessment of MMPI profiles of male batterers. *Violence and Victims, 6,* 309–320.

Flynn, C. P. (1996). Normative support for corporal punishment: Attitudes, correlates, and implications. *Aggression and Violent Behavior, 1,* 47–55.

Focus: Call for help. (1994, June 23). *MacNeil/Lehrer NewsHour* [Transcript]. Overland Park, KS: Strictly Business.

Follette, V. M., & Alexander, P. C. (1992). Dating violence: Current and historical correlates. *Behavioral Assessment, 14,* 1–3.

Follette, V. M., Polusny, M. A., Bechtle, A. E., & Naugle, A. E. (1996). Cumulative trauma: The impact of child sexual abuse, adult sexual assault, and spouse abuse. *Journal of Traumatic Stress, 9,* 25–35.

Follette, V. M., Polusny, M. A., & Milbeck, K. (1994). Mental health and law enforcement professionals: Trauma history, psychological symptoms, and impact of providing services to child sexual abuse survivors. *Professional Psychology: Research and Practice, 25,* 275–282.

Follingstad, D. R., Bradley, R. G., Helff, C. M., & Laughlin, J. E. (2002). A model for predicting dating violence: Anxious attachment, angry temperament, and need for relationship control. *Violence and Victims, 17,* 35–47.

Follingstad, D. R., & DeHart, D. D. (2000). Defining psychological abuse of husbands toward wives. *Journal of Interpersonal Violence, 15,* 891–920.

Follingstad, D. R., Runge, M. M., Ace, A., Buzan, R., & Helff, C. (2001). Justifiability, sympathy level and internal/external locus of the reasons battered women remain in abusive relationships. *Violence and Victims, 16,* 621–643.

Fontana, V. J., & Alfaro, J. (1987). *High risk factors associated with child maltreatment fatalities.* New York: Mayor's Task Force on Child Abuse and Neglect.

Fontana, V. J., & Moohnan, V. (1994). Establish more crisis intervention centers. In D. Bender & B. Leone (Eds.), *Child abuse: Opposing viewpoints* (pp. 227–234). San Diego, CA: Greenhaven.

Fontes, L. A. (2002). Child discipline and physical abuse in immigrant Latino families: Reducing violence and misunderstandings [Electronic version]. *Journal of Counseling & Development, 80,* 31–41.

Foo, L., & Margolin, G. (1995). A multivariate investigation of dating aggression. *Journal of Family Violence, 10,* 351–377.

Forbes, G. B., & Adams-Curtis, L. (2001). Experiences with sexual coercion in college males and females. *Journal of Interpersonal Violence, 16,* 865–889.

Ford, D. A. (1999, July). *Coercing victim participation in domestic violence prosecutions.* Paper presented at the Sixth International Family Violence Research Conference, Durham, NH.

Ford, D. A., & Regoli, M. J. (1992). The preventive impact of policies for prosecuting wife batterers. In E. S. Buzawa & C. G. Buzawa (Eds.), *Domestic violence: The changing criminal justice response* (pp. 181–207). Westport, CT: Greenwood.

Ford, J. D., Racusin, R., Daviss, W. B., Ellis, C. G., Thomas, J., Rogers, K., et al. (1999). Trauma exposure among children with attention deficit hyperactivity disorder and oppositional defiant disorder. *Journal of Consulting and Clinical Psychology, 67,* 786–789.

Ford, J. P., Rompf, E. L., Faragher, T. M., & Weisenfluh, S. M. (1995). Case outcomes in domestic violence court: Influence of judges. *Psychological Reports, 77,* 587–594.

Fortin, A., & Chamberland, C. (1995). Preventing the psychological maltreatment of children. *Journal of Interpersonal Violence, 10,* 275–295.

Fortunata, B., & Kohn, C. S. (2003). Demographic, psychosocial, and personality characteristics of lesbian batterers. *Violence and Victims, 18,* 557–568.

Foshee, V. A. (1996). Gender differences in adolescent dating abuse prevalence, types and injuries. *Health Education Research, 11,* 275–286.

Foshee, V. A., Bauman, K. E., Arriaga, X. R., Helms, R. W., Koch, G. G., & Linder, G. F. (1998). An evaluation of Safe Dates, an adolescent prevention program. *American Journal of Public Health, 88,* 45–50.

Foshee, V. A., Bauman, K. E., Greene, W. F., Koch, G. G., Linder, G. F., & MacDougall, J. E. (2000). The Safe Dates program: 1-year follow-up results. *American Journal of Public Health, 90,* 1619–1622.

Foshee, V. A., & Linder, G. F. (1997). Factors influencing service providers' motivation to help adolescent victims of partner violence. *Journal of Interpersonal Violence, 12,* 648–664.

Foshee, V. A., Linder, G. F., MacDougall, J. E., & Bangdiwala, S. (2001). Gender differences in the longitudinal predictors of adolescent dating violence. *Preventive Medicine, 32,* 128–141.

Foubert, J. D., & Marriott, K. A. (1997). Effects of a sexual assault peer education program on men's belief in rape myths. *Sex Roles, 36,* 257–266.

Foubert, J. D., & McEwen, M. K. (1998). An all-male rape prevention peer education program: Decreasing fraternity men's behavioral intention to rape. *Journal of College Student Development, 39,* 548–556.

Fowler, W. E., & Wagner, W. G. (1993). Preference for and comfort with male versus female counselors among sexually abused girls in individual treatment. *Journal of Counseling Psychology, 40,* 65–72.

Francis, W. M. (1993). Integrated responses to family violence: Implications for law enforcement. *Family Violence and Sexual Assault Bulletin, 9*(3), 25–28.

Fraser, M. W., Walton, E., Lewis, R. E., Pecora, P.J. (1996). An experiment in family reunification: Correlates of outcomes at one-year follow-up. *Children and Youth Services Review, 18,* 335–361.

Frasier, P. Y., Slatt, L., Kowlowitz, V., & Glowa, P. T. (2001). Using the stages of change model to counsel victims of intimate partner violence. *Patient Education and Counseling, 43,* 211–217.

Frazier, P. A., Byer, A. L., Fischer, A. R., Wright, D. M., & DeBord, K. A. (1996). Adult attachment style and partner choice: Correlational and experimental findings. *Personal Relationships, 3,* 117–136.

Frazier, P. A., Conlon, A., & Glaser, T. (2001). Positive and negative life changes following sexual assault. *Journal of Consulting and Clinical Psychology, 69,* 1048–1055.

Freed, L. H., Gupta, R., Hynes, C., & Miller, E. (2003). Detecting adolescent dating violence in the clinical setting. *Journal of Adolescent Health, 32,* 151–152.

Freedner, N., Freed, L. H., Yang, Y. W., & Austin, S. B. (2002). Dating violence among gay, lesbian, and bisexual adolescents: Results from a community survey. *Journal of Adolescent Health, 31,* 469–474.

Freeman, L. N., Mokros, H., & Poznanski, E. O. (1993). Violent events reported by normal urban school-aged children: Characteristics and depression correlates. *Journal of the American Academy of Child and Adolescent Psychiatry, 32,* 419–423.

Freund, K., & Langevin, R. (1976). Bisexuality in homosexual pedophilia. *Archives of Sexual Behavior, 5,* 415–423.

Frias-Armenta, M. (2002). Long-term effects of child punishment on Mexican women: A structural model. *Child Abuse & Neglect, 26,* 371–386.

Friedrich, W. N. (1990). *Psychotherapy of sexually abused children and their families.* New York: Norton.

Friedrich, W. N. (1993). Sexual victimization and sexual behavior in children: A review of recent literature. *Child Abuse & Neglect, 17,* 59–66.

Friedrich, W. N., Dittner, C. A., Action, R., Berliner, L., Butler, J., Damon, L., et al. (2001). Child Sexual Behavior Inventory: Normative, psychiatric and sexual abuse comparisons. *Child Maltreatment, 6,* 37–49.

Friedrich, W. N., Grambusch, P., Broughton, D., Kuiper, J., & Beilke, R. L. (1991). Normative sexual behavior in children. *Pediatrics, 88,* 456–464.

Friedrich, W. N., Grambusch, P., & Damon, L. (1992). The Child Sexual Behavior Inventory: Normative and clinical findings. *Journal of Consulting and Clinical Psychology, 60,* 303–311.

Friedrich, W. N., Luecke, W. M., Beilke, R. L., & Place, V. (1992). Psychotherapy outcome of sexually abused boys. *Journal of Interpersonal Violence, 7,* 396–409.

Frieze, I. H. (2003). Violence in close relationships: Development of a research area: Comment on Archer (2000). *Psychological Bulletin, 126,* 681–684.

Frieze, I. H., & Browne, A. (1989). Violence in marriage. In L. Ohlin & M. Tonry (Eds.), *Family violence* (pp. 163–218). Chicago: University of Chicago Press.

Frisch, M. B., & MacKenzie, C. J. (1991). A comparison of formerly and chronically battered women on cognitive and situational dimensions. *Psychotherapy, 28,* 339–344.

Frodi, A., & Lamb, M. (1980). Child abusers' responses to infant smiles and cries. *Child Development, 51,* 238–241.

Frommer, F. J. (2002, December 19). Group cites video-game makers for violence against women [Associated Press article].

Fry, P. S., & Barker, L. A. (2001). Female survivors of violence and abuse: Their regrets of action and inaction in coping. *Journal of Interpersonal Violence, 16,* 320–342.

Fulmer, T. T. (1990). The debate over dependency as a relevant predisposing factor in elder abuse and neglect. *Journal of Elder Abuse & Neglect, 2*(1/2), 51–71.

Fulmer, T. T. (1991). Elder mistreatment: Progress in community detection and intervention. *Family and Community Health, 14*(2), 26–34.

Fulmer, T. T., & O'Malley, T. A. (1987). *Inadequate care of the elderly.* New York: Springer.

Fulmer, T. T., Ramirez, M., Fairchild, S., Holmes, D., Koren, M. J., & Teresi, J. (1999). Prevalence of elder mistreatment as reported by social workers in a probability sample of adult day health care clients. *Journal of Elder Abuse & Neglect, 11*(3), 25–36.

Fyfe, J. J., Klinger, D. A., & Flavin, J. M. (1997). Differential police treatment of male-on-female spousal violence. *Criminology, 35,* 455–473.

Gaarder, E., & Belknap, J. (2002). Tenuous borders: Girls transferred to adult court. *Criminology, 40,* 481–517.

Gagan, R. J., Cupoli, J. M., & Watkins, A. H. (1984). The families of children who fail to thrive: Preliminary investigations of parental deprivation among organic and nonorganic cases. *Child Abuse & Neglect, 8,* 93–103.

Galloro, V. (2001). Watching out for nursing home residents. *Modern Healthcare, 31*(20), 24–26.

Gamache, E. (1991). Domination and control: The social context of dating violence. In B. Levy (Ed.), *Dating violence: Young women in danger* (pp. 69–83). Seattle: Seal.

Ganaway, G. K. (1989). Historical versus narrative truth: Clarifying the role of exogenous trauma in the etiology of MPD and its variants. *Dissociation, 2,* 205–220.

Ganley, A. L. (1981). *Court mandated counseling for men who batter: A three-day workshop for mental health professional* [Participants' manual]. Washington, DC: Center for Women's Policy Studies.

Ganley, A. L. (1989). Integrating feminist and social learning analyses of aggression: Creating multiple models for intervention with men who batter. In P. L. Caesar & L. K. Hamberger (Eds.), *Treating men who batter: Theory, practice, and programs* (pp. 195–235). New York: Springer.

Garbarino, J. (1992). *Children in danger: Coping with the consequences of community violence.* San Francisco: Jossey-Bass.

Garbarino, J. (1995). *Raising children in a socially toxic environment.* San Francisco: Jossey-Bass.

Garbarino, J., & Crouter, A. (1978). Defining the community context for parent-child relations: The correlates of child maltreatment. *Child Development, 49,* 604–616.

Garbarino, J., Guttman, E., & Seely, J. (1986). *The psychologically battered child.* San Francisco: Jossey-Bass.

Garcia, J. L., & Kosberg, J. I. (1992). Understanding anger: Implications for formal and informal caregivers. *Journal of Elder Abuse & Neglect, 4*(4), 87–99.

Garmezy, N., & Rutter, M. (1985). Acute reactions to stress. In M. Rutter & L. Hersov (Eds.), *Child and adolescent psychiatry: Modern approaches* (2nd ed., pp. 152–176). Oxford: Blackwell Scientific.

Garner, J. H., & Clemmer, E. (1986). *Danger to police in domestic disturbances: A new look.* Washington, DC: U.S. Department of Justice.

Garner, J. H., & Maxwell, C. D. (2000). What are the lessons for the police arrest studies? In S. K. Ward & D. Finkelhor (Eds.), *Program evaluation and family violence research* (pp. 83–114). Binghamton, NY: Haworth.

Garrity-Rokous, F. E. (1994). Punitive legal approaches to the problem of prenatal drug exposure. *Infant Mental Health Journal, 15,* 218–237.

Gartner, R. (1993). Methodological issues in cross-cultural large-survey research on violence. *Violence and Victims, 8,* 199–215.

Gates, D. (1994, December 12). History of the orphanage. *Newsweek, 124,* 33.

Gaudin, J. M. (1993). Effective intervention with neglectful families. *Criminal Justice and Behavior, 20,* 66–89.

Gazmararian, J. A., Lazorick, S., Spitz, A. M., Ballard, T. J., Saltzman, L. E., Marks, J. S. (1996). Prevalence of violence against pregnant women. *Journal of the American Medical Association, 275,* 1915–1920.

Geffner, R., & Rosenbaum, A. (1990). Characteristics and treatment of batterers. *Behavioral Sciences and the Law, 8,* 131–140.

Gelles, R. J. (1973). Child abuse as psychopathology: A sociological critique and reformulation. *American Journal of Orthopsychiatry, 43,* 611–621.

Gelles, R. J. (1980). A profile of violence toward children in the United States. In G. Gerbner, C. J. Ross, & E. Zigler (Eds.), *Child abuse: An agenda for action* (pp. 82–105). New York: Oxford University Press.

Gelles, R. J. (1983). An exchange/social control theory. In D. Finkelhor, R. J. Gelles, G. T. Hotaling, & M. A. Straus (Eds.), *The dark side of families: Current family violence research* (pp. 151–165). Beverly Hills, CA: Sage.

Gelles, R. J. (1989). Child abuse and violence in single-paren families: Parent absence and economic deprivation. *American Journal of Orthopsychiatry, 59,* 492–501.

Gelles, R. J. (2000). Controversies in family preservation programs *Journal of Aggression, Maltreatment, & Trauma, 3,* 239–252.

Gelles, R. J., & Cornell, C. P. (1990). *Intimate violence in families* (2n ed.). Newbury Park, CA: Sage.

Gelles, R. J., & Hargreaves, E. (1981). Maternal employment and violence towards children. *Journal of Family Issues, 2,* 509–530.

Gelles, R. J., & Harrop, J. (1989). *The risk of abusive violence among children with nonbiological parents.* Paper presented at the annual meeting of the National Council on Family Relations New Orleans.

Gelles, R. J., & Loseke, D. R. (1993). Conclusions: Social problem social policy, and controversies on family violence. I R. J. Gelles & D. R. Loseke (Eds.), *Current controversies o family violence* (pp. 357–366). Newbury Park, CA: Sage.

Gelles, R. J., & Straus, M. A. (1979). Determinants of violence in th family: Toward a theoretical integration. In W. R. Burr, R. Hil F. I. Nye, & I. Reiss (Eds.), *Contemporary theories about th family* (pp. 549–581). New York: Free Press.

Gelles, R. J., & Straus, M. A. (1987). Is violence toward childre increasing? A comparison of 1975 and 1985 national surve rates. *Journal of Interpersonal Violence, 2,* 212–222.

Gelles, R. J., & Straus, M. A. (1988). *Intimate violence.* New Yor Simon & Schuster.

Gennetian, L. A. (2003). Welfare policies and domestic abuse amo single mothers. *Violence and Victims, 9,* 1171–1190.

George, C., Kaplan, N., & Main, M. (1984). *Attachment interview f adults.* Unpublished manuscript, University of Californi Berkeley.

George, M. J. (2003). Invisible touch. *Aggression and Violent Behavi 8,* 23–60.

George, R., Wulczyn, F., & Fanshel, D. (1994). A foster care resear agenda for the 90s. *Child Welfare, 73,* 525–549.

Gerard, A. B. (1994). *Parent-Child Relationship Inventory (PC manual.* Los Angeles: Western Psychological Services.

Gerard, M. (2000). Domestic violence: How to screen and interve *RN, 63*(12), 52–57.

Gerow, J. R. (1989). *Psychology: An introduction* (2nd ed.). Glenvi IL: Scott, Foresman.

Gershoff, E. T. (2002a). Corporal punishment by parents and asso ated child behaviors and experiences: A meta-analytic a theoretical review. *Psychological Bulletin, 128,* 539–579.

Gershoff, E. T. (2002b). Corporal punishment, physical abuse, and burden of proof: Reply to Baumrind, Larzelere, and Cow (2002), Holden (2002), and Parke (2002). *Psycholog Bulletin, 128,* 602–611.

Getting new Social Security numbers for battered women. (19 April/May). *Domestic Violence Report, 4,* 52.

Giarretto, H. (1982). A comprehensive child sexual abuse treatm program. *Child Abuse & Neglect, 6,* 263–278.

Gibbs, N. (1993, January 18). 'Til death do us part. *Time, 141,* 40–45.

Gibson, J. W., & Gutierrez, L. (1991). A service program for safe-ho children. *Families in Society, 72,* 554–562.

Gidycz, C. A., Layman, M. J., Rich, C. L., Crothers, M., Gyls, J., Mato A., et al. (2001). An evaluation of an acquaintance rape prev tion program. *Journal of Interpersonal Violence, 16,* 1120–11

Gil, D. G. (1970). *Violence against children: Physical child abuse in United States.* Cambridge, MA: Harvard University Press.

Gilbert, N. (1993). Examining the facts: Advocacy research overstates the incidence of date and acquaintance rape. In R. J. Gelles & D. R. Loseke (Eds.), *Current controversies on family violence* (pp. 120–132). Newbury Park, CA: Sage.

Gilbert, N. (1998). Realities and mythologies of rape [Electronic version]. *Society, 35,* 356–362.

Giles-Sims, J. (1983). *Wife battering: A systems theory approach.* New York: Guilford.

Gillham, B., Tanner, G., Cheyne, B., Freeman, I., Rooney, M., & Lambie, A. (1998). Unemployment rates, single parent density, and indices of child poverty: Their relationship in different categories of child abuse and neglect. *Child Abuse & Neglect, 22*(2), 79–90.

Ginsburg, H., Wright, L. S., Harrell, P. M., & Hill, D. W. (1989). Childhood victimization: Desensitization effects in the later lifespan. *Child Psychiatry and Human Development, 20,* 59–71.

Giorgio, G. (2002). Speaking silence: Definitional dialogues in abusive lesbian relationships. *Violence Against Women, 8,* 1233–1259.

Giovannoni, J., & Becerra, R. (1979). *Defining child abuse.* New York: Free Press.

Glaser, D. (2002). Emotional abuse and neglect (psychological maltreatment): A conceptual framework. *Child Abuse & Neglect, 26,* 697–714.

Glasser, M., Kolvin, I., Campbell, D., Glasser, A., Leitch, I., & Farrelly, S. (2001). Cycle of child sexual abuse: Links between being a victim and becoming a perpetrator. *British Journal of Psychiatry, 179,* 482–494.

Gleason, W. J. (1993). Mental disorders in battered women: An empirical study. *Violence and Victims, 8,* 53–68.

Gleason, W. J. (1995). Children of battered women: Developmental delays and behavioral dysfunction. *Violence and Victims, 10,* 153–160.

Glendenning, F. (1993). What is elder abuse and neglect? In P. Decalmer & F. Glendenning (Eds.), *The mistreatment of elderly people* (pp. 1–34). London: Sage.

Glisson, C. (1996). Judicial and service decisions for children entering state custody: The limited role of mental health. *Social Service Review, 70,* 257–279.

Glod, C. A. (1993). Long-term consequences of childhood physical and sexual abuse. *Archives of Psychiatric Nursing, 7*(3), 163–173.

Glowa, P. T., Frasier, P. Y., & Newton, W. P. (2002). Increasing physician comfort level in screening and counseling patients for intimate partner violence: Hands-on practice. *Patient Education and Counseling, 46,* 213–220.

Godenzi, A., & De Puy, J. (2001). Overcoming boundaries: A cross-cultural inventory of primary prevention programs against wife abuse and child abuse. *Journal of Primary Prevention, 21,* 455–475.

Godkin, M. A., Wolf, R. S., & Pillemer, K. A. (1989). A case-comparison analysis of elder abuse and neglect. *International Journal of Aging and Human Development, 28,* 207–225.

Goergen, T. (2001). Stress, conflict, elder abuse and neglect in German nursing homes: A pilot study among professional caregivers. *Journal of Elder Abuse & Neglect, 13*(1), 1–26.

Gold, S. N., Lucenko, B. A., Elhai, J. D., Swingle, J. M., & Sellers, A. H. (1999). A comparison of psychological/psychiatric symptomatology of women and men sexually abused as children. *Child Abuse & Neglect, 23,* 683–692.

Gold, S. R., Sinclair, B. B., & Balge, K. A. (1999). Risk of sexual revictimization: A theoretical model. *Aggression and Violent Behavior, 4,* 457–470.

Goldberg-Ambrose, C. E. (1992). Unfinished business in rape law reform. *Journal of Social Issues, 48*(1), 173–185.

Golden, A., Roos, B. A., Silverman, M. A., & Beber, C. (2000). Nursing home "abuse" litigation is instructive. *Geriatrics, 55*(2), 11, 15–16.

Goldenson, R. M. (Ed.). (1970). *The encyclopedia of human behavior: Psychology, psychiatry, and mental health* (Vol. 1). Garden City, NY: Doubleday.

Goldenson, R. M. (Ed.). (1984). *Longman dictionary of psychology and psychiatry.* New York: Longman.

Golding, J. M. (1999). Intimate partner violence as a risk factor for mental disorders: A meta-analysis. *Journal of Family Violence, 14,* 99–132.

Goldman, J. D. G., & Padayachi, U. K. (2000). Some methodological problems in estimating incidence and prevalence in child sexual abuse research. *Journal of Sex Research, 4,* 305–314.

Goldner, V., Penn, P., Sheinberg, M., & Walker, G. (1990). Love and violence: Gender paradoxes in volatile attachments. *Family Process, 29,* 343–364.

Goldstein, D., & Rosenbaum, A. (1985). An evaluation of self-esteem of maritally violent men. *Family Relations, 34,* 425–428.

Gomby, D., Culross, P., & Behrman, R. (1999). Home visiting: Recent program evaluations—analysis and recommendations. *Future of Children, 9*(1), 4–26.

Gomes-Schwartz, B., Horowitz, J. M., & Cardarelli, A. P. (1990). *Child sexual abuse: The initial effects.* Newbury Park, CA: Sage.

Gondolf, E. W. (1988a). *Battered women as survivors: An alternative to treating learned helplessness.* Lexington, MA: Lexington.

Gondolf, E. W. (1988b). The effect of batterer counseling on shelter outcome. *Journal of Interpersonal Violence, 3,* 275–289.

Gondolf, E. W. (1997). Batterer program: What we know and need to know. *Journal of Interpersonal Violence, 12,* 83–98.

Gondolf, E. W. (1998a). *Assessing woman battering in mental health services.* Thousand Oaks, CA: Sage.

Gondolf, E. W. (1998b). Service contract and delivery of a shelter outreach project. *Journal of Family Violence, 13,* 131–145.

Gondolf, E. W. (1998c). The victims of court-ordered batterers. *Violence Against Women, 4,* 659–676.

Gondolf, E. W. (2000a). How batterer program participants avoid reassault. *Violence Against Women, 6,* 1204–1222.

Gondolf, E. W. (2000b). Mandatory court review and batterer program compliance. *Journal of Interpersonal Violence, 15,* 428–437.

Gondolf, E. W. (2001). Limitations of experimental evaluation of batterer programs. *Trauma, Violence, & Abuse, 2,* 79–88.

Gondolf, E. W. (2002). Service barriers for battered women with male partners in batterer programs. *Journal of Interpersonal Violence, 17,* 217–227.

Gondolf, E. W., & Foster, R. A. (1991). Pre-program attrition in batterer programs. *Journal of Family Violence, 6,* 337–349.

Gondolf, E. W., & Heckert, D. A. (2003). Determinants of women's perceptions of risk in battering relationships. *Violence and Victims, 18,* 371–386.

Gondolf, E. W., Heckert, D. A., & Kimmel, C. M. (2002). Nonphysical abuse among batterer program participants. *Journal of Family Violence, 17,* 293–314.

Gondolf, E. W., & White, R. J. (2000). "Consumer" recommendations for batterers programs. *Violence Against Women, 6,* 198–217.

Good, G. E. (1998). Men and masculinities: The good, the bad, and the ugly. *SPSMM Bulletin, 3*(4), 1–3.

Good, G. E., Heppner, M. J., Hillenbrand-Gunn, T. L., & Wang, L. (1995). Sexual and psychological violence: An exploratory study of predictors in college men. *Journal of Men's Studies, 4,* 59–71.

Goodkind, J. R., Gillum, T. L., Bybee, D. I., & Sullivan. (2003). The impact of family and friends' reactions on the well-being of women with abusive partners. *Violence Against Women, 9,* 347–373.

Goodman, G. S., Bottoms, B. L., Redlich, A., Shaver, P. R., & Diviak, K. R. (1998). Correlates of multiple forms of victimization in religion-related child abuse cases. *Journal of Aggression, Maltreatment, & Trauma, 2,* 273–295.

Goodman, G. S., Bottoms, B. L., & Shaver, P. R. (1994). *Characteristics and sources of allegations of ritualistic child abuse* (Executive summary of the final report to the National Center on Child Abuse and Neglect, Grant No. 90CA1405). Washington, DC: National Center on Child Abuse and Neglect.

Goodman, G. S., Hirschman, J., Hepps, D., & Rudy, L. (1991). Children's memory for stressful events. *Merrill-Palmer Quarterly, 37,* 109–158.

Goodman, G. S., Taub, E. P., Jones, D. P. H., England, T., Port, L. K., Rudy, L., et al. (1992). Testifying in criminal court. *Monographs of the Society for Research in Child Development, 57*(5, Serial No. 229).

Goodman, L. A., Bennett, L., & Dutton, M. A. (1999). Obstacles to victims' cooperation with the criminal prosecution of their abusers: The role of social support. *Violence and Victims, 14,* 427–444.

Goodman, L. A., Dutton, M. A., Weinfurt, K., & Cook, S. (2003). The Intimate Partner Violence Strategies Index. *Violence Against Women, 9,* 163–186.

Goodyear-Smith, F. A., & Laidlaw, T. M. (1999). Aggressive acts and assaults in intimate relationships: Towards an understanding of the literature. *Behavioral Sciences and the Law, 17,* 285–304.

Gordon, M. (2000). Definitional issues in violence against women: Surveillance and research from a violence research perspective. *Violence Against Women, 6,* 747–783.

Gordon, R. A., Holmes, M., & Maly, C. (1999). Research productivity in the areas of child abuse and domestic violence. *Psychological Reports, 84,* 887–898.

Gore-Felton, C., Gill, M., Koopman, C., & Spiegel, D. (1999). A review of acute stress reactions among victims of violence: Implications for early intervention. *Aggression and Violent Behavior, 4,* 203–306.

Gottesman, I. I. (2001). Psychopathology through a life span-genetic prism. *American Psychologist, 56,* 867–878.

Gottman, J. M., Jacobson, N. S., Rushe, R. H., Shortt, J. W., Babcock, J., La Tallade, J. J., et al. (1995). The relationship between heart rate reactivity, emotionally aggressive behavior, and general violence in batterers. *Journal of Family Psychology, 9,* 227–248.

Gough, H. G. (1975). *Manual for the California Psychological Inventory.* Palo Alto, CA: Consulting Psychologists Press.

Gover, A. R., MacDonald, J. M., & Alpert, G. P. (2003). Combating domestic violence: Findings from an evaluation of a local domestic violence court. *Criminology & Public Policy, 3,* 109–132.

Graham, D. L. R., Rawlings, E., & Rimini, E. (1988). Survivors of terror: Battered women, hostages, and the Stockholm syndrome. In K. A. Yllö & M. Bograd (Eds.), *Feminist perspectives on wife abuse* (pp. 217–233). Newbury Park, CA: Sage.

Graham-Bermann, S. A. (2002). Child abuse in the context of domestic violence. In J. E. B. Myers, L. Berliner, J. Briere, C. T. Hendrix, C. Jenny, & T. A. Reid (Eds.), *The APSAC handbook on child maltreatment* (2nd ed., pp. 119–129). Thousand Oaks, CA: Sage.

Graham-Bermann, S. A., & Hughes, H. M. (2003). Intervention for children exposed to interparental violence (IPV): Assessment of needs and research priorities. *Clinical Child and Family Psychology Review, 6,* 189–204.

Graham-Bermann, S. A., & Levendosky, A. A. (1998). Traumatic stress symptoms in children of battered women. *Journal of Interpersonal Violence, 14,* 111–128.

Graham-Kevan, N., & Archer, J. (2003a). Intimate terrorism and common couple violence: A test of Johnson's predictions in four British samples. *Journal of Interpersonal Violence, 18,* 1247–1270.

Graham-Kevan, N., & Archer, J. (2003b). Physical aggression and control in heterosexual relationships: The effect of sampling. *Violence and Victims, 18,* 181–196.

Grasley, C., Wolfe, D. A., & Wekerle, C. (1999). Empowering youth to end relationship violence. *Children's Services, 2,* 209–223.

Grasmick, H. G., Blackwell, B. S., Bursik, R. J., & Mitchell, S. (1993). Changes in perceived threats of shame, embarrassment, and legal sanctions for interpersonal violence, 1982–1992. *Violence and Victims, 8,* 313–325.

Gray, E. (1993). *Unequal justice: The prosecution of child sexual abuse.* New York: Free Press.

Gray, H. M., & Foshee, V. A. (1997). Adolescent dating violence: Differences between one-sided and mutually violent profiles. *Journal of Interpersonal Violence, 12,* 126–141.

Grayston, A. D., & De Luca, R. V. (1999). Female perpetrators of child sexual abuse: A review of the clinical and empirical literature. *Aggression and Violent Behavior, 4,* 93–106.

Graziano, A. M. (1994). Why we should study subabusive violence against children. *Journal of Interpersonal Violence, 9,* 412–419.

Graziano, A. M., & Mills, J. (1992). Treatment for abused children: When is a partial solution acceptable? *Child Abuse & Neglect, 16,* 217–228.

Graziano, A. M., & Namaste, K. A. (1990). Parental use of physical force in child discipline: A survey of 679 college students. *Journal of Interpersonal Violence, 5,* 449–463.

Green, A. H. (1984). Child abuse by siblings. *Child Abuse & Neglect, 8,* 311–317.

Green, A. H. (1998). Factors contributing to the generational transmission of child maltreatment. *Journal of the American Academy of Child and Adolescent Psychiatry, 37,* 1334–1336.

Greenberg, J. R., McKibben, M., & Raymond, J. A. (1990). Dependent adult children and elder abuse. *Journal of Elder Abuse & Neglect, 2*(1/2), 73–86.

Greenfeld, L. A. (1996). *Child victimizers: Violent offenders and their victims* (NCJ Publication No. 153258). Washington, DC: U.S. Department of Justice.

Greenfeld, L. A., Rand, M. R., Craven, D., Klaus, P. A., Perkins, C. A., Ringel, C., et al. (1998). *Violence by intimates* (NCJ Publication No. 167237). Washington, DC: U.S. Department of Justice.

Greenwood, G. L., Relf, M. V., Huang, B., Pollack, L. M., Canchola, J. A., & Catania, J. A. (2002). Battering victimization among a probability-based sample of men who have sex with men. *American Journal of Public Health, 92,* 1964–1969.

Gregory, C., & Erez, E. (2002). The effects of batterer intervention programs. *Violence Against Women, 8,* 206–232.

Griffing, S., Ragin, D. F., Sage, R. E., Madry, L., Bingham, L. E., & Primm, B. J. (2002). Domestic violence survivors' self-identified reasons for returning to abusive relationships. *Journal of Interpersonal Violence, 17,* 306–319.

Grigsby, N., & Hartman, B. R. (1997). The barriers model: An integrated strategy for intervention with battered women. *Psychotherapy, 34,* 484–497.

Gross, A. B., & Keller, H. R. (1992). Long-term consequences of childhood physical and psychological maltreatment. *Aggressive Behavior, 18,* 171–185.

Gross, A. M., Bennett, T., Marx, B. P., Sloan, L., & Juergens, J. (2001). The impact of alcohol and alcohol expectancies on male perception of female sexual arousal in a date rape analog. *Experimental and Clinical Psychopharmacology, 9,* 380–388.

Grossman, S. E., & Lundy, M. (2003). Use of domestic violence services across race and ethnicity by women aged 55 and older. *Violence Against Women, 9,* 1442–1452.

Groves, B. M. (2002). *Children who see too much.* Boston: Beacon.

Groves, B. M., & Zuckerman, B. (1997). Interventions with parents and caregivers of children who are exposed to violence. In J. D. Osofsky (Ed.), *Children in a violent society* (pp. 183–201). New York: Guilford.

Gruber, K. J., & Jones, R. J. (1983). Identifying determinants of risk of sexual victimization of youth: A multivariate approach. *Child Abuse & Neglect, 7,* 17–24.

Grunbaum, J. A., Kann, L., Kinchen, S. A., Williams, B., Ross, J. G., Lowry, R., et al. (2002). Youth Risk Behavior Surveillance— United States, 2001. *Journal of School Health, 72,* 313–326.

Guterman, N. B. (2001). *Stopping child maltreatment before it starts: Emerging horizons in early home visitation services.* Thousand Oaks, CA: Sage.

Hackett, G., McKillop, P., & Wang, D. (1988, December 12). A tale of abuse. *Newsweek, 117,* 56–61.

Hahm, H., & Guterman, N. (2001). The emerging problem of physical child abuse in South Korea. *Child Maltreatment, 6,* 169–179.

Haj-Yahia, M. M. (1998a). Beliefs about wife beating among Palestinian women. *Violence Against Women, 4,* 533–558.

Haj-Yahia, M. M. (1998b). A patriarchal perspective of beliefs about wife-beating among Arab Palestinian men from the West Bank and Gaza Strip. *Journal of Family Issues, 19,* 595–621.

Haj-Yahia, M. M. (2000). Implications of wife abuse and battering for self-esteem, depression, and anxiety as revealed by the Second Palestinian National Survey on Violence Against Women. *Journal of Family Issues, 21,* 435–463.

Halicka, M. (1995). Elder abuse and neglect in Poland. In J. I. Kosberg & J. L. Garcia (Eds.), *Elder abuse: International and cross-cultural perspectives* (pp. 157–169). Binghamton, NY: Haworth.

Hall, C. C. I. (1997). Cultural malpractice: The growing obsolescence of psychology with the changing U.S. population. *American Psychologist, 52,* 642–651.

Hall, D. M. (1998). The victims of stalking. In J. R. Meloy (Ed.), *The psychology of stalking: Clinical and forensic perspectives* (pp. 115–136). New York: Academic Press.

Halligan, S. L., Michael, T., Clark, D. M., & Ehlers, A. (2003). Posttraumatic stress disorder following assault: The role of cognitive processing, trauma memory, and appraisals. *Journal of Consulting and Clinical Psychology, 71,* 419–431.

Halpern, C. T., Oslak, S. G., Young, M. L., Martin, S. L., & Kupper, L. L. (2001). Partner violence among adolescents in opposite-sex relationships: Findings from the National Longitudinal Study of Adolescent Health. *American Journal of Public Health, 91,* 1679–1685.

Hamarman, S., & Bernet, W. (2000). Evaluating and reporting emotional abuse in children: Parent-based, action-based focus aids in clinical decision-making. *Journal of the American Academy of Child and Adolescent Psychiatry, 39,* 928–930.

Hamarman, S., Pope, K. H., & Czaja, S. J. (2002). Emotional abuse in children: Variations in legal definitions and rates across the United States. *Child Maltreatment, 7,* 303–311.

Hamberger, L. K. (1994). Domestic partner abuse: Expanding paradigms for understanding and intervention. *Violence and Victims, 9,* 91–94.

Hamberger, L. K., & Ambuel, B. (1998). Dating violence. *Pediatric Clinics of North America, 45,* 381–390.

Hamberger, L. K., & Arnold, J. (1989). Dangerous distinctions among "abuse," "courtship violence," and "battering." *Journal of Interpersonal Violence, 4,* 520–522.

Hamberger, L. K., & Arnold, J. (1991). The impact of mandatory arrest on domestic violence perpetrator counseling services. *Family Violence Bulletin, 6*(1), 11–12.

Hamberger, L. K., & Barnett, O. W. (1995). Assessment and treatment of men who batter. In L. Vandecreek, S. Knapp, & T. L. Jackson (Eds.), *Innovations in clinical practice: A source book* (Vol. 14, pp. 31–54). Sarasota, FL: Professional Resource Press.

Hamberger, L. K., & Guse, C. E. (2002). Men's and women's use of intimate partner violence in clinical samples. *Violence Against Women, 8,* 1301–1331.

Hamberger, L. K., & Hastings, J. E. (1986). Personality correlates of men who abuse their partners: A cross-validation study. *Journal of Family Violence, 1,* 323–341.

Hamberger, L. K., & Hastings, J. E. (1989). Counseling male spouse abusers: Characteristics of treatment completers and dropouts. *Violence and Victims, 4,* 275–286.

Hamberger, L. K., & Hastings, J. E. (1990). Recidivism following spouse abuse abatement counseling: Treatment implications. *Violence and Victims, 5,* 157–170.

Hamberger, L. K., & Hastings, J. E. (1991). Personality correlates of men who batter and nonviolent men: Some continuities and discontinuities. *Journal of Family Violence, 6,* 131–147.

Hamberger, L. K., Lohr, J. M., Bonge, D., & Tolin, D. F. (1996). A large sample empirical typology of male spouse abusers and its relationship to dimensions of abuse. *Violence and Victims, 11,* 277–292.

Hamberger, L. K., & Potente, T. (1994). Counseling heterosexual women arrested for domestic violence: Implications for theory and practice. *Violence and Victims, 9,* 125–137.

Hamby, S. L. (1995). *Dominance Scale.* Durham: University of New Hampshire Press.

Hamby, S. L. (1996). The Dominance Scale: Preliminary psychometric properties. *Violence and Victims, 11,* 199–212.

Hamby, S. L. (1998). Partner violence: Prevention and intervention. In J. L. Jasinski & L. M. Williams (Eds.), *Partner violence: A comprehensive review of 20 years of research* (pp. 210–256). Thousand Oaks, CA: Sage.

Hamby, S. L., Poindexter, V. C., & Gray-Little, B. (1996). Four measures of partner violence: Construct similarity and classification differences. *Journal of Marriage and the Family, 58,* 127–139.

Hampton, R. L., & Newberger, E. H. (1988). Child abuse incidence and reporting by hospitals: Significance of severity, class, and race. In G. T. Hotaling, D. Finkelhor, J. T. Kirkpatrick, & M. A. Straus (Eds.), *Coping with family violence: Research and policy perspectives* (pp. 212–221). Newbury Park, CA: Sage.

Hanley, R. (1998, July 1). Neighbor accused of firing at house of paroled rapist [Electronic version]. *New York Times,* p. B6.

Hanna, C. (1996). No right to choose: Mandated victim participation in domestic violence prosecutions. *Harvard Law Review, 109*, 1850–1909.

Hannon, R., Hall, D. S., Nash, H., Formanti, J., & Hopson, T. (2000). Judgments regarding sexual aggression as a function of sex of aggressor and victim. *Sex Roles, 5–6*, 311–322.

Hansen, M., Harway, M., & Cervantes, N. (1991). Therapists' perceptions of severity in cases of family violence. *Violence and Victims, 6*, 225–235.

Hanson, R. K., Gizzarelli, R., & Scott, H. (1994). The attitudes of incest offenders. *Criminal Justice and Behavior, 21*, 187–202.

Hanson, R. K., & Wallace-Capretta, S. (1998, July). *Attitudinal support for wife assault: New findings and cumulative evidence.* Paper presented at Program Evaluation and Family Violence Research: An International Conference, Durham, NH.

Hanson-Breitenbecher, K. (2001). Sexual revictimization among women: A review of the literature focusing on empirical investigations. *Aggression and Violent Behavior, 6*, 415–432.

Hardesty, J. L. (2002). Separation assault in the context of postdivorce parenting: An integrative review of the literature. *Violence Against Women, 8*, 597–621.

Hare, R. D. (1980). A research scale for the assessment of psychopathy in criminal populations. *Personality and Individual Differences, 1*, 111–117.

Harmon, P. A. (2001). Why do men batter women? Assessing empathy, self-regard and narcissism levels, and attitudes toward women, men's roles and family of origin experiences among middle to upper class male batterers. *Dissertation Abstracts International, 62*(12), 6023B. (UMI No. 9315947)

Harned, M. S. (2001). Abused women or abused men? An examination of the context and outcomes of dating violence. *Violence and Victims, 16*, 269–285.

Harris, H. N., & Valentiner, D. P. (2002). World assumptions, sexual assault, depression, and fearful attitudes toward relationships. *Journal of Interpersonal Violence, 17*, 286–305.

Harris, J. A. (1999). Review and methodological considerations in research on testosterone and aggression. *Aggression and Violent Behavior, 4*, 273–291.

Harris, J. A., Vernon, P. A., & Boomsma, D. I. (1998). The heritability of testosterone: A study of Dutch adolescent twins and their parents. *Behavior Genetics, 28*, 165–171.

Harris, M. B. (1991). Effects of sex of aggressor, sex of target, and relationship on evaluations of physical aggression. *Journal of Interpersonal Violence, 6*, 174–186.

Harris, N. (1990). Dealing with diverse cultures in child welfare. *Protecting Children, 7*(3), 6–7.

Harris, R., Stickney, J., Grasley, C., Hutchinson, G., Greaves, L., & Boyd, T. (2001). Searching for help and information: Abused women speak out. *Library & Information Science Research, 23*, 123–141.

Harris, S. B. (1996). For better or for worse: Spouse abuse grown old. *Journal of Elder Abuse & Neglect, 8*(1), 1–33.

Hart, B. (1986). Lesbian battering: An examination. In K. Lobel (Ed.), *Naming the violence: Speaking out about lesbian battering* (pp. 173–189). Seattle: Seal.

Hart, B. J. (1996). Battered women and the criminal justice system. In E. S. Buzawa & C. G. Buzawa (Eds.), *Do arrests and restraining orders work?* (pp. 98–114). Thousand Oaks, CA: Sage.

Hart, J., Gunnar, M., & Cicchetti, D. (1996). Altered neuroendocrine activity in maltreated children related to symptoms of depression. *Developmental Psychopathology, 8*, 201–214.

Hart, S. D., Hare, R. D., & Forth, A. E. (1993). Psychopathy as a risk marker for violence: Development and validation of a screening version of the Revised Psychopathy Checklist. In J. Monahan & H. Steadman (Eds.), *Violence and mental disorder: Developments in risk assessment* (pp. 81–98). Chicago: University of Chicago Press.

Hart, S. N., & Brassard, M. R. (1989). *Developing and validating operationally defined measures of emotional maltreatment: A multimodal study of the relationships between caretaker behaviors and child characteristics across three developmental levels* (Grant No. DHHS 90CA1216). Washington, DC: U.S. Department of Health and Human Services.

Hart, S. N., & Brassard, M. R. (1991). Psychological maltreatment: Progress achieved. *Development and Psychopathology, 3*, 61–70.

Hart, S. N., & Brassard, M. R. (1993). Psychological maltreatment. *Violence Update, 3*(7), 4, 6–7, 11.

Hart, S. N., Brassard, M. R., Binggeli, N. J., & Davidson, H. A. (2002). Psychological maltreatment. In J. E. B. Myers, L. Berliner, J. Briere, C. T. Hendrix, C. Jenny, & T. A. Reid (Eds.), *The APSAC handbook on child maltreatment* (2nd ed., pp. 79–103). Thousand Oaks, CA: Sage.

Hart, S. N., Brassard, M. R., & Karlson, H. C. (1996). Psychological maltreatment. In J. Briere, L. Berliner, J. A. Bulkley, C. Jenny, & T. A. Reid (Eds.), *The APSAC handbook on child maltreatment* (pp. 72–89). Thousand Oaks, CA: Sage.

Hart, S. N., Germain, R., & Brassard, M. R. (1987). The challenge: To better understand and combat psychological maltreatment of children and youth. In M. R. Brassard, R. Germain, & S. N. Hart (Eds.), *Psychological maltreatment of children and youth* (pp. 3–24). New York: Pergamon.

Hartley, C. C. (2002). The co-occurrence of child maltreatment and domestic violence: Examining both neglect and child physical abuse. *Child Maltreatment, 7*, 349–358.

Hartman, C. R., & Burgess, A. W. (1988). Information processing of trauma. *Journal of Interpersonal Violence, 3*, 443–457.

Hartmann, H. I., Laurence, L., Spalter-Roth, R., & Zuckerman, D. M. (1997). *Measuring the costs of domestic violence against women and the cost-effectiveness of interventions: An initial assessment and proposal for further research.* Washington, DC: Institute for Women's Policy Research. Retrieved from Institute for Women's Policy Research Web site: http://www.iwpr.org

Harway, M., Geffner, R., Ivey, D., Koss, M. P., Murphy, B. C., Mio, J. S., et al. (2002). *Intimate partner abuse and relationship violence.* Washington, DC: American Psychological Association.

Harway, M., & O'Neil, J. M. (Eds.). (1999). *What causes men's violence against women?* Thousand Oaks, CA: Sage.

Hasday, J. E. (2000). Contest and consent: A legal history of marital rape [Electronic version]. *California Law Review, 88*, 1373–1505.

Haskett, M. (1990). Social problem-solving skills of young physically abused children. *Child Psychiatry and Human Development, 21*, 109–118.

Hastings, B. M. (2000). Social information processing and the verbal and physical abuse of women. *Journal of Interpersonal Violence, 15*, 651–664.

Hastings, J. E., & Hamberger, L. K. (1988). Personality characteristics of spouse abusers: A controlled comparison. *Violence and Victims, 3*, 31–48.

Hastings, J. E., & Hamberger, L. K. (1994). Psychosocial modifiers of psychopathology for domestically violent and nonviolent men. *Psychological Reports, 74*, 112–114.

Hathaway, J. E., Mucci, L. A., Silverman, J. G., Brooks, D. R., Mathews, R., & Pavlos, C. A. (2000). Health status and health care use of Massachusetts women reporting partner abuse. *American Journal of Preventive Medicine, 19,* 302–307.

Hathaway, J. E., Silverman, J. G., Brooks, D. R., Mucci, L. A., Tavares, B., Keenan, H., et al. (1998, July). *Utilization of police, civil restraining order and medical care services by female survivors of partner violence.* Paper presented at Program Evaluation and Family Violence Research: An International Conference, Durham, NH.

Hathaway, P. (1989). Failure to thrive: Knowledge for social workers. *Health and Social Work, 14,* 122–126.

Hathaway, S. R., & McKinley, J. C. (1989). *MMPI-2 (Minnesota Multiphasic Personality Inventory).* Minneapolis: University of Minnesota Press.

Haugaard, J. J. (2000). The challenge of defining child sexual abuse. *American Psychologist, 55,* 1036–1039.

Haugaard, J. J., & Reppucci, N. D. (1988). *The sexual abuse of children.* San Francisco: Jossey-Bass.

Hawkins, J. D. (1995). Controlling crime before it happens: Risk-focused prevention. *National Institute of Justice, 229,* 10–18.

Hawley, T. L., Halle, T. G., Drasin, R. E., & Thomas, N. G. (1995). Children of addicted mothers: Effects of the crack epidemic on the caregiving environment and the development of preschoolers. *American Journal of Orthopsychiatry, 65,* 364–379.

Hay, T., & Jones, L. (1994). Societal interventions to prevent child abuse and neglect. *Child Welfare, 73,* 379–403.

Hayashino, D. S., Wurtele, S. K., & Klebe, K. J. (1995). Child molesters: An examination of cognitive factors. *Journal of Interpersonal Violence, 10,* 106–116.

Hayward, H. (2002). Preparing for the future: Incorporating a disability perspective in psychological science. *APS Observer, 15*(2), 21–22, 49.

Hazzard, A. (1993). Trauma-related beliefs as mediators of sexual abuse impact in adult women survivors: A pilot study. *Journal of Child Sexual Abuse, 2*(3), 55–69.

Healey, K. M. (1995). *Victim and witness intimidation: New developments and emerging responses* (NCJ Publication No. 156555). Washington, DC: U.S. Department of Justice.

Healey, K. M., Smith, C., & O'Sullivan, C. (1998, February). *Batterer intervention: Program approaches and criminal justice strategies* (NCJ Publication No. 168638). Washington, DC: U.S. Department of Justice.

Healthy Families America. (1994). *Violence Update, 5*(2), 1–4.

Hebert, M., Lavoie, F., & Parent, N. (2002). An assessment of outcomes following parents' participation in a child abuse prevention program. *Violence and Victims, 17,* 355–372.

Hechler, D. (1988). *The battle and the backlash: The child sexual abuse war.* Lexington, MA: Lexington.

Hegar, R. L., & Yungman, J. J. (1989). Toward a causal typology of child neglect. *Children and Youth Services Review, 11,* 203–220.

Hegar, R. L., Zuravin, S. J., & Orme, J. G. (1994). Factors predicting severity of physical child abuse injury. *Journal of Interpersonal Violence, 9,* 170–183.

Helfer, R. E. (1990, June). The neglect of our children. *The World & I,* pp. 531–541.

Hemenway, D., Solnick, S., & Carter, J. (1994). Child-rearing violence. *Child Abuse & Neglect, 18,* 1011–1020.

Hemmens, C., Strom, K., & Schlegel, E. (1998). Gender bias in the courts: A review of the literature. *Sociological Imagination, 35,* 22–42.

Henderson, A. J. Z., Bartholomew, K., & Dutton, D. G. (1997). He loves me; he loves me not: Attachment and separation resolution of abused women. *Journal of Family Violence, 12,* 169–191.

Henning, K. R., Jones, A., & Holdford, R. (2003). Treatment needs of women arrested for domestic violence: A comparison with male offenders. *Journal of Interpersonal Violence, 18,* 839–856.

Henning, K. R., & Klesges, L. M. (July, 1999). *Evaluation of the Shelby County domestic violence court.* Paper presented at the Sixth International Family Violence Research Conference, Durham, NH.

Henning, K. R., & Klesges, L. M. (2003). Prevalence and characteristics of psychological abuse reported by court-involved battered women. *Journal of Interpersonal Violence, 18,* 857–871.

Henning, K. R., Leitenberg, H., Coffey, P., Turner, T., & Bennett, R. T. (1996). Long-term psychological and social impact of witnessing physical conflict between parents. *Journal of Interpersonal Violence, 11,* 35–51.

Henry, J. (1997). System intervention trauma to child abuse victims following disclosure. *Journal of Interpersonal Violence, 12,* 499–512.

Hensey, O. J., Williams, J. K., & Rosenbloom, L. (1983). Intervention in child abuse: Experiences in Liverpool. *Developmental Medicine and Neurology, 25,* 606–611.

Hensing, G., & Alexanderson, K. (2000). The relation of adult experience of domestic harassment, violence, and sexual abuse to health and sickness absence. *International Journal of Behavioral Medicine, 7,* 1–18.

Heppner, M. J., Humphrey, C. F., DeBord, K. A., & Hillenbrand-Gunn, T. L. (1995). The differential effects of rape prevention programming on attitudes, behavior, and knowledge. *Journal of Counseling Psychology, 42,* 508–518.

Herbert, T. B., Silver, R. C., & Ellard, J. H. (1991). Coping with an abusive relationship: How and why do women stay? *Journal of Marriage and the Family, 53,* 311–325.

Herdt, G. (1987). *The Sambia: Ritual and gender in New Guinea.* New York: Holt, Rinehart & Winston.

Herek, G. M. (1990). The context of anti-gay violence: Notes on cultural and psychological heterosexism. *Journal of Interpersonal Violence, 5,* 316–333.

Herman, J. L. (1992). *Trauma and recovery.* New York: Basic Books.

Herman, J. L., & Schatzow, E. (1987). Recovery and verification of memories of childhood sexual trauma. *Psychoanalytic Psychology, 4,* 1–14.

Herrenkohl, E. C., Herrenkohl, R. C., Egolf, B. P., & Russo, M. J. (1998). The relationship between early maltreatment and teenage parenthood. *Journal of Adolescence, 21,* 291–303.

Herrenkohl, E. C., Herrenkohl, R. C., Rupert, L. J., Egolf, B. P., & Lutz, J. G. (1995). Risk factors for behavioral dysfunction: The relative impact of maltreatment, SES, physical health problems, cognitive ability, and quality of parent-child interaction. *Child Abuse & Neglect, 19,* 191–203.

Herrenkohl, R. C., Egolf, B. P., & Herrenkohl, E. C. (1997). Preschool antecedents of adolescent assaultive behavior: A longitudinal study. *American Journal of Orthopsychiatry, 67,* 422–432.

Herrenkohl, R. C., Herrenkohl, E. C., Egolf, B. P., & Wu, P. (1991). The developmental consequences of abuse: The Lehigh longitudinal study. In R. H. Starr & D. A. Wolfe (Eds.), *The effects of child abuse and neglect: Issues and research* (pp. 57–85). New York: Guilford.

Herrenkohl, T. I., Huang, B., Tajima, E., & Whitney, S. D. (2003). Examining the link between child abuse and youth violence:

An analysis of mediating mechanisms. *Journal of Interpersonal Violence, 18,* 1189–1208.

Hersch, K., & Gray-Little, B. (1998). Psychopathic traits and attitudes associated with self-reported sexual aggression in college men. *Journal of Interpersonal Violence, 13,* 456–471.

Hesse, E., & Main, M. (2000). Disorganized infant, child, and adult attachment: Collapse in behavioral and attentional strategies. *Journal of the American Psychoanalytic Association, 48,* 1097–1127.

Hewitt, B., Podesta, J. S., & Longley, J. (2002, June 3). No time to wait. *People, 57,* 21.

Hewitt, S. K. (1998). *Small voices: Assessing allegations of sexual abuse in preschool children.* Thousand Oaks, CA: Sage.

Heyman, R. E., Feldbau-Kohn, S. R., Ehrensaft, M. K., Langhinrichsen-Rohling, J., & O'Leary, K. D. (2001). Can questionnaire reports correctly classify relationship distress and partner physical abuse? *Journal of Family Psychology, 15,* 334–346.

Heyman, R. E., & Neidig, P. H. (1999). A comparison of spousal aggression prevalence rates in U.S. Army and civilian representative samples. *Journal of Consulting and Clinical Psychology, 67,* 239–242.

Hickox, A., & Furnell, J. R. G. (1989). Psychosocial and background factors in emotional abuse of children. *Child: Care, Health and Development, 15,* 227–240.

Higgins, D. J., & McCabe, M. P. (2000). Multi-type maltreatment and the long-term adjustment of adults. *Child Abuse Review, 9,* 6–18.

Higgins, D. J., & McCabe, M. P. (2001). Multiple forms of child abuse and neglect: Adult retrospective reports. *Aggression and Violent Behavior, 6,* 547–578.

Hightower, D., Heckert, A., & Schmidt, W. (1990). Elderly nursing home residents' need for public guardianship services in Tennessee. *Journal of Elder Abuse & Neglect, 2*(3/4), 105–122.

Hildyard, K. L., & Wolfe, D. A. (2002). Child neglect: Developmental issues and outcomes. *Child Abuse & Neglect, 26,* 679–695.

Hill, J. B., & Amuwo, S. A. (1998). Understanding elder abuse and neglect. In N. A. Jackson & G. C. Oates (Eds.), *Violence in intimate relationships: Examining sociological and psychological issues* (pp. 195–223). Woburn, MA: Butterworth-Heinemann.

Hill, M. S., & Fischer, A. R. (2001). Does entitlement mediate the link between masculinity and rape-related variables? *Journal of Counseling Psychology, 48,* 39–50.

Hillson, J. M. C., & Kupier, N. A. (1994). A stress and coping model of child maltreatment. *Clinical Psychology Review, 14,* 261–285.

Hilton, N. Z. (1992). Battered women's concerns about their children witnessing wife assault. *Journal of Interpersonal Violence, 7,* 77–86.

Hilton, N. Z. (1994). The failure of arrest to deter wife assault: What now? *Violence Update, 4*(5), 1–2, 4, 10.

Hilton, N. Z., Harris, G. T., & Rice, M. E. (1998). On the validity of self-reported rates of interpersonal violence. *Journal of Interpersonal Violence, 16,* 865–889.

Hines, D. A., & Saudino, K. J. (2002). Intergenerational transmission of partner violence. *Trauma, Violence, & Abuse, 3,* 210–225.

Hines, D. A., & Saudino, K. J. (2003). Gender differences in psychological, and sexual aggression among college students using the revised Conflict Tactics Scale. *Violence and Victims, 18,* 197–217.

Hines, T. (2003). *Pseudoscience and the paranormal* (2nd ed.). Amherst, NY: Prometheus.

Hinrichsen, G. A., Hernandez, N. A., & Pollack, S. (1992). Difficulties and rewards in family care of depressed older adults. *Gerontologist, 32,* 486–492.

Hird, M. J. (2000). An empirical study of adolescent dating aggression in the UK. *Journal of Adolescence, 23,* 69–78.

Hirsch, C. H., Stratton, S., & Loewy, R. (1999). The primary care of elder mistreatment. *Western Journal of Medicine, 170,* 353–358.

Hirschfeld, R. M., Klerman, G. L., Chodoff, P., Korchin, S., & Barrett, J. (1976). Dependency–self-esteem–clinical depression. *Journal of the American Academy of Psychoanalysis, 4,* 373–388.

Hirschi, T. (1969). *Causes of delinquency.* Berkeley: University of California Press.

Hockenberry, S. L., & Billingham, R. E. (1993). Psychological reactance and violence within dating relationships. *Psychological Reports, 73,* 1203–1208.

Hoefnagels, C., & Baartman, H. (1997). On the threshold of disclosure: The effects of a mass media field experiment. *Child Abuse & Neglect, 21,* 557–573.

Hoefnagels, C., & Mudde, A. (2000). Mass media and disclosures of child abuse in the perspective of secondary prevention: Putting ideas into practice. *Child Abuse & Neglect, 2,* 1091–1101.

Hoelting, J., Sandell, E., Letourneau, S., Smerlinder, J., & Stranik, M. (1996). The MELD experience with parent groups. *Zero to Three, 16*(6), 9–18.

Hofeller, K. (1982). *Social, psychological and situational factors in wife abuse.* Palo Alto, CA: R&E Research Associates.

Hoffman, N. D., Swann, S., & Freeman, K. (2003). Communication between health care providers and gay, lesbian, bisexual, transgender, and questioning youth. *Journal of Adolescent Health, 32,* 131.

Hofford, M., & Harrell, A. D. (1993). *Family violence: Interventions for the justice system.* Washington, DC: Bureau of Justice Assistance.

Holcomb, D. R., Savage, M. P., Seehafer, R., & Waalkes, D. M. (2002). A mixed-gender date rape prevention intervention targeting freshmen college athletes. *College Student Journal,* 165–180.

Holden, G. W. (1998). Introduction: The development of research in another consequence of family violence. In G. W. Holden, R. Geffner, & E. N. Jouriles (Eds.), *Children exposed to marital violence: Theory, research, and applied issues* (pp. 1–18). Washington, DC: American Psychological Association.

Holden, G. W. (2002). Perspectives on the effects of corporal punishment: Comment on Gershoff (2002). *Psychological Bulletin, 128,* 590–595.

Holden, G. W. (2003). Children exposed to domestic violence and child abuse: Terminology and taxonomy. *Clinical Child and Family Psychology Review, 6,* 151–160.

Holden, G. W., Geffner, R. A., & Jouriles, E. N. (Eds.). (1998). *Children exposed to marital violence: Theory, research, and applied issues.* Washington, DC: American Psychological Association.

Holden, G. W., & Ritchie, K. L. (1991). Linking extreme marital discord, child rearing, and child behavior problems: Evidence from battered women. *Child Development, 62,* 311–327.

Holiman, M. J., & Schilit, R. (1991). Aftercare for battered women: How to encourage the maintenance of change. *Psychotherapy, 28,* 345–353.

Holland, L. R., Kasraian, K. R., & Leonardelli, C. A. (1987). Elder abuse: An analysis of the current problem and potential role the rehabilitation professional. *Physical & Occupational Therapy in Geriatrics, 5*(3), 41–50.

Holloway, M. (1994, August). Trends in women's health: A global view. *Scientific American,* pp. 76–83.

Holmes, W. C., & Slap, G. B. (1998). Sexual abuse of boys: Definition, prevalence, correlates, sequelae, and management. *Journal of the American Medical Association, 280,* 1855–1862.

Holmes, W. M. (1993). Police arrests for domestic violence. *American Journal of Police, 12,* 101–125.

Holt, V. L., Kernic, M. A., Wolf, M., & Rivara, F. P. (2003). Do protection orders affect the likelihood of future partner violence and injury? *American Journal of Preventive Medicine, 24,* 16–21.

Holtzworth-Munroe, A., Bates, L., Smutzler, N., & Sandin, E. (1997). A brief review of the research on husband violence: Part I. Maritally violent versus nonviolent men. *Aggression and Violent Behavior, 2,* 65–99.

Holtzworth-Munroe, A., & Hutchinson, G. (1993). Attributing negative intent to wife behavior: The attributions of maritally violent versus nonviolent men. *Journal of Abnormal Psychology, 102,* 206–211.

Holtzworth-Munroe, A., Meehan, J. C., Stuart, G. L., Herron, K., & Rehman, U. (2000). Testing the Holtzworth-Munroe and Stuart (1994) batterer typology. *Journal of Consulting and Clinical Psychology, 68,* 1000–1019.

Holtzworth-Munroe, A., Meehan, J. C., Stuart, G. L., Herron, K., & Rehman, U. (2003). Do subtypes of maritally violent men continue to differ over time? *Journal of Consulting and Clinical Psychology, 71,* 728–740.

Holtzworth-Munroe, A., Rehman, U., & Herron, K. (2000). General and spouse-specific anger and hostility in subtypes of maritally violent men and nonviolent men. *Behavior Therapy, 31,* 603–630.

Holtzworth-Munroe, A., & Stuart, G. L. (1994). Typologies of male batterers: Three subtypes and the differences among them. *Psychological Bulletin, 116,* 476–497.

Holtzworth-Munroe, A., Stuart, G. L., & Hutchinson, G. (1997). Violent versus nonviolent husbands: Differences in attachment patterns, dependency, and jealousy. *Journal of Family Psychology, 11,* 314–331.

Honeycutt, T. C., Marshall, L. L., & Weston, R. W. (2001). Toward ethnically specific models of employment, public assistance and victimization. *Violence Against Women, 7,* 126–140.

Hong, S. M., & Page, S. V. (1989). A psychological reactance scale: Development, factor structure, and reliability. *Psychological Reports, 64,* 1323–1326.

Horkan, E. M. (1995). Elder abuse in the Republic of Ireland. In J. I. Kosberg & J. L. Garcia (Eds.), *Elder abuse: International and cross-cultural perspectives* (pp. 119–137). Binghamton, NY: Haworth.

Horn, J. L., & Trickett, P. K. (1998). Community violence and child development: A review of research. In P. K. Trickett & C. J. Schellenbach (Eds.), *Violence against children in the family and the community* (pp. 103–138). Washington, DC: American Psychological Association.

Horne, S. (1999). Domestic violence in Russia. *American Psychologist, 54,* 55–61.

Horrific images of woman reveal shame of elder abuse. (2003, August 20). *Alameda Times-Star,* op-ed sec., p. 1.

Horton, A. L., & Johnson, B. L. (1993). Profile and strategies of women who have ended abuse. *Families in Society, 74,* 481–492.

Horton, C. B., & Cruise, T. K. (2001). *Child abuse and neglect: The school's response.* New York: Guilford.

Horwitz, A. V., Widom, C. S., McLaughlin, J., & White, H. R. (2001). The impact of childhood abuse and neglect on adult mental health: A prospective study. *Journal of Health and Social Behavior, 42,* 184–201.

Hotaling, G. T., Straus, M. A., & Lincoln, A. J. (1990). Intrafamily violence and crime and violence outside the family. In M. A. Straus & R. J. Gelles (Eds.), *Physical violence in American families: Risk factors and adaptations to violence in 8,145 families* (pp. 431–470). New Brunswick, NJ: Transaction.

Hotaling, G. T., & Sugarman, D. B. (1986). An analysis of risk markers in husband to wife violence: The current state of knowledge. *Violence and Victims, 1,* 101–124.

Hotaling, G. T., & Sugarman, D. B. (1990). A risk marker analysis of assaulted wives. *Journal of Family Violence, 5,* 1–13.

Houskamp, B. M., & Foy, D. W. (1991). The assessment of post-traumatic stress disorder in battered women. *Journal of Interpersonal Violence, 6,* 367–375.

Howe, D. (1995). Pornography and the paedophile: Is it criminogenic? *British Journal of Medical Psychology, 68*(1), 15–27.

Howes, C., & Espinosa, M. P. (1985). The consequences of child abuse for the formation of relationships with peers. *Child Abuse & Neglect, 9,* 397–404.

Hoyle, C., & Sanders, A. (2000). Police response to domestic violence: From victim choice to victim empowerment? *British Journal of Criminology, 40,* 14–36.

Huber, R., Borders, K. W., Badrak, K., Netting, F. E., & Nelson, H. W. (2001). National standards for the long-term care ombudsman program and a tool to assess compliance: The Huber Badrak Borders Scales. *Gerontologist, 41,* 264–271.

Hudson, M. F. (1991). Elder mistreatment: A taxonomy with definitions by Delphi. *Journal of Elder Abuse & Neglect, 3*(2), 1–20.

Hudson, M. F. (1994). Elder abuse: Its meaning to middle-aged and older adults—Part II: Pilot results. *Journal of Elder Abuse & Neglect, 6*(1), 55–82.

Hudson, M. F., Beasley, C., Benedict, R. H., Carlson, J. R., Craig, B. F., & Mason, S. C. (2000). Elder abuse: Some Caucasian-American views. *Journal of Elder Abuse & Neglect, 12*(1), 89–114.

Hudson, M. F., & Carlson, J. R. (1999). Elder abuse: Its meaning to Caucasians, African Americans, and Native Americans. In T. Tatara (Ed.), *Understanding elder abuse in minority populations* (pp. 187–204). Washington, DC: Taylor & Francis.

Hudson, W. W. (1982). *The clinical measurement package: A field manual.* Belmont, CA: Dorsey.

Huesmann, L. R., Moise-Titus, J., & Podolski, C. (2003). Longitudinal relations between children's exposure to TV violence and their aggressive and violent behavior in young adulthood: 1977–1992. *Developmental Psychology, 39,* 201–221.

Hughes, D. (1996). Sex tours via the Internet. *Agenda: Empowering Women for Equality, 28,* 71–76.

Hughes, H. M. (1992). Impact of spouse abuse on children of battered women: Implications for practice. *Violence Update, 2*(17), 1, 9–11.

Hughes, H. M., & Luke, D. A. (1998). Heterogeneity in adjustment among children of battered women. In G. W. Holden, R. A. Geffner, & E. N. Jouriles (Eds.), *Children exposed to marital violence: Theory, research, and applied issues* (pp. 185–221). Washington, DC: American Psychological Association.

Hughes, H. M., Parkinson, D., & Vargo, M. (1989). Witnessing spouse abuse and experiencing physical abuse: A "double whammy"? *Journal of Family Violence, 4,* 197–209.

Hughes, P. P., Marshall, D., & Sherrill, C. (2003). Multidimensional analysis of fear and confidence of university women relating to crimes and dangerous situations. *Journal of Interpersonal Violence, 18,* 33–49.

Humphrey, S. E., & Kahn, A. S. (2000). Fraternities, athletic teams, and rape: Importance of identification with a risky group. *Journal of Interpersonal Violence, 15,* 1313–1322.

Humphreys, J. C., Lee, K. A., Neylan, T. C., & Marmar, C. R. (1999a). Sleep patterns of sheltered battered women. *Image: Journal of Nursing Scholarship, 31*(Pt. 2), 139–143.

Humphreys, J. C., Lee, K. A., Neylan, T. C., & Marmar, C. R. (1999b). Trauma history of sheltered battered women. *Issues in Mental Health Nursing, 20,* 319–332.

Hunt, P., & Baird, M. (1990). Children of sex rings. *Child Welfare, 69,* 195–207.

Hunter, J. A., Goodwin, D. W., & Becker, J. V. (1994). The relationship between phallometrically measured deviant sexual arousal and clinical characteristics in juvenile sexual offenders. *Behavior Research and Therapy, 32,* 533–538.

Hunter, R. S., Kilstrom, N., Kraybill, E. N., & Loda, F. (1978). Antecedents of child abuse and neglect in premature infants: A prospective study in a newborn intensive care unit. *Pediatrics, 61,* 629–635.

Huss, M. T., & Langhinrichsen-Rohling, J. (2000). Identification of the psychopathic batterer: The clinical, legal, and policy implications. *Aggression and Violent Behavior, 5,* 403–422.

Huston, T. L., & Vangelisti, A. L. (1991). Socioemotional behavior and satisfaction in marital relationships: A longitudinal study. *Journal of Personality and Social Psychology, 61,* 721–733.

Hutchison, I. W. (1999a). Alcohol, fear, and woman abuse. *Sex Roles, 40,* 893–920.

Hutchison, I. W. (1999b). *Influence of alcohol and drugs on women's utilization of the police for domestic violence* (NCJ Publication No. 179277). Washington, DC: U.S. Bureau of Justice Statistics.

Hutchison, I. W., & Hirschel, J. D. (1998). Abused women: Help-seeking strategies and police utilization. *Violence Against Women, 4,* 436–456.

Hutchison, I. W., Hirschel, J. D., & Pesackis, C. E. (1994). Family violence and police utilization. *Violence and Victims, 9,* 299–313.

Hyden, M. (1999). The world of the fearful: Battered women's narratives of leaving abusive husbands. *Feminism and Psychology, 9,* 449–469.

Hyman, A., Schillinger, D., & Lo, B. (1995). Laws mandating reporting of domestic violence: Do they promote patient well-being? *Journal of the American Medical Association, 273,* 1781–1787.

Hyman, S. E. (2000). The needs for database research and for privacy collide. *American Journal of Psychiatry, 157,* 1723–1724.

The impact of arrest on domestic violence: Results from five policy experiments. (1999, October). *National Institute of Justice Journal,* pp. 27–28.

Intagliata, K. L. (2002). Improving the quality of care in nursing homes: Class action impact litigation. *University of Colorado Law Review, 73,* 1013–1045.

Irvine, J. (1990). Lesbian battering: The search for shelter. In P. Elliott (Ed.), *Confronting lesbian battering* (pp. 25–30). St. Paul: Minnesota Coalition for Battered Women.

Isaac, N. E. (1998). Corporate sector response to domestic violence. In National Institute of Justice & American Bar Association, *Legal interventions in family violence: Research findings and policy implications* (NCJ Publication No. 171666, pp. 76–77). Washington, DC: U.S. Department of Justice.

Isaac, N. E., & Enos, V. P. (2001, September). *Documenting domestic violence: How health care providers can help victims* (NCJ Publication No. 188564). Washington, DC: U.S. Department of Justice.

Itzin, C. (1997). Pornography and the organization of intra- and extrafamilial child sexual abuse. In G. K. Kantor & J. L. Jasinski (Eds.), *Out of the darkness: Contemporary perspectives on family violence* (pp. 58–79). Thousand Oaks, CA: Sage.

Jackels, N. (1997). *Hispanic immigrant women and domestic violence* [CD-ROM]. Abstract obtained from ProQuest File: Dissertation Abstracts Item 1383003

Jackson, S. (2003). Analyzing the studies. In S. Jackson, L. Feder, D. R. Forde, R. C. Davis, C. D. Maxwell, & B. G. Taylor, *Batterer intervention programs: Where do we go from here?* (NCJ Publication No. 195079, pp. 23–29). Washington, DC: National Institute of Justice.

Jackson, S. M. (1998). Issues in the dating violence research: A review of the literature. *Aggression and Violent Behavior, 4,* 233–247.

Jackson, S. M., Cram, F., & Seymour, F. W. (2000). Violence and sexual coercion in high school students' dating relationships. *Journal of Family Violence, 15,* 23–36.

Jacobson, N. S. (1994a). Contextualism is dead; long live contextualism. *Family Process, 33,* 97–100.

Jacobson, N. S. (1994b). Rewards and dangers in researching domestic violence. *Family Process, 33,* 81–85.

Jacobson, N. S., & Gottman, J. M. (1993, August). *New picture of violent couples emerges from UW study.* Paper presented at the annual meeting of the American Psychological Association, Toronto.

Jacobson, N. S., Gottman, J. M., Gortner, E., Berns, S., & Shortt, J. W. (1996). Psychological factors in the longitudinal course of battering. *Violence and Victims, 11,* 625–629.

Jacobson, N. S., Gottman, J. M., Waltz, J., Rushe, R., Babcock, J. C., & Holtzworth-Munroe, A. (1994). Affect, verbal content and psychophysiology in the arguments of couples with a violent husband. *Journal of Consulting and Clinical Psychology, 62,* 982–988.

Jaffe, P. G., & Geffner, R. A. (1998). Child custody disputes and domestic violence: Critical issues for mental health, social service, and legal professionals. In G. W. Holden, R. A. Geffner, & E. N. Jouriles (Eds.), *Children exposed to marital violence: Theory, research, and applied issues* (pp. 371–396). Washington, DC: American Psychological Association.

Jaffe, P. G., Hastings, E., & Reitzel, D. (1992). Child witnesses of woman abuse: How can schools respond? *Response, 79*(2), 12–15.

Jaffe, P. G., Sudermann, M., Reitzel, D., & Killip, S. M. (1992). An evaluation of a secondary school primary prevention program on violence in intimate relationships. *Violence and Victims, 7,* 129–146.

Jaffe, P. G., Wolfe, D. A., & Wilson, S. K. (1990). *Children of battered women.* Newbury Park, CA: Sage.

Jakupcak, M. (2003). Masculine gender role stress and men's fear of emotions as predictors of self-reported aggression and violence. *Violence and Victims, 18,* 533–541.

Jang, K. L., Vernon, P. A., & Livesley, W. J. (2001). Behavioural-genetic perspectives on personality function. *Canadian Journal of Psychiatry, 46,* 234–244.

Jankowski, M. K., Leitenberg, H., Henning, K. R., & Coffey, P. (1999). Intergenerational transmission of dating aggression as a function of witnessing only same sex parents vs. opposite sex parents vs. both parents as perpetrators of domestic violence. *Journal of Family Violence, 14,* 267–279.

Janosick, E., & Green, E. (1992). *Family life.* Boston: Jones & Bartlett.

Jean, P. J., & Reynolds, C. R. (1980). Development in Bias in Attitudes Survey: A sex-role questionnaire. *Journal of Psychology, 104,* 269–277.

Jehu, D., Klassen, C., & Gazan, M. (1986). Cognitive restructuring of distorted beliefs associated with childhood sexual abuse. *Journal of Social Work and Human Sexuality, 4,* 49–69.

Jenkins, E. J., & Bell, C. C. (1994). Violence exposure, psychological distress, and high risk behaviors among inner-city high school students. In S. Friedman (Ed.), *Anxiety disorders in African-Americans* (pp. 76–88). New York: Springer.

Jennings, J. L., & Murphy, C. M. (2000). Male-male dimensions of male-female battering: A new look at domestic violence. *Psychology of Men & Masculinity, 1*(1), 21–29.

Jensen, G. F., & Karpos, M. (1993). Managing rape: Exploratory research on the behavior of rape statistics. *Criminology, 31,* 363–385.

Jervis, L. L., Jackson, M. Y., & Manson, S. M. (2002). Need for, availability of, and barriers to the provision of long-term care services for older American Indians. *Journal of Cross-Cultural Gerontology, 17,* 295–311.

Jogerst, G. J., Dawson, J. D., Hartz, A. J., Ely, J. W., & Schweitzer, L. A. (2000). Community characteristics associated with elder abuse. *Journal of the American Geriatric Society, 48,* 513–518.

Johns, S., & Hydle, I. (1995). Norway: Weakness in welfare. In J. I. Kosberg & J. L. Garcia (Eds.), *Elder abuse: International and cross-cultural perspectives* (pp. 139–156). Binghamton, NY: Haworth.

Johnson, B., Li, D., & Websdale, N. (1998). Florida mortality review project: Executive summary. In National Institute of Justice & American Bar Association, *Legal interventions in family violence: Research findings and policy implications* (NCJ Publication No. 171666, pp. 40–42). Washington, DC: U.S. Department of Justice.

Johnson, E. H., & Greene, A. F. (1992). The interview method for assessing anger: Development and validation. In E. H. Johnson, W. D. Gentry, & S. Julius (Eds.), *Personality, elevated blood pressure, and essential hypertension.* Washington, DC: Hemisphere.

Johnson, I. M. (1988). Wife abuse: Factors predictive of the decision-making process of battered women. *Dissertation Abstracts International, 48,* 3202A. (UMI No. 8803369)

Johnson, I. M., Crowley, J., & Sigler, R. T. (1992). Agency response to domestic violence: Services provided by battered women. In E. C. Viano (Ed.), *Intimate violence: Interdisciplinary perspectives* (pp. 191–202). Bristol, PA: Taylor & Francis.

Johnson, I. M., & Sigler, R. T. (2000). Forced sexual intercourse among intimates. *Journal of Family Violence, 15,* 95–108.

Johnson, J. G., Cohen, P., & Smailes, E. M. (2001). Childhood verbal abuse and risk for personality disorders during adolescence and early adulthood. *Comprehensive Psychiatry, 42,* 16–23.

Johnson, J. G., Smailes, E. M., Cohen, P., Brown, J., & Bernstein, D. P. (2000). Associations between four types of childhood neglect and personality disorder symptoms during adolescence and early adulthood: Findings of a community-based longitudinal study. *Journal of Personality Disorders, 14,* 171–187.

Johnson, J. M., & Bondurant, D. M. (1992). Revisiting the 1982 church response survey. *Studies in Symbolic Interaction, 13,* 287–293.

Johnson, M. P. (1995). Patriarchal terrorism and common couple violence: Two forms of violence against women. *Journal of Marriage and the Family, 57,* 283–294.

Johnson, M. P. (2000). Conflict and control: Images of symmetry and asymmetry in domestic violence. In A. Booth, A. C. Crouter, & M. Clements (Eds.), *Couples in conflict.* Mahwah, NJ: Lawrence Erlbaum.

Johnson, M. P., & Ferraro, K. J. (2000). Research on domestic violence in the 1990s: Making distinctions. *Journal of Marriage and the Family, 62,* 948–963.

Johnson, R. M., Kotch, J. B., Catellier, D. J., Winsor, J. R., Dufort, V., Hunter, W., et al. (2002). Adverse behavioral and emotional outcomes from child abuse and witnessed violence. *Child Maltreatment, 7,* 179–186.

Johnson, S., & Lebow, J. (2000). The "coming of age" of couples therapy. *Journal of Marital and Family Therapy, 26,* 23–38.

Johnson, T. A. (2003, January/February). Police accountability: A European perspective. *ACJS Today, 26,* 7–9.

Johnson, T. C. (1989). Female child perpetrators: Children who molest other children. *Child Abuse & Neglect, 13,* 571–585.

Johnson, T. F. (1986). Critical issues in the definition of elder mistreatment. In K. A. Pillemer & R. S. Wolf (Eds.), *Elder abuse: Conflict in the family* (pp. 167–196). Dover, MA: Auburn House.

Joint Commission on Accreditation of Healthcare Organizations. (2002). *How to recognize abuse and neglect.* Oakbrook Terrace, IL: Author.

Jones, A. S. (2000). The cost of batterer programs: How much and who pays? *Journal of Interpersonal Violence, 15,* 566–586.

Jones, D. P. H. (1986). Individual psychotherapy for the sexually abused child. *Child Abuse & Neglect, 10,* 377–385.

Jones, D. P. H. (1991). Ritualism and child sexual abuse. *Child Abuse & Neglect, 15,* 163–170.

Jones, D. P. H. (1994). Editorial: The syndrome of Munchausen by proxy. *Child Abuse & Neglect, 18,* 769–771.

Jones, D. P. H., & McGraw, J. M. (1987). Reliable and fictitious accounts of sexual abuse to children. *Journal of Interpersonal Violence, 2,* 27–45.

Jones, J. E. (1992). State intervention in pregnancy: Comment. *Louisiana Law Review, 52,* 1159–1160.

Jones, L. M., & Finkelhor, D. (2003). Putting together evidence on declining trends in sexual abuse: A complex puzzle. *Child Abuse & Neglect, 27,* 133–135.

Jones, N. T., Ji, P., Beck, M., & Beck, N. (2002). The reliability and validity of the Revised Conflict Tactics Scale (CTS2) in a female incarcerated population. *Journal of Family Issues, 23,* 441–457.

Jones, R. L., & Jones, J. M. (1987). Racism as psychological maltreatment. In M. R. Brassard, R. Germain, & S. N. Hart (Eds.), *Psychological maltreatment of children and youth* (pp. 146–158). New York: Pergamon.

Jones, R. L., & Kaufman, L. (2003, May 1). Foster care caseworkers' errors are detailed in New Jersey. *New York Times.*

Jonker, F., & Jonker-Bakker, P. (1991). Experiences with ritualistic child sexual abuse: A case study from the Netherlands. *Child Abuse & Neglect, 15,* 191–196.

Jonson-Reid, M. (2003). Foster care and future risk of maltreatment. *Children and Youth Services Review, 25,* 271–294.

Jordan, C. E., Logan, T., Walker, R., & Nigoff, A. (2003). Stalking: An examination of the criminal justice response. *Journal of Interpersonal Violence, 18,* 148–165.

Jordan, C. E., Quinn, K., Jordan, B., & Daileader, C. R. (2000). Stalking: Cultural, clinical, and legal considerations. *Brandeis Law Journal, 38*, 513–579.

Joseph, C. (1995). Scarlet wounding: Issues of child prostitution. *Journal of Psychohistory, 23*(1), 2–17.

Jouriles, E. N., McDonald, R., Stephens, N., Norwood, W. D., Spiller, L. C., & Ware, H. S. (1998). Breaking the cycle of violence: Helping families departing from battered women's shelters. In G. W. Holden, R. A. Geffner, & E. N. Jouriles (Eds.), *Children exposed to marital violence: Theory, research, and applied issues* (pp. 337–369). Washington, DC: American Psychological Association.

Jouriles, E. N., & Norwood, W. D. (1995). Physical aggression toward boys and girls in families characterized by the battering of women. *Journal of Family Violence, 9*, 69–78.

Judge OKs retrial in alleged abuse case. (2003, February 1). *Los Angeles Times*, p. B3.

Julian, T. W., & McHenry, P. C. (1993). Mediators of male violence toward female intimates. *Journal of Family Violence, 8*, 39–56.

Justice, B., & Calvert, A. (1990). Family environment factors associated with child abuse. *Psychological Reports, 66*, 458.

Justice, B., & Justice, R. (1979). *The broken taboo*. New York: Human Sciences.

Kalichman, S. C., Craig, M. E., & Follingstad, D. R. (1989). Factors influencing the reporting of father-child sexual abuse: Study of licensed practicing psychologists. *Professional Psychology: Research and Practice, 20*, 84–89.

Kalmuss, D. S. (1984). The intergenerational transmission of marital aggression. *Journal of Marriage and the Family, 46*, 11–19.

Kalmuss, D. S., & Straus, M. A. (1990). Wife's marital dependency and wife abuse. In M. A. Straus & R. J. Gelles (Eds.), *Physical violence in American families: Risk factors and adaptations to violence in 8,145 families* (pp. 369–382). New Brunswick, NJ: Transaction.

Kalu, W. J. (1993). Battered spouses as a social concern in work with families in two semi-rural communities in Nigeria. *Journal of Family violence, 8*, 361–373.

Kandel, E., & Mednick, S. A. (1991). Perinatal complications predict violent offending. *Criminology, 29*, 519–529.

Kandel-Englander, E. (1992). Wife battering and violence outside the family. *Journal of Interpersonal Violence, 7*, 462–470.

Kane, R. (1999). Patterns of arrest in domestic violence encounters: Identifying a police decision-making model. *Journal of Criminal Justice, 27*, 65–80.

Kane, T. A., Staiger, P. K., & Ricciardelli, L. A. (2000). Male domestic violence: Attitudes, aggression, and interpersonal dependency. *Journal of Interpersonal Violence, 15*, 16–29.

Kanin, E. J. (1957). Male aggression in dating-courting relations. *American Journal of Sociology, 63*, 197–204.

Kantor, G. K., Jasinski, J. L., & Aldarondo, E. (1994). Sociocultural status and incidence of marital violence in Hispanic families. *Violence and Victims, 9*, 207–222.

Kantor, G. K., & Little, L. (2003). Defining the boundaries of child neglect: When does domestic violence equate with parental failure to protect? *Journal of Interpersonal Violence, 18*, 338–355.

Kaplan, M. S., Becker, J. V., & Martinez, D. F. (1990). A comparison of mothers of adolescent incest versus non-incest perpetrators. *Journal of Family Violence, 5*, 209–214.

Kaplan, S. J., Pelcovitz, D., & Labruna, V. (1999). Child and adolescent abuse and neglect research: A review of the past 10 years: Part I. Physical and emotional abuse and neglect. *Journal of the American Academy of Child and Adolescent Psychiatry, 38*, 1214–1222.

Kaplan, S. J., Pelcovitz, D., Salzinger, S., Mandel, F. S., & Weiner, M. (1997). Adolescent physical abuse and suicide attempts. *Journal of the American Academy of Child and Adolescent Psychiatry, 36*, 799–808.

Kashani, J. H., & Allan, W. D. (1998). *The impact of family violence on children and adolescents*. Thousand Oaks, CA: Sage.

Kasian, M., & Painter, S. L. (1992). Frequency and severity of psychological abuse in a dating population. *Journal of Interpersonal Violence, 7*, 350–364.

Kaslow, N. J., Thompson, M. P., Meadows, L. A., Jacobs, D., Chance, S., Gibb, B., et al. (1998). Factors that mediate and moderate the link between partner abuse and suicidal behavior in African American women. *Journal of Consulting and Clinical Psychology, 66*, 533–540.

Kassinove, H., & Tafrate, R. C. (2002). *Anger management: The complete treatment guidebook for practitioners*. Atascadero, CA: Impact.

Katz, J., Carine, A., & Hilton, A. (2002). Perceived verbal conflict behaviors associated with physical aggression and sexual coercion in dating relationships: A gender-sensitive analysis. *Violence and Victims, 17*, 93–109.

Katz, R. C. (1990). Psychosocial adjustment in adolescent child molesters. *Child Abuse & Neglect, 14*, 567–575.

Kauffman, J. (2002). Looking at the past and the future of diversity and aging: An interview with E. Percil Stanford and Fernando Torres-Gil. *Generations, 26*(3), 74–78.

Kaufman, J., & Cicchetti, D. (1989). The effects of maltreatment on school-aged children's socioemotional development: Assessments in a day-camp setting. *Developmental Psychology, 25*, 516–524.

Kaufman, J., & Zigler, E. (1987). Do abused children become abusive parents? *American Journal of Orthopsychiatry, 57*, 186–192.

Kaufman, J., & Zigler, E. (1993). The intergenerational transmission of abuse is overstated. In R. J. Gelles & D. R. Loseke (Eds.), *Current controversies on family violence* (pp. 209–221). Newbury Park, CA: Sage.

Kaufman, J. G., & Widom, C. S. (1999). Childhood victimization, running away, and delinquency. *Journal of Research in Crime and Delinquency, 36*, 347–370.

Kaufman, L., & Kocieniewski, D. (2003, January 10). Caseworkers say overload makes it risky for children. *New York Times*, p. B6.

Kaukinen, C. (2002). The help-seeking decisions of violent crime victims: An examination of the direct and conditional effects of gender and the victim-offender relationship. *Journal Interpersonal Violence, 17*, 432–456.

Keilitz, S. L. (1994). Civil protection orders: A viable justice system tool for deterring domestic violence. *Violence and Victims*, 79–84.

Keilitz, S. L., Davis, C., & Eikeman, H. S. (1998). *Civil protection orders: Victims' views on effectiveness*. Washington, DC: U. Department of Justice.

Kelleher, K., Chaffin, M., Hollenberg, J., & Fischer, E. (1994). Alcohol and drug disorders among physically abusive and neglectful parents in a community-based sample. *American Journal Public Health, 84*, 1586–1590.

Kelley, S. J. (1989). Stress responses of children to sexual abuse and ritualistic abuse in day care centers. *Journal of Interpersonal Violence, 4*, 502–513.

Kelley, S. J. (1996). Ritualistic abuse of children. In J. Briere, L. Berliner, J. A. Bulkley, C. Jenny, & T. A. Reid (Eds.), *The APSAC handbook on child maltreatment* (pp. 90–99). Thousand Oaks, CA: Sage.

Kelley, S. J. (2002). Child maltreatment in the context of substance abuse. In J. E. B. Myers, L. Berliner, J. Briere, C. T. Hendrix, C. Jenny, & T. A. Reid (Eds.), *The APSAC handbook on child maltreatment* (2nd ed., pp. 105–117). Thousand Oaks, CA: Sage.

Kelley, S. J., Brant, R., & Waterman, J. (1993). Sexual abuse of children in day care centers. *Child Abuse & Neglect, 17,* 71–89.

Kelling, G. L. (1999). *"Broken windows" and police discretion* (NCJ Publication No. 178259). Washington, DC: U.S. Department of Justice.

Kellogg, N. D., Burge, S., & Taylor, E. R. (2000). Wanted and unwanted sexual experiences and family dysfunction during adolescence. *Journal of Family Violence, 15,* 55–68.

Kemp, A., Green, B. L., Hovanitz, C., & Rawlings, E. I. (1995). Incidence and correlates of posttraumatic stress disorder in battered women: Shelter and community samples. *Journal of Interpersonal Violence, 10,* 43–55.

Kempe, C. H., & Helfer, R. E. (Eds.). (1972). *Helping the battered child and his family.* Philadelphia: J. B. Lippincott.

Kempe, C. H., Silverman, F. N., Steele, B. F., Droegemueller, W., & Silver, H. K. (1962). The battered child syndrome. *Journal of the American Medical Association, 17,* 17–24.

Kempe, R. S., Cutler, C., & Dean, J. (1980). The infant with failure-to-thrive. In C. H. Kempe & R. E. Helfer (Eds.), *The battered child* (3rd ed., pp. 163–182). Chicago: University of Chicago Press.

Kempe, R. S., & Goldbloom, R. B. (1987). Malnutrition and growth retardation ("failure to thrive") in the context of child abuse and neglect. In R. E. Helfer & R. S. Kempe (Eds.), *The battered child* (4th ed., pp. 312–335). Chicago: University of Chicago Press.

Kendall-Tackett, K. A., & Eckenrode, J. (1996). The effects of neglect on academic achievement and disciplinary problems: A developmental perspective. *Child Abuse & Neglect, 20,* 161–169.

Kendall-Tackett, K. A., Williams, L. M., & Finkelhor, D. (1993). Impact of sexual abuse on children: A review and synthesis of recent empirical studies. *Psychological Bulletin, 113,* 164–180.

Kennan, B. (1998). Evolutionary biology and strict liability for rape. *Law and Psychology Review, 22,* 131–177.

Kent, A., & Waller, G. (1998). The impact of childhood emotional abuse: An extension of the child abuse and trauma scale. *Child Abuse & Neglect, 22,* 393–399.

Kent, A., & Waller, G. (2000). Childhood emotional abuse and eating psychopathology. *Clinical Psychology Review, 20,* 887–903.

Kerr, M. A., Black, M. M., & Krishnakumar, A. (2000). Failure-to-thrive, maltreatment and the behavior and development of 6-year-old children from low-income, urban families: A cumulative risk model. *Child Abuse & Neglect, 24,* 587–598.

Kershaw, S. (2003, October 20). Elder care Americanized. *Los Angeles Daily News,* p. 12.

Kesner, J. E., Julian, T., & McKenry, P. C. (1997). Application of attachment theory to male violence toward female intimates. *Journal of Family Violence, 12,* 211–228.

Kesner, J. E., & McKenry, P. C. (1998). The role of childhood attachment factors in predicting male violence toward female intimates. *Journal of Family Violence, 13,* 417–432.

Kessler, A. (2002). State laws on human research subjects. *APS Observer, 15*(8), 9–10.

Kessler, R. C., Borges, G., & Walters, E. E. (1999). Prevalence of and risk factors for lifetime suicide attempts in the National Comorbidity Survey. *Archives of General Psychiatry, 56,* 617–625.

Kessler, R. C., McGonagle, K. A., Zhao, S., Nelson, C. B., Hughes, M., Eshelman, S., et al. (1994). Lifetime and 12-month prevalence of *DSM-III-R* psychiatric disorders in the United States: Results from the National Comorbidity Survey. *Archives of General Psychiatry, 51,* 8–19.

Kessler, R. C., Molnar, B. E., Feurer, I. D., & Appelbaum, M. (2001). Patterns and mental health predictors of domestic violence in the United States: Results from the National Comorbidity Survey. *International Journal of Law and Psychology, 24,* 487–508.

Ketsela, T., & Kedebe, D. (1997). Physical punishment of elementary school children in urban and rural communities in Ethiopia. *Ethiopian Medical Journal, 35,* 23–33.

Khan, F. I., Welch, T. L., & Zillmer, E. A. (1993). MMPI-2 profiles of battered women in transition. *Journal of Personality Assessment, 60,* 100–111.

Kim, K. I., & Cho, Y. G. (1992). Epidemiological survey of spousal abuse in Korea. In E. C. Viano (Ed.), *Intimate violence: Interdisciplinary perspectives* (pp. 277–282). Bristol, PA: Taylor & Francis.

Kim, N. S., & Ahn, W. (2002). Clinical psychologists' theory-based representations of mental disorders predict their diagnostic reasoning and memory. *Journal of Experimental Psychology: General, 131,* 451–476.

Kinard, E. M. (1996). Conducting research on child maltreatment: Effects on researchers. *Violence and Victims, 11,* 65–70.

Kinard, E. M. (2001). Recruiting participants for child abuse research: What does it take? *Journal of Family Violence, 16,* 219–236.

Kindermann, C., Lynch, J., & Cantor, D. (1997). *Effects of the redesign on victimization estimates* (NCJ Publication No. 164381). Washington, DC: U.S. Bureau of Justice Statistics.

Kingma, J. (1999). Repeat victimization of violence: A retrospective study from a hospital emergency department for the periods 1971–1995. *Journal of Interpersonal Violence, 14,* 79–90.

Kirkpatrick, L. A., Waugh, C. E., Valencia, A., & Webster, G. D. (2002). The functional domain specificity of self-esteem and the differential prediction of aggression. *Journal of Personality and Social Psychology, 82,* 756–767.

Kiser, L. J., Pugh, R. L., McColgan, E. B., Pruitt, D. B., & Edwards, N. B. (1991). Treatment strategies for victims of extrafamilial child sexual abuse. *Journal of Family Psychotherapy, 2*(1), 27–39.

Kitchener, K. S. (2000). *Foundations of ethical practice, research, and teaching in psychology.* Mahwah, NJ: Lawrence Erlbaum.

Kitzmann, K. M., Gaylord, N. K., Holt, A. R., & Kenny, E. D. (2003). Child witnesses to domestic violence: A meta-analytic review. *Journal of Consulting and Clinical Psychology, 71,* 330–352.

Kivela, S. L. (1995). Elder abuse in Finland. In J. I. Kosberg & J. L. Garcia (Eds.), *Elder abuse: International and cross-cultural perspectives* (pp. 31–44). Binghamton, NY: Haworth.

Klaus, P. A. (2000). *Crimes against persons age 65 or older, 1992–97* (NCJ Publication No. 176352). Washington, DC: U.S. Department of Justice. Retrieved December 8, 2003, from http://www.ojp.usdoj.gov/bjs/pub/pdf/cpa6597.pdf

Klein, C. F. (1995). Full faith and credit: Interstate enforcement of protection orders under the Violence Against Women Act of 1994. *Family Law Quarterly, 29,* 253–271.

Klein, E., Campbell, J. C., Soler, E., & Ghez, M. (1997). *Ending domestic violence: Changing public perceptions/halting the epidemic.* Thousand Oaks, CA: Sage.

Knight, R. A., & Hatty, S. E. (1992). Violence against women in Australia's capital. In E. C. Viano (Ed.), *Intimate violence: Interdisciplinary perspectives* (pp. 255–264). Bristol, PA: Taylor & Francis.

Knopp, F., Freeman-Longo, R., & Stevenson, W. (1992). *Nationwide survey of juvenile and adult sex-offender treatment programs and model.* Orwell, VT: Safer Society.

Kodjo, C., Auinger, P., & Ryan, S. (2002). Barriers to adolescents accessing mental health services. *Journal of Adolescent Health, 30,* 101–102.

Kolbo, J. R., Blakely, E. H., & Engleman, D. (1996). Children who witness domestic violence: A review of empirical literature. *Journal of Interpersonal Violence, 11,* 281–293.

Kolko, D. J. (1987). Treatment of child sexual abuse: Programs, progress, and prospects. *Journal of Family Violence, 2,* 303–318.

Kolko, D. J. (1992). Characteristics of child victims of physical violence. *Journal of Interpersonal Violence, 7,* 244–276.

Kolko, D. J. (1996a). Clinical monitoring of treatment course in child physical abuse: Child and parent reports. *Child Abuse & Neglect, 20,* 23–43.

Kolko, D. J. (1996b). Individual cognitive behavioral treatment and family therapy for physically abused children and their offending parents: A comparison of clinical outcomes. *Child Maltreatment, 1,* 322–342.

Kolko, D. J. (1998). Treatment and intervention for child victims of violence. In P. K. Trickett & C. J. Schellenbach (Eds.), *Violence against children in the family and the community* (pp. 213–249). Washington, DC: American Psychological Association.

Kolko, D. J. (2002). Child physical abuse. In J. E. B. Myers, L. Berliner, J. Briere, C. T. Hendrix, C. Jenny, & T. A. Reid (Eds.), *The APSAC handbook on child maltreatment* (2nd ed., pp. 21–54). Thousand Oaks, CA: Sage.

Kolko, D. J., Moser, J., & Hughes, J. (1989). Classroom training in sexual victimization awareness and prevention skills: An extension of the Red Flag/Green Flag People program. *Journal of Family Violence, 4,* 25–45.

Korbin, J. E. (2002). Culture and child maltreatment: Cultural competence and beyond. *Child Abuse & Neglect, 26,* 637–644.

Korbin, J. E., Anetzberger, G. J., & Austin, C. (1995). The intergenerational cycle of violence in child and elder abuse. *Journal of Elder Abuse & Neglect, 7*(1), 1–15.

Korbin, J. E., Anetzberger, G. J., Thomasson, R., & Austin, C. (1991). Abused elders who seek legal recourse against their adult offspring: Findings from an exploratory study. *Journal of Elder Abuse & Neglect, 3*(3), 1–18.

Korbin, J. E., Coulton, C. J., Lindstrom-Ufuti, H., & Spilsbury, J. (2000). Neighborhood views on the definition and etiology of child maltreatment. *Child Abuse & Neglect, 24,* 1509–1527.

Kosberg, J. I. (1988). Preventing elder abuse: Identification of high risk factors prior to placement decisions. *Gerontologist, 28,* 43–50.

Kosberg, J. I., & Cairl, R. E. (1986). The Cost of Care Index: A case management tool for screening informal care providers. *Gerontologist, 26,* 273–278.

Kosberg, J. I., & Garcia, J. L. (1995a). Common and unique themes on elder abuse from a world-wide perspective. In J. I. Kosberg & J. L. Garcia (Eds.), *Elder abuse: International and cross-cultural perspectives* (pp. 183–197). Binghamton, NY: Haworth.

Kosberg, J. I., & Garcia, J. L. (1995b). Introduction to the book. In J. I. Kosberg & J. L. Garcia (Eds.), *Elder abuse: International and cross-cultural perspectives* (pp. 1–12). Binghamton, NY: Haworth.

Kosberg, J. I., & Nahmiash, D. (1996). Characteristics of victims and perpetrators and milieus of abuse and neglect. In L. A. Baumhover & S. C. Beall (Eds.), *Abuse, neglect, and exploitation of older persons: Strategies for assessment and intervention* (pp. 31–49). Baltimore: Health Professions Press.

Koss, M. P. (1985). The hidden rape victim: Personality, attitudinal, and situational characteristics. *Psychology of Women Quarterly, 9,* 193–212.

Koss, M. P. (1988). Hidden rape: Sexual aggression and victimization. In A. W. Burgess (Ed.), *Rape and sexual assault* (Vol. 2, pp. 3–25). New York: Garland.

Koss, M. P. (1989). Hidden rape: Sexual aggression and victimization in a national sample of students in higher education. In M. A. Pirog-Good & J. E. Stets (Eds.), *Violence in dating relationships: Emerging social issues* (pp. 145–168). New York: Praeger.

Koss, M. P. (1990). The women's mental health research agenda. *American Psychologist, 45,* 374–380.

Koss, M. P. (1992a). Defending date rape. *Journal of Interpersonal Violence, 7,* 122–126.

Koss, M. P. (1992b). The underdetection of rape: Methodological choices influence incidence estimates. *Journal of Social Issues, 48*(1), 61–76.

Koss, M. P. (1993). Detecting the scope of rape. *Journal of Interpersonal Violence, 8,* 198–222.

Koss, M. P. (2000). Blame, shame, and community justice: Responses to violence against women. *American Psychologist, 55,* 1332–1343.

Koss, M. P., & Cook, S. L. (1993). Facing the facts: Date and acquaintance rape are significant problems for women. In R. J. Gelles & D. R. Loseke (Eds.), *Current controversies on family violence* (pp. 104–119). Newbury Park, CA: Sage.

Koss, M. P., & Gaines, J. A. (1993). The prediction of sexual aggression by alcohol use, athletic participation, and fraternity affiliation. *Journal of Interpersonal Violence, 8,* 94–108.

Koss, M. P., & Gidycz, C. A. (1985). Sexual Experiences Survey: Reliability and validity. *Journal of Consulting and Clinical Psychology, 53,* 422–423.

Koss, M. P., Gidycz, C. A., & Wisniewski, N. (1987). The scope of rape: Incidence and prevalence of sexual aggression and victimization in a national sample of higher education students. *Journal of Consulting and Clinical Psychology, 55,* 162–170.

Koss, M. P., Goodman, L. A., Browne, A., Fitzgerald, L. F., Puryear Keita, G., & Russo, N. F. (1994). *Male violence against women at home, at work, and in the community.* Washington, DC: American Psychological Association.

Koss, M. P., & Oros, C. J. (1982). Sexual Experiences Survey: A research instrument investigating sexual aggression and victimization. *Journal of Consulting and Clinical Psychology, 50,* 455–457.

Kovacs, M. (1992). *Children's Depression Inventory.* North Tonawanda, NY: Multi-Health System.

Krajewski, S. S. (1996). Results of a curriculum intervention with seventh graders regarding violence in relationships. *Journal of Family Violence, 11,* 93–112.

Krantz, G., & Ostergren, P. O. (2000). The association between violence victimisation and common symptoms in Swedish women. *Journal of Epidemiology and Community Health,* 815–821.

Kratcoski, P. C. (1984). Perspectives on intrafamily violence. *Human Relations, 37,* 443–453.

Kravets, D. (2003, January 7). When she says "no," it's rape. *Los Angeles Daily News*, p. 4.

Kreston, S. S. (2002). On-line crimes against children. *Section on Child Maltreatment Newsletter, 7*(2), 13.

Krishnan, S. P., Hilbert, J. C., & Pase, M. (2001). An examination of intimate partner violence in rural communities: Results from a hospital emergency department study from Southwest United States. *Family and Community Health, 24*(1), 1–14.

Kropp, P. R., & Hart, S. D. (1997). Assessing risk of violence in wife assaulters: The Spousal Assault Risk Assessment Guide. In C. D. Webster & M. A. Jackson (Eds.), *Impulsivity: Theory, assessment, and treatment* (pp. 302–325). New York: Guilford.

Kropp, P. R., & Hart, S. D. (2000). The Spousal Assault Risk Assessment (SARA) Guide: Reliability and validity in adult male offenders. *Law and Human Behavior, 24*, 101–118.

Kropp, P. R., Hart, S. D., Webster, C. W., & Eaves, D. (1995). *Manual for the Spousal Assault Risk Assessment Guide* (2nd ed.). Vancouver: Institute of Family Violence.

Krueger, R. F., Moffitt, T. E., Caspi, A., Bleske, A., & Silva, P. A. (1998). Assortive mating for antisocial behavior: Developmental and methodological implications. *Behavior Genetics, 23*, 173–186.

Krug, E. G., Dahlberg, L. L., Mercy, J. A., Zwi, A. B., & Lozano, R. (Eds.). (2002). *World report on violence and health*. Geneva: World Health Organization.

Krugman, R. D. (1995). Future directions in preventing child abuse. *Child Abuse & Neglect, 19*, 272–279.

Kruttschnitt, C., & Dornfeld, M. (1992). Will they tell? Assessing preadolescents' reports of family violence. *Journal of Research in Crime and Delinquency, 29*, 136–147.

Kubany, E. S., Hill, E. E., & Owens, J. A. (2003). Cognitive trauma therapy for battered women with PTSD: Preliminary findings. *Journal of Traumatic Stress, 16*, 81–91.

Kuleshnyk, I. (1984). The Stockholm syndrome: Toward an understanding. *Social Action and the Law, 10*(2), 37–42.

Kurrle, S. E., & Sadler, P. M. (1993). Australian service providers: Responses to elder abuse. *Journal of Elder Abuse & Neglect, 5*(1), 57–76.

Kurtz, P. D., Gaudin, J. M., Howing, P. T., & Wodarski, J. S. (1993). The consequences of physical abuse and neglect on the school age child: Mediating factors. *Children and Youth Services Review, 15*, 85–104.

Kurtz, P. D., Gaudin, J. M., Wodarski, J. S., & Howing, P. T. (1993). Maltreatment and the school-aged child: School performance consequences. *Child Abuse & Neglect, 17*, 581–589.

Kury, H., & Ferdinand, T. (1997). The victim's experience and fear of crime. *International Review of Victimology, 5*, 93–140.

Kurz, D. (1989). Social science perspective on wife abuse. *Gender & Society, 3*, 489–505.

Kurz, D. (1991). Corporal punishment and adult use of violence: A critique of "Discipline and deviance." *Social Problems, 35*, 155–161.

Kurz, D. (1993). Physical assaults by husbands: A major social problem. In R. J. Gelles & D. R. Loseke (Eds.), *Current controversies on family violence* (pp. 88–103). Newbury Park, CA: Sage.

Kwan, A. Y. (1995). Elder abuse in Hong Kong. In J. I. Kosberg & J. L. Garcia (Eds.), *Elder abuse: International and cross-cultural perspectives* (pp. 65–80). Binghamton, NY: Haworth.

Lacayo, R., Barovick, H., Cloud, J., & Duffy, M. (1998, October 26). The new gay struggle. *Time, 152*, 32–36.

Lachenmeyer, J. R., & Davidovicz, H. (1987). Failure to thrive: A critical review. In B. B. Lahey & A. E. Kazdin (Eds.), *Advances in clinical psychology* (Vol. 10, pp. 335–359). New York: Plenum.

Lachnit, C. (1991, April 13). "Satan trial": Jurors rule for two sisters. *Orange County Register* (California), p. 26.

Lachs, M. S., & Pillemer, K. A. (1995). Abuse and neglect of elderly persons. *New England Journal of Medicine, 332*, 437–443.

Lachs, M. S., Williams, C., O'Brien, S., Hurst, L., & Horwitz, R. (1997). Risk factors for reported elder abuse and neglect: A nine-year observational cohort study. *Gerontologist, 37*, 469–474.

Lachs, M. S., Williams, C., O'Brien, S., Pillemer, K. A., & Charlson, M. (1998). The mortality of elder mistreatment. *Journal of the American Medical Association, 280*, 428–432.

Lackie, L., & de Man, A. F. (1997). Correlates of sexual aggression among male university students. *Sex Roles, 37*, 451–457.

Ladner, J. A. (2000). *Children in out-of-home placements* (Children's Roundtable report). Retrieved from Brookings Institution Web site: http://www.brookings.edu/comm/childrensroundtable/issue4.htm

Laffaye, C., Kennedy, C., & Stein, M. (2003). Post-traumatic stress disorder and health-related quality of life in female victims of intimate partner violence. *Violence and Victims, 18*, 227–238.

Lahey, B. B., Conger, R. D., Atkeson, B. M., & Treiber, F. A. (1984). Parenting behavior and emotional status of physically abusive mothers. *Journal of Consulting and Clinical Psychology, 52*, 1062–1071.

Lambert, L. C., & Firestone, J. M. (2000). Economic context and multiple abuse techniques. *Violence Against Women, 6*, 49–67.

Landenburger, K. M. (1998). The dynamics of leaving and recovering from an abusive relationship. *Journal of Obstetric, Gynecologic, and Neonatal Nursing, 27*, 684–691.

Landsman, M. J., Nelson, K., Allen, M., & Tyler, M. (1992). *The Self-Sufficiency Project: Final report*. Iowa City, IA: National Resource Center on Family Based Services.

Lane, G., & Russell, T. (1989). Second-order systemic work with violent couples. In P. L. Caesar & L. K. Hamberger (Eds.), *Treating men who batter* (pp. 134–162). New York: Springer.

Lang, D. (1974, November 25). A reporter at large: The bank drama. *New Yorker*, pp. 56–126.

Lang, R. A., Flor-Henry, P., & Frenzel, R. R. (1990). Sex hormone profiles in pedophilic and incestuous men. *Annals of Sex Research, 3*, 59–74.

Lang, R. A., & Frenzel, R. R. (1988). How sex offenders lure children. *Annals of Sex Research, 1*, 303–317.

Langeland, W., & Hartgers, C. (1998). Child sexual and physical abuse and alcoholism: A review. *Journal of Studies on Alcohol, 59*, 336–348.

Langevin, R., Lang, R. A., & Curnoe, S. (1998). The prevalence of sex offenders with deviant fantasies. *Journal of Interpersonal Violence, 13*, 315–327.

Langford, D. R. (1996). Predicting unpredictability: A model of women's processes of predicting battering men's violence. *Scholarly Inquiry for Nursing Practice, 10*, 371–385.

Langhinrichsen-Rohling, J., & Dostal, C. (1996). Retrospective reports of family-of-origin divorce and abuse and college student's preparenthood cognitions. *Journal of Family Violence, 11*, 331–346.

Langhinrichsen-Rohling, J., Huss, M. T., & Ramsey, S. (2000). The clinical utility of batterer typologies. *Journal of Family Violence, 15*, 37–53.

Langhinrichsen-Rohling, J., Monson, C. M., Meyer, K. A., Caster, J., & Sanders, A. (1998). The associations among family-of-origin violence and young adults' current depressed, hopeless, suicidal, and life-threatening behavior. *Journal of Family Violence, 13,* 243–261.

Langhinrichsen-Rohling, J., Neidig, P., & Thorn, G. (1995). Violent marriages: Gender differences in levels of current violence and past abuse. *Journal of Family Violence, 10,* 159–176.

Langhinrichsen-Rohling, J., Smutzler, N., & Vivian, D. (1994). Positivity in marriage: The role of discord and physical aggression against wives. *Journal of Marriage and the Family, 56,* 69–79.

Lanktree, C. B., Briere, J., & Zaidi, L. Y. (1991). Incidence and impacts of sexual abuse in a child outpatient sample: The role of direct inquiry. *Child Abuse & Neglect, 15,* 447–453.

Lanning, K. V. (1991). Ritual abuse: A law enforcement view or perspective. *Child Abuse & Neglect, 15,* 171–173.

Lanning, K. V. (2002). Criminal investigation of sexual victimization of children. In J. E. B. Myers, L. Berliner, J. Briere, C. T. Hendrix, C. Jenny, & T. A. Reid (Eds.), *The APSAC handbook on child maltreatment* (2nd ed., pp. 329–347). Thousand Oaks, CA: Sage.

Lanning, K. V., & Burgess, A. W. (1984, January). Child pornography and sex rings. *FBI Law Enforcement Bulletin,* pp. 10–16.

Laor, N., Wolmer, L., & Cohen, D. J. (2001). Mother's functioning and children's symptoms 5 years after a SCUD missile attack. *American Journal of Psychiatry, 158,* 1020–1026.

Largen, M. A. (1987). A decade of change in the rape reform movement. *Response, 10*(2), 4–9.

Larson, C. S., Terman, D. L., Gomby, D. S., Quinn, L. S., & Behrman, R. E. (1994). Sexual abuse of children: Recommendations and analysis. *Future of Children, 4*(2), 4–30.

Larzelere, R. E. (1996). A review of outcomes of parental use of nonabusive or customary physical punishment. *Pediatrics, 98,* 824–828.

Larzelere, R. E. (2000). Child outcomes of non-abusive and customary physical punishment by parents: An updated literature review. *Clinical Child and Family Psychology Review, 3,* 199–221.

Lash, S. J., Copenhaver, M. M., & Eisler, R. M. (1998). Masculine gender-role stress and substance abuse among substance-dependent males. *Journal of Gender, Culture, and Health, 3,* 183–191.

Lash, S. J., Eisler, R. M., & Schulman, R. S. (1990). Cardiovascular reactivity to stress in men: Effects of masculine gender-role stress appraisal and masculine performance challenge. *Behavior Modification, 14,* 3–20.

Laub, A. (1996, February 1). Perspective on child protection; Punishment by public penury. *Los Angeles Times,* p. B9.

Laumann, E., Gagnon, J., Michael, R., & Michaels, S. (1994). *The social organization of sexuality: Sexual practices in the United States.* Chicago: University of Chicago Press.

Launius, M. H., & Jensen, B. L. (1987). Interpersonal problem-solving skills in battered, counseling, and control women. *Journal of Family Violence, 2,* 151–162.

Lauritsen, J. L. (1999). Limitations in the use of longitudinal self-report data: A comment. *Criminology, 37,* 687–694.

Lauritsen, J. L., & White, N. A. (2001). Putting violence in its place: The influence of race, ethnicity, gender, and place on the risk for violence. *Criminology & Public Policy, 1,* 37–59.

Laviola, M. (1992). Effects of older brother–young sister incest: A study of the dynamics of 17 cases. *Child Abuse & Neglect, 16,* 409–421.

LaViolette, A. D., & Barnett, O. W. (2000). *It could happen to anyone: Why battered women stay* (2nd ed.). Thousand Oaks, CA: Sage.

LaViolette, A. D., Barnett, O. W., & Miller, C. L. (1984, August). *A classification of wife abusers on the Bem Sex-Role Inventory.* Paper presented at the Second Family Violence Research Conference, Durham, NH.

Lavoie, F., Vezina, L., Piche, C., & Boivin, M. (1995). Evaluation of a prevention program for violence in teen dating relationships. *Journal of Interpersonal Violence, 10,* 516–524.

Law Enforcement Research Center. (1996). *Police and people with disabilities.* Minneapolis: Author.

Lawrence, E., & Bradbury, T. N. (2001). Physical aggression and marital dysfunction: A longitudinal analysis. *Journal of Family Psychology, 15,* 135–154.

Laws, D. R., & Marshall, W. L. (1990). A conditioning theory of the etiology and maintenance of deviant sexual preferences and behavior. In W. L. Marshall, D. R. Laws, & H. E. Barbaree (Eds.), *Handbook of sexual assault: Issues, theories, and treatment of the offender* (pp. 209–229). New York: Plenum.

Lawson, C. (1993). Mother-son sexual abuse: Rare or underreported? A critique of the research. *Child Abuse & Neglect, 17,* 261–269.

Lawson, D. M., Dawson, T. E., Kieffer, K. M., Perez, L. M., Burke, J., & Kier, F. J. (2001). An integrated feminist/cognitive-behavioral and psychodynamic group treatment for men who abuse partners. *Psychology of Men & Masculinity, 2*(1), 86–99.

Lee, J. K. P., Jackson, H. J., Pattison, P., & Ward, T. (2002). Developmental risk factors for sexual offending. *Child Abuse & Neglect, 26,* 73–92.

Leeder, E. (1988). Enmeshed in pain: Counseling the lesbian battering couple. *Women & Therapy, 7*(1), 81–99.

Leifer, M., Shapiro, J. P., & Kassem, L. (1993). The impact of maternal history and behavior upon foster placement and adjustment in sexually abused girls. *Child Abuse & Neglect, 17,* 755–766.

LeJeune, C., & Follette, V. M. (1994). Taking responsibility: Sex differences in reporting dating violence. *Journal of Interpersonal Violence, 9,* 133–140.

Lemon, N. K. D. (2002, October/November). Sonoma County, California, sheriff's department settles domestic violence murder case for one million dollars. *Domestic Violence Report, 8,* 1, 11–12, 14–16.

Lempert, L. B. (1996). Women's strategies for survival: Developing agency in abusive relationships. *Journal of Family Violence, 11,* 269–289.

Leonard, J. (2001, September 12). Sheriff's sergeant accused of child abuse. *Los Angeles Times,* p. B1

Leonard, K. E., & Senchak, M. (1993). Alcohol and premarital aggression among newlywed couples. *Journal of Studies on Alcohol, 11,* 96–108.

Lerner, C. F., & Kennedy, L. T. (2000). Stay-leave decision making in battered women: Trauma, coping and self-efficacy. *Cognitive Therapy and Research, 24,* 215–232.

Lesch, K. P., & Merschdorf, U. (2000). Impulsivity, aggression, and serotonin: A molecular psychobiological perspective. *Behavioral Sciences and the Law, 18,* 581–604.

Lesnik-Oberstein, M., Koers, A. J., & Cohen, L. (1995). Parental hostility and its sources in psychologically abusive mothers: A test of the three-factor theory. *Child Abuse & Neglect, 19,* 33–49.

Letellier, P. (1996). Twin epidemics: Domestic violence and HIV infection among gay and bisexual men. In C. M. Renzetti & C. H. Miley (Eds.), *Violence in gay and lesbian domestic partnerships* (pp. 69–82). Binghamton, NY: Haworth.

Letendre, L. A. (2000). Beating again and again: Why Washington needs a new rule of evidence admitting prior acts of domestic violence. *Washington Law Review, 75*, 973–1004.

Levant, R. F. (1994, August). *Male violence against female partners: Roots in male socialization and development.* Paper presented at the annual meeting of the American Psychological Association, Los Angeles.

Levant, R. F. (1995). *Masculinity reconstructed.* New York: Dutton.

Levendosky, A. A., Huth-Bocks, A. C., Semel, M. A., & Shapiro, D. L. (2002). Trauma symptoms in preschool-age children exposed to domestic violence. *Journal of Interpersonal Violence, 17*, 150–164.

Levendosky, A. A., Lynch, S. M., & Graham-Bermann, S. A. (2000). Mothers' perceptions of the impact of woman abuse on their parenting. *Violence Against Women, 6*, 247–271.

Levenson, J. S., & Morin, J. W. (2001). *Treating nonoffending parents in child sexual abuse cases.* Thousand Oaks, CA: Sage.

Levesque, R. J. R. (1997). Dating violence, adolescents, and the law. *Virginia Journal of Social Policy, 4*, 339–379.

Levesque, R. J. R. (2000). Cultural evidence, child maltreatment, and the law. *Child Maltreatment, 5*, 146–160.

Levesque, R. J. R. (2001). *Culture and family violence.* Washington, DC: American Psychological Association.

Levin, R. (1999). Participatory evaluators. *Violence Against Women, 5*, 1213–1227.

Levinson, D. (1988). Family violence in a cross-cultural perspective. In V. B. Van Hasselt, R. L. Morrison, A. S. Bellack, & M. Hersen (Eds.), *Handbook of family violence* (pp. 435–456). New York: Plenum.

Levitan, R. D., Parikh, S. V., Lesage, A. D., Hegadoren, K. M., Adams, M., Kennedy, S. H., et al. (1998). Major depression in individuals with a history of childhood physical or sexual abuse: Relationship to neurovegetative features, mania and gender. *American Journal of Psychiatry, 155*, 1746–1752.

Levitt, N. (2002, June). APA tells the Senate why we need more geropsychologists. *APA Monitor on Psychology, 33*, 17.

Levy, B. (1991). *Dating violence: Young women in danger.* Seattle: Seal.

Levy, B. (1997). Common stereotypes contribute to invisibility of battered lesbians. *Update* (Newsletter of the Statewide California Coalition for Battered Women), *3*(1), 1, 6.

Lewis, D. O., Lovely, R., Yeager, C., & Femina, D. D. (1989). Toward a theory of the genesis of violence: A follow-up study of delinquents. *Journal of the American Academy of Child and Adolescent Psychiatry, 28*, 431–436.

Lewis, S. F., & Fremouw, W. J. (2001). Dating violence: A critical review of the literature. *Clinical Psychology Review, 21*, 105–127.

Lia-Hoagberg, B., Kragthorpe, C., Schaffer, M., & Hill, D. L. (2001). Community interdisciplinary education to promote partnerships in family violence prevention. *Family and Community Health, 24*(1), 15–27.

Lieber, J., & Steptoe, S. (1994, June 27). Fatal attraction. *Sports Illustrated*, pp. 15–31.

Limbaugh, R. (1994, January 24). No tears for Lorena. *Newsweek, 124*, 56.

Lindsey, D., Martin, S., & Doh, J. (2002). The failure of intensive casework services to reduce foster care placements: An examination of family preservation studies. *Children and Youth Services Review, 24*, 743–775.

Lipovsky, J. A., & Elliott, A. N. (1993). Individual treatment of the sexually abused child. *APSAC Advisor, 6*(3), 15–18.

Lipschitz, D. S., Kaplan, M. L., Sorkenn, J. B., Faedda, G. L., Chorney, P., & Asnis, G. M. (1996). Prevalence and characteristics of physical and sexual abuse among psychiatric outpatients. *Psychiatric Services, 47*, 189–191.

Lithwick, M., Beaulieu, M., Gravel, S., & Straka, S. M. (1999). The mistreatment of older adults: Perpetrator-victim relationships and interventions. *Journal of Elder Abuse & Neglect, 11*(4), 95–112.

Lloyd, J. C., & Sallee, A. L. (1994). The challenge and potential of family preservation services in the public child welfare system. *Protecting Children, 10*(3), 3–6.

Lloyd, S. A. (1988, November). *Conflict and violence in marriage.* Paper presented at the annual meeting of the National Council on Family Relations, Philadelphia.

Lloyd, S. A. (1991). The dark side of courtship: Violence and sexual exploitation. *Family Relations, 40*, 14–20.

Locke, H. J., & Wallace, K. M. (1959). Short Marital Adjustment and Prediction Tests: Their reliability and validity. *Journal of Marriage and Family Living, 21*, 251–255.

Lockhart, L. L., White, B. W., Causby, V., & Isaac, A. (1994). Letting out the secret: Violence in lesbian relationships. *Journal of Interpersonal Violence, 9*, 469–492.

Loeber, R., & Farrington, D. P. (1997). Strategies and yields of longitudinal studies on antisocial behavior. In D. M. Stoff, J. Breiling, & J. D. Maser (Eds.), *Handbook of antisocial behavior* (pp. 125–139). New York: John Wiley.

Loftus, E. (1993). The reality of repressed memories. *American Psychologist, 48*, 518–537.

Loftus, E. (2003). Our changeable memories: Legal and practical implications. *Nature Reviews, 4*, 231–234.

Loftus, E., & Ketcham, K. (1991). *Witness for the defense: The accused, the eyewitness, and the expert who puts memory on trial.* New York: St. Martin's.

Lohr, B. A., Adams, H. E., & Davis, M. J. (1997). Sexual arousal to erotic and aggressive stimuli in sexually coercive and noncoercive men. *Journal of Abnormal Psychology, 106*, 230–242.

Lombardi, L. (1998). *A survey of formerly battered women's perceptions of professional response to domestic violence* [CD-ROM]. Abstract obtained from ProQuest File: Dissertation Abstracts Item 9829189

London, M. (2003, May/June). Crafting support services for older women. *Victimization of the Elderly and Disabled, 6*, 5–6.

Longres, J. F. (1992). Race and type of maltreatment in an elder abuse system. *Journal of Elder Abuse & Neglect, 4*(3), 61–83.

Lonsway, K. A., & Conis, P. (2003, October). Officer domestic violence. *Law and Order, 51*, 132–134.

Lonsway, K. A., & Fitzgerald, L. A. (1994). Rape myths: In review. *Psychology of Women Quarterly, 18*, 133–164.

Lopez, M. A., & Heffer, R. W. (1998). Self-concept and social competence of university student victims of childhood physical abuse. *Child Abuse & Neglect, 22*, 183–195.

Loring, M. T. (1994). *Emotional abuse.* Lexington, MA: Lexington.

Loring, M. T., Smith, R. W., & Bolden, T. (1997). Distal coercion: Case studies. *Psychology: A Journal of Human Behavior, 34*, 10–14.

Los Angeles County Department of Community and Senior Citizen Services. (1994). *Abuse by others: 1/93 through 6/93.* Los Angeles: Author.

Los Angeles County Medical Association. (1992). *Diagnostic and treatment guidelines on elder abuse and neglect.* Los Angeles: Author.

Los Angeles Department of Probation. (1998). *Los Angeles Department of Probation approved batterers' programs.* Los Angeles: Author.

Loseke, D. R. (2003). *Thinking about social problems: An introduction to constructionist perspectives* (2nd ed.). New York: Aldine de Gruyter.

Lottes, I. L., & Weinberg, M. S. (1997). Sexual coercion among university students: A comparison of the United States and Sweden. *Journal of Sex Research, 34,* 67–78.

Lowenstein, A. (1995). Elder abuse in a forming society: Israel. In J. I. Kosberg & J. L. Garcia (Eds.), *Elder abuse: International and cross-cultural perspectives* (pp. 81–100). Binghamton, NY: Haworth.

Lucente, S. W., Fals-Stewart, W., Richards, H. J., & Goscha, J. (2001). Factor structure and reliability of the Revised Conflict Tactics Scales for incarcerated female substance abusers. *Journal of Family Violence, 16,* 437–450.

Lundy, M., & Grossman, S. (2001). Clinical research and practice with battered women. *Trauma, Violence, & Abuse, 2,* 120–141.

Luntz, B., & Widom, C. S. (1994). Antisocial personality disorder in abused and neglected children grown up. *American Journal of Psychiatry, 151,* 670–674.

Lutzker, J. R. (1990a). Behavioral treatment of child neglect. *Behavior Modification, 14,* 301–315.

Lutzker, J. R. (1990b). Project 12-Ways: Treating child abuse and neglect from an ecobehavioral perspective. In R. F. Dangel & R. F. Polster (Eds.), *Parent training: Foundations of research and practice.* New York: Guilford.

Lutzker, J. R., Bigelow, K. M., Doctor, R. M., Gershater, R. M., & Greene, B. F. (1998). An ecobehavioral model for the prevention and treatment of child abuse and neglect. In J. R. Lutzker (Ed.), *Handbook of child abuse research and treatment* (pp. 239–266). New York: Plenum.

Lutzker, J. R., Campbell, R. V., & Watson-Perczel, M. (1984). Using the case study method to treat several problems in a family indicated for child neglect. *Education and Treatment of Children, 7,* 315–333.

Lutzker, J. R., Megson, D. A., Dachman, R. S., & Webb, M. E. (1985). Validating and training adult-child interaction skills to professionals and to parents indicated for child abuse and neglect. *Journal of Child and Adolescent Psychotherapy, 2,* 91–104.

Lutzker, S. Z., Lutzker, J. R., Braunling-McMorrow, D., & Eddleman, J. (1987). Prompting to increase mother-baby stimulation with single mothers. *Journal of Child and Adolescent Psychotherapy, 4,* 3–12.

Lynch, M. A., & Roberts, J. (1982). *Consequences of child abuse.* London: Academic Press.

Lynch, S. M., & Graham-Bermann, S. A. (2000). Woman abuse and self-affirmation. *Violence Against Women, 6,* 178–197.

Lyon, E. (1993). Hospital staff reactions to accounts by survivors of childhood abuse. *American Journal of Orthopsychiatry, 63,* 410–416.

Lyon, T. D. (1999). The new wave of suggestibility research: A critique. *Cornell Law Review, 73,* 1004–1087.

Lyons, T. J., & Oates, R. K. (1993). Falling out of bed: A relatively benign occurrence. *Pediatrics, 92,* 125–127.

Lyons-Ruth, K., Connell, D. B., Grunebaum, H. U., & Botein, S. (1990). Infants at social risk: Maternal depression and family support services as mediators of infant development and security of attachment. *Child Development, 61,* 85–98.

Mace, N. L. (1981). *The 36-hour day: A family guide to caring for persons with Alzheimer's disease, related dementing illness, and memory loss in later life.* Baltimore: Johns Hopkins University Press.

MacEwen, K. E. (1994). Refining the intergenerational transmission hypothesis. *Journal of Interpersonal Violence, 9,* 350–365.

Macfie, J., Cicchetti, D., & Toth, S. L. (2001). The development of dissociation in maltreated preschool-aged children. *Development and Psychopathology, 13,* 233–254.

Machin, E. (1984). A survey of the behavior of the elderly and their supporters at home. In C. Gilleard (Ed.), *Living with dementia.* London: Croom Helm.

MacLeod, J., & Nelson, G. (2000). Programs for the promotion of family wellness and the prevention of child maltreatment: A meta-analytic review. *Child Abuse & Neglect, 24,* 1127–1149.

MacMillan, V. M., Olson, R. L., & Hansen, D. J. (1991). Low and high deviant analogue assessment of parent-training with physically abusive parents. *Journal of Family Violence, 6,* 279–301.

Madonna, P. G., Van Scoyk, S., & Jones, D. P. H. (1991). Family interactions within incest and non-incest families. *American Journal of Psychiatry, 148,* 46–49.

Madu, S. N. (2001). Prevalence of child psychological, physical, emotional, and ritualistic abuse among high school students in Mpumalanga Province, South Africa. *Psychological Reports, 89,* 431–444.

Magdol, L., Moffitt, T. E., Caspi, A., Newman, D. L., Fagan, J. A., & Silva, P. A. (1997). Gender differences in partner violence in a birth cohort of 21-year-olds: Bridging the gap between clinical and epidemiological approaches. *Journal of Consulting and Clinical Psychology, 65,* 68–78.

Magdol, L., Moffitt, T. E., Caspi, A., & Silva, P. A. (1998). Hitting without a license: Testing explanations for differences in partner abuse between young adult daters and cohabitors. *Journal of Marriage and the Family, 60,* 41–55.

Maguire, K., & Pastore, A. L. (Eds.). (1994). *Sourcebook of criminal justice statistics: 1993.* Washington, DC: U.S. Department of Justice.

Mahlstedt, D., & Keeny, L. (1993). Female survivors of dating violence and their social networks. *Feminism and Psychology, 3,* 319–333.

Maiuro, R. D., Cahn, T. S., & Vitaliano, P. P. (1988). Anger, hostility, and depression in domestically violent versus generally assaultive men and nonviolent control subjects. *Journal of Consulting and Clinical Psychology, 56,* 17–23.

Majdan, A. (1998, March). *Prevalence and personality correlates of women's aggressive behaviors against male partners.* Poster presented at the biennial meeting of the American Psychology-Law Society, Redondo Beach, CA.

Makepeace, J. M. (1981). Courtship violence among college students. *Family Relations, 30,* 97–102.

Maker, A. H., Kemmelmeier, M., & Peterson, C. (1998). Long-term psychological consequences in women of witnessing parental physical conflict and experiencing abuse in childhood. *Journal of Interpersonal Violence, 13,* 574–589.

Malamuth, N. M. (1989). Predictors of naturalistic sexual aggression. M. A. Pirog-Good & J. E. Stets (Eds.), *Violence in dating relationships: Emerging social issues* (pp. 219–240). New York: Praeger.

Malamuth, N. M., & Briere, J. (1986). Sexual violence in the media: Indirect effects on aggression against women. *Journal of Social Issues, 42*(3), 75–92.

Malatack, J. J., Wiener, E. S., Gartner, J. C., Zitelli, B. J., & Brunetti, (1985). Munchausen by proxy: A new complication of central venous catheterization. *Pediatrics, 75,* 523–525.

Maletzky, B. M., & Field, G. (2003). The biological treatment of dangerous sexual offenders, A review and preliminary report the Oregon pilot Depo-Provera program. *Aggression Violent Behavior, 8,* 391–412.

Malinosky-Rummell, R., & Hansen, D. J. (1993). Long-term consequences of childhood physical abuse. *Psychological Bulletin, 114,* 68–79.

Maluccio, A. N. (2002). Family preservation or adoption? An essay review. *Children and Youth Services Review, 24,* 287–292.

Man found guilty in Megan's killing. (1997, May 31). *Sacramento Bee.* Retrieved from http://www.sacbee.com

Man held after wife found chained [Associated Press article]. (2003, April 5). *Los Angeles Daily News,* p. 15.

Mankowski, E. S., Haaken, J., & Silvergleid, C. S. (2002). Collateral damage: An analysis of the achievements and unintended consequences of batterer intervention programs and discourse. *Journal of Family Violence, 17,* 167–184.

Manly, J. T., Kim, J. E., Rogosch, F. A., & Cicchetti, D. (2001). Dimensions of child maltreatment and children's adjustment: Contributions of development timing and subtype. *Development and Psychopathology, 13,* 759–782.

Mannarino, A. P., & Cohen, J. A. (1996a). Abuse-related attributions and perceptions, general attributions, and locus of control in sexually abused girls. *Journal of Interpersonal Violence, 11,* 162–180.

Mannarino, A. P., & Cohen, J. A. (1996b). A follow-up study of factors that mediate the development of psychological symptomatology in sexually abused girls. *Child Maltreatment, 1,* 246–260.

Marans, S., & Cohen, D. (1993). Children and inner-city violence: Strategies for intervention. In L. Leavitt & N. Fox (Eds.), *Psychological effects of war and violence on children* (pp. 281–302). Hillsdale, NJ: Lawrence Erlbaum.

Marciak, B. J., Guzman, R., Santiago, A., Villalobos, G., & Israel, B. A. (1999). Establishing LA VIDA: A community-based partnership to prevent violence against women. *Health Education and Behavior, 26,* 821–840.

Marcus, R. F., & Swett, B. (2002). Violence and intimacy in close relationships. *Journal of Interpersonal Violence, 17,* 570–586.

Marcus, R. F., & Swett, B. (2003). Multiple-precursor scenarios: Predicting and reducing campus violence. *Journal of Interpersonal Violence, 18,* 553–571.

Marech, R. (2003, August 24). When help fails. *San Francisco Chronicle Magazine,* p. 12.

Marenin, O. (1997). Victimization surveys and the accuracy and reliability of official crime data in developing countries. *Journal of Criminal Justice, 25,* 463–475.

Margolin, G. (1998). Effects of domestic violence on children. In P. K. Trickett & C. J. Schellenbach (Eds.), *Violence against children in the family and the community* (pp. 57–101). Washington, DC: American Psychological Association.

Margolin, G., & Burman, B. (1993). Wife abuse versus marital violence: Different terminologies, explanations, and solutions. *Clinical Psychology Review, 13,* 59–73.

Margolin, G., Burman, B., & John, R. S. (1989). Home observations of married couples reenacting naturalistic conflicts. *Behavioral Assessment, 11,* 101–118.

Margolin, G., John, R. S., & Foo, L. (1998). Interactive and unique risk factors for husbands' emotional and physical abuse of their wives. *Journal of Family Violence, 13,* 315–341.

Margolin, G., John, R. S., & Gleberman, L. (1988). Affective responses to conflictual discussions in violent and nonviolent couples. *Journal of Consulting and Clinical Psychology, 56,* 24–33.

Margolin, L., & Craft, J. L. (1990). Child abuse by adolescent caregivers. *Child Abuse & Neglect, 14,* 365–373.

Margolin, L., Moran, P. B., & Miller, M. (1989). Social approval for violations of sexual consent in marriage and dating. *Violence and Victims, 4,* 45–55.

Marino, R., Weinman, M. L., & Soudelier, K. (2001). Social work intervention and failure to thrive in infants and children. *Health and Social Work, 26,* 90–98.

Marques, J., Nelson, C., West, M. A., & Day, D. M. (1994). The relationship between treatment goals and recidivism among child molesters. *Behavior Research and Therapy, 32,* 577–588.

Marshall, A. D., & Holtzworth-Munroe, A. (2002). Varying forms of husband sexual aggression: Predictors and subgroup differences. *Journal of Family Psychology, 16,* 286–296.

Marshall, C. E., Benton, D., & Brazier, J. M. (2000). Elder abuse: Using clinical tools to identify clues of mistreatment. *Geriatrics, 55*(2), 42, 44, 47–50, 53.

Marshall, L. L. (1994). Physical and psychological abuse. In W. R. Cupach & B. H. Spitzberg (Eds.), *The dark side of interpersonal communication* (pp. 281–311). Hillsdale, NJ: Lawrence Erlbaum.

Marshall, L. L., & Rose, P. (1990). Premarital violence: The impact of family of origin violence, stress, and reciprocity. *Violence and Victims, 5,* 51–64.

Marshall, L. L., Weston, R., & Honeycutt, T. C. (2000). Does men's positivity moderate or mediate the effects of their abuse on women's relationship quality? *Journal of Social and Personal Relationships, 17,* 660–675.

Marshall, W. L., & Barbaree, H. E. (1988). The long-term evaluation of a behavioral treatment program for child molesters. *Behavior Research and Therapy, 26,* 499–511.

Marshall, W. L., Barbaree, H. E., & Butt, J. (1988). Sexual offenders against male children: Sexual preferences. *Behavior Research and Therapy, 26,* 383–391.

Marshall, W. L., Barbaree, H. E., & Christophe, D. (1986). Sexual offenders against female children: Sexual preferences for age of victims and type of behaviour. *Canadian Journal of Behavioural Science, 18,* 424–439.

Marshall, W. L., & Eccles, A. (1993). Pavlovian conditioning processes in adolescent sex offenders. In H. E. Barbaree, W. L. Marshall, & S. Hudson (Eds.), *The juvenile sex offender* (pp. 118–142). New York: Guilford.

Marshall, W. L., Jones, R., Ward, T., Johnston, P., & Barbaree, H. E. (1991). Treatment outcome with sex offenders. *Clinical Psychology Review, 11,* 465–485.

Marshall, W. L., & Marshall, L. E. (2000). The origins of sexual offending. *Trauma, Violence, & Abuse, 1,* 250–263.

Marshall, W. L., & Pithers, W. (1994). A reconsideration of treatment outcome with sex offenders. *Criminal Justice and Behavior, 21,* 10–27.

Marshall, W. L., Serran, G. A., & Cortoni, F. A. (2000). Childhood attachments, sexual abuse, and their relationship to adult coping in child molesters. *Sexual Abuse, 12*(1), 17–26.

Martin, J. A., & Elmer, E. (1992). Battered children grown-up: A follow-up study of individuals severely maltreated as children. *Child Abuse & Neglect, 16,* 75–87.

Martin, M. E. (1997). Double your trouble: Dual arrest in family violence. *Journal of Family Violence, 12,* 139–157.

Martin, P. Y., & Hummer, R. A. (1995). Fraternities and rape on campus. In P. Searles & R. J. Berger (Eds.), *Rape and society: Readings on the problem of sexual assault* (pp. 139–151). Boulder, CO: Westview.

Martinez, P., & Richters, J. E. (1993). The NIMH Community Violence Project: Children's distress symptoms associated with violence exposure. In D. Reiss, J. E. Richters, M. Radke-Yarrow, & D. Scharff (Eds.), *Children and violence* (pp. 82–95). New York: Guilford.

Mash, E. J., Johnston, C., & Kovitz, K. (1983). A comparison of the mother-child interactions of physically abused and non-abused children during play and task situations. *Journal of Clinical Child Psychology, 12,* 337–346.

Massachusetts Department of Education. (2001, September 16). *Updated guidelines for schools on addressing teen dating violence.* Retrieved from http://www.doe.edu/hs/tdv/tdv1.html

Mastrofski, S. D., Parks, R. B., Reiss, A. J., & Worden, R. E. (1998). *Policing neighborhoods: A report from Indianapolis.* Washington, DC: U.S. Department of Justice.

Mathes, E. W., & Severa, N. (1981). Jealousy, romantic love, and liking: Theoretical considerations and preliminary scale development. *Psychological Reports, 49,* 23–31.

Matlaw, J. R., & Spence, D. M. (1994). The hospital elder assessment team: A protocol for suspected cases of elder abuse and neglect. *Journal of Elder Abuse & Neglect, 6*(2), 23–37.

Maxfield, M. G., & Widom, C. S. (1996). The cycle of violence: Revisited six years later. *Archives of Pediatrics and Adolescent Medicine, 150,* 390–395.

Maxwell, C. D., Garner, J. H., & Fagan, J. A. (June, 2001). *The effects of arrest on intimate partner violence: New evidence from the Spouse Assault Replication Program* (NCJ Publication No. 188199). Washington, DC: U.S. Department of Justice.

Mayseless, O. (1991). Adult attachment patterns and courtship violence. *Family Relations, 40,* 21–28.

Mazerolle, P., & Piquero, A. (1997). Violent responses to strain: An examination of conditioning influences. *Violence and Victims, 12,* 323–343.

Mazzeo, S. E., & Espelage, D. L. (2002). Association between childhood physical and emotional abuse and disordered eating behaviors in female undergraduates: An investigation of the mediating role of alexithymia and depression. *Journal of Counseling Psychology, 49,* 86–100.

McCarroll, J. E., Thayer, L. E., Liu, X., Newby, J. H., Norwood, A. E., Fullerton, C. S., et al. (2000). Spouse abuse recidivism in the U.S. Army by gender and military status. *Journal of Consulting and Clinical Psychology, 68,* 521–525.

McCarroll, J. E., Ursano, R. J., Liu, X., Thayer, L. E., Newby, J. H., Norwood, A. E., et al. (2000). Deployment and the probability of spousal aggression by U.S. Army soldiers. *Military Medicine, 165,* 41–44.

McCarthy, G., & Taylor, A. (1999). Avoidant/ambivalent attachment style as a mediator between abusive childhood experiences and adult relationship difficulties. *Journal of Child Psychology & Psychiatry & Allied Disciplines, 40,* 465–477.

McCloskey, L. A., & Bailey, J. A. (2000). The intergenerational transmission of risk for child sexual abuse. *Journal of Interpersonal Violence, 15,* 1019–1035.

McCloskey, L. A., Figueredo, A. J., & Koss, M. P. (1995). The effects of systemic family violence on children's mental health. *Child Development, 66,* 1239–1261.

McCloskey, L. A., & Lichter, E. L. (2003). The contribution of marital violence to adolescent aggression across different relationships. *Journal of Interpersonal Violence, 18,* 390–412.

McClung, J. J., Murray, R., & Braden, N. J. (1988). Intentional ipecac poisoning in children. *American Journal of Diseases in Children, 142,* 637–639.

McCormick, T. (1999). Convicting domestic violence abusers when the victim remains silent. *BYU Journal of Public Law, 13,* 427–449.

McCourt, J., Peel, J. C. F., & O'Carroll, P. (1998). The effects of child sexual abuse on the protecting parent(s): Identifying a counseling response for secondary victims. *Counseling Psychology Quarterly, 11,* 283–299.

McCray, J. A., & King, A. R. (2003). Personality disorder attributes as supplemental goals for change in interpersonal psychotherapy. *Journal of Contemporary Psychotherapy, 33,* 79–92).

McCurdy, K., & Daro, D. (1993). *Current trends in child abuse reporting and fatalities: The results of the 1992 annual fifty state survey.* Chicago: National Center on Child Abuse Prevention Research.

McCurdy, K., & Daro, D. (1994a). Child maltreatment: A national survey of reports and fatalities. *Journal of Interpersonal Violence, 9,* 75–94.

McCurdy, K., & Daro, D. (1994b). *Current trends in child abuse reporting and fatalities: The results of the 1993 annual fifty state survey.* (Available from the National Committee to Prevent Child Abuse, 332 South Michigan Ave., Suite 1600, Chicago, IL 60604)

McDermott, T. (1997, November 16). Letourneau and Billie: Similar cases but different outcomes. *Seattle Times.* Retrieved from http://www.seattletimes.com

McFall, C. (2000, March/April). Rainbow services: A new beginning for older battered women. *Victimization of the Elderly and Disabled, 2,* 86.

McFarlane, J., Campbell, J. C., & Watson, K. (2002). Intimate partner stalking and femicide: Urgent implications for women's safety. *Behavioral Sciences and the Law, 20,* 51–68.

McGee, R. A., & Wolfe, D. A. (1991). Psychological maltreatment: Toward an operational definition. *Development and Psychopathology, 3,* 3–18.

McGreevy, P. (1997, July 19). LAPD called lax on violence by its own. *Los Angeles Daily News,* p. 3.

McGreevy, P. (1998, April 10). Valley called soft on abusers. *Los Angeles Daily News,* pp. 1, 17.

McGuire, T., & Feldman, K. (1989). Psychological morbidity of children subjected to Munchausen syndrome by proxy. *Pediatrics, 83,* 289–292.

McHale, S. M., & Pawletko, T. M. (1992). Differential treatment of siblings in two family contexts. *Child Development, 63,* 68–91.

McHenry, P. C., Julian, T. W., & Gavazzi, S. M. (1995). Toward a biopsychosocial model of domestic violence. *Journal of Marriage and the Family, 57,* 307–320.

McKay, M. M. (1994). The link between domestic violence and child abuse: Assessment and treatment considerations. *Child Welfare, 73,* 29–39.

McKell, A. J., & Sporakowski, M. J. (1993). How shelter counselors' views about responsibility for wife abuse relate to services they provide. *Journal of Family Violence, 8,* 101–112.

McKenzie, R. B. (Ed.). (1998). *Rethinking orphanages for the 21st century.* Thousand Oaks, CA: Sage.

McLeer, S. V., Dixon, J. F., Henry, D., Ruggiero, K., Escovitz, K., Niedda T., et al. (1998). Psychopathology in non-clinically referred sexually abused children. *Journal of the American Academy of Child and Adolescent Psychiatry, 37,* 1326–1333.

McLeod, J. D., & Kessler, R. C. (1990). Socioeconomic status differences in vulnerability to undesirable life events. *Journal of Health and Social Behavior, 31,* 162–172.

McNair, D. M., Lorr, M., & Droppelman, L. F. (1971). *EDITS manual for the Profile of Mood States.* San Diego, CA: Educational and Industrial Testing Service.

McNally, R. J., Bryant, R. A., & Ehlers, A. (2003, November). Does early psychological intervention promote recovery from posttraumatic stress? *Psychological Science in the Public Interest, 4,* 45–79.

McNutt, L. A., Carlson, B. E., Rose, I. M., & Robinson, D. A. (2002). Partner violence intervention in the busy primary care environment. *American Journal of Preventive Medicine, 22,* 84–91.

McSkimming, M. J., Sever, B., & King, R. S. (2000). The coverage of ethics in research methods textbooks. *Journal of Criminal Justice Education, 11,* 51–63.

McWhirter, P. T. (1999). Domestic violence in Chile. *American Psychologist, 54,* 47–40.

Meadow, R. (1977). Munchausen syndrome by proxy: The hinterland of child abuse. *Lancet, 2,* 343–345.

Meadow, R. (1990). Suffocation, recurrent apnea, and sudden infant death. *Journal of Pediatrics, 117,* 351–356.

Mears, D. P. (2003). Research and interventions to reduce domestic violence revictimization. *Trauma, Violence, & Abuse, 4,* 127–147.

Mears, J. (2003). Survival is not enough: Violence against older women in Australia. *Violence Against Women, 9,* 1478–1489.

Meddaugh, D. I. (1990). Reactance: Understanding aggressive behavior in long-term care. *Journal of Psychosocial Nursing and Mental Health Services, 28*(4), 28–33.

Meichenbaum, D. (1977). *Cognitive-behavior modification: An integrative approach.* New York: Plenum.

Meisel, J., Changler, D., & Rienzi, B. M. (2003). Domestic violence prevalence and effects on employment in two California TANF populations. *Violence Against Women, 9,* 1191–1212.

Melton, G. B. (2002). Chronic neglect of family violence: More than a decade of reports to guide US policy. *Child Abuse and Neglect, 26,* 569–586.

Melton, G. B., & Barry, F. D. (1994). Neighbors helping neighbors: The vision of the U.S. Advisory Board on Child Abuse and Neglect. In G. B. Melton & F. D. Barry (Eds.), *Protecting children from abuse and neglect* (pp. 1–13). New York: Guilford.

Melton, H. C., & Belknap, J. (2003). He hits, she hits: Assessing gender differences and similarities in officially reported intimate partner violence. *Criminal Justice and Behavior, 30,* 328–348.

Menio, D., & Keller, B. H. (2000). CARIE: A multifaceted approach to abuse prevention in nursing homes. *Generations, 24*(2), 28–32.

Mennen, F. E., & Meadow, D. (1994). A preliminary study of the factors related to trauma in childhood sexual abuse. *Journal of Family Violence, 9,* 125–142.

Mennen, F. E., & Meadow, D. (1995). The relationship of abuse characteristics to symptoms in sexually abused girls. *Journal of Interpersonal Violence, 10,* 259–274.

Merrill, G. S., & Wolfe, V. A. (2000). Battered gay men: An exploration of abuse, help seeking and why they stay. *Journal of Homosexuality, 39*(2), 1–30.

Merrill, L. L., Hervig, L. K., & Milner, J. S. (1996). Childhood parenting experiences, intimate partner conflict resolution, and adult risk for child physical abuse. *Child Abuse & Neglect, 20,* 1049–1065.

Merrill, L. L., Newell, C. E., Thomsen, C. J., Gold, S. R., Milner, J. S., Koss, M. P., et al. (1999). Childhood abuse and sexual revictimization in a female navy recruit sample. *Journal of Traumatic Stress, 12,* 211–225.

Merschman, J. C. (2001). The dark side of the Web: Cyberstalking and the need for contemporary legislation. *Harvard Women's Law Journal, 24,* 255–292.

Mertin, P. G. (1992). An adaptation of the Conflict Tactics Scales. *Australian Journal of Marriage and the Family, 13,* 166–169.

Mertin, P. G., & Mohr, P. B. (2001). A follow-up study of posttraumatic stress disorder, anxiety, and depression in Australian victims of domestic violence. *Violence and Victims, 16,* 645–653.

Mesch, G. S. (2000). Women's fear of crime: The role of fear for the well-being of significant others. *Violence and Victims, 15,* 323–336.

Messman-Moore, T. L., & Long, P. J. (2000). Child sexual abuse in the form of adult sexual abuse, adult physical abuse, and adult psychological abuse. *Journal of Interpersonal Violence, 15,* 489–502.

Mian, M., Marton, P., & LeBaron, D. (1996). The effects of sexual abuse on 3- to 5-year-old girls. *Child Abuse & Neglect, 20,* 731–745.

Migliaccio, T. A. (2002). Abused husbands. *Journal of Family Issues, 23,* 26–52.

Mihalic, S. W., & Elliott, D. (1997). A social learning theory model of marital violence. *Journal of Family Violence, 12,* 21–47.

Milberger, S., Israel, N., LeRoy, B., Martin, A., Potter, L., & Patchak-Schuster, P. (2003). Violence against women with physical disabilities. *Violence and Victims, 18,* 581–590.

Miles, A. (2002). Holding Christian men accountable for abusing women. *Journal of Religion & Abuse, 4*(3), 15–27.

Millburn, M. A., Mathes, R., & Conrad, S. D. (2000). The effects of viewing R-rated movie scenes that objectify women on perceptions of date rape. *Sex Roles, 43,* 645–664.

Miller, B., & Marshall, J. (1987). Coercive sex on the university campus. *Journal of College Student Development, 28,* 38–47.

Miller, J., & Bukva, K. (2001). Intimate violence perceptions: Young adults' judgments of abuse escalating from verbal arguments. *Journal of Interpersonal Violence, 16,* 133–150.

Miller, L. (1999). Child abuse brain injury: Clinical, neuropsychological, and forensic considerations. *Journal of Cognitive Rehabilitation, 17*(2), 10–19.

Miller, L. C. (1984). *Louisville Behavior Checklist manual* (Rev. ed.). Los Angeles: Western Psychological Services.

Miller, S. L., & Simpson, S. S. (1991). Courtship violence and social control: Does gender matter? *Law & Society Review, 2,* 335–365.

Miller-Perrin, C. L. (1998). Sexually abused children's perceptions of sexual abuse: An exploratory analysis and comparison across ages. *Journal of Child Sexual Abuse, 7*(1), 1–22.

Miller-Perrin, C. L., & Perrin, R. D. (1997). *Unifying the field of family violence.* Paper presented at the meeting of the American Professional Society on the Abuse of Children, Miami, FL.

Miller-Perrin, C. L., & Perrin, R. D. (1999). *Child maltreatment: An introduction.* Thousand Oaks, CA: Sage.

Miller-Perrin, C. L., & Wurtele, S. K. (1988). The child sexual abuse prevention movement: A critical analysis of primary and secondary approaches. *Clinical Psychology Review, 8,* 313–329.

Millon, T. (1983). *Millon Clinical Multiaxial Inventory manual.* Minneapolis: Interpretive Scoring Systems.

Millon, T. (1987). *MCMI-II, Millon Clinical Multiaxial Inventory–II.* Minneapolis: National Computer Systems.

Mills, L. G. (1999). Killing her softly: Intimate abuse and the violence of state interventions. *Harvard Law Review, 113,* 551–613.

Mills, L. G., & Yoshihama, M. (2002). Training children's service workers in domestic violence assessment and intervention: Research findings and implications for practice. *Children and Youth Services Review, 24,* 561–581.

Milner, J. S. (1993). Social information processing and physical child abuse. *Clinical Psychology Review, 13,* 275–294.

Milner, J. S. (1998). Individual and family characteristics associated with intrafamilial child physical and sexual abuse. In P. K. Trickett & C. J. Schellenbach (Eds.), *Violence against children in the family and the community* (pp. 141–170). Washington DC: American Psychological Association.

Milner, J. S., & Chilamkurti, C. (1991). Physical child abuse perpetrator characteristics: A review of the literature. *Journal of Interpersonal Violence, 6,* 336–344.

Milner, J. S., & Dopke, C. (1997). Child physical abuse: Review of offender characteristics. In D. A. Wolfe, R. J. McMahon, & R. D. Peters (Eds.), *Child abuse: New directions in prevention and treatment across the lifespan* (pp. 27–54). Thousand Oaks, CA: Sage.

Milner, J. S., & Robertson, K. R. (1990). Comparison of physical child abusers, intrafamilial sexual child abusers, and child neglecters. *Journal of Interpersonal Violence, 5,* 37–48.

Min, P. G. (2001). Changes in Korean immigrants' gender role and social status, and their marital conflicts. *Sociological Forum, 16,* 301–320.

Miner, M., Marques, J., Day, D. M., & Nelson, C. (1990). Impact of relapse prevention in treating sex offenders: Preliminary findings. *Annals of Sex Research, 3,* 165–185.

Miranda, R., Jr., Meyerson, L. A., Marx, B. P., & Simpson, S. M. (2002). Sexual assault and alcohol use: Exploring the self-medication hypothesis. *Violence and Victims, 17,* 205–217.

Mirrlees-Black, C. (1999). *Domestic violence: Findings from a new British Crime Survey self-completion questionnaire* (Publication No. 191). London: Home Office Research Study.

Mitchell, J., & Morse, J. (1998). *From victims to survivors: Reclaimed voices of women sexually abused in childhood by females.* Washington, DC: Accelerated Development.

Mixson, P. M. (1991). Self-neglect: A practitioner's perspective. *Journal of Elder Abuse & Neglect, 3*(1), 35–42.

Model law on family violence includes strict arrest policy. (1994). *Criminal Justice Newsletter, 25*(10), 1–2.

Moe, A. M., & Bell, M. P. (2004). Abject economics: The effects of battering and violence on women's work and employability. *Violence Against Women, 10,* 29–55.

Moeller, T. P., Bachmann, G. A., & Moeller, J. R. (1993). The combined effects of physical, sexual, and emotional abuse during childhood: Long-term health consequences for women. *Child Abuse & Neglect, 17,* 623–640.

Moffitt, T. E. (1997). *Partner violence among young adults.* Washington, DC: U.S. Department of Justice.

Moffitt, T. E., & Caspi, A. (1999). *Findings about partner violence from the Dunedin Multidisciplinary Health and Development Study* (NCJ Publication No. 170018). Washington, DC: U.S. Department of Justice.

Moffitt, T. E., Caspi, A., Krueger, R. F., Magdol, L., Margolin, G., Silva, P. A., et al. (1997). Do partners agree about abuse in their relationship? A psychometric evaluation of interpartner agreement. *Psychological Assessment, 9,* 47–56.

Moffitt, T. E., Caspi, A., Rutter, M., & Silva, P. A. (2001). *Sex differences in antisocial behaviour: Conduct disorder, delinquency and violence in the Dunedin Longitudinal Study.* Cambridge: Cambridge University Press.

Moffitt, T. E., Krueger, R. F., Caspi, A., & Fagan, J. A. (2000). Partner abuse and general crime: How are they the same? How are they different? *Criminology, 38,* 199–231.

Mohr, W. K. (1998, August/September). Bringing together the town and the gown: NIJ initiative for practitioner synthesis. *Domestic Violence Report, 3,* 89.

Molidor, C. E. (1995). Gender differences of psychological abuse in high school dating relationships. *Child and Adolescent Social Work Journal, 12,* 119–134.

Molidor, C. E., & Tolman, R. M. (1998). Gender and contextual factors in adolescent dating violence. *Violence Against Women, 4,* 180–194.

Mollerstrom, W. W., Patchner, M. A., & Milner, J. S. (1992). Family functioning and child abuse potential. *Journal of Clinical Psychology, 48,* 445–454.

Monahan, K., & Lurie, A. (2003). Disabled women sexually abused in childhood: Treatment considerations. *Clinical Social Work Journal, 31,* 407–418.

Monahan, K., & O'Leary, K. D. (1999). Head injury and battered women: An initial inquiry. *Health and Social Work, 24,* 269–278.

Monson, C. M., & Langhinrichsen-Rohling, J. (1998). Sexual and nonsexual marital aggression: Legal considerations, epidemiology, and an integrated typology of perpetrators. *Aggression and Violent Behavior, 3,* 369–389.

Montgomery, N. (1996, July 9). Sex charges against teachers still shock, but not so unusual. *Seattle Times.* Retrieved from http://www.seattletimes.com

Montoya, J. (1993). Something not so funny happened on the way to conviction: The pretrial interrogation of child witnesses. *Arizona Law Review, 35,* 927.

Moon, A., & Benton, D. (2000). Tolerance of elder abuse and attitudes toward third-party intervention among African American, Korean American, and White elderly. *Journal of Multicultural Social Work, 8,* 283–303.

Moon, A., & Williams, O. J. (1993). Perceptions of elder abuse and help-seeking patterns among African-American, Caucasian American, and Korean-American elderly women. *Gerontologist, 33,* 386–395.

Moore, T. M., Eisler, R. M., & Franchina, J. J. (2000). Causal attributions and affective responses to provocative female partner behavior by abusive and nonabusive males. *Journal of Family Violence, 15,* 69–80.

Moos, R. H. (1974). *Family Environment Scale.* Palo Alto, CA: Consulting Psychologists Press.

Morency, N. L., & Krauss, R. M. (1982). The nonverbal encoding and decoding of affect in first and fifth graders. In R. S. Feldman (Ed.), *Development of nonverbal behavioral skill.* New York: Springer-Verlag.

Morgan, A. B., & Lilienfeld, S. O. (2000). A meta-analytic review of the relation between antisocial behavior and neuropsychological measures of executive function. *Clinical Psychology Review, 20,* 113–136.

Morganthau, T., Springen, K., Smith, V. E., Rosenberg, D., Beals, G., Bogert, C., et al. (1994, December 12). The orphanage. *Newsweek, 124,* 28–32.

Morrow, K. B. (1991). Attributions of female adolescent incest victims regarding their molestation. *Child Abuse & Neglect, 15,* 477–482.

Morton, E., Runyan, C. W., Moracco, K. E., & Butts, J. (1998). Partner homicide-suicide involving female homicide victims: A population-based study in North Carolina, 1988–1992. *Violence and Victims, 13,* 91–106.

Morton, N., & Browne, K. D. (1998). Theory and observation of attachment and its relation to child maltreatment: A review. *Child Abuse & Neglect, 22,* 1093–1104.

Mosher, D. L., & Sirkin, M. (1984). Measuring a macho personality constellation. *Journal of Research in Personality, 18,* 150–163.

Moskowitz, S. (1997). Private enforcement of criminal mandatory reporting laws. *Journal of Elder Abuse & Neglect, 9*(3), 1–22.

Moss, V. A., Pitula, C. R., Campbell, J. C., & Halstead, L. (1997). The experience of terminating an abusive relationship from an Anglo and African American perspective: A qualitative descriptive study. *Issues in Mental Health Nursing, 18,* 433–454.

Mount Sinai/Victim Services Agency, Elder Abuse Project. (1988). *Elder mistreatment guidelines for health care professionals: Detection, assessment, and intervention.* New York: Author.

Mouradian, V. E. (2001). Applying schema theory to intimate aggression: Individual and gender differences in representation of contexts and goals. *Journal of Applied Social Psychology, 31,* 376–408.

Mouton, C., Rovi, S., Furniss, K., & Lasser, N. (1999). The association between health and domestic violence in older women: Results of a pilot. *Journal of Women's Health and Gender-Based Medicine, 9,* 1173–1179.

Movsas, T. Z., & Movsas, B. (1990). Abuse versus neglect: A model to understand the causes of and treatment strategies for mistreatment of older persons. *Issues in Law & Medicine, 6,* 163–173.

Mowat-Leger, V. (2002). Risk factors for violence: A comparison of domestic batterers and other violent and nonviolent men. *Dissertation Abstracts International, 63*(04), 2046B. (UMI No. NQ67053)

Muehlenhard, C. L. (1989). Misinterpreted dating behaviors and the risk of date rape. In M. A. Pirog-Good & J. E. Stets (Eds.), *Violence in dating relationships: Emerging social issues* (pp. 241–256). New York: Praeger.

Muldary, P. S. (1983). Attribution of causality of spouse assault. *Dissertation Abstracts International, 44,* 1249B. (UMI No. 8316576)

Mulhern, S. (1991). Satanism and psychotherapy: A rumor in search of an inquisition. In J. Richardson, J. Best, & D. Bromley (Eds.), *The satanism scare* (pp. 145–174). New York: Aldine de Gruyter.

Mulhern, S. (1994). Satanism, ritual abuse, and multiple personality disorder: A sociohistorical perspective. *International Journal of Clinical and Experimental Hypnosis, 42*(4), 265–288.

Mullen, P. E., Martin, J. L., Anderson, J. C., Romans, S. E., & Herbison, G. P. (1996). The long-term impact of the physical, emotional, and sexual abuse of children: A community study. *Child Abuse & Neglect, 20,* 7–21.

Mullin, C. R., & Linz, D. (1995). Desensitization and resensitization to violence against women: Effects of exposure to sexually violent films on judgments of domestic violence victims. *Journal of Personality and Social Psychology, 69,* 449–459.

Municipal liability for domestic violence homicides. (1998, August/September). *Domestic Violence Report, 3,* 90.

Munkel, W. I. (1994). Neglect and abandonment. In A. E. Brodeur & J. A. Monteleone (Eds.), *Child maltreatment: A clinical guide and reference* (pp. 241–257). St. Louis, MO: Medical Publishing.

Muram, D., Miller, K., & Cutler, A. (1992). Sexual assault of the elderly victim. *Journal of Interpersonal Violence, 7,* 70–76.

Murdoch, J. B. (2000). Is imminence really necessity? Reconciling traditional self-defense doctrine with the battered woman syndrome. *Northern Illinois University Law Review, 20,* 191–218.

Murphy, C. M., & Blumenthal, D. R. (2000). The mediating influence of interpersonal problems on the intergenerational transmission of relationship aggression. *Personal Relationships, 7,* 203–218.

Murphy, C. M., & Dienemann, J. A. (1999). Informing the research agenda on domestic abuser intervention through practitioner-research dialogues. *Journal of Interpersonal Violence, 14,* 1314–1326.

Murphy, C. M., Meyer, S. L., & O'Leary, K. D. (1993). Family of origin violence and MCMI-II psychopathology among partner assaultive men. *Violence and Victims, 8,* 227–238.

Murphy, C. M., Meyer, S. L., & O'Leary, K. D. (1994). Dependency characteristics of partner assaultive men. *Journal of Abnormal Psychology, 103,* 729–735.

Murphy, C. M., Morrel, T. M., Elliott, J. D., & Neavins, T. M. (2003). A prognostic indicator scale for the treatment of partner abuse perpetrators. *Journal of Interpersonal Violence, 18,* 1087–1105.

Murphy, C. M., Stosny, S., & Morrel, T. M. (in press). Change in self-esteem and physical aggression during treatment for partner violent men. *Journal of Family Violence.*

Murphy, E. M. (2003). Being born female is dangerous for your health. *American Psychologist, 58,* 205–210.

Murray, B. (1999, October). Cultural insensitivity leads to unfair penalties. *APA Monitor on Psychology.* Retrieved October 4, 2002, from http://apa.org/monitor/oct99/mv2.html

Murray, S. L., Bellavia, G. M., Rose, P., & Griffin, D. W. (2003). Once hurt, twice hurtful: How perceived regard regulates daily marital interactions. *Journal of Personality and Social Psychology, 84,* 126–147.

Murray, S. L., Rose, P., Bellavia, G. M., Holmes, J. G., & Kusche, A. G. (2002). When rejection stings: How self-esteem constrains relationship-enhancement processes. *Journal of Personality and Social Psychology, 83,* 556–573.

Murrin, M. R., & Laws, D. R. (1990). The influence of pornography on sexual crimes. In W. L. Marshall, D. R. Laws, & H. E. Barbaree (Eds.), *Handbook of sexual assault: Issues, theories, and treatment of the offender* (pp. 73–91). New York: Plenum.

Murty, K. S., & Roebuck, J. B. (1992). An analysis of crisis calls by battered women in the city of Atlanta. In E. C. Viano (Ed.), *Intimate violence: Interdisciplinary perspectives* (pp. 61–81). Bristol, PA: Taylor & Francis.

Mydans, S. (1994, June 3). Prosecutors are rebuked on child sex abuse case. *New York Times,* p. A7.

Myers, J. E. B. (1992). *Evidence in child abuse and neglect cases.* New York: John Wiley.

Myers, J. E. B. (1993). Commentary: A call for forensically relevant research. *Child Abuse & Neglect, 17,* 573–579.

Myers, J. E. B. (1994). Adjudication of child sexual abuse cases. *Future of Children, 4*(2), 84–101.

Myers, J. E. B. (1998). *Legal issues in child abuse and neglect practice* (2nd ed.). Thousand Oaks, CA: Sage.

Myers, J. E. B. (2002). The legal system and child protection. In J. E. B. Myers, L. Berliner, J. Briere, C. T. Hendrix, C. Jenny, & T. A. Reid (Eds.), *The APSAC handbook on child maltreatment* (2nd ed., pp. 305–327). Thousand Oaks, CA: Sage.

Myers, J. E. B., & Peters, W. D. (1987). *Child abuse reporting and legislation in the 1980s.* Denver, CO: American Humane Association.

Nabi, R. L., & Horner, J. R. (2001). Victims with voices: How abused women conceptualize the problem of spousal abuse and implications for intervention and prevention. *Journal of Family Violence, 16,* 237–253.

Nadon, S. M., Koverola, C., & Schludermann, E. H. (1998). Antecedents to prostitution: Childhood victimization. *Journal of Interpersonal Violence, 13,* 206–221.

Nahmiash, D., & Reis, M. (2000). Most successful intervention strategies for abused older adults. *Journal of Elder Abuse & Neglect, 12*(3/4), 53–70.

Nasjleti, M. (1980). Suffering in silence: The male incest victim. *Child Welfare, 59,* 269–275.

National Center for Injury Prevention and Control. (2000). *Dating violence.* Retrieved from http://www.cdc.gov/ncipc/factsheets/datviol.htm

National Center for Injury Prevention and Control. (2002). *CDC injury research agenda.* Atlanta, GA: Centers for Disease Control and Prevention.

National Center for Injury Prevention and Control. (2003). *Costs of intimate partner violence against women in the United States.* Atlanta, GA: Centers for Disease Control and Prevention.

National Center for Missing and Exploited Children. (n.d.). Pornographic images of children. In *Child sexual exploitation.* Retrieved January 25, 2004, from http://www.ncmec.org/missingkids/servlet

National Center for Prosecution of Child Abuse. (1993). *Legislation requiring sex offenders to register with a government agency.* Alexandria, VA: Author.

National Center for Victims of Crime. (2002, January). Enforcement of protective orders (NCJ Publication No. 189190). *VC Legal Series Bulletin, 4,* 1–7.

National Center on Child Abuse and Neglect. (1978). *Child sexual abuse: Incest, assault, and sexual exploitation.* Washington, DC: U.S. Department of Health and Human Services.

National Center on Child Abuse and Neglect. (1993). *National child abuse and neglect data system* (Working paper 2, 1991 summary data component). Washington, DC: U.S. Department of Health and Human Services.

National Center on Elder Abuse. (1998). *The national elder abuse incidence study: Final report.* Madison, WI: Author.

National Clearinghouse on Child Abuse and Neglect Information. (1998a). *Administration for Children and Families: Principles for implementing the Adoption and Safe Families Act of 1997.* Retrieved from http://www.calib.com/nccanch/asfa.html

National Clearinghouse on Child Abuse and Neglect Information. (1998b). *NCCAN lessons learned: The experience of nine child abuse and neglect prevention programs.* Retrieved from http://www.calib.com/nccancn/pubs/lessons/prevcomp.html

National Clearinghouse on Child Abuse and Neglect Information. (2001). *In focus: The risk and prevention of maltreatment of children with disabilities.* Retrieved November 6, 2003, from http://nccanch.acf.hhs.gov/pubs/prevenres/focus.cfm

National Clearinghouse on Child Abuse and Neglect Information. (n.d.). *Statutes-at-a-glance.* Retrieved November 6, 2003, from http://nccanch.acf.hhs.gov/general/legal/statutes/statutes-glance.cfm

National Coalition of Anti-Violence Programs. (2001). *Lesbian, gay, bisexual and transgender domestic violence in 2000.* New York: Author.

National Council of Juvenile and Family Court Judges. (1994). *Model code on domestic and family violence.* Reno, NV: Author.

National Institute of Justice & American Bar Association. (1998). *Legal interventions in family violence: Research findings and policy implications* (NCJ Publication No. 171666). Washington, DC: U.S. Department of Justice.

National Institute on Disability and Rehabilitation Research. (2003). *Long-range plan 1999–2003.* Washington, DC: U.S. Department of Education.

National Low Income Housing Commission. (1998). *Women and housing.* Retrieved from http://www.nilhc.org/backgrd? htm#rural

National Opinion Research Center. (1998). *General Social Survey 1972–2000 cumulative codebook.* Retrieved May 17, 2002 from http://www.icpsr.umich.edu/GSS

National Research Council. (1993). *Understanding child abuse and neglect.* Washington, DC: National Academy Press.

Naumann, P., Langford, D., Torres, S., Campbell, J., & Glass, N. (1999) Woman battering in primary care practice. *Family Practice 16,* 343–352.

Nayak, M. B., & Milner, J. S. (1998). Neuropsychological functioning Comparison of mothers at high- and low-risk for child abuse *Child Abuse & Neglect, 22,* 687–703.

Nazoo, J. (1995). Uncovering gender differences in the use of marital violence: The effect of methodology. *Sociology, 29,* 475–494.

Neff, J. A., Holamon, B., & Schluter, T. D. (1995). Spousal violence among Anglos, Blacks, and Mexican Americans: The role of demographic variables, psychosocial predictors, and alcohol consumption. *Journal of Family Violence, 10,* 1–21.

Neidig, P., Friedman, D., & Collins, B. (1986). Attitudinal family violence characteristics of men who have engaged in spousal abuse. *Journal of Family Violence, 1,* 223–233.

Nelson, D. (2002). Violence against elderly people: A neglected problem. *Lancet, 360,* 1094.

Nelson, H. W. (2000). Injustice and conflict in nursing homes: Toward advocacy and exchange. *Journal of Aging Studies, 14,* 39–61

Nelson, K. (1994). Innovative service models in social service *Journal of Clinical Child Psychology, 23,* 26–31.

Nelson, K., Saunders, E., & Landsman, M. J. (1990). *Chronic neglect: A perspective: A study of chronically neglecting families in a large metropolitan county.* Oakdale: University of Iowa School of Social Work, National Resource Center on Family Based Services.

Nelson, W. M., & Finch, A. J. (2000). *Children's Inventory of Anger.* Los Angeles: Western Psychological Services.

Nerenberg, L. (1995). LAPD's fiduciary SWAT team. *Nexus, 1*(2), 4–

Nerenberg, L. (1996). *Older battered women.* Washington, DC: National Center on Elder Abuse.

Nerenberg, L. (2000). Forgotten victims of financial crime and abuse: Facing the challenge. *Journal of Elder Abuse & Neglect, 12*(2), 49–73.

Nerenberg, L. (2003). *Daily money management programs: A protection against elder abuse.* Washington, DC: National Center on Elder Abuse.

Neuger, C. C. (2002). Premarital preparation: Generating resistance to marital violence. *Journal of Religion & Abuse, 4*(3), 43–5

Neumann, D. A., Houskamp, B. M., Pollock, V. E., & Briere, J. (1996). The long-term sequelae of childhood sexual abuse in women: A meta-analytic review. *Child Maltreatment, 1,* 6–16.

Neumann, R. (2000). The causal influences of attributions on emotions: A procedural priming approach. *Psychological Science, 11,* 179–182.

New Jersey State Attorney General's Office. (2000). *Attorney general guidelines for law enforcement for the implementation of sex offender registration and community notification laws.* Retrieved December 9, 2003, from http://www.state.nj lps/dcj/megan1.pdf

Newberger, C. M., Gremy, I. M., Waternaux, C. M., & Newberger, E. H. (1993). Mothers of sexually abused children: Trauma and repair in longitudinal perspective. *American Journal of Orthopsychiatry, 63,* 92–102.

Newcomb, M. D., & Locke, T. F. (2001). Intergenerational cycle of maltreatment: A popular concept obscured by methodological limitations. *Child Abuse & Neglect, 25,* 1219–1240.

Newmark, L., Harrell, A., & Adams, W. P. (1995). *Evaluation of police training conducted under the family violence prevention and services act* (NCJ Publication No. 157306). Washington, DC: U.S. Department of Justice.

Newton-Taylor, B., DeWit, D., & Gliksman, L. (1998). Prevalence and factors associated with physical and sexual assault of female university students in Ontario. *Health Care for Women International, 19,* 155–164.

Ney, P. G., Fung, T., & Wickett, A. R. (1994). The worst combinations of child abuse and neglect. *Child Abuse & Neglect, 18,* 705–714.

NiCarthy, G. (1987). *The ones who got away.* Seattle: Seal.

Nichols, L., & Feltey, K. M. (2003). "The woman is not always the bad guy": Dominant discourse and resistance in the lives of battered women. *Violence Against Women, 9,* 784–806.

Nicole, J. (1997). *Hispanic immigrant women and domestic violence* [CD-ROM]. Abstract obtained from ProQuest File: Dissertation Abstracts Item 1383003

Niebuhr, G. (1998, June 10). Baptists laud submission by women. *Los Angeles Daily News,* pp. 8, 10.

Nielsen, J. M., Endo, R. K., & Ellington, B. L. (1992). Social isolation and wife abuse: A research report. In E. C. Viano (Ed.), *Intimate violence: Interdisciplinary perspectives* (pp. 40–59). Bristol, PA: Taylor & Francis.

Noll, J. G., Horowitz, L. A., Bonnano, G. A., Trickett, P. K., & Putnam, F. W. (2003). Revictimization and self-harm in females who experienced childhood sexual abuse. *Journal of Interpersonal Violence, 18,* 1452–1471.

Noll, J. G., Trickett, P. K., & Putnam, F. W. (2003). A prospective investigation of the impact of childhood sexual abuse on the development of sexuality. *Journal of Consulting and Clinical Psychology, 71,* 575–586.

Norman, P., & Finan, E. (2001, November 12). Veil of tears. *People, 56,* 107–110.

Norman, R. L. (2000). How do I prevent burnout? In H. Dubowitz & D. DePanfilis (Eds.), *Handbook for child protection practice* (pp. 582–584). Thousand Oaks, CA: Sage.

North American Man/Boy Love Association. (2002). *Statement of purpose.* Retrieved May 14, 2002, from http://qrd.tcp.com/qrd/orgs/NAMBLA/statement.of.purpose

North American Council on Adoptable Children. (n.d.). *How to adopt.* Retrieved March 2003 from http://www.nacac.org

Nosek, M. A., & Howland, C. A. (1998). *Abuse of women with disabilities.* Minneapolis: Minnesota Center Against Violence and Abuse.

Nosek, M. A., Howland, C. A., & Young, M. E. (1997). Abuse of women with disabilities: Policy implications. *Journal of Disability Policy Studies, 8,* 157–175.

Novaco, R. (1975). *Anger control: The development and evaluation of an experimental treatment.* Lexington, MA: Lexington.

Nurius, P. S., Furrey, J., & Berliner, L. (1992). Coping capacity among women with abusive partners. *Violence and Victims, 7,* 229–243.

Nutt, R. L. (1999). Women's gender-role socialization, gender-role conflict, and abuse: A review of predisposing factors. In M. Harway & J. M. O'Neil (Eds.), *What causes men's violence against women?* (pp. 117–134). Thousand Oaks, CA: Sage.

Nuttall, R., & Jackson, H. (1994). Personal history of childhood abuse among clinicians. *Child Abuse & Neglect, 18,* 455–472.

Oates, R. K., & Bross, D. C. (1995). What have we learned about treating child physical abuse? A literature review of the last decade. *Child Abuse & Neglect, 19,* 463–474.

O'Brien, M. (1991). Taking sibling incest seriously. In M. Patton (Ed.), *Family sexual abuse: Frontline research and evaluation* (pp. 75–92). Newbury Park, CA: Sage.

O'Brien, M., John, R. S., Margolin, G., & Erel, O. (1994). Reliability and diagnostic efficacy of parents' reports regarding children's exposure to marital aggression. *Violence and Victims, 9,* 45–62.

Ockleford, E., Barnes-Holmes, Y., Morichelli, R., Moriaria, A., Scocchera, F., Furniss, F., et al. (2003). Mistreatment of older women in three European countries. *Violence Against Women, 9,* 1453–1464.

O'Donnell, C. J., Smith, A., & Madison, J. R. (2002). Using demographic risk factors to explain variations in the incidence of violence against women. *Journal of Interpersonal Violence, 17,* 1239–1262.

O'Donohue, W., Yeater, E. A., & Fanetti, M. (2003). Rape prevention with college males. *Journal of Interpersonal Violence, 18,* 513–531.

O'Farrell, T. J., Fals-Stewart, W., Murphy, M., & Murphy, C. M. (2003). Partner violence before and after individually based alcoholism treatment for male alcoholic patients. *Journal of Consulting and Clinical Psychology, 71,* 92–102.

O'Farrell, T. J., & Murphy, C. M. (1995). Marital violence before and after alcoholism treatment. *Journal of Consulting and Clinical Psychology, 63,* 256–262.

O'Farrell, T. J., Murphy, C. M., Neavins, T. M., & Van Hutton, V. (2000). Verbal aggression among male alcoholic patients and their wives in the year before and two years after alcoholism treatment. *Journal of Family Violence, 15,* 295–310.

Office for Victims of Crime. (1999). *Breaking the cycle of violence: Recommendations to improve the criminal justice response to child victims and witnesses.* Washington, DC: U.S. Department of Justice.

Office for Victims of Crime. (2002a). *First response to victims of crime who have a disability* (NCJ Publication No. 195500). Washington, DC: U.S. Department of Justice.

Office for Victims of Crime. (2002b). *Strengthening antistalking statutes* (NCJ Publication No. 189192). Washington, DC: U.S. Department of Justice.

Office of Juvenile Justice and Delinquency Prevention. (1995). *OJJDP fact sheet* (No. 21). Rockville, MD: Juvenile Justice Clearinghouse.

Ogg, J., & Bennett, G. C. J. (1992). Elder abuse in Britain. *British Medical Journal, 305,* 998–999.

O'Hagan, K. (1993). *Emotional and psychological abuse of children.* Toronto: University of Toronto Press.

O'Hagan, K. (1995). Emotional and psychological abuse: Problems of definition. *Child Abuse & Neglect, 19,* 449–461.

O'Hearn, R. E., & Davis, K. E. (1997). Women's experience of giving and receiving emotional abuse. *Journal of Interpersonal Violence, 12,* 375–391.

Ohlin, L., & Tonry, M. (1989). Family violence in perspective. In L. Ohlin & M. Tonry (Eds.), *Violence in marriage* (pp. 1–18). Chicago: University of Chicago Press.

O'Keefe, M. (1994). Adjustment of children from maritally violent homes. *Families in Society, 75,* 403–415.

O'Keefe, M. (1997). Predictors of dating violence. *Journal of Interpersonal Violence, 12,* 546–568.

O'Keefe, M. (1998). Factors mediating the link between witnessing interparental violence and dating violence. *Journal of Family Violence, 13,* 39–57.

O'Keefe, M., & Treister, L. (1998). Victims of dating violence among high school students. *Violence Against Women, 4,* 195–223.

Okun, L. E. (1986). *Woman abuse: Facts replacing myths.* Albany: State University of New York Press.

Oldham, J., Clarkin, J., Appelbaum, A., Carr, A., Kernberg, P., Lotterman, A., et al. (1985). A self-report instrument for borderline personality organization. In T. H. McGlasham (Ed.), *The borderline: Current empirical research* (pp. 1–18). Washington, DC: American Psychiatric Press.

Olds, D. L. (1997). The Prenatal/Early Infancy Project: Preventing child abuse and neglect in the context of promoting maternal and child health. In D. A. Wolfe, R. J. McMahon, & R. D. Peters (Eds.), *Child abuse: New directions in prevention and treatment across the lifespan* (pp. 130–154). Thousand Oaks, CA: Sage.

Olds, D. L., Henderson, C. R., Tatelbaum, R., & Chamberlain, R. (1986). Preventing child abuse and neglect: A randomized trial of nurse home visitation. *Pediatrics, 78,* 65–68.

O'Leary, K. D. (1993). Through a psychological lens: Personality traits, personality disorders, and levels of violence. In R. J. Gelles & D. R. Loseke (Eds.), *Current controversies on family violence* (pp. 7–30). Newbury Park, CA: Sage.

O'Leary, K. D. (1996). Physical aggression in intimate relationships can be treated within a marital context under certain circumstances. *Journal of Interpersonal Violence, 11,* 450–452.

O'Leary, K. D. (1999). Psychological abuse: A variable deserving critical attention in domestic violence. *Violence and Victims, 14,* 3–23.

O'Leary, K. D., Barling, J., Arias, I., Rosenbaum, A., Malone, J., & Tyree, A. (1989). Prevalence and stability of physical aggression between spouses: A longitudinal analysis. *Journal of Consulting and Clinical Psychology, 57,* 263–268.

O'Leary, K. D., & Curley, A. D. (1986). Assertion and family violence: Correlates of spouse abuse. *Journal of Marital and Family Therapy, 12,* 281–289.

O'Leary, K. D., Slep, A. M. S., & O'Leary, S. (2000). Co-occurrence of partner and parent aggression: Research and treatment implications. *Behavior Therapy, 31,* 631–648.

Olinger, J. P. (1991). Elder abuse: The outlook for federal legislation. *Journal of Elder Abuse & Neglect, 3*(1), 43–52.

Olson, D. H. L. (1985). *FACES III.* Minneapolis: University of Minnesota Press.

Olson, G. (n.d.). *So you want to be a foster parent?* National Foster Parent Association. Retrieved December 5, 2003, from http://www.nfpainc.org

Olson, J. M., Vernon, P. A., Jang, K. L., & Harris, J. A. (2001). The heritability of attitudes: A study of twins. *Journal of Personality and Social Psychology, 80,* 845–860.

O'Malley, H. C., Segel, H. D., & Perez, R. (1979). *Elder abuse in Massachusetts: Survey of professionals and paraprofessionals.* Boston: Legal Research and Services to the Elderly.

Ondersma, S. J., Simpson, S. M., Brestan, E. V., & Ward, M. (2000). Prenatal drug exposure and social policy: The search for an appropriate response. *Child Maltreatment, 5,* 93–108.

O'Neal, M. F., & Dorn, P. W. (1998). Effects of time and an educational presentation on student attitudes toward wife-beating. *Violence and Victims, 13,* 149–157.

O'Neil, J. M., & Harway, M. (1999). Revised multivariate model explaining men's risk factors for violence against women. In M. Harway & J. M. O'Neil (Eds.), *What causes men's violence against women?* (pp. 207–241). Thousand Oaks, CA: Sage.

O'Neill, D. (1998). A post-structuralist review of the theoretical literature surrounding wife abuse. *Violence Against Women, 4,* 457–490.

Orb, A., Eisenhauer, L., & Wynaden, D. (2000). Ethics in qualitative research. *Journal of Nursing Scholarship, 33,* 93–96.

Orchowsky, S., & Weiss, J. (2000). Domestic violence and sexual assault data collection systems in the United States. *Violence Against Women, 6,* 904–911.

Orgata, S. (1988). *Familial Experiences Interview.* Unpublished manuscript, University of Michigan, Ann Arbor.

Orlov, R. (1997, July 24). Violence may cost officers. *Los Angeles Daily News,* p. 4.

Orr, D. A. (2000). *Weind v. State* and the battered woman syndrome: The toothless tigress can now roar. *Florida Coastal Law Journal, 2,* 125–139.

Ortiz, E. T. (1998). Female genital mutilation and public health: Lessons from the British experience. *Health Care for Women International, 19,* 119–129.

Osherson, S., & Krugman, S. (1990). Men, shame, and psychotherapy. *Psychotherapy, 27,* 327–339.

Osmond, M., Durham, D., Leggett, A., & Keating, J. (1998). *Treating the aftermath of sexual abuse: A handbook for working with children in care.* Washington, DC: Child Welfare League of America.

Osofsky, J. D. (1995). The effects of violence exposure on young children. *American Psychologist, 50,* 782–788.

Osofsky, J. D. (Ed.). (1997). *Children in a violent society.* New York: Guilford.

Osofsky, J. D. (1998). Children as invisible victims of domestic and community violence. In G. W. Holden, R. A. Geffner, & E. N. Jouriles (Eds.), *Children exposed to marital violence: Theory, research, and applied issues* (pp. 95–117). Washington, DC: American Psychological Association.

Osofsky, J. D. (1999). The impact of violence on children. *Future of Children, 9*(3), 33–49.

Osofsky, J. D. (2003). Prevalence of children's exposure to domestic violence and child maltreatment: Implications for prevention and intervention. *Clinical Child and Family Psychology Review, 6,* 161–170.

Osofsky, J. D., Wewers, S., Hann, D., & Fick, A. (1993). Chronic community violence: What is happening to our children? *Psychiatry, 56,* 36–45.

Ost, J. (2003). Seeking the middle ground in the "memory wars." *British Journal of Psychology, 94,* 125–139.

Ostroff, C., & Atwater, L. E. (2003). Does whom you work with matter? Effects of referent group gender and age composition on managers' compensation. *Journal of Applied Psychology, 88,* 725–740.

Otiniano, M., Herrera, C., & Teasdale, T. (1998). Hispanic elder abuse. In Archstone Foundation (Ed.), *Understanding and combating elder abuse in minority communities.* Long Beach, CA: Archstone Foundation.

Otto, J. M. (2000, May/June). Fitting elder abuse into the family violence continuum. *Victimization of the Elderly and Disabled, 3,* 5–6.

Otto, J. M., & Quinn, K. (1999, January/February). The National Elder Abuse Incidence Study: An evaluation by the National Association of Adult Protective Services Administrators. *Victimization of the Elderly and Disabled, 2,* 4.

Otto, R. K., & Melton, G. B. (1990). Trends in legislation and case law on child abuse and neglect. In R. T. Ammerman & M. Hersen (Eds.), *Children at risk: An evaluation of factors contributing to child abuse and neglect* (pp. 55–83). New York: Plenum.

Overholser, J. C., & Beck, S. J. (1989). The classification of rapists and child molesters. *Journal of Offender Counseling, Services & Rehabilitation, 13,* 15–25.

Overman, W. H. (1992). Preventing elder abuse and neglect through advance legal planning. *Journal of Elder Abuse & Neglect, 3*(4), 5–21.

Padgett, T. (2002, July 22). Is Florida bad for kids? *Time,* p. 27.

Pagelow, M. D. (1981). *Woman-battering: Victims and their experiences.* Beverly Hills, CA: Sage.

Pagelow, M. D. (1984). *Family violence.* New York: Praeger.

Pagelow, M. D. (1992). Adult victims of domestic violence. *Journal of Interpersonal Violence, 7,* 87–120.

Paget, K. D., Philp, J. D., & Abramczyk, L. W. (1993). Recent developments in child neglect. In T. H. Ollendick & R. J. Prinz (Eds.), *Advances in clinical child psychology* (Vol. 15, pp. 121–174). New York: Plenum.

Palmer, S., Brown, R., & Barrera, M. (1992). Group treatment program for abusive husbands: Long-term evaluation. *American Journal of Orthopsychiatry, 62,* 276–283.

Pan, H. S., Neidig, P. H., & O'Leary, K. D. (1994). Predicting mild and severe husband-to-wife physical aggression. *Journal of Consulting and Clinical Psychology, 62,* 975–981.

Paolucci, E. O., Genuis, M. L., & Violato, C. (2001). A meta-analysis of the published research on the effects of child sexual abuse. *Journal of Psychology, 135,* 17–36.

Paquet, J., Damant, D., Beaudoin, G., & Proulx, S. (1998, July). *Domestic violence: Legal process and process of empowerment.* Paper presented at Program Evaluation and Family Violence Research: An International Conference, Durham, NH.

Parents guilty in child-abuse case. (2003, August 21). *Richmond Times Dispatch,* p. B2.

Paris, J. (2001). Why behavioral genetics is important for psychiatry [Editorial]. *Canadian Journal of Psychiatry, 46,* 223–224.

Parish, R. A., Myers, P. A., Brandner, A., & Templin, K. H. (1985). Developmental milestones in abused children, and their improvement with a family-oriented approach to the treatment of child abuse. *Child Abuse & Neglect, 9,* 245–250.

Parke, R. D. (2002). Punishment revisited: Science, values, and the right question—Comment on Gershoff (2002). *Psychological Bulletin, 128,* 596–601.

Parke, R. D., & Collmer, C. W. (1975). Child abuse: An interdisciplinary analysis. In E. M. Hetherington (Ed.), *Review of child development research* (Vol. 5, pp. 509–590). Chicago: University of Chicago Press.

Parker, G., & Lee, C. (2002). Predictors of physical and emotional health in a sample of abused Australian women. *Journal of Interpersonal Violence, 17,* 987–1001.

Parker, J. G., & Herrera, C. (1996). Interpersonal processes in friendship: A comparison of abused and nonabused children's experiences. *Developmental Psychology, 32,* 1025–1038.

Parker, L. S. (1997). A "brutal case" or "only a family jar"?: Violence against women in San Diego County, 1880–1900. *Violence Against Women, 3,* 294–318.

Parrott, D. J., & Zeichner, A. (2003). Effects of hypermasculinity on physical aggression against women. *Psychology of Men & Masculinity, 4*(1), 70–78.

Paschall, M. J., & Fishbein, D. H. (2002). Executive cognitive functioning and aggression: A public health perspective. *Aggression and Violent Behavior, 7,* 215–235.

Passantino, G., Passantino, B., & Trott, J. (1990). Satan's sideshow. *Cornerstone, 90,* 24–28.

Patterson, G. R. (1982). *Coercive family process.* Eugene, OR: Castalia.

Paulozzi, L. J., Saltzman, L. E., Thompson, M. P., & Holmgreen, P. (2001, October 12). Surveillance for homicide among intimate partners—United States, 1981–1998. *Morbidity and Mortality Weekly Report, 50,* 1–15.

Paveza, G. J. (1988). Risk factors in father-daughter child sexual abuse: A case-control study. *Journal of Interpersonal Violence, 3,* 290–306.

Paveza, G. J., Cohen, D., Eisdorfer, C., Freels, S., Semla, T., Ashford, J. W., et al. (1992). Severe family violence and Alzheimer's disease: Prevalence and risk factors. *Gerontologist, 32,* 493–497.

Pearce, J. W., & Pezzot-Pearce, T. D. (1997). *Psychotherapy of abused and neglected children.* New York: Guilford.

Pearlman, L. A., & MacIan, P. S. (1995). Vicarious traumatization: An empirical study of the effects of trauma work on trauma therapists. *Professional Psychology: Research and Practice, 26,* 558–565.

Pearson, J., Thoennes, N., & Griswold, E. A. (1999). Child support and domestic violence: The victims speak out. *Violence Against Women, 5,* 427–448.

Peduzzi, J. J., Watzlaf, V. J. M., Rohrer, W. M., III, & Rubinstein, E. N. (1997). A survey of nursing home administrators' and ombudsmen's perceptions of elderly abuse in Pennsylvania. *Topics in Health Information Management, 18*(1), 68–76.

Pelcovitz, D., Kaplan, S., Goldenberg, B., & Mandel, F. (1994). Posttraumatic stress disorder in physically abused adolescents. *Journal of the American Academy of Child and Adolescent Psychiatry, 33,* 305–312.

Peled, E., & Davis, D. (1995). *Groupwork with children: A practitioner's manual.* Thousand Oaks, CA: Sage.

Peled, E., & Edleson, J. L. (1992). Multiple perspectives on groupwork with children of battered women. *Violence and Victims, 7,* 327–346.

Peled, E., Eisikovits, Z., Enosh, G., & Winstok, Z. (2000). Choice and empowerment for battered women who stay. *Social Work, 45,* 9–25.

Peled, E., Jaffe, P. G., & Edleson, J. L. (Eds.). (1994). *Ending the cycle of violence: Community responses to children of battered women.* Thousand Oaks, CA: Sage.

Pelligrini, K. L. (2000). Analysis of a violence intervention program: Population, treatment compliance and recidivism. *Dissertation Abstracts International, 60*(10), 5231B.

Pelton, L. H. (1982). Personalistic attributions and client perspectives in child welfare cases: Implications for service delivery. In T. A. Willis (Ed.), *Basic processes in helping relationships* (pp. 81–101). New York: Academic Press.

Pelton, L. H. (1994). The role of material factors in child abuse and neglect. In G. B. Melton & F. D. Barry (Eds.), *Protecting children from abuse and neglect* (pp. 166–181). New York: Guilford.

Pence, D., & Wilson, C. (1994). *Team investigation of child sexual abuse: Uneasy alliance.* Thousand Oaks, CA: Sage.

Pence, E., & Paymar, M. (1993). *Education groups for men who batter: The Duluth model.* New York: Springer.

Penley, J. A., Tomaka, J., & Wiebe, J. S. (2002). The association of coping to physical and psychological health outcomes: A meta-analytic review. *Journal of Behavioral Medicine, 25,* 551–603.

Perez, C. M., & Widom, C. S. (1994). Childhood victimization and long-term intellectual and academic outcomes. *Child Abuse & Neglect, 18,* 617–633.

Perilla, J. L., Bakeman, R., & Norris, F. H. (1994). Culture and domestic violence: The ecology of abused Latinas. *Violence and Victims, 9,* 325–339.

Perrin, R. D., & Miller-Perrin, C. L. (2004). *Statistical claims-making in family violence advocacy.* Paper presented at the annual meeting of the Pacific Sociological Association, San Francisco.

Perris, C., Jacobsson, L., Lindstrom, H., von Knorring, L., & Perris, H. (1980). Development of a new inventory for assessing memories of parental rearing behavior. *Acta Psychiatrica Scandinavica, 61,* 265–274.

Perry, N. W., & McAuliff, B. D. (1993). The use of videotaped child testimony: Public policy implications. *Notre Dame Journal of Law, Ethics, and Public Policy, 7,* 387–422.

Perry, N. W. (1992). How children remember and why they forget. *APSAC Advisor, 5*(3), 1–2, 13–16.

Peters, D., & Range, L. (1995). Childhood sexual abuse and current suicidality in college women and men. *Child Abuse & Neglect, 19,* 335–341.

Peters, J., Dinsmore, J., & Toth, P. (1989). Why prosecute child abuse? *South Dakota Law Review, 34,* 649–659.

Peters, J. M. (1989). Criminal prosecution of child abuse: Recent trends. *Pediatric Annals, 18,* 505-509.

Peterson, E. S. L. (1999). Murder as self-help: Women and intimate partner homicide. *Homicide Studies, 3,* 30–46.

Peterson, L., Tremblay, G., Ewigman, B., & Saldana, L. (2003). Multilevel selected primary prevention of child maltreatment. *Journal of Consulting and Clinical Psychology, 71,* 601–612.

Peugh, J., & Belenko, S. (2001). Examining the substance use patterns and treatment needs of incarcerated sex offenders. *Sexual Abuse, 13*(3), 179–195.

Pfeifer, S. (2002, November 21). Tough love or abuse? *Los Angeles Times,* p. A1.

Pfeifer, S., & Anton, M. (2002, December 17). Parents' action not conspiracy, jury says. *Los Angeles Times,* p. B1.

Pfohl, S. J. (1977). The "discovery" of child abuse. *Social Problems, 24,* 310–323.

Phelan, P. (1995). Incest and its meaning: The perspectives of fathers and daughters. *Child Abuse & Neglect, 19,* 7–24.

Phillips, L. R. (1996) *Final report of the causal and cultural factors affecting the quality of family caregiving project.* Unpublished manuscript, University of Arizona, Tucson.

Phillips, L. R., Torres de Ardon, E., & Briones, G. S. (2000). Abuse of female caregivers by care recipients: Another form of elder abuse. *Journal of Elder Abuse and Neglect, 12*(3/4), 123–143.

Phillipson, C. (1992). Confronting elder abuse: Fact and fiction. *Generations Review, 2,* 3.

Phillipson, C. (1993). Abuse of older people: Sociological perspectives. In P. Decalmer & F. Glendenning (Eds.), *The mistreatment of elderly people* (pp. 88–101). London: Sage.

Physical violence and injuries in intimate relationships—New York, Behavioral Risk Factor Surveillance System, 1994. (1996). *Morbidity and Mortality Weekly Report, 45,* 765–767.

Pianta, R. C., & Egeland, B. (1994). Relation between depressive symptoms and stressful life events in a sample of disadvantaged mothers. *Journal of Consulting and Clinical Psychology, 62,* 1229–1234.

Pierce, R., & Pierce, L. (1985). The sexually abused child: A comparison of male and female victims. *Child Abuse & Neglect, 9,* 191–199.

Pierce, R. L. (1984). Child pornography: A hidden dimension of child abuse. *Child Abuse & Neglect, 8,* 483–493.

Piers, M. W. (1978). *Infanticide: Past and present.* New York: Norton.

Pillemer, K. A. (1986). Risk factors in elder abuse: Results from a case-control study. In K. A. Pillemer & R. S. Wolf (Eds.), *Elder abuse: Conflict in the family* (pp. 236–263). Dover, MA: Auburn House.

Pillemer, K. A. (1993). The abused offspring are dependent: Abuse is caused by the deviance and dependence of abusive caregivers. In R. J. Gelles & D. R. Loseke (Eds.), *Current controversies on family violence* (pp. 237–249). Newbury Park, CA: Sage.

Pillemer, K. A., & Bachman, R. (1991). Helping and hurting: Predictors of maltreatment of patients in nursing homes. *Research on Aging, 13,* 74–95.

Pillemer, K. A., & Finkelhor, D. (1988). The prevalence of elder abuse A random sample survey. *Gerontologist, 28,* 51–57.

Pillemer, K. A., & Hudson, B. (1993). A model abuse prevention program for nursing assistants. *Gerontologist, 33,* 128–131.

Pine, D. S., & Cohen, J. A. (2002). Trauma in children and adolescents Risk and treatment of psychiatric sequelae. *Biological Psychiatry, 51,* 519–531.

Pipher, M. (1994). *Reviving Ophelia: Saving the selves of adolescent girls.* New York: Ballantine.

Pirog-Good, M. A., & Stets, J. E. (1986). Programs for abusers: Who drops out and what can be done. *Response, 9*(2), 17–19.

Pithers, W., & Kafka, M. (1990). Relapse prevention with sex aggressors: A method for maintaining therapeutic gain and enhancing external supervision. In W. L. Marshall, D. R. Laws, & H. E. Barbaree (Eds.), *Handbook of sexual assault: Issues theories, and treatment of the offender* (pp. 343–361) New York: Plenum.

Pitsiou-Darrough, E. N., & Spinellis, C. D. (1995). Mistreatment of the elderly in Greece. In J. I. Kosberg & J. L. Garcia (Eds., *Elder abuse: International and cross-cultural perspective* (pp. 45–64). Binghamton, NY: Haworth.

Pittman, A. L., Wolfe, D. A., & Wekerle, C. (1998). Prevention during adolescence: The Youth Relationship Project. In J. R. Lutzke (Ed.), *Handbook of child abuse research and treatment* (pp. 341–356). New York: Plenum.

Pittman, F. (1987). *Turning points: Treating families in transition and crisis.* New York: Norton.

Pitzner, J. K., & Drummond, P. D. (1997). The reliability and validity of empirically scaled measures of psychological/verbal control and physical/sexual abuse: Relationship between mood and history of abuse independent of other negative events. *Journal of Psychonomic Research, 43,* 125–142.

Pizzey, E. (1974). *Scream quietly or the neighbours will hear.* Harmondsworth: Penguin.

Pleck, E. (1987). *Domestic tyranny: The making of American social policy against family violence from colonial times to present.* New York: Oxford University Press.

Pledger, C. (2003). Discourse on disability and rehabilitation issues Opportunities for psychology. *American Psychologist, 5* 279–284.

Podnieks, E. (1992). National survey on abuse of the elderly Canada. *Journal of Elder Abuse & Neglect, 4*(5), 5–58.

Poertner, J., Bussey, M., & Fluke, J. (1999). How safe are out-of-home placements? *Children and Youth Services Review, 21,* 549–563.

Poitras, M., & Lavoie, F. (1995). A study of the prevalence of sexual coercion in adolescent heterosexual dating relations in a Quebec sample. *Violence and Victims, 10,* 299–313.

Polansky, N. A., Ammons, P. W., & Gaudin, J. M. (1985). Loneliness and isolation in child neglect. *Social Casework, 66,* 38–47.

Polansky, N. A., Ammons, P. W., & Weathersby, B. L. (1983). Is there an American standard of child care? *Social Work, 28,* 341–346.

Polansky, N. A., Chalmers, M. A., & Williams, D. P. (1987). Assessing adequacy of rearing: An urban scale. *Child Welfare, 57,* 439–448.

Polansky, N. A., Gaudin, J. M., Ammons, P. W., & Davis, K. B. (1985). The psychological ecology of the neglectful mother. *Child Abuse & Neglect, 9,* 265–275.

Polansky, N. A., Gaudin, J. M., & Kilpatrick, A. C. (1992). The maternal characteristics scale: A cross-validation. *Child Welfare League of America, 71,* 271–280.

Polansky, N. A., & Williams, D. P. (1978). Class orientation to child neglect. *Social Work, 23,* 397–401.

Police agencies lack experience investigating cyberstalking. (2001). *Criminal Justice Newsletter, 31*(19), 6–7.

Pollack, D. (1995). Elder abuse and neglect cases reviewed by appellate courts. *Journal of Family Violence, 10,* 413–424.

Pollak, S. D., Cicchetti, D., Hornung, K., & Reed, A. (2000). Recognizing emotion in faces: Developmental effects of child abuse and neglect. *Developmental Psychology, 36,* 679–688.

Pontius, A. A. (2002). Impact of fear-inducing violence on neuropsychological visuo-spatial test in warring hunter-gatherers: Analogies to violent Western environments. *Aggression and Violent Behavior, 7,* 69–84.

Popejoy, L. L., Rantz, M. J., Conn, V., Wipke-Tevis, D., Grando, V. T., & Porter, R. (2000). Improving quality of care in nursing facilities. *Journal of Gerontological Nursing, 26*(4), 6–13.

Porch, T. L., & Petretic-Jackson, P. A. (1986, August). *Child sexual assault prevention: Evaluating parent education workshops.* Paper presented at the annual meeting of the American Psychological Association, Washington, DC.

Portwood, S. G. (1999). Coming to terms with a consensual definition of child maltreatment. *Child Maltreatment, 4,* 56–68.

Powers, J. L., & Eckenrode, J. (1988). The maltreatment of adolescents. *Child Abuse & Neglect, 12,* 189–199.

Prendergast, W. E. (1979). The sex offender: How to spot him before it is too late. *Sexology,* pp. 46–51.

Preston, S. (1984). Children and elderly in the U.S. *Scientific American, 251*(6), 44–49.

Price, J. L., Hilsenroth, M. J., Petretic-Jackson, P. A., & Bonge, D. (2001). A review of individual psychotherapy outcomes for adult survivors of childhood sexual abuse. *Clinical Psychology Review, 21,* 1095–1121.

Prino, C. T., & Peyrot, M. (1994). The effect of child physical abuse and neglect on aggressive, withdrawn, and prosocial behavior. *Child Abuse & Neglect, 18,* 871–884.

Procci, W. R. (1990). *Medical aspects of human sexuality.* New York: Cahners.

Ptacek, J. (1999). *Battered women in the courtroom: The power of judicial responses.* Boston: Northeastern University Press.

Public health and aging: Nonfatal physical assault-related injuries among persons aged > 60 years treated in hospital emergency departments—United States, 2001. (2003). *Morbidity and Mortality Weekly Report, 52,* 812–816.

Pulido, M. L., & Gupta, D. (2002). Protecting the child and the family: Integrating domestic violence screening into a child advocacy center. *Violence Against Women, 8,* 917–933.

Purewal, J., & Ganesh, I. (2000). Gender violence, trauma, and its impact on women's mental health. *Journal of Indian Social Work, 61,* 542–557.

Purillo, K. M., Freeman, R. C., & Young, P. (2003). Association between child sexual abuse and sexual revictimization in adulthood among women sex partners of injection drug users. *Violence and Victims, 18,* 493–484.

Putnam, F. W. (1991). The satanic ritual abuse controversy. *Child Abuse & Neglect, 15,* 175–179.

Putnam, F. W., Helmers, K., & Trickett, P. K. (1993). Development, reliability, and validation of a child dissociation scale. *Child Abuse & Neglect, 17,* 731–740.

Putnam, R. (2000). *Bowling alone: The collapse and revival of American community.* New York: Simon & Schuster.

Pynoos, R. S., Frederick, C., Nader, K., & Arroyo, W. (1987). Life threat and posttraumatic stress in school-age children. *Archives of General Psychiatry, 44,* 1057–1063.

Quigley, M. M., & Tedeschi, J. T. (1996). Mediating effects of blame attributions on feelings of anger. *Personality and Social Psychology Bulletin, 22,* 1280–1288.

Quin, A. S. (1999). Imposing federal criminal liability on nursing homes: A way of deterring inadequate health care and improving the quality of care delivered. *Saint Louis University Law Journal, 43,* 653–693.

Quinn, M. J. (1985). Elder abuse and neglect. *Generations, 10*(2), 22–25.

Quinsey, V. L., Chaplin, T. C., & Carrigan, W. F. (1979). Sexual preferences among incestuous and nonincestuous child molesters. *Behavior Therapy, 10,* 562–565.

Quinsey, V. L., Harris, G. T., Rice, M. E., & Lalumiere, M. L. (1993). Assessing treatment efficacy in outcome studies of sex offenders. *Journal of Interpersonal Violence, 8,* 512–523.

Quittner, A. L., & Opipari, L. C. (1994). Differential treatment of siblings: Interview and diary analyses comparing two family contexts. *Child Development, 65,* 800–814.

Rabinowitz, D. (1990, May). From the mouths of babes to a jail cell: Child abuse and the abuse of justice—a case study. *Harper's, 280,* 52–63.

Radke-Yarrow, M., & Klimes-Dougan, B. (2002). Parental depression and offspring disorders: A developmental perspective. In S. H. Goodman & I. H. Gotlib (Eds.), *Children of depressed parents: Mechanisms of risk and implications for treatment* (pp. 155–173). Washington, DC: American Psychological Association.

Radosevich, A. C. (2000). Thwarting the stalker: Are anti-stalking measures keeping pace with today's stalker? *University of Illinois Law Review, 2000,* 1371–1395.

Raine, A. (1993). *The psychopathology of crime: Criminal behavior as a clinical disorder.* San Diego, CA: Academic Press.

Raj, A., & Silverman, J. (2002). Violence against immigrant women: The roles of culture, context, and legal immigrant status on intimate partner violence. *Violence Against Women, 8,* 367–398.

Ramsey-Klawsnik, H. (1991). Elder sexual abuse: Preliminary findings. *Journal of Elder Abuse & Neglect, 3*(3), 73–90.

Rand, M. R. (1997). *Violence-related injuries treated in hospital emergency departments* (NCJ Publication No. 156921). Rockville, MD: U.S. Department of Justice.

Randolf, M. K., & Conkle, L. K. (1993). Behavioral and emotional characteristics of children who witness parental violence. *Family Violence and Sexual Assault Bulletin, 9*(2), 23–27.

Rapaport, K., & Burkhart, B. R. (1984). Personality and attitudinal characteristics of sexually coercive college males. *Journal of Abnormal Psychology, 93,* 216–227.

Raphael, J., & Tolman, R. M. (1997). *Trapped by poverty/trapped by abuse: New evidence documents the relationship between domestic violence and welfare* (A research compilation from the Project for Research on Welfare, Work, and Domestic Violence, a collaborative project). Ann Arbor: Taylor Institute and University of Michigan.

Rathus, J. H., & O'Leary, K. D. (1997). Spouse-Specific Dependency Scale: Scale development. *Journal of Family Violence, 12,* 159–168.

Rausch, S. L., van der Kolk, B. A., Fisler, R. F., & Alpert, N. M. (1996). A symptom provocation study of posttraumatic stress disorder using positron emission tomography and script-driven imagery. *Archives of General Psychiatry, 53,* 380–387.

Rawlings, E. I., Allen, G., Graham, D. L. R., & Peters, J. (1994). Chinks in the prison wall: Applying Graham's Stockholm syndrome theory in the treatment of battered women. In L. Vandecreek, S. Knapp, & T. L. Jackson (Eds.), *Innovations in clinical practice: A source book* (Vol. 13, pp. 401–417). Sarasota, FL: Professional Resource Press.

Ray, K. C., Jackson, J. L., & Townsley, R. M. (1991). Family environments of victims of intrafamilial and extrafamilial child sexual abuse. *Journal of Family Violence, 6,* 365–374.

Reay, A. C., & Browne, K. D. (2002). The effectiveness of psychological interventions with individuals who physically abuse or neglect their elderly dependents. *Journal of Interpersonal Violence, 17,* 416–431.

Rebovich, D. J. (1996). Prosecution response to domestic violence: Results of a survey of large jurisdictions. In E. S. Buzawa & C. G. Buzawa (Eds.), *Do arrests and restraining orders work?* (pp. 176–191). Thousand Oaks, CA: Sage.

Records show uneven domestic violence effort. (1994, September 25). *Boston Globe,* pp. 1, 28–29.

Reed, D. (1999). Where's the penalty flag? A call for the NCAA to promulgate an eligibility rule revoking a male student-athlete's ability to participate in intercollegiate athletics for committing violent acts against women. *Women's Rights Law Reporter, 21,* 41–56.

Regehr, C. (1990). Parental responses to extrafamilial child sexual assault. *Child Abuse & Neglect, 14,* 113–120.

Regoczzi, W. C. (2001). Exploring racial variations in the spousal sex ratio of killing. *Violence and Victims, 16,* 591–606.

Reis, M. (2000). The IOA Screen: An abuse-alert measure that dispels myths. *Generations, 24*(6), 13–16.

Reitan, R. M. (1984a). *Aphasia and sensory-perceptual deficits in adults.* Tucson, AZ: Reitan Neuropsychology Laboratory.

Reitan, R. M. (1984b). *Aphasia and sensory-perceptual deficits in children.* Tucson, AZ: Neuropsychology Press.

Reitan, R. M. (1988). *Halstead-Reitan Neuropsychological Test batteries.* Tucson, AZ: Reitan Neuropsychology Laboratories.

Reitzel-Jaffe, D., & Wolfe, D. A. (2001). Predictors of relationship abuse among young men. *Journal of Interpersonal Violence, 16,* 99–115.

Religion; Psychiatrist's appointment to abuse panel criticized; Catholics: Some victims' advocates oppose the expert, who is against patient therapy based on recovered memory. (2002, September 14). *Los Angeles Times,* p. B23.

Rempel, J. K., Holmes, J. G., & Zanna, M. P. (1985). Trust in clos relationships. *Journal of Personality and Social Psychology, 49* 95–112.

Rendon, R., & Horswell, C. (2003, August 23). CPS fires caseworke for not reporting abuse tip. *Houston Chronicle,* p. A1.

Renk, K., Liljequist, L., Steinberg, A., Bosco, G., & Phares, V. (2002 Prevention of child sexual abuse: Are we doing enough *Trauma, Violence, & Abuse, 3,* 68–84.

Renninger, S. M., Veach, P. M., & Bagdade, P. (2002). Psychologist knowledge, opinions, and decision-making processes regard ing child abuse and neglect reporting laws. *Profession Psychology: Research and Practice, 33,* 19–23.

Rennison, C. M. (2001). *Intimate partner violence and age of victi 1993–1999* (NCJ Publication No. 187635). Washington D U.S. Department of Justice.

Rennison, C. M. (2003). *Intimate partner violence, 1993–2001* (N Publication No. 197838). Washington, DC: U.S. Department Justice.

Rennison, C. M., & Planty, M. (2003). Nonlethal intimate partner vi lence: Examining race, gender, and income patterns. *Violen and Victims, 18,* 433–443.

Rennison, C. M., & Welchans, S. (2000). *Intimate partner violen* (NCJ Publication No. 178247). Washington, DC: U. Department of Justice.

Reno, J. (1994). Foreword. *APSAC Advisor, 7*(4), 1.

Renzetti, C. M. (1992). *Violent betrayal: Partner abuse in lesbian rel tionships.* Newbury Park, CA: Sage.

Reppucci, N. D., Land, D., & Haugaard, J. J. (1998). Child sexual abu prevention programs that target young children. In P. Trickett & C. J. Schellenbach (Eds.), *Violence against childr in the family and the community* (pp. 317–337). Washingt DC: American Psychological Association.

Reulbach, D. M., & Tewksbury, J. (1994). Collaboration between pr tective services and law enforcement: The Massachuse model. *Journal of Elder Abuse & Neglect, 6*(2), 9–21.

Rew, L., & Esparza, D. (1990). Barriers to disclosure among sexua abused male children. *Journal of Child and Adolesc Psychiatric and Mental Health Nursing, 3,* 120–127.

Reyes, K. (1999, Spring). Domestic violence prevention for cle proves slow-going. *Focus, 4,* 1–3.

Reyna, P. (1999). Confronting violence against women with disab ties. *Update* (Newsletter of the Statewide California Coaliti for Battered Women), *5*(6), 13.

Rhodes, N. R., & McKenzie, E. B. (1998). Why do battered wor stay? Three decades of research. *Aggression and Viol Behavior, 3,* 391–406.

Rice, F. P. (1998). *Human development: A lifespan approach* (3rd e Upper Saddle River, NJ: Prentice Hall.

Rich, A. (1976). *Of woman born.* New York: Norton.

Richardson, D. R., Hammock, G. S., Smith, S. M., Gardner, W. Signo, M. (1994). Empathy as a cognitive inhibitor of aggr sion. *Aggressive Behavior, 20,* 275–289.

Richardson, J., Best, J., & Bromley, D. (Eds.). (1991). *The satan scare.* New York: Aldine de Gruyter.

Richters, J. E., & Martinez, P. (1990). *Things I have seen and hear structured interview for assessing young children's viole exposure.* Rockville, MD: National Institute of Mental Heal

Richters, J. E., & Martinez, P. (1993a). The NIMH Commur Violence Project: Children as victims and witnesses to lence. In D. Reiss, J. E. Richters, M. Radke-Yarrow, & D. Sc (Eds.), *Children and violence* (pp. 7–21). New York: Guilfo

Richters, J. E., & Martinez, P. (1993b). Violent communities, family choices, and children's chances: An algorithm for improving the odds. *Development and Psychopathology, 5,* 609–627.

Richters, J. E., & Saltzman, W. (1990). *Survey of children's exposure to community violence: Parent report.* Rockville, MD: National Institute of Mental Health.

Rickert, V. I., Sanghvi, R., & Wiemann, C. M. (2002). Is lack of sexual assertiveness among adolescent and young adult women a cause for concern? *Perspectives on Sexual and Reproductive Health, 34,* 178–183.

Ridington, J. (1989). *Beating the "odds": Violence and women with disabilities* (Position paper). Vancouver: DisAbled Women's Network.

Riedel, M., & Best, J. (1998). Patterns in intimate partner homicide: California, 1987–1996. *Homicide Studies, 2,* 305–320.

Rigakos, G. S. (1995). Constructing the symbolic complainant: Police subculture and the nonenforcement of protection orders for battered women. *Violence and Victims, 10,* 227–247.

Riggs, D. S. (1993). Relationship problems and dating aggression: A potential treatment target. *Journal of Interpersonal Violence, 8,* 18–35.

Riggs, D. S., & Caulfield, M. B. (1997). Expected consequences of male violence against their female dating partners. *Journal of Interpersonal Violence, 12,* 229–240.

Riggs, D. S., Caulfield, M. B., & Street, A. E. (2000). Risk for domestic violence: Factors associated with perpetration and victimization. *Journal of Clinical Psychology, 56,* 1289–1316.

Riggs, D. S., Dowdall, D., & Kuhn, E. (1999, July). *Posttraumatic stress disorder, anger and relationship conflict as predictors of marital violence.* Paper presented at the Sixth International Family Violence Research Conference, Durham, NH.

Riggs, D. S., Kilpatrick, D. G., & Resnick, H. S. (1992). Long-term psychological distress associated with marital rape and aggravated assault: A comparison to other crime victims. *Journal of Family Violence, 7,* 283–296.

Riggs, D. S., Murphy, C. M., & O'Leary, K. D. (1989). Intentional falsification in reports of interpartner aggression. *Journal of Interpersonal Violence, 4,* 220–232.

Riggs, D. S., O'Leary, K. D., & Breslin, F. C. (1990). Multiple correlates of physical aggression in dating couples. *Journal of Interpersonal Violence, 5,* 61–73.

Riley, N. E. (1996). China's "missing girls": Prospects and policy [Electronic version]. *Population Today, 24*(2), 4.

Rind, B., Tromovitch, P., & Bauserman, R. (1998). A meta-analytic examination of assumed properties of child sexual abuse using college samples. *Psychological Bulletin, 124,* 22–53.

Rindfleisch, N., & Nunno, M. (1992). Progress and issues in the implementation of the 1984 out-of-home care protection amendment. *Child Abuse & Neglect, 16,* 693–708.

Ritter, J., Stewart, M., Bernet, C., Coe, M., & Brown, S. A. (2002). Effects of childhood exposure to familial alcoholism and family violence on adolescent substance use, conduct problems, and self-esteem. *Journal of Traumatic Stress, 15,* 113–122.

Rix, K. (2001). Battered woman syndrome and the defense of provocation: Two women with something more in common. *Journal of Forensic Psychiatry, 12,* 131–139.

Robbins, K. (1999). No-drop prosecution of domestic violence: Just good policy, or equal protection mandate? *Stanford Law Review, 52,* 205–233.

Roberts, R. N., Wasik, B. H., Casto, G., & Ramey, C. T. (1991). Family support in the home: Programs, policy, and social change. *American Psychologist, 46,* 131–137.

Robinson, A. L., & Chandek, M. S. (2000). The domestic violence arrest decision: Examining demographic, attitudinal, and situational variables. *Crime & Delinquency, 46,* 18–37.

Robinson, M. B. (2002, November/December). An analysis of 2002 ACJS papers: What members presented about and they ignored. *ACJS Today, 22,* 1, 3–6.

Rodriguez, E., Lasch, K. E., Chandra, P., & Lee, J. (2001). Family violence, employment status, welfare benefits, and alcohol drinking in the United States: What is the relation? *Journal of Epidemiology and Community Health, 55,* 172–178.

Rodriguez, G., & Cortez, C. (1988). The evaluation experience of the Avanc, Parent-Child Education Program. In H. Weiss & F. Jacobs (Eds.), *Evaluating family programs* (pp. 287–302). New York: Aldine.

Rodriguez, S. F., & Henderson, V. A. (1995). Intimate homicide: Victim-offender relationship in female-perpetrated homicide. *Deviant Behavior, 16,* 45–57.

Rogan, M. T. (1997). Fear conditioning induces associative long-term potentiation in the amygdala. *Nature, 390,* 604–607.

Rogers, P., Krammer, L., Podesta, J. S., & Sellinger, M. (1998, August 31). Angry and hurt, but no quitter. *People,* pp. 61–62, 64.

Rogge, R. D., & Bradbury, T. N. (1999). Till violence does us part: The differing roles of communication and aggression in predicting adverse marital outcome. *Journal of Clinical and Consulting Psychology, 67,* 340–351.

Rogosch, F., Cicchetti, D, & Abre, J. L. (1995). The role of child maltreatment in early deviations in cognitive and affective processing abilities and later peer relationships problems. *Development and Psychopathology, 7,* 591–609.

Rohrbeck, C. A., & Twentyman, C. T. (1986). Multimodal assessment of impulsiveness in abusing, neglecting, and nonmaltreating mothers and their preschool children. *Journal of Consulting and Clinical Psychology, 54,* 231–236.

Roiphe, K. (1993). *The morning after: Sex, fear and feminism.* London: Hamish Hamilton.

Rollstin, A. O., & Kern, J. M. (1998). Correlates of battered women's psychological distress: Severity of abuse and duration of the postabuse period. *Psychological Reports, 82,* 387–394.

Roloff, M. E., Soule, K. P., & Carey, C. M. (2001). Reasons for remaining in a relationship and responses to relational transgressions. *Journal of Social and Personal Relationships, 18,* 362–385.

Romano, E., & De Luca, R. V. (2001). Male sexual abuse: A review of effects, abuse characteristics, and links with later psychological functioning. *Aggression and Violent Behavior, 6,* 55–78.

Romano, J. L., & Hage, S. M. (2000). Prevention and counseling psychology: Revitalizing commitments for the 21st century. *Counseling Psychologist, 28,* 733–763.

Romero, D., Chavkin, W., Wise, P. H., & Smith, L. A. (2003). Low-income mothers' experience with poor health, hardship, work, and violence. *Violence Against Women, 9,* 1231–1244.

Romero, J., & Williams, L. (1995). Recidivism among convicted sex offenders: A 10-year follow-up study. *Federal Probation, 49*(1), 58–64.

Romito, P., & Saurel-Cubizolles, M. J. (2001). The relationship between parents' violence against daughters and violence by other perpetrators. *Violence Against Women, 7,* 1429–1463.

Rondfeldt, H. M., Kimmerling, R., & Arias, I. (1998). Satisfaction with relationship power and perception of dating violence. *Journal of Marriage and the Family, 60,* 70–78.

Rorty, M., Yager, J., & Rossotto, E. (1994). Childhood sexual, physical, and psychological abuse in bulimia nervosa. *American Journal of Psychiatry, 151,* 1122–1126.

Roscoe, B., Goodwin, M. P., & Kennedy, D. (1987). Sibling violence and antagonistic interactions experienced by early adolescents. *Journal of Family Violence, 2,* 121–137.

Rose, L. E., Campbell, J., & Kub, J. (2000). The role of social support and family relationships in women's responses to battering. *Health Care for Women International, 21,* 27–30.

Rose, S., & Meezan, W. (1995). Child neglect: A study of the perceptions of mothers and child welfare workers. *Children and Youth Services Review, 17,* 471–486.

Rosen, K. H., & Stith, S. M. (1995). Women terminating abusive dating relationships: A qualitative study. *Journal of Social and Personal Relationships, 12,* 155–160.

Rosen, L. N., Kaminski, R. J., Parmley, A. M., Knudson, K. H., & Fancher, P. (2003). The effects of peer group climate on intimate partner violence among married male U.S. Army soldiers. *Violence Against Women, 9,* 1045–1071.

Rosen, L. N., Parmley, A. M., Knudson, K. H., & Fancher, P. (2002). Intimate partner violence among married males U.S. army soldiers: Ethnicity as a factor in self-reported perpetration and victimization. *Violence and Victims, 17,* 607–622.

Rosenbaum, A. (1988). Methodological issues in marital violence research. *Journal of Family Violence, 3,* 91–104.

Rosenbaum, A., & Hoge, S. K. (1989). Head injury and marital aggression. *American Journal of Psychiatry, 146,* 1048–1051.

Rosenbaum, A., & O'Leary, K. D. (1981). Marital violence: Characteristics of abusive couples. *Journal of Consulting and Clinical Psychology, 49,* 63–76.

Rosenberg, D. A. (1987). Web of deceit: A literature review of Munchausen syndrome by proxy. *Child Abuse & Neglect, 11,* 547–563.

Rosenberg, M. (1979). *Conceiving the self.* New York: Basic Books.

Rosenberg, M. S. (1987). New directions for research on psychological maltreatment of children. *American Psychologist, 42,* 166–171.

Rosenblatt, D. E. (1996). Documentation. In L. A. Baumhover & S. C. Beall (Eds.), *Abuse, neglect, and exploitation of older persons: Strategies for assessment and intervention* (pp. 145–161). Baltimore: Health Professions Press.

Rosenfeld, A. A., Bailey, R., Siegel, B., & Bailey, G. (1986). Determining incestuous contact between parent and child: Frequency of children touching parents' genitals in a nonclinical population. *Journal of the American Academy of Child Psychiatry, 25,* 481–484.

Rosenfeld, A. A., Siegel, B., & Bailey, R. (1987). Familial bathing patterns: Implications for cases of alleged molestation and for pediatric practice. *Pediatrics, 79,* 224–229.

Rosenfeld, B. D. (1992). Court-ordered treatment of spouse abuse. *Clinical Psychology Review, 12,* 205–226.

Rosenfeld, B. D. (2000). Assessment and treatment of obsessional harassment. *Aggression and Violent Behavior, 5,* 529–549.

Rosenthal, J. A., Motz, J. K., Edmonson, D. A., & Groze, V. (1991). A descriptive study of abuse and neglect in out-of-home placement. *Child Abuse & Neglect, 15,* 249–260.

Rosenthal, P. A., & Doherty, M. B. (1984). Serious sibling abuse by preschool children. *Journal of the American Academy of Child Psychiatry, 23,* 186–190.

Rosler, A., & Witzum, E. (2000). Pharmacotherapy of paraphilias in the next millennium. *Behavioral Sciences and the Law, 18,* 43–56.

Ross, S. M. (1996). Risk of physical abuse to children of spouse abusing parents. *Child Abuse & Neglect, 20,* 589–598.

Rossman, B. B. R. (1994). Children in violent families: Current diagnostic and treatment considerations. *Family Violence and Sexual Assault Bulletin, 10*(3/4), 29–34.

Rossman, B. B. R. (2001). Longer term effects of children's exposure to domestic violence. In S. A. Graham-Bermann & J. L. Edleson (Eds.), *Domestic violence in the lives of children* (pp. 35–65). Washington, DC: American Psychological Association.

Rossman, B. B. R., & Ho, J. (2000). Posttraumatic response and children exposed to parental violence. *Journal of Aggression, Maltreatment, & Trauma, 3,* 85–106.

Roth, A. (1998, June 8). Jailing the victim. *Los Angeles Daily News,* pp. 1, 9.

Roth, S., & Newman, E. (1991). The process of coping with sexual trauma. *Journal of Traumatic Stress, 4,* 279–297.

Rothbaum, F., Weisz, J., Pott, M., Miyake, K., & Morelli, G. (2000). Attachment and culture: Security in the United States and Japan. *American Psychologist, 55,* 1093–1104.

Rotheram-Bokes, M. J., Rosario, N., & Koopman, C. (1991). Minority youths at high risk: Gay males and runaways. In M. E. Colton & S. Gore (Eds.), *Adolescent stress: Causes and consequences* (pp. 181–200). New York: Aldine de Gruyter.

Roy, M. (1982). *The abusive partner: An analysis of domestic battering.* New York: Van Nostrand.

Royce, L., & Coccaro, E. (2001). The neuropsychopharmacology of criminality and aggression. *Canadian Journal of Psychiatry, 46,* 35–43.

Rubin, A. (1991). The effectiveness of outreach counseling and support groups for battered women: A preliminary evaluation. *Research on Social Work Practice, 1,* 332–357.

Rudin, M. M., Zalewski, C., & Bodmer-Turner, J. (1995). Characteristics of child sexual abuse victims according to perpetrator gender. *Child Abuse & Neglect, 19,* 963–973.

Ruggiero, K. J., McLeer, S. V., & Dixon, J. F. (2000). Sexual abuse characteristics associated with survivor psychopathology. *Child Abuse & Neglect, 24,* 951–964.

Runge, R. R., & Hearn, M. E. (2000, December/January). Employment rights advocacy for domestic violence victims. *Domestic Violence Report, 5,* 17–18, 26–29.

Runyan, D. K., Curtis, P. A., Hunter, W. M., Black, M. M., Kotch, J. B., Bangdiwala, S., et al. (1998). LONGSCAN: A consortium for longitudinal studies of maltreatment and the life course of children. *Aggression and Violent Behavior, 3,* 275–285.

Runyan, D. K., Hunter, W. M., & Everson, M. D. (1992). *Maternal support for child victims of sexual abuse: Determinants and implications* (Grant No. 90–CA-1368). Washington, DC: National Center on Child Abuse and Neglect.

Runyan, D. K., Hunter, W. M., Socolar, R. R. S., Amaya-Jackson, L. English, D., Landsverk, J., et al. (1998). Children who prosper in unfavorable environments: The relationship to social capital. *Pediatrics, 101,* 12–18.

Rural Women's Work Group of the Rural Task Force of the American Psychological Association. (2000). *The behavioral health care needs of rural women.* Retrieved from American Psychological Association Web site: http://www.apa.org/rural

Rush, F. (1980). *The best kept secret: Sexual abuse of children.* Englewood Cliffs, NJ: Prentice Hall.

Russell, B. L., & Oswald, D. L. (2002). Sexual coercion and victimization of college men. *Journal of Interpersonal Violence, 17,* 273–285.

Russell, D. E. H. (1982). *Rape in marriage.* New York: Macmillan.

Russell, D. E. H. (1983). The incidence and prevalence of intrafamilial and extrafamilial sexual abuse of female children. *Child Abuse & Neglect, 7,* 133–146.

Russell, D. E. H. (1988). Pornography and rape: A causal model. *Political Psychology, 9,* 41–73.

Russell, D. E. H. (1990). *Rape in marriage* (Rev. ed.). Bloomington: Indiana University Press.

Russo, N. F. (Ed.). (1985). *A women's mental health agenda.* Washington, DC: American Psychological Association.

Rust, J. O., & Troupe, P. A. (1991). Relationships of treatment of child sexual abuse with school achievement and self-concept. *Journal of Early Adolescence, 11,* 420–429.

Ryan, G., & Lane, S. (Eds.). (1991). *Juvenile sexual offending.* Lexington, MA: Lexington.

Sacramento Police Department. (n.d.). *How to obtain and use sex offender information.* Retrieved December 4, 2003, from Sacramento Police Department Web site: http://sacpd.org

Sagrestano, L. M., Heavey, C. L., & Christensen, A. (1999). Perceived power and physical violence in marital conflict. *Journal of Social Issues, 55*(1), 65–79.

Saillant, C., & Dirmann, T. (2002, June 2). Officials seek Latino foster homes. *Los Angeles Times.*

St. Joan, J. (2001). Building bridges, building walls: Collaboration between lawyers and social workers in a domestic violence clinic and issues of client confidentiality. *Clinical Law Review, 7,* 403–467.

Salomon, A., Bassuk, S. S., & Huntington, N. (2002). The relationship between intimate partner violence and the use of addictive substances in poor and homeless single mothers. *Violence Against Women, 8,* 785–815.

Salter, A. C. (1988). *Treating child sex offenders and victims: A practical guide.* Newbury Park, CA: Sage.

Saltzman, L. E., Fanslow, J. L., McMahon, P. M., & Shelley, G. A. (1999). *Intimate partner violence surveillance: Uniform definitions and recommended data elements* (Version 1.0). Retrieved from Centers for Disease Control and Prevention Web site: http://www.cdc.gov/ncipe

Salzinger, S., Feldman, R. S., Hammer, M., & Rosario, M. (1993). The effects of physical abuse on children's relationships. *Child Development, 64,* 169–187.

Salzinger, S., Kaplan, S., Pelcovitz, D., Samit, C., & Krieger, R. (1984). Parent and teacher assessment of children's behavior in child maltreating families. *Journal of the American Academy of Child Psychiatry, 23,* 459–464.

Sanders, B., & Moore, D. L. (1999). Childhood maltreatment and date rape. *Journal of Interpersonal Violence, 14,* 115–124.

Sanders, M. J., & Bursch, B. (2002). Forensic assessment of illness falsification, Munchausen by proxy, and factitious disorder, NOS. *Child Maltreatment, 7,* 112–124.

Sanderson, M. (2000, May/June). Building training partnerships. *Victimization of the Elderly and Disabled, 3,* 1–2, 14–15.

Sandnabba, N. K., Santtila, P., Wannas, M., & Krook, K. (2003). Age and gender specific sexual behaviors in children. *Child Abuse & Neglect, 27,* 579–605.

Santana, A. (1998, March 15). Imprisoned Letourneau is pregnant. *Seattle Times.* Retrieved from http://www.seattletimes.com

Sappington, A. A., Pharr, R., Tunstall, A., & Rickert, E. (1997). Relationships among child abuse, date abuse, and psychological problems. *Journal of Clinical Psychology, 53,* 318–329.

Saradjian, J. (1996). *Women who sexually abuse children: From research to clinical practice.* Chichester, Eng.: John Wiley.

Sarason, I. G., Johnson, J. H., & Siegel, J. M. (1978). Assessing the impacts of life change: Development of the life experience survey. *Journal of Consulting and Clinical Psychology, 46,* 932–946.

Sarber, R. E., Halasz, M. M., Messmer, M. C., Bickett, A. D., & Lutzker, J. R. (1983). Teaching menu planning and grocery shopping to a mentally retarded mother. *Mental Retardation, 21,* 101–106.

Saunders, B. E. (2003). Understanding children exposed to violence: Toward an integration of overlapping fields. *Journal of Interpersonal Violence, 18,* 356–376.

Saunders, B. E., Kilpatrick, D. G., Hanson, R. F., Resnick, H. S., & Walker, M. E. (1999). Prevalence, case characteristics, and long-term psychological correlates of child rape among women: A national survey. *Child Maltreatment, 4,* 187–200.

Saunders, D. G. (1992). A typology of men who batter: Three types derived from cluster analysis. *American Journal of Orthopsychiatry, 62,* 264–275.

Saunders, D. G. (1994). Posttraumatic stress symptom profiles of battered women: A comparison of survivors in two settings. *Violence and Victims, 9,* 31–44.

Saunders, D. G. (1995). The tendency to arrest victims of domestic violence: A preliminary analysis of officer characteristics. *Journal of Interpersonal Violence, 10,* 147–158.

Saunders, D. G. (1996). Feminist-cognitive-behavioral and process-psychodynamic treatments for men who batter: Interactions of abuser traits and treatment model. *Violence and Victims, 11,* 393–414.

Saunders, D. G. (2002). Are physical assaults by wives and girlfriends a major social problem? *Violence Against Women, 8,* 1424–1448.

Saunders, D. G., Lynch, A., Grayson, M., & Linz, D. (1987). The Inventory of Beliefs about Wife Beating: The construction and empirical validation of a measure of beliefs and attitudes. *Violence and Victims, 2,* 39–55.

Saveman, B., Astrom, S., Bucht, G., & Norberg, A. (1999). Elder abuse in residential settings in Sweden. *Journal of Elder Abuse & Neglect, 10*(1/2), 43–60.

Saywitz, K. J., Goodman, G. S., & Lyon, T. D. (2002). Interviewing children in and out of court. In J. E. B. Myers, L. Berliner, J. Briere, C. T. Hendrix, C. Jenny, & T. A. Reid (Eds.), *The APSAC handbook on child maltreatment* (2nd ed., pp. 349–377). Thousand Oaks, CA: Sage.

Saywitz, K. J., Mannarino, A. P., Berliner, L., & Cohen, J. A. (2000). Treatment for sexually abused children and adolescents. *American Psychologist, 55,* 1040–1049.

Saywitz, K. J., & Nathanson, R. (1993). Children's testimony and their perceptions of stress in and out of the courtroom. *Child Abuse & Neglect, 17,* 613–622.

Saywitz, K. J., & Snyder, L. (1993). Improving children's testimony with preparation. In G. S. Goodman & B. L. Bottoms (Eds.), *Child victims, child witnesses: Understanding and improving testimony* (pp. 117–146). New York: Guilford.

Scarce, M. (1997). Same-sex rape of male college students. *Journal of American College Health, 45,* 171–173.

Scavo, R. R. (1989). Female adolescent sex offenders: A neglected treatment group. *Social Casework, 70,* 114–117.

Schaaf, K. K., & McCanne, T. R. (1998). Relationship of childhood sexual, physical, and combined sexual and physical abuse to adult victimization and posttraumatic stress disorder. *Child Abuse & Neglect, 22,* 1119–1133.

Schaefer, C. (1997). Defining verbal abuse of children: A survey. *Psychological Reports, 80,* 626.

Schafer, J. (1996). Measuring spousal violence with the Conflict Tactics Scale. *Journal of Interpersonal Violence, 11,* 572–585.

Schafer, J., Caetano, R., & Clark, C. (1998). Rates of intimate partner violence in the United States. *American Journal of Public Health, 88,* 1702–1704.

Schauben, L. J., & Frazier, P. A. (1995). Vicarious trauma: The effects on female counselors of working with sexual violence survivors. *Psychology of Women Quarterly, 19,* 49–64.

Schechter, S. (1988). Building bridges between activists, professionals, and researchers. In K. A. Yllö & M. Bograd (Eds.), *Feminist perspectives on wife abuse* (pp. 299–312). Newbury Park, CA: Sage.

Schellenbach, C. J. (1998). Child maltreatment: A critical review of research on treatment for physically abusive parents. In P. K. Trickett & C. J. Schellenbach (Eds.), *Violence against children in the family and the community* (pp. 251–268). Washington, DC: American Psychological Association.

Schene, P. (1996). Child abuse and neglect policy: History, models, and future directions. In J. Briere, L. Berliner, J. A. Bulkley, C. Jenny, & T. A. Reid (Eds.), *The APSAC handbook on child maltreatment* (pp. 385–397). Thousand Oaks, CA: Sage.

Schetky, D. H., & Green, A. H. (1988). *Child sexual abuse: A handbook for health care and legal professionals.* New York: Brunner/Mazel.

Schewe, P. (Ed.). (2002). *Preventing violence in relationships: Interventions across the life span.* Washington, DC: American Psychological Association.

Schindehette, S. (1998, September 7). High infidelity. *People,* pp. 52–59.

Schmitt, B. D. (1987). The child with nonaccidental trauma. In R. E. Helfer & R. S. Kempe (Eds.), *The battered child* (4th ed., pp. 178–196). Chicago: University of Chicago Press.

Schneider, E. M. (1986). Describing and changing: Women's self-defense work and the problem of expert testimony on battering. *Women's Rights Law Reporter, 9*(3/4), 195–222.

Schneider, E. M. (2000). *Battered women and feminist lawmaking.* New Haven, CT: Yale University Press.

Schollenberger, J., Campbell, J. C., Sharps, P. W., O'Campo, P., Gielen, A. C., Dienemann, J., et al. (2003). African American HMO enrollees: Their experiences with partner abuse and its effect on their health. *Violence Against Women, 9,* 599–618.

Schornstein, S. L. (1997). *Domestic violence and health care: What every professional needs to know.* Thousand Oaks, CA: Sage.

Schreier, H. A. (1997). Factitious presentation of psychiatric disorder by proxy. *Child Psychology and Psychiatry Review, 2,* 108–115.

Schubot, D. B. (2001). Date rape prevalence among female high school students in a rural midwestern state during 1993, 1995, and 1997. *Journal of Interpersonal Violence, 16,* 291–296.

Schuler, M. E., & Nair, P. (1999). Brief report: Frequency of maternal cocaine use during pregnancy and infant neurobehavioral outcome. *Journal of Pediatric Psychology, 24,* 511–514.

Schumacher, J. A. (2002). Battering and common couple violence: A construct validation. *Dissertation Abstracts International, 63*(03), 1573B. (UMI No. 3044966)

Schumacher, J. A., Feldbau-Kohn, S., Slep, A. M. S., & Heyman, R. E. (2001). Risk factors for male-to-female partner physical abuse. *Aggression and Violent Behavior, 6,* 281–352.

Schumacher, J. A., Slep, A. M. S., & Heyman, R. E. (2001a). Risk factors for child neglect. *Aggression and Violent Behavior, 6,* 231–254.

Schumacher, J. A., Slep, A. M. S., & Heyman, R. E. (2001b). Risk factors for male-to-female partner psychological abuse. *Aggression and Violent Behavior, 6,* 255–268.

Schwartz, I. M., AuClaire, P., & Harris, L. J. (1991). Family preservation services as an alternative to out-of-home placement of adolescents. In K. Wells & D. E. Biegel (Eds.), *Family preservation services: Research and evaluation* (pp. 33–46). Newbury Park, CA: Sage.

Schwartz, M. (2000). *Elder abuse law: Elder abuse, nursing homes, and fiduciaries.* Retrieved September 5, 2003, from http://www.elderabuselaw.com

Schwartz, M., O'Leary, S. G., & Kendziora, K. T. (1997). Dating aggression among high school students. *Violence and Victims, 12,* 295–305.

Schwartz, M. D. (2000). Methodological issues in the use of survey data for measuring and characterizing violence against women. *Violence Against Women, 6,* 815–838.

Schwartz, M. D., & Nogrady, C. A. (1996). Fraternity membership, rape myths, and sexual aggression on a college campus. *Violence Against Women, 2,* 148–162.

Schwartz, M. D., & Pitts, V. (1995). Exploring a feminist routine activities approach to explaining sexual assault. *Justice Quarterly, 12,* 9–31.

Schwartz, R. H., Milteer, R., & LeBeau, M. A. (2000). Drug-facilitated sexual assault ("date rape"). *Southern Medical Journal, 93,* 558–561.

Scott, K. L., & Wolfe, D. A. (2000). Change among batterers: Examining men's success stories. *Journal of Interpersonal Violence, 8,* 827–842.

Scott, K. L., & Wolfe, D. A. (2003). Readiness to change as a predictor of outcome in batterer treatment. *Journal of Consulting and Clinical Psychology, 71,* 879–889.

Sedlak, A. J. (1990). *Technical amendment to the study finding: National incidence and prevalence of child abuse and neglect 1988.* Rockville, MD: Westat.

Sedlak, A. J. (1991). *National incidence and prevalence of child abuse and neglect: 1988: Revised report.* Rockville, MD: Westat.

Sedlak, A. J. (1997). Risk factors for the occurrence of child abuse and neglect. *Journal of Aggression, Maltreatment, & Trauma,* 149–187.

Sedlak, A. J., & Broadhurst, D. D. (1996). *Third National Incidence Study on child abuse and neglect.* Washington, DC: U.S. Department of Health and Human Services.

Sedlar, G., & Hansen, D. J. (2001). Anger, child behavior, and family distress: Further evaluation of the Parental Anger Inventory. *Journal of Family Violence, 16,* 361–373.

Segal, S. R., & Iris, M. A. (1989). Strategies for service provision: The use of legal interventions in a systems approach to casework. In R. Filinson & S. R. Ingman (Eds.), *Elder abuse: Practice and policy* (pp. 104–116). New York: Human Sciences Press.

Segal, Z. V., & Stermac, L. E. (1990). The role of cognition in sexual assault. In W. L. Marshall, D. R. Laws, & H. E. Barbaree (Eds.), *Handbook of sexual assault: Issues, theories, and treatment of the offender* (pp. 161–174). New York: Plenum.

Seidman, B. T., Marshall, W. L., Hudson, S. M., & Robertson, P. J. (1994). An examination of intimacy and loneliness in sex offenders. *Journal of Interpersonal Violence, 9,* 518–534.

Seith, C. (2001). Security matters: Domestic violence and public social services. *Violence Against Women, 7,* 799–820.

Sellers, C. S., Folts, W. E., & Logan, K. M. (1992). Elder mistreatment: A multidimensional problem. *Journal of Elder Abuse & Neglect, 4*(4), 5–23.

Semel, E. (1997). Counterpoint: Megan's law is a knee-jerk reaction to a senseless personal tragedy [Electronic version]. *Corrections Today, 59*(6), 21.

Seneca Falls Convention, Seneca Falls, New York, July 19–20, 1848, including the Declaration of Sentiments and Resolutions. (1848). Retrieved November 10, 2003, from E. C. DuBois Web site: http://www.sscnet.ucla.edu/history/dubois/classes/995/98F/doc5.html

Sengstock, M. C., Hwalek, M., & Petrone, S. (1989). Services for aged abuse victims: Service types and related factors. *Journal of Elder Abuse & Neglect, 1*(4), 37–56.

Senn, C. Y., Desmarais, S., Verberg, N., & Wood, E. (2000). Predicting coercive sexual behavior across the lifespan in a random sample of Canadian men. *Journal of Social and Personal Relationships, 17,* 95–113.

Serbin, L., & Karp, J. (2003). Intergenerational studies of parenting and the transfer of risk from parent to child. *Current Directions in Psychological Science, 12,* 138–142.

Sgroi, S. M. (1982). Family treatment of child sexual abuse. *Journal of Social Work and Human Sexuality, 1,* 109–128.

Shah, G., Veedon, R., & Vasi, S. (1995). Elder abuse in India. In J. I. Kosberg & J. L. Garcia (Eds.), *Elder abuse: International and cross-cultural perspectives* (pp. 101–118). Binghamton, NY: Haworth.

Shahar, G. (2001). Maternal personality and distress as predictors of child neglect. *Journal of Research in Personality, 35,* 537–545.

Shainess, N. (1979). Vulnerability to violence: Masochism as process. *American Journal of Psychotherapy, 33,* 174–189.

Shakeshaft, C., & Cohan, A. (1995). Sexual abuse of students by school personnel [Electronic version]. *Phi Delta Kappan, 76,* 512.

Shakoor, B. H., & Chalmers, D. (1991). Co-victimization of African American children who witness violence and the theoretical implications of its effects on their cognitive, emotional, and behavioral development. *Journal of the National Medical Association, 83,* 233–238.

Shalansky, C., Ericksen, J., & Henderson, A. (1999). Abused women and child custody: The ongoing exposure to abusive ex-partners. *Journal of Advanced Nursing, 29,* 416–426.

Sharhabani-Arzy, R., Amir, M., Kotler, M., & Liran, R. (2003). The toll of domestic violence: PTSD among battered women in an Israeli sample. *Journal of Interpersonal Violence, 18,* 1335–1346.

Shepard, M. F. (1992). Predicting batterer recidivism five years after community intervention. *Journal of Family Violence, 7,* 167–178.

Shepard, M. F., & Campbell, J. A. (1992). The Abusive Behavior Inventory: A measure of psychological and physical abuse. *Journal of Interpersonal Violence, 7,* 291–305.

Shepard, M. F., & Pence, E. L. (1988). The effect of battering on the employment status of women. *Affilia, 3*(2), 55–61.

Shepard, M. F., & Pence, E. L. (Eds.). (1999). *Coordinating community responses to domestic violence: Lessons from Duluth and beyond.* Thousand Oaks, CA: Sage.

Sheppard, J. (1997). Double punishment. *American Journalism Review, 19*(9), 36–41.

Sheridan, L. P., Blaauw, E., & Davies, G. M. (2003). Stalking: Knowns and unknowns. *Trauma, Violence, & Abuse, 4,* 148–162.

Sheridan, L. P., Gillett, R., Blaauw, E., Davies, G. M., & Patel, D. (2003). "There's no smoke without fire": Are male ex-partners perceived as more "entitled" to stalk than stranger or acquaintance stalkers? *British Journal of Psychology, 94,* 87–98.

Sherman, L. W., & Berk, R. (1984). The specific deterrent effects of arrest for domestic assault. *American Sociological Review, 49,* 261–272.

Sherman, L. W., Smith, D. A., Schmidt, J. D., & Rogan, D. P. (1992). Crime, punishment, and stake in conformity: Legal and informal control of domestic violence. *American Sociological Review, 57,* 680–690.

Shields, A., Ryan, R. M., & Cicchetti, D. (2001). Narrative representations of caregivers and emotion dysregulation as predictors of maltreated children's rejection by peers. *Developmental Psychology, 37,* 321–337.

Shir, J. S. (1999). Battered women's perceptions and expectations of their current and ideal marital relationship. *Journal of Family Violence, 14,* 71–82.

Shor, R. (2000). Child maltreatment: Differences in perceptions between parents in low income and middle income neighbourhoods. *British Journal of Social Work, 30,* 165–178.

Short, L. M., McMahon, P. M., Chervin, D. D., Shelley, G. A., Lezin, N., Sloop, K. S., et al. (2000). Survivors' identification of protective factors and early warning signs for intimate partner violence. *Violence Against Women, 6,* 272–285.

Shotland, R. L. (1992). A theory of the causes of courtship rape: Part 2. *Journal of Social Issues, 48*(1), 127–143.

Shuman-Austin, L. A. (2000). Is leaving work to obtain safety "good cause" to leave employment? Providing unemployment insurance to victims of domestic violence in Washington State. *Seattle University Law Review, 23,* 797–847.

Sidebotham, P., Golding, J., & ALSPAC Study Team. (2001). Child maltreatment in the "children of the nineties": A longitudinal study of parental risk factors. *Child Abuse & Neglect, 25,* 1177–1200.

Sidebotham, P., & Heron, J. (2003). Child maltreatment in the "children of the nineties": The role of the child. *Child Abuse & Neglect, 27,* 337–352.

Siegel, J. M. (1986). The multidimensional anger inventory. *Journal of Personality and Social Psychology, 51,* 191–200.

Siegel, L. J. (1995). *Criminology.* St. Paul, MN: West.

Sierra, L. (1997). Representing battered women charged with crimes for failing to protect their children from abusive partners. *Double-Time* (Newsletter of the National Clearinghouse for the Defense of Battered Women), *5*(1/2), 1, 4–7.

Sigler, R. T. (1989). *Domestic violence in context: An assessment of community attitudes.* Lexington, MA: Lexington.

Silbert, M. (1982). Prostitution and sexual assault: Summary of results. *International Journal for Biosocial Research, 3,* 69–71.

Silbert, M., & Pines, A. M. (1983). Early sexual exploitation as an influence in prostitution. *Social Work, 28,* 285–289.

Silverman, A. B., Reinherz, H. Z., & Giaconia, R. M. (1996). The long-term sequelae of child and adolescent abuse: A longitudinal community study. *Child Abuse & Neglect, 8,* 709–723.

Silverman, J. G., Raj, A., Mucci, L. A., & Hathaway, J. E. (2001). Dating violence against adolescent girls and associated substance use, unhealthy weight control, sexual risk behavior, pregnancy, and suicidality. *Journal of the American Medical Association,* 286, 572–579.

Silvern, L., Karyl, J., Waelde, L., Hodges, W. F., Starek, J., Heidt, E., et al. (1995). Retrospective reports of parental partner abuse: Relationships to depression, trauma symptoms and self-esteem among college students. *Journal of Family Violence,* 10, 177–202.

Simon, L. M. (1995). A therapeutic jurisprudence approach to the legal processing of domestic violence cases. *Psychology, Public Policy, and Law, 1,* 43–79.

Simon, T. R., Anderson, M., Thompson, M. P., Crosby, A. E., Shelley, G., & Sacks, J. J. (2001). Attitudinal acceptance of intimate partner violence among U.S. adults. *Violence and Victims, 16,* 115–126.

Simoneti, S., Scott, E. C., & Murphy, C. M. (2000). Dissociative experiences in partner-assaultive men. *Journal of Interpersonal Violence, 15,* 1262–1283.

Simons, R. L., Lin, K., & Gordon, L. C. (1998). Socialization in the family of origin and male dating violence. *Journal of Marriage and the Family, 60,* 467–478.

Simons, R. L., Whitbeck, L. B., Conger, R. D., & Wu, C.-I. (1991). Intergenerational transmission of harsh parenting. *Developmental Psychology, 27,* 159–171.

Simons, R. L., Wu, C.I., Johnson, C., & Conger, R. D. (1995). A test of various perspectives on the intergenerational transmission of domestic violence. *Criminology, 33,* 141–170.

Simpson, J. A., Rholes, S. W., & Phillips, D. (1996). Conflict in close relationships: An attachment perspective. *Journal of Personality and Social Psychology, 71,* 899–914.

Singer, D. (2002). *Quality of care project.* Denver, CO: Denver Regional Council on Government Aging Services.

Singer, M. T., & Nievod, A. (2003). New age therapies. In S. O. Lilienfeld, S. J. Lynn, & J. M. Lohr (Eds.), *Science and pseudoscience in clinical psychology* (pp. 176–204). New York: Guilford.

Sirles, E. A., & Franke, P. J. (1989). Factors influencing mothers' reactions to intrafamily sexual abuse. *Child Abuse & Neglect, 13,* 131–139.

Slep, A. M. S., & Heyman, R. E. (2001). Where do we go from here? Moving toward an integrated approach to family violence. *Aggression and Violent Behavior, 6,* 353–356.

Sleutel, M. R. (1998). Women's experiences of abuse: A review of qualitative research. *Issues in Mental Health Nursing, 19,* 525–539.

Smallbone, S. W., & Dadds, M. R. (2001). Further evidence for a relationship between attachment insecurity and coercive sexual behavior in nonoffenders. *Journal of Interpersonal Violence, 16,* 22–35.

Smalley, S., & Braiker, B. (2003, January 30). Suffer the children. *Newsweek,* pp. 32–33.

Smith, A., & Chiricos, T. (2003). Structural antecedents of aggravated assault: Exploratory assessment of female and male victimization. *Violence and Victims, 18,* 55–70.

Smith, B. E., Hillenbrand, S. W., & Goretsky, S. R. (1990). *The probation response to child sexual abuse offender: How is it working?* Chicago: American Bar Association.

Smith, H., & Israel, E. (1987). Sibling incest: A study of the dynamics of 25 cases. *Child Abuse & Neglect, 11,* 101–108.

Smith, J. P., & Williams, J. G. (1992). From abusive household to dating violence. *Journal of Family Violence, 7,* 153–165.

Smith, M. (1999, March 2). Judge dismisses charges in "false memories" case. *Houston Chronicle,* p. A1.

Smith, M., & Pazder, L. (1980). *Michelle remembers.* New York: Crongdon & Lattes.

Smith, M. D. (1991). Male peer support of wife abuse. *Journal of Interpersonal Violence, 6,* 512–519.

Smith, P., Perrin, S., Yule, W., & Rabe-Hesketh, S. (2001). War exposure and maternal reactions in the psychological adjustment of children from Bosnia-Hercegovina. *Journal of Child Psychology and Psychiatry, 42,* 395–404.

Smith, P., & Welchans, S. (2000). Peer education: Does focusing on male responsibility change sexual assault attitudes? *Violence Against Women, 6,* 1255–1268.

Smith, P. H., Earp, J. L., & DeVellis, R. (1995). Measuring battering: Development of the Women's Experience with Battering (WEB) Scale. *Women's Health, 1,* 273–288.

Smith, P. H., Edwards, G., & DeVellis, R. (1998). *Intimate partner violence: Prevalence, co-occurrence, and health consequences.* Washington, DC: American Public Health Association.

Smith, P. H., Smith, J. B., & Earp, J. L. (1999). Beyond the measurement trap: A reconstructed conceptualization and measurement of women battering. *Psychology of Women Quarterly, 23,* 179–195.

Smith, P. H., Thornton, G. E., DeVellis, R., Earp, J. L., & Coker, A. (2002). A population-based study of the prevalence and distinctiveness of battering, physical assault, and sexual assault in intimate relationships. *Violence Against Women, 10,* 1208–1232.

Smith, S. M. (1975). *The battered child syndrome.* London: Butterworth.

Smith, S. M., Hanson, R., & Noble, S. (1974). Social aspects of the battered baby syndrome. *British Journal of Psychiatry, 125,* 568–582.

Smith, W. L. (1994). Abusive head injury. *APSAC Advisor, 7*(4), 16–21.

Smith, W. R. (1988). Delinquency and abuse among juvenile sexual offenders. *Journal of Interpersonal Violence, 3,* 400–413.

Smolak, L., & Murnen, S. K. (2002). A meta-analytic examination of the relationship between child sexual abuse and eating disorders. *International Journal of Eating Disorders, 31,* 136–150.

Smolowe, J. (1995, December 11). Making the tough calls. *Time, 1,* 40–44.

Snow, B., & Sorenson, T. (1990). Ritualistic child abuse in a neighborhood setting. *Journal of Interpersonal Violence, 5,* 474–487.

Snow, D. A. (2001). Extending and broadening Blumer's conceptualization of symbolic interactionism. *Symbolic Interactionism, 24,* 367–377.

Snyder, D. K. (1996). *Marital Satisfaction Inventory (MSI)–Revised.* Los Angeles: Western Psychological Services.

Snyder, J. (2003, September/October). Elder fraud pilot project introduced in Philadelphia. *Victimization of the Elderly & Disabled, 6,* 33, 45–46.

Sobsey, D. (1994). *Violence in the lives of people with disabilities.* Baltimore: Paul H. Brookes.

Sobsey, D., & Doe, T. (1991). Patterns of sexual abuse and assault. *Sexuality and Disability, 9,* 243–260.

Social Services Inspectorate. (1992). *Confronting elder abuse: An London Region Survey.* London: Her Majesty's Stationery Office.

Soeken, K. L., McFarlane, J., Parker, B., & Lominack, M. C. (1998). The Abuse Assessment Screen: A clinical instrument to measure frequency, severity, and perpetrator of abuse against women. In J. C. Campbell (Ed.), *Empowering survivors of abuse: Health care for battered women and their children* (pp. 195–203). Thousand Oaks, CA: Sage.

Soler, H., Vinayak, P., & Quadagno, D. (2000). Biosocial aspects of domestic violence. *Psychoneuroendocrinology, 25,* 721–739.

Somer, E., & Braunstein, A. (1999). Are children exposed to interparental violence being psychologically maltreated? *Aggression and Violent Behavior, 4,* 449–456.

Sommer, R., Barnes, G. E., & Murray, R. P. (1992). Alcohol consumption, alcohol abuse, personality and female perpetrated spouse abuse. *Personality and Individual Differences, 13,* 1315–1323.

Sonkin, D. J. (2000). *Court-mandated perpetrator assessment and treatment handbook.* Sausalito, CA: Author.

Soos, J. N., Sr. (2000, September/October). Gray murders: Undetected homicides of the elderly plus one year. *Victimization of the Elderly and Disabled, 3,* 33–34, 42.

Sorenson, S. B., Stein, J. A., Siegel, J. M., Golding, J. M., & Burnam, M. A. (1987). Prevalence of adult sexual assault: The Los Angeles Epidemiologic Catchment Area Study. *American Journal of Epidemiology, 126,* 1154–1164.

Sorenson, S. B., & Telles, C. A. (1991). Self-reports of spousal violence in a Mexican-American and non-Hispanic white population. *Violence and Victims, 6,* 3–15.

Sousa, C. A. (1999). Teen dating violence: The hidden epidemic. *Family and Conciliation Courts Review, 37,* 356–374.

Sovinski, C. J. (1997). The criminalization of maternal substance abuse: A quick fix to a complex problem. *Pepperdine Law Review, 25*(1), 107–139.

Spaccarelli, S., & Fuchs, C. (1997). Variability in symptom expression among sexually abused girls: Developing multivariate models. *Journal of Clinical Child Psychology, 26,* 34–35.

Spaccarelli, S., Sandler, I. N., & Roosa, M. (1994). History of spouse violence against mother: Correlated risks and unique effects in child mental health. *Journal of Family Violence, 9,* 79–98.

Spanier, G. B. (1976). Measuring dyadic adjustment: New scales for assessing the quality of marriage and similar dyads. *Journal of Marriage and the Family, 38,* 15–28.

Sparr, L. E. (1996). Mental defense and posttraumatic stress disorder: Assessment of criminal intent. *Journal of Traumatic Stress, 9,* 405–425.

Spears, J. W., & Spohn, C. G. (1997). The effect of evidence factors and victim characteristics on prosecutors' charging decisions in sexual assault cases. *Justice Quarterly, 14,* 501–524.

Spector, M., & Kitsuse, J. I. (1977). *Constructing social problems.* Menlo Park, CA: Benjamin Cummings.

Spencer, J. W., & Knudsen, D. D. (1992). Out-of-home maltreatment: An analysis of risk in various settings for children. *Children and Youth Services Review, 14,* 485–492.

Spielberger, C. D. (1988). *Manual for the State-Trait Anger Expression Inventory.* Odessa, FL: Psychological Assessment Resources.

Spielberger, C. D. (1991). *State-Trait Anger Expression Inventory: Professional manual* (Rev. research ed.). Odessa, FL: Psychological Assessment Resources.

Spillane-Grieco, E. (2000). From parent verbal abuse to teenage physical aggression? *Child and Adolescent Social Work Journal, 17,* 411–430.

Spitzberg, B. (2002). The tactical topography of stalking victimization and management. *Trauma, Violence, & Abuse, 30,* 261–288.

Spitzer, R. L., Williams, J. B., Gibbon, M., & First, M. B. (1990). *User's guide for the Structured Clinical Interview for DSM-III-R.* Washington, DC: American Psychiatric Press.

Spohn, C. G., & Holleran, D. (2001). Prosecuting sexual assault: A comparison of charging decisions in sexual assault cases involving strangers, acquaintances, and intimate partners. *Justice Quarterly, 18,* 651–688.

Sprecher, S. (2001). Equity and social exchange in dating couples: Associations with satisfaction, commitment, and stability. *Journal of Marriage and Family, 63,* 599–613.

Springs, F. E., & Friedrich, W. N. (1992). Health risk behaviors and medical sequelae of childhood sexual abuse. *Mayo Clinic Proceedings, 67,* 527–532.

Stacey, W. A., & Shupe, A. (1983). *The family secret.* Boston: Beacon.

Stark, E. (1993). Mandatory arrest of batterers: A reply to critics. *American Behavioral Scientist, 36,* 651–680.

Stark, E. (2002). The battered mother in the child protective service caseload: Developing an appropriate response. *Women's Rights Law Reporter, 23,* 107–131.

Starr, R. H., Jr. (1982). A research-based approach to the prediction of child abuse. In R. H. Starr, Jr. (Ed.), *Child abuse prediction: Policy implications* (pp. 105–134). Cambridge, MA: Ballinger.

State of California, Department of Justice (2003). *Registered sex offenders.* Retrieved May 2003 from http://caag.state.ca.us/megan

State of Oregon, Children's Services Division. (1991). *Mental injury: The hidden hurt* [Brochure]. Salem: Author.

Staudt, M., & Drake, B. (2002a). Intensive family preservation services: Where's the crisis? *Children and Youth Services Review, 24,* 777–795.

Staudt, M., & Drake, B. (2002b). Research on services to preserve maltreating families. *Children and Youth Services Review, 24,* 645–652.

Steele, B. F., & Alexander, H. (1981). Long-term effects of sexual abuse in childhood. In P. B. Mrazek & C. H. Kempe (Eds.), *Sexually abused children and their families* (pp. 223–233). New York: Pergamon.

Steele, B. F., & Pollock, C. B. (1968). A psychiatric study of parents who abuse infants and small children. In R. E. Helfer & C. H. Kempe (Eds.), *The battered child* (pp. 89–133). Chicago: University of Chicago Press.

Steffensmeir, D., & Hayne, D. L. (2000). The structural sources of urban female violence in the United States. *Homicide Studies, 4,* 107–134.

Stehno, S. M. (1982). Differential treatment of minority children in service systems. *Social Work, 27,* 39–45.

Steiger, H., & Zanko, M. (1990). Sexual traumata among eating disordered, psychiatric, and normal female groups: Comparison of prevalence and defense styles. *Journal of Interpersonal Violence, 5,* 74–86.

Stein, K. (1991). A national agenda for elder abuse and neglect research: Issues and recommendations. *Journal of Elder Abuse & Neglect, 3*(3), 91–108.

Stein, T. J. (1993). Legal perspectives on family violence against children. In R. L. Hampton, T. P. Gullotta, G. R. Adams, E. H. Potter III, & R. P. Weissberg (Eds.), *Family violence: Prevention and treatment* (pp. 179–197). Newbury Park, CA: Sage.

Steinman, M. (1991). The public policy process and woman battering: Problems and potentials. In M. Steinman (Ed.), *Woman battering: Policy responses* (pp. 1–18). Cincinnati, OH: Anderson.

Steinmetz, S. K. (1977). The battered husband syndrome. *Victimology, 2,* 499–509.

Steinmetz, S. K. (1982). A cross-cultural comparison of sibling violence. *International Journal of Family Psychiatry, 2,* 337–351.

Steinmetz, S. K. (1987). Family violence: Past, present, and future. In M. B. Sussman & S. K. Steinmetz (Eds.), *Handbook of marriage and the family* (pp. 725–765). New York: Plenum.

Steinmetz, S. K. (1993). The abused elderly are dependent: Abuse is caused by the perception of stress associated with providing care. In R. J. Gelles & D. R. Loseke (Eds.), *Current controversies on family violence* (pp. 222–236). Newbury Park, CA: Sage.

Stephens, B. J., & Sinden, P. G. (2000). Victims' voices: Domestic assault victims' perceptions of police demeanor. *Journal of Interpersonal Violence, 15,* 534–547.

Stermac, L., Del Bove, G., & Addison, M. (2001). Violence, injury, and presentation patterns in spousal sexual assaults. *Violence Against Women, 7,* 1218–1233.

Stermac, L., Hall, K., & Henskens, M. (1989). Violence among child molesters. *Journal of Sex Research, 26,* 450–459.

Sternberg, K. J., Lamb, M. E., Greenbaum, C., Cicchetti, D., Dawud, S., Cortes, R. M., et al. (1993). Effects of domestic violence on children's behavior problems and depression. *Developmental Psychology, 29,* 44–52.

Sternberg, K. J., Lamb, M. E., Greenbaum, C., Dawud, S., & Cortes, R. M. (1994). The effects of domestic violence on children's perceptions of their perpetrating and non-perpetrating parents. *International Journal of Behavioral Development, 17,* 779–795.

Stets, J. E., & Straus, M. A. (1989). The marriage license as a hitting license: A comparison of assaults in dating, cohabiting, and married couples. In M. A. Pirog-Good & J. E. Stets (Eds.), *Violence in dating relationship: Emerging social issues* (pp. 33–52). New York: Praeger.

Stewart, A. (2000). Who are the respondents of domestic violence protection orders? *Australian and New Zealand Journal of Criminology, 33,* 77–90.

Stewart, A., & Maddren, K. (1997). Police officers' judgments of blame in family violence: The impact of gender and alcohol. *Sex Roles, 37,* 921–933.

Stiegel, L. A. (2001). *Financial abuse of the elderly: Risk factors, screening techniques, and remedies.* Chicago: American Bar Association, Commission on Legal Problems of the Elderly. Retrieved December 8, 2003, from http://www.abanet.org/elderly/financial_abuse_of_the_elderly.doc

Stiegel, L. A. (2003, July/August). Washington report. *Victimization of the Elderly and Disabled, 6,* 19–20.

Stiegel, L. A., Heisler, C. J., Brandl, B., & Judy, A. (2000, November/December). Developing services for older victims of domestic or sexual assault: The approach of Wisconsin coalitions. *Victimization of the Elderly and Disabled, 3,* 49–50, 58–60.

Stiehm, J. (2003, August 19). Great-grandmother charged with abuse of 8-month-old. *Baltimore Sun,* p. 3B.

Stith, S. M., & Farley, S. C. (1993). A predictive model of male spousal violence. *Journal of Family Violence, 8,* 183–201.

Stith, S. M., Jester, S., & Bird, G. (1992). A typology of college students who use violence in their relationships. *Journal of College Student Development, 33,* 411–421.

Stith, S. M., Rosen, K. H., Middleton, K. A., Busch, A. L., Lundberg, K., & Carlton, R. P. (2000). The intergenerational transmission of spouse abuse: A meta-analysis. *Journal of Marriage and the Family, 62,* 640–654.

Stoesz, D. (2002). It's time to charter welfare departments. *Families in Society, 83,* 398–399.

Stone, A. E., & Fialk, R. J. (1999, December/January). Backlash against the abused victim in custody disputes. *Domestic Violence Report, 4,* 1, 26–27.

Stoneberg, T. (2002). Moving from vulnerability to empowerment. *Journal of Religion & Abuse, 4*(3), 61–73.

Stop Prisoner Rape. (2002, October 30). *Stop Prisoner Rape accuses FBI of ignoring male rape in new crime report* [Press release]. Retrieved November 16, 2003, from Stop Prisoner Rape Web site: http://www.spr.org

Stordeur, R. A., & Stille, R. (1989). *Ending men's violence against their partners: One road to peace.* Newbury Park, CA: Sage.

Stosny, S. (1995). *Treating attachment abuse: A compassion approach.* New York: Springer.

Stouthamer-Loeber, M., van Kammen, W., & Loeber, R. (1992). Researchers' forum: The nuts and bolts of implementing large-scale longitudinal studies. *Violence and Victims, 7,* 63–78.

Straight, E. S., Harper, F. W. K., & Arias, I. (2003). The impact of partner psychological abuse on health behaviors and health status in college women. *Journal of Interpersonal Violence, 18,* 1035–1054.

Strand, V. C. (2000). *Treating secondary victims: Intervention with the nonoffending mother in the incest family.* Thousand Oaks, CA: Sage.

Stratford, L. (1988). *Satan's underground.* Eugene, OR: Harvest House.

Straus, M. A. (1976). Sexual inequality, cultural norms, and wife beating. *Victimology, 1,* 54–76.

Straus, M. A. (1979). Measuring intrafamily conflict and aggression: The Conflict Tactics Scale (CT). *Journal of Marriage and the Family, 41,* 75–88.

Straus, M. A. (1980). Societal stress and marital violence in a national sample of American families. *Annals of the New York Academy of Sciences, 347,* pp. 229–250.

Straus, M. A. (1983). Ordinary violence, child abuse, and wife beating: What do they have in common? In D. Finkelhor, R. J. Gelles, G. T. Hotaling, & M. A. Straus (Eds.), *The dark side of families: Current family violence research* (pp. 213–234). Beverly Hills, CA: Sage.

Straus, M. A. (1991a, September). *Children as witness to marital violence: A risk factor for life long problems among a nationally representative sample of American men and women.* Paper presented at the Ross Roundtable on Children and Violence Washington, DC.

Straus, M. A. (1991b). Conceptualization and measurement of battering: Implications for public policy. In M. Steinman (Ed.), *Woman battering: Policy responses* (pp. 19–47). Cincinnati OH: Anderson.

Straus, M. A. (1991c). Discipline and deviance: Physical punishment of children and violence and other crime in adulthood. *Social Problems, 38,* 133–154.

Straus, M. A. (1991d). New theory and old canards about family violence research. *Social Problems, 38,* 180–197.

Straus, M. A. (1992). Children as witnesses to marital violence: A risk factor for life-long problems among a nationally representative sample of American men and women. In *Children and violence: A report of the Twenty-Third Ross Roundtable of Initial Approaches to Common Paediatric Problems.* Columbus OH: Ross Laboratories.

Straus, M. A. (1993). Physical assaults by wives: A major social problem. In R. J. Gelles & D. R. Loseke (Eds.), *Current controversies on family violence* (pp. 67–87). Newbury Park, CA: Sage.

Straus, M. A. (1994). *Beating the devil out of them: Corporal punishment in American families.* Lexington, MA: Lexington.

Straus, M. A. (1999). The controversy over domestic violence by women: A methodological, theoretical, and sociology of science analysis. In X. Arriaga & S. Oskamp (Eds.), *Violence in intimate relationships* (pp. 17–44). Thousand Oaks, CA: Sage.

Straus, M. A. (2000). Corporal punishment and primary prevention of physical abuse. *Child Abuse and Neglect, 24*, 1109–1114.

Straus, M. A. (2001). *Beating the devil out of them: Corporal punishment in American families and its effects on children* (2nd ed.). New Brunswick, NJ: Transaction.

Straus, M. A., & Gelles, R. J. (1986). Societal change and change in family violence from 1975 to 1985 as revealed by two national surveys. *Journal of Marriage and the Family, 48*, 465–479.

Straus, M. A., & Gelles, R. J. (Eds.). (1990). *Physical violence in American families: Risk factors and adaptations to violence in 8,145 families.* New Brunswick, NJ: Transaction.

Straus, M. A., Gelles, R. J., & Steinmetz, S. K. (1980). *Behind closed doors: Violence in the American family.* Garden City, NY: Doubleday.

Straus, M. A., Hamby, S. L., Boney-McCoy, S., & Sugarman, D. B. (1995). *The Revised Conflict Tactics Scales (CTS2): Development and preliminary psychometric data.* Durham, NH: Family Violence Research Laboratory.

Straus, M. A., Hamby, S. L., Finkelhor, D., Moore, D. W., & Runyan, D. (1998). Identification of child maltreatment with the Parent-Child Conflict Tactics Scales: Development and psychometric data for a national sample of American parents. *Child Abuse & Neglect, 22*, 249–270.

Straus, M. A., & Mouradian, V. E. (1998). Impulsive corporal punishment by mothers and antisocial behavior and impulsiveness of children. *Behavioral Sciences and the Law, 16*, 353–374.

Straus, M. A., & Smith, C. (1990). Family patterns of primary prevention of family violence. In M. A. Straus & R. J. Gelles (Eds.), *Physical violence in American families: Risk factors and adaptations to violence in 8,145 families* (pp. 507–526). New Brunswick, NJ: Transaction.

Straus, M. A., Sugarman, D. B., & Giles-Sims, J. (1997). Spanking by parents and subsequent antisocial behavior of children. *Archives of Pediatric and Adolescent Medicine, 151*, 761–767.

Street, A. E. (1998). Psychological abuse and posttraumatic stress disorder in battered women: Examining the role of shame. *Dissertation Abstracts International, 59*(05), 2438B. (UMI No. 9908648)

Streissguth, A. (1997). *Fetal alcohol syndrome: A guide for families and communities.* Baltimore: Paul H. Brookes.

Stress undercuts flu shots. (1996). *Science News, 149*(15), 231.

Stuart, G. L., Ramsey, S. E., Moore, T. M., Kahler, C. W., Farrell, L. E., Recupero, P. R., et al. (2003). Reductions in marital violence following treatment for alcohol dependence. *Journal of Interpersonal Violence, 18*, 1113–1131.

Stubben, J. D. (2001). Working with and conducting research among American Indian families. *American Behavioral Scientist, 44*, 1466–1481.

Studer, M. (1984). Wife-beating as a social problem: The process of definition. *International Journal of Women's Studies, 7*, 412–422.

Sturgeon, V. H., & Taylor, J. (1980). Report of a five year follow-up study of mentally disordered sex offenders released from Atascadero State Hospital in 1973. *Criminal Justice Journal, 4*, 41–63.

Suarez, K. E. (1994). Teenage dating violence: The need for expanded awareness and legislation. *California Law Review, 82*, 423–471.

Successes seen in making arrests for Internet-related sex crimes. (2003, November 17). *Criminal Justice Newsletter*, pp. 1–2.

Sudermann, M., & Jaffe, P. G. (1997). Children and youth who witness violence: New directions in intervention and prevention. In D. A. Wolfe, R. J. McMahon, & R. D. Peters (Eds.), *Child abuse: New directions in prevention and treatment across the lifespan* (pp. 55–78). Thousand Oaks, CA: Sage.

Sudia, C. (1986). Preventing out-of-home placement of children: The first steps to permanency planning. *Children Today, 15*(6), 4–5.

Sugarman, D. B., & Frankel, S. L. (1993, August). *A meta-analytic study of wife assault and patriarchal beliefs.* Paper presented at annual meeting of the American Psychological Association, Toronto.

Sugarman, D. B., & Hotaling, G. T. (1989). Dating violence: Prevalence, context, and risk markers. In M. A. Pirog-Good & J. E. Stets (Eds.), *Violence in dating relationships: Emerging social issues* (pp. 3–32). New York: Praeger.

Sugarman, D. B., & Hotaling, G. T. (1997). Intimate violence and social desirability: A meta-analytic review. *Journal of Interpersonal Violence, 12*, 275–290.

Sullivan, P. M., & Knutson, J. F. (1998). The association between child maltreatment and disabilities in a hospital-based epidemiological study. *Child Abuse & Neglect, 22*, 271–288.

Sundram, C. J. (2000, January/February). Sex and mental disability: A responsible approach. *Victimization of the Elderly and Disabled, 2*, 67–68.

Sundram, C. J. (2003, September/October). Discovering quality assurance documents. *Victimization of the Elderly and Disabled, 6*, 33–34, 47.

Sutliff, J. A. (1995). *Avoidance coping strategies and symptomatology of victims of violence* [CD-ROM]. Abstract obtained from ProQuest File: Dissertation Abstracts Item 9518035

Swagerty, D. L., Takahashi, P. Y., & Evans, J. M. (1999). Elder mistreatment. *American Family Physician, 59*, 2804–2808.

Swart, L., Seedat, M., Stevens, G., & Ricardo, I. (2002). Violence in adolescents' romantic relationships: Findings from a survey amongst school-going youth in a South African community. *Journal of Adolescence, 25*, 385–395.

Sweeney, P. M. (2003, July/August). Exploitation of adults on the Internet. *Victimization of the Elderly and Disabled, 6*, 17, 29–30.

Swenson, C. C., & Kolko, D. J. (2000). Long-term management of the developmental consequences of child physical abuse. In R. M. Reece (Ed.), *Treatment of child abuse: Common ground for mental health, medical, and legal practitioners* (pp. 135–154). Baltimore: Johns Hopkins University Press.

Swett, C., Surrey, J., & Cohen, C. (1990). Sexual and physical abuse histories and psychiatric symptoms among male psychiatric outpatients. *American Journal of Psychiatry, 147*, 632–636.

Symposium on domestic violence. (1997). *Willamette Law Review, 33*, 767–998.

Taft, C. T., Murphy, C. M., Elliott, J. D., & Morrel, T. M. (2001). Attendance-enhancing procedures in group counseling for domestic abusers. *Journal of Counseling Psychology, 48*, 51–60.

Tamraz, D. N. (1996). Non-offending mothers of sexually abused children: Comparison of opinions and research. *Journal of Child Sexual Abuse, 5*(4), 75–99.

Tan, C., Basta, J., Sullivan, C. M., & Davidson, W. S. (1995). The role of social support in the lives of women exiting domestic violence shelters. *Journal of Interpersonal Violence, 10,* 437–451.

Tang, C. S. (1997). Psychological impact of wife abuse: Experiences of Chinese women and their children. *Journal of Interpersonal Violence, 12,* 466–478.

Tang, C. S. (1998). The rate of child abuse in Chinese families: A community survey in Hong Kong. *Child Abuse & Neglect, 22,* 381–391.

Tang, C. S., Cheung, F. M., Chen, R., & Sun, X. (2002). Definition of violence against women. *Journal of Interpersonal Violence, 17,* 671–688.

Tarasoff v. Regents of the University of California, 529 P.2d 553 (Cal. 1974), vac., reheard in bank and aff'd, 131 Cal Rptr. 14, 551 P.2d 334 (1976).

Tatara, T. (1993). Understanding the nature and scope of domestic elder abuse with the use of state aggregate data: Summaries of the key findings of a national survey of state APS and aging services. *Journal of Elder Abuse & Neglect, 5*(4), 35–57.

Tatara, T., & Kusmeskus, L. (1999). *Types of elder abuse in domestic settings.* Washington, DC: National Center on Elder Abuse.

Taylor, B. G., Davis, R. C., & Maxwell, C. D. (2001). The effects of a group batterer treatment program: A randomized experiment in Brooklyn. *Justice Quarterly, 18,* 171–201.

Teaster, P. B. (2003). *A response to the abuse of vulnerable adults: The 2000 survey of State Adult Protective Services.* Washington, DC: National Center on Elder Abuse.

Tebbutt, J., Swanston, H., Oates, R. K., & O'Toole, B. I. (1997). Five years after child sexual abuse: Persisting dysfunction and problems of prediction. *Child & Adolescent Psychiatry, 36,* 330–339.

Teicher, M. H. (2002, March). Scars that won't heal: The neurobiology of child abuse. *Scientific American,* pp. 68–75.

Tellegen, A., & Waller, N. G. (2000). Exploring personality through test construction: Development of the Multidimensional Personality Questionnaire. In S. R. Briggs & J. M. Cheek (Eds.), *Personality measures: Development and evaluation.* Greenwich, CT: JAI.

Testa, M., & Dermen, K. H. (1999). The differential correlates of sexual coercion and rape. *Journal of Interpersonal Violence, 14,* 548–561.

Thigpen, S. M., & Bonner, B. L. (1994). Child death review teams in action. *APSAC Advisor, 7*(4), 5–8.

Thomas, J. N. (1998). Community partnerships: A movement with a mission. *APSAC Advisor, 11,* 2–3.

Thomas, W. I., & Thomas, D. S. (1928). *The child in America: Behavioral problems and programs.* New York: Knopf.

Thompson, C. (1989). Breaking through walls of isolation: A model for churches in helping victims of violence. *Pastoral Psychology, 38,* 35–38.

Thompson, K. D. (1995). *Officially reported characteristics of spouse abuse victims seeking assistance in Utah, 1992* [CD-ROM]. Abstract obtained from ProQuest File: Dissertation Abstracts Item 1358266

Thompson, M. P., Kaslow, N. J., Kingree, J. B., Rashid, A., Puett, R., Jacobs, D., et al. (2000). Partner violence, social support, and distress among inner-city African-American women. *American Journal of Community Psychology, 28,* 127–143.

Thompson, R. A., Laible, D. J., & Robbennolt, J. K. (1997). Child care and preventing child maltreatment. In C. J. Dunst & M. Wolery (Eds.), *Advances in early education and day care* (pp. 173–202). Greenwich, CT: JAI.

Thompson, R. A., & Wilcox, B. L. (1995). Child maltreatme research: Federal support and policy issues. *Americc Psychologist, 50,* 789–793.

Three deputies get domestic violence convictions sealed. (1997, Ma 1). *Los Angeles Daily News,* p. 6.

Thurston, W. E., Cory, J., & Scott, C. M. (1998). Building a feminist th oretical framework for screening of wife-battering: Key issu to be addressed. *Patient Education and Counseling, 33,* 299–30

Tiedens, L. Z. (2001). Anger and advancement versus sadness ar subjugation: The effect of negative emotion expressions c social status conferral. *Journal of Personality and Soci Psychology, 80,* 86–94.

Tiff, L. L. (1993). *Battering of women: The failure of intervention ar the case for prevention.* Boulder, CO: Westview.

Tilden, V. P. (1989). Response of the health care delivery system battered women. *Issues in Mental Health Nursing, 10,* 309–32

Timmons-Mitchell, J., Chandler-Holtz, D., & Semple W. E. (199€ Post-traumatic stress symptoms in mothers followin children's reports of sexual abuse: An exploratory stuc *American Journal of Orthopsychiatry, 66,* 463–467.

Timnick, L. (1985, August 25). 22% in survey were child abu victims. *Los Angeles Times,* p. 1.

Tinsley, C. A., Critelli, J. W., & Ee, J. S. (1992, August). *The percepti of sexual aggression: One act, two realities.* Paper presented the annual meeting of the American Psychologic Association, Washington, DC.

Tjaden, P., & Thoennes, N. (1992). Predictors of legal intervention child maltreatment cases. *Child Abuse & Neglect, 16,* 807–82

Tjaden, P., & Thoennes, N. (1998a). *Prevalence, incidence, and cons quences of violence against women: Findings from the Natior Violence Against Women Survey* (NCJ Publication No. 17283? Washington, DC: U.S. Department of Justice.

Tjaden, P., & Thoennes, N. (1998b). *Stalking in America: Findir from the National Violence Against Women Survey* (N Publication No. 169592). Washington, DC: U.S. Department Justice.

Tjaden, P., & Thoennes, N. (2000a). *Extent, nature, and consequenc of intimate partner violence* (NCJ Publication No. 18186? Washington, DC: U.S. Department of Justice.

Tjaden, P., & Thoennes, N. (2000b). *Full report of the prevalence, in dence, and consequences of violence against women: Findir from the National Violence Against Women Survey* (N Publication No. 183781). Washington, DC: U.S. Department Justice.

Toews, M. L., McHenry, P. C., & Catless, B. S. (2003). Male-initiat partner abuse during marital separation prior to divorc *Violence and Victims, 18,* 387–402.

Tolan, P. H., & Guerra, N. (1998). Societal causes of violence agair children. In P. K. Trickett & C. J. Schellenbach (Eds.), *Violer against children in the family and the commun* (pp. 195–209). Washington DC: American Psychologic Association.

Tollefson, D. R. (2002, March). Factors associated with batterer trea ment success and failure. *Dissertation Abstracts Internation 62,* 3191A. (UMI No. 3026165)

Tolman, R. M. (1989). The development of a measure of psycholog cal maltreatment of women by their male partners. *Violer and Victims, 4,* 159–178.

Tolman, R. M., & Bennett, L. W. (1990). A review of quantitati research on men who batter. *Journal of Interpersonal Violen 5,* 87–118.

Tomita, S. K. (1990). The denial of elder mistreatment by victims and abusers: The application of neutralization theory. *Violence and Victims, 5,* 171–184.

Tomita, S. K. (2000). Elder mistreatment: Practice modifications to accommodate cultural differences. *Journal of Multicultural Social Work, 8,* 305–326.

Tomkins, A. J., Mohamed, S., Steinman, M., Macolini, R. M., Kenning, M. K., & Afrank, J. (1994). The plight of children who witness woman battering: Psychological knowledge and policy implications. *Law and Psychology Review, 18,* 137–187.

Tomz, J. E., & McGillis, D. (1997). *Serving crime victims and witnesses* (2nd ed.) (NCJ Publication No. 163174). Washington, DC: U.S. Department of Justice.

Tonizzo, S., Howells, K., Day, A., Reidpath, D., & Froyland, I. (2000). Attributions of negative partner behavior by men who physically abuse their partners. *Journal of Family Violence, 15,* 155–167.

Torry, W. I. (2000). Culture and individual responsibility: Touchstones of the cultural defense. *Human Organization, 59,* 58–71.

Toth, S. L., Cicchetti, D., Macfie, J., Maughan, A., & Vanmeenen, K. (2000). Narrative representations of caregivers and self in maltreated preschoolers. *Attachment and Human Development, 2,* 271–305.

Towns, A., & Adams, P. (2000). "If I really loved him enough, he would be okay." *Violence Against Women, 6,* 558–585.

Travis, C. (1993, January). Beware the incest-survivor machine. *New York Times,* p. 1.

Trebino, J. L. (1997). The effect of violence in the family of origin on college dating relationships: A meta-analysis of the intergenerational transmission of dating violence. *Dissertation Abstracts International, 35*(02), 456A. (UMI No. 1382653).

Tremblay, C., Hebert, M., & Piche, C. (1999). Coping strategies and social support as mediators of consequences in child sexual abuse victims. *Child Abuse & Neglect, 23,* 929–945.

Trepiccione, M. A. (2001). At the crossroads of law and social science: Is charging a battered mother with failure to protect her child an acceptable solution when her child witnesses domestic violence? *Fordham Law Review, 69,* 1487–1522.

Trickett, P. K., Aber, J. L., Carlson, V., & Cicchetti, D. (1991). Relationship of socioeconomic status to the etiology and developmental sequelae of physical child abuse. *Developmental Psychology, 27,* 148–158.

Trickett, P. K., & Kuczynski, L. (1986). Children's misbehaviors and parental discipline strategies in abusive and nonabusive families. *Developmental Psychology, 22,* 115–123.

Trickett, P. K., McBride-Chang, C., & Putnam, F. W. (1994). The classroom performance and behavior of sexually abused females. *Development and Psychopathology, 6,* 183–194.

Trickett, P. K., & Putnam, F. W. (1998). Developmental consequences of child sexual abuse. In P. K. Trickett & C. J. Schellenbach (Eds.), *Violence against children in the family and the community* (pp. 39–56). Washington, DC: American Psychological Association.

Trimpey, M. L. (1989). Self-esteem and anxiety: Key issues in an abused women's support group. *Issues in Mental Health Nursing, 10,* 297–308.

Trull, T. J. (2001). Structural relations between borderline personality disorder features and putative etiological correlates. *Journal of Abnormal Psychology, 110,* 471–481.

Truman-Schram, D. M., Cann, A., Calhoun, L., & Vanwallendael, L. (2000). Leaving an abusive dating relationship: An investment model comparison of women who stay versus women who leave. *Journal of Social and Clinical Psychology, 19,* 161–183.

Trupin, E., Tarico, V., Low, B., Jemelka, R., & McClellan, J. (1993). Children on child protective service caseloads: Prevalence and nature of serious emotional disturbance. *Child Abuse & Neglect, 17,* 345–355.

Trute, B. (1998). Going beyond gender specific treatments in wife battering: Pro-feminist couple and family therapy. *Aggression and Violent Behavior, 3,* 1–5.

Tsukada, N., Saito, Y., & Tatara, T. (2001). Japanese older people's perceptions of "elder abuse." *Journal of Elder Abuse & Neglect, 13*(1), 71–89.

Tucker, J. S., & Anders, S. L. (1999). Attachment style, interpersonal perception accuracy, and relationship satisfaction in dating couples. *Personality and Social Psychology Bulletin, 25,* 403–412.

Tuel, B. D., & Russell, R. K. (1998). Self-esteem and depression in battered women: A comparison of lesbian and heterosexual survivors. *Violence Against Women, 4,* 344–362.

Turell, S. C. (2000). A descriptive analysis of same-sex relationship violence for a diverse sample. *Journal of Family Violence, 15,* 281–294.

Turner, R. J., & Noh, S. (1983). Class and psychological vulnerability among women: The significance of social support and personal control. *Journal of Health and Social Behavior, 33,* 10–24.

Turner, S. F., & Shapiro, C. H. (1986). Battered women: Mourning the death of a relationship. *Social Work, 31,* 372–376.

Turney, D. (2000). The feminizing of neglect. *Child and Family Social Work, 5,* 47–56.

Tuteur, J. M., Ewigman, B. E., Peterson, L., & Hosokawa, M. C. (1995). The maternal observation matrix and Mother-Child Interaction Scale: Brief observational screening instruments for physically abusive mothers. *Journal of Clinical Child Psychology, 24,* 55–62.

Tweed, R. G., & Dutton, D. G. (1998). A comparison of impulsive and instrumental subgroups of batterers. *Violence and Victims, 13,* 217–230.

Twentyman, C. T., & Plotkin, R. C. (1982). Unrealistic expectations of parents who maltreat their children: An educational deficit that pertains to child development. *Journal of Clinical Psychology, 38,* 497–503.

Tyler, K. A. (2002). Social and emotional outcomes of childhood sexual abuse: A review of recent research. *Aggression and Violent Behavior, 7,* 567–589.

Tyler, R. P., & Stone, L. E. (1985). Child pornography: Perpetuating the sexual victimization of children. *Child Abuse & Neglect, 9,* 313–318.

Tyrell, D. E. (2002). Understanding the coping strategies of men who batter through a stress and coping framework. *Dissertation Abstracts International, 63*(02), 1053B. (UMI No. 3043418)

Uchida, C. D., Putnam, C. A., Mastrofski, J., Solomon, S., & Dawson, D. (2001). *Evaluating a multi-disciplinary response to domestic violence: The DVERT program in Colorado Springs* (NCJ Publication No. 190230). Washington, DC: U.S. Department of Justice.

Ullman, S. E. (1999). Social support and recovery from sexual assault: A review. *Aggression and Violent Behavior, 4,* 343–358.

Ulrich, Y. C., Cain, K. C., Sugg, N. K., Rivara, F. P., Rubanovice, D. M., & Thompson, R. S. (2003). Medical care utilization patterns in women with diagnosed domestic violence. *American Journal of Preventive Medicine, 24,* 9–15.

Umberson, D., Anderson, K., Glick, J., & Shapiro, A. (1998). Domestic violence, personal control, and gender. *Journal of Marriage and the Family, 60,* 442–452.

Urban, B. Y., & Bennett, L. W. (1999). When the community punches a time clock. *Violence Against Women, 5,* 1178–1193.

Urquiza, A. J., & Goodlin-Jones, B. L. (1994). Child sexual abuse and adult revictimization with women of color. *Violence and Victims, 9,* 223–232.

Urquiza, A. J., & Timmer, S. G. (2002). Patterns of interaction within violent families: Use of social interaction research methodology. *Journal of Interpersonal Violence, 17,* 824–835.

Urquiza, A. J., Wyatt, G. E., & Goodlin-Jones, B. L. (1997). Clinical interviewing with trauma victims: Managing interviewer risk. *Journal of Interpersonal Violence, 12,* 759–772.

Urwin, C. A., & McCrory, J. (2000, September/October). Expanding an APS training program through collaboration. *Victimization of the Elderly and Disabled, 3,* 33, 43–45.

U.S. Advisory Board on Child Abuse and Neglect. (1990). *First report of the U.S. Advisory Board on Child Abuse and Neglect.* Washington, DC: U.S. Department of Health and Human Services and National Council on Child Abuse and Neglect.

U.S. Advisory Board on Child Abuse and Neglect. (1993). *Neighbors helping neighbors: A new national strategy for the protection of children.* Washington, DC: Government Printing Office.

U.S. Bureau of the Census. (1997). *Statistical abstract of the United States* (117th ed.). Washington, DC: U.S. Department of Commerce.

U.S. Bureau of the Census. (2000). *U.S. population estimates, by age, sex, race, and Hispanic origin* (Current Population Reports No. P25-1095). Retrieved December 8, 2003, from http://www.census.gov/population/estimates/nation/intfile2-1.txt

U.S. Bureau of Justice Statistics. (1992a). *Census of state and federal correctional facilities, 1990* (NCJ Publication No. 137003). Washington, DC: U.S. Department of Justice.

U.S. Bureau of Justice Statistics. (1992b). *Criminal victimization in the United States, 1991* (NCJ Publication No. 139563). Washington, DC: U.S. Department of Justice.

U.S. Bureau of Justice Statistics. (1994). *Violence between intimates* (NCJ Publication No. 149259). Washington, DC: U.S. Department of Justice.

U.S. Bureau of Labor Statistics. (1999). *Usual weekly earnings of wage and salary workers: Fourth quarter 1998* (USDL Publication No. 99-15). Washington, DC: U.S. Department of Labor.

U.S. Conference of Mayors. (1998). *A status report on hunger and homelessness in America's cities.* Washington, DC: Author.

U.S. Department of Health and Human Services. (2002). *Appropriateness of minimum nurse staffing ratios in nursing homes.* Retrieved May 27, 2002, from http://www.house.gov/reform/min

U.S. Department of Health and Human Services, Administration on Children, Youth and Families. (1981). *Study findings: National study of the incidence and severity of child abuse and neglect* (DHHS Publication No. OHDS 81-30325). Washington, DC: Government Printing Office.

U.S. Department of Health and Human Services, Administration on Children, Youth and Families. (1988). *Study findings: Study of national incidence and prevalence of child abuse and neglect* (DHHS Publication No. ADM 20-01099). Washington, DC: Government Printing Office.

U.S. Department of Health and Human Services, Administration on Children, Youth and Families. (1993). *A report on the maltreatment of children with disabilities* (DHHS Contract No. 105-89-1630). Washington, DC: Government Printing Office.

U.S. Department of Health and Human Services, Administration on Children, Youth and Families. (1994). *Child maltreatment 1992: Reports from the states to the National Center on Child Abuse and Neglect.* Washington, DC: Government Printing Office.

U.S. Department of Health and Human Services, Administration on Children, Youth and Families. (1996). *Child maltreatment 1994: Reports from the states to the National Child Abuse and Neglect Data System.* Washington, DC: Government Printing Office.

U.S. Department of Health and Human Services, Administration on Children, Youth and Families. (1997, July 30). *Foster care and adoption statistics current reports.* Retrieved from http://www.acf.dhhs.gov/programs/cb/stats/afcars/index.htm

U.S. Department of Health and Human Services, Administration on Children, Youth and Families. (1998). *Child maltreatment 1996: Reports from the states to the National Child Abuse and Neglect Data System.* Washington, DC: Government Printing Office.

U.S. Department of Health and Human Services, Administration on Children, Youth and Families. (2000). *Child maltreatment 1998.* Washington, DC: Government Printing Office. Retrieved May 3, 2003, from http://www.acf.hhs.gov/programs/cb/publications/cm00/outcover.htm

U.S. Department of Health and Human Services, Administration on Children, Youth and Families. (2001). *Child maltreatment 1999.* Washington, DC: Government Printing Office.

U.S. Department of Health and Human Services, Administration on Children, Youth and Families. (2002a). *The AFCARS report.* Retrieved November 20, 2003, from http://www.acf.hhs.gov/programs/cb/publications/afcars/report7.htm

U.S. Department of Health and Human Services, Administration on Children, Youth and Families. (2002b). *National Child Abuse and Neglect Data System (NCANDS) summary of key findings from calendar year 2000.* Retrieved May 16, 2002, from http://www.calib.com/nccanch/ prevmnth/scope/ncands.cfm

U.S. Department of Health and Human Services, Administration on Children, Youth and Families. (2003a). *Child maltreatment 2001.* Washington, DC: Government Printing Office.

U.S. Department of Health and Human Services, Administration on Children, Youth and Families. (2003b, May 19). *Foster care and adoption statistics current reports.* Retrieved from http://www.acf.dhhs.gov/programs/cb/publications/index.htm

U.S. Department of Justice. (1996). *The validity and use of evidence concerning battering and its effects in criminal trials* (NCJ Publication No. 160972). Washington, DC: Author.

U.S. Department of Justice. (2000). *Measuring violence against women: Recommendations from an interagency workshop* (NCJ Publication No. 184447). Washington, DC: Author.

U.S. Department of Justice, Federal Bureau of Investigation. (2002). *Crime in the United States 2001: Uniform crime report.* Washington DC: Government Printing Office.

U.S. General Accounting Office. (1991). *Elder abuse: Effectiveness report laws and other factors* (Publication No. HRD-91-74). Washington, DC: Government Printing Office.

U.S. General Accounting Office. (2002a). *Gun control: Opportunities to close loopholes in the National Instant Criminal Background Check System* (Publication No. GAO-02-720). Washington, DC: Government Printing Office.

U.S. General Accounting Office. (2002b). *Nursing homes: More can be done to protect residents from abuse.* Retrieved May 27, 2002, from http://aging.senate.gov/hr78.htm

U.S. House of Representatives, Select Committee on Aging. (1990, May 1). *Elder abuse: A decade of shame and inaction* (Hearings). Washington, DC: Government Printing Office.

Vaillant, G. E., & Milofsky, E. S. (1982). The etiology of alcoholism: A prospective viewpoint. *American Psychologist, 37,* 494–503.

Valentiner, D. P., Foa, E. B., Riggs, D. S., & Gershuny, B. S. (1996). Coping strategies and posttraumatic stress disorder in female victims of sexual and nonsexual assault. *Journal of Abnormal Psychology, 105,* 455–458.

Valera, E. M., & Berenbaum, H. (2003). Brain injury in battered women. *Journal of Consulting and Clinical Psychology, 71,* 797–804.

Vandello, J. A., & Cohen, D. (2003). Male honor and female fidelity: Cultural scripts that perpetuate domestic violence. *Journal of Personality and Social Psychology, 84,* 997–1010.

van den Boom, D. C. (1994). The influence of temperament and mothering on attachment and exploration: An experimental manipulation of sensitive responsiveness among lower-class mothers with irritable infants. *Child Development, 65,* 1457–1477.

van den Boom, D. C. (1995). Do first-year intervention effects endure? Follow-up during toddlerhood of a sample of Dutch irritable infants. *Child Development, 66,* 1798–1816.

van den Bree, M. B. M., Svikis, D. S., & Pickens, R. W. (1998). Genetic influences in antisocial personality and drug use disorders. *Drug and Alcohol Dependence, 49,* 177–187.

VanderMeer, J. L. (1992). Elder abuse and the community health nurse. *Journal of Elder Abuse & Neglect, 4(4),* 37–45.

Van Hightower, N. R., Gorton, J., & DeMoss, C. (2000). Predictive models of domestic violence and fear of intimate partners among migrant and seasonal farm workers. *Journal of Family Violence, 15,* 137–154.

Van Wie, V. E., & Gross, A. M. (2001). The role of women's explanations for refusal on men's ability to discriminate unwanted sexual behavior in a date rape scenario. *Journal of Family Violence, 16,* 331–344.

Varia, R., Abidin, R. R., & Dass, P. (1996). Perceptions of abuse: Effects on adult psychological and social adjustment. *Child Abuse & Neglect, 20,* 511–526.

Varvaro, F. F. (1991). Using a grief response assessment questionnaire in a support group to assist battered women in their recovery. *Response, 13(4),* 17–20.

Vaselle-Augenstein, R., & Ehrlich, A. (1992). Male batterers: Evidence for psychopathology. In E. C. Viano (Ed.), *Intimate violence: Interdisciplinary perspectives* (pp. 139–154). Bristol, PA: Taylor & Francis.

Vass, J. S., & Gold, S. R. (1995). Effects of feedback on emotion in hypermasculine males. *Violence and Victims, 10,* 217–226.

Vazquez, C. I. (1996). Spousal abuse and violence against women: The significance of understanding attachment. *Annals of the New York Academy of Sciences, 789,* 119–128.

Weinsrideris, M. E. (2000). The prospective effects of modifying existing law to accommodate preemptive self-defense by battered women. *University of Pennsylvania Law Review, 149,* 613–644.

Wellinga, M. L. (1997, February 2). Crackdown on sex offenders raises tough questions. *Sacramento Bee.* Retrieved from http://www.sacbee.com

Veneziano, C., Veneziano, L., & LeGrand, S. (2000). The relationship between adolescent sex offender behaviors and victim characteristics with prior victimization. *Journal of Interpersonal Violence, 15,* 363–374.

Verhoek-Oftedahl, W., Pearlman, D. N., & Babcock, J. C. (2000). Improving surveillance of intimate partner violence by use of multiple data sources. *American Journal of Preventive Medicine, 19,* 308–315.

Victor, J. S. (1993). *Satanic panic.* Chicago: Open Court.

Vinton, L. (1991). Factors associated with refusing services among maltreated elderly. *Journal of Elder Abuse & Neglect, 3(2),* 89–103.

Vinton, L. (1998). A nationwide survey of domestic violence shelters' programming for older women. *Violence Against Women, 4,* 559–571.

Vinton, L. (2003). A model collaborative project toward making domestic violence centers elder ready. *Violence Against Women, 9,* 1504–1513.

Vinton, L., Altholz, J. A., & Lobell, T. (1997). A five-year follow-up study of domestic violence programming for battered older women. *Journal of Women and Aging, 9,* 3–15.

Violence Against Women Office. (2000). *The Violence Against Women Act of 2000 (VAWA 2000).* Retrieved from http://www.ojp. usdoj.gov/ vawo/laws/vawa_summary2.htm

Violence in families leads to delinquency, OJJDP study finds. (1995). *Criminal Justice Newsletter, 26(3),* 6–7.

Virginia Coalition for the Homeless. (1995). *1995 shelter provider survey.* Richmond: Author.

Virginia Department of Social Services. (2003). Internet crime against children. *Virginia Child Protection Newsletter, 68,* 2–17.

Virkkunen, M., Rawlings, R., Tokola, R., Poland, R. E., Giuidotti, A., Nemeroff, C., et al. (1994). CSF biochemistries, glucose metabolism, and diurnal activity rhythms in alcoholic, violent offenders, fire setters, and healthy volunteers. *Archives of General Psychiatry, 51,* 20–27.

Vissing, Y. M., Straus, M. A., Gelles, R. J., & Harrop, J. W. (1991). Verbal aggression by parents and psychosocial problems of children. *Child Abuse & Neglect, 15,* 223–238.

Vivian, D., & Malone, J. (1997). Relationship factors and depressive symptomatology associated with mild and severe husband-to-wife physical aggression. *Violence and Victims, 12,* 3–18.

Vladescu, D., Eveleigh, K., Ploeg, J., & Patterson, C. (1999). An evaluation of a client-centered case management program for elder abuse. *Journal of Elder Abuse & Neglect, 11(4),* 5–22.

Vogel, L. C. M., & Marshall, L. L. (2001). PTSD symptoms and partner abuse: Low income women at risk. *Journal of Traumatic Stress, 14,* 569–584.

Vogt, W. P. (1993). *Dictionary of statistics and methodology: A nontechnical guide for the social sciences.* Newbury Park, CA: Sage.

Volavka, J. (1995). *Neurobiology of violence.* Washington, DC: American Psychiatric Association.

Waaland, P., & Keeley, S. (1985). Police decision making in wife abuse: The impact of legal and extralegal factors. *Law and Human Behavior, 9,* 355–366.

Wade, K. A., Garry, M., Read, J. D., & Lindsay, D. S. (2002). A picture is worth a thousand lies: Using false photographs to create false childhood memories. *Psychonomic Bulletin and Review, 9,* 597–603.

Wagar, J. M., & Rodway, M. R. (1995). An evaluation of a group treatment approach for children who have witnessed wife abuse. *Journal of Family Violence, 10,* 295–306.

Waldner-Haugrud, L. K. (1999). Sexual coercion in lesbian and gay relationships: A review and critique. *Aggression and Violent Behavior, 4,* 139–149.

Waldner-Haugrud, L. K., Gratch, L. V., & Magruder, B. (1997). Victimization and perpetration rates of violence in gay and lesbian relationships: Gender issues explored. *Violence and Victims, 12,* 173–184.

Walker, C. E., Bonner, B. L., & Kaufman, K. L. (1988). *The physically and sexually abused child.* New York: Pergamon.

Walker, E., Downey, G., & Bergman, A. (1989). The effects of parental psychopathology and maltreatment on child behavior: A test of the diathesis-stress model. *Child Development, 60,* 15-24.

Walker, L. E. (1977). Battered women and learned helplessness. *Victimology, 2,* 525–534.

Walker, L. E. (1979). *The battered woman.* New York: Harper & Row.

Walker, L. E. (1983). The battered woman syndrome study. In D. Finkelhor, R. J. Gelles, G. T. Hotaling, & M. A. Straus (Eds.), *The dark side of families: Current family violence research* (pp. 31–48). Beverly Hills, CA: Sage.

Walker, L. E. (1984). *The battered woman syndrome.* New York: Springer.

Walker, L. E. (1985, June 7). *Psychology of battered women.* Symposium conducted at the Laguna Human Options Conference, Laguna Beach, CA.

Walker, L. E. (1991). Post-traumatic stress disorder in women: Diagnosis and treatment of battered woman syndrome. *Psychotherapy, 28,* 21–29.

Walker, L. E. (1993). The battered woman syndrome is a psychological consequence of abuse. In R. J. Gelles & D. R. Loseke (Eds.), *Current controversies on family violence* (pp. 133–153). Newbury Park, CA: Sage.

Wall, C. E. (1993). *Battered women and their batterers: Personality variables and attitudes toward violence* [CD-ROM]. Abstract obtained from ProQuest File: Dissertation Abstracts Item 9324523

Wallace, R., & Nosko, A. (1993). Working with shame in the group treatment of male batterers. *International Group Psychotherapy, 43,* 45–61.

Wallen, J., & Rubin, R. H. (1997). The role of the family in mediating the effects of community violence on children. *Aggression and Violent Behavior, 2,* 33–41.

Waltermaurer, E. S., Ortega, C. A., & McNutt, L. A. (2003). Issues in estimating the prevalence of intimate partner violence. *Journal of Interpersonal Violence, 18,* 959–974.

Walters, G. D. (1992). A meta-analysis of the gene-crime relationship. *Criminology, 30,* 595–613.

Walton, E., Fraser, M. W., Lewis, R. E., & Pecora, P. (1993). In-home family-focused reunification: An experimental study. *Child Welfare, 72,* 473–487.

Wan, A. M. (2000). Battered women in the restraining order process: Observations on a court advocacy program. *Violence Against Women, 6,* 606–632.

Wang, C. T., & Daro, D. (1996). *Current trends in child abuse reporting and fatalities: The results of the 1995 annual fifty state survey.* Chicago: National Committee to Prevent Child Abuse.

Wang, C. T., & Daro, D. (1997). *Current trends in child abuse reporting and fatalities: The results of the 1996 annual fifty state survey.* Chicago: National Center on Child Abuse Prevention Research.

Wang, C. T., & Daro, D. (1998). *Current trends in child abuse reporting and fatalities: The results of the 1997 annual fifty state survey.* Chicago: National Center on Child Abuse Prevention Research.

Ward, M. J., Lee, S. S., & Lipper, E. G. (2000). Failure-to-thrive is associated with disorganized infant-mother attachment and unresolved maternal attachment. *Infant Mental Health Journal, 21,* 428–442.

Warnken, W. J., Rosenbaum, A., Fletcher, K. E., Hoge, S. K., & Adelman, S. A. (1994). Head-injured males: A population at risk for relationship aggression. *Violence and Victims, 9,* 153–166.

Washington State Coalition Against Domestic Violence. (2000). *Honoring their lives, learning from their deaths.* Seattle: Author.

Wasik, B., & Roberts, R. N. (1994). Survey of home visiting programs for abused and neglected children and their families. *Child Abuse & Neglect, 18,* 271–283.

Waterman, J., Kelly, R. J., Oliveri, M. K., & McCord, J. (1993). *Behind the playground walls: Sexual abuse in preschools.* New York: Guilford.

Waters, M. (2000, June). Guidelines urge researchers to take a less superficial look at minorities. *APA Monitor on Psychology, 31,* 12.

Watkins, G. (2003, September/October). Martha's story. *Victimization of the Elderly and Disabled, 6,* 39–43.

Watson, C. G., Barnett, M., Nikunen, L., Schultz, C., Randolph-Elgin, T., & Mendez, C. M. (1997). Lifetime prevalences of nine common psychiatric/personality disorders in female domestic abuse survivors. *Journal of Nervous and Mental Disease, 185,* 645–647.

Watson, J. M., Cascardi, M., Avery-Leaf, S., & O'Leary, K. D. (2001). High school students' responses to dating aggression. *Violence and Victims, 16,* 339–348.

Wattendorf, G. (1996). Prosecuting cases without victim cooperation. *FBI Law Enforcement Bulletin, 65*(4), 18–20.

Wauchope, B. A., & Straus, M. A. (1990). Physical punishment and physical abuse of American children: Incidence rates by age, gender, and occupational class. In M. A. Straus & R. J. Gelles (Eds.), *Physical violence in American families: Risk factors and adaptations to violence in 8,145 families* (pp. 133–148). New Brunswick, NJ: Transaction.

Waxman, L., & Trupin, R. (1997). *A status report on hunger and homelessness in America's cities: 1997.* Washington, DC: U.S. Conference of Mayors.

Weaver, T. L., & Clum, G. A. (1995). Psychological distress associated with interpersonal violence: A meta-analysis. *Clinical Psychology Review, 15,* 115–140.

Weber, T. (1991, April 13). Tearful jurors say they'll never forget horrifying testimony. *Orange County Register,* p. 26.

Webersinn, A. L., Hollinger, C. L., & DeLamtre, J. E. (1991). Breaking the cycle of violence: An examination of factors relevant to treatment follow-through. *Psychological Reports, 68,* 231–244.

Websdale, N. (1995). Rural woman abuse: The voices of Kentucky women. *Violence Against Women, 1,* 309–338.

Wechsler, D. (1997). *WAIS-III, Wechsler Adult Intelligence Scale.* San Antonio, TX: Psychological Corporation.

Wechsler, H., Lee, J. E., Kuo, M., & Lee, H. (2000). College binge drinking in the 1990s: A continuing problem. Results of the Harvard School of Public Health 1999 college alcohol study. *Journal of American College Health, 48,* 199–210.

Weinberg, S. K. (1955). *Incest behavior.* New York: Citadel.

Weiner, A. (1991). A community-based education model for identification and prevention of elder abuse. *Journal of Gerontological Social Work, 16*(3/4), 107–119.

Weinhardt, L. S. (1999). Sexual coercion among women living with severe and persistent mental illness: Review of the literature and recommendations for mental health providers. *Aggression and Violent Behavior, 4,* 307–317.

Weis, J. G. (1989). Family violence research methodology and design. In L. Ohlin & M. Tonry (Eds.), *Family violence* (pp. 117–162). Chicago: University of Chicago Press.

Weis, L. (2001). Race, gender, and critique: African-American women, White women, and domestic violence in the 1980s and 1990s. *Signs, 27,* 139–159.

Weiss, E. L., Longhurst, J. G., & Mazure, C. M. (1999). Childhood sexual abuse as a risk factor for depression in women: Psychosocial and neurobiological correlates. *American Journal of Psychiatry, 156,* 816–828.

Weisz, A. N., & Black, B. M. (2001). Evaluating a sexual assault and dating violence prevention program for urban youth. *Social Work Research, 25,* 89–100.

Weitzman, P. F., & Weitzman, E. A. (2003). Promoting communication with older adults: Protocols for resolving interpersonal conflicts and for enhancing interactions with doctors. *Clinical Psychology Review, 23,* 523–535.

Wekerle, C., & Wolfe, D. A. (1993). Prevention of child abuse and neglect: Promising new directions. *Clinical Psychology Review, 13,* 501–540.

Wekerle, C., & Wolfe, D. A. (1996). Child maltreatment. In E. J. Mash & R. A. Barkley (Eds.), *Child psychopathology* (pp. 492–537). New York: Guilford.

Wekerle, C., & Wolfe, D. A. (1998). Windows for preventing child and partner abuse: Early childhood and adolescence. In P. K. Trickett & C. J. Schellenbach (Eds.), *Violence against children in the family and the community* (pp. 339–369). Washington, DC: American Psychological Association.

Wekerle, C., & Wolfe, D. A. (1999). Dating violence in mid-adolescence: Theory, significance, and emerging prevention initiatives. *Clinical Psychology Review, 19,* 435–456.

Welbourne, A., Lipschitz, D. S., Selvin, H., & Green, R. (1983). A comparison of the sexual learning experiences of visually impaired and sighted women. *Journal of Visual Impairment and Blindness, 77,* 256–259.

Wells, R. D., McCann, J., Adams, J., Voris, J., & Ensign, J. (1995). Emotional, behavioral, and physical symptoms reported by parents of sexually abused, nonabused, and allegedly abused prepubescent females. *Child Abuse & Neglect, 19,* 155–163.

Wells, S. J. (1994). Child protective services: Research for the future. *Child Welfare League of America, 123,* 431–447.

Werner-Wilson, R. J., Zimmerman, T. S., & Whalen, D. (2000). Resilient response to battering. *Contemporary Family Therapy, 22,* 161–188.

Wesch, D., & Lutzker, J. R. (1991). A comprehensive 5-year evaluation of Project 12-Ways: An ecobehavioral program for treating and preventing child abuse and neglect. *Journal of Family Violence, 6,* 17–35.

Wesley, J. K., Allison, M. T., & Schneider, I. E. (2000). The lived body experience of domestic violence survivors: An interrogation of female identity. *Women's Studies International Forum, 23,* 211–222.

West, A., & Wandrei, M. L. (2002). Intimate partner violence: A model for predicting interventions by informal helpers. *Journal of Interpersonal Violence, 17,* 972–986.

West, J. A. (2002). Public service advertising in the 21st century: Exploration of unintended effects of domestic violence campaigns. *Dissertation Abstracts International, 63*(04), 1174A. (UMI No. 3049494)

Westrup, D., Fremouw, W. J., Thompson, R. N., & Lewis, S. F. (1999). The psychological impact of stalking on female undergraduates. *Journal of Forensic Sciences, 44,* 554–557.

Wetzel, L., & Ross, M. A. (1983). Psychological and social ramification of battering: Observations leading to a counseling methodology for victims of domestic violence. *Personnel and Guidance Journal, 61,* 423–428.

Wexler, D. B., & Bruce, J. W. (Eds.). (1996). *Law in a therapeutic key: Developments in therapeutic jurisprudence.* Durham, NC: Carolina Academic Press.

Whalen, M. (1996). *Counseling to end violence against women: A subversive model.* Thousand Oaks, CA: Sage.

Whatley, M. A., & Riggio, R. E. (1991, August). *Attributions of blame for female and male victims.* Paper presented at the annual meeting of the American Psychological Association, San Francisco.

Whatule, L. J. (2000). Communication as an aid to resocialization: A case of men's anger groups. *Small Group Research, 31,* 424–446.

Whipple, E. E., & Webster-Stratton, C. (1991). The role of parental stress in physically abusive families. *Child Abuse & Neglect, 15,* 279–291.

Whipple, E. E., & Wilson, S. R. (1996). Evaluation of a parent education and support program for families at risk of physical child abuse. *Families in Society, 77,* 227–239.

White, J. W., & Koss, M. P. (1991). Courtship violence: Incidence in a national sample of higher education students. *Violence and Victims, 6,* 247–256.

White, J. W., Smith, P. H., Koss, M. P., & Figueredo, A. J. (2000). Intimate partner aggression: What have we learned? Comment on Archer 2000. *Psychological Bulletin, 126,* 690–696.

White, R. J., & Gondolf, E. W. (2000). Implications of personality profiles for batterer treatment. *Journal of Interpersonal Violence, 15,* 467–488.

White Ribbon Campaign. (n.d.). *The White Ribbon Campaign.* Retrieved from http://www.whiteribbon.com

Widom, C. S. (1989a). Child abuse, neglect, and violent criminal behavior. *Criminology, 27,* 251–271.

Widom, C. S. (1989b). Does violence beget violence? A critical examination of the literature. *Psychological Bulletin, 106,* 3–28.

Widom, C. S. (1995, March). Victims of childhood sexual abuse: Later criminal consequences. *National Institute of Justice Journal,* pp. 1–8.

Widom, C. S. (1999). Posttraumatic stress disorder in abused and neglected children grown up. *American Journal of Psychiatry, 156,* 1223–1229.

Widom, C. S., Ireland, T. O., & Glynn, P. J. (1995). Alcohol abuse in abused and neglected children followed-up: Are they at increased risk? *Journal of Studies on Alcohol, 56,* 207–217.

Widom, C. S., & Kuhns, J. B. (1996). Childhood victimization and subsequent risk for promiscuity, prostitution, and teenage pregnancy: A prospective study. *American Journal of Public Health, 86,* 1607–1612.

Widom, C. S., & Maxfield, M. G. (2001). *An update on the "Cycle of Violence"* (NCJ Publication No. 184894). Washington, DC: U.S. Department of Justice.

Wiehe, V. R. (1990). *Sibling abuse: Hidden physical, emotional, and sexual trauma.* Lexington, MA: Lexington.

Wiehe, V. R. (1997). *Sibling abuse: Hidden physical, emotional, and sexual trauma* (2nd ed.). Thousand Oaks, CA: Sage.

Wiese, D., & Daro, D. (1995). *Current trends in child abuse reporting and fatalities: The results of the 1994 annual fifty state survey.* Chicago: National Committee to Prevent Child Abuse.

Wiist, W. H., & McFarlane, J. (1998). Utilization of police by abused pregnant Hispanic women. *Violence Against Women, 4,* 677–693.

Wilber, K. H., & McNeilly, D. P. (2001). Elder abuse and victimization. In J. E. Birren & K. W. Schai (Eds.), *Handbook of the psychology of aging* (5th ed., pp. 569–591). San Diego, CA: Academic Press.

Wild, N. J. (1989). Prevalence of child sex rings. *Pediatrics, 83,* 553–558.

Wilkens, S. L. (2002). The social problem-solving skills of preschoolers who witness domestic violence as measured by the MacArthur Story-Stem Battery. *Dissertation Abstracts International, 63*(01), 555B. (UMI No. 3040112)

Williams, K. R. (1992). Social sources of marital violence and deterrence: Testing an integrated theory of assaults between partners. *Journal of Marriage and the Family, 54,* 620–629.

Williams, L. M. (1994). Recall of childhood trauma: A prospective study of women's memories. *Journal of Consulting and Clinical Psychology, 62,* 1167–1176.

Williams, L.M. (2003). Understanding child abuse and violence against women: A life course perspective. *Journal of Interpersonal Violence, 18,* 441–451.

Williams, L. M., & Finkelhor, D. (1990). The characteristics of incestuous fathers: A review of recent studies. In W. L. Marshall, D. R. Laws, & H. E. Barbaree (Eds.), *Handbook of sexual assault: Issues, theories, and treatment of the offender* (pp. 231–255). New York: Plenum.

Williams, M. B. (1993). Assessing the traumatic impact of child sexual abuse: What makes it more severe? *Journal of Child Sexual Abuse, 2*(1), 41–59.

Williamson, G. M., & Silverman, J. G. (2001). Violence against female partners: Direct and interactive effects of history, communal orientation, and peer-related variables. *Journal of Social and Personal Relationships, 18,* 535–549.

Williamson, J. M., Borduin, C. M., & Howe, B. A. (1991). The ecology of adolescent maltreatment: A multilevel examination of adolescent physical abuse, sexual abuse, and neglect. *Journal of Consulting and Clinical Psychology, 59,* 449–457.

Willis, D. J., & Silovsky, J. (1998). Prevention of violence at the societal level. In P. K. Trickett & C. J. Schellenbach (Eds.), *Violence against children in the family and the community* (pp. 401–416). Washington, DC: American Psychological Association.

Willson, P., McFarlane, J., Malecha, A., Watson, K., Lemmey, D., Schultz, P., et al. (2000). Severity of violence against women by intimate partners and associated use of alcohol and/or illicit drugs by perpetrators. *Journal of Interpersonal Violence, 15,* 996–1008.

Wilson, C. (1998). Are battered women responsible for protection of their children in domestic violence cases? *Journal of Interpersonal Violence, 13,* 289–293.

Wilson, D. G., & Wilson, A. V. (1991). *Spousal abuse cases: Perceptions and attitudes of service providers* (Report prepared for Attorney General's Task Force on Domestic Violence Crime). Louisville: Kentucky Criminal Justice Statistical Analysis Center.

Wilson, M. I., & Daly, M. (1992). Who kills whom in spouse killings? On the exceptional sex ratio of spousal homicides in the United States. *Criminology, 30,* 189–215.

Wilson, M. N., Baglioni, A. J., Jr., & Downing, D. (1989). Analyzing factors influencing readmission to a battered women's shelter. *Journal of Family Violence, 4,* 275–284.

Wind, T. W., & Silvern, L. (1992). Type and extent of child abuse as predictors of adult functioning. *Journal of Family Violence, 7,* 261–281.

Wind, T. W., & Silvern, L. (1994). Parenting and family stress as mediators of the long-term effects of child abuse. *Child Abuse & Neglect, 18,* 439–453.

Wingood, G. M., DiClemente, R. J., Bernhardt, J. M., Harrington, K., Davies, S. L., Robillard, A., et al. (2003). A prospective study of exposure to rap music videos and African American female adolescents' health. *American Journal of Public Health, 93,* 437–439.

Wingood, G. M., DiClemente, R. J., & Raj, A. (2000). Identifying the prevalence and correlates of STDs among women residing in domestic violence shelters. *Women & Health, 30*(4), 15–26.

Winton, M. A. (1990). An evaluation of a support group for parents who have a sexually abused child. *Child Abuse & Neglect, 14,* 397–405.

Wisner, C. L., Gilmer, T. P., & Saltzman, L. E. (1999). Intimate partner violence against women: Do victims cost health plans more? *Journal of Family Practice, 6,* 439–443.

Witt, D., & Sheinwald, J. (1992). *The Family Empowerment Program: A social group work model of long-term, intensive, and innovative strategies to reduce the incidence of chronic neglect for at risk parents* (Project report, FY88 Grant No. 90CA1392 National Center on Child Abuse and Neglect). Pontiac, MI: Oakland Family Services.

Wodarski, J. S., Kurtz, P. D., Gaudin, J. M., & Howing, P. T. (1990). Maltreatment and the school age child: Major academic, socioemotional, and adaptive outcomes. *Social Work, 35,* 506–513.

Wolf, M. E., Ly, U., Hobart, M. A., & Kernic, M. A. (2003). Barriers to seeking police help for intimate partner violence. *Journal of Family Violence, 18,* 121–129.

Wolf, R. S. (2000). The nature and scope of elder abuse. *Generations, 24*(2), 6–12.

Wolf, R. S., & Donglin, L. (1999). Factors affecting the rate of elder abuse reporting to state protective services programs. *Gerontologist, 39,* 222–228.

Wolf, R. S., & Pillemer, K. A. (1988). Intervention, outcome, and elder abuse. In G. T. Hotaling, D. Finkelhor, J. T. Kirkpatrick, M. A. Straus (Eds.), *Coping with family violence* (pp. 257–274). Newbury Park, CA: Sage.

Wolf, R. S., & Pillemer, K. A. (1989). *Helping elderly victims: The reality of elder abuse.* New York: Columbia University Press.

Wolf, R. S., & Pillemer, K. A. (1997). The older battered woman: Wives and mothers compared. *Journal of Mental Health and Aging, 3,* 325–336.

Wolf, R. S., & Pillemer, K. A. (2000). Elder abuse and case outcome. *Journal of Applied Gerontology, 19,* 203–220.

Wolfe, D. A. (1987). *Child abuse: Implications for child development and psychopathology.* Newbury Park, CA: Sage.

Wolfe, D. A. (1991). *Preventing physical and emotional abuse of children.* New York: Guilford.

Wolfe, D. A. (1999). *Child abuse: Implications for child development and psychopathology* (2nd ed.). Thousand Oaks, CA: Sage.

Wolfe, D. A., Crooks, C. V., Lee, V., McIntyre-Smith, A., & Jaffe, P. (2003). The effects of children's exposure to domestic violence: A meta-analysis and critique. *Clinical Child and Family Psychology Review, 6,* 171–187.

Wolfe, D. A., Edwards, B., Manion, I., & Koverola, C. (1988). Early intervention for parents at risk of child abuse and neglect: A preliminary investigation. *Journal of Consulting and Clinical Psychology, 56,* 40–47.

Wolfe, D. A., & Jaffe, P. G. (1999). Emerging strategies in the prevention of domestic violence. *Future of Children, 9*(3), 133–141.

Wolfe, D. A., & Wekerle, C. (1993). Treatment strategies for child physical abuse and neglect: A critical progress report. *Clinical Psychology Review, 13,* 473–500.

Wolfe, D. A., Wekerle, C., Reitzel-Jaffe, D., & Lefebvre, L. (1998). Factors associated with abusive relationships among maltreated and nonmaltreated youth. *Development and Psychopathology, 10,* 61–85.

Wolfe, D. A., Wekerle, C., & Scott, K. (1997). *Alternatives to violence: Empowering youth to develop healthy relationships.* Thousand Oaks, CA: Sage.

Wolfe, D. A., Wekerle, C., Scott, K., Straatman, A. L., Grasley, C., & Reitzel-Jaffe, D. (2003). Dating violence prevention with at-risk youth: A controlled outcome evaluation. *Journal of Consulting and Clinical Psychology, 71,* 279–291.

Wolfe, D. A., Wolfe, V. V., & Best, C. L. (1988). Child victims of sexual abuse. In V. B. Van Hasselt, R. L. Morrison, A. S. Bellack, & M. Hersen (Eds.), *Handbook of family violence* (pp. 157–185). New York: Plenum.

Wolfner, G. D., & Gelles, R. J. (1993). A profile of violence toward children: A national study. *Child Abuse & Neglect, 17,* 197–212.

Wolman, B. B. (1973). *Dictionary of behavioral science.* New York: Van Nostrand Reinhold.

Wolock, T., & Horowitz, B. (1984). Child maltreatment as a social problem: The neglect of neglect. *American Journal of Orthopsychiatry, 54,* 530–542.

Woods, S. J. (1999). Normative beliefs regarding the maintenance of intimate relationships among abused and nonabused women. *Journal of Interpersonal Violence, 14,* 479–491.

Woods, S. J., & Isenberg, M. A. (2001). Adaptation as a mediator of intimate abuse and traumatic stress in battered women. *Nursing Science Quarterly, 14,* 213–221.

Worchester, N. (2002). Women's use of force. *Violence Against Women, 8,* 1390–1415.

Worden, H. A. (2002). The effects of race and class on women's experience of domestic violence. *Dissertation Abstracts International, 62*(12), 4346A. (UMI No. 3034787)

Worling, J. R. (1995). Adolescent sibling-incest offenders: Differences in family and individual functioning when compared to adolescent nonsibling sex offenders. *Child Abuse & Neglect, 19,* 633–643.

Wuest, J., & Merritt-Gray, M. (1999). Not going back: Sustaining the separation in the process of leaving abusive relationships. *Violence Against Women, 5,* 110–133.

Wurtele, S. K. (1993). The role of maintaining telephone contact with parents during the teaching of a personal safety program. *Journal of Child Sexual Abuse, 2*(1), 65–82.

Wurtele, S. K. (2002). School-based child sexual abuse prevention. In P. A. Schewe (Ed.), *Preventing violence in relationships: Interventions across the life span* (pp. 9–26). Washington, DC: American Psychological Association.

Wurtele, S. K., Kast, L. C., & Melzer, A. M. (1994). Sexual abuse prevention education for young children: A comparison of teachers and parents as instructors. *Child Abuse & Neglect, 16,* 865 876.

Wurtele, S. K., Kvaternick, M., & Franklin, C. F. (1992). Sexual abuse prevention for preschoolers: A survey of parents' behaviors, attitudes, and beliefs. *Journal of Child Sexual Abuse, 1*(1), 113–128.

Wurtele, S. K., & Miller-Perrin, C. L. (1992). *Preventing child sexual abuse: Sharing the responsibility.* Lincoln: University of Nebraska Press.

Wyatt, G. E. (1985). The sexual abuse of Afro-American and White-American women in childhood. *Child Abuse & Neglect, 9,* 507–519.

Yan, E., & Tang, C. S. (2001). Prevalence of psychological impact of elder abuse. *Journal of Interpersonal Violence, 16,* 1158–1174.

Yan, E., & Tang, C. S. (2003). Proclivity to elder abuse: A community study on Hong Kong Chinese. *Journal of Interpersonal Violence, 18,* 999–1017.

Yanagida, E. H., & Ching, J. W. (1993). MMPI profiles of child abusers. *Journal of Clinical Psychology, 49,* 569–576.

Yegidis, B. L. (1992). Family violence: Contemporary research findings and practice issues. *Community Mental Health Journal, 28,* 519–529.

Yelsma, P. (1996). Affective orientation of perpetrators, victims, and functional spouses. *Journal of Interpersonal Violence, 11,* 141–161.

Yick, A. G., & Agbayani-Siewert, P. (2000). Dating violence among Chinese American and White students: A sociocultural context. *Journal of Multicultural Social Work, 8,* 101–129.

Yllö, K. A. (1993). Through a feminist lens: Gender, power, and violence. In R. J. Gelles & D. R. Loseke (Eds.), *Current controversies on family violence* (pp. 47–62). Newbury Park, CA: Sage.

Yorukoglu, A., & Kemph, J. P. (1966). Children not severely damaged by incest with a parent. *Journal of the American Academy of Child Psychiatry, 5,* 111–124.

Yoshihama, M. (2001). Immigrants-in-context framework: Understanding the interactive influence of socio-cultural contexts. *Evaluation and Program Planning, 24,* 307–318.

Yoshihama, M. (2002). The definitional process of domestic violence in Japan. *Violence Against Women, 8,* 339–366.

Yoshihama, M., & Gillespie, B. W. (2002). Age adjustment and recall bias in the analysis of domestic violence data: Methodological improvements through the application of survival analysis method. *Journal of Family Violence, 17,* 199–221.

Yoshihama, M., & Sorenson, S. B. (1994). Physical, sexual, and emotional abuse by male intimates: Experiences of women in Japan. *Violence and Victims, 9,* 63–77.

Yoshioka, M. R., DiNoia, J., & Ullah, K. (2001). Attitudes toward marital violence: An examination of four Asian communities. *Violence Against Women, 7,* 900–926.

Young, M., Barker-Collo, S., & Harrison, R. (2002). Evaluating and overcoming barriers to taking abuse histories. *Professional Psychology: Research and Practice, 32,* 407–414.

Young, M. E., Nosek, M. A., Howland, C. A., Chanpong, G., & Rintala, D. H. (1997). Prevalence of abuse of women with physical disabilities. *Archives of Physical Medicine and Rehabilitation, 78*(12, Suppl. 5), S34–S38.

Young, R. E., Bergandi, T. A., & Titus, T. G. (1994). Comparison of the effects of sexual abuse on male and female latency-aged children. *Journal of Interpersonal Violence, 9,* 291–306.

Youngblade, L. M., & Belsky, J. (1990). Social and emotional consequences of child maltreatment. In R. T. Ammerman & M. Hersen (Eds.), *Children at risk: An evaluation of factors contributing to child abuse and neglect* (pp. 109–140). New York: Plenum.

Yuan, Y. T., & Struckman-Johnson, D. L. (1991). Placement outcomes for neglected children with prior placements in family preservation programs. In K. Wells & D. E. Biegel (Eds.), *Family preservation services: Research and evaluation* (pp. 92–118). Newbury Park, CA: Sage.

Zanarini, M. C., Ruser, T. F., Frankenburg, F. F., Hennen, J., & Gunderson, J. G. (2000). Risk factors associated with the dissociative experiences of borderline patients. *Journal of Nervous and Mental Disease, 188,* 26–30.

Zellman, G. L., & Fair, C. C. (2002). Preventing and reporting abuse. In J. E. B. Myers, L. Berliner, J. Briere, C. T. Hendrix, C. Jenny, & T. A. Reid (Eds.), *The APSAC handbook on child maltreatment* (2nd ed., pp. 449–475). Thousand Oaks, CA: Sage.

Zezima, K. (2003, August 25). News of ex-priest's death evokes range of emotions. *New York Times,* p. A8.

Zillmann, D. (1990). The interplay of cognition and excitation in aggravated conflict among intimates. In D. D. Cahn (Ed.), *Intimates in conflict: A communication perspective* (pp. 187–208). Hillsdale, NJ: Lawrence Erlbaum.

Zimny, G. H., & Diamond, J. A. (1993). Judicial evaluation of recommendations for improving monitoring of guardians. *Journal of Elder Abuse & Neglect, 5*(3), 51–67.

Zingraff, M. T., Leiter, J., Myers, K. A., & Johnsen, M. C. (1993). Child maltreatment and youthful problem behavior. *Criminology, 31,* 173–202.

Zink, T., Regan, S., Jacobson, C. J., Jr., & Pabst, S. (2003). Cohort, period, and aging effects: A qualitative study of older women's reasons for remaining in abusive relationships. *Violence Against Women, 9,* 1429–1441.

Zlotnick, C. K., Kohn, R., Peterson, J., & Pearlstein, T. (1998). Partner physical victimization in a national sample of American families. *Journal of Interpersonal Violence, 13,* 156–166.

Zorza, J. (1994). Woman battering: High costs and the state of the law. *Clearinghouse Review, 28,* 383–395.

Zorza, J. (1995). Recognizing and protecting the privacy and confidentiality needs of battered women. *Family Law Quarterly, 29,* 273–311.

Zorza, J. (1998, June/July). Batterer manipulation and retaliation in the courts: A largely unrecognized phenomenon sometimes encouraged by court practices. *Domestic Violence Report, 3,* 67–68, 75–76.

Zorza, J. (2003, April/May). Battered mothers speak out: Part II. The recommendations. *Domestic Violence Report, 4,* 49, 57–60.

Zorza, J., & Woods, L. (1994). *Mandatory arrest.* Washington, DC: National Center on Women and Family Law.

Zorza, R., & Klemperer, J. (1999, April/May). The Internet-based domestic court preparation project: Using the Internet to overcome barriers to justice. *Domestic Violence Report, 4,* 49–50, 59–60.

Zubretsky, T. M., & Digirolamo, K. M. (1994). Adult domestic violence: The alcohol connection. *Violence Update, 4*(7), 1–2, 4, 8.

Zuravin, S. J. (1987). Unplanned pregnancies, family planning problems, and child maltreatment. *Family Relations, 36,* 135–139.

Zuravin, S. J. (1988). Child abuse, child neglect, and maternal depression: Is there a connection? In National Center on Child Abuse and Neglect (Ed.), *Child neglect monograph: Proceedings from a symposium.* Washington, DC: National Clearinghouse on Child Abuse and Neglect Information.

Zuravin, S. J. (1989). The ecology of child abuse and neglect: Review of the literature and presentation of data. *Violence and Victims, 4,* 101–120.

Zuravin, S. J. (1991). Research definitions of child physical abuse and neglect: Current problems. In R. H. Starr, Jr., & D. A. Wolfe (Eds.), *The effects of child abuse and neglect: Research issues* (pp. 100–128). New York: Guilford.

Zuravin, S. J., & DiBlasio, F. A. (1992). Child-neglecting adolescent mothers: How do they differ from their nonmaltreating counterparts? *Journal of Interpersonal Violence, 7,* 471–487.

Zweig, J. M., Schlichter, K. A., & Burt, M. R. (2002). Assisting women victims of violence who experience multiple barriers to services. *Violence Against Women, 8,* 162–180.

AUTHOR INDEX